Proceedings of the

FOURTH EUROMICRO WORKSHOP ON PARALLEL AND DISTRIBUTED PROCESSING

– PDP '96 –

Proceedings of the

Fourth Euromicro Workshop on Parallel and Distributed Processing

– PDP '96 –

January 24 – 26, 1996

Braga, Portugal

IEEE Computer Society Press
50 Years of Service • 1946-1996

Los Alamitos, California

Washington • Brussels • Tokyo

IEEE Computer Society Press
10662 Los Vaqueros Circle
P.O. Box 3014
Los Alamitos, CA 90720-1264

IEEE Computer Society Press Order Number PR07376
ISBN 0-8186-7376-1
ISSN 1066-6192

Additional copies may be ordered from:

IEEE Computer Society Press
Customer Service Center
10662 Los Vaqueros Circle
P.O. Box 3014
Los Alamitos, CA 90720-1264
Tel: +1-714-821-8380
Fax: +1-714-821-4641
Email: cs.books@computer.org

IEEE Computer Society
13, Avenue de l'Aquilon
B-1200 Brussels
BELGIUM
Tel: +32-2-770-2198
Fax: +32-2-770-8505
euro.ofc@computer.org

IEEE Computer Society
Ooshima Building
2-19-1 Minami-Aoyama
Minato-ku, Tokyo 107
JAPAN
Tel: +81-3-3408-3118
Fax: +81-3-3408-3553
tokyo.ofc@computer.org

Editorial production by Mary E. Kavanaugh
Cover production by Joseph Daigle
Printed in the United States of America by KNI, Inc.

The Institute of Electrical and Electronics Engineers, Inc.

Table of Contents

Session 5 — Interconnection of Networks

Chair: G. Sechi

Session 6 — Parallel Database Systems

Chair: A. Proenca

Open Forum Session II

Chair: E. Luque

Open Forum Session III

Chair: R. Beivide

Session 10 — Parallel Performance, Models, and Simulation

Chair: A. Tyrrell

Program and Organizing Chairs' Message

These are the proceedings of the Fourth Euromicro Workshop on Parallel and Distributed Processing (PDP 96). This series of workshops began in January 1993 and has continued without interruption since then. After Gran Canaria, Malaga, and San Remo, it is now time for Braga and Portugal to host the group of experts in the field of parallel and distributed processing that always meet at the PDP event.

Following the spirit of its predecessors, PDP 96 aims at providing a forum for the following:

- assessment of the current situation of parallel computing
- presentation of recent developments in this area
- identification of major trends for future research

There were 110 papers submitted to the workshop from academic, industrial, and research institutions. These papers were reviewed by a board of highly qualified referees, including some of the most prestigious experts in parallel computing. After the reviewing process, the program committee selected 39 full papers and 32 posters. The issues covered in these works include numerical algorithms, communications, programming tools, parallel languages, and environments.

The organization of such an event requires the cooperation of many people. We would like to thank the authors, reviewers, program committee members, and session chairmen for their contributions. A word of thanks and acknowledgment is also due the Keynote Speakers, Professors Michael Gerndt and Heitor Pina. We also express here our gratitude to all those who spent many hours putting together PDP 96, as well as those who helped with the publicity, financial, local arrangements, proceedings preparation, and registration aspects of the workshop.

Finally, we are grateful to the following organizations for their sponsorship of the workshop:

Universidade do Minho
FCCN
JNICT

Welcome to PDP 96 and Portugal!

Emilio López Zapata
Departamento de Arquitectura de Computadores
Universidad de Malaga
ezapata@atc.ctima.uma.es

Rui Ralha
Departamento de Matematica
Universidade do Minho
r_ralha@math.uminho.pt

Program and Organizing Committee

Program Chair

Emilio López Zapata
Departamento de Arquitectura de Computadores
Universidad de Malaga

Deputy Program Chair

Pablo Pérez Trabado
Departamento de Arquitectura de Computadores
Universidad de Malaga

Program Committee

Jose Cardoso e Cunha
Universidade Nova de Lisboa

Filomena Dias d'Almeida
Faculdade de Engenharia do Porto

Mario Dal Cin
Universität Erlangen-Nürnberg

Fausto Distante
Politecnico di Milano

Jose B.A. Fortes
Purdue University

Antonio Gonzalez
Universidad Politecnica de Catalunya

Paulo Guedes
INESC – Portugal

Peter Kacsuk
KFKI Research Institute – Hungary

Emilio Luque Fadon
Universidad Autonoma de Barcelona

Francisco Moura
Universidade do Minho

Peter Milligan
Queen's University of Belfast

Lakshmi V. Narasimhan
DSTO – Australia

Gabor Nemeth
Budapest Technical University

David Padua
Illinois University

Edwige Pissaloux
Universite Paris XI

Oscar Plata
Universidad de Santiago de Compostela

Alberto J. Proenca
Universidade do Minho

Rui Ralha
Universidade do Minho

Lutz Richter
Universität Zürich

Joel Saltz
University of Maryland

Nello Scarabottolo
Università degli Studi di Modena

Giacomo Sechi
IFCTR-CNR – Italy

Joao Gabriel Silva
Polo II - Universidade

Henk J. Sips
Delft University of Technology

Francisco Tirado
Universidad Complutense de Madrid

Jose María Troya
Universidad de Malaga

Mateo Valero
Universidad Politecnica de Catalunya

Harry Wijshoff
Leiden University

Stephen Winter
University of Westminster

Hans Zima
Universität Wien

Organizing Chair

Rui Ralha
Departamento de Matematica
Universidade do Minho

Deputy Organizing Chair

Maria Antonia Forjaz
Departamento de Matematica
Universidade do Minho

Referees

A.W.G. Duller
Alfredo Bautista
Andreas Krumme
Andy Tyrrell
Antonio González
Antonio M. Vidal
Arjan J.C. van Gemund
Barbara Chapman
Bernd Wender
Carlos Aliagas
Chris Jesshope
Christoph W. Kessler
Dylan Banarse
Edwige Pissaloux
Emilio López Zapata
Emilio Luque
Enric Pastor
Enrique Alba
Enrique Quintana
Ernesto Pimentel
Ernst A. Heinz
Fausto Distante
Filomena Dias d'Almeida
Francisco Arguello
Francisco F. Rivera
Francisco Moura
Francisco Tirado
François Irigoin
G.A. Kohring
Gabor Nemeth
Gerardo Bandera
Giacomo Sechi
Graham Horton
Guy Robinson
Hans Zima
Henk Sips
Javier Bruguera
Joao Gabriel Silva
Jose B.A. Fortes
Jose Cardoso e Cunha
Jose Duato
Jose Ignacio Martin Llorente
Jose M. Cela
Jose María Troya
Jose Miguel Alonso
Jose R. González de Mendívil
Josep Larriba
Juan Carlos Fabero
Juan J. Navarro Guerrero
Juan López
Julio Ortega Lopera
Julio Villalba
Ko-Yang Wang
Lakshmi Narasimhan
Luís Díaz de Cerio
Luís Felipe Romero
Luís Moura e Silva
Lutz Richter
Manuel Costa
Manuel Díaz Rodríguez
Mario Dal Cin
Mateo Valero
Michael Gerndt
Miguel Valero García
Nello Scarabottolo
Nemeth Zsolt
Nicolás Guil
Oscar Plata

Oswaldo Trelles
Pablo Pérez Trabado
Paulo Guedes
Pedro de Miguel
Peter Kacsuk
Peter Milligan
Rafael Asenjo
Ramón Beivide
Rudolf Berrendorf
Rui Ralha
S. Benkner
Stephen Winter
Thomas Fahringer
Thomas Rauber
Tom Lake
Vicente Hernández
Víctor Sánchez Canga
Xavier Martorell
Zina Ben Miled

❖ KEYNOTE SESSION I ❖

"Programming Shared Virtual Memory Multiprocessors"

Speaker

M. Gerndt

Programming Shared Virtual Memory Multiprocessors

Michael Gerndt
Central Institute for Applied Mathematics
Research Centre Jülich (KFA)
D-52425 Jülich, Germany
email: m.gerndt@kfa-juelich.de

Abstract

Highly parallel machines needed to solve compute intensive scientific applications are based on the distribution of physical memory across the compute nodes. The drawback of such systems is the difficult message passing programming model. Therefore, a lot of research in simplifying the programming model is going on. This article investigates the combination of a task parallel programming model implemented on top of a shared virtual address space provided by the operating system of the parallel machine.

1 Programming Models for Massively Parallel Systems

A large number of numerical simulations require highly parallel computing systems for reasonable turnaround times. Current architectures are based on the distribution of memory across the compute nodes to provide the necessary memory bandwidth. The scalability of centralized shared memory systems is limited by the network and the memory bandwidth.

Programming languages and tools for distributed memory systems and thus for the underlying programming models hide to a different extent the two important properties of such systems: parallelism and memory distribution.

Currently three programming models are available for distributed memory multiprocessors: message passing, data parallel, and task parallel.

All models are based on a static process concept: A set of processes is created at the beginning of the application and run until its end. In the message passing model, the user has to provide local code for each process and a process can access only private data. Access to remote data has to be programmed in form of message passing.

In the data parallel programming model, the program is written in a global style with a single thread of control and parallel operations on data structures. Data are accessed in parallel operations via simple variable references. The distribution of data structures determines the distribution of parallel computations.

In the task parallel programming model, the program is also written in a global style. Tasks, for example parallel sections or iterations of parallel loops, are distributed onto the processes. Processes can access shared and private data via variable references.

All three programming models force the user to specify parallelism. Automatic parallelization tools can be used to detect parallelism in sequential codes and express it in the data parallel or the task parallel programming model.

Due to the shared address space in the data parallel and the task parallel programming model, and the support of global parallel code, i.e. vector operations or parallel loops, coding parallel algorithms is much easier than in the message passing model. Of course, in both models the user has to be aware of the physical distribution of memory and has to ensure that computations are done by the processor which has the accessed data in its local memory already.

Mapping computation and data in an optimal way has to be performed manually by the user. The two models provide different concepts for this task: the data distribution concept and the work distribution concept. While data distributions determine explicitly the data layout across the physical memories and implicitly the work distribution via the owner-computes rule, the work distribution is explicitly specified in the task parallel model. The programmer simply has to map computations accessing the same data[1] to the same processor to ensure data locality instead of worrying about the individual distributions of all the data structures of a program.

The most well-known programming language based

[1] Typically, these are computations for the same object in the physical domain of the application, and the work distribution directly results from the domain decomposition selected for parallelization.

on the data parallel model is HPF [HPF 94]. It was designed for *distributed private memory multiprocessors* which do not support a global address space on system level. The HPF compiler has to generate message passing code, i.e. the program is translated into local code executed on each processor and remote references have to be translated into explicit message passing. Both tasks require precise knowledge of the distributions of data structures and an analysis of the access patterns. This requirement lead to a very restrictive design of the language.

With the advent of *distributed shared memory systems (DSM systems)*, the implementation of HPF was simplified. DSM systems support a global address space, either in hardware or in software. Distributed arrays can be mapped into the global address space and no message passing is required to access remote data. But still the compiler has to understand the distribution of data structures to determine the distribution of parallel operations.

Due to the global address space in DSM systems, on such machines the much more flexible task parallel model can be implemented. The work distribution specification in this model eliminates the second implementation problem mentioned above. As stated previously, the model is based on the dynamic exploitation of local memory if data is reused in a processor. This is offered in DSM systems either by big caches in the individual nodes, we call these systems *cache-coherent remote memory access systems (CC-RMA systems)* or by migrating the data on demand into the local memory, as it is done in *shared virtual memory systems (SVM systems)*.

2 Shared Virtual Memory Systems

In CC-RMA systems like the Convex Exemplar, DASH and Flash [LLGW 92], each address has a fixed home memory. Remote addresses can be cached and thus reuse of a remote address in a processor may result in a local access. If a remote address is evicted from the cache, it is written back to its fixed home memory. The concept of caching has at least two important aspects: First, the coherence of copies in the caches of multiple processors has to be guaranteed, and second, the cache has to be large enough to avoid premature eviction of data. The second aspect is particularly important for scientific codes with their big arrays. The cache coherence problem has been studied in a lot of research projects, and several different techniques have been developed. Recently, a cache coherence protocol was standardized in the IEEE SCI-Bus [JLGS 90].

In SVM systems, a virtual address does not have a fixed home memory. If a currently remote address is accessed, a block of memory[2] including this address is transfered into the local memory of the node. Therefore, the next accesses to this address range in the processor are serviced with high probability by the local memory. In addition, an address that is evicted from the processor cache due to capacity problems is always written back to the local memory.

Most SVM systems are implemented in software based on the memory management hardware of the processor. The systems from Kendall Square were the only hardware implementation of SVM. In this article we focus on software SVM systems that can be implemented on top of every distributed private memory architecture.

Similar to CC-RMA systems, SVM systems have to solve the coherence problem for multiple copies of pages in different memories. Due to the lack of a fixed home location, SVM systems have to manage the dynamically changing virtual address mapping of pages.

The basis for all SVM implementations is the dissertation of Kai Li [Li 86]. His implementation called IVY demonstrated the feasibility of this concept [Li 88]. He described the implementation of strong coherence via an invalidation approach[3] and introduced several manager algorithms for the administration of pages.

The manager algorithms vary in their network requirements and the load balance of the overhead. In the *broadcast distributed manager algorithm*, a request for a page is broadcasted to all processors and served by the processor responsible for the page. A single processor keeps all the information and services all the requests in the *centralized manager algorithm*. In the *fixed distributed manager algorithm* the responsibility for pages is cyclically distributed among processors. The approach taken by most SVM implementations is the *dynamic distributed manager algorithm*, which distributes the responsibility dynamically according to the access patterns and thus leads to optimal results for static communication patterns.

Besides network contention and load balance, the memory requirements of the algorithms are very important. This aspect was studied in a recent SVM-implementation for the Intel Paragon, the *Advanced Shared Virtual Memory system (ASVM)* [ZTM 96, Zeis 93]. In the dynamic distributed manager algorithm each processor has to maintain for each page in the global address space some administration infor-

[2] Typically, this is done on page or cache line basis.

[3] This protocols guarantees coherence by allowing multiple read copies but only one copy if a processor writes to a page

mation, which limits the number of nodes in an SVM system. In the ASVM the dynamic distributed manager algorithm is based on a cache for administration information to reduce its memory requirements. If no information is available in the cache, other protocols are applied to obtain the required information.

The strong coherent memory based on the big granularity of pages stresses a problem also known from CC-RMA systems, *false sharing.* Although processors access different locations on a page, the page is migrated between the processors. One way to reduce this problem are weaker coherence protocols also known from CC-RMA systems. The first SVM system supporting a weak coherence protocol is the *KOAN* implementation [BoPr 92] on the iPSC/2. Pages in a weak coherent address range may have multiple write copies. Only when the address range is explicitly made coherent, the write copies are merged to form again a single copy of the page.

A new approach in implementing SVM is *BLIZZARD-E* on the CM-5 [SFL 94]. In addition to the page-based techniques described above, BLIZZARD-E uses the *error correcting code bits (ECC bits)* of the memory to implement much finer-grain coherence units. The ECC bits are modified such that an exception occurs if an address is accessed which does not have appropriate permissions. In addition to the new functionality, the ECC bits still fulfill in most points their original purpose.

3 Programming Languages Supporting the Task Parallel Model

Task parallel programming languages are more general than data parallel programming languages. With respect to scientific applications they offer functional parallelism for implementing multi-disciplinary applications and more flexible work distribution features. As mentioned above, the important feature with respect to SVM systems is the ability to specify the work distribution.

First language constructs for work distribution were implemented in KSR Fortran [KSRF 92]. Parallel loops could be annotated with regular distribution strategies, such as block and cyclic. In addition, the affinity region concept was provided with the following notation:

```
C*KSR* affinity region ( parameter list )
  code including multiple parallel loops
C*KSR* end affinity region
```

The parameter list allows the programmer to specify the distribution of an iteration space onto the processors. The iteration spaces of parallel loops within the affinity region are distributed onto the processors according to that specification. The affinity region has the very interesting property of defining a work distribution in a global way for a specified code region. It neither supports the usage of multiple work distributions in the same code region nor global work distribution across subroutine boundaries, and does not support work distribution for functional parallelism.

Another drawback of KSR Fortran was the underlying fork-join model. In the fork-join model new processes are dynamically created for parallel regions and thus scheduling work onto processes does not guarantee locality. Fortran-S [BKP 93] instead was based on a static set of processes created at the beginning of the application and terminated at its end. It is the programming interface for the KOAN implementation on the iPSC/2 and the successor MYOAN on the Intel Paragon. Fortran-S provides similar work distribution concepts as KSR Fortran but, due to the static process concept, the resulting mapping is much more intuitive to the user.

The limitations of the work distribution concept in both languages triggered the design of a new language called SVM-Fortran [BeGe 95]. SVM-Fortran is one component of the SVM-Fortran programming environment which is based on the ASVM on the Intel Paragon and additionally provides performance analysis and optimization tools[4].

SVM-Fortran borrowed the concepts of processor arrangements and templates from HPF as tools to specify scheduling decisions globally through template distributions. In contrast to the affinity region of KSR, individual templates can be used for different objects in the application domain and scheduling strategies can be defined for the whole program.

Due to the implementation requirements, the template concept in HPF is very restrictive. SVM-Fortran, targeting SVM systems, uses templates in a much more flexible way. Templates can not only be distributed with simple standard strategies, i.e. block and cyclic, but the general-block strategy known from Vienna Fortran and an element-wise irregular distribution can be used. The irregular distribution is very useful for unstructured grid applications.

In addition, templates do not have static distributions by default. Since the distributions are evaluated at runtime, the compiler does not have to know the distribution. Therefore, templates can be redistributed at any time during the computation. Due

[4]More information about the SVM-Fortran project can be accessed via the world wide web: http://www.kfa-juelich.de/zam/PT/ReDec/ProgLangc/SVM.html

```
      SUBROUTINE G(....,T,N,...)
CSVM$ TEMPLATE::  T1(N,N)
CSVM$ PROCESSORS::  P(2,NUMPROC()/2)
CSVM$ DISTRIBUTE (BLOCK,BLOCK) ONTO P::T1

CSVM$ PDO(LOOPS(I,J),
CSVM$*    STRATEGY(ON_HOME(T1(I,J))))
      DO I=1,M
         DO J=1,M
            ...
         ENDDO
      ENDDO
```

Figure 1: SVM-Fortran example program

to the same reasons, templates can be passed to subroutines as arguments and thus, a distribution can be defined globally in the main program and need not be specified in each subroutine separately.

Template distributions determine the work distribution for parallel loops in *predefined scheduling* which assigns loop iterations to processors according to the distribution of the template.

In addition to scheduling loops based on a template's distribution, the template's distribution can also result from scheduling a loop. This is especially useful for codes with unbalanced work load and with irregular accesses. For example, loops can be scheduled with dynamic strategies and the resulting work distribution can be stored after the execution of the parallel loop in form of a template distribution. The same approach can be used for irregular codes to schedule computation onto the same processor when accessing data in the same coherence unit [BeGe 95a]. This *aligned-scheduling* is based on the performance monitoring support of the ASVM explained below.

The example in Figure 1 illustrates the usual usage of the work distribution features of SVM-Fortran. The parallel loop is scheduled via the distribution of template `T1`.

Besides the work distribution features of task parallel languages, several runtime mechanisms proved to be very useful, i.e. prefetching, poststore, page locking, and reduction handling.

Reduction operations are very important in scientific codes. All task parallel languages, KSR Fortran, Fortran-S, and SVM-Fortran provide an additional annotation to parallel loops to identify reduction variables. For example, in SVM-Fortran a parallel loop provides the option `reduction(var-name)` which defines the specified variable to be a reduction variable. The variable can be a scalar or an array and it is the task of the compiler to determine the reduction operation from the loop body. Instead of implementing a reduction variable as a shared variable using appropriate synchronization, each processor performs a local reduction on a private copy and the copies are merged into a global value at the end of the loop.

Page locking is also provided in all mentioned languages. In some codes it is necessary to implement atomic operations on data structures. This can be done via a critical section, but here, a portion of the code is defined to be atomic and thus only one processor can execute the code. This is too restrictive. The synchronization has to ensure that operations on the same data structure are atomic, but the same operation on other data structures can be executed in parallel, e.g. for different array elements. This is implemented by page locking which allows to lock all variables on a page.

SVM-Fortran as well as KSR Fortran provide prefetching of variables to hide memory access latency. While both languages allow to annotate individual references to a variable with a prefetch operation, SVM-Fortran also provides an interesting prefetch library, which monitors the page faults occuring in a parallel loop and stores the page faults in a *prefetch list*. Prefetch lists do have a unique index and a prefetch operation can be performed for a prefetch list everywhere in the program. This concept allows the programmer to provide additional overlap between prefetching and computation. An example for the usage of the SVM-Fortran prefetch library is shown in Figure 2. In the first incarnation of the parallel loop, the prefetch list with index `1` is constructed. During the subsequent executions of this code, the pages are prefetched and the `create_pfl` routines return immediatly since the prefetch list is already defined.

In addition to prefetching of variables also broadcasting a variable in advance to potential readers can help in optimizing applications with a single producer multiple consumer situation. This concept was introduced in KSR Fortran and called *poststore*. The potential readers can either be all processors or the subset of processors that had a read copy of the variable.

4 Performance Analysis

Programming SVM systems is not as simple as one could expect. Still the problem of access latency to remote adresses dominates program development. The user has to carefully tune his application to reduce

```
csvm$ replicated_region
100   call prefetch_pfl(1)
      ...
      call create_pfl_start(1,u,n*n*4)
csvm$ pdo(loops(j))
      do j=2,n-1
         do i=2,n-1
            uhelp(i,j)=..u(i-1,j)+u(i+1,j)
         enddo
      enddo
      call create_pfl_stop(1)
csvm$ replicated_region_end
```

Figure 2: SVM-Fortran prefetching library

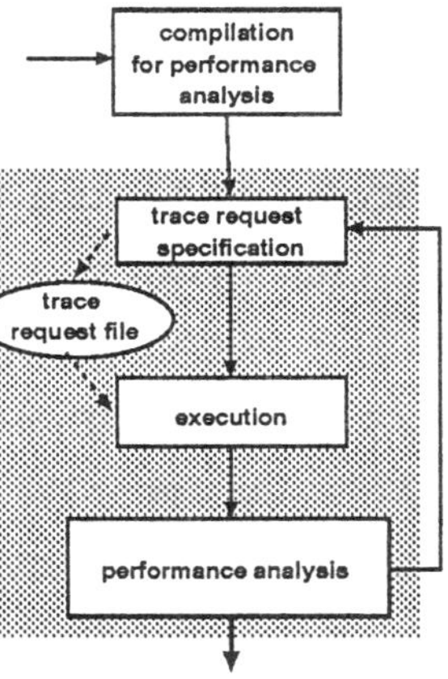

Figure 3: Incremental performance analysis

remote accesses resulting from true and false sharing. There are at least two important advantages compared to programming DM systems with HPF.

First, the program can be ported to the new architecture in an incremental approach. This approach is not applicable for HPF since the memory of a node severely limits the amount of data replication usually occuring for non-optimized code sections.

Second, during code optimization the user need not switch to another programming model. Optimizing HPF codes requires from the user a deep understanding of the generated message passing code while the users motivation for using HPF was to avoid message passing. Tools for optimizing programs for SVM systems can instead be implemented based on the source code of the application.

On SVM systems as well as on other systems standard profiling tools can be used to analyze the execution profile of an application. Usually, this information is not precise enough to understand the performance problems of an application.

In addition to a graphical profiling tool, KSR provided a trace-based performance analysis tool for visualizing start and stop events for program regions, such as parallel loops and parallel sections. Beyond this functionality, programming SVM systems requires a precise understanding of data movement and synchronization overhead. This precise knowledge cannot be obtained from statistics for the whole program printed at the end of a program run. A much finer granularity of information is required with a finer resolution in space as well as time, i.e. selectively gathered for code sections and different incarnations of these sections.

Gathering much finer information selectively for different incarnations is known as *tracing*. This technique is implemented in a number of performance analysis tools for the message passing model [Hond 95]. The tools trace information about message transfers and visualize the information graphically in form of graphical statistics and space-time diagrams. The two major deficiencies of these tools are the lack of source code information and the amount of data gathered at run time.

In the Fortran-S/Koan project, the trace-based performance visualization tool SVMview was developed based on the visualization widgets of the Pablo environment. The tool is based on a trace format which includes start and stop events for program regions and events for individual page faults. Based on the region events, the execution point in the source code can be visualized and based on the page fault information, different visualizations of the data movement are supported. This environment does not include features for reducing the amount of generated data.

In SVM systems tracing individual page faults leads to very big trace files which cannot be generated efficiently and also not be handled efficiently by the performance analysis tools.

In the SVM-Fortran project a modified approach is used to do performance analysis. The tool OPAL (Optimizer and Performance Analyzer) [GKO 95] allows to incrementally analyze the performance of a program. Instead of generating every information in a single run and selecting useful information afterwards in the analysis tool, very specific information can be requested from a program run. The incremental performance analysis concept is outlined in Figure 3.

The SVM-Fortran program is compiled once for performance analysis. The compiler inserts hooks which may call the performance analysis monitor SAM

(SVM-Fortran Application Monitor). Whether the hooks call the monitor is determined by a *trace request file*. In the trace request file the user specifies which information should be traced. Examples for such requests are:

request (∗) *local *.reg_no(*): RPFsum, WPFsum*
request (∗) *local foo.reg_(5): RPFsum(A,B)*
request (∗) *local foo.reg_no(5): RPF(A)*

The first request specifies that in all processors and all regions, i.e. parallel loops, parallel sections, and subroutines, the sums of the read and write page faults have to be traced. Thus, for each incarnation of the section the information including an identification of the section is written to a trace file. This demonstrates two features of the SVM-Fortran trace format: source code support and a hierarchy of trace information. The requested sums allow to determine regions with high page fault rates and, more precisely, the incarnations with high page fault rates.

The second request determines for a specific region in subroutine `foo` the individual page fault sums for specific arrays. This typically leads to the array responsible for a large number of page faults.

The last request generates individual events for each page fault. This precise information is used in the analysis of the program behaviour to determine exactly the array element access responsible for a page fault.

The requested information is generated either directly by SAM or SAM instruments the ASVM to trace information only available to the kernel. For example, region start and stop events are generated by SAM while page fault events are generated by the ASVM. To reduce intrusion, the events are collected in a trace buffer and flushed to files when the trace buffer is filled. SAM checks the fill rate of the buffer at every barrier and every region exit. Since the threshold for the fill rate at a barrier is lower than for a region, the buffer is typically flushed in barriers, disturbing all processes in the same way.

OPAL assists the user in all performance analysis phases on the basis of a source-code-related view. Program units are accessible through a graphical visualization of the call graph. The source code can be folded such that only introductory directives of parallel regions are visible, and comments can be hidden. These techniques allow the user to achieve a good overview of his program code.

OPAL supports a menu-driven specification of trace requests that frees the user from the subtle specification syntax. OPAL extracts the most useful statistical data, but does not store all the trace information in memory. These statistical data can be visualized as annotations to the source code in a separate performance column in the main window. This way of presenting information does provide a good overview of the performance results.

If the user needs more information on individual trace regions, he can mark a trace region and request a list of all trace events of a specific type. For example, OPAL presents all shared variables accessed in the selected trace region, and the user can select specific variables for which he would like to see individual page faults. The tool then extracts from the trace file of an individual processor only the pagefault information for these variables and the selected program region. Due to the source code information in the trace files, all the information can be requested and presented in form of trace regions and program variables, e.g. the faulting address is translated into the array name and the indices of the array element.

Thus, the tool allows to instrument selected regions of the source code to obtain certain information. Starting from statistical data for these program regions also incarnation-specific information can be analyzed for regions of the source code. Of course, sometimes time dependent information can better be visualized in a graphical manner. Therefore, the SVM-Fortran programming environment includes the state-of-the-art visualization tool PARvis (Parallel Visualization Environment). PARvis is mainly used for visualizing performance information of message passing codes. It also provides special displays supporting SVM-Fortran programs, e.g. an extension of the time line display with page movement information. Especially the time line display is extremly useful for obtaining a detailed understanding of the movement of individual pages. The required and provided interface technology is flexible zooming and scrolling of the time line which is implemented only in this tool.

The major drawback of such an environment is that still the user has to navigate through the large number of analysis choices and has to detect bottlenecks by himself. Future tools have to include user guidance as well as the ability to automatically analyze program performance. For frequently occuring performance bugs, the tool should be able to automatically proof the existence of these bugs by incrementally analyzing the program behaviour.

5 Program Optimization

Although the parallelization of applications is significantly simplified with the task parallel programming model on top of SVM systems, programs suffer from several performance bottlenecks. Performance critical areas are data locality, load balance, and synchronization.

Reasons for imperfect data locality are true and false sharing. Required communication among processes due to data dependences is implemented in form of access to remote data. The resulting data migration is a consequence of true data sharing.

Reduction of true sharing can be implemented by elimination of data dependences or by localizing data dependences. In the literature a large number of loop transformations is known for this purpose. In addition to loop transformations, changing the work distribution to localize data dependences is an important technique. Automatic data and work distribution techniques play a central role in this context. In addition to static optimizations, run time optimization can be applied. Based on performance monitoring, the current page distribution can be determined and parallel iterations be executed on the processor owning the data due to previous computations. This aligned scheduling technique was first implemented in the SVM-Fortran project.

If communication cannot be avoided, prefetching and poststore are well known techniques to hide access latencies. As long as the access latency in SVM systems is very high, the prefetch operations have to be executed early before the access to allow enough overlapping of computation and communication. Prefetching can also eliminate double page faults, i.e. a write page fault following immediatly a read page fault for the same location.

Data migration also results from access to the same coherence unit without accessing the same data, i.e. false sharing. This problem is more important with larger coherence units, but it is well-known also in CC-RMA systems based on cache lines. Several techniques have been developed to reduce false sharing in programs. Again, most of the techniques optimize the work distribution, such as loop blocking and aligned scheduling. In addition to these techniques, transformations of the data mapping are applied, such as aligning arrays at page boundaries, array padding, dimension interchanging, and general linear transformations on the array shapes [AAL 95, BGM 95]. For irregular access patterns an element-wise reordering can be applied, such as renumbering techniques for finite element nodes [ToAb 94]. As mentioned at the beginning, also weak coherence protocols can be applied to reduce false sharing.

The second performance bottleneck is load balancing. Optimization of load balance should be done statically. If dynamic techniques, such as self-scheduling are applied, careful consideration of the impact on data locality is necessary. Therefore, more global techniques, such as redistribution of templates are preferable over loop-level techniques since a single page fault resulting from the migration of work will distort the comutation time due to high access latency.

A specific problem of the task parallel programming model is the amount of barrier synchronization. Barriers are executed before and after each parallel operation. At least languages have to provide annotations to eliminate barrier operations but it is preferable to perform barrier reduction automatically in the compiler. The techniques can either be based only on dependence information or can also take distribution information into account [BoBo 95, Tseng 95]. In the latter case, only dependences across processor shall not exist.

Besides elimination of barriers, barriers can also be replaced by pointwise synchronization. This is related very much to HPF compilation techniques, but has not been investigated in the context of task parallel languages. The problem of barrier overhead can of course be significantly reduced by faster barriers, as they are implemented in hardware on the Cray T3D system.

6 Summary

Shared virtual memory systems, either implemented in software or in hardware, are special distributed shared memory systems. The important characteristic is the migration of data among the physical memories, extending the concept of caching beyond the relatively small processor and secondary caches.

Programming languages based on the task parallel programming model, which is more general than the data parallel model, can be implemented in a straightforward way. Nevertheless, due to the physical distribution of memory, careful programming is necessary to obtain efficient codes. This programming has to be supported by adequate high-level programming tools for performance analysis and program optimization. Without these tools, which in our opinion are easier to build compared to similar tools for HPF, programming DSM systems is not much simpler than message passing programming. But, this is true for all high-level programming models trying to hide intricate details of parallel architectures.

References

[AAL 95] J.M. Anderson, S.P. Amarasinghe, M.S. Lam, *Data and Computation Transformations for Multiprocessors*, Proceedings of Fifth ACM SIG-

PLAN Symposium on Principles and Practice of Parallel Programming (PPoPP '95), Santa Barbara, pp. 134-143, 1995

[BGM 95] F. Bodin, E.D. Granston, T. Montaut, *Page-level Affinity Scheduling for Eliminating False Sharing*, Proceedings Fifth Workshop on Compilers for Parallel Computers, Malaga, pp. 175-186, 1995

[BKP 93] F. Bodin, L. Kervella, T. Priol, *Fortran-S: A Fortran Interface for Shared Virtual Memory Architectures*, Proceedings of Supercomputing 93, Portland, pp. 274-283, November 1993

[BeGe 95] R. Berrendorf, M. Gerndt, *SVM-Fortran Reference Manual Version 1.4*, Internal Report KFA-ZAM-IB-9510, Central Institute for Applied Mathematics, Research Centre Jülich, 1995

[BeGe 95a] R. Berrendorf, M. Gerndt, *Compiling Data Parallel Languages for Shared Virtual Memory Systems*, Internal Report KFA-ZAM-IB-9517, Central Institute for Applied Mathematics, Research Centre Jülich, 1995

[BoBo 95] M. O'Boyle, F. Bodin, *Compiler Reduction of Synchronization in Shared Virtual Memory Systems*, Proceedings ICS 95, Barcelona, pp. 318-327, 1995

[BoPr 92] F. Bodin, T. Priol, *Overview of the KOAN Programming Environment for the iPSC/2 and Performance Evaluation of the BECAUSE Test Program 2.5.1*, Proc. of BECAUSE European Workshop, Sophia-Antipolis, Oct. 1992

[GKO 95] M. Gerndt, A. Krumme, S. Özmen, *Performance Analysis for SVM-Fortran with OPAL*, submitted for publication to International Conference on Parallel and Distributed Processing Techniques and Applications (PDPTA'95), Georgia, 1995

[HPF 94] HPFF, *High Performance Fortran Language Specification, Version 1.1, November 1994*, Rice University, Houston, Texas, November 1994

[Hond 95] A. Hondroudakis, *Performance Analysis Tools for Parallel Programs*, Edingburgh Parallel Computing Centre, The University of Edingburgh, 1995

[JLGS 90] D.V. James, A.T. Laundrie, S. Gjessing, G.S. Sohi, *Distributed-Directory Scheme: Scalable Coherent Interface*, IEEE Computer, Vol. 23, No. 6, pp. 74-77, 1990

[KSRF 92] Kendall Square Reserach Corporation, *KSR Fortran Programming Manual*, Kendall Square Research, 1992

[LLGW 92] D. Lenoski, J. Laudon, K. Gharachorloo, W. Weber, A. Gupta, J. Hennessy, M. Horowitz, M. Lam, *The Standford Dash Multiprocessor*, IEEE Computer, pp. 63-79, March 1992

[Li 86] K. Li, *Shared Virtual Memory on Loosely Coupled Multiprocessors*, Ph.D. Dissertation, Yale University 1986, Technical Report YALEU/DCS/RR-492

[Li 88] K. Li, *IVY: A Shared Virtual Memory System for Parallel Computing*, ICPP 1988, Vol II, pp. 94-101, 1988

[SFL 94] I. Schoinas, B. Falsafi, A.R. Lebeck, S.K. Reinhardr, J.R. Larus, D.A. Wood, *Fine-grain Access Control for Distributed Shared Memory*, Proceedings ASPLOS-VI, ACM Operating Systems Review, 28(5), pp. 297-306, December 1994

[ToAb 94] K.A. Tomko, S.G. Abraham, *Data and Program Restructuring of Irregular Applications for Cache-Coherent Multiprocessors*, Proceedings ICS94, Manchester, pp. 214-225, 1994

[Tseng 95] C.-W. Tseng, *Compiler Optimizations for Eliminating Barrier Synchronization*, Proceedings PPOPP'95, ACM SIGPLAN Notices, Vol. 30, No. 8, pp. 144-155, August 1995

[ZTM 96] S. Zeisset, S. Tritscher, M. Mairandres, *A New Approach to Distributed Memory Management in the Mach Microkernel*, to appear in: Proceedings of the USENIX 1996 Technical Conference, San Diego, California, January 1996

[Zeis 93] S. Zeisset, *Evaluation and Enhancement of the Paragon Multiprocessor's Shared Virtual Memory System*, Diploma Thesis, Technische Universität München, 1993

❖ SESSION 1 ❖

Numerical Algorithms I

Chair

F. Tirado

Parallel Simulation of a Multi-Dimensional Computational Fluid Dynamics Problem

P. W. Grant, M. F. Webster and X. Zhang
Department of Computer Science
University of Wales, Swansea
Swansea SA2 8PP, UK

Abstract

The simulation of computational fluid dynamics problems in two and more dimensions involves computations of multiple degrees of freedom, such as the components of velocity, which are an obvious source of parallelism. Further to our previous investigation in this area, we report on our current experiences in extracting such parallelism on a distributed network platform. A finite element method for simulating incompressible viscous flows is parallelised using a domain decomposition approach. Various issues that arise in this implementation are discussed in the light of our experimental results.

1 Introduction

A finite element method has been adopted to transform the solution of the generalised incompressible Navier-Stokes equations [1] into a time-stepping solution process on a set of linear equation systems. This approach may be used to model the flow of Newtonian and non-Newtonian fluids. The finite element method subdivides and discretises the problem domain into a mesh of elements, taken here in triangular form. A nodal solution vector is then obtained with components at the mesh nodes; interpolation on the shape functions provides the solution at other locations. For velocity interpolation, the interpolation function is quadratic with degrees of freedom defined at six nodes, three vertex nodes and three mid-side nodes. Pressure interpolation is of a linear form defined on the three vertex nodes. This provides piecewise continuous interpolation to the solution on the domain and a Galerkin weighted residual method completes the spatial discretisation.

Finite element algorithms are inherently suitable for exploiting parallelism as data dependency is localised within the elements of the mesh. As a special case, a problem domain can be partitioned into subregions for a distributed parallel solution, requiring only interprocessor communication on subdomain boundaries. Our previous experience reported in [2] has shown that this parallelisation approach can be extremely effective for such problems. In this paper, we investigate yet another alternative source of parallelism over components of multiple vectors. Since computations over the various solution vector components are often identical, this type of parallelism can be easily derived with little program modification. We report an initial implementation of this parallelisation approach superimposed on the domain partition approach and comment on how further improvement can be achieved.

2 A Taylor-Galerkin/pressure-correction finite element scheme

In the case of incompressible flows, the Navier-Stokes equations can be discretised by a transient semi-implicit Taylor-Galerkin/pressure-correction (TGPC) finite element scheme [3, 4, 5] of the form:

$$(\frac{2\rho\mathbf{M}}{\Delta t}+\frac{\mathbf{S}_\mu}{2})(U^{(n+\frac{1}{2})}-U^{(n)})=\frac{F^{(n)}+F^{(n+\frac{1}{2})}}{2}+\{\mathbf{L}^TP-[\mathbf{S}_\mu+\rho\mathbf{N}(U)]U\}^{(n)} \quad (1)$$

$$(\frac{\rho\mathbf{M}}{\Delta t}+\frac{\mathbf{S}_\mu}{2})(U^{(*)}-U^{(n)})=\frac{F^{(n)}+F^{(n+1)}}{2}+\{\mathbf{L}^TP-\mathbf{S}_\mu U\}^{(n)}-[\rho\mathbf{N}(U)U]^{(n+\frac{1}{2})} \quad (2)$$

$$\frac{\Delta t\mathbf{K}}{2\rho}(P^{(n+1)}-P^{(n)})=\mathbf{L}U^{(*)} \quad (3)$$

$$\frac{2\rho\mathbf{M}}{\Delta t}(U^{(n+1)}-U^{(*)})=\mathbf{L}^T(P^{(n+1)}-P^{(n)}) \quad (4)$$

where $\mathbf{M}$ is a constant mass matrix; μ is the viscosity of the fluid; $\mathbf{S}_\mu$ is a diffusion matrix; $\mathbf{K}$ is a pressure difference stiffness matrix; $\mathbf{N}(N)$ is a convection matrix; $\mathbf{L}$ is a divergence/pressure gradient matrix; F is a force function vector due to boundary conditions; U is the velocity solution vectors and P is the pressure solution vector. The entries of $\mathbf{N}(U)$, $\mathbf{N}_{ij}(U)$, appearing in the right-hand-sides of equations (1) and (2) takes the form

$$\mathbf{N}_{ij}(U) = \int_\Omega \phi_i(\phi_l U_k^l \frac{\partial \phi_j}{\partial x_k}) r d\Omega \quad (5)$$

where x_1 and x_2 indicate radial and axial axes, r and z respectively; ϕ is the interpolation function; $(U_1, U_2) = U$ and the double index l indicates an implied summation. The tensorial entries of matrix $\mathbf{S}_\mu$, $(\mathbf{S}_\mu)_{ij}$, appearing in both the right-hand-sides and

1066-6192/96 $5.00 © 1996 IEEE
Proceedings of PDP '96

left-hand-sides of equations (1) and (2) takes the form

$$(\mathbf{S}_\mu)_{ij} = [S_{lm}]_{ij}, \quad l,m = 1,2 \tag{6}$$

$$(S_{11})_{ij} = \int_\Omega \mu(2\frac{\delta\phi_i}{\partial r}\frac{\partial\phi_j}{\partial r} + \frac{\partial\phi_i}{\partial z}\frac{\partial\phi_j}{\partial z} + 2\frac{\phi_i\phi_j}{r^2})rd\Omega \tag{7}$$

$$(S_{12})_{ij} = \int_\Omega \mu(\frac{\partial\phi_i}{\partial z}\frac{\partial\phi_j}{\partial r})rd\Omega \tag{8}$$

$$(S_{21})_{ij} = (S_{12})_{ji} \tag{9}$$

$$(S_{22})_{ij} = \int_\Omega \mu(\frac{\partial\phi_i}{\partial r}\frac{\partial\phi_j}{\partial r} + 2\frac{\partial\phi_i}{\partial z}\frac{\partial\phi_j}{\partial z})rd\Omega \tag{10}$$

For the simulation of the fluid flows under investigation, their evaluation involves numerical integration; the numerical integration loops over seven Gauss integration points per element and is costly but unavoidable. In equations (1), (2) and (4), the right-hand-sides (RHSs) and solutions are multiple vectors, corresponding to individual velocity components of the continuous solution. The parallel evaluation of these vectors forms the theme of this paper. The RHS and solution in (3) are, however, single vectors representing the scalar pressure solution component. The order of computation on each time step is to start with equations (1) and (2) to produce $U^{(*)}$ from $(U^{(n)}, P^{(n)})$, then equation (3) computes $P^{(n+1)}$ and finally equation (4) computes $U^{(n+1)}$. Matrices $\mathbf{M}$, $\mathbf{S}_\mu$ and $\mathbf{K}$ are sparse, *symmetric*, and *positive definite* under appropriate imposed boundary conditions.

A preconditioned version of a Jacobi iterative method [6], which does not require explicit assembly of system matrices, is used for the solution of equations (1), (2) and (4) which are all of the same type. The relevant RHSs are assembled once and stored for use in the following Jacobi iteration sweeps. This method has been shown to be well-suited to the solution of such augmented mass matrix equations, due to their favourable conditioning, requiring few iterations [7]. The method is also highly parallelisable; each vector component of the nodal solution is completely independent of the remainder within a single Jacobi iteration sweep. The matrix $\mathbf{K}$ is a constant matrix of relatively small proportions compared with the overall system size. Its attributes recommend a direct method of solution for equation (3), such as a Choleski method [8].

The main computation involved in the solution of equations (1)–(4) comprises

1. assembly of RHS vectors of equations (1), (2) and (4) accumulating local contributions,
2. implicit assembly of system matrices $\mathbf{M}$ and $\mathbf{S}_\mu$,
3. the Jacobi iteration,
4. assembly of RHS vector (3),
5. assembly and factorisation of matrix $\mathbf{K}$, and
6. the Choleski solution.

Operations 1–3 are performed in the solution of equations (1), (2) and (4), and operations 4–6 relate only to the solution of equation (3). The solution of equation (3) is insignificant in the overall computation and not a major consideration in this paper. Further details however can be found in [2]. In the following sections, the parallelisation of operations 1–3 are discussed in some detail.

3 A distributed parallel implementation

3.1 Domain decomposition approach

The fundamental parallelism in this implementation is realized by decomposing the finite element mesh into a number of connected subregions. Arbitrary distribution of computation does not normally result in a satisfactory parallel performance on distributed platforms as communication among processors is unlikely to be minimised. Assuming the computations concerned are mainly element based, a simple and sensible way to distribute workload is to partition spatial problem domains into subblocks and assign element computations within a connected region to the same processor. Such a distribution will produce some boundary nodes which are shared by several processors, requiring some interprocessor communication to accumulate contributions from different subblocks on these nodes. There are many techniques which partition spatial domains, the one used here is a Recursive Spectral Bisection (RSB) method [9]. RSB attempts to minimise the total length of subblock boundaries and therefore reduces interprocessor communication.

Each RHS vector entry associates with a specific mesh node. It is formed by accumulating contributions from elements to which the corresponding node is attached. The assembly of RHSs can be performed in a element-wise fashion; each time the process computes a small contribution vector of a particular element, and accumulates corresponding entries into a global vector. It is not difficult to appreciate that the domain decomposition approach can be easily incorporated into the assembly of RHSs.

The main computations in a Jacobi iteration are system matrix and vector multiplications. As the system matrices $\mathbf{M}$ and $\mathbf{S}_\mu$ can be viewed as an accumulation of element contribution matrices, these multiplications can actually be performed as the summation of multiplications of element matrices and vectors. This permits the possibility of convoluting the multiplications with the assembly of matrices $\mathbf{M}$ and $\mathbf{S}_\mu$ (hence avoiding explicit assembly of $\mathbf{M}$ and $\mathbf{S}_\mu$ and providing a significant saving in storage) and executing the multiplications in parallel, in the same manner as performed for the assembly process.

Some computations in operation 1–3 are however node oriented. These include vector addition and subtraction, and diagonal matrix and vector multiplication. They are distributed according to whichever subdomain a node belongs to. On boundary nodes, these operations are simply duplicated.

3.2 Parallelism over multiple degrees of freedom

To enable parallelism over multiple degrees of freedom, we assign statically one processor to each degree of freedom (this approach we refer to as a DOF approach below). This is a hybrid approach – imposed upon the domain decomposition approach in a direct fashion on a single domain process. As the assembly and solution of equation (3) only requires one processor per subdomain, the remaining processors lie idle. Under present circumstances this does not lead to a significant waste of resource as the duration is comparatively short.

Extra interprocessor communication is also necessary. The first step for the solution of our equations is the assembly of RHSs. The fact that each RHS component in equations (1)–(4) depends on all solution components of its previous fractional step implies that the solution computed by a particular processor should generally be broadcast within its subdomain (including that on boundary nodes). Notice that each $(\mathbf{S}_\mu)_{ij}$ itself is a 2×2 matrix. This implies that terms appearing in equations (1) and (2) are dependent on all degrees of freedom of (ΔU) through products with components of $\mathbf{S}_\mu$. Therefore similar broadcasts are introduced at the beginning of each Jacobi sweep, when equations (1) and (2) are solved.

3.3 Interprocessor communication

There are two types of interprocessor communication involved in the context of this paper. The first is associated with the accumulation of boundary contributions, the second with the broadcast of individual components of multiple vectors within a subdomain.

In an unstructured domain mesh, the connectivity of boundary nodes is unbounded. It is therefore possible for a boundary node to be shared by a large number of subdomains. Accumulating boundary contributions from all subdomains requires the knowledge of boundary node global connectivity and corresponding interprocessor communication. It is appropriate to resort to an extra processor to handle the accumulation of all boundary contributions and as the total number of boundary nodes is unlikely to be large, one boundary processor should be sufficient. This approach has the following two advantages over distributing the task among subdomain processors. Firstly, each subdomain processor needs only to communicate with the boundary processor reducing the number of its communication connections to a minimum. On a broadcasting network, which is the case here, establishing a physical network connection is likely to be expensive. Therefore reduction of communication connection should take a high priority. Secondly, a centralised communication configuration is much easier to program and manage than a distributed one. To make this process more efficient, the computation on boundary elements is performed prior to that on internal elements so that boundary contributions can be delivered to the boundary processor and the accumulated results can be returned in parallel with the evaluation on elements internal to the subdomain. The communication cost can be hidden provided there are sufficient internal elements.

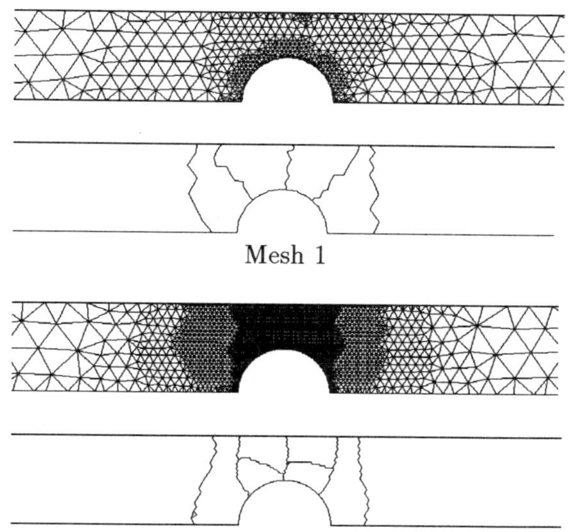

Figure 1: Two test meshes and their associated subdomains

As the number of degrees of freedom is never large, we allow direct dialogue between each pair of processors within a subdomain. Unfortunately, in this application, it is difficult to perform the second type of communication in parallel with numerical computation. Since the overall message length of all such communications is proportional to the size of the problem domain, for large test problems, this type of communications may incur a measurable communication cost.

4 Experimental results and concluding remarks

A test platform of a network of nineteen diskless Sun Sparc-1 workstations has been used, employing the PVM3 [10] library for network message passing. These workstations run SunOS (UNIX) operating system, and are interconnected by an Ethernet network.

Simulations for steady constant viscosity flow past a rigid sphere in a tube have been conducted, under an axisymmetric frame of reference using this generalised Newtonian scheme. Two processors are assigned to each subdomain when the DOF approach is adopted. Two meshes of 1535 elements (`Mesh 1`) and 5764 elements (`Mesh 2`) have been tested. In the vicinity of the sphere, the central portions of these meshes and their associated subdomain partitions (indicated by plotting all edges whose both end nodes are on a boundary) generated by the RSB algorithm, are displayed in Figure 1. One of the nineteen workstations is used as a boundary processor. For experiments adopting the DOF approach, two processors are employed for each subdomain, in other cases only one processor is used.

First of all, it has been found that the DOF approach does not introduce any significant influence on the effectiveness of the domain decomposition approach. In other words, a DOF test run with n (≤ 9) subdomain partitions is roughly n times as fast as that without domain partitioning. Tests also reveal that speedup due to the DOF approach is mesh size sensitive, but insensitive to the number of subdomains. For `Mesh 1` the improvement is about 10% and for `Mesh 2` it is only 1%. These figures are very low compared with the ideal performance of 100%. A careful analysis of the program has revealed the time consuming evaluations of equations (5) and (6) are not parallelisable by the DOF approach, because the major part of the computation involved is necessary for each degree of freedom (although this is not strictly true for equation (6), the amount of possible saving is not seen to be significant). In this implementation, the computation is actually duplicated on each processor, and this is believed to be the principal reason for the inefficiency. A possible solution to this difficulty is to parallelise instead through the quadrature over the seven point Gauss rule employed in all domain integral evaluation. On a networked platform, this can be implemented by employing seven processors, each being responsible for a particular Gauss point over all elements. Since the total amount of extra communication introduced by the DOF approach between the processors associated with each individual degree of freedom is proportional to the size of meshes, `Mesh 2` results in more data traffic. It is this that we link with the further performance degradation (10% to 1%).

In conclusion, this hybrid DOF approach has not been found an effective strategy for this particular application on networked computers, although the approach extracts coarse grained parallelism. The fundamental reason is that this application introduces extra network communication due to the fact that some terms in equations (1)–(4) are dependent on all degrees of a solution vector at a previous stage. Provided each degree of freedom is distributed to a different processor, the total amount of data involved in such communication within a time step is of $O(m^2n)$ (m being the total number of degrees of freedom and n being the total number of mesh nodes), irrespective of how many subdomains the original problem domain has been partitioned into. Transmitting this amount of data on computer clusters connected by broadcasting networks does not make the approach easily scalable to problems with larger n or m values. It is obvious that, to achieve maximal speedup of the DOF approach alone, the optimal number of processors, equivalent to the number of degrees of freedom, is bounded by m. Nevertheless, this does not necessary prevent us from extracting other scalable parallelism as an additional layer superimposed upon the DOF approach. In fact, our results for the hybrid DOF approach show that extra processors can be utilised to effectively realise a DOF domain decomposition approach. Also, there are many engineering circumstances which involve the simulation of large-scale Newtonian flows. For the simulation of such flows, their corresponding diffusion matrix may be represented in block diagonal form, which in turn avoids the need for data communication at the beginning of each Jacobi sweep. In these cases, the DOF approach would reflect better performance characteristics. In contrast on a shared-memory platform, such data dependency does not present a significant problem.

Acknowledgements

This research has been supported by a grant from the UK EPSRC (GR/J12321).

References

[1] R. Temam. *Navier-Stokes Equations: Theory and Numerical Analysis*. North-Holland Publishing Company, Amsterdam, 1977.

[2] P.W. Grant, M.F. Webster, and X. Zhang. Solving computational fluid dynamics problems on unstructured grids with distributed parallel processing. In A. Ferreira and J. Rolim, editors, *Parallel Algorithms for Irregularly Structured Problems*, volume 980 of *Lecture Notes in Computer Science*, pages 187 – 197, Lyon, France, September 1995. Springer-Verlag. (Tech. Report CSR 8-95, Dept. of Computer Science, University of Wales, Swansea).

[3] P. Townsend and M.F. Webster. An algorithm for the three-dimensional transient simulation of non-Newtonian fluid flows. In G.N. Pande and J. Middleton, editors, *Proc. Int. Conf. Num. Meth. Eng.: Theory and Applications*, volume II, pages T12/1–11, Swansea, 1987. NUMETA, Nijhoff, Dordrecht.

[4] D.M. Hawken, H.R. Tamaddon-Jahromi, P. Townsend, and M.F. Webster. A Taylor-Galerkin-based algorithm for viscous incompressible flow. *Int. J. Num. Meth. Fluids*, 10:327–351, 1990.

[5] D. Ding, P. Townsend, and M.F. Webster. Computer modelling of transient thermal flows of non-Newtonian fluids. *J. Non-Newtonian Fluid Mechanics*, 47:239–265, 1993.

[6] L.A. Hageman and D.M. Young. *Applied Iterative Methods*. Academic Press, London, 1981.

[7] D. Ding, P. Townsend, and M.F. Webster. Iterative solutions of Taylor-Galerkin augmented mass matrix equations. *Int. J. Num. Meth. Eng.*, 35:241–253, 1992.

[8] J.H. Wilkinson and C. Reinsch. *Handbook for Automatic Computation, Linear Algebra*, volume II. Springer-Verlag, New York, 1971.

[9] H.D. Simon. Partitioning of unstructured problems for parallel processing. *Computer Systems in Engineering*, 2:135–148, 1991.

[10] A. Geist, A. Beguelin, J. Dongarra, W. Jiang, R. Manchek, and V. Sundream. PVM3 user's guide and reference manual. Technical report, Oak Ridge National Laboratory, 1993.

Computing the Singular Values of the Product of two Matrices in Distributed Memory Multiprocessors

Manuel Mollar

Dpto. de Informática
Univ. Jaume I
Aptdo. 242, 12071-Castellón (SPAIN)

Vicente Hernández

Dpto. de S. Inf. y Computación
Univ. Politécnica de Valencia
Aptdo. 22012, 46071-Valencia (SPAIN)

Abstract

A parallel algorithm for computing the singular values of the product of two matrices A and B has been developed. The algorithm is based on the Kogbetliantz method. We use a simple and efficient data distribution, adequate for multicomputers. The application of the rotations is done in a simple order that shows the same convergence rate as the sequential and the odd - even orderings. Also, this convergence is tested in a reliable manner, very easy to implement. On every step of the computation, only a row of A and a column of B are transferred between adjacent processors, and a total interchange of rotation parameters is done in blocks of $2n/p$ elements. The parallel algorithm has been implemented on a linear ring of T805 transputers using Parallel C, and on a *Meiko* multicomputer using PVM3, obtaining high efficiencies in both cases.

Keywords: Control theory, product singular value decomposition, Kogbetliantz algorithm, plane rotations, Parallel C, PVM, transputer, distributed memory multiprocessors.

1 Introduction

This paper describes a parallel algorithm for computing the singular values of the product of two matrices and its implementation on two different multicomputers. The product singular value decomposition (PSVD) is defined as follows. For any given matrices, $A \in \Re^{m\times n}, B \in \Re^{n\times p}$, there exist two matrices $U \in \Re^{m\times n}$ and $V \in \Re^{n\times p}$ with orthogonal columns, an orthogonal matrix $Q \in \Re^{n\times n}$ and a full rank upper triangular matrix $R \in \Re^{n\times n}$, such that

$$A = U\Sigma_A RQ^T \ , \quad B = QR^{-1}\Sigma_B V^T \tag{1}$$

with

$$\Sigma_A = \mathrm{diag}(\alpha_1,\ldots,\alpha_n),\ \Sigma_B = \mathrm{diag}(\beta_1,\ldots,\beta_n). \tag{2}$$

The n pairs (α_i,β_i) are called the product singular values of (A,B) and the singular values of the product AB are the products $\alpha_i\beta_i$, for $i = 1,\ldots,n$.

The PSVD was introduced by Fernando and Hammarling [5] as a new generalization of the SVD, based on the product AB^T. It complements the generalized singular value decomposition (GSVD) introduced by Van Loan [15] and Paige and Sanders [13], now called quotient-SVD (QSVD), as proposed in [3]. The parallel computation of the GSVD has been treated in [1, 2]. A complete study of the properties of the PSVD can be found in [4].

In this paper we present a parallel algorithm to compute the product singular values of (A,B), and we start by considering A and B in upper triangular form. Such a problem arises from the computation of Balanced Realizations of Control Linear Systems using the method proposed by Laub et al. [9]. In general, if we start from a dense matrix, it can be transformed to triangular form using the QR decomposition. Parallel implementations on distributed memory architectures of this decomposition can be found in [1], where the topological considerations and the distribution of data among the processors are similar to those exposed here.

The rest of this paper is organized as follows. Section 2 describes the basic Kogbetliantz algorithm to compute the PSVD. Section 3 discusses the parallel algorithm, and in sections 4 and 5 the particular considerations for two implementations are described, one with point to point communications using Parallel C, and the other using PVM3. Section 6 shows the performance and efficiency of the results obtained in both implementations.

1066-6192/96 $5.00 © 1996 IEEE
Proceedings of PDP '96

2 Basic Algorithm

Considering $A, B \in \Re^{n\times n}$ upper triangular matrices, we want to compute the decomposition $U^TAQ = \Sigma_A R$, $Q^TBV = R^{-1}\Sigma_B$, described in the Introduction. The algorithm is an implicit Kogbetliantz method [5, 8]. If $A_{ij} = A\begin{pmatrix} i,j \\ i,j \end{pmatrix}$, two matrix sequences $\{A_k\}$ and $\{B_k\}$ are generated from the expressions:

$$\begin{aligned} A_{k+1} &= J(\theta,i,j)^T A_k L(\varphi,i,j) \\ B_{k+1} &= L(\varphi,i,j)^T B_k K(\phi,i,j), \end{aligned} \tag{3}$$

where J and K are plane rotations, chosen such that the matrix $C_{ij} = A_{ij}B_{ij}$ is diagonal.

First, the updates J^TA_k and B_kK destroy the triangularity of the matrices. In order to perform the next step, the triangularity is returned by computing the plane rotation L.

Step by step, the product A_kB_k goes to the diagonal form, and

$$A_k \to \Sigma_A R \quad \text{and} \quad B_k \to R^{-1}\Sigma_B \quad \text{as} \quad k\to\infty.$$

In [2] Luk suggests that for Kogbetliantz algorithms it is enough to set $j = i+1$, $i = 1,\dots,n-1$ to obtain the final diagonal form. Considering that the method only works with the elements $c_{i,i+1}$ and produces the complete diagonalization of C, testing only these elements will be enough to determine the convergence.

To compute J and K, two steps are necessary ([10]). Suppose that $C_{ij} = \begin{pmatrix} w & x \\ 0 & z \end{pmatrix}$. We find a rotation $S(\psi)$ that converts the matrix to the symmetric form:

$$S(\psi)\begin{pmatrix} w & x \\ 0 & z \end{pmatrix} = \begin{pmatrix} p & q \\ q & r \end{pmatrix}. \tag{4}$$

To do this, if $x = 0$ we take $\psi = 0$, otherwise we compute:

$$\rho = \frac{w+z}{x} \equiv \cot\psi, \quad \sin\psi = \frac{\text{sign}(\rho)}{\sqrt{1+\rho^2}}, \quad \cos\psi = \rho\sin\psi. \tag{5}$$

Then we diagonalize the symmetric matrix:

$$K(\phi)^T\begin{pmatrix} p & q \\ q & r \end{pmatrix}K(\phi) = \begin{pmatrix} d_1 & 0 \\ 0 & d_2 \end{pmatrix}.$$

If $q = 0$ then $\phi = \frac{\pi}{2}$. Otherwise ϕ can be obtained from

$$\tan\phi = \frac{\text{sign}\rho}{|\rho| + \sqrt{1+\rho^2}}, \tag{6}$$

where $\rho = \cot 2\phi = \frac{r-p}{2q}$.

This expression gives the largest angle, as we want to perform "outer rotations". The rotation J is given by $J^T = K^TS^T$. The sequential algorithm follows.

Algorithm 1
repeat
  conv= true
  for $i = 1,\dots,n-1$ **do**
    if $C_{ij} \leftarrow A_{ij}B_{ij}$ is not diagonal **then**
      conv= false
      compute $J(\theta,i,j)$ and $K(\phi,i,j)$ using C_{ij}
      $A \leftarrow J(\theta,i,j)^TA$ and $B \leftarrow BK(\phi,i,j)$
      compute $L(\psi,i,j)$ using A or B
      $A \leftarrow AL(\psi,i,j)$ and $B \leftarrow L(\psi,i,j)^TB$
until *conv* **or** the maximum number of iterations is reached.

The experimental results show that the number of iterations is function of n, and usually lower than $5n$ for a reasonable precision.

3 Parallel Algorithm

The previous algorithm is inherently sequential. For a given i, to compute the rotation $J(\theta,i,i+1)$ the elements $a_{i,i}$, $a_{i,i+1}$ and $a_{i+1,i+1}$ are employed, and then they are updated by the application of the rotation. The next step also implies the element $a_{i+1,i+1}$ to compute $J(\theta,i+1,i+2)$, so the parallelism is inhibited. The difficulty is centered in the order of the application of the rotations.

To compute the rotation $J(\theta,i+2,i+3)$, the implied elements are $a_{i+2,i+2}$, $a_{i+2,i+3}$ and $a_{i+3,i+3}$, and when updating, the updated rows of A are $i+2$ and $i+3$. Thus, this computation does not interfere with the computation of $J(\theta,i,i+1)$ and the corresponding updating, that involves rows i and $i+1$ of A.

In [2, 11] Luk et al. present a new ordering based on this property, called the *odd-even* ordering. Basically the rotations $J(\theta,i,i+1)$ for odd i can be computed and performed simultaneously. Then, on the next step, the "even" rotations are computed and applied. Also the rotations J and K can be managed at the same time, as they affect different matrices. The scheme of the algorithm is:

Algorithm 2
repeat
  for $i = 1, 3, \ldots, (i \text{ odd})$ **do**
    compute $J(\theta, i, j)$ and $K(\phi, i, j)$
    $A \leftarrow J(\theta, i, j)^T A$ and $B \leftarrow BK(\phi, i, j)$
  for $i = 1, 3, \ldots, (i \text{ odd})$ **do**
    compute $L(\psi, i, j)$
    $A \leftarrow AL(\psi, i, j)$ and $B \leftarrow L(\psi, i, j)^T B$
  for $i = 2, 4, \ldots, (i \text{ even})$ **do**
    ⋮
until *conv* **or** the maximum number of iterations is reached.

The algorithm presented in this paper is a coarse grain algorithm, initially designed for a ring of processors. It is strongly related with the data distribution that we introduce now. For simplicity, we assume that n is a multiple of the number of processors p (otherwise zero rows can be added). Using the triangular structure of A and B, they can be stored in a single array:

$$M = \begin{pmatrix} B^T & \begin{matrix} 0 & 0 & & & \\ & 0 & 0 & & \\ & & \ddots & \ddots & \\ & & & 0 & 0 \end{matrix} & A \end{pmatrix}.$$

This array is distributed by blocks of consecutive rows. On p processors, processor P_i holds rows with index $\frac{n}{p} \times i + j$, with $j = 1, \ldots, \frac{n}{p} - 1$. For example, for 6 rows and 2 processors:

$$\begin{array}{c} \\ \\ \text{proc 0} \\ \hline \text{proc 1} \\ \\ \\ \end{array} \left(\begin{array}{ccccccccc} b_{11} & 0 & 0 & a_{11} & a_{12} & a_{13} & a_{14} & a_{15} & a_{16} \\ b_{12} & b_{22} & 0 & 0 & a_{22} & a_{23} & a_{24} & a_{25} & a_{26} \\ b_{13} & b_{23} & b_{33} & 0 & 0 & a_{33} & a_{34} & a_{35} & a_{36} \\ \hline b_{14} & b_{24} & b_{34} & b_{44} & 0 & 0 & a_{44} & a_{45} & a_{46} \\ b_{15} & b_{25} & b_{35} & b_{45} & b_{55} & 0 & 0 & a_{55} & a_{56} \\ b_{16} & b_{26} & b_{36} & b_{46} & b_{56} & b_{66} & 0 & 0 & a_{66} \end{array}\right).$$

The scheme offers an optimal balance of storage and the most efficient physical memory use, and will produce a quasi-optimal balance of computation.

Using the odd-even algorithm and this data distribution, only one row of M (by processor), containing a row of A and a column of B, needs to be interchanged between adjacent processors. Figure 1 shows the computation sequence for n=12. The "-" symbol relates the two rows of M involved on a rotation.

	proc 0	proc 1	proc 2
Odd	1-2 3-4	5-6 7-8	9-10 11-12
Even	1 2-3	4-5 6-7	8-9 10-11 12
	proc 0	proc 1	proc 2

Fig. 1

This implementation exhibits a good load balance, only broken by processor P_0 in the even step. But for $n = 15$ the balance is worse, as we see in figure 2. Also the direction of row transfers between processors is opposite to that in figure 1, increasing the implementation difficulties.

	proc 0	proc 1	proc 2
Odd	1-2 3-4	5-6 7-8 9-10	11-12 13-14 15
Even	1 2-3 4-5	6-7 8-9 10-11	12-13 14-15
	proc 0	proc 1	proc 2

Fig. 2

The case $n = 15$ can be improved by breaking the odd-even ordering and performing some rotations in sequential ordering, as is shown in figure 3.

	proc 0	proc 1	proc 2
Step 1	1-2 3-4-5	6-7 8-9-10	11-12 13-14-15
Step 2	1 2-3 4	5-6 7-8 9	10-11 12-13 14 15
	proc 0	proc 1	proc 2

Fig. 3

This serialization can be extended to all the rows, as figure 4 shows, becoming the structure employed in our algorithm.

	proc 0	proc 1	proc 2
Step 1	1-2-3-4	5-6-7-8	9-10-11-12
Step 2	1 2 3	4-5 6 7	8-9 10 11 12
	proc 0	proc 1	proc 2

Fig. 4

In the first step all the local computation is performed in every processor using sequential order. To complete the iteration, a row transfer is made, and the second step is performed, returning the updated row to its original location. Figure 5 shows that the scheme is independent of n.

	proc 0	proc 1	proc 2
Step 1	1-2-3-4-5	6-7-8-9-10	11-12-13-14-15
Step 2	1 2 3 4	5-6 7 8 9	10-11 12 13 14 15
	proc 0	proc 1	proc 2

Fig. 5

The parallel algorithm for one iteration is:

Algorithm 3

In P_k, $k = 0, \dots, p-1$

(1.1 local computation)

for $i = 1, 2, \dots, \frac{n}{p} - 1$ **do** /* local index */

if $C_{ij} \leftarrow A_{ij} B_{ij}$ is not diagonal **then**

compute J and K

$A \leftarrow J^T A$ and $B \leftarrow BK$

compute L and store it

apply L to the fragments of columns of A and rows of B stored in this processor

(1.2 distributed computation)

send the stored rotations L to the rest of processors

receive the rotations L from the rest of processors and apply them to the corresponding fragments of columns of A and rows of B stored in this processor

(1.3 distributed computation)

In P_k, $k = 0, \dots, p-2$

send to P_{k+1} the last row of M stored in this processor

In P_k, $k = 1, \dots, p-1$

receive the incoming row

(2.1 local computation)

In P_k, $k = 1, \dots, p-1$

$i = 0$

compute J, JA, K, BK and L as in step 1

(2.2 distributed computation)

In P_k, $k = 0, \dots, p-1$

apply the rotations L as in step 1

(2.3 distributed computation)

In P_k, $k = 1, \dots, p-1$

return the row to P_{k-1}

After every iteration, global convergence must be tested using the appropriate algorithm, as we explain in the next section. The computational cost of algorithm 3 can be estimated by $(6(2n+4)+35)(n-1)$.

4 Implementation using Parallel C

The algorithm has been tested using a board with sixteen T805 transputers [14] and a Parallel C compiler [7]. On this platform, only point to point communications are possible without the use of additional software. The topology employed is a ring of processors. Here, the transfer of rows of M between adjacent processors is easy to implement.

Three aspects are implementation dependent:

4.1 Initial data distribution.

The corresponding blocks of the initial matrices A and B are sent from processor P_0 to the rest of processors. Processor P_i receives data for processors $P_i, \dots, P_p$ and sends data to $P_{i+1}, \dots, P_p$.

4.2 Distributed application of L (algorithm 3, steps 1.2 and 2.2).

Using the ring topology, this computation is performed in $p-1$ steps. At every step, the rotations are sent from one processor to the next, applying them to the corresponding block stored on it. Figure 6 shows the process for $p = 4$.

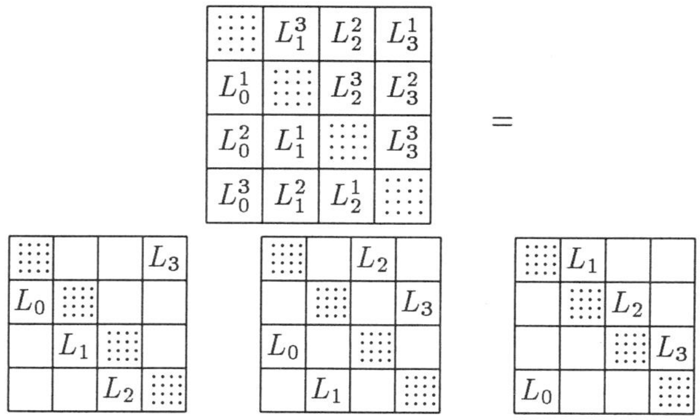

step 1 step 2 step 3

Fig. 6

The algorithm follows.

Algorithm 4

In P_k:

for $ip = 1, \dots, k$ **do**

send $L_{k-ip+1 \oplus p}$ to P_{k+1}

receive $L_{k-ip \oplus p}$ from P_{k-1}

apply to rows $(k-ip)\frac{n}{p}, \dots, (k-ip+1)\frac{n}{p} - 1$ of B

for $ip = k+1, \dots, p-1$ **do**

send $L_{k-ip+1 \oplus p}$ to P_{k+1}

receive $L_{k-ip \oplus p}$ from P_{k-1}

apply to columns $n - (ip-k)\frac{n}{p} + 1, \dots, n - (ip-k-1)\frac{n}{p}$ of A

This algorithm has a good parallelism if the pairs (send,receive) can be performed simultaneously, needing in this case only one communication step for every value of ip. On the other hand, using the rendezvous scheme of Parallel C, the algorithm loses the parallelism on the communications (computations remain parallel), needing $p-1$ steps for every ip to perform the (send,receive) operations. Also, one processor needs to invert the order of the operations to avoid deadlock. We designate this approach as *seq-sr* method and the experimental results are presented in section 6.

The effort necessary to implement simultaneous communications using explicit concurrency can be reduced using a simple strategy: processors $P_1, P_3, \ldots$ will perform (send,receive) operations and processors $P_2, P_4, \ldots$ will do (receive,send) ones. The communication is then always performed in two steps. We call it *alt-sr* method and the experimental results appear in section 6.

The previous discussion can also be applied to steps 1.3 and 2.3 of algorithm 3. If α is the cost of the communication set up, and β is the cost per byte, the communication costs are estimated in table 1.

method / step	1.2 & 2.2	1.3 & 2.3
seq-sr	$(p-1)^2(\alpha+\beta\frac{n}{p})$	$(p-1)(\alpha+\beta(n+2))$
alt-sr	$2(p-1)(\alpha+\beta\frac{n}{p})$	$2(\alpha+\beta(n+2))$

Table 1: comm. costs

4.3 Convergence test.

After every iteration, a processor has determined the local convergence of the algorithm, and needs to know if the rest of the processors have finished their work, to determine the global convergence. If *conv* holds the local convergence, an algorithm follows.

Algorithm 5

In P_0:
  if *conv* **then**
    send *conv* to P_1
    receive *conv* from P_{p-1}
    send *conv* to P_1
    if *conv* **then**
      receive *conv* from P_{p-1}
  else
    send *conv* to P_1
    receive *conv* from P_{p-1}
In P_k, $k = 1, \ldots, p-1$:
  test = *conv*
  receive *conv* from P_{k-1}
  if *conv* **then**
    conv = *test*
    send *conv* to P_{k+1}
    receive *conv* from P_{k-1}
    if *test* **then**
      send *conv* to P_{k+1}
  else
    send *conv* to P_{k+1}

Then, *conv* holds the global convergence. This algorithm, implemented without concurrent communications, is rather sequential, but the final impact is negligible (see section 6). The communication cost is $(p-1)(\alpha+\beta)$ when *conv* is false (will be true only in the last iterations). The algorithm can be improved as in the previous subsection.

5 Implementation using PVM3

The algorithm has also been implemented on a Meiko multicomputer with eight Sun Sparc processors [12] using PVM3 [6]. This interface allows direct communication between any two processors, and the Meiko architecture guarantees a constant bandwidth across the network. This will result in an easier implementation that we designate *mult-s* method:

5.1 Data distribution.

Processor P_0 distributes the blocks of M directly to the rest of processors.

5.2 Distributed application of L.

Using the *multicast* facility of PVM, the algorithm follows:

Algorithm 6

In P_k:
  multicast L_k to the rest of processors
  for $ip = 0, \ldots, k-1$ **do**
    receive L_{ip} from P_{ip}
    apply L_{ip} to rows $ip\frac{n}{p}, \ldots, (ip+1)\frac{n}{p}-1$ of B
  for $ip = k+1, \ldots, p-1$ **do**
    receive L_{ip} from P_{ip}
    apply L_{ip} to columns $ip\frac{n}{p}, \ldots, (ip+1)\frac{n}{p}-1$ of A

Using PVM, the approximate communication costs for the three methods are exposed in table 2.

method / step	1.2 & 2.2	1.3 & 2.3
seq-sr	$(p-1)(\alpha+\beta\frac{n}{p})$	$\alpha+\beta(n+2)$
alt-sr	$2(p-1)(\alpha+\beta\frac{n}{p})$	$2(\alpha+\beta(n+2))$
mult-s	$(p-1)(\alpha+\beta\frac{n}{p})$	$\alpha+\beta(n+2)$

Table 2: comm. costs

Due to the concurrent nature of communications, the *alt-sr* method gives worse performance than the *seq-sr* method, which gives results of the same order than the *mult-s* one. This results are presented in section 6.

5.3 Convergence test.

The algorithm follows:

Algorithm 7

In P_0:

multicast *conv* to the rest of processors

if *conv* **then**

receive convergence from the rest of processors, perform an OR operation on them and store the result in *conv*

multicast *conv* to the rest of processors

In P_k:

test = *conv*

receive *conv* from P_0

if *conv* **then**

send *test* to P_0

receive *conv* from P_0

Except in the last iterations, this algorithm is performed in one parallel step, with an approximated cost of $(\alpha + \beta)$.

6 Experimental Results

The efficiencies of the *seq-sr* implementation on the T805 ring multiprocessor are shown in table 3, where rows represent the matrix sizes and columns the number of processors. Efficiencies greater than one come from cache usage, as a consequence of the high degree of parallelism.

	2	3	4	5	6	8	10	12	15
60	0.97	0.95	0.91	0.87	0.81	....	0.59	0.49	0.37
120	0.98	0.97	0.95	0.92	0.89	0.84	0.76	0.68	0.56
240	1.01	1.00	0.99	0.98	0.96	0.93	0.88	0.82	0.74
360	1.00	1.00	0.99	1.01	1.00	0.97	0.94	0.90	0.83
480	....	1.00	1.00	0.99	0.98	0.99	0.96	0.93	0.88

Table 3: *seq-sr* impl. (T805)

Table 4 represents the weights of the different parts of the *alt-sr* implementation on the T805, for $n = 60$, obtained with a simulator ([13]).

Processors	2	3	4	5	6	10	12	15
Step 1.1	74%	63%	57%	52%	47%	33%	28%	21%
Step 1.2	22%	30%	33%	35%	36%	37%	36%	35%
Step 1.3	0%	1%	1%	2%	3%	5%	7%	9%
Step 2.1	1%	2%	3%	4%	4%	6%	7%	7%
Step 2.2	2%	3%	4%	5%	6%	11%	13%	17%
Step 2.3	1%	1%	2%	2%	3%	6%	7%	9%
Conv. test	0%	0%	0%	0%	1%	2%	2%	2%

Table 4: Simulation of the *alt-sr* impl. (T805, $n = 60$)

In the *alt-sr* implementation, the communication improvements produce higher efficiencies as the number of processors grows, obtaining 3.38 MFlops of peak performance, for $n = 480, p = 15$. The results appear in table 5.

	2	3	4	5	6	8	10	12	15
60	0.97	0.95	0.92	0.89	0.86	....	0.70	0.62	0.51
120	0.99	0.97	0.96	0.94	0.92	0.89	0.83	0.78	0.69
240	1.01	1.00	1.00	0.99	0.98	0.95	0.92	0.89	0.83
360	1.00	1.00	0.99	1.01	1.00	0.99	0.97	0.94	0.90
480	....	1.00	1.00	0.99	0.99	1.00	0.98	0.96	0.93

Table 5: *alt-sr* impl. (T805)

Tables 6 and 7 show the results of the PVM implementation on the Meiko multiprocessor. The peak performance is 34.16 MFlops, obtained for $n = 600, p = 8$.

	2	3	4	5	6	8
120	0.90	0.79	0.69	0.54	0.46	0.32
240	1.00	0.96	0.92	0.85	0.79	0.63
360	1.02	1.01	1.01	1.01	0.99	0.91
480	1.00	1.01	1.00	0.98	0.95	0.95
600	1.03	1.04	1.04	1.03	1.02	0.99

Table 6: *seq-sr* implementation (Meiko)

	2	3	4	5	6	8
120	0.90	0.78	0.70	0.49	0.42	0.31
240	1.01	0.97	0.93	0.86	0.73	0.64
360	1.02	1.02	1.01	0.99	0.97	0.94
480	1.02	1.02	1.01	0.97	0.95	0.94
600	1.02	1.04	1.04	1.03	1.02	0.98

Table 7: *mult-s* implementation (Meiko)

References

[1] Bai, Z: *A Parallel Algorithm for Computing the Generalized Singular Value Decomposition.* Journal of Parallel and Distributed Computing, 20, pp. 280-288 (1994).

[2] Brent, R., Luk, F. and van Loan, C.: *Computation of the generalized singular value decomposition using mesh connected processors.* Proc. SPIE, Vol. 431, Real time signal processing VI, pp. 66-71 (1983).

[3] De Moor, B. and Golub, G. H.: *Generalized Singular Value Decompositions: A proposal for a standardized nomenclature.* Num. Anal. Proj. Report 89-04, Comput. Sci. Dept., Stanford University (1989).

[4] De Moor, B.: *On the structure and geometry of the PSVD.* Num. Anal. Project, NA-89-05, Comput. Sci. Dept., Stanford University (1989).

[5] Fernando, K. and Hammarling, S.: *A generalized singular value decomposition for a product of two matrices and balanced realization.* NAG Technical Report TR1/87, Oxford (1987).

[6] Geist, A., Beguelin, A. et al.: *PVM 3 User's Guide and Reference Manual.* ORNL/TM-12187, Oak Ridge National Laboratory, Oak Ridge, Tennesse 37831, (1994).

[7] INMOS Limited: *ANSI C toolset language reference.* (1990).

[8] Kogbetliantz, E.: *Solution of linear equations by diagonalization of coefficients matrix.* Quart. Appl. Math., 13, pp. 123-132 (1955).

[9] Laub, A., Heath, M., Paige, C. and Ward, R.: *Computation of system balancing transformations and other applications of simultaneous diagonalization algorithms.* IEEE Trans. Aut. Control, Vol. AC-32, No. 2 (1987)

[10] Luk , F.: *A triangular processor array for computing singular values.* Linear Algebra Appl., 77, pp. 259-273 (1986).

[11] Luk, F.: *A parallel method for computing the generalized singular value decomposition.* Journal of Parallel and Dist. Comput., Vol. 2, pp. 250-260 (1985).

[12] Meiko Limited: *Computing Surface - User's Guide.* (1994).

[13] Mollar, M.: *A Small Parallel C Simulator.* Proc. 4th Euromicro Workshop on Par. and Dist. Comp. (1996)

[14] Paige, C. and Sanders, M.: *Towards a generalized singular value decomposition.* SIAM J. Numer. Anal., 18 pp., 398-405, (1981).

[15] Transtech Parallel Sys. Ltd.: *Transtech TMB08 PC TRAM motherboard, TMB08MAN0690.* (1991).

[16] Van Loan, C.: *Generalizing the singular value decomposition. SIAM J. Numer.* Anal. 13, p. 76-83 (1976).

A Latency-hiding MIMD Wavelet Transform

G.Seaman
SCSISE
University of Westminster
London W1M 8JS

Abstract

The Discrete Wavelet Transform (DWT) may be used for applications in which real time execution is critical but data sizes are very large. Real-time execution can only be achieved through a parallel implementation. Published parallel implementations are suitable only for systems with very many (SIMD) processors or very few, specialized (systolic) processors. Neither approach is satisfactory for most MIMD systems, for which the algorithm used should be scaleable across small to medium numbers of processors.

The DWT has a tree-based structure which lends itself naturally to data-parallel SIMD implementations. Such implementations involve large amounts of synchronous, fine-grained communication. MIMD systems, especially those based on message-passing, cannot efficiently support the levels of communication demanded by SIMD algorithms without retailoring of the algorithm. A data driven algorithm which masks communication latency with computation is proposed as an alternative.

1 Introduction

The Discrete Wavelet Transform (DWT) is commonly used for applications in which real time execution is critical but data sizes are very large, such as image compression. If the data is to be analyzed in more than one dimension using multiple passes of a separable DWT, then the only way to meet the real-time requirement is through a parallel implementation. However, published parallel implementations of the DWT are either SIMD, depending on very large numbers of processors for their effectiveness, or systolic, and limited to very small numbers of specialized processors. Neither approach is satisfactory for most MIMD systems, for which the algorithm used should be scaleable across small to medium numbers of processors.

The Discrete Wavelet Transform can be executed in many different ways. It may be carried out using matrix multiplication, involving $O(N)^2$ computational steps (where N is the data size), or by means of the Fourier transform, using $O(N \log N)$ steps. Standard methods for parallelizing both these methods are commonplace. However, it is generally recognized that the most efficient implementations (in terms of number of operations required) for typical applications are based on Mallat's recursive algorithm [Mall89], which is $O(N)$, so this should be the starting point for a parallel implementation.

2 Mallat's Algorithm

Mallat's algorithm generates wavelet transform coefficients recursively; the output coefficients $h_j(k)$ at each level are generated from the values $l_j(k)$ of the previous level, where $l_0(k)$ (for image compression purposes) can be considered to be the original sampled data values. $h_j(k)$ and $l_j(k)$ are generated from $l_{j-1}(k)$ through convolution with two FIR filters, $c(n)$ and $g(n)$ (which are low-pass and high-pass respectively), followed by decimation:

$$l_j(k) = \sqrt{2}\sum_n c(n)l_{j-1}(n-2k) \qquad (1)$$

$$h_j(k) = \sqrt{2}\sum_n g(n)l_{j-1}(n-2k) \qquad (2)$$

That is, given $l_0(k)$, convolve it with $g(n)$ and downsample by two to produce the first set of outputs, $DWT_{0,k}$. Convolve the $l_0(k)$ with $c(n)$ and downsample by two to produce the input sequence for the next recursion (Figure 1). The recursion may be stopped after any number of iterations; for images, 3–5 iterations is a typical figure.

The two filters have a simple relationship to one another:

$$g(n) = (-1)^n c(1-n) \qquad (3)$$

which gives scope for reducing the total number of operations.

Inverting the transform involves recombining the two sequences $l_j(k)$ and $h_j(k)$:

$$l_{j-1}(n) = \sqrt{2}\sum_k \left(c(n-2k)l_j(k) + g(n-2k)h_j(k)\right) \qquad (4)$$

That is, one stage of the transform is reversed by convolving $l_j(k)$ and $h_j(k)$ with the reversed and upsampled filter pair, and adding the results.

The dataflow diagram for the inverse transform is simply the transpose of the diagram for the forward transform, so that once an efficient implementation of the transform in either direction has been found, an implementation of the transform in the reverse direction is given (semi-) automatically.

The algorithm can be applied both to one-dimensional and n-dimensional signals (eg, with $n = 2$,

1066-6192/96 $5.00 © 1996 IEEE
Proceedings of PDP '96

images, and with $n = 3$, video sequences). In the case of n-dimensional signals, if the wavelet basis used is separable the algorithm may either be applied directly to the n-dimensional signal or may be applied once in each dimension. The direct approach requires a far higher operation count than that which operates on successive dimensions, so that the second approach is normally to be preferred.

There are various possible methods of dealing with the data boundaries, but the basic algorithm uses circular convolution, which is assumed here.

3 Previous Approaches

The time complexity of a sequential implementation of Mallat's algorithm is $O(N)$, where N is the amount of data to be processed. More exactly, the algorithm requires $2LND$ computational steps, where L is the filter length and D is the number of dimensions, in addition to the operations required for data management and housekeeping.

Published parallel implementations of Mallat's algorithm have taken one of two approaches. The first looks at the overall structure of the algorithm. The algorithm is tree-structured, as can be seen in figure 1.

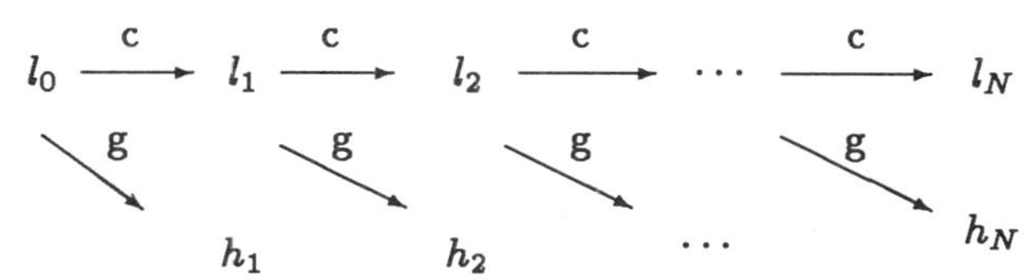

Figure 1: Mallat's algorithm: forward transform

The achievable parallel time complexity is therefore $\Theta(\log N)$, giving a maximum speedup of $\Theta(N/\log N)$. The natural approach for SIMD style parallel systems is to achieve this maximum by allocating one PE for each convolution operation at each level in the transform. This approach was presented in Lu [Lu93]. However, Lu's method depends on having sufficient PEs available, and performance degrades rapidly in an unpredictable, operating-system dependent way as several PEs functions are multiplexed onto one when the volume of data exceeds the number of PEs.

Furthermore, since the SIMD approach requires $2N$ PEs each carrying out L operations with an overall time of $L \log N$, even when there *are* sufficient PEs available the efficiency will only be $2LN/(2N \times L \log N) = 1/\log N$. This low efficiency is typical of tree-based algorithms, where only one level of the tree is active at any time. The inefficiency may be reduced by pipelining if a continuous stream of data blocks to be transformed is available [Lee94]; however the method still involves a large amount of interprocessor communication which increases when the algorithm is used in more than one dimension, since a large amount of data movement is required to map a multi-dimensional tree onto a grid, the most common underlying SIMD structure. The sheer volume of communication involved in the SIMD approach makes it inappropriate for adaptation to a MIMD structure.

The second approach has been followed by designers more concerned with ease of implementation in VLSI. This approach takes advantage of the structure of the core operations of the algorithm. The key point is the presence of the shift by 2 within the convolution (equation 2). This implies that only every second output of the convolution is to be retained. This feature has traditionally been used in VLSI signal processing to allow a reduction of the clock speed required by two, using 'polyphase filtering' [Vaid93]. Here the filter is split into an odd and an even section, only one of which is active during any clock cycle.

An alternative to reducing the clock rate which is more appropriate for parallel systems is to use the 'idle' half of the filter to produce the higher level output values before the full set of first level output values has been generated. Since there are $N/2$ first level values and $N/4 + N/8 + N/16 \ldots + 1 = N/2$ higher level values, the entire set of values from all levels can be calculated in N filter steps. Figure 2 shows a 16-leaf tree 'collapsed' into a linear list in this way.

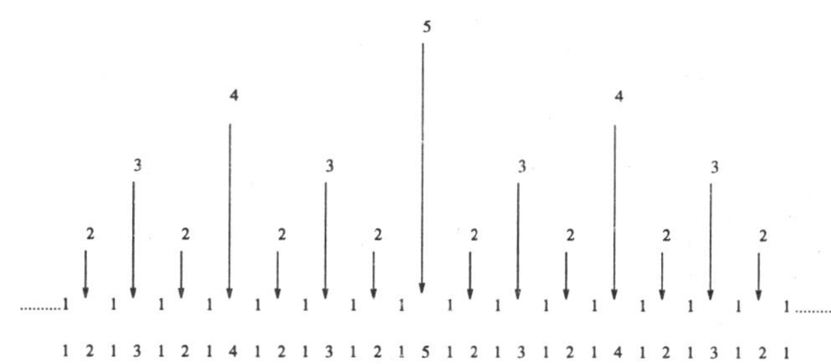

Figure 2: Collapsed tree

Each individual multiplication involved in the pair of convolutions in equation 2 can be further assigned to a single processor, giving a speedup of $2L$ and reducing the time complexity to exactly N (for one dimension).

This general method was first suggested by Knowles [Know90], while variations on the theme have been followed up by several authors; e.g. [Par93, Lang94, Frid94, Frid94b]. Some of this work is summarized in [Chak95].

Like the SIMD approach this method is not easily adapted for MIMD systems. The speedup of $2L$ cannot be exceeded, and except in VLSI or systolic systems the overheads involved in such fine-grain parallelism are likely to outweigh the gains.

4 A MIMD Implementation

Neither the SIMD nor the Systolic approaches are suitable for direct use in most MIMD systems, where there is often a large penalty for the fine-grained communications on which these approaches depend. In addition, most MIMD systems do not have the very large numbers of processors typical of SIMD systems, forcing a more coarse-grained approach. For most available parallel systems it is realistic to assume that the number of processors available will be far fewer than the number of data points input to the transform.

It is therefore necessary to allocate relatively large data sections to each processor. This should enable near-linear speedup and good efficiency. The fact that the wavelet transform is largely a local one, in contrast to the DFT and other common transforms, means that this goal should be achievable.

The requirements for an effective transfer of the algorithm to MIMD systems include:

- Taking advantage of all available locality in the data and the algorithm structure to maximize the ratio of computation to communication.
- The overlapping of communications with computation to mask the communication latencies involved.
- The distribution of communication in time to avoid communication bursts which may saturate the communication medium.
- The distribution of communication in place to reduce the distances traversed by each message (this last point is obviously dependent on the underlying network structure, and so is to some extent system specific)

An ideal implementation should give as close as possible to linear speedup on any reasonable number of processors (in the following, the number of processors is restricted to powers of two).

4.1 Maximizing Locality

The first decision to be made is the placement of the data. Since each level of the transform involves a pair of convolutions on a series of data points, and convolution is essentially a local operation, the original ordering of this data has to be maintained within each subpart allocated to a separate processor. The data can therefore simply be broken into sections of equivalent size for each processor. The communication involved is then at the boundaries of these data segments.

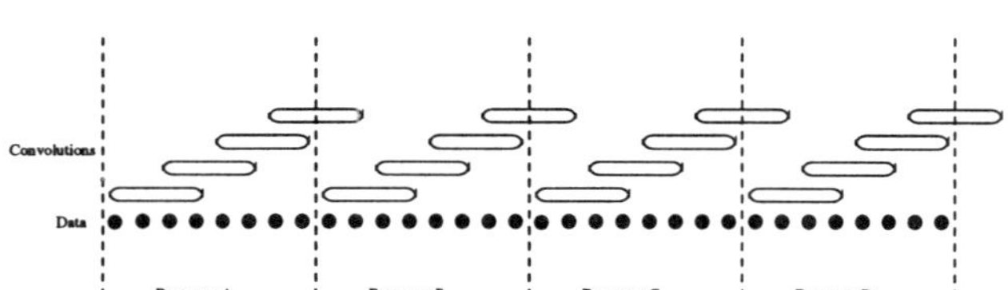

Figure 3: Data overlap during convolution

Since this communication takes place at the boundaries between segments, it can be minimized by placing the input data in such a way as to allocate each processor the same amount of data while minimizing the total boundary between PEs; in other words, the volume of data allocated to each PE has to be at a maximum relative to its surface area.

For one dimension there is only one way to allocate each PE P/N contiguous data items, but for more dimensions there are many different possible ways to partition the data while maintaining contiguity. The most intuitive method for an image would seem to be to allocate each PE a group of scan lines; however, although this minimizes communication for the horizontal transform, communication is maximized for the vertical transform.

For a general n-dimensional transform, since communication depends on the surface area of each n-dimensional polygon into which the n-dimensional input data matrix is divided, and the ratio of surface area to volume is at a minimum when the polygon is a cube, total communication will be at a minimum when each partition is as close as possible to an n-dimensional cube.

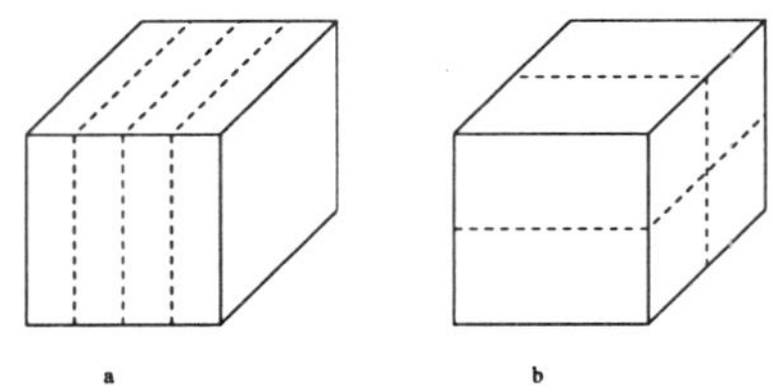

Figure 4: a) Inefficient data partition; b) Efficient data partition

A simple algorithm which will generate this partition is to recursively halve the length of the remaining longest side of the polygon $\log_2(P)$ times.

4.2 Latency Masking

For parallel convolution in one dimension the data is simply broken into P contiguous segments, as shown in figure 3. The figure illustrates convolution and downsampling on 32 data points with a filter length L of 4. From the figure it is evident that communication is needed between neighbouring PEs at the points of overlap, and that the degree of overlap will depend on the filter length. In general, if the PEs are numbered $0 \ldots P-1$, each PE_i needs to send its $L-2$ leftmost data to PE_{i-1}. For circular convolution, PE_0 needs to send this data to PE_{P-1}.

Figure 3 shows convolution with the low-pass filter. The definition of the high pass filter (equation 3) makes this a non-causal filter: that is, since this is a circular convolution, PE_0 must wait for data supplied by PE_P before carrying out its own first high-pass convolution operation. Similarly, PE_1 needs data from PE_0, etc.: all the computation is dependent on the communication step at each level. If the high-pass filter is shifted to become causal (creating a corresponding $(L-2)/2$-point shift right in the output) then the two filters are aligned and each PE calculates and transmits its own overlap data for the next transform level at the *start* of the computation of the preceding level, but only requires overlap data from the next PE at the *end* of its computation of each transform level. The larger the amount of data allocated to each PE the more likely it is that this computation time will completely mask out the communication time.

This latency-hiding technique becomes less effective as the number of PEs increases, meaning that it is also necessary to try to spread the communications to avoid the 'bursty' message passing suggested so far, where all messages are sent shortly after the start of the computation of a new transform level.

4.3 Communication Timing

The communication discussed so far is at least fairly local. However, the convolution overlap shown in figure 3 does not simply repeat at each level, since the data is decimated following each filtering operation, while the filter length stays constant.

As soon as the PEs hold less than $L/2$ data inputs (i.e., after the first $\lfloor \log_2 \left(\frac{N/P}{L/2}\right) \rfloor$ layers), the filters overlap the data held in more than one neighbouring PE. This is illustrated in figure 5 for $L = 6$, where the multiple overlap begins following level 2.

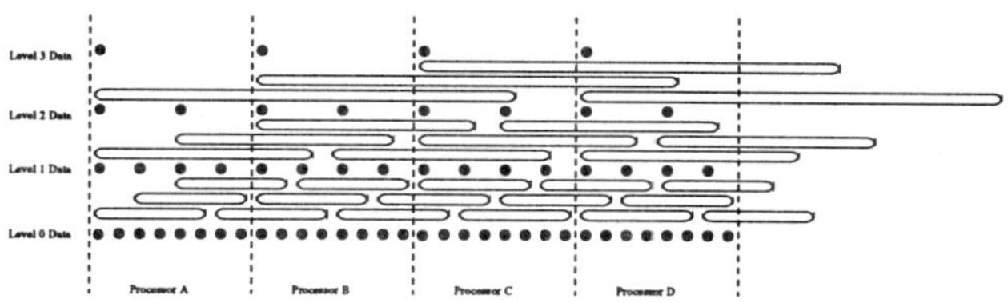

Figure 5: Data overlap with multiple layers

The higher levels therefore require relatively more communication. However, with the conventional ordering of the algorithm, working successively upwards through the levels, by the time the higher levels have been reached there is very little further computation to do in order to mask this communication.

To hide the communication it is necessary to reorder the computation. Collapsing the tree into a linear list as shown in figure 2 reorders the computation so that the first elements of the higher transform levels are now calculated at most half-way through the computation of the first level, which contains the majority of the computation. This maximizes the time available for data communication, and allows some masking of the communication latency.

However, this simple reordering is deterministic so that variable delays in messages will cause computation stalls. An alternative reordering which takes potential delays into account can be generated following the simple rule: 'of all the levels waiting to be processed, chose the highest first'. This gives the (default) sequence (for 16 inputs and $L = 2$):

1 1 2 1 1 2 3 1 1 2 1 1 2 3 4 1 1 2 1 1 2 3
1 1 2 1 1 2 3 4 5 ...

Data from each level can be transmitted to neighbouring PEs as soon as it has been generated, effectively interleaving the communication at all levels with computation and allowing masking of most of the higher-level communication.

This is a data-driven method which removes the timing constraints on the calculation of the transform coefficients by allowing variable ordering of message arrival and so succeeds both in reducing computation stalls and in reducing the bursty communication required by the deterministic algorithm.

4.4 Revenge of the Tree

Trees have deep roots and are difficult to remove completely. The first source of communication in the MIMD Wavelet algorithm is convolution overlap; the second source of communication comes from the tree-based nature of the algorithm, which cannot be completely suppressed. Figure 6 illustrates the problem. Here, each dot represents a single convolution operation, with data partitioned among 8 PEs.

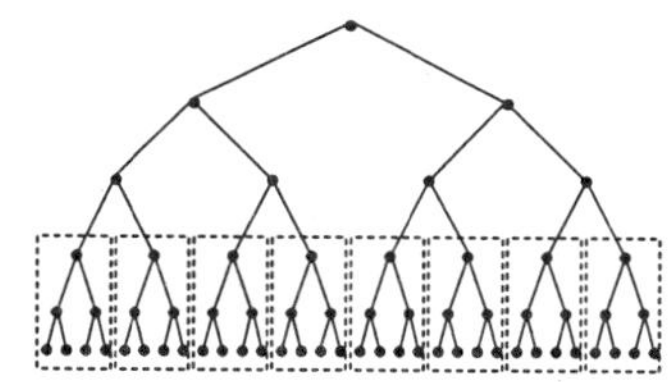

Figure 6: Tree partition with 8 PEs

It can be seen that computation is local only for the first $\log_2(N/P)$ levels. This is the first level where each PE holds less than 2 data inputs. Above this level the global nature of the transform comes into play: the tree structure reasserts itself, some PEs have to drop out of the computation, while others are transmitting messages in steps of powers of two. this additional communication is an inherent feature of the algorithm which cannot be removed. However, there are only $P-1$ convolution sums involved at this stage, as against the $2N-P$ carried out in parallel. Provided P is fairly small relative to N, this final stage does not have have a major impact on overall performance.

The final stage is often avoided completely in practice since the topmost levels of the transform are rarely computed; the output values from a circular convolution have little meaning once the number of inputs has shrunk to less than the filter length.

5 Implementation

The different versions of the algorithm were tested using *pvm* running on a network of SPARC workstations. This is not an ideal platform, in particular due to the lack of parallel I/O in such a system and the absence of performance tuning tools. However, using the graphical interface *xpvm* it was possible to draw qualitative conclusions about performance.

As expected, the execution times of the naive algorithm were dominated by the time spent waiting for messages to arrive, due to the exceptionally large latency in message passing in such a system.

In the latency-hiding algorithm, this waiting time was almost completely covered by computation. However, the high overhead associated with message creation and sending in *pvm* meant that actual execution times were not much reduced; some of the masking of the message latency was actually due to the additional computation introduced in order to handle the non-deterministic algorithm, and some to the overheads of the *pvm* library calls. These overheads could be reduced by bundling data to be sent between processes into larger packets, but very large packet sizes again increased waiting time. Waiting time was also increased by the introduction of a barrier call between processing of each dimension.

6 Conclusions

A reorganization of Mallat's algorithm for parallel systems which minimizes message passing and maximizes latency-hiding of messages has been suggested. The reorganized algorithm has a data-flow style, where convolution operations take place once they are demanded by the availability of the necessary subset of the data.

Attemps to implement this algorithm using *pvm* have not been highly successful, mainly due to the high overheads (both in computation and in library calls) involved with this system.

However, it is hoped to use this experience in the future in developing custom systolic processors to be used as part of a parallel system for video compression. In a custom-designed system the overheads associated both with message-passing and with non-sequential computation can be minimized.

References

[Chak95] C.Chakrabarti and M.Vishwanath, *Efficient Realizations of the Discrete and Continuous Wavelet Transforms: From Single Chip Implementations to Mappings on SIMD Array Computers*, IEEE Trans. Signal Proc. Vol 43, No. 3, Mar. 1995

[Frid94] J.Fridman and E.S.Manolakos, *On the synthesis of regular VLSI architectures for the 1-D discrete wavelet transform*, SPIE Conf. on Mathematical Imaging: Wavelet Applications in Signal and Image Processing II, San Diego CA, July 1994

[Frid94b] J. Fridman and E.S. Manolakos, *Distributed Memory and Control VLSI Architectures for the 1-D Discrete Wavelet Transform*, IEEE Trans. VLSI Signal Processing Oct. 94

[Geist94] A. Geist et al., *PVM: Parallel Virtual Machine; A Users' Guide and Tutorial for Networked Parallel Computing*, MIT Press 1994

[Know90] G.Knowles: *VLSI Architecture for the Discrete Wavelet Transform*, Electronics Letters, 26(15) July 1990

[Lang94] R. Lang, E. Plesner, H. Schröder, A. Spray, *An efficient systolic architecture for the one-dimensional wavelet transform*, SPIE Vol. 2242 Wavelet Applications (1994)

[Lee94] H.Lee, J.Liu, A.Chan, C.Chui, *Parallel Implementation of Wavelet Decomposition/Reconstruction Algorithms*, SPIE Vol. 2242 Wavelet Applications (1994)

[Lu93] Jian Lu, *Parellelizing Mallat's Algorithm for 2-D Wavelet Transforms*, Information Processing Letters Vol. 45 pp. 255-9 1993

[Mall89] S.Mallat,*A Theory for Multiresolution Signal Decomposition: The Wavelet Representation*, IEEE Trans. Pat. Rec. & Mach. Int., Vol. 11, No. 7, July 1989

[Par93] K.K.Parhi and T. Nishitani: *VLSI Architectures for Discrete Wavelet Transforms*, IEEE Trans. VLSI Systems Vol 1 No. 2 June 1993

[Quinn94] M.J. Quinn, *Parallel Computing: Theory and Practice*, McGraw-Hill 1994

[Soren93] H.Sorensen and C.Burrus, *Fast DFT and Convolution Algorithms*, in S.Mitra and J.Kaiser (Eds) *Handbook for Digital Signal Processing*, John Wiley 1993

[Vaid93] P.P. Vaidyanathan, *Multirate Systems and Filter Banks*, Prentice-Hall, Englewood Cliffs NJ, 1993

Simulation of Chaotic Iterative Processes in Speed-Independent Computing Networks

N.M.Goubareni
Instytute of Mathematics and Computer Science
Technical University of Chęstochowa
Chęstochowa, POLAND, 42-200

Abstract

Mathematical simulation of selforganizing chaotic processes in networks with speed independent processes by means of asynchronous method of chaotic relaxations with delay using the Monter-Carlo method is considered. This method allows to imitate effectively the fulfilment of chaotic computing process depending on spread of time parameters of speed independent processors. Every speed independent processor is nonsynchronous computing device in which duration of transient process is a random variable. In this work it is assumed that the random variable has normal distribution as far as duration of work of logical elements has namely such law of distribution. It is considered behaviour of network consisted from interacting speed independent processors, local strategy of which is defined by durations of transient processes in them and control over transparency of fixing elements at input and output of processors are fulfilled by circurts defining end moment of transient processes. For computer simulation it was chosen solving the Dirichlet problem for Laplace's equation on rectangular domain of R^2. Numerical calculations for solving this problem, comparing evaluations of errors and speed of convergence of computing processes arising in networks with speed independent processors are presented.

1 Introduction

Most of investigations concerning the organization of computing processes in parallel systems are devoted to synchronous programmed realization of these processes. Their complexity is much enough and increases with increase of system dimension. It is well known [1] that interaction of computing blocks according to principle of speed independent circuits doesn't require application of method of synchronization and provides system speed with maximal possibility.

Necessity of complicate programmed realization of computing processes in parallel system, low effect of using speed of elementary base, considerable consumption of energy spending to support function of synchronous system are those defects which force to elaborate asynchronous selforganizing methods and adaptate them into parallel systems. Fruitful idea of speed independent networks didn't obtain wide application owing to lack of effective methods for fixing end moment of transient processes in elements of network. However there exist some perspectives in elaboration of method for fixing end moment of transient processes in computing elements of parallel computing system. One of such approach is based on analyzis of behaviour of Boolean derivatives of all logical variables of global-parallel computing device [2], [3].

It is important that realization of strategy of local interaction of computing blocks on the basis of ideology of speed independence leads to arise of selforganizing computing processes. In sluggishless systems property of selforganization reveals itself in establishment of chaotic iterative processes.

2 Basic mathematical notions

We are using the basic notions of the theory of asynchronous iterative methods developing by Baudet [5]. The important significance in this theory has the notion of chaotic iteration which is originally due to Chason and Miranker [4] who introduced it at first during the investigation of asynchronous iterative algorithms for solving systems of linear algebraic equations.

Definition 1.

A sequence of nonempty subsets $I = \{I_k\}_{k=0}^{\infty}$ of set $\{1, 2, ..., n\}$ is a sequence of chaotic sets if

$$\limsup_{j\to\infty} I_j = \{1, 2, ..., n\}$$

Assume that speed independent computing network (SICN) consists from n processors working independently one from another. In this case sequence of chaotic sets has simple interpretation: it sets the time diagram of work for each nonsynchronous computing element (NCE) during nonsynchronous work of SICN. Let the sequence of iteration $\{\mathbf{y}^k\}_{k=1}^{\infty}$ is calculated on SICN, then subset I_k is the set of number of those NCE which take place really at the calculation of vector coordinates $\mathbf{y}^k$ on the k-th step of iteration.

As it is shown at work [5] the sequence of chaotic sets $I = \{I_k\}_{k=1}^{\infty}$ is characterized by such important property: for every $i \in N$ there exists such $p \in N$ that there are fulfilled the conditions:

$$\bigcup_{i=j+1}^{j+p} I_i = \{1, 2, ..., n\}$$

1066-6192/96 $5.00 © 1996 IEEE
Proceedings of PDP '96

$$\bigcup_{i=j+1}^{j+p-1} I_i \neq \{1,2,...,n\}. \qquad (1)$$

Assume that it is given the operator equation

$$\mathbf{y} = \mathbf{F}\mathbf{y} \qquad (2)$$

where $\mathbf{y} = \{y_1, y_2, ..., y_n\} \in R^n$; $\mathbf{F} : R^n \to R^n$ - nonlinear operator, which is represented by coordinate functions:

$$F\{y_1, y_2, ..., y_n\} = \left\{ \begin{array}{l} f_1(y_1, y_2, ..., y_n) \\ f_2(y_1, y_2, ..., y_n) \\ \dots\dots\dots\dots \\ f_n(y_1, y_2, ..., y_n) \end{array} \right\}. \qquad (3)$$

In this case the operator equation (2) can be rewritten in coordinate form:

$$y_i = f_i(y_1, y_2, ..., y_n) \qquad (i = 1,2,...,n). \qquad (4)$$

Definition 2.

Let $\mathbf{F} : R^n \to R^n$ - operator which is given in the form (3), $\mathbf{y}^0 \in R^n$. Asynchronous method of chaotic relaxations with limited delay for operator $\mathbf{F}$ is a method of building sequence of vectors $\{\mathbf{y}^k\}_{k=0}^{\infty}$, which is given recursively by

$$y_i^k = \begin{cases} y_i^{k-1} & \text{if } i \notin I_k; \\ f_i(y_1^{\sigma_1(k)}, y_2^{\sigma_2(k)}, ..., y_n^{\sigma_n(k)}) & \text{if } i \in I_k. \end{cases} \qquad (5)$$

where $I = \{I_k\}_{k=1}^{\infty}$ is a sequence of chaotic sets and $J = \{\sigma(k)\}_{k=1}^{\infty}$ is a sequence of n-dimensional vectors with integer coordinates satisfying for every $i = 1,2,...,n$ and $k \in N$ such properties:

$$0 \leq \sigma_i(k) \leq k;$$

$$\exists s \in N \quad \text{that} \quad 0 \leq \sigma_i(k) \leq s. \qquad (6)$$

The number s defines the depth of using iterations and in fact reflects the possibilities of concrete computer system by which the method is realized. Later on the sequence $J = \{\sigma(k)\}_{k=1}^{\infty}$ will be called the delay sequence and the number s - delay.

In the work [4] it was proved a sufficient condition on the operator F for the convergence of any asynchronous iteration. In particular if $\mathbf{F}$ is a contracting operator with linear majorant on a subset D of R^n (i.e. there exists nonnegative matrix $\mathbf{A}$ with spectrum radius $\rho(\mathbf{A}) \leq 1$ such that $| \mathbf{F}\mathbf{y}_1 - \mathbf{F}\mathbf{y}_2 | < \mathbf{A} | \mathbf{y}_1 - \mathbf{y}_2 |$ for every $\mathbf{y}_1, \mathbf{y}_2 \in D$) then the sequence $\{\mathbf{y}^k\}_{k=0}^{\infty}$ starting with $\mathbf{y}^0 \in D$ and obtained by means of asynchronous iterative method converges to unique fixed point $\mathbf{y}^*$ of operator $\mathbf{F}$ in D.

3 Mathematical simulation of work of speed independent computing network

It is possible to organize work of SICN by means of asynchronous iterations. Assume that SICN consists from n processors. Let $I = \{I_k\}_{k=0}^{\infty}$ is a sequence of chaotic sets, $J = \{\sigma(k)\}_{k=1}^{\infty}$ is a delay sequence and it is given increasing sequence of time $\{t_k\}_{k=0}^{\infty}$. Then for obtaining the sequence of iterations $\{\mathbf{y}^k\}_{k=0}^{\infty}$ it is possible to fulfil the computation in SICN by such diagram. At the time moment t_k processors calculate those components of iterative vector $\mathbf{y}^k$ which numbers belong to set I_k. In this case there are used the values of component of known previous iterations with numbers of corresponding components of vector $\sigma(k)$. After fulfilment of computing by formula (5) the processors write obtaining values to memory and begin the new calculations corresponding to moment of time t_{k+1} .

It is more interesting other question: how for really working asynchronous SICN to build the sequence of chaotic sets and delay sequence, in other words how to simulate the work of such device? In this work it is presented solution of such problem for some SICN working in parallel regime of computing and described the work of such SICN.

Assume that on the plane R^2 it is given some mesh domain $D \subset R^2$ consisting from n points - mesh points. Introduce discrete time $T = \{t_k\}_{k=0}^{\infty}$, where $t_k = k\Delta t$, $\Delta t = const > 0$. We consider that at the beginning moment of time $t_0 = 0$ in every point $\theta_i \in D$ it is given some beginning value $y_i^0 \in R$ $(i = 1,2,...,n)$. Let $y_i^k = y_i(t_k)$ - value of mesh point $\theta_i \in D$ at the time moment $t_k \in T$, which is a real number depending on θ_i and t_k. We will consider that it is given operator $\mathbf{F} : R^n \to R^n$ in the form (3) according to which calculations are fulfilled in every mesh point. Now assume that change from state y_i^k to state y_i^{k+1} fulfils by means of SICN consisting from n processors working in asynchronous regime. In this case the work of every processor is fulfilled mutually independently and takes different intervals of time which are defined by codes of numbers on which the processors fulfil computations in every mesh point at definite moment of time.

We will consider that every processor has speed of responce in the interval from Δt to $l\Delta t$, where l - some positive integer and value $1 \leq i \leq l$ for every processor is defined at random. Work of every processor depends on full group of pairwise incompatible events $A_1, A_2, ..., A_l$. In this case event A_j indicates that for computation of necessary value processor has to work during the time $j\Delta t$ $(j = 1,2,...,l)$ and then returns to initial state.

For building of mathematical model imitating the work of such SICN we use the Monte-Carlo method.

Let $\omega^k = \{\omega_1^k, \omega_2^k, ..., \omega_n^k\}$ - the sequence of independent discrete random variables; ω_i^k - discrete random variable concerning to work of i-th processor and $\omega_i^k = j$ if the event A_j takes place for i-th processor at the time moment t_k.

At every time moment t_k the work of SICN is defined by means of a sequence of independent discrete random variables

$$\xi^k = \{\xi_1^k, \xi_2^k, ..., \xi_n^k\}$$

where $\xi_i^1 = \omega_i^1$, and if $k > 1$ then

$$\xi_i^k = \begin{cases} \omega_i^k & \text{if } \xi_i^{k-1} = 1; \\ \xi_i^{k-1} - 1 & \text{if } \xi_i^{k-1} \neq 1. \end{cases} \quad (7)$$

for $i = 1, 2, ..., n$.

At every time moment t_k the sequence ξ^k shows at what phase of work every processor is. In this case if $\xi_i^{k-1} = 1$ then new computation is fulfilled in i-th mesh point on k-th step, i. e. mesh point is restored; calculating value is put into memory and new information is put into i-th processor for which work it is required time equals to ω_i^k. If $\xi_i^{k-1} \neq 1$ then processor continues its work and value in i-th mesh point isn't changed, i. e. $y_i^k = y_i^{k-1}$.

Calculations in every mesh point are defined by formula (5) using the sequence of chaotic sets $I = \{I_k\}_{k=1}^{\infty}$ and delay sequence $J = \{\sigma(k)\}_{k=1}^{\infty}$, which are built by means of sequence $\{\xi^k\}_{k=1}^{\infty}$. Chaotic set I_k is built by vector ξ^k in such way:

$$I_k = \{j \in (1, 2, ..., n) \mid \xi_j^k = 1\} \quad (8)$$

i. e. set I_k is consisted from those numbers j on which places in vector ξ^k there is 1. So if $\xi_j^k = 1$ then $j \in I_k$ and if $\xi_j^k \neq 1$ then $j \notin I_k$. Therefore $I_k \subset \{1, 2, ..., n\}$.

From the building of vector ξ^k and assumption that for every $i = 1, 2, ..., n$ and $k \in N$, $\omega_i^k \leq l$ it follows that for every $k \in N$ it is fulfilled the condition:

$$\bigcup_{i=k}^{k+l} I_i = \{1, 2, ..., n\}. \quad (9)$$

This condition signifies that at every time interval with length $(l+1)\Delta t$ every coordinate of iterative vector is restored if only one time.

Coming from sequence $I = \{I_k\}_{k=1}^{\infty}$ we will build the sequence of indexes $\{k_p\}_{p=1}^{\infty}$ which is satisfied the conditions:

1. $k_{p_1} < k_{p_2}$ if $p_1 < p_2$;

2. for every $p \geq 1$ there are fulfilled the conditions:

$$\bigcup_{i=k_p+1}^{k_{p+1}} I_i = \{1, 2, ..., n\};$$

$$\bigcup_{i=k_p+1}^{k_{p+1}-1} I_i \neq \{1, 2, ..., n\}. \quad (10)$$

Such sequence always exists in according to condition (1), is defined uniquely and called minimal sequence. With regard to condition (9) we have $k_{p+1} - k_p \leq l + 1$.

Consider the sequence of iteration $\{\mathbf{y}^r\}_{r=k_{p+1}}^{k_p+1}$ for which in vector $\mathbf{y}^{k_p+1}$ each component is restored if only one time in comparison with vector $\mathbf{y}^{k_p}$. Such sequence of vectors is called macroiteration, and number p - the number of macroiterations.

Coming from a real work of SICN the delay sequence $J = \{\sigma(k)\}_{k=1}^{\infty}$ is been building in such way:

1. if $k = 1$ then $\sigma(k) = 0$;

2. if $1 < k \leq p_1$ and $p_r + 1 < k \leq p_{r+1}$ then

$$\sigma_i(k) = \begin{cases} \sigma_i(k-1) & \text{if } i \in I_k \\ \sigma_i(k-1) + 1 & \text{if } i \notin I_k \end{cases} \quad (11)$$

3. if $k = p_r + 1$ then

$$\sigma_i(k) = \begin{cases} k-2 & \text{if } i \in I_k \\ k-1 & \text{if } i \notin I_k \end{cases},$$

where $i = 1, 2, ..., n$.

From this building it is obviously that $0 \leq \sigma_i(k) \leq k-1$ and $\sigma_i(k) \geq \sigma_i(k-1) \geq ... \geq k-l$, i. e. it is fulfilled inequality $k - \sigma_i(k) \leq l$ for every $k \in N$ and $i = 1, 2, ..., n$. So the sequence $\{\sigma(k)\}_{k=1}^{\infty}$ satisfies to conditions (6) and number $l = s$ defines the delay of system.

So work of SICN can be characterized by means of calculations by formula (5), and the sequence of chaotic sets $I = \{I_k\}_{k=1}^{\infty}$ is defined by (8) and the delay sequence $J = \{\sigma(k)\}_{k=1}^{\infty}$ is defined by (11).

Consider the problem connected with the choice of sequence of independent discrete random variables $\omega^k = \{\omega_1^k, \omega_2^k, ..., \omega_n^k\}$ each of them ω_i^k has finite number of values $1, 2, ..., l$.

Assume the discrete random variable $\omega_i^k = \omega$ has value j with probability

$$\mathbf{P}\{\omega = j\} = p_j. \quad (12)$$

Its mathematical expectation is given by

$$\mathbf{M}\omega = \sum_{j=1}^{l} j p_j,$$

where

$$\sum_{j=1}^{l} p_j = 1$$

and its distribution function has form

$$\mathbf{F}_\omega(x) = \sum_{i<x} p_i.$$

We will say that a continuous random variable $\eta(t)$ with distribution function $\mathbf{G}_\eta(x)$ approximates a discrete random variable ω which has finite number of values $1, 2, ..., l$ if $\mathbf{G}_\eta(j) = \mathbf{F}_\omega(j)$ for $j = 1, 2, ..., l-1$.

For simulation of work of SICN assume that approximating random variable $\eta(t)$ has normal distribution. We will show how with the help of $\eta(t)$ can be built the discrete variable ω which is approximated by $\eta(t)$.

Define a random variable ω in such way:

$$\omega = \begin{cases} 1 & \text{if } \eta(t) \leq 1; \\ j+1 & \text{if } j < \eta(t) \leq j+1, \quad \text{j=1,2,...,l-2;} \\ l & \text{if } \eta(t) > l-1. \end{cases}$$

Let $\mathbf{G}_\eta(x)$ - distribution function of random variable $\eta(t)$. Denote by $p_j = \mathbf{P}\{\omega = j\}$ for $j = 1, 2, ..., l$. We will calculate the distribution function $\mathbf{F}_\eta(x)$ for $x = j$ and show that $\mathbf{F}_\eta(j) = \mathbf{G}_\eta(j)$ for $j = 1, 2, ..., l-1$. Indeed, $p_1 = \mathbf{F}_\omega(1) = \mathbf{P}\{\omega = 1\} = \mathbf{P}\{\eta(t) \leq 1\} = \mathbf{G}_\eta(1)$. For $j = 1, 2, ..., l-1$ we have $p_{j+1} = \mathbf{P}\{\omega = j+1\} = \mathbf{P}\{j < \eta(t) \leq j+1\} = \mathbf{G}_\eta(j+1) - \mathbf{G}_\eta(j)$. And so for $j = 2, 3, ..., l-1$

$$\mathbf{F}_\omega(j) = \sum_{i \leq j} p_i = \mathbf{G}_\eta(j).$$

Thus continuous random variable $\eta(t)$ approximates discrete random variable ω and

$$p_l = 1 - \mathbf{F}_\omega(l-1) = 1 - \sum_{j \leq l-1} p_j.$$

Therefore $\sum_{i=1}^{l} p_i = 1$ and the random variable ω has probability distribution in the form (12).

To give a random variable $\eta(t)$ with normal distribution it is required to define its mathematical expectation $\mathbf{M}\eta$ and standard deviation σ. Coming from the connection of random variables $\eta(t)$ and ω it is naturally to consider $\mathbf{M}\eta = l/2$. For definition of standard deviation σ we will use so-called three sigma rule. As far as the variable $\eta(t)$ approximates the random variable ω on interval from 1 to $l-1$ it is required to consider that event $| \eta - \mathbf{M}\eta | < \mathbf{M}\eta$ is to be practically reliable. It is known that probability of such event is defined by formula:

$$\mathbf{P}\{| \eta - \mathbf{M}\eta | < \mathbf{M}\eta\} = 2\mathbf{\Phi}(\frac{\mathbf{M}\eta}{\sigma})$$

where

$$\mathbf{\Phi}(x) = \frac{1}{\sqrt{2\pi}} \int_0^x \exp^{-\frac{y^2}{2}} dy$$

is well-known and tabulated Laplace function. As far as $2\mathbf{\Phi} \approx 0.997$ then for $\sigma = \mathbf{M}\eta/3$ event $| \eta - \mathbf{M}\eta | < \mathbf{M}\eta$ is fulfilled with probability closed to 1. Thus it is possible to choise standard deviation of variable $\eta(t)$ which equals to $l/6$.

4 Computer simulation and experimental results

For computing experiment consider boundary value Dirichler problem for Laplace differential equation in domain $D \cup \Gamma$, where D is square with side a; $D = \{(x, y) \in R^2 \mid 0 \leq x, y \leq a\}$, Γ is boundary of this square:

$$\frac{\delta^2 u(x,y)}{\delta x^2} + \frac{\delta^2 u(x,y)}{\delta y^2} = 0 \tag{13}$$

$$u(x,y) \mid_\Gamma = g(x,y) \tag{14}$$

where $g(x, y)$ is known function which is given on boundary Γ .

We use the finite-difference method for numerical solution of this boundary value problem. For this aim we cover domain $D \cup \Gamma \subset R^2$ by mesh with step $h = a/(N-1)$. Coordinates of mesh points $x_i = ih$, $y_j = jh \quad (i, j = 0, 1, ..., N-1)$; for short we denote by u_{ij}, g_{ij} values $u(x_i, y_j), g(x_i, y_j)$. In inner mesh point (i, j) problem (13) is changed by finite-difference equation:

$$u_{i,j} = \frac{1}{4}(u_{i-1,j} + u_{i+1,j} + u_{i,j-1} + u_{i,j+1}). \tag{15}$$

In boundary mesh points it is supposed

$$u_{i,j} = g_{i,j} \tag{16}$$

Regulate components of vector $\mathbf{v}$ of unknowns naturally:

$$\mathbf{v} = (u_{00}, u_{10}, ..., u_{N-1,0}, u_{01}, u_{11}, ..., u_{N-1,N-1}).$$

Then finite-difference problem can be written in matrix form

$$\mathbf{v} = \mathbf{L}\mathbf{v} + \mathbf{b} \tag{17}$$

where $\mathbf{L}$ - matrix of finite-difference Laplace operator; $\mathbf{b}$ - vector consisting from components of vector of boundary conditions g, and $b_{ij} = g_{ij}$ if (i, j) is boundary mesh point and $b_{ij} = 0$ otherwise.

It is known that all eigenvalues of matrix $\mathbf{L}$ by absolute value is less than 1, i. e. $\rho(\mathbf{L}) < 1$. And so for solving of system of linear algebraic equations (17) we can apply the asynchronous method of chaotic relaxations with delay by formula (5), and coordinate function f_α for inner mesh point α is defined by equality (15) and for boundary mesh point - by equality (16).

We represent results of computer simulation for function $g(x, y)$ of such form

$$g(x,y) = \begin{cases} 1/2 & \text{if } (x,y) = (0, a-b), (b, a); \\ -1/2 & \text{if } (x,y) = (a-b, 0), (a, b); , \\ 0 & \text{otherwise.} \end{cases}$$

where $b = a/(N-1)$.

The important characteristics of iterative methods are speed of convergence and speed of response of the method. Remind that speed of convergence of sequence $\{\mathbf{y}^k\}_{k=1}^{\infty}$ to fix point $\mathbf{y}^*$ is called lower limit

$$\Psi = \liminf_{k\to\infty} \frac{-\lg \|\mathbf{y}^k - \mathbf{y}^*\|}{k}$$

if this limit exists.

Using speed of convergence it is possible to obtain approximate value of number of iterations n which are required for reduction norm of initial error $\epsilon^0 = \mathbf{y}^0 - \mathbf{y}^*$ in ξ^{-1} times:

$$n \approx -\frac{\lg(\xi)}{\Psi}.$$

Denote by

$$\tau = \frac{-\lg \|\mathbf{y}^k - \mathbf{y}^*\|}{k}.$$

It was studing dependence τ on number of iterations and macroiterations for different values N and l. Discretization number N of mesh with size NxN and delay number of SICN l were varied from 8 to 32. We also conducted the computer simulations for this problem (13) by means of method of simple iteration, simple Seidel's method and Seidel's method with relaxation parameters $\omega_1 = 1$ and $\omega_2 = 1.27$. Computer simulation was conducted also by method of asynchronous chaotic relaxations with delay using relaxation parameter ω_2 in such way:

$$v^{k+1} = v^k - \omega_2(v^k - v^{k+\frac{1}{2}}),$$

where $v^{k+\frac{1}{2}}$ is calculated by formula (5). The results of these simulations are given in the form of graphs on Fig.1 and Fig.2 for $N = 32$.

The figure 1 shows the dependence τ on number of makroiterations for method of asynchronous chaotic relaxations with delay for different number of delay. It is shown that the speed of convergence for this method is reducing with the increase of the number of delay. But with increase of the number of macroiterations that difference is becoming insignificant. The figure 2 shows the dependence τ on the number of iteration for numerical solution of problem (13),(14) by different methods. It is shown that the method of asynchronous chaotic relaxations with delay has approximately such speed of convergence as method of simple iteration and some less one than Seidel's method. But taking into account that fulfilment time of each macroiteration for method of asynchronous chaotic relaxations is considerably less we can say that the equivalent speed of network consisted from speed independent processors will be considerably higher.

At the work of D.Chason and W.Miranker [4] there given the estimates of speed of convergence of iterative sequences obtained by asynchronous methods. If $\{k_p\}_{p=1}^{\infty}$ is a minimal sequence for method of chaotic relaxation with delay then

$$\Psi \geq -(\liminf_{k\to\infty} \frac{k(p)}{k}) \lg \rho(L),$$

where $k(p) = p$, $k_p \leq k < k_{p+1}$.

In fact

$$\liminf_{k\to\infty} \frac{k(p)}{k}$$

is a lower limit of ratio of number of macroiterations to full number of iterations.

These estimates are obtained the full support at the result of conducted computer simulation.

5 Conclusion

Conducted investigations show that chaotic self-organizing processes arising in speed independence networks can be simulated by means of sequences of chaotic sets. There exist convergent selforganizing chaotic algorithmical processes in networks with speed independent processes which don't require programmed work of parallel structure. Arising in them chaotic processes for contracting operators have speed of convergence which is not worse than known methods have.

Recently we considered also the parallel algorithms for image reconstructions by method of asynchronous chaotic relaxations with delay using the Monte-Carlo method, which imitate the fulfilment of chaotic computing processes in networks consisted from speed independent processors. It was conducted their computer simulation with application to tomographic reconstruction from incomplete data. Also it was shown that they give good results by comparison with corresponding synchronous well known iterative algebraic algorithms.

These investigations prove some perspectives for development of networks with speed independent processors like medium in which selforganizing computer processers arise.

6 Acknowledgment

The author is grateful to A.Katkow for formulation of a question, useful discussions and constant attention to this work.

References

[1] D.E.Muller, " Infinite sequences and finite Machines," *Proc. Fourth Ann. IEEE Symp. on Switch. Circuit Th. Log. Design*, S-156, pp.9-16, 1963.

[2] A.Katkov, V.Romantsov, A.Novicky, *Fixation device for transient process in digital circuit,* Autor's Sertificate USSR N1200249 G0513 23/02, 1985.

[3] A.Katkov, *Digital simulating machines,* Kiev: Naukova Dumka, 1989.

[4] D.Chason, W.Miranker, "Chaotic relaxation," *Linear Algebra Appl.*, Vol.2, pp.199-222, 1969.

[5] G.M.Baudet, "Asynchronous iterative methods for multiprocessors," *J. Assoc. Comput. Mach.*, Vol.25 pp.226-244, 1978.

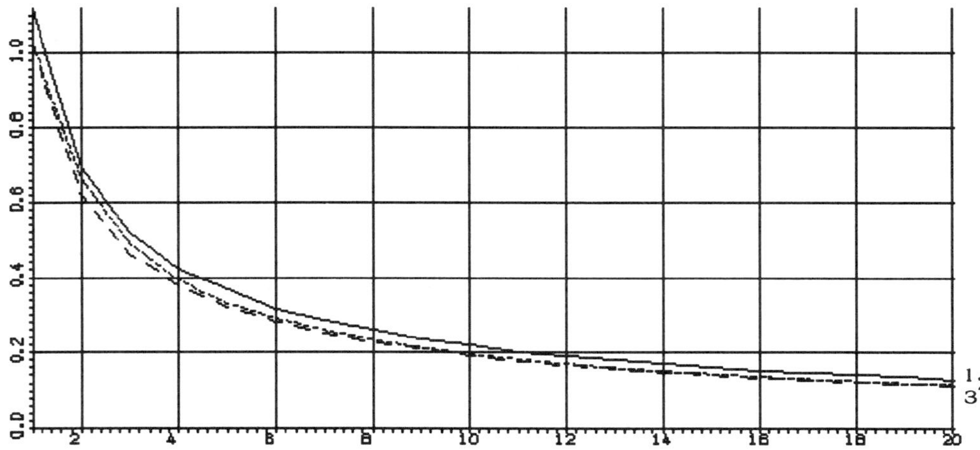

Figure 1: Graphs of dependence τ on number of macroiterations for numerical solution of problem (13),(14) by method of asynchronous chaotic relaxations with delay if $\omega_1 = 1.27$ accordingly for: 1- $l = 4$, 2 - $l = 8$, 3-$l = 16$

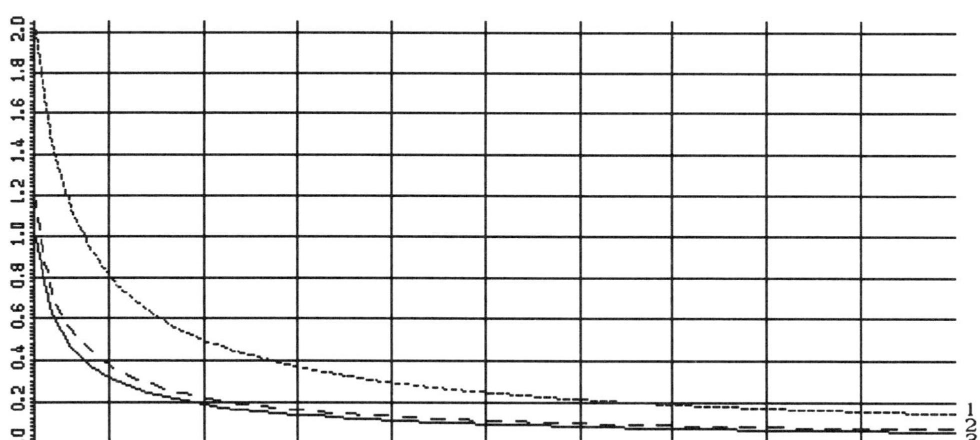

Figure 2: Graphs of dependence τ on number of iterations (macroiterations) for numerical solution of problem (13),(14) by: 1 - Seidel's method if $\omega_1 = 1$; 2 - method of asynchronous chaotic relaxations with delay if $\omega_1 = 1$; 3 - method of simple iteration

Sparse Householder QR Factorization on a Mesh

Ramón Doallo, Juan Touriño

Dept. Electrónica y Sistemas
Universidad de La Coruña
Campus de Elviña s/n
15071 La Coruña, Spain
E-mail: {esdoallo,juan}@udc.es

Emilio L. Zapata

Dept. Arquitectura de Computadores
Universidad de Málaga
Plaza El Ejido s/n
29013 Málaga, Spain
E-mail: ezapata@atc.ctima.uma.es

Abstract

In this document we are going to analyze the parallelization of QR factorization by means of Householder transformations. This parallelization will be carried out on a machine with a mesh topology (a 2-D torus to be more precise). We use a cyclic distribution of the elements of the sparse matrix M we want to decompose over the processors. Each processor represents the nonzero elements of its part of the matrix by a one-dimensional doubly linked list data structure. Then, we describe the different procedures that constitute the parallel algorithm. As an application of QR factorization, we concentrate on the least squares problem and finally we present a evaluation of the efficiency of this algorithm for a set of test matrices from the Harwell-Boeing sparse matrix collection.

1 Introduction

In many scientific fields it is necessary to solve large systems of linear equations: fluid dynamics, molecular chemistry, aeronautic simulation... In many cases, these systems are sparse, feature we can use in order to reduce the computation time and the memory necessary for the solution of these problems. We can use iterative methods [3], such as the conjugate gradient algorithm or direct methods [7], mainly based on Gaussian elimination. In this document we consider a direct method based on orthogonalization: QR decomposition. It basically consists in the decomposition of a matrix M of dimensions $A * B$ (with $A \geq B$) into the product of two matrices: $Q * R$, where Q is an orthogonal matrix (that is, the columns of Q are orthogonal and of unit length; consequently, $Q^T * Q = I$, that is, $Q^T = Q^{-1}$) and R is upper triangular.

LU decomposition is more widely employed for the solution of sparse linear equation systems because it is less costly in computation time and memory despite the better numerical stability of QR decomposition. However, the main use of QR decomposition is in the various applications it has in linear algebra, such as eigenvalue calculation and the least squares problem. There are several algorithms for finding this decomposition: Householder reflections or transformations, Givens rotations and Modified Gram-Schmidt algorithm. Different results obtained for dense matrices can be found in [4, 18, 16, 17] on distributed-memory machines; or for sparse matrices in [15, 13, 9, 14].

The algorithm we will implement is the one based on Householder transformations [10, chapter 5] with column pivoting in order to contemplate those cases in which the rank of matrix M is not maximum (B). Pivoting will also be used in order to provide numerical stability. This algorithm obtains a matrix Q of dimensions $A * A$ and a matrix R of dimensions $A * B$, in which the elements of the last A-B rows of this matrix are zero.

The parallel algorithm has been programmed for Fujitsu's *AP1000* MIMD distributed-memory computer and previously debugged using the software simulator called CASIM [6]. This supercomputer has a 2-D torus topology. It consists of 64 to 1024 processing elements or cells (*SPARC* processors) and three independent communication networks: the *torus network (T-net)* for point to point communications between cells; the *broadcast network (B-net)* for 1 to N communications between the host and the cells as well as for the distribution and recollection of the data; and the *synchronization network (S-net)* for the barrier synchronization. For more details on this architecture consult [12]. To all this we must add a specific instruction set [1] for the distribution and recollection of the data (very adequate for working with dense matrices) and reduction instructions for obtaining sums, maxima and minima of the elements in different cells. We are going to assume, in the notation, a general configuration of $m * n$ processing elements or cells. Each cell is going to be identified by coordinates *(idx,idy)*, with $0 \leq idx < n$ and $0 \leq idy < m$; m identifies the number of cells in the Y axis and n the number of cells in the X axis.

2 Data storage structure

In general, we will say that a matrix is sparse if it is advantageous to exploit the null elements. As in the sparse QR decomposition problem the structure of the

1066-6192/96 $5.00
Proceedings of PDP '96

matrices varies (due to the *fill-in*), it is convenient to use dynamic structures for the storage of the data in the cells that support the changes in the disposition of the nonzero elements. The main factor we have taken into account in the selection of the data storage structure has been the nature of the algorithm. Thus, as we will later see, we are only going to need column access to the matrix (except in the least squares problem). Consequently, we have chosen to use doubly linked lists, each one of which represents a column of the matrix. Their structure is given by the following code:

```
typedef struct item {
  index i;
  type mij;
  struct item *up;
  struct item *down; } item;
```

where *index* is the data type of the row index i of the matrix element (an integer, for example) and *type* is the data type of the element of the matrix. This list is arranged in growing order of the index i. We also need two pointers per list, one at the beginning and another one at the end:

```
item *startcr[MAXSIZE];
item *lastcr[MAXSIZE];
```

where $MAXSIZE$ is a constant that represents the maximum number of local rows or columns.

An important fact is that we only require efficient access by columns in this algorithm; this implies large memory savings. Thus, in a LU decomposition for sparse matrices [5], we would need a data structure that facilitated access both by rows and by columns, such as a two-dimensional doubly linked list, and in order to do this we would need to store, in addition to what we have indicated, the j index of each element and two additional pointers (one to the previous row element and another to the next). On the other hand, the time needed for managing this structure would increase.

The parallel algorithm uses several routines for insertion and deletion in the lists in order to optimize their handling. As an example, there is an *insertion* procedure that contemplates an insertion at the end of the list or in the middle, and as a complement there is another procedure *fast_insertion* that only takes into account insertions at the beginning of the list. The division of insertion into two procedures is due to the fact that in certain steps of the algorithm we are only going to need insertions at the beginning of the lists and this way computation times can be reduced.

3 The parallel algorithm

The parallel algorithm developed has been generalized for any dimension of the mesh and any dimension of matrix M, so that the execution for a single processor is going to be equivalent to the sequential algorithm.

3.1 Data distribution

We have chosen a cyclic distribution of the data, also known as *grid* distribution and *scattered square* decomposition. Element (I,J) of the original matrix M is located in a cell $(idx,idy)=(J \bmod n, I \bmod m)$. The original matrix M is distributed among the local matrices (lists) and, after executing the corresponding parallel algorithm, we will obtain a piece of the matrix R in each one of them. It is therefore an *in-place* algorithm. From the global indices (I,J) that identify the elements of the matrix, we can obtain the local indices (i,j) in each cell: $i=\lfloor \frac{I}{m} \rfloor$, $j=\lfloor \frac{J}{n} \rfloor$. If the dimension of matrix M is $A * B$, the dimension of the local matrices once the distribution has been carried out would be $a * b$ (the dimension will vary depending on the cell we consider): $a = \lfloor \frac{A}{m} \rfloor + idy < A \bmod m$; $b= \lfloor \frac{B}{n} \rfloor + idx < B \bmod n$. The logical expressions $idy < A \bmod m$, $idx < B \bmod n$ will return one if they are fulfilled and zero otherwise. In a similar way, we can reconstruct the global indices of the matrix from the local indices: $I = (i * m) + idy, J = (j * n) + idx$. This is necessary for the result recollection stage (matrix R and the solution vector of the least squares problem). The selection of this distribution responds to two reasons: data balancing and load balancing.

So, this is a problem of reducing the index space. The algorithm is made up of as many steps as columns in the original matrix (unless the rank is smaller). Let us assume that in a given moment we are in step k of the algorithm. Then, as we will later see, elements (α,μ) of matrix R, will be updated with $k \leq \alpha < A$; $k \leq \mu < B$. It is clear that if we employed a consecutive distribution of the data, as the algorithm was executed, a large number of the cells would be inactive because the elements of the matrix that have to be updated would be concentrated in a few cells. This is prevented using a cyclic distribution.

3.2 Main procedure of the program

In what follows we present the main body of the parallel algorithm. This code is the same for all the cells of the computer.

cell_main()

```
1    Receiving_Data_from_Host();
2    rank=B;
3    Norms();
4    for (current_index=0;current_index<B;
          current_index++) {
5      Pivot_Element();
6      if (fabs(pivot)<EPSILON) {
7        rank=current_index;
8        break; }
9      Column_Swap();
10     Householder_Vector();
11     Householder_Product(); }
12   Sending_Data_to_Host();
```

(1-2) The cells receive the submatrices corresponding to the original matrix M according to a cyclic distribution scheme; *rank* indicates the rank of this original matrix. The maximum rank for *M* is *B* (number of columns), as $A \geq B$.

(3) This procedure finds the square of the euclidean norms of the columns of matrix *M* and stores them in vector *norm*. The fact that each list represents one column of the matrix favours the calculation. Each cell obtains the local norms corresponding to the column segments (local lists) it contains. By means of the reduction instruction *y_fsum* of the *AP1000* (sum by columns), the *norm* vector of a given cell is going to contain the norms of the global columns corresponding to the original matrix *M*.

We go through the columns of the matrix and perform all the following actions:

(5-8) Obtain in variable *pivot* the pivot element, which is the maximum of the norms of the columns whose order is higher than or equal to *current_index* (iteration we are currently processing) of our global matrix. The index of the global column containing the pivot element is called *pivot_index*. Both values (*pivot* and *pivot_index*) will be contained in all the cells. If the pivot element is zero (*EPSILON* is the required precision), the rank of the matrix is given by the value *current_index* and the algorithm ends. Initially, we calculate the local maximum of each cell (this value is going to be the same for each cell column). The global maximum is obtained by means of a reduction instruction (*x_fmax*) which finds the maximum by cell rows.

(9) If the pivot is different from zero, we perform a swap of the column we are processing with the column of the pivot element in matrix *R* and of their corresponding norms.

(10-11) Once the pivoting has been carried out, we apply the Householder transformations, updating the appropriate elements of matrix *R*, as well as the corresponding norms. In the following sections we describe the last three procedures in more detail.

(12) The local results of the cells are sent to the host in order to reconstruct the global results.

3.3 Column_Swap procedure

A swap of the square of the norm and of the column of matrix *R* with global index *current_index* (current column we are processing) with the norm and column corresponding to the global index *pivot_index* (column of the pivot element) is carried out. This can be observed in figure 1.

The cell column that contains the current column exchanges this column of matrix *R* (as well as the corresponding norm) with the cell column that contains the pivot column. Consequently, we have to send a local list to another cell (which can be the same one). In order to carry out this process of sending information to another cell, we have to indicate the start memory address where this information is located and the size. This implies that the information we send has to occupy consecutive memory positions, situation that obviously does not happen with the information contained in a data structure such as a list. This would imply a great temporal cost, since we would

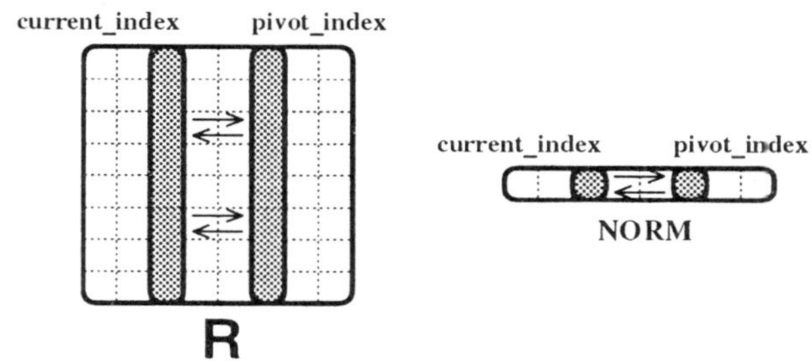

Figure 1: Column swap (pivoting)

have to establish as many connections (for sending the data) as components of the list. In the *AP1000* computer, the communication time *T* can be modelled by an affine function so that for a message of *N* bytes, $T = t_0 + t_b * N \mu s$, where t_0 is a fixed overhead in establishing the communication and t_b is the transfer time per byte. In point to point communications (using the *T-net*), $t_0 = 6.9\mu s$ and $t_b = 0.069\mu s$. In the *B-net* these values vary depending on several conditions: $t_0 = 43 - 60\mu s$ and $t_b = 0.026 - 0.042\mu s$. In [11] we find numerous experiments and measures of the communication times of the *AP1000*. Therefore, it would be interesting to send all the components of the list in a single message and this way we would save the fixed overhead in each one of the communications. In order to implement this solution, we will use a special structure, a *packed vector* [7, chapter 2] that is going to act as a buffer for sending the necessary information.

As we show in figure 2, the procedure is the following: we go through the local list corresponding to the column of matrix *R* from the end; as we go through it, we store each one of the elements in the buffer and erase the element from the list. The management of the erasure has been optimized: we use a specific routine for erasing the last element of the list. As header of this exchange buffer, we indicate the value of the square of the norm of that column. As a conclusion, with a single pass over the local list, it is completely erased and its content written in the swap buffer. As a result, we have our information in consecutive memory positions and we send the corresponding column of *R*, as well as the square of the norm in a single message. The receiving cell will reconstruct the new local list for *R* by means of a function for insertion. This insertion has also been optimized: we always insert at the beginning of the local list we are constructing, as the buffer is arranged according to a decreasing order of the row index.

3.4 Householder_Vector procedure

By means of this procedure we are going to get the *Householder vector (v)*, of length *dim=A-current_index*, so that *v[current_index]* (the first component of the vector) is 1 and the product $(I - 2vv^T/v^Tv)\delta$ is zero in all of the components except the first one. *I* is the identity matrix, of dimensions

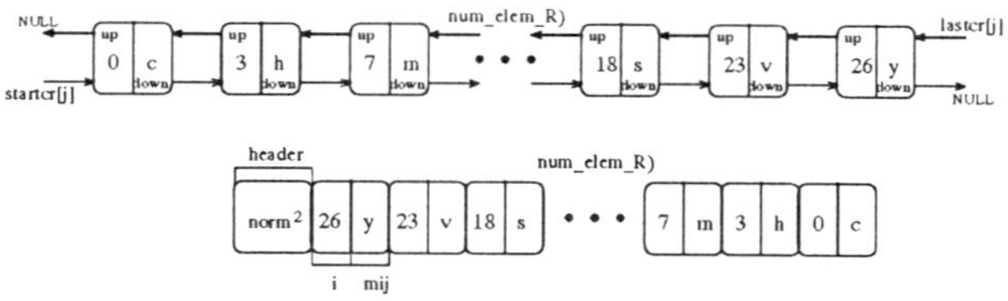

Figure 2: Buffer for sending local lists

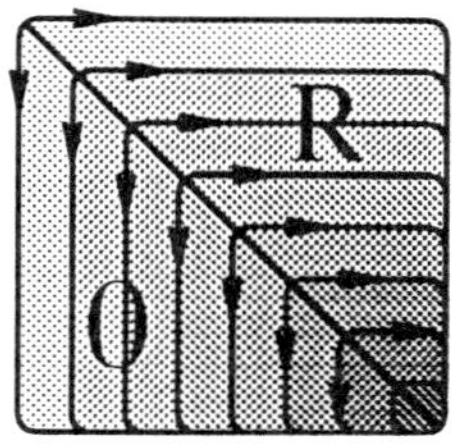

Figure 3: Process of obtaining matrix R from the original matrix M

*dim*dim* and δ is the subcolumn *(α,current_index)* of our matrix, *current_index* $\leq \alpha < A$. We call matrix $P = I - 2vv^T/v^Tv$, of dimensions *dim*dim*, Householder matrix.

In order to get vector v we only require accessing the current column (access by columns) and divide it by a given value. Once this is completed, each cell column will contain vector v in a cyclic distribution. As the *Householder vector* is going to contain many null elements and is going to be broadcast to all the cells of the mesh, we are going to store it in a packed vector. Nonetheless, so as not to complicate the notation, we reference it as if it was a conventional vector.

In this procedure, only the processor column that contains the current column we are processing is going to be working.

3.5 Householder_Product procedure

In this procedure we are going to update matrix M, in particular, the submatrix S of dimensions *(A-current_index)*(B-current_index)*, made up of elements (α, μ), *current_index* $\leq \alpha < A$ and *current_index* $\leq \mu < B$, so that we will substitute the original submatrix S by the product $P{*}S$, being P the Householder matrix. This product $P{*}S$ is equivalent to performing the operation $S + vw^T$, with $w = \beta S^T v$ and β a floating point number equal to $-2/v^Tv$. Remember that the global vector v starts in index *current_index* and ends in *A-1*. On the other hand, the global vector w also starts in position *current_index* and ends in *B-1*.

As we have calculated the Householder vector in the previous procedure, the updating of S as $S{=}P{*}S$ would make all the elements of subcolumn *(α,current_index)*, *current_index* $< \alpha < A$ of our matrix zero. Thus, once all the iterations (B iterations) of the algorithm have been carried out, we will get the upper triangular matrix R, as shown in figure 3.

The cyclic distribution of the data is going to allow us to follow an optimal path through submatrix S distributed in the cells. The strategy consists in going through the columns (local lists) corresponding to this submatrix, starting from the last column. When we reach a column whose global index is less than *current_index*, we end the process. Also, in order to process each column, we go through the corresponding list from the end until we reach a row whose global index is less than *current_index*.

In the first place, we obtain in all the cells the value β. After this, we calculate vector $w = \beta S^T v$, from element *w[current_index]* to *w[B-1]* (its length is therefore, *B-current_index*). It is not necessary to transpose S due to the disposition of the data. Each cell row will contain vector w which is distributed in a cyclic manner. We will update submatrix S, as $S = S + vw^T$. For this, we place ourselves in element S_{ij} of matrix S which is the one we are going to update and make $S_{ij} = S_{ij} + v_i w_j$. When this sum is carried out, it may happen that $S_{ij} = 0$ and $v_i, w_j \neq 0$, so that an element of submatrix S which was initially null, now takes a nonzero value (fill-in); we therefore insert it in the corresponding local list. It may also happen that element S_{ij} takes a value of zero and consequently, we will have to eliminate it from the corresponding local list (the opposite phenomenon to the fill-in).

This section of code is optimized because when it updates a column of submatrix S, the corresponding local list is going to suffer a single pass, always starting from the last one of its elements and until an element with a global row index lower than *current_index* is found. In addition, we have taken into account that when we perform an insertion at the beginning of a local list (due to the fill-in), all the rest of the insertions will also be at the beginning of the list. In this procedure the norms of the columns will also be updated.

We must point out that once the algorithm has ended, what we really get is a $M * \Pi = Q * R$ factorization, where Π is a permutation $B * B$, made up by the product of *rank* elementary permutations: $\Pi = \pi_0 * \pi_1 * \ldots * \pi_{rank-1}$, being each π_i, with *i=0,...,rank-1*, the identity matrix or a matrix resulting from swapping two of its columns. This is due to the pivoting we carry out in the *Column_Swap* procedure. In general, obtaining matrix Q in an explicit manner is not going to be necessary. It can be obtained by previously storing it in a factorized format. It consists in storing the Householder vectors as they are obtained, in the lower triangular part of matrix R. Each Householder vector will have a length of *A-current_index*. However, the first element (*v[current_index]*), as we have obtained it, will always be one and it will not be necessary to store it. Consequently, we will use column *current_index* of matrix R, from row *current_index+1* to row *A-1* in order to store the corresponding Householder vector. And, from this factorized format, an algorithm can be applied (***backward accumulation***) in order to get Q in an explicit way (see [10, chapter 5] for more details).

4 An application: the least squares problem

As an application example of the QR decomposition, we are going to approach a standard problem in linear algebra: the least squares problem. It consists in calculating a vector x of length B that minimizes $||Mx - z||_2$ (euclidean norm), where M is a matrix of dimensions $A * B$ (with $A \geq B$) and z is a vector of length A. If the rank of M is maximum (B), the least squares problem is going to have a unique solution (x_{LS}). In any other case, it is going to have an infinite number of solutions x_{SOL}, out of which there will only be one whose norm is minimum and which we will also denote as x_{LS}: $x_{LS} = x_{SOL}/||x_{SOL}||_2$ *is minimum*. In the case where A=B, the least squares problem is equivalent to solving a linear equation system $Mx = z$ as, obviously, $||Mx - z||_2 = 0$ (minimum norm).

The solution of this problem can be approached adapting the parallel algorithm that carries out the QR decomposition of matrix M. In particular, the least squares problem is going to be equivalent to solving the upper triangular system: $R\Pi^T x = Q^T z$. This approach is adequate due to the good numerical stability of the QR factorization. With this algorithm we will get the unique solution to the least squares problem when $rank(M) = B$. In the case where $rank(M) < B$, we will get one of the infinite solutions: the one called basic solution, which will have a maximum of *rank* nonzero elements and that in general will not coincide with the minimum norm solution x_{LS}.

4.1 Obtaining vector $Q^T z$

Once vector z has been cyclicly distributed in each cell column, the product $Q^T z$ can be calculated at the same time we perform the Householder transformations. In order to get this product it is not necessary to have physically a vector z, as we store it directly in vector *qtz* and through an iterative process, in the end we will obtain in *qtz* the $Q^T z$ product we desire (in-place algorithm). Consequently, initially, vector *qtz* will contain vector z (of length A). And, in each one of the iterations (B, if the rank is maximum) of our parallel algorithm we will carry out the following actions for the elements of vector *qtz* and v, from component *current_index* to component *A-1*: $\lambda = \beta qtz^T v$; $qtz = qtz + v\lambda$.

Once all the iterations of the algorithm have ended, we will get the product $Q^T z$ in vector *qtz*, from index *0* to index *B-1*. Now we will add two procedures to the main body of the program: *Back_Substitution()* and *Permutation()*.

4.2 Back_Substitution procedure

By means of this procedure we will solve the upper triangular system $Rx = Q^T z$. The corresponding sequential algorithm is the following:

for (i=rank-1;i≥0;i- -)

$$x_i = (qtz_i - \sum_{j=i+1}^{rank-1} r_{ij} x_j)/r_{ii};$$

being r_{ij} element *(i,j)* of matrix R. It is a loop with data dependencies, and thus this loop must be maintained in the parallel code without any possibility of distributing it among the cells. In addition, it is necessary to access the elements of matrix R by rows. This implies a big drawback, as matrix R is stored by columns. We solve it using an auxiliary pointer vector with as many components as columns in the matrix. This would permit access to matrix R (from bottom to top) by rows going through the linked lists corresponding to the columns of the matrix only once.

Once the backsubstitution is carried out we get, in each cell row, the solution vector x of global length B cyclicly distributed, so that the global component J of vector x will be replicated in the cell column with *idx=J mod n*.

4.3 Permutation procedure

Due to the column swap carried out in the QR factorization, in order to obtain the final solution to the least squares problem we will have to apply the Π permutation to the components of vector x obtained in the previous procedure, so that we overwrite x with vector: Πx. All the cells will have a vector called *permut*, of local length B (it is the only global vector whose components are not distributed among the cells, but is completely stored in them). This vector will contain the index of the swapped column (pivot column) in each iteration. For this, we will add as first command of the *Column_Swap* procedure:

```
permut[current_index]=pivot_index;
```

This way, applying the swaps stored in vector *permut* starting from the end, we obtain the elements of vector x in the correct order.

5 Evaluation of the algorithm and conclusions

In order to carry out several temporal measurements of the parallel algorithm we have made use of the *Performance Analyzer* of the *AP1000* computer [2], which analyzes performance during execution and provides several temporal measures: times of the task, of inactivity of the cells, of interruptions, of calls to libraries, average, maximum and minimum values of these times for all the cells, information on various events, etc.

The sparse matrices we have used for the evaluation of the algorithm were obtained from the *Harwell-Boeing* collection [8]. Table 1 shows a description of the matrices we have selected. $A*B$ indicates the dimensions of the matrix; *El(M)* the number of nonzero elements and *El(R)* the number of nonzero elements of matrix R. The selection of these matrices is due to the fact that all of them include vector z, necessary for solving the least squares problem and,

Matrix	Origin	A*B	El(M)	El(R)
WELL1033	Least squares problems in surveying	1033*320	4732	13832
WELL1850	Least squares problems in surveying	1850*712	8758	52303
SHERMAN1	Oil reservoir simulation	1000*1000	3750	66187

Table 1: Harwell-Boeing sparse matrices for the evaluation

Matrix	1*1	2*2	4*4	8*8
WELL1033	112.31	47.13	16.10	6.41
WELL1850	1515.07	408.13	120.71	35.93
SHERMAN1	574.14	185.91	62.78	26.70

Table 2: Execution times (in seconds)

in particular, matrices *WELL1033* and *WELL1850* are specific for the solution of this problem.

Table 2 shows the execution times (in seconds) for some of the configurations of the mesh. All the measures depicted include the time required for carrying out the QR factorization and solving the least squares problem. The times required for the distribution and recollection of the data are not included because we assume that the problem of solving least squares is a possible subproblem within a wider program.

Figure 4 shows the efficiency and the speed-up obtained for these sparse matrices. Observe that the results are better for larger sizes of the matrix. This is because with larger matrices there are more calculations and thus the parallelism is more efficiently used. Small sizes of matrix M result in low efficiencies because the calculation time of the task itself is small with respect to the additional time required by communications (message passing) and other factors. In addition, a larger number of nonzero elements (as is the case of matrix *WELL1850*) also provides longer effective calculation times and the parallelism applied motivates that the calculation time of the task in each processor is large with respect to the times that are not related with the task itself.

The factors that are going to influence the fill-in of a given sparse matrix are the following: the dimension and rank of the matrix, the degree of sparsity (number of null elements) and a factor of great importance but difficult to model, the pattern of the matrix, that is, the location of the nonzero elements. Thus, with the same dimension, rank and degree of dispersion for two matrices, the fill-in may vary significantly, depending on how the nonzero elements are placed. Consequently, there will also be large variations in the execution times and efficiencies. The reduction of the fill-in is the work we are currently carrying out. As a conclusion, the sparse approach to the QR factorization we have presented is more adequate with respect to the dense approach the bigger the dimension of matrix M and the smaller the number of nonzero elements (high degree of sparsity).

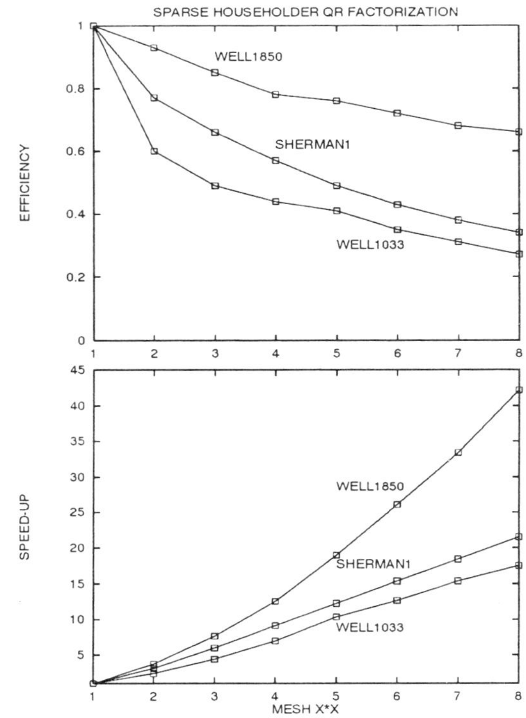

Figure 4: Efficiency and speed-up measures

Acknowledgements

We gratefully thank to the Fujitsu Parallel Computing Research Centre (Japan) and the Galician Supercomputing Centre (Spain) for giving us access to the AP1000 machine.

References

[1] *AP1000 Program Development Guide*, Fujitsu Laboratories Ltd., 3rd edition, July 1993.

[2] *AP1000 User's Guide*, Fujitsu Laboratories Ltd., June 1993.

[3] R. Barret, M. Berry, T. Chan, J. Demmel, J. Donato, J. Dongarra, V. Eijkhout, R. Pozo, C. Romine and H. Van der Vorst, *Templates for the Solution of Linear Systems: Building Blocks for Iterative Methods*, 1993.

[4] C.H. Bischof, Adaptive Blocking in the QR Factorization, *The Journal of Supercomputing*, Vol.3, pp.193-208, 1989.

[5] R.H. Bisseling, J.G.G. Van de Vorst and A.F. Van der Stappen, Parallel Sparse LU Decomposition on a Mesh Network of Transputers, *SIAM J. Matrix Anal. Appl.*, Vol.14, n.3, pp.853-879, July 1993.

[6] *CASIM User's Guide*, Fujitsu Laboratories Ltd., 4th edition, August 1991.

[7] I.S. Duff, A.M. Erisman and J.K. Reid, *Direct Methods for Sparse Matrices*, Clarendon Press, 1986.

[8] I.S. Duff, R.G. Grimes and J.G. Lewis, *User's Guide for the Harwell-Boeing Sparse Matrix Collection*, Technical Report TR-PA-92-96, CERFACS, October 1992.

[9] J.A. George and M.T. Heath, Solution of Sparse Linear Least Squares Problems using Givens Rotations, *Linear Algebra Appl.*, Vol.34, pp.69-83, 1980.

[10] G.H. Golub and C.F. Van Loan, *Matrix Computations*, The Johns Hopkins University Press, 2nd edition, 1989.

[11] H. Ishihata, T. Horie, S. Inano, T. Shimizu, S. Kato and M. Ikesaka, Third Generation Message Passing Computer AP1000, *Proceedings of ISS'92*, pp.46-55, November 1992.

[12] H. Ishihata, T. Horie and T. Shimizu, Architecture for the AP1000 Highly Parallel Computer, *Fujitsu Sci. Tech. Journal*, Vol.29, n.1, pp.6-14, March 1993.

[13] S.G. Kratzer, Sparse QR Factorization on a Massively Parallel Computer, *The Journal of Supercomputing*, Vol.6, pp.237-255, 1992.

[14] J.H.W. Liu, On General Row Merging Schemes for Sparse Givens Transformations, *SIAM J. Sci. Statist. Computing*, Vol.7, pp.1190-1211, 1986.

[15] P. Matstoms, *Sparse QR Factorization with Applications to Linear Least Squares Problems*, PhD thesis, Department of Mathemathics, Linköping University, Sweden, 1994.

[16] A. Pothen and P. Raghavan, Distributed Orthogonal Factorization: Givens and Householder Algorithms, *SIAM J. Sci. Statist. Computing*, Vol.10, pp.1113-1134, 1989.

[17] E.L. Zapata, J.A. Lamas, F.F. Rivera and O.G. Plata, Modified Gram-Schmidt QR Factorization on Hypercube SIMD Computers, *Journal of Parallel and Distributed Computing*, Vol.12, pp.60-69, 1991.

[18] B.B. Zhou and R.P. Brent, *Parallel Implementation of QRD Algorithms on the Fujitsu AP1000*, Technical Report TR-CS-93-12, Computer Sciences Laboratory, The Australian National University, Canberra, ACT 0200, Australia, November 1993.

❖ Session 2 ❖

Virtual Shared Memory

Chair

M. Gerndt

The Role of Associative Memory in Virtual Shared Memory Architectures: A Price-Performance Comparison*

Henk L. Muller† Paul W.A. Stallard David H.D. Warren

Department of Computer Science, University of Bristol, UK.
Working at PACT/SRF, 10 Priory Road, Bristol. BS8 1TU, UK.
e-mail: {henkm,paul,warren}@pact.srf.ac.uk

Abstract

In designing a virtual shared memory architecture, an important consideration is whether the main memory should be conventional or (set-) associative. This is the main distinction between so-called CC-NUMA and COMA architectures. In this article we investigate the consequences on price and performance of different choices of component in the memory hierarchy, assuming a main memory which is either conventional or set-associative. We use analytic models driven by accurate miss ratios determined from actual parallel executions of a range of realistic benchmarks. We make cost assumptions based on published figures for different types of storage components.

Our results show that, for many programs, CC-NUMA machines need a large coherent cache, often equalling the size of the main memory, in order to achieve good price-performance. As a consequence, optimal CC-NUMA and COMA configurations tend to need set-associative memories of similar size, and show rather little difference in price-performance. Optimal COMA configurations tend to be more general purpose, as one can find a configuration that is nearly optimal in price-performance for all applications that we used, while optimal CC-NUMA configurations tend to be more application specific.

1 Introduction

Virtual shared memory (VSM) provides a globally shared memory (single address space) on physically distributed memory systems. One of the design issues in the design of a VSM is whether to bind data to certain physical locations in the machine, or to allow the data to migrate freely. The first approach is taken by (amongst others) the DASH [1], MIT-Alewife [2] and Galactica [3], the second approach is the one that is used in the design of the KSR-1 [4] and DDM [5]. The first three machines have a conventional memory at the processor nodes for the main data storage. Caches are used to store frequently used data, coming from either the local memory or from remote nodes. Each data item has a *fixed* home location in one of the nodes. In the second group of machines, each node is equipped with a *(set-)associative main memory*, in which an (arbitrary) subset of the data can be stored. In these machines, data is not associated with any node in particular and migrates to the nodes where it is needed. These machines typically also have (optional) set-associative caches to reduce the number of accesses to the main memory.

In this article, we evaluate some of the design choices in the memory hierarchy of a VSM architecture. In particular, we evaluate the use of conventional versus set-associative memory for the main storage at each node. The first group of machines is said to be simpler in design and hence cheaper, the second group of machines is said to be more expensive but faster and more flexible because of data migration. It follows directly that performance should not be the only issue in the comparison, the price is equally important. The comparison presented here is therefore a comparison based on the price-performance.

A direct comparison of two machines, one from each of the two groups, is very interesting, but does not tell us if dispensing with the conventional memory is an advantage or not. The machines may have a different network, directory structure, protocol, or consistency scheme [6]. The analysis presented here is therefore abstracted above this level of detail. Using real (measured) figures for real programs running on various configurations, we model the performance under the assumption that the machines are built using the same network interconnect, and using the same directory structure. In Section 2, the range of architectures to be evaluated is defined. The price and performance models used are discussed in Sections 3 and 4. Section 5 presents the results of the evaluation and and analysis. More detailed results are presented in a technical report [7],

*Work supported by ESPRIT P7249, OMI/HORN.

† Authors are ordered alphabetically.

2 Set-associative vs conventional memory

A fast memory system is essential for processors to operate at anything like full speed. Because fast memory is expensive, there are typically one or more caches between the processor and the memory. A cache is a small, fast and transparent component that is used to store the data that is used most frequently. Because of locality of reference, most accesses are satisfied directly in the first level cache, the main memory is accessed only rarely and can thus be implemented using cheap and slow components. The sizes, cycle times and degree of associativity of the caches must be balanced so that the system has good performance "on average", without being excessively expensive.

In a virtual shared memory system, the use of set-associative memories introduces an extra degree of freedom in the design space. The conventional memory at the end of the cache hierarchy of each node can itself be replaced by a set-associative memory. In many ways this set-associative memory is just like a level $n+1$ cache. However, it is not an optional component and is therefore not strictly a cache—instead we call this the associative main memory. An architecture with a conventional memory is known as a CC-NUMA (for Cache Coherent Non Uniform Memory Architecture). We will use the term NUMA for brevity and because we do not insist on the presence of the coherent cache. An architecture with an associative memory has been called a COMA (for Cache Only Memory Architecture, a misnomer since, as we have just argued, the last level is not strictly a cache).

An arbitrary example of a NUMA architecture is the Galactica [3]. The Galactica has one level of write-through cache, one level of coherent cache and a conventional memory. The Galactica is clustered: four nodes are connected by a fast bus to the main memory of a cluster, reducing the costs of the directory. We could compare this with an arbitrary instance of a COMA, for example the HORN-DDM, a particular implementation of the DDM architecture. The HORN-DDM [5] is a scalable COMA: the directories are structured in a hierarchy so data distribution and invalidation can be implemented with only $O(\log n)$ costs.

A straightforward comparison between two specific instances is interesting in its own right, but will not show us whether a COMA is a good idea or not. It might tell us whether hierarchical directories are an advantage, weak consistency has better performance, or whether these two compensate for each other [6]. For this reason we will compare COMA and NUMA architectures under the assumption that they are implemented with the same network, consistency model, and consistency protocol.

A comparison of clustering processors on a leaf node (used in the DASH and the Galactica) in order to share the protocol overhead by more processors and to increase effectiveness of memory usage is presented by Nayfeh [8]. We assume that nodes are not clustered.

It is reasonable to believe that these two architectures can be implemented with the same directory and network structure. It is entirely feasible to build a COMA with a mesh, or a NUMA with a Banyan interconnect; an example of a COMA without a hierarchical network is the COMA-F [9] (this article also quantifies the *performance* differences between NUMA and COMA architectures with specific protocols for the NUMA and COMA). We have abstracted from the network and assumed in both cases that there is a relatively large miss-penalty if the data isn't available locally.

We have assumed for our measurements that the architectures have a sequential consistency model. This was mainly done for practical reasons: our set of benchmark programs expect sequential consistency, and our platform to measure the essential characteristics such as hit ratios is sequentially consistent. We cannot abstract from the consistency issue in that we cannot show that going to a weaker consistency model would give a structural advantage to either COMA or NUMA architectures.

Given the fact that both machines use the same consistency model, it is justified to assume that they can be implemented using almost the same protocol. The difference between a NUMA and COMA protocol is the fact that data that is displaced in a COMA must be stored at another node—there is no conventional memory where the data can be stored in such a case. This difference causes a very small complication in the COMA protocol, and causes differences in hit-ratios of the associative memories of a COMA in comparison with the hit-ratio of equally sized coherent caches of a NUMA. We account for the resulting difference in performance. The choice of using, for example, an updating or an invalidating protocol has performance consequences on both machines, we do not believe that it will have structurally different effects on a NUMA or a COMA. All figures presented in this paper are measured with an invalidating protocol.

Given the above restrictions, this paper presents a price-performance study to compare COMA and NUMA architectures. The study has been performed over a range of architectures with the following specifications:

- A 100 MIPS processor, with a write buffer.
- An instruction cache sufficiently large to allow us to ignore instruction references.
- An optional write-through data cache, of between 4 and 128 Kbytes, with 16 byte lines, followed by two optional copy-back caches of between 64 and 2048 Kbytes each with 64 byte lines.

Type	Access time	Price per Mbyte
SRAM	10 ns	$ 400 per MByte
SRAM	35 ns	$ 100 per MByte
DRAM	90 ns	$ 50 per MByte
DRAM	120 ns	$ 25 per MByte

Table 1: Price-performance options for conventional memory [11, page 455].

Size, Access time, Type	Price
16K, 15 ns, SRAM, 4-way, 16 byte line	$ 10.35
128K, 40 ns, SRAM, 4-way, 64 byte line	$ 18.85
2M, 120 ns, DRAM, conventional memory	$ 50.00
2M, 125 ns, DRAM, 4-way, 64 byte line	$ 64.45

Table 2: Sample price-performance options for various type of storage.

- A conventional (NUMA) or associative (COMA) memory large enough to hold the data set of the program.

All caches and associative memories are 4-way set-associative. All caches and memories (including the associative memories) have a size that is a power of 2. The price of each architecture is determined following the price model that is presented in Section 3. The price is eventually expressed in dollars.

Following the performance model of Section 4 the system performance is calculated for a number of applications on each memory hierarchy. The performance of a specific program running on a specific architecture is expressed as a MIPS rating (which is application specific, and is used to compare the performance of an identical program running on two different memory hierarchies).

The majority of applications come from the SPLASH suite [10]. Details on the other applications can be found in the complete paper [7]. The data sets have been chosen to be large enough to get useful cache performance information, but small enough so that we would get results in a reasonable time. In all cases the programs would run in the order of a few seconds of real time. We will come back to the size of the data sets in Section 5.

Finally, dividing the MIPS rate of an application/machine-pair over the price of the machine shows how many MIPS one can buy for a dollar for this particular program running on this particular architecture. These price-performance figures are presented and compared in Section 5.

3 The price model

The price calculations assume a very simple model. The price of a machine is given by the sum of the base price (the processor, with all its external interfaces, memory management, networking, PCB and power supply), and a price per memory or cache. All prices are expressed in dollars. We assume that parts are produced in sufficient quantity so that we can ignore the development costs.

To determine the price of the memory hierarchy we start with a table of memory prices of existing memory technology. Table 1 shows the price and performance of four types of memory. The two faster and more expensive memories are typical SRAM technology, the two others represent DRAM technology. The performance of the memory is expressed as the average random access time of the memory. This is the time needed to retrieve the first word of data. Assuming that there is enough time to recover, the cycle time of DRAM's can be ignored. The price is quoted as dollars per Megabyte.

From these figures the price of all memories are derived. For associative memories, (used for the caches and the COMA main memory), there is an additional cost associated with the tag storage, and the lookup and replacement hardware.

The data storage can be built with any of the memories listed in Table 1. Using a slow data storage leads (obviously) to a slow associative memory. The price of this data storage is calculated using Table 1. We assume that the tags must be stored in faster memory. For the DRAM-based associative memories the slower SRAM suffices for the tags, for the SRAM-based caches the tag lookup needs to be in faster SRAM. The price of the tag storage is again calculated using Table 1. We assume that an address has 48 bits.

For the comparison, selection and replacement logic, we assume the price is the equivalent of 6 Kbytes of fast memory for write-through caches—a price that is comparable to the one assumed by Nayfeh [8]. For copy-back caches and the COMA associative memory we assume an equivalent of 8 Kbytes of fast memory. Note that this price does not depend on the size of the cache because the tag storage is accounted separately. The cost of the coherency protocol is accounted for in the general price of the machine.

We have assumed the associative memory will be 5 ns slower than the raw speed of the memory from which it is built. This allows the tag-logic the time to perform the selection. Note that one can argue that DRAM based associative memories do not need the selection overhead and are consequently a bit cheaper and faster than we assume, but we have chosen not to go into this level of detail. Some sample price-performance options are given in Table 2. Notice for example that the price of the fast 16 Kbyte cache is equivalent to $0.66 per Kbyte ($10.35 / 16), that is

26 times more expensive per Kbyte than the 2 Mbyte slow DRAM.

We realise that the assumptions are debatable. There are, for example, discretisation effects in a real world system. As an example, alongside a processor there might be room left to fit a 32K cache—a 64K cache will be disproportionally more expensive, and going to a 16K cache might not make the system much cheaper. Although these effects must be taken into account when determining the final design parameters of a system [8], we ignore them here because we think that this will not cause a structural bias towards either COMA or NUMA architectures. Another arguable issue is that this model will simply predict a price for an arbitrarily large 15 ns cache (e.g. 2 Mbytes), which is not easy to construct. The price of such a cache (about $ 1000) will however prevent it from ever being used in an architecture that is meant to have good price-performance.

For the price of the base system (processor, PCB, network etc) we have assumed a constant cost per node of $400. This figure is a free interpretation of Hennessy and Patterson [12, page 63]. For a different base price the price-performance balance shifts. If the base price becomes very high, the price of the memory hierarchy is negligible, so an arbitrary amount of money can be spent to get a good price-performance ratio. If the base price approaches zero, the cheapest memory hierarchy possible will be chosen. In the discussion we will see that for reasonable architectures (with good price performance) the memory price accounts for about 10% of the total price. This is in line with breakdown figures from the literature [1, 12], and price quotations for state of the art parallel machines.

The base price incorporates the price of implementing the coherency protocol. We cannot easily estimate the extra overhead of the coherency protocol of the COMA over that of a NUMA. Both have to replace data, but the COMA has to deal with the possibility of placement of data that has been evicted at another node. In the DDM-HORN protocol about 1% of the protocol code is dedicated to this task. If we assume that 5% of the base price is for protocol hardware [1], the difference would be around 1% of 5%, or $0.20 in the base cost. The difference in price-performance would therefore be roughly 0.05%. We have chosen to ignore this, but the reader should bear in mind that a slight overhead must be added.

4 The performance model

For each architecture we need to obtain a reliable estimation of its performance. We estimate this performance with an analytical model that uses measured numbers of memory accesses and misses. We measure the miss ratios of both types of architecture using the HORN-DDM emulator [13]. The emulator emulates the DDM and provides timing results as well as statistics on the numbers and types of misses in the data cache and the associative memory. To predict miss ratios for NUMA architectures, we have extended the emulator to include a coherent cache that is maintained alongside the associative memory. The NUMA hit ratio assumes that the program would execute along the same execution path.

The analytical model is able to estimate the effect of adding extra levels of caching between the (measured) processor cache and coherent cache or associative memory. It assumes that the miss ratio of caches does not depend on the speed of the cache, or on the speed and size of the rest of the memory hierarchy. This is a valid first order approximation. Since the various cache memories in the hierarchy include each other, the absolute number of misses at any level depends only on the size (or the associativity) of the cache at that level. A second order effect can cause more or less misses because a faster running node might experience a different number of misses (since other nodes in the parallel machine might have invalidated a local copy). This effect is ignored.

These models are a simplification of the real performance. Most notably, all losses due to synchronisation primitives such as barriers and locks are not properly modelled. Although the memory accesses needed for these operations (scalable spin-locks and barriers) are accounted for in the hit and miss ratios, the time spend waiting for the lock or barrier is not accounted for. The model is therefore not useful to predict the performance of a specific application, but it can serve to compare two different memory hierarchies. We believe that neither a COMA or NUMA will have structural difficulties in executing synchronisation primitives, or will disproportionally penalise the use of synchronisation primitives.

For each program, we have run the emulator with different sizes of NUMA caches, different sizes of COMA memory, and different sizes of write-through (processor) caches. The measured numbers of misses are then used to estimate the performance of the architecture, using Equations 1 and 2 defined below.

To estimate the performance of the system we calculate the average instruction cycle time based on the number of instructions executed, the number of references to memories and the hit ratio and speed of the caches that are being used. For a COMA this is expressed in the following formula:

$$\text{COMA-Time} = IT_I + M_n T_N + \sum_{i=1}^{n-1} M_{i-1} T_{C,i} \quad (1)$$

where I is the number of instructions, T_I is the time per instruction, M_k is the number of misses in the level k cache (M_0 is the number of accesses performed by the processor),

$T_{C,i}$ is the access time of the cache at level i, and T_N is the response time of the network.

In a NUMA some of the last level misses, M_n, will be serviced from the local portion of the global memory and the remainder from some remote memory. The fraction of accesses that hit the local memory is denoted α ($\alpha = 0$ means that all accesses are remote, $\alpha = 1$ means that all accesses are satisfied locally). This means that the last term of the COMA-run-time, $M_n T_N$ is replaced with a term $M_n(\alpha T_M + (1 - \alpha)T_N)$.

$$\text{NUMA-Time} = IT_I + M_n(\alpha T_M + (1 - \alpha)T_N) + \sum_{i=1}^{n-1} M_{i-1} T_{C,i} \quad (2)$$

where T_M is the access time of the local conventional memory. Note that the M_i values in this equation are different from the M_i values of the COMA, because thrashing due to forced placement of evicted data does not occur in a NUMA. All effects due to differences in the efficiency in memory usage between COMA and NUMA architectures [14] are accounted for in these miss-ratios, as measured by the emulator.

The equations above assume that all memory operations always block until the operation has been completed. This is a fair assumption for read operations (except for the presence of possible delay slots), but not for write operations. In the context of a sequentially consistent machine successive operations can be queued and handled asynchronously (one after each other). Read operations must wait until all write operations have completed in order to retain sequential consistency[1]. We model a single write buffer in our model by assuming a different miss penalty for write operations:

$$M_i^{write} = M_i - (1 - e^{-M_i/f})f \quad (3)$$

where f is the average time between memory operations. This model for the write penalty assumes that memory operations are uniformly distributed over the run. This write buffer results, as expected, in some performance improvement: little for programs with frequent misses (as for example Mp3d, 15.6 MIPS to 16.2 MIPS on a specific architecture), more for programs with less frequent misses (as for example Barnes from 56 to 65 MIPS on the same architecture).

None of the programs that we use allocates memory explicitly on certain nodes. This means that they will exhibit a small α, which we can assume is approximately $1 / P$. In order to get a feeling for what might happen if the programmer invests time in physically grouping the data, or if the compiler does a clever job in allocating the data, we have done experiments with $\alpha = 1$ (the unattainable ideal).

To judge the quality of this model, the performance of eight COMA configurations has been estimated with the model and compared to the performance measured on the emulator. Because the latter includes synchronisation timings, the performance figures cannot be compared directly. There is a good linear relation between the time estimated by the model and the time predicted by the emulator. The error was always less than 5% and in most of the cases within 1 or 2%.

5 Results

For all architectures that can be constructed given the constraints in Section 2, the price (dollars), performance (MIPS), and value for money (MIPS per dollar) figure can be calculated for each application program. The MIPS per dollar figure is used to define that one machine is *better* than another. We have attempted to answer three questions, described in the sections below: what machine is best on a per application basis; what machine is best on average; and can the results be generalised for other input parameters. We evaluated 8- and 32-node systems, the detailed results of the latter are shown in the full report [7]

5.1 The best architecture per application

Table 3 shows, per application, the best COMA, the best NUMA (best being defined as the highest MIPS per dollar figure), and the architecture with the highest performance, for 8-node machines. Price and performance figures are given in \$ per node and MIPS per node. The memory hierarchy of each configuration is shown with the first level left, and the last level right. Wt, Cb, and Sa stand for Write-through, Copy-back and Set-associative. The last component of the NUMA line is the conventional memory. The $\rightarrow$ indicates the architecture with the best price-performance. The figures show that the differences for the optimal price-performance COMA and NUMA is relatively small. In some cases a NUMA is better, in others a COMA is better. The largest differences occur when trying to design an 8-node Mp3d machine (NUMA is 9% better), or an 8-node Wang machine (COMA is 15% better). The performance figures for machines with optimal price-performance are all close to the maximum performance figure (that is obtained without regard to the price and therefore on a machine using huge, very expensive, caches). Another reference point is the cheapest machine with worst performance. One can build a COMA without caches for little more than \$400 that performs a factor of 2 or 3 worse, or a NUMA without caches that performs a few orders of magnitude worse.

[1] Under processor consistency read operations may continue as long as they peek in the write queue [15].

Architecture	Price	Perf	MIPS/$
aurora.tina: maximum performance (and cost)	913.28	74.5	0.082
NUMA 8K:15:Wt-SRAM 128K:40:Cb-SRAM 512K:120:DRAM	434.96	69.1	0.159
→ COMA 64K:15:Cb-SRAM 512K:125:Sa-DRAM	444.53	73.1	0.164
locus.Primary1.grin: maximum performance (and cost)	1213.28	61.9	0.051
→ NUMA 8K:15:Wt-SRAM 128K:40:Cb-SRAM 256K:120:DRAM	428.71	59.7	0.139
COMA 64K:15:Cb-SRAM 256K:125:Sa-DRAM	437.60	57.2	0.131
cholesky.bcsstk14: maximum performance (and cost)	1213.28	53.1	0.044
→ NUMA 16K:15:Wt-SRAM 128K:40:Cb-SRAM 256K:120:DRAM	432.28	51.4	0.119
COMA 64K:15:Cb-SRAM 256K:125:Sa-DRAM	437.60	49.7	0.114
water.343: maximum performance (and cost)	554.00	78.7	0.142
→ NUMA 8K:15:Wt-SRAM 64K:40:Cb-SRAM 256K:120:DRAM	421.68	76.4	0.181
COMA 64K:15:Cb-SRAM 256K:125:Sa-DRAM	437.60	77.6	0.177
wave.240: maximum performance (and cost)	658.20	75.6	0.115
NUMA 8K:15:Wt-SRAM 512K:40:Cb-SRAM 512K:120:DRAM	476.66	73.4	0.154
→ COMA 64K:15:Cb-SRAM 512K:125:Sa-DRAM	444.53	73.1	0.164
wang.100000: maximum performance (and cost)	913.28	71.1	0.078
NUMA 8K:15:Wt-SRAM 1024K:40:Cb-SRAM 1024K:120:DRAM	544.24	67.0	0.123
→ COMA 64K:15:Cb-SRAM 1024K:125:Sa-DRAM	458.30	66.0	0.144
barnes.4000: maximum performance (and cost)	913.28	84.5	0.092
NUMA 8K:15:Wt-SRAM 256K:40:Cb-SRAM 256K:120:DRAM	442.68	78.2	0.177
→ COMA 64K:15:Cb-SRAM 512K:125:Sa-DRAM	444.53	82.3	0.185
mp3d.30000: maximum performance (and cost)	913.28	19.5	0.021
→ NUMA 8K:15:Wt-SRAM 256K:40:Cb-SRAM 256K:120:DRAM	442.68	18.9	0.043
COMA 64K:15:Cb-SRAM 256K:125:Sa-DRAM	437.60	17.3	0.039

Table 3: The price-performance of COMA and NUMA architectures, for 8 nodes.

A very interesting observation from Table 3 is that the best price-performance figures for many applications running on a NUMA require a cache to be (almost) the same size as the conventional memory. This explains why in these cases a COMA has a better price-performance: it does not have the conventional memory. Not all applications however require a large coherent cache, programs like Water are quite happy with a smaller cache. Barnes needs a COMA memory larger than the memory of the NUMA because of its sharing requirement, and the possibility of evicted data overwriting valuable data in other nodes [14]. Despite that, the COMA has a better price-performance.

In the case of the 32-node figures [7], the differences are even smaller, a few percent at most. We should note here that not all programs show good speedup on so many processors. Cholesky on this input matrix and the program running on Aurora do not have sufficient parallelism beyond 10 nodes, so we should not take these figures too seriously. Mp3d has steadily increasing (albeit very low) speedup, while Locus has a slowdown on this number of processors.

The other thing to remark on is that we have used programs with small data sets. Many programs require larger data sets for a serious run, Barnes for example will require about 16K elements [10], giving rise to a 25 times larger data set. We do not expect a seriously different behaviour in the locality behaviour for many of these programs. Many programs tend to use a small fraction of the data frequently (thus requiring a small first level cache) and a fraction $1/P$ of the data in a very uniform manner (thus requiring a large second level cache). This is independent of the data size.

5.2 The on-average best architecture

Building application-specific machines is not the goal of computer design. Instead we want to design a machine that does well on an "average set of programs". The MIPS rate (or MIPS/$) is not suitable for comparing different programs, since programs have different instruction mixes. For this reason we have normalised all price-performance figures per application: the best architecture is rated 1, all others are rated at a number denoting the fraction of the best price-performance. Note that there is only one best architecture: either a COMA or a NUMA. Both NUMA and COMA machines are given a rating relative to the single best price-performance. This comparison is performed for NUMA and COMA configurations with various main memory sizes, so we can find the on-average best 512 Kbyte per node machine, the on-average best 1 Mbyte per node machine and so on.

For each memory size, we use the relative price-

Application / Machine	aurora MIPS	aurora rel p/p	locus MIPS	locus rel p/p	cholesky MIPS	cholesky rel p/p	water MIPS	water rel p/p	wave MIPS	wave rel p/p	wang MIPS	wang rel p/p	barnes MIPS	barnes rel p/p	mp3d MIPS	mp3d rel p/p	average rel p/p
NUMA-256K			59.2	0.958	51.2	0.969	76.9	0.954					78.2	0.953	18.9	1.000	0.967
Better			59.7	1.000	51.0	1.000	76.4	1.000									
COMA-256K			57.2	0.939	49.7	0.953	77.6	0.976					79.3	0.980	17.3	0.926	0.955
Better			55.0	0.940													
NUMA-512K	70.8	0.959	59.2	0.945	51.2	0.956	76.9	0.941	60.7	0.821			78.2	0.939	18.9	0.986	0.935
Better	69.1	0.970	59.7	0.986	51.0	0.986	76.4	0.985	68.3	0.931							
COMA-512K	73.1	1.000	56.4	0.909	50.0	0.943	77.6	0.959	73.1	1.000			82.3	1.000	17.5	0.920	0.962
Better																	
NUMA-1024K	70.8	0.875	60.2	0.877	51.5	0.877	76.9	0.859	73.4	0.907	57.6	0.815	80.8	0.886	19.1	0.910	0.876
Better	69.1	0.943	59.7	0.958	51.0	0.958	76.4	0.958			67.0	0.844	78.2	0.914	18.9	0.960	
COMA-1024K	73.2	0.969	56.5	0.881	50.4	0.919	77.6	0.928	73.1	0.967	66.0	1.000	82.4	0.968	17.5	0.891	0.940
Better																	
NUMA-2048K	70.8	0.833	60.2	0.835	51.5	0.835	76.9	0.818	73.4	0.863	57.6	0.776	80.8	0.844	19.1	0.866	0.834
Better	69.1	0.893	59.7	0.908	51.4	0.908	76.4	0.906			67.0	0.808	78.2	0.868	18.9	0.911	
COMA-2048K	73.3	0.911	57.7	0.844	50.2	0.859	77.6	0.870	73.1	0.908	66.0	0.938	82.4	0.908	17.5	0.837	0.884
Better																	

Table 4: Average best COMA and NUMA with 256K–2048K memory per node, for 8 nodes.

Suboptimality for	aurora	locus	cholesky	water	wave	wang	barnes	mp3d
NUMA-aurora, locus, cholesky	0.0	0.0	0.0	1.0	27.6	52.2	15.5	4.2
NUMA-water	6.6	4.1	1.0	0.0	38.7	55.4	34.0	10.8
NUMA-wave	7.2	8.4	8.5	10.3	0.0	3.4	3.0	5.2
NUMA-wang	17.3	17.2	17.9	20.1	11.0	0.0	13.6	15.4
NUMA-barnes, mp3d	1.0	4.1	3.0	4.3	11.9	43.6	0.0	0.0

Table 5: Nearly optimal configurations and the loss in price-performance in percent.

Configuration	Price
256K machines	
NUMA: 8K:15:Wt-SRAM 256K:40:Cb-SRAM 256K:120:DRAM	$ 447
COMA: 64K:15:Cb-SRAM 256K:125:Am-DRAM	$ 441
512K machines	
NUMA: 8K:15:Wt-SRAM 256K:40:Cb-SRAM 512K:120:DRAM	$ 453
COMA: 64K:15:Cb-SRAM 512K:125:Am-DRAM	$ 448
1024K machines	
NUMA: 8K:15:Wt-SRAM 512K:40:Cb-SRAM 1024K:120:DRAM	$ 497
COMA: 64K:15:Cb-SRAM 1024K:125:Am-DRAM	$ 464
2048K machines	
NUMA: 8K:15:Wt-SRAM 512K:40:Cb-SRAM 2048K:120:DRAM	$ 522
COMA: 64K:15:Cb-SRAM 2048K:125:Am-DRAM	$ 494

Table 6: Specification of the configurations of Table 4.

performance figures to select configurations that give good price-performance over all applications with equal weighting. These configurations are presented in Table 4.

For each size of memory, the on-average best COMA and NUMA configuration are shown (a missing entry indicates that the program cannot run in this little memory). For each application the absolute performance figure and the relative price-performance figure for that specific application are given. In some cases a better machine of the given type and memory size exists for a certain application program. These machines are shown in a smaller font in the row labelled "Better". A description of the average best configurations is presented in Table 6.

Notice that the differences are only very small: for a 1024K machine, the on-average best COMA is 6% from optimal, the on-average best NUMA is 12% from optimal, so the difference is about 6% in this case. A very interesting observation from the on-average best configurations is that the COMA configurations tend to be more general: the best COMA on-average is identical to the best COMA for each specific application program, while for the NUMA configurations there are better alternatives for many programs. These are not selected as the on-average best one, because they have bad price-performance for at least one of the other programs.

This is shown in detail in Table 5, which displays the deviation from optimal price-performance for four 8-node 1024K NUMA configurations. Each row lists an configuration that is best for a set of applications, the columns list for each applications the deviation from optimal price-performance. The machine that is optimal for Aurora, is very suboptimal for Wang (by a factor of 2). The machine best for Wang is 15-20% suboptimal for 5 other applications. NUMA configurations that are very reasonable according to one application can have devastating price-performance for another application (never use one application to evaluate an architectures).

The Wave architecture is a reasonable compromise, being only 5-10% suboptimal. There was no machine that was better than this one on-average, so it is this machine which was selected as the best 8 node 1024K NUMA. (Note that for the COMA architectures all applications preferred the same 1024K machine.)

5.3 Generalising the results

The α parameter of Equation 2 was set to a value that represents a random distribution of data over the memories in the NUMA, i.e. $1 / p$. This is reasonable if we assume that neither the compiler nor the programmer has performed an

Number of Nodes		Memory sizes 128	256	512	1024	2048
8 Nodes	Difference COMA NUMA %	0.0±0.0	-1.4±1.7	2.2±2.0	5.1±2.5	4.0±2.5
	Generality NUMA	1.0±0.0	0.3±0.1	0.2±0.1	0.1±0.1	0.1±0.1
	Generality COMA	1.0±0.0	0.7±0.3	0.8±0.2	0.8±0.2	0.9±0.2
	NUMA more general	0%	2%	1%	0%	0%
	COMA more general	0%	86%	97%	99%	100%
	Equally general	100%	12%	2%	1%	0%
32 Nodes	Difference COMA NUMA %	-1.8±0.8	1.6±1.6	1.9±1.9	1.4±1.9	0.1±2.0
	Generality NUMA	0.4±0.1	0.3±0.1	0.3±0.1	0.4±0.1	0.4±0.1
	Generality COMA	0.7±0.2	0.6±0.2	0.7±0.2	0.7±0.2	0.8±0.2
	NUMA more general	4%	6%	2%	1%	0%
	COMA more general	86%	85%	94%	96%	98%
	Equally general	10%	10%	4%	3%	2%

Table 7: Results after a variation in parameters.

explicit allocation of memory. A higher α results in much better performance figures for NUMA machines. We have (merely as a consistency test) run tests where α equals one, representing the case that the memory is always located in the correct place, i.e. there is no interprocessor communication. Because the data is always local, the program will run faster, and the machine will be cheaper since the coherent cache is not necessary. Consequently the price-performance increases. The difference is largest for Mp3d (a factor 6), while others gain less (between 10% for Barnes and 50% for Locus). Notice that a high value for α means that a COMA architecture will have better performance as well (the hit-ratio on the COMA memory must approach 1), but a COMA cannot be made cheaper. The net result is that NUMA architectures will have around 10% better price-performance. The case of $\alpha = 1$ is a hypothetical situation and this potential advantage can only be realised if the programmer (or the compiler) is very clever in its data distribution and the algorithm requires only negligible interprocessor communication.

The tables before sketch the difference between NUMA and COMA architectures for only one point in the design space: a 100-MIPS processor with 48 address bits and assuming the price structure shown in Table 1. We have repeated the experiment 400 times where all price and performance parameters were randomly varied by up to a factor of 1.6 larger or smaller. We have kept α and the speed of the processor constant. This experiment resulted in 400 of the tables shown earlier which are summarised in Table 7.

The first row shows the average difference in relative price-performance of COMA and NUMA architecture over the 400 experiments as a percentage—a positive number means "COMA better". This means that for a 512K machine with 8 nodes the COMA is on-average 2.2% better with a standard deviation of 2. These figures are very close to zero indeed, although one can clearly see a trend. For machines with a very small memory the NUMA is better, for machines with more memory the COMA is better, and for machines with unnecessary large memory one can project that the NUMA will be better again. This is not surprising because memory is purchased that will not be used, it is better to buy cheap conventional memory instead of more expensive associative memory.

The second and third row of the table shows the generality of the architectures. The generality is defined as the number of application programs for which the average best architecture is also the best for that particular application, divided by total number of applications (the generality is thus defined to be between 0 and 1). As an example, the generality of the COMA-256K in Table 4 is $4 / 5 = 0.8$, the generality of the NUMA-256K in the same table is $2/5 = 0.4$. The generality is again averaged over the 400 experiments and presented along with the standard deviation. On average, a COMA machine tends to be more general than a NUMA.

These figures are amplified a bit in the fourth, fifth and sixth row, which show respectively: per point of the design space, if a COMA was more general than a NUMA; the other way around or; they were equally general. These figures more clearly support our conclusion that a NUMA is less general (or the other way around: one can build an application specific machine with better price-performance for many applications), while a COMA is relatively application independent.

6 Conclusions

We have investigated the effect on price-performance of different design choices in the memory hierarchy of a virtual shared memory architecture. In particular, our study enables us to compare NUMA machines, where the main memory is conventional, with COMA machines, where the main memory is set-associative. Performance figures were estimated using measured miss ratio figures and an analytic model for calculating average performance. The price figures were obtained using a table of basic memory prices and a set of relations to calculate the prices of caches and memories.

For half of our benchmark set (Barnes, Mp3d, Wang, Wave), a NUMA needs a large coherent cache (approaching the size of its main memory) in order to have comparable price-performance with the best COMA configurations. At this point the COMA is cheaper (because it dispenses with the conventional main memory), while offering equal performance. On other benchmarks (Aurora, Cholesky, Locus, Water), a NUMA works well with a smaller cache (2 to 4 times smaller than the main memory), giving the NUMA a more favourable price-performance. In all cases, the difference in price-performance between the optimal NUMA and COMA configurations is small.

We find that COMA architectures tend to be less application specific: it is possible to find COMA configurations which produce close to the the best price-performance for the majority of applications, while the best NUMA configurations for the applications are all different. Overall, we find that a COMA configuration produces the best average price-performance across all the benchmarks for both 8-node and 32-node machines, but only by a small margin (2-6%) compared with the best NUMA configuration. Although the differences are small, and obviously depend on the precise assumptions made in the modelling, we believe the trend is clear; it still holds when we vary the parameters of our model to reflect other prices for caches and memories.

Our main conclusion is that any virtual memory architecture needs a large set-associative memory, whether it be used as a cache (as in a NUMA) or as a main memory (as in a COMA). Given this fact, the differences between a NUMA and a COMA can be seen as not so great in practice.

References

[1] D. Lenoski, J. Laudon, T. Joe, D. Nakahira, L. Stevens, A. Gupta, and J. Hennessy. The DASH Prototype: Logic Overhead and Performance. *IEEE Transactions on Parallel and Distributed Systems*, 4(1):41–61, January 1993.

[2] D. Chaiken, J. Kubiatowicz, and A. Agarwal. LimitLESS Directories: A Scalable Cache Coherence Scheme. In *Proceedings of the Fourth International Conference on Architectural Support for Programming Languages and Operating Systems, ASPLOS-IV*, pages 224–234, April 1991.

[3] Andrew W. Wilson jr., Richard P. LaRowe jr., Robert J. Ionta, Ralph P. Valentino, Beeching Hu, Peter R. Breton, and Pocheong Lau. Update Propagation in the Galactica Net Distributed Memory Architecture. In *Proceedings of the International Workshop on Support for Large Scake Shared Memory Architectures*, pages 18–31, Cancun, Mexico, April 1994.

[4] KSR. *KSR Technical Summary*. Kendall Square Research, Waltham, MA, 1992.

[5] Henk L. Muller, Paul W. A. Stallard, and David H. D. Warren. The Data Diffusion Machine with a Scalable Point-to-Point Network. Technical Report CSTR-93-17, Department of Computer Science, University of Bristol, October 1993.

[6] Jaswinder Pal Singh, Truman Joe, Anoop Gupta, and John L. Hennessy. An Empirical Comparison of the Kendall Square Research KSR-1 and Stanford DASH Multiprocessors. In *Proceedings of Supercomputing '93*, pages 214–225. Association for Computing Machinery, 1993.

[7] Henk L. Muller, Paul W. A. Stallard, and David H. D. Warren. The Role of Associative Memory in VSM Architectures: A Price-Performance Comparison. Technical Report CSTR-95-009, Department of Computer Science, University of Bristol, May 1995.

[8] Basem A. Nayfeh and Kunle Olukotun. Exploring the Design Space for a Shared-Cache Multiprocessor. In *Proceedings of the 21st Annual International Symposium on Computer Architecture*, pages 166–175, Chicago, Illinois, April 1994. IEEE Computer Society Press.

[9] P. Stenström, T. Joe, and A. Gupta. Comparative Performance Evaluation of Cache-Coherent NUMA and COMA Architectures. In *Proceedings of the 19th Annual International Symposium on Computer Architecture*, pages 80–91, Gold Coast, Australia, May 1992. ACM Press.

[10] Jaswinder Pal Singh, Wolf-Dietrich Weber, and Anoop Gupta. SPLASH: Stanford Parallel Applications for Shared-Memory. Technical report, Computer Systems Laboratory, Stanford University, 1991.

[11] D.A. Patterson and J.L. Hennessy. *Computer Architecture, the Hardware Software Interface*. Morgan Kaufman, San Mateo, California, 1994.

[12] J.L. Hennessy and D.A. Patterson. *Computer Architecture, A quantitative approach*. Morgan Kaufman, San Mateo, California, 1990.

[13] Henk L. Muller, Paul W. A. Stallard, David H. D. Warren, and Sanjay Raina. Parallel Evaluation of a Parallel Architecture by means of Calibrated Emulation. In *Proceedings of the 8th International Parallel Processing Symposium*, pages 260–267, Cancun, Mexico, April 1994. IEEE Computer Society Press.

[14] Truman Joe and John L. Hennessy. Evaluating the Memory Overhead Required for COMA Architectures. In *Proceedings of the 21st Annual International Symposium on Computer Architecture*, pages 82–93, Chicago, Illinois, April 1994. IEEE Computer Society Press.

[15] James R. Goodman. Cache Consistency and Sequential Consistency. Technical Report WISCN-1006, Dept. of Comp. Science, University of Wisconsin, Madison, March 1989.

Implementing Distributed Shared Memory on top of MPI: the DSMPI Library

Luis M. Silva
João Gabriel Silva

University of Coimbra
Portugal
Email: luis@eden.dei.uc.pt

Simon Chapple

Edinburgh Parallel Computing Centre
Scotland
Email: simonc@epcc.ed.ac.uk

Abstract

Distributed shared memory has been recognized as an alternative programming model to exploit the parallelism in distributed memory systems since it provides a higher level of abstraction than simple message passing. DSM combines the simple programming model of shared-memory with the scalability of distributed memory machines.

This paper presents DSMPI, a parallel library that runs atop of MPI and provides a Distributed Shared Memory abstraction. It provides an easy-to-use programming interface, is flexible, portable and supports heterogeneity. Moreover, it supports different coherence protocols and models of consistency. We present some performance results taken in a network of workstations and in a Cray T3D which show that DSMPI can be competitive with MPI for some applications.

1. Introduction

Distributed Shared Memory (DSM) systems provide the shared memory programming model on top of distributed memory systems (i.e. distributed memory multiprocessors or networks of workstations). DSM is appealing because it combines the performance and scalability of distributed memory systems with the ease of programming of shared-memory machines. In the DSM paradigm processes communicate with each other through shared variables that are placed somewhere in the system but the programmer does not have to worry about where the data is. With message passing the programmer has to be aware of the data movements between processes, and each process has to know when to communicate, with whom to communicate and what data should be sent in a message. There are many algorithms for which the message passing implementation is non-trivial, tedious and error-prone. The DSM system hides the remote communication from the application programmer and provides a simpler abstraction that the programmer understands well. As a consequence, the code written for DSM becomes more compact and easy to read than the same code written for message passing. In short, DSM is an appealing programming model because it facilitates the task of programming in parallel and allows an easy porting of existing sequential codes based on concurrent programming to distributed-memory machines.

Distributed Shared Memory has received much attention in the past decade and several DSM systems have been presented in the literature [1-3]. Basically, they can be classified in four main approaches:

(i) Hardware implementations, where the cache coherency and DSM protocols are supported by the hardware. Examples include the DASH multiprocessor [4], PLUS [5] and the KSR-1 machine [6].

(ii) Operating system implementations, that extend the virtual memory-management mechanisms to access remote data. Some relevant examples are the IVY system [7], Mirage [8] and Clouds [9].

(iii) Compiler implementations, where all the data distribution and management is implemented by the compiler and a run-time system. Interesting examples of languages are Orca [10], Amber [11] and COOL [12].

(iv) Library implementations. In this approach, the DSM abstraction is completely implemented by a run-time library that is linked with the application program. Systems like Munin [13], TreadMarks [14] and ADSMITH [15] can be included in this category.

1066-6192/96 $5.00 © 1996 IEEE
Proceedings of PDP '96

DSMPI is included in this latter class. The library provides a C interface and the programmer calls the DSMPI functions in the same way it calls any MPI routine.

The main aim of this library is to provide an easy-to-use programming interface based on the abstraction of a globally accessed shared memory that can be read and/or written by any process of a MPI application. The most important guidelines that we took into account during the design of the library were:

(i) assure full portability of DSMPI programs;

(ii) provide an easy-to-use and flexible programming interface;

(iii) support heterogeneous computing platforms;

(iv) optimize the DSM implementation to allow execution efficiency.

The library was implemented without using any special features of the underlying operating system. It does not require any special compiler, pre-processor or linker. This is a key feature to obtain portability. In this point, we depart from the approach that was followed by other library-level implementations of DSM, like Munin [13] or TreadMarks [14], since those systems make use of some memory-management facilities provided by the underlying operating system. Munin, for instance, requires a special preprocessor and a modified linker. Those systems provide transparent access to the shared data but at the expense of lack of portability. In our case, we sacrificed transparency to achieve portability.

This means that all shared data and the read/write operations should be declared explicitly by the application programmer. The sharing unit is a program variable or a data structure. For this reason, DSMPI can be classified as a structure-based DSM system, as opposed to other DSM systems that are implemented in a page basis and make use of the operating system virtual memory facilities. Page-based DSM systems (like IVY [7], and Mirage [8]) are prone to the problem of false sharing. When different processes want to write different variables that are located in the same page the system has to send the page back and forth between them resulting in unnecessary coherence traffic and lack of efficiency. Munin and TreadMarks alleviate the problem of false-sharing by allowing multiple writers to the same page and by using a complex scheme to merge the changes at the synchronization points.

DSMPI does not provide full transparency since it does not make use of any memory-management facility of the operating system, neither requires the use of any special compiler. It does not incur in the problem of false sharing because the unit of shared data is completely dynamic and related to existing objects (or data structures) of the application.

At the same time, it allows the use of heterogeneous computing platforms while most of the other DSM systems are limited to homogeneous platforms. It is complicated to support heterogeneity in page-based DSM systems. Mermaid [27] is an example of a system that supports Heterogeneous DSM: memory is shared in pages, but each page can only contain one type of data. This is a enormous drawback and seems to be the only way to support heterogeneity in page-based DSM systems. DSMPI is a Heterogeneous DSM system since the library knows the exact format of each shared data object, and the library makes use of the MPI features to support heterogeneous computing platforms.

Finally, DSMPI allows the coexistence of both programming models (message passing and shared data) within the same application. This has been considered recently as the optimum solution for parallel programming [16-17].

Concerning absolute performance, we can expect applications that use DSM to perform worse than their message passing counterparts. However, this is not always true. It really depends on the memory-access pattern of the application and on the way the DSM system manages the consistency of replicated data.

In DSMPI we tried to optimize the accesses to shared data by introducing three different protocols of data replication and three different models of consistency that can be adapted to each particular application in order to exploit its semantics. With such facilities we expect DSM programs to be competitive with MPI programs in terms of performance.

The rest of the paper is organized as follows: section 2 describes the general organization of DSMPI. Section 3 presents the replication protocols and section 4 describes the models of consistency that were implemented. The programming interface is presented in Section 5. Section 6 shows some performance results and finally section 7 concludes the paper.

2. DSMPI Organization

In DSMPI there are two kinds of processes: application processes and daemon processes. The latter ones are responsible for the management of replicated data and for the protocols of consistency. Since the current implementations of MPI [18] are not thread-safe we had to implement the DSMPI daemons as separate processes. This is a limitation of the current version of DSMPI that will be relaxed as soon as there is some thread-safe implementation of MPI. All the communication between daemons and application processes is done by message passing. Each application process has access to a local cache that is located in its own address space and where it keeps the copies of replicated data objects. The daemon processes maintain the master copies of the shared objects. DSMPI maintains a two-level memory hierarchy: a local cache and a remote shared memory that is located in and managed by the daemons. Figure 1 presents the virtual organization of DSMPI.

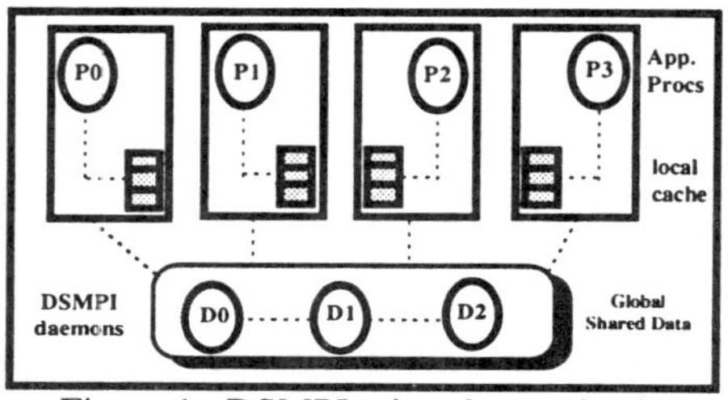

Figure 1: DSMPI virtual organization

The number of daemons used by an application is chosen by the programmer as well as its location, by using a configuration file (`dsmconf`) that is read by the DSMPI initialization routine. This approach gives to the user the freedom to choose the most convenient mapping of daemon processes according to the application needs. In practice, there is a notion of virtual domains where each daemon is responsible by some tasks of one or more application processes. One of the daemons is elected as the Master Daemon and will be responsible by some tasks that require some centralized responsibility.

The ownership of the data objects is implemented through a static distributed scheme. While a centralized scheme would introduce a bottleneck, a dynamic distributed policy would require the use of broadcasts to determine the current owner of a data object [19]. In the static distributed policy, the owner daemon of each object is chosen by the run-time system during the startup of the application and never changes during the program execution. Each process maintains a local directory containing the location of each object in the system. This static distribution strategy requires less control messages than the dynamic strategy and does not introduce the congestion of a central server.

The mapping of data objects to daemons can also be chosen by the application programmer. When the process creates a shared object the assigned owner will be the associated daemon. This facility can enhance the performance of the applications when correctly used, but if the mapping provided by the programmer is completely inadequate it would certainly degrade the performance of the application. The next version of DSMPI will have an adaptive mapping strategy based on run-time heuristics that will adapt the mapping of the data objects to daemon processes accordingly to the observed communication patterns of the application. Such facility could alleviate or adjust some wrong decision taken by the application programmer. The current version of DSMPI is still limited in this aspect.

3. Replication Protocols

The library allows the programmer to chose the replication strategy for each shared object among three possible choices. Shared objects can be classified as `WRITE_MOSTLY`, `READ_WRITE` or `READ_MOSTLY`. The first class represents those objects that are frequently written. In such a case is not worthwhile to replicate the object among the processes. Only one copy is maintained by one of the daemons.

In the other two classes (`READ_WRITE` and `READ_MOSTLY`) the objects are replicated among the caches of the processes that use them. Data replication is one way of exploiting parallelism, since multiple reads can be executed in parallel. For these two classes of objects the ratio between the number of reads and writes should justify the replication of data. Each daemon that keeps the ownership of a replicated object maintains a list (*copy-set*) of the processes that have a copy in its local cache. A process is included in that list when it issues a remote read request. After that and in the absence of write operations, the process reads the object from its local cache.

Each daemon is responsible for the consistency of the replicated objects that it owns. There is a considerable difference between the protocols that implement those two classes. For READ_WRITE objects, the system implements a write-invalidation protocol. This means that on a write operation all the cached copies of the object are invalidated from the local caches. Only the process that writes to the object maintains an updated copy in its local cache. When some of the other processes wants to read or write that object it gets a *cache-miss*, and it has to fetch the object remotely from the daemon that maintains its ownership.

For READ_MOSTLY objects the library uses a write-update protocol. This means that all the cached copies of the object are updated atomically after each write operation. This scheme does not incur in cache-misses as the write-invalidation protocol but in the case of large size objects it requires the sending of large size messages that carry the update notices.

Both protocols have advantages and disadvantages [19]. Invalidation-based protocols have the advantage of using smaller consistency-related messages than update-based protocols since they only specify the object that needs to be invalidated and not the data itself. The write-update protocols reduce the likelihood of a *cache-miss*. The choice between these protocols clearly depends on the ratio of read/write accesses and on the size of the data object.

The application programmer has the freedom to choose between those three classes when it creates a particular shared object. It has been argued in [19] that no single algorithm for DSM will be suitable for most applications. Shared objects have different characteristics, thus it is important to select the coherence protocols that best match the application characteristics.

The replication of data and the placement of shared objects is an important feature to improve the efficiency of the application. DSMPI is not the only system that provides more than one class of objects. Munin [13] is another system that provides several classes of objects. Through the use of annotations the programmer can choose among seven different coherence protocols tailored for different types of data. The type of the data objects remains static once specified, and this means that Munin, as well as DSMPI, cannot dynamically adjust the coherence protocols to possible changes in the behaviour of the application.

The study presented in [20] also considers multiple coherence protocols but presents a self-adjusting scheme where the run-time system monitors the usage pattern of each data object and performs a protocol adjustment to the objects that have a different behaviour than was specified previously through the user annotations. It has been proved to be a very interesting technique with quite good results and we plan to include such facility in the next version of DSMPI.

4. Models of Consistency

In order to exploit further efficiency, we have implemented three different models of consistency: Sequential consistency (SC), Release Consistency (RC) and Lazy Release consistency (LRC). The SC model was proposed in the IVY system [7], where all the operations in shared data are performed as if they were following a sequential order. This is the normal model of consistency, that in some particular cases does not perform very well in DSM systems implemented on networks like Ethernet. For such cases, the programmer can make use of the RC model, that in our case implements the protocol of the DASH multiprocessor [4]. In this model, it is assumed that all the accesses are protected by synchronization primitives (*acquire* and *release*, corresponding to lock/unlock operations). It attempts to mask the latency of write operations by allowing them to be performed in the background with the computation. The process is only stalled when executing a *release*, at which time it must wait for all its previous writes to perform. However, this model does not attempt to reduce the high cost of moving data across the system. It only tries to reduce the latency of write operations.

Another Release Consistency model has been implemented in Munin [14], where all the write notices from a process are collected and only sent when the processor reaches a synchronization release point. This does not introduce a significant improvement over the Dash Release Consistency protocol, and by this reason we choose the previous one.

To reduce the message traffic the programmer can use the LRC model of consistency. DSMPI implements a similar protocol as proposed in the TreadMarks system [14]. This model relaxes the Release Consistency protocol by further postponing the sending of write notices until the next acquire. When a process writes into a replicated data object, rather than sending update/invalidate notices to all potentially interested processes (i.e. those that belong to the *copy-set* list), it keeps a record of the objects that it updated and informs the acquiring process of all those write notices that are in the logical past of the releaser but yet in the logical past of the acquirer. In other words, the LRC scheme keeps track of the causal dependencies between write operations, acquires and releases, allowing it to propagate the write notices lazily only when they are needed. To implement this scheme we have used the Vector Time mechanism, and the resulting protocol, albeit complex, reduces considerably the number of messages and the amount of data exchanged on behalf of the replication protocols [21-22].

Another model of consistency was proposed in the Midway system (the Entry Consistency model) [23]. This model simplifies the implementation of the consistency protocol but demands more effort from the application programmer, since it requires the association of each lock to the data objects that it protects.

5. Programming Interface

The current version only provides a interface for C. A Fortran interface is planned for the next release. The routines provided by DSMPI are represented in Figure 2.

```
- DSMPI_Startup(comm);
- DSMPI_Exit(void);
- DSMPI_Decl_SO(name,count,
                data_type, *shobj);
- DSMPI_Create_SO(shobj, access_type);
- DSMPI_Read(shobj,buf, model);
- DSMPI_Write(shobj, buf, model);
- DSMPI_ReadSome(shobj, buf, count,
                 offset, model);
- DSMPI_WriteSome(shobj, buf, count,
                  offset, model);
- DSMPI_Lock(lock_id);
- DSMPI_UnLock(ock_id);
- DSMPI_Wait(sem_id);
- DSMPI_Signal(sem_id,N);
- DSMPI_Barrier(barrier_id,N);
```

Figure 2: DSMPI primitives.

Initialization and Termination

To start a DSMPI application all the processes must invoke `DSMPI_Startup()`. This function returns a MPI communicator that can be used by the application processes to communicate directly through message passing. To terminate correctly a DSMPI application all the processes have to call `DSMPI_Exit()`.

Declaration and Creation of Shared Objects

The set of shared objects used in the application should be declared explicitly by all the processes at the beginning of the application through the routine `DSMPI_Decl_SO()`. With this routine the programmer has to specify the data type of the object, and the number of elements. It returns a shared object identifier that should be used in any further reference to that object. To create one shared object a process has to call the `DSMPI_Create()` primitive. In this call, the programmer has the freedom to chose the replication strategy for the shared objects by indicating the access_type among the three options: `WRITE_MOSTLY`, `READ_WRITE` and `READ_MOSTLY`.

Read and Write Operations

Communication between processes is made by using explicit read and write operations on shared objects. The programmer just calls `DSMPI_Read()` or `DSMPI_Write()` and does not need to be aware of the location of the object. Maybe the object is read from its local cache, or maybe it is read or written remotely.

In the current version, the programmer has the freedom to specify the required model for data consistency among three choices: `DSM_SC`, `DSM_DRC` and `DSM_LRC`, where `DSM_SC` corresponds to Sequential Consistency, `DSM_DRC` corresponds to the Dash Release Consistency protocol, and finally `DSM_LRC` corresponds to Lazy Release Consistency

To read or write only parts of some object the programmer may find the following routines very useful: `DSMPI_ReadSome()` and `DSMPI_WriteSome()`. The programmer has only to specify the offset within the object and the number of basic elements he wants to read (or write). These routines have been proved to be very effective to operate in large size objects (like arrays and vectors) when the program only wants to read or update a small part of the object.

Synchronization Primitives

To control the concurrent access to shared variables the programmer has to use some synchronization primitives. DSMPI provides locks, semaphores and barriers. These are the usual synchronization primitives provided by most DSM systems.

The library also provides support for checkpointing through the use of three additional primitives, that are not presented herein since it is out of the scope of this paper. More details about the checkpointing scheme can be obtained in [24].

6. Performance Results

The main question to be answered is: what is the price in terms of performance the users of DSMPI have to pay when comparing with MPI ?

Applications that use any DSM system are expected to perform worse than if they use message passing directly because DSM is implemented on top of message passing. However, there are some claims [25] that DSM can be competitive with message passing for many applications. We present some results that corroborate those claims.

Ideally, the number of messages exchanged in a software implementation of DSM should be equal to the number of messages exchanged in a message passing implementation of the same application. This hardly happens, but the DSM system should be optimized to achieve a competitive level of performance. The performance of a DSM system is directly affected by several factors, like:

(I) the memory-access pattern of the application; (ii) the replication of shared data and the protocol that assures its consistency; (iii) the implementation of relaxed models of consistency; (iv) other optimizations that try to reduce the exchange of DSM data through the communication network.

In this section we evaluate the overhead of using DSMPI against message passing. For that, we have implemented two versions of the following six applications:

- *TSP*: solves the Traveling Salesman Problem using a branch-and-bound algorithm. It uses a Master/slave programming paradigm. The program uses a task queue that is a shared object globally accessed to all the slave processes. There are two other shared objects which are replicated among the slave processes: one that keeps the minimum path, and the other that maintains the best route. The minimum value is frequently read and is used to prune part of the search tree. When a slaves finds a new solution it updates these two variables. The DSMPI version used locks to protect the access to the shared objects.
- *NQUEENS*: solves the placement problem of N-queens in a N-size chessboard. It also follows the Master/Worker programming model. The DSMPI version made use of locks to protect the task queue structure and other shared objects that keep the number of solutions achieved.
- *SOR*: successive overrelaxation its an iterative method to solve Laplace's equation on a regular grid. The grid is partitioned into regions, each containing a band of rows of the global grid. Each region is assigned to a process. The DSMPI program uses a set of shared objects to exchange the row boundaries. This application used only barriers as synchronization variables.
- *GAUSS*: solves a system of linear equations using the method of Gauss-elimination. The algorithm uses partial pivoting and distributes the columns of the input matrix among the processes in an interleaved way to avoid imbalance problems. At each iteration of the algorithm, one of the processes finds the pivot element and sends the pivot column to all the other processes. The DSMPI used a shared object to store the pivot column and the indication of the pivot. A semaphore is used to protect the access to those shared objects. At the end of each iteration all the processes have to execute a barrier synchronization.
- *ASP*: solves the All-pairs Shortest Paths problem, i.e. it finds the length of the shortest path from any node i to any other node j in a given graph with N nodes using Floyd's algorithm. In each iteration there is one of the slaves which has the pivot row. It broadcast its value by writing it to a shared object that is read by the other slaves. The DSMPI program uses locks to protect the access to that object and a barrier at the end of each iteration.
- *NBODY*: this program simulates the evolution of a system of bodies under the influence of gravitational forces. The original algorithm used a ring structure for communication and at the end of each iteration it uses a collective operation to calculate a minimum value among the processes. The DSMPI version makes use of semaphores to synchronize the communicating objects and a barrier at the end of each iteration.

First we measured the performance in a network of workstations composed by 4 Sun4 machines connected by a 10 Mb/s Ethernet. The overhead is represented in Table 1.

Table 1: Performance Results in a NOW

APPLICATION	MPI Version	DSMPI Version	DSMPI/MPI
TSP (18)	5 min 09 sec 941	5 min 12 sec 780	1.0091
NQUEENS (13)	2 min 57 sec 124	2 min 59 sec 558	1.0137
SOR (1024,2001)	6 min 21 sec 555	6 min 44 sec 043	1.0589
GAUSS (2048)	15 min 28 sec 479	18 min 23 sec 996	1.1890
ASP (1024)	10 min 03 sec 562	10 min 37 sec 376	1.0560
NBODY (4000)	10 min 05 sec 652	10 min 06 sec 342	1.0011

For some of the applications (TSP, NQUEENS, and NBODY) the overhead of the DSMPI version is almost negligible (0.91%, 1.37% and 0.11%, respectively). The DSMPI version of SOR and ASP still has an acceptable overhead (5.89% and 5.60%) but the overhead for the GAUSS application was already considerable (18.90%). The reason for that difference is due to the extensive use of semaphores and large size shared objects.

These kind of results are similar to the ones obtained in the implementation of the Munin system [13] that achieved performance within 90-95% of the hand-coded message-passing implementations of the same application.

Another study presented in [25] compared the performance of TreadMarks [13] with PVM [26] and concluded that TreadMarks performed nearly identical to PVM for programs that have a high ratio of computation/communication and large granularity of sharing. For programs with little access locality and a large amount of shared data Treadmarks performed within 50% of PVM. For the remaining applications it performed within 75% of PVM.

The study presented in [27] shows that with current processors, the bandwidth of the 10 Mb/sec Ethernet becomes a bottleneck, limiting the speedup and the efficiency of the applications. With 100 Mb/sec ATM networks, that are now appearing on the market, those authors achieved considerable improvements in the performance of their DSM system.

To corroborate the idea that the bandwidth of the communication network is a feature of paramount importance we conducted a similar experiment in the CRAY T3D machine of the EPCC[1]. The results are shown in Table 2.

The first two applications used 8 processors: the DSMPI version used 7 workers and one daemon process, while the MPI counterpart used 7 workers and 1 master process. The remaining applications used 16 workers. The corresponding DSMPI version used 4 additional processors to run the daemon processes. Additional processors were required because the operating system (UNICOS) of the Cray only permits one process per processor.

Table 2: Performance Results in the Cray T3D

APPLICATION	MPI Version	DSMPI Version	DSMPI/MPI
TSP (18)	1 min 46 sec 445	1 min 46 sec 176	0.9974
NQUEENS (14)	7 min 43 sec 863	7 min 41 sec 685	0.9953
SOR (2048,5001)	1 min 57 sec 803	2 min 02 sec 323	1.0383
GAUSS (2048)	1 min 37 sec 946	1 min 38 sec 791	1.0086
ASP (1024)	1 min 38 sec 068	1 min 44 sec 369	1.0642
NBODY (4000)	52 sec 498	43 sec 821	0.8347

Surprisingly, three of the applications (TSP, NQUEENS and NBODY) performed better when using DSMPI than using MPI: 0.26%, 0.47% and 16.53%, respectively. Reasons to explain such improvement include the replication of data through the local caches, the reduction of synchronization that exists in message passing and the correct mapping of the shared objects.

This set of results in the T3D suggest that when the underlying communication system is fast we can expect DSMPI to be directly competitive with message passing (at least for some applications).

7. Conclusions and Future Work

DSMPI is a DSM parallel library that does not require any special feature from the operating system, uses a standard compiler, and assures full-portability across all the platforms that support MPI. It also provides support for two additional but important features: fault-tolerance (see [24]) and heterogeneity.

Another interesting feature of DSMPI is the possibility of integrating shared-data and message passing within the same program. The mixture of both programming models in the same program can be a very effective solution for parallel programming.

The current version of DSMPI still presents some drawbacks, as pointed out within the text. We plan to overcome some of these drawbacks in the next release. Despite these limitations we consider DSMPI an easy-to-use and flexible library that presents an interesting level of efficiency and can be effectively used together with MPI.

[1] Edinburgh Parallel Computing Centre, Scotland.

Acknowledgments

The work herein presented was made when the first author was a visitor at EPCC. The visit was made possible due to the TRACS programme, and the first author would like to thank the TRACS team, in special, to Andy Sanwell, Elspeth Minty and Brian Fletcher for their support. The first author is supported by JNICT on behalf of the "Programa Ciência" (BD-2083-92-IA).

References

[1] M.R. Eskicioglu. "A Comprehensive Bibliography of Distributed Shared Memory", TR-95-01, Univ. of New Orleans, May 1995

[2] S. Raina. "Virtual Shared Memory: A Survey of Techniques and Systems", CSTR-92-36, University of Bristol, December 1992

[3] B. Nitzberg, V. Lo. "Distributed Shared Memory: A Survey of Issues and Algorithms", IEEE Computer, Vol. 24, No. 8, pp. 52-60, 1991

[4] D. Lenoski, J. Laudon, K. Gharachorloo, A. Gupta, J. Henessy. "The Directory-based Cache Coherence Protocol for the DASH Multiprocessor", Proc. 17th Annual International Symposium on Computer Architecture, pp. 148-159, 1990

[5] R. Bisiani, M.Ravishankar. "PLUS: a Distributed Shared-Memory System", Proc. 17th Int. Symposium on Computer Architecture, pp. 115-124, 1990

[6] J. Rothnie. "Overview of the KSR-1 Computer System", Technical Report TR-9202001, Kendal Square Research, 1992

[7] K. Li, P.Hudak. "Memory Coherence in Shared Virtual Memory Systems", ACM Transactions Computer Systems, Vol. 7, No. 4, pp. 321-359, Nov. 1989

[8] B.Fleish, G.Popek. "Mirage: a Coherent Distributed Shared Memory Design", Proc. 14th ACM Symp. Operating System Principles, pp. 211-223, 1989

[9] U.Ramachnadran, M.Y. Khalidi. "An Implementation of Distributed Shared Memory", Software - Practice and Experience, Vol. 21 (5), pp. 443-464, May 1991

[10] M.Kaashoek, H.Bal, A.Tanenbaum. "Orca: a Language for Parallel Programming of Distributed Systems", IEEE Trans. on Software Engineering, Vol. 18(3), March 1992

[11] J.Chase, F.Amador, E.Lazowska, h.Levy, R.Littlefield. "The Amber System: Parallel Programming on a Network of Multiprocessors", Proc. 12th ACM Symposium on Operating System Principles, pp. 147-158, Dec. 1989

[12] R.Chandra, A.Gupta, J.L.Hennessy. "COOL: An Object-Based Language for Parallel Programming", IEEE Computer, pp. 13-26, Aug.94

[13] J.Carter, J.Bennet, W.Zwaenepoel. "Implementation and Performance of Munin", ACM Symposium on Operating System Principles, pp. 152-164, October 1991

[14] P.Keleher, A.Cox, S.Dwarkadas, W.Zwaenepoel. "TreadMarks: Distributed Shared Memory on Standard Workstations and Operating Systems", Proc. Winter 94 USENIX Conference, pp. 115-131, January 1994

[15]W.Y. Liang. "ADSMITH: a Structure-based Heterogeneous Distributed Shared Memory on PVM", Technical Report Institute of Computer Science National Tsing Hua University, Taiwan, June 1994

[16] R.J.Harrison. "Moving Beyond Message Passing: Experiments with a Distributed-Data Model", Technical Report Argonne National Laboratory, 1991

[17] D.Kranz, K.Johnson, A.Agarwal. "Integrating Message-Passing and Shared-Memory: Early Experience", Proc. 5th ACM SIGPLAN Symposium on Principles and Practice of Parallel Programming, pp. 54-63, May 1993

[18] MPI Forum. MPI Forum. "A Message Passing Interface Standard". May 1994, Available on **netlib.**

[19] M.Stumm, S.Zhou. "Algorithms Implementing Distributed Shared Memory", IEEE Computer, Vol. 23 (5), pp. 54-64, May 1990

[20] H.H.Wang, R.C.Chang. "A Distributed Shared Memory System with Self-Adjusting Coherence Scheme", Parallel Computing, Vol. 20, pp. 1007-1025, 1994

[21] P.Keleher, A.Cox, W.Zwaenepoel. "Lazy Release Consistency for Software Distributed Shared Memory", Proc. 19th Annual Int. Symposium on Computer Architectures, pp. 13-21, May 1992

[22] S.Dwarkadas, P.Keleher, A.Cox, W.Zwaenepoel. "Evaluation of Release Consistent Software Distributed Shared Memory on Emerging Network Technology", ACM Computer Architecture News, Vol. 21, No. 2, pp. 144-155, May 1993

[23] B.N.Bershad, M.J.Zekauskas. "Midway: Shared Memory Parallel Programming with Entry Consistency for Distributed Memory Multiprocessors", Technical Report CMU-CS-91-170, September 1991

[24] L.M.Silva, S.Chapple, J.G.Silva. "Checkpointing DSMPI Programs", Technical Report University of Coimbra, (submitted for publication).

[25] S.Chandra, J.Larus, A.Rogers. "Where is Time Spent in Message-Passing and Shared-Memory Programs ?", Proc. ACM ASPLOS VI, October 1994

[26] R.Bisiani, A.Forin. "Multilingual Parallel Programming of Heterogeneous Machines", IEEE Transactions on Computers, Vol. 37(9), pp. 930-945, 1988

[27] S.Zhu, M.Stumm, K.Li, D.Wortman. "Heterogeneous Distributed Shared Memory", IEEE Transactions on Parallel and Distributed Systems, Vol. 3, No. 5, pp. 540-554, September 1992

Open Forum Session I

Chair

F. d'Almeida

Modelling Agents in C++CL for Content-Based Image Retrieval

P. Charlton, B. Huet and G. Justog
S.C.S.I.S.E.
University of Westminster
115 New Cavendish St
London W1M 8JS
England
{charltp, huetb, justog}@wmin.ac.uk

Abstract

In this paper, we describe a hybrid system for dealing with content-based retrieval [8, 7] from a library of images. An agent architecture is used in conjunction with a neural network to match and retrieve images. We explain how we define and use our image indices which allows us to treat the problem in a distributed fashion. We combine the indices with a multiple agent approach to help reduce our search space and to retrieve an image as a parallel action. The resulting system is one which is flexible but controlled.

A neural network is used to generate a feature vector from the images which is used by the agents. The agents are based on the theories behind Lilies. Lilies (Localisation and InterLeaving stragIES [4, 6, 3]) was developed to deal with multiple agents for planning environment. Lilies was used to prototype the initial representation of the agents used for searching the database.

Although an implementation of the **search-agents** *has been developed in Lilies, we also describe in this paper the design to convert the agent model to C++CL platform. C++CL is an object oriented framework layered on top of PVM which allows planned and unplanned reconfiguration of distributed systems. Basically, this paper introduces two issues about distributed systems: (i) a neural net for image compression and (ii) the design of an agent searching architecture using C++CL [18, 19].*

1 Introduction

We consider a new approach to the problem of content-based image retrieval by addressing the application as distributed. To make the images distributed we use neural nets to organise the image data into eigenvectors. We then operate on the eigenvectors using multiple agents as implemented in *Lilies*.

Lilies is a system which allows multiple agents to communicate in order to develop solutions to planning problems. The system gives a representation which builds on the blackboard structure [10]. However, the original application required that the system should be more flexible than the blackboard architecture offered. Part of the extension of *Lilies* is in creating localisations for an agent based system. Reflection [3, 4, 6] is used to deal with adaption in the case of the original application having to deal with change and partial plans. We have taken the theories developed through *Lilies* and applied them to deal with a distributed problem of content-based image retrieval. In the original application, *Lilies* was used to simulate a physical agent based planning system, here we do not have the overhead of dealing with reactive planning. This means that the interleaving of planning and execution is not so constrained.

1.1 Overview of the Image Retrieval System

We combine two distributed architectures for dealing with Image Retrieval: (i) A neural net and (ii) an agent architecture. Using a Neural Network approach to solve the problem of indexing shapes allows a very efficient transformation of the raw 2D shape data into an index (Eigenvector) directly usable as an index for the retrieval process. However the Principal Component Analysis (PCA) performed by the network is not able to cope with changes in the orientation of the shape under consideration. Some techniques involving separating PCA extraction (one for the whole shape database and one specific to each shape under various viewing conditions) have been used to overcome this problem [23]. Having used the neural network approach to extract a compressed images in the form of eigen vectors, we then use an agent architecture, initially, as a simple search engine. We take advantage of the flexibility of an agent architecture [5] to improve the search and matching operations. This is possible because an agent architecture allows both containment in terms of problem solving scope and adaptability within this scope.

Figure 1 summarises how our image retrieval system works. Firstly the user provides an image to search on. The shape entered is then processed by a neural network to extract relevant features. The goal allocation agent receives the eigenvector for the image to search on, the list of eigenvalues to allocate to agents and the range threshold (which determines the selectiveness of the retrieval process).

The goal allocation agent assigns the list of eigenvalues of the images to be searched and the range threshold value to each search-agent. Each search-agent then proceeds to find a match on the range given, this range is just a min-max configuration. When an agent finds a match the pointer to the image is posted to the global database. Each agent has a local blackboard [3, 4] to allow local adaption.

In our original prototyping of the image retrieval system, our agents only dealt with local adaption [8]. A distributed system requires a communication protocol if adaption is to occur across the agents as well as in localisations. Communication between agents has a number of problems in distributed systems [30, 20]. We have been able to overcome some of these problems due to (i) the organisation of the domain (the distributed compression of images through the use of neural nets) and (ii) the use of the observer as a communicator [3, 2].

The paper covers the following points: (i) compressing shape images, (ii) retrieving shape images using *Lilies* and (iii) Converting agents represented in *Lilies* to C++CL.

2 Content-Based Retrieval of Images

Most of the image database systems currently available only use keywords associated to each image in order to retrieve images. The major drawback of this technique is that the same image can be described using different words, and even if the database is able to deal with synonyms, the search is exclusively limited to the initial text information provided for this image.

As the size and content of image database grow dramatically, new techniques for efficient and intelligent retrieval need to be investigated. The images in a database (or only a small area of an image) can be indexed using three different criteria (or features) [24, 27, 16, 12, 14]. The first feature that can be extracted is **colour**. The colour feature allows queries such as "Find all images that contain *Colour* as principal colour", where the *Colour* can be selected from another image or from a colour table. A reduced image histogram technique [28] is commonly used to perform such a task. We are using feed-forward neural networks to generate the reduced image "histogram" from the complete one.

The second feature is the **texture**.The coarseness, contrast, and direction are extracted from the selected image area (or the whole image) and are used for indexing. Several algorithms for texture extraction may be used [29] to perform this task. However, we are now using a neural network based extraction of the texture in the image.

The third feature, the one on which we will concentrate, is **shape**. Again, a neural network performs a Principal Component Analysis on a thresholded version of the image [24, 31, 1]. The eigenvector generated from the principal component analysis for each of the images is stored in a database. A query based on the shape of an object is resolved by comparing eigenvectors from the database with the shape under consideration. Figure 2 shows how the image database is created.

2.1 Neural Network for Shape Feature Extraction

There are various techniques of performing shape recognition [21, 9]. However, Principal Component Analysis (PCA) has several advantages over those techniques. Performing PCA on a thresholded image results in Feature selection or Feature extraction. Feature selection is the process of transforming a data space into a feature space of the same dimension. The effectiveness of feature selection resides in the possible reduction of the number of "relevant" features. In other words, the data set (a shape in our case) is subject to a reduction of dimension [13].

This reduction is performed by discarding the principal components (eigenvalues) that have a small variance and retaining only those that have a large variance. Fortunately, there is a close correspondence between the statistical method of PCA and the behavior of self-organized Artificial Neural Networks (ANN). Using the Hebbian-type learning rule for the ANN synaptic connections can evolve into a filter for the first principal component of the input distribution [25].

The neural network is a two-layer linear feed-forward network with 64x64 input units and 18 output units (see Figure 3). The training is to be performed using a simple unsupervised learning rule called generalized Hebbian algorithm [13].

The ANN is trained using a large set of randomly generated shapes as well as some clip-art images [15]. The network outputs generate the eigenvector required to distinguish between input patterns. Using artificial neural network to extract the shape feature from an image object allows the dimensionality reduction aspect of the shape recognition process to be distributed.

2.2 Content-Based Retrieval as a Distributed Problem

Object-recognition, pattern matching and feature extraction have proven to be difficult and require a large amount of computing resources. Therefore, instead of computing the eigenvector for each entry of the image database during the search procedures the eigenvector will be stored as an associated image entry. The eigenvector can be regarded as being a compressed version of the original image. It is not viable to do an extensive search in the whole database in order to satisfy a query. A solution is to perform some off-line indexing of the database population.

The indexing is performed by ordering each eigenvalue in the eigenvector of the whole database. Using this method, the search by each agent (the agent is discussed in more detail in section 3) is made more effective. In order to minimize the database access bottleneck at the beginning of a query, the database will be decomposed into multiple files. Each eigenvalue will be stored in a separate file. Our system will be therefore composed of 18 sub-databases (one for each eigenvalue of the eigenvector). By distributing the search for each feature of the eigenvector, using multiple agents, the relevant database entry is rapidly selected.

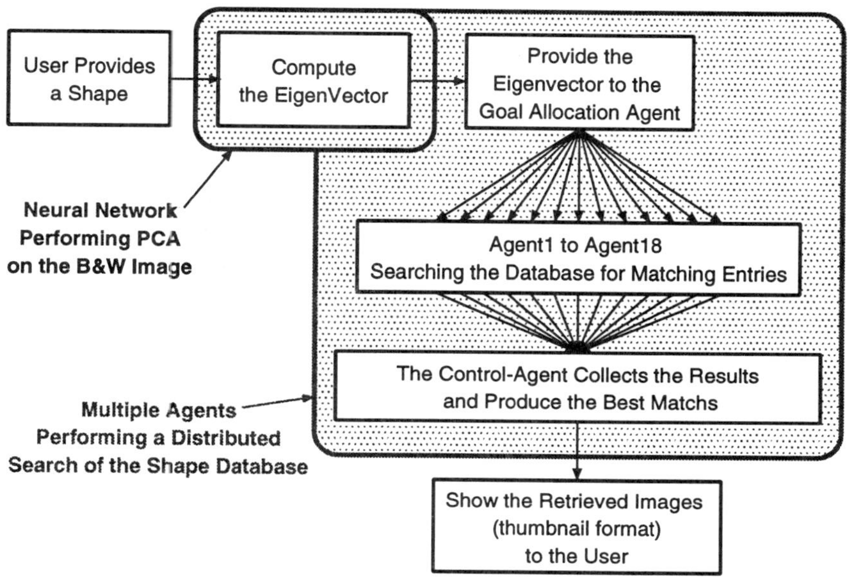

Figure 1: Image Retrieval System Overview

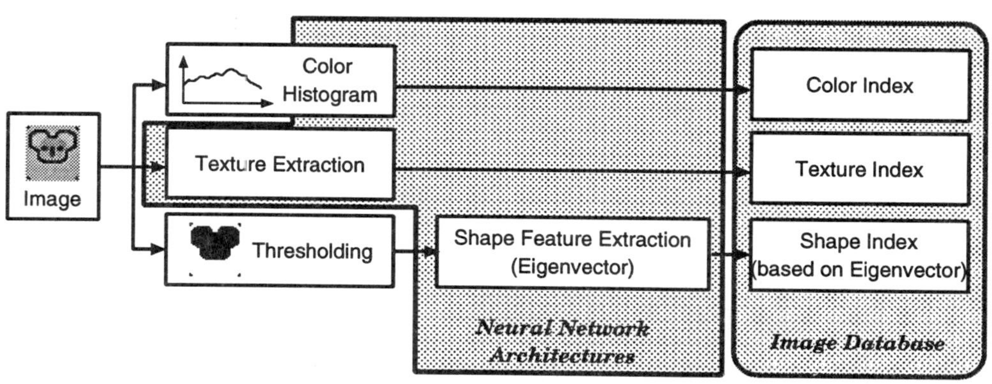

Figure 2: Content-Based Retrieval of Images

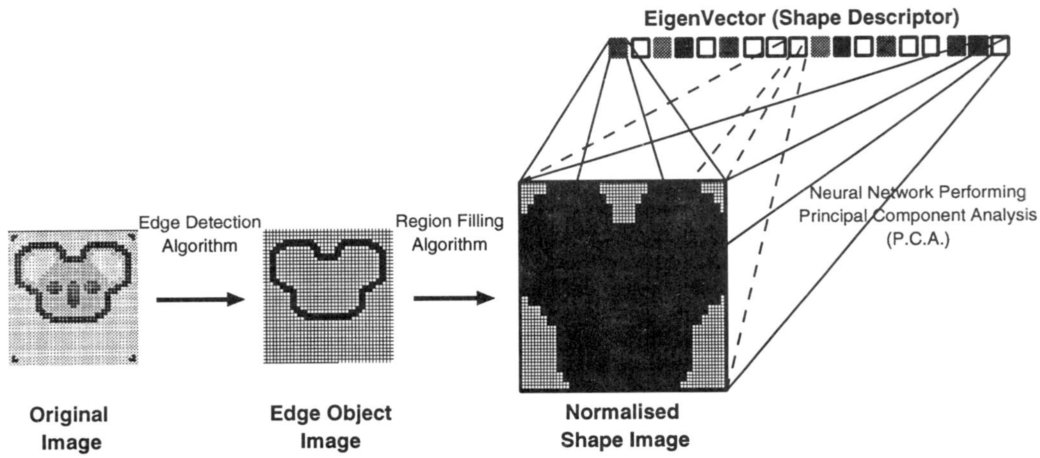

Figure 3: Generating the Shape Index

3 Using an Agent Architecture

There is an increasing amount of work being done in using agent based architectures from theory, design, to performance testing. The term agent has taken on a number of definitions. Before going any further we will define the term agent. There are two main categories for an agent: *autonomous agents* and *acting-agents* [32, 22]. Autonomous agents have motivations as well as goals. An acting-agent just has goals and when the agent is no longer *acting* the agent is classified as an object.

Within an agent there are structures which may be classified as process-agents (integrated reasoning processes [26]). This nesting of classified agents can occur at many levels in *Lilies*. Thus, an **agent** can be composed of autonomous-agents, and/or acting-agents, and/or process-agents. This gives one abstraction level of the applications activity and each layer can be unwrapped to show more detail of the localised activity. The context of the localisation being determined by the collection of structures.

3.1 How to Use a Multiple Agent System for Content-based Image Retrieval

Lilies creates an environment which allows each agent to have a blackboard type problem solver. *Lilies* is able to deal with adaption and change, these aspects of the system are exploited by this application at this stage of the development. Some flexibility of the system is through the controller agent which collates the results.

The application has been designed to use (i) 18 **search-agents** for the management and the search for the retrieval of images based on shape, (ii) a **goal allocation agent** which posts the task to each **search-agent**, each agent receives a list on the type of vector organisation, this speeds up the processing with the use of a threshold range, and (iii) a **control-agent** which receives and displays the solution set. An overview of the system is presented in figure 4. The control-agent uses the intermediate local blackboards to determine the solution set. The entries posted are pointers to image files and are not the actual images. Once the list of solutions is in place, the selected images can be retrieved and displayed to the user. Each agent is like a mini-blackboard system, generating local solutions to the criteria specified by the goal allocation agent and the user threshold. Each agent acts as a heuristic defined by a knowledge source structure. The setup procedure is as described in [6, 4]. Each agent can act independently while generating a solution set.

The control-agent can be triggered once the search-agents have started to process the image information. A delay can be set or the default is until all the agents are finished. One of the advantages in this design is the localisation approach of the blackboard. The localisations are achieved by an agent name extension. As the local blackboards can be accessed by one agent the control-agent, it is the entries we are interested in. We can be selective or general as the application dictates. There are a number of ways the database of agents information can be accessed:

1. The control-agent has the list of pointers stored as a file as part of the knowledge level.

2. The control-agent keeps a counter for each eigenvalue.

3. The *PROPOSE*[1] structure to keep an agent-value and the level can become the pointer. For each pointer we can add the next agent-value entry.

[1] The PROPOSE structure is used in the classical blackboard architecture (BB1 [10]) to update the blackboard database.

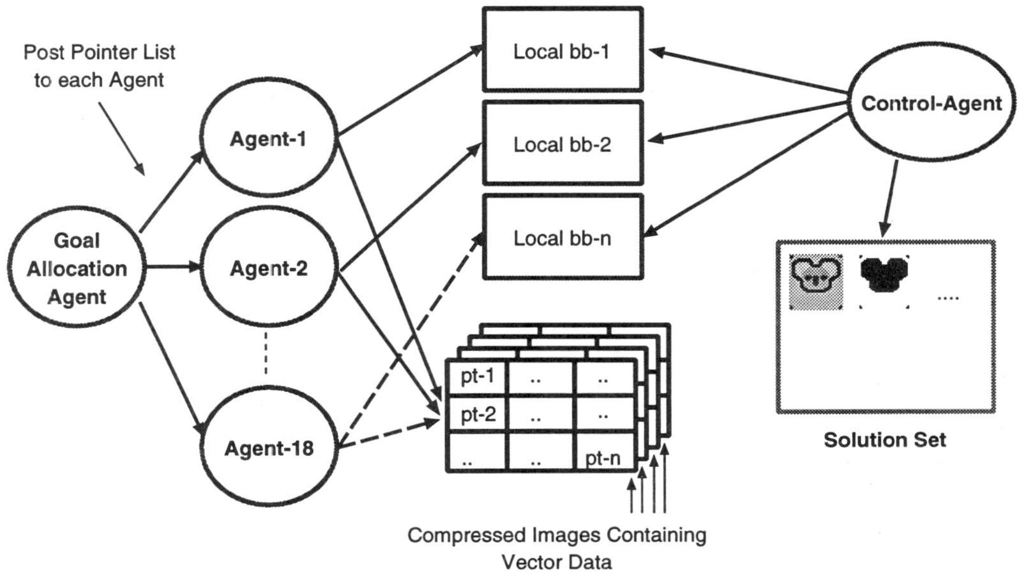

Figure 4: An Overview of the Agent Architecture

We are using option 3, as we can take advantage of the blackboard functions and *Lilies* by considering each localisation as a whole. We simply do an operation of $ENTRIES-IN-LEVEL[2] pointer-value and a list is returned. The comparison for a complete list of agent contribution or a sub-list can now be done depending on the application requirements.

During the setup phased an index list is posted onto the agent's blackboard and is maintained by a counter. The index list means we can stop processing once the threshold has been passed. For example, if we get the first value in the list we return a pointer to an image which contains the lowest eigenvalue[3] (see figure 5). The object contains the compressed image. The agent-value is an index to the eigenvalue required from the object. This value is returned and compared with the threshold value being operated on. The file of pointers also contains the eigenvalue, so we do not need to access the image database until the relevant number of matches is found.

4 C++CL and Lilies

4.1 An Overview of C++CL

The philosophy behind C++CL is to provide a tool for developing reconfigurable systems which are simple and portable. The simplicity of C++CL is achieved by implementing the model as a C++ application framework. This means that a reconfigurable distributed system is produced by creating objects from the classes provided.

C++CL works like an O-O specification of an operational semantics for CL [17, 18] applications where the classes denote CL are semantical entities and the actions denote CL operations on that entity[4]. This makes the framework not only extensible at the application level where certain classes can be stylised for particular applications but also it can be used to implement other models by modifying the semantical entities and their operations. Certainly, the approach is more suitable for reconfigurable system models but it can be applied to many parallel and distributed models. In this paper, we show how the framework is applied to the development of distributed agents.

Further to the portability supported by C++, the framework also allows portability at the communication level. This is achieved by implementing the communication system on the top of PVM [11] which provides an interface that runs on different platforms.

C++CL basically consists of components such as *configuration*, *task*, *configuration table*, and the *communication interface*. Certain components such as configuration table and communication interface are not user-level components but they are essential parts of the model.

A task contains a collection of ports which are used for communication. These ports interact with the interface component which provides the high-level communication. At the lower-level, the communication is provided by the communication component which is implemented in PVM.

[2] A blackboard operation.

[3] Remember that the list of pointers the agent is dealing with is for all the images at that eigenvalue position.

[4] In CL the processes are task modules. The task modules communicate by message passing. Processes do not share any kind of information except that defined by the messages.

A configuration can have ports if it is a subconfiguration. It can create and destroy (task and configuration) instances and perform configuration operations. Most of these operations are registered in the configuration table. The configuration can also query the configuration table for information about the configuration state.

The construction of an application using the framework is very simple. First, the task components are created, and then the configuration components, which use those tasks, are created. In order to create a task component, a derived class **Task** must be created, and its ports must be declared in its interface. To illustrate how this is done, the class *Agent* is defined. The declaration of the interface of the class *Agent* is presented in Figure 5, where the C++CL keywords are written in boldface letters. Two **Port** objects *in* and *out* of type *RecordIn* and *RecordOut* respectively are declared. Only two member functions are declared, the constructor *Agent* and **TaskBody** where the computation performed by the task is defined.

Figure 5 also shows the implementation of the class *Agent*. In the constructor of the class, the **Port** objects are initialised, and their directions are defined. That is, *in* is defined as an **EntryPort** and *out* as an **ExitPort**. In the **TaskBody** function, *in* is used to receive a message and *out* is used to output a message.

4.2 Converting Agents Represented in Lilies to C++CL

Lilies is based on a classical blackboard architecture [10]. The system extends the blackboard approach and allows the concept of localisations within a unified framework. This fits in well with the C++CL framework [18, 19] which has a configuration class and a process class (for programming-in-the-large and programming-in-the-small respectively). The first design crossover is to consider the extended blackboard interpreter as a general configuration object and the processes as a basic collection of knowledge source structures.

However, *Lilies* supports an agent structure which is like a local blackboard. The agents are nested within the global blackboard, but have their own local scope. The global blackboard is like the environment the agents are executing in. The representation of the communication and the environment can be modeled using the C++CL **Configuration** class. The processes representation allows a local scope which can be used to model the agents and will contain the following structures: (i) knowledge sources, (ii) local blackboard and (iii) the local agenda for knowledge source control. In the initial development for this domain, the local blackboard will not be used only a global blackboard held by the control-agent.

The communication between the agents for the image retrieval domain has initially been simplified. Also we anticipate "unplanned" configurations which will be applied during the image searching, for example when the current threshold value has no matches.

A simple agent class is defined in Figures 5 following the framework outlined in [19].

Each agent takes the same format and the goal-agent is defined as the **Configuration** object. The search-agents and the control-agent are defined as **Tasks** and are the imported into the **Configuration** object to be instantiated. Virtual nodes are define for each module and follows closely to the definition given in [19]. Each search-agent is passed three parameters, these are: (i) a filename to the list of pointers and eigenvalue (ii) the minimum eigenvalue and (iii) the maximum eigenvalue value.

In using C++CL we lose some of the explicit agent modeling which was inherent in *Lilies*, such as the local blackboard structure which is unified in and represented as part-of the global blackboard. There is the option of each agent maintaining its own local blackboard and once a number of matches have been achieved this local blackboard could be passed as a structure to the control-agent. This approach may, however, require more maintenance especially when using unplanned configuration.

As the goal-agent is now part of the configuration, we can use its representation to retain some of the flexibility when changes are required to the search-agents.

5 Conclusion

The organisation of our data gives us immediate interest in considering altering the threshold values. *Lilies* allows unplanned reconfiguration, not only at a global architecture point but also from an agent perspective. C++CL is more restrictive from a reconfiguration view due to the unknown requirements of the user, internal "process" reconfiguration is currently not allowed. However, our agent architecture does adhere to a structure which may be used later to allow for unplanned configuration in the small. Although we are currently focusing on typical use of the C++CL language for the general process configuration. This allows the following adaptive properties of the system: (i) change the number of eigenvalues to be used in the data retrieval – instead of using eighteen we could chose to use more values, (ii) modify the system to the results of the threshold analysis and (iii) the main advantages of the approach is the flexibility of the system for viewing alternative combinations of conditions.

This representation gives us flexibility over the type of analysis on the data set. The set can be expanded or truncated according to the user requests which adapts the algorithm for solution formation for the goal allocating agent and the controller agent. The advantage of using the agents means we can benefit from using both a parallel and adaptive context.

We have discussed our new approach to image retrieval as a distributed problem using two distributed frameworks, these being neural networks and intelligent agents system. We have provided our initial ideas on:

1. The ability of our system to improve the retrieval performance of the search process by using distributed agents. Although, the system is able to run on a single processor, its design makes

```
class Agent: public Task
{
  private:
    // Declare the ports (istream * filename,
    // double minimum, double maximum)
    Port<RecordIn> *in;
    // (char *imagefilename, int agentID)
    Port<RecordOut> *out;
    // Define the number of parameters
    int _arg ;
  protected:
    virtual void TaskBody
        (unsigned int, char**);
  public:
    Agent(char*,int);
};
```

```
// The InterfaceComponent of the Task
extern InterfaceComponent *theInterface;
Agent::Agent(char *name, int arg):
        Task(name, arg, task)
{
    _arg = arg;
    in = new Port<RecordIn> ( EntryPort );
    out = new Port<RecordOut> ( ExitPort );
}
Agent::TaskBody
    (unsigned argc, char** argv)
{
  RecordIn aRecordIn;
  RecordOut aRecordOut;
  in->receive(&aRecordIn);
    find-matches
      get-first eigenvalue within range
        loop while still in range
          out->send(aRecordOut);
};
Agent *thisTask= new Agent("Agent",0);
```

Figure 5: An outline of the class *Agent*

it powerful and efficient when running on multi-processor or distributed architecture. One of the advantages of the application is its low inter-agent communication, and so improved performance can be obtained using the approach explained here.

2. Using adaption and simulation to further improve the system performance - this heuristic adequate approach to incremental change and look ahead which *Lilies* is already capable of in a typical planning frame. The configuration language will be used for this.

3. Using *Lilies* as a rapid prototyping system. We can use this system as a consistency checker for our agents, in terms of representation and operation.

We have discussed large scale analysis, parallelism of the controller aspects and adaption. For further details on reflection as an adaptive approach see [4, 6].

References

[1] C.K. Chan and M.B. Sandler. A complete shape recognition system using the hough transform and neural network. *IEEE Proceeding on Information Retrieval*, 1992.

[2] P Charlton. Building reflective strategic rules for planning. *12th UK Planning and Scheduling special interest group*, 1993.

[3] P Charlton. A reflective strategic problem solving model. *Springer Verlag - Lecture Notes in Artificial Intelligence*, 1993.

[4] P Charlton. Lilies - a framework for building multiple agents for adaptive planning. *AAAI spring-symposium 1995 -Lessons Learned from Implemented Software Architectures for Physical Agents. To be published in a Special AAAI Journal*, 1995.

[5] P. Charlton. Self-configurable software agents. *Workshop on Advances in Meta object Protocols and Reflection at ECOOP '95, Springer-Verlag*, August 1995.

[6] P. Charlton. *Reflective Lilies for Planning.* PhD thesis, Maths, Bath University, Bath, In preparation.

[7] P. Charlton and B. Huet. Intelligent agents for image retrieval. *A Forum on Research and Technology Advances in Digital Libraries (ADL95) - To be published in Springer Verlag*, 1995.

[8] P. Charlton and B. Huet. Using multiple agents for content-based image retrieval. *European Research Seminar on Advances in Distributed Systems*, April 1995.

[9] J.P. Eakins. SAFARI - a shape retrieval system for engineering drawings. *Proceedings of 11th BCS Information Retrieval Specialist Group Research Group Colloquium on Information Retrieval*, 1989.

[10] R. Englemore and T. Morgan. *Blackboard Systems.* Addison and Wesley, 1988.

[11] A. Geist, A. Beguelin, J. J. Dongarra, W. Jiang, R. Manchek, and V. S. Sunderam. Pvm 3 user's

guide and reference manual. Technical report, Oak Ridge National Laboratory, May 1993.

[12] T. Gevers and A.W.M. Smeulders. $\sum$nigma: An image retrieval system. *International Conference on Pattern Recognition (ICPR) 1992*, 1992.

[13] S. Haykin. *Neural Networks A Comprehensive Foundation.* Macmillan, 1994.

[14] K. Hirata and T. Kato. Query by visual example. *Advances in Databases Technology EDBT 92*, 1992.

[15] B. Huet. Shape encoding for image database. *Submitted to the Second Asian Conference on Computer Vision*, December 1995. Singapore.

[16] D. Davis J. Oakley and R. Shann. Manchester visual query language. *Image and Vision Storage and Retrieval*, 1993.

[17] G. R. R. Justo and P. R. F. Cunha. Dynamic configuration as a paradigm to develop flexible and robust system. In *ICYCS'91*, pages 46–50, Beijing, China, 1991. Int. Academic Press.

[18] G. R. R. Justo and P. R. F. Cunha. Programming distributed systems with configuration languages. In *Int. Workshop on Configurable Distributed Systems*, pages 118–127. IEE, London, 1992.

[19] G. R. R. Justo and P. R. F. Cunha. C++CL: An object-oriented framework for the development of reconfigurable distributed systems. Technical report, School of Computer Science, University of Westminster, London, 1994.

[20] H. Kitano and J. Hendler. *Massively Parallel Artificial Intelligence.* The AAAI press, 1994.

[21] V.F. Learver. *Shape Detection in computer vision using hough transform.* Springer-Verlag, 1990.

[22] M. M. Luck and M. d'Inverno. A formal framework for agency and autonomy. *First International Conference on Multiagent Systems - IMCAS '95*, 1995.

[23] H. Murase and S.K. Nayar. Visual learning and recognition of 3d objects from appearance. *International Jouranl of Computer Vision*, 14:5–24, 1995.

[24] W. Niblack, R. Barber, W. Equitz, M. Flickner, E. Glasman, D. Petkovic, P. Yanker, C. Faloutsos, and G. Taubin. The QBIC project: Querying images by content using color, texture and shape. *Image and Vision Storage and Retrieval*, 1993.

[25] E. Oja. A simplified neuron model as a principal component analyzer. *Journal of Mathematical Biology*, pages 267–273, 1982.

[26] Doug Riecken. M: An architecture of integrated agents. *Communications of the ACM*, 37(7):107–116, July 1994.

[27] M. J. Swain. Interactive indexing into image databases. *Image and Vision Storage and Retrieval*, 1993.

[28] M. J. Swain and D.H. Ballard. Color indexing. *Journal of Information Processing (Japan)*, 1991.

[29] H. Tamura, S. Mori, and T. Yamawaki. Texture features corresponding to visual perception. *IEEE Transactions on Systems, Man and Cybernetics*, 1978.

[30] G. Tel. *Introduction to Distributed Algorithms.* Press Syndicate of the University of Cambridge, 1994.

[31] M. Turk and A. Pentland. Eigenfaces for recognition. *Journal of Cognitive Neuroscience*, 1990.

[32] Shoham. Yoav. Agent-oriented programming. Technical Report STAN-CS-90-1335, Department of Computer Science, stanford University, 1991.

CPVM - Extending PVM for Consistent Checkpointing

Andrea Clematis
IMA, CNR
Via De Marini, 6
16149 Genova Italy

Vittoria Gianuzzi
DISI, Univ. Genova
Viale Benedetto XV, 3
16132 Genova Italy

Abstract

This paper presents CPVM, a library that provides the user with a support to implement non blocking, blobal checkpoint- restart algorithms for applications written using PVM thereby achieving fault-tolerance.

A salient feature of CPVM is the way in which, solely on the basis of a simple set of new PVM primitives, it provides several advanced facilities useful to solve different problems.

CPVM can also be used as a platform on top of which to implement different algorithms to detect stable properties such as deadlocks and termination, and to support job-swapping and migration in an environment where there previously was none.

1 Introduction

Distributed systems are more and more used as parallel machines, thus making programs more prone to failure, debugging more complex, and load balancing a necessary facility. All these problems are often thightly related and require the same set of basic facilities.

The situation is however not uniform and the same problem can be addressed from different points of view. Let us consider a distributed application programmed using a communication library like Linda, Express, PVM, or MPI. In the following, the attention will be concentrated on message passing libraries. There are at least two aspects that influence the definition of a suitable strategy e.g. for fault tolerance and load balancing. The first point is the intrinsic structure of the application, the second one is the type of event that we want to consider.

As far as it concerns application structure a parallel application exibiths very often a regular communication pattern and behaves like an SPMD program. These two points can be used to design simple and efficient fault tolerance and load balancing strategies, as discussed in [Silv95, Clem94]. Also the set of facilities which are necessary is very reduced. Using communication libraries it is possible to design structured (e.g. processor farm) fault tolerant and load balanced applications.

The type of event that is considered has also an influence. Two basic different types of event can be considered: friendly and unfriendly manifesting. In the first category planned manteinance operations, dynamically changing load conditions are included. Unfriendly events are e.g. node faults. Some communication libraries provide suitable interfaces (e.g. Piranha for Linda) to deal with friendly events. To deal with unfriendly events a true fault tolerance strategy is necessary.

Despite the large part of applications exibith a regular structure, there are applications of pratical interest (e.g. a distributed discrete simulation) which have a general structure and an unpredictable communication pattern. For these applications the problem of fault tolerance is especially important and general strategies have to be used [Gian95]. A possibility to provide fault tolerance to such applications is to use a distributed checkpointing algorithm. Distributed checkpointing has been widely considered, and the key point in its implementation is the availability of a suitable protocol to take a consistent cut.

A consistent cut is necessary for the correct recording of intermediate process and channel states. The concept of consistent cut will be formalized in Section

1066-6192/96 $5.00 © 1996 IEEE
Proceedings of PDP '96

3. Intuitively, looking at a time space diagram, as that presented in Figure 1 a consistent cut is one in which arrows that cross the cut line have their starting point on the left and the ending point on rigth side of the cut. Hence C2 is consistent, while C1 is unconsistent. We define *cut protocol* a distributed algorithm that permits to obtain a consistent cut and to conveniently mark all messages in transit during the cut protocol execution.

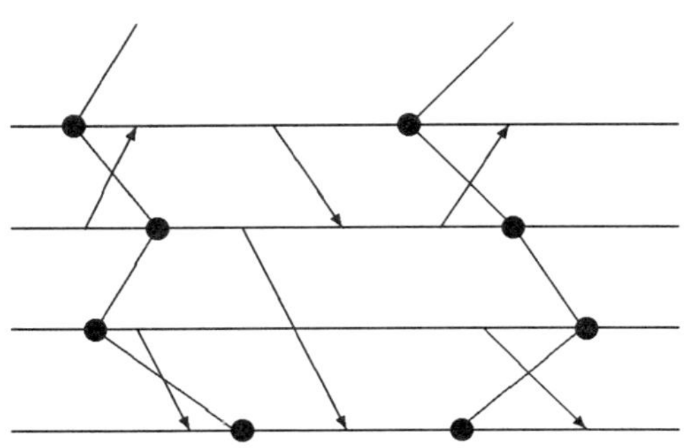

Figure 1: Non consistent (C1) and consistent (C2) cuts.

Consistent cut protocols are of interest in the implementation of different facilities like:
1. Distributed checkpointing,
2. Process migration for load balancing,
3. Job swapping,
4. Global snapshot,
5. Debugging.

In the first three cases it is necessary to save process and channel states at the cut instant and then to collect messages in transit. In case 4 and 5 it is sufficient to compute and transmit values of interest at the cut instant. Hence in cases 1, 2 and 3 the efficiency of the cut protocol is important but not crucial since the saving operations have usually a dominant cost. However it is important that the algorithm is reliable, possibly simple and reasonably efficient. In cases 4 and 5 the cut operation could be repeated very often, and represents usually the dominant cost. Efficiency is then very important.

Further looking to checkpointing it is necessary to provide primitive operations which permit to save the state of a process, the message in transit and to restart computation.

Moreover, the words "state of the process" has different meaning depending on the problem (checkpoint, global function evaluation, termination detection, etc.) faced. Even in case of checkpointing algorithm, the state can be an image of the main memory (the CORE used in [Stel94]) or a restricted part of it, depending on the application. The system proposed here provides a protocol which implements a Consistent Cut, that is which defines the cut event for each process, and records the messages in transit (hereafter referred as Cut Algorithm). Moreover, it also provides procedures and primitives to support the restart of the application from a checkpoint. Other operations (recording of the states, recording on stable storage or replicas implementation and so on) are not considered here. Even if there has been much research on snapshot and checkpoint algorithms for parallel and distributed systems, few implementations are available, we shortly survey the situation for consistent cut algorithms in Section 4.

The paper is organized in the following way. In Section 2 we shortly discuss fault tolerant issues in PVM. In Section 3 the general model of computation we are coinsidering is described. Section 4 presents consistent cut protocols in some details. Section 5 describe the architecture of CPVM a modified PVM version which provides consistent cut facilities and primitives to restart computation after a failure or a reconfiguration. Finally in Section 6 experimental results are presented.

2 PVM and Fault Tolerance

PVM (Parallel Virtual Machine) is a well know communication library for the development of portable parallel applications. It is based on the message passing communication model and it is composed by two parts the PVM library and the daemon process. Here we consider those PVM features related to fault tolerance.

The Parallel Virtual Machine is organized as a master-node machine, where it exists a single master which starts the computation, and controls the machine. Moreover there exists a group of nodes which belong to the virtual machine. A copy of PVM system is present on each node. A configured virtual machine can be used to execute parallel program, or in turn a parallel program can configure its own virtual machine.

By the point of view of fault tolerance PVM provides facilities to keep alive the Virtual Machine despite node failures. This does not mean that a PVM application is implicitely able to tolerate a node failure. If the master fails then both the application and the Virtual Machine fail. Node fault detection and recovery inside the Virtual Machine originate in the daemon to daemon transmission protocol [Geis94], and it is based on time out on communications. Hence any node is able to tolerate any other node failure. When a node detects the master failure it automatically shut down itself, thus the master failure implies the Virtual Machine failure. Since no possibility is provided to backup the master on a remote node, this behaviour avoids the Virtual Machine partitioning in two partial machines. Master failure remains a point of weakness for PVM. We do not address master failure in this paper.

By the application point of view three functions are provided which can be used to detect node failure. The correct use of these primitives and the recovery actions are left to the programmer of the application. However well defined limits exist on the possibility of the application to tolerate faults. The primitives suitable for node fault detection are: pvm_notify (), pvm_mstat(), and pvm_pstat().

The notify function has a behaviour similar to that of a signal handler. A node may ask to be notified when a certain event occurs. The event may be a node deleting operation. The notification occurs through a message, and in consequence of notification a proper code may be executed. The stat function return the state of a node (mstat) or the state of a process (pstat) to the caller. These functions may be used as well for node failure detection.

These functions are useful only for failure detection, while recovery is not supported. However they are sufficient to tolerate workers fault in processor farm computation in which workers exibith a functional behaviour. Here our attention is devoted to provide facilities to tolerate fault in a general application.

3 Model description

The target considered is an asynchronous distributed system, that is, a set of processes, dynamically created and terminated, communicating by means of messages sent through channels. Each process is in principle allowed to communicate with one other, then the logical topology of a distributed system is a strongly connected graph. Moreover, the system does not have a global clock.

Each process p in the process set P is represented by its state $S(p)$, and each channel ch in the channel set C is represented by the set of messages $M(ch)$ sent but not yet delivered to the destination process. $m(s,d)$ is a message sent by s to process d.

A distributed computation is the collection of the local computations, where a local computation of a process is the sequence of locally happened events (that is, send, receive and internal events). The events are partially ordered in the distributed computation by the relation *Happened Before* relation denoted by $\prec$, defined by Lamport, that is: $e_i \prec e_j$ if e_i and e_j are local to the same process and the time associated with e_i is smaller than the time associated with event e_j, or if e_i is the sending and e_j is the receiving event for the same message.

Each process is considered to run on a host (workstation), connected through a communication network. Communications are handled by a subsystem providing at least the following features:

1. each process is able to communicate with each other, and every message is delivered once and correctly, with unpredictable delay (reliable all-pair point-to-point communications property).
2. host and task failures are partly handled by the system, that is, the failure of a component does not cause the failure of the whole system, and messages sent to a failed process are discarded by the network (fault detection and handling property).
3. A failure notification is reported to processes which require such service (failure report property).

The implementation here proposed is based on PVM, which supports the above features, but that fails if the master host fails. For the sake of simplicity, only a statically defined set of processes will be considered, even if PVM allows their dynamic management. The processes must be created initially by the user inside a *starter* process, residing on the master host, which maintains the knowledge of the system and acts as coordinator for the cut and restart algorithms. This solution, however, does not exclude the possibility of implementing a completely distributed algorithm, managing also the creation and termination of processes, for example connecting processes with a logical ring.

4 Consistent Cut Algorithm

A *Cut* for a distributed system is usually defined as the union of local histories for all processes in P, until some clock value, possibly different for each process. Then, the *pseudo event cut* is an internal event occurred at time $clock_k$ for each process p_k. An event occurred before its local cut event is said to be in the past of the cut, in the future otherwise.

A cut is *Consistent* if between any two events e_i and e_j, respectively occurred in the future and in the past of the cut, the Happened Before relation is not established [Chan85], that is $e_i \not\prec e_j$.

Given a Consisten Cut C, a *Global Snapshot* for C is defined as:

$$\cup_{p_i \in P} S(p_i) \bigcup \cup_{ch_j \in C} M(ch_j)$$

where $S(p_i)$ is the state of process p_i at its local cut event, and $M(ch_j)$ is the set of messages in transit through the cut line, that is, sent in the past and received in the future of the cut.

The Cut Algorithm is a total algorithm, that is, it is composed by:
- a local algorithm which defines the cut event and collects the messages in transit, and
- a global algorithm which coordinates the local cuts.

The most known among the algorithms for performing a consistent snapshot, and probabily the unique widely implemented, is also the first one proposed which does not require the freezing of the computation, that is, the Chandy- Lamport algorithm [Chan85]. Such an algorithm sends a *marker* through every logical channel in order to ensure the consistency of the cut. In a network in which each process is allowed to communicate with each other, the number of markers is $O(n^2)$, where n is the number of processes. Such method has been used in [Stel94] to implement a checkpoint algorithm for the system CODINE. It can be optimized, but using additional memory structures and augmenting the execution time of the algorithm. A comparison among three algorithms (the sync-and-stop algorithm which freezes the program, and two versions of the Chandy Lamport algorithm) is reported in [Plan94].

In the CPVM system, a different algorithm for the local cut algorithm has been implemented, that is the Lai and Yang algorithm [Lai87], extended in order to allow a correct restart after failure.

4.1 The extended Lai Yang algorithm

The cut algorithm can be viewed as a computation superimposed on the basic one [Tel91], then, distinction is made between *basic* messages, sent by the underlying application, and *control* messages, sent by the cut algorithm.

In the original Lai-Yang algorithm, each process is assegned a *color*, white or red, and a 1 bit piggybacking is also required for every message to carry the color of the process at sending time. On the contrary, the algorithm presented in the following needs 3 colors (one more for the restart protocol implementation), chosen among white, red and green, corresponding to a 2 bit piggybacking. Moreover, each process has a *status* which assumes one out of 3 values: *restart* when the process is in the restarting phase, *computing* during the normal computation, *cut* during the cut evaluation.

Different choices can be performed in order to implement the global algorithm. In the CPVM algorithm, a *starter* process broadcasts messages to every other process. Such a starter is aware of all processes' identities. The control messages sent by the starter to a process in order to perform a cut are: *ctr_start* to start the local cut and *ctr_trm* to inform the process that no message is still in transit. Every process with *status* = *cut* sends *ctr_cnt* and *ctr_ack* control messages to the starter when necessary.

Initially, each process has *color* = *white* and *status* = *computing*. The following actions are implemented in each process p:

1. Three counters are maintained for the sent and received basic messages, separately for each color. A counter is incremented on receipt of a message, decremented on sending.

2. Upon the receipt of a basic or control message *msg*, if the following condition holds:
   (*status* = *computing*) $\wedge$ (((*msg is basic*)

$\wedge$ (*color(msg)* $\neq$ *color*)) $\vee$ (*msg is ctr_start*)) then: a *ctr_cnt* message carrying the value *count(color)* is sent to the starter, *status* is set to *cut*, *color* to its successor and *count(color)* to 1 if the message is basic, to 0 on the contrary. If the control message *ctr_start* is received when *status* $\neq$ *computing*, it is discarded.

3. Upon the receipt of a basic message *msg*, if *status* = *cut* and *color(msg)* $\neq$ *color* then the message is in transit. An acknowledge message *ctr_ack* is sent to the starter process.

4. Upon the receipt of the *ctr_trm* message, the process sets *status* to *computing*.

The starter starts the cut operation broadcasting *ctr_start* to every process, then it collects the counter values sent by each process adding them: the resulting value is the number of messages in transit. After the receipt of the same number of *ctr_ack* no more message is still in transit, then the starter sends *ctr_trm* to inform the processes that the cut algorithm is terminated.

The message complexity of such a scheme is $O(n+M)$ where n is the number of processes and M is the number of messages in transit.

Let us now consider the situation in case of task or node failure. The failure is discovered by the starter process, then the computation can be restarted from the last taken checkpoint. A problem arising at restart time is that messages belonging to the failed computation can be still in transit (see Figure 2).

Two cases must be considered:

1. Messages sent to a failed process. PVM automatically discards these messages, without any problem for the sending process.

2. Messages sent to a non failed process. These messages must be discarded, that is, a process must be able to understand whether a channel from a faulty or non faulty process holds messages belonging to a previous phase. If the sender process s is a non faulty one, a marker can be sent by s to each other process in order to flush the PVM FIFO channels (whith a message complexity of $O(n^2)$), but if s is the failed process, such markers cannot be sent.

The message coloring provides a simple means in order to solve the last problem, due to the presence

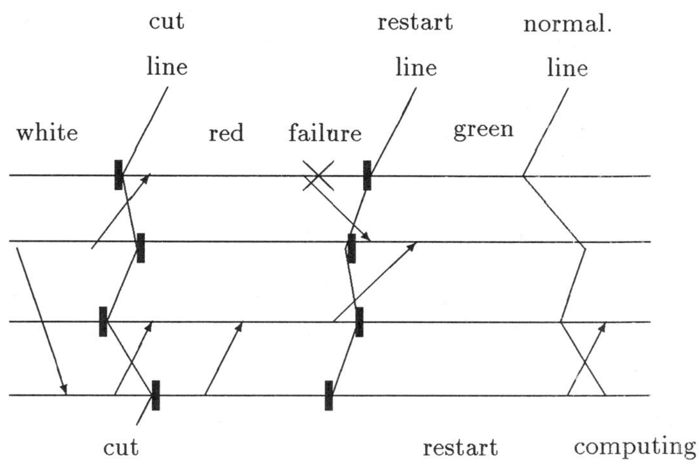

Figure 2. Computation restart after failure.

of the third color. Since a failure could happen during a normal execution interval or during the cutting interval, messages in transit can be colored with no more than two colors. Then, if the processes in the restarting phase are painted with a third color, they can recognize the old messages and discard them. A timeout must be set, to signal the end of the restarting phase.

The starter process coordinates the restarting phase by means of 3 kinds of control messages: *ctr_stop* to stop the computation after failure discovery, *ctr_rst* to restart a computation with a new color, and *ctr_nrm*, to force *status* to *computing*. The actions to be performed upon the receipt of a *ctr_stop* message are not presently been completely implemented. In such a case, the local part of CPVM should halt the execution, delete all the messages, excepts the messages in transit recorded during the last completed cut, allows the user to restore the checkpointed memory status and sets the *status* to *restart*.
Deletion of messages is possible using the function *pvm_cut_delete (cut_id)* which deletes all the messages marked with the specified *cut_id*.

The effect of the *ctr_rst* control message is to restart the computation, ignoring messages painted with a different color, until the receipt of the *ctr_nrm* control message, which "normalize" the behaviour of the process.

The actions performed by the starter process and by the user processes are shown in the Appendix. The user process actions are performed by CPVM, that is, they belong to the superimposed computation, and are hidden to the user.

5 The CPVM architecture

Let us consider the changes performed on the original PVM code and the new primitives and procedures provided by CPVM. The features of the architecture are summarized in Figure 3.

Application level	starter process
CPVM library	*cpvm_init_starter()* *cpvm_inquiry()* *cpvm_cut_delete()* *cpvm_forward()* *cpvm_cut()*
PVM modified functions	*pvm_nrecv()* *pvm_send()* *other send/rec funct.*

Figure 3: the CPVM architecture

5.1 Implementation of the cut algorithm

The user is not aware of the control messages set by the superimposed algorithm, nor of the color of the basic messages. The starter code is provided by the CPVM system but it can be easily changed following different user needs. The control messages are PVM messages, with reserved tag fields.

CPVM also provides the procedures which are activated by these control messages and that must be included in each process. Only the *ctr_stop* procedure is not provided, since it is application dependent. As consequence of such procedure each process must restore the last taken checkpoint, and create new replicas, if necessary.

The 2 bits required to color the message are obtained from the tag field, then without any additional transmission cost. The color is added when an output message is built after a call to pvm_initsend(), and it is filtered when received by PVM, so that the user is not aware of it.

Since generally more than one cut is performed during the computation, but only a limited number of them must be recorded at a time, every cut is identified by a positive integer, incremented at each round of the cut algorithm. Messages flowing through the cut line have the additional field *in_transit* set to this value, while non in transit message has this field set to 0. Messages in transit are not deleted from PVM buffers, as usually happens in PVM when the application program unpacks the data carried by them, in order to minimize the time needed to record the checkpoint. An additional primitive, *cpvm_cut_delete(cut_id)* allows to delete the messages marked by such an identifier when this checkpointed cut is no more needed.

Other additional fields have also been added for each process, that is: the color, the status, the three message counters and the identifier of the last cut. Each one of these values can be known by means of specialized *cpvm_inquiry* primitives.

6 Experimental Results

Experiments with CPVM are currently under development and early results are now available. These early experiences are aimed to assess the possibility of using CPVM without introducing a relevant overhead. Tests have been executed to measure this overhead for computation that uses CPVM but does not activate the cut algorithm (normal), and for computation that uses CPVM and the cut algorithm.

In Table 1 are summarized data relative to overheads in normal computation. Send and receive data are obtained by reapetedly trasmitting 1 byte between two Sparcl workstation connected by ethernet. Global Communication Overehead (GCO) is the overhead measured for a network of 4 processes distributed on 4 different workstation, and continuosly communicating using a random communication pattern. The

	overehead in %
send	+1.30
receive	+0.28
GOC	+0.05

Table 1: Overheads for some type of communications using CPVM without consistent cut algorithm

overheads are expressed in percentage with respect to PVM computation.

In Table 2 results relative to overheads measured for different bencmark programs, which execute a cut every 15 seconds, are summarized. The benchmarks programs are: a general network of processes, a master slave program, and a grid computation.

benchmark	overehead in %
general network	−1.81
master slave	−0.26
grid computation	−0.54

Table 2: Overheads for benchmark programs executing a cut every 15 second on a long lasting computation

References

[Geis94] A. Geist et al., "PVM: Parallel Virtual Machine A Users' Guide and Tutorial for Networked Parallel Computing", *The MIT Press* 1994

[Chan85] K. Chandy, L. Lamport, "Distributed snapshots: determining global states of distributed systems. *ACM Trans. Comput. Systems*, 3(1), pp.63-75, 1985.

[Clem94] A. Clematis, "Fault Tolerant Programming for Network Based Parallel Computing", *Microprocessing and Microprogramming* 40 (1994), 765-768

[Dikk94] L. Dikken, F. v.d. Linden, J. Vesseur, P. Sllot, "Dynamic PVM", *Proc. HPCN Europe*, LNCS 797, Vol.2, pp.273-277, 1994.

[Gian95] V. Gianuzzi, F. Merani, "Using PVM to implement a Distributed Dependable Simulation System", *3rd Euromicro Workshop on Parallel and Distributed Processing*, IEEE Comp. Soc., 1995.

[Lai87] T.-H. Lai, T.-H. Yang, "On distributed snapshots", Inform. Process. Lett., 25, pp.153-158, 1987.

[Matt93] F. Mattern, "Efficient Algorithms for distributed snapshots and global virtual time approximation", *J. of Parall. and Distrib. Comp.*, 18, pp.423-434, 1993.

[Maty94] L. Matyska, K. Taft, "Fault tolerant PVM application? - A case study with D-CICADA(FT). *Proc. 2nd PVM Europ. Meet.*, Roma 1994.

[Plan94] J.S. Plank, Kai Li, "ickp: A Consistent Checkpointer for Multicomputers", *IEEE Parallel & Distributed Technology*, 2(2), Summer 1994.

[Silv95] L.M. Silva, J.G. Silva, S. Chapple, L. Clarke, "Fault Tolerance on Regular Decomposition Grid Applications", *3rd Euromicro Workshop on Parallel and Distributed Processing*, IEEE Comp. Soc., 1995.

[Stel94] G. Stellner, "Consistent checkpoints of PVM applications", *Proc. 2nd PVM Europ. Meet.*, Roma 1994.

[Tel91] G. Tel, *Topics in distributed algorithms*, Cambridge Univ. Press, 1991.

Appendix

Actions of the starter process:

```
CIs: (* upon snapshot request *)
  begin
    color := succ(color);
    for every process p do send ctr_ckp to p
    count := 0;
    for every process p do begin
      receive ctr_cnt < c >;
      count := count + c end ;
    while count ≠ 0 do receive ctr_ack;
    for every process p do send ctr_trm to p
  end ;

CFs: (* Upon failure notification *)
begin
  color := succ(color);
```

```
    send ctr_stop to all processes;
    send ctr_rst < list of failed tasks > to all processes;
    sleep for timeout time;
    send ctr_nrm to all processes;
end
```

Actions of the user process.

```
Sp: (* send regular message msg through (p, q) *)
    begin
        color(msg) := color;
        count(color) := count(color)+1;
        send msg to q
    end ;

Rp: (* Upon receipt of a regular message msg *)
    begin
        if color(msg) ≠ color then
        case cut_status of
            restart: discard message;
            cut: msg_in_transit;
            computing: begin
                            cut_event;
                            msg_in transit end
            end
        else receive msg from q;
        count(color) := count(color) - 1;
    end ;

    procedure msg_in_transit;
    begin
        receive msg from q;
        send ctr_ack to p_starter;
        mark(msg, in_transit);
    end ;

    procedure cut_event;
    begin
        in_transit := in_transit + 1;
        cut_user_procedure
        send ctr_cnt < count(color) > to p_starter;;
        color := succ(color);
        count(color) := 0;
        cut_status := cut;
    end :

CCi: (* Upon ctr_ckp receipt *)
        if cut_status = computing then cut_event;

CMp: (* Upon ctr_trm receipt *)
        cut_status := computing;

CRi: (* Upon ctr_rst receipt *)
        if cut_status = restart then begin
            color := color(msg);
            execute code     end

CNp: (* Upon ctr_nrm receipt *)
        cut_status := cut
```

Delay-Insensitive Synchronization on a Message-Passing Architecture with an Open Collector Bus

H. Bekker

Department of Computing Science,
University of Groningen,
9700 AV Groningen, The Netherlands

E.J. Dijkstra

Department of Computing Science,
University of Groningen,
9700 AV Groningen, The Netherlands

Abstract

The performance of some algorithms, running on a message passing computer, is limited by the high latency of global communications. To increase the performance, a simple open collector bus, operated by delay insensitive programs running on each processor can be used. We illustrate this by an example: the constraint algorithm SHAKE as used in Constraint Molecular Dynamics (M.D.) simulation. We present a parallelizable SHAKE algorithm and show how it can be implemented on a ring architecture. On a large ring the use of message passing to synchronize SHAKE iterations may take up to 40% of the total time. We show how the communication time can be reduced by adding a very simple open collector bus, operated by a delay insensitive algorithm. In this way the time spent on the synchronization of SHAKE iterations will be negligible.

We want to emphasize that this kind of open collector bus can be used with many delay insensitive algorithms. To show this we will mention other possible applications.

Key words: synchronization, delay insensitive algorithm, open collector bus, constraint dynamics.

1 Introduction

Message passing systems consisting of a large number of processors, connected by a sparse interconnection topology (e.g. a ring or a mesh) prove to be a cost effective solution for many practical applications. These systems offer local communication with a high bandwidth and a low latency, but their global communication falls short in two respects: bandwidth and latency. This may give problems for the following classes of algorithms:

(i): Algorithms limited by the sustained bandwidth of the architecture. These algorithms often require local or global communication of large amounts of data followed by calculations which take up less time. This paper is not about this class of algorithms but about:

(ii): Algorithms limited by the latency of the communications. These algorithms often require global communication of very small amounts of data followed by some calculations. An important instance of such an algorithm is the synchronization of a fine grained iterative process.

This paper is about a simple hardware extension, solving the class of problems described in (ii). To be more specific, we will show that a very simple open collector bus, (O.C.-bus) running along all the processors, may be used to improve the performance of the algorithms in (ii).

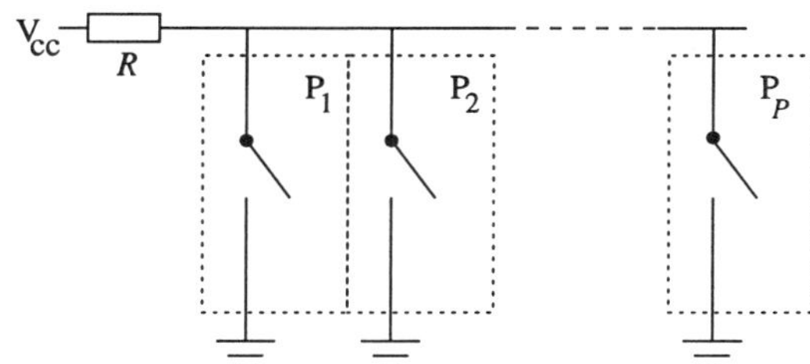

Figure 1: Open collector line, running along P processors. The value read at every processor is the same. It is the logical **and** of the values written at all processors, where True(False) corresponds to an open(closed) gate.

The O.C.-bus consists of a few (4...8) lines, without any further lines for clocking or control. (See figure 1). Each of these lines is memory mapped, which means that by clearing or setting a specific bit in memory every processor can clamp (pull down) respectively unclamp the line. By reading a specific bit in memory, every processor can obtain the logical value of each line. This value is the same on every processor, and is the logical **and** of the values written on that line.

We will show that delay insensitive algorithms are very suitable to operate this bus. By using delay insensitive algorithms a low quality implementation of the O.C.-bus is acceptable: no bus terminators are required, no characteristic impedance, etc. Moreover, the use of delay insensitive algorithms, also called self timed algorithms, makes it possible to operate the O.C.-bus without clock or control lines.

The rest of this paper consists of a worked out example of molecular dynamics simulation on a message passing system. First a general introduction of constraint molecular dynamics is given. Then it is shown that running this algorithm on a ring architecture leads to the type of problem described in (ii). Finally, it is shown how the use of an O.C.-bus, operated by a delay insensitive algorithm solves this problem. Also two similar applications of the O.C.-bus are mentioned.

1066-6192/96 $5.00 © 1996 IEEE
Proceedings of PDP '96

2 Constraint Molecular Dynamics simulation

Molecular Dynamics (M.D.) Simulation is a method to simulate the behaviour of a many particle (atom) system by numerically integrating Newton's equation of motion. M.D. simulation is performed as follows: the initial system state S_0, that is, the position $\mathbf{r}_i$ and velocity $\mathbf{v}_i$ of every particle i in the system at time t_0 is given. By integrating Newton's law $\mathbf{F}_i = m \cdot \mathbf{a}_i$ for every particle, subsequent states $S_1, S_2, \ldots, S_n$ are calculated where $S_n \equiv S(t_0 + n\Delta t)$. To calculate S_{n+1} from S_n, first the total force $\mathbf{F}_i(t_0 + n\Delta t)$ on every particle i due to all other particles in the system is calculated. Then this force $\mathbf{F}_i(t_0 + n\Delta t)$ is used to calculate for every particle the new velocity $\mathbf{v}_i(t_0 + (n+1)\Delta t)$. Using this velocity, the new position $\mathbf{r}_i(t_0 + (n+1)\Delta t)$ of every particle is calculated. Repeating this procedure gives the time development of the system.

Every timestep, during the force calculations, many types of interaction-forces are evaluated: Coulomb forces, Lennard-Jones forces, covalent forces, etc. Some of these interactions are very rigid. The most rigid interaction in an M.D. simulation is the covalent interaction. This means that two particles having a covalent interaction, have an almost constant distance. Put in another way: covalent interactions have a high eigenfrequency. The maximal allowed timestep used in an M.D. simulation is dictated by the allowed numerical drift of the integration algorithm, so it is dictated by the highest frequency in the system, and should be approximately $1/(40\times$*highest frequency*$)$. However, the behaviour of covalent interactions is not part of the physics of interest of an M.D. simulation. Leaving out frequencies above 1/4 to 1/2 the highest frequency does not influence the outcome of an M.D. simulation. So, it is a waste of computer time to use a timestep based on covalent eigenfrequencies. For that reason, nowadays in most M.D. programs, the covalent interactions are handled using *constraint dynamics*, which means that the distance between particles with a covalent bond is kept constant. Then the timestep may be as high as 1/20 to 1/10 ($\times$*highest frequency*). In this way an M.D. simulation runs two to four times faster.

Because an atom may have covalent interactions with a number of atoms[1], substituting covalent interactions by length constraints will in general result in a set of connected length constraints with a, possibly cyclic, graph like structure. Covalent interactions are bonded interactions, so, no constraints are created or broken during a simulation.

The introduction of length-constraints has no consequences for the force calculations, except of course that the forces of covalent interactions are not calculated. However, the introduction of length-constraints has severe consequences for the algorithm in which Newton's law is integrated, resulting in a matrix equation. As the rank of the matrix is the number of constraints in the system, for systems with many constraints, solving this equation directly on a parallel computer is complex. There exists however a fast, iterative method called SHAKE [1], to solve the matrix equation. The special thing about SHAKE is that its iterative way of solving the matrix equation is directly reflected in iterative adjustment of pairs of particle positions. This last interpretation of the SHAKE method has become so familiar that it is almost forgotten that it is a matrix solver in disguise. We will adhere to this habit, and in what follows write about the SHAKE algorithm as pairwise adjusting particle positions to constraint conditions in an iterative way.

SHAKE is used as follows. Every timestep, the interaction forces, the new velocities and new positions are calculated as if no constraints exist, except that no covalent interaction forces are evaluated. Clearly, particle positions obtained in this way do not fulfill the distance constraints between particles. Then SHAKE is invoked. In SHAKE, particle positions are corrected in an iterative way, such that finally all length-constraints are fulfilled within a predefined tolerance. So, at the end of every timestep many SHAKE iterations have to be done.

SHAKE is implemented as follows. The particle numbers of every pair of particles between which a distance constraint exists, are kept in a constraint-list (CL). So, in CL, every constraint is represented by two particles. (In this article we assume that the constraint distance is the same for every constrained pair of particles, so we need not store this in CL.) In every iteration, SHAKE goes through CL once; the order in which items of CL are processed does not matter. Processing an item of CL means that the positions of the particles of this pair are adjusted such that their relative distance becomes the required constraint distance.[2] Because a particle may have more than one constraint interaction, repositioning a particle due to one constraint may disturb another, previously adjusted constraint. Therefore, after every iteration of adjusting positions of particle pairs, the constraint conditions are checked. If these conditions are not fulfilled within a predefined tolerance, another iteration is done, in which all constraints in CL are processed once again. Typically, at the end of every timestep SHAKE does 4...40 iterations, but for large molecules, some hundreds of iterations may be required. On a single processor, SHAKE typically takes 5...20% of the total CPU time of an M.D. simulation.

In the SHAKE algorithm as we presented it, two particle *positions* are adjusted when processing an item from CL. When processing the next item from CL, a possibly previously adjusted particle position is adjusted further. So, items from CL cannot be processed simultaneously. Fortunately, the SHAKE algorithm can be restated without these dependencies. When processing an item from CL, instead of immediately adjusting the two particle positions, the resulting particle *displacements* are accumulated.[3] After processing the whole CL, particles are displaced over their accumulated displacements. In pseudo code, the parallelizable SHAKE algorithm looks like:

[1]In a typical M.D. system the number of constraints is of the same order as the number of particles.

[2]Although not relevant for this paper, adjusting positions goes as follows. The particles of the constrained pair a, b, with positions $\mathbf{r}_a$ and $\mathbf{r}_b$, are reset in the direction of $\mathbf{r}_a(t-\Delta t) - \mathbf{r}_b(t-\Delta t)$, such that the center of mass of this pair does not change, and their distance becomes the constraint distance.

[3]This cannot be derived by transformations of the algorithm, but is a matter of numerical mathematics.

```
procedure SHAKE;
type rvec= array[1..3] of real;
   partId=1..N; { number of particles is N }
var
   r, displ: array [partId] of rvec;
   CL: array [1..nr_constr] of
                    record a,b: partId end;
begin
repeat
   clear(displ);
   for i:=1 to nr_constr do begin
      displ[CL[i].a] += .... ; { See footnote² }
      displ[CL[i].b] += .... ; { See footnote² }
   end;
   for i:=1 to N do r[i] += displ[i];
until all_constraints_within_tolerance;
end;
```

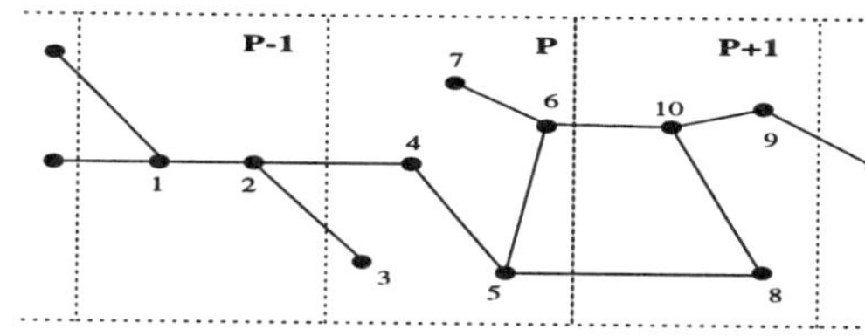

Figure 2: The lists NCCI, LCI and PCCI on processor p for the part of some constraint graph mapped near processor p. NCCI= (3,2); (4,2). LCI= (4,5); (5,6); (6,7). PCCI= (6,10); (5,8). On processor p constraint interactions in NCCI and LCI are evaluated.

3 SHAKE on a ring architecture

At the departments of physical chemistry, and computer science in Groningen, the M.D. simulation package GROMACS [2,3] has been implemented on a custom-built ring architecture, consisting of 32 i860 processors. Each i860 board plugs into a collective PC bus, and has two eight bits wide parallel interfaces (2 Mb/sec) to connect the board in the ring. Also on the PC bus is an i486, running UNIX, which serves as a host. This host uses the PC bus to load code and initial data on the i860 processors, and for I/O purposes.

In the GROMACS ring implementation, particles are statically allocated on processors. An M.D. system of N particles, numbered from 1 to N, is mapped on P (in our case $P = 32$) processors by allocating the first N/P particles on processor 1, the second N/P on processor 2, etc. The processor H_i on which particle i is allocated is called its *home processor*. The home processor of particle i calculates the final position of i after a timestep (constrained and unconstrained). As will be clear, the particle numbering determines the home processor of every particle.

For the force calculations it does not matter how particles are allocated on the processors. That is because every particle potentially interacts with every other particle. Therefore, at the beginning of every timestep, the position of every particle i is, starting from its home processor H_i, distributed over half the ring, in say the positive direction. Distribution over half the ring is sufficient because in this way every position pair $\mathbf{r}_i, \mathbf{r}_j$ is present on at least one processor. After this distribution stage, interaction forces are calculated. Then the interaction forces on every particle i are communicated [4] in the negative direction to H_i where they are summed to the net force on particle i. Finally, on the home processor of each particle its new, unconstrained velocity and position is calculated. Now SHAKE is invoked. Because between any two particles there may be a constraint, in principle for every SHAKE iteration, as in the force calculations, particle positions would have to be distributed over half the ring. However, this would take far too much time. In [4] we proposed a method, to minimize communication during SHAKE calculations. It is based on the bandwidth reduction algorithm of Gibbs, Poole and Stockmeyer. The essence of the method is that particles are numbered in such a way that particles between which a length constraint exists, get close numbers, so, are mapped on close processors. In fact, with this method, even for rather complex molecules, particles between which a constraint exists, are mapped on the same or on directly adjacent processors.[5] So, during SHAKE only communication between very near processors is required.

Most parallel implementations of the M.D. algorithm do not include constraint dynamics. In those cases where it is included [5,6] no use is made of accumulated displacements to parallelize SHAKE, nor the bandwidth reduction method to minimize communication during SHAKE iterations.

We are now almost ready to write down the SHAKE algorithm as it runs on every processor of the ring, but first we will explain how the global constraint list CL, as introduced in section 1, is distributed over processors, and how on every processor this partial list is partitioned into even smaller parts.

The contents of CL do not change during a simulation, so an almost perfect load balance for parallel SHAKE calculations can be accomplished by assigning the same number of items of CL to every processor. On every processor the constraint interactions assigned to that processor are stored in LCL (Local Constraint List). The list LCL is subdivided still further into three sublists (see figure 2): NCCI, LCI, and PCCI (Negative-Crossing, Local-, and Positive-Crossing Constraint Interactions). On processor p, NCCI (PCCI) contains those constraint interactions of which particle b is home on processor $p-1$ ($p+1$), and particle a is home on p. LCI contains interactions of which both particles are home on p. So on p, the list PCCI contains the same number-pairs, but in reverse order, as the list NCCI on $p+1$. The data structures NCCI, LCI and PCCI can be used to define which constraint interactions are evaluated by which processor: *processor p evaluates the constraints in its NCCI and LCI list.* Then the SHAKE algorithm as it runs on every processor is as follows:

[4] On the GROMACS ring architecture this communication, together with the foregoing communication to distribute particle positions takes about 5% to 10% of the total time.

[5] If this is not the case, the particles are still mapped on very close processors. Such a case can be handled by a straightforward extension of the method we propose, but we did not encounter molecules with constraint structures of this complexity.

```
procedure SHAKE;
{ parallel SHAKE on a ring architecture,
   see also figure 2 }
type rvec= array[1..3] of real;
partId=1..N; { N is the number of particles }
var
r, displ: array [partId] of rvec;
NCCI: array [1..nr_NCCI] of record a,b: partId end;
      { home(a)= p, home(b)=p−1 }
PCCI: array [1..nr_PCCI] of record a,b: partId end;
      { home(a)=p, home(b)=p+1 };
LCI: array [1..nr_LCI] of record a,b: partId end;
      { home(a)=p, home(b)=p };
begin
send PCCI_b_positions to posdir;
receive NCCI_b_positions from negdir;
repeat
  clear(displ);
  calculate displacements;
      { due to constraints in NCCI and LCI}
  send NCCI_b_displacements to negdir;
  receive PCCI_b_displacements from posdir;
  sum displacements and add to r;
      {for particles home on this processor}
  send PCCI_b_positions to posdir;
  receive NCCI_b_positions from negdir;
  LCWT:=check_local_constraints;
      {Local_Constraints_Within_Tolerance}
until ACWT;
    {All_Constraints_Within_Tolerance}
end;
```

With this, the parallel SHAKE algorithm is completely specified, except for the last few statements with LCWT and ACWT (Local- and All Constraints Within Tolerance), which concern the evaluation of the global stop criterion of SHAKE iterations during the current timestep. This will be discussed in the next section.

4 The function ACWT implemented with the open collector bus

SHAKE iterations should be stopped when on every processor the constraints in the lists NCCI and LCI are within tolerance, i.e. when on every processor the boolean variable LCWT is true. Representing LCWT on processor p by $LCWT_p$, the function ACWT can be specified as ACWT:=$LCWT_1$ **and** $LCWT_2$ **and** ... **and** $LCWT_P$.

On a message passing ring architecture such as GROMACS, the function ACWT can be implemented in three ways.

(i) By sending a single message around the whole ring twice. First the message accumulates the logical **and** of all LCWT, and in a second round this result is passed to all processors as ACWT.

(ii) As P messages, all moving around the whole ring once. At every processor one message is released which returns to that same processor. While moving around the ring, the message evaluates the logical **and** of all LCWT. When arriving at the processor from which it was released, this processor inspects the contents of the message to see if another iteration of SHAKE is required.

(iii) The third implementation uses the PC bus and the host computer. Every processor sends its LCWT to the host. There, the logical **and** is evaluated and transmitted back to the individual processors.

As will be clear, each of these methods takes at least P communications. On our GROMACS ring implementation, we measured that sending a minimal message (1 byte) from a processor to an adjacent processor, or from a processor to the host, takes $\sim 150\,\mu$sec, mainly due to startup overhead. So, for $P = 32$, evaluating ACWT takes at least $32 \times 15 \times 10^{-5} = 4.8 \times 10^{-3}$ sec. We also measured that the *calculations* of one SHAKE iteration take the same amount of time. (20 SHAKE iterations, without communication can take 10% of the total time. One timestep takes 0.1...1 sec, let us say 1 sec, then one SHAKE iteration takes about 5×10^{-3} sec.) On the present architecture the one-to-one ratio of the time spent in SHAKE calculations and its synchronization is however no problem because SHAKE typically takes only 10% of the total time, so spending an additional 10% in ACWT is no major problem. However, when the same type of simulation is done on a ring consisting of twice as many processors, the total time spent on calculations is halved while the time spent in ACWT doubles. So, about 40% of the total time will be spent in ACWT.

To solve this problem we will equip our next architecture with an eight line O.C.-bus as described in the introduction. The function ACWT can be implemented using four of these lines. We will call these four lines "valid", "accepted", "next", and "data". We name the values written on these lines: l_valid, l_accepted, l_next, l_data; and the values read: g_valid, g_accepted, g_next, g_data. The prefixes l and g stand for local and global. The local variables are write-only and the global variables are read-only. The signals "valid", "accepted" and "next" will serve as global control signals. In [7] it is explained why at least three control signals are required. A delay insensitive implementation of ACWT which runs on each processor, is straightforward:

```
function ACWT;
begin
  l_data:= LCWT;
  l_accepted:=False; l_valid:=True;
  repeat until g_valid;
  ACWT:=g_data;
    {ACWT:= LCWT1 and ... and LCWTP}
  l_next:=False l_accepted:=True;
  repeat until g_accepted;
  l_valid:=False; l_next:=True;
  repeat until g_next;
end;
```

After the first repeat, "data" is valid. After the second repeat, "data" has been accepted by all processors. The third repeat is necessary to return to the neutral state. Initially, l_valid (g_valid) must be False. It can be seen that after g_valid becomes true, i.e. after the slowest process has evaluated its LCWT and assigned it to l_data, the evaluation of the function ACWT proceeds without delay. On every processor, immediately after finishing the function ACWT the next SHAKE iteration is started, or SHAKE iterations are stopped.

5 Discussion

In our particular case, that is, constraint molecular dynamics on a ring architecture, adding a small O.C.-bus is a sensible investment because the price of this feature is low (a few hundred dollars) compared to the price of the whole computer ($\approx$ \$100,000), while the speed increase is much higher than this ratio. Moreover, the hardware risk that goes with this feature, that is, the risk of destabilizing an otherwise well functioning architecture, is very small.

In our opinion, there are many other useful applications of an O.C.-bus in a message passing computer. Especially the combination of an O.C.-bus with delay insensitive algorithms looks promising. We will briefly mention two other applications.

The first example we want to mention is process arbitration. On every processor a number is generated. Process arbitration means that on every processor it is decided whether the highest number is on this processor. A delay insensitive arbitration algorithm, using four wired **or** lines has been designed (unpublished) by C.E. Molnar. This way of process arbitration will be much faster than using the message passing mechanism.

The second example is the TRIMOSBUS [7]. The TRIMOSBUS is a general purpose bus, operated with a delay insensitive algorithm. It consists of at least four open collector lines, three of which are used for sequencing, and the other ones as data lines. It may be used for arbitrary point to point communications, and for broadcasting. In this way, on a parallel computer, small amounts of data may be exchanged between processors much faster than with the usual message passing mechanism.

The research field of "delay insensitive" algorithms and hardware is thriving nowadays. Many delay insensitive algorithms are conceived, and experimental, delay insensitive hardware is designed. Of both, the correctness can be proved by delay insensitive algebra [8,9]. How delay insensitive algorithms and hardware will develop is not clear at this moment. We do feel however, that a simple O.C.-bus connecting the processors of a parallel message passing architecture, combined with delay insensitive algorithms, is a simple and fast general purpose feature, which may be used to increase the performance of algorithms which cannot be implemented efficiently or elegantly with the message passing mechanism. Obviously, an O.C.-bus cannot replace the usual communication and routing hardware of message passing systems, but for a number of applications it can increase the performance in a straightforward way. Because the price/performance ratio of the O.C.-bus is low, and because it is a simple and robust piece of hardware, it is worth considering to add this hardware feature to sparsely connected parallel computers.

A reviewer remarked that the synchronization mechanism described in this article strongly resembles the barrier synchronization mechanism of the CRAY T3D architecture.

6 Conclusions

A small O.C.-bus, operated by delay insensitive algorithms, is a fast and simple mechanism, which on message passing systems can be used to increase the performance of many applications.

An example of such an application is constraint M.D. implemented with the SHAKE algorithm. A SHAKE iteration can be parallelized by accumulating the *displacements* of every particle and adding the total displacement to the particle position at the end of the iteration.

Synchronizing iterations and the termination of SHAKE on a message passing ring architecture, proves to be relatively time-consuming due to the latency of message passing. SHAKE becomes less time-consuming by extending the hardware with a small O.C.-bus. Synchronization can then be done by a simple delay insensitive algorithm.

Acknowledgments

We want to thank M.K.R. Renardus for carefully reading and commenting this text, J.T. Udding for his expertise in the field of delay insensitive algorithms, and the reviewer for making useful remarks.

Literature

[1] J.P. Ryckaert, G. Ciccotti, H.J.C. Berendsen, Numerical integration of the Cartesian equations of motion of a system with constraints: molecular dynamics of n-alkanes. *Journal of Comp. Phys.* **23**, 327-341, 1977.

[2] H. Bekker, H.J.C. Berendsen, E.J. Dijkstra, S. Achterop, R. v. Drunen, D. v.d. Spoel, A. Sijbers, H. Keegstra, B. Reitsma and M.K.R. Renardus, GROMACS: a parallel computer for molecular dynamics simulation. *Conf. Proc. Physics Computing '92*, pages 252-256, World Scientific Publishing Co. Singapore, New York, London, 1993.

[3] H. Bekker, E.J. Dijkstra, H.J.C. Berendsen. Molecular Dynamics simulation on an i860 based ring architecture. *Supercomputer* 54, X-2, 4–10, 1993.

[4] H. Bekker, E.J. Dijkstra, H.J.C. Berendsen. Mapping molecular dynamics simulation calculations on a ring architecture. In *Parallel Computing: From Theory to Sound Practice*, ed. W. Joosen and E. Milgrom, pages 268–279, IOS Press, Amsterdam, 1992.

[5] A.R.C. Raine. Systolic loop methods for molecular dynamics simulation, generalized for macromolecules. *Molecular Simulation*, Vol. 7, pages 59-69, 1991.

[6] S.E. DeBolt, P. Kollman. AMBERCUBE MD, Parallelization of AMBER's Molecular Dynamics Module for Distributed-Memory Hypercube Computers. *Journal of Comp. Chem.*, Vol. 14, No. 3, 312-329, 1993.

[7] I.E. Sutherland, C.E. Molnar, C.E. Sproull, J.C. Mudge. The TRIMOSBUS. *Proc. of the Caltech Conf. on VLSI*, January 1979.

[8] L. Lavagro and A. Sargiovanni-Vincentelli. Algorithms for Synthesis and Testing of Asynchronous circuits, Kluwer Academic Publishers, 1993.

[9] M.B. Josephs, J.T. Udding. An overview of Delay Insensitive Algebra. In *Proc. of the* 26th *Annual Hawaii Int. Conf. on System Sciences*, ed. T.N. Mudge, V. Milutinovic, L. Hunter, 329-338, IEEE Computer Society Press, 1993.

Object-Oriented Model of Parallel Programs

Henryk Krawczyk, Bogdan Wiszniewski
Faculty of Electronics, Telecommunications and Informatics
Technical University of Gdansk
80-952 Gdansk, POLAND

Abstract

The aim of this paper is to investigate an object oriented model of parallel programs in a distributed memory environment that is structural and yet has reduced complexity in dealing with parallel software. The presented model enables integration of well-known methods based on the common concept of a program control flow. A parallel program is described by a multi-flow graph, being an extension of an ordinary flow-graph. It allows developers to design structural tests, to assess test coverage and to estimate quality parameters.

1 Introduction

Structural representations of computer programs utilize a common approach based on flow-graphs [5]. By drawing a control flow graph for a given program developers can get insight into the control data flow issues avoiding the unnecessary detail of the underlying programming language syntax. Flow-graphs provide a convenient abstraction for evaluating program quality and for generating tests.

A control flow-graph uses two basic kinds of objects: *processing nodes*, representing a sequence of assignment statements, and *decision nodes*, representing points in a program at which the control flow can diverge. Program executions are represented in this model as paths going through nodes of the corresponding control flow-graph. Normally, control flow-graphs are intended to model individual sequential programs.

Structural representations of parallel programs are more difficult to grasp than their sequential counterparts, since many paths may be followed in a system in parallel. Moreover, some specific nodes of component flow-graphs may correspond to communication statements that depend on one another, making paths hard to express.

One possible solution to capturing parallelism is the Petri net model, with a number of tokens representing control flow of component processes as they progress through the system. Unfortunately, analysis of a Petri net seems to be more abstract to programmers than the intuitively simpler flow-graph, and requires a great deal of formalism [1].

Another solution is provided by finite state machines modeling component processes [2]. A parallel system can be represented then by a product machine with a set of states being a Cartesian product of sets of states of all component machines. Although FSMs seem to be intuitively close to flow-graphs with respect to the ability of representing serial executions of program statements, the usual problem of state explosion makes the realistic analysis of product machines impossible.

In our model we aim at retaining the intuitive simplicity of flow-graphs, but also want to capture the ability of Petri nets to represent multiple flows of control, as well as provide an FSM-like mechanism for ordering program statements related to state transitions.

2 Objects in parallel systems

Figure 1 specifies a hierarchy of node objects for building flow-graphs with multiple flows of control; along with graphical representations of node classes we present their respective specifications using C++. These specifications introduce schematically basic characteristics of node objects used in our model.

Nodes may be connected to one another, i.e., each exit of any node may be connected to some entry of another node; we mark this in our model by labeling each exit with a label of the entry that exit is connected to. Labels of entries are unique, i.e., there are no two entries with the same label at any node. In general there is no precedence of connected nodes, as one node may be connected to many nodes by the respective entries (exits). Entries of a single node may be associated with different flows of control, therefore each node may be entered in parallel by more than one program. After leaving that node many nodes may be visited in parallel since exits of a single node may also correspond to different flows of control.

1066-6192/96 $5.00 © 1996 IEEE
Proceedings of PDP '96

Visiting of nodes by flows of control in sequential programs is intended normally to represent execution of program statements (processing nodes) or evaluating predicates (decision nodes). These statements are either *assignment statements* or *conditional statements*. Nodes in our model reflect that fact by associating two types of expressions with node exits. One is a 'conditional-statement', and another is an 'assignment-expression', as shown in Figure 1.

Objects from the assignment and conditional classes of nodes allow for multiple flows of control to enter and/or exit them in parallel. At each entry of a single node from either class flows of control cause the evaluation of the respective expression. Note, that an entry in some node not connected to any preceding exit of some other node represents a *start* point in a related sequential program control flow (process creation point). Similarly, an exit in some node not connected to any following entry of some other node represents an *end* point in a related sequential program control flow (process termination point). Exits of nodes from either class that correspond to termination points of respective processes may also have assignment or, respectively, conditional expressions to be evaluated there. If assignment or conditional nodes do not require multiple flows of control, then they correspond to ordinary nodes of sequential control flow graphs.

Multiple flows of control constitute just one feature of nodes in parallel program flow-graphs. Another feature is the interaction of flows at selected points of component programs, what is due to communication statements. Owing to this feature, a node allowing for many flows to arrive at its entries in parallel may provide some internal "processing" of flows in order to determine what particular flows can exit this node. Therefore such a class of nodes has properties of the conditional node. It also has properties of the assignment node, since interaction of flows may result in some data objects (values) being transferred in between flows. Multiple inheritance of this class of nodes is shown in Figure 1.

3 Encapsulation of communication events

Internal processing of control flows is performed by finite state protocol machines, determining a specific order of executing communication actions involved in establishing the corresponding connection between processes. This enables encapsulation of interprocess communication in the form of communication events and has been made possible by the modular design of parallel programs, when processes can communicate with one another only through a well-defined set of interface points.

Based on the classification of nodes developed so far one can view a set of sequential programs running in parallel as a set of interconnected instantiations of the node class objects.

Parallel systems are usually viewed as sets of *event-driven* activities associated with individual programs called *processes*. Processes define basic interconnected components of a system and are viewed as independent units that communicate through a set of well defined interface "access points". Interface between parallel system components involves synchronization and exchange of data. Rules for communicating processes are established by *protocols*, which control ordering of selected events. Implementation is aimed at expressing specified system units (processes) and their interface in terms of a selected programming language and the language's underlying interprocess communication model.

Based on the assumption that processes are physically distributed and independent modules communicating through service access points one may distinguish nodes in a system control flow graph that are associated with "internal actions" (of individual processes) from nodes associated with "external actions" dealing with interprocess communication. Relative ordering of nodes associated with internal actions belonging to different threads of control is therefore irrelevant, as these objects are truly independent.

On the other hand, in a distributed environment like TCP/IP [3] or PVM [4], processes constitute physically separated units, and the use of communication statements by processes is limited to a manageable and small set of access points (ports). In other words, external actions form special sets of actions related to specific connections being established between cooperating processes. Typically, for any connection being established, there is only one corresponding protocol, and that protocol determines a specific set of related external actions. We refer to each single set of such actions as a *communication event*. A communication event is unique and can be distinguished from other communication events by distinguishing actions constituting them. For each communication event one can construct a finite state protocol machine by specifying all possible orders of executing actions from the corresponding event.

Actions from different events are independent, since they manipulate different data objects which are associated with separate access points in component processes. Therefore, communication event node objects cannot influence each other's ordering of actions. This encapsulation of protocol machines eliminates the problem of combinatorial explosion when the parallel system is viewed as a collection of automata, since it constitutes in our approach a sum of protocol machines of all communication event node objects and respective FSMs representing component processes. A sum machine is much simpler to analyze and understand than a product machine mentioned before, and its set of states is of smaller cardinality, i.e., as of the union of component processes' states rather then the Cartesian product of such sets; it can be shown that the total number of states in a sum machine can be bound by a linear function of the total number of processes and the total number of actions in a parallel system [7].

Careful analysis of application protocols in various parallel programming environments indicates that the number of *different* protocol machines is reasonably low. For example, typical network oriented application platforms based on message passing, like TCP/IP or PVM mentioned before distinguish two types of communication statements for sending: one is point-to-point, when a single process sends a single message to some other process, and another is broadcast, when a single process sends a single message to a group of processes. Communication statements for sending may be either blocking or non-blocking. A blocking send forces the sender to wait until receiver is ready to read a message being sent, while a non-blocking send puts the message to some buffer regardless of the state of the receiver. TCP/IP provides both types of the send communication statement, while PVM just the non-blocking one.

There are also two types of communication statements in TCP/IP and PVM for receiving: in either blocking or non-blocking mode. In each mode, a receiver may want to receive a message from a specific sender or just any sender.

This defines three basic classes of application protocols: one-to-one, many-to-one, one-to-many. If we distinguish blocking and non-blocking send statements, as well as blocking and non-blocking receive statements there are twelve kinds of protocol machines in total.

Note, that the number of internal states in any machine of one of the kinds characterized above is usually one per each respective pair of "matching" communication statements. Each such internal state may be simply labeled as "communication engaged", and for which there is only one preceding state and one successor state, being respectively initial and final states. The set of internal states of all protocol machines in a given communication event node object determines all possible sequences of communication actions constituting the corresponding event.

4 A big example

In this example we consider a parallel program consisting of three processes: a referee and two players, who play a game similar to black jack. Source code of the example processes is shown in Figure 2.

Player processes are sending bids to the referee by selecting an arbitrary number from 1 to 9. The referee process waits for bids from each player, and upon receiving, the bid is added to the score. The score is initially set to zero. The first player initiates the game by sending its first bid to the referee. The referee updates a score and sends it to the second player. Bids are being sent until the score reaches 100. The referee notifies a winner, kills both players and terminates.

Lines of this example source code are aligned to correspond to the individual flow-graphs of component programs. The left column of the text consists of comments corresponding to the adjacency matrix of each respective flow-graph.

This relatively simple program is potentially very complex, what is due to rather liberal use of interprocess communication statements in PVM. By introducing communication events that encapsulate communication actions a great deal of structuring can be imposed upon a program of interest to facilitate control flow analysis and test design. This structuring concept can be provided for program design to keep under control the number of possible interprocess communications in the target code [6], as well as for static concurrency analysis of existing programs when designing structural tests [7].

A multi-flow-graph corresponding to this example parallel program is presented in Figure 3. It consists of three threads, with the middle one representing the referee. Note, that node objects not involved in creating processes nor in any interprocess communication belong to just one thread; such objects in one thread are independent from their counterparts in other threads, and they are connected as ordinary flow-graph nodes. There is one node object involved in creating two players by the referee with entries forming a set: {`0.2`, `1.1`, `2.1`}, and six communication event node objects forming sets: {`1.2`, `0.6`}, {`0.8`, `2.2`}, {`1.8`, `1.15`, `0.11`}, {`0.15`, `2.10`}, {`0.16`, `2.15`}, and {`1.10`, `0.20`}. Only these objects are involved in communications between the referee and each single player, providing a specific set of access points to the related processes. No other interaction between processes is possible except these points.

It can be seen from Figure 3 that the multi-flow graph representation of the example parallel program from Figure 2 is almost like an ordinary flow-graph. Sequential nodes in each flow-graph can be executed independently, thus in parallel, to other flow-graphs. Interaction, i.e., communication, between flow-graphs is encapsulated by a few nodes having a well defined purpose, protocol and location in the overall program structure.

5 Conclusions

We have outlined our object oriented model of parallel programs that provides encapsulation of interprocess communication by node objects. Owing to this encapsulation, structures of parallel program computations and control flows can be made more understandable and visible for a user.

Classes of nodes specified here can be implemented in any object oriented language to provide a database for a parallel program developer and/or tester. With such a database the program structure can be better visualized with intuitively simple graph drawing using predefined objects. This structure may be used for program detailed design (forward engineering), test design for various structural tests or re-engineering already implemented programs to improve their structure.

In its current form, the model has been adopted for the testing tool being developed for the Copernicus Software Engineering for Parallel Processing (SEPP) European programme [8].

References

[1] Peterson, J.: *Petri Net Theory and the Modeling of Systems.* Prentice-Hall, Englewood Cliffs, N.J., 1981.

[2] Sidhu, D.P., Leung, T.K.: Formal methods for protocol testing - a detailed study. *IEEE Trans. Software Eng.* **SE-15**, 413-426 (1989).

[3] Comer, D.: *Internetworking with TCP/IP Vol.1: Principles, Protocols, and Architecture*, 2nd ed., Prentice-Hall, New Jersey, 1991.

[4] Geist, A., *et al.*: PVM 3 user's guide and reference manual. Oak Ridge National Lab, Oak Ridge, Tennessee, 1994.

[5] Hecht, M.S.: *Flow Analysis of Computer Programs.* North-Holland, 1977.

[6] Krawczyk, H., Wiszniewski, B.: Design for Testability of Parallel Programs. In Proc. Software Quality Conference SQC'95, Dundee, UK, July 1995.

[7] Szczerba, A., Wiszniewski B. A tool for testing communication events in TCP/IP environments. In Proc. Parallel Computing Conference ParCo'95, Ghent, Belgium, September 1995.

[8] Winter, S., Kacsuk, P.: Software engineering for parallel processing. Proc. 8th Symp. on Microcomputer and Microprocessor Applications, 12-14 October, Budapest, Hungary, 285-293 (1994).

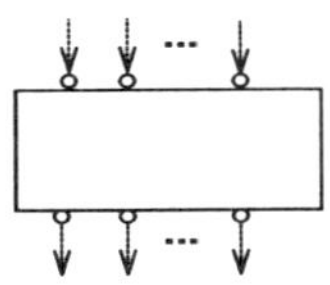

```
class Vector; class Action;
class Node {
  public:
    int N; // no of entries
    int K; // no of exits
    Action *entries; // entries labeled by current actions
    Action *exits;   // exits labeled by successor actions
    Vector initial;  // entries holding incoming tokens
    Vector final;    // exits holding outgoing tokens
    // abstract Node execution
    virtual Vector& step(Vector&)=0;
};
```

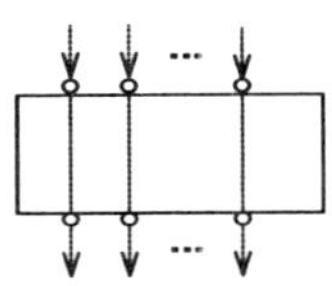

```
class Statement;
class Assignment: public Node {
  public:
    Statement *expression; // assignments at exits
};
```

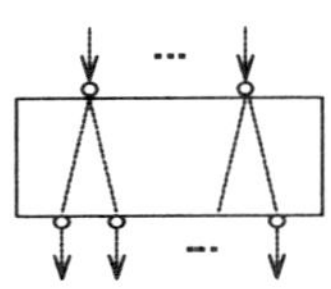

```
class Statement;
class Conditional: public Node {
  public:
    Statement *predicate; // predicates at exits
};
```

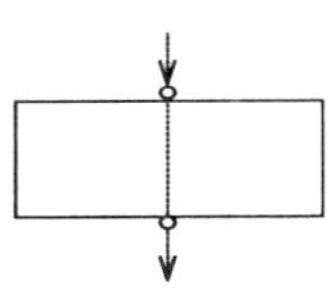

```
class Expression: public Assigment {
  public:
    const static int N=K=1;
};
```

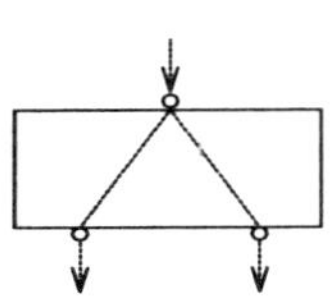

```
class Decision: public Conditional{
  public:
    const static int N=1;
};
```

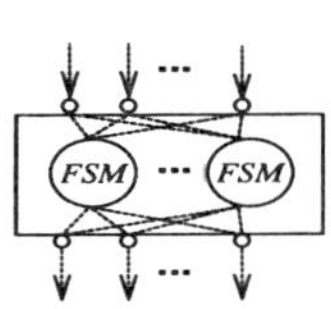


```
class FSM;
class CommunicationEvent: public Conditional, public Assignment {
  private:
    FSM **machines // array of lists of machines at each entry
};
```

Figure 1: Multi-flowgraph objects

```
#include "players.h"
/* #.1: #.2 */          main(){/* process #=0 (REFEREE) starts here */
                        const int nproc = 2; /* no of players */
                        int tids[2]; /* players */
                        int s_msgtype, r_msgtype;
                        int numt, player, score, bid, mytid;
                        mytid = pvm_mytid();
                        s_msgtype = 200; r_msgtype = 201;
                        /* start players */
/* #.2: #.3 */          numt = pvm_spawn("player",(char **)0,0,"",nproc,tids);
/* #.3: #.4 #.5 */      if (numt < 2)
/* #.4: */              {printf("...cannot start players");
                        pvm_exit(); exit(1); }
                        /* REFEREE code */
/* #.5: #.6 */          score = 0;
                        player = 1; /* send PLAYER_1 its no */
/* #.6: #.7 */          pvm_initsend(PvmDataRaw);
                        pvm_pkint(&player,1,1);
                        pvm_send(tids[0],s_msgtype);
                        /* send PLAYER_2 its no */
/* #.7: #.8 */          player = 2; /* send PLAYER_2 its no */
/* #.8: #.9 */          pvm_initsend(PvmDataRaw);
                        pvm_pkint (&player,1,1);
                        pvm_send(tids[1],s_msgtype);
/* #.9: #.10 */         printf("...starting the game.");
/* #.10: #.11 #.21 */   while(score < 100)
                        /* receive bid from PLAYER_1 */
/* #.11: #.12 */        pvm_recv(tids[0],r_msgtype);
                        pvm_upkint(&bid,1,1);
                        pvm_upkint(&player,1,1);
                        /* check new score */
/* #.12: #.13 */        score += bid;
/* #.13: #.14 #.15 */   if (score >= 100)
/* #.14: #.21 */        printf ("...and the winner is %d !",player);
                        /* send score to PLAYER_2 */
/* #.15: #.16 */        else {pvm_initsend(PvmDataRaw);
                        pvm_pkint(&score,1,1);
                        pvm_send(tids[1],s_msgtype);
                        /* receive bid from PLAYER_2 */
/* #.16: #.17 */        pvm_recv(tids[1],r_msgtype);
                        pvm_upkint(&bid,1,1);
                        pvm_upkint(&player,1,1);
/* #.17: #.18 */        printf("...referee has %d from player %d.",bid,player);
                        /* check new score again */
                        score += bid;
                        printf("...score is now %d",score);
/* #.18: #.19 #.20 */   if (score >= 100)
/* #.19: #.21 */        printf ("...and the winner is %d !",player);
                        /* send score to PLAYER_1 */
/* #.20: #.10 */        else {pvm_initsend(PvmDataRaw);
                        pvm_pkint(&score,1,1);
                        pvm_send(tids[0],s_msgtype);
                        }}}
                        /* terminate players */
/* #.21: */             pvm_kill(tids[0]); pvm_kill(tids[1]);
                        /* stop REFEREE */
                        pvm_exit(); return(0);
                        }
```

```
#include "players.h"
                        main() {/* process PLAYER_#, #=1,2 starts here */
/* #.1: #.2 */          FILE *in, *out;
                        int referee, player_no;
                        int score, bid, mytid;
                        mytid = pvm_mytid();
                        referee = pvm_parent(); /* know the REFEREE */
/* #.2: #.3 */          pvm_recv(referee,r_msgtype);
                        pvm_upkint(&player_no,1,1);
                        /* PLAYER_1 starts the game */
/* #.3: #.4 #.9 */      if (player_no == 1)
/* #.4: #.5 */          {out = fopen(CONSOLE,"w"); in = fopen (CONSOLE,"r");
                        bid = 0; /* get bid */
/* #.5: #.6 #.7 */      while(!((bid > 0) && (bid < 10)))
/* #.6: #.5 */          {fprintf(out,"...initial bid from PLAYER_1 ?");
                        fscanf (in,"%d",&bid);}
/* #.7: #.8 */          fclose(out); fclose(in);
                        /* send bid to REFEREE */
/* #.8: #.9 */          pvm_initsend(PvmDataRaw);
                        pvm_pkint(&bid,1,1); pvm_pkint(&player_no,1,1);
                        pvm_send(referee,s_msgtype);}
/* #.9: #.10 */         while(1) /* infinite loop */
                        /* current score from REFEREE */
/* #.10: #.11 */        {pvm_recv(referee,r_msgtype);
                        pvm_upkint(&score,1,1);
/* #.11: #.12 */        out = fopen(CONSOLE,"w"); in = fopen(CONSOLE,"r");
                        fprintf(out,"...score is %d;",score);
                        bid = 0; /* get bid */
/* #.12: #.13 #.14*/    while(!((bid > 0) && (bid < 10)))
/* #.13: #.12 */        {fprintf (out,"...bid from PLAYER_%d ?",player_no);
                        fscanf(in,"%d",&bid);}
/* #.14: #.15 */        fclose(out); fclose(in);
                        /* send bid to REFEREE */
/* #.15: #.9 */         pvm_initsend(PvmDataRaw);
                        pvm_pkint(&bid,1,1); pvm_pkint(&player_no,1,1);
                        pvm_send(referee,s_msgtype);}
                        }
```

Figure 2: PVM example source files

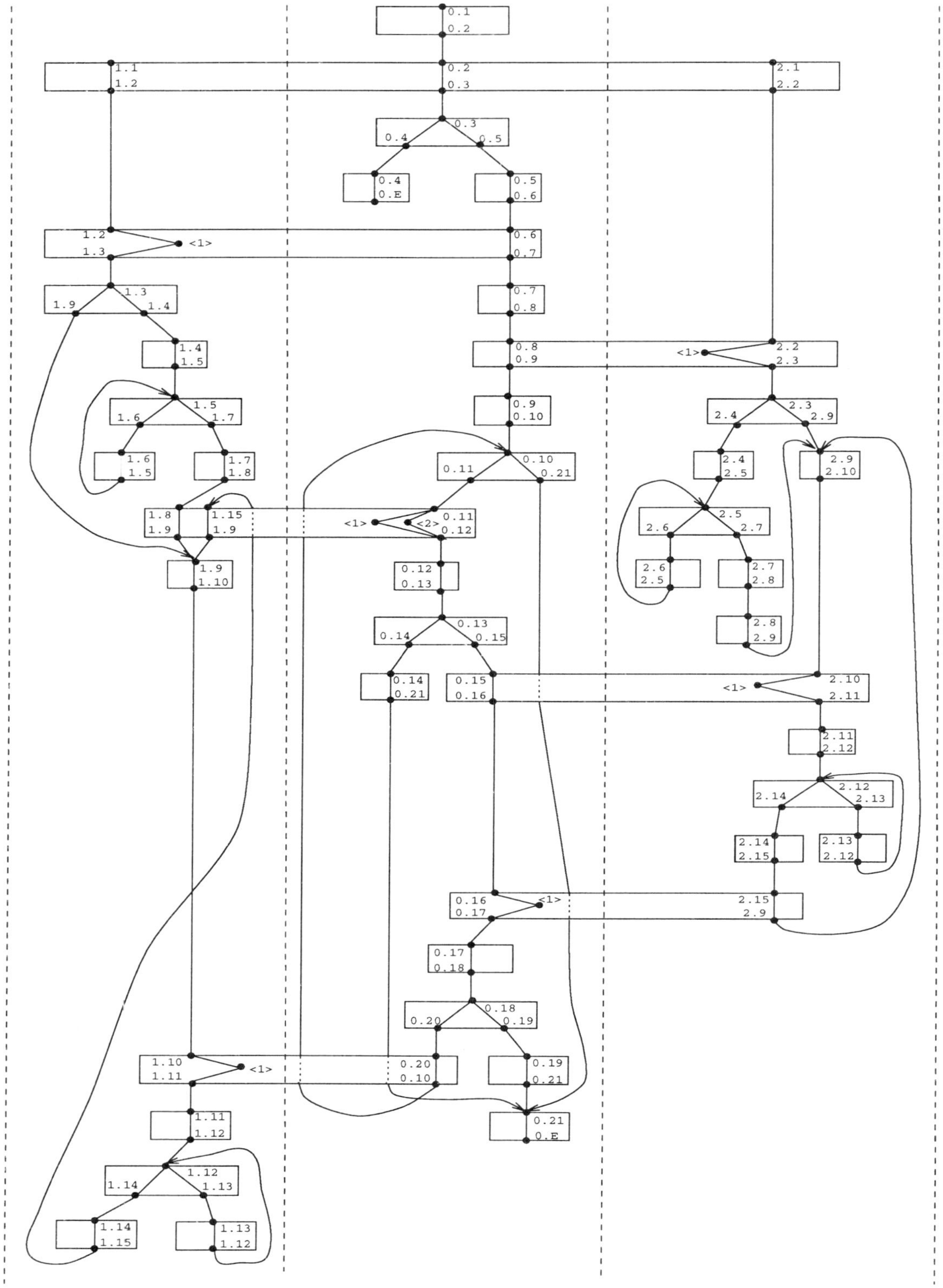

Figure 3: A multi-flowgraph of players

Concurrent Object-Oriented Programming Techniques in a Term Graph Rewriting Framework

George A. Papadopoulos

Department of Computer Science
University of Cyprus
75 Kallipoleos Str.
Nicosia, P.O. Box 537, CY 1678
CYPRUS

Email: george@turing.cs.ucy.ac.cy

Abstract

The relationship between the generalised computational model of Term Graph Rewriting (TGRS) and Object-Oriented Programming (OOP) is explored and exploited by extending the TGRS model with records where access to parameters is done by naming rather than position. Records are then used as the basis for expressing object-oriented techniques such as delegation and (various forms of) inheritance. The effect is that TGRS with records can now be used as an implementation model for a variety of (concurrent) object-oriented (functional, logic or otherwise) languages but also as a common formalism for comparing various related techniques (such as different forms of inheritance).

Keywords: Term Graph Rewriting; Records; Delegation; Inheritance; (Concurrent) Object-Oriented Programming Techniques.

1. Introduction

The generalised computational model of Term Graph Rewriting Systems ([1]) has been used extensively as an implementation vehicle for a number of, often divergent, programming paradigms ranging from the traditional functional programming ones ([6,8]) to the (concurrent) logic programming ones ([5,10]). The model is also capable of supporting imperative programming techniques such as destructive assignment which is needed frequently for modelling object behaviour (say, the changing of an object's state); in addition, the notion of sharing, a fundamental concept in the graph rewriting world, corresponds directly to the notion of reusability. However, there has not been so far a coherent attempt to use TGRS as an implementation model for Object-Oriented Programming (OOP) techniques.

In this paper we explore and exploit the relationship between TGRS and OOP by means of extending the TGRS framework with records where access to parameters is done by naming rather than position. Records are then used as the basis for expressing OOP techniques such as delegation and (various forms of) inheritance ([2,11]). Furthermore, if we also enforce a programming methodology where all functions defined and used in a program access their parameters via the use of a single record we end up with a framework where all pattern matching and function application is done based on named rather than positional parameters. This enhanced framework of "TGRS with records" (or "TGRS with names") provides a powerful formalism able to play the role of a generalised implementation model for a variety of (possibly concurrent) OOP languages but also act as a common platform for comparing the various OOP techniques and assessing their usefulness with respect to each other.

In particular, using as a vehicle the intermediate compiler target language Dactl ([4,3]) based on TGRS and playing the role of a high-level machine language in the FLAGSHIP project ([7]), we first show how records can be implemented in the language without the need to extend the semantics of the associated TGR computational model; then, we use records as the basis for implementing a variety of OOP techniques. The rest of the paper is organised as follows: the next section introduces the TGRS model and the language Dactl and the third one extends Dactl with records; the fourth section introduces the methodology of using solely records for function definition and application and the fifth one provides a number of techniques for modelling fundamental OOP techniques such as delegation and inheritance. The paper ends with a discussion of current, future and related research.

2. Term Graph Rewriting Systems and the Associated Language Dactl

The TGRS model of computation is based around the notion of manipulating term graphs or simply graphs. In particular, a program is composed of a set of graph rewriting rules 'L=>R' which specify the transformations that could be performed on those parts of a graph (redexes) which match some LHS of such a rule and can thus evolve to the form specified by the corresponding RHS. Usually ([1]), a graph G is represented as the tuple $<N_G, root_G, Sym_G, Succ_G>$ where:

- N_G is the set of nodes for G
- $root_G$ is a special member of N_G, the root of G

1066-6192/96 $5.00 © 1996 IEEE
Proceedings of PDP '96

- Sym_G is a function from N_G to the set of all function symbols
- $Succ_G$ is a function from N_G to the set of tuples $N_G{}^*$, such that if $Succ(N) = (N_1...N_k)$ then k is the arity of N and $N_1...N_k$ are the arguments of N.

Note that the arguments of a graph node are identified by position and in fact we write `Succ(N,i)` to refer to the `i`th argument of N using a left-to-right ordering. The context-free grammar for describing a graph could be something like

```
graph  ::=   node | node+graph
node   ::=   A(node,...,node) |identifier |
             identifier:A(node,...,node)
```

where `A` ranges over a set of function symbols and an `identifier` is simply a name for some node.

In the associated compiler target language Dactl, a graph G is represented as the tuple $<N_G, root_G, Sym_G, Succ_G, NMark_G, AMark_G>$ where in addition to those parts of the tuple described above we also have:

- $NMark_G$ which is a function from N_G to the set of node markings $\{\varepsilon, *, \#^n\}$
- $AMark_G$ which is a function from N_G to the set of tuples of arc markings $\{\varepsilon, \hat{}\}^*$

A Dactl rule is of the form

$$\text{Pattern} \to \text{Contractum}, \quad x_1{:=}y_1,\ldots,x_i{:=}y_i, \quad \mu_1 z_1,\ldots,\mu_j z_j$$

where after matching the `Pattern` of the rule with a piece of the graph representing the current state of the computation, the `Contractum` is used to add new pieces of graph to the existing one and the redirections $x_1{:=}y_1,\ldots,x_i{:=}y_i$ are used to redirect a number of arcs (where the arc pointing to the root of the graph being matched is usually also involved) to point to other nodes (some of which will usually be part of the new ones introduced in the `Contractum`); the last part of the rule $\mu_1 z_1,\ldots,\mu_j z_j$ specifies the state of some nodes (idle, active or suspended).

In order to illustrate some of Dactl's features which are important for understanding the rest of the paper we present below the equivalent Dactl program for a non-deterministic merge as it would be written in any state-of-the-art concurrent (constraint) logic programming language.

```
merge([X|XS],YS,ZS] :-
    ZS=[X|ZS1], merge(XS,YS,ZS1).
merge(XS, [Y|YS],ZS) :-
    ZS=[Y|ZS1], merge(XS,YS,ZS1).
merge([],YS,ZS) :- ZS=YS.
merge(XS,[],ZS) :- ZS=XS.
```

```
MODULE Merge;
IMPORTS Arithmetic; Logic;
SYMBOL REWRITABLE PUBLIC CREATABLE Merge;
SYMBOL OVERWRITABLE PUBLIC OVERWRITABLE Var;
SYMBOL CREATABLE PUBLIC CREATABLE Cons; Nil;
PATTERN PUBLIC
    PAIR = Cons[head:ANY tail:ANY];
    LIST = (PAIR+Nil);
RULE
    Merge[Cons[x xs] ys zs:Var] =>
       *Merge[xs ys zs1],
       zs:=*Cons[x zs1:Var]|
    Merge[xs l:PAIR zs:Var] =>
       *Merge[xs l.tail zs1],
       zs:=*Cons[l.head zs1:Var]|
    Merge[Nil ys zs:Var] => *True, zs:=*ys|
    Merge[xs Nil zs:Var] => *True, zs:=*xs;
    (Merge[p1 p2 p3]&
     Merge[Var ANY ANY]+Merge[ANY Var ANY]) =>
       #Merge[^p1 ^p2 p3];
    Merge[ANY ANY ANY] => *False;
ENDMODULE Merge;
```

The first four Dactl rules implement the corresponding ones of the original program. Note here the use of '`=>`' instead of '`->`' for root overwriting and the use of '`:=`' to model assignment. Note also the selection operator '`.`' used for illustrative purposes in the second rule where `x.y` is used to refer to a node `y` of some pattern `x` (in other words, the first two rules illustrate an explicit and an implicit, respectively, way for performing pattern matching).

The fifth rule models the suspension of the process if none of its first two input arguments is instantiated yet; here note the use of the pattern operators '`&`' (conjunction) and '`+`' (sum) where `A&B` must match both `A` and `B` and `A+B` can match either `A` or `B`. Therefore, what this rule says is that if both the two input arguments of `Merge` are still unistantiated (i.e. `Var`) then the process suspends.

Finally, the last rule reports failure if the input arguments have been instantiated to anything other than a `Cons` or `Nil`. Rules separated by a '`|`' can be tested in any order whereas those separated by a '`;`' will be tested sequentially. So, in describing the previous rule we said "both" although the rule formulation suggested "either of" because the sequential operator used there guaranteed that if either input argument was instantiated then one of the first four rules would have been matched.

Another thing to note is that the nodes of a graph are labelled with symbols for which an associated access class is specified. In particular, a `REWRITABLE` symbol (such as `Merge`) can be rewritten only by means of ordinary root redirections whereas an `OVERWRITABLE` symbol (such as `Var`) can be rewritten only by means of non-root redirections; also a `CREATABLE` symbol can only be used as the name implies. An overwritable symbol can be "assigned" values by means of non-root overwrites as many times as it is required, and can thus play the role of either a declarative single-assignment variable or the usual imperative one.

3. Term Graph Rewriting with Records

In order to be able to model some fundamental OOP techniques we propose the introduction of records where the aim is to support standard record manipulation operations such as record creation, selection and updating of a record's elements, etc. without the need to extend the semantics of the underlying TGR model of computation. In particular, a record is a data structure of the form

```
Record["string_name"
       Name1[value1]   ...   Namen[valuen]]
```

where the following symbol declarations have been defined.

```
SYMBOL CREATABLE
PUBLIC CREATABLE Record; Unbound;

SYMBOL OVERWRITABLE
PUBLIC OVERWRITABLE Name1; ... ;Namen;

PATTERN PUBLIC
    RECORD = (Record[STRING]+
              Record[STRING ANY]+
              Record[STRING ANY ANY]+
              Record[STRING ANY ANY ANY]+  ...);
    NAME = (Name1+ ... +Namen);
```

In other words, a record is a data structure comprising a string (its name id), and a sufficient number of overwritable symbols (possibly none if the record denotes a constant value) which represent the fields of the record. In `Name[value]`, `value` can be any value (even another record or a function invocation) including the special (`OVERWRITABLE`) symbol `Unbound` with the obvious meaning. The following fundamental operations are allowed on records.

```
CreateRecord[rec_name:STRING
             Names[name1 ... namen]
             Values[value1 ... valuen]]
    => *Record[rec_name
              Name1[value1]   ...   Namen[valuen]];

RecordElement[rec:RECORD name:NAME] => *value;

SetRecordElement[rec:RECORD name:NAME value] =>
    *True, name:=*value;
```

Note that in selecting the value of a record element in the second rule, if `Name` is not a field of the record the rule returns `False` as the answer. However, an attempt to update a record field which does not exist (third rule) is considered a null operation; `SetRecordElement` will still return `True` but of course no field will be updated. This is a typical approach when named parameters or variables are involved in a computation ([2,11]).

All these three operations on records are implemented at a lower level in the language but in a way that adheres to the already established semantics for TGRS. Name comparison, for instance, is done by mapping the respective symbols onto their equivalent string values and checking for string equality. As it has already been mentioned, records in Dactl are updatable objects where the value of a (named) field can be changed multiple times by virtue of the semantics of non-root redirections supported by the underlying TGR model.

4. Term Graph Rewriting with Names

If the use of records is coupled with an enforced programming methodology where function parameters are encapsulated within a record and operations such as pattern matching are viewed as field selections, a compact formalism is yielded able to accommodate fully the needs of OOP such as support for software composition. A user program, for instance, does not have to rely on knowing information like the arity of a function or the full range of parameters it takes. In addition, reusability comes for free due to the inherent notion of sharing available in a graph rewriting framework.

We show the principles of programming in "TGRS with names" by encoding some well known list manipulation functions using records.

```
SYMBOL OVERWRITABLE
PUBLIC OVERWRITABLE Head; Tail;
PATTERN PUBLIC Nil  = Record["Nil"];
               Cons = Record["Cons" Head[ANY]
                                    Tail[ANY]];

Length[rec:Nil] => *0|
Length[rec:Cons] =>
    #IAdd[1 ^#Length[^*RecordElement[rec Tail]]];

Append[rec1:Nil rec2] => *rec2|
Append[rec1:Cons rec2] =>
    #Cons[^*RecordElement[rec Head]
        #Append[^*RecordElement[rec Tail] rec2]];
```

A call to `Length`, for instance, could take the following form (where `INITIAL` denotes the first rule to be tried in a Dactl program).

```
INITIAL => #Length[^record_list],
          record_list:#CreateRecord["Cons"
                      Names[Head Tail]
                      ^#Values[1 ^tail1]],
          tail1:#CreateRecord["Cons"
                      Names[Head Tail]
                      ^#Values[2 ^tail2]],
          tail2:*CreateRecord["Nil"
                      Names[] Values[]];
```

Note in the second rule for `Append` the concurrent building of both the head and the tail of the appended list. The use of names introduces extra verbosity in the code which, however, can be taken care of by means of syntactic sugar extensions. We can define, for instance, a field selection operator '°' and rewrite `Append`, say, as follows:

```
Append[rec1:Nil rec2] => *rec2|
Append[rec1:Cons rec2] =>
    *Cons[rec1°Head *Append[rec1°Tail rec2]];
```

In order to reduce verbosity in the rhs of some rule during the creation of a new record, we can define a "record template" and use '°' again to instantiate its named parameters. So assuming the following list template declaration

```
PATTERN PUBLIC LIST = Record["Cons"
                             Head[Unbound]
                             Tail[Unbound]];
```

the rule for `INITIAL` can be written as follows.

```
INITIAL => *Length[list], list:LIST,
          list°Head:=1, list°Tail:=list1:LIST,
          list1°Head:=2, list1°Tail:=Nil;
```

Other similar syntactic extensions are also possible. For instance, we can write

```
F[rec°X:'A' ...] => ...|
F[rec°Y:(Unbound+INT) ...] => ...;
```

where the pattern matching for F will succeed if its first argument is a record having either a field named X with value 'A' or a field named Y whose value is the symbol Unbound or some integer. All these syntactic extensions can be translated to the core subset of the language using the fundamental operations on records and a sufficient number of auxiliary rules. In the rest of the paper, however, we use this core subset only (even at the expense of rendering sometimes the code less readable) to highlight the fact that everything we do requires no semantic extensions to the underlying TGR model.

5. Delegation and Inheritance in TGRS with Names

We now show the principles of expressing delegation and inheritance in our framework. The first subsection describes the basic strategy for achieving object encapsulation and representation which is subsequently used to model these OOP techniques.

5.1 Object Encapsulation and Representation

The extended with records framework provides the required mechanism needed for object encapsulation and representation and acts as the basis for modelling delegation and inheritance. There are a number of ways ([2]) to achieve encapsulation (and hence inheritance) and here for lack of space we concentrate our attention on only two of them; as an example we use as object the unavoidable 2-dimensional point with a number of elementary methods associated with it.

```
SYMBOL CREATABLE
PUBLIC CREATABLE
    SetX; SetY; Move; Clear;          { methods

SYMBOL REWRITABLE
PUBLIC CREATABLE Point2D;             { object

SYMBOL REWRITABLE Point2D_aux;
SYMBOL OVERWRITABLE PUBLIC OVERWRITABLE
    XCoord; YCoord;                   { parameters

PATTERN PUBLIC
    POINT = Record["Point2D"
                   XCoord[ANY]
                   YCoord[ANY]];      { class
    NAME = (XCoord+YCoord);

Point2D[rec:POINT Nil] => *rec|
Point2D[rec:POINT Cons[message rest]] =>
    #Point2D[^*Point2D_aux[rec message] rest]|
Point2D[rec:POINT fun:REWRITABLE] =>
    #Point2D[rec ^*fun]|
Point2D[rec:POINT var:OVEWRITABLE] =>
    #Point2D[rec ^var];
Point2D[ANY ANY] => *False;
```

```
Point2D_aux[rec name:NAME] =>
    *RecordElement[rec name]|
Point2D_aux[rec SetX[dx:INT]] =>
    *SetRecordElement[rec XCoord dx]|
Point2D_aux[rec SetY[dy:INT]] =>
    *SetRecordElement[rec YCoord dy]|
Point2D_aux[rec Move[dx:INT dy:INT]] =>
    ##Wait[rec ^update1 ^update2],
    update1:#SetRecordElement[rec XCoord ^new_x],
     new_x:#IAdd[^*RecordElement[rec XCoord] dx],
    update2:#SetRecordElement[rec YCoord ^new_y],
     new_y:#IAdd[^*RecordElement[rec YCoord] dy]|
Point2D_aux[rec Clear] =>
    ##Wait[rec ^update1 ^update2],
        update1:*SetRecordElement[rec XCoord 0],
        update2:*SetRecordElement[rec YCoord 0];
```

A number of points should be cleared before we continue the discussion. A 2-dimensional point is represented by means of an appropriate record. The corresponding object is represented by means of a recursive function comprising two arguments: the record and a stream parameter accepting a list of messages to this object. Each message in the list is handled by an associated auxiliary function which returns the updated record. Note the third and fourth rules in Point2D where we model synchronisation. Depending on whether the paradigm is functional or other (concurrent logic say), the stream of messages may be a function application needed to be fired (if the paradigm supports lazyness) or a logical variable waiting to be instantiated by some message producer. The last rule reports failure if the object is invoked with the wrong type of arguments.

In the fourth and fifth rules for Point2D_aux note the following points. First, we use imperative techniques to update the record fields rather than a "more proper" declarative approach where a fresh record is generated and returned with updated fields; this is done, of course, for the sake of efficiency by exploiting the power of repeatable non-root overwrites. Second, the updating operations of different fields in the record are done concurrently, exploiting here the high degree of fine grain parallelism available in the TGR model. The auxiliary function Wait is simply waiting for both updating operations to complete before returning the record as its result. Third, messages like Move should, strictly speaking, also be records so that the textual position of their componens (and possibly other information such as their number) need not be known by the object handling them. We choose the ordinary positional approach however for the sake of keeping the complexity of the presentable code down to a manageable level.

Finally, note that the above implementation of methods for a 2-dimensional point can also be used for any other type of point (3-dimensional, etc.), simply by extending the pattern definition of POINT.

```
PATTERN PUBLIC POINT = (Record["Point2D"
                        XCoord[ANY] YCoord[ANY]]
                       +
                        Record["Point3D" ...]
                       +
                        Record["Point3DColour" ...]
                       + ...);
```

This is possible because the use of records renders the update operations polymorphic and independent of, say, the number and names of arguments in other types of points.

The above approach achieves object encapsulation and reuse of methods by instances of other similar classes. However, an even more flexible approach is the following where the record itself is extended with a `Class` parameter denoting the class of the object and allowing the extracting of a method from a class and its direct application to instances of subclasses. We present only that part of the code which is different from the one shown above.

```
SYMBOL CREATABLE PUBLIC CREATABLE
    GetX; GetY; SetX; SetY; Move; Clear;

SYMBOL OVERWRITABLE PUBLIC OVERWRITABLE
    Class; XCoord; YCoord;

PATTERN PUBLIC
       POINT = Record["Point2D"
                      Class[Point2D]
                      XCoord[ANY]
                      YCoord[ANY]];
       METHOD = (GetX+GetY+SetX+SetY+Move+Clear);


Point2D[method:METHOD] => *Point2D_aux[method]|
Point2D[Nil] => *Nil|
Point2D[Cons[message rest]] =>
    #Point2D[^*Point2D_aux[message] rest]|
Point2D[fun:REWRITABLE] => #Point2D[^*fun]|
Point2D[var:OVEWRITABLE] => #Point2D[^var];
Point2D[ANY] => *False;

Point2D_aux[GetX[rec:POINT]] =>
    *RecordElement[rec XCoord]|
Point2D_aux[GetY[rec:POINT]] =>
    *RecordElement[rec YCoord]|
Point2D_aux[SetX[rec:POINT dx:INT]] =>
    *SetRecordElement[rec XCoord dx]|
Point2D_aux[SetY[rec:POINT dy:INT]] =>
    *SetRecordElement[rec YCoord dy]|
Point2D_aux[Move[rec:POINT dx:INT dy:INT]] =>
    ##Wait[rec ^update1 ^update2],
    update1:#SetRecordElement[rec XCoord ^new_x],
     new_x:#IAdd[^*RecordElement[rec XCoord] dx],
    update2:#SetRecordElement[rec YCoord ^new_y],
     new_y:#IAdd[^*RecordElement[rec YCoord] dy]|
Point2D_aux[Clear[rec:POINT]] =>
    ##Wait[rec ^update1 ^update2],
        update1:*SetRecordElement[rec XCoord 0],
        update2:*SetRecordElement[rec YCoord 0];
```

Note that in order to use this approach the appropriate class must be selected first followed by a selection of the required method. Here we make use of the following "metarule" available in Dactl.

```
Apply_To[f:FUNCTION_NAME param_1 ... param_n] =>
    *F[param_1 ... param_n];
```

A typical query now takes the following form (where `MovedPoint` is an instance of `Point2D`).

```
MovedPoint[rec:POINT messages] =>
     #Apply_To[^*RecordElement[rec Class]
               messages];
INITIAL => #MovedPoint[^*CreateRecord["Point2D"
                        Names[Class XCoord YCoord]
                        Values[Point2D 0 0]]
                        messages];
```

where we assume that `messages` denotes a list of messages where their first argument is the record to be updated.

5.2 Delegation

Delegation using records can be expressed by representing the values of some of its parameters as selection functions of fields in other records as in the following example.

```
Delegator[rec:RECORD] =>
    *CreateRecord["Delegator" Names[X Y Z]
                  Values[2 5 RecordElement[rec Z]]];
```

where the value of the `Z` field in `Delegator` is taken to be that of the corresponding field in `rec`. Dynamic delegation involving a variable set of named parameters is also possible although some preprocessing is required. In the following delegation construct

```
Delegator[rec:RECORD] =>
    *CreateRecord["Delegator" Names[X Y Other]
             Values[2 5 RecordElement[rec Other]]];
```

`Other` is a special name which stands for all names involved or a subset of them. There is the need to enhance the functionality of the basic record manipulation operations so that they can substitute `Other` with the right name parameter but since the set of these names is finite this can be done with reasonable programming effort.

5.3 Inheritance

The second technique for object encapsulation and representation discussed in section 5.1 can be used as the basis for modelling inheritance where methods defined in a certain class are applied to instances of some other class. In order to illustrate this ability we define a 3-dimensional point which inherits the methods of its 2-dimensional counterpart (some pattern definitions must be redefined and their new values are also shown below).

```
SYMBOL CREATABLE
PUBLIC CREATABLE GetZ; SetZ; Move2D; Move3D;

SYMBOL REWRITABLE PUBLIC CREATABLE Point3D;

SYMBOL REWRITABLE Point3D_aux;

SYMBOL OVERWRITABLE PUBLIC OVERWRITABLE ZCoord;

PATTERN PUBLIC
    POINT = (Record["Point2D" Class[Point2D]
                    XCoord[ANY] YCoord[ANY]]
              +
             Record["Point3D" Class[Point3D]
                    XCoord[ANY] YCoord[ANY]
```

```
                                    ZCoord[ANY]]);
    METHOD2D = (GetX[ANY]+GetY[ANY]+
                SetX[ANY]+SetY[ANY]);
    METHOD = (METHOD2D+GetZ[ANY]+SetZ[ANY]+
              Move2D[ANY ANY ANY]+
              Move3D[ANY ANY ANY ANY]);
```

Point3D is the same as Point2D

```
Point3D_aux[GetZ[rec:POINT]] =>
    *RecordElement[rec ZCoord]|
Point3D_aux[SetZ[rec:POINT dz:INT]] =>
    *SetRecordElement[rec ZCoord dz]|
Point3D_aux[method:Move2D[rec:POINT dx:INT
                                    dy:INT]] =>
    *Point2D[Move[rec dx dy]]|
Point3D_aux[Move3D[rec:POINT dx:INT dy:INT
                                    dz:INT]]
    => ##Wait[rec ^update12 ^update3],
       update12:*Point2D[Move[rec dx dy]],
       update3:#SetRecordElement[rec ZCoord
                                       ^new_z],
       new_z:#IAdd[^*RecordElement[rec ZCoord]
                                       dz]|
Point3D_aux[method:METHOD2D] => *Point2D[method];
```

In the example above, Point3D renames Move to Move2D and inherits its code from Point2D in order to implement a Move3D operation, defines new methods for accessing and updating the third argument, and delegates all the other messages to Point2D. This is sufficient for modelling inheritance based on static binding. However, it is also possible to model more flexible forms of inheritance based on dynamic binding by noting that: i) instead of mentioning explicitly class (and super class) names we can get them from the record information, and ii) methods such as Move and Move3D can in fact be implemented in terms of more elementary methods such as GetX, etc. defined in the same class. So assuming that Point3D is now of the form

```
Record["Point3D" Class[Point3D] Super[Point2D]
       XCoord[INT] YCoord[INT] ZCoord[INT]]
```

its implementation can be defined as follows.

```
Point3D_aux[GetZ[rec:POINT]] =>
    *RecordElement[rec ZCoord]|
Point3D_aux[SetZ[rec:POINT dz:INT]] =>
    *SetRecordElement[rec ZCoord dz]|
Point3D_aux[method:Move2D[rec:POINT dx:INT
                                    dy:INT]]
    => #Apply_TO[^*RecordElement[rec Super]
                 Move[rec dx dy]]|
Point3D_aux[Move3D[rec:POINT dx:INT dy:INT
                                    dz:INT]]
    => ##Wait[rec ^update12 ^update3],
       update12:#Apply_TO[^*RecordElement[rec
                                    Super]
                          Move[rec dx dy]],
       update3:#SetRecordElement[rec ZCoord
                                    ^new_z],
       new_z:#IAdd[^#Apply_TO[^*RecordElement[rec
                              Class] GetZ] dz]|
Point3D_aux[method:METHOD2D] =>
    #Apply_TO[^*RecordElement[method Super]
                                    method];
```

where we rely again on the functionality of the Apply_To metarule to create dynamically function applications. Note that the classes involved (Point2D and Point3D) are not mentioned explicitly and are derived by means of retrieving the appropriate values from the parameters Class and Super. These classes can, of course, be changed dynamically as in the following example

```
Point[rec:POINT] =>
    *Point3D[rec],
    *SetRecordElement[rec Super Point3DColour];
```

where all references to super will now use the methods in the class Point3DColour.

Admittedly, the programs produced are verbose but they can be viewed as being written in the kernel form of the language, the high level one being similar to the syntactic sugaring discussed at the end of section 4.

6. Conclusions; Current, Further and Related Work

We have extended the framework of TGRS to support record manipulation and we have shown how this extended framework can be used as the basis for modelling OOP techniques such as delegation and inheritance in a TGR framework. Thus, such an extended model of TGRS with records (or TGRS with names) can play the same role that the ordinary TGRS model has played for the past decade wrt (concurrent) logic ([5,10]) and functional ([6,8]) languages, namely to provide an implementation vehicle for a number of OOP languages. In addition, as it was again the case for other declarative formalisms ([3]), it is possible to use TGRS as a common basis for comparing various OOP languages but perhaps more importantly for studying and comparing different approaches regarding object encapsulation, inheritance, etc.

The use of named parameters as the basis for providing OOP capabilities has been used in a number of computational models ranging from (constraint or otherwise) logic ([11]) to functional ([2]) paradigms. In fact, the work reported in [2] which introduces λN (λ-calculus with names) was the initial inspiration for conducting this research.

In the more general setting of Rewriting Systems, one must mention the work of Meseguer ([9]) who defines a theory of concurrent objects within the framework of the concurrent functional object-oriented language Maude, an extension of OBJ. The developed framework is very powerful but the underlying execution model is multiset rewriting which requires the use of a special Rewrite Rule Machine using associative memory. Also, Maude seems to allow multi-headed lhs of rules which is a very powerful albeit difficult to implement formalism. Our approach, driven from practical considerations, is more modest, admittedly narrower in scope, but also easier to implement.

We are currently defining a high-level syntax aiming at reducing program verbosity and we study the extension of the current framework with a suitable type system. Also, we investigate the interaction of parallelism and non-determinism with the OOP extensions.

References

[1] H. P. Barendregt, M. C. J. D. Eekelen, J. R. W. Glauert, J. R. Kennaway, M. J. Plasmeijer and M. R. Sleep, Term Graph Rewriting, *PARLE'87*, Eindhoven, The Netherlands, June 15-19, LNCS 259, Springer Verlag, pp. 141-158.

[2] L. Dami, *Software Composition: Towards an Integration of Functional and Object-Oriented Approaches*, Ph.D. Thesis, Department of Computer Science, University of Geneva, Switzerland, 1994.

[3] J. R. W. Glauert, K. Hammond, J. R. Kennaway and G. A. Papadopoulos, Using Dactl to Implement Declarative Languages, *CONPAR'88*, Manchester, UK, Sept. 12-16, Cambridge University Press, pp. 116-124.

[4] J. R. W. Glauert, J. R. Kennaway, and M. R. Sleep, *Final Specification of Dactl*, Internal Report SYS-C88-11, School of Information Systems, University of East Anglia, Norwich, UK, 1988.

[5] J. R. W. Glauert and G. A. Papadopoulos, A Parallel Implementation of GHC, *FGCS'88*, Tokyo, Japan, Nov. 28 - Dec. 2, Vol. 3, pp. 1051-1058.

[6] K. Hammond, *Parallel SML: A Functional Language and its Implementation in Dactl*, Ph.D. Thesis, School of Information Systems, University of East Anglia, Norwich, UK, published by Pitman Publishers, 1990.

[7] J. A. Keane, An Overview of the Flagship System, *Journal of Functional Programming*, Vol. 4 (1), pp. 19-45, January 1994.

[8] J. R. Kennaway, Implementing Term Rewrite Languages in Dactl, *CAAP'88*, Nancy, France, March 21-24, LNCS 299, Springer Verlag, pp. 117-131; extended version in *Theoretical Computer Science*, Vol. 72, 1990, pp. 225-250.

[9] J. Meseguer, A Logical Theory of Concurrent Objects, *OOPSLA/ECOOP'90*, Ottawa, Canada, Oct. 21-25, ACM/SIGPLAN, pp. 101-115.

[10] G. A. Papadopoulos, A Fine Grain Parallel Implementation of Parlog, *TAPSOFT'89*, Barcelona, Spain, March 13-17, LNCS 352, Springer Verlag, pp. 313-327.

[11] G. Smolka and R. Treinen, Records for Logic Programming, *The Journal of Logic Programming*, Vol. 18 (3), April, 1994, pp. 229-258.

Specifying Almost-Real Concurrent Object-Oriented Programs

Denis Roegel
CRIN-CNRS & INRIA-Lorraine
Campus scientifique — BP 239
54506 Vandœuvre-lès-Nancy cedex, France
roegel@loria.fr

Abstract

Parallel programming is difficult. The need for correct and efficient parallel programs is important and one way to meet this requirement is to work on the refinement chain. Beginning with a specification written in TLA$^+$ (for instance), we can transform it – or refine it – into finer grained specifications. At some step, enough structure will have appeared so that we can bridge a gap to fix this structure. We introduce a more concrete *version of TLA$^+$, CTLA, where structuring concerns are to be expressed, but where distributing, mapping or implementation problems are avoided. Indeed, we firmly believe that it is a mistake to go immediately from TLA$^+$ to a real language like CC++, since the ditch is still too wide. A numerical example supports our claim.*

1 Introduction

Parallel programming is difficult. Proving parallel programs correct may even be more difficult. Proving some property of a program is usually done for simple programs whose formalization is straightforward.

There is a need for a framework allowing formal derivations of concurrent programs. Such a framework should guarantee the correctness of the implementation, and provide some kind of encapsulation making the reuse of produced code if not straightforward, at least easier.

Correctness can be formalized in logic and we consider the Temporal Logic of Actions [3]. Encapsulation, modularity, reusability are provided in object-oriented languages. Concurrent object-oriented design is not easy [6]. We propound a design methodology by pairing a generic and powerful specification language and an object-oriented programming language.

The paper goes as follows: we first motivate the introduction of an intermediate language. Then we give a short account of the specification language and the programming language. An example introduces TLA$^+$. We do then define the CTLA language and explain its relationship with TLA$^+$. We address the refinement of specifications, study a computation example involving matrices and conclude.

2 Task separation

Usually, getting a concurrent program out of a specification involves several operations:

- finding an *algorithm* which permits to satisfy the specification; this includes turning TLA$^+$ actions into an *operational* form;
- *structuring* the specification in order to exploit the parallelism;
- refining the *data structures*;
- *distributing* tasks over processes;
- trying to get an *efficient* program;
- handling various *implementation details*, such as rounding problems, finite range of values, etc.
- transforming the program in order to *improve readability*.

We believe that it is unreasonable to try to achieve all these tasks at once. Actually, we propose to group the tasks into two main steps:

1. A step introducing an algorithm and its structure;
2. A step handling data refinement, efficiency, implementation problems, tuning, etc.

The intermediate state consists of the CTLA language.

3 The specification language

Our purpose is to use a generic specification language and not some *ad hoc* language. TLA$^+$ is a specification language defined by Lamport in [5]. It is basically TLA [3]

Proceedings of PDP '96

with modularity and definition mechanisms. TLA stands for Temporal Logic of Actions. A specification in TLA is a set of behaviours, that is, a set of sequences of states. A state is a valuation of variables. TLA is a linear and discrete-time temporal logic.

A TLA specification has the form $\exists x : Init \wedge \Box_v[\mathcal{N}] \wedge L$ where *Init* is a state predicate constraining the first state of a behaviour, $\mathcal{N}$ is an action, that is, a relation on pairs of successive states, and L is a liveness property. Intuitively, such a specification only *retains* the behaviours satisfying *Init* initially, where every pair of successive states satisfies $\mathcal{N}$ or does not change v, and whose infinite behaviours are constrained by L, which says that some actions must be executed if they are enabled from a certain point on. L is as a matter of fact a conjunction of weak and strong fairness assumptions, and we refer the reader to [3] for more details. Finally, the existentially quantified variable x represents an internal variable, that is, a *local* variable. Quantification is *hiding*.

The module in figure 1 gives a brief introduction to TLA$^+$. Besides parameters which can be instanciated by other modules, the module structure encapsulates various definitions, classified according their "temporal type" and their value. The first definition, *Init*, is a *predicate*. It is true or false in a given state. The second definition, *A*, is an *action*. It contains a reference to a primed variable. This means a reference to the next state of the computation. A is true in a given state, if $x > y$ in this state and the value of x in the next state is the current value of x to which we subtract the current value of y. The temporal formula is a formula true for some traces. We may view this formula as something that *selects* some traces among others. The traces that make *Spec* true are the *good* (i.e. acceptable) traces.

Besides these categories, there are also state functions, transition functions, theorems, etc. Some of them will be seen in the forthcoming example describing a matrix multiplication algorithm.

4 The target language: Concrete TLA (CTLA)

4.1 The language definition: CTLA

CTLA resembles CC++ [1; 8; 9; 2] and hence C++, but it is not a subset of CC++. We summarize here interesting changes which were introduced in order to cope with TLA$^+$.

module M

parameters

x, y : VARIABLE

$Init \triangleq x > 0$

action

$A \triangleq (x > y) \wedge (x' = x - y)$

temporal

$Spec \triangleq Init \wedge \Box[A]_x \wedge \mathrm{WF}_x(A)$

Figure 1: TLA$^+$ example

4.1.1 Typing: sets and structures

CTLA is a typed language where a type is any set definable in Zermelo-Fraenkel set theory [7] to which Hilbert's ε is added in the form of the `CHOOSE` operator. Typing corresponds to set membership in TLA.

There is no `struct` mechanism in CTLA. Functions whose domain is the set of field names can replace the `structs`.

A few types are predefined in CTLA. These are:

- $\mathbb{Z}$ (positive and negative integers, infinite precision): `int`;
- $\mathbb{R}$ (positive and negative reals, infinite precision): `real`;
- strings: `string`; this is a shorthand for the set of tuples of characters.

Other types can easily be defined using `set`, similar to C's `typedef`. For instance, here is how one would define the type of binary trees where nodes are strings:

```
set node = string;
set btree =
    CHOOSE t :
        (:A: x :in: t :
              (:E: n,l,r : (n :in: node)
                         /\ (l :in: t)
                         /\ (r :in: t)
                         /\ (x = <<n,l,r>>)
              )
        );
```

The sets occuring in a set construction can be either predefined sets, or sets constructed using the standard TLA operators ($\rightarrow$,...).

In the previous example, the type `node` is a set initialized to the string type (set). the type `btree` is defined as a set `t` satisfying the predicate on the right of `CHOOSE`. In this predicate, the same notations as in TLA are used, viz. `:A:`, `:E:`, `:in:` and `/\` denote respectively $\forall$, $\exists$, $\in$ and $\wedge$. An alternative notation for `x :in: y` might be `x:y`, but we reserve it for quantification.

Hence, a variable of type `btree` is a tuple of three elements. The first one is of type `node` which is an alias for the predefined type `string`. The second and third one are elements of type `btree`. When these two elements are equal to $\varnothing$, the node is a leaf. Note that `btree` also covers the infinite binary trees.

We may also have dependent types. For instance, here we define the set of elements of `E` which lie between 0 and 1:

```
set zero_one[E] = {x :in: E : (x>0) /\ (x<1)};
```

The types that have been defined may later on, in further refinement steps, become classes or structures, for instance in CC++.

4.1.2 Variables

Variables are simply declared in the usual way, giving their (possibly dependent) type. They can be defined anywhere, not necessarily at the beginning.

Variables can be synchronization variables if their type is preceded by `sync`. This is as in CC++.

4.1.3 Classes

CTLA has classes as well as member functions. Classes have constructors as in C++, but no destructors, because we do not need to free memory. Examples can be found further. CTLA classes will always correspond to TLA$^+$ modules, never to set declarations in TLA$^+$.

We do not allow an object (an instance of a class) to be a parameter of a function, simply because a class corresponds to a TLA$^+$ module, and modules are not used as arguments. Also, a function can not give an object as its result. This does not mean that the idea is not interesting, but that we want CTLA to be close to TLA$^+$.

The `public`/`private` distinction is maintained. This is useful because we can make `public` variables correspond to parameters in a TLA$^+$ module. `private` variables will be quantified variables in a TLA$^+$ module.

4.1.4 Functions and parameter passing

When a function is called with parameters, the parameter itself is passed. It corresponds to the `VAR` tag of PASCAL. We do never use pointers to pass arguments. Examples can be found later in this paper.

The types of the parameters and of the result are any types allowed by CTLA.

4.1.5 Dynamic data structures

We have no dynamic creation of data structures using `new` and `delete`, because they are not needed with CTLA's abstract data structures. There is no primitive concept of memory, and in particular of a finite memory.

4.1.6 Actions

Actions in TLA are relations between a current state and a next state, for instance: $(x' = x+1) \vee (x' = x-1)$. There is no notion of an action in CTLA, but the CTLA functions (assignments) which correspond to actions must be operational and therefore computable. This does not mean that they have to be deterministic, of course.

Hence, CTLA can be seen as an executable version of TLA$^+$.

4.1.7 CC++ extensions

- The `par`, `parfor` and `spawn` statements which specify concurrent execution in CC++, either structured or not, are also part of CTLA.

```
par {
    <statement1>;
    <statement2>;
    ...
    <statementN>;
    }
```

- The same applies to `sync` variables — which are used to synchronize thread executions, and to `atomic` functions. We won't use these features in this paper.

It is to be noted that when a non-`sync` variable is a parameter of two functions called in parallel, none of the two functions has the right to modify it.

4.1.8 CC++ features dropped

Many CC++ constructs were of no concern to us because they help improve efficiency, or readability, but don't influence correctness. We didn't keep them for the intermediate language CTLA and we also avoided redundancy as much as possible. For instance, we forgot about function prototypes. These features help catch errors in programs but this is no longer necessary in our design method. A more detailed list of dropped features appears elsewhere.

In spite of these withdrawals, sufficiently interesting features remain: the class structure of C++ and the parallel structuring operators of CC++.

5 Correspondance between programming and specification language

We can establish a correspondance between a CTLA class and a TLA$^+$ module.

A CTLA program can be viewed as a TLA$^+$ specification where control structures have been added and where actions are computable. This structuring of the specification prepares the real program, but it is not yet the real program, since we do for instance keep all TLA$^+$ data structures and expressiveness.

The semantics of CTLA is no longer the same as that of TLA$^+$. We have no longer a trace semantics with global states.

We can easily draw some parallel between these two languages. In general, a CTLA class is made of some data structure and operations to manipulate them. A CTLA class can be parameterized, that is, some of its variables can be initialized through a constructor.

A TLA$^+$ module can also define data structures, can be parameterized and defines predicates and actions local to the module.

Finally, a CTLA object instanciates a class and this instanciation corresponds to inclusion of modules in TLA$^+$ using the `INCLUDE` construct.

Inheritance in C++ corresponds to the use of the `IMPORT` directive within TLA$^+$. However, when using `IMPORT`, one can not redefine an object. We have no overloading in TLA$^+$. Whereas in C++, one can redefine a member function in a derived class. So, that is why we do not allow redefinition of member functions in CTLA.

6 Refining the specifications

Given a TLA$^+$ specification of a parallel program, the derivation of a CTLA program from this specification is made of transformation steps. We do have a sequence of specifications as shown in figure 2.

The first specification Π_0 is merely a pre-post condition. In the chain depicted in figure 2, Π_i defines a set of behaviours. So does Π_{i+1}. Asserting that Π_i is refined in Π_{i+1} means that the set of behaviours defined by Π_{i+1} is included in the set of behaviours defined by Π_i. This relation is also expressed by the implication of the temporal formulas: $\Pi_{i+1} \Rightarrow \Pi_i$. Proofs in TLA and in particular proving refinements is a topic that has already been studied to some depth. We refer the reader to [4] for more details.

6.1 Action refinement

An important task of the refinement process is what we call the *action refinement*. It is the operation by which an action is refined in an other one, or in several "smaller" (or finer) actions. In the sequel, we will see several such operations.

6.2 Decomposing actions

The action refinement process will make heavy use of two transformations:

- Action A is refined into action B, if $B \Rightarrow A$, B being possibly of the form $B_1 \circ B_2$;
- If A_1 is refined into A_2 and B_1 into B_2, then $A_1 \circ B_1$ is refined into $A_2 \circ B_2$; this follows from $(A_2 \Rightarrow A_1) \wedge (B_2 \Rightarrow B_1) \Rightarrow (A_2 \circ B_2 \Rightarrow A_1 \circ B_1)$.

7 An example: multiplication of matrices

We consider square matrices with the number of rows and columns being a power of 2. Such a matrix will be divided in four square submatrices(and lead to independant computations which can be done in parallel.

7.1 Initial TLA$^+$ modules

We first define some useful sets (figure 3): the set of positive integers and the set of square matrices of size a power of 2. A square matrix is a tuple of three elements, the first of which is a function called *element_function*. Eventually, *element_function* will for example be mapped (implemented) onto an array.

Next, we define the multiplication module *Matrix_product* (figure 4) using the predicate *compatible_matrix* and the function *DotProd*. *compatible_matrix* is a predicate checking that two matrices can be multiplied. The components of a tuple are accessed by means of the '.' notation.

The modules defined so far give us the action *mult_a*[1] which can be used to build up more complex specifications. However, this action is not yet suited for implementation, and especially not parallel implementation.

7.2 Refined modules

The module *Matrix_product* is refined into the *Matrix_product2* module (figure 6).

In this module, several useful state functions are defined:

[1] In order to clearly identify them with respect to similar functions or definitions, we let all actions end with '_a'.

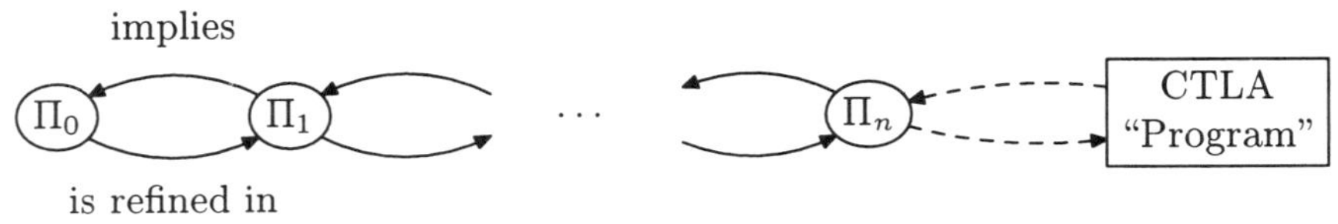

Figure 2: Refinement of a TLA$^+$ specification

module *Matrix*

$Nat^+ \triangleq Nat \setminus \{0\}$

$sqmatrix[E] \triangleq \{\langle f, n, E\rangle : (f \in [Nat^+ \rightarrow [Nat^+ \rightarrow E]]) \wedge (n \in Nat^+) \wedge (\exists\, p \in Nat : n = 2^p)\}$

Figure 3: The definition of a square matrix of 2^p lines

- *add* computes the sum of two compatible square matrices; this is just defined as being the matrix whose element function is the sum of the element functions of the two matrices;
- *rest* (restriction) yields a sub-block of a given matrix, from row r_1 to r_2 and column c_1 to c_2;
- *build* takes four blocks, and puts them together to form a square matrix twice as big;

All these operations consist merely in the definition of the appropriate element functions.

Then *mult* uses these definitions in order to express the matrix multiplication as a composition of smaller matrix multiplications. The action *mult_a* is the *operational* equivalent of the *mult* function.

All what we have done was to give an equivalent but more detailed definition of the *mult* function in module *Matrix_product*. This definition is recursive and corresponds to the block decomposition of the matrix. This is a first step towards task separations.

The next step is to split the action *mult_a* in order to mirror the split of the function *mult*.

The module *Matrix_product2* is eventually refined into the *Matrix_product5* module (figure 7).

This last refinement takes the dependencies between variables into account.

This new module features a new "bulleted list", similar to conjunction or disjunction lists: it is the composition list, using the '$\circ$' separator. This means that the items are composed using the relation composition.

7.3 CTLA code

We sketch some parts of the CTLA code corresponding to the module *Matrix_product*. First, here is a simple implementation of the Nat^+ type:

```
set Natp = {x :in: int : x > 0}
```

`Natp` is the set of positive integers. This corresponds to the Nat^+ definition of module *Matrix*.

Figure 8 shows the `sqmatrix` type definition.

All the TLA$^+$ definitions seen so far are only type definitions and had a simple CTLA counterpart[2]. Module *Matrix_product5* however is different for it has actions. Such a module will correspond to a CTLA class. This class is sketched in figure 5.

8 Conclusion

The big advantage in linking TLA$^+$ and CTLA is the structural correspondance between the languages. It seemed appealing to try to "map" TLA$^+$ modules on classes of an object-oriented programming language.

TLA$^+$ is also a generic specification language, with powerful definition abilities. Its modular structure seemed interesting for reuse and composition.

Another important advantage is the abstractness of CTLA with respect to data structures. We don't have to deal with implementation problems, roundings, etc. Therefore, it is easier to prove the correctness of CTLA programs. The study of our example should convince the reader of the usefulness of this separation.

[2]Because CTLA's data structures are essentially TLA$^+$'s ones.

module *Matrix_product*

import *Matrix*

parameters

E : CONSTANT

predicate

$$compatible\_matrix(A, B) \triangleq \wedge (A \in sqmatrix[E]) \vee (B \in sqmatrix[E]) \\ \wedge A.2 = B.2 \\ \wedge (A.3 = Real) \vee (A.3 = Complex)$$

state function

$$DotProd[i \in Nat^+][j \in Nat^+][k \in Nat^+][A \in sqmatrix[E]][B \in sqmatrix[E]] \triangleq \\ \textbf{if } k = 0 \textbf{ then } 0 \\ \textbf{else } DotProd[i][j][k-1][A][B] + A[i][k] * A[k][j]$$

$$mult[A \in sqmatrix[E]][B \in sqmatrix[E]] \triangleq \textbf{let } g[i][j] \triangleq DotProd[i][j][A.2][A][B] \\ \textbf{in } \langle g, A.2, A.3 \rangle$$

actions

$$mult\_a(A, B, C) \triangleq \wedge compatible\_matrix(A, B) \\ \wedge C' = mult[A][B]$$

Figure 4: *Matrix_product* module

```
class Matrix_product
  {
  private:
    set e;
  public:
    Matrix_product(set E){e=E} // constructor
    sqmatrix[e] add(...){...};
    sqmatrix[e] rest(...){...};
    sqmatrix[e] build(...){...};
    sqmatrix[e] mult(...){
             ...
             sqmatrix[e] a11,a12,a21,a22,b11,b12,b21,b22;
             par {a11=rest(...); ...;b22=rest(...);}
             sqmatrix[e] a,b,c,d;
             par {a=add(mult(a11,b11),mult(a12,b21));...;d=...;}
             return build(a,b,c,d);
             };
  }

Matrix_product M(E);
sqmatrix[E] C;
C=M.mult(A,B);
```

Figure 5: Class Matrix_product

References

[1] K. Mani Chandy and Carl Kesselman. CC++: A Declarative Concurrent Object Oriented Programming Notation, 1993.

[2] Ian T. Foster. *Designing and Building Parallel Programs – Concepts and Tools for Parallel Software Engineering.* Addison-Wesley Publishing Company, 1995.

[3] Leslie Lamport. The Temporal Logic of Actions. *ACM Transactions on Programming Languages and Systems*, 16(3):872–923, May 1994.

[4] Leslie Lamport. TLA WWW page: http://

module *Matrix_product2*

import *Matrix*

parameters
E : CONSTANT

...

state function

$$
\begin{aligned}
&add(A,B) \triangleq \wedge\ compatible\_matrix(A,B)\\
&\qquad\qquad\quad \wedge\ \textbf{let } s[i][j] \triangleq (A.1)[i][j] + (B.1)[i][j] \textbf{ in } \langle s, A.2, A.3\rangle\\
&rest(A, r1, r2, c1, c2) \triangleq \textbf{let } f[i][j] \triangleq (A.1)[i + r1 - 1][j + c1 - 1]\\
&\qquad\qquad\qquad\qquad\quad \textbf{in } \langle f, r2 - r1 + 1, A.3\rangle\\
&build(A,B,C,D) \triangleq\\
&\quad \textbf{let } f[i][j] \triangleq \textbf{if } i \le A.2 \textbf{ then if } j \le A.2 \textbf{ then } (A.1)[i][j] \textbf{ else } (B.1)[i][j - A.2 + 1]\\
&\qquad\qquad\qquad\qquad \textbf{else if } j \le A.2 \textbf{ then } (C.1)[i - A.2 + 1][j] \textbf{ else } (D.1)[i - A.2 + 1][j - A.2 + 1]\\
&\quad \textbf{in } \langle f, 2 * A.2, A.3\rangle\\
&mult[A \in sqmatrix[E]][B \in sqmatrix[E]] \triangleq\\
&\quad \textbf{if } A.2 = B.2 = 1\\
&\qquad \textbf{then let } f[i][j] \triangleq ((A.1)[1][1]) * ((B.1)[1][1]) \textbf{ in } \langle f, 1, A.3\rangle\\
&\qquad \textbf{else}\\
&\qquad\quad \textbf{let } A11 \triangleq rest(A, 1, (A.2)/2, 1, (A.2)/2)\\
&\qquad\qquad\ A12 \triangleq rest(A, 1, (A.2)/2, (A.2)/2 + 1, A.2)\\
&\qquad\qquad\ A21 \triangleq rest(A, (A.2)/2 + 1, A.2, 1, (A.2)/2)\\
&\qquad\qquad\ A22 \triangleq rest(A, (A.2)/2 + 1, A.2, (A.2)/2 + 1, A.2)\\
&\qquad\qquad\ B11 \triangleq rest(B, 1, (B.2)/2, 1, (B.2)/2)\\
&\qquad\qquad\ B12 \triangleq rest(B, 1, (B.2)/2, (B.2)/2 + 1, B.2)\\
&\qquad\qquad\ B21 \triangleq rest(B, (B.2)/2 + 1, B.2, 1, (B.2)/2)\\
&\qquad\qquad\ B22 \triangleq rest(B, (B.2)/2 + 1, B.2, (B.2)/2 + 1, B.2)\\
&\qquad\quad \textbf{in } build(add(mult[A11][B11], mult[A12][B21]), add(mult[A11][B12], mult[A12][B22]),\\
&\qquad\qquad add(mult[A21][B11], mult[A22][B21]), add(mult[A21][B12], mult[A22][B22]))
\end{aligned}
$$

actions

$$mult\_a(A,B,C) \triangleq compatible\_matrix(A,B) \wedge (C' = mult[A][B])$$

Figure 6: *Matrix_product2* module

`www.research.digital.com/SRC/personal/Leslie_Lamport/tla/tla.html`, 1995.

[5] Leslie Lamport and Stephan Merz. Specifying and Verifying Fault-Tolerant Systems. In *Proceedings of the Third International Symposium on Formal Techniques in Real Time and Fault Tolerant Systems, 19–23 September 1994, Lübeck, Germany*, 1994.

[6] Bertrand Meyer. Systematic Concurrent Object-Oriented Programming. *Communications of the ACM*, 36(9):56–80, 1993.

[7] J. R. Shoenfield. Axioms of Set Theory. In Jon Barwise, editor, *Handbook of Mathematical Logic*, chapter B.1, pages 321–344. North-Holland Publishing Company, 1977.

[8] Paolo A. G. Sivilotti. A Verified Integration of Parallel Programming Paradigms in CC++. In H.J. Siegel, editor, *8th International Parallel Processing Symposium (IPPS 94), Cancun*, pages 44–50. IEEE, April 1994.

[9] Paul A. G. Sivilotti and Peter A. Carlin. A Tutorial for CC++. Technical Report Caltech CS-TR-94-02, Compositional Systems Research Group, Department of Computer Science, California Institute of Technology, Caltech Mail Stop 256-80, Pasadena, California 91125, 1994.

module *Matrix_product5*

...

actions

$$
\begin{array}{l}
add\_a(A,B,C) \triangleq \land\ compatible\_matrix(A,B) \\
\qquad\qquad \land \exists s : ((s[i][j] = (A.1)[i][j] + (B.1)[i][j]) \land (C' = \langle s, A.2, A.3\rangle)) \\
rest\_a(A, r1, r2, c1, c2, C) \triangleq \exists f : \land f[i][j] = (A.1)[i + r1 - 1][j + c1 - 1] \\
\qquad\qquad \land\ C' = \langle f, r2 - r1 + 1, A.3\rangle \\
build\_a(A,B,C,D,M) \triangleq \\
\quad \textbf{let}\ f[i][j] \triangleq \textbf{if}\ i \le A.2\ \textbf{then if}\ j \le A.2\ \textbf{then}\ (A.1)[i][j] \\
\qquad\qquad\qquad\qquad\qquad\qquad \textbf{else}\ (B.1)[i][j - A.2 + 1] \\
\qquad\qquad\qquad\qquad \textbf{else if}\ j \le A.2\ \textbf{then}\ (C.1)[i - A.2 + 1][j] \\
\qquad\qquad\qquad\qquad\qquad\qquad \textbf{else}\ (D.1)[i - A.2 + 1][j - A.2 + 1] \\
\quad \textbf{in}\ \ M' = \langle f, 2 * A.2, A.3\rangle \\
mult\_a(A,B,C) \triangleq \land\ compatible\_matrix(A,B) \\
\qquad \land \lor (A.2 = B.2 = 1) \land (\exists f : \land f[i][j] = ((A.1)[1][1]) * ((B.1)[1][1]) \\
\qquad\qquad\qquad\qquad\qquad \land\ C' = \langle f, 1, A.3\rangle) \\
\qquad \lor \exists A11, A12, A21, A22, B11, B12, B21, B22, \\
\qquad\ M1111, M1221, M1112, M1222, M2111, M2221, M2112, M2222, \\
\qquad\ AA1, AA2, AA3, AA4 : \\
\qquad\quad \circ \land rest\_a(A, 1, (A.2)/2, 1, (A.2)/2, A11) \\
\qquad\qquad \land rest\_a(A, 1, (A.2)/2, (A.2)/2 + 1, A.2, A12) \\
\qquad\qquad \land rest\_a(A, (A.2)/2 + 1, A.2, 1, (A.2)/2, A21) \\
\qquad\qquad \land rest\_a(A, (A.2)/2 + 1, A.2, (A.2)/2 + 1, A.2, A22) \\
\qquad\qquad \land rest\_a(B, 1, (B.2)/2, 1, (B.2)/2, B11) \\
\qquad\qquad \land rest\_a(B, 1, (B.2)/2, (B.2)/2 + 1, B.2, B12) \\
\qquad\qquad \land rest\_a(B, (B.2)/2 + 1, B.2, 1, (B.2)/2, B21) \\
\qquad\qquad \land rest\_a(B, (B.2)/2 + 1, B.2, (B.2)/2 + 1, B.2, B22) \\
\qquad\quad \circ \land (M1111' = mult[A11][B11]) \land (M1221' = mult[A12][B21]) \\
\qquad\qquad \land (M1112' = mult[A11][B12]) \land (M1222' = mult[A12][B22]) \\
\qquad\qquad \land (M2111' = mult[A21][B11]) \land (M2221' = mult[A22][B21]) \\
\qquad\qquad \land (M2112' = mult[A21][B12]) \land (M2222' = mult[A22][B22]) \\
\qquad\quad \circ \land (AA1' = add(M1111, M1221)) \land (AA2' = add(M1112, M1222)) \\
\qquad\qquad \land (AA3' = add(M2111, M2221)) \land (AA4' = add(M2112, M2222)) \\
\qquad\quad \circ\ C' = build(AA1, AA2, AA3, AA4)
\end{array}
$$

Figure 7: *Matrix_product5* module

```
set sqmatrix[E] = {<<f,n,E>> : (f :in: [Natp -> [Natp -> E]])
                              /\ (n :in: Natp) /\ (:E: p :in: Nat : n=2^p)}
```

Figure 8: `sqmatrix[E]` set

Parallel Formulations of Matrix-Vector Multiplication for Matrices with Large Aspect Ratios

John Lloyd (Member IEEE)
Department of Computation
University of Manchester Institute of Science and Technology
Manchester M60 1QD, United Kingdom
jlloyd@ap.co.umist.ac.uk

Abstract

Matrix-vector multiplication is an important component of a large number of parallel algorithms. Over the years, many parallel formulations of matrix-vector multiplication have been proposed. However, they all tend to suffer from the same basic problem: while they may perform well for square matrices, or matrices with moderate aspect ratios, their efficiency deteriorates considerably for matrices with large aspect ratios.

This paper proposes novel techniques for improving the efficiency of matrix-vector multiplication for matrices with large aspect ratios. The basic approach involves partitioning the matrix and vector over a logical array of processors, which is then embedded in the physical architecture. The dimensions of the logical array are chosen so as to minimise the communication overhead associated with the algorithm. Two popular families of parallel architectures are considered: square meshes with wraparound connections, and hypercubes.

Theoretical results show that, for large numbers of processors, and for matrices with large aspect ratios, the new schemes perform significantly better than existing ones.

1 Introduction

Matrix-vector multiplication is an important component of a large number of parallel algorithms. Over the years, many parallel formulations of matrix-vector multiplication have been proposed [1, 2]. However, they all tend to suffer from one basic problem: while they may perform well for square matrices, or matrices with moderate aspect ratios (the ratio of the longest side of the matrix, to the shortest side), their efficiency deteriorates considerably for matrices with large aspect ratios.

This paper proposes novel techniques for improving the efficiency of matrix-vector multiplication for matrices with large aspect ratios. We specifically consider the case where the matrix has few non-zero entries (in other words, the matrix is dense). Sparse matrix-vector multiplication is discussed by Cook and Sadecki [3], and Ferng and others [4]. The basic approach involves partitioning the matrix and vector over a logical array of processors which is then embedded in the physical architecture. The dimensions of the logical array are chosen so as to minimise the communication overhead associated with the algorithm.

Two popular families of parallel architectures are considered: square meshes with wraparound connections, and hypercubes. In particular we consider mesh-connected and hypercube-connected parallel computers that employ store-and-forward routing with single-port communication [2]. The time to deliver an m-word message between two processors that are l connections apart is $t_s + t_w ml$, where t_s is the startup time and t_w is the per-word transfer time (the inverse of the bandwidth).

Theoretical results show that, for large numbers of processors, and for matrices with large aspect ratios, the new schemes perform significantly better than the existing ones.

The remainder of this paper is organised as follows. Section 2 reviews some common parallel formulations of matrix-vector multiplication and obtains expressions for their parallel execution time on mesh and hypercube-connected architectures. Section 3 describes techniques for improving the efficiency of matrix-vector multiplication for matrices with large aspect ratios and compares their theoretical performance with that of the original algorithms. Section 4 contains some conclusions and suggestions for further work.

2 Parallel Formulations of Matrix-Vector Multiplication

In this section we review some common parallel algorithms for multiplying a dense $m \times n$ matrix with an $n \times 1$ vector. At least four distinct parallel formulations of matrix-vector multiplication are possible, depending on the way in which the matrix and vector elements are partitioned among the processors.

2.1 Row Partitioning

One of the simplest parallel formulations of matrix-vector multiplication is based on a rowwise partitioning of the matrix among p processors [2, 5]. Each processor is initially assigned m/p complete rows of the matrix and

1066-6192/96 $5.00 © 1996 IEEE
Proceedings of PDP '96

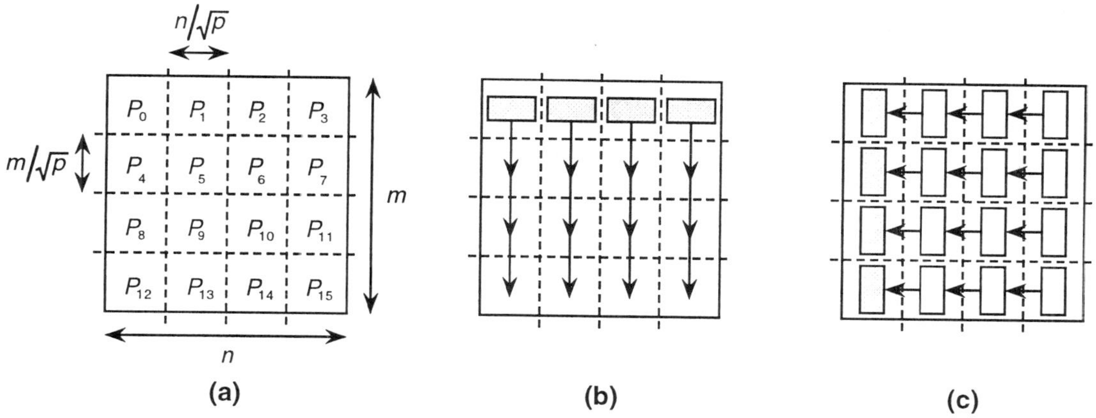

Figure 1 Block-partitioned matrix-vector multiplication with non-uniform distribution of the vector.

n/p elements of the vector. Since the vector has to be multiplied with each row of the matrix, every processor needs the entire vector. To accomplish this, each processor broadcasts its portion of the vector to every other processor in an all-to-all broadcast operation. After this communication step, each processor has the vector available locally and m/p rows of the matrix. Using these, it computes m/p elements of the product vector.

On a mesh, the all-to-all broadcast takes time $2t_s\sqrt{p}+t_w n$ [2]. Assuming that a single multiplication and addition takes t_c units of time to perform, each processor spends $t_c\, mn/p$ units of time in multiplying its m/p rows with the vector. Hence, the parallel execution time for this procedure is

$$T_P = t_c \frac{mn}{p} + 2t_s\sqrt{p} + t_w n \tag{1}$$

On a hypercube, the all-to-all broadcast takes time $t_s \log p + t_w n$ [2]. As the time spent performing computation is still $t_c\, mn/p$, the parallel execution time is

$$T_P = t_c \frac{mn}{p} + t_s \log p + t_w n \tag{2}$$

2.2 Column Partitioning

While the previous scheme involved partitioning the rows of the matrix, an alternative approach involves partitioning the columns among the processors [2, 5]. Each processor is initially assigned n/p complete columns of the matrix and the n/p elements of the vector corresponding to those columns. As the vector is already aligned along the rows of the matrix, no initial communication is required. Each processor multiplies its m partial rows of the matrix with its portion of the vector to obtain m partial product-sums. The partial product-sums are then accumulated using a multinode accumulation operation [2] so that each processor ends up with m/p elements of the product vector.

First, consider the case for the mesh. Assuming that a single multiplication-addition pair takes t_c units of time, each processor spends $t_c\, mn/p$ units of time in multiplying its m partial rows with n/p elements of the vector. Ignoring the time required to perform additions, a multinode accumulation of messages of size m/p among p processors takes time $2t_s\sqrt{p}+t_w m$ [2]. Hence, the parallel execution time for the entire procedure is

$$T_P = t_c \frac{mn}{p} + 2t_s\sqrt{p} + t_w m \tag{3}$$

On a hypercube, the multinode accumulation can be performed in time $t_s \log p + t_w m$ [2]. As the time spent performing computation is unchanged, the parallel execution time is

$$T_P = t_c \frac{mn}{p} + t_s \log p + t_w m \tag{4}$$

When $m < n$, this scheme has a lower communication overhead than the row-partitioned scheme.

2.3 Block Partitioning with Non-Uniform Distribution of the Vector

Another widely-used parallel formulation is based on a two-dimensional partitioning of the matrix [2]. Figure 1 illustrates the data partitioning and communication for this scheme. The $m \times n$ matrix is partitioned among p processors so that each processor receives a block of size $m/\sqrt{p} \times n/\sqrt{p}$ (Figure 1(a)). When the matrix is partitioned in this way it is convenient to regard the processors as being configured as a $\sqrt{p} \times \sqrt{p}$ array. The $n \times 1$ vector is partitioned over the topmost row of the array so that each processor receives $n/\sqrt{p}$ elements. In the first step, the processors in the topmost row broadcast their portions of the vector to all the other processors in their respective columns (Figure 1(b)). After this columnwise one-to-all broadcast, the vector is aligned along the rows of the matrix. Each processor then

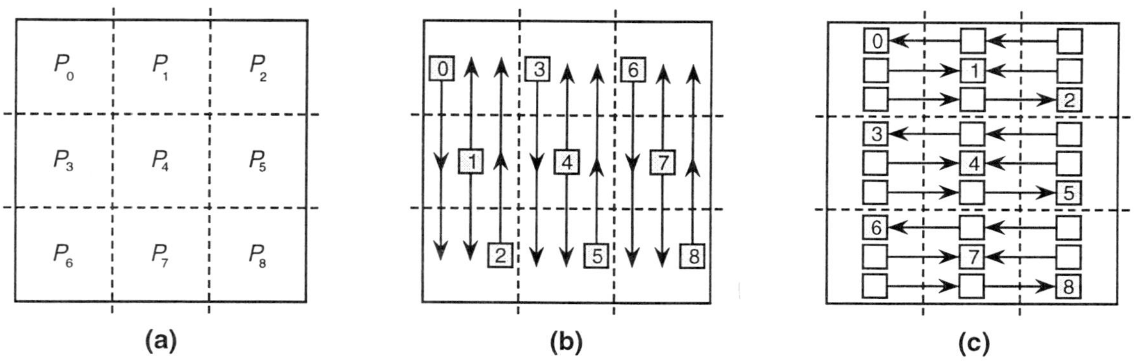

Figure 2 Block-partitioned matrix-vector multiplication with uniform distribution of the vector.

multiplies its $m/\sqrt{p} \times n/\sqrt{p}$ block of the matrix with the portion of the vector received during the first step to produce $m/\sqrt{p}$ partial product-sums. The partial product-sums are then accumulated along each row to obtain the product vector. Hence, the last step of the algorithm is a single-node accumulation [2] of the $m/\sqrt{p}$ values in each row, with the leftmost processor of the row as the destination (Figure 1(c)).

On a $\sqrt{p} \times \sqrt{p}$ mesh of processors, the columnwise one-to-all broadcast can be performed in time $t_s\sqrt{p} + t_w n$ [2]. Assuming that a single multiplication-addition pair takes t_c units of time, each processor spends about $t_c\, mn/p$ time in multiplying its block of the matrix with the portion of the vector received during the first step. Ignoring the time required to perform additions, the final rowwise single-node accumulation can also be performed in time $t_s\sqrt{p} + t_w n$ [2]. Hence, the parallel execution time for the entire procedure is

$$T_P = t_c \frac{mn}{p} + 2t_s\sqrt{p} + t_w(m+n) \tag{5}$$

This algorithm can also be mapped quite easily onto a hypercube using a well-known embedding of a $\sqrt{p} \times \sqrt{p}$ array in a $p = 2^{2k}$ processor hypercube [6]. The processors in each row and column of the array form a $2^k = \sqrt{p}$ processor hypercube. Also, the communication subnetworks corresponding to the different rows and columns are disjoint. So the columnwise one-to-all broadcasts and rowwise single-node accumulations can be implemented using hypercube-based algorithms. The columnwise one-to-all broadcast requires $t_s \log\sqrt{p} + t_w n \log\sqrt{p}/\sqrt{p}$ time to perform [2]. The time spent performing computation is the same as for the mesh. Ignoring the time needed to perform additions, the final rowwise single-node accumulation takes time $t_s \log\sqrt{p} + t_w m \log\sqrt{p}/\sqrt{p}$ [2]. Hence, the overall parallel execution time is

$$T_P = t_c \frac{mn}{p} + t_s \log p + t_w(m+n)\frac{\log p}{2\sqrt{p}} \tag{6}$$

The main advantage of this scheme over the row-partitioned and column-partitioned schemes is that it exploits a greater degree of concurrency and can therefore use more processors to run the same-sized problem faster. For hypercubes with large numbers of processors, the block-partitioned formulation is also faster than either of the other two schemes.

2.4 Block Partitioning with Uniform Distribution of the Vector

For large problem sizes, the simple one-to-all broadcast and single-node accumulation algorithms which are assumed to be used in the previous section become very inefficient. This is because they fail to balance the communication load evenly among the processors. One way of achieving a more balanced communication load is by using pipelined or hybrid communication algorithms [2, 7, 8]. Alternatively, we can distribute the vector among the processors in such a way that the communication load is intrinsically more balanced [1, 5]. Figure 2 shows an example of this type of approach. The $m \times n$ matrix is block-partitioned among p processors such that each processor receives a block of size $m/\sqrt{p} \times n/\sqrt{p}$ (Figure 2(a)). The vector is uniformly partitioned among the processors so that each processor receives n/p vector elements. The portions of the vector are mapped onto the $\sqrt{p} \times \sqrt{p}$ array in a column-major order (Figure 2(b)). Notice that each column of processors collectively contains the vector elements corresponding to the columns of the matrix that reside in it.

In the first step, each processor broadcasts its portion of the vector to the other processors in the same column. This involves performing a columnwise all-to-all broadcast with messages of size n/p (Figure 2(b)). After this communication step, the vector is aligned along the rows of the matrix. Each processor then multiplies its $m/\sqrt{p} \times n/\sqrt{p}$ block of the matrix with the vector elements received during the previous step, to produce $m/\sqrt{p}$ partial product-sums. The partial sums are then be accumulated along each row to obtain the product vector. This is achieved using a rowwise multinode accumulation;

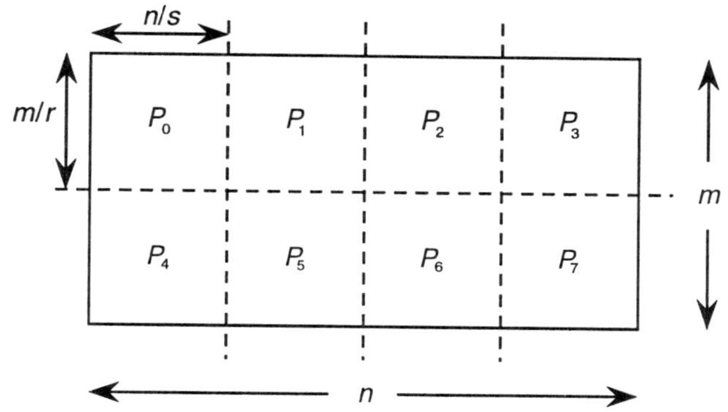

Figure 3 Block partitioning an $m \times n$ matrix over a $r \times s$ array ($r = 2$, $s = 4$).

each processor ends up with m/p elements of the product vector (Figure 2(c)).

On a $\sqrt{p} \times \sqrt{p}$ mesh of processors the columnwise all-to-all broadcast takes time $t_s\sqrt{p} + t_w n/\sqrt{p}$ [2]. Each processor spends approximately $t_c mn/p$ time in multiplying its $m/\sqrt{p} \times n/\sqrt{p}$ block of the matrix with the $n/\sqrt{p}$ vector elements received during the first step. Ignoring the time required to perform additions, the final rowwise multinode accumulation can be performed in $t_s\sqrt{p} + t_w m/\sqrt{p}$ time [2]. Hence, the parallel execution time for the entire procedure is

$$T_P = t_c \frac{mn}{p} + 2t_s\sqrt{p} + t_w \frac{m+n}{\sqrt{p}} \qquad (7)$$

On a p-processor hypercube, the columnwise all-to-all broadcast and rowwise multinode accumulation can be implemented using hypercube-based communication procedures. The columnwise all-to-all broadcast requires $t_s \log\sqrt{p} + t_w n/\sqrt{p}$ time to perform [2]. As, in the case of the mesh, each processor spends approximately $t_c mn/p$ time in multiplying its $m/\sqrt{p} \times n/\sqrt{p}$ block of the matrix with the $n/\sqrt{p}$ vector elements received during the first step. Ignoring the time required to perform additions, the final rowwise multinode accumulation takes $t_s \log\sqrt{p} + t_w m/\sqrt{p}$ time [2]. Hence, the parallel execution time for the entire procedure is

$$T_P = t_c \frac{mn}{p} + t_s \log p + t_w \frac{m+n}{\sqrt{p}} \qquad (8)$$

While this scheme does have a smaller communication overhead than the former block-partitioned scheme, it can only be used when the problem size is sufficiently large compared with the number of processors.

3 Improving Efficiency for Matrices with Large Aspect Ratios

In the previous section, four basic algorithms for performing matrix-vector multiplication were described. For matrices with moderate aspect ratios, the block-partitioned schemes tend to result in smaller communication overheads. However, as the aspect ratio is increased, they become increasingly more inefficient. The source of this inefficiency is the factor $m+n$ that appears in coefficient of the per-word transfer time t_w in Equations (5) to (8); this term increases as the matrix aspect ratio increases. To illustrate just how dramatic this effect can be, consider a matrix with an aspect ratio of 1000. Matrices with this sort of aspect ratio are not uncommon in some types of neural network model [9]. For such a matrix, the term $m+n$ is over 30 times larger than that associated with a square matrix having the same number of elements.

This section describes techniques for improving the efficiency of block-partitioned algorithms for matrices with large aspect ratios. These techniques basically involve block-partitioning the matrix over a rectangular array of processors, and then embedding the rectangular array in a hypercube or mesh.

3.1 Improving Efficiency on a Hypercube

Both of the block-partitioned approaches described in the Section 2 can be extended by partitioning the $m \times n$ matrix over an $r \times s$ array (where $rs = p = 2^{2k}$) such that each processor receives a block of size $m/r \times n/s$. Figure 3 illustrates this for a 2×4 array. The $r \times s$ array is then embedded in a hypercube [6]. The processors in each column of the embedded array correspond to an r-processor hypercube and the processors in each row correspond to an s-processor hypercube.

In the first of the two block-partitioned algorithms, the vector is uniformly distributed over the topmost row of the array so that each processor receives n/s elements. The initial columnwise one-to-all broadcasts take place among r processors with messages of size n/s. The time required for this operation is $(t_s + t_w n/s)\log r$. [2] Assuming that a single multiplication-addition pair takes t_c units of time, each processor spends about $t_c mn/p$ time in multiplying its $m/r \times n/s$ block of the matrix with the n/s vector elements received during the first step. The final rowwise single-node accumulations take place among s processors

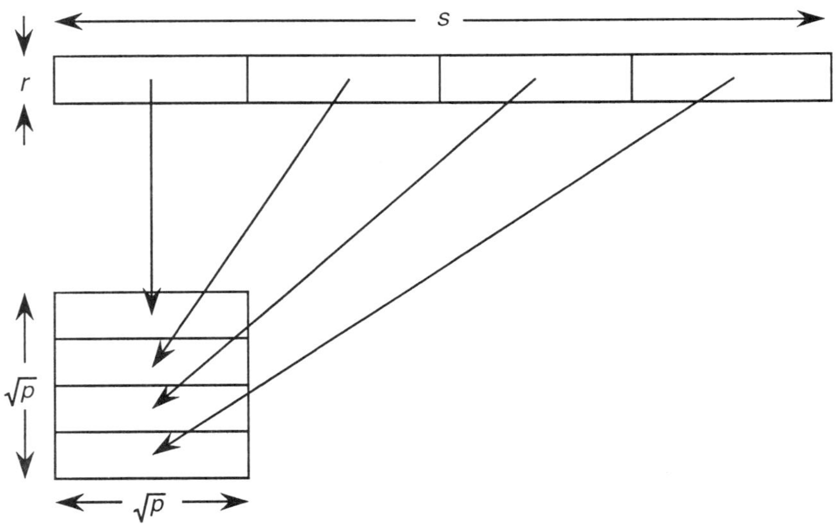

Figure 4 Embedding an $r \times s$ array in a $\sqrt{p} \times \sqrt{p}$ mesh $(s > r)$.

with messages of size m/r. Ignoring the time needed to perform additions, the time required for this operation is $(t_s + t_w m/r)\log s$ [2]. After this communication step, each processor in the leftmost column contains m/r elements of the product vector. The parallel execution time for the overall procedure is

$$T_P = t_c \frac{mn}{p} + t_s \log p + t_w \left(\frac{n \log r}{s} + \frac{m \log s}{r} \right) \quad (9)$$

By applying some elementary calculus we can show that the coefficient of t_w is minimised when

$$\frac{r(\ln r + 1)}{s(\ln s + 1)} = \frac{m}{n} \quad (10)$$

For a matrix aspect ratio of $m/n = 1/1000$ and $p = 4096$, the optimal configuration for the array is 4×1024. This configuration reduces the coefficient of t_w by a factor of over 20 times that associated with a square array configuration.

In the second block-partitioned algorithm, the vector is uniformly partitioned into blocks of size n/p. These blocks are then allocated to the $r \times s$ array in column-major order. The initial columnwise all-to-all broadcasts take place among r processors with messages of size n/p. The time required for this operation is $t_s \log r + t_w n/s$ [2]. Assuming that a single multiplication-addition pair takes t_c units of time, each processor spends about $t_c mn/p$ time in multiplying its $m/r \times n/s$ block of the matrix with the n/s vector elements received during the first step. The final rowwise multinode accumulations take place among s processors with messages of size m/p. Ignoring the time needed to perform additions, the time required for this operation is $t_s \log s + t_w m/r$ [2]. After this communication step, each processor contains m/p elements of the product vector. The parallel execution time for the overall procedure is

$$T_P = t_c \frac{mn}{p} + t_s \log p + t_w \left(\frac{n}{s} + \frac{m}{r} \right) \quad (11)$$

Again, applying some elementary calculus, we can show that the coefficient of t_w is minimised when

$$\frac{r}{s} = \frac{m}{n} \quad (12)$$

In other words, the communication overhead is minimised when the aspect ratio of the array matches the aspect ratio of the matrix. For a matrix aspect ratio of $m/n = 1/1000$ and $p = 4096$, the optimal configuration for the array is 2×2048. This configuration reduces the coefficient of t_w by a factor of over 15 times that associated with a square array configuration.

3.2 Improving Efficiency on a Mesh

Whereas it is relatively easy to embed rectangular arrays in a hypercube, the same does not hold true for the mesh. A number of techniques have been developed for embedding rectangular arrays into square meshes [10] but they are fairly complex and involve irregular patterns of communication. A simpler technique for embedding an $r \times s$ array in a $\sqrt{p} \times \sqrt{p}$ mesh (where $s > r$ and $rs = p = 2^{2k}$) is illustrated in Figure 4. In this scheme, the $r \times s$ array is sliced into blocks of size $r \times \sqrt{p}$ which are then stacked one on top of the other in the $\sqrt{p} \times \sqrt{p}$ mesh. The situation where $r > s$ is dealt with similarly by slicing the $r \times s$ array into blocks of size $\sqrt{p} \times s$, which are then stacked side by side in the $\sqrt{p} \times \sqrt{p}$ mesh.

For the first of the two block-partitioned algorithms, the vector is uniformly distributed over the topmost row of

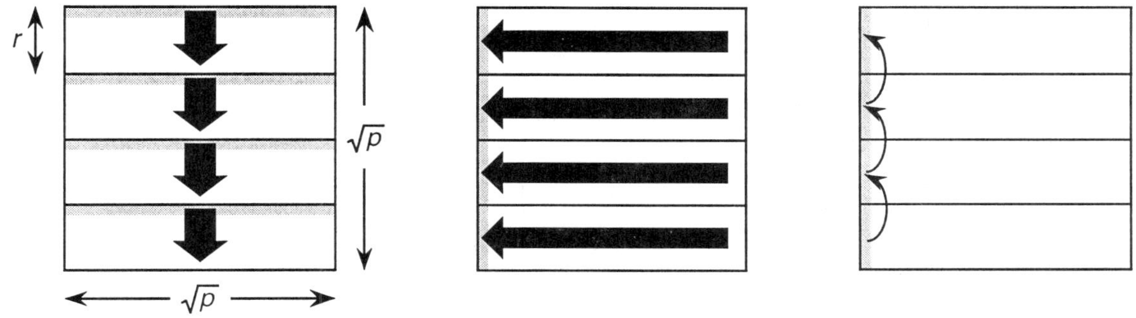

(a) (b) (c)

Figure 5 Block-partitioned matrix-vector multiplication with non-uniform distribution of the vector.

processors in the embedded rectangular array such that each processor receives n/s elements. The initial columnwise one-to-all broadcasts in the embedded array (Figure 5(a)) are non-interfering and can be performed in approximately $r(t_s + t_w n/s)$ time [2]. Assuming that a single multiplication-addition pair takes t_c units of time, each processor spends about $t_c mn/p$ in multiplying its $m/r \times n/s$ block of the matrix with the n/s vector elements received during the first step.

The rowwise single-node accumulations in the embedded array are performed in two phases. In the first phase, rowwise single-node accumulations are performed in each row of the mesh with the processor in the leftmost column as the destination (Figure 5(b)). These accumulations are non-interfering and can be performed in approximately $\sqrt{p}(t_s + t_w m/r)$ time [2]. At the end of this phase, each processor in the leftmost column contains m/r partial product-sums . These partial product-sums are then accumulated over the corresponding processors in each of the stacked blocks, leaving the product vector distributed uniformly over the leftmost column of processors in the topmost block (Figure 5(c)). This communication is implemented by shifting the partial sums in the leftmost column, upwards, r steps at a time. Ignoring the time needed to perform additions, each r-step shift takes $r(t_s + t_w m/r)$ time [2]. Since there are $\sqrt{p}/r - 1$ such shift steps, this phase of the communication takes time $(\sqrt{p} - r)(t_s + t_w m/r)$. The parallel execution time for the entire procedure is

$$T_P = t_c \frac{mn}{p} + 2t_s\sqrt{p} + t_w\left(\frac{nr}{s} + \frac{2m\sqrt{p}}{r} - m\right) \quad (13)$$

By applying some elementary calculus we can show that the coefficient of t_w is minimised when

$$\frac{r}{s} = \left(\frac{m}{n}\right)^{2/3} \quad (14)$$

For a matrix aspect ratio of $m/n = 1/1000$ and $p = 4096$, the optimal aspect ratio of the array is $r/s = 1/100$. Under the assumptions made above, we have two possible choices for the configuration: either 8×512 or 4×1024. In fact, the former of these two configurations gives the lower communication overhead. By embedding an 8×512 array in the mesh using the technique described above, we can reduce the coefficient of t_w by a factor of over 30 times that associated with a square array configuration.

For the second block-partitioned algorithm, the vector is uniformly partitioned into blocks of size n/p. These blocks are then allocated to the embedded rectangular array in column-major order. The initial columnwise all-to-all broadcasts in the embedded array (Figure 6(a)) are non-interfering and can be performed in approximately $2r(t_s + t_w n/p)$ time using shift-based communication [2]. If a single multiplication-addition pair takes t_c units of time, each processor spends about $t_c mn/p$ time in multiplying its $m/r \times n/s$ block of the matrix with the n/s vector elements received during the first step. Each processor now contains m/r partial sums which must be accumulated over the rows of the embedded array to obtain the product vector.

The rowwise multinode accumulations in the embedded array are performed in two phases. In the first phase, rowwise multinode accumulations are performed in each row of the mesh so that each processor ends up with $m/r\sqrt{p}$ partial product-sums (Figure 6(b)). These accumulations are non-interfering and, ignoring the time required to perform additions, can be performed in approximately $t_s\sqrt{p} + t_w m/r$ time [2]. The partial product-sums are then accumulated over the corresponding processors in each of the stacked blocks, so that each processor ends up with m/p elements of the product (Figure 6(c)). This involves shifting the partial sums around the mesh in a vertical direction, r steps at a time. Ignoring the time required to perform additions, each r-step shift takes $r(t_s + t_w m/p)$ time [2]. Since there are $\sqrt{p}/r - 1$ such shift steps, this phase of the communication takes time $(\sqrt{p} - r)(t_s + t_w m/p)$.

The parallel execution time for the entire procedure is

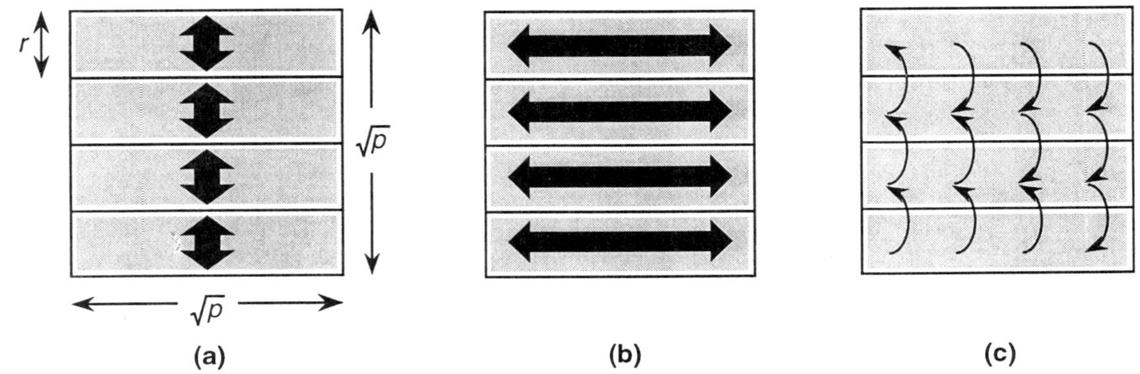

Figure 6 Block-partitioned matrix-vector multiplication with uniform distribution of the vector.

$$T_P = t_c \frac{mn}{p} + t_s\left(2\sqrt{p} + r\right) + t_w\left(\frac{m}{\sqrt{p}} + \frac{2n-m}{s} + \frac{m}{r}\right) \quad (15)$$

By applying some elementary calculus we can show that the coefficient of t_w is minimised when

$$\frac{r}{s} = \frac{m}{2n-m} \quad (16)$$

For a matrix aspect ratio of $m/n = 1/500$ and $p = 4096$, the optimal configuration for the array is approximately 2×2048. By embedding the 2×2048 array in the square array using the technique described above, we can reduce the coefficient of t_w by a factor of over 10 times that associated with a square array configuration.

4 Conclusions

In this paper we have seen that the efficiency of many existing parallel formulations of matrix-vector multiplication deteriorates for matrices with large aspect ratios. Novel techniques have been proposed for improving the efficiency in this situation. The basic approach has involved partitioning the matrix and vector over a logical array of processors which is then embedded in the physical architecture. The dimensions of the logical array are chosen so as to minimise the communication overhead associated with the algorithm. The process of selecting an optimal configuration for the array is non-trivial and depends not only on the aspect ratio of the matrix, but also on the type of communication used in the parallel algorithm.

Theoretical results show that, for large numbers of processors, and for matrices with large aspect ratios, the new schemes perform significantly better than the existing ones. We are in the process of implementing these algorithms on a Parsys SN9500 multicomputer.

5 References

1. Fox, G.C., et al., *Solving Problems on Concurrent Processors*, Vol. 1, 1988, Englewood Cliffs, NJ, Prentice Hall.
2. Kumar, V., et al., *Introduction to Parallel Computing: Design and Analysis of Algorithms*, 1994, Redwood City, CA, Benjamin/Cummings Publishing Company Inc.
3. Cook, R. and J. Sadecki, "Sparse Matrix-Vector Product on Distributed Memory MIMD Architectures," in *Proceedings of the Sixth SIAM Conference on Parallel Processing for Scientific Computing*, 1993, Norfolk, Virginia, SIAM.
4. Ferng, W., et al., "Basic Sparse Matrix Computations on Massively Parallel Computers," 1992, Army High Performance Computing Research Center, 92-084, July 1992.
5. Mathur, K.K. and S.L. Johnsson, "All-to-All Communication on the Connection Machine CM-200," 1993, Center for Research in Computing Technology, Harvard University, Technical Report TR-02-93, January 1993.
6. Saad, Y. and M.H. Schultz, "Topological Properties of Hypercubes," *IEEE Transactions on Computers*, 1988, **37**(7), p. 867-872.
7. Saad, Y. and M.H. Schultz, "Data communication in parallel architectures," *Parallel Computing*, 1989, **11**, p. 131-150.
8. Johnsson, S.L. and C.-T. Ho, "Optimum Broadcasting and Personalized Communication in Hypercubes," *IEEE Transactions on Computers*, 1989, **38**(9), p. 1249-1268.
9. Ienne, P., "Architectures for Neuro-Computers," 1993, École Polytechnique Fédérale de Lausanne, Technical Report 93/21, January 1993.
10. Aleliunas, R. and A.L. Rosenberg, "On Embedding Rectangular Grids in Square Grids," *IEEE Transactions on Computers,* 1982, **31**(9), p. 907-913.

Ab-initio Molecular Dynamics Calculations: A Parallel Implementation of the Car-Parrinello Method

R. Di Felice
INFM - Dipartimento di Fisica, Università di Roma *Tor Vergata*
Via della Ricerca Scientifica 1, I-00133 Roma, Italy

M.L. Mantovani
CICAIA - Università di Modena
Via Campi 213/A, I-41100 Modena, Italy

C. M. Bertoni
INFM - Dipartimento di Fisica, Università di Modena
Via Campi 213/B, I-41100 Modena, Italy

Abstract

We present a parallel implementation of the Car-Parrinello method [1, 2] for first principles molecular dynamics simulations, in the Parallel Virtual Machine (PVM, version 3.3.4) environment on the CRAY-T3D computer. Parallelism is achieved at the Single Program Multiple Data (SPMD) level, dividing among processors the calculations on different columns of a large matrix, containing the electronic wavefunctions of a condensed matter system object of the simulation, written in a plane-wave basis. Fast Fourier Tranforms (FFT's) of these electronic states are the heaviest computations in the program. Communications are avoided in most of the code, except where the columns must be orthogonalized among each other. Even if it is not possible to make parallel the whole code, we have reached a parallel implementation of the most time-consuming part. We get an excellent behaviour of this part, and a satisfactory global behaviour.

1 Introduction

The Car-Parrinello method is a Molecular Dynamics (MD) scheme which can describe the electronic structure in the time-evolution of a system: it can be applied to simulations of condensed matter in its liquid, amorphous [3] and solid [4] states. MD is an alternative to Monte Carlo and other techniques to describe the statistical behavior of systems. It consists of solving the equations of motion of atoms in order to describe their trajectory, and the statistical averages can then be found as time-averages. Classical schemes are based on the calculation of the ionic forces from empirical potentials, which often do not account for many-body interactions and for the correlations existing between the ionic and the electronic subsystems. In the Car-Parrinello scheme, on the contrary, the forces are calculated without imposing any experimental constraints, but from the exact total-energy-functional determined on the basis of the instantaneous electronic configuration. That makes the dynamical simulation much heavier, since one has to store and evolve a larger phase space made up not only with the ionic coordinates, but also with the electronic degrees of freedom, which are the sampled wavefunctions of the occupied states: they are evolved in time on the same footing of the ionic coordinates, through classical equations of motion, but they describe in themselves the quantomechanical nature of the electrons.

The method has been applied to a large variety of systems in the past decade; recently complex systems become of interest for which larger and larger supercells are necessary: the feasibility of *ab-initio* MD simulations for such systems depends on the evolution of the computational means. Enlarging the physical dimension of the simulation cell, *i.e.* the number of atoms that it contains, implies enlarging the number of electronic states to include in the calculation, and this finds a strict limitation in the memory and speed of nowadays computers. Parallel implementations of the original code allow to overcome both these limitations. It is possible to choose different ways for parallelization: none of them gives perfect scaling, in that a lot of sections in the program are implicitly scalar, but it is possible to reach good results.

We shall describe in the next sections the basic algorithm and our parallel implementation, and lately we will show some results as concerning execution-times gain, efficiency and speedup, from some tests made on a sample system.

2 The Method

A detailed description of the method can be found in Ref.'s [1] and [2]. Here we try to focus its practi-

1066-6192/96 $5.00 © 1996 IEEE
Proceedings of PDP '96

cal implementation with main attention to the sections that we have parallelized. We want to describe a condensed matter system made up with nuclei and electrons; we work in the pseudopotential approach [5], so only valence electrons are considered, while the electrons of internal shells form an ion together with their nucleus. The total energy $E = K_e + K_I + E_{e,e} + E_{I,I} + E_{e,I}$ from which ionic forces are derived is a functional of the electronic charge density, on the basis of the Density Functional Theory (DFT) [6], which is written as a sum over the electronic states.

$$\rho_e(\mathbf{r}) = \sum_{\mathbf{k}} w_{\mathbf{k}} \sum_{i=1}^{N} f_{i,\mathbf{k}} \left|\psi_{i,\mathbf{k}}(\mathbf{r})\right|^2 \qquad (1)$$

N is the total number of electronic states, $\mathbf{k}$ indicates some points in the first Brillouin Zone (I-BZ) associated with the simulation supercell, and $w_{\mathbf{k}}$ are the weights of the $\mathbf{k}$-points included in the summation [7]. K_e is the electronic kinetic energy, K_I the ionic kinetic energy; $E_{e,e}$ is the energy coming from the electron-electron interaction, $E_{I,I}$ the one from the ion-ion interaction, and $E_{e,I}$ the one from the electron-ion interaction. In the whole program, the $\psi_{i,\mathbf{k}}(\mathbf{r})$'s are written in a plane-wave basis-set

$$\psi_{i,\mathbf{k}}(\mathbf{r}) = e^{i\mathbf{k}\cdot\mathbf{r}} \sum_{\mathbf{g}} c_{i,\mathbf{k}}(\mathbf{g}) e^{i\mathbf{g}\cdot\mathbf{r}} \qquad (2)$$

where the $\mathbf{g}$'s are reciprocal-space vectors. $c_{i,\mathbf{k}}(\mathbf{g})$ is the Fourier coefficient of the ith electronic state associated to the $\mathbf{g}$ vector and to the $\mathbf{k}$ point. These coefficients are explicitly initialized and updated in the program, not the wavefunctions in $\mathbf{r}$-space. So, in order to calculate the electronic charge density from equation (1) at each step of the dynamical evolution, FFT's of these $\mathbf{g}$-functions are to be performed for each index i. After building up the $\rho_e(\mathbf{r})$, the total potential $V[\rho_e(\mathbf{r})]$ and the total energy $E[\rho_e(\mathbf{r})]$ are calculated, and then the ionic forces $\nabla_{\mathbf{R}_I} E$. As the electronic degrees of freedom have to be dynamically evolved on the same footing of the ionic ones, the forces on the part of the classical phase space describing electrons have to be calculated, too. They are given by the formula:

$$\begin{aligned} \mu \ddot{c}_{i,\mathbf{k}}(\mathbf{g}) &= -\frac{1}{2} \frac{\partial E\left[\{\mathbf{R}_I\}, \left\{c_{i,\mathbf{k}}(\mathbf{g})\right\}\right]}{\partial c^*_{i,\mathbf{k}}(\mathbf{g})} + o.\ c. \\ &= -\hat{H} c^*_{i,\mathbf{k}}(\mathbf{g}) + o.\ c. \end{aligned} \qquad (3)$$

μ is the *mass* associated with the evolution of the electronic states in the enlarged phase space, chosen in such a way that the combined dynamics works well, *i.e.* the system does not present a drift from the instantaneous minimum total energy functional. The calculation of the electronic forces is a hard step and implies, for each value of i, a backward and a forward FFT. The evaluation of the charge density and of the electronic forces together take the largest portion of the computation. Eq. (3) includes orthonormality constraints (*o. c.*), which have to be imposed on the $c_{i,\mathbf{k}}(\mathbf{g})$ at each time-step: the ith state has to be orthogonal to all the other j^{th} states. After that, ionic and electronic equations of motions are solved and the program goes to the following time-step. In Tab. 1 the implemented scheme of the *ab-initio* MD is illustrated. We want to point out that, if we use the special symmetry which can be recovered if the single Γ point in the I-BZ is used in the simulation, the number of FFT's necessary for the transformation of the wavefunctions is not equal to the number of states, but to the half of this number. In this condition, one can choose real wavefunctions $\psi_{i,\mathbf{k}}(\mathbf{r})$, having the following symmetry for their Fourier components:

$$c^*_{i,\mathbf{k}}(\mathbf{g}) = c_{i,\mathbf{k}}(-\mathbf{g}) \qquad (4)$$

initial guess for $c^*_{i,\mathbf{k}}(\mathbf{g})$ for equation (2)
calculation of $\rho_e(\mathbf{r})$ according to equation (1) $N/2$ FFT's: $c_{i,\mathbf{k}}(\mathbf{g}) \longrightarrow \psi_{i,\mathbf{k}}(\mathbf{r})$
calculation of the potential $V[\rho_e(\mathbf{r})]$ (1 FFT) and of the ionic forces $\nabla_{\mathbf{R}_I} E$
electronic forces ($2\times N/2$ FFT's) $N/2$ FFT's: $c_{i,\mathbf{k}}(\mathbf{g}) \longrightarrow \psi_{i,\mathbf{k}}(\mathbf{r})$ $V(\mathbf{r})\psi_{i,\mathbf{k}}(\mathbf{r})$ $N/2$ FFT's: $V(\mathbf{r})\psi_{i,\mathbf{k}}(\mathbf{r}) \longrightarrow \left[V \cdot c_{i,\mathbf{k}}\right](\mathbf{g})$
integration of the electronic equations of motion (3)
orthonormalization $\sum_{\mathbf{g}} c^*_{i,\mathbf{k}}(\mathbf{g}) c_{j,\mathbf{k}}(\mathbf{g}) = \delta_{i,j}$
integration of the ionic equations of motion $M_I \ddot{\mathbf{R}}_I = -\nabla_{\mathbf{R}_I} E$
next time-step $t + \Delta t$ or statistical averages

Table 1: Scheme of an *ab-initio* MD run. N is the number of electronic states accounted for.

Eq. (4) allows to store the $c_{i,\mathbf{k}}$ on only half the necessary **g**-space (saving memory occupation) and to perform an FFT for two states simultaneously (saving computation time). In order to keep this feature in the parallel implementation, we shall always work with an even number of states on each processor.

3 Parallel implementation: electronic states are divided among processors

We have modified the described algorithm in such a way that a single processor makes FFT calculations and other updating calculations only on a certain number *n_per_proc* = *N/N$PES* of states, where N is the total number of electronic states and *N$PES* is the number of available processors.

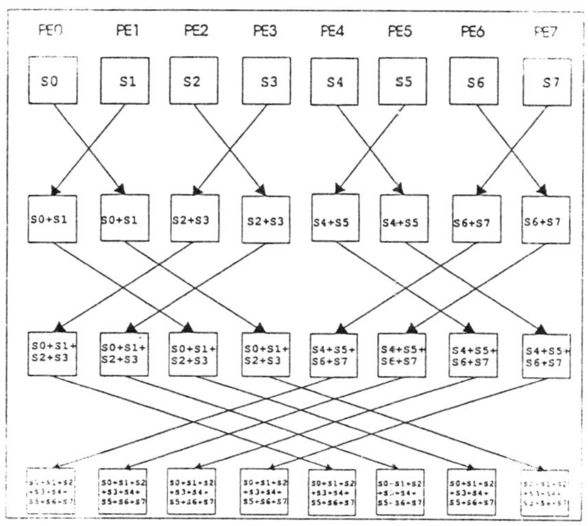

Fig. 1: Schematic representation of the algorithm written to perform the total sum over all the processors of a very large array on a grid. It is an iterative procedure in which each processor sends and receives a partial sum updated at each step, and ends when all processors have got the total sum. This is an example on eight processing units, but it works for any number of CPU's being a power of 2. s# in the boxes of the table indicates the partial sum calculated by processor #. The first row enumerates the CPU's and the others contain the operations performed by a given CPU.

So, when calculating the charge density (eq. (1)), each processor, after evaluating the FFT's of its states, makes a partial sum

$$\sum_{\mathbf{k}} w_{\mathbf{k}} \sum_{i=1}^{n\_per\_proc} f_{i,\mathbf{k}} \left|\psi_{i,\mathbf{k}}(\mathbf{r})\right|^2$$

and then communications among all processors follow to update the total $\rho_e(\mathbf{r})$ together with two real variables containing the total electronic kinetic energy and

# of CPU's	Parallel time(s)	Orthonormalization time(s)	Total time(s)
1	1170.38	30.23	1238.86
2	585.53	30.69	653.07
4	293.31	20.59	350.71
8	147.36	13.76	197.91
16	74.57	10.27	121.63
32	38.35	9.40	84.57
64	20.40	8.95	66.24

Table 2: Execution times of different code sections varying the number of working CPU's. The Total time is the job total time minus the time of the initialization and writing operations made once for each job. The Parallel time comprehends the calculation of the electronic charge density and of the forces on the electronic degrees of freedom. The Orthonormalization time is the time spent in the orthonormalization procedure.

the total number of electrons calculated as a **g**-space sum $\sum_{\mathbf{k}} w_{\mathbf{k}} \sum_{i,\mathbf{g}} f_{i,\mathbf{k}} \left|c_{i,\mathbf{k}}(\mathbf{g})\right|^2$. At the end all processors contain the right charge density matrix on a grid in real space and a single FFT of this matrix follow in order to build up the potential. We sketch in Fig. 1 a diagram of the algorithm chosen for communication, which works for a number of processors being a power of 2.

After this section the run of the code goes on scalarly until the computation of the electronic forces has to be performed. A subroutine dedicated to such a task was called for each electronic state i in the original version. In our present version each processing unit has to call it just *n_per_proc* times and there is no need for communicating an updated $c_{i,\mathbf{k}}(\mathbf{g})$ to all CPU's. In principle, this part of the whole calculation should have a perfectly linear scaling, and we will show in the next section that this is the case.

The only problem is the existence of orthonormality constraints in the evolution of the electronic subsystem. Furthermore, there exist in the code two orthonormalization algorithms: one that ensures the fulfilling of the orthonormality constraints at each dynamical step, and the other that does not take into account the dynamics, and consequently is valid only when the Car-Parrinello method is applied in its minimization approach [2]. Up to now we have only implemented the second one in a parallel version. In the scalar (or vectorial) execution the algorithm has the following structure: within the loop (do i=1,N) over the electronic states, at the ith step the ith state is orthogonalized *simultaneously* to all the jth states with j = 1,i-1 (through matrix-vector multiplication library subroutines), and then normalized. In the parallel version this algorithm is to be modified substantially, in that a single processor never stores the whole matrix of *all* the states. Our implementation is the following: within the loop over the number of active processing units (do $io = 1, N\$PES$), at the io^{th} step the io^{th} CPU orthonormalizes the states living on it with the previously described algorithm. Then it sends its updated states to all the other jo^{th} ($jo = io+1$, $N\$PES$) CPU's, which orthonormalize the states living on them *simultaneoulsy* to all the received states. In summary, the orthonormalization of the states stored on processor *io* begins at the first iteration and ends at iteration *io*. The scheme of the algorithm is shown in Fig. 2.

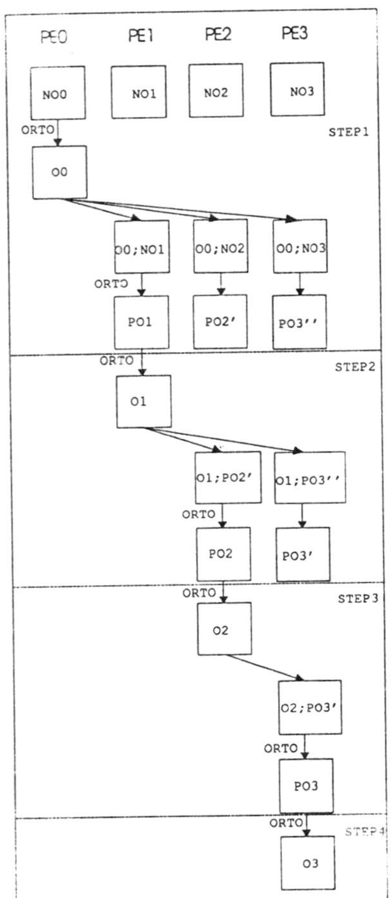

Fig. 2: Orthonormalization algorithm in our parallel implementation. This is an example on 4 CPU's, but it works for any number of processors (power of 2). NO# is the matrix of the Non-Orthonormalized states on processor #. PO# is the matrix of the Partially-Orthonormalized states on processor #. O# is the matrix of the Orthonormalized states on processor #. The *primes* indicate intermediate partial orthonormalizations.

4 Results

We present now some preliminary results concerning execution times, obtained from runs of 10 iterations (on the CRAY-T3D parallel computer) on a test system made up with 64 Si atoms in a simple cubic supercell, in the minimization approach. The physical results are correct, compared with other scalar computations, but we will not care about them in this paper. In Tab. 2 we show total CPU time, the time spent in the parallel parts (calculation of the charge density + calculation of the forces on the electronic degrees of freedom), and the time spent in the orthonormalization subroutine. The total CPU time is the actual total execution time minus the initialization time and the time used in writing the output files: these operations are performed once for each job, independent on the number of steps, so their times become meaningless in the interesting runs which comprehend thousands of iterations. In Tab. 3 the efficiency and speedup for the previously mentioned excution times are reported. The graphical representations of the quantities in Tab. 2 and in Tab. 3 are shown in Fig. 3, Fig. 4 and Fig. 5. The speedup and the efficiency on M working processors are defined as:

$$Speedup(M) = CPU(1)/CPU(M)$$

$$Efficiency(M) = Speedup(M)/M$$

As it was argued, the parts that have been implemented in a parallel way present a good-scaling behaviour. Their speedup increases linearly with the number of processors up to 32 processors, and the value at 64 processors is 57. Their efficiency is almost constant, approximately 1.

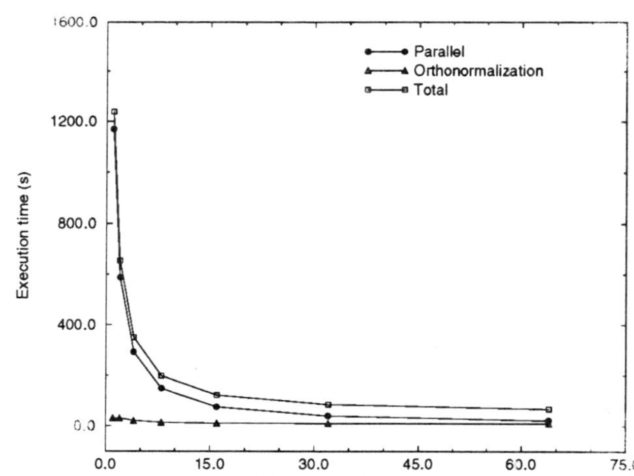

Fig. 3: Plots of the execution times reported in Tab. 2. It is possible to note that the Total time is only slightly higher than the time spent in the parallel calculations, that justifies our present implementation.

#	1	2	4	8	16	32	64
PE PS	1.00 1.00	1.00 2.00	1.00 3.99	0.99 7.94	0.98 15.70	0.95 30.52	0.90 57.37
OE OS	1.00 1.00	0.49 0.99	0.37 1.47	0.27 2.20	0.18 2.94	0.10 3.22	0.05 3.38
TE TS	1.00 1.00	0.95 1.90	0.88 3.53	0.78 6.26	0.64 10.19	0.46 14.65	0.29 18.70

Table 3: Efficiency and speedup, as defined in the text, for the times reported in Tab. 2. PE is the efficiency for the parallel execution; OE for the orthonormalization procedure; TE for the total execution. Analogous abbreviations are used for the speedup (PS, OS, TS). # is the number of active processors.

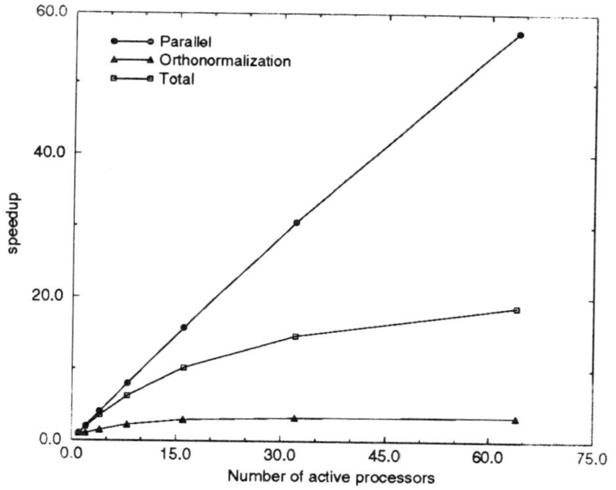

Fig. 4: Plots of the speedup for the various execution times reported in Tab. IV.

The total CPU time does not present such a satisfactory behaviour, because it contains the bias of the different scalar operations. The efficiency decreases to 50% when using 32 processors. The orthonormalization subroutine shows a slight decrease in the execution time with increasing the number of CPU's used, as we could expect because of the high number of communications in the procedure. The most interesting feature to note in Fig. 3 is that actually the time spent in the calculations that we have parallelized is the highest fraction of the total computation time.

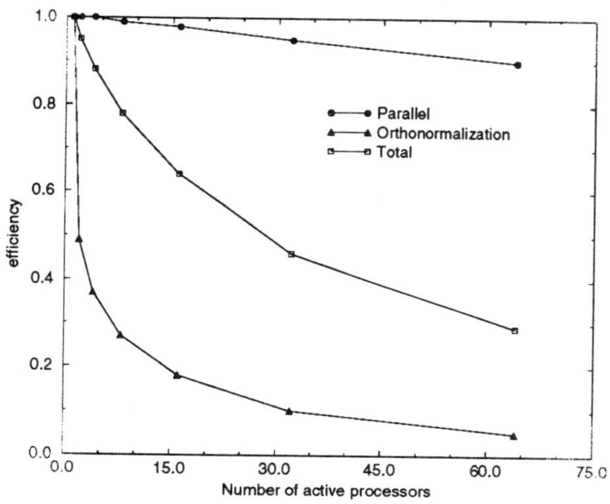

Fig. 5: Plots of the efficiency for the various execution times reported in Tab. IV.

5 Future developments

In the immediate future, our main goal is to go beyond PVM using the hardware facilities of the CRAY-T3D parallel paradigm (*work sharing*). Before doing that, some other problems are to be solved before having a program really able to perform MD runs which give meaningful results. We remember that in our actual parallel implementation the execution gives exact results for the procedure of minimizing the total energy only with respect to the electronic wavefunctions, *i.e.* it is possible to calculate the total energy of a system in which the ionic configuration is fixed. So we have in mind the following further steps:

- adjustment of the loops in which arrays for the ionic forces are calculated, in order to have the correct description of the ionic motion and consequently correct results for the combined minimization of the ionic and electronic degrees of freedom (first order equations of motion);
- parallel implementation of the orthonormalization subroutine which solves the dynamical constraints [8], in order to perform true dynamical runs, with second order equations of motion, and obtain the trajectory of a system and analyze its statistical behaviour;
- some other technicalities to improve speed, such as the use of Cray-optimized FFT subroutines and a real decrease in memory occupation of the arrays which depend on the electronic states (up to now they are still dimensioned to the total number of states, even if the calculations are divided among processors).

6 Conclusions

We have presented a parallel implementation of the Car-Parrinello method for *ab-initio* Molecular Dynamics on the CRAY-T3D computer system. We have shown that the possibility of obtaining a perfectly linear scaling of the total execution time is affected from a bias due to the precence of code sections which are implicitly scalar. Nonetheless one can get very good results for the parallel parts. We can say that within our parallelization scheme it is worth while to increase the number of processors up to 32: for higher numbers the gain is not substantial. Anyway, this allows to increase the physical dimension of the system to be studied, opening the way to investigation of systems that cannot be presently stored on even the largest and most powerful computers.

Acknowledgements.

We thank CINECA (Inter-Univesity Computer Centre of the North-East Italy) for allowing us to use the CRAY-T3D available there under a scientific grant.

References

[1] R. Car and M. Parrinello, from *"Simple Molecular Systems at Very High Density"*, edited by A. Polian, P. Lubeyre, and N. Boccara, Plenum Publishing Corporation (1989).

[2] R. Car and M. Parrinello, *Phys. Rev. Lett.* **55**, 2471 (1985).

[3] F. Finocchi, G. Galli, M. Parrinello, and C.M.Bertoni, *Phys. Rev. Letters* **68**, 4044 (1992).

[4] R. Di Felice, A.I. Shkrebtii, F. Finocchi, C.M. Bertoni, and G. Onida, *Journal of Electron Spectroscopy* **64/65**, 697 (1993).

[5] J.C. Phillips and L. Kleinman, *Phys. Rev. 116*, 287 (1959); W.E. Pickett, *Comp. Phys. Rep. 9*, 115 (1989).

[6] P. Hohemberg and W. Kohn, *Phys. Rev.* **136**, B864 (1964); W. Kohn and L.J. Sham, *Phys. Rev.* **140**, A1133 (1965); W. Kohn and P. Vashista, from *"Theory of the Inhomogeneous Electron Gas"*, edited by S. Lundqvist and N.H. March, Plenum Press, New York (1983).

[7] A. Baldereschi, *Phys. Rev. B* **7**, 5212 (1973); D.J. Chadi and M.L. Cohen, *Phys. Rev B* **8**,5747 (1973); H.J. Monkhorst and J.D. Pack, *Phys. Rev. B* **13**, 5188 (1976).

[8] J.P. Ryckaert, G. Ciccotti, and H.J.C. Berendsen, *J. Comp. Phys.* **23**, 327 (1977).

A Parallel Processing System for Simulations of Vortex Blob Interactions

**G. Braschi, *G. Danese, *I. De Lotto, *D. Dotti, **M. Gallati, *F. Leporati, *M. Mazzoleni
*Dip. Informatica e Sistemistica - **Dip. Ingegneria Idraulica e Ambientale
Università degli Studi di Pavia - Italia - Via Ferrata, 1 - 27100 Pavia
Tel. +39/382/505350 - Fax +39/382/505373 - e-mail gianni@ipvvis.unipv.it

Abstract

The vortex method in the simulation of 2D incompressible flows with complex interacting circulations is very attractive if compared with other nowadays widespread methods. However, the vortex method is computationally very expensive and suggests the adoption of suitably powerful computing units.

Our group analysed some parallelisation techniques of the algorithm, in order to obtain the best performances on a dedicated parallel architecture. A promising architecture was simulated in a PVM (Parallel Virtual Machine) environment to identify correctness and efficiency of the selected choices. The implementation of the most promising one on a Special Purpose Computer (SPC) based on i860 Risc Intel units is in progress.

The porting of the parallelised algorithm into the SPC will result into a low-cost system, completely available to the user, with expected performances comparable to those of modern supercomputers.

Introduction

In the field of fluid mechanics, many flow fields can be conveniently analysed by means of models based on the definition of vorticity, but at expense of high computational load, since deterministic and random interactions have to be computed in order to simulate the continuously changing patterns of velocity in the bulk of the fluid. In effect, a wide portion of fluid flow must be simulated, for a time long enough to extract, from the analysis, meaningful average values for the most important parameters.

Simulation runs and experimental sessions must be repeatedly interleaved, with the purpose of optimising the simulation algorithm, both as for its adherence to the reality and for the processing efficiency. This is a typical situation where easy availability of a powerful computing unit takes on the maximum importance for achieving a satisfactory operating efficiency.

While in one of the Departments of our University this problem was faced with classical simulation tools, in another Department experience was gained in the development of a parallel Special Purpose Computer (SPC), targeted to the simulation of systems of interacting particles; thus it was only a matter of occasional meetings between neighbours to verify the convenience of cooperation that could provide an efficient work tool for one group, while widening the experience of the other. It turned out that the processing element, based on the Intel i860 Risc unit, could be retained without major changes, while the architecture of the connections could be easily adapted in order to better meet the requirements of the new problem; thus, a powerful processing tool, with expected performances comparable to those of a two-unit Cray YMP C90, will be made easily available to the experimenters.

This paper first describes the flow dynamics problem and the adopted simulation algorithm; then the connection architecture best fitted to the algorithm is identified, experimenting parallelised versions of the algorithm in the PVM (Parallel Virtual Machine) environment. The expected simulation efficiency is evaluated, comparing the expected processing time to those already obtained with a workstation and obtainable with other wide-spread number crunching machines. At last some conclusions are drawn.

The physical problem

The 2D equations of an incompressible viscous flow may be written in term of velocity and vorticity in cartesian coordinates x,y [1]:

$$\mathrm{div}\mathbf{V} = 0 \qquad (1) \qquad\qquad \frac{D\omega}{Dt} = \nu \,\mathrm{div}\,\mathrm{grad}\,\omega \qquad (2)$$

with the proper boundary conditions.

In these equations $\mathbf{V}=[u,v]$ is the velocity vector, $\omega\mathbf{k} = (\partial v/\partial x - \partial u/\partial y)\mathbf{k}$ is the vorticity vector (where **k** is the unit vector perpendicular to the x-y plane) and ν is the kinematic viscosity.

The incompressibility condition is implicitly taken into account by the definition of the stream function ψ related to the velocity and vorticity by:

$$\mathbf{V} = -\mathrm{rot}\,(\psi\,\mathbf{k}) \quad (3a) \qquad\qquad \nabla^2 y = -\,\omega \quad (3b)$$

The differential system made up of equations (2) and (3b), with the proper boundary conditions, when numerically integrated over an eulerian mesh, gives the value of velocity and vorticity in each point of the computational domain.

The solution of equation (3b), in an infinite domain, may be written as [2]:

$$\psi(z,t) = -\frac{1}{2\pi}\int \ln|\mathbf{z}-\mathbf{z}'|\,\omega(\mathbf{z}',t)\,d\mathbf{z}' \quad (4)$$

where $z=(x,y)$ and $dz=dxdy$.

The velocity field may then be calculated by derivation, according to equation (3a) :

$$V(z,t) = \frac{\mathbf{k}}{2\pi}\times\int\frac{\mathbf{z}-\mathbf{z}'}{|\mathbf{z}-\mathbf{z}'|^2}\,\omega(\mathbf{z}',t)\,d\mathbf{z}' \quad (5)$$

Equation (5) (well-known in electrodynamics as Biot-Savart law), defines the relation between velocity and vorticity and, together with equation (2), completely describes the velocity field in an infinite domain. Following the classical method, at each time-step the equation of convection and diffusion of vorticity (2) is splitted into two parts:

$$\left(\frac{\partial\omega}{\partial t}\right)_c = -\mathbf{V}\cdot\text{grad}\,\omega \quad (6)$$

$$\left(\frac{\partial\omega}{\partial t}\right)_d = \nu\,\text{div grad}\,\omega \quad (7)$$

which describe separately the convection and the diffusion effects. A corresponding decomposition is necessary in the boundary conditions.

Equation (6) may be written:

$$\frac{D\omega}{Dt} = 0 \quad (6a)$$

which states the invariability of the vorticity of each particle of the fluid during the motion. The boundary conditions for this equation are relevant only on the velocity components perpendicular to the borders of the computational domain.

Equation (6), the well-known heat equation, is consistent with the no slip boundary condition over solid walls.

Simulation of the convective effect

The solution of the eulerian problem defined by equations (6a) and (5) over an infinite domain consists in the calculation, from an initial situation, of the trajectories of the "vortex particles" moving with a velocity given by equation (5) and conveying their vorticity unaltered. In particular, the initial continuous distribution of vorticity is discretized using a finite number of "elementary" vortices, moving without distortion according to the velocity of their center.

The vorticity may be considered concentrated in a geometrical point (where it reaches an infinite value). However, for computational reasons, it is better to avoid singularities in the center of the vortex and it is preferable to consider such particles as "vortex blobs", with a vorticity simmetrically distributed around the center, over an area scaling with a parameter ε (the "vortex radius") and satisfying the following condition (considering the origin of the coordinate system in the center of the vortex):

$$\omega(r) = \Gamma f_\varepsilon(r) \quad (8)$$

where Γ is the circulation associated with the vortex, given by the Stokes theorem:

$$\Gamma = 2\pi\int r\omega(r)\,dr \quad (9)$$

This equation is integrated where $|\omega|$ is not null.

The "core function" $f_\varepsilon(r)$ defines the distribution of vorticity around the center of the vortex and has the same meaning of the shape function in the finite element method. Using this definition the distribution of vorticity $\omega(z,t)$ may be discretized using N vortices:

$$\omega(z,t) = \sum_{j=1}^{N}\Gamma_j f_\varepsilon(\mathbf{z}-\mathbf{z}_j(t)) \quad (10)$$

This expression, introduced in equation (5), gives the velocity induced in point $\mathbf{z}$ by the N vortices [3]:

$$\mathbf{V}(z,t) = \sum_{j=1}^{N}\Gamma_j\,\mathbf{K}(\mathbf{z}-\mathbf{z}_j(t)) \quad (11a)$$

$$\mathbf{K}(z) = \frac{k}{2\pi}\times\frac{\mathbf{z}}{|\mathbf{z}|^2}\,g(|z|) \quad (11b)$$

$$g(r) = 2\pi\int_0^r s\,f_\varepsilon(s)\,ds \quad (11c)$$

These expressions give the velocity of the vortex located in the point $\mathbf{z}_i$, at the time t, induced by the velocity field generated by all the other vortices:

$$\mathbf{V}_i(t) = \sum_{j=1}^{N}\Gamma_j\,\mathbf{K}(\mathbf{z}_i-\mathbf{z}_j(t)) \quad (12)$$

A potential field $\mathbf{V}_{0i}$ may be added to this value, in order to take into account the boundary conditions. The value of g(r) depends upon the core function used. If the vortices are considered as point vortices, the core vorticity is given by the Dirac function: $f_\varepsilon(r)=\delta(r)/2\pi$ so as $g(r)=1$ and the function $\mathbf{K}$ has a singularity in the origin. The choice of suitable core functions allows to eliminate the singularity; if we assume [3]:

$$f_\varepsilon(r) = \frac{\varepsilon^2}{\pi\left(r^2 + \varepsilon^2\right)^2} \quad (13)$$

the singularity is avoided by modifying the denominator in the origin:

$$K_\varepsilon(z) = \frac{k}{2\pi} \times \frac{z}{|z|^2 + \varepsilon^2} \quad (14)$$

Hald (1987) et al. demonstrated that as N tends to infinity, so as to reduce the distance between the vortices, and ε approaches zero, but in such a way to allow the vortices to overlap, the solution obtained with the vortex method tends to the exact solution of the Euler equations. It is possible to demonstrate that the simmetry of the core function implies a second order accuracy and that, with a suitable choice, the accuracy may reach higher orders [4] .

Simulation of the diffusive effect

The methods used by different authors in order to simulate the diffusive effect caused by the viscosity in a Lagrangian calculation are of two kinds.

The methods based on vortex "age" either reduce its circulation [5] or increase its radius [6] proportionally to its age. It has been demonstrated, however, that these techniques produce a result not converging to the solution of equation (2).

The method of "random-vortex", proposed by Chorin [7], simulates the diffusive effect in a statistical way, by adding an appropriate gaussian noise to the convective motion. The theoric basis of this technique [8] lies in the observation that the Green function of equation (7) is identical to the probability density function of a gaussian random variable η characterized by null mean and standard deviation $\sqrt{2\nu\, dt}$.

According with the algorithm based on this observation, a random translation 2νdtη (where $\eta=[\eta_x,\eta_y]$ represents a couple of random numbers, extracted from a gaussian distribution with zero mean and unit variance) is added to the convective displacement of each vortex.

Time integration

In order to displace the i-th vortex in the time interval dt, the Adam-Bashforth formula is used:

$$z_i^{n+1} = z_i^n + dt\,(3V_i^n - V_i^{n-1})/2 + h_i \sqrt{2\nu\, dt} \quad (15)$$

This scheme combines the second order precision with computational economy, since it requires, compared with first order scheme, only the storage of the velocity field at two consecutive instants.

The particular problem considered: 2D interaction of a uniform stream with circular shaped obstacles, at high Reynolds number

The boundaries of the solid obstacles force to zero the flow velocity: as a consequence, a high velocity gradient region (boundary layer) takes place between the free stream and the solid surface (the higher the velocity, the thinner the layer).

The Reynolds number Re is the parameter governing the phenomenon:

$$Re = \frac{VD}{\nu} \quad (16)$$

where:

V is the stream velocity;

D the diameter of the obstacle;

ν the kinematic viscosity of the fluid.

If Re is higher than a critical value (supercritical condition) the boundary layer separates from the solid wall in the rear part of the cylinder, generating a wake characterized by the periodic detaching of turbulent circulations.

The unknown position of the separation point affects the characteristics of the wake and hence the characteristics of the whole flow field.

It is thus necessary that the calculation accurately simulates the flow dynamics in the region where the separation occurs.

From the engineering point of view, it is necessary to compute the pressure distribution over the obstacles surface, its characteristic fluctuation (Strouhal number) and its integrals in the flow direction and normal to it (drag and lift forces).

When the obstacles are more then one, it is necessary to take into account their interaction, i.e. the effects of the mutual interference, which depend upon the reciprocal distance and the alignment with the stream direction: an example of what happens is showed by Fig.1.

Wind-engineering problems usually deal with the impact of the stream on several neighbouring structures, and the flow field is strongly influenced by their reciprocal interferences.

The vortex method seems suitable for the simulation of this flow field where the vorticity born at the solid surface moves far away from its points of origin.

Simulation of the vortex method

We execute a software simulation of the behaviour of the vortices generated by the interaction of a uniform stream with one cylindric obstacle: each vortex is characterized by its coordinates, velocity components, age and power. Fig. 2 includes a flow-chart showing the phases of the simulation:

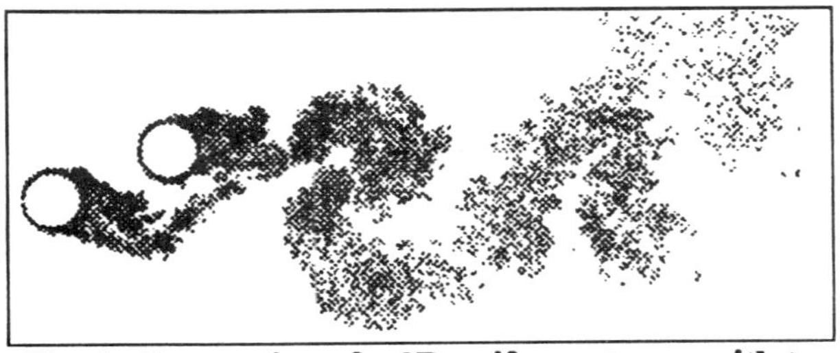

Fig. 1 - Interaction of a 2D uniform stream with two cylindric obstacles

- an input phase defining the geometric parameters of the simulated system and the vortex generation points on the surface of the cylindric obstacle;
- a preliminary phase with the inizialization of the global variables with absolute values or those coming from the last interrupted simulation;
- a vortex loop (repeated with a user-defined period dt) consisting of the following steps:
  a) the vorticity produced at the solid boundaries is computed and discretized in a number of elementary vortices to be added to the others, already present (vortex generation);
  b) the velocity of each vortex is computed adding the contribution of each other vortex (convective velocity evaluation);
  c) the effect of the convective velocity on each vortex is considered (convective velocity evaluation);
  d) a random displacement is added to consider the diffusive effect (diffusive velocity evaluation and vortex displacement);
  e) some statistical calculations are made on the iteration data, for the successive analysis;
  f) a "coalescing phase" is made to reduce the number of the existent vortices in the simulated space (coalescence);
- a final phase to store the resulting data for the successive analysis.

The most heaviest computationally speaking phase is the vortex loop. Fig. 3 shows the different sub-phases of the loop with their dependence from the number N of vortices; the most onerous is the calculation of the convective component of the velocity of each vortex because it involves the evaluation of interaction between each vortex and all the others.

Also the "coalescing phase", which will be explained below, depends on N^2 but it is executed periodically (i. e. every 10 iterations) and consists of few instructions, so its computational weight is not too high.

In this case, the computational load grows with the square of the number of the vortices in the system as showed by (17):

$$c * \sum_{1}^{k_{max}} \left(k * N_g\right)^2 \cong \frac{c * k^3{}_{max} * N_g^2}{3} \quad (17)$$

where:
k = iteration index [1...k_{max}=4000];
c = number of operations (on single precision data) for each iteration;
N_g = number of vortices generated in each iteration;

To avoid a quick saturation of the available memory, the simulation program executes the coalescence by which it reduces the number of existent vortices: the space is subdivided in bands within which the vortices, whose distance is less than a prefixed value, are replaced with a single term where the new velocity and coordinates are the average of the original ones and the new power is the sum of the original powers.

The prefixed value of the distance depends on the considered band of the vortices.

As an example a program generates 72 vortices per iteration and executes 4000 loops, but at the end of the execution the system has only 40000 vortices with a significant reduction in the use of memory and in computing time.

Also referring to Fig. 2-3, the time due for a single iteration can be expressed by :

$$N_g * t_{vb} + N^2 * t_{vc} + N * t_{vd} + N * t_{vm} + N * t_s + N^2 t_{co} \quad (18)$$

where:
t_{vb} = time for generation of one vortex;
t_{vm} = time for the displacement of one vortex;
t_{vc} = time for evaluation of the convective component of the velocity of one vortex;
t_{vd} = time for evaluation of the diffusive component of the velocity of one vortex;
t_s = time for statistics calculation on vortex parameters;
t_{co} = time for coalescing phase of a couple of vortices;
N_g = number of generated vortices;
N = total number of the vortices.

Program execution times with different numbers of iterations on a Silicon Graphics XS24 workstation initially increase with the cube of the number of iterations, as expected from (17); then the dependence slows down, approaching proportionality, because the effect of the coalescence is more sensible. Considering the birth of 72 vortices for iteration, for only 90 iterations the execution runs for 20 minutes, but the same program takes nearly three days for a significant simulation of 4000 iterations.

The execution profiling shows that with only 90 iterations the convective velocity evaluation routine corresponds to the 95% of the total computing time; thus a parallelisation method aiming to its subdivision among different processing units can reduce significantly the total computational time.

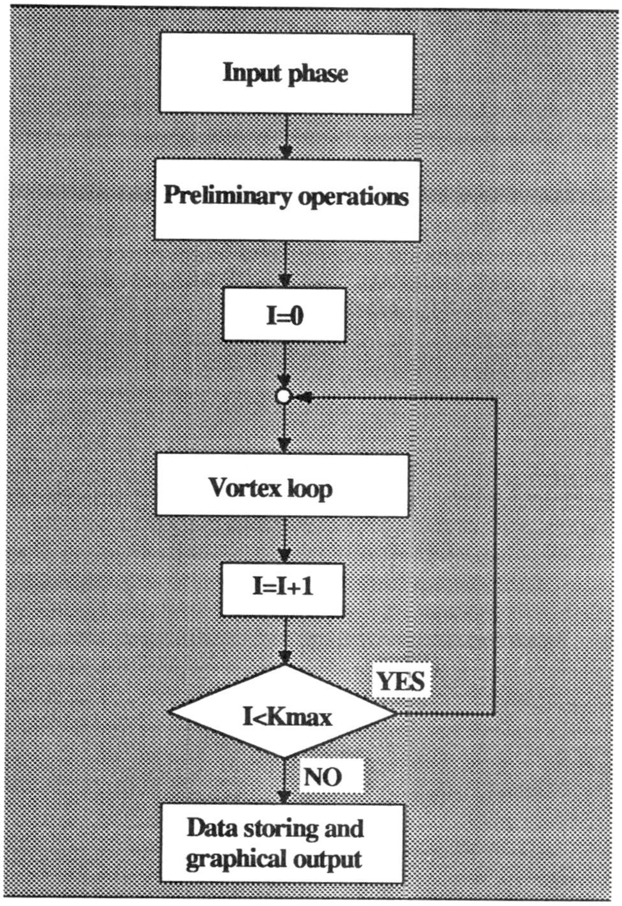

Fig. 2 - Flow-chart of the simulation program

Parallelisation method proposed

We concentrate our attention on the parallelisation of the heaviest phase of the simulation, the vortex loop: to distribute the computational load we first choose to fractionate the vortices among the Processing Elements; at each time step each PE evaluates the interactions between its local vortices and those received from the other PE's.

On the basis of these considerations we identified a ring of PE's as the most promising architecture for the parallelisation of the vortex method: the reason is in the fact that the proposed solution requires that the same information (the vortex coordinates) is transmitted to all the PE's for the elaboration; with this topology of connection, at each step of communication data arrive where they are effectively processed.

Within the ring, a master node is defined, which starts each operation of the algorithm; in particular, it breeds the vortices.

The times required by the previously described phases of the program change as follows:

1) the first operation is the generation of the vortices and the communication of their coordinates to all the PE's. This operation employs a time:

$$N_g * (t_{vb} + t_c) \qquad (19)$$

where:

t_{vb} is the time for the generation of one vortex;

t_c is the time for the communication of the parameters of one vortex;

N_g is the number of vortices generated at each iteration;

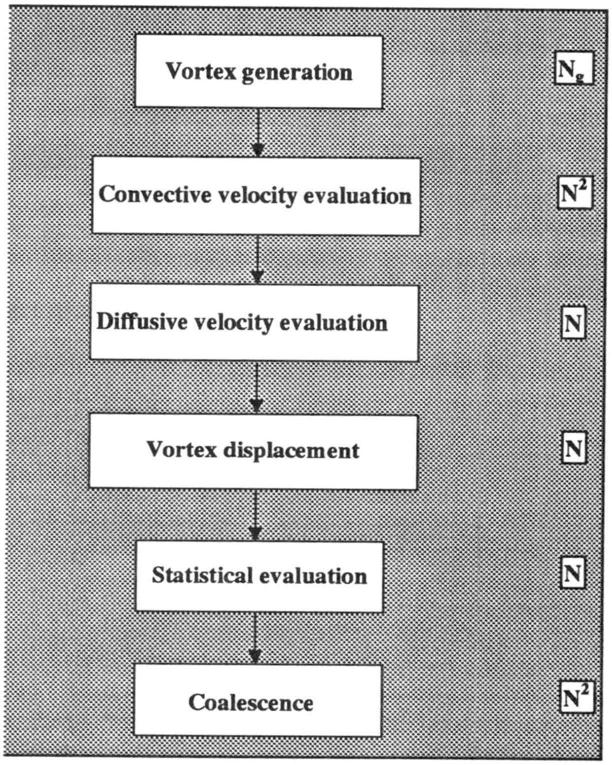

Fig. 3 - Flow-chart of the vortex loop with the dependence on the number of vortices

2) the convective component of the velocity is due to the effect of each vortex on all the others in the field. At first each PE evaluates the effect due to the interactions between its local vortices; then it sends along the ring the coordinates of its vortices and receives from the previous PE in the ring the coordinates of the vortices stored in that PE; now it calculates the effect of the interactions between the received vortices and its ones.

This procedure is repeated M times (M is the number of processors); thus, finally each PE has considered the effect of all the distributed vortices on its local own.

The time needed for this elaboration is :

$$\frac{N^2}{M} * tvc + tce * M \qquad (20)$$

where:

t_{vc} = time for the evaluation of the convective component of one vortex (due to one interaction);

t_{ce} = time for the communication of the vortex coordinates;

N = total number of vortices;

3) as previously seen the diffusive velocity component is evaluated by multiplication of constant terms by a random number, thus this phase can be executed locally on each PE with a time

$$\frac{N}{M} * tvd \qquad (21)$$

where t_{vd} = time needed for the evaluation of the diffusive component of the velocity for one vortex;

4) the same considerations apply to the space displacement of the vortices and the time contribution is in this case:

$$\frac{N}{M} * tvm \qquad (22)$$

where t_{vm} is the time needed for the space displacement of one vortex;

5) with regard to the coalescing phase, we first describe the sequential operations executed by the program and then the parallelised solution proposed. The serial program saves the parameters of each considered vortex (coordinates, velocity and power) in temporary vectors and operates as follows:

a) each vortex is assigned to a band on the basis of the value of its x coordinate;

b) steps from c) to i) are executed for each vortex i;

c) vortex i with null power is not considered;

d) vortex i belonging to the band containing the cylindric obstacle is not subjected to the coalescing phase; its parameters are directly transferred to the temporary vectors;

e) alternatively, for each vortex j (j>i) within the distance characteristic for the band considered, the steps f)-h) are executed;

f) the coordinates and the powers of all the vortices j are summed;

g) the number of vortices j is evaluated;

h) for each vortex j, its power is set to zero;

i) if the total power of the vortex i and the vortices j is not null, the average coordinates and the sum of the powers is saved in the temporary vectors;

l) the temporary vectors are transferred into the working vectors with a substantial reduction of the number of vortices.

The parallelisation must respect the sequentiality of the operations previously described: this consideration prevents from the parallel coalescing of one vortex on each PE. In the described procedure, if one divides the order number of a vortex by the number of the PE's, the remainder identifies the owner PE while the quotient indicates the order number of the vortex inside the PE itself.

The proposed solution consists of the following phases:

a) after the coalescing phase each vortex may be stored in a position different from the starting one, so the program creates one pointer for the *source* vortex i and one pointer for the *target* vortex k; at the beginning either pointers point to the first vortex considered;

b) for each source vortex i, steps c)-h) are executed;

c) the following operations are executed if the vortex power is not null;

d) the vortex coordinates are dispatched to all the PE's;

e) the nodes create a counter and temporary variables for the vortices subjected to the coalescing phase. The variables are initialised with the parameters of the considered vortex and the counter is set to 1 in the owner PE, while all of them are set to 0 in the other PE's;

f) each PE evaluates the distance of each local vortex j from the considered vortex i, with j>i; if this value is lower than the distance characteristic of the band considered, the parameters of the vortex j are accumulated in the temporary variables of that PE, the coalescing counter is incremented and the vortex power is set to zero;

g) the temporary variables are dispatched to the PE owner of the target vortex k. Each PE receives the set of variables, sums its own and sends the updated set to the following PE in the ring; the last PE evaluates the average of the coordinates of the velocity and the sum of the power for the target vortex;

h) if the total power is not null, these variables are stored and the pointer to the target vortex k is updated.

These operations allow also the sorting of the coagulated vortices, removing the "holes" created in the original sequence of the vortices.

Experimentation environment and porting into a Special Purpose Computer

In the previous section we already described the parallelisation techniques for the vortex blob algorithm.

Now we describe the computing platform we are using to estimate the efficiency of a parallel system charged with execution of the parallel version of the algorithm; as a result a load balance among the Processing Elements of the system will be analyzed so as to reach the best exploitation of the computing power of the system itself.

At last we discuss the design of a SPC based on the parallelisation techniques discussed in order to reach performance comparable to that of supercomputers, but featuring a low implementation cost and a complete availability for the users.

The experimentation environment is based on PVM 3.3.6 (Parallel Virtual Machine) software system that runs on a workstation network made up of HP 705 computers [9]. PVM permits the simulation of parallel machines based on different architectures thanks to a user library containing routines for spawning processes and managing the communications between them.

Furthermore, PVM gives information about the exploitation time of each Processing Element (PE) of the simulated architecture, the time spent waiting for messages coming from other PE's, and so on. The goal of that part of the work is related to the optimization of the parallel version of an algorithm and to the identification of architectures suitable to map the algorithm in the best way.

A SPC based on that architecture can be designed and the problem of the parallel algorithm porting can be easily faced.

In particular the translation process needed for running the programs on the PE's of the SPC requires the compilation of the source code producing an object code for the target processors. Furthermore it is necessary to replace the PVM communication routines with those suited to the SPC.

Our group already experimented the design strategy described above: problems related to particle system simulations were successfully faced designing and assembling an instrument purposely devoted to those problems [10].

The first implementation was related to Montecarlo Metropolis simulations of liquid crystals during their phase transition [11]. The simulated system is made up of a few thousands of rotating particles in a two-dimensional lattice-gauge with two-body interactions [12].

An accurate study of the algorithm also considering the computing weight of each part of the algorithm itself permitted to identify a double ring architecture of processing elements, as the most promising one. The resulting computation system is made up of a double ring of PE's described below and of a Front-End Computer (Fig. 4). The system is able to operate as a stand-alone unit (Fig. 4a), but the Front-End computer allows to interface the system with an Ethernet LAN, controlling it from a Host Computer (Fig. 4b). The tasks attributed to the Front End Computer are the development of the operating programs and the user interface.

If we consider as a sample a physical system with 10000 particles and long-range interactions, a SPC based on 8 PE's is 3 times faster than a two-processor Cray YMP C90 and 6 times than the Convex 8320 when executing a version of the algorithm compiled without optimization; in the case of optimized compilation our system becomes 2.6 times slower than Cray and 1.2 times faster than Convex. The reason for this should be found in the preliminary version of the optimized compiler available with our i860 SW development kit.

Other applications are in progress; all of them exploit the same PE, while adapting the inter-connection scheme to each parallel algorithm.

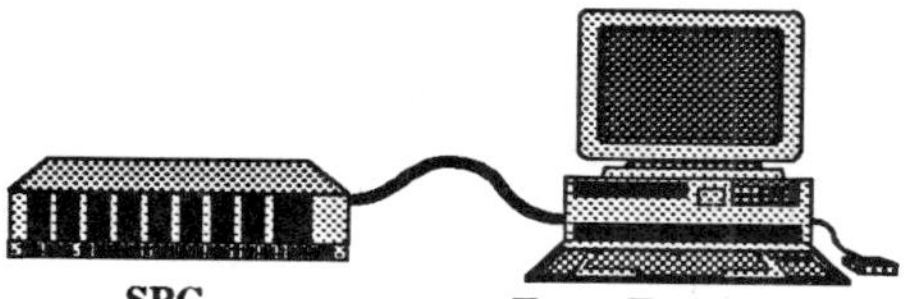

Fig. 4a

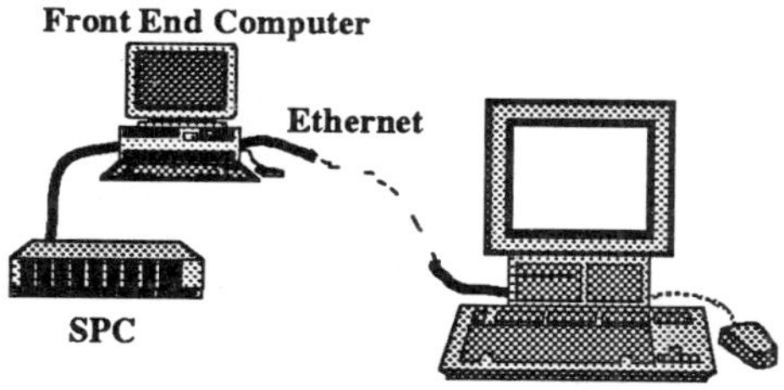

Fig. 4b

Fig. 4 - The computing system

Each PE is made up by a sandwich of two Eurocard boards properly connected. Two CPU's are present: the Intel i860 microprocessor is the main one charged with simulation program execution; it includes a fast floating point unit able to reach a peak performance of 80 MFlops on single precision data [13].

The second one is a Motorola Single Chip Computer (SCC) which initializes and monitors the PE; furthermore a serial link interfaces the SCC to the Front End Computer to centralize diagnostic informations. Communications between the PE's take place through First In First Out buffers reducing transfer problems between PE's. Inside each board are also present a Rom containing the firmware for initializing the PE and a static Ram sized to contain processing programs as well as data. On the basis of the previous considerations the resulting block scheme is given in Fig. 5.

The main CPU, namely the i860, is placed at the centre of the figure; it is connected to the Fifo's and to parallel receivers through a data bus and proper control lines. It is also connected to the bootstrap Rom and to program and data Ram. The other CPU (SCC) initialises the PE and manages a serial bus interface, with control purposes, which connects all the PE's and the Host Computer. The SCC recognizes also the PE name (board address), reads the status flags of the Fifo's and drives the front panel LED's.

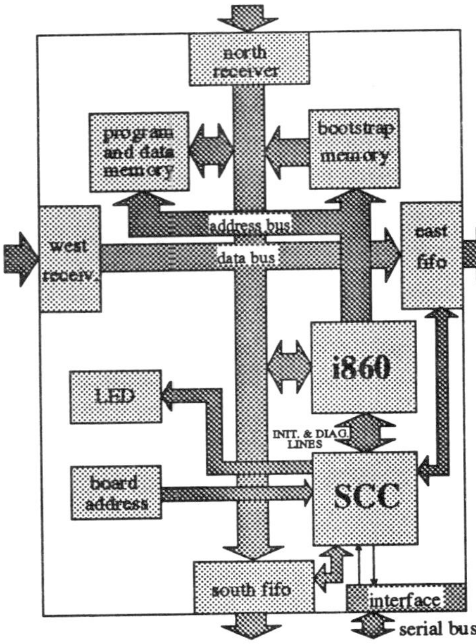

Fig. 5 - The processing node

Conclusions

The simulation program developed in Fortran by the researchers of the Hydraulic Dept. group was deeply analysed, in order to show the most computationally onerous routines; it was thus possible to establish that more than 95% of the computing time is devoted to the evaluation of the convective term of the vortex motion, considering realistic simulation conditions. Then the parallelisation of the algorithm has been faced, and is taking place, through the following steps:

1) the simulation program has been run in a PVM environment, yet retaining the sequential mode;
2) a first parallelisation has been experimented, with every operation retained in the master node, but with the vortex coordinates distributed to a set of slave PE's;
3) the final parallelisation is at present under test, with the distribution of the computer code to all the available PE's, following the above described lines.

The porting to the SPC environment will then be achieved in a short time, as it was our experience with the preceeding simulation algorithm, and experimental results are expected to demonstrate increased processing speed, compared to those obtained with the powerful previously used workstation, by an order of magnitude.

Bibliography

[1] H. Lamb, "Hydrodynamics", Cambridge University Press, 6th ed., 1932.

[2] A.F. Ghoniem, Y. Cagnon, "Vortex simulation of laminar recirculating flow", Journ. Comp. Physics, 68, 346-377, (1987).

[3] A. Leonard, "Vortex method for flow simulation", Journ. Comp. Physics, 37,289-335, (1980).

[4] J.T. Beale, A. Majda, "High order accurate vortex methods with explicit velocity kernels", Journ. Comp. Physics, 58, 188-208, (1985).

[5] W. T. Ashurst , "Numerical simulation of turbulent mixing layers via vortex dynamics", Turbulent shear flows I, Springer-Verlag (1977).

[6] C. Greengard, "The core spreading vortex method approximates the wrong equation", Journ. Comp. Physics, 61, 345-348, (1985).

[7] J. A. Chorin, "Numerical study of slightly viscous flow", Journ.Fluid Mech. 57, 785-796, (1973).

[8] A.F. Ghoniem, F.S. Sherman, "Grid-free simulation of diffusion using random walk methods", Journ. Comp. Physics, 61, 1-37, (1985).

[9] A. Geist, A. Beguelin, J. Dongarra et al., "PVM 3 User's guide and reference manual", University of Tennessee, Oak Ridge National Laboratory, Emory University, May 1993.

[10]G. Danese, I. De Lotto, D. Dotti et al., "An instrument for Computational Physics", Genova, Internal report of INFM Institute, November 1994.

[11]N. Metropolis, A. Rosenbluth, M. Rosenbluth et al., "Equation of state calculations by fast computing methods", The Journal of Chemical Physics, vol. 21, pp. 11-16, June 1953.

[12]S. Romano, "Computer simulation study of a disordered plane-rotator system in two dimensions, with long range ferromagnetic interactions", Physical Rewiew, vol. 42, pp. 8647-8650, 1990.

[13]L. Kohn, N. Margulis, "Introducing the Intel i860 64-bit Microprocessor", IEEE Micro, August 1989, pp. 15-30.

A Small Parallel C Simulator

Manuel Mollar
Depto. de Informática
Universidad Jaume I
Aptdo. 242, 12071 Castellón, Spain

Abstract

The C language is an interesting choice for parallel programming with the transputer. We present a module built in C that allows a program written in INMOS Parallel C to be run in any computer with minor changes, using a sequential compiler. Only the language is simulated, not the architecture, providing fast execution and reasonably accurate timing.

1 Introduction.

Our simulator allows the compilation and execution of parallel programs written in Parallel C using our favorite programming toolset in the corresponding computer. The main goal is the *simulation of the language*, not the architecture. In consequence, the debugging facilities will be those of the programming tool, so the training effort is minimum. In short, the main advantages of the built simulator are four: debugging facilities, high execution speed, deadlock detection and the possibility of running without the transputer hardware. It has been written in ANSI C to guarantee portability. After having developed it using the Borland C IE on a PC-clone, it has been compiled under HP UX without any change.

In §2 we describe the simulation guidelines and give some definitions, in §3 and §4, the necessary changes to program source are described. In §5 and §6 the basic simulation strategy and algorithms are given, showing the debugging possibilities in §8 and §9. In §7 we explain the available multiprogramming features.

2 The simulation.

The simulator is constructed as two include files and one module that must be linked with the parallel program. It provides the routines for communication, and a transparent concurrence mechanism to simulate the parallelism. The chosen concurrence strategy is based in a co-routine scheme built using the *setjmp* C package. Of course, a round-robin scheduler would be more realistic, but the difficulties and the loss of portability are evident. Furthermore, most debuggers will not run with this scheme. Co-routine based concurrent execution is far from the behavior of the parallel program. However, once the transfer strategy has been understood, the sequential trace of the program is very convenient for a good tracking of the parallel algorithm.

For every processor, the simulator distinguishes (and can compute) among *Total Time (TT)*, *Input Waiting Time (IWT)*, *Output Waiting Time (OWT)*, *Communication Time (CMT)*, and *Computation Time (CPT)*. Last one is the employed by the simulating processor (in all that follows, the host processor) in executing any no-communication instruction. A scale factor is computed to return the real transputer times (T805).

The communication costs (CMT) are estimated with a usual theoretical model: estimate the cost of the link set up and the cost of the transmission of one byte. The total cost is: cost of set up + cost per byte * no. of bytes. Both can be manual or automatically adjusted. Setting them to 0,0, the simulator will show the degree of parallelism of the algorithm. The communication costs are only accounted in the processor that does the output operation (in all that follows, the output processor); in the input processor, it is accounted as Input Waiting Time, defined as the time from the input operation request to its completion. By Output Waiting Time we designate the expired one from the output request till the input operation beginning.

Always, we know the Total Time per processor, so the maximum one is the time of the parallel algorithm. We also know the total computation time, as the addition of the Computation Time of every processor. Then, the simulator can compute the *speed up* of the algorithm for any given number of processors respect to the same algorithm executed in one processor.

In the simulation, a processor executes its code sequentially until it requires to communicate with another. Depending on the situation of the other, execution is transferred to it. The transfer routine ac-

1066-6192/96 $5.00 © 1996 IEEE
Proceedings of PDP '96

counts the expended CPU time. The algorithmic effort is centered in the communication routines, as we will explain.

The number of physical links in the transputer can be extended in the simulation to any number. So, an algorithm designed for a n-cube that runs directly in the T805 transputer for $n = 1,2,3$, can be tested for any value of n, to prove its correction, simply increasing the number of links at configuration time.

3 The tailored program.

In the transputer system, configured executable code may be constituted by different programs for the different processors [1]. Now, by evident reasons, only a program can be present. The solution is that *each simulated processor executes a routine of the tailored program*. This routine does not need to be different for every processor, the configuration mechanism allows to allocate the same routine for several processors.

Thus, the first tailoring operation is to join the original programs into a single one, maintaining the multiple file structure, if desired. To do it, all the *main* routines must be renamed. Then, a new *main* routine must be created, intended to configure the network and to start the simulation. To avoid the construction of a parser for the files accepted by *icconf* [1], the simulator includes a set of routines that implements the configuration task.

The joining process has a drawback concerning to global variables. Suppose that in the transputer network configuration, a program must be shared by several processors. In the tailored code, we want to allocate the same routine for these processors. Then, all the global variables from the original program must be converted into local ones to the renamed routine. The presence of global data in the tailored program implies the simulation of a shared memory. The only alternative is the replication of the variables, with the corresponding naming task or the inclusion in a vector, but this is not a serious approach.

To avoid having a program for the simulator and others for the transputer, we can use the C preprocessor. Using the #ifdef directive, code can be tailored at compilation time, using the appropriate definitions. For example, suppose that we want to run a program in processor 0 and another in the rest of processors. We can write the code for a single file like this:

```
/* Here the headers for all the processors */
#ifndef procR
/* Here special headers for processor 0 */
#endif
#ifndef procR
#ifdef proc0
  int main()
#else
  void RoutineFor0 ()
#endif
/* Here the code for processor 0 */
#endif /* #ifndef */
#ifndef proc0
#ifdef procR
  int main()
#else
  void RoutineForRest ()
#endif
/* Here the code for the rest of processors */
#endif /* #ifndef */
#ifdef InSimulator
  void main()
  /* Here the code for configuring */
#endif
```

In this example, for the real machine, we must define *proc0* at compiling time to generate code for processor 0, define *procR* to generate code for the rest of processors. When in the simulator, *InSimulator* is already defined, allowing code generation for the simulator. So, the tailoring process becomes automatic. If the multiple file scheme is maintained, a more simple use of the preprocessor will give the correct result. Using the *#ifdef* directive for the *main* and selecting the files at link time, will be enough.

4 The configuration routines.

These procedures are similar to those used by *icconf* to make them easy to use. The main difference comes from the tailored program: each simulated processor holds a routine of the program, not a different program (like in the original occurs). Furthermore, no distinction is made between process and processor, so the original sentences *place* and *use* are joined in a single one, *Place*. It sets which routine is allocated in what processor, with an estimate of the extra workspace that the routine needs (in the stack), as we will explain. Another parameter to *Place* is the result to a call to *Interface*. This routine implements partially the original interface: only I/O channels and integer values are supported as parameters. The process Id is treated as a special case, to economize memory. A call to *Place*, will be, for example:

Place(*rout, extra, proc,*
Interface(5,iPId,iInpChan,East,iOutChan,East,
iInpChan,West,iOutChan,West)),

which will place a routine *rout* in processor *proc* with the extra stack *extra* and with an interface including five parameters: the PID, an input process (designed by iInpChan) for link East (1), an output process for the same link, and the same for link West.

Channel specification in the interface implies explicit determination of the physical link on which the channel will be placed, so the original *place* sentence applied to channels is not necessary (and not implemented). To connect two processors, the *Connect* procedure is used, specifying the two processors and the two links. Establishing connection between two processors by a determined link implies the existence of two channels for each processor, which can be used by the placed routine if they are specified in the interface construction.

Despite the differences with the original configuration process may seem substantial, this simplified scheme allows in practice setting up most of the configuration schemes, in the desired way: the use of *get_param* by the program does not need to be modified.

Furthermore, dynamic creation of interfaces is possible, allowing their construction at run time. Using this facility, a set of built in topologies is given with the simulator, included in *misc.h*, allowing quickly starting:

- A bi-directional ring of processors,
- A crossbar of any number of processors,
- A full tree with any number of sons by node and any deepth,
- A wrapped mesh with any number of dimensions with any number of processors by dimension, and
- A hypercube of any dimension.

Obviously, when more than four links are needed, the algorithms cannot be directly implemented in the T805 transputer. Here, the interface is constructed using the links in the order 1,2,3,0,4,5, ... So, compatibility is maintained when possible.

A complete description may be found in the include file *misc.h*.

5 Process management.

Each processor is simulated with a co-routine that executes one of the renamed routines. Each processor has its local clock. *Process work space is allocated in the stack*, including the local data. Only three procedures implement process management. The routine *StartSystem* called when the configuration task is done, assigns a PID to itself (we refer to it as the initial process) and transfers to the processor 1. Using an informal notation, the algorithm is simple:

set the initial time
transfer(1)
repeat
  for every non finished process **do**
    transfer to it
until no process

The *Transfer* routine *is only called internally by the communication routines*, so context switching is transparent to the user. The algorithm for *Transfer(PID)* follows.

localclock+= current time of host processor -
  previous *initialtime*
if process with this PID does not exist **then**
  set the work space for the current process
  call the placed routine
  exit_terminate(0)
else if process has finished **then** error
else *initialtime*= current time of host processor
  transfer to the process with this PID

The other routine is *exit_terminate*, that simply marks the process as terminated and transfers execution to the initial process, entering the previous repeat loop, transferring control to any other non finished process. This loop is also intended to schedule any process that performs some action after the last call to some communication routine, because process scheduling is *only carried out by the communication routines*.

It is usual that the first simulated routine called by any program is *get_param*. This is not necessary in the real machine, but it is in the simulator. The first time that a program calls *get_param*, it does its expected work, and then starts the next process. The declared local variables are already allocated in the stack, so the extra stack is only intended to allow possible calls to other routines, and acts as a work space for the process. The process creation ordering is 1, 2, ..., n-1, 0, so the remaining of the stack is available for proc. 0, despite its extra stack (the specified). This is very convenient, because proc. 0 may need a great amount of stack to perform I/O.

6 The communication routines.

The data structure for every process is an array of channel descriptors. One input channel and another output one are allocated for each physical link, no matter if they were not specified in the interface, for simplicity. Each descriptor holds what link in what processor is connected to it. The communication strategy is a simple buffer operation: the data passed to ChanOut are copied into a buffer pointed by the input channel descriptor of the connected processor. ChanIn will deallocate the buffer after copying it to its destination.

When a process calls ChanIn, data may be not ready. In our concurrence scheme, waiting for the message consists in transferring control to the partner process, from which data are expected. Calling ChanOut by the output process, execution is transferred to the input process. The specification for ChanIn is given in [2] and the basic algorithm may be:

```
if message not received then
   transfer to the output process
/* execution continues here if a transfer to this
                                    process occurs */
if data have been received then
   copy information
   deallocate buffer
else deadlock
```

And for ChanOut:

```
allocate buffer
copy message to it
transfer to the input process
if data not deallocated then
   deadlock
```

However this is not valid. Deadlocks will be detected where they do not occur, due that the control may be transferred to the input process by another process. For example, suppose this situation:

Process 0	Process 1	Process 2
ChanIn from 1	ChanOut to 2	ChanIn from 1
ChanIn from 2	ChanOut to 0	ChanOut to 0

Starting from processor 0, control will return to it from processor 2, and data are not ready in the channel to proc. 1. If control is **another time** transferred to proc. 1, the second ChanOut (to proc. 0) will be performed, and the example communication will terminate.

Deadlock detection is possible establishing the maximum number of transfers (always to the same processor). Observe that anyway, with three processors at most two transfers will be necessary to schedule the system. With n processors, if processor 0 performs a ChanIn to communicate with proc. 1, at most the other n-2 procs. can demand communication with proc. 0 without knowing for certain that deadlock will occur, so at most n-2 extra transfers can be admitted, no matter from which processor come. If the last transfer does not carry the message, deadlock occurs. So the algorithm for ChanIn is this:

```
while (message not received) and
        (number of transfers is less than n) do
   transfer to the output process
if data not received then
   deadlock
else ...
```

Observe that during the extra transfers, control pass through processes that can be doing output, so a similar loop must appear in ChanOut.

For each input channel, IWT and the number of input operations (NIO) are accounted. For each output channel, OWT, the number of output operations (NOO) and the number of transferred bytes (NTB) are registered. The values NOO and NTB are accounted in order to give complete information to the user. Communication times are no explicitly accumulated. So, the computation time (CPT) is obtained from:

$$TT = CPT + \sum_{Channel}[IWT + OWT + NOO * (\text{channel set up time}) + NTB * (\text{time per byte})].$$

While TT is measured in the transfer operation, considering the previous algorithms, the communication times must be determined in the ChanIn routine. Transfer operations in ChanIn and ChanOut will cause undesired CPU time spent. So, considering the high performance of the original Parallel C routines, the algorithmic CPU time is discarded and the computation time for ChanIn and ChanOut is reduced to the minimum updating directly TT for the process. Supposing the data received and TI the processor time at which ChanIn begins and TO the (different) processor time at which the corresponding ChanOut begins, the algorithm for time measuring is:

```
if TI < TO then
   /* input process is waiting */
   wait = TO - TI + CMT
   TO+ = CMT
   TI = TO
   IWT+ = wait
else
   wait = TI - TO
   TO = TI + CMT
   TI = TO
   IWT+ = CMT
   OWT+ = wait
```

The routines *ChanInChanFail* and *ChanOutChanFail* described in [2] have not been implemented. However, *ChanInTimeFail* or *ChanOutTimeFail*, are very interesting for asynchronous parallel programming. Now, suppose that *timeI* is the max. waiting time for ChanInTimeFail and *timeO* the same for ChanOut-TimeFail, the algorithm for ChanInTimeFail follows.

```
repeat  /* to handle a ChanOutTimeFail that fails */
  repeat perform transfers
  until data received or deadlock condition
  if no data received then
    if timeI >= 0 then
      TI+ = timeI
      IWT+ = timeI
      return failure
    else
      deadlock
  else
    compute CMT
    if TI <= TO then
      wait = TO - TI
      if (timeI >= 0) and (timeI < wait) then
        /* failing */
        aux = TI + timeI
        wait = timeI
        failI =true
      else
        aux = TO + CMT
        wait = aux - TI
        TO = aux
      IWT+ = wait
      TI = aux
    else
      wait = TI - TO
      if (timeO >= 0) and (timeO < wait) then
        aux = TO + timeO
        wait = timeO
        failO = true
        CMT = 0
      else
        aux = TI + CMT
      OWT+ = wait
      TO = aux
      IWT+ = CMT
      TI+ = CMT
  if not failI then
    copy data and deallocate
until failI or not failO
return failI
```

Observe that the previous algorithm for ChanIn is embedded in this one. So, ChanInTimeFail is the basic input routine: ChanIn is ChanInTimeFail with *timeI = -1*. The same applies for ChanOut and ChanOutTimeFail, where simpler changes are made to return failure when deadlock or not message in *timeO*.

7 Multiprogramming features.

The first requirement for an optimal simulator is that any program written in Parallel C may run on the simulator. However, this is not true here. The simulator does not support multiprogramming in a transputer. So all the calls relative to process management are not supported, except those of time measuring. Really, we have originally designed the simulator to *develop and test* some numerical parallel algorithms. In this context, one process per processor is a usual practice, to obtain greater efficiencies.

However, several multiprogramming features have been implemented, as follows. The fact that the simulator does not support explicit multiprogramming, inhibits the possibility of performing concurrent I/O. Concurrent input, for example, is useful to make simultaneous input from different links. Even in a single link communication, concurrent I/O can be very useful to increase efficiency by means an intermediate message buffering. This possibility is valid for any parallel program. Then, in the simulator, an additional option is available at configuration time to stay that all I/O is handled by an intermediate buffering process for every channel. The code executed by this virtual process follows.

For input operations:

```
repeat forever
  read message into auxiliary buffer (at time Ti)
  send it to the user process (at time TI)
```

For output operations:

```
repeat forever
  read message from user process into auxiliary
        buffer (at time TO)
  send it to the partner (at time To)
```

In the real machine, the communication times may be strongly improved, but additional memory will be needed. In the simulation, no process is created, and no memory is needed for buffers. Simply, ChanIn will compute times in a different way. Although in the transputer process contention will disappear in most cases (using the buffering), the simulated behavior is the same that without the buffering, by obvious reasons.

The suggested use of this option follows: when the program works, activate the option and then, compare execution times; if they are really improved, building the buffering with auxiliary processes in the transputer may be justified.

In the simulator, concurrent mode is not compatible with time fail routines. Considering than $Ti \leq TI$ and $TO \leq To$, three situations are possible: $Ti \leq TI < To$, $To < Ti \leq TI$ and $Ti \leq To \leq TI$. The algorithm for ChanIn follows:

```
if TI < To then
   IWT+ = To - TI + TC
   To+ = TC
   TI = To
else
   if To < Ti then
      To = Ti + TC
      if To > TI then
         IWT+ = To - TI
         TI = To
   else
      To+ = TC
      if To > TI then
         IWT+ = To - TI
         TI = To
Ti = TI
```

The WT is incremented in ChanOut, that, before transfering does:

```
if To   /* previous, actualized by ChanIn */
      > TO   /* actual */ then
   OWT+ = To - TO
   TO = To
else
   To = TO /* for the next */
```

8 Debugging facilities.

The simulator has a trace mode in which several events are logged to the output. The events are mainly the relatives to communication activity, including waiting times. Combining the trace with the possibility of using *printf* instructions from any processor, a classical debugging method is obtained.

Of course, we prefer the possibilities given by interactive symbolic debuggers. The use of the step by step execution founds here a similar situation to those that appears in event-driven programs: a step may result in an excessive number of operations for debugging purpose. Suppose that a call to *ChanOut* is executed. It will perform a transfer to the input process, that in its turn can cause another transfers. So, when control returns to the next instruction, a lot of work may be done, and if we search for some error, it may appear in this step.

Breakpoints are the recommended tool. If we put them in the critical points of the program, each time that the control passes through the breakpoint, execution will stop. If several processors share a same routine (it is usual), the breakpoint will affect to the first processor that arrives to it. When conditional breakpoints are available, the processor selection is allowed using the variable *Process*, which returns the current process. Evidently, this variable must not be used into the program.

For debugging purposes, synchronization is an important task. In the transputer, under *idebug*, putting breakpoints in the different processors allows pausing all the processors at the desired point. Without the debugger, synchronization usually needs to be done in the transputer by means of message passing. In the simulator, only one process will arrive at his breakpoint at a time, due the sequential nature of the simulation; so another way of synchronization is necessary. The routine *Synchronize*, located in the desired points, simulates such a message passing, without any channel use. Processes are blocked inside *Synchronize* until every one calls it. Then execution continues in processor 0. But *Synchronize*, in contrast with message passing, does not affect CPU time; it can appear in the source code as it is needed, without changing timing results.

9 Profiling.

Several routines use *Synchronize*, in particular those of time information. Suppose that a segment of the parallel algorithm has a portion of code in different processors. To obtain partial execution times, this portion can be selected. The routine *BeginProfile (Profile Variable)* called from processor 0 marks the beginning of the portion to be measured; the end is marked by *EndProfile*, also in the proc. 0. In the other procs., the equivalent portions are marked by two calls to *Synchronize*, which must be done in all the processors. If no code corresponding to the parallel algorithm is present, it will simply be called twice. The pair *BeginProfile* - *EndProfile* accumulates execution data in the variable, and then, in any point of the source code, the routine *ShowProfile* will write a report on the output. The returned data are the mentioned $CPT, IWT, OWT, NIO, NOO, NTB$ and TT, detailed by channel if proceeds and desired.

Similar action performs the pair *SynchronizeCPU* - *ShowCPU*, which, using the previous routines, marks the begin and the end of a report, showing data. The main differences are: no accumulation is performed, an implicit profile variable is used, and, when synchronizing, CPU times of all processors are set to be equal to the greatest CPU time. The increased CPU time is accounted as IWT in a virtual channel. Observe that it is a valid approach, due that to obtain the CPU time of a portion of the algorithm, in the real machine, the mentioned message passing strategy needs to be used, obtaining the same results.

As auxiliary routines, *LockCPU* and *UnLockCPU* mark a portion of code in any processor that do not consumes CPU time. None of the simulator routines can be called between them. This is a good mechanism to write on the output without CPU consumption.

10 Implementation details.

The time estimate features are based on the possibility of high precision time measuring in the host computer. The *clock* C function returns the desired times, but usually its resolution is very poor. For example, in a PC, time counter is incremented 18.2 times per second; in most of the Unix systems, time is returned in microseconds, but with intervals of 0.01 seconds. On these situations, the simulator runs, but the time estimate is bad.

So, to set up the simulator in a machine, two routines must be implemented. The routine *SetInstant* must obtain the actual time of day, or CPU time (of the host), and store it in a variable of type *TyInstant.* This type must be defined for convenient storage. Another one, *Interval,* computes the interval between two previous measured instants, returning the difference in microseconds, stored in a long int. The general specification and the implementation for the PC (with $3\mu s$ of precision) of this routines is given in the distribution kit.

11 Experimental results.

In order to experiment with the simulator a set of programs has been prepared. Communication and wait times have been tested with them. Also, several programs test the built topologies. The distribution kit holds a user manual containing a complete example to show the time measuring in several cases. Also, two real programs have been used to experiment: one to calculate the Hessenberg reduction of a matrix, and another to compute the product singular value decomposition (PSVD) of two matrices.

The simulator performance depends strongly on the power of the host processor. Experimental results show that the i80486/33 processor is about twice faster than the T805 transputer running at 20 MHz. The processor of our HP Apollo is 8 times faster than the same transputer.

But the true determinant of the real time needed for the simulation is the complexity of communications. A communication that in the transputer can take few microseconds, in the simulation may involve hundreds of transfers in the process scheduling from the communication routines. The simulated time will be rather exact, but the time employed in the simulation may be many times larger.

To simulate transputer times with precision, a scaling factor is computed by the simulator at run time, to establish the relation of performance between the mentioned transputer and the host processor. Of course, this factor is not very exact, and user can determine it manually, experimenting with true programs. With the correct factor, we have experimented over the mentioned processors to compute the PSVD of matrices with different sizes over different number of processors. Results differ about 10% with the real times. Also, the computed speed up holds this percentage referred to the true one.

In the PC under DOS, Borland C exhibits a very powerful and quick debugger, but stack size is limited to 64kbytes, which reduces the number of processors that can be simulated to nearly 300, with a very small program. In front, under HP UX, lower memory constraints allow big simulations. Here, 4095 processors are started to compute $\Sigma_{i=x}^{y} i$ with a fan-in algorithm implemented over a binary tree of processors, involving about two seconds of simulation.

References

[1] INMOS Limited, "ANSI C toolset user manual", 1990.

[2] INMOS Limited, "ANSI C toolset language reference", 1990.

Parallel Programming with CAPSE - A Case Study *

B. Gruber, G. Haring
University of Vienna
Institute of Applied Computer Science
and Information Systems
Dept. of Advanced Computer Engineering
Lenaugasse 2/8, A-1080 Vienna, Austria
Tel: +43 1 408 63 66 10
Fax: +43 1 408 04 50
e-mail: *gruber@ani.univie.ac.at*

D. Kranzlmüller, J. Volkert
Johannes Kepler University Linz
Institute of Computer Science
Dept. for Graphics and
Parallel Processing
Altenbergerstr. 69, A-4040 Linz, Austria
Tel: +43 732 2468 9499
Fax: +43 732 2468 9496
e-mail: *kranzlmueller@gup.uni-linz.ac.at*

Abstract

The CAPSE environment for Computer Aided Parallel Software Engineering is intended to assist the developer in the crucial task of parallel programming. The methodology of CAPSE is based on direct manipulative graphical creation and editing of scalable workload characterizations of MIMD algorithms. This paper presents the basic concepts of this methodology and an example of a parallel Poisson solver. The workload characterization representing the computation and communication behavior of the algorithm is based on directed acyclic task graphs, which achieve scalability by composing the task graph of scalable basic patterns instead of single nodes and arcs. The composition and the usage of these basic patterns is described in the light of designing the Poisson solver algorithm. The resulting task graph is used to predict the program's performance on a nCUBE 2 distributed memory machine with the PAPS simulator.

1 Introduction

To exploit the full power of parallel computers, programs are necessary, which can be distributed equally over the available resources, keeping the processors working and the communication overhead as well as the waiting times minimum. The selection of appropriate algorithms and their efficient implementation is crucial for the performance of the resulting program.

The CAPSE approach (Computer Aided Parallel Software Engineering) [4] is intended to assist the developer during this challenging task by providing tools for performance prediction in early stages of the software development cycle. This prediction mainly depends on the communication structures, according to the great impact of communication on the performance of parallel programs.

The development of an efficient algorithm implementation is based on the design of a task graph which describes the computation and communication behavior of the algorithm. In contrast to various tools, like PSEE (Parallel System Evaluation Environment) [2] or Qsolver [7] [5], which offer the possibility of graphical workload characterizations without a mechanism to scale these characterizations to different problem sizes, the task graph description is created graphically and is scalable in terms of problem size and architecture size. The algorithm is described with communication patterns which are treated as individual geometrical objects.

A main part of the CAPSE environment is the PatternTool [3], an interactive tool for creating scalable hierarchical graphs. The user enters a task graph based model of the algorithm in terms of scalable patterns. The design of PatternTool allows the user to describe regular communication patterns easily.

The performance evaluation of the designed algorithm is done by simulation with the PAPS toolset (Performance Prediction of Parallel Systems) [8] [9]. PAPS can be parameterized for different computer systems by defining petri net models for task execution and communication behavior. At present such parameterizations are provided with PAPS for the nCUBE 2 and the Intel Paragon. Further parameterizations will be added in the future.

The current implementations of PatternTool and PAPS are running on SUN workstations with UNIX operating system. The graphical user interface is based

*This work was funded by the Austrian Federal Ministry of Science and Research (research grant GZ 613.562/1-II/6/93).

on X-Windows.

This paper is organized as follows. First we give a short overview of PatternTool and its basic concepts. Section 3 introduces the case study, which is an example Poisson solver, and the target architecture of the resulting implementation. In section 4 we describe how the example algorithm is modeled with the CAPSE toolset. The resulting design is presented and the predicted behavior is compared to an actual implementation on the nCUBE 2 multiprocessor. We conclude with a short summary and future aspects of this project.

2 PatternTool

The description of algorithms with PatternTool is based on scalable acyclic task graphs. These task graphs consist of nodes which represent sequential processing and directed arcs. Arcs between nodes mapped on different processors represent communications, arcs between nodes mapped on the same processor represent control flow. The semantics of each node are as follows:

- Input (control flow or data) is passed to the node along the arcs pointing to it.
- Each node starts the sequential processing of the data after all incoming communication is finished.
- Afterwards output (control flow or data) is send along the outgoing arcs.

The design of algorithms is based on this simple model. The nodes do not contain the actual coding, but only the execution times of the activities on the nodes and the amount of data transfered across the arcs as parameters. This means that the task graph only describes the program flow of the algorithm, but does not contain any implementation details for processing the data. Therefore the model can be applied as soon as the computation and communication behavior of the algorithm has been defined, which happens early in a hierarchical design process.

2.1 Scalability

A major feature of the PatternTool is the scalability of the model according to problem size. For scalability analysis, it is useful to build models which describe the algorithm with small problem sizes, and later scale it up for various problem sizes and different numbers of processors. Especially for modeling massively parallel algorithms it is not appropriate to be forced to draw thousands of nodes and arcs manually. Instead the model is constructed graphically for one problem size small enough to fit on a computer screen or a sheet of paper. Afterwards it is scaled to realistic sizes.

The scaling-mechanism of PatternTool is based on the following four items:

- Basic patterns
- Selection operations
- Relational operations
- Macro nodes

2.2 Basic patterns

The scalability is achieved if task graphs are constructed from scalable *basic patterns* of nodes and groups of arcs between these patterns. The patterns define the relative number, relative position and relative indices of the appropriate nodes as well as all operations applicable to the pattern. During the design the actual number of nodes is given as a parameter to the pattern. If this parameter is changed, the number of the nodes in the pattern is changed automatically. Currently the following basic patterns are implemented:

- One and two dimensional arrays,
- Triangles (half of a two dimensional array cut off at the diagonal),
- Butterfly networks,
- Binary and arbitrary trees.

It is possible to treat user defined graphs just like the predefined basic patterns. They inherit all the operations defined for the patterns, which they are derived from. It is also possible for the user to define his own operations for them, which improves their usage.

2.3 Selection operations

For each of these patterns, special *selection operations* are defined. For example, one dimensional arrays allow the selection of ranges. In two dimensional arrays rows and columns can be selected. Furthermore the selections represent patterns again, i.e. the rows and columns of a two dimensional array are one dimensional arrays with all their applicable operations as for example range selections.

All operations always refer to the actual selection and are performed for all nodes of this selection. If all nodes of a pattern are selected with an operation like `selectAll` it is obvious, that the following operations always refer to all nodes of the pattern, even if the number of nodes changes. On contrary for example, if all nodes of a pattern (i.e. three nodes of a pattern with three nodes) are selected separately, it is not possible to expand this pattern automatically (i.e. when expanding the three-node pattern it is not clear if the user has the first three nodes, the last three nodes or all nodes in mind). To distinguish these cases, several selection operations are provided.

2.4 Relational operations

Another item which supports the scaling of task graphs are *relational operations*. They are provided to access nodes by their relative position to other nodes (i.e. `left`, `right`, `up` and `down` in two dimensional arrays). The user is prevented from cumbersome index operations and especially from exception handling at the borders of the patterns. The main advantage of using relational operations occurs when defining communications.

2.5 Macro nodes

The composition of more complex patterns from the basic patterns are introduced by the *macro nodes* mechanism. The macro nodes are collections which contain a pattern of nodes. Since this subpattern may also contain macro nodes, arbitrary complex patterns are possible. Each node may be converted into a macro node, thus providing support for hierarchical modeling and stepwise refinement. During the design on the screen the user can control, if the pattern contained in a macro node should be visible or not. This gives the possibility of viewing the same model at different levels of detail.

Replications of subpatterns are easily achieved by selecting several nodes at once to be macro nodes containing the same subpattern. PatternTool provides the possibility of conditionally inserting subpatterns. The user can specify a subpattern to use if the condition is true and a different one to use if it is false. By using a random number generator this feature can be used to model dynamic, data dependent behavior. PatternTool always shows one example of such a dynamic graph. For performance prediction lots of examples can be simulated. Loops with an unknown number of iterations can be modeled by an array with a parameter from the random number generator.

2.6 Communication

The definition of communications is established between two selections. Each communication consists of a source selection, a target selection and a relational operation defining the index transformation between the selections. It is represented by arcs between the nodes of the two selections. The arcs between macro nodes contain a communication between selections of the patterns contained in the macro nodes.

2.7 User Interface

The specification is done interactively with a graphical user interface. The graph is visible in each phase of its definition. Nodes and arcs can be selected by simply clicking on the appropriate graphical object. All operations applicable to the current selection are available by menus and dynamically changed list boxes.

To visualize the task graph for different problem sizes, its layout is calculated automatically. Therefore a layout is defined for each basic pattern. The nodes of one dimensional arrays are aligned horizontally from left to right, whereas the nodes of two dimensional arrays or a triangle are aligned in rows and columns. In trees the root node is placed in the middle over its subtrees. These rules are applied recursively.

The macro nodes surround their contained patterns. Therefore the size of a macro node is determined by the size of its contained pattern. Since the nodes in a pattern can be macro nodes, the automatic layout is able to deal with nodes of different sizes in the same pattern. Arcs always connect nodes directly.

Since the automatic layout mechanism does not always achieve optimal results (especially arcs may overlap easily), the user has the possibility to influence the generated layout. It is possible to shift, rotate, mirror, enlarge and reduce nodes. With hiding and unhiding it is possible to control the level of abstraction. For macro nodes all these operations affect the contained pattern accordingly.

3 Case Study: Poisson Solver

In this paper the use of the CAPSE environment is illustrated with a case study. The example is an implementation of a parallel Poisson solver algorithm for a distributed memory machine like the nCUBE 2 multiprocessor system.

3.1 Jacobi Iteration Algorithm

The Poisson solver algorithm works on the *Poisson equation* on the unit square, a linear partial differential equation [1]:

$$\frac{\delta^2 f}{\delta x^2}(x,y) + \frac{\delta^2 f}{\delta y^2}(x,y) = g(x,y) \qquad (x,y) \in [0,1]^2$$

where $g : [0,1]^2 \rightarrow \Re$ is a known function. The goal is to find a function $f : [0,1]^2 \rightarrow \Re$ that satisfies

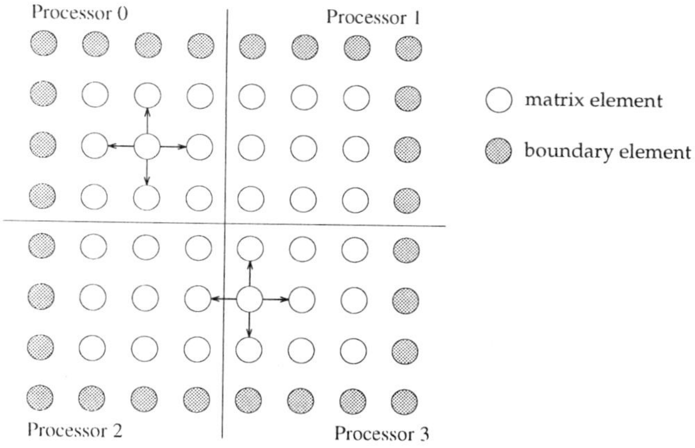

Figure 1: Poisson solver on fcur processors

the Poisson equation and has prescribed values on the boundary of the unit square. The numerical solver algorithm of this equation considers the values of f only on a finite grid of points in the unit square. The basic part of the solver is an iteration that calculates the following approximation, which is called the Jacobi Iteration method [1]:

$$f_{i,j}^{t+1} = \frac{1}{4}\left(f_{i+1,j}^{t} + f_{i-1,j}^{t} + f_{i,j+1}^{t} + f_{i,j-1}^{t}\right) - g(i,j)$$

The parallel implementation is straightforward. We assign each processor to a block of the $n \times n$ matrix, which is surrounded by a constant boundary. During each iteration the processors calculate their part of the matrix using the equation above (see figure 1). The iterations continue as long as the difference between two successive values of each element are beyond a certain threshold ε or after a fixed number of iteration steps. The only problem occurs with elements that have neighbors on different processors. The solution is to use an overlap area, in this case one row or one column of the neighboring processor. The introduction of the overlap areas forces the implementation of an update step, which exchanges the overlap areas with the new results after each iteration. Therefore the Poisson solver can be implemented as follows:

```
/* Parallel Poisson Solver */
begin
  do
    compute value f_{i,j}^{t+1} for each matrix element
    compute maximum difference of f_{i,j}^{t+1} and f_{i,j}^{t}
    if maximum difference > ε then
      exchange overlap areas
    endif
  while maximum difference > ε
end
```

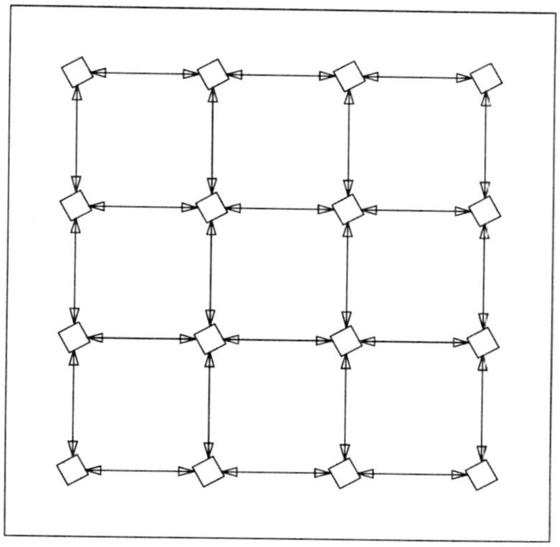

Figure 2: Main pattern of Poisson solver algorithm

Although the Jacobi Iteration is usually not used for practical purposes, we stick to it for didactical reasons. Of course Red-Black Gauss-Seidel Iteration could be used instead.

3.2 Target System: nCUBE 2

The target system for the implementation of the Poisson solver is a nCUBE 2 multiprocessor [6], which is a MIMD distributed memory machine with up to 2^{13} processing nodes arranged in a hypercube topology. Each node consists of a nCUBE 2 processor and 1 to 64 MBytes of memory. The nCUBE 2 processor contains a general purpose 64-bit CPU, an error correcting memory management unit (MMU) and a network communication unit (NCU). The CPU is rated at 7.5 MIPS and has a FPU with a peak performance of 2.3 MFLOPS in 64-bit precision mode.

The NCU consists of 14 bidirectional serial links that are able to transmit up to 2.2 MByte/s in both directions. It provides automatic cut-through message routing with the so-called wormhole switching technique. Message propagation and computations can be performed at the same time, as the NCU operation does not interfere with computation on the host.

The operating system on the nCUBE 2 nodes is VERTEX, a small UNIX version. C and FORTRAN are the available programming languages. The communication primitives are supported by functions in a library.

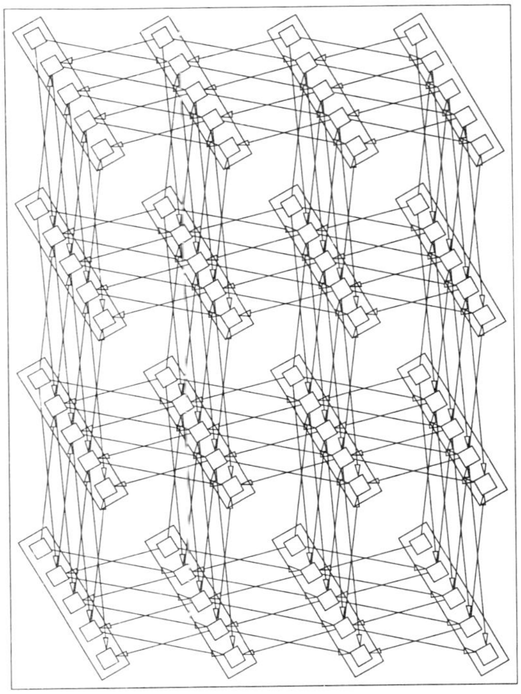

Figure 3: Poisson solver algorithm with 5 steps

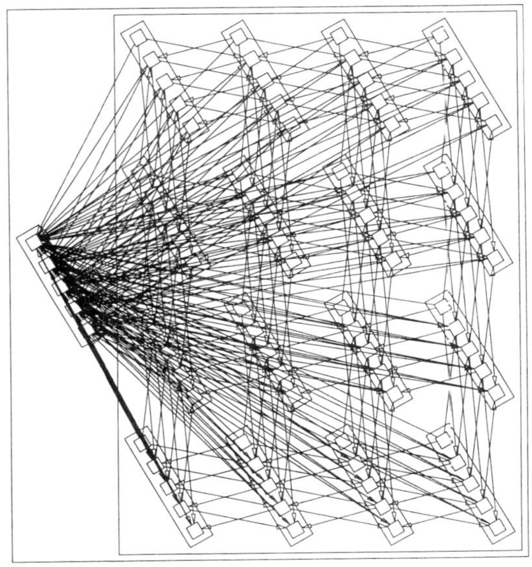

Figure 4: Poisson algorithm with central master

4 Modeling with CAPSE

In this section the PatternTool is used to create a performance model of the parallel Poisson solver.

In the model, according to the structure of the algorithm, the calculation of the $f_{i,j}^{t+1}$ is thought to be done on a grid of virtual processors, which will be mapped on the physical processors of the nCUBE 2.

The first step in creating a model with PatternTool is to identify the scaling parameters. For the Poisson algorithm these are the number of rows and columns of the processor grid, the number of rows and columns of the input matrix and the number of iterations that will be performed. These scaling parameters are entered and initial values have to be provided by the user.

In our example implementation we will use 2^p processors of a nCUBE 2 with $p = 0, 2, 4, 6$ and $n \times n$ matrices with $0 < n \leq 1600$. The number of iterations is set to a constant value of 5.

4.1 Main Task Graph Pattern

The main pattern of the algorithm is constructed as visualized in figure 2. It consists of a two dimensional array of nodes, which can be seen as the virtual processors, all communicating with their neighbors. All communications are realized with the relational operations (section 2.4). The two dimensional array is parameterized with the number of rows and columns of the processor grid. In this example 4×4 virtual processors are used.

Since we planned to do five iterations, each node is assigned a one dimensional array of five nodes, which represents one step of the algorithm each. The communications are refined to connect all nodes of the macro nodes permuted by the relational operation `right`. This means that the indices are increased by one. If the resulting node does not exist, like for all last nodes in the macros, the arc is omitted automatically. This prevents the user from taking special care for the last iteration step. An analogy to the `if maximum difference` $> \varepsilon$ construct in the pseudo code is therefore not necessary. The result is shown in figure 3.

4.2 Complete Task Graph Model

To complete the model of the algorithm, it is necessary to model the comparison of all the local differences against the threshold ε. This is done by adding a new task with five steps which is communicating with all the other tasks as shown in figure 4.

The screenshot already contains a lot of graphical objects. This indicates that we have chosen a too large initial problem size. It might be better to use a smaller one, if the complexity of the task graph is further increased.

In figure 5 each step of the algorithm is divided into two parts. The first part represents the calculation of the value $f_{i,j}^{t+1}$ for each matrix element. Then the

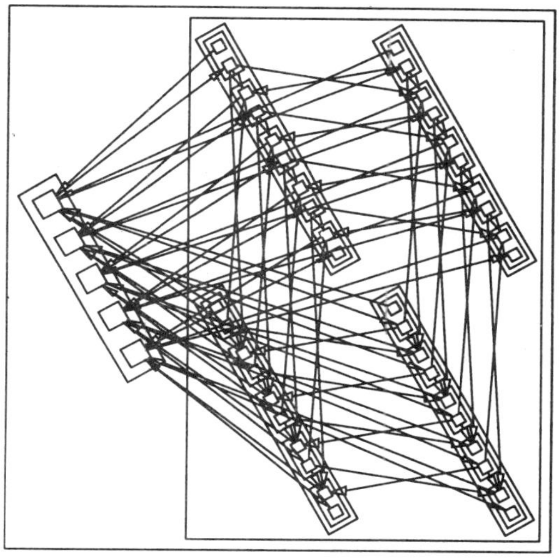

Figure 5: Poisson algorithm with refined steps

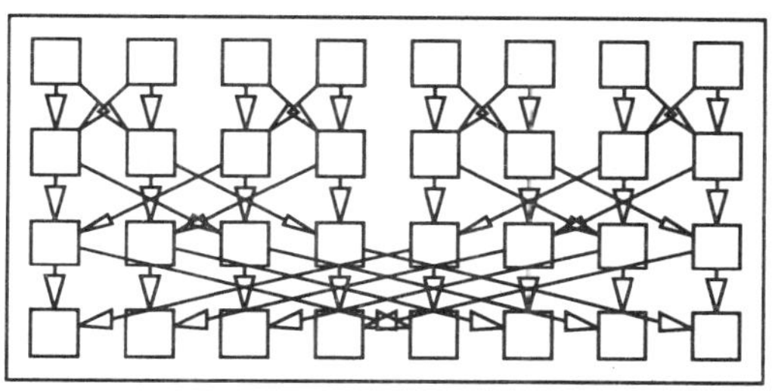

Figure 6: Global operation on the nCUBE 2

difference between $f_{i,j}^{t+1}$ and $f_{i,j}^{t}$ is evaluated. The second part represents the preparation of the communication with the neighbors. This partitioning considers the fact, that the communication with the master task is done before the communication with the neighbors, and not at the same time as in figure 4. To reduce the complexity of the figure, the algorithm is now shown for only four processors.

As a last improvement the centralized check of the differences is replaced by a global distributed maximum operation. Figure 6 shows the pattern of the global operation scaled for a hypercube of dimension 3, i.e. 2^3 processors. This global maximum operation can be developed separately and used here just like a basic pattern. A collection of such fundamental algorithms and their parameterizations for specific computer systems can be stored and reused as basic patterns in future algorithms.

Figure 7 contains the resulting task graph for 2×2 virtual processors with the global maximum operation.

Different variants of the algorithm can be modeled

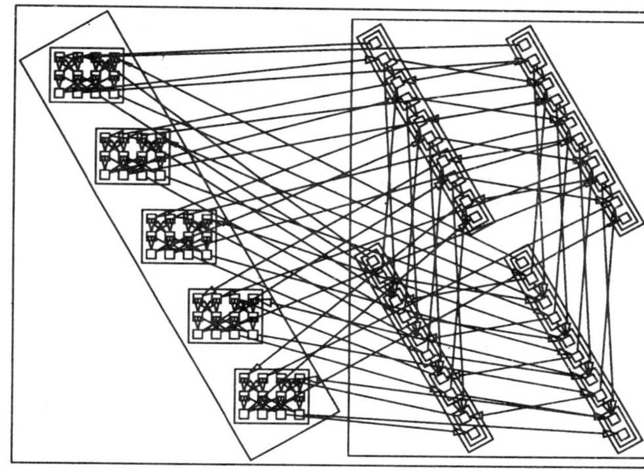

Figure 7: Poisson algorithm with global operation

analogously. Actually Figure 5 and Figure 7 can be seen as two implementation variants of the same algorithm and performance predictions can be compared.

4.3 Parameterization

The next step is the parameterization of the task graph nodes, that do not contain subpatterns, to be able to predict the performance of the poisson solver, using PAPS. These atomic nodes are attributed with the execution time of the activities they are representing. Since performance prediction is intended to be done at very early stages of the software development cycle, this assignment can be accomplished by rough estimates, sufficient for initial performance oriented compromises of design decisions.

In a first approach the time needed for one operation was assumed to be 1μsec. This can lead to following parameterizations.

- part1: 5 operations to calculate $f_{i,j}^{t+1}$ and 1 to calculate the difference to $f_{i,j}^{t}$ per matrix element $\Rightarrow 6 \times ldim^2$.
- part2: prepare 4 overlap areas, which are 1 row or 1 column each $\Rightarrow 4 \times ldim$.

ldim represents the dimension of the blocks assigned to individual processors.

The communication represented by the arcs between the nodes of part1 and part2 of different virtual processors are parameterized with the number of bytes that are transfered, one row or column of double precision floating point values giving $8 \times ldim$. The arcs representing the global operation are parameterized with a constant value of 8, representing the sending of one

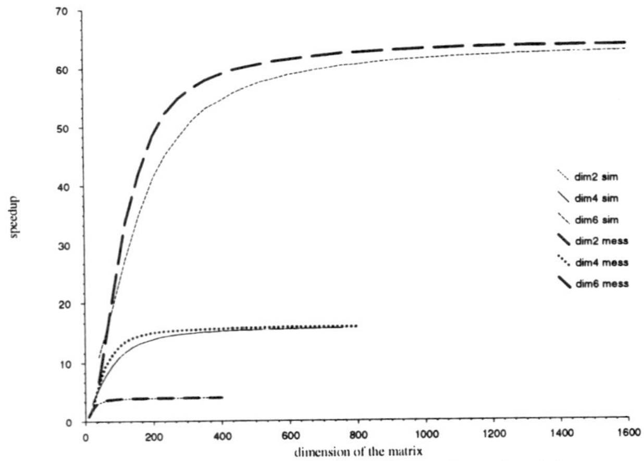

Figure 8: Speedup measured and predicted with parameterization based on rough estimates

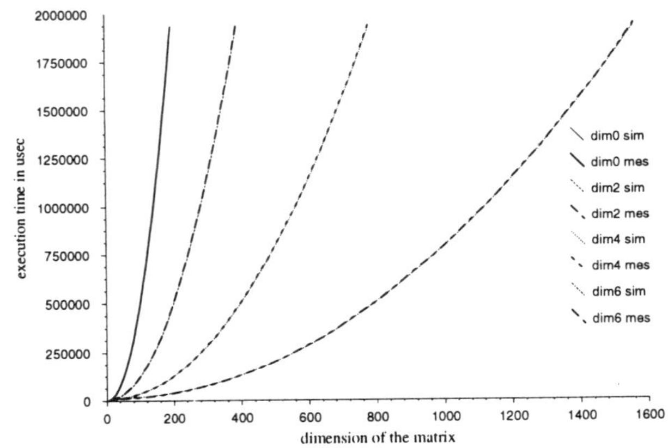

Figure 9: Execution time measured and predicted with exact parameterization

double precision floating point value (8 bytes). The arcs coming back from the global collection are parameterized with 1 representing just a flag byte. The arcs between the nodes of part1 and part2 on the same virtual processor need no parameterization, because they only define a control flow and no actual communications.

The parameterization of the global operation was done by running a small benchmark program measuring the actual execution time of the global maximum operation on the nCUBE 2. Since this pattern was created to be part of a collection of fundamental algorithms it should be parameterized as precisely as possible to allow correct performance prediction results.

4.4 Mapping

Now all the atomic task nodes have to be mapped to the physical processors of the target machine. This is done by assigning appropriate mapping functions to each atomic task node, which return the number of the physical processor, where the node will be mapped to. For all task nodes inside the right box (the nodes representing part1 and part2), the mapping function is: $index(0) + index(1) \times$ *rows of virtual processors* , giving the physical processor number for the simulation. (index(x) gives the index of the node in the x-th dimension of its pattern.)

For all task nodes inside the left box (the nodes representing the global maximum operations), the mapping function is simply $index(0)$. This mapping can be supplied with the pattern for the global operation, so that the user will not have to worry about the correct mapping when using it.

4.5 Validation

This model of the algorithm resulted in execution time predictions that clearly could not be very exact. On the other hand it shows the same characteristic scaling behavior like measurements of an actual implementation of the algorithm. Therefore predictions based on this very inexact parameterization can already give a good impression of the qualitative behavior of the algorithm. Especially the speedup predictions as shown in figure 8 are quite close to the correct values.

4.6 Improvement of the Parameterization

As a further improvement the sequential parts of the algorithm distinguished in the model were measured separately and approximated with least square deviance. This lead to the following parameterizations:

part1: $315 - 52.5 \times ldim + 9.81 \times ldim^2$.
part2: $59.7 + 8.16 \times ldim + 0.392 \times ldim^2$.

The parameterizations of the arcs needed no changes, because calculations of the execution times of the communications are reflected accordingly by the simulation method. Also the mappings need no changes. Figure 9 shows the prediction of the execution time based on these parameterizations compared to the measured execution time of the implementation. The difference between simulation and measurement is below ±5% for nearly the whole range.

The great relative errors (figure 10) for small matrix dimensions come from the fact, that the parameters are wrong by up to 100% for very small matrices. The reason for this is inexact parameterization.

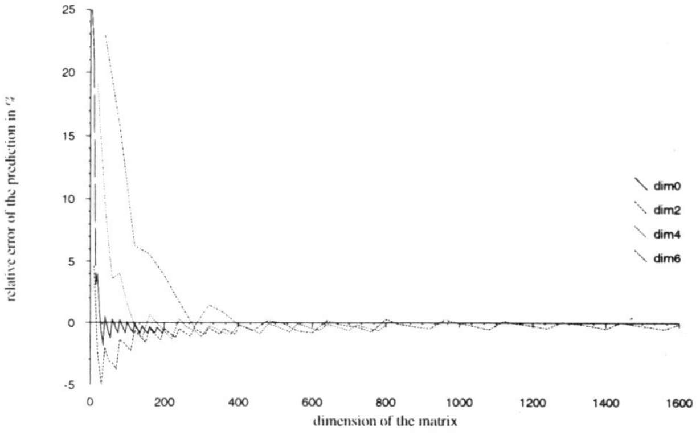

Figure 10: Relative error of prediction based on exact parameterization

5 Conclusions and Future Work

With PatternTool it is possible to define the communication patterns and control flows of algorithms by means of geometrical patterns of nodes and patterns of arcs connecting them. A user with moderate experience with the tool can do this in a reasonable amount of time. Compared to textual specification methods, especially the time needed to verify the communication patterns is much shorter, because it can be graphically seen which tasks are communicating and no sending to nonexistent targets will ever happen.

The main concepts of these definitions have been presented and their application has been shown in a case study for a Poisson solver. Simulation results have been presented for different parameterizations and a validation of the simulation results was done by comparing them to measurements of an actual implementation, showing the quality of the predictions as well as the usability of the CAPSE tools for performance predictions in early stages of the software development cycle.

The current versions of PatternTool and PAPS can only handle algorithms with statically defined structure and mapping. Future versions are intended to be able to handle algorithms with dynamic load balancing and irregular communication patterns, like e.g. a parallel raytracer.

Libraries of models of fundamental algorithms will have to be build together with library managing capabilities of the tool. Such a library should cover multicasts, global operations and parallel subroutines. The models should be parameterized for various different target machines.

Additionally it will be necessary to provide possibilities for the verification of the scalability of a graph. It should be possible to see the dependencies of the shape of the graph from the various scaling parameters. In the current version the only possibility to check the scaling behavior of a graph is to change one or more scaling parameters and to see what happens to the graph.

References

[1] D.P. Bertsekas and J.N. Tsitsiklis. *Parallel and Distributed Computation - Numerical Methods.* Prentice Hall, Inc., Englewood Cliffs, 1989.

[2] Departament d'Informàtica, Universitat Autònoma de Barcelona. *Parallel System Evaluation Environment User's Guide*, 1992.

[3] A. Ferscha and B. Gruber. Prototype graphical communication pattern editor. Technical Report PACT/CEI - Deliverable D6H/2 (GZ 308.926), obtainable from the anonymous ftp-server ftp.ani.univie.ac.at, /pub/CEI/D6H-2.ps.gz, Institute of Applied Computer Science and Information Systems, Department of Advanced Computer Engineering, 1995.

[4] G. Haring and A. Ferscha. Performance oriented development of parallel software with capse. In *Proc. of the Workshop on Environments and Tools for Parallel Scientific Computing, May 25-27, Blackberry-Inn, Walland/Tennessee, 1994*, 1994.

[5] Teemo Kerola. Qsolver, a modular environment for solving queueing network models. In *Proceedings of the 5th international conference on Modelling Techniques and Tools for Computer Performance Evaluation*, pages 409–420, 1991.

[6] nCUBE. *nCUBE 2 Programmer's Guide.* nCUBE Corporation, 1990.

[7] Päivi Purovesi Teemo Kerola and Erkki Hietalahti. Qsolver user guide. Technical Report C-1990-32, Department of Computer Science, University of Helsinki, 1990.

[8] H. Wabnig and G. Haring. Paps - the parallel program performance prediction toolset. pages 284–304. G. Haring, G. Kotsis (eds.): Computer Performance Evaluation - Modelling Techniques and Tools, Proc. of the 7th Intern. Conf., Vienna, Springer Verlag, Lecture Notes in Computer Science 794, 1994.

[9] H. Wabnig, G. Haring, D. Kranzlmüller, and J Volkert. Communication pattern based performance prediction of multiprocessor systems. In *Proc. of CONPAR'94 VAPP VI, (Linz, Austria, September 6-8, 1994) Springer Verlag, Lecture Notes in Computer Science 854*, pages 41–52, 1994.

❖ Session 3 ❖

Routing

Chair

N. Scarabottolo

Liveness Conditions for a Safe Distributed Deadlock Resolution Algorithm*

J. R. González de Mendívil[1], F. Fariña[2], J. Villadangos[1], J. R. Garitagoitia[2]
[1] Department of Automatic Control, Electronics and System Engineering; Public University of Navarra; Campus Arrosadia s/n, 31006 Pamplona, SPAIN; e.mail:<jrmendi@tsc.upna.es>
[2] Department of Mathematics and Computation; Public University of Navarra; Campus Arrosadia s/n, 31006 Pamplona, SPAIN; e.mail:<joserra@upna.es>

Abstract

Although the problem of deadlock detection and resolution in distributed systems has been studied in detail during the last years, it is still an open and difficult problem for all but the simplest models. One of the main difficulties in finding adequate solutions in the Multiple-Request model resides in the need to avoid false deadlock resolutions. In this paper we show a distributed solution with the Strong Safety Condition of "only true deadlocks must be detected/resolved". The algorithm was proved to satisfy this safety condition in [1] and now we study the liveness conditions the algorithm supports.

1. Introduction

The Deadlock Problem has been studied in detail during the last years [2] [3], but it is still a very difficult problem in the area of Distributed Systems. Recently, different formal frameworks [4] [5] have been presented in order to characterize deadlocks in various resource allocation models and to define the correctness criteria that Distributed Deadlock Detection/Resolution (DDD/R) algorithms must verify. The classical intuitive criteria of correctness: Strong Safety Condition (SSC): "*only true deadlocks must be detected/resolved*"; and Strong Liveness Condition (SLC): "*every deadlock must be detected/resolved in finite time*"; are satisfied only for very restricted models of resource management —as the Single-Request model [6] [7]. One of the main difficulties in dealing with deadlocks in complex resource allocation models is that certain operations over a particular deadlock situation —the resolution via aborting a process— affect to another deadlocks of the system. Some published works for complex models are directed to the design of DDD/R algorithms in which liveness and high performance are the desired properties [8] [9]. However, those works usually forget the issue of the SSC by relaxing such a property. They use different Weak Safety Conditions (WSC) which allow to resolve some kinds of false deadlocks.

Recently, we have proposed a new DDD/R algorithm for the Multiple-Request (MR) model [1] which verifies the SSC. The proposed solution is probe-based [2], that is, it uses special messages, called probes, to detect deadlocks. The algorithm uses priority of processes to select the victims; and simple information of the probes is stored to guarantee the resolution of only true deadlocks.

In this paper, we are interested on the study of the liveness conditions the algorithm verifies. In order to give a formal way to prove the properties, the algorithm abstraction is expressed by using the *Input/Output Automata Model* [10] [11]. We prove that the proposed DDD/R algorithm verifies the SLC when the re-entrance of aborted processes is finite; and in the infinite case, it verifies the Weak Liveness Condition (WLC): *"Deadlocks are resolved while there exist deadlocks in the system"*. This starvation is due by the required SSC.

The rest of the paper is organized as follows. Section 2 presents the environment and the specifications of the problem. Section 3 is devoted to show the resolution algorithm. Section 4 deals with the correctness proof. Finally, concluding remarks end the work.

2. Specifications

A Distributed System can be considered as a collection of sites interconnected by a communication network. In order to simplify the discussion, we consider only one process or resource for each site. A process requests to its local manager for the resources it needs. The manager sends the requests to the sites where the resources stand. If a resource is allocated to the process which have requested

* This work has been partially supported by the Basque Government under the scholarship number BFI.95.037 and by the CICYT under the research grant TIC 93-304.

it, then the local manager of that resource sends a grant message. We are not interested in modelling the relation among local managers, but capturing the global behaviour of the *wait for* relations among processes and resources of the system. In this work, the real behaviour is simulated by using a special graph, called the *Communication-Wait For Graph* (CWFG) [1] [5].

2.1 The Manager of the system

In this work, the distributed deadlock in MR model is studied. The model assumes that each process can perform several requests each time, and then, it waits for a reply to each request. The changes in the *wait for* relations among processes and resources can be modelled by the executions of the automaton M [1], which abstract the MR model.

Let $N=\{1, 2,\ldots, n,\ldots\}$ be a countable set of non-zero positive integers, called *nodes*. An element of N can be interpreted in several ways: the identifier, or the priority of a process or resource, or the site where they act. The total order of N yields to consider the values as priorities of nodes —in order to ensure the algorithm only selects processes as candidates to resolve deadlocks, it is assumed that their priority is lower than the priority of resources—. The fact that N be countable avoids the discussion about re-entrance of victims. —it is simulated by assigning new values in N to re-entrant processes.

The set $E=\{e_{ij} / i\neq j \wedge i, j\in N\}$ represents the set of *intermediate nodes*. A subset $E_i=\{e_{ij} / i\neq j \wedge i, j\in N\}$ can be interpreted as the possible *wait for* relations that node i may maintain with another nodes j.

The CWFG is a pair $(N \cup E, Arcs)$ where the set $Arcs \subseteq \{\langle i, e_{ij}\rangle, \langle e_{ij}, j\rangle / i\neq j \wedge i, j\in N\}$. The arcs represent the partial knowledge about the *wait for* relations different nodes can find at their sites. A generic arc of the graph will be denoted $\langle n, n'\rangle$. A value $version(\langle n, n'\rangle)$ counts the number of appearances of arc $\langle n, n'\rangle$ on the graph.

Finally the set *victims* contains the aborted nodes in the history of the system.

A state $s\in states(M)$ is defined by the values of the variables: $s.Arcs$, $s.victims$ and $\forall i, j\in N$: $s.version(\langle i, e_{ij}\rangle)$ and $s.version(\langle e_{ij}, j\rangle)$. Initially $s.Arcs = s.victims = \emptyset$ and $s.version(\langle i, e_{ij}\rangle) = s.version(\langle e_{ij}, j\rangle)=0$.

The action signature of the M is: $in(M)=\{abort(i)\}$ and $out(M)=\{\forall i, j\in N: \forall needed(i)\in 2^{E_i}:: add(i, needed(i)); add(e_{ij}, j), del(e_{ij}, j), del(i, e_{ij})\}$.

The steps of M are given with the preconditions/effects formalism [10].

add(i, *needed*(i))
prec: $d^+(i)=0 \wedge i\notin victims.$ // $d^+(i) \equiv$ *outdegree of node i.*
eff: $Arcs \leftarrow Arcs \cup \{\langle i, e_{ij}\rangle / e_{ij}\in needed(i)\}$;
FOR e_{ij} IN *needed*(i) DO
$version(\langle i, e_{ij}\rangle) \leftarrow version(\langle i, e_{ij}\rangle) + 1.$

An add(i, *needed*(i)) action means that process i has requested a set of resources. This action only can be performed if process i is not waiting for other resource and is not a victim. If node i represents a resource, the action means that the resource has been allocated to the process contained in *needed*(i). This action only can be performed if the resource is not being held by other process. The action is always local to the site of the node i and implies a request/grant message to be delivered.

add(e_{ij}, j)
prec: $version(\langle e_{ij}, j\rangle)= version(\langle i, e_{ij}\rangle) - 1 \wedge j\notin victims.$
eff: $Arcs \leftarrow Arcs \cup \{\langle e_{ij}, j\rangle\}$;
$version(\langle e_{ij}, j\rangle) \leftarrow version(\langle e_{ij}, j\rangle) + 1.$

An add(e_{ij}, j) action means that resource j knows the request of process i, or that the no victim process j knows that resource i is waiting its release. In both cases, the reception of the request/grant messages sent by the previous action is implicitly included. Therefore, this action cannot be executed if an action add(i, *needed*(i)) has not been performed.

del((e_{ij}, j)
prec: $d^+(j)=0 \vee i\in victims$
eff: $Arcs \leftarrow Arcs - \{\langle e_{ij}, j\rangle\}.$

The action del(e_{ij}, j) means that process j is sending to resource i its release, so process j cannot be blocked. If j is a resource then it means that j is going to be allocated to process i, so it cannot be allocated to other process. In both cases, this action implies the sending of a release/grant message to node i. This action also can mean that resource j has received a *withdrawing* message [3] which was created when i aborted.

del(i, e_{ij})
prec: $i\in victims \vee (d^+(e_{ij})=0 \wedge (j\in victims \vee version(\langle e_{ij}, j\rangle)= version(\langle i, e_{ij}\rangle) - 1)).$
eff: $Arcs \leftarrow Arcs - \{\langle i, e_{ij}\rangle\}.$

A del(i, e_{ij}) action can mean that process i has received a grant from resource j or it is withdrawing its requests because it is a victim, or that resource i has received a release message from process j or it has received a message indicating that its holder j has aborted.

abort(i)
eff: $victims \leftarrow victims \cup \{i\}$;
$Arcs \leftarrow Arcs - incoming(i).$

As the I/O automata are input enabled, input actions have not preconditions. The effects of this action are clear.

Remark 1 [1]: It is simple to prove that, in absence of abort(.) actions, the existence of a circuit in the state of M is a stable property. Therefore, deadlocks can be characterized by the existence of circuits in the graph, that is, $\exists C \subseteq s.Arcs \Leftrightarrow$ there exists a deadlock in the system.

Remark 2 [1]: Only the performance of abort(.) actions can break circuits, then those are the actions which *resolve* the deadlocks of the system. Therefore, the performance of an abort(i) action is an event of *deadlock resolution* if and only if that action breaks a circuit in the graph. If no circuit is broken by its performance then the event is a *false deadlock resolution*.

It is easy to see that the executions of M satisfy the following lemma that says how a circuit is created.

Lemma 1: Let $\alpha = s_0 \pi_1 s_1 \ldots \pi_n s_n \ldots$ be a fair execution of M. $\exists\ C :: (C \subseteq s_k.Arcs \wedge C \not\subset s_{k-1}.Arcs \Rightarrow \pi \in \{\forall\ i, j \in N :: \text{add}(e_{ij}, j)\})$.

2.2 The Specification of the Algorithm

The specification of the algorithm is given by the automaton A_0 defined as follows:

A state s$\in$ *states*(A_0) is defined by the values of : s.*Arcs* and s.*victims*. Initially s.*Arcs*= s.*victims* = Ø

The action signature of A_0 is: $out(A_0)$={abort(i)} and $in(A_0)$= {$\forall$i, j$\in$ N: $\forall$*needed*(i)$\in 2^{E_i}$:: add(i, *needed*(i)); add(e_{ij}, j), del(e_{ij}, j), del(i, e_{ij})}.

The steps of A_0 are the following:

abort(i)
prec: $\exists\ C \subseteq Arcs \wedge$ i= min(*Nodes*(*C*) $\cap$ *N*) // *min ≡ minimum*
eff: *victims* ← *victims* ∪ {i};
Arcs ← *Arcs* - *incoming*(i);

add(i, *needed* (i))
eff: *Arcs* ← *Arcs* ∪ {⟨i, e_{ij}⟩/ e_{ij}∈ *needed*(i)};

add(e_{ij}, j)
eff: *Arcs* ← *Arcs* ∪ {⟨e_{ij}, j⟩};

del((e_{ij}, j)
eff: *Arcs* ← *Arcs* – {⟨e_{ij}, j⟩};

del(i, e_{ij})
eff: *Arcs* ← *Arcs* – {⟨i, e_{ij}⟩};

The partition on *local*(A_0) has one class A^0= $out(A_0)$= {$\forall$ i $\in$ N :: abort(i)}. This partition implies that the fair executions of A_0 verify the property:

Property 1: Let $\alpha = s_0 \pi_1 s_1 \ldots \pi_n s_n \ldots$ be a fair execution of A_0. $\exists\ C \subseteq s_k.Arcs \Rightarrow \exists$ k'>k :: $\pi_{k'} \in out(A_0)$.

Proof: The existence of a circuit in the graph enables one abort(.) action —each circuit have a node verifying the condition of being the node with lower priority in the circuit— and these actions belong to the class A^0. Only the breaking of the circuit can disable the class, so it will be enabled until the execution of one of its actions. Therefore, by fairness, one action of A^0= out(A_0) will be eventually performed.

This property expresses the WLC . If the system is assumed to be finite —*N* finite—, it is simple to show that WLC implies SLC.

Lemma 2: Let $\alpha = s_0 \pi_1 s_1 \ldots \pi_n s_n$ be a fair execution of A_0. $\exists C \subseteq s_k.Arcs \Rightarrow \exists$ k'>k, i$\in$ *Nodes*(*C*) :: $\pi_{k'}$= abort(i).

Proof: By contradiction. Assume the property is false, that is: $\exists C \subseteq s_k.Arcs$ verifying $\forall$ k'>k :: $C \subseteq s_{k'}.Arcs$. The function d(s): $\{s\ /\ C \subseteq s.Arcs\} \rightarrow Z^+$ is defined as d(s) = $|N|$ - $|s.victims|$ - $|C|$. The execution of actions of A^0 makes this function decrease. No action can increase it so this function is monotonally decreasing. As C remains in the graph, Property 1 ensures that the actions of A^0 have to be performed, so d(s) must decrease during the execution. As function d(s) is upper bounded, there exist one state $s_{k'}$ verifying d($s_{k'}$) = 0. That is N - $s_{k'}.victims$ = *Nodes*(*C*). Since circuit C remains, A^0 is enabled and one of their actions must be eventually performed. Only the actions abort(i) with i belonging to *Nodes*(*C*) can be enabled —a victim node cannot be aborted again—, so eventually one abort(i) action with i $\in$ *Nodes*(*C*) must be executed. However, this action would break C and, therefore, the initial assumption does not hold.

3. The Deadlock Resolution Algorithm

The algorithm will be defined by the automaton A_1. Some definitions used in their state were given above.

There are state variables associated with each node, n: *status*(n), *version*(n), *create*(n), *transmitted*(n) and *to_reply*(n). The variable *status*(n) indicates the status of the node with respect to the deadlock resolution algorithm. This variable has one of the following values: *running* if the node does not maintain *wait for* relations, *blocked* if the node waits for another node and has not been selected to break a deadlock, *candidate* if the node has been selected to break a circuit and *victim* if the node has been aborted. The variables *version*(n) are counters that allow to distinguish obsolete information. A set *create*(n) contains all intermediate nodes for which n has to create a probe. A set *transmitted*(n) records the probes that have been transmitted by n; and the set *to_reply*(n) registers the nodes from which an information message has arrived while n is in candidate status.

The algorithm works with three kinds of messages: *probes*, *information messages* and *reply messages*. A probe has six fields, m= (det, init, version, to, v, v'). The first field identifies the kind of the message; *init* is the priority of the node which created the probe; *version* is the value of *version*(init) when the probe was created; *to* is the intermediate node to which the probe was sent when it was created, being v the version of the arc ⟨to, init⟩ when the probe was created. The field v' is the only field that is modified in a probe by the rest of nodes; it is the version of the arc where a node transmits the probe when this transmission is performed. The set containing all possible probes in the executions of the algorithm is called D. The *information* and *reply messages* have two fields: the identifier of the kind of message —*inf* for information messages and *rep* for reply messages— and the priority of the node that creates the message. The set of all possible information messages in the executions of the algorithm is called I, and the set of all reply messages, R.

The state variables, *mess*(possible arc), are FIFO lists which contain the messages that are travelling from a particular node to an intermediate node or vice versa.

Therefore, a state $s \in states(A_1)$ is defined by the values of the variables: s.*Arcs*, $\forall i \in N$: s.*status*(i), s.*version*(i), s.*create*(i), s.*transmitted*(i), s.*to_reply*(i), and $\forall i, j \in N$: s.*version*(⟨i, e_{ij}⟩), s.*version*(⟨e_{ij}, j⟩), s.*mess*(i, e_{ij}) and s.*mess*(e_{ij}, j). Initially s.*Arcs*= s_0.*victims*= Ø; $\forall i \in N$: s.*create*(i)= s.*transmitted*(i)= s.*to_reply*(i)= Ø, s.*status*(i)= *running*, s.*version*(i)= 0, and $\forall i, j \in N$: s.*version*(⟨i, e_{ij}⟩)= s.*version*(⟨e_{ij}, j⟩)= 0, s.*mess*(i, e_{ij})= s.*mess*(e_{ij}, j)= ε.

3.2 Actions of A_1

The automaton A_1 reflects the performance of the algorithm under a MR manager, so its action signature can be seen as partitioned into two groups: The actions of communication between the algorithm and the manager and the actions defining the performance of the algorithm.

Formally the automaton action signature is:

in(A_1)={ $\forall i, j \in N$: $\forall$*needed*(i)$\in 2^{E_i}$: add(i, *needed*(i)); add(e_{ij}, j), del(e_{ij}, j), del(i, e_{ij})}

out(A_1)= {$\forall i \in N$: abort(i)}

int(A_1)= {$\forall i, j \in N$: create(i, j), handle_det(i, e_{ij}), handle_inf(i, e_{ij}), handle_rep(i, e_{ij}), detect(i), $\forall m \in D \cup I \cup R$: send(j, e_{ij}, m)}

The actions are given in the following.

add(i, *needed*(i))
eff: *Arcs* ← *Arcs* ∪ {⟨i, e_{ij}⟩/ $e_{ij} \in$ *needed*(i)};
    status(i) ← blocked;
    FOR e_{ij} IN *needed*(i) DO
        version(⟨i, e_{ij}⟩) ← *version*(⟨i, e_{ij}⟩) + 1.

add(e_{ij}, j)
eff: *Arcs* ← *Arcs* ∪ {⟨e_{ij}, j⟩};
    version(⟨e_{ij}, j⟩) ← *version*(⟨e_{ij}, j⟩) + 1;
    IF *status*(j)≠ candidate THEN
        create(j) ← *create*(j) ∪ {e_{ij}}.

del(i, e_{ij})
eff: *Arcs* ← *Arcs* – {⟨i, e_{ij}⟩};
    IF d^+(i)= 0 THEN
        status(i) ← running;
        version(i) ← *version*(i) + 1;
        create(i) ← Ø.

If d^+(i)= 0 then i cannot belong to any circuit, so the action makes obsolete its previous probes and empties the set *create*(i).

del(e_{ij}, j)
eff: *Arcs* ← *Arcs* – {⟨e_{ij}, j⟩};
    create(j) ← *create*(j) – {e_{ij}}.

create(i, j)
prec: *status*(i)= blocked ∧ $e_{ji} \in$ *create*(i);
eff: *mess*(e_{ji}, i) ← *mess*(e_{ji}, i)•(det, i, *version*(i), e_{ji}, *version*(⟨e_{ji}, i⟩), *version*(⟨e_{ji}, i⟩));
    create(i) ← *create*(i) – {e_{ji}}.

The action create(i, j) creates a probe of node i and sends it towards node j. That probe appears in the arc from e_{ji} to i because the probes go in a backward direction through the arcs of the graph.

send(j, e_{ij}, m)
prec: *mess*(e_{ij}, j) = m • μ ∧ m ∈ $D \cup I \cup R$.
eff: *mess*(e_{ij}, j) ← μ;
    mess(i, e_{ij}) ← *mess*(i, e_{ij}) • m.

The actions send(j, e_{ij}, m) model the reliable communication among the sites. These actions always pass a message of the algorithm from a site to another one. The rest of the actions are commented at the end of the presentation.

handle_det(i, e_{ij})
prec: *mess*(i, e_{ij})= (det, init, vn, to, v, v') • μ ∧ (init= i ⇒ (⟨to,init⟩∉ *Arcs* ∨ v≠ *version*(⟨to,init⟩) ∨ *version*(i)≠vn ∨ ⟨i,e_{ij}⟩∉*Arcs* ∨ v'≠*version*(⟨i,e_{ij}⟩))).
eff: *mess*(i, e_{ij}) ← μ;
    IF ⟨i, e_{ij}⟩∈ *Arcs* AND v'= *version*(⟨i, e_{ij}⟩ AND
        status(i)= blocked AND
        incoming(i)≠ Ø THEN // *else the probe is lost.*
      IF init < i THEN //*Case transmission.*
        FOR ⟨e_{ki}, i⟩ IN *incoming*(i) DO
            mess(e_{ki}, i) ← *mess*(e_{ki}, i) •
                (det, init, vn, to, v, *version*(⟨e_{ki}, i⟩);
            transmitted(i) ← *transmitted*(i) ∪ {init}.
      IF init ≥ i THEN // *Regeneration of probes.*
        FOR ⟨e_{ki}, i⟩ IN *incoming*(i) DO
            create(i) ← *create*(i) ∪ {e_{ki}}.

detect(i)
prec: ∃⟨i, e_{ij}⟩∈ *Arcs* / *mess*(i,e_{ij})= (det, i, *version*(i), to, *version*(⟨to,i⟩), v) • μ ∧ *status*(i)= blocked ∧ ⟨to,i⟩∈ *Arcs* ∧ v= *version*(⟨i, e_{ij}⟩);
eff: *mess*(i, e_{ij}) ← μ;
    status(i) ← candidate;
    create(i) ← Ø;
    FOR k IN *transmitted*(i) DO
        mess(e_{ki}, i) ← *mess*(e_{ki}, i) • (inf, i).

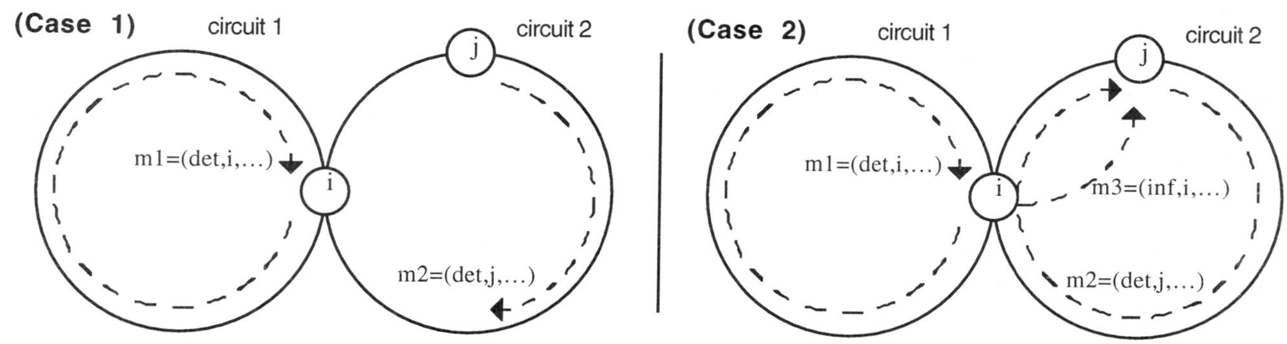

Figure 1. Possible executions of A_1 when there exist a knot in the CWFG.

The action handle_det(i, e_{ij}) is enabled if one probe has arrived to node i unless this probe would be a probe enabling detect(i). The former action checks the conditions that can make the probe irrelevant; if it decides the probe is relevant, it can transmit this probe to its predecessors in the graph, or send to them its own probes by enabling its create(.) actions. If the probe is relevant to the node and is one of its own probes, then the action detect(i) is enabled. This action makes the node to enter the second phase of the algorithm. It can be shown [1] that this action ensures the existence of a deadlock in the system which can be resolved only by node i, so node i is a candidate and informs to the nodes that need it about this new situation.

handle_inf(i, e_{ij})
prec: *mess*(i, e_{ij})= (inf, j) • μ.
eff: *mess*(i, e_{ij}) ← μ;
IF *status*(i)= candidate THEN *// Permission denied.*
to_reply(i) ← *to_reply*(i) ∪ {j}.
ELSE *// Giving permission to j.*
mess(e_{ji}, i) ← *mess*(e_{ji}, i) • (rep, i);
IF *status*(i)= blocked THEN
version(i) ← *version*(i) + 1.

handle_rep(i, e_{ij})
prec: *mess*(i, e_{ij})= (rep, j) • μ.
eff: *mess*(i, e_{ij}) ← μ;
transmitted(i) ← *transmitted*(i) – {j}.

abort(i)
prec: *status*(i)= candidate ∧ *transmitted*(i)= Ø.
eff: *status*(i) ← victim;
Arcs ← *Arcs* – *incoming*(i);
FOR k IN *to_reply*(i) DO
mess(e_{ki}, i) ← *mess*(e_{ki}, i) • (rep, i).

When node i knows, by the execution of a handle_inf(i, e_{ij}) action, that node j is a candidate, then it can reply that the abortion is allowed and modify its *version* —all previously sent probes will be irrelevant after this modification— or, if the node is another candidate it delays the reply until its abortion. This second case avoids a kind of false resolutions. The reception of a reply message by the handle_rep(i, e_{ij}) action only causes the candidate i to erase a node from which it will wait for the permission to abort.

Finally, an abort(i) action transforms process i into a victim. A victim process does not maintain any resource, so arcs with i as terminal endpoint are deleted. The actions abort(i) together with the performance of handle_inf(k, e_{ki}) and handle_rep(i, e_{ik}) actions assure the local knowledge about the circuits and candidates before the abortion is consistent.

The partition on local(A_1) is composed by the classes: A^1; ∀ i ∈ N :: $D^1{}_i$; and ∀ i, j ∈ N :: $H^1{}_{ij}$, $S^1{}_{ij}$ and $C^1{}_{ij}$ being A^1= out(A_1)= {∀ i ∈ N :: abort(i)}; $D^1{}_i$= {detect(i)}; $S^1{}_{ij}$= {∀m ∈ $D \cup I \cup R$ :: send(e_{ij}, m)}; $C^1{}_{ij}$ = {create(j, i)} and finally $H^1{}_{ij}$= {handle_det(i, e_{ij}), handle_inf(i, e_{ij}), handle_rep(i, e_{ij})}; .

The Figure 1 helps the reader to obtain an intuitive vision of the behaviour of the algorithm. The nodes i and j are the lowest priority node of circuit 1 and 2 respectively. In case 1, the node i detects the circuit 1 before it receives the probe m_2 of the node j. In case 2, the node i detects circuit 1 after it has transmitted the probe m_2 of the node j.

The probes have the mission of detecting circuits and identifying the node with minimum priority of each circuit as a candidate to resolve it —in Figure 1 the messages (det, ...) represent the probes—. Each node only let pass through it the probes created by lower priority nodes —in Figure 1, case 2 only is possible if j < i—, and stores information about the probes it has transmitted. When a node is selected as a candidate to break a circuit —when m_1 reaches i—, this node can perform two actions. If no probe has been transmitted by it then it knows that it is the lowest priority node of a circuit and it can proceed to abort —case 1 of Figure 1, i detects circuit 1 and can abort itself; the abortion resolves circuits 1 and 2, but as m_2 cannot reach j no false deadlock can be resolved—. In the other case, the initiators of the probes that have been transmitted by the candidate node do not know that this node is going to abort. This fact could promote a posterior false resolution —if m_2 reaches node j in Figure 1, case 2 after the abortion of node i—. This is avoided by the introduction of an invalidation mechanism. Before aborting a candidate node, it sends information messages to the nodes that created the message it has transmitted. These messages have the mission of reporting that previous probes of receptor nodes are no longer valid —in Figure 1 case 2, i informs to j that it is going to abort; after the reception of m_3 by j, m_2 is not considered as relevant by node j—. The candidate node waits for a reply for each inf message before aborting. During this delay no probe passes through the candidate node. If a candidate receives an information message, then it stores that message and only sends the corresponding reply when aborting —in Figure 1 if m_2 reaches j before m_3, then j is candidate when it receives the information message. Until its abortion, j will not send the reply to i, so i cannot abort.

The automaton A_1 is the result of the composition of the automata of each site, which represent an instance of the DDD/R algorithm, and the communication network after hiding the communication actions —{send(j, e_{ij}, m)}—. The automaton A_1 reflects the global behaviour of the DDD/R algorithm in the distributed system.

4. Proof of Correctness

In [1], we have provided the complete proof for the SSC: "*only true deadlocks must be detected/resolved*". Basically, that work shows that if $\alpha \in execs(A_1)$ and the action π_k = abort(i) then $\exists C \subseteq s_{k-1}.Arcs$ verifying that i = min($Nodes(C) \cap N$). The proof is based in the existence of a possibilities mapping [10], *h* defined as follows:

Definition 1: h: $states(A_1) \rightarrow 2^{states(A_0)}$ is defined as the mapping such that $t \in h(s) \Leftrightarrow s.victims = t.victims \wedge s.Arcs = t.Arcs$.

To prove that *h* is a possibilities mapping the main idea was the use of the definition of a *relevant probe*:

Definition 2: m= (det, init, vn, to, v, v') is a relevant probe of an arc ⟨n, n'⟩, with n, n'$\in N \cup E$, at state s of A_1 if and only if the following conditions hold:

(i) s.*mess*(n, n')= $\mu \bullet m \bullet \mu'$
(ii) ⟨n, n'⟩$\in$ s.*Arcs*
(iii) ⟨to, init⟩$\in$ s.*Arcs*
(iv) s.*version*(init)= vn
(v) s.*version*(⟨to, init⟩)= v
(vi) s.*version*(⟨n, n'⟩)= v'
(vii) s.*status*(n)$\neq$ victim
(viii) s.*status*(i)= blocked

The following result is the key for the proof and it can be made by simple induction over the length of the execution:

Let α be an execution of A_1, $\alpha = s_0\pi_1 s_1 \ldots \pi_k s_k \ldots$ If m= (det, init, vn, to, v, v') is a relevant probe of the arc ⟨n, n'⟩ at state s_k then there exists a path $P \subseteq s_k.Arcs$ such that: $First(P)$= n $\wedge$ $Last(P)$= init $\wedge$ $\forall$l$\in$ (($Nodes(P)$-{init, n}) $\cap N$):: (l>init $\wedge$ init$\in$ $s_k.transmitted$(l)).

In the particular case of a relevant probe fires the performance of π_k = detect(i), it implies $\exists C \subseteq s_{k-1}.Arcs$ such that i = min($Nodes(C) \cap N$). In addition, the order established by sets transmitted(.) and to_reply(.) allows to prove that SSC is verified.

At this point, we are interested on the liveness of the algorithm.

4.1. Liveness

Since the fair behaviours of A_0 verify WLC (SLC if N is finite), we only have to prove that the fair behaviours of A_1 are included into the set of fair behaviours of A_0 [10]. Some previous Lemmas are needed. All of them assume that $\alpha = s_0 \pi_1 s_1 \ldots \pi_n s_n \ldots$ is a fair execution of A_1

Firstly, Lemmas 3 and 4 prove that the messages of the algorithm reach their destination. The actions and partition of A_1 assume the channels are secure and FIFO, so the proof of these lemmas is obvious.

Lemma 3: $s_k.mess(i, e_{ij}) = \omega\ m\ \omega' \Rightarrow \exists\ k' \geq k :: s_{k'}.mess(i, e_{ij}) = m\ \omega''$. ($\omega$, ω' and $\omega'' \in (D \cup I \cup R)^*$).

Lemma 4: $s_k.mess(e_{ij}, j) = \omega\ m\ \omega' \Rightarrow \exists\ k' \geq k :: s_{k'}.mess(e_{ij}, j) = m\ \omega''$. ($\omega$, ω' and $\omega'' \in (D \cup I \cup R)^*$).

The following invariant can be easily proved by induction over the length of the executions. It says that while there exist circuits in the system one locally controlled action of A_1 must be enabled. That is while there exist deadlocks the algorithm is trying to detect them.

Lemma 5: $\exists\ C \subseteq s_k.Arcs \Rightarrow \exists\ \langle e_{ij}, j\rangle \in C$ :: enabled(s_k, create(j, i)) $\vee \exists \langle n, n'\rangle \in C :: s_k.mess(n, n') \neq \varepsilon$ $\vee$ ($\exists$ i $\in$ $Nodes(C)$ :: $s_k.status$(i)= candidate $\wedge$ $s_k.transmitted$(i) = $\emptyset$)

The following Lemmas ensure that the existence of a circuit in the graph imply a subsequent detection of a circuit —the same or another. Firstly, when a circuit appears, if it doesn't contains any candidate, the creation of probes of one of its nodes is enabled.

Lemma 6: $\exists\ C :: (C \not\subset s_{k-1}.Arcs \wedge C \subseteq s_k.Arcs) \Rightarrow$ ($\exists\langle e_{ij}, j\rangle \in C$ :: (enabled(s_k, C^1_{ij}))$\vee$ $s_k.status$(j)= candidate)

Proof: By Lemma 1, π_k= add(e_{ij}, j). The effects of such an action ensure that the Lemma holds.

Once the class C^1_{ij} is enabled, only the deletion of some arcs or the selection of i as candidate can avoid the execution of its action.

Lemma 7: enabled(s_k, C^1_{ij}) $\Rightarrow \exists$ k' > k :: ($\pi_{k'} \in$ {detect(i), create(j, i), del(e_{ij}, j)} $\vee\ \forall\ e_{jl}$ :: ⟨j, e_{jl}⟩ $\notin s_{k'}.Arcs$).

Proof: By definition of fairness, either one action of C^1_{ij} is executed or the class is disabled. In the first case, as create(j, i) is executed, the Lemma holds. In the second case one of the conditions of the Lemma must be true to disable the class.

It can be ensured that the existence of circuits in the system leads to the execution of detect(.) actions, that is, to the appearance of candidates.

Lemma 8: $\exists\ C :: (C \subseteq s_k.Arcs \wedge i = \min(Nodes(C)) \wedge \exists e_{ji} :: \langle e_{ji}, i\rangle \in C) \Rightarrow \exists\ k' > k :: \pi_{k'}= \text{create}(i, j) \vee \{l\in N / s_k.status(l)= \text{candidate}\}\neq \emptyset$.

Proof: Assume that never there are candidates in the system —in other case the proof is trivial. Lemmas 6 and 7 ensure the creation of a probe after the appearance of the circuit. Lemmas 3 and 4 assure that this probe reaches their destination enabling classes H^1_{kl}. Fairness says that the probes are eventually handled. It is easy to see that the actions that handle the probes, if the node belongs to a circuit, either transmit them or enable the creation of new probes until the detection of the circuit. Therefore one probe of the circuit will eventually reach node i enabling C^1_{ij}. By lemma 7, as C remains —only candidates can abort— create(i, j) action will be eventually performed.

Lemma 9: $\exists\ C :: C \subseteq s_k.Arcs \Rightarrow \exists\ k' \geq k :: \{l\in N / s_{k'}.status(l)= \text{candidate}\}\neq \emptyset$.

Proof: Assume the Lemma does not hold. In such a case, Lemma 8 ensures that the probe of node i will be created, being $i = \min(Nodes(C))$. As there are not candidates and the circuit remains the same reasoning of the proof of Lemma 8 lets assure that the probe will eventually reach i detecting C and changing the status of node i to candidate. Therefore, the initial assumption is false and the Lemma holds.

Finally the following Lemmas will let assure that the existence of candidates leads to deadlock resolutions.

Lemma 10: $i \in s_k.to\_reply(j) \Rightarrow s_k.status(j)= \text{candidate} \wedge j < i$.

Proof: $i \in s_k.to\_reply(j)$ implies that j has received an (inf, i) message. This message was sent by i when it was selected as candidate. Node i sent the message to the elements of *transmitted*(i). It is easy to see that if j belonged to that set then j < i. In addition, the sets *to_reply*(n) are empty unless n is a candidate.

Lemma 11: $s_k.status(i)= \text{candidate} \Rightarrow \exists\ k' \geq k :: s_{k'}.transmitted(i)= \emptyset \vee \exists\ j \neq i :: i \in s_{k'}.to\_reply(j)$.

Proof: Node i sent (inf, i) messages to the elements of its set *transmitted*(i) when it was selected as candidate. By Lemmas 3 and 4, these messages reach their destination. If some receivers of those messages are candidate, then i will be added to their sets *to_reply*(.) making the Lemma true. In the other case, by the effects of the action handle_inf(), (rep, .) messages will be sent to i. All those reply messages will reach i by Lemmas 3 and 4. Node i will empty its set *transmitted*(i) when it will have handled all those messages.

The following Lemma assumes that there are not infinite deadlocks at any time in a system.

Lemma 12: $s_k.status(i)= \text{candidate} \Rightarrow \exists\ k' \geq k :: \text{enabled}(s_{k'}, A^1)$.

Proof: By Lemma 11 either $s_k.transmitted(i)= \emptyset$ and consequently abort(i) is enabled or $\exists\ j :: i \in s_{k'}.to\_reply(j)$. In this case, by Lemma 10, j < i and *status*(j) = candidate. As the same arguments can be used recursively, we can build an ordered sequence of candidates $i < j_1 < j_2 < \ldots$. That sequence cannot be infinite and, therefore, there will exist j_n such $transmitted(j_n)$ is empty enabling the class of abort actions A^1.

In order to finish this proof of correctness only rest to show that the fair behaviours of A_1 are a subset of the fair behaviours of A_0. That is, the fair behaviours of A_1 verify the same liveness conditions as the fair behaviours of A_0. The proof is going to be presented uses some results of the I/O Automata model about execution correspondences [10]. The main result is the following Theorem.

Theorem 1: Let A and B be two I/O automata and h a possibilities mapping from A to B. If $(\forall\ \alpha \in fairexecs(A) \wedge \forall\ \beta \in execs(B)) :: (\beta\ C_h\ \alpha \Rightarrow \beta \in fairexecs(B))$ then $fairbehs(A) \subseteq fairbehs(B)$.

Proof: It is proved in [10] that $\beta\ C_h\ \alpha \Rightarrow sched(\alpha) \mid acts(B) = sched(\beta)$. We can restrict both sequences to the set $ext(B)$ and, as $acts(B) \mid ext(B) = ext(B)$, we obtain $sched(\alpha) \mid ext(B) = sched(\beta) \mid ext(B)$. Since $\beta\ C_h\ \alpha$ also implies that $ext(A) = ext(B)$ the previous expression is the same as $sched(\alpha) \mid ext(A) = sched(\beta) \mid ext(B)$. Therefore, by definition of behaviour, we obtain $beh(\alpha)= beh(\beta)$. In conclusion if β is fair, α have to be also fair.

Lemma 13: $fairbehs(A_1) \subseteq fairbehs(A_0)$

Proof: By Theorem 1, we only must show that $(\forall\ \alpha \in fairexecs(A_1) \wedge \forall\ \beta \in execs(A_0)) :: (\beta\ C_h\ \alpha \Rightarrow \beta \in fairexecs(A_0))$. This property is going to be showed by contradiction. Assume the existence of two executions α and β such that $\beta\ C_h\ \alpha$ being $\alpha\in fairexecs(A_1)$ and $\beta \notin fairexecs(A_0)$. We are going to study four cases.

A) $\alpha= s_0\pi_1\ldots\pi_k s_k$ and $\beta= t_0\varphi_1\ldots\varphi_i t_i$ are finite: If β is not fair then A^0 is enabled at t_i and therefore $\exists C \subseteq t_i.Arcs$. As, by definition [10], $t_i\in h(s_k)$ then $\exists C \subseteq s_k.Arcs$. Therefore by Lemma 5 some class of $part(A_1)$ is enabled at t_i and α cannot be fair.

B) $\alpha= s_0\pi_1\ldots\pi_k s_k\ldots$ is an infinite execution while $\beta= t_0\varphi_1\ldots\varphi_i t_i$ is finite: If β is not fair then A^0 is enabled at t_i and therefore $\exists C \subseteq t_i.Arcs$. As $\beta\ C_h\ \alpha$ then [10] $\exists k :: \forall\ k' \geq k :: t_i\in h(s_{k'})$. Therefore $\forall\ k' \geq k :: \exists\ C \subseteq s_{k'}.Arcs$. By Lemmas 9 and 12, there exist k", k < k' < k", such that the class A^1 is enabled in $s_{k''}$. Only the execution of one of these actions can disable such a class. However, no action of A^1 can be performed because its actions are also actions of A_0 and in other case it should appear in β. Therefore

$\exists$ k'' such that $\forall$ k' $\geq$ k'' the class A^1 is enabled and no action of this class is executed. Consequently the execution α is not fair.

C) $\alpha = s_0\pi_1 \ldots \pi_k s_k \ldots$ and $\beta = t_0\varphi_1 \ldots \varphi_i t_i$ are infinite. If β is not fair then there must exist one class of $part(A_0)$ and one state s_k such that $\forall$ i' $\geq$ i the class A^0 is enabled and none of its actions appears in the execution. That is, there exist always circuits in the graph but there are not resolutions. Assume that s_k is the first state such that $t_i \in h(s_{k'})$. Therefore $\forall$ k' $\geq$ k :: $\exists$ $C \subseteq s_{k'}.Arcs$ and $\pi_{k'} \notin A^1$. In such a case Lemmas 9 and 12 ensure that there exist k'', k < k' < k'', such that the class A^1 is enabled in $s_{k''}$. As only the execution of one of its actions can disable that class and no action of A^1 can be performed—its actions are also actions of A_0, so it should appear in β—, α cannot be fair.

D) $\alpha = s_0\pi_1 \ldots \pi_k s_k$ is finite being $\beta = t_0\varphi_1 \ldots \varphi_i t_i$ infinite: As β C_h α, then $sched(\alpha) \mid acts(A_0) = sched(\beta)$. Therefore β cannot be higher than α.

5. Conclusions

In this paper, a Distributed algorithm for Deadlock Detection/Resolution in a system with Multiple-Request model has been introduced. The main goal has been the design of a distributed solution which verifies the Strong Safety Condition: "*only true deadlocks are resolved*". We show that the proposed DDD/R algorithm verifies the Strong Liveness Condition of "*every deadlock is resolved in finite time*" when the re-entrance of aborted processes is finite; and in the infinite case, it verifies the Weak Liveness Condition of "*Deadlocks are resolved while there exist deadlocks in the system*". In order to provide a formal correctness proof of the algorithm, we have used the I/O Automata Model as the basis for the formalism. Several aspects of our work require further discussion: (a) It is obvious the cost in messages for detecting deadlocks can be of importance, about $O(l^2)$ for a circuit of l nodes [5]. However, it is possible to reduce it by eliminating the symmetry on the generation of probes for each node, in a similar way as in [4]. This fact could have important impact for practical purposes but we have avoided it in the present work because the complexity it implies in the development of the solution and in the proofs is very high. (b) In the finite case, the proposed solution verifies both SSC and SLC. However, the latency of a deadlock strongly depends on the invalidation mechanism of probes and the mechanism of handling candidates. Candidates wait for other ones because the probes they transmitted are of importance to assure safety. In order to find another approach, it would be of interest to study the relations between circuits and candidates at high level of abstraction as it was proposed in [12] for the design of a DDD/R algorithm. (c) In the infinite case, the main problem is the possibility of the starvation of a circuit because its minimum node is not able to reach the status candidate due by resolutions of candidates related with it. Since in general the frequency of deadlock appearance is low, this problem is rarely found in practice. However, the consideration of the times one node have been re-entered as part of its priority is a possibility to assure the deadlocks are always detected and resolved.

References

[1] F. Fariña, J. R. González de Mendívil, C. F. Alastruey, J. R. Garitagoitia, "A Safe Distributed Deadlock Resolution Algorithm for the Multiple-Request Model"; *Proceedings of the EUROMICRO95 Conference*; 595-602, Como, Italy; 4-7 Sep. 1995.

[2] E. Knapp; "Deadlock Detection in Distributed Databases"; *ACM Computing Surveys*; vol. 19; no. 4; pp. 303-328; Dec. 1987.

[3] M. Singhal; "Deadlock Detection in Distributed Systems"; *IEEE Computer*; pp. 37-48; Nov .1989.

[4] A. D. Kshemkalyani, M. Singhal; "On Characterization and Correctness of Distributed Deadlock Detection"; *Technical Report*: OSU-CISRC-6/90 TR 15; The Ohio State University, Jan. 1993.

[5] J. R. González de Mendívil, J. Bernabeu, J. R. Garitagoitia, F. Fariña; "A Deadlock Resolution Algorithm Based on the Input/Output Automata Model"; *Technical Report*: DSIC-II-9/94; Politechnic University of Valencia; 1994.

[6] A. D. Kshemkalyani, M. Singhal; "Invariant-Based Verification of a Distributed Deadlock Detection Algorithm"; *IEEE Transactions on Software Engineering*; vol. 17; no. 8; pp. 789-799; Aug. 1991.

[7] J. R. González de Mendívil, J. Bernabeu, A. Demaille, J. R. Garitagoitia; "Correctness of a Distributed Deadlock Resolution Algorithm for the Single Request Model"; *Proceedings of the 3rd. Euromicro Workshop in Parallel and Distributed Systems*; pp. 254-261; San Remo, Italy; 25-27 Jan 1995.

[8] A. D. Kshemkalyani, M. Singhal; "Efficient Detection and Resolution of Generalized Distributed Deadlocks"; *IEEE Transactions on Software Engineering*; vol. 20; no. 1; pp. 43-53, Jan. 1994.

[9] M. Roesler, W. A. Burkhard; "Resolution of Deadlocks in Object-Oriented Distributed Systems"; *IEEE Transactions on Computers*; vol. 38; no. 8; pp. 1212-1224; Aug. 1989.

[10] N. A. Lynch, M. R. Tuttle; "Hierarchical Correctness Proofs for Distributed Algorithms"; *Technical Report*: MIT/LCS/TR-387; M. I. T. Laboratory for Computer Science; 1987.

[11] N. A. Lynch, M. R. Tuttle; "An Introduction to Input/Output Automata"; *CWI Quarterly*, vol. 2; no. 3; pp. 219-246; Sep. 1989.

[12] J. R. González de Mendívil, "Formal Solutions for the Deadlock Detection Problem"; Ph. D. Dissertation; University of the Basque Country; Mar. 1993. (In Spanish).

TransCom: a Communication Microkernel for Transputers

J.C. Moure Daniel Franco Elisa Heymann Emilio Luque
Unidad de Arquitectura de Ordenadores
Departamento de Informática
Universidad Autónoma de Barcelona
08193 - Bellaterra, Barcelona, Spain
E-mail: iinfd@cc.uab.es

Abstract

If parallel computers have to become general purpose tools, it is necessary to develop services that make transparent its internal characteristics and make parallel programming easier. Trying to fulfil this goal and to have a platform for the test and evaluation of mechanisms for a parallel architecture, a microkernel called TransCom *has been designed for a distributed-memory multiprocessor.*

The microkernel includes services to virtualise the communication network, *which provides a parallel programming model based on message passing. It has been designed in two steps: a tiny system core called* TransRouter *providing simple functions for data transport and routing, but without protocol services, and a basic set of communication primitives, on top of the* TransRouter *and including its own communication protocols, to make up the* TransCom. *Concurrently with the development of the microkernel, some studies and simulations have been undertaken in order to* virtualise the "processor resource" *through the load distribution among the processors.*

1. Introduction

The properties which an application programmer demands from a computer system are basically: fast and easy development of programs, reliable execution, help for error debugging, easy portability and rapid execution either with present or with upcoming computers. Parallel computers are not an exception. Nowadays, they look like very much earlier sequential computers regarding the lack of facilities to use them. The challenge for a parallel computer's designer is to provide a high-level and simple view of the computer, making the internal characteristics of its architecture transparent. This new view of the computer, a mixture of physical components (hardware) and system programs (software) is known as a *virtual* computer.

The computer's designer is faced with with different and conflicting goals. On the one hand, the virtual computer must provide general services increasing usability, reliability, productivity and portability for a wide range of applications. On the other hand, execution will not be as fast as if application and architecture had been directly tuned. In fact, some services can be a dead weight for many applications that do not use them. This overhead imposed by the system software could be stretched out by allowing the programmer to access the 'actual' architecture, instead of accessing the virtual architecture. Nevertheless, two factors decrease the importance of obtaining high performance from a couple application-architecture: any strategy a programmer uses to tune application and computer can be embodied into the virtual computer in the future and any software service can be implemented by hardware, improving its performance.

To sum up, in the same way as the address translation mechanisms (virtual memory) and the automatic data movement through the memory hierarchy (cache memory) have prevailed as essential characteristics of any sequential computer, (in spite of some loss of performance in specific situations), it will be necessary to find general mechanisms for parallel computers, where its benefits surpass its drawbacks.

This work was supported by the Spanish Comisión Interministerial de Ciencia y Tecnología (CICYT) under contract number TIC 95/0868, and partially sponsored by the EU's Copernicus Programme under Contract number CIPA-C1-93-0251

The two basic goals of our work are the study of improvements to the internal architecture and the development of a high level environment for parallel programming. In this framework, a microkernel for a distributed-memory multiprocessor, called *TransCom,* has been designed. It includes services to *virtualise the communication network* among processors. The microkernel joins the flexibility to change, modify and include services with the possibility of executing real applications to obtain precise results to validate the mechanisms and to measure its performance. The final results can be extrapolated to calculate the incidence of implementing the services in hardware. Additionally, the microkernel is the foundation to build a complete environment for parallel programming that would allow to experiment at all levels, from the internals of the architecture to the development of applications, and including the programming model.

Concurrently with the development of the microkernel some studies and simulations have been undertaken in order to *virtualise the load distribution* among the parallel computer. Simulation is another interesting option when studying the incidence of architectural improvements, specially when there is no idea about the advantages and disadvantages of a particular mechanism, because it allows a fast prototype development to generate earlier results. Also, it is useful to test mechanisms that, given their high cost of implementation or physical limitations, are unrealisable.

The rest of the paper is organised as follows. In the first place, there is a description of how the microkernel virtualise communications. Sections 3 and 4 present the two layers making up the microkernel, the inner layer is called *TransRouter*, [14], and the upper layer, build on top of the TransRouter, that constitutes the whole microkernel or *TransCom,* [5]. The studies about load balancing and its integration into the microkernel are explained in section 5. Finally, we conclude by discussing related work and some conclusions.

2. The virtualisation of the communications

The microkernel, or *TransCom,* represents the first step to obtain a general-purpose parallel computer, because it makes transparent the topological characteristics of the communication network, providing a virtual architecture where all the processors are directly connected to each other and all the (logical) connections do provide the same communication capability (named effective bandwidth and latency).

The microkernel has been designed in two steps. Firstly, a tiny system core called *TransRouter*, [14], has been developed to provide simple functions for data transport and routing, but without protocol services. It provides the foundation for modular extensions of more complex communication models. The second step was the design and development of a basic set of communication primitives, including its own communication protocols, on top of the *TransRouter* to make up what we called the *TransCom,* [5]. *TransCom* provides a parallel programming model based on message passing (CSP [7]) and described in [11]. The software is implemented in a Tandem Supernode [16] from Parsys, with 32 T8-transputers [8] connected through a statically reconfigurable network.

The *TransRouter* software is a data transport kernel. It is not intended for general use, instead it is designed as a foundation for modular extensions of more complex communication primitives. It provides services to move packets of data between processors, but lacks protocol services to synchronise the sending and receiving of the packets. Protocols have to be provided by an upper layer and implemented upon the *TransRouter* to fit it with a particular programming model(s), for example, synchronous channels, asynchronous buffers like PVM, [17], active messages, [4], shared virtual memory, etc. Also, the communication primitives address processors, which are the basic entities of computation, and not processes, which can be embedded in the system by an upper layer.

The *TransCom* offers message passing between any number of processes. Variable length messages, communication channels and processes are the new entities introduced by the *TransCom*. Processes invoke explicit primitives upon logical channels. There are different types of channels that allow the communication among two or more processes, offering high level communication mechanisms to the programmer. The basic channel protocol is synchronous as shown in section 4.

3. TransRouter

The basic goals in the *TransRouter*'s design are:

- To provide a virtual communication system where all processors exchange data as if they were directly connected to each other (to make transparent the topology of the network to the user).
- The virtualisation of the underlying interconnection hardware has to be achieved not only at the functional or logical level but even at the performance level: the data transfer capability has to be the same for any couple of processors in the system.

Figure 1 presents the actual architecture, where each processor is connected to up to four processors, and the virtual architecture where all processors are connected to each other. In the first case, each connection has the same bandwidth and latency (or distance) but between non-neighbour processors, the bandwidth and latency consumed by a packet transmission are multiplied by the number of links that data have to traverse. In the second case, all the logical links have the same bandwidth and latency, and all processors are at the same distance.

The data transport service is reliable, deadlock-free and starvation-free. It uses the virtual channel's approach described by Dally [2], consisting on breaking the cycles of the static routing algorithm with virtual channel. Anyway, packets delivered by the routing system must be immediately read by the processor or discarded, because they will be overwritten. Protocols can not restrain packets from being receipt or they must assure that cyclic dependencies are not allowed. There is no control with regard to a wrong use of the services. Also, order is not guaranteed among packets sent from the same source processor to the same destination processor. A protocol can be build on top of the *TransRouter* to provide packet reordering when necessary.

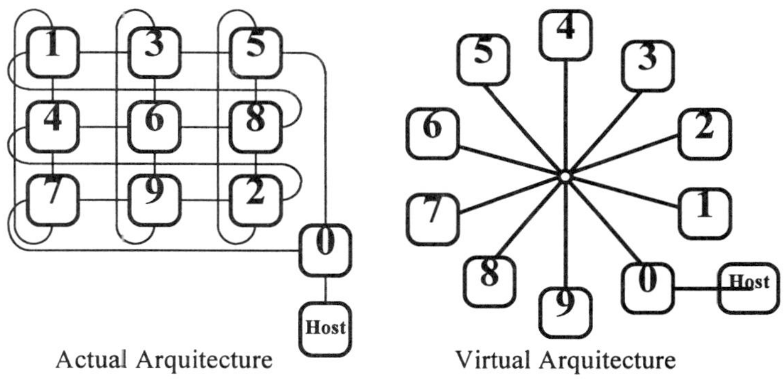

Figure 1. Virtualisation of the Communication Network

In the current implementation, the efficient use of the communication resources (physical links and DMA's) has higher priority than the efficient use of the CPU. The concurrent use of all the links is preferred even if that means that more time is spent by the CPU serving communication. Furthermore, efficient use of bandwidth is preferred than low latency, because the incidence of latency is expected to be reduced by multithreading, overlapping communication and computation.

3.1. TransRouter characteristics

The unit of information transmitted among processors is a fixed-length packet, made up by an information part and a header identifying the destination processor and containing routing information. The communication functions reference the processor identifiers, from zero upwards, and not topological characteristics of the network. The 0 identifier is reserved to the processor directly connected to the host.

It is possible to send data to a given processor or to broadcast data to all the processors simultaneously. This characteristic allows the simple and efficient implementation of all kind of primitives for global transport of messages and global synchronisation.

The interconnection topology selected for the current implementation is called midimew [1], but both the number of processors and the topology can be changed easily. The performance of the communication system, both the bandwidth and the latency, is uniform and does not depend on the particular processors that communicate but on the average load of the network. The performance will also depend on the topology's connectivity degree. Given the current system characteristics (transputer), a Store&Forward flow control is used.

3.2. Interface specification

The *TransRouter* primitives are shown in table 1. When an upper layer uses the *TransRouter* to send a packet to some processor, first it has to obtain a free buffer to store the packet using the *TrRout.Buffer.Request* function, which can block the requesting process. After copying the desired information, the upper layer will invoke the *TrRout.Send* or *TrRout.Broadcast* functions to send the packet to a suitable processor or to all the processors in the system (including the source processor).

Constants:

Packet.Size/* Maximum size (in bytes) of a packet of data */

Send Calls:

TrRout.Buffer.Request (*B*)/* Request a buffer *B*. Blocking primitive */

TrRout.Send (*P*)/* Send the last requested buffer to processor *P* */

TrRout.Broadcast ()/* Send the last requested buffer to all the processors */

Receive Calls:

TrRout.Receive (*B*)/* Wait and receive a buffer. Blocking primitive */

TrRout.Receive.Release ()/* Release received buffer */

Information Calls:

TrRout.WhoAmI ()/* Returns current processor identifier */

TrRout.N.Proc ()/* Returns the number of processors in the system */

TrRout.MemStart ()/* Returns the start address of the free memory area */

TrRout.MemEnd () /* Returns the end address of the free memory area */

Table 1. TransRouter functions

The upper layer has to declare a server process to manage the input packets and implement the suitable protocol, which will be invoked by the TransRouter when a data packet arrives to its destination. The server process defines its entry point calling the *TrRout.Receive* function and blocks until the arrival of a packet. It then completes the actions corresponding to the protocol associated with the packet, awaking other internal processes if necessary, and returning control to the *TransRouter* as soon as possible calling the *TrRout.Receive.Release* function. The buffer will be reused by the system, so it is essential that the server process copies the information in other location, if it must be preserved.

Finally, there are four functions for obtaining information about the only aspects of the actual architecture that an upper layer can access: the number of processors, the current processor's identifier, and the start and end of the free memory area.

3.3. Obtaining homogeneous performance

With the current static routing algorithm, communication latency is bounded provided that collisions never occur between packets using the same physical link. Unfortunately, in any sparse communication network, some communication patterns can not be realised without collisions, and this collisions can reduce system performance drastically. The problem is not the lack of resources but an inappropriate use of them, because some links will be always busy while other will be under-used.

A solution to this problem was presented by M.D. May and P.W. Thompson in [13], based on a work made by L.G. Valiant [18]. The work indicates that it is possible to design a universal routing system that can implement all communication patterns with an efficient bandwidth and bounded message latency (proportional to *log*(number of processors)). To eliminate the network hot-spots, two-phase routing is employed. Every packet is first dispatched to a randomly chosen intermediate destination and then to its final destination. In the two phases the static routing algorithm is used. The average values of latency and bandwidth are doubled but, with a very high probability, hot-spots are evenly distributed over the links for all communication patterns and resources are efficiently used. Also, the current values of latency and bandwidth barely differ with respect to the theoretical values.

4. TransCom

A new layer is implemented over the packet service *TransRouter*, previously explained, making up the complete *TransCom* microkernel. It provides a message-passing mechanism based on the CSP programming model. A programming model has the advantage of including a program methodology, which gives a set of rules to help the programmer write his program. Next, a brief description of the programming model, fully introduced in [11] is outlined.

The programmer designs his application by means of expressing parallelism as a collection of processes. A process is a bit of sequential code with its own internal data (variables). Processes are executed concurrently and collaborate to solve a common problem exchanging information by message-passing. Channels are used to carry out the message-passing. A channel is a program entity that links two or more processes and transports information. The data type of the information, the protocol used on transmission and the buffering capability are defined in the channel structure. Explicit communication primitives are called by processes to perform a communication action. These primitives are supplied by the kernel.

The source and destination specification is determined in a indirect way by the identifier of the channel which links the processes. Therefore, internal process code creation and definition of the links through channels are managed independently. This feature can help the programmer because the application is written in two steps: first, the process graph which defines the links and the parallel application structure and, second, the internal code.

To begin with, channels can be thought of as unidirectional, point-to-point and their protocol is synchronous. This means that processes involved in the communication are blocked until each one has executed its corresponding communication primitive. From this moment on, the information is transferred and both processes can continue its execution. Because it is known that each data sent is consumed by the receiver, a synchronous protocol guarantees a transparent and safe semantic.

- *Many-to-one* communication: where each sender process sends a different message to a receive-only process. Each receive primitive receives only one message from one of the senders.
- *One-of-many* communication: where one process send messages to a set of processes. Each primitive sends one message to one of the receivers. There exists two possibilities: the destination process is specified or is the first ready process.
- *Many-to-many* communication: where a set of sender processes send messages to a set of receivers processes. Again, the destination process can be specified or can be the first ready process.
- *One-to-many* communication (*multicast*): the same message is sent to all the members of a process group.

This set of channel types gives the programmer higher level programming structures, which make the programming language more powerful. For instance, MPI-like data-movement primitives, [15], the "worker-farmer" paradigm or global broadcast operations can be easily implemented.

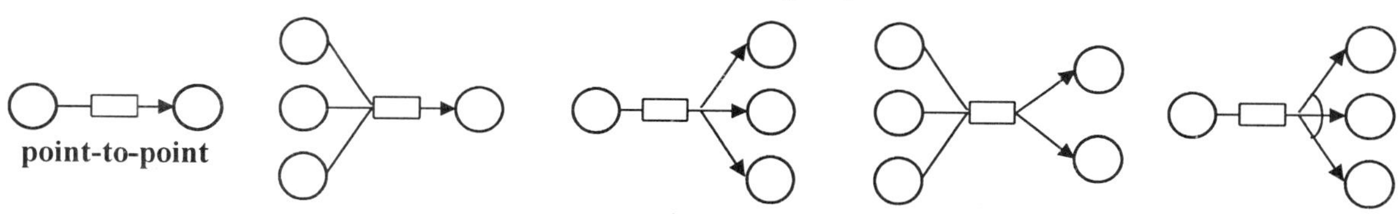

Figure 2. Channel types

4.1. Interface Specification

Basic primitives are send, receive, and detect message.

> **Send** (int *Channel*, void * *P*) /* Sends the message in *P* to *Channel* */
>
> **Receive** (int *Channel*, void * *P*) /* Receives a message from *Channel* on *P* */
>
> **Test** (int *Channel*) /* Tests whether if there is a message waiting on *Channel* */

The synchronous, point-to-point, communication is the simplest one. In addition, higher-level communication types are defined through different channel types. These types offer the programmer useful programming structures. The different channel types for communication among several processes are explained below:

Furthermore, there is the possibility of changing the channel protocol by adding buffering capability to the channels. This is a way to decouple the sending and receiving of messages, allowing different rates in the sending and receiving operations. This allows a certain level of asynchronous operation, since process blocking is not possible while data buffer is not full. In this sense, semisynchronous or asynchronous PVM-like protocols can be implemented, [17].

4.2. Implementation

Message service implementation has been carried out by means of concurrent processes. Fig. 3 shows *TransCom* internal process structure and their relationship. Each user process (*User*) has associated two handler processes (*HandSend* and *HandRecv*) whose function is to interface with the User process in order to send and receive messages. This interface is done by using transputer internal software channels (*UserHandSend* and *UserHandRecv*) without sharing common data. Furthermore, there is a *SendMess* process which sends messages packet by paquet to the network through the *TransRouter* and another process *RecvMess* which collects packets delivered by the *TransRouter*. These two processes communicate with the others using internal software channels and also accessing to common data structures (*ChannOutput* and *ChannInput*).

decide which process must be migrated, when and where must be moved (migration policies), and, on the other, a migration technique must be developed for the particular system (migration mechanisms).

Migration policies can be classified in relation to several criteria as described in [12]: whether they are centralised or not, whether independent or overlapped domain, whether local or global and if they are based on heuristic approximations or on iterative methods that can be mathematically analysed, like those based on diffusion schemes.

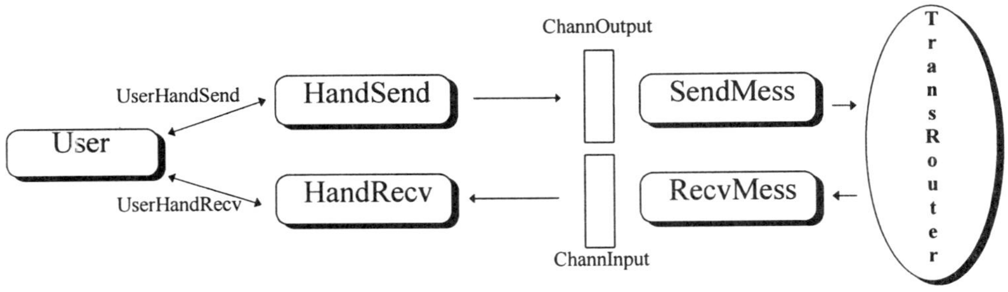

Figure 3. TransCom: Process Diagram

5. Load balancing and process migration

In addition to the processor interconnection network virtualisation, another parallel computer feature that seems suitable to be virtualised is the processor resource. Processor management has a great impact on the computer performance. Process distribution among processors should achieve a high rate of process usability during the execution time. This is difficult to get through a static process distribution because the computing load and communication patterns are not known at compile time.

Therefore, due to the computing volume of each process and their dependencies some processors can have no process ready while other processors have ready processes waiting to be executed. The goal would be a system able to dynamically distribute processes in order to balance the load of each processor. In this way, the programmer would see the parallel computer as a "virtual processor" resource made of all the physical processors in the system. That is, a virtual processor where the load would be automatically distributed among physical processors, flowing from the heaviest loaded processors to the less loaded processors.

To achieve this goal, dynamic process migration mechanisms must be provided. There will be two phases to solve. On the one hand, the system must be able to

Migration mechanisms involve two tasks: firstly, one related to code migration and, secondly, another related to process communication. The first task implies interrupting the process, to move code and data to a different position in the memory of a different processor, and, finally, to continue its execution in the new processor. Process interruption and reassume is not difficult in transputers thanks to its microprogrammed scheduler. However, code reallocation to a new memory location cause many problems because code generated by the compiler (INMOS C Toolset [9]) is position-dependent. The problems are absolute memory references generated at execution time when a function is called, or in using pointers, or global variables or calling library functions. Two kind of solutions have been adopted: do not allow language features which use absolute references or create a server process which monitors absolute references creation and does the necessary translation. See [6]

The second task consist of achieving that the migrated process will continue receiving messages in its new destination. At this point, three different situations may appear: messages sent to a process that are in the network when the process is going to migrate, messages generated while the process is migrating, and messages generated after the process has migrated. Several techniques can be distinguished which have different impact on the global performance. Each technique adopts a different solution on each of the above cases. A comparison has been carried out in [6] where six techniques are shown: full protocol, message rejection, message forwarding, use of an initial direction, centralised scheme and mailbox, and where a simulation has been carried out to show the impact of each technique in the communications performance.

6. Related work and discussion

There are some works closely related to our approach in the design of a communication service. The *Universal Packet Routing Interface* [3] is an "interface to a packet-routing facility for global communications in a locally-connected message-passing machine". It has been also implemented in a network of T8-series transputers and provides a view where all processors are connected to each other but without considering homogeneous performance. *Active Messages* [4] also takes a minimalist approach, but it is a complete message passing model available to the programmer and its goal is to reduce the cost imposed to the communication latency by many operating systems. Finally, the T9000 processor and the C104 router, [10] and [13], represent a hardware approach to build general purpose interconnection networks. Its goal is very similar to ours but it does not address the implementation of a broadcast service.

To conclude, a communication microkernel called *TransCom* has been designed and implemented. It offers a complete virtualisation of the communication network in a parallel computer and has two main goals:

- to have a platform for testing and evaluating different solutions in a parallel architecture design. An open question is to find which services have to be included in a general parallel computer. A future task consists of modelling the current parallel environment and obtaining system parameters in order to evaluate its performance and extrapolate the results to study the appropriate level of integration (hardware, firmware, or software) of each service provided by the microkernel.
- to be the foundation of a user-friendly parallel programming environment. The microkernel supports message passing between processes and makes the machine characteristics transparent to the user. In the future, it is expected that load balancing services using process migration will be included. This work is part of a general project called SEPP (Software Engineering for Parallel Processing) [19], the major interests of which comprise tools for program design, simulation, run-time support and behaviour analysis in parallel systems.

7. References

[1] R. Beivide, E. Herrada, J.L. Balcázar, and J. Labarta, "Optimized mesh-connected networks for SIMD and MIMD architectures", Proc. 14th Int. Symp. on Comput. Archit., June 1987, pp. 163-170.

[2] W. J. Dally "Virtual Channel Flow Control" 17th Int. Symp. on Comp. Arch., 1990, pp. 60-68.

[3] M. Debbage, M. B. Hill, "ParaPET: A Parallel Programming Environment Toolkit" Technical Report ESPRIT Project P5404, University of Southampton, November 1992.

[4] T. Eicken, D. Culler, S. Goldstein and K. Schauser, "Active Messages: A mechanism for integrated communication and computation", in: Proc. Nineteenth Int. Symp. on Computer Architecture (ACM Press, New York, 1992)

[5] D.Franco, J.C. Moure, E. Heymann, E.Luque "TransCom: Communication services for a transputer-based multicomputer" Technical Report, Computer Science Department. Universitat Autonoma de Barcelona. 1995

[6] E. Heymann "Soporte para la migración de procesos en computadores paralelos de memoria distribuida" Master Thesis, Computer Science Department. Universitat Autonoma de Barcelona. 1995

[7]C.A.R.Hoare "Communicating Sequential Processes", Prentice-Hall Int. 1985

[8] "The Transputer Reference Book", Third Edition, Inmos Ltd. 1992

[9] INMOS. Ansi C Toolset. 1992

[10] "The T9000 Transputer Hardware Reference Manual", Inmos Ltd. 1993

[11] E. Luque et al. "A Parallel Programming Model for Distributed Systems" Technical Report. Computer Science Department. Universidad Autonoma de Barcelona. 1994

[12] E.Luque, A.Ripoll, A.Cortés, T.Margalef "A distributed diffusion method for dynamic load balancing on parallel computers" Proceedings of the Euromicro Workshop on Parallel and Distributed Processing. IEEE Press 1995. pp.43-50

[13] M.D. May, P.W. Thompson, P.H. Welch "Networks, Routers and Transputers: Function, Performance and Applications" IOS Press, 1993.

[14] J.C. Moure, D.Franco, E. Heymann, E.Luque "TransRouter: a data transport microkernel for transputers" Technical Report, Computer Science Department. Universitat Autonoma de Barcelona. 1995

[15] "MPI. A Message-Passing Interface Standard". Message Passing Interface Forum. 1994

[16] "*Hardware Reference for the Parsys SN1000 Series*" Technical Reference, Parsys Ltd, September 1989.

[17] A.Geist et al. "PVM. User's Guide and Reference Manual". Oak Ridge National Laboratory. 1994

[18], L.G. Valiant, "A scheme for fast parallel communication" SIAM J. on Computing 11 (1982) pp. 350-361.

[19] S.C. Winter and P. Kacsuk, "Software Engineering for Parallel Processing" Proceedings of the 8th symposium of microcomputer and microprocessor applications, vol 1,pp. 285-303, Budapest, 1994.

Rule-based Routing in Massively Parallel Systems[1]

Werner Brockmann, Thomas Kosch, Erik Maehle
Medizinische Universität zu Lübeck
Institut für Technische Informatik
Ratzeburger Allee 160
D-23538 Lübeck, Germany

Abstract

In order to increase the performance of an interconnection network, efficient routing schemes are required which adapt to the system state. In this paper an approach to routing hardware is introduced which allows to tailor it flexibly to different routing algorithms and to incorporate different kinds of information easily within a routing decision. The key concept is to use a rule-based specification to represent the routing algorithm which is executed by a fixed rule-interpreter with an interchangeable rule-base. This allows to provide an universal routing chip with a highly flexible and efficient hardware implementation even of sophisticated routing algorithms. Three different examples illustrate the application of such a rule-based router. The discussion of implementation issues shows that a rule-based router is well suited for an implementation with state-of-the-art VLSI-technologies, e.g. a single-chip ASIC.

1: Introduction

In order to design a balanced massively parallel system, the performance of the interconnection network has to meet the performance of the computing nodes. On the commercial market, most new parallel computers provide fat nodes with very high computing power making the performance of the interconnection network a critical issue. Thus it is necessary to maximize its throughput as well as to minimize its latency by balancing network topology, the routing algorithm, flow control scheme and switching technique. In particular the interdependencies between topology and routing algorithm are a main topic and need further investigations.

A routing algorithm in general has to meet several requirements. First of all, it must be deadlock- and livelockfree. To minimize the network latency, it should preferably use shortest paths. But the shortest path is not always the fastest one because of congestion. As most topologies of interconnection networks offer several alternative paths from a source to a destination node, the routing algorithm has to select one path out of them according to the load and availability of the corresponding links. It is determined by environmental parameters representing e.g. hot spots, congestions, partition boundaries or faults. The more knowledge about the topology and the state of the machine can be used, the greater usually is the achieveable performance.

In general, oblivious routing, adaptive routing and randomized routing are distinguished. **Oblivious routing algorithms**, like dimension-ordered routing (xy-routing for grids (see chapter 3.2 for a rule-based implementation), e-cube routing for hypercubes [1]) and interval routing [2], use predefined paths from a source to a destination node. If a packet leaves the source node, the path is determined in advance and cannot be changed within the network. Thus the oblivious schemes do not consider dynamically changing environmental variables. Therefore oblivious schemes cannot bypass link failures, congestions or hot spots.

Adaptive routing algorithms offer the freedom of choosing among alternative paths from a source to a destination node. If the routing algorithm is able to detect link failures or congestions, it can consider these events for the routing decision. Therefore adaptive schemes are able to react flexibly to changes of the system state. E.g. [3] introduces a fault-tolerant algorithm which rerouts in case of failures.

In [4] the dimension reversal routing algorithm is presented. In order to prevent deadlocks, a message is adaptively routed along suitably numbered and dimension-ordered virtual channels in a decreasing way. This algorithm significantly improves throughput for non-uniform traffic patterns, but it shows only little difference on the performance with random traffic. As channels fail, the performance of the interconnection network gracefully degrades with the dimension reversal algorithm.

The turn model, proposed by [5], provides a systematic approach to the developement of maximally adaptive routing algorithms for n-dimensional meshes and k-ary n-cubes. The resulting routing algorithms offer adaptivity and deadlock freedom by prohibiting a minimum number of turns to avoid cycles among packets. Compared to the dimension-ordered xy-routing for two-dimensional grids, this routing scheme is partially adaptive. One possibility of prohibiting two turns leads to north last routing [5] (see chapter 3.3). If the path length should be minimal, this algorithm is fully adaptive for a destination in the south of the source because multiple paths are allowed; for a

[1] sponsored by the DFG (MA 1412/3-1) in cooperation with SFB 1511 „Massive Parallelität"

1066-6192/96 $5.00 © 1996 IEEE
Proceedings of PDP '96

northern destination it is oblivious because a message which is once directed to the north has to proceed into the northern direction until it reaches its destination. The algorithm is also adaptive in this case if longer paths are allowed, due to detouring to the south. A combination of north-last and south-last routing using virtual networks is proposed in [6]. This algorithm is fully adaptive.

The goal of **random routing algorithms** is to distribute the communication load of the interconnection network uniformly. The routing is thus based on a random variable, e.g. messages are routed to a randomly selected intermediate destination node and then further to the original destination. One effect of this load distribution is that the buffer space necessary at each node is reduced [7]. Another randomized approach is the Chaos Router [8] (see chapter 3.4). This routing algorithm is superior to oblivious routing, because it is able to route around congestions and failures. Moreover the chaos routing algorithm uses randomization for eliminating livelocks.

The more flexible a routing algorithm, the more difficult it is to specify and to implement. Most routing chips available today only support oblivious routing and are restricted to special topologies. Routing algorithms, which take a more global system state into account, normally have to be implemented in software due to their complexity. But software schemes cause a network latency which is prohibitively high for state-of-the-art communication bandwidth above 100 Mbps, especially for short messages. Hence, flexible, adaptive routing strategies are needed which take into account the system state as far as possible and which can be implemented easily in hardware. Additionally, they should be tailored to different network topologies or even network partitions with minimum effort, although they are implemented in hardware. As a promising approach for such routers, a rule-based approach is introduced in the following part of this paper. It is based on the ARON-technique which allows a high speed hardware implementation. Typical examples show a rule-based specification of different routing algorithms in order to give an impression of the applicability of rule-based systems to realistic routing schemes. The first two examples assume wormhole routing [9] which works with minimal buffering, but bears the risk of temporal message blockings. The example of chaos routing demonstrates that rule-based routing is also applicable to routing with packet buffers. Finally some implementational issues are discussed.

2: Rule-based routing approach

In recent years, knowledge-based systems like expert systems showed a way to get an implementation which is very easily tailored to a specific application. They are based on a strict separation of the application-specific knowledge and a fixed interpreter, which depends only on the knowledge representation, but not on the knowledge itself. This general feature of knowledge-based systems is the starting point for the rule-based routing approach as it allows universal and highly flexible routers whose behavior may be completely changed by reloading the rule-base. The rule-based approach also offers the opportunity to incorporate expert knowledge directly. Thus knowledge about the system topology and about dealing with congestions, faults etc. is implemented in an intuitive way.

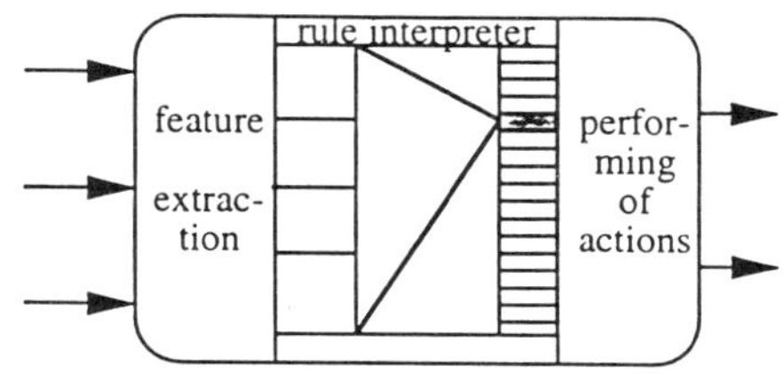

Fig. 1: Structure of a rule-based system

A rule-based system in general consists of three stages (Fig. 1), namely feature extraction, rule interpreter and performing of actions. In case of rule-based routing, feature extraction and performing of actions build the interfaces to the interconnection network itself. The first stage extracts those features out of the input signals which are evaluated by the rule-base. They may be a numerical quantity or even of linguistical type. Input variables or features of numerical type are e.g. node numbers, source or target addresses, priority of messages or Boolean variables representing the blocking of an output link, link failure or overload situation. Linguistic variables like 'small', 'medium' or 'large' may describe for instance a queue or message length. The performing of actions part provides the signals for controlling router components like input or output multiplexers, buffers or queues.

The second stage is the rule-interpreter. There are several ways to build it. The most simple and intuitive approach is based on a rule-based specification without a complicated inference procedure. The rules thus have the following structure:

IF premise **THEN** conclusion.

Each premise evaluates the features representing the system state. If it is true, the entire rule is able to fire, i.e. the action specified within the conclusion is performed by the third stage. Such actions may be for instance the selection of an output link or a buffer. If multiple rules with different conclusions fire at a time, an appropriate action has to be selected. This conflict resolution is normally a time-consuming task. According to the ARON-technique [10, 11], our conflict resolution uses rule-priorities and is performed off-line by a compilation of the rule-base. Through this compilation, an unequivocal conclusion is related to each possible input state. The ARON-technique exploits this fact to store the compiled rule-base within a completely filled one-dimensional table-structure which assigns exactly one action to each input state. A simple RAM is then loaded with the compiled rule-base. A routing decision is thus related to the system state by calculating a corresponding index and accessing the entire table item. This allows a fast and direct selection of the rule under consideration instead of search in the rule-base because its interpretation is reduced to a simple index computation.

Determining this index is nothing but a weighted summation. Because this is a fixed scheme, independant from the rule-base and the system state, the rule-interpreter can be easily and efficiently implemented in hardware. As long as the first and third stage of the rule-based router provide all needed features and actions, the routing implementation is extremely flexible and can easily be adapted to different topologies and various routing algorithms by only changing the rule-base. Rule-based routing is thus well suited for balancing the performance of an interconnection network and processing nodes.

3: Examples of rule-based routing

3.1: Basic Structure

In order to give an impression of the potentials of a rule-based formulation of routing algorithms, rule-based routing algorithms are introduced by reimplementing state-of-the-art routing examples, namely an oblivious, an adaptive and a randomized routing scheme, using a rule-based specification.

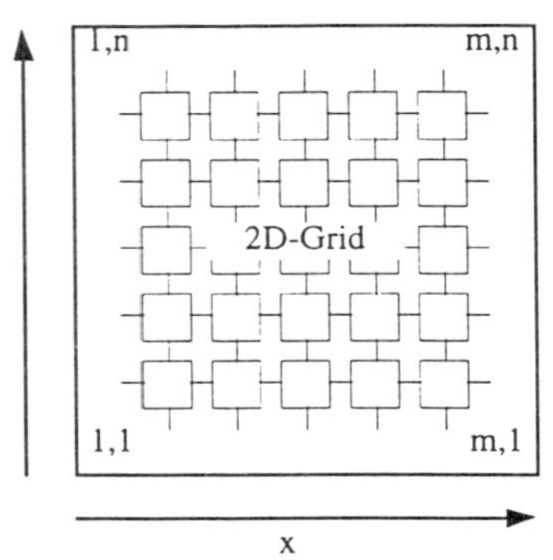

Fig. 2: Arrangement of nodes in a 2D-grid

Because k-ary n-cubes have found widespread use as a topology for massively parallel systems, the starting point for the reflection is the arrangement of the routers in a 2D-grid with n lines and m columns (Fig. 2). A single rule-based router (RBR) has one bidirectional link in each of the four directions (i.e. north, south, east and west) and an additional home link which connects the computing node to the interconnection network (Fig. 3).

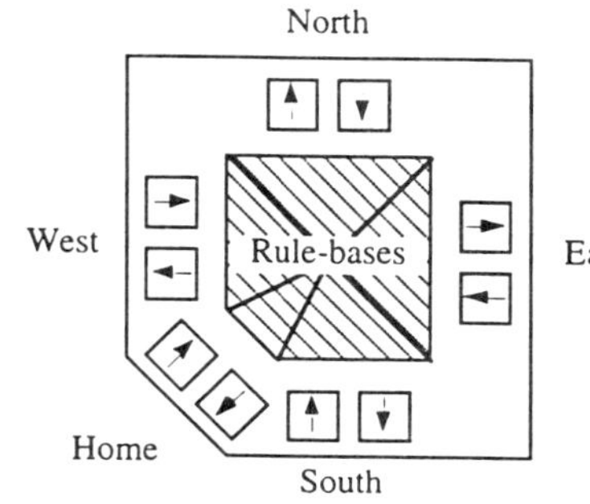

Fig. 3: Block diagram of the RBR within a node

3.2: Rule-Based XY-Routing

XY-routing belongs to the dimension-ordered routing schemes. So, in the case of a 2D-grid, a message is routed from the source node starting in the x-direction (along a row) towards the column of the destination node. Having arrived at the appropriate column, the message travels in y-direction along the column to the destination node.

IF zx = px AND zy < py	**THEN** south
IF zx = px AND zy = py	**THEN** home

Fig. 4: Rule-base for xy-routing (northern input)

As an example the rule-base for the northern input of a xy-router is shown in Fig. 4. This input is only addressed by messages which are in the right column and which have a destination south of the source node. Two rules are sufficient here because each incoming message is appointed to the entire node or to a node in the southern direction only. Any other destination indicates a fault. The rules for other inputs which are not listed here are similar.

In the premise of the rules *zx* and *zy* represent the coordinates of the destination node, whereas *px*, *py* stand for the coordinates of the particular computing node connected to the RBR. The symbolic names in the conclusion part of the rules stand for sending the message to the corresponding output link, if the particular rule fires. Note that the rule-base is represented within the rule-based router such that exactly one rule fires for each situation, making an efficient hardware implementation by the ARON-technique straight forward. I.e. for any case which is not covered by the rule-base an error signal is generated by a default-rule. This relies on the assumption that all necessary routing decisions are explicitly specified. If appropriate rules are defined, specific errors may also be discriminated because each router may check the destination and direction of a message versus its own position within the interconnection network and within the routing-chip itself.

3.3: Rule-Based North-Last Routing

To illustrate the flexibility of the method and to demonstrate that the system state can be easily considered in a rule-based approach, the rules for the partially adaptive north-last routing are formulated. The north-last algorithm is derived from the turn model mentioned before. It avoids cycles by allowing only six out of eight possible turns.

IF zx > px AND Ceast = ok **THEN** east
IF zx > px AND Ceast <> ok AND Csouth = ok **THEN** south
IF zx > px AND Ceast <> ok AND Csouth <> ok AND Cwest = ok **THEN** west
IF zx > px AND Ceast <> ok AND Csouth <> ok AND Cwest <> ok **THEN** fail_stop
IF zx < px AND Cwest = ok **THEN** west
IF zx < px AND Cwest <> ok AND Csouth = ok **THEN** south
IF zx < px AND Cwest <> ok AND Csouth <> ok AND Ceast = ok **THEN** east
IF zx < px AND Ceast <> ok AND Csouth <> ok AND Cwest <> ok **THEN** fail_stop
IF zx = px AND zy < py AND Csouth = ok **THEN** south
IF zx = px AND zy < py AND Csouth <> ok AND Cwest = ok **THEN** west
IF zx = px AND zy < py AND Csouth <> ok AND Cwest <> ok AND Ceast = ok **THEN** east
IF zx = px AND zy < py AND Csouth <> ok AND Cwest <> ok AND Ceast <> ok **THEN** fail_stop
IF zx = px AND zy = py AND Chome = ok **THEN** home
IF zx = px AND zy = py AND Chome <> ok **THEN** node_failure

Fig. 5: Rule-base for north-last routing (northern input)

Fig. 5 shows the rule-base of the northern input (same link as for the xy-routing, Fig. 4), expanded with features to implement adaptivity which is used for fault tolerance in this case. The rules for the other directions read similarly (see Appendix). In order to achieve fault tolerance, one additional Boolean input variable per direction and two additional conclusions specifying detected faults must be provided. In the example the *Cdir* variable represents the state of the outgoing link into the *dir* direction. The contents of this variable is *ok* if the corresponding link is not faulty. The activation of the *fail_stop* action must halt the system for reconfiguration because all output links to neighbours of the actual router, except the bidirectional incoming link, are faulty and the message cannot be moved towards its destination. The *node_failure* action indicates that the computing node belonging to the appropriate router cannot be reached and has to be reported as faulty to a diagnosis software.

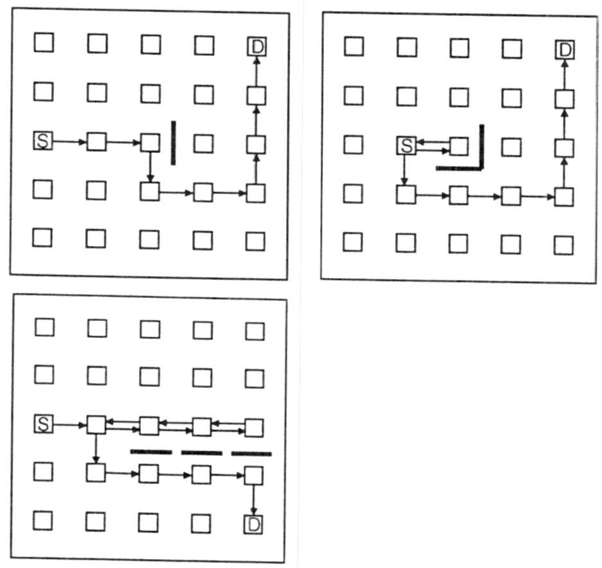

Fig. 6: Example paths of a north-last algorithm (Link failures are marked by thick lines.)

Otherwise a faulty link respectively faulty node is bypassed in the south. In order to illustrate this, Fig. 6 illustrates several examples of paths which are chosen by the algorithm in the case of link failures. If no failures occur, adaptivity is not necessary and the algorithm behaves like the known xy-routing.

3.4: Rule-Based Chaos Routing

Fig. 7 shows the block diagram of a chaos router. Each of the links has a buffer for a single message (*Odir*, *Idir*, with *dir* = north, south, east, west, home) which is expanded with a full/empty bit representing the buffer state for handshaking. The *central queue* contains the messages which are waiting for an empty output buffer.

When a message leaves an output buffer, because it is received by an adjacent node, the central queue is examined whether it contains another message specified for this output. If such an entry is found, the message is dequeued and stored in the corresponding output buffer. Then the input buffer of the same direction is read and if it is not empty, the message is enqueued and tagged with the desired output or if the destination is reached, the message is not enqueued and delivered via the home link. If no message determined for the output link is found in the central queue but central queue as well as corresponding input buffer are full, the message of a randomly selected entry is dequeued first and stored in the empty output buffer, i.e. it is derouted. Then the incoming message is enqueued in order to prevent a congestion.

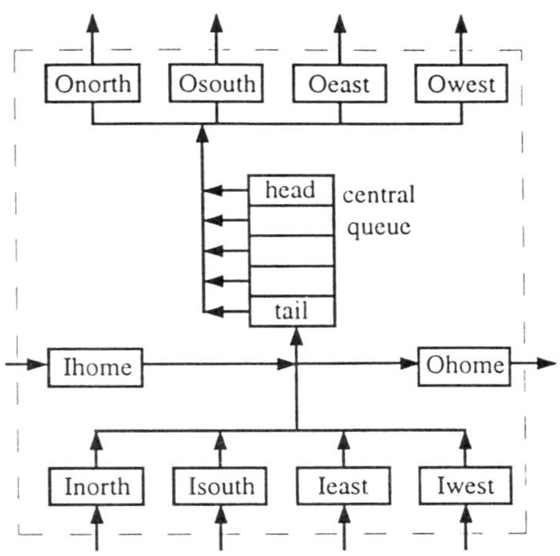

Fig. 7: Block diagram of a chaos router

The computing node is only allowed to inject a new message via the *Ihome* buffer, if the queue length is below a certain threshold value. This value may be defined before the rule-base is compiled or otherwise remains changeable at run-time in order to control the injection of messages. By means of this *threshold* input variable, the communication load of the network can be controlled.

The following input variables respectively actions must be available:

- *Odir* gets the status (full, empty) of the output buffer in the given *dir* direction.
- *Idir* gets the status (full, empty) of the input buffer in the given *dir* direction.
- *match(dir)* tests whether the queue contains a message for *Odir*
- *dequeue(dir)* dequeues the first (before matched) message for *Odir*
- *enqueue(dir)* appends the message read from the actual input buffer (which is marked empty afterwards) to the central queue tagged with the outgoing direction *dir*.
- *deroute(dir)* selects randomly a message entry in the queue and sends the message along the *dir* link.
- *thres* defines the threshold value for steering the message injection.

IF Onorth=empty AND match(north)=true
THEN dequeue(north)

/* analogous for Osouth, Oeast, Owest */

IF Onorth=empty AND zx<px AND match(north)=false AND Inorth=full AND queue=full
THEN deroute(north) AND enqueue(west)

IF Onorth=empty AND zx>px AND match(north)=false AND Inorth=full AND queue=full
THEN deroute(north) AND enqueue(east)

IF Onorth=empty AND zx=px AND zy<py AND match(north)=false AND Inorth=full AND queue=full
THEN deroute(north) AND enqueue(south)

IF Onorth=empty AND zx=px AND zy>py AND match(north)=false AND Inorth=full AND queue=full
THEN deroute(north) AND enqueue(north)

/* analogous for Osouth, Oeast, Owest */

IF Inorth=full AND zx=px AND zy=py AND Ohome=empty **THEN** home

IF Inorth=full AND zx<px AND queue<>full
THEN enqueue(west)

IF Inorth=full AND zx>px AND queue<>full
THEN enqueue(east)

IF Inorth=full AND zx=px AND zy<py AND queue<>full **THEN** enqueue(south)

IF Inorth=full AND zx=px AND zy>py AND queue<>full **THEN** enqueue(north)

/* analogous for Isouth, Ieast, Iwest */

Fig. 8: Rule-base for chaos routing (northern part)

Fig. 8 gives the rule-base for the northern, Fig. 9 for the home input of a chaos router. If no derouting takes place, the behavior of this algorithm is comparable to the xy-routing.

IF Ihome=full AND zx<px AND queue<thres
THEN enqueue(west)

IF Ihome=full AND zx>px AND queue<thres
THEN enqueue(east)

IF Ihome=full AND zx=px AND zy<py AND queue<thres **THEN** enqueue(south)

IF Ihome=full AND zx=px AND zy>py AND queue<thres **THEN** enqueue(north)

Fig. 9: Rule-base for chaos routing (home input)

This implementation of chaos routing prevents deadlocks because it follows the north-last strategy. Due to selecting derouted messages randomly, livelocks are also resolved after a while.

4: Implementational Issues

4.1: General questions

A suitable implementation of a rule-based routing chip has to consider a lot of different constraints which are very closely related. Two different views have to be matched, namely communication demands and implementational restrictions. Their interrelation is manifold.

The network topology determines the number of links for each routing chip and thus the complexity of the routing itself and of the routing chip. Because limits given by the implementation must be taken into account, routing strategies have to be elaborated achieving an optimal balance of implementational costs on one hand and efficiency and flexibility on the other hand.

The key is to find suitable features which are evaluated by rule-bases. To improve performance, a more global system view is needed. It is achieved by cooperating with neighboring routing chips through exchanging local information about their internal states. Appropriate features may thus achieve a more global system view recursively by exchanging information about the (local) state of links, e.g. their activity, faults or priorities of messages which are transmitted or blocked. Buffering routing schemes may additionally use information about the queue lengths of neighboring links. For instance by considering the message type and priority as well as the load state, the action of a routing decision may also influence the buffering, e.g. by selecting a suitable buffer or derouting messages.

Rule-based routing therefore offers a great potential to increase flexibility and thus performance in a simple way. But the applied routing algorithm also has a strong impact on message formats, and vice versa. Additional potential arises if the routing decision also supports system services like virtual networks, priorities, broadcasts, fault-tolerance etc. It thus has to evaluate features like message priorities and length, may combine multiple messages for the same destination or control the buffer management. If needed, this may also be implemented by a separate rule-based system in order to make a routing-chip as flexible as possible.

In order to increase the reusability of a routing chip, it has to be highly flexible in spite of its implementation in hardware. The key problem is that routing decisions depend on the network topology as well as on the position of the routing chip within the communication network and on the routing algorithm itself. Thus reconfigurability should be used, for instance to configure a buffer pool to adapt to different message formats. Reloading a rule-base is another step which requires a RAM memory. But feature extraction and performing of actions should also be tailored to a specific network or routing algorithm by reconfiguration. Either a superset of all possible features and actions is implemented and suitable ones are selected, or reprogrammable hardware is used as known from recent FPGA technologies (see [12] for more details). Whereas such features are implemented straightforward on a software basis, a hardware implementation has to take limits concerning chip size, pin-count, power consumption and so forth into account. Memory for buffers as well as for rule-bases and thus the number of features is also limited. The different routing aspects thus have to be carefully considered and balanced, in order to achieve minimal latency and an optimal communication bandwidth. The various design parameters have to be carefully evaluated before a routing chip can be built.

4.2: Rule-interpreter

Compared to other hardware routers, the two key features concerning costs of rule-based routing are latency and memory demands of the rule-interpreter. Latency results from evaluating the features, addressing the table, accessing the entire action and performing the action.

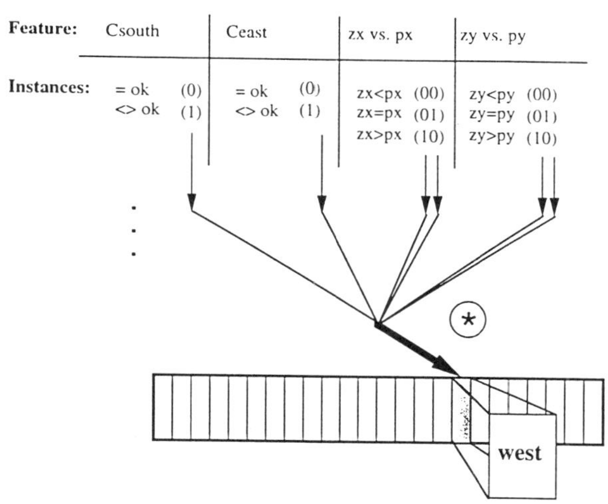

Fig. 10: Address computation by concatenation

According to the ARON-technique, evaluating the features is done by simply coding the different instances of each feature. This causes very small delay because in a hardware implementation coding is done in parallel. Out of the entire codes the index is computed. In order to minimize latency caused by that, a special variant of the ARON-technique should be used preferably which exploits concatenation instead of a weighted summation to determine the index for accessing the firing table item (Fig.

10). Address computation thus causes no additional latency, but may increase memory demands if a feature has a number of instances which is not a power of 2. The time for accessing the entire item only depends on the size and implementation of memory. In order to minimize it, memory should be as small as possible and static RAM-technology should be used. Performing the entire actions is nothing but steering multiplexers or setting flags. It causes only propagation delays and is thus not very time-consuming. If coding of features is also done by memory in order to achieve a very flexible hardware implementation, the latency time for the routing decision may yield down to two memory access times. A first ivestigation on a FPGA-implementation of a rule-interpreter on a Xilinx 4003 showed a latency time below 150 ns for the routing decision. In an ASIC-implementation it will probably be less than 50 ns.

$$S = \prod_{i=1}^{m} n_i \qquad (1)$$

with S: memory demands, m: number of features
n_i: number of instances of feature i

According to the ARON-technique each feature is treated as being orthogonal to each other. After compilation, it relates to an individual dimension in a completely filled, multi-dimensional rule-matrix. This is linearized and stored in a (RAM-)memory. The memory demands for a rule-base increases thus exponetially with the number of features which are used (1). But decomposition may reduce memory demands significantly. I.e., instead of a single rule-base evaluating all features, a cascade structure is used in which each rule-base evaluates only a subset of features. This is illustrated in Fig. 11 for the northern input of the north-last routing algorithm according to Fig. 5.

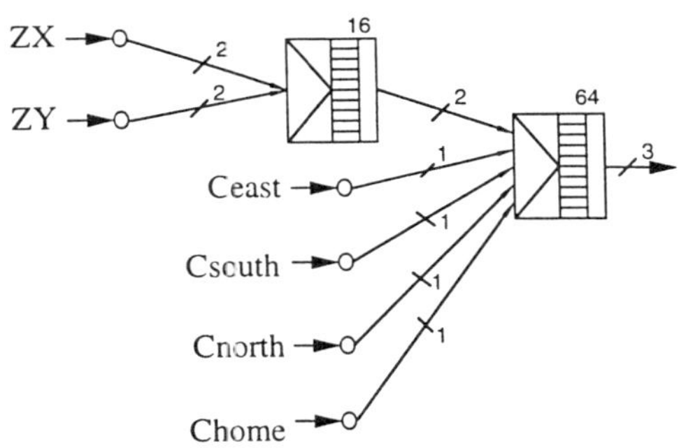

Fig. 11: Decomposed north-last router (northern input)

In this case, decomposition is done into groups of features concerning destination coordinates and concerning the system state. The first stage determines the desired direction. The second stage matches it with the entire system state and performs the entire action. This decompostion reduces memory demands from 256*3 bit to 16*2+64*3 bit and also chip size at the cost of one additional memory access

5: Concluding Remarks

In this paper the concept of rule-based routing in massively parallel systems is introduced. It relies on the rule-based formulation of routing algorithms and the interpretation of the rules by a fixed rule interpreter which can be efficiently implemented in hardware by the ARON-technique. In this way even sophisticated adaptive routing algorithms are well suited for a hardware implementation which adapts to load situations and faults. Because system-specific knowledge is implemented to a great deal in an exchangeable rule-base, a rule-based routing chip may be tailored universally to different routing algorithms, network topologies and node architectures by reloading and reconfiguration and is still very fast.

The rule-based specification is an intuitive interface to domain experts. It allows to evaluate many differrent kinds of information about the system state. Rule-based routing may thus react flexibly on congestions, faults and so forth. It also bears a great potential to incorporate additional knowledge about the system architecture or about different classes of application algorithms in order to optimize the performance of an interconnection network. It furthermore allows to check the flow of messages for consistency and to integrate not only fault detection but also fault diagnosis.

Future work is directed towards a VLSI-implementation. It will focus especially on two cross-coupled aspects. The first one is to find appropriate routing algorithms and design parameters which gain an optimal improvement compared to conventional techniques by exploiting more information and acting more flexibly. It addresses also questions of message formats and buffer strategies. The second aspect is to find an architecture for the router which guarantees a high performance, flexibility and universality on one hand, but is within reach of state-of-the-art VLSI-technology.

6: References

[1] H. Sullivan, T.R. Bashkow: A Large Scale, Homogeneous, Fully Distributed Parallel Machine. Proc. 4th Symp. on Computer Architecture, Vol. 5, 105-124, 1977

[2] J. van Leeuven, R.B. Tan: Interval Routing. The Computer Journal, Vol. 30, No. 4, 298-307, 1987

[3] B. Bieker, G. Deconinck, E. Maehle, J. Vounckx: Reconfiguration and Checkpointing in Massively Parallel Systems. Proc. 1st European Dependable Computing Conference EDCC-1, 353-370, Berlin 1994

[4] W.J. Dally, H. Aoki: Deadlock-Free Adaptive Routing in Multicomputer Networks Using Virtual Channels. IEEE Trans. on Parallel and Distributed Systems, Vol. 4, No. 4, 466-475, 1993

[5] C.J. Glass, L.M. Ni: The Turn Model for Adaptive Routing. Proc. 19th International Symposium on Computer Architecture, 278-287, 1992

[6] C.M. Cuningham, D.R. Avresky: Fault-Tolerant Adaptive Routing for Two-Dimensional Meshes. First Int. Symp. on High Performance Computing Architecture, Raleigh, North Carolina, USA, 1995

[7] T. Leighton: Introduction to Parallel Algorithms and Architectures: Arrays, Trees, Hypercubes. Morgan Kaufmann Publishers, Inc. 1992

[8] S. Konstantinidou, L. Snyder: The Chaos Router: A Practical Application of Randomization in Network Routing. Proc. Symposium on Parallel Algorithms and Architectures, 21-30, 1990

[9] L.M. Ni, P.K. McKinley: A Survey of Wormhole Routing Techniques in Direct Networks. IEEE Computer, Vol. 26, No. 2, 62-76, 1993

[10] W. Brockmann: Real-Time Architecture for Knowledge Processing Systems. Proc. Euromicro '91 Workshop on Real-Time Systems, 52-60, IEEE Computer Society Press, Los Alamitos 1991

[11] W. Brockmann: Combining Real-Time with Knowledge Processing Techniques. Proc. 5th Int. Conf. on Industrial and Engineering Applications of Artificial Intelligence and Expert Systems IEA-AIE, 594-603, Paderborn 1992

[12] W. Brockmann, T. Kosch, E. Maehle: Regelbasiertes Routing mit lokaler Adaptivität. To appear in: Proc. 14th PARS-Workshop (Parallel-Algorithmen, -rechnerstrukturen und -systemsoftware), Stuttgart 1995

Appendix

Additional rule-bases for north-last-routing

```
/*************** West Router ***************/
W1: if ZX>PX & Ceast=OK  then EAST
W2: if ZX>PX & Ceast<>OK & Csouth=OK then SOUTH
W3: if ZX>PX & Ceast<>OK & Csouth<>OK
     & Cwest=OK then WEST
W4: if ZX>PX & Ceast<>OK & Csouth<>OK
     & Cwest<>OK then FAIL_STCP
W5: if ZX<PX & Csouth=OK  then SOUTH
W6: if ZX<PX & Csouth<>OK & Ceast=OK then EAST
W7: if ZX<PX & Csouth<>OK & Ceast<>OK
    then FAIL_STOP
W8: if ZX=PX & ZY<PY & Csouth=OK then SOUTH
W9: if ZX=PX & ZY<PY & Csouth<>OK & Cwest=OK
    then WEST
W10: if ZX=PX & ZY<PY & Csouth<>OK & Cwest<>OK
      & Ceast=OK then EAST
W11: if ZX=PX & ZY<PY & Csouth<>OK & Cwest<>OK
      & Ceast<>OK then FAIL_STOP
W12: if ZX=PX & ZY>PY & Cnorth=OK  then NORTH
W13: if ZX=PX & ZY>PY & Cnorth<>OK
      then FAIL_STOP
W14: if ZX=PX & ZY=PY & Chome=OK then HOME
W15: if ZX=PX & ZY=PY & Chome<>OK
      then NODE_FAILURE
/*************** East Router ***************/
E1: if ZX<PX & Cwest=OK then WEST
E2: if ZX<PX & Cwest<>OK & Csouth=OK then SOUTH
E3: if ZX<PX & Cwest<>OK & Csouth<>OK
     & Ceast=OK then EAST
E4: if ZX<PX & Cwest<>OK & Csouth<>OK
     & Ceast<>OK then FAIL_STOP
E5: if ZX>PX & Csouth=OK  then SOUTH
E6: if ZX>PX & Csouth<>OK & Cwest=OK then WEST
E7: if ZX>PX & Csouth<>OK & Cwest<>OK
    then FAIL_STOP
E8: if ZX=PX & ZY<PY & Csouth=OK then SOUTH
E9: if ZX=PX & ZY<PY & Csouth<>OK & Cwest=OK
    then WEST
E10: if ZX=PX & ZY<PY & Csouth<>OK & Cwest<>OK
      & Ceast=OK then EAST
E11: if ZX=PX & ZY<PY & Csouth<>OK & Cwest<>OK
      & Ceast<>OK then FAIL_STOP
E12: if ZX=PX & ZY>PY & Cnorth=OK then NORTH
E13: if ZX=PX & ZY>PY & Cnorth<>OK
     then FAIL_STOP
E14: if ZX=PX & ZY=PY & Chome=OK then HOME
E15: if ZX=PX & ZY=PY & Chome<>OK
     then NODE_FAILURE
/*************** South Router ***************/
S1: if ZX=PX & ZY>PY & Cnorth=OK then NORTH
S2: if ZX=PX & ZY>PY & Cnorth<>OK
    then FAIL_STOP
S3: if ZX=PX & ZY=PY & Chome=OK then HOME
S4: if ZX=PX & ZY=PY & Chome<>OK
    then NODE_FAILURE
/*************** Home Router ***************/
H1: if ZX<PX & Cwest=OK then WEST
H2: if ZX<PX & Cwest<>OK & Csouth=OK then SOUTH
H3: if ZX<PX & Cwest<>OK & Csouth<>OK
     & Ceast=OK then EAST
H4: if ZX<PX & Cwest<>OK & Csouth<>OK
     & Ceast<>OK then FAIL_STOP
H5: if ZX>PX & Ceast=OK then EAST
H6: if ZX>PX & Ceast<>OK & Csouth=OK then SOUTH
H7: if ZX>PX & Ceast<>OK & Csouth<>OK
     & Cwest=OK then WEST
H8: if ZX>PX & Ceast<>OK & Csouth<>OK
     & Cwest<>OK then FAIL_STOP
H9: if ZX=PX & ZY<PY & Csouth=OK then SOUTH
H10: if ZX=PX & ZY<PY & Csouth<>OK & Cwest=OK
     then WEST
H11: if ZX=PX & ZY<PY & Csouth<>OK & Cwest<>OK
      & Ceast=OK then EAST
H12: if ZX=PX & ZY<PY & Csouth<>OK & Cwest<>OK
      & Ceast<>OK then FAIL_STOP
H13: if ZX=PX & ZY>PY & Cnorth=OK then NORTH
H14: if ZX=PX & ZY>PY & Cnorth<>OK
      then FAIL_STOP
```

Overlapping Computations and Communications in Torus Networks

Alvaro Suárez, C.N. Ojeda-Guerra*

Dpto. de Electrónica y Telecomunicación
Universidad de Las Palmas de Gran Canaria
Campus Universitario de Tafira (Pabellón A)
35017 - Las Palmas de G.C.
phone:+34 28 451239/458987
fax:+34 28 451243
e-mail: {alvaro,cnieves}@cic.teleco.ulpgc.es

Abstract

A fundamental aspect in the design of parallel applications consist in minimizing communications: reducing the number of messages or overlapping computations and communications. The objective of this paper is the design of parallel algorithms that use processors and expensive resources such as communications efficiently. We present a partial embedding of computation and communication graphs that have a cubic or planar structure, onto 2-D or 1-D torus graphs. With this embedding good values for normal embedding metrics are obtained, and its advantage is that it allows an initial data distribution between PEs (Processing Element) that makes overlapping computations and communications possible. To start with we obtain parallel algorithms with a number of processes dependent on the number of processors in the torus. Then we modify the embedding in order to execute problems with matrices whose size is independent of the number of processors of the torus multicomputer.

1 Introduction

The implementation of any parallel algorithm on a multicomputer [1] with a certain interconnection topology is highly influenced by the characteristics of this algorithm. Characteristics such as the movement of data, the communication between processes, initial distribution of data and others influence the choosing of the topology used. On the other hand, the utilization of the processors and the communication time are two important considerations in designing parallel algorithms. Communication is one of the most expensive resources in a multicomputer and the efficient management of it is important. The modelation of computations and communications with a graph G is important in order to study this communication. In a similar way the parallel architecture (in which the parallel algorithm will be executed) can be modelled with another graph H [2].

The embedding of the graph G (that represents a determinated interconnection between processes) onto another graph H (that represents the interconnection between processors) consists in mapping the nodes of G onto nodes of H, such as the edges of G match with one or more edges of H. In order to measure the effectiveness of the embedding 4 metrics have been used traditionally: dilation, expansion, congestion and maximum load [3].

The results of the embedding graphs have several important applications in parallel processing. They provide a theoretical base for evaluating the performance of parallel architectures. Moreover, these results can be used for comparing different architectures. The functions of embeddings can be implemented in these architectures to allow the re-configuration of the network and the automatic mapping of algorithms. In [4] an embedding function is implemented between tori and meshes of different dimensions onto IBM Victor multicomputer. The objective of this embedding is to minimize the dilation. In [5] an embedding algorithm of hypercube graphs onto torus multicomputers is presented. In addition to measuring the traditional metrics, parallel algorithms for the FFT are generated. In these algorithms the overlapping of computations and communications is presented and good results are obtained [6].

In this paper we study the generation of parallel

*Centre For Applied Microelectronic member.

1066-6192/96 $5.00 © 1996 IEEE
Proceedings of PDP '96

algorithms for linear algebra problems. To solve this problems in a parallel way is important because they are a frequently used kernel in scientific applications that require a very low execution time. The graphs of these applications are cubic or planar in general. We present a partial embedding of these graphs on 1-D or 2-D tori. Our main objective is to obtain an initial data distribution that enables us to overlap computations and communications. The steps of our methods (in order to generate the parallel algorithm) are the following: 1) Generation of the computation and communication graph starting with the sequential algorithm. 2) Partial embedding of this graph onto torus multicomputer. Initial distribution of data. 3) Computation distribution with no restriction over the number of necessary processors. 4) Reduction of the number of processors: Consider again the steps 2 and 3. As an example we use the matrix multiplication problem in order to illustrate our method.

In section 2 we present the sequential algorithm for matrix multiplication. In section 3 the embedding is defined and the initial data distribution is studied. In section 4 we discuss the computation distribution. In section 5 the implementation of the parallel algorithm in a 2-D torus is presented. In section 6 the experimental results are presented. Finally in section 7 we present some conclusion and future work.

2 Sequential algorithm

Let $A(a_{i,j})$, $B(b_{i,j})$ and $C(c_{i,j})$ be matrices of $n \times n$ elements. A sequential algorithm with $O(n^3)$ complexity that solves the multiplication of equation 1 is given in equation 2.

$$c_{i,j} = \sum_{r=0}^{n-1} a_{i,r} \times b_{r,j} \ , \qquad \forall\ i,j = 0..n-1 \qquad (1)$$

$$\begin{aligned}
&do\ i = 0, n-1\\
&\quad do\ j = 0, n-1\\
&\quad\quad do\ r = 0, n-1\\
&\quad\quad\quad c_{i,j} = c_{i,j} + a_{i,r} \times b_{r,j}\\
&\quad\quad enddo\\
&\quad enddo\\
&enddo
\end{aligned} \qquad (2)$$

In order to relax the total order of execution of the sequential computations we consider the relation (R) between the $a_{i,r}$ and $b_{r,j}$ $(a_{i,r}\ R\ b_{r,j})$ $(\forall r = 0..n-1)$. All the elements belongings to one row of matrix A and the ones belongings to a column of matrix B are related [8]. It is important to take into account this relation because it will help us to obtain the initial distribution of data in the PEs memories.

3 Embedding and initial data distribution

In the sequential algorithm there are 3 nested loops and one statement that belongs to the inner loop. We consider the iteration space [7] (IS) of this algorithm. The coordinates of this IS are the variables of the loops and each point represents a computation (corresponding to a particular combination of values of the variables of the loops). We suppose that each point is a process that can be executed in parallel with other processes. The parallelism is limited by the dependencies. In this algorithm the dependencies are produced by the computation and reuse of the elements $c_{i,j}$. For each constant value $i = i_1$ and $j = j_1$ and for each value of loop variable r, the $c_{i_1 j_1}$ is reused. That is to say, in the iteration $r+1$ the element computed in iteration r is computed again to obtain a new value for it. So, the iteration r must always be executed before the iteration $r+1$. Each process must have in its local memory the elements of the matrices to be used in the represented point. It would be necessary to store an element of a matrix in more than one process.

For example, in figure 1.a the 3-D IS for the matrix multiplication algorithm is presented. We have supposed, for simplicity, that an inner point is connected to its 6 neighbours; however there are only dependencies in the r coordinate. The matrix A is replicated in each plane $\pi(i,r)$; matrix B is replicated in the planes $\pi(r,j)$. In figure 1.b the dependencies are shown (originally, the matrix C is in the plane $\pi(i,j,r=0)$. As an example, the processes that compute c_{00} have been indicated.

Let $G(P_c, D)$ be the graph that represents the IS, where P_c is a matrix of processes and matrix D stands for the dependencies (column vectors) in the IS. We additionally suppose an identity matrix for edges because we suppose that the points of the IS are totally connected with its neighbours. In matrix multiplication sequential algorithm matrix D is the column vector $\vec{d_1} = (0,0,1)$.

Let $H(P_d, C_o)$ be the graph that represents the plane of processors, where $P_d(\vec{i},\vec{j})$ are the nodes (PEs) and $C_o(\vec{i},\vec{j})$ are the physical connections between PEs. We applied an embedding of graph G onto graph H so as to obtain good values of: dilation, expansion, congestion and maximum load. An additional objective is to get the overlapping of computations and communications:

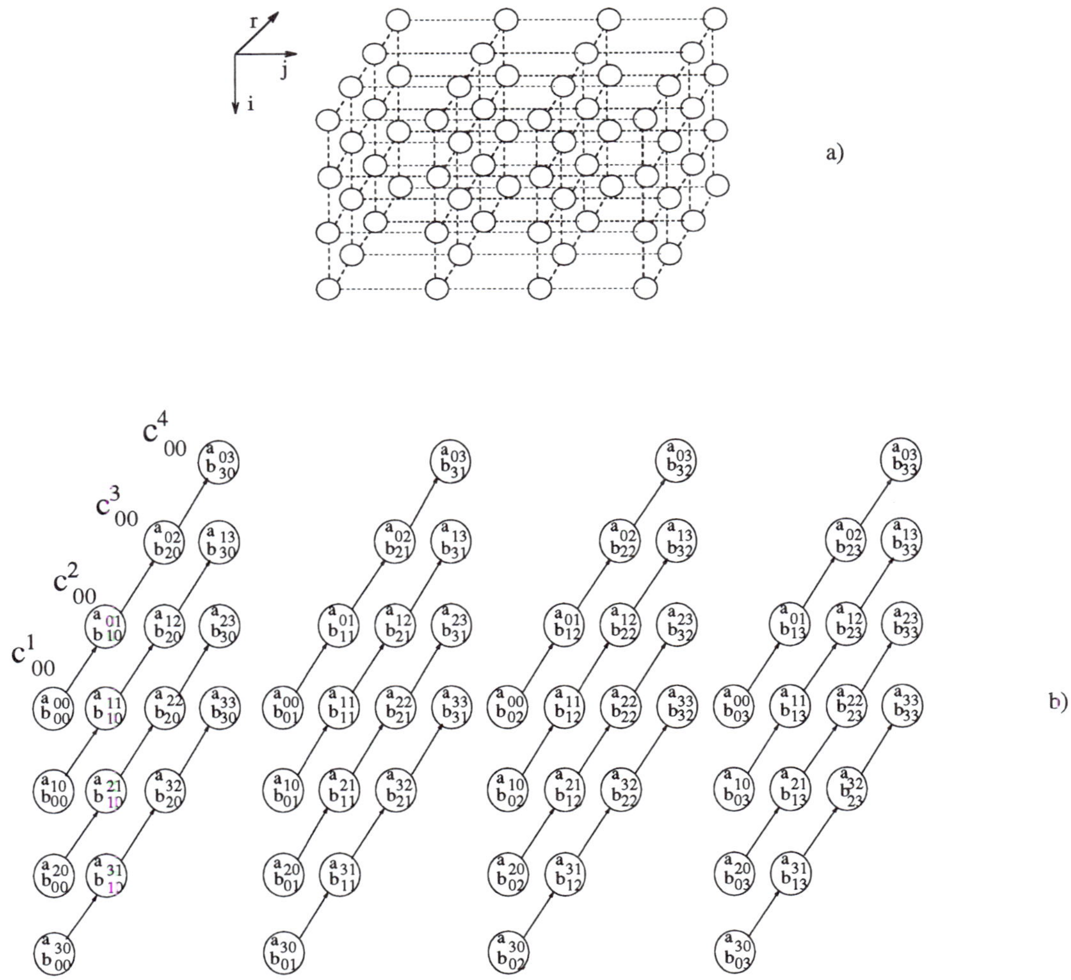

Figure 1: **a) 3-D IS for the matrix multiplication algorithm. b) Dependencies.**

par

... computations

... communications

endpar

Initially, the embedding we propose can be formulated in the following form:

$$I' = T \times I \qquad (3)$$

where: a) T is a $n' \times n'$ [7] in which the first $n'-1$ rows are the direction vectors of a projection plane (n' is the number of nested loops). We choose a projection plane perpendicular to the vector $\vec{d_1}$. This will allow us to overlap the computations and the communications because computed data in the PEs won't have to be communicated. The n' row of T can be chosen as a vector with at least one element set to one. This vector isn't relevant to the embedding. In the matrix multiplication example $n'= 3$ and since $\vec{d_1} = (0,0,1)$ we choose the projection plane $\pi((1,0,0),(0,1,0))$. The third row of matrix T is chosen to $(0,0,1)$. b) $I(n' \times 1)$ is the coordinate vector of the processes (graph G). The $n'-1$ first elements of vector I' are the coordinates of the PEs (graph H).

The expansion of the graph H is n because we project the 3-D IS in a processor plane. The dilation is 1 because processes with distance 1 will be set to distance 1 in the plane. The congestion is n and the maximum load is n.

With this embedding the i' row of A is repeated in the PEs ($i', j' = 0..n-1$). Moreover, the column j' of B is repeated in the PEs ($i' = 0..n-1, j'$). In order to eliminate this data redundancy we modify the embedding so that the projected points will satisfy the following restriction:

$$r = (i + j) \ mod \ n \quad (4)$$

That is to say, the PE (i', j') will be associated with one of the processes in the dimension r subject to the restrictions (3) and (4) simultaneously. In figure 2.a the processes in black are the ones considered by the partial embedding for $n = 4$.

With this partial embedding we obtain an optimal initial data distribution. That is to say, the PE (i', j') stores the elements $a_{i',r}, b_{r,j'}$ and computes $c_{i',j'}$. This data distribution is coherent with the relation between the elements of matrices A, B and C.

In figure 2.b the initial data distribution in the plane of PEs is shown for matrix multiplication for $n = 4$. Let us note that with this distribution of data the elements of A and B can be communicated to the neighbour PEs at the same time as an element of C is computed.

4 Distribution of computations in the PEs

After the distribution of data has been done we distribute computation guided by the data distribution. This computation distribution can be derived directly from the sequential algorithm. Given that the set of processes has been mapped in the PEs (i', j') (that we'll name (i, j) from now on for simplicity) and that these PEs do computations in parallel we can assume that the variables of (i, j) loops represent to the PEs (doall loops [9]). The r variable loop will be replicated between PEs in function of the data distribution. Specifically, the first computation that the PE (i, j) does is the one that is done in the sequential for $r = (i+j) \ mod \ n$. In [10] a more complete study of the code transformation of the sequential code is made for systolic arrays. The results of that work can be modified to be applied to our embedding. The rest of the values of r (for each PE) must be ordered such as:

a) several PEs don't use the same element of A or B in the same instant of time to compute an element of C.

b) The elements of A and B that are necessary (for successive values of r) are stored in the memories of the neighbouring PEs. An ordination of r values, for the PE (i, j) that satisfies this restrictions is:

$$r = (i + j + l) \ mod \ n$$
$$\forall \ l = 1..n - 1$$

The computations that perform the PE (i, j) are:

$$\begin{aligned}
&do \ l = 0, n - 1 \\
&\quad r = (i + j + l) \ mod \ n \\
&\quad c_{i,j} = c_{i,j} + a_{i,r} \times b_{r,j} \\
&enddo
\end{aligned}$$

We can realize that this ordination is obtained from the sequential algorithm introducing an auxiliary variable l and the reorganization of the r values.

For example, from the figure 2.b we can deduce that the PE $(0, 0)$ computes the product $c_{0,0} = a_{0,0} \times b_{0,0} + c_{0,0}$, for the value $l = 0$. For $l = 1$, it neccesitates $a_{0,1}$ and $b_{1,0}$ that are in the memories of the neighbouring PEs and they won't be used by other PE. For this value of l, the PE$(0, 3)$ needs the value $a_{0,0}$ and the PE$(3, 0)$ needs $b_{0,0}$. So these two PEs must be connected to PE$(0, 0)$ by different links.

5 Implementation onto torus multicomputer

In the 2-D torus multicomputer each processor has two neighbours in each dimension with direct independent links. Let Co be the $n'{-}1 \times n'{-}1$ matrix connections of the torus multicomputer. These connections can be obtained as $Co = T' \times I_{n}' \times T'^{t}$, where I_{n}' $(n' \times n')$ is the identity matrix. T' $(n'{-}1 \times n'{-}1)$ is the identity matrix concatenated with the column vector $\vec{0}(n'{-}1 \times 1)$, $T' = [I_{n'-1 \times n'-1} | \vec{0}(n'{-}1 \times 1)]$.

This transformation matrix is chosen because the plane of PEs is $\pi(i, j)$. This plane of connections is the subset of the connections represented by I_{n}' and that with this transformation are described with through matrix Co. In general, matrix T' can be computed according to the projection plane of T or the projection vectors of $G(\vec{d}_1)$.

Given a PE $I' = (i, j, r, ...)^t$ and let $\vec{Co}_i$ be the column vectors of the connection matrix Co, the neighbour PEs of PE I' are $I'' = (I' \pm \vec{Co}_i) \ mod \ n$ $(\forall \ i = 1..n'{-}1)$. For example, for matrix multiplication Co the identity matrix is 2×2 and the 4 neighbours PEs of the PE $I' = (i, j)$ are $((i \pm 1) \ mod \ n, j), (i, (j \pm 1) \ mod \ n)$. So, for the constant value of $l = l_1$, the $P_c(i, j)$: a) Will send the $a_{i,r}$ to $P_c((i, j) - \vec{Co}_2)$, because it will need this value to do a computation when $l = l_1 + 1$ and the value $b_{r,j}$ to $P_c((i, j) - \vec{Co}_1)$ where $r = (i + j + l_1) \ mod \ n$. b) Will receive from PE $P_c((i, j) + \vec{Co}_2)$ the value $a_{i,r}$ and from PE $P_c((i, j) + \vec{Co}_1)$ the value $b_{r,j}$ where $r = (i + j + l_1 + 1) \ mod \ n$.

The initial stored data in the PEs will go through it so that after $n - 1$ communications all the $a_{i,r}$, $b_{r,j}$ data implied in the computation of $c_{i,j}$ will be processed. In the following sections we will study two parallel algorithms. For the first one we will suppose that the

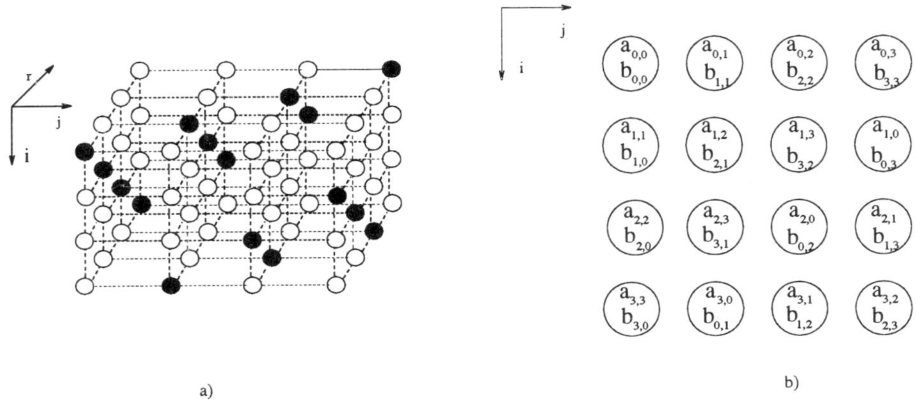

Figure 2: **a) Partial embedding of G onto H. b) Initial distribution for $n = 4$.**

number of PEs (m) in the i (j) dimension of the torus is equal to the number of rows (columns) of the matrices (n). For the second one we will suppose that $m < n$.

5.1 Parallel algorithm for $n = m$

In order to design the parallel algorithm, for a generic PE (i, j), we take into account: the applied embeddings, the initial data distribution, the connection matrix and the overlapping of computation and communication. In this algorithm the PEs must index the elements of the matrices in their local memories. So they will use 3 memory cells for storing $a_{i,r}$, $b_{r,j}$ and $c_{i,j}$.

The PE communicates data using point o point channels. The message passing primitives specify the channel of communication and the variable to be communicated. The PE (i, j) can use the connection matrix Co for communicating the data to its neighbour PEs (see section 5). Is the parallel algorithm for the PE (i, j). Follows:

```
cij=0
do z = 1,n − 1
      par
         send(((i,j) − C⃗o2) mod n,air)
         send(((i,j) − C⃗o1) mod n,brj)
         receive(((i,j) + C⃗o2) mod n,Air)
         receive(((i,j) + C⃗o1) mod n,Brj)
         cij = cij + air × brj
      endpar
      air = Air; brj = Brj
enddo
cij = cij + air × brj
```

In this algorithm we have used two auxiliary variables (Air, Brj), for overlapping the computations and communications. Let us note that there will be $n-1$ overlapped computations and communications. Finally, all the PEs do $n-1$ copies of data in their local memories and a final computation of the element cij. In figure 3 the movement of data between PEs is shown. There are only 3 steps (z) for $n = 4$.

5.2 Embedding for $m < n$

Problems in the real world require matrices with a great amount of elements by rows. This implies that the number of PEs in the multicomputer is very high (for $n = m$). On the other hand, the utilization of the PEs is relatively low: n multiplications and $n-1$ communications. The objective we have now is to reduce the number of PEs increasing the number of computations they do. For this, we must find an embedding and an initial data distribution that allows us to overlap the computations and communications.

The problem to adapt algorithm to architectures with a lower number of PEs than the originated with the original embedding is known as partitioning. In the design of systolic arrays there is a big amount of published works. In [11] a simple method of partitioning is proposed in which the results of the original embedding are used in order to obtain the data and computation distribution in the new PEs. In our embedding this scheme isn't applicable because the new computations and communications can't be overlapped. So, we modify our original embedding in order to make this restriction effective.

In what follows we explain the new embedding for a number of PEs ($m \times m$) lower than ($n \times n$). The matrices A and B are divided in $p \times p$ submatrices being $p = \lceil \frac{n}{m} \rceil$. If the matrices have no $p \times p$ elements, we add new rows and columns with all of their elements to 0. In the new embedding, the elements $a_{i,r}$ and $b_{r,j}$ initially stored can not be repeated in other

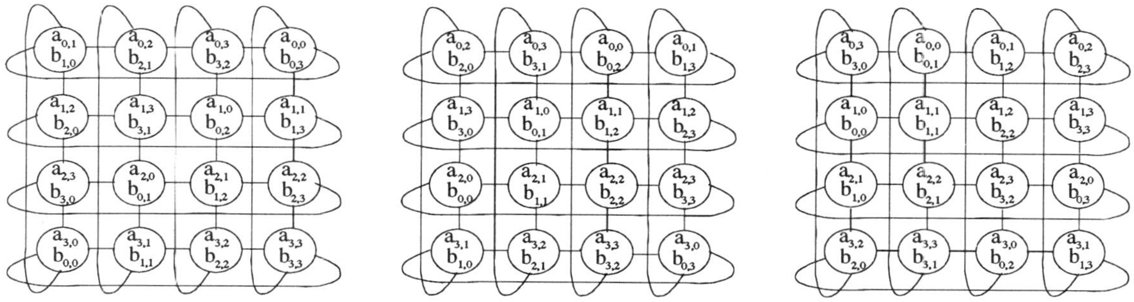

a) b) c)

Figure 3: **Movement of data between PEs. a)** $z = 1$. **b)** $z = 2$. **c)** $z = 3$.

local memory of the PEs of the row i and the column j (the $p \times p$ set of values of each PE must be different to the set of the rest of available PEs). Futhermore, the values stored inside a PE can not be repeated. In order to make the new embedding and the initial data distribution effective we apply (3) subject to the following restrictions:

```
For all PE (x = x1,y = y1)
    where x = 0..m − 1, y = 0..m − 1,
apply (3) to the process (i,j,r) of G so:
    i = x1 × p...x1 × p + (p − 1) and
    j = y1 × p...y1 × p + (p − 1)
subject to the restriction:
    r = (i + j) mod p + r0, where r is in the
    rank [r0..r0 + p − 1], and
    where r0 = [(x + y) mod m] × p
```

For the matrix multiplication example, the IS is divided in cubic portions of size $p \times p \times p$. From this portions we choose $p \times p$ processes that will be mapped in one PE.

In figure 4.a we show the IS of the figure 1 where the points in black are the ones that will be mapped in the PEs. In figure 4.b we show the new initial data distribution in the PEs.

Now the maximum load increases to $(p \times p)$, leaving several nodes of G to distance 0 and the congestion is 1. At cubic portions level, nodes that were to distance 2 now are to distance 0.

5.3 Parallel algorithm

The parallel algorithm is obtained from the results of the section bellow. The connections are directly obtained from matrix Co. In this case, the PEs must index submatrices A, B and C of dimension $p \times p$ in its local memories. Moreover, they must compute the product of submatrices and communicate the submatrices A and B to their neighbours. The submatrices of A and B are communicated in the same way as the individual elements of A and B were communicated (for $n = m$, section 5.1) taking into account that now there are $m \times m$ PEs. The computation of the submatrix multiplication (inside a PE) and the communications are done in parallel. The ordination (z) of the computation of different matrices multiplications (inside a PE) can be deduced in the same way as for the original embedding. Following we show the algorithm for a generic PE (x, y).

```
p = ⌈n/m⌉; c(0 : p − 1, 0 : p − 1) = 0
do z = 1, m − 1
   par
      send(((x, y) − Co2)) mod m,a)
      send(((x, y) − Co1)) mod m,b)
      receive(((x, y) + Co2)) mod m,A)
      receive(((x, y) + Co1)) mod m,B)
      do i = 0, p − 1
         do j = 0, p − 1
            do r = 0, p − 1
               c(i, j) = a(i, r) × b(r, j) + c(i, j)
            enddo
         enddo
      enddo
   endpar
   a(0:p-1,0:p-1)=A(0:p-1,0:p-1)
   b(0:p-1,0:p-1)=B(0:p-1,0:p-1)
enddo
do i = 0, p − 1
   do j = 0, p − 1
      do r = 0, p − 1
         c(i, j) = a(i, r) × b(r, j) + c(i, j)
      enddo
   enddo
enddo
```

Inside a PE the matrix multiplication is done in the same way as in the sequential algorithm. We have used

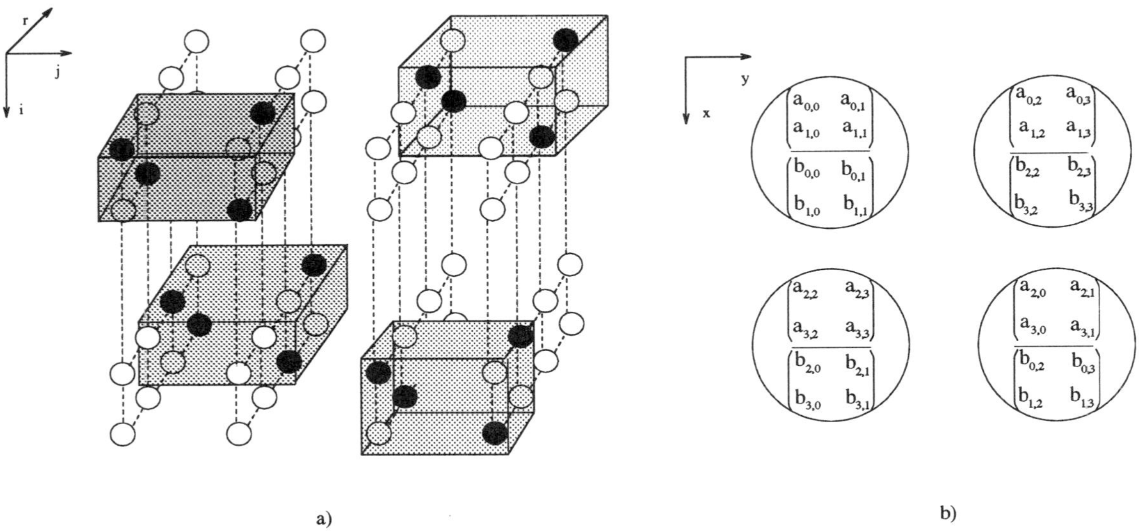

Figure 4: **a) Partial embedding of G onto H for $m < n$. b) Initial data distribution for $m = 2$ and** $n = 4$.

auxiliary submatrices A and B in order to overlap the computations and communications.

6 Experimental results

We have implemented the parallel algorithm of section 5.3 in a T800 Transputer[1] based multicomputer with 16 PEs with 1Mbyte of local memory by transputer. The hardware platform was a B008 motherboard. This motherboard is externally connected to a memory in a PC computer and to another B012 board. Also we have implemented our algorithm in a SN-1000 Transputer based multicomputer in the Centro Europeo de Paralelismo de Barcelona (C.E.P.B.A.)[2]. In this configuration the transputers have 4Mbyte of local memory. We have used this new machine in order to consider bigger matrices sizes.The data of the matrices A and B originally are in the memory of the PC computer. We have used OCCAM2 parallel language for programming it with INMOS toolsets and the sequential and parallel programs have been optimized.

For measuring the time of the parallel algorithm we have taken into account the time spent in distributing the data stored in the PC memory into the local memories of Tranputers. Moreover we have included the time spent downloading the results of the multiplication (C) back to the PC memory. This isn't usually taken into account in other works in this area. In figure 5, we show the results of the efficiency of the parallel algorithm as opposed to the size of the matrices (n), for the two machines.

The ascendent slope of the efficiency curves and the lower efficiency in the SN-1000 must be noted.

7 Conclusions and future work

In this paper we have presented an embedding of cubic or planar processes graphs onto 2-D torus multicomputers with planar or linear structure. This embedding has the advantage (as opposed to others embeddings and partitioning methods) that computations and communications can be overlapped. We have added conditions to the points of the IS that are mapped in the PEs and we have modified the embedding for a reduced number of PEs in the torus multicomputer. This embedding has been ilustrated with the linear algebra matrix multiplication algorithm. But this embedding can be used for other complex algorithm such as Triangular System of Equations, matrix-vector multiplication, and so on. The good experimental results have been obtained in a T800 Transputer based multicomputer with 16 PEs. We have tried some other algorithms with good results. Guided by this results we will continue in the development of more complex algorithms based on our embedding technique. We are planning a software platform for parallelizing sequential algorithms in a systematic way guided by our embedding technique.

References

[1] Athas, W.C., Seitz C.L. *Multicomputer. Message passing concurrent computers. IEEE computer,*

[1]Thanks to Ricardo Pérez García (Falcultad de Informática U.L.P.G.C.)

[2]Thanks to Maite Ortega and Judit Gimenez (C.E.P.B.A.)

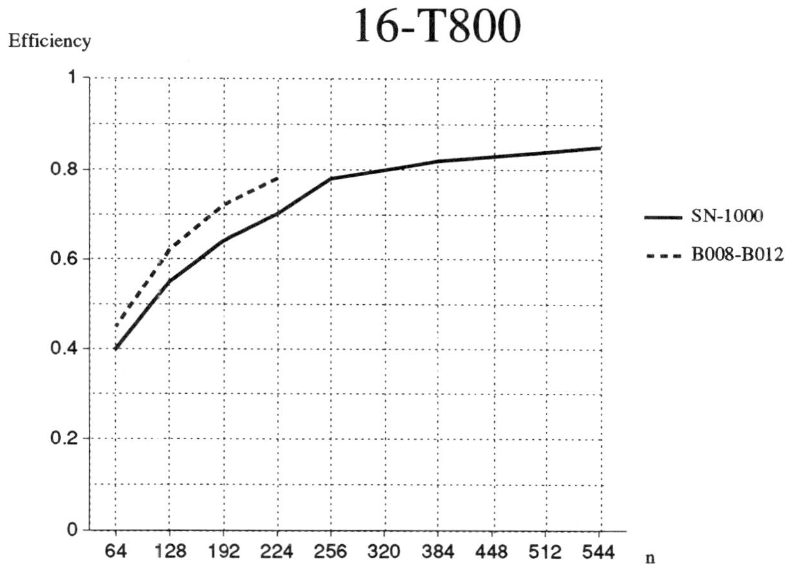

Figure 5: **Efficiency of the prallel algorithm.**

Agost. 1988,pp. 9-24.

[2] Ho C., Jonhsson S.L. *On embedding of arbitrary meshes in boolean cubes with expansion two dilation two. Proc. international conf. Parallel processing, 1987, pp. 188-191.*

[3] Varma A., Ragavendra C.S. *Interconection networks for multiprocessors and multicomputers. Theory and Practice (chapter 9), IEEE computer society press, pp. 430-436.*

[4] Ma Eva, Tao Lixin. *Embeddings among meshes and tori. J. Parallel and Distributed Computing, Vol. 18, 1993, pp. 44-55.*

[5] González Antonio, Valero-García Miguel, Díaz de Cerio Luis. *Embedding Hypercubes onto Rings and Toruses. DAC/UPC Report No. RR-93/01, January 1993.*

[6] Díaz de Cerio Luis, Valero-García Miguel, González Antonio. *A study of the Communication Cost of the FFT on Torus Multicomputers. DAC/UPC Report No. RR-94/25, November 1994.*

[7] Moldovan, D.I. *The design of algoritms for VLSI Systolic Arrays. Proceedings of the IEEE, vol. 1, no. 1. January, 1983.*

[8] Quinn Michael J. *Parallel computing. Theroy and Practice. McGraw-Hill International editions. Computer Science Series. 1994.*

[9] Wolfe M. *Massive Parallelism through program restructuring. Technical Report No. CS/E 90-009. Oregon Graduate Institute, Department of Computer Science and Engineering. June 1990.*

[10] Suárez Alvaro. *Ejecución entrelazada de las particiones en algoritmos sistólicos particionados. Tesis, Departamento de Arquitectura de Computadores, Universidad politécnica de Cataluña. Septiembre. 1993.*

[11] Moldovan D.I., Fortes J.A.B. *Partitioning and mapping algorithms into fixed systolic arrays. IEEE transactions on computers, vol. C-35, no. 1. January. 1986.*

Dynamic Slicing of Parallel Message-Passing Programs

Mariam Kamkar, Patrik Krajina, Peter Fritzson

Department of Computer and Information Science
Linköping University, S-581 83 Linköping, Sweden
Email: marka@ida.liu.se, patkr@ida.liu.se, petfr@ida.liu.se
Fax: +46 13 282666 Phone: +46 13 281000

Abstract

As software applications grow larger and more complex, program maintenance activities such as adding new functionality, debugging, and testing consume an increasing amount of available resources for software development. This is especially true for distributed systems communicating via message-passing. In order to cope with this increased complexity, programmers need effective computer-supported methods for decomposition and dependence analysis of programs, to understand dependencies between different parts of software systems and to find the sources of errors.

Program slicing is one method for such decomposition and dependence analysis. A program slice with respect to a specified variable at some program point consists of those parts of the program which may directly or indirectly affect the value of that variable at the particular program point.

In this paper we present an algorithm for dynamic slicing of distributed/parallel programs and some results from an implementation for a parallel MIMD computer.

1 Introduction

As software applications grow larger and more complex, program maintenance activities such as adding new functionality, debugging, and testing consume an increasing amount of available resources for software development. In order to cope with this increased complexity, programmers need effective computer-supported methods for decomposition and dependence analysis of programs [6, 5, 13, 8].

Program slicing is one method for such decomposition and dependence analysis. A program slice with respect to a specified variable at some program point consists of those parts of the program which may directly or indirectly affect the value of that variable at the particular program point. This is useful for understanding dependences within programs. A *static* program slice [15] is computed through static data and control flow analysis and is valid for all possible executions of the program. Static slices are often imprecise, i.e., they contain unnecessarily large parts of the program. In contrast, *dynamic* program slicing [9] considers only a particular execution of a program. The main application of dynamic program slicing is hence in program debugging. This is due to the fact that program debugging is used to analyze a particular execution of a program, the one that shows the existence of a bug in the program. Given an incorrect value of a variable of interest, dynamic program slicing can present a dynamic slice to the debugger (human or system) for further investigation.

As an example consider the program in Figure 1(I) which computes sum of the integers `1` to `n`. Figure 1(II) shows a static slice of this program with respect to the value of variable `sum` that is computed at statement `printf("%\n", sum)`. This slice consists of all statements in the program that are needed to compute the final value of `sum` in any execution, in this example the static slice is equal to the original program. Figure 1(III) shows a dynamic slice of the program in Figure 1(I) with respect to the final value of `sum` for the specific test case `n=0`.

The concept of dynamic slicing has been introduced originally for sequential programs (for a survey of program slicing techniques see [7, 14]). Distributed programs introduce several problems which do not exist in sequential programs (e.g., non-reproducible behaviors, non-deterministic selection of communication events, etc.). Several methods for dynamic slicing of distributed programs have been proposed [10, 3, 2]. Previously we have developed an interprocedural dynamic slicing algorithm, which works at the procedure abstraction level [11], and which here has been generalized to handle communicating, message-passing parallel programs.

In this paper we present an algorithm for dynamic slicing

1066-6192/96 $5.00 © 1996 IEEE
Proceedings of PDP '96

(I)

```
main()
{ int N, i, sum;
  iread(0, &N);
  sum = 0;
  i = 1;
  while (i <= N) {
    sum += i;
    i++;
  }
  printf("%i\n", sum);}
```

(II)

```
main()
{ int N, i, sum;
  iread(0, &N);
  sum = 0;
  i = 1;
  while (i <= N) {
    sum += i;
    i++;
  }
  printf("%i\n", sum);}
```

(III)

```
main()
{ int N, i, sum;

  sum = 0;







  printf("%i\n", sum);}
```

Figure 1 : (I) Example program. (II) Static slice of the program with respect to the final value of variable `sum`. (III) Dynamic slice of the program with respect to the final value of variable `sum` for input `n=0`.

of distributed/parallel programs, and some results from an implementation for a parallel MIMD computer. We introduce the notion of Distributed Dynamic Dependence Graph (DDDG) which represents control, data and communication dependences in a distributed program. This graph is built at run-time and used to compute slices of the program through graph traversals.

The rest of the paper is structured as follows: Section 2 describes the programming language under consideration; Section 3 defines the dynamic slicer for distributed programs; The general overview of the parallel distributed dynamic slicer is presented in Section 4; Section 5 gives some results from an implementation for the parallel MIMD computer. Section 6 describes the construction of the Distributed Dynamic Dependence Graph (DDDG) used in the algorithm which is introduced in Section 7; Related work and Conclusions are discussed in Section 8 and 9.

2 The Programming Language under Consideration

In the current implementation we are using the ANSI-C programming language both as the slicing system implementation language and the supported language for software to be analyzed, but similar languages, like Pascal, Fortran, Modula-2 etc., could also be supported using the same technique. In this implementation, the following C data types and program constructs can be handled: all kinds of variables including scalars, arrays, records, pointers, dynamic structures, global variables etc.; assignment statements; conditional (**if**, **switch**) statements; loops (**for**, **while**, **do**); function calls (with/without return values, in and out parameters); type casting; message handling by **send** and **receive** statements.

The syntax and semantics of send and receive statements are as follows:

`SendMessage (TopId, ProcId, Data, Size)`: Execution of a send statement results in the transmission of the message stored in `Data` to the process identified by `ProcId`.

`RecvMessage(TopId, ProcId, Data, Size)`: Execution of a receive statement causes the assignment of a sent message to `Data`. The receive statement is blocking.

Currently the implemented dynamic slicer does not support macros, include files, libraries, shared variables, i.e., global variables shared between processes.

3 Dynamic Slices for Distributed Programs

A distributed program consists of a set of processes that communicate through message passing primitives. As in the sequential program, there exist data and control dependences between statements in a distributed program [4]. There is a data dependence between two statements whenever a variable appearing in one statement may have an incorrect value if the two statements are reversed. For example, given the following sequence of statements, `s2` is data dependent on `s1`.

```
s1)x = y + z
s2) w = x / a
```

A control dependence exists between a statement and the predicate whose value immediately controls the execution of that statement. In the following sequence of statements, `s2` is control dependent on the predicate `p` in `s1`.

```
s1)if (p) then
s2)x = y + z
   endif
```

There is an additional dependence relation in distributed programs which arises as the result of communications between processes through send and receive statements. A receive statement is communication dependent on its send statement partner. In the following set of statements, s2 is communication dependent on its communicating partner s1; the statement s2 is receiving a message in &x from the process with ProcId 1, sent by statement s1 through the message denoted by &x.

```
s1)SendMessage(top_id,1 (void*) &x,
 sizeof(x));
s2)RecvMessage(top_id,1,(void*) &x,
 sizeof(x));
```

Given a distributed program $P = \{p_1, p_2, \ldots p_n\}$ where p_i is a process in P, we define a distributed dynamic slice on program P to be $\text{ProgSlice} = \{<p_1, s_1>, <p_2, s_2> \ldots <p_n, s_n>\}$ where s_i is a subset of statements of process p_i and contains all statements which directly or indirectly affect the computation of a specific statement (called slicing criterion) in a specific process.

A distributed slicing criterion is a non-empty set defined to be:

$C = \{<s_i, x_i> |$ where s_i is a selected statement in process p_i with test case $x_i\}$.

The criterion contains at least one element and at most equal to the number of processes in the program i.e., one element per process.

Figure 2 (I) shows a simple example program which consists of two processes, process Send-Receive with ProcId 0 and process Receive-Send with ProcId 1. This program computes the square of the value of variable x through these processes. Process 0 initializes x with integer 17 and then sends it to process 1 for further computation. Process 1, after receiving the value 17, computes its square and returns it to process 0. Process 0 receives the square of 17 and prints it out. Considering statement 11 in process 0 (which prints out the square of 17) as a slicing criterion, those statements which participates in the computation of the square of 17 are statements 8,9,10, and 11 in process 0 and statements 8,10, and 11 in process 1, i.e., all the highlighted statements in Figure 2 (I). As a result for the program Prog, consisting of two processes:

```
Prog = {Send-Receive, Receive-Send}
```

the distributed slice will be:

```
ProgSlice = {<Send-Receive,{8,9,10,11}>,
 <Receive-Send, {8,10,11}>}
```

In order to analyze communication behavior in distributed programs we have also considered information about communication events in a program and its slice. For a distributed program $\text{Prog} = \{p_1, p_2, \ldots p_n\}$, the set ProgCom of all communication events is:

```
ProgCom ={(<p,rec>, <q,snd>) | where rec
 in process p is communication
 dependent on snd in process q}.
```

Figure 2 (II) shows the communication events of the program in Figure 2 (I). A communication slice ComSlice is a subset of ProgCom which consists of those communication events appear in the ProgSlice of the program. In Figure 2(II), the program communication events are as follows:

```
ProgCom={(<Receive-Send,8>,
 <Send-Receive,9>),
 (<Send-Receive,10>,<Receive-Send,11>}
```

The ComSlice in this example is the same as the ProgCom of the program.

4 General Overview of the Dynamic Slicer

We have implemented the Dynamic Slicer shown in Figure 3 on a parallel MIMD machine, a Parsytec GC PowerPlus-128 machine with 128 PowerPC 601 processors and a communications network including 256 T805 transputers.

To construct the Distributed Dynamic Dependence Graph (DDDG) the slicer system first instruments the distributed program by calls to data and communication dependency collecting routines. These routines construct the Data and Communication Dependence Graph (*DataComDep*) at run time and the Control Dependence Graph (*ContDep*) at compile time. Then the instrumented program is compiled into object code (as a future solution the instrumentation can be built into the compiler and therefore eliminate the need of a separate instrumented source code file). When the object code is executed, the *DataComDep* is created on-the-fly and dumped into a trace file.

The above mentioned steps are performed for and by each process. The slicing can now be done by the slicing system by accessing all trace files, source code files and control dependences files through the file system.

4.1 The Slicer System

Automatic Instrumenting & Instrumented code

The automatic instrumentor instruments the target C program. This part has not been implemented yet. The instrumentation is currently being done by hand.

Input: Target C program

Output: Instrumented target C program and a file containing *ContDep*.

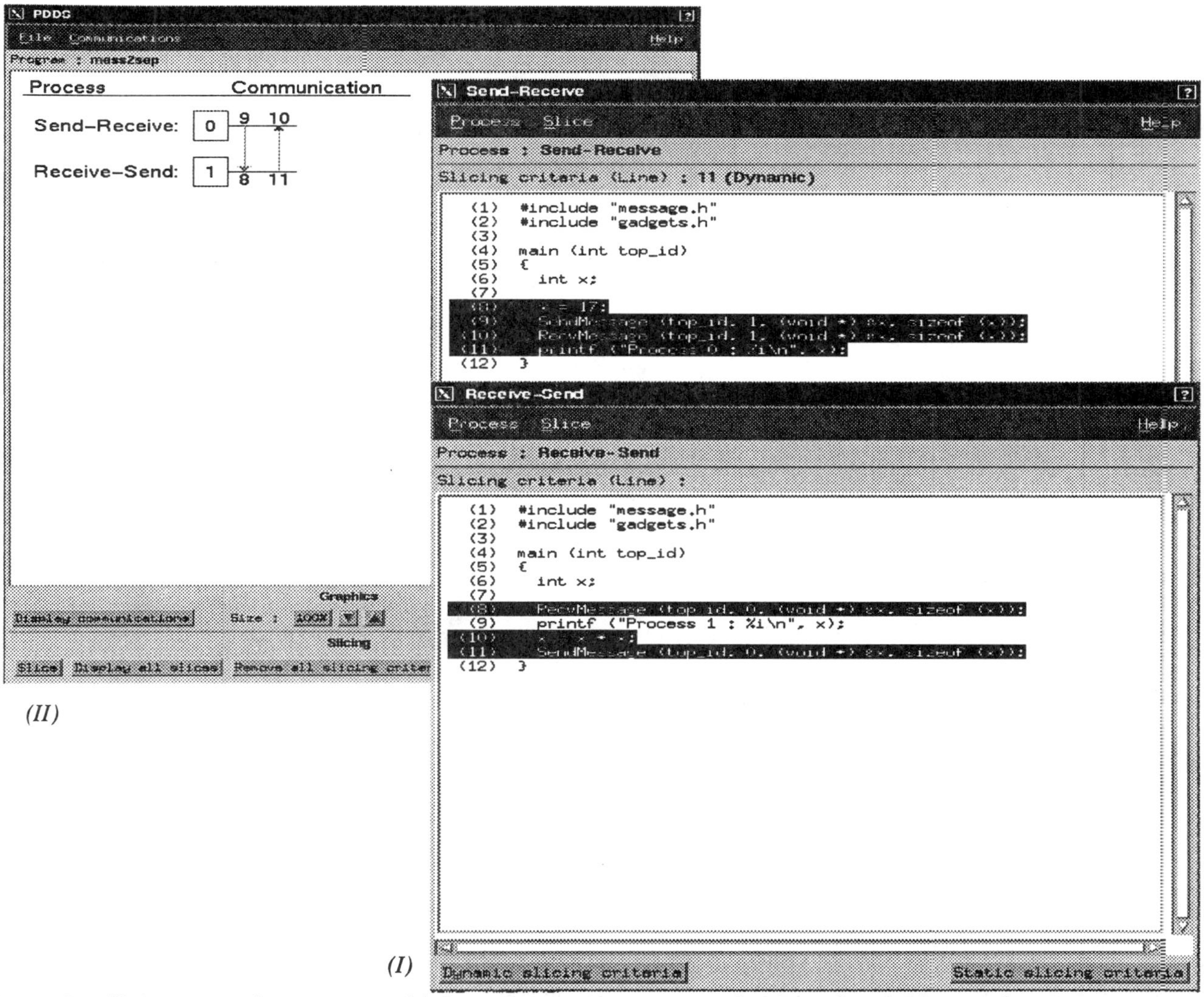

Figure 2 : (I) An example program which computes the square of value of variable x, using two processes Send-Receive with ProcId 0 and Receive-Send with ProcId 1. (II) Communication dependences between processes Send-Receive and Receive-Send.

Compiling & Object Code

An ANSI-C compiler from Motorola which cross-compiles to the Parsytec GC is used.

Input: Instrumented target C program
Output: Object code

Executing & Trace file

The program runs on the Parsytec GC and generates a trace file containing the *DataComDep*.

Input: None
Output: The *DataComDep* as a trace file

User Input: User data
User Output: User data

The Slicer

The slicing criterion, which is a statement in a specific process, is sent from the slicer GUI by a socket. A sequential algorithm is used and the slice is sent to the GUI. It is written in sequential C.

Input: DDDG: DataComDep in a trace file and the file containing the ContDep
Socket Input: Slicing criterion
Socket Output: Statements and messages in the slice

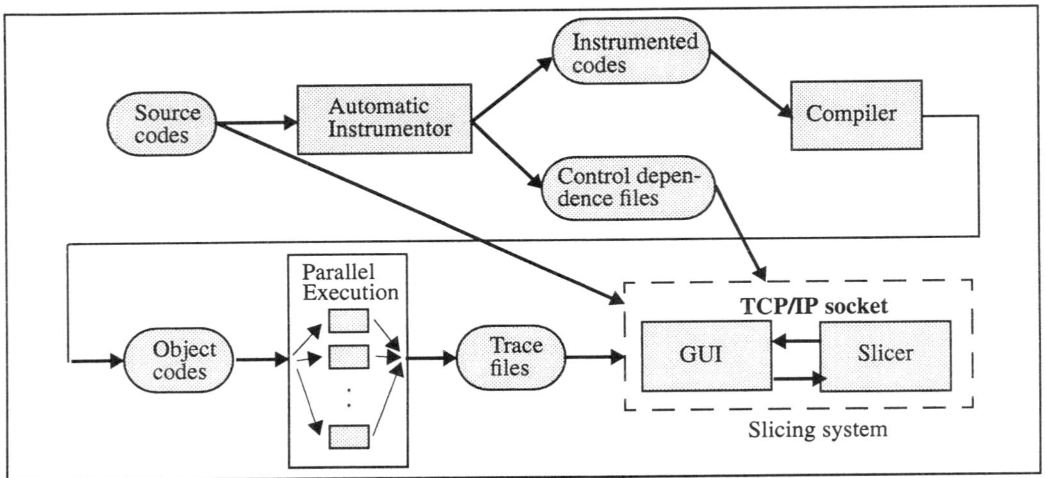

Figure 3 : General overview of the Dynamic Slicer system

The GUI

This is the Graphical User Interface of the slicer. The slicing criterion is defined here and sent by a socket to the slicer and the computed slice from the slicer is presented graphically. It has been implemented in sequential C, employing the Motif user interface component library.

Socket Input: Statements and messages in the slice
Socket Output: Slicing criterion
User Input: Slicing criterion
User Output: Graphical view of the statements and messages in the slice

5 Performance Measurements

The scalability and performance of the implemented slicing system has been measured when applied to a small parallel array processing application running on the Parsytec GC/PowerPlus-128 MIMD computer with 128 processors and a node memory of 32 Mbyte. We have measured the latency for a 1 byte message on this computer to approximately 140 microseconds. The data rate between two pairs of processors varies between 2 and 3.5 Mbyte/second depending on the message size. On the other hand, a given node can send data to 4 neighbors simultaneously. A 6-way parallel file system is also available on this machine, with a measured performance of approximately 10 Mbytes/second for both reading and writing.

The results for the small array application are shown in Table 1. It was not possible to run the application on only one processor with instrumentation on, since the produced trace overflowed the node memory of 32 Mbyte. Here we have only measured the elapsed time without and with instrumentation, since producing the trace is the dominant cost of performing dynamic slicing. The computation of the actual slice is currently done on a workstation in a post-mortem manner, and is independent on the number of processors which produced the trace file. We are planning to replace this sequential slicing computation by a parallel version in the future.

Table 1: Scalability when slicing a small array application

Number of processors	Time without instrumentation (milliseconds)	Speedup (without instr)	Time with instrumentation (milliseconds)	Speedup (with instr)
1	2475	1 (assigned)	–	1 (assigned)
2	1275	1.94	5281	2 (assigned)
4	658	3.76	3417	3.09
8	353	7.01	2481	4.26
16	218	11.35	2024	5.75
32	149	16.61	1786	5.91

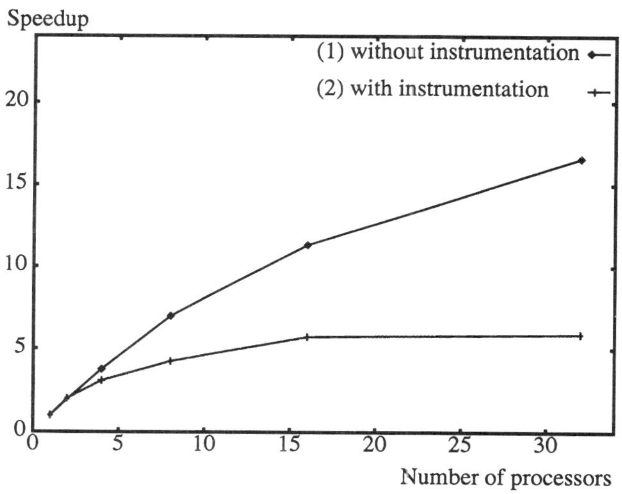

Figure 4 : Speedup curves for a small array application, (1) without instrumentation and (2) including instrumentation to produce trace data for dynamic slicing using the slicer system.

Figure 4 shows the two speedup curves produced from the data in Table 1.

The scalability of the "pure", un-instrumented application is reasonable up to approximately 16 processors where the latency and message passing time is starting to become significant compared to the computing work done on each processor. Surprisingly enough, the scalability of the instrumented application is worse despite the fact that more work is done on each processor, which might have resulted in better scalability. The explanation is that the sequential work performed by the master node (1.5 seconds part of all the times shown in the column for time with instrumentation) increased relatively more than in the slaves because of the instrumentation, since many simple assignment statements were instrumented in the master.

The tracing overhead introduced by the instrumentation varies between a factor of 4 on 2 processors to a factor of 12 on 32 processors. This is high, but not unreasonable price, that may be worth to pay for locating some hard-to-find bugs.

6 Distributed Dynamic Dependence Graph (DDDG)

In this section we discuss a data structure called Distributed Dynamic Dependence Graph (DDDG) which is used in computing distributed dynamic slices. The DDDG consists of two graphs, the Control Dependence Graph (ContDep), and the Data and Communication Dependence Graph (DataComDep).

6.1 Control Dependence Graph (ContDep)

A Control Dependence Graph, `ContDepG = (CDG`$_1$`, CDG`$_2$`,...,CDG`$_n$`)`, of a distributed program `Prog = (p`$_1$`, p`$_2$`,...,p`$_n$`)` is a set of subgraphs `CDG`$_i$`=(V`$_i$`,C`$_i$`)`; where `V`$_i$ is the set of vertices corresponding to simple statements and predicate expressions in process `p`$_i$ and `C`$_i$ is the set of edges that reflect control dependences between vertices in `V`$_i$. The Control Dependence Graph is constructed at compile time since control dependences are not dependent on a particular execution. Control dependences from this graph is then used at run-time together with data and communication dependences to include dependent statements when computing slices.

6.2 Data and Communication Dependence Graph (DataComDep)

A Data and Communication Dependence Graph of a distributed program `Prog=(p`$_1$`,p`$_2$`,...,p`$_n$`)` is a distributed graph `DataComDepG=(DCDG`$_1$`,DCDG`$_2$`,...,DCDG`$_n$`)` where `DCDG`$_i$ represents the data and communication dependences for process `i`.

The DataComDep graph is constructed during the execution of the program on-the-fly and contains data and communication dependences. It can be constructed in several ways. We present three methods:

1. Complete statement instance-based graph
2. Reduced statement instance-based graph
3. Statement-based graph

The selected method

For the first prototype implementation, we have used the first method, *complete statement instance-based graph* in the implementation of the Dynamic Slicer. The reasons for this choice is that the first method gives accurate slices and it is simpler to implement than the second choice. Also, since most of the implementation work needed for method 1 can be re-used as part of a future implementation of the second method, method 1 was a natural choice for a first implementation.

The definition of the Data and Communication Dependence Graph for each process is as follows:

`DataComDep(p)=`<`V,E`>, where
`V={s|s` is a statement instance in process `p}`
`E` = a set of dependence edges divided in two groups:
`DataDep`: a `DataDep` edge connects two statement instances `s`$_i$`,s`$_j$ in process `p` and shows that the computation of `s`$_i$ is data dependent on `s`$_j$.
`ComDep`: a `ComDep` edge connects a receive statement

instance s_i in process p to a send statement instance s_j in process q to represent a communication dependence between s_i and s_j.

7 An Incremental Dynamic Slicing Algorithm

Given the Distributed Dynamic Dependence Graph, the slice can be computed in two ways: by a parallel algorithm or by a sequential slicing algorithm. In this paper we consider a sequential algorithm for performing the slicing through a trace traversal, even though the construction of the trace has been done in parallel.

Definition 1: A $\rightarrow$ B means that A is dependent on B, of type data or control dependence.

Definition 2: (p, r) $\rightarrow$ (q, s) means that (receive) node r in process p is communication dependent on (send) node s in process q.

The general idea behind the algorithm is that all messages come in the form of (p, r) $\rightarrow$ (q, s), i.e., node pairs. This communication dependence is stored at the receive node, i. e., (q, s) is stored at (p, r).

A sequential program can easily be sliced incrementally, because all nodes of the DDDG can be stored in a linear linked list and they are data and/or control dependent on earlier nodes (i.e., nodes executed earlier) during a backward slicing. However, for slicing of parallel programs this cannot be done as easily. When the slicing algorithm reaches the send node (q, s) (see definition 2 above), it is not clear yet if this node will be included in the slice or not until the receive node (p, r) has been sliced. This algorithm suspends the slicing of a certain process if a send node is reached and this message has not yet been encountered, i. e., the corresponding receive node has not yet been sliced. The algorithm computes accurate dynamic slices.

8 Related Work

The concept of dynamic slicing has been originally introduced for sequential programs. Distributed programs introduce several problems which do not exist in sequential programs (e.g., non-reproducible behaviors, non-deterministic selection of communication events, etc.). Several methods for dynamic slicing of distributed programs have been proposed.

Duesterwald and et al. [3] introduce a Distributed Dependence Graph for representation of distributed programs. A distributed program consists of a set of processes. Communication between processes is assumed to be synchronous and non-deterministic send and receive statements. Their Distributed Dependence Graph contains a single vertex for each statement and control predicate in the program. Control dependences between statements are determined statically while data and communication dependences are added to the graph at run-time. Slices are computed by determining the set of vertices from which the vertices specified in the criterion can be reached. This approach deals with non-determinism by replacing non-deterministic communication statements in the program with deterministic communication statements in the slice.The slicing algorithm may compute inaccurate slices in the presence of loops due to the fact that a single vertex is used for all occurrences of a statement in the execution history.

Korel and Ferguson [10] extend the dynamic slicing method of Korel and Laski [9] to distributed programs with Ada-type rendezvous communication. They formalize the execution history as a distributed program path and introduce the notion of communication influence to capture the interdependence between tasks (in addition to Definition-Use, Test-Control and Identity relations from the previous work). A dynamic slice is defined to be an executable projection of the original program that is obtained by deleting statements from it. The program is only guaranteed to preserve the behavior of the program if the rendezvous in the slice occur in the same relative order as in the program. This approach requires a mechanism for replaying rendezvous in the slice in the same relative order as they appeared in the original program.

Cheng [2] proposes a program representation, Process Dependence Net (PDN), for concurrent programs. PDN, in addition to the usual control and data dependence, represents selection, synchronization and communication dependences. Cheng's algorithm for computing dynamic slices is basically a generalization of the initial approach by Agrawal and Horgan [1] which computes a dynamic slice based on a static graph. Consequently, the slicing algorithm may compute inaccurate slices.

To summarize Korel and Ferguson [10] and Duesterwald et al. [3] compute slices that are executable programs, but deal with non-determinism in a different way. Approaches presented in this paper and by Cheng [2] do not consider this problem because the computed slices are not executable programs. The dynamic slicing method by Duesterwald et al. [3] and Cheng [2] use static dependence graphs for computing dynamic slices. Although this is more space-efficient than the other approaches, the computed slices are inaccurate. The algorithms by Korel and Ferguson and the one used in our approach both require an amount of space that depends on the number of executed statements. Korel and Ferguson require their slices to be executable; therefore these slices contain more statements than those computed by our algorithm.

9 Conclusions

In this paper we have presented an algorithm for distributed dynamic slicing and a tool (the Dynamic Slicer) for performing slicing on parallel and distributed message-passing based application. The slicer has an easy-to-use window-oriented user interface that clearly marks the parts of the program which contributes to some selected (faulty) computational result.The need for tools to help the programmer understand dependencies and interactions is more pressing in parallel software compared to conventional sequential software. This is especially true for message-passing based software.

This is the first prototype implementation of the slicer, which gives a tracing overhead of a factor of 4 (on 2 processors) to a factor of 12 (on 32 processors) in increase of execution time. A reasonable, but not perfect scalability of the combination of slicer and application is currently achieved. A number of rather small adjustments in the tracing mechanism of the slicing tools is expected to improve the scalability properties.

However, to be useful for large applications further improvements in the efficiency of the tracing part of the slicing mechanism are needed. For example, the parallel version of the slicing algorithm mentioned in this paper should be implemented, static analysis of loops to reduce the amount of tracing should be utilized. Finally, the slicing tool itself should be integrated with a full parallel debugger, for example DETOP [12], which supports multi-processor, multi-thread and multi-program debugging. We have recently started a cooperation with the originators of DETOP towards this goal.

References

[1] Hiralal Agrawal and Joseph R. Horgan. Dynamic Program Slicing. In *Proceedings of the ACM SIGPLAN'90 Conference on Programming Language Design and Implementation*, pages 246–256, New York, June 1990.

[2] Jingde Cheng. Slicing Concurrent Programs - a graph-theoretical approach. *In proceeding of the First international workshop on Automated and Algorithmic Debugging (1993)*, P. Fritzson, Ed., vol. 749 of Lecture notes in computer science, springer-verlag, pp. 223-240, 1993.

[3] Evelyn Duesterwald, Rajiv Gupta, and Mary Lou Soffa. Distributed Slicing and Partial Re-execution for Distributed Programs. In *Proceedings of the Fifth Workshop on Languages and Compilers for Parallel Computing*, New Haven Connecticut, August 1992.

[4] Jeanne Ferrante, Karl J. Ottenstein, and Joe D. Warren. The Program Dependence Graph and its Use in Optimization. *ACM Transactions on Programming Languages and Systems*, 9(3):319–349, July 1987.

[5] Keith B. Gallagher and James Lyle. Using Program Slicing in Software Maintenance. *IEEE Transaction on Software Engineering*, 17, 8, pp. 751-761, 1991.

[6] Susan Horwitz, Jan Prins, and Thomas Reps. Integrating Non-Interfering Versions of Programs. In *Proceedings of the ACM SIGSOFT/SIGPLAN Symposium on Principles of Programming Languages*, San Diego, California, January 1988.

[7] Mariam Kamkar. Interprocedural dynamic Slicing with Applications to Debugging and Testing. Ph.D. thesis (No. 297), Department of Computer and Information Science, Linköping University, April 93.

[8] Mariam Kamkar, Peter Fritzson, Nahid Shahmehri: Interprocedural Dynamic Slicing with Applications to Interprocedural Data Flow Testing. In *Proc of the IEEE Conf. on Software Maintenance, CSM-93*, San Diego, Sept. 1993.

[9] Bogdan Korel and Janusz Laski. Dynamic Slicing of Computer Programs. *The Journal of Systems and Software*, 1990.

[10] Bogdan Korel and Roger Ferguson. Dynamic Slicing of Distributed Programs. *Applied Mathematics and Computer Science* Vol. 2, No. 2, pp. 199-215, 1992.

[11] Mariam Kamkar, Nahid Shahmehri, Peter Fritzson: Three Approaches to Interprocedural Dynamic Slicing. In Proc. of *EUROMICRO'93 (Journal of Microprocessing and Microprogramming)*, vol. 38, No 1-5, Sept. 1993. Published by North-Holland.

[12] Michael Oberhuber and Roland Wismuller: DETOP - An Interactive Debugger for PowerPC based Multicomputers. *In Proc. of ZEUS'95 workshop on Parallel Programming and Computing*, Linköping, Sweden, May 17-19, 1995. Published by IOS Press.

[13] Nahid Shahmehri, Mariam Kamkar, and Peter Fritzson: Semi-Automatic Bug Localization in Software Maintenance. In *Proc. of the IEEE Conf. on Software Maintenance, CSM'90*, San Diego, Nov. 1990.

[14] Frank Tip. Generation of Program analysis Tools. Ph.D. thesis (series; 1995-5), Institute for Logic, Language and Computation, Amsterdam, Netherlands, 1995.

[15] Mark Weiser. Program Slicing. *IEEE Transactions on Software Engineering*, SE–10(4):352–357, July 1984.

❖ SESSION 4 ❖

Programming Tools

Chair

P. Milligan

Systematic Assessment of the Overhead of Tracing Parallel Programs*

Alain Fagot and Jacques Chassin de Kergommeaux

APACHE project
IMAG Institute, 46, avenue Félix Viallet
F-38031 Grenoble Cedex 1, FRANCE
{Alain.Fagot,Jacques.Chassin}@imag.fr

Abstract

Instant Replay is a classical technique developed to help programmers to cope with transient errors occurring in non-deterministic executions of parallel programs. Enough information is recorded during an initial recording phase to be able to force subsequent re-executions to be deterministic with respect to the initial one. If the time overhead of the initial recording is sufficiently low, recording can be used as a normal execution mode of parallel programs.

This article describes the method used to assess systematically the overhead of the recording phase of an Instant Replay tool implemented for an RPC-based programming model named ATHAPASCAN. *Evaluation was done using synthetic programs generated from program models of classical parallel algorithms. The generality of the method comes from the possibility of generating multiple program instances from a single algorithm model. Experimental results confirm the efficiency of the tested execution replay tool.*

1 Introduction

This paper presents the methodology used to systematically assess the overhead induced by tracing parallel programs and the results of this assessment. The framework of the experiments is the ATHAPASCAN parallel programming model, based on remote procedure call (RPC). ATHAPASCAN is developed in the APACHE project whose aim is to build a complete software environment combining portability *and* efficiency for the development of parallel applications [10]. Portability and efficiency will be achieved through automatic load balancing facilities adapting to the exploitable granularity of the target parallel system and to the resources available at run-time.

Many parallel programs present a non-deterministic behavior, even if they produce deterministic computation results. Non-deterministic execution behaviors originate mainly in execution environments of programs. Such an environment depends on a large number of factors that cannot be controlled by the programmer, such as the initial contents of cache memories, the initial state of the operating system or the simultaneous execution of demon processes on the same multiprocessor. Programs adapting to the execution environment for efficiency reasons, using dynamic load balancing techniques for example, are very prone to exhibit non-deterministic execution behaviors. Non-deterministic execution behavior of erroneous parallel programs may result in transient errors which appear infrequently or vanish when debugging tools are used, because of changes introduced by these tools in the causal relationship between parallel processes.

The most classical technique used to catch transient errors appearing during executions of parallel programs is to *record* an initial execution and to *force* subsequent executions to be deterministic with respect to the initial execution, using the recorded information. Debugging an erroneous program then amounts to record an erroneous execution and to apply cyclic debugging techniques during subsequent replayed executions. In order for this technique to be effective, the perturbation resulting from the recording operation ought to be kept sufficiently low so that errors appearing in unrecorded executions do not vanish in recorded ones and vice-versa. If this overhead is low enough, recording can be left active during each execution of a parallel program, so that an error occurring infrequently can be captured and subsequently reproduced. Systematic measurements of the overhead induced by tracing with the depicted mechanism should produce two informations. First, a measure of the mean perturbation observed for the selected algorithms. Second, the potential existence of pathological cases for which the recording mechanism would induce a severe perturbation. Expected results are a low overhead for all cases and no such pathological situations.

Estimating the overhead induced for a limited number of applications is not sufficient since it does not guarantee that any application will suffer the same overhead as the one observed for the few tests. The overhead assessment must be done for a large spectrum of applications covering enough cases to be representative of most possible situations. The main characteristics of the ATHAPASCAN applications are the general structure of their flow of control and the volume of exchanged data. Combining many different possibilities leads to a great number of applications to be studied. Rather than manually writing a specific

*This work was partially sponsored by the EU's Copernicus programme under contract number CIPA-C193-0251 and by the French Ministry of Research under the inter-PRC project Trace.

1066-6192/96 $5.00 © 1996 IEEE
Proceedings of PDP '96

application for each case, benefit can be taken from the existing *ANDES* tool allowing the generation of synthetic programs. Synthetic programs are commonly used for performance analysis [6]. Their advantage is to offer easy adaptability to emulate various application and system characteristics without requiring complete rewriting of benchmark applications.

After a presentation of the execution replay technique developed for the ATHAPASCAN programming model in section 2, the performance evaluation method is described in section 3. The experimentation protocol and the results follow in section 4. Further developments are sketched in the conclusion.

2 Execution replay mechanism

2.1 The Athapascan programming model

In ATHAPASCAN, the execution of parallel programs is performed by a set of identical *virtual processors* operating asynchronously [3]. Expression of parallelism is achieved by non-blocking remote procedure calls (requests), thereby hiding the underlying communication protocols under the parameters and results transmission mechanisms. Thus the ATHAPASCAN model is well suited for expressing control parallelism. Each virtual processor includes several *Entry Points*, which are the targets of remote procedure calls (see Figure 1). No other communications are available in ATHAPASCAN.

A remote procedure call results in the execution of a light-weight process (thread) within the virtual processor holding the target entry point. This thread may in turn create new threads by issuing remote procedure calls. Several light-weight processes execute concurrently within each virtual processor to hide the latency of communications in parallel systems. ATHAPASCAN remote procedure calls are issued with the *Spawn* primitive. The *WaitSpawn* primitive waits for the completion of remote procedure calls. A prototype of ATHAPASCAN was implemented as a set of operators used from a host language (currently C) using PVM [12] as communication library and several thread libraries [2]. A record-replay mechanism is included in this prototype [4].

2.2 Execution replay in Athapascan

The principle of the control driven replay is to record the order of accesses to shared resources. Classical implementations of Instant Replay record the order of accesses to shared variables [8] or system-level primitives for passing messages [9]. In the ATHAPASCAN model, shared resources are entry points, accessed by requests. Our record-replay mechanism exploits the properties of the computational model to record events at an intermediate level of abstraction where several system-level events can be abstracted in one, thereby reducing the number of records while being independent of the underlying communication system.

Each call to an entry point results in a typical sequence of such "abstract" events. Figure 1 represents a complete sequence of events generated by a call to an entry point, from the request emission (event **a**) to the result receipt (event **d**) passing through the request receipt (event **b**) and the result emission (event **c**). A replay can be driven by forcing the execution order of request receipts (event **b**). Since an entry point controls racing requests, it can be responsible for recording the order in which it serves incoming requests.

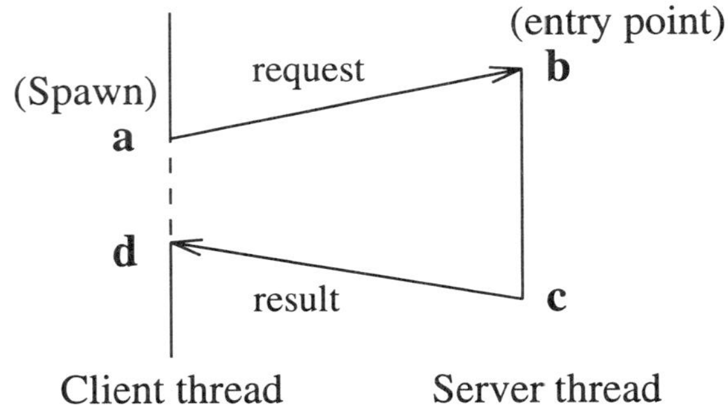

Figure 1: Sequence of events for a call to an entry point.

Each entry point is responsible for recording its request receipt history (event **b**). This history contains the order of request unique identifiers. A request identifier is constructed independently by the client thread emitting the request in a deterministic way: in particular, it is independent of the other threads sharing the same virtual processor. For the ATHAPASCAN model, it has the following form: ⟨VirtualProcessorID, EntryPointID, ThreadID, RequestID⟩.

The simplifications brought to the classical models result from the communication simplicity of the ATHAPASCAN model. Processes obey a Client-Server protocol which is a sub-class of the model of communicating processes. To each request corresponds a result and a result is emitted only after a request was received. The proposed techniques can be applied to Client-Server programming models. The ATHAPASCAN request and result transmissions can be implemented in several different ways without consequences on the design of the record-replay mechanism. This independence leads to a reduction of the number of trace-points for some implementations, up to a factor of six relative to the classical solution of implementing the record-replay at the system level. This reduction factor is obtained at low cost since no additional information is appended to messages.

3 Time-overhead measurement method

The evaluation of the overhead arising from the collection of traces, was done using the performance evaluation methodology and tools developed for the APACHE project [13]. The aim of this methodology is to be able to predict the performances of parallel algorithms executed on a class of distributed memory parallel machines. The measurement methodology includes several stages: quantitative modeling of parallel algorithms, generation of parallel synthetic programs from the models and performance measurements of the execution of synthetic programs on parallel computers (see figure 2). These three phases are detailed in the following.

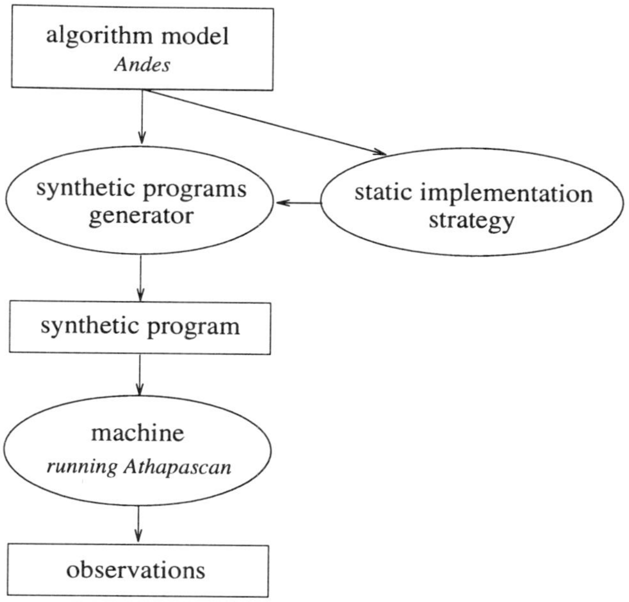

Figure 2: Evaluation chain.

3.1 Modeling parallel algorithms using *ANDES*

The *ANDES* (Algorithms aNd DEScription) modeling language of parallel algorithms [7] is targeted towards control parallelism and models basic control structures, precedence, computation costs, data dependency costs, global data movements, hierarchical model refinement and message passing.

In *ANDES*, a program is modeled as a directed graph (called *DG-ANDES*) whose vertices model *computation nodes* and arcs model the nodes *precedence order* (see figure 3). Each computation vertex is composed of three *logics* of different kinds: an *input* logic, a *computation* logic and an *output* logic. Input and output logics are used to describe the interdependency relations between computation nodes, mainly the interdependencies of tasks precedences and communications. The computation logic models part of the computation performed by the application.

Input and output logics can be of several types. The most common types are boolean logics and the logics associated to global operations. For example, if a computation node has an *OR* input logic, execution of the node computation logic will start as soon as the first input communication of the node will take place; on the contrary, computation of nodes having an *AND* input logic will only start after the execution of all input communications. A global operation logic can be used to model global communications such as diffusions. An output logic modeling a diffusion is equivalent to an *AND* output logic where the same data is associated to all the communications.

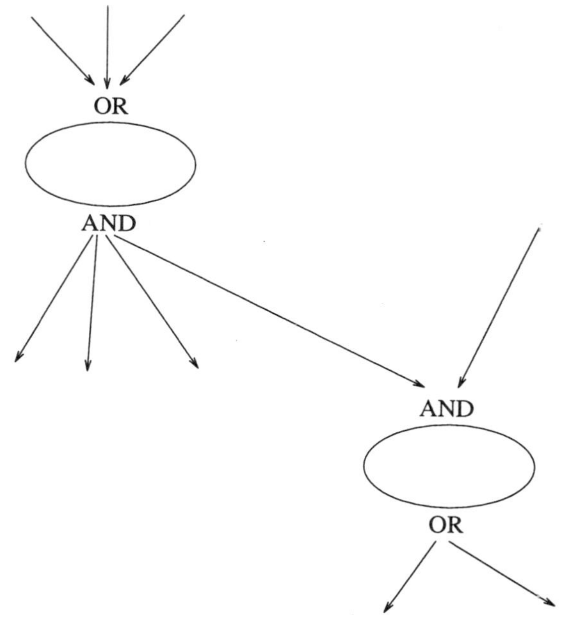

Figure 3: *ANDES* input and output logics

ANDES being used for quantitative performance evaluation, numerical functions can be associated with logics to model the resource needs of the machine. Communication costs are associated to input and output logics while computation costs are associated to computation logics. These costs can be constants or random functions or they can depend on other characteristics of the graph. Random functions are used to model costs that cannot be predicted. *Depending costs* are used to model computations such as those whose costs depend on the size of the input data. *ANDES* will also support the development of regular and hierarchical program models.

A computation logic can model sequential code or another parallel computation expressed by a *DG-ANDES*. Vertices can model another *DG-ANDES* therefore allowing hierarchical representations of programs: this feature can be useful when analyzing the computation granularity and its effect on performance. The more detailed is the *DG-ANDES*, the "finer grained" is the model. When a computation logic models sequential code, a cost is associated with this logic. This cost models the number of basic operations of the code, a basic operation being defined outside the model (a floating-point operation, an integer operation, etc.). Input/output logics represent the data interdependence among computation nodes as well as the precedence relations. Costs are also associated with input/output logics, representing data sizes.

It is possible to derive different instantiations of a parallel algorithm from a model of this algorithm in *ANDES* by changing the granularity of parallel activities (tasks) or the way work is split. An *ANDES* model of algorithm thus represents a complete set or class of algorithms.

3.2 Performance evaluation of *ANDES* models

Three different techniques can be considered to evaluate the performances of an *ANDES* model of a parallel algorithm: analytical modeling, simulation or performance measurements on an actual parallel computer. The first technique requires to solve mathematically a model and is potentially very complex. Realistic simulation of a parallel program is usually very slow. Performance measurements of parallel programs was therefore the technique retained to evaluate the performances of *ANDES* models of parallel algorithms, the programs produced from *ANDES* models being indeed *synthetic* parallel programs.

A synthetic parallel program is a real program whose resources consumption (processor, memory and communication) can be easily controlled. Synthetic programs can be generated automatically from descriptions written in the *ANDES* modeling language [7] of parallel algorithms. Synthetic programs emulate the behaviors described in the models. Synthetic programs are executed on a real multiprocessor in order to obtain execution performance measurements as close as possible from the results of the corresponding actual implementations of the algorithm. The *ANDES* synthetic program generator was first targeted at transputer-based Supernode multiprocessor and later adapted to IBM SP1.

From a model of algorithm written in *ANDES*, it is possible to generate a wide range of different synthetic programs with different structures and costs. For example for a *Divide and Parallelize* algorithm, it is possible to change the branching factor of the nodes or the depth of the tree. Once the structure of the control flow is fixed, it remains possible to vary the parameters influencing computation and communication costs. According to the model, parameters related to both structure and costs can be made interdependent, for example by making the branching factor dependent on the volume of received data.

3.3 Adapting *ANDES* to Athapascan

The definition of the input/output logics depends on the computational model for which synthetic programs are to be produced. Only deterministic programs were used for the evaluation of the trace recording overhead (see section 4.2). Therefore, only the *Spawn* and *WaitSpawn* operators were required to model deterministic ATHAPASCAN programs in *ANDES*. New input and output logics had to be defined to model ATHAPASCAN programs (see figure 4):

Input logics:

- **REQ:** a single input representing an ATHAPASCAN request.
- **WAIT:** one input indicating the continuation of the execution thread and one or several inputs representing the expected results from previous vertices.
- **COMP:** a single input representing the continuation of the execution thread.

Output logics:

- **RES:** a single output to represent the result.
- **SPAWN:** one output indicating the continuation of the execution thread and one or several outputs representing requests to be sent.
- **CONT:** a single output representing the continuation of the execution thread.

Some compositions of vertices and edges were not allowed since they have no semantics in the ATHAPASCAN programming model and could hinder the generation of correct synthetic programs.

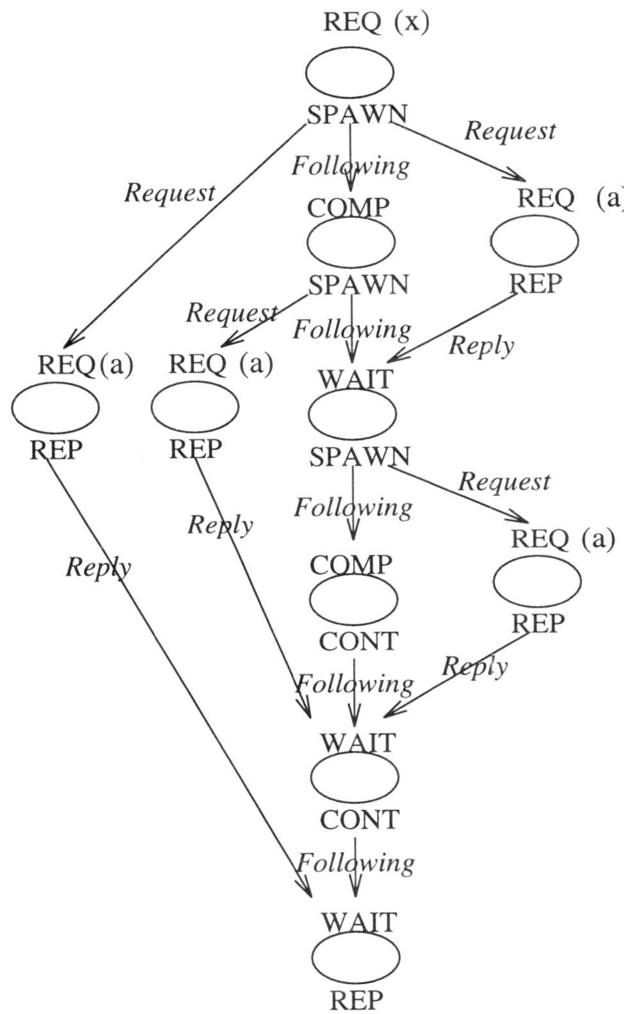

Figure 4: Graph of an Athapascan program representing all feasible connections.

4 Measurements of the trace recording overhead

The aim of the performance measurements was to evaluate systematically the intrusion of the recording of traces necessary for re-executing deterministically ATHAPASCAN programs. The expected result of these measurements was a confirmation of preliminary results indicating that the overhead of trace recording remained sufficiently low for trace recording to be considered as the normal ATHAPASCAN execution mode. Another potential result from these measurements was the identification of "pathological" programs if any.

4.1 Benchmark programs

The overhead of trace recording was evaluated by measuring the execution times of synthetic programs, generated from *ANDES* models of algorithms. Synthetic programs being "real" programs, they can be used as any "real benchmark" to measure the overhead of trace recording. The selected models include algorithm models extracted from "real benchmarks" or constructed from well known algorithms of the literature.

Paradoxically, we had to restrict ourselves to program models having a deterministic behavior. The behavior of a non-deterministic program can indeed be so different for each of its executions that comparisons become impossible. This was experienced with a process-farm implementation of the N-queens problem where some executions recording traces ran faster than un-monitored executions. For programs whose behavior is non-deterministic, it is not possible to apply a statistical measurement method, based on the hypothesis that observed executions have similar behaviors.

The set of selected algorithms is composed of the following structures of algorithms *Divide and Parallelize* (balanced tree), *Prolog-like Search Tree* (unbalanced tree), *Regular Iteration* (same number of forks in each step), *Master-Slaves* (variable number of forks in each step) and *Strassen's Matrix Product* [11] (recursive numerical algorithm). The choice of a combination of computation and communication costs in a model determines a specific algorithm.

Six computation/communication ratios were considered for each algorithm model. They range from very inefficient use of the system (10 times more communication time than computation time) to more favorable use (30 times more computation time than communication time). Intermediate values in the range were logarithmically spaced to obtain ratio values close to 0.1, 0.3, 1, 3, 10, 30. The computation/communication ratios of synthetic programs were adjusted by tuning the values of the costs parameters (computation and communication) of the models while the structural ones, such as branching factor for example, were left unchanged.

Experiments were performed by generating a synthetic program for each model of algorithm and each of the selected ratios. Execution threads defined in the models were mapped, on the virtual processors executing the synthetic programs, by one of the greedy algorithms of the mapping toolbox of the APACHE project [1]. From these mappings and the *ANDES* models of algorithms, synthetic ATHAPASCAN programs were generated.

4.2 Experimental method

To measure the time overhead of the recording, the execution times of synthetic programs were measured "with" and "without" the recording mode set. For each benchmark, enough measures were done to guarantee, with a probability greater or equal to 95%, that the real mean execution time be enclosed within an interval (confidence range), smaller than 3% of its value and centered around the estimated mean value. Each overhead ($\overline{over}$) was computed as the ratio of the difference of mean execution time "with" recording mode set ($\bar{t}_r$) and mean execution time "without" recording mode set ($\bar{t}_u$), divided by the mean execution time "without" recording mode set:

$$\overline{over} = \frac{\bar{t}_r - \bar{t}_u}{\bar{t}_u} = \frac{\bar{t}_r}{\bar{t}_u} - 1$$

If we assume the overhead to be low, which was confirmed by the experimental results (see figure 5), the confidence range can be approximated to a fixed value of 6% (see appendix section A). Because of the ratio between two results known with a certitude of 95% each, the certitude over the precision of the overheads is limited to 90%.

Synthetic programs were executed by a prototype of the ATHAPASCAN kernel running on a 32 nodes IBM SP1 operated by the AIX Unix operating system. To limit the perturbations arising from the execution of Unix processes not involved in the experiments, the system was reserved for the measures, with no other user allowed to run another application simultaneously. Results obtained when these experimental conditions were not guaranteed, by simultaneous execution of another parallel program on the SP1 for example, could not be used because of their unstable behaviors. However, it proved difficult to eliminate all perturbations, some arising for example from the simultaneous execution of system processes or from the computation of unwanted PVM processes, "left" on the computer by previous users. Therefore, some measures collected with a "moderately" perturbated computing environment were kept, when the statistical instability remained sufficiently low to reach the desired precision.

The number of measures n necessary to obtain a given precision (3%) with a probability greater or equal to 95% is given by the formula

$$\frac{\sigma \times 1.96}{\sqrt{n}} \leq 0.03$$

where σ is the standard deviation of the measures [6]. To obtain the desired precision, we observed that 40 different measures were sufficient for any program instance and for most experimental conditions, both with and without the recording mode set. To ease the experiments, the same number of measures were done for all benchmarks, even when the desired precision could have been reached with a lower number of measures. Therefore, the confidence range of the mean execution time of most benchmarks was better than 3% and thus the confidence range of the overhead

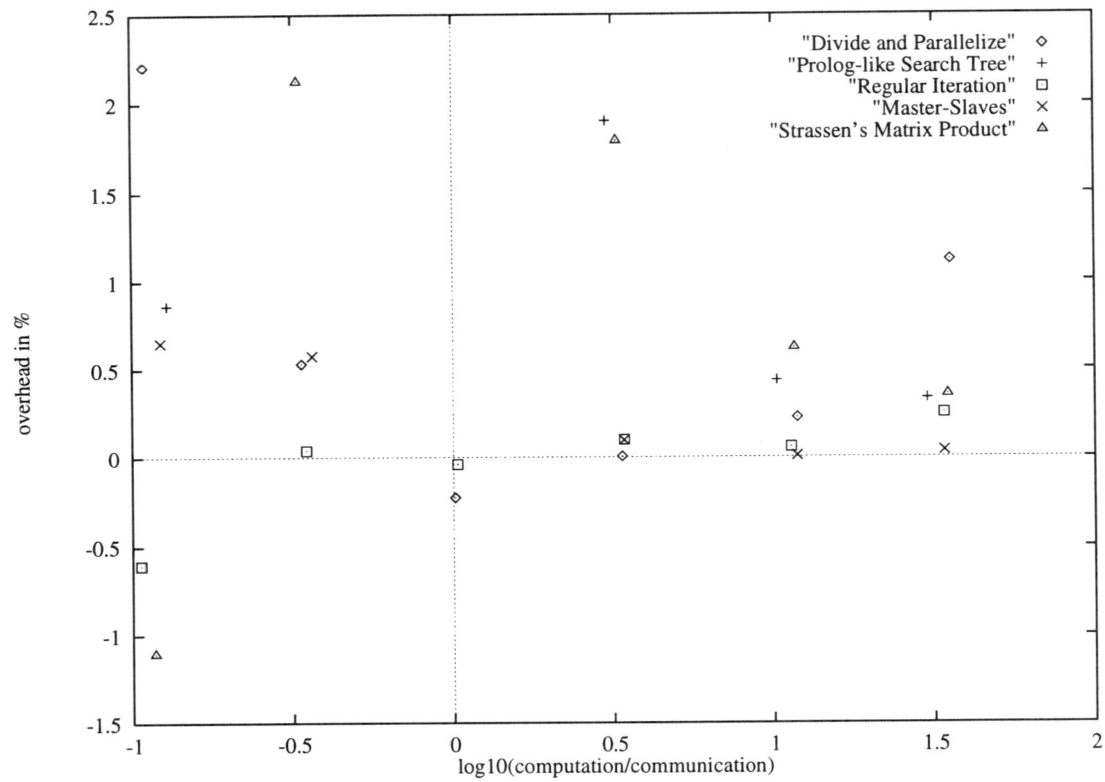

Figure 5: Percentage of tracing time overhead.

For each of the selected models, the mean measured percentage of time overhead is given.

lower than 6%. This explains the differences between the precisions of the results given in figure 6. The whole experiment represented over 2400 different executions of ATHAPASCAN programs, performed mostly overnight!

4.3 Time overhead measurement results

Measurement results are summarized on figures 5 and 6 which display the measured recording overheads with their confidence ranges. The main outcome from these measures is that recording overheads are lower than 5%, even for the improbable cases where communication costs represent 10 times computation costs. No algorithm seems pathological with respect to the time overhead of recording. There seems to be no simple rule relating the distribution of time overhead induced by the tracing mechanism. The less disturbed model is the *Regular Iteration* but this cannot be generalized to other regular schemes.

5 Conclusion

A record-replay mechanism was included in an ATHAPASCAN prototype implementation. The overhead due to tracing was systematically measured by using synthetic programs. The methodology is based on the ALPES methodology, using the *ANDES* tool developed in the APACHE project. This tool allows a rapid construction of a great number of applications with desired characteristics. The use of a synthetic program generator avoids the necessity of manually writing the whole set of applications being used as benchmarks. The obtained results confirm experimentally the low intrusiveness of the recording mechanism, with a time overhead of less than 5% of the total execution time in the worst case.

Based on these indications, we have sufficient confidence to set the "record" mode as the default execution mode of ATHAPASCAN. The record-replay mechanism will serve as a basis for the development of the debugging tool which is currently being designed. Thus it will be possible to correct even the most transient errors, by capturing them as soon as they occur and debugging them using a cyclic method.

ANDES algorithm models developed for these measures are currently being used for a systematic comparison of static mapping versus dynamic scheduling. For these experiments, the same algorithm is used for the generation of statically mapped synthetic programs (as it was done for the above described measures) and dynamically mappable synthetic programs [5]. The expected result is a relation between the characteristics of the tested applications and their behavior under the different mapping strategies.

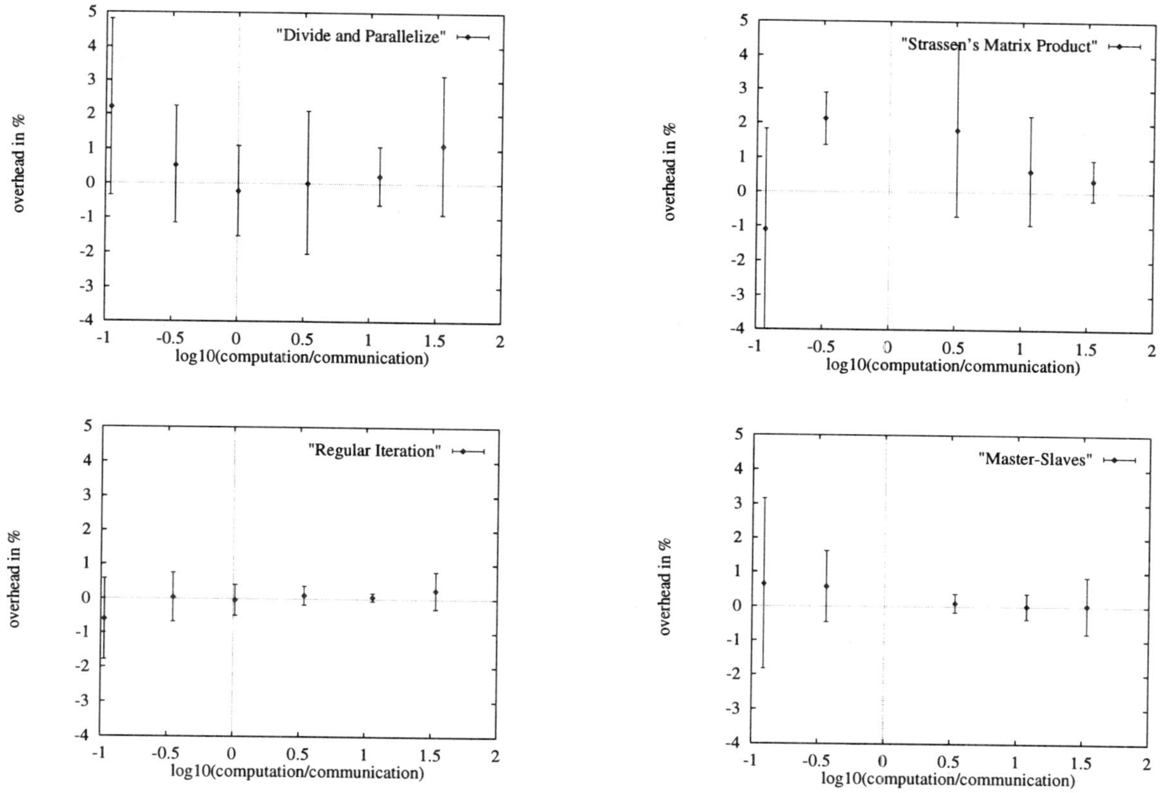

Figure 6: Percentage of tracing time overhead.

Most of the mean execution times were computed with a confidence range lower than 3%, leading to smaller overhead confidence range.

Acknowledgements

João Paulo Kitajima designed and implemented the *ANDES* tool and adapted the models of algorithms used for these measures. Jean-Marc Vincent taught us the basics of statistics necessary for this work.

References

[1] P. Bouvry, J. Chassin de Kergommeaux, and D. Trystram. Efficient solutions for mapping parallel programs. In S. Haridi, K. Ali, and P. Magnusson, editors, *EuroPar'95 Parallel Processing*, volume 966 of *LNCS*, pages 379–390. Springer-Verlag, August 1995.

[2] M. Christaller. Athapascan-0a sur PVM3 : définition et mode d'emploi. Rapport APACHE 11, IMAG, Grenoble, February 1994. In French. At `ftp.imag.fr:imag/APACHE/RAPPORTS`.

[3] M. Christaller. ATHAPASCAN-0A control parallelism approach on top of PVM. In *Proc PVM User's group meeting*. University of Tennessee, Oak Ridge, 1994.

[4] A. Fagot and J. Chassin de Kergommeaux. Formal and experimental validation of a low-overhead execution replay mechanism. In S. Haridi, K. Ali, and P. Magnusson, editors, *Euro-Par'95 Parallel Processing*, volume 966 of *LNCS*, pages 167–178. Springer-Verlag, August 1995.

[5] A. Fagot, J.P. Kitajima, and A. Vermeerbergen. Systematic Comparison of the Performance of Static Mapping and Dynamic Scheduling. In *ParCo'95*, Gent, Belgium, 1995.

[6] Raj Jain. *The art of computer systems performance analysis: techniques for experimental design, measurement, simulation, and modeling.* Wiley Professional Computing. John Wiley and Sons, New York, 1991.

[7] J. P. Kitajima and B. Plateau. Modelling parallel program behaviour in *ALPES*. *Information and Software Technology*, 36(7):457–464, July 1994.

[8] T.J. LeBlanc and J.M. Mellor-Crummey. Debugging Parallel Programs with Instant Replay. *IEEE Transactions on Computers*, C-36(4):471–481, April 1987.

[9] E. Leu and A. Schiper. Execution replay: a mechanism for integrating a visualization tool with a symbolic debugger. In Y. Robert, L. Bougé, M. Cosnard, and D. Trystram, editors, *CONPAR 92 - VAPP V*, volume 634 of *LNCS*. Springer-Verlag, September 1992.

[10] B. Plateau. Présentation d'APACHE. Rapport APACHE 1, IMAG, Grenoble, December 1994. In French. Available at `ftp.imag.fr:imag/APACHE/RAPPORTS`.

[11] V. Strassen. Gaussian Elimination is not Optimal. *Numerische Mathematik*, Band 13(Heft 4):354–356, 1969.

[12] V.S. Sunderam. PVM: A Framework for Parallel Distributed Computing. *Concurrency: Practice and Experience*, 2(4):315–339, December 1990.

[13] C. Tron, Y. Arrouye, J. Chassin de Kergommeaux, J.P. Kitajima, E. Maillet, B. Plateau, and J.-M. Vincent. Performance Evaluation of Parallel Systems: the ALPES environment. In *Proceedings of ParCo93*. Elsevier Science Publishers, 1993.

A Confidence range and certitude over the time overhead

Let t_r be the mean execution time "with" recording mode set, t_u the mean execution time "without" recording mode and *over* the percentage of time overhead caused by the recording.

The measures of average execution times $\bar{t}_r$ and $\bar{t}_u$ are done with a 3% precision, that is:

$$t_r \in [\bar{t}_r - c \times \bar{t}_r \ , \ \bar{t}_r + c \times \bar{t}_r]$$

and

$$t_u \in [\bar{t}_u - c \times \bar{t}_u \ , \ \bar{t}_u + c \times \bar{t}_u]$$

with $c = 0.015$.

Therefore:

$$over \in \left[\frac{\bar{t}_r - c \times \bar{t}_r - (\bar{t}_u + c \times \bar{t}_u)}{\bar{t}_u + c \times \bar{t}_u} \ , \ \frac{\bar{t}_r + c \times \bar{t}_r - (\bar{t}_u - c \times \bar{t}_u)}{\bar{t}_u - c \times \bar{t}_u}\right]$$

The lower bound of the interval can be written:

$$\frac{\bar{t}_r}{\bar{t}_u} \times \frac{1-c}{1+c} - 1$$

c being small, $\frac{1-c}{1+c}$ can be approximated by:

$$(1-c) \times (1-c)$$

that is $1 - 2c$ if we neglect the c^2 term.

Therefore the lower bound can be approximated by:

$$\frac{\bar{t}_r}{\bar{t}_u} - 1 - 2c \times \frac{\bar{t}_r}{\bar{t}_u}$$

If the overhead is low, $\frac{\bar{t}_r}{\bar{t}_u}$ is close to 1, and the lower bound of the interval can be minored with its approximate value:

$$\frac{\bar{t}_r}{\bar{t}_u} - 1 - 2c$$

Similarly we can approximate the upper bound of the interval. It comes:

$$over \in \left[\frac{\bar{t}_r}{\bar{t}_u} - 1 - 2c \ , \ \frac{\bar{t}_r}{\bar{t}_u} - 1 + 2c\right]$$

The confidence range can therefore be approximated by 4c which is 0.06, that is a fixed value of 6%, independent of the measured overhead value. Of course, the above is an upper bound and is a good approximation only if the measured overhead remains low, which is verified by the measures.

We can also compute the probability for the measured overhead $\overline{over}$ to belong to the confidence range. Starting from:

$$\overline{over} = \frac{\bar{t}_r}{\bar{t}_u} - 1$$

we know that for the measured overhead to fall *outside* the confidence range, it is necessary that one of the measured averages $\bar{t}_r$ or $\bar{t}_u$ does not belong to its confidence range (3%). These two measurements being independent, the probability for the measured overhead to fall *outside* the confidence range is the sum of the probabilities for the two measured values to fall outside their confidence range. Since enough measures were done to obtain a certitude of 95% for the measured execution times of $\bar{t}_r$ and $\bar{t}_u$, each of these probabilities is 5% and their sum is 10%. And thus $\overline{over}$ belongs to the confidence range with a probability of 90%.

Visualisation of Reduced Abstracted Behaviour as a Design Tool

Antti Valmari, Konsta Karsisto & Manu Setälä

Tampere University of Technology, Software Systems Laboratory
PO Box 553, FIN-33101 Tampere, FINLAND

Abstract

This article presents a user-friendly formal method for obtaining comprehensive feedback from the behaviour of a design of a distributed system. The method consists of abstracting and reducing the behaviour and showing the result in a graphical form on a computer screen. Deadlocks, livelocks, incorrect actions and many other kinds of design errors can often be easily discovered from the graphical representation. The method differs from animation, simulation and testing in that it analyses ***all*** *possible behaviours simultaneously. For instance, if the graphical representation does not contain a deadlock, then the system is* ***guaranteed*** *to be free from deadlocks. The method is illustrated by using it in the development of a well-known communication protocol. This article concentrates on the use of the method; the underlying theory and computer tools have been discussed elsewhere.*

1 Introduction

Correctly behaving distributed software is notoriously difficult to design. A typical distributed system has to be able to process input arriving at almost any time and perhaps simultaneously from many sources. The relative execution speeds of the different units (often called *processes*) of the system are usually impossible to predict accurately, and they may vary because of changes in workload. Messages sent by a process to another may get lost. As a consequence, the execution of a typical distributed system may proceed in numerous different ways, and the total behaviour consisting of all possible executions is very complicated.

A human being can seldom properly comprehend the total behaviour of a distributed system. A designer typically analyses the executions where everything goes as expected, and after that investigates a small number of error situations, such as loss of a message or a premature input. But even if he tries to be careful, he can cover only a small proportion of all possible executions, because there are so many of them. The same holds for testing. Consequently, many executions remain unchecked, and the system may behave incorrectly.

The above-mentioned problems have caused several researchers to believe that trustworthy distributed systems cannot be designed without formal correctness proofs or formal correctness-preserving development techniques. Indeed, many formal approaches to distributed system design have been developed. Unfortunately, most of them require significant mathematical background and skills from their users, perhaps more than can be expected from an average system designer. Furthermore, formal methods can seldom be used for fast checking of design ideas, because theorem proving and correctness-preserving design steps tend to require lots of time and effort.

The purpose of this article is to demonstrate that formal methods need not be unfriendly. We will show that *abstraction*, *reduction* and *visualisation* of behaviour can be used as a fast and easy way of getting extensive feedback of design ideas. We will illustrate our approach by showing a step-by-step development of a nontrivial distributed system, namely an advanced version of the well-known alternating bit communication protocol [1]. We develop first the original version of the protocol where there is no upper limit to the number of retransmissions. Although this version is very well-known, many interesting observations will be made from its design process. Then we add a retransmission counter to the protocol and find out that the protocol does not work correctly after error situations. Finally we add a recovery mechanism and obtain a correct protocol.

Our abstraction, reduction and visualisation approach is based on *process algebraic* theories such as CSP [4]. In them, the notion of "abstraction" is formalised by defining a suitable *semantic model* or *equivalence*. We use *Chaos-Free Failures Divergences Equivalence* [12, 13]. It is related to the standard equivalence in CSP, but is not exactly the same. We use our own equivalence because, as is explained in [8, 11], better known equivalencies either throw some essential information away, or are not suitable for visualisation (yield too big pictures). Our reduction

1066-6192/96 $5.00 © 1996 IEEE
Proceedings of PDP '96

algorithm resembles those suggested for CSP-style equivalencies (e.g. [3]), and is described in [12]. The computer tool we used in our case study is called *ARA* or *Advanced Reachability Analysis* [6, 9]. It accepts system descriptions written in a variant of the formal specification language Lotos [2]. Lotos has been standardised by ISO [5]. Overall introductions of the use of CFFD-equivalence and ARA in validation and verification were given in [7, 10].

Lack of space prevents us from describing CFFD-equivalence or other theoretical background of our approach in any detail in this article. This is not a major problem, though, because one of our present goals is to demonstrate that abstraction, reduction and visualisation can be used without knowing the theory — at least to some extent. Of course, one should not attempt to make far-reaching conclusions from reduced abstracted behaviour before studying the theory. Therefore, the approach presented in this article should not be considered as a verification method, but only as a method of getting comprehensive, but not decisive feedback. The use of abstraction, reduction and visualisation as a verification method has been discussed in [11].

2 First version: processes, LTSs and global behaviour

The goal in our case study is to develop a communication protocol with the architecture shown in Figure 1. The purpose of the protocol is to implement reliable transmission of data using unreliable channels. The customer at the sending site requests the protocol to transmit the message *msg* to the other customer by executing the action *send⟨msg⟩*. After successful transmission, the protocol should deliver the message to the receiving customer with the action *rec⟨msg⟩*. At this stage, we do not yet know what actions concerning the channels are needed, so we have shown them as question marks "??" in Figure 1.

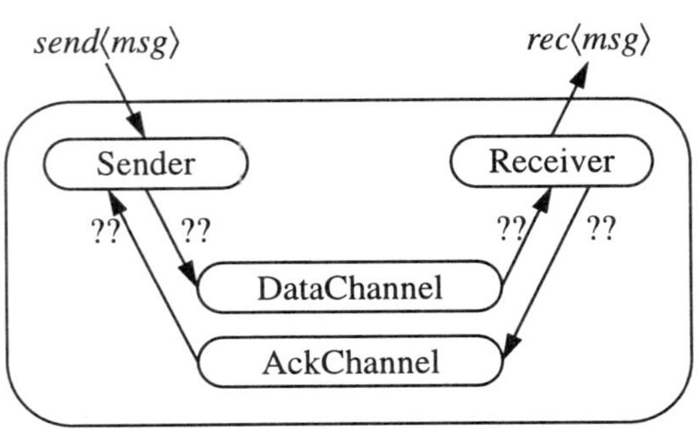

Fig. 1 The architecture of the example protocol

The experience we have had with visualisation of behaviour and ARA shows that one should not attempt to design a system in full before starting to use the tool. Otherwise, the design will usually be so badly wrong and its behaviour will be so complicated that ARA cannot handle it, and even if it could, the user could not understand the visualised behaviour. It is much better to start with something very simple, proceed in small steps, and check every step with the tool before continuing. We formulate this observation as our first two guidelines.

> **Guideline 1: Start with a very simple system.**
>
> Start with a system which is so small and simple that you are sure that it behaves correctly. Check its behaviour with the tool. If necessary, make the system even simpler, until you get the behaviour you expect.

> **Guideline 2: Proceed in small steps.**
>
> Add more features to the system one by one. Check the result of each modification immediately with the tool before adding more functionality.

```
$sort data_type is (m1, m2)
process Version1[ send, rec, sdata, rdata,
                          sack, rack, losedata, loseack ] :=
    Sender[ send, sdata, rack ]
        |[ sdata, rack ]|
    ( DataChannel[ sdata, rdata, losedata ] |||
    AckChannel[ sack, rack, loseack ] )
        |[ rdata, sack ]|
    Receiver[ rec, rdata, sack ]
where
    process Sender[ send, sdata, rack ] :=
        send ? msg : data_type; sdata ! msg; rack;
        Sender[ send, sdata, rack ]
    endproc
    process Receiver[ rec, rdata, sack ] :=
        rdata ? msg : data_type; rec ! msg; sack;
        Receiver[ rec, rdata, sack ]
    endproc
    process DataChannel[ sdata, rdata, losedata ] :=
        sdata ? msg : data_type; (
            rdata ! msg; DataChannel[ sdata, rdata, losedata ]
                []
            losedata; DataChannel[ sdata, rdata, losedata ]
        )
    endproc
    process AckChannel[ sack, rack, loseack ] :=
        sack; (
            rack; AckChannel[ sack, rack, loseack ]
                []
            loseack; AckChannel[ sack, rack, loseack ]
        )
    endproc
endproc
```

Fig. 2 First version of the protocol in ARA Lotos

In accordance to Guideline 1, our first version of the protocol does not have retransmissions or sequence numbers. In it Sender accepts a sending request from the local customer via action *send*, sends the message through DataChannel by executing action *sdata*, waits for and receives an acknowledgement from Receiver (*rack*), and starts again from the beginning. The message may have two different values: m_1 and m_2. Receiver delivers an arriving message (*rdata*) to the customer (*rec*), and sends an acknowledgement (*sack*). The channels receive a message for transmission (*sdata* and *sack*) and then either deliver it (*rdata* and *rack*) or lose it (*losedata* and *loseack*). Sender, Receiver and DataChannel store the message in their local variables *msg*. The protocol is shown in the ARA tool variant of Lotos in Figure 2.

Because our approach is not Lotos-dependent (although our current tools are), in Figure 3 we have shown the behaviours of the component processes of the protocol also in another form, namely as *labelled transition systems* (*LTS*). LTSs are essentially finite-state automata without acceptance states, so Figure 3 should be easily understandable. Figure 3 was obtained from the specification in Figure 2 almost automatically with ARA (the graphical representation has been stylized manually).

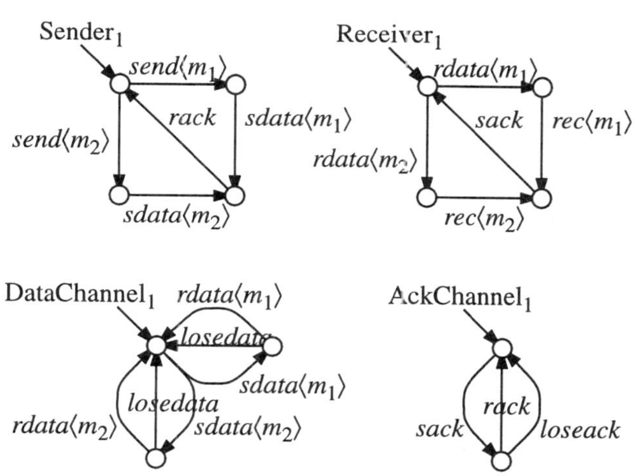

Fig. 3 Processes of the first protocol version in LTS form

The behaviour of the protocol as a whole is determined by the behaviours of the component processes and the semantics of inter-process communication. Like in process algebras and Lotos, in our approach processes communicate synchronously. For instance, transmission of message m_1 from Sender to DataChannel is represented by simultaneous execution of the action *sdata*$\langle m_1 \rangle$ by Sender and DataChannel. The global behaviour of the protocol is shown in Figure 4 in LTS form. Figure 4 shows a *send-sdata-rdata-rec-sack-rack*-cycle for both possible values of messages, and a deadlock which is reached after loss of message or acknowledgement.

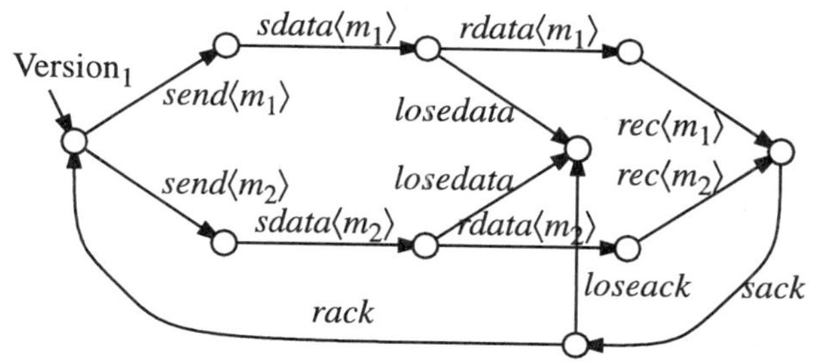

Fig. 4 Global behaviour of first protocol version

Figure 4 is reasonably readable, but only because the system whose behaviour it shows is exceptionally simple.

3 Second version: abstraction and reduction of behaviour

To get rid of the deadlock in Figure 4 we add retransmission to the protocol. For simplicity, we start with unlimited retransmission. The corresponding version of Sender is shown in Figure 5.

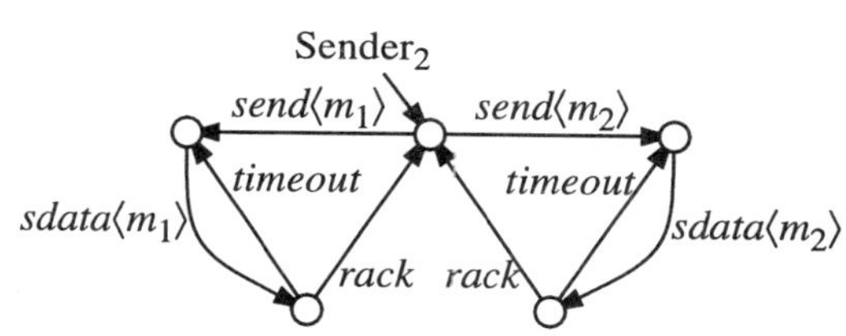

Fig. 5 Sender with unlimited retransmission

This relatively simple modification makes the global behaviour of the protocol much more complicated. The LTS showing the global behaviour has now 92 states and 265 transitions. It is too big for inspection.

Apparently lot of the complexity of the current version is caused by different combinations of the two messages m_1 and m_2 stored in Sender, Receiver and DataChannel. Since the logic of the protocol is — or at least should be — independent of the content of the message, and we have not yet got the logic to work correctly, we may try to reduce the complexity by dropping the other message type. We can put it back later when the protocol has started to work well with one message type. This modification reduces the global LTS significantly: to 34 states and 89 transitions.

> **Guideline 3: Remove details which are not essential for the current problem.**
>
> You can put them back later when everything else works.

The global behaviour is now small enough for ARA visualiser tool to show it on a computer screen. However, the resulting picture is far from readable. Therefore, we start to use the two other main tools of our approach: abstraction and reduction.

> **Guideline 4: Restrict your view to a small set of interesting actions.**
>
> Choose a small set of interesting actions, and abstract and reduce according to it. If necessary, reduce the set further. Again, you can put the removed actions back, when you have got the behaviour correct with respect to the smaller set.

It is natural to investigate a communication protocol from the point of view of its clients. Considering our example protocol and Guideline 4, this implies that we should choose the set {*send*, *rec*} as the set of interesting actions. So we abstract the other actions away by converting them *invisible*, that is, by *hiding* them. At the Lotos level this is achieved by adding the following line after the third line of the Lotos text in Figure 2:

hide *sdata*, *rdata*, *sack*, *rack*, *losedata*, *loseack*, *timeout* **in**

(Furthermore, the names of the hidden actions may be removed from the process definition gate list at lines 2 and 3, but this is not necessary.) It is customary to denote invisible actions by the special symbol "τ" in LTSs.

Abstraction alone does not modify the size of an LTS. It only replaces "τ" for the names of some transitions. However, an abstracted LTS can usually be reduced significantly. ARA contains a tool which takes an LTS as input, and produces another, typically much smaller LTS, which is equivalent to the input LTS as far as an external observer can see. That is, the reduced LTS preserves all possible orderings in which visible actions may be executed, and it preserves also some deadlock and livelock information, but it does not preserve invisible actions any more than absolutely necessary for presenting deadlocks and livelocks. The reduced LTS corresponding to our current version of the protocol is shown in Figure 6.

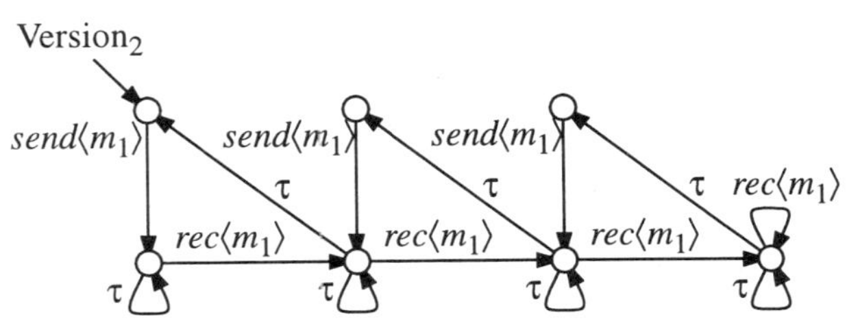

Fig. 6 Reduced LTS of protocol with unbounded retransmission and one message type

Figure 6 is fairly readable. From it we can see that the protocol does not work correctly: the first *send*$\langle m_1\rangle$ may be followed by more than one *rec*$\langle m_1\rangle$, implying that the protocol can deliver the same message more than once. Actually, it can deliver it an infinite number of times! This is, of course, due to unlimited retransmission and absence of sequence numbers. But our point here was not to show how protocols should be built. Our point was to show that behavioural errors — such as duplication of messages — may be easily spotted from LTSs showing reduced abstracted behaviour.

Certain aspects of Figure 6 may need some explanation. The τ-loops adjacent to some of the states in Figure 6 denote infinite invisible activity, or livelock. They are caused by endless repetition of retransmissions and loss of data or acknowledgements. The τ-transitions leading from the states in the lower row to the states in the upper row may seem unnecessary, as they do not affect the orderings in which visible actions may be performed. Their purpose is to show that the protocol may avoid or exit the τ-loop and thus commit itself to execute *send*$\langle m_1\rangle$. This happens when an acknowledgement reaches Sender. Although it is not apparent in this example, commitment information is necessary for reasoning about deadlocks when a system is used as a component of a bigger system.

It may seem peculiar that Figure 6 contains three copies of the same structure and then a *rec*-loop. The reason for the repeating structure is that after many enough retransmissions, the system may be able to execute three but no more than three *send*-actions in a row without an intervening *rec*-action. This, in turn, derives ultimately from the structures of Sender and Receiver and the ability of Ack-Channel of storing at most one acknowledgement. But we need not bother ourselves now with this kind of details. We have already seen that this version of the protocol duplicates messages, so it is not correct anyway.

4 Adding sequence numbers

Duplication of messages in the previous version of the protocol is caused by the fact that Receiver cannot distinguish an original data message from its retransmissions. Therefore, if the acknowledgement is lost or delayed, Sender may send the same message twice (actually, any number of times), and both copies may reach Receiver and be delivered to the customer. To prevent this from happening, we attach sequence numbers to messages. The alternating bit protocol has sequence numbers in both data messages and acknowledgements [1], but, just to see what will happen, we try first with sequence numbers only in the data messages. The resulting reduced behaviour is shown in Figure 7. We can see that the first transmission (i.e. *send*-*rec*-sequence) proceeds correctly. However, after it the protocol may execute any number of *send*-actions without *rec*-actions, that is, it may lose an arbitrary number of messages.

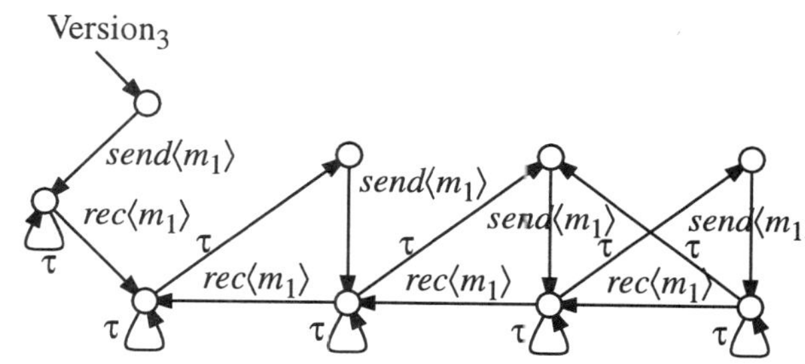

Fig. 7 Reduced behaviour when only data messages have sequence numbers

Figure 8 shows Sender and Receiver after adding sequence numbers to both data messages and acknowledgements. The resulting reduced global behaviour is shown in Figure 9 (a). Figure 9 (a) is remarkably simple. It shows that the protocol cannot lose or duplicate messages, but it may livelock.

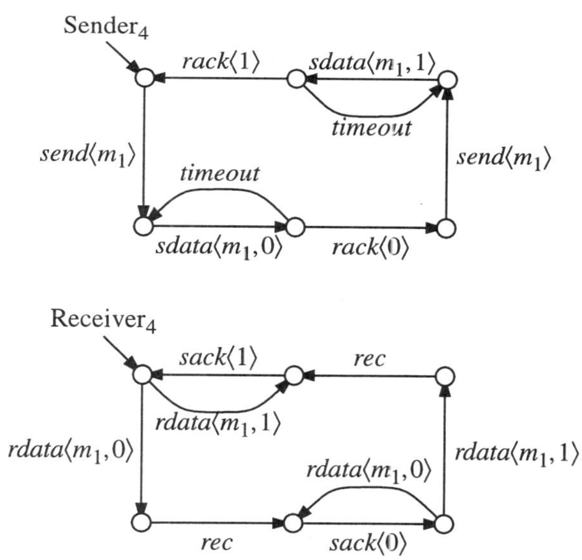

Fig. 8 Sender and Receiver with sequence numbers in both directions

We can now fulfil our earlier promise of adding more message types later. Figure 9 (b) shows the reduced global behaviour with three message types.

Now that we have a satisfactorily working protocol, it can be used as a component of a bigger system. Actually, the theory underlying our approach guarantees that it does not matter whether we use the original protocol or its

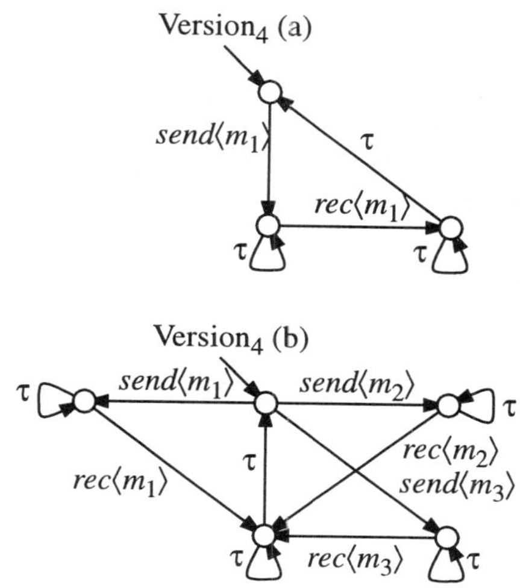

Fig. 9 Reduced behaviour of alternating bit protocol with (a) 1 (b) 3 different messages

reduced behaviour when investigating the bigger system. This justifies our last guideline.

Guideline 5: Develop and check big systems hierarchically.

First develop and check its subsystems. When checking the whole system, you may replace the subsystems by their reduced LTSs (this often dramatically speeds up computer runs).

5 Adding upper bound to retransmissions

The protocol we have developed so far is essentially the alternating bit protocol from [1]. It works well except that it may livelock before or after any *rec*-action. In particular, the protocol is guaranteed to livelock if either of the two channels it relies on is totally broken.

In order to demonstrate the usefulness of reduction and visualisation with more complicated systems, we develop the protocol further. We try to prevent livelocks by modifying Sender so that it makes at most a fixed finite number of transmission attempts for each sending request. If timeout occurs after the last transmission attempt, Sender gives up and indicates failure by executing an *err*-action.

Figure 10 shows the reduced global behaviour of this version of the protocol. The lower part of Figure 10 contains a nice *send*-*rec*-τ-cycle, which obviously corresponds to successful operation of the protocol. This cycle may be exited by executing an invisible action before or after the *rec*-action. If the cycle is exited, an error indication *err* is given, as is appropriate. We see that the message may be lost altogether, in which case the protocol returns to its initial state soon after giving the error indication. This is what we would expect. It is also possible that the message is delivered to the destination (*rec*), but an error indication is given either before or after the delivery. This kind of behaviour results if the message gets through the channel, but acknowledgements are lost or delayed, so that Sender is not informed about success before it declares failure. Since we cannot guarantee that acknowledgements do not get lost, we have to accept this outcome.

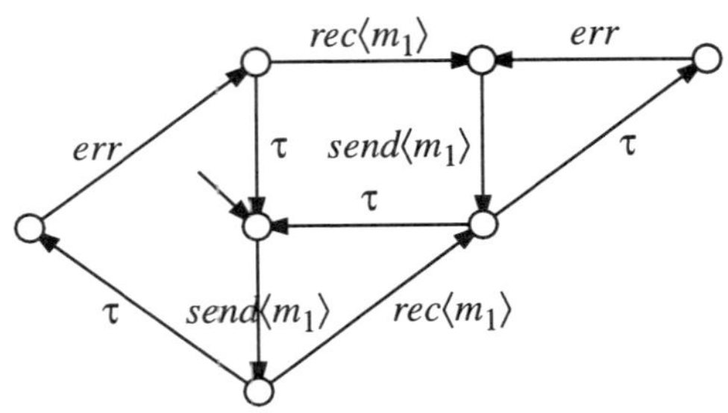

Fig. 10 Protocol with bounded number of retransmissions

However, the behaviour of the protocol after a *send*-τ-*err*-*rec*- or *send*-*rec*-τ-*err*-sequence is not acceptable. The protocol is then in the middle state in the top row of Figure 10, and is ready to accept a new sending request. This request (*send*) will cause it to execute either an invisible action leading to the initial state, or an invisible action and error indication taking it back to where it was. In neither case the message is delivered. In other words, if an error indication was given for the previous message but the message was actually delivered, then the next message is guaranteed to get lost! Furthermore, although the message is lost, error indication is not necessarily given (the *send*-τ-path to initial state), which is unforgivable. Apparently something is wrong in the current version of the protocol.

The problem with the protocol is that if a message reaches Receiver but its acknowledgement is lost, then Receiver changes its sequence number, but Sender does not. Therefore, Receiver will interpret the next message as a retransmission of the previous message, and will thus acknowledge it without delivering it. To prevent this from happening we add a new message type *sync* to the system. *Sync* is used only for synchronising the sequence numbers. Receiver will acknowledge it in the ordinary way, but will not deliver it to the customer. Whenever Sender is not sure of synchronisation, it sends *sync* and waits for its acknowledgement before sending the actual message. To increase reliability, we assume that Sender cannot initially rely on synchronisation. The modified Sender and Receiver are shown in Figure 11. For simplicity, Sender tries transmission only once in the figure.

The reduced joint behaviour of the sender and receiver

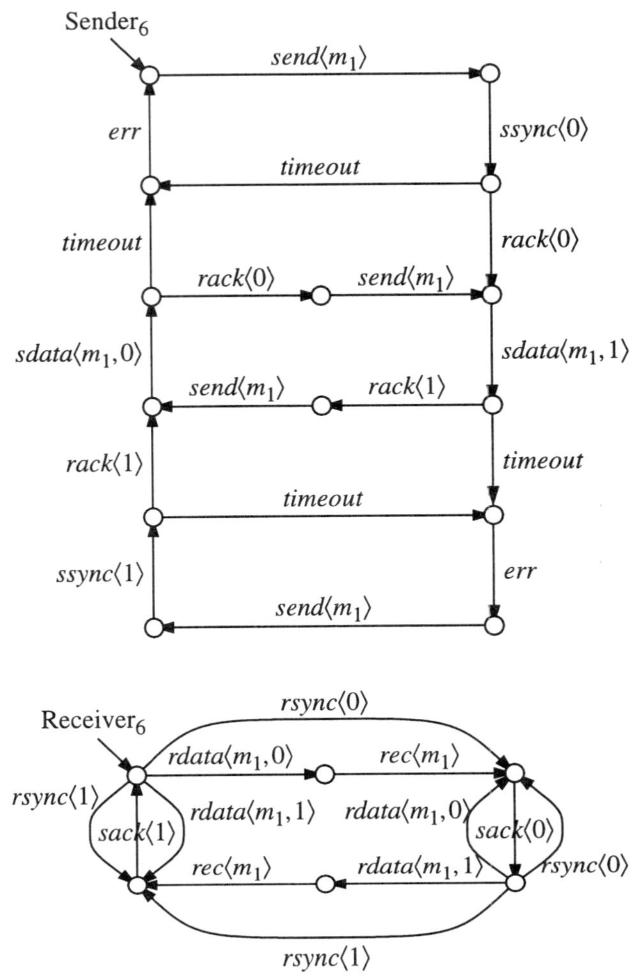

Fig. 11 Final Sender and Receiver

in Figure 11 with appropriate data and acknowledgement channels is shown in Figure 12. It contains two *send*-transitions. Both of them are followed by either *rec* or *err*, so the protocol cannot any more lose messages without notice, and is never in a state where failure is predetermined. In fact, most of the behaviour shown in Figure 12 is acceptable. The only worrying sequence is *send*-τ-*err*-τ-*send*-*rec*-*rec*; it looks like a message may be duplicated. On the other hand, the same sequence results if the message sent first is not lost, but delayed so much that it is delivered only after the next sending request. So it is impossible to say on the basis of Figure 12 whether the protocol is now correct.

To get final confirmation, we construct a reduced abstracted behaviour for the protocol with two message types and, adhering to Guideline 4, we leave visible only the actions *send*⟨m_2⟩ and *rec*⟨m_2⟩. The result is shown in

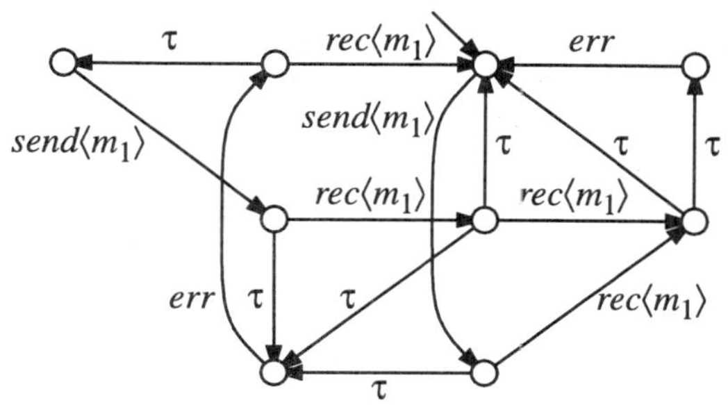

Fig. 12 Reduced behaviour of final protocol

Figure 13. From it we see that at any instant of time, the number of delivered m_2-messages is at most the number of m_2-messages that have been given to the protocol. A similar picture is obtained if only m_1-messages are left visible. Thus the final protocol does not duplicate messages, and is correct.

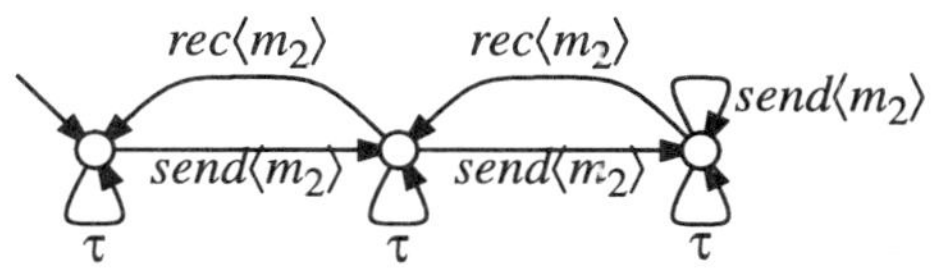

Fig. 13 Checking message duplications

6 Discussion

The goal of this article was to show how abstraction, reduction and visualisation can be used to obtain comprehensive feedback from the global behaviour of a design. We demonstrated that design errors (such as loss or duplication of messages) can be easily spotted from LTSs representing reduced behaviour. We also gave some guidelines for the design process using our approach.

Sometimes LTS pictures give new insight to the behaviour of a system. For instance, Figure 10 reveals that the version of the protocol with bounded retransmission may lose a message *after* giving an error indication. This observation enabled us to develop a simple error recovery scheme guaranteeing that the protocol is not confused by losses of messages. In this way LTS figures give the designer valuable feedback which may be extremely difficult to obtain with other means.

Our approach, as it was presented in this article, should be considered as an intermediate form between testing and verification. In principle, the information shown in an LTS picture is comprehensive. If the picture does not contain any deadlocks, then the system cannot deadlock. In this sense our approach is a verification approach.

On the other hand, the user of our approach can get misled in at least three different ways. Firstly, he may misread LTS pictures. In particular, the *absence* of some action may easily go unnoticed. Secondly, because synchronous communication does not specify whether an action is executed by a system or its environment, one may easily make wrong conclusions about the progress properties of the system. For instance, Figure 9 (a) seems to suggest that $send\langle m_1\rangle$ is guaranteed to occur eventually, but this is in contradiction with the liberty of the sending customer of never sending anything. And finally, an LTS picture shows the behaviour of the model the designer wrote, not of the model he intended to write. Errors in Sender and Receiver would very likely have been apparent in the reduced global behaviour, but would we have noticed it if we forgot to model loss of messages in AckChannel? These issues should be given serious consideration before our method deserves to be called a verification method. Such consideration was given in [11].

We did not talk much about our computer tools in this article. This was intentional. The tools have been described in earlier articles (e.g. [6, 7, 9, 12]). In the present article we wanted to concentrate on the use of abstraction, reduction and visualisation in system development, using just any suitable tools. Because of similar reasons, we did not emphasise the use of Lotos. Indeed, our approach does not depend on Lotos — any language which uses synchronous communication and can be given an operational semantics in terms of LTSs can be used. Users of Lotos, CSP, CCS, Occam, or even Ada can easily implement the final protocol in their favourite languages, because we specified the behaviours of its component processes by showing their LTSs.

Although we did not want to concentrate on tools in this article, there is one question we should not ignore: how big systems can be handled with our approach? The honest answer is that we do not know. Most of the computer runs we did for this article took less than two minutes. The versions of the alternating bit protocol developed in Section 5 were by no means trivial. We have tried our approach also to other systems, such as Peterson's mutual exclusion algorithm [7, 11] and a star-like master-slave protocol for avoiding collisions in the Ethernet. In our experience, performance of the tools becomes a major problem when systems become more complicated. On the other hand, our tools can certainly be improved.

There are fundamental results in computational complexity theory implying that the performance problem is unlikely to ever go totally away. These results apply to *all* verification, not just our approach. Verification researchers have taken the performance problem seriously and have developed many ingenious techniques that alleviate it. Some of them can be applied to our approach (and indeed have been, although not in this article). We believe that with them, our abstraction, reduction and visualisation approach will become feasible for industrial use.

Acknowledgements

The work of Konsta Karsisto was funded by the Technical Research Centre of Finland (VTT) and the Technology Development Centre of Finland (TEKES), and is part of the ESPRIT III BRA project REACT (6021). Manu Setälä was supported by the Academy of Finland, project REFORM.

References

[1] Bartlett, K. A., Scantlebury, R. A. & Wilkinson, P. T.: "A Note on Reliable Full-Duplex Transmission over Half-Duplex Links", *Communications of the ACM* 12 (5) 1969, pp. 260–261.

[2] Bolognesi, T. & Brinksma, E.: "Introduction to the ISO Specification Language LOTOS", *Computer Networks and ISDN Systems* 14, 1987, pp. 25–59.

[3] Cleaveland, R. & Hennessy, M.: "Testing Equivalence as a Bisimulation Equivalence", *Proc. Workshop on Automatic Verification Methods for Finite State Systems*, LNCS 407, Springer-Verlag 1990, pp. 11–23.

[4] Hoare, C. A. R.: *Communicating Sequential Processes*, Prentice-Hall 1985, 256 p.

[5] International Organization for Standardization: "Information processing systems — Open Systems Interconnection — LOTOS — A formal description technique based on the temporal ordering of observational behaviour", *International standard ISO 8807*, 1989, 142 p.

[6] Savola, R.: "A State Space Generation Tool for LOTOS Specifications", *VTT Publications* 241, Technical Research Centre of Finland (VTT), Espoo, Finland 1995, 107 p.

[7] Setälä, M. & Valmari, A.: "Validation and Verification with Weak Process Semantics", *Proc. Nordic Seminar on Dependable Computing Systems 1994*, Lyngby, Denmark, August 1994, pp. 15–26.

[8] Valmari, A.: "Failure-Based Equivalences are Faster than Many Believe", *Proc. Structures in Concurrency Theory 95*, Workshops in Computing Series, Springer-Verlag, 1995, pp. 326–340.

[9] Valmari, A., Kemppainen, J., Clegg, M. & Levanto, M.: "Putting Advanced Reachability Analysis Techniques Together: the "ARA" Tool", *Proc. Formal Methods Europe '93: Industrial-Strength Formal Methods*, LNCS 670, Springer-Verlag 1993, pp. 597–616.

[10] Valmari, A. & Savola, R.: "Verification of the Behaviour of Reactive Software with CFFD-semantics and Ara Tools", to appear in *Proc. ESA International Symposium on On-Board Real-Time Software*, Noordwijk, The Netherlands, Nov. 1995, European Space Agency, 8 p.

[11] Valmari, A. & Setälä, M.: *Visual Verification of Safety and Liveness*, Tampere University of Technology, Software Systems Laboratory, Report 17, Tampere, Finland, September 1995, 20 p.

[12] Valmari, A. & Tienari, M.: "An Improved Failures Equivalence for Finite-State Systems with a Reduction Algorithm", *Protocol Specification, Testing and Verification XI* (Proc. 11th International IFIP WG 6.1 Symposium on Protocol Specification, Testing and Verification, Stockholm, Sweden, June 1991), North-Holland 1991, pp. 3–18.

[13] Valmari, A. & Tienari, M.: "Compositional Failure-Based Semantic Models for Basic LOTOS", In print in *Formal Aspects of Computing*, 1995, 29 p.

❖ Session 5 ❖

Interconnection of Networks

Chair

G. Sechi

Performance Analysis of Multipath Multistage Interconnection Networks with Nonuniform Output Traffic Distribution *

Byungho Kim Boseob Kwon Hyunsoo Yoon Seungryul Maeng Jungwan Cho

Department of Computer Science
Korea Advanced Institute of Science and Technology
373-1 Kusung-Dong, Yusung-Gu, Taejon 305-701, Korea

Abstract

The paper develops the analysis of output buffers in multipath multistage interconnection networks. The delay-throughput performance of output buffers in multipath multistage interconnection networks is closely related to the output traffic distribution *which is the packet arrival rates at each output link connected to a given output module. Many multipath networks produce nonuniform output traffic distributions even if the input traffic pattern is uniform. We propose in this paper the performance model for output buffer analysis with respect to the nonuniform output traffic distribution and analyze the output buffer performance of several multipath networks by our proposed analysis model. It is shown that the output traffic distributions are different to the various multipath networks and the output buffer performance such as packet loss probability and delay gets better as nonuniformity of the output traffic distribution becomes higher.*

1 Introduction

Multistage Interconnection Networks have been well researched as an interconnection mechanism between processors and memory modules of parallel machines [1, 2, 3, 4]. Most of them are blocking networks as like the banyan network [5]. In the blocking networks, packets may collide with each other in the network even if their destinations are different. Resource contentions arise if more than one cell needs to access the same link or the same internal buffer location. Although these networks have simple structure, the internal packet conflicts degrade the performance in the network as the dimension of the network becomes larger. In the nonblocking networks as like the Crossbar [6] and the Batcher-banyan network [7], packets with distinct destination addresses can be forwarded to the destinations without any contention in the network. Although internal blocking dose not occur in nonblocking networks, blocking can occur if more than one packet is destined to the same destination.

*This work was partially supported by *Center for Artificial Intelligence Research* of KAIST and *Electronics and Telecommunications Research Institute.*

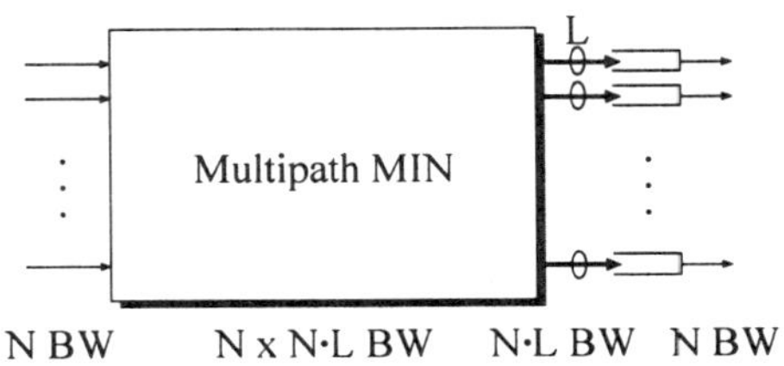

Figure 1. The multipath multistage interconnection network

Nonblocking networks are divided into two categories according to the position of the buffers: input queueing networks with buffers at the sources of the network and output queueing networks with buffers at the destinations of the network. In the nonblocking network with input queueing, the throughput performance is approximately 58% under uniform traffic [6]. This degradation is due to packet blocking in the head of line buffers at the inputs. To cope with this problem, networks with larger bandwidth are required. In recent years, there have been many proposals for output-queued networks which take advantage of multiple paths available in the networks to improve the performance. These multipath networks can support higher bandwidth than those of nonblocking networks by passing multiple packets to the same destination simultaneously as shown in Figure 1. Examples of multipath networks are the replicated or dilated banyan network [8], the tandem banyan network [9], and the multistage shuffle network [10].

In the multipath networks, the performances of the output buffer such as the mean delay and the packet loss probability are determined by several parameters, which are size of the output buffer, throughput of the switching network fed into the output buffer, and the number of the output links. While there have been many isolated studies of the network performance for individual architecture, studies of the performance analysis of the output buffer with respect to the multiple output links of the multipath networks have been relatively few. In this paper, as a noticeable factor that affects the performance of the output buffer in the multipath networks, we introduce the *output traffic distribution*, which means the packet arrival rates on each output link connected to a given output module, and propose an analytical performance model for the output buffer analysis focusing on the nonuniform output traffic distribution. To evaluate our proposed performance model, we analyze performance of the output buffer for several existing multipath networks such as the tandem banyan network [9], the multistage shuffle network [10], and the multipath crossbar [11].

Analysis results show that the output traffic distribution is different according to the particular network architecture. Many multipath networks produce nonuniform output traffic distribution even if the input traffic pattern is uniform, and the degree of nonuniformity varies also with the different network architectures. We identify in this paper the relationship between the output traffic distribution and the performance of the output buffer quantitatively.

The remainder of this paper is organized as follows. In Section 2, we propose a performance model for output buffer analysis. In Section 3, we briefly illustrate three network architectures considered for the performance comparison. In Section 4, we compute the output traffic distribution of each network and analyze the performance of the output buffer using the proposed model. Conclusions are presented in Section 5.

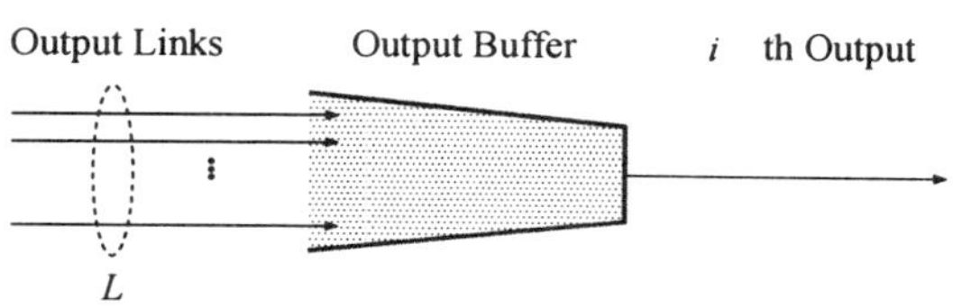

Figure 2. The model of an output module for multipath networks

2 Performance Model for Output Buffer Analysis

2.1 Traffic Model

We consider two types of traffic models; the uniform traffic and the favorite request pattern as a nonuniform traffic. Under the uniform traffic pattern, a multipath network is assumed to be loaded by a purely random and balanced traffic; that is, at the front of the network, the following assumption holds:

1) a packet is received with the same probability in each time unit;

2) packet arrival events at different input links in the same time units are mutually independent;

3) packet arrival events at an input link or at different input links in different time units are mutually independent;

4) each packet is given an output address that uniformly loads all the network output modules.

Under the favorite request, assumption 4) is replaced by the following one, while the other assumptions are remained same:

4) each packet in the i-th input link is destined to the j-th output module with the predetermined favorite rate, f, where $i = j$, or is uniformly loaded all output modules, where $i \neq j$.

Let λ denotes the input load, then the probability of a packet having an output module address under the favorite request pattern is represented by

$$\begin{aligned} p_{i,j} &= \lambda f & for\ \ i = j \\ p_{i,j} &= (\lambda - \lambda f)/(N-1) & for\ \ i \neq j, \end{aligned}$$

where $0 \leq f \leq 1$. In the following, the traffic pattern considered for the network evaluation is uniform traffic basically. The favorite request pattern is applied to the analysis of the multipath crossbar.

2.2 Performance Model

An output module for a multipath network can be viewed as shown in Figure 2 which is independent of a particular network architecture. The output module consists of a finite size of output buffer and multiple *output links.* For the general operation of the output module, we consider the following basic assumptions :

- Output buffer can accept multiple packets destined to the same output module simultaneously.
- One packet is removed out of the output buffer at each unit time as long as there is a packet to be transferred.

The performance of the output buffer can be regarded as a function of the number of output links and the packet arrival rates on each output link under the given size of output buffer. Let us define some parameters related to the output buffer analysis:

$\mathcal{L}$: Number of output links connected to an output module,

m : Size of the output buffer,

$\mathcal{T}(i)$: Packet arrival rate on the ith output link, for $1 \leq i \leq \mathcal{L}$, and

$\alpha(i)$: Probability of having i packet arrivals at a given time all destined for a same output module, for $0 \leq i \leq \mathcal{L}$.

The *output traffic distribution* means the distribution patterns of all $\mathcal{T}(i)$.

Input arguments for the performance model are $\mathcal{L}$ and $\mathcal{T}(i)$. We model the output buffer as a discrete time Markov chain. With the buffer size of m, let Q_t denote the number of packets in a given output buffer just after the tth time unit, and A_t denote the number of packet arrivals during tth time unit, then,

$$Q_t = \min(\max(0,\ Q_{t-1} + A_t - 1),\ m). \quad (1)$$

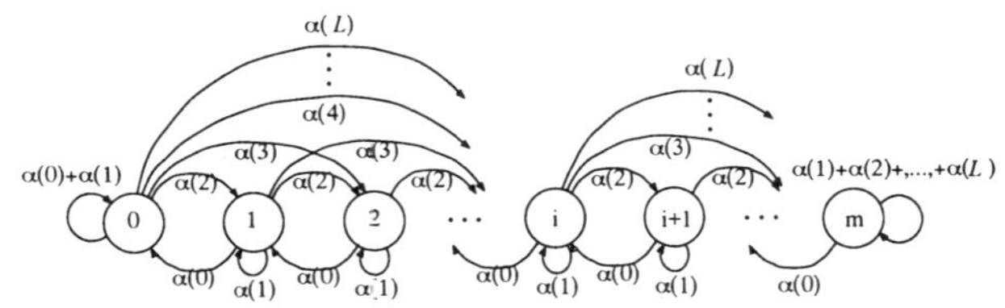

Figure 3. Markov chain state transition diagram of the output buffer.

Let Q denote the steady-state buffer size obtained from Q_t. Figure 3 shows the Markov chain state transition diagram. The transition probabilities are in terms of $\alpha(i)$. When the output traffic distribution has nonuniform pattern, that is, all $\mathcal{T}(i)$ are different, we can obtain $\alpha(i)$ by considering all of the possible events. Assume an experiment which satisfies the following conditions 1 - 4 :

1. The experiment consists of a sequence of n trials, where n is fixed in advance of the experiment.
2. The trials are identical, and each trial can result in one of the two possible outcomes, which we denote true (T) or false (F).
3. The trials are independent, so that the outcome on any particular trial dose not influence the outcome on any other trial.
4. The probability that a true trial occurs after the last true trial is random from an experiment to the following experiment; we denote these probabilities by τ_i, for $1 \le i \le n$.

This experiment is identical to the binomial experiment [12] except the condition 4. An event of the output module (shown in Figure 2) occurred in a time slot can be approximated into the experiment; in which, considering the number of output links $\mathcal{L}$ as n, the possibility of the packet arrival at the output link i as a trial, and the $\mathcal{T}(i)$ as τ_i. Let v_i denote $1-\tau_i$, then, a simple product, $\prod_{i=1}^{n}(\tau_i + v_i)$, can be represented by

$$\prod_{i=1}^{n}(\tau_i + v_i) \quad = \quad \sum_{i=0}^{n} group(i), \tag{2}$$

where $group(i)$ is the probability that i of n trials are true. $group(i)$ is obtained by assigning each trial of n to an element in the set $\{0,1\}$. Thus,

$$group(i) \quad = \quad \sum_{\Omega(n,i)} \left(\prod_{k=1}^{n} {\tau_k}^{\omega_k} \cdot {v_k}^{1-\omega_k} \right), \tag{3}$$

where

$$\Omega(n,i) \quad = \quad \{(\omega_1, \omega_2, \ldots, \omega_n) \mid \sum_{k=1}^{n} \omega_k = i, \quad for\ \omega_k = \{0,1\}\}.$$

Thus, replacing the $group(i)$ as $\alpha(i)$ and τ_k as $\mathcal{T}(k)$, we can obtain following equation,

$$\alpha(i) \quad = \quad \sum_{\Omega(\mathcal{L},i)} \left(\prod_{j=1}^{\mathcal{L}} \mathcal{T}(j)^{\omega_j} \cdot (1-\mathcal{T}(j))^{1-\omega_j} \right) \quad for \quad 0 \le i \le \mathcal{L}. \tag{4}$$

In case the output traffic distribution has uniform pattern, that is, all $\mathcal{T}(i)$ are identical, above equation can be reduced to the following one presented by Yeh [13].

$$\alpha(i) = \binom{N}{i} (\frac{\lambda}{N})^i (1-\frac{\lambda}{N})^{N-i} \ \ for\ 0 \le i \le \mathcal{L}, \tag{5}$$

where λ is the offered input load with dimension of N.

From the state transition diagram, we obtain the following balance equations.

$$q_0 \simeq Pr(Q=0) \quad = \quad (\alpha(0)+\alpha(1))q_0 + \alpha(0)q_1, \tag{6}$$

$$q_i \simeq Pr(Q=i) \quad = \quad \sum_{j=0}^{i+1} \alpha(i+1-j)q_j \quad for \quad 1 \le i < \mathcal{L}, \tag{7}$$

$$q_i \simeq Pr(Q=i) \quad = \quad \sum_{j=(i-\mathcal{L}+1)}^{i+1} \alpha(i+1-j)q_j \quad for \quad \mathcal{L} \le i < m, \tag{8}$$

$$q_m \simeq Pr(Q=m) \quad = \quad \sum_{j=(m-\mathcal{L}+1)}^{m-1} \alpha(m+1-j)q_j + \sum_{j=1}^{\mathcal{L}} \alpha(j)q_m. \tag{9}$$

Rather than using the Z transform of Q, we obtain the steady-state buffer size probabilities directly by the transition matrix for the Markov chain from above equations with the replacement of the last equation by

$$\sum_{j=0}^{m} q_j = 1. \tag{10}$$

The normalized throughput ρ is then

$$\rho \quad = \quad 1 - q_0\alpha(0), \tag{11}$$

and the probability of the packet loss in the output buffer is

$$Pr\ [packet\ loss\ in\ output\ buffer] = \frac{1}{\lambda} \sum_{i=2}^{\mathcal{L}} \left(q_{m+2-i} \cdot \sum_{j=i}^{\mathcal{L}} (j-i+1) \cdot \alpha(j) \right) = 1 - \frac{\rho}{\lambda}, \tag{12}$$

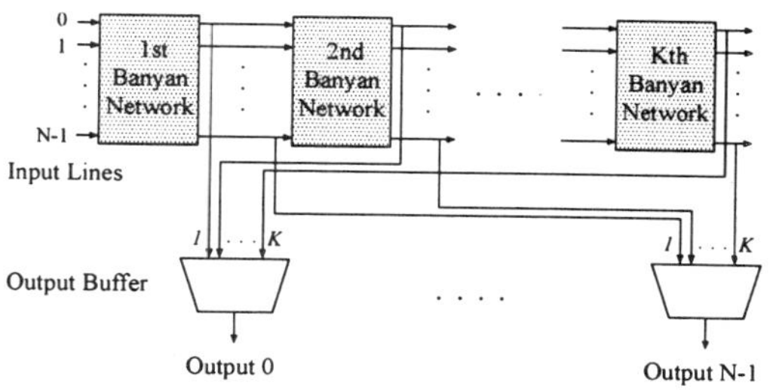

Figure 4. The tandem banyan network.

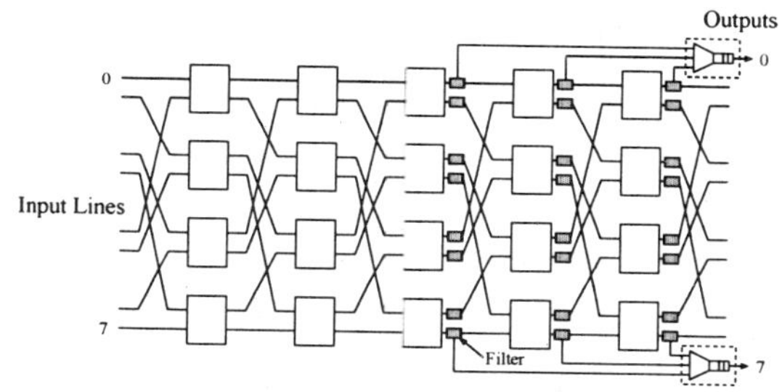

Figure 5. An 8 × 8 multistage shuffle network with 5 stages.

where

$$\lambda = \sum_{i=1}^{\mathcal{L}} \mathcal{T}(i), \tag{13}$$

which is identical to the offered input load. The mean buffer length is

$$\overline{Q} = \sum_{i=1}^{m} iq_i \tag{14}$$

and the mean waiting time in the output buffer is obtained using the Little's formula as follows

$$\overline{W} = \frac{\overline{Q}}{\rho}. \tag{15}$$

3 Multipath networks

We consider three kinds of multipath networks which employ different concepts to provide multiple paths; the tandem banyan network [9], the multistage shuffle network [10], and the multipath crossbar. The multipath crossbar is considered as an ideal multipath network which can produce the most nonuniform output traffic distribution.

A. Tandem Banyan Network

The tandem banyan network consists of multiple banyan networks placed in series as shown in Figure 3, such that each output of every banyan network is connected to both corresponding input of the following network and the corresponding output module. Upon a conflict between two packets at a switching element, one of the two packets is properly routed, while the other is routed to the wrong way. The packet which gets misrouted is marked and at the end of a banyan network it is fed into the following banyan network for further processing.

B. Multistage Shuffle Network

The multistage shuffle network is constructed using $H(\geq n = log_2 N)$ stages, each with $N/2$ unbuffered switching elements. Successive stages are interconnected through the perfect shuffle pattern. At the stages after the $log_2 N$th stage, all packets which have succeeded in reaching their desired destination proceed to the output modules. Figure 5 shows an 8 × 8 multistage shuffle network with $H = 5$.

C. Multipath Crossbar

The multipath crossbar [11] provides L disjoint paths between each source and destination. An output module can accept up to L packets having the same destination address simultaneously, while at most one packet is accepted at each output module in the original Crossbar. These L packets are packed into the output links logically ordered. For example, when one packet is arrived in the given output module, the packet is passed always through the specific output link in which the output traffic in the output link becomes the highest one. It is impossible to build such a network in the real world, however, the multipath crossbar with the packing assumption can provide the upper bound of the nonuniformity of output traffic distribution.

4 Performance Analysis

The analysis in this section is performed under uniform input traffic model. For the fair comparison of the performance of the output buffer, we decide $\mathcal{L}$ and $\mathcal{T}(i)$ of each network which are resulted in the throughput analysis of the switching networks.

4.1 Analysis of Output Traffic Distributions

Firstly, the output traffic distribution of all $\mathcal{T}(i)$ is obtained from the analysis of the switching network. In the following, we analyze the throughputs of each switching network for $\mathcal{T}(i)$.

A. Analysis of Tandem Banyan Network

For an n-stage banyan network built of k by k unbuffered switching elements, the probability p_m that there are some packets on any particular input at the

mth stage of the network is approximated by [14]

$$p_m = \frac{2k}{(k-1)m + \frac{2k}{\lambda}}, \quad (16)$$

where λ is the input load. The input load for the ith banyan network in the tandem banyan network is defined as the remained packets which get misrouted in the preceding banyan networks. Thus, with $m = log_2 N$ stages and $k = 2$, the throughput at the ith banyan network, $\mathcal{T}(i)$, is obtained by

$$\mathcal{T}(i) = \frac{4}{log_2 N + \frac{4}{p - \sum_{j=1}^{i-1} \mathcal{T}(j)}}, \quad where\ 1 \le i \le K. \quad (17)$$

B. Analysis of Multistage Shuffle Network

The analysis of the multistage shuffle network is based on Awdeh's work [10]. In the multistage shuffle network, packets are delivered to the output module out of the stages n $(= log_2 N)$ to H. A packet in the switching network has own counter field C, which represents the number of remained stages to the correct output. Thus, a packet can be in any of $n+1$ states, ranging from $C = n$ (which corresponds to a packet n stages far from its destination), to $C = 0$ (which corresponds to a packet that has reached its destination, *or there is no packet*). The corresponding state transition diagram is shown in Figure 4.1. A packet in state i $(1 \le i \le n)$ can move to state $i-1$ in case of correct routing, or to state n in case of deflection.

Let $q(i,k)$ be the probability that an output link of stage k $(0 \le k \le H)$ carries a packet with $C = i$ $(0 \le i \le n)$; $q(i,0)$ refers to an input link of the first stage. Defining $w(i,k)$ as the probability that a packet with $C = i$ at an output link of stage k $(0 \le k < H)$ does not misrouted by a switching element in stage $k+1$, then,

$$w(i,k) = \begin{cases} 1 - q(i,k)/4 & \text{if } i = 1 \\ 1 - \frac{1}{2}\sum_{j=1}^{i-1} q(j,k) - \frac{1}{4}q(i,k) & \text{if } 2 \le i \le n. \end{cases} \quad (18)$$

From the balance equations of the transition diagram of Figure 4.1, the following equations are obtained,

$$\left.\begin{aligned} q(0,k+1) &= q(0,k) + q(1,k)w(1,k) \\ q(i,k+1) &= q(i+1,k)\cdot w(i+1,k), \\ q(n,k+1) &= \sum_{j=1}^{n} q(j,k)[1 - w(j,k)] \end{aligned}\right\} \quad (19)$$

for $0 \le k < H$, where

$$q(i,0) = \begin{cases} 1-\lambda & \text{if } i = 0 \\ 0 & \text{if } 0 < i < n \\ \lambda & \text{if } i = n \end{cases} \quad (20)$$

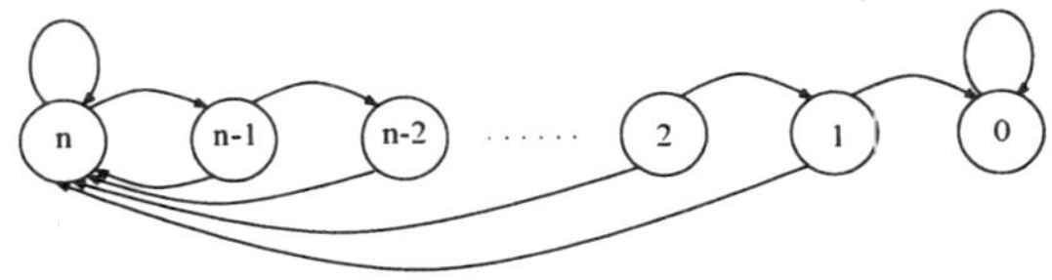

Figure 6. The state transition diagram of a packet in the multistage shuffle network.

for the offered input traffic λ. $q(i,k)$ is obtained by recursively solving the above equations starting from the input stage. Thus, $\mathcal{T}(i)$ for the multistage shuffle network is obtained by

$$\mathcal{T}(i) = q(0, n+i-1) - q(0, n+i-2) \quad (21)$$

where $1 \le i \le H - n + 1$.

C. Analysis of Multipath Crossbar

In the multipath crossbar, we assume that if there is at least one packet destined to a given output module, the packet is to be passed always through the first output link logically ordered. Accordingly, the second output link in the logical order can deliver a packet when there are at least two packets destined to the output module. Therefore, the packets in front of each output module are packed into the output links with logical ordering. Firstly, let $\mathcal{A}(i)$ denote the probability of i packet arrivals destined to a given output module without regard to the packing assumption, then, $\mathcal{T}(i)$ is obtained by

$$\mathcal{T}(i) = 1 - \sum_{j=0}^{i-1} \mathcal{A}(j). \quad (22)$$

Under the uniform traffic pattern, $\mathcal{A}(i)$ is described by

$$\mathcal{A}(i) = \binom{N}{i}\left(\frac{\lambda}{N}\right)^i\left(1 - \frac{\lambda}{N}\right)^{N-i} \quad for\ 1 \le i < \mathcal{L}. \quad (23)$$

However, under the favorite request pattern, $\mathcal{A}(i)$ can be obtained by considering the favorite request and the non-favorite requests separately as follows:

$$\mathcal{A}(i) = P_A(i) + P_B(i), \quad (24)$$

where

$$P_A(i) = \binom{N-1}{i}(p)^i(1-p)^{N-1-i}\cdot(1-\lambda f) \quad (25)$$

$$P_B(i) = \binom{N-1}{i-1}(p)^{i-1}(1-p)^{N-1-(i-1)}\cdot\lambda f \quad (26)$$

$$for\ \ p = \frac{(\lambda - \lambda f)}{(N-1)}.$$

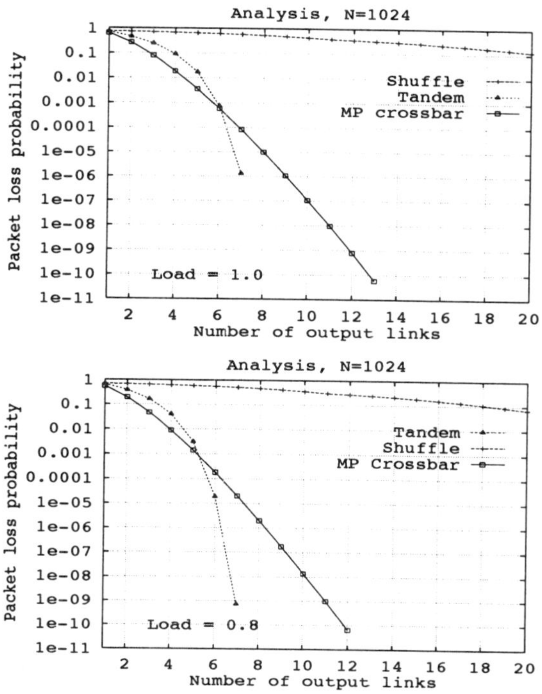

Figure 7. Number of output links versus packet loss probability.

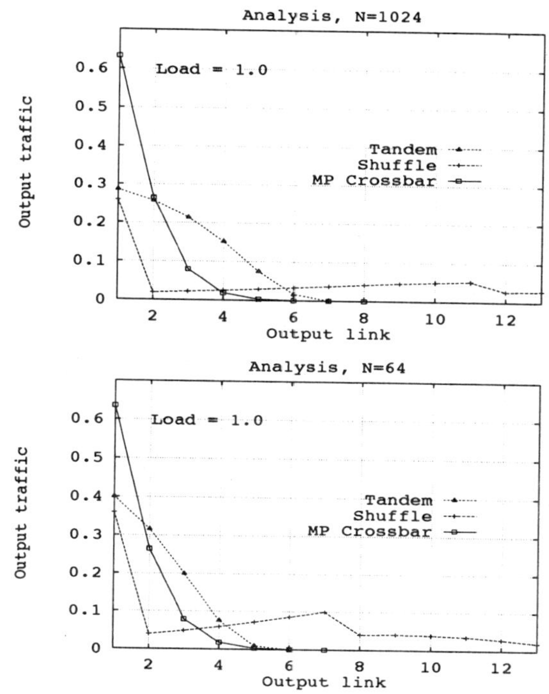

Figure 8. Output traffic distributions.

4.2 Performance Results

For the fair comparison of the output buffer performance, we have to decide each $\mathcal{L}$ of the networks under the condition that their throughputs on the switching networks are equal. Thus, we first show the throughputs on each switching network and decide their $\mathcal{L}$. Following performance results consist of two parts; the output traffic distributions on each $\mathcal{L}$ output link and delay-throughput performances of the output buffer.

4.2.1 Output Traffic Distributions

Figure 7 represents the number of output links versus the probability of packet loss curve in the switching networks. If we consider the probability of packet loss less than 10^{-7} with 100% load or 10^{-9} with 80% load, the corresponding $\mathcal{L}$ for each network is 8 for the tandem banyan network, 45 for the multistage shuffle network, and 11 for the multipath crossbar.

Figure 4.2.1 shows the output traffic distributions for each network (obtained by Equation (4)). Estimating the degree of the nonuniformity as the standard deviation of the curve, the figure exhibits that the multipath crossbar has the most nonuniform output traffic distribution and the tandem banyan network follows.

4.2.2 Output Buffer Performance

Figure 9 shows the packet loss probability versus the output buffer size curve, especially the graph with 80% load on the right side shows for both analysis (lines) and simulation (symbols). We notice that the analytical results are in an agreement with the simulation ones. The multipath crossbar having the most nonuniform output traffic distribution shows the best performance of packet loss probability. For an example, to achieve packet loss probability less than 10^{-9} for 1024 $\times$ 1024 networks with 80% load, the multipath crossbar requires 23 packet buffers, while the tandem banyan network and the multistage shuffle network require 33 and 39 packet buffers respectively. Such results are analogous to the analysis results of the output traffic distribution consistently.

Figure 10 shows the load versus delay curve (obtained by Equation (15)) under the buffer size of 40. The figure shows that all of the networks have relatively small delay up to 90% load.

4.2.3 Performance Results under Nonuniform Traffic Model

Figure 11 shows the output traffic distributions of the multipath crossbar under the favorite request pattern in which the favorite request rates, f, vary from 0.2 to 0.8 compared to the result of uniform traffic pat-

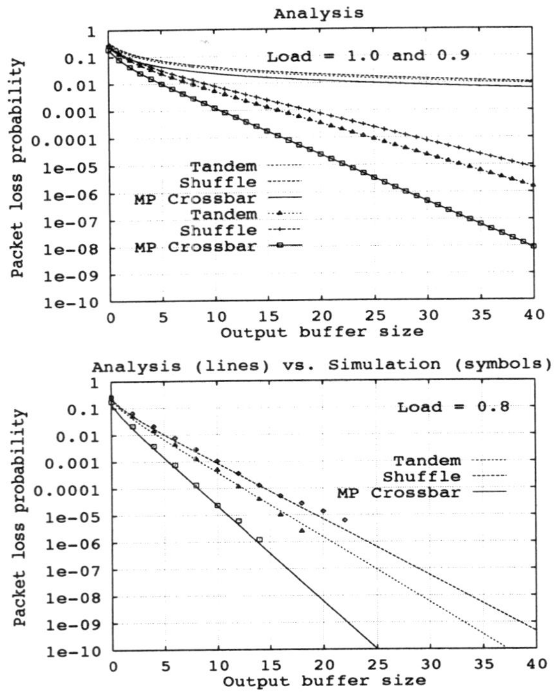

Figure 9. Packet loss probability of the output buffer.

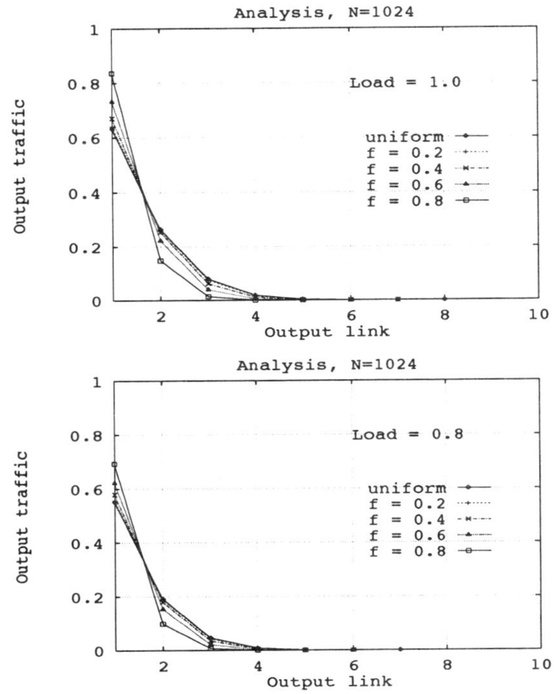

Figure 11. Output traffic distributions under the favorite request pattern.

tern. Figure 12 shows the packet loss probability of the output buffer under the favorite request pattern corresponded to the parameters of Figure 11. These figures show that the performance of the output buffer gets better as the favorite request rate grows, that is, as the input traffic pattern is more nonuniform.

5 Conclusions

This paper proposed a performance model for the output buffer analysis in multipath networks with respect to the nonuniform output traffic distribution. To demonstrate our proposed performance model, we investigated three multipath networks: the tandem banyan network, the multistage shuffle network, and the multipath crossbar. It has shown that the delay-throughput performance of the output buffer is analogous to the output traffic distribution, and moreover the output buffer performance is better as the nonuniformity of the output traffic distribution becomes higher.

The multipath crossbar has been considered as an ideal multipath network which can get the upper bound of the nonuniformity of output traffic distributions. As shown in the analysis results, the multipath crossbar represents the ideal performance of output buffer. So, we have applied the favorite request pattern as a nonuniform input traffic to only the multipath crossbar.

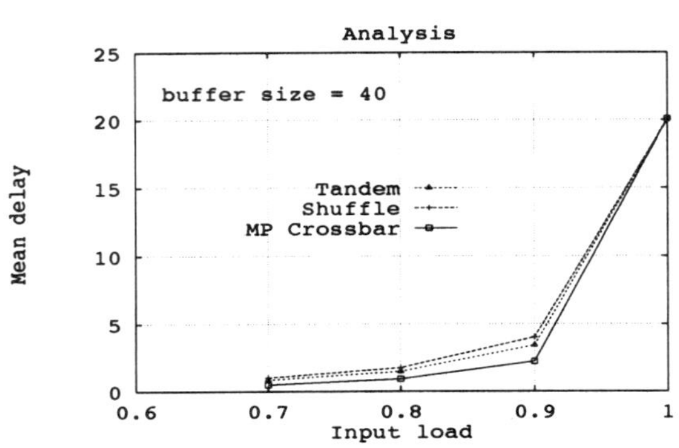

Figure 10. Load versus delay of the output buffer.

References

[1] J. H. Patel, "Performance of Processor-Memory Interconnections for Multiprocessors," *IEEE Transaction on Computers*, vol. C-30, pp. 771–780, Oct. 1981.

[2] G. Broomell and J. R. Health, "Classification Categories and Historical Development of Circuit Switching Topologies," *ACM Computing Surveys*, vol. 15, Jun. 1983.

[3] H. Yoon, K. Y. Lee, and M. T. Liu, "Performance Analysis of Multibuffered Packet-Switching Networks in Multiprocessor Systems," *IEEE Transaction on Computers*, vol. 39, pp. 319–327, Mar. 1990.

[4] T. Hanawa, H. Amano, and Y. Fujikawa, "Multistage Interconnection Networks with Multiple Outlets," in *Proc. 1994 International Conference on Parallel Processing*, pp. 1–8, 1994.

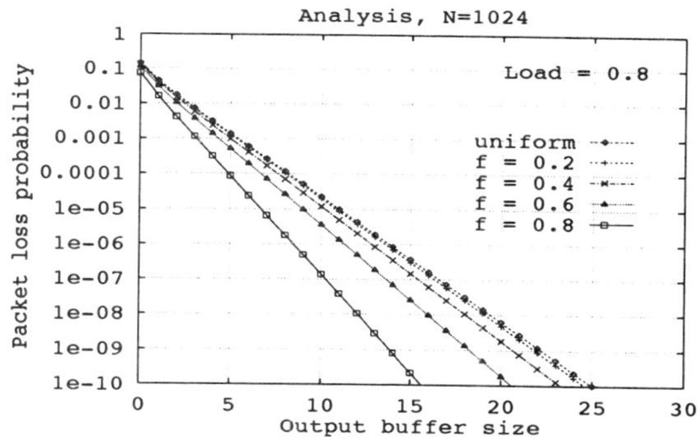

Figure 12. Packet loss probability of the output buffer under the favorite request pattern.

[5] L. R. Goke and G. J. Lipovski, "Banyan Networks for Partitioning Multiprocessor System," in *Proc. 1st Ann. Sympo. Comp. Archi.*, pp. 21–28, 1973.

[6] M. J. Karol, M. G. Hluchjy, and S. P. Morgan, "Input Versus Output Queueing on a Space-Division Packet Switch," *IEEE Transaction on Communications*, vol. COM-35, pp. 1347–1356, Dec. 1987.

[7] J. Hui and E. Arthurs, "A Broadband Packet Switch for Integrated Transport," *IEEE Journal on Selected Areas in Communications*, vol. SAC-5, pp. 1264–1273, Oct. 1987.

[8] T. H. Szymanski and V. C. Hamacher, "On the Permutation Capability of Multistage Interconnection Networks," *IEEE Transaction on Computers*, vol. C-36, pp. 810–822, Jul. 1987.

[9] F. A. Tobagi, T. Kwok, and F. M. Chiussi, "Architecture, Performance, and Implementation of the Tandem Banyan Fast Packet Switch," *IEEE Journal on Selected Areas in Communications*, vol. 9, pp. 1173–1193, . 1991.

[10] R. Y. Awdeh and H. T. Mouftah, "Design and Performance Analysis of an Output Buffering ATM Switch with Complexity of $O(Nlog_2N)$," in *Proc. of INFOCOM'94*, pp. 420–424, 1994.

[11] B. Kim, J. Kim, B. Kwon, H. Yoon, and J. Cho, "Nonuniform Output Traffic Distributions in Multipath Multistage Interconnection Networks," in *Proc. of Int. Sympo. on Parallel and Distributed Supercomputing*, pp. 112–118, Sep. 1995.

[12] J. L. Devore, *Probability and Statistics for Engineering and the Sciences.* Books/Cole Publishing Company, 1990.

[13] Y. S. Yeh, M. G. Hluchyj, and A. S. Acampora, "The Knockout Switch: A Simple, Modular Architecture for High-Performance Packet Switching," *IEEE Journal on Selected Areas in Communications*, vol. SAC-5, pp. 1274–1283, Oct. 1987.

[14] C. P. Kruskal and M. Snir, "The Performance of Multistage Interconnection Networks for Multiprocessors," *IEEE Transaction on Computers*, vol. C-32, pp. 1091–1098, Dec. 1983.

Tree-Based Communication Model for WK-Recursive Networks

A. Iazzetta ° - C. Sanges ° - U. Scafuri *

°Istituto per la Ricerca sui Sistemi Informatici Paralleli (IRSIP) - CNR
via P. Castellino, 111 - 80131 Napoli - Italy
*Centro per il Calcolo Parallelo ed i Supercalcolatori (CPS) - CNR
via Diocleziano, 328 - 80124 Napoli - Italy
E-mail: carlo@irsip.na.cnr.it

Abstract

WK-Recursive networks constitute a class of interconnection network topologies for massively parallel systems purposely devised by the Authors. These networks are constructed in a recursive fashion to achieve a fully scalable structure. Starting from the peculiar structure of these networks, the present paper describes a tree-based communication model, which allowed to handle in a very simple and efficient way several form of collective communications such as multicast and broadcast. Because efficient collective communications are closely associated with the structure of the multiple paths concurrently engaged in the network, this communication model, directly tied to the WK interconnection network topologies, represents a good solution to design collective communication mechanisms.

1: Introduction

Since their introduction WK-Recursive networks [1],[2] have drawn much attention in literature [3],[4],[5] because they offer a high degree of regularity, scalability and symmetry which very well conform to a modular design and implementation of distributed systems involving a large number of computing elements. Nowadays the challenge for WK-networks, as for any networks is to meet satisfactorily the need of efficiently supporting several forms of collective communication. These are commonly used in all areas of parallel computing ranging from neural networks to linear algebra. For example nCUBE-2 directly supports broadcast and special multicast in which the destination nodes form a subcube. The adoption of such special mechanisms derives from the need for the user to rely on communication mechanisms as an alternative to the traditional but not always effective point-to-point communication. The taking into account of the intrinsic characteristics of the interconnection network permits the system designer to keep the implementation simpler and make the deadlock problems more affordable. The present paper is intended to describe a communication model, valid for the whole class of WK-Recursive topologies, which suggested the definition of a new communication mechanism, termed WK-multicast (WKm), for implementing a special multicast feature in which the set of destination nodes forms a virtual node.

The paper is organized as follows. In section 2, we first present our notation and terminology, followed by the graph theoretical model of the WK-Recursive topologies, then a network partitioning strategy based on the trees encompassed in the WK-networks is also reported as well. Section 3, contains the description of the tree-based communication model. This model constitutes the basis for the WKm communication mechanism, formally described in section 4. In section 5, a simple WKm based implementation of multicast and broadcast is depicted and, finally, sections 6 and 7 give some concluding remarks.

2: WK-Recursive Network

A class of modular networks, named WK-Recursive, has been proposed and used at IRSIP Institute for building up the Pina2 prototype, a massively parallel MIMD system. WK-Recursive networks offer a high degree of regularity and scalability which very well conforms to both a modular design and the realization of distributed systems involving a large number of computing elements.

A WK-Recursive network is characterized by a pair (K,L), where K is the node degree and L the expansion level. The network interconnects K^L physical nodes and is constructed as follows: each node is identified by L

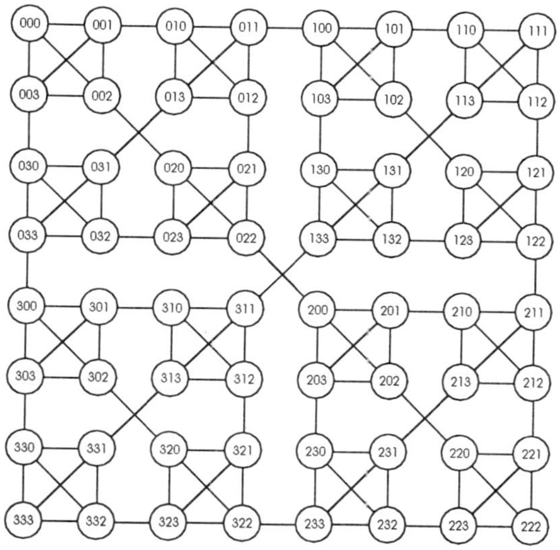

Fig. 1: WK-network (K = 4, L = 3)

coordinates $n_L \ldots n_2 n_1$, where $0 \le n_i < K$ for $1 \le i \le L$. Two nodes $A = (a_L \ldots a_2 a_1)$ and $B = (b_L \ldots b_2 b_1)$ are connected - hence becoming neighbors - if and only if there exists an integer w $(1 \le w \le L)$ such that

$$\begin{array}{lllll} a_w \neq b_w & & & & \\ a_\ell = b_\ell & \ell = L,\ldots,w+1 & \text{if } w < L & & \\ a_i = b_w & i = w-1,\ldots,1 & \text{if } w > 1 & & (1) \\ b_i = a_w & i = w-1,\ldots,1 & \text{if } w > 1 & & \end{array}$$

WK-networks give real "handy" scalability in terms of both hardware and software implementation. Such networks can be built in arbitrarily large sizes, independently of the node degree. Existing links are left undisturbed when the network grows in size, and the communication software remains unchanged.

Fig. 1 shows a member of the class of these topologies with K = 4 and L = 3 for a total number of nodes equal to 64. In the sequel we shall refer to this particular network to illustrate graphically the properties of the entire class of topologies as they are being characterized.

As far as the communication link indexing is concerned, it is local to each node: each of its K bidirectional links is numbered (0,1,..,K-1) according to the index of the other node it is connected to. Referring to (1), the link connecting A and B is numbered b_w on node A and a_w on node B, where w we define *weight* of the link. With these assumptions, each link has two different associated indices.

Let us note that the weight of a link numbered c by the node N can be easily obtained by comparing the digits of N with c, because w is equal to the i-th position of the least significant digit n_i different from c, i.e. $w = i$. As a result (K-1) links will have weight $w = 1$. In addition, for a given link of weight w, n_w is the number assigned

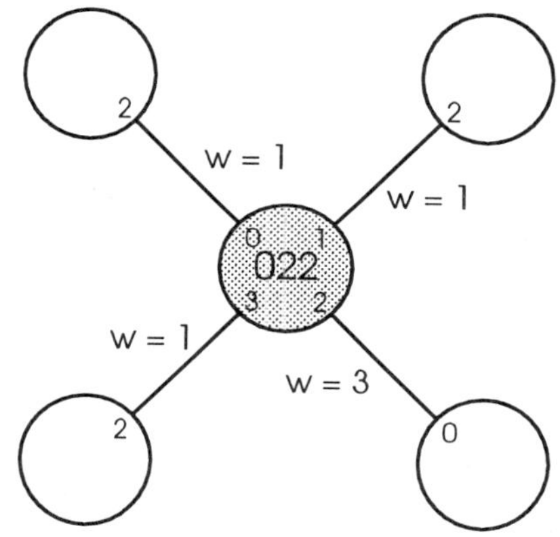

Fig. 2: Link indexing for the neighbors of 022

by the neighbor to this link. In Fig. 2 is shown the numbers assigned by the neighbors to the links of a given node.

In our analysis of the communication mechanisms for WK-networks, it has been very useful to consider the trees embedded in the network. Obviously, the links and nodes of a WK-network can be considered as arcs and vertices of a graph; hence, we shall borrow graph theory terminology when necessary for the sake of clarity.

Let us consider an undirected graph whose vertices are all the nodes in the WK-network, and whose edges are all the links which can be numbered i on one of the two connected nodes. Let us name this graph G_i. It is possible to give G_i an orientation by considering each edge as directed from the node which assigned the number i to such an edge to the other node. We call the directed graph thus obtained (Fig. 3b) *Reverse Tree Graph* (RTG_i). If the orientation in RTG_i is inverted, another directed graph - which we call *Direct Tree Graph* (DTG_i) - is obtained (Fig. 3a).

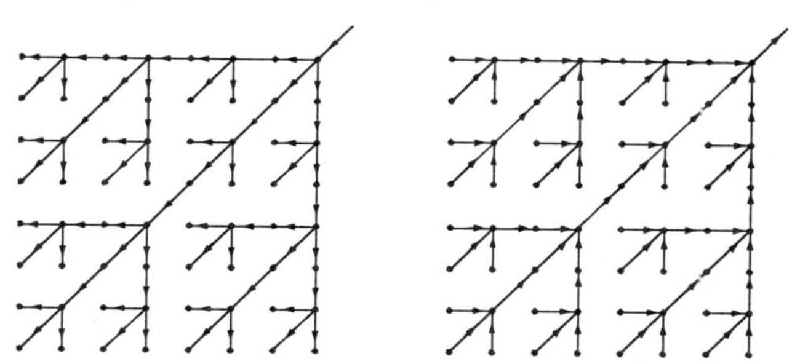

a) DTG_1 b) RTG_1

Fig. 3: Direct Tree and Reverse Tree Graphs

In this way, on a WK-network it is possible to map as many as K *DTG*'s and K *RTG*'s [6],[7]. It is easy to see that both the *DTG*'s and *RTG*'s don't have any path in common. Note that the RTG_i has the property that its nodes have only the edge i as output, and all input edges, if any, satisfying the condition $n_{w\_inp} = i$ where *w_inp* is the weight of the input edge; likewise, the nodes of DTG_i have as input only the edge *i*, and outputs the edges satisfying the condition $n_{w\_out} = i$. In accordance with these properties, on a WK communication network, we can give two conditions which ensure that the message communication path lies on a particular WK tree-structured graph.

For a given node N in the WK-network, let *l_inp* be the link through which a message reaches the node, and, likewise, *l_out* be one of the links through which the message can be forwarded. Let us consider the following conditions:

a) $l\_out = n_{w\_inp}$

b) $n_{w\_out} = l\_inp$

When a message reaches the current node N, a communication algorithm evaluating a), for each output link, ensures that the communication path lies on the *RTG* where the message was injected. Likewise, condition b) ensures that the communications path lies on the *DTG*. Let us note that the message does not need to carry any information about the chosen tree.

3: WK tree-based communication model

WK-networks can be obtained by recursively expanding a basic fully connected structure to form higher-level *virtual* nodes. If K is the node degree, using K nodes we can build a fully connected configuration still having K free links. This structure can be viewed as being virtually similar to each component node of degree K. Therefore, it constitutes a *first-level virtual node* of cardinality W, formed by W=K fully connected real nodes which can serve as a building block for expanded configurations. Once an origin and an orientation have been arbitrarily fixed, each real node is given an index $n_1 \in \{0,1,..,W-1\}$. Likewise, each of the W first-level virtual nodes constituting a second-level virtual node is given an index n_2. In general, each (ℓ-1)-th level virtual node composing an ℓ-th level virtual node is assigned an index n_l.

The indexing scheme for nodes, adopted in (1), can be established as follows. If L is the network expansion level, every node is given L digits: n_1 represents the position occupied by the real node within the first-level virtual node, n_2 represents the position occupied by this first-level virtual node within the second level virtual node and so on.

Virtual nodes and their recursive structure suggested the devising of a *level-ordered* model of communication in order to implement a point-to-point communication valid for the whole class of WK-Recursive topologies. It is based on the concept of *Smallest Virtual Node* (*SVN*) defined as the lowest level virtual node containing a pair of given nodes, so that each current node through which a message is routed identifies, together with the destination node, a specific ℓ-level *SVN*. This level-ordered model imposes the routing through *SVN*'s of decreasing levels until the *SVN* coincides with the destination node, as depicted in Fig. 4.

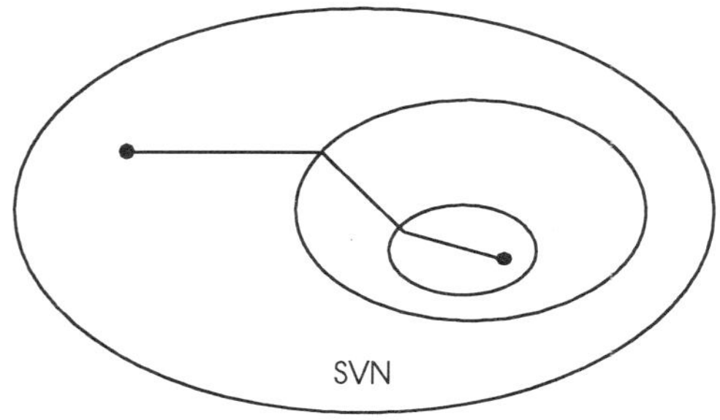

Fig. 4: WK *level-ordered* communication model

A distributed self-routing algorithm was proposed in [1] where the message routing advances through *SVN*'s in a strictly decreasing level-ordered. A message has the destination node address embedded into, which is compared with the current node address for routing decisions: *the message is routed through the link number equal to the most significant digit of the destination node index different from the current node index.*

Since the left-most digit position in which the current and destination node addresses differ represents the level of the current *SVN*, the algorithm is consistent with the level-ordered communication model.

Even though this algorithm does not always guarantee the shortest paths, it nonetheless is well suited for simple and efficient implementation. Moreover, it paves the way to an approach where the visibility of the actual communication paths play a key role in the definition of a new communication model.

Given a pair of communicating nodes A and B, if the pertaining *SVN* has level ℓ, there are two ℓ-1 level virtual nodes - among the K composing the *SVN* - which contain A and B respectively. We call the ℓ-1 level virtual node containing the source node A *virtual source node* (*VSN*), and the ℓ-1 virtual node containing the destination node B *virtual destination node* (*VDN*). There exists only one link, having weight $w = \ell$, connecting *VSN* to *VDN*. This link connects the real node C of *VSN* to the real node D of *VDN* and, according to the link indexing, it is numbered $i = d_\ell$ on node C and $j = c_\ell$ on node D. Since all the real nodes belonging to *VSN* and *VDN* have the same ℓ-th digit of their index respectively, we have $c_\ell = a_\ell$ and $d_\ell = b_\ell$. According to *RTG* and *DTG* definitions, the link can be viewed as belonging to the RTG_i in the *VSN* and to the DTG_j in the *VDN*, where $i = b_\ell$ and $j = a_\ell$.

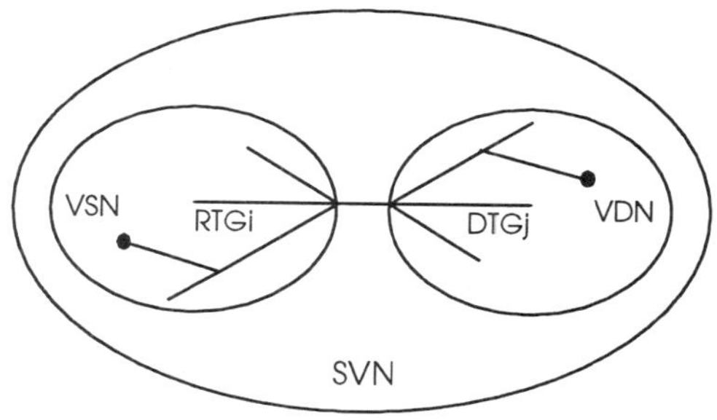

Fig. 5: WK *tree-based* communication model

Consequently, we can adopt a *tree-based* model where communications are organized in two phases: the output phase, occurring in the *VSN*, involves a reverse tree-based communication, whereas the input phase, in the *VDN*, involves a direct tree-based communication, as illustrated in Fig 5. The level of the *VSN* and *VDN* in which such phases occur respectively, is defined *confinement level* L_c, and is equal to the left most-digit position in which the current and destination node addresses differ (level of the *SVN*) reduced by 1.

The tree-based model is useful to devise routing strategies which allow the implementation of efficient and reliable mechanisms for communication among groups of nodes belonging to virtual nodes. For example, if a message injected in a *VDN* has to be broadcast to all its real nodes, the only parameter L_c - computed once at message preparation time - shall suffice to route the message.

4: An alternative communication mechanism

Let $\mathfrak{s}$ be a real node of a WK-network and S the virtual node of level $\ell < L$, where $\mathfrak{s} \in S$. Let j be the position occupied by S within the $(\ell+1)$-th level virtual node N. S is connected to the remaining (K-1) virtual nodes of level ℓ belonging to N. We denote each of them by D_i^ℓ where i is the position they hold in N. For a given $\mathfrak{s}$, we define the set $D_\mathfrak{s}$ of the virtual nodes D_i^ℓ associated to $\mathfrak{s}$, as:

$$D_\mathfrak{s} = \{ D_i^\ell \mid 0 \le \ell < L, 0 \le i < K \text{ and } i \neq j \} \qquad (2)$$

We can consider one D_i^ℓ as destination for a message originated in $\mathfrak{s}$ when this message must be delivered to all nodes belonging to D_i^ℓ. This communication mechanism is hereinafter referred to as WK-multicast (WKm) and is characterized by the triplet $(\mathfrak{s}, i, \ell)$.

Given $\mathfrak{s} \in S$ and $d \in D_i^\ell$, recalling that *VSN* is the virtual source node and *VDN* is the virtual destination node for a communication from $\mathfrak{s}$ to d, we note that

$$S \equiv VSN \quad \text{and} \quad D_i^\ell \equiv VDN \qquad (3)$$

Because of these correspondences, a WKm routing can be easily implemented on WK-networks by using the tree-based communication approach. A message traveling from $\mathfrak{s}$ to D_i^ℓ lies on the RTG_i until the weight of the input link of the current node is less than ℓ, and then, by using DTG_i, it is delivered to all the real nodes of *VDN*, i.e., D_i^ℓ.

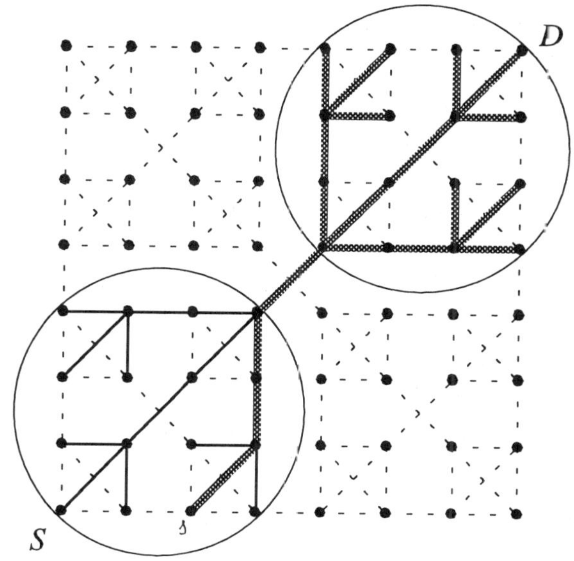

Fig. 6: WKm communication ($\mathfrak{s}$ = 323, i = 1, ℓ = 2)

Fig. 6 shows the paths assigned to a WKm message originated in the real node $\mathfrak{s}$ and addressed to the virtual node D_1^2.

A WKm routing algorithm can be easily implemented in a distributed fashion. A message is formatted at the source node by labeling it with the level ℓ of the virtual destination node. A preliminary routing step, at the source node, determines which link the message has to be sent to, thus selecting the appropriate *RTG* Two successive steps, for output and input phase, lead the message to reach its destinations. According to the confinement conditions, described in the previous section, the distributed routing algorithm results:

< output phase >

IF ($w\_inp \le L_c$) THEN

forward through l_out : $l\_out = n_{w\_inp}$

< input phase >

IF ($w\_out \le L_c$) THEN

forward through all l_out : $n_{w\_out} = l\_inp$

In the output phase, the clause THEN corresponds to the condition a) above mentioned.

The condition $w\_inp \leq L_c$ becomes false when the message reaches the first node of *VDN*, i.e. the communication occurred between *VSN* and *VDN*, and the input phase is taking place. In the input phase, the condition $w\_out \leq L_c$ ensures the confinement of the message within the *VDN*, where the message is routed on the current *DTG* according to the above condition b). Note that the parameters required by the tree-based communication model strictly depend upon the link's attributes.

5: WKm for Multicast and Broadcast

The tree-based model for WK-networks can be profitably adopted to easily implement the routing of messages for more general communication mechanisms such as multicast or broadcast.

The simplest way to implement multicast relies on multiple point-point communications, but this method creates too much unnecessary traffic and is likely to cause message delay and network congestion. An efficient multicast routing algorithm should transmit the message to each destination node in the shortest time and on the fewest channels possible. Further it should deliver messages along a path as most common as possible, then branch them to each destination node [8]. The tree-based model, here proposed, very well conforms to an easy and efficient implementation of such a communication mechanism. Actually it suggests to organize the entire set of destination nodes in subsets, according to *VDN*'s of different levels.

A graph theoretical model for multicast communication in multicomputers can be formally defined as follows. Let $G(V,E)$ be a graph corresponding to the interconnection topology under consideration and $D = (d_1, d_2, \ldots, d_n) \subseteq V$ denote the set of n destination nodes in a multicast.

In order to implement a multicast routing on WK-networks we can partition the D set into subsets S_D each containing all the destination nodes belonging to the same *VDN*, given the source node $\mathfrak{s}$. Because each *VDN* corresponds to one D_i^t, by using as many WKm communications as subsets of D, all destination nodes can be reached. Since $S_D \subseteq D_i^t$, a message must itself transport all the information necessary to reach single destinations. Moreover, the destination nodes of S_D can be grouped in lower level virtual nodes belonging to that *VDN*. Thus, at message preparation time, clever techniques can be used to compress the destination addresses in order to have messages as short as possible.

As described earlier on the input phase the WKm algorithm forks the message on the *DTG* according to condition b), which ensures the communication paths lie on the pertaining *DTG*. By taking into account the compression technique, an augmented condition b) can be profitably used to select the appropriate communication paths on the *DTG*.

WKm offers a simple solution to implement the broadcast communication too [9]. Since $\mathfrak{s} \cup D_\mathfrak{s}$ constitutes the whole set of the WK real nodes, $D_\mathfrak{s}$ represents a partitioning of all destination nodes for the broadcasting operations originated in $\mathfrak{s}$.

According to (2) (Section 4) the broadcast can be easily implemented using as many WKm communications as the cardinality of $D_\mathfrak{s}$, i.e. (K-1)∗L WKm messages. In this case, each message need not to transport any routing information to reach its single destinations; the only notion of the L_c level is sufficient to route the message. More in detail, given a real source node $\mathfrak{s}$, we have only (K-1)∗L possible partners of a WKm communication for $\mathfrak{s}$, against the (K^L-1) real destination nodes of a point-to-point communication. It is simple to verify that given the pair $(\mathfrak{s}, i)$ its WKm partners result sorted by increasing levels of *VDN*'s as distances increase. Moreover, there are K node-disjoint and edge-disjoint paths between the root node $\mathfrak{s}$ and the remaining nodes in the network, such that each path lies along a different spanning tree.

These considerations lead to a suitable approach to parallelize the transmission of messages. The source node can transmit in a concurrent fashion the whole set of (K-1)∗L messages on its K outgoing channels. Also, in order to establish a pipelined communication along each of the K sub-trees, it is necessary that the broadcasting algorithm outputs the messages bond to a given channel according to a *farthest-destination-first* basis [10], i.e. in decreasing-distance-order to their *VDN*'s partners. Note that the above discussion implies that the algorithm is time-optimal. Indeed, the proposed algorithm implements at all the parallelism of the message's transmission, even though it introduces some traffic overhead due to the number of the message replications which is obviously greater than the K messages that would suffice to perform a straight broadcasting communication [2].

The tree-based communication model here proposed has hence provided for a parallel-oriented approach for the transmission of messages. This issue in fact draws much attention in the literature, where the general problem consists in covering certain networks with edge-disjoint trees [11].

6: Wormholed WKm

One attractive feature of the WKm communication algorithm is that it uses only the output channel i in the

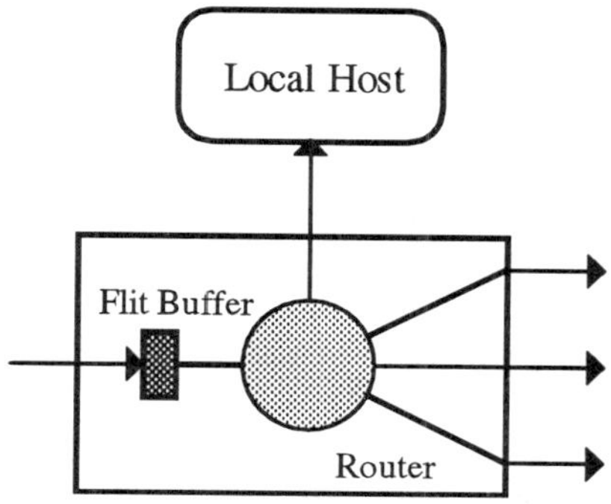

Fig. 7: Message replication

VSN and only the input channel *j* in the *VDN*. In a previous work [7], we exploited these properties in order to solve the deadlock problem for wormholed point-to-point communication by considering a direct WK communication network as constituted by two acyclic networks: one called WK-output, constituted by the K *RTG*'s, and the other called WK-input, constituted by K *DTG*'s. In order to transport messages from the WK-output to the WK-input, an additional unidirectional channel for each pair of corresponding nodes was provided. As a result, the directed graph of the whole communication network is cycle-free, thus avoiding deadlocks. Such arrangement can be profitably used to implement deadlock-free WKm based wormholed communications too [12].

In order to support these forms of collective communication, the WK-input must be enhanced with the functionality of *message replication*. This allows flit-by-flit replication of the message onto multiple outgoing channels of the *DTG* in the *VDN* and the channel connecting the router with the local processor, effectively producing a tree-like message worm (Fig. 7).

Note that if a header flit in the *VDN* is blocked in one busy channel, the progress of flits in the whole routing tree is stopped. This situation can occur when another message is injected into the *VDN* on a sub-tree contended by the first message. Because of the acyclicity of the *DTG*, we only have a temporary block if we suppose the messages are always removed from the network once they reach their destination. Assuming that the number of concurrent channels connecting each local processor to its router is equal to K, i.e., referring to a K-port model [9], the last condition is satisfied, thus avoiding deadlock [12].

In general, for tree-like wormholed communication, channel contention greatly increases the network congestion. If we consider multiple concurrent WKm messages engaged into the WK-input network, the network performances can considerably degrade. In order to cope with such a problem, we can exploit the virtual channel concept [13]. Recalling that any *VSN*/*VDN* pair identifies an ℓ-level WKm communication, it is possible to subdivide WKm messages into L classes. Consequently, we can split the WK-input network into L independent virtual networks, each of which provides all possible paths for any of the message classes. Mapping these virtual networks onto the physical network [6],[14] and ensuring that each WKm communication involves the pertaining virtual network, multiple WKm simultaneous communications of different levels can progress concurrently, because flits pertaining to messages of different classes may be interleaved over the same physical link, thus avoiding the above congestion problems. Obviously, mapping virtual networks onto a physical network requires L flit buffers and a flit-level flow control at each node of the network.

A different solution, based on a communication scheduling discipline, can be adopted. A time partitioning technique could be used to implement the L virtual sub-networks, so that at any given time only WKm communications pertaining to a given level are allowed. This is an interesting issue and deserves further study.

7: Conclusion

The tree-based communication model proposed here has been specifically conceived for WK-Recursive interconnection networks. This model provides for efficient and reliable mechanisms for distributing data over groups of nodes by fully exploiting the recursive nature of WK-networks and their organization in virtual nodes. It allowed us to define a special multicast, named WKm, which is a restricted form of multicasting in which the destinations are constituted by the real nodes belonging to a WK virtual node. Finally, we have also verified that the WKm can be used as a basic component of very popular forms of collective communication such as multicast and broadcast.

In [15] this model of communication has been adopted to define another form of collective communication among virtual nodes useful in the execution of descend/ascend algorithms on the WK-Recursive networks [16]. From the system designer's point of view a model taking into account the intrinsic characteristics of the interconnection network permits to confront with the manifold problems arising from the implementation of efficient and deadlock-free wormhole routing algorithms [12].

At present, we are studying the suitability of the tree-based model for operations of gathering and scattering on WK-networks.

References

[1] G. Della Vecchia and C. Sanges. A Recursively Scalable Network VLSI Implementation. *Future Generation Computer Systems*. **4**(3) (1988) 235-243.

[2] G. Della Vecchia and C. Sanges. An Optimized Broadcasting Technique For WK-Recursive Topologies. *Future Generation Computer Systems*. **5**(4) (1990) 353-358.

[3] R. Fernandes. Recursive Interconnection Networks for Multicomputer Networks. *Proceedings of International Conference on Parallel Processing*. **1** (1992) 76-79.

[4] R. Fernandes and A. Kanevsky. Substructure Allocation in Recursive Interconnection Networks. *Proceedings of International Conference on Parallel Processing*. **1** (1993) 319-322.

[5] D. R. Duh and G. H. Chen. On the combinatorial properties of WK-Recursive networks. *Journal of Parallel and Distributed Computing*. **23** (1994) 468-474.

[6] A. Iazzetta and C. Sanges. Partitioning WK-Recursive Networks. *EC Newsletter*. Laterza. **4**(3) (1992) 15-23.

[7] A. Iazzetta, C. Sanges, and U. Scafuri. A Routing Strategy for WK-Networks. *Proceedings of Conference on Massively Parallel Computing Systems*. IEEE Computer Society. Ischia, Italy (1994).

[8] Y. Lan, A.-H. Esfahanian and L. M. Ni. Multicast in Hypercube Multiprocessors. *Journal of Parallel and Distributed Computing*. **8** (1990) 30-41.

[9] S. L. Johnsson and C.-T. Ho. Optimum broadcasting and personalized communication in hypercubes. *IEEE Transactions on Computer*. **38**(9) (1989) 1249-1268.

[10] S. N. Bhatt, G. Pucci, A. Ranade, A. L. Rosenberg. Scattering and Gathering Messages in Networks of Processors. *IEEE Transactions on Computer*. **42**(8) (1993) 938-949.

[11] D. S. Greenberg and S. N. Bhatt. Routing multiple paths in hypercubes. *Math. Syst. Theory*. **24** 295-321.

[12] A. Iazzetta, C. Sanges, and U. Scafuri. Special Multicast wormhole Routing for WK-Networks. Submitted to *Networks*.

[13] W.J. Dally. Virtual-Channel Flow Control. *IEEE Transactions on Parallel and Distributed Systems*. **3**(2) (1992) 194-205.

[14] P.R. Miller, C.R. Jessophe, J.T. Yantchev. The Mad Postman Network Chip. *Proceedings of Transputing '91*. IOS Press. Sunnyvale, CA (1991) 517-536.

[15] C. Sanges and U. Scafuri. Virtual Nodes Communication on WK-Networks. *Proceedings of ParCo'95 Conference*, Gent (BE) (1995).

[16] G. H. Chen and D. R. Duh. Topological properties, Communication, and Computation on WK-Recursive Networks. *Networks*. **24** (1994) 303-317.

Interconnection Network Design: A Statistical Analysis of Interactions between Factors

R. Alcover P. López J. Duato L. Zúnica

Facultad de Informática
Universidad Politécnica de Valencia
P.O.B. 22012. 46071 - Valencia, SPAIN
E-mail: {rosa,plopez,jduato}@gap.upv.es

Abstract

Interconnection network performance depends on several parameters, including network design parameters, network size, message traffic and message length. Simulation is the methodology usually followed in evaluation studies, because the model can more faithfully represent hardware implementation, taking into account more details. Nevertheless, the number of parameter combinations is often high, and simulations also take long to complete. Therefore, evaluation studies must choose a subset of the parameters and restrict the variability of each of them.

In a previous paper [20], we have proposed a methodology for evaluating interconnection networks. It is based on experimental design used in statistical studies. Using this methodology, we can study network behavior considering many parameters, running only a subset of the simulations required to study all the combinations. In addition, the methodology permits to quantify the effect of interactions among the parameters. In this paper, we make use of the second advantage of this methodology, analyzing the effect of node design parameters and their interactions for a 8-ary 3-cube with adaptive wormhole routing.

1 Introduction

Many research effort has been dedicated during the last decade to improve the performance of multicomputers [2]. A key architectural issue is the interconnection network. From the performance point of view, the objective of the network designer is to minimize latency (time required to deliver a message) and maximize throughput (maximum data rate accepted by the network). To meet this objective, the designer manipulates three independent variables [10]: topology, routing algorithm and flow-control mechanism, as well as several chip design parameters.

From the topology point of view, direct networks have become a popular architecture to build massively parallel computers because they scale well. The prototypical direct network is the k-ary n-cube. A k-ary n-cube has n dimensions. Each of them has k nodes connected in a ring fashion. Assuming constraints on the bisection width, node delays, wire delays and pin count, several studies [9, 1, 28] show that low-dimensional k-ary n-cubes are often the best choice.

Second generation multicomputers use wormhole flow-control [8]. Each message is serialized into a sequence of parallel data units, called flow control units, or flits. The flit at the head of a message determines the route. As the header flit is routed, the remaining flits follow it in a pipeline fashion. This technique makes the message latency largely insensitive to the distance in the message-passing network.

Lacking a completely connected topology, the routing algorithm decides the path selected by a packet to reach its destination. Routing can be classified as deterministic or adaptive. In the former case, the path is completely determined by the source and destination nodes. In the latter case, given the source and destination nodes, the path selected by a particular packet depends on dynamic network conditions, such as the presence of congested or faulty channels. Efficient routing is critical to the performance of direct networks. In addition, the routing algorithm must be deadlock-free. Many authors have proposed deadlock-free routing algorithms [8, 18, 12, 16, 13].

Once the topology, flow-control and routing algorithm have been chosen, performance measures of the interconnection network depend on a large number of parameters, including network and node design parameters, message traffic, and message length. Concerning network and node design parameters, the network can be evaluated with a varying number of vir-

[0]This work was supported by the Spanish CICYT under Grant TIC94–0510–C02–01.

tual channels per physical channel. Also, it can be considered several delays of the basic components of the node, several input and output buffer sizes, several flit and phit sizes, several network sizes, ... Concerning messages, the choices are even larger. Several distributions of message generation rate, and of message destination nodes can be considered together with distinct message sizes. Traces from parallel applications can also be considered.

Instead of analytic modeling, simulation is often used to evaluate the approach considered, because the model can more faithfully represent hardware implementation, taking into account details like channel multiplexing, delays in blocked messages, and so on. The drawback is the long time required by each simulation. Several researches have focused on reducing the simulation time. The use of parallel simulators [22] is one of the most common approaches.

Due to the simulation time, evaluation studies usually take into account only a subset of the meaningful variables or factors. It is usual to consider only two sizes (or even only one) for message length, only large interconnection networks, only a fixed number of dimensions for a given size, and so on. For instance, in [13] we evaluated adaptive algorithms for 3D-tori considering only one network size, and a fixed message length. In addition, the adaptive algorithms were evaluated using only one level for the number of virtual channels.

In a previous paper [20], we have proposed a methodology for evaluating interconnection networks. The purpose of this methodology is twofold. First, it allows us to run only a subset of the total number of simulations required for estimating the effect of all the factors considered, without a noticeable loss in precision. Secondly, we can figure out the most significant effects (single effects and interactions) of the factors with a given level of significance. In [20], we have applied this methodology to reduce the number of simulations required to obtain the optimal levels for the number of virtual channels and some node design parameters, such as input and output buffer size, for a 8-ary 3-cube with adaptive routing. In this paper, we apply this methodology to analyze the effect of these factors and their interactions, without reducing the number of simulations.

In section 2, we informally present the basic concepts of experimental design. In order to apply the above methodology to a practical case, in section 3 the multicomputer model assumed is presented. Then, the chosen parameters and their levels are defined in section 4. The simulation results are discussed in section 5. Finally, some conclusions are drawn.

2 Basic concepts of experimental design

The goal of a proper experimental design [4, 23, 21, 17] is to obtain the maximum information with the minimum number of experiments. This saves considerable labor that would have been spent gathering data. A proper analysis of experiments also helps in separating out the effects of various factors that might affect performance. Also, it allows to determine if a factor has a significant effect or if the observed deviation is simply due to random variations caused by measurement errors and out-of-control parameters.

Next, we are going to summarize the statistical terms that are frequently used in the design and analysis of experiments:

- Experiment. Set of tests whose objective is to obtain information to improve the process, task or product under study.
- Response variable. It is what we want to optimize.
- Controlled factors. Parameters that have an impact on the response variable and whose effects need to be quantified. For each one, several alternative values are chosen and evaluated.
- Levels. The values that a factor can take are called its levels. In other words, each factor level constitutes one alternative for that factor.
- Treatment. Each combination of factor levels that is going to be analyzed in a test is called a treatment.
- Replication. Repetition of all or some treatments is called replication.
- Design. An experimental design consists of specifying the response variable(s), its measurement units, the factors and their levels to include in the experiment, the number of tests and the treatment to apply in each test, organizing all the experimental tasks, and, once the results have been obtained, going on to their statistical analysis.
- Interaction. Two factors A and B are said to interact if the effect of A depends upon the level of B or vice versa.

It can be thought that if several factors are simultaneously modified, then it is not possible to isolate the effects of each one on the response variable. The basic idea that allows us this possibility is the orthogonality property [4, 23, 21, 17, 25, 26]. Two factors I and J, with i and j levels or variants, respectively, are orthogonal if, in the tests for each one of the i levels of I, every level j of J is used in the same proportion. Thus, the estimated effect of a factor is not affected by the effect of the remaining factors. This allows us to isolate the single effects of all studied factors. The orthogonality among the single effects can be easily extended over the double, triple, ..., interactions among factors.

An experimental design is balanced if each possible treatment is assayed the same number of times, k. If $k > 1$, the design is called replicated, otherwise the design is non-replicated. If each possible treatment between factors is evaluated, the design is a full factorial design. If either the number of factors or their levels is large, the number of tests required for a full factorial design is too large. In such cases, it is possible to evaluate only a subset of the full factorial design. These designs are called fractional factorial designs [4, 29, 17, 25, 26]. However, the information obtained from a fractional factorial design is smaller than the one obtained from a full factorial design. For instance, it may not be possible to compute the interactions among the factors.

3 Multicomputer model

The network is a 8-ary 3-cube with bidirectional channels. Each node of the network consists of a processor, its local memory and a communication controller. This controller consists of a router, a switch, and several channels. A three-port architecture [24] is considered.

The router decides the output channel for a message as a function of its destination node, the current node and the output channel status. The router can only process one message header at a time. It is assigned to waiting messages in a demand-slotted round-robin fashion (including those messages generated by the local processor). When a message gets the router but it cannot be routed because all the alternative output channels are busy, it must wait in the input buffer until its next turn. Partially or fully adaptive routing can be used. The algorithms used were proposed in [13]. These algorithms can be implemented using a different number of virtual channels per physical channel, being the minimal number of virtual channels 2 and 3, respectively. In the partially adaptive algorithm, dimensions are crossed in increasing order, choosing any virtual channel. The fully adaptive routing algorithm is based on the partially adaptive one with 2 virtual channels per physical channel. Dimensions can be crossed out of order using the additional virtual channels.

The switch is a crossbar. So, it allows multiple messages traversing it simultaneously without interference. It is configured by the router each time a successful routing is made.

Physical channels can be split into several virtual channels. Virtual channels are assigned to the physical link using a demand-slotted round-robin arbitration scheme. Each virtual channel has an associated buffer. This buffer is divided into two halves, one associated with the output port of the switch, and another one associated with the input to the next node's switch.

We assume that all operations inside each node are synchronized by its local clock signal. To compute the clock frequency of a node, we will use the delay model proposed in [6]. It assumes 0.8 micron CMOS gate array technology for the implementation. We have already used this model to evaluate adaptive routing in [13].

- Router. Routing a message involves the following operations: Address decoding, routing decision, and header selection. The first operation extracts the message header and generates requests of acceptable outputs (2.7 ns). The routing decision logic takes as inputs the possible output channels generated by the address decoder, and the status of the output channels. This circuit has a delay equal to $0.6 + 0.6 \log F$ ns, F being the number of options offered by the routing algorithm. Finally, the router must compute the new header. New headers can be calculated in parallel with the routing decision, but the appropriate one must be selected. This operation has a delay equal to $1.4 + 0.6 \log F$ ns.

  Therefore, total routing time will be the sum of all delays, yielding:

  $T_r = 2.7 + 0.6 + 0.6 \log F + 1.4 + 0.6 \log F = 4.7 + 1.2 \log F$ ns.

  Notice that the header flit is not transferred to the output channel during the routing operation. This transfer will be performed later by the switch.

- Switch. The time required to transfer a flit from one input channel to the corresponding output channel is the sum of the delay involved in the internal flow control unit (2.2 ns), the delay of the crossbar ($0.4 + 0.6 \log P$ ns), and the setup time of the output channel latch (0.8 ns), P being the number of ports of the switch.

  Therefore, switch time is:

$T_s = 2.2 + 0.4 + 0.6 \log P + 0.8 = 3.4 + 0.6 \log P$ ns.

- Channels. The time required to transfer a flit across a physical channel includes the off-chip delay across the wires, and the time required to latch it onto the destination. This time is equal to 4.9 ns. If virtual channels are used, the time required to arbitrate and select one of the ready flits must be added ($1.24 + 0.6 \log V$), V being the number of virtual channels per physical channel.

  Then, total channel delay yields:

  $T_c = 4.9 + 1.24 + 0.6 \log V = 6.14 + 0.6 \log V$ ns.

Next, we will instantiate these times for every routing algorithm used:

1. Partially adaptive routing. The number of routing choices is equal to the number of virtual channels. Because dimensions are crossed in order, the switch can be built by cascading several low size crossbars, one per dimension. Substituting $F = V$, $P = 2V + 3$:

   $T_r = 4.7 + 1.2 \log V$ ns.

   $T_s = 3.4 + 0.6 \log (2V + 3)$ ns.

   $T_c = 6.14 + 0.6 \log V$ ns.

2. Fully adaptive routing. Now, the number of routing choices is $F = 3(V - 2) + 2$, because we have $V - 2$ channels in each dimension that can be used to cross the dimensions in any order, and also the two channels provided by the basic partially adaptive algorithm. As there are two channels per dimension, with V virtual channels per physical channel, plus three memory channels, the switch has a number of ports $P = 6V + 3$. Substituting:

   $T_r = 4.7 + 1.2 \log (3V - 4)$ ns.

   $T_s = 3.4 + 0.6 \log (6V + 3)$ ns.

   $T_c = 6.14 + 0.6 \log V$ ns.

Assuming that the three operations must be performed in one clock cycle, the clock period is determined by the slowest operation. Hence:
$T = \max(T_r, T_s, T_c)$

4 Experimental design

We have evaluated the behavior of both partially and fully adaptive routing algorithms, considering a router design based on the model presented in section 3.

The response variable to minimize is message latency, measured in nanoseconds.

Four factors have been chosen to analyze their effect on the latency:

- Number of virtual channels per physical channel. It is well-known that virtual channels affect performance of routing algorithms [11, 19, 15]. Taking into account that a higher number of virtual channels per physical channel decreases the bandwidth available to each channel and increases node delay considerably, we have used only two levels for this factor. The lowest level is the minimum number of virtual channels required for that particular algorithm, and the highest level is one unit higher. Thus, the levels are 2 and 3 for the partially adaptive algorithm, 3 and 4 for the fully adaptive algorithm.

- Input/Output channel buffer size. These factors are usually neglected in performance evaluation studies. Clearly, there is a minimum buffer size depending on the particular implementation. For instance, in our model a 2-flit buffer is required to avoid bubbles when messages are advancing. In some studies [11, 19, 13], there is a total amount of buffering associated with each physical channel, and the size of the buffer associated with each virtual channel decreases when the number of virtual channels increases. In this paper, considering that a large buffering associated with each physical channel is expensive and difficult to implement without an increase in the time required to latch data into the buffer, we have bounded the buffer size to 4 flits. Thus, three levels have been considered: 2, 3, and 4 flit buffers.

- Traffic rate. To apply experimental design techniques, factor levels must be fixed. So, the same values of traffic rate must be used in all the experiments of each design. However, given a particular routing algorithm, the throughput of the network depends on the number of virtual channels and buffer sizes. On the other hand, loads near saturation are useless. Thus, we have analyzed a range of traffic high bounded by the lowest throughput achieved by a given routing algorithm. In particular, four levels have been assayed for the partially adaptive algorithm, and eight levels have been assayed for the fully adaptive algorithm.

As we want to obtain the effect of the interactions among factors, all the possible treatments have been analyzed. Thus, we have used a full-factorial, balanced and non-replicated design.

Message traffic and message length depend on applications and operating system. For each treatment, we have considered that message generation rate is constant and the same for all the nodes. Message length is fixed to 16 flits. Finally, message destination is randomly chosen among all the nodes. This pattern has been widely used in other performance evaluation studies [11, 5, 3, 13].

5 Results

The statistical analysis of the results obtained in each design has been done by means of the analysis of variance technique (ANOVA). It is a powerful statistical tool for studying the effect of factors on the average value of the response variable [27].

Basically, this technique decomposes the observed total variability of a set of data into several items. Each item is associated with one of the studied factors and their interactions, plus a residual (error) part. Thus, the importance of a factor is measured by the proportion of the total variation in the response that is explained by the factor.

The sample variance of y can be computed as follows [4, 23, 21, 17, 26]:

$$S_y^2 = \frac{\sum_{i=1}^{N}(y_i - \overline{y})^2}{N-1}$$

where N denotes the number of tests and $\overline{y}$ denotes the mean of the response variable from all tests. The numerator is called total variation of y or sum of squares total (SS_T). In our design, SS_T can be computed as follows:

$SS_T = SS_{\text{Main effects}} + SS_{\text{Interactions}} + SS_{\text{Residual}}$

These sums of squares for the simulations we have run are shown in table 1, which have been computed using an statistical package (STATGRAPHICS). The percentage of variation explained by an effect (factor or interaction) can be used to measure the importance of that effect.

To statistically test the significance of a factor, we first divide its sum of squares by its corresponding degree of freedom (d.f.) to get the mean square (MS). The d.f. of a factor is its number of levels minus one. The d.f. of an interaction is the product among the d.f. of the factors that interact. The total d.f. is the number of tests minus one. Finally, residual d.f. is the difference between the total d.f. and the d.f. sum of all effects.

Next, a F test (Fisher-Snedecor) is used [14, 4, 23, 21, 26]. For this, all the F-ratios are computed. The F-ratio to test the significance of a factor A is:

F-ratio$_A = \frac{MS_A}{MS_{\text{Residual}}}$

Source	SS	d.f.	MS	F-ratio	F-table
Main Effects:					
A(V. channels)	7561.5	1	7561.5	1882.3	4.03
B(Input buffer)	721.3	2	360.6	89.8	3.18
C(Output buffer)	82.0	2	41.0	10.2	3.18
D(Traffic)	38905.1	3	12968.3	3228.2	2.79
Interactions:					
AD	301.1	3	100.4	25.0	2.79
BC	60.8	4	15.2	3.8	2.56
BD	117.8	6	19.6	4.9	2.29
Residual:	200.9	50	4.0	-	-
Total:	47950.3	71	675.4	-	-

Table 1: Variance analysis for the partially adaptive routing algorithm

Thus, the factor A is considered significant at a significance level if its computed F-ratio is greater than the value from the F-table [14, 4, 23, 21, 26] for this significance level. We have worked with a significance level of 95 %.

Table 1 shows the ANOVA results for the partially adaptive routing algorithm. Only the significant effects are shown. For the sake of shortness, we will not show the ANOVA table for the fully adaptive one.

When the effect of a factor is significant, it is necessary to analyze the nature of that effect. For instance, the effect of a three-level factor can be significant because the three levels lead to different average values of the response variable or because only one level has an impact on the response variable. A simple method proposed in [17, 26, 7] is to analyze the difference among average values corresponding to factor levels, building LSD (Least Significative Difference) intervals. This method is associated with the ANOVA procedure in statistical packages. Using these intervals, we can obtain two probabilistic bounds for each factor level. It must be emphasized that these intervals are not confidence intervals for the effects. They are obtained from the confidence intervals for the difference of two average values.

Once the LSD intervals have been represented, the difference between two levels is considered significant if their respective intervals (one for each factor level) do not overlap.

Next, the simulation results are presented. For the sake of clarity, the LSD intervals are only shown for the single effects. Figures 1, 2, 3, and 4 show the results for the partially and fully adaptive routing algorithm. In figures 1 and 3 single effects are shown, whereas figures 2 and 4 show double interactions of factor effects.

Applying the expression derived in section 3, clock

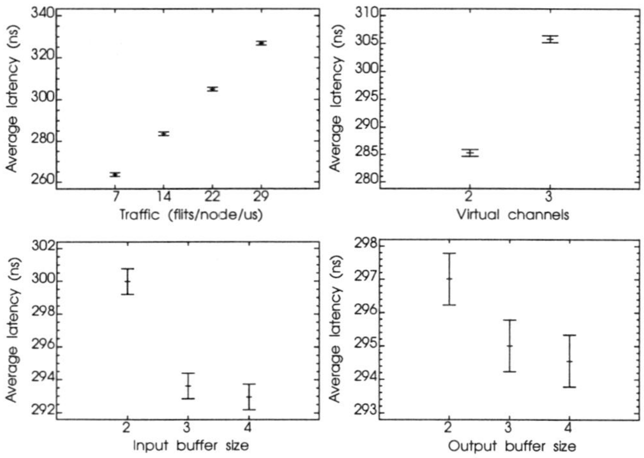

Figure 1: Single effects of factors on the latency for the partially adaptive algorithm

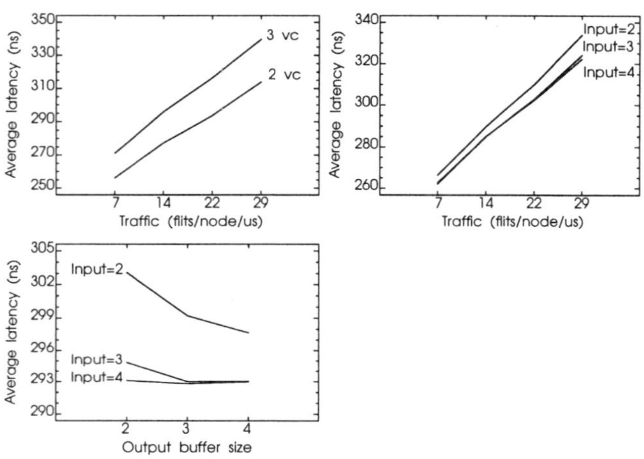

Figure 2: Double interactions of factor effects on the latency for the partially adaptive algorithm

period is 6.74 and 7.09 ns for the partially adaptive routing algorithm with 2 and 3 virtual channels per physical channel, respectively. For the fully adaptive routing algorithm, clock period is 7.49 and 8.3 ns for 3 and 4 virtual channels per physical channel, respectively.

Message latency increases with traffic. Both a positive and statistically significant linear and quadratic effects are detected. This effect is more pronounced in the case of the fully adaptive routing algorithm, because more values of traffic have been considered. For the partially adaptive routing algorithm, two virtual channels per physical channel is the best choice. In addition, this choice is the best for the full range of traffic analyzed. For the fully adaptive routing algorithm, the

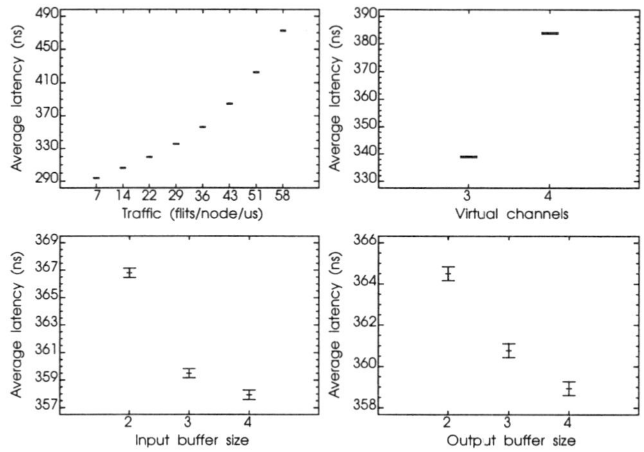

Figure 3: Single effects of factors on the latency for the fully adaptive algorithm

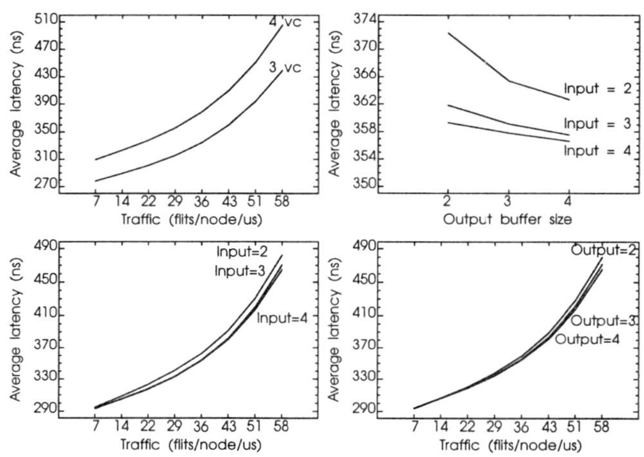

Figure 4: Double interactions of factor effects on the latency for the fully adaptive algorithm

optimal level for the number of virtual channels is also the minimum one. Although increasing the number of virtual channels adds routing flexibility, it also decreases clock frequency. For the network we analyzed, it is not interesting.

With respect to input and output buffering, the greater the size of the buffers, the lower message latency achieved, as it was obviously expected. In the partially adaptive routing algorithm the interactions plot between the input and output buffer size is very meaningful. When 4 flits input buffers are used, making output buffers deeper than 2 flits serves no purpose. It must be also noticed that there is not significant interaction between output buffer size and traffic. Therefore, it has not been shown. In the fully adaptive routing algorithm, there is little gain when buffer size is increased from three to four flits. Therefore, we conclude that three flit buffers can be used for input and output, for both routing algorithms.

Finally, it must be pointed out that an analysis of variance provides accurate results only if some hypotheses are satisfied: The observations must be independent, normally distributed and with constant variance. We have used the necessary techniques to verify these assumptions.

6 Conclusions

In a previous paper [20], we have proposed a statistical methodology to analyze interconnection network performance. Its advantages are twofold. In first place, running only a subset of the simulations required in a conventional evaluation study, network behavior can be estimated with a high degree of accuracy, saving time, resources, and, most important, design time. In second place, the methodology allows us to obtain with high precision the effects of each considered factor, and their interactions. Interactions are not easily obtained by conventional methods.

In this paper, we make use of the second advantage of this methodology to analyze the effects of some node design parameters such as number of virtual channels, input and output buffer sizes and their interactions for a 512-node 3D-torus with adaptive (both partially and fully) wormhole routing. A delay model has been considered for the multicomputer node.

Concerning virtual channels, two levels have been analyzed. Although increasing the number of virtual channels adds routing flexibility, it also decreases clock frequency. In our case, both routing algorithms achieve better performance when the minimum number of virtual channels per physical channel are used. Concerning buffer sizes, three levels have been analyzed, obtaining that the intermediate one (three flits) achieves the best cost-performance tradeoff. It must be noticed that the results could be different if another node model was considered.

References

[1] A. Agarwal, "Limits on interconnection network performance", *IEEE Trans. Parallel Distributed Syst.*, vol. 2, no. 4, pp. 398–412, Oct. 1991.

[2] W.C. Athas and C.L. Seitz, "Multicomputers: Message-passing concurrent computers," *IEEE Comput. Mag.*, vol. 21, no. 8, pp. 9–24, Aug. 1988.

[3] R.V. Bopana, and S. Chalasani, "A comparison of adaptive wormhole routing algorithms," in *Proc. 20th Annu. Int. Symp. Comput. Architecture*, May 1993.

[4] G.E. Box, W.G. Hunter and J.S. Hunter *Statistics for experimenters*, New York, Wiley, 1978.

[5] A.A. Chien and J.H. Kim, "Planar-adaptive routing: Low-cost adaptive networks for multiprocessors," in *Proc. 19th Annu. Int. Symp. Comput. Architecture*, May 1992.

[6] A.A. Chien, "A cost and speed model for k-ary n-cube wormhole routers," in *Proc. Hot Interconnects'93*, Aug. 1993.

[7] J.L. Coronado et al, *Estadística aplicada con statgraphics*, Madrid, Ra-ma, 1994.

[8] W.J. Dally and C.L. Seitz, "Deadlock-free message routing in multiprocessor interconnection networks," *IEEE Trans. Comput.*, vol. C-36, no. 5, pp. 547–553, May 1987.

[9] W.J. Dally, "Performance analysis of k-ary n-cube interconnection networks," *IEEE Trans. Computers*, Vol. C-39, No. 6, pp. 775-785, June 1990.

[10] W.J. Dally, "Network and processor architecture for message-driven computers", in R. Suaya and G. Birtwistle (ed), *VLSI and parallel computation*, Morgan Kauffman, pp. 140-222, 1990.

[11] W.J. Dally, "Virtual-channel flow control," *IEEE Trans. Parallel Distributed Syst.*, vol. 3, no. 2, pp. 194–205, Mar. 1992.

[12] J. Duato, "Deadlock-free adaptive routing algorithms for multicomputers: evaluation of a new algorithm," in *Proc. 3rd IEEE Int. Symp. Parallel Distributed Processing*, Dec. 1991.

[13] J. Duato and P. López, "Performance evaluation of adaptive routing algorithms for k-ary n-cubes," in *Proc. Parallel Computer Routing and Communication Workshop*, May 1994.

[14] R.A. Fisher, *The design of experiments*, Edimburg, Oliver Boyd, 1953.

[15] P.T. Gaughan and S. Yalamanchili, "Adaptive routing protocols for hypercube interconnection networks," *IEEE Comput. Mag.*, vol. 26, no. 5, pp. 12–23, May 1993.

[16] C.J. Glass and L.M. Ni, "The turn model for adaptive routing," in *Proc. 19th Annu. Int. Symp. Comput. Architecture*, May 1992.

[17] R. Jain, *The art of computer systems performance analysis*, New York, Wiley, 1991.

[18] C.R. Jesshope, P.R. Miller, and J.T. Yantchev, "High performance communications in processor networks," in *Proc. 16th Annu. Int. Symp. Comput. Architecture*, May–June 1989.

[19] P. López and J. Duato, "Deadlock-free adaptive routing algorithms for the 3D-torus: limitations and solutions," in *Proc. Parallel Architectures Languages Europe 93*, June 1993.

[20] P. López, R. Alcover, J. Duato and L. Zúnica, "A Methodology to Speed-up the Evaluation of Interconnection Networks", *IEEE Computer Society TCCA Newsletter*, August 1995, pp. 32–37.

[21] R. Mason, R.F. Gunst and J.L. Hess, *Statistical design and analysis of experiments*, New York, Wiley, 1989.

[22] J. Miguel, A. Arruabarrena, C. Izu, "Parallel simulation of message routing networks," *Proc. 3rd Euromicro Workshop in Parallel and Distributed Processing*, Jan. 1995.

[23] D.C. Montgomery, *Design and analysis of experiments*, New York, Wiley, 1984.

[24] P.K. McKinley, H. Xu, A. Esfahanian and L.M. Ni, "Unicast-based multicast communication in wormhole-routed networks," in *Proc. 1992 Int. Conf. Parallel Processing*, Aug. 1992.

[25] D. Peña, *Estadística, modelos y métodos*, Madrid, Alianza, 1992.

[26] R. Romero, L. Zúnica, *Estadística*, Valencia, SPUPV, 1994.

[27] H. Scheffé, *The analysis of variance*, New York, Wiley, 1959.

[28] S.L. Scott, J.R. Goodman, "The impact of pipelined channels on *k*-ary *n*-cube networks," *IEEE Comput. Mag.*, vol. 5, no. 1, pp. 2–16, Jan. 1994.

[29] G. Taguchi and Y.I. Wu, *Introduction to off-line quality control*, Central Japan Quality Control Association, 1984.

An Empirical Evaluation of Techniques for Parallel Discrete-Event Simulation of Interconnection Networks

José Miguel[1,2], Agustín Arruabarrena[2], Ramón Beivide[3] and José A.B. Fortes[1]

[1]School of Electrical and Computer Engineering
Purdue University
West Lafayette, IN 47907, USA

[2]Dep. de Arquitectura y Tecnología de Computadores
UPV/EHU
Apdo. 649
20080 San Sebastián, Spain

[3]Departamento de Electrónica
Universidad de Cantabria
Av. de los Castros s/n
39005 Santander, Spain

acpmialj@si.ehu.es, acparfra@si.ehu.es, beivide@ccucvx.unican.es, fortes@ecn.purdue.edu

Abstract

Three parallel discrete-event simulators—synchronous, conservative and optimistic—implemented on an Intel Paragon multicomputer are comparatively evaluated. Parallelism is achieved by model decomposition, distributing the simulation among a set of collaborative logical processes. The three simulators differ in the way those processes synchronize to obey causal restrictions in the simulation of events. Message passing network models are used to study these simulation alternatives. A set of experiments are carried out to understand how model parameters influence simulator performance. Experimental evidence leads to the conclusion that the optimistic simulator is not a viable tool for the analysis of this kind of models. The opposite conclusion applies to the other two: if the workload assigned to each logical process is above a certain threshold then the synchronization overhead is comparatively low and the simulators perform and scale well up to a large number of processors. Performance threshold is influenced by some parameters of the simulated model (size of the network, load level and message length), as well as by the number of processors used by the simulators.

J. Miguel is currently a Visiting Scholar at the School of Electrical and Computer Engineering, Purdue University.

This work has been done under the partial support of the CICYT, Spain, under contract TIC95-0378, and the National Science Foundation, USA, under grants MIP-9500673 and CDA-9015696.

1: Introduction

Computer simulation is often required to validate, verify or complement analytical models of complex systems. Multiprocessors offer the possibility of large-scale systems simulation as long as efficient parallel processing implementations are adopted. Out of three possible approaches, this paper identifies two efficient discrete-event based parallel simulation techniques for simulation of message passing torus interconnection networks. Experiments conducted on an Intel Paragon multicomputer provide the empirical basis of the conclusions of this paper.

In [8, 9] parallel simulation techniques were analyzed using very simplistic models as benchmarks: torus networks of FCFS servers, traversed by a fixed number of jobs. Four different simulators were used: sequential event-driven, sequential time-driven, parallel conservative event-driven (with deadlock avoidance via null messages) and parallel optimistic event-driven [2, 3, 4, 7]. For the models under consideration it was found in [8, 9] that speedups up to 10 could be obtained for the conservative simulator on a network of 16 transputers. The performance of the optimistic simulator was not such good, in part due to an inefficient implementation of the algorithm.

After this preliminary evaluation performed with a toy model, a realistic model was selected to work with. In [1] a fairly complete set of measurements of the characteristics of some interconnection networks can be found, obtained with a sequential simulator. A small set of these well-known models were selected to test the actual performance of the synchronous, conservative and optimistic parallel simulators working with a useful workload.

The details of the selected model can also be found in [1]. It is basically a torus network of message routing elements (routers). Each router (Figure 1) is connected to four neighbors and to a processing element, via bi-directional channels. All the messages have the same length. The flow-control mechanism is cut-through and, for this reason, message queues are needed, which are associated to each output channel. Operation of the network is assumed to be synchronous. It takes a *cycle* to move a flit from port/queue to port/queue, in the same or in different router. This means that timestamps of events are always integer values.

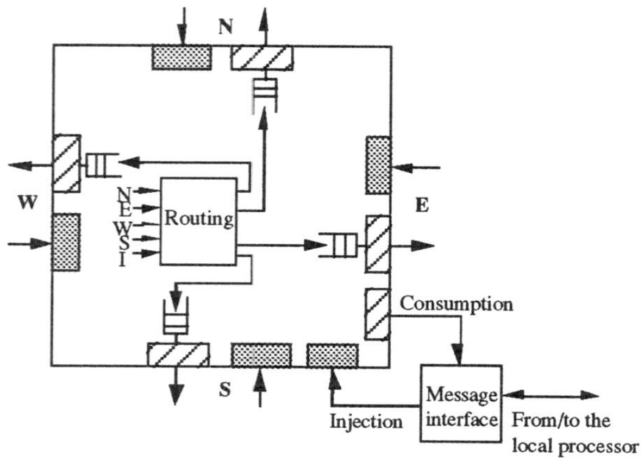

Figure 1. Model of message router.

Three parallel simulators have been implemented and tested on the Paragon multicomputer at Purdue University: CMB (Chandy-Misra-Bryant [2,3]), TW (Time Warp [7]) and SPED (Synchronous Parallel Event Driven [11]). They have in common the fact that parallelism is exploited by model decomposition: the model to simulate is divided into several parts, and each part is assigned to a Logical Process (LP). Those LPs can run concurrently, each one simulating its part of the whole. However, in order to maintain the causal relationships among the events in the simulation, a synchronization mechanism is needed. Here is where the three simulators differ.

The SPED simulator executes events in non-decreasing timestamp order. Only those events with the same timestamp are executed concurrently. The synchronous nature of SPED comes from the fact that all the LPs share the same vision of time, and they barrier-synchronize each time the simulation clock advances.

The other two simulators, CMB and TW, are asynchronous: each LP has its own local view of time. In order to perform a simulation that is globally correct, each LP needs to obey the following rule: execute all the incoming events in non-decreasing timestamp order. This rule is not easy to follow because, after executing a sequence of events, a new one might arrive from other LP, with a timestamp smaller than that of the last executed event, thus impeding the receiver LP to obey the stated rule. A CMB simulator never allows these situations to happen. To do so, LPs block before executing an event, until it is totally safe to proceed. This kind of synchronization is known as *conservative*. A TW simulator allows erroneous situations to arise, but those are detected and a *rollback* is done to jump to an error-free point in the (simulated) past. This kind of synchronization is known as *optimistic*.

A problem with CMB simulators is that the blocking synchronization mechanism can lead to the deadlocks. For this reason, CMB has to be enhanced with a method to resolve deadlocks. A deadlock avoidance mechanism based on an interchange of null messages [3] is used for this purpose.

The rest of the paper assumes that the reader has a knowledge of the above-mentioned synchronization mechanisms. A good source of information about the topic is [4].

The paper is structured as follows. First some general characteristics of the performed experimental work are described. The actual experiments carried out for the simulators evaluation are then described, followed by specific analysis of the results for each of the simulators: conservative (CMB), optimistic (TW) and synchronous (SPED). The paper ends with some conclusions.

2: Overview of the experiments

The performed set of experiments uses the following parameters of the model:

- *Message length*: 4 and 32-*flit* (flow-control digit) messages were considered. It is assumed that a flit advances from one router to another in one cycle (of simulated time).
- *Load of the network*: amount of information generated by the processing nodes, measured from 0 (none) to 100 (theoretical maximum). The maximum (100) corresponds to the bisection bandwidth (in flits) of the network, that is, to a situation where the channels of the network bisection are continuously utilized. A given load level can be reached with many short messages or with few long messages.
- *Size of the network*: most of the experiments assume a network of 16×16 routers, but some results for other network sizes are also reported.

Other parameters such as the size of the router queues, the communication patterns and the routing strategy were fixed, although they could be easily changed (if the purpose of the study was to analyze the model, instead of the simulators). The transit queues can hold 10 messages, while the injection queue has enough room for 4 messages. A random communication pattern was used: a node can send messages to any of the other nodes, with the same probability. The (time) separation between messages generated at a given node is exponentially distributed, with a mean that is directly proportional to the message length and inversely proportional to the network size and load. The routing strategy is oblivious in order of dimension (first X, then Y), following a technique described in [1, 6] to avoid communication deadlocks. This is needed because the topology is a torus.

To perform a parallel simulation the simulated network is divided into squares of the same size, and each square is assigned to a logical process. This means that each LP simulates an aggregate of routers, instead of only one. The size of the square depends on the number of available processing elements (PEs): exactly one LP is mapped onto each PE.

No special effort is done to exploit the lookahead ability of this model, for the case of CMB [4]. It is possible to obtain lookahead when a LP simulates just a model element (a router). However, when a LP simulates an aggregate of routers the obtained lookahead is very low and the potential benefit does not pay for the effort of computing it. Fortunately, a lookahead of 1 cycle is always available, so deadlocks are conveniently avoided.

A sequential event-driven simulator was also implemented, in order to have a reference point to assess the achieved performance of the parallel simulators under different configurations and workloads. After measuring the execution time of a sequential and a parallel simulation of the same model, a speedup figure can be computed. The model simulated by the sequential and parallel programs are basically the same but, in order to make fair comparisons, some optimizations were included in the sequential version, which take advantage of the use of a single memory space.

3: Experiments with CMB

This section presents the results of seven experiments performed with CMB. Table 1 summarizes the parameters used in the experiments: the first three parameters (network size, message length and load) are related to the model. The fourth is the number of processing elements (and, thus, of LPs) used by the simulator. The obtained results, in the form of speedup curves, are plotted in Figures 2, 3 and 4.

Before analyzing the results, the purpose of these experiments is described. Experiments **1P—4P** deal with a relatively small model of 16×16 routers, with message length 4 or 32, and running on 4 or 16 PEs. The goal was to confirm some results obtained in previous experiments with a toy model [9]. In particular, the objective was to test the following hypothesis:

1 The simulator scales well, that is, the speedup with 16 PEs is better than the speedup with 4 PEs. This should be confirmed by comparing **1P** with **2P**, and **3P** with **4P**.

2 Results are better with 4-flit messages than with 32-flit messages. With the same level of load, 4-flit messages means at least 8 times more simulation events than 32-flit messages. Execution times should be larger for the sequential and CMB simulators, but the latter will have more opportunities to self-synchronize without needing many null messages, reducing the synchronization overhead. This should be confirmed by comparing **1P** with **3P** and **2P** with **4P**.

3 Performance improves for higher loads. Again, the higher the load the larger the number of events managed by the simulator, giving more synchronization opportunities. This should be confirmed by the four experiments.

Experiments **5P** and **6P** deal with a model four times larger than that used in the previous set. The goal is to confirm that CMB performance improves with the imposed workload. In this case it is not necessary to use a synthetic workload (as was the case with the toy model), because the natural way of increasing the work performed by a LP is increasing the number of routers it simulates, and this is achieved simulating larger networks.

Experiment **7P** is a more complete scalability test. A medium-size model of 24×24 routers is simulated, using 4, 9, 16, 36 and 64 PEs.

For all the experiments the simulator ran for 4000 cycles. It should be noticed that some of these experiments are not well dimensioned for the Paragon. Execution times are very short (less than 3 seconds in some cases), and a minimum variation in the run time given by the system can result in a significant variation of speedup, so trends are more significant than actual values.

	1P	2P	3P	4P	5P	6P	7P
Network size	16×16	16×16	16×16	16×16	32×32	32×32	24×24
Message length	4	4	32	32	4	32	4
Load	5—90	5—90	5—90	5—90	5—90	5—90	50
Number of PEs	4	16	4	16	16	16	4—64

Table 1. Experiments performed with CMB-DA in the Paragon.

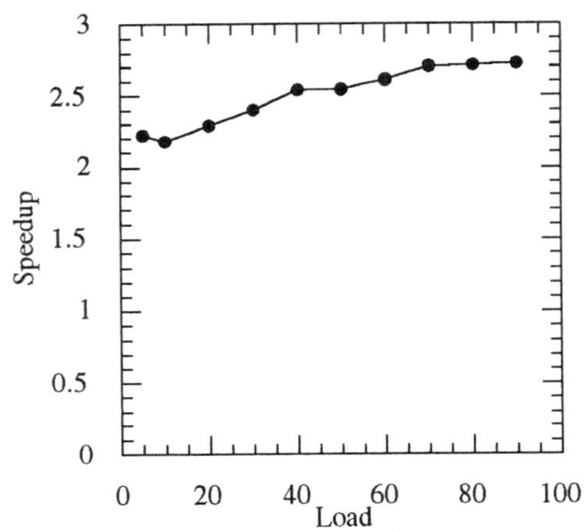

Experiment **1P**. 4-flit messages, 4 PEs

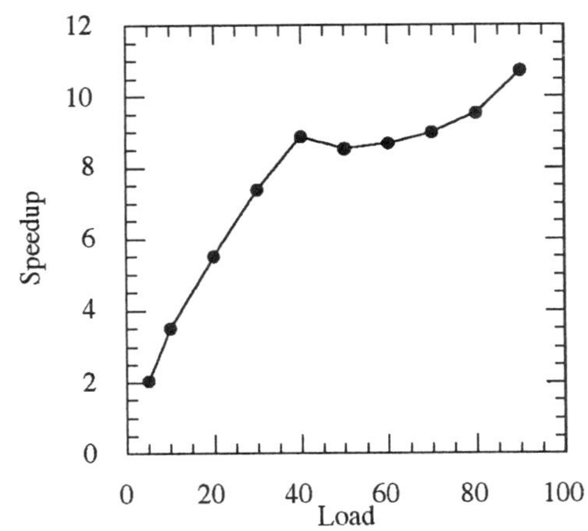

Experiment **2P**. 4-flit messages, 16 PEs

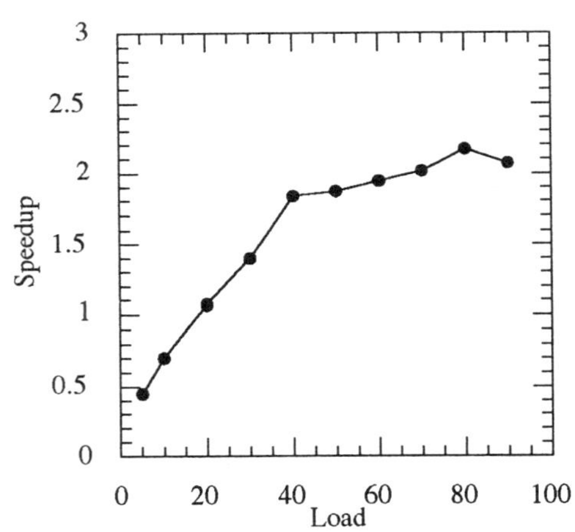

Experiment **3P**. 32-flit messages, 4 PEs

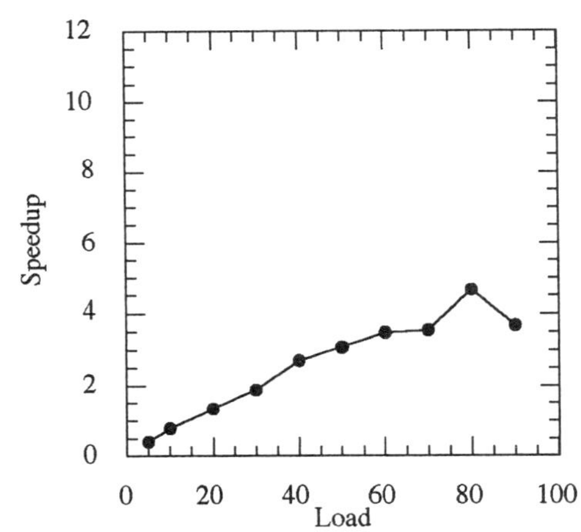

Experiment **4P**. 32-flit messages, 16 PEs

Figure 2. Results of experiments 1P—4P with CMB. Simulation of a network of 16×16 routers.

The results shown in Figures 2 and 3 confirm the initial hypothesis: the best performance is obtained with large, highly loaded models managing short messages. These scenarios are a challenge for sequential simulators, while CMB distributes the load quite evenly, effectively exploiting the available parallelism.

The results of experiment 7P, plotted in Figure 4 (right), shows that CMB scales very well, being the plot almost a straight line. The event density is high enough to keep all the PEs busy most of their time, even for the case of 64 PEs.

Figure 5 shows the contribution of computation and synchronization to LP execution time when running experiment **7P** with CMB. **Tsim** is the effective time performing simulations of events, plus the time needed to send non-null messages. **Trec** is the time spent receiving messages, useful or null. As the receive operation is blocking, Trec mainly accounts for the time LPs are awaiting for messages, not for the actual fact of reading a received message. **Thn** represents the time a LP spends sending null messages and checking if there is any message able to be consumed.

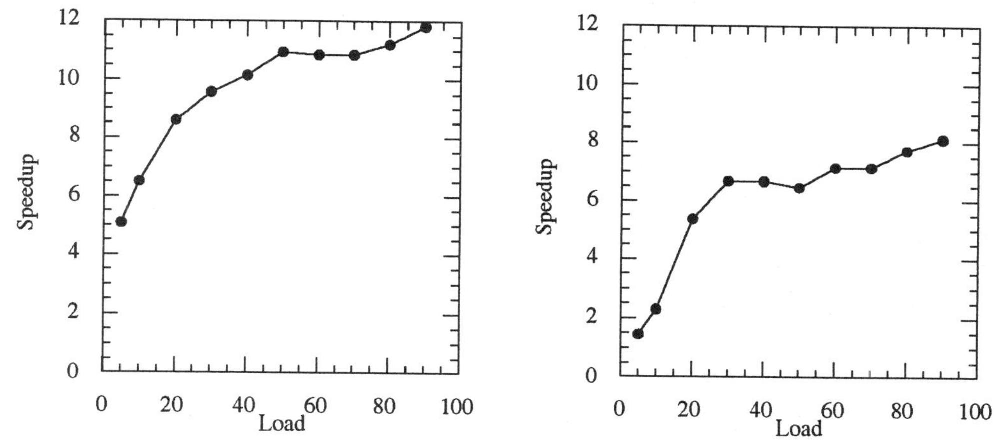

Experiment **5P**. 4-flit messages   Experiment **6P**. 32-flit messages

Figure 3. Results of experiments 5P and 6P with CMB. Simulation of a network of 32×32 routers in 16 PEs.

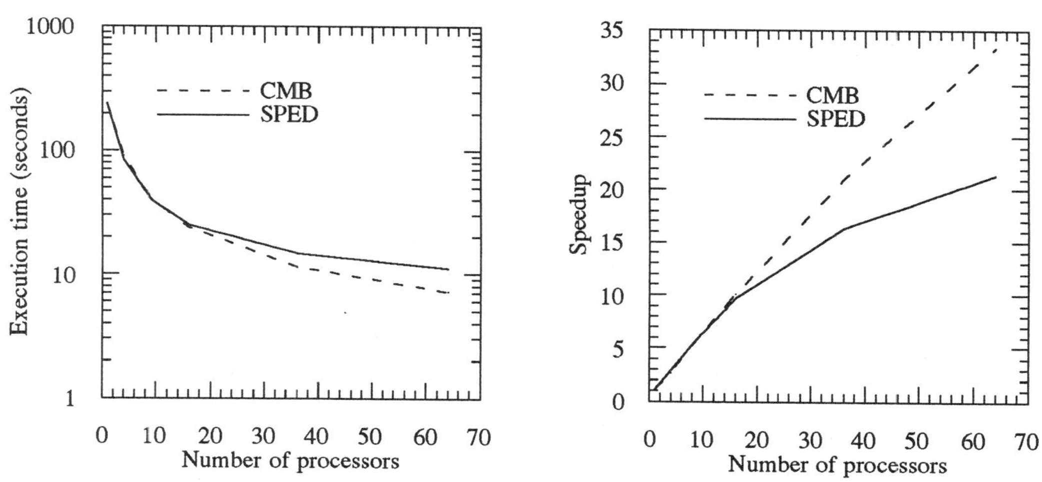

Figure 4. Execution times (left) and achieved speedups (right) of SPED and CMB running experiment 7P.

Clearly, if the model is distributed among a large number of LPs, the amount of work assigned to each LP decreases, and the synchronization demands increases. This can be seen very clearly in the Figure 5: when only 4 LPs are used, 85% of the execution time is simulation, and 15% is synchronization. When the number of LPs is increased to 64, these figures change to 55% and 45% respectively.

It is clear that if more PEs were utilized the proportion of synchronization time would increase, resulting in a performance degradation. However, for a big enough problem, it pays to use all the available PEs.

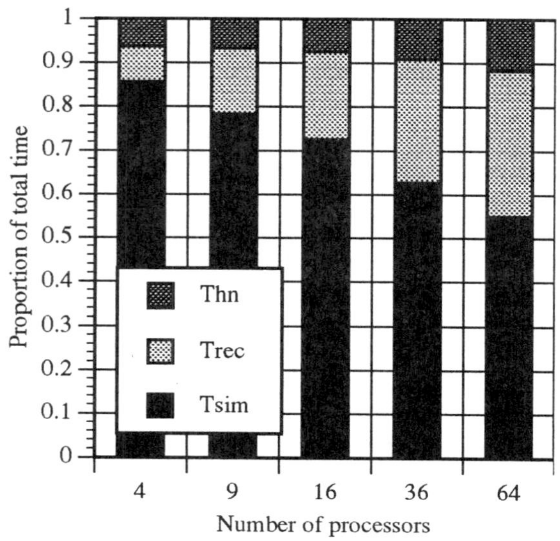

Figure 5. Distribution of the execution time of the LPs in CMB among simulation and synchronization.

4: Experiments with TW

Preliminary tests done with an implementation of TW using *conservative time windows* gave very poor performance figures, much worse than it was expected from [9]. This was (partly) caused by the large size of the state to be saved before executing each event: the state of the LP is the combination of all the state variables that represent the collection of routers assigned to the LP, plus a small number of variables for statistics gathering. This is excessive, because an event only modifies the state of one router, plus the statistics.

This fact led to the implementation of an optimization known as *incremental state saving*. Before executing an event, only the part of the state that is affected by that event is saved, making a copy of the full state only every N events. The interval N can be a static value or, as is the case for our implementation, dynamically adjusted. This optimization doubled execution speed, but performance remains inferior to that of CMB. In fact, for all the performed tests, the sequential simulator *was always much faster* that TW, independently of the number of PEs.

From this particular experience, it is concluded that TW is not a suitable approach to the study of the particular kind of model presented here. Execution monitoring revealed that almost all the events executed in a speculative way have to be undone. The result is that the simulator looses most of its time doing these "management" activities:

- Storing state copies and antimessages.
- Traversing the input queue to locate messages to annihilate, or to find the right place to insert a message belonging to the past.
- Coast-forwarding to reconstruct appropriate state versions.
- Sending and managing antimessages.
- Computing the global virtual time.

In the list of sources of overhead, insertion of future events and extraction of events to simulate, have not been included, because those activities have to be done in any simulator. However, as many of those insertions and extractions are speculative and have to be undone an done again, they also contribute to the overall overhead.

It is interesting to observe that, despite the good deal of effort devoted to the implementation of the TW simulator in a distributed memory environment, its performance remains discouragingly low. This seems to be an exception to the observations by Fujimoto in [5], one of the most comprehensive evaluations of TW: "*thus far, the experience of researchers (with TW) has been that (situations where most of the time is spent executing incorrect computations and rolling them back) are seldom encountered in practice, and, when discovered, usually points to a correctable flaw in the implementation rather than any fundamental flaw in the algorithm*". It should be mentioned that these observations were made in the context of a shared memory implementation of TW.

As also pointed out in [5], state saving overhead seems to be the root cause of this poor performance. Fujimoto concludes that "*State-saving overhead limits the effectiveness of TW to applications where the amount of computation required to process an event can be made significantly larger that the cost of saving a state vector.*" This is not the case for this particular application: the cost of executing an event is very low, while the state size is huge. Even when incremental state saving is used the amount of data moved for state saving is several times larger than the data moved to execute an event.

It can be concluded that TW is not a viable approach for the kind of parallel computer and the domain of models presented in this study. This must be said without implying that TW is not viable in any context: many references can be found in the literature that report successful application of this synchronization method, in different hardware platforms and with different problem domains.

5: Experiments with SPED

After performing a series of experiments with the SPED simulator in the Paragon, it was observed that it behaves very much like CMB, with only a significant difference: SPED degrades sooner when the load of the LPs is reduced. Figure 4 (left) shows the execution time of these two simulators when running experiment **7P** (see Table 1). The scale is logarithmic to better appreciate the differences. Figure 4 (right) shows the speedups achieved by both simulators as a function of the number of PEs. For small number of PEs, SPED performs slightly better than CMB. However, when the number of PEs increases (and, therefore, the workload of each LP decreases) CMB performs better than SPED.

Figure 6 shows the contribution of computation and synchronization to LP execution time when running experiment **7P** with SPED. **Tsim** is the time devoted to simulate events and send messages. **Trec** is the time spent awaiting and receiving messages. **Tbar** is the time spent barrier-synchronizing. The Figure is self-explanatory: the problem size of experiment **7P** is large enough to keep 4 PEs busy most of the time but, when distributed along 64 nodes, each node needs most of its time for synchronization (60%), performing useful computation only a 40% of the time.

An experiment like **7P**, but simulating a network of 90×90 nodes, has also been done with SPED and CMB. The results indicate that, for this case, SPED performs slightly better than CMB, even using 100 Paragon PEs, and that both simulators scale equally well. The reason is that for this size of model the workload is large enough to keep all the LPs busy, performing useful computation most of the time and minimizing the (relative) effort devoted to synchronization.

The number of barriers executed by the LPs was observed to be 4000 in all the cases, that is, as many barriers as simulation cycles. The reason for this is simple: the density of events is big enough to have always at least one event per cycle. Only for some particular cases with small models and very low loads (less than 5) the number of barriers was found to be less than the number of cycles.

A good characteristic of this simulator is that obtains reasonable speedups using a very simple algorithm, without the complicated memory management strategies of TW, and without some the restrictions of CMB (no cycles with zero timestamp increment).

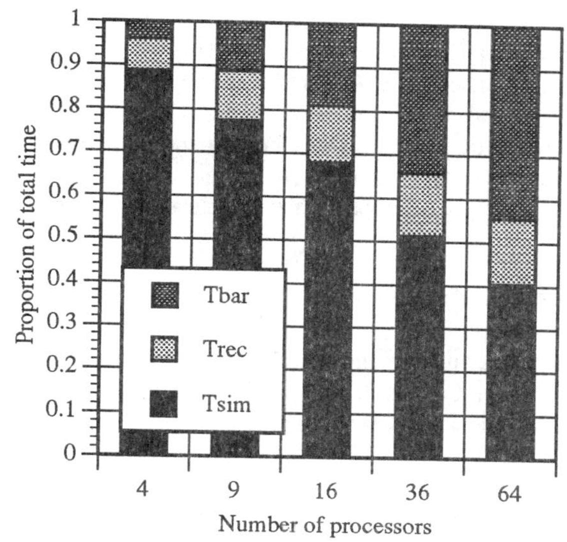

Figure 6. Distribution of the execution time of the LPs in SPED among simulation and synchronization.

6: Conclusions

In this paper a comparative experimental evaluation of three parallel discrete-event simulators for the study a model of a message passing network has been presented. The knowledge obtained from previous experiments with a toy model has been applied, when possible, to this, more realistic, model.

In general, preliminary ideas on which characteristics of the simulated model help to improve the performance of the conservative parallel simulator have been confirmed. In order to take advantage of CMB, a model with a high degree of internal communication is needed, which allows processes to remain synchronized without needing null messages. In the model used in this study, this happens when network size is large, load is high and messages are short. These three parameters have the strongest influence in the performance of the simulator. It is interesting to observe that, conveniently, the best scenario for the CMB simulator is the worst for the sequential event-driven simulator: speedups are best precisely when they are most needed, and are poor only in cases where simulation runs are very short in the sequential but also in the parallel version.

The experience with optimistic synchronization has been quite discouraging. The performance of the tested TW implementation is very poor, even after introducing a series of optimizations. The conclusion is that TW is not the right tool for the kind of study presented here.

Finally, the experience with SPED, the synchronous parallel simulator, has been very positive. It performs worse than CMB only for very lowly loaded systems, being as efficient as CMB (or even more efficient) for medium and highly loaded systems. It has the additional advantage of a more simple implementation, and can be used in environments were CMB is not applicable because of the presence of loops with zero timestamp increment.

Acknowledgments

Many thanks to the personnel at Purdue University Computing Center, Research Computing Division, for their technical support using the Paragon.

References

[1] Arruabarrena A. 1993. *Análisis y evaluación de sistemas de interconexión para procesadores masivamente paralelos*. PhD Dissertation, Dept. of Computer Architecture and Technology, University of the Basque Country.

[2] Bryant, R.E. 1977. *Simulation of packet communications architecture computer systems*. MIT-LCS-TR-188, Massachusetts Institute of Technology.

[3] Chandy, K.M. and Misra, J. 1979. "distributed simulation: a case study in design and verification of distributed programs" *IEEE Transactions on Software Engineering SE-5*, no. 5 (Sept.), 440—452.

[4] Fujimoto, R.M. 1990. "Parallel discrete event simulation". *Comm. of the ACM 33*, no. 10 (Oct.) 31—53.

[5] Fujimoto, R.M. 1990 "Optimistic approaches to parallel discrete event simulation". *Trans. of The Society for Comp. Simulation*, Vol. 7, No. 2, 153—191.

[6] Izu, C. 1994. *Análisis, evaluación y aportaciones al diseño de arquitecturas para encaminadores de mensajes*. PhD Dissertation, Dept. of Computer Architecture and Technology, University of the Basque Country.

[7] Jefferson, D.R. 1985. "Virtual time". *ACM Trans. on Programming Languages and Systems 7*, no. 3 (July) 405—425.

[8] Miguel, J.; Arruabarrena A. and Beivide, R. 1993. "Conservative parallel discrete event simulation in a transputer-based multicomputer". In *Transputer Applications and Systems '93*. R. Grebe et al. (Eds.) IOS Press, 636—650.

[9] Miguel, J.; Arruabarrena A. and Beivide, R. 1994. "Conservative and optimistic distributed simulation in massively parallel computers: a comparative study." In *Proc. of the Conference on Massively Parallel Computing Systems MPCS'94* (Ischia, Italy, Sept.), 528—532.

[10] Miguel, J.; Arruabarrena, A. and Beivide, R. 1995. "Parallel simulation of message routing networks". In *Proc. 3rd. Euromicro Workshop on Parallel and Distributed Processing PDP'95* (San Remo, Italy, Jan.), 138—145.

[11] Soulé, L. 1992. Parallel logic simulation: an evaluation of centralized-time and distributed-time algorithms. PhD dissertation. Stanford Univ. Technical Report CSL-TR-92-527.

A New Efficient Submesh Allocation Strategy for Mesh Multicomputers*

Geunmo Kim Jinchun Kim Hyunsoo Yoon

Department of Computer Science
Korea Advanced Institute of Science & Technology (KAIST)
Taejon, 305-701, Korea

Abstract

The submesh allocation problem is to recognize and locate a free submesh that can accommodate a request for a submesh of a specified size. This paper proposes a new best-fit submesh allocation strategy. The proposed strategy maintains and uses a free submesh list to get global information for free submeshes. For an allocation request, the proposed strategy tries to allocate a best-fit submesh which causes the least amount of potential fragmentation so as to preserve the large free submeshes as many as possible and to prevent processor fragmentation for later requests. For this purpose, we introduce a novel function for quantifying the degree of potential fragmentation of submeshes. The proposed strategy has the complete submesh recognition capability. Extensive simulation is carried out to compare the proposed strategy with the previous strategies and experimental results indicate that the proposed strategy exhibits the best performance along with about 30% average improvement over the best previous strategy.

1 Introduction

The mesh has been drawing considerable attention as a topology of multicomputer due to its simple, regular, and scalable structure. Based on this topology, several prototypes and commercial systems have been built or marketed, such as Intel Touchstone Delta [1], Intel Paragon XP/S [2], Tera Computer System [3], Fujitsu AP-100 [4], Sanyo Edden/Cyberflow System [4], Parsytec GC [5], and PASM [6].

In a mesh multicomputer supporting multitasking environment, numerous parallel tasks can be assigned to independent submeshes and executed simultaneously. A host computer connected to the mesh multicomputer is responsible for allocating submeshes to incoming tasks and releasing them on completion of tasks for later use. Since tasks request the submeshes of various sizes, efficient submesh allocation, in order to make the mesh system to accommodate as many tasks as possible, is an important issue for achieving high performance on a mesh multicomputer.

The goal of submesh allocation is to maximize processor utilization by minimizing *fragmentation* — *internal* and *external*. Internal fragmentation occurs if a larger submesh is allocated to a task than that is required. External fragmentation occurs when even if a sufficient number of processors are available, they do not form a submesh large enough to accommodate the incoming request. External fragmentation also occurs when allocation strategy cannot recognize some available submeshes because the strategy dose not have complete recognition capability. Such fragmentation results in the degradation of system utilization.

In the last few years, several submesh allocation strategies have been reported in the literature [7, 8, 9, 10, 11]. These strategies are classified into two approaches, *first-fit* and *best-fit*. In the first-fit approach [7, 8, 9, 10], submeshes are searched in a fixed sequence and the first free submesh is allocated. On the other hand, the best-fit approach [9, 11] is intended to allocate an appropriate submesh by considering the contributions of submeshes to the external fragmentation for the mesh system. All the strategies except [7] can successfully eliminate internal fragmentation by allocating the submesh of the exact size requested. These strategies, however, quite suffer from external fragmentation resulted from the nature of their allocation policies — incomplete recognition capability and/or first-fit behavior. To solve this problem, a best-fit strategy with complete recognition capability is proposed recently [11], and this strategy shows better performance than all the previous strategies. This strategy, however, has the drawback that it is only applicable to somewhat specific situations owing to the limitation of its heuristic.

In this paper, we propose a new best-fit submesh allocation strategy with complete recognition capability, called *Free Submesh List* (*FSL*) strategy. The proposed strategy maintains and uses a free submesh list keeping all of the different free submeshes available in the system. The basic idea of our approach is to allocate a submesh which can preserve the large free submeshes as many as possible and to maintain the high availability of the wide range of submeshes, for later tasks. This approach would be able to reduce the external fragmentation, especially prevent the 'unnecessary' external fragmentation occurring by an inefficient allocation. From simulation study, the proposed strategy

*This work was supported in part by *Center for Artificial Intelligence Research* in KAIST.

achieves about 30% average improvement over the best previous strategy. While the proposed strategy can be easily extended to the meshes of higher dimensions, our discussion here is limited to the two-dimensional meshes, for simplicity.

Section 2 presents notations and definitions used by the proposed strategy. Section 3 introduces the proposed strategy. Presented and discussed in Section 4 are the simulation results. Conclusion is given in Section 5.

2 Preliminaries

A two dimensional mesh $M(L_X, L_Y)$ is an $L_X \times L_Y$ rectangular grid which consists of $L_X \cdot L_Y$ nodes. A *node* in a mesh system refers to a processor. So the terms *node* and *processor* are used interchangeably in this paper. A node in a mesh is identified by its coordinate $< x, y >$ from the lower-leftmost position $< 0,0 >$ of the mesh, where $0 \leq x \leq L_X - 1$ and $0 \leq y \leq L_Y - 1$. Fig. 2 presents a 10×10 mesh.

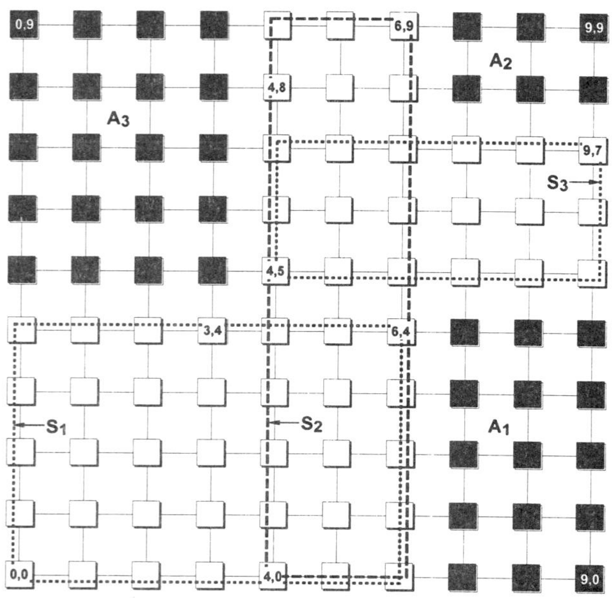

Fig. 1. Example of a 10×10 **mesh** $M(10, 10)$

A *submesh* $S(l_x, l_y)$ in the mesh $M(L_X, L_Y)$, $1 \leq l_x \leq L_X$ and $1 \leq l_y \leq L_Y$, is an $l_x \times l_y$ rectangular grid which belongs to $M(L_X, L_Y)$ with $l_x \cdot l_y$ nodes. The address of a submesh is denoted by a quadruple ($< x, y >, < x', y' >$), where $< x, y >$ indicates its lower-leftmost coordinate and $< x', y' >$ its upper-rightmost one. A *free submesh* is a submesh in which all the processors are currently free. An *allocated submesh* is a submesh in which all the processors are currently allocated to a task. For example, $S_1(< 3,0 >, < 9,4 >)$ in Fig. 2 denotes a free submesh of 7×5 and $A_1(< 0,8 >, < 2,9 >)$ an allocated submesh of 3×2. We specify a incoming request for a submesh of size $a \times b$ or $b \times a$ by (a, b).

Definition 1 A free submesh is said to be *dominant* if it is not covered by (i.e., not a submesh of) any other free submeshes. Dominant free submeshes may not be disjoint each other, that is, they may share common regions (said to be *overlapping*).

Definition 2 The *free submesh list* (*FSL*) is a sorted list of dominant free submeshes in non-increasing order of size, i.e., the number of nodes. If two free submeshes are of the same size, one of them closer to square submesh is prior to the other.

In a 10×10 mesh as shown in Fig. 2, for example, there are three dominant free submeshes, $S_1(< 0,0 >, < 6,4 >)$, $S_2(< 4,0 >, < 6,9 >)$, and $S_3(< 4,5 >, < 9,7 >)$ of sizes $35(7 \times 5)$, $30(3 \times 10)$, and $18(6 \times 3)$, respectively. In this case, FSL is sorted in sequence S_1, S_2, and S_3, from the largest free submesh to the smallest one.

Definition 3 For an request (a, b), a *candidate submesh* is a free submesh of size $a \times b$ or $b \times a$.

Definition 4 The *reservation factor* of a submesh $S(< x_1, y_1 >, < x_2, y_2 >)$ against a submesh $S'(< x'_1, y'_1 >, < x'_2, y'_2 >)$ of size $l'_x \times l'_y$ is referred to $rf(S, S')$ and is defined as the size of the largest submesh formed from S' except the overlapping region as follows (see Fig. 2):

$$rf(S,S') = \begin{cases} max\{\ (x_1 - x'_1) \cdot l'_y,\ (x'_2 - x_2) \cdot l'_y, \\ \quad l'_x \cdot (y_1 - y'_1),\ l'_x \cdot (y'_2 - y_2)\ \}, \\ \quad\quad if\ S\ and\ S'\ are\ overlapping, \\ l'_x \cdot l'_y\ (=\ size\ of\ S'), \quad otherwise. \end{cases}$$

where $max\{*\}$ is a function that returns the largest non-negative value.

In Fig. 2, $rf(S_2(< 4,0 >, < 6,9 >), S_1(< 0,0 >, < 6,4 >)) = 20\ (= max\{\ 4 \cdot 5,\ 0,\ 0,\ -5 \cdot 7\ \})$, since the largest submesh constructed from S_1 except the overlapping region $(< 4,0 >, < 6,4 >)$ is $(< 0,0 >, < 3,4 >)$ of size 4×5.

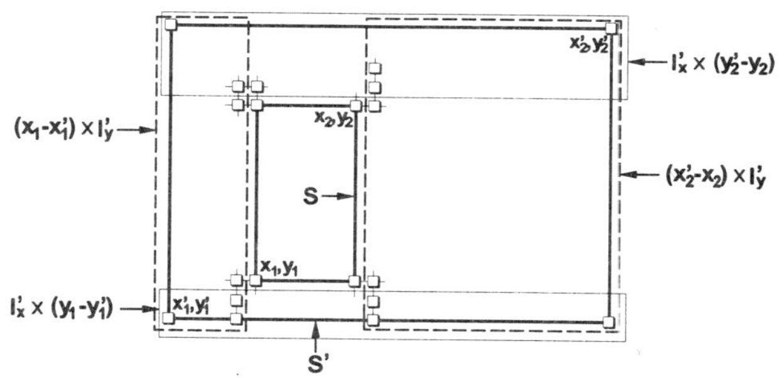

Fig. 2. Reservation Factor : Reserved Submeshes by S

3 The Proposed Strategy

In the following, we propose a new best-fit allocation strategy with complete recognition capability based on the FSL. The proposed strategy uses the *rf* to estimate the potential external fragmentation of candidate submeshes and allocates the candidate with the largest *rf*'s against all the free submeshes. The proposed strategy offers the best solution to date which can effectively reduce the external fragmentation.

3.1 Allocation Algorithm

For an allocation request (a, b), first, the proposed allocation algorithm generates candidate submeshes of the size either $a \times b$ or $b \times a$ from four corners of free submeshes in FSL. Consider a free submesh $S(<x_1, y_1>, <x_2, y_2>)$ in FSL accommodating the request. As shown in Fig. 3 (a), candidate submeshes of types $a \times b$ and/or $b \times a$ can be generated at each corner of S. One approach, we adopt, is to consider only the candidates of a type with the larger rf value against S when candidates of both types can be generated. Although many other candidate submeshes may be possible, considering only the above candidates is sufficient because, with regard to the submesh S, they have the largest rf value and conserve the largest submeshes than any other candidates. This approach is expected to cause less external fragmentation in the choice of candidate submeshes by preventing the large free submesh from being fragmented to several smaller submeshes. Fig. 3 (b) presents all candidate submeshes for the request (3,2) on the case of Fig. 2, where C_k^* denote candidate submeshes originated from the free submesh S_k in Fig. 2.

On the completion of generating candidate submeshes, the algorithm evaluates the rf of each candidate submesh against the first free submesh of FSL and then rejects candidate submeshes except those which have the largest rf value, and, evaluates candidate submeshes not rejected against the second free submesh of FSL and then rejects candidate submeshes except those which have the largest rf value, and, so on. The rf is used for evaluating the potential external fragmentation of candidate submeshes. The candidate submesh with large rf values can conserve larger free submeshes than the one with small rf values. Since the free submeshes in FSL are sorted in non-increasing order of size, the above evaluation process using rf chooses the candidate submesh reserving free submeshes as large as possible for later tasks. This may prevent 'unnecessary' external fragmentation and alleviate the overall external fragmentation. For example, suppose in Fig. 3 (b) that the two tasks $t_1 = (3, 2)$ and $t_2 = (7, 5)$ are submitted to the system in that order. If either one of C_1^* or C_2^1 is allocated to the task t_1, the subsequent task t_2 cannot be allocated due to the external fragmentation. This is an instance of 'unnecessary' external fragmentation arising because of an inefficient allocation. On the other hand, allocating one of C_2^2 or C_3^* to the task t_1 can accommodate the task t_2 in the submesh $(<0, 0>, <6, 4>)$. In this case, the proposed algorithm allocates C_3^2 to the task t_1, since C_3^2 has the largest rf values against all the free submeshes (see Example 1).

After the evaluation for the candidates, if two or more candidates are remained, the algorithm performs the evaluation for the candidates against the entire mesh $(<0, 0>, <L_X - 1, L_Y - 1>)$. The rf value of a candidate against the entire mesh indicates the

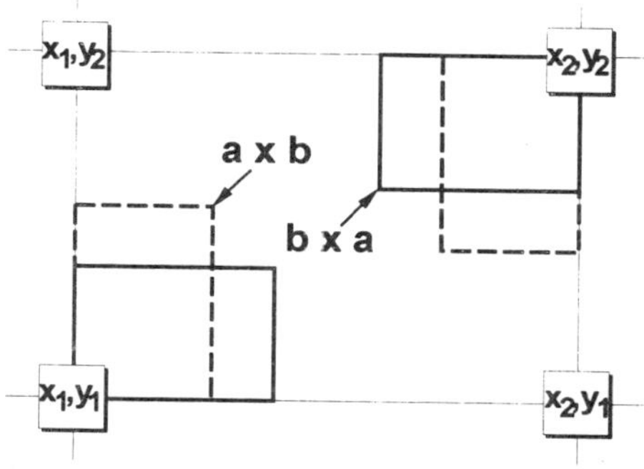

(a)

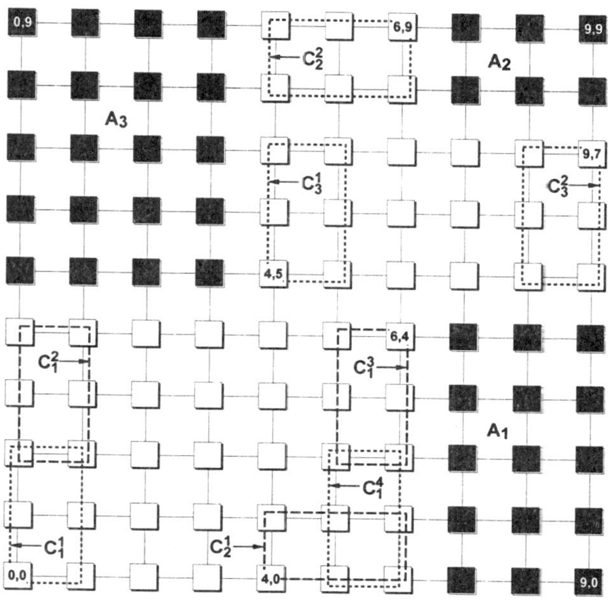

(b)

Fig. 3. (a) Candidate submeshes from a free submesh for the request (a, b). (b) Candidate Submeshes for the request (3,2)

size of a potential free submesh reserved by the candidate. The algorithm chooses the candidate which has the largest rf value, so that the already allocated submeshes on being released may be merged each other or together with free submeshes into large free submesh(es). The formal allocation algorithm is presented in Fig. 3.1. The symbols used by the algorithm means that: *cand_list* denotes the list of candidate submeshes being considered; *free_list* denotes FSL, the list of free submeshes; *alloc_list* denotes the list of allocated submeshes; *best* denotes the best candidate submesh. The following example illustrates allocation process for a request (3,2) in the situation of Fig. 2.

Example 1 Initially, FSL = $\{S_1, S_2, S_3\}$. The algorithm, from free submeshes S_1, S_2, and S_3, generates candidate submeshes $\{C_1^1, C_1^2, C_1^3, C_1^4, C_2^1, C_2^2, C_3^1, C_3^2\}$ as shown in Fig. 3 (b). Then, the algorithm

```
Alloc( a, b ) /* Request (a, b) */
{
/* Step 1 */   cand_list = φ;
               for all free submesh S ∈ free_list do
                   if (S can accommodate the request a × b or b × a)
                     Generate candidate submeshes from the four corners of S and
                     store them to cand_list;
               if (cand_list == φ)
                  Stop and wait until a submesh is released;
/* Step 2 */   for all free submesh S ∈ free_list do {
                   Evaluate the rf of each candidate submesh in cand_list against S;
                   Reject candidate submeshes except those which have the largest rf value;
                   if (There is only one candidate submesh in cand_list)
                     Assign it to best and goto Step 3;
               }
               Select the candidate submesh which has the largest rf value against the mesh
               (< 0,0 >, < L_X − 1, L_Y − 1 >) and assign it to best;
/* Step 3 */   for all free submesh S ∈ free_list do
                   if (S is overlapping with best) {
                     Delete S from free_list;
                     Generate new submeshes by decomposing S and
                     insert them into free_list if they are dominant submeshes;
                   }
               Allocate submesh best to the request and insert it into alloc_list;
}
```

Fig. 4. Allocation Algorithm

evaluates the rf's of candidate submeshes against the first free submesh S_1: $rf(C_1^1, S_1) = rf(C_1^2, S_1) = 25$ (= size of $(< 2,0 >, < 6,4 >)$ of 5×5), $rf(C_1^3, S_1) = rf(C_1^4, S_1) = 25$ (= size of $(< 0,0 >, < 4,4 >)$ of 5×5), $rf(C_2^1, S_1) = 21$ (= size of $(< 0,2 >, < 6,4 >)$ of 7×3), and, $rf(C_2^2, S_1) = rf(C_3^1, S_1) = rf(C_3^2, S_1) =$ **35** (= size of S_1). Excepting candidate submeshes C_2^2 and C_3^* with the largest rf value of 35, the algorithm rejects other candidate submeshes. Again, the algorithm evaluates the rf's of candidates C_2^2 and C_3^* against the second free submesh S_2: $rf(C_2^2, S_2) = 24$ (= size of $(< 4,0 >, < 6,7 >)$ of 3×8), $rf(C_3^1, S_2) = 15$ (= size of $(< 4,0 >, < 6,4 >)$ of 3×5), and, $rf(C_3^2, S_2) =$ **30** (= size of S_2). The algorithm rejects C_2^2 and C_3^1. Now that only one candidate submesh C_3^2 remains (which is the best under the current situation), the algorithm does not perform evaluation for the third free submesh S_3. In step 3, because S_3 is overlapping with the best candidate C_3^2, the algorithm decomposes S_3 into free region(s) and an allocated one, and generates a submesh $(< 4,5 >, < 7,7 >)$ (denoted as S'). Since S' is a dominant submesh, S' is inserted into FSL and finally FSL = $\{S_1(< 0,0 >, < 6,4 >), S_2(< 4,0 >, < 6,9 >), S'(< 4,5 >, < 7,7 >)\}$.

3.2 Deallocation Algorithm

Once a submesh is released after the corresponding task is completed, the deallocation algorithm starts from the initial mesh $(< 0,0 >, < L_X - 1, L_Y - 1 >)$ and generates a new set of dominant free submeshes by decomposing the initial mesh with the allocated submeshes. Fig. 3.2 describes the deallocation algorithm. For a released submesh R, first (step 1), if FSL (*free_list*) is empty, the released submesh is inserted into FSL; otherwise, if the allocation list (*alloc_list*) is empty, all the submeshes in FSL are removed and FSL is set to the initial list $\{(< 0,0 >, < L_X - 1, L_Y - 1 >)\}$ because all the nodes of mesh system are free. Otherwise, that is, if both FSL and the allocation list are not empty, FSL is set to the initial list $\{(< 0,0 >, < L_X - 1, L_Y - 1 >)\}$, and the algorithm decomposes submesh(es) in FSL for all the allocated submeshes in the allocation list with the same way as in step 3 of allocation algorithm. After completion of step 2, FSL is set to the dominant free submeshes including all the nodes of the released submesh R.

Example 2 Consider the situation of Fig. 2 again. Initially, FSL = $\{S_1, S_2, S_3\}$ and *alloc_list* = $\{A_1, A_2, A_3\}$. When the allocated submesh A_3 is released, A_3 is removed from *alloc_list*, and *alloc_list* = $\{A_1, A_2\}$. In step 2, FSL is reset to the initial state $\{S(< 0,0 >, < 9,9 >)\}$. For the allocated submesh A_1, S is decomposed into two submeshes S_1' and S_2' as shown in Fig. 3.2, and so FSL = $\{S_1'(< 0,0 >, < 6,9 >), S_2'(< 0,5 >, < 9,9 >)\}$. For the allocated submesh A_2, since S_2' is overlapping with A_2, S_2' is removed from FSL and is decomposed into two free submeshes $S_3'(< 0,5 >, < 9,7 >)$ and $S_4'(< 0,5 >, < 6,9 >)$.

```
Dealloc( R ) /* R is a released submesh */
{
/* Step 1 */  if (free_list == φ) { free_list = {R};  return; }
              if (alloc_list == φ) { free_list = {(< 0,0 >, < L_X − 1, L_Y − 1 >)};  return; }
/* Step 2 */  free_list = {(< 0,0 >, < L_X − 1, L_Y − 1 >)};
              for all allocated submesh S ∈ alloc_list do
              for all free submesh S' ∈ free_list do
                 if (S is overlapping with S') {
                    Delete S' from free_list and generate new submeshes by decomposing S';
                    Insert the new submeshes into free_list if they are currently dominant;
                 }
}
```

Fig. 5. Deallocation Algorithm

Since S'_3 is dominant and S'_4 is covered by S'_1, S'_3 is inserted into FSL and finally FSL $= \{S'_1(<0,0>,<6,9>), S'_3(<0,5>,<9,7>)\}$.

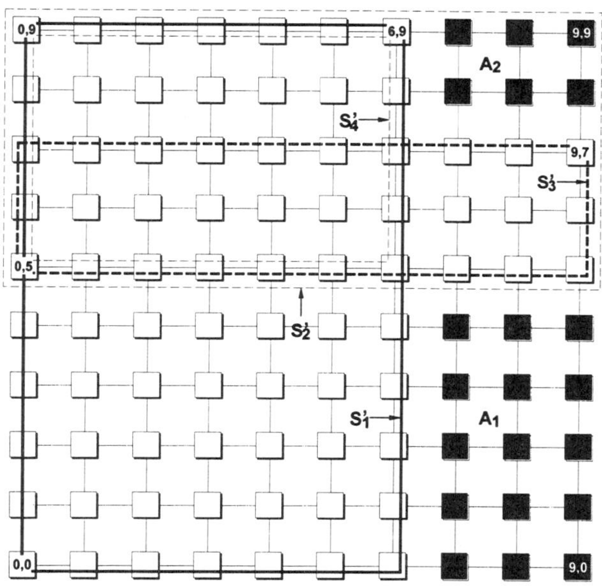

Fig. 6. Example of Deallocation Algorithm

3.3 Algorithm Analysis

We first analyze the time complexity of the allocation algorithm in the worst case. In step 1, if we assume that the number of free submeshes in FSL is N_f, candidate submeshes can be generated from at most N_f free submeshes. The time complexity of step 1 is $O(N_f)$. In step 2, at most $4 \cdot N_f$ candidate submeshes are evaluated for N_f submeshes in FSL. So step 2 has the time complexity of $O(N_f^2)$. In step 3, N_f submeshes in FSL may be overlapping with the *best* submesh, and they are decomposed into at most four free submeshes which are inserted into FSL if they are dominant. The time complexity of step 3 is $O(N_f^2)$. Therefore, the allocation algorithm takes $O(N_f^2)$ time complexity in the worst case.

Let us analyze the time complexity of the deallocation algorithm in the worst case. The time complexity of step 1 is $O(1)$ when either FSL or the allocation list is empty. In step 2, if we assume that the number of allocated submeshes in *alloc_list* is N_a, then from the following theorem, the maximum number of dominant free submeshes (N_f) is less than $4 \cdot N_a$. Since the time complexity of the body of *if*-statement of step 2 is $O(N_f)$, that of step 2 is $O(N_a \cdot N_f^2) = O(N_a^3)$. Therefore, the deallocation algorithm takes $O(N_a^3)$ time complexity.

Theorem 1 *If there exist $k(\geq 1)$ allocated submeshes in a mesh, then the maximum number of dominant free submeshes is less than or equal to $4 \cdot k$.*

Proof. If k allocated submeshes exist in a mesh, the mesh can be divided into k arbitrary independent (i.e., non-overlapped) regions (submeshes), each of which must include only one allocated submesh. Then, each region includes at most four free submeshes, each of which may not be really a dominant free submesh. If a free submesh in a region is not a dominant free submesh, it is a part (submesh) of a dominant free submesh. Since there exist at most $4 \cdot k$ free submeshes in k regions and a dominant free submesh may be counted more than once if it is divided into the parts of one or more regions, the maximum number of dominant free submeshes is less than or equal to $4 \cdot k$. ■

4 Simulation Study

Two previous strategies, the Busy-List[1] and AS strategies, are compared with our FSL strategy, since they show the better performance than any other strategies [10, 11]. The workload considered on sim-

[1] The source code of the busy-list strategy was provided by D.D.Sharma and D.K.Pradhan [11].

ulation is characterized by the distributions of job arrival, job size (submesh size), and job residence (service) time. The job arrival pattern is assumed to follow Poisson distribution with an arrival rate λ. The job residence time is assumed to follow exponential distribution with a given mean residence time. The job size (the side lengths of submesh) is assumed to follow a given distribution: *uniform*, *normal*, and *exponential*. Under normal distribution, the mean of each side length were selected as $(1 + L_X)/2$ and $(1 + L_Y)/2$, and the variances as half of the mean, i.e., $(1 + L_X)/4$ and $(1 + L_Y)/4$ for $L_X \times L_Y$ mesh. The exponential distribution has the same mean as the normal distribution. Values drawn from the distributions outside of the range were ignored. For a given *system load* ρ $(0.0 < \rho \leq 1.0)$, the job arrival rate (λ) is determined as follows:

$$job\ arrival\ rate(\lambda) = \frac{\rho \cdot N}{m \cdot r}$$

where N is the number of processors contained in the mesh $(N = L_X \cdot L_Y)$, m is the mean number of processors in a submesh request, and r is a given mean residence time.

As is commonly assumed when studying the performance of processor allocation strategies, we assume a FCFS job scheduling discipline. The performance of strategies is measured in terms of the mean waiting delay (WD), allocation miss (AM), and mean search time (MST) for 100,000 requests per run of simulation under 95% confidence level with the error range of $\pm 3\%$, which are defined as follow: $\underline{WD}$, the time that elapses from the moment a job initially arrives to the system until it is allocated to a submesh; $\underline{AM}$, the percentage of allocation miss for valid requests, where a request is valid if there are enough nodes available; $\underline{MST}$, the average cpu time elapsed on allocation(s) and deallocation per job (the allocation attempt for a job may be done more than once).

The first experiment was performed to measure the mean waiting delay by changing the size of mesh from 16×16 to 512×512. The offered load and the mean residence time were given 0.47 and 10 seconds, respectively. Fig. 4 gives the results of experiment for the uniform and exponential distributions. The proposed strategy outperforms the other strategies. The proposed strategy shows the nearly similar performance for both distributions, while the Busy-List and AS strategies show the somewhat dependent results on the type of load. For the uniform distribution, the proposed strategy improves the mean waiting delay about 31% to 56% over the AS strategy and 14% to 26% over the Busy-List strategy. For the exponential distribution, the proposed strategy achieves 46% to 91% and 16% to 39% improvements over the AS and the Busy-List strategies, respectively. These results are due to relative efficiency of the heuristic of the proposed strategy over the first-fit policy of the AS strategy and the heuristic of the Busy-List strategy.

The second experiment was performed to measure the mean waiting delay by changing the offered load from 0.1 to 1.0 for 64×64 mesh. Fig. 4 gives the results of experiment for the uniform and normal distributions with the range of the load from 0.3 to 0.55, to obtain

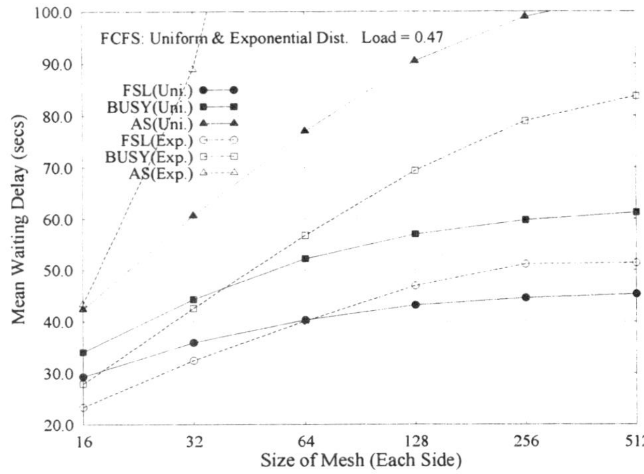

Fig. 7. WD vs. Size of Mesh

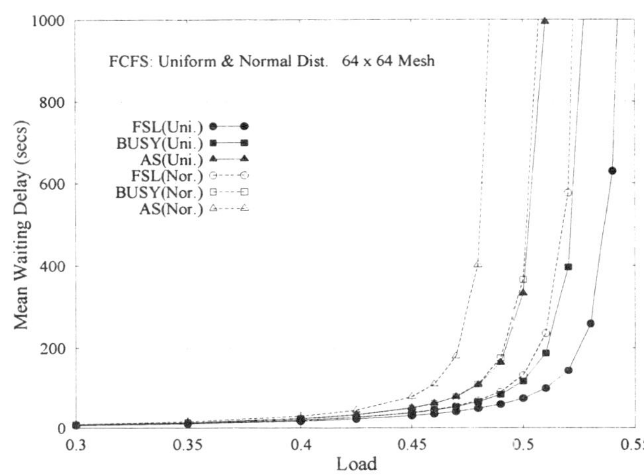

Fig. 8. WD vs. Load

better scaling factor because all the strategies saturated over the load 0.55. The proposed strategy performs the best under all the loads. Only the proposed strategy can sustain the load over 0.5, nearly up to 0.55, for both uniform and normal distributions.

To observe a picture of the optimality of the strategies, the third experiment was performed to gauge the percentage of the allocation miss for valid requests. Fig. 4 presents the result for the uniform distribution. The proposed strategy exhibits the lowest miss percentage compared to the other strategies. The allocation miss for a valid request is due to the external fragmentation including the unnecessary external fragmentation resulted from the decision in the previous allocation step, as already explained in the previous section. The experimental results demonstrate that our strategy provides more optimal allocation than the other strategies.

The fourth experiment was performed to compare

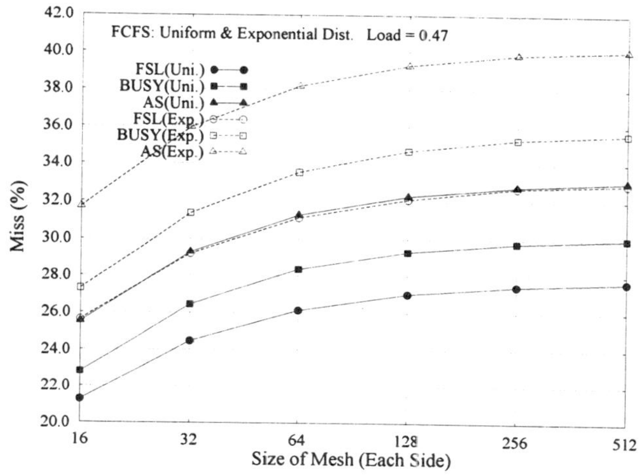

Fig. 9. AM vs. Size of Mesh

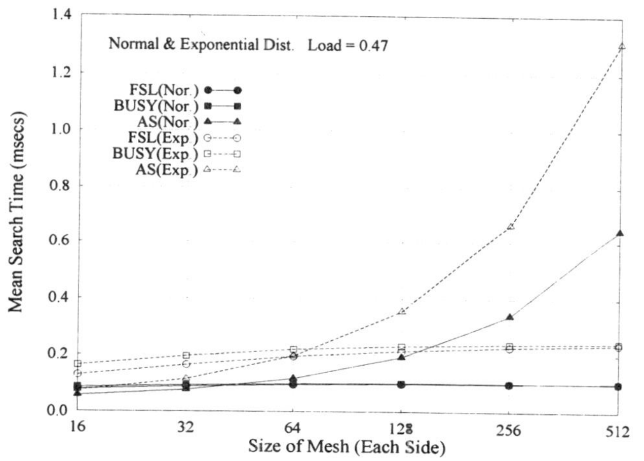

Fig. 10. MST vs. Size of Mesh

the run-time overheads, i.e., the mean search times, of strategies. The experimental results are given in Fig. 4. It shows that the Busy-List and our strategy give the nearly constant mean search times, regardless of the size of mesh, while our strategy exhibits slightly lower than the Busy-List strategy. The AS strategy, however, provides the mean search time increasing proportional to the size of mesh.

5 Conclusion

The performance of mesh multicomputer possessing hundreds or thousands of processors is subject to the efficient use of its processors. An efficient submesh allocation strategy is essential for achieving the high performance on mesh multicomputer. In this paper, we introduced a new best-fit submesh allocation strategy for mesh multicomputers. Simulation results show that the proposed strategy leads to the lowest waiting delay, allocation miss, and run-time overhead compared to other strategies for meshes of various sizes under various kinds of system loads. The proposed strategy offers the most efficient and practical solution for mesh multicomputers.

References

[1] Intel Corp., *A Touchstone DELTA System Description*, 1991.

[2] Intel Corp., *Paragon XP/S Product Overview*, 1991.

[3] R. Alverson et al., "The Tera computer system," in *Proc. of 1990 Int'l Conf. on Supercomputing*, pp. 1–6, 1990.

[4] D. K. Kahaner and U. Wattenberg, "Japan: a competitive assessment," *IEEE Spectrum*, pp. 42–47, Sept. 1992.

[5] G. Zorpette, "The power of parallelism," *IEEE Spectrum*, pp. 28–33, Sept. 1992.

[6] T. E. Bell, "Beyond today's supercomputers," *IEEE Spectrum*, pp. 72–75, Sept. 1992.

[7] K. Li and K. H. Cheng, "A Two Dimensional Buddy System for Dynamic Resource Allocation in A Partitionable Mesh Connected System," in *Proc. ACM Computer Science Conf.*, pp. 22–28, 1990.

[8] P. Chuang and N. Tzeng, "An Efficient Submesh Allocation Strategy for Mesh Computer Systems," in *Proc. of 11th Int'l Conf. on Distributed Computing Systems*, pp. 256–262, 1991.

[9] Y. Zhu, "Efficient Processor Allocation Strategies for Mesh-Connected Parallel Computers," *Journal of Parallel and Distributed Computing*, vol. 16, pp. 328–337, Dec. 1992.

[10] J. Ding and L. N. Bhuyan, "An Adaptive Submesh Allocation Strategy for Two-Dimensional Mesh Connected Systems," in *Proc. of Int'l Conf. on Parallel Processing*, vol. II, pp. 193–200, 1993.

[11] D. D. Sharma and D. K. Pradhan, "A Fast and Efficient Strategy for Submesh Allocation in Mesh-Connected Parallel Computers," in *IEEE Symp. on Parallel and Distributed Processing*, pp. 682–689, 1993.

❖ SESSION 6 ❖

Parallel Database Systems

Chair

A. Proenca

Extendible Hashing for Concurrent Insertions and Retrievals

Yasuhiro HIRANO, Fumiaki MIURA, and Tetsuji SATOH

NTT Information and Communication Systems Laboratories, Yokosuka, 238-03 Japan

Abstract

We propose an improved extendible hashing and bucket multi-versioning, achieving a higher concurrency. In our improved extendible hashing, the global depth and directory entries are asynchronously modified to reduce lock conflicts on the directory. Furthermore, bucket multi-versioning enables read only access to a bucket which is being split. Simulation studies show that these two methods provide speedup in proportion to the number of processors, and enable concurrent insertions and retrievals to be performed without either one affecting the other.

1 Introduction

Indexes, which are used to quickly retrieve and insert records, are required to keep stable performance even when the number of records significantly varies. Dynamic hashing schemes have been proposed [2], that can flexibly adapt to changes in the number of records. Extendible hashing [4] and linear hashing [6] are two examples of such dynamic hashings.

In addition, the concurrent access algorithms on an index have been studied (e. g., [5]), and a technique for proving such concurrent algorithms was proposed [8]. For treating large amounts of data and obtaining high performance, the use of parallel and distributed computation was also studied [3], [7]. This paper describes a concurrent access to an extendible hashing on shared everything multiprocessors.

The extendible hashing has a strong point, which is when a bucket is full the extendible hashing splits the bucket and does not make any overflow buckets, in contrast to linear hashing which splits buckets in a previously decided order and makes some overflow buckets. In the original extendible hashing, global depth and directory entries must be read or written atomically. Unfortunately, since many directory entries must be modified when a bucket is split, the critical section elongates and concurrency is reduced. Furthermore, splitting a bucket makes it inaccessible to other transactions.

This paper proposes an improved extendible hashing that enables (a) asynchronous updating of global depth and directory entries, and (b) bucket multi-versioning by which splitting and referring to the same bucket can be done simultaneously by different transactions.

2 Extendible Hashing

To obtain an address of a record including a specified key, k, a pseudo key, h, is calculated by applying a hash function, $h(k)$, to the key. Suppose that a pseudo key, h, consists of n bits and is described as

$$h = \sum_{i=0}^{n-1} h_i 2^i. \tag{1}$$

In this paper, we represent the least significant m bits of pseudo key, h, as

$$LSB(h,m) = \begin{cases} 0 & (m=0) \\ \sum_{i=0}^{m-1} h_i 2^i & (m>0) \end{cases}, \tag{2}$$

and the most significant m bits as

$$MSB(h,m) = \begin{cases} 0 & (m=0) \\ \sum_{i=1}^{m} h_{n-i} 2^{m-i} & (m>0) \end{cases}. \tag{3}$$

An example of an extendible hashing [4] is shown in Fig. 1 (a). An extendible hashing consists of a directory and buckets. The directory has global depth, GD, and 2^{GD} entries $E[0] \cdots E[2^{GD}-1]$. Each bucket, B, has a local depth, $B.LD$, and contains records.

A record is retrieved from a bucket obtained by

$$B = E[LSB(h(k), GD)] \tag{4}$$

when a pseudo key is used from the least significant bits, or

$$B = E[MSB(h(k), GD)] \tag{5}$$

when a pseudo key is used from the most significant bits. In Figure 1, equation (4) is used.

To insert a record, a candidate bucket is found using the above algorithm. When the bucket is full, it is split into two buckets and their local depths are increased by one. If the old local depth is less than the global depth ($B.LD < GD$), some directory entries are modified to indicate the new buckets (e.g., Fig. 1 (b)). If the old local depth is equal to the global depth ($B.LD = GD$), the directory is doubled in size and the global depth is increased by one (e.g., Fig. 1 (c)).

For concurrent access of extendible hashing, global depth and directory entry references must be an atomic operation to avoid extension of the directory between the two references. To shorten the time the directory is locked, a lock-coupling [8] technique can be used, i.e., lock the directory, refer to the global depth and entry, lock the bucket and then unlock

1066-6192/96 $5.00 © 1996 IEEE
Proceedings of PDP '96

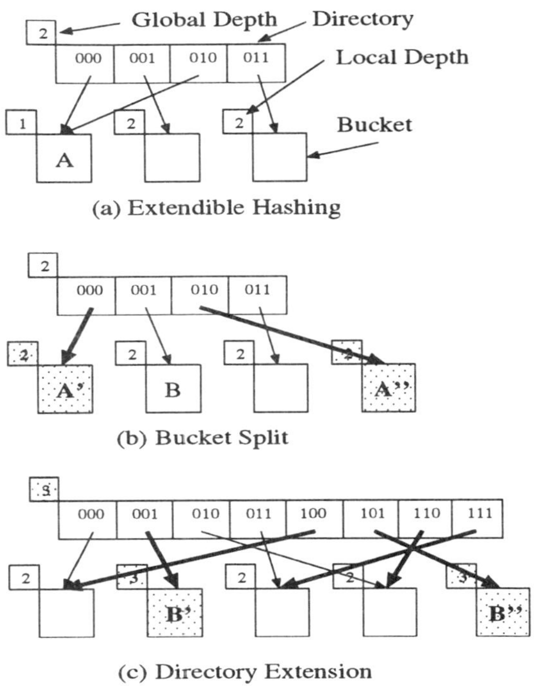

Figure 1: Extendible Hashing

the directory. When some buckets are simultaneously split, the entries to be modified for each bucket are distinct except in the case of directory extension. Thus, multiple buckets can be concurrently split by locking the directory in an exclusive mode for directory extension and in a shared mode for the other cases.

In an extendible hashing, a bucket is indicated by $2^{GD-B.LD}$ entries. Splitting a bucket requires at least half of these entries to be modified, and extending the directory requires modification of the global depth and 2^{GD} entries. Therefore, the critical section can be a long procedure, lowering concurrency.

3 Improved Extendible Hashing

3.1 Structure

We propose an improved extendible hashing in which global depth and directory entries can be asynchronously referred to and modified, and fewer entries need to be modified when splitting a bucket.

The structure of our improved extendible hashing is shown in Fig. 2. As the figure shows, it consists of a directory and buckets. The differences between the proposed hashing and the original extendible hashing are (1) the least significant bits of the pseudo key are used, (2) the number of entries pointing to one bucket is no more than that of an extendible hashing, because some directory entries may not be used, and (3) global depth means that entries whose indices are less than 2^{GD} must be used but other entries may or may not be used.

Difference (1) is because during directory extension all entries except one, which indicates the bucket causing directory extension, are just copied and can be accessed when the least significant bits are used, while some of the entries are modified and cannot be accessed during directory extension when the most significant bits are used.

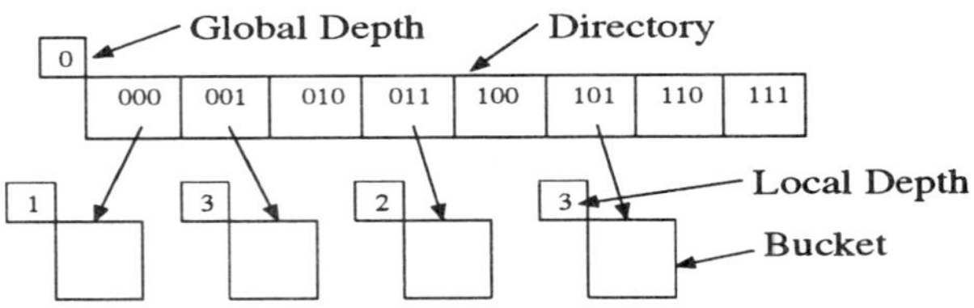

Figure 2: Improved Extendible Hashing

```
begin
    i := GD
    loop
        B := E[LSB(h(k), i)]
        if B.LD > i
        then i ++
        else
            Retrieve Record from Bucket B
            Finish Processing
    endloop
end
```

Figure 3: Find Algorithm

3.2 Find Algorithm

Figure 3 illustrates the find algorithm. Until the number of pseudo key bits used to determine an entry is more than or equal to the local depth, the directory reference and comparison are repeated with the incremented number of bits.

The comparison makes it possible to detect the occurrence of directory extension between references of global depth and directory entry, and the repeated reference and comparison make it possible to recover from incorrect navigation. Therefore, the global depth and directory entry references do not have to be an atomic operation.

3.3 Insert Algorithm

Figure 2 (a) shows examples of insert operations. No global depth updates are necessary, because the find algorithm does not require a correct global depth value. Insert operations update fewer directory entries than they do in the original extendible hashing, because only one entry must indicate each bucket. Therefore, the critical section of the proposed hashing is shorter than that of the original extendible hashing.

3.4 Directory Maintenance

The find algorithm must repeat directory and local depth references at most $\{\max(B.LD) - GD\}$ times. To reduce the number of repeated references, i.e., to increase the speed of the find algorithm, global depth can be increased by modifying the entries which are not used. This operation is called "directory maintenance".

Figure 2 (b) shows examples of directory maintenance. This maintenance can be done at any time.

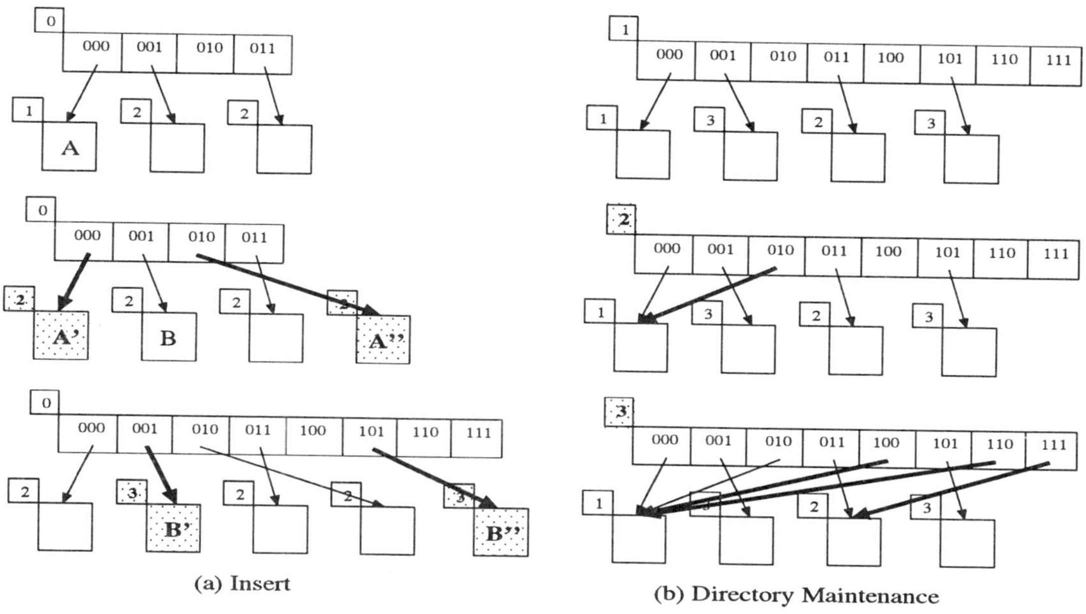

Figure 4: Improved Extendible Hashing

Unlike the original extendible hashing, no synchronization of the insert and maintenance is necessary.

Directory maintenance requires that all the entries whose indices are less than 2^{GD} point to the correct buckets. If the global depth is greater than the minimum value of the local depth, then some buckets are indicated by more than one entry and the critical section elongates, but it still remains shorter than that of the original extendible hashing.

3.5 Concurrent Algorithm

In the improved extendible hashing, as in the original extendible hashing, multiple buckets can be concurrently split by locking the directory in the exclusive mode for directory maintenance and in the shared mode for other cases.

Since the number of entries updated in the critical section is less than that in the original extendible hashing, concurrency is higher. Furthermore, because the directory maintenance is optional, omitting it further enhances its concurrency, especially in creating a hash structure when buckets are frequently split.

If references or updates of global depth or directory entry are all atomic operations, keeping the global depth no greater than the minimum value of the local depth enables references to and updates of the directory to be done concurrently, because comparing the number of bits with the local depth can detect the splitting of a bucket. The last comparison must follow the locking of the bucket to avoid further splitting of the bucket. In this case, because referring to the directory does not require the directory to be locked, high concurrency can be obtained.

Figure 5 shows the concurrent insert algorithm with directory maintenance. The technique in which a directory reference is repeated when the number of bits is less than the local depth or when the bucket is locked in the exclusive mode is categorized as a give-up technique [8].

4 Bucket Multi-Versioning

Concurrency between insertions and retrievals is reduced by the fact that while a bucket is being split it cannot be read because some records in it would be removed to a new bucket. To solve this problem, we introduce a method that allocates two new buckets and copies records into these buckets so that the old bucket can be read. This method can be used for both the proposed and original extendible hashings. This new method for splitting a bucket is called *bucket multi-versioning*, and the original method is *bucket single-versioning*.

An example of this method is shown in Fig. 6. The bucket is split through the following steps.

(1) Lock the bucket in the exclusive mode (Fig. 6 (a)). Hereafter, lock requests to this bucket must not wait for the lock to be released, i.e., the requester starts over again from the directory reference step.

(2) Allocate two new buckets and copy records into these buckets (Fig. 6 (b)).

(3) Modify directory entries to indicate these buckets (Fig. 6 (c), (d)).

(4) As described below, the find algorithm does not have to lock any buckets and thus, the old bucket can be read by transactions other than the one who locked the bucket in the exclusive mode. The old bucket may be removed after no transaction refers to it (Fig. 6 (e)). This can be done by counting the number of transactions referring to each bucket, or by using time stamps to determine whether there are any transactions which

```
begin
    i := GD
    loop
        Shared-Lock Directory
        B_A := E[LSB(h(k), i)]
        if B_A.LD > i
        then i++
        else
            if Shared-Lock Bucket B_A failed
            then Unlock Directory and continue
            else
                Unlock Directory
                if B_A.LD > i
                then
                    i++
                    Unlock Bucket B_A and continue
                else
                    if Bucket B_A has Space for Record
                    then
                        Insert Record into B_A
                        Unlock B_A and Finish Processing
                    else
                        if Exclusive-Lock Bucket B_A failed
                        then Unlock Bucket B_A and continue
                        else exitloop
    endloop
    Allocate two new Buckets (called Bucket B_B)
    B_B.LD := B_A.LD + 1
    Shared-Lock Bucket B_B
    Move Records whose pseudo key satisfy h_{B_A.LD} = 1
        from B_A to B_B
    Shared-Lock Directory
    E[LSB(h(k), B_A.LD) + 2^{B_A.LD}] := B_B
    if Exclusive-Lock Directory succeed
    then Directory Maintenance
    Unlock Directory
    B_A.LD++
    Unlock Bucket B_B
    Unlock Bucket B_A
end
```

Figure 5: Concurrent Insert Algorithm

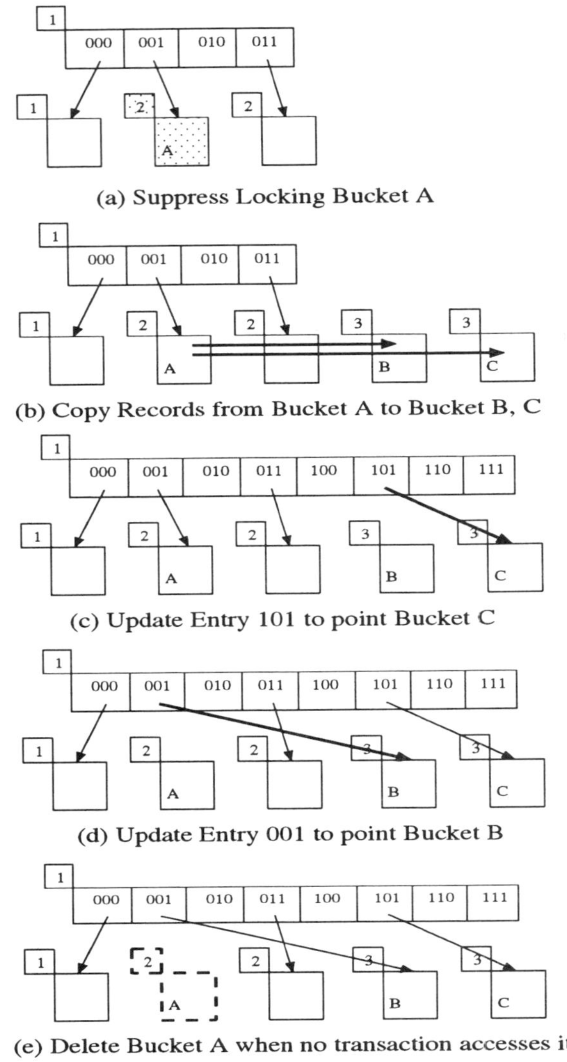

Figure 6: Bucket Multi-Versioning

started before all the entries were modified so as not to indicate the bucket.

Using this algorithm, the bucket can be read while it is being split. For example, in Fig. 6, bucket A can be referred to between (a) and (c), and buckets B and C can be referred to in (d). Therefore, it is unnecessary for the find algorithm to lock any buckets. Thus, bucket multi-versioning enhances concurrency between insertions and retrievals.

It is not necessary for insert algorithm to compare the number of bits with local depth again after the bucket is locked, because the local depth is not modified.

In the original extendible hashing, directory locking can be released before locking a bucket by restarting from the directory reference when locking the bucket fails.

Moreover, if references or updates of global depth or directory entry are all atomic operations, the original hashing allows concurrent referring to and updating of the directory except for directory extension, and the proposed hashing makes directory locking unnecessary when referring to the directory.

Therefore, bucket multi-versioning enhances concurrency in the directory as well as in the buckets.

5 Implementation and Performance Evaluation

In this section, we compare the performance of the original extendible hashing and our improved extendible hashing.

We implemented a main memory database prototype with the proposed and original extendible hashings on a Sun Sparc Station. However, performance in parallel processing environments must be compared by means of a simulation study, because we do not have multiprocessor environments.

Two types of transactions on shared memory multiprocessors, inserting a record into a main memory database and retrieving a record, are simulated. Each process sequentially executes the transactions.

The processing times of the operations, which actually are the number of instructions obtained by

Table 1: Processing Times used in Simulations

Processing	Time (# of Instructions)
Start Transaction	200
Insert Record	800
Hash Function	300
Refer Directory	100
Lock, Unlock	300
Allocate and Initialize Bucket	200
Compare Keys	100
Update Directory Entry	50
Refer/Update Global Depth	20
Refer/Update Local Depth	20
Finish Transaction	500

measuring inserts and retrievals of the Wisconsin databases [1] on our main memory database prototype on the Sun Sparc Station, are shown in Table 1. Referring to or updating a global depth or directory entry are all assumed to be atomic operations.

Each bucket contains no more than six records. Keys are unique random sequences, and therefore retrievers stop searching the records in the bucket when either a record is found or all records have been searched.

We use the following abbreviations where global depth maintenance is a kind of directory maintenance, keeping the global depth equal to the minimum value of local depths.

P: Proposed Extendible Hashing
O: Original Extendible Hashing
MV: Bucket Multi-Versioning
SV: Bucket Single-Versioning
NGD: No Global Depth Maintenance
GD: with Global Depth Maintenance

5.1 Response Time

Figure 7 shows the elapsed times for inserting 10,000 records using one and 32 processors. The number of processes executing the transactions is equal to the number of processors. The inclination of each graph shows the average response time at each point.

5.1.1 Single Processor

The proposed hashings with global depth maintenance (P-SV-GD, P-MV-GD) are the fastest, and the proposed hashings without global depth maintenance (P-MV-NGD, P-SV-NGD) are as fast as the original extendible hashing (O-MV, O-SV). This is because repeated reference to the directory or modifying many directory entries take more time than modifying global depth and the small number of references to the directory.

In the proposed extendible hashing, single-versioning (P-SV-GD, P-SV-NGD) is faster than multi-versioning (P-MV-GD, P-MV-NGD) because the latter requires more work, such as the initializing and locking of buckets.

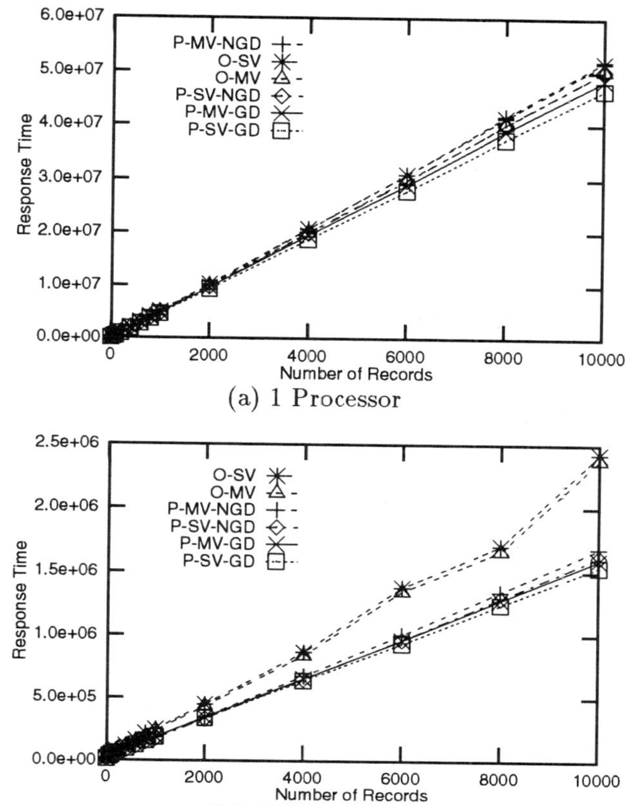

(a) 1 Processor

(b) 32 Processors

Figure 7: Response Time

The fact that all the graphs are almost straight shows that the average response time of each hashing does not depend on whether each hashing stores few records (initial state) or many records (steady state).

5.1.2 Multiple Processors

With 32 processors, the proposed hashing is always faster because the waiting time for referencing the directory in ordinary hashing exceeds that for repeated reference to the directory in the proposed hashing.

While the average response time of the ordinary hashing depends on the number of records in it, that of the proposed hashing does not. This is addressed in Section 5.3.

5.2 Speedup Ratio

5.2.1 Effect of the number of Processors

Figure 8 shows the speedup ratio when varying the number of processors for inserting 10,000 records. The number of processes executing transactions is equal to the number of processors. The proposed extendible hashing achieves speedup proportional to the number of processors for up to 32 processors.

The proposed hashing without global depth maintenance (P-SV-NGD, P-MV-NGD) provides a somewhat higher speedup than that with global depth

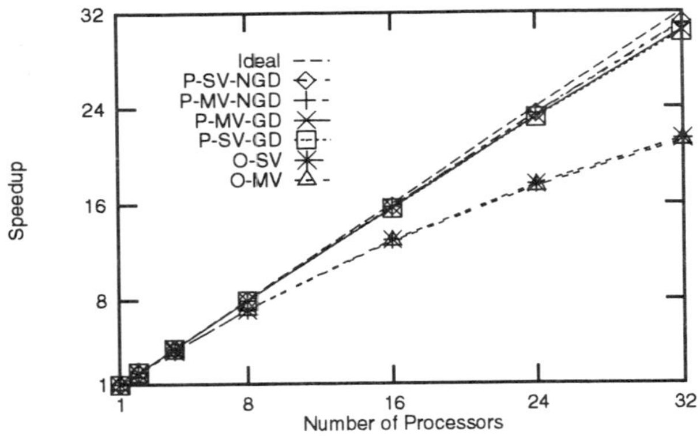

Figure 8: Effect of the number of Processors

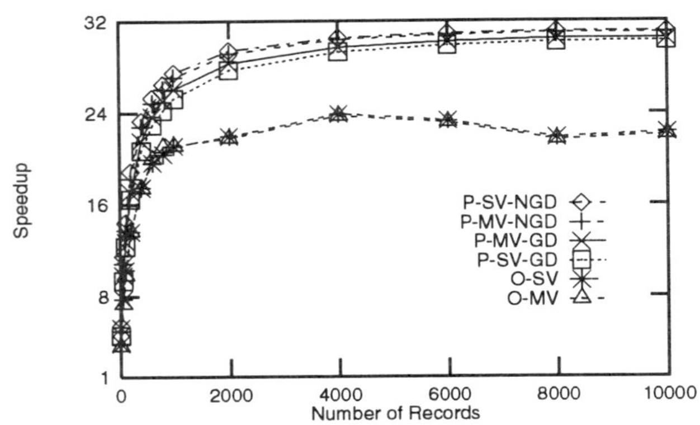

Figure 9: Effect of Number of Records

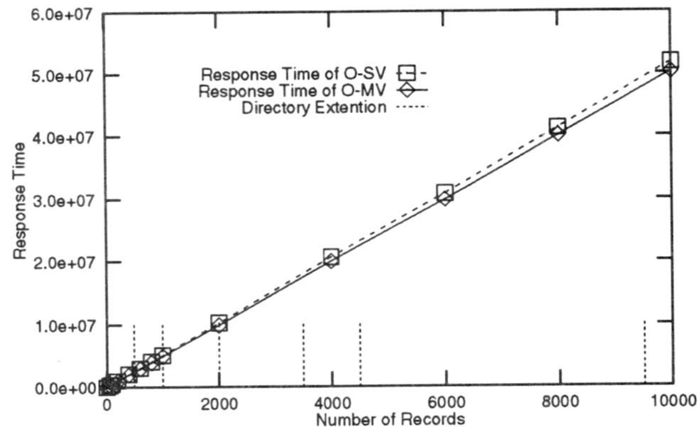

(a) 1 Processor

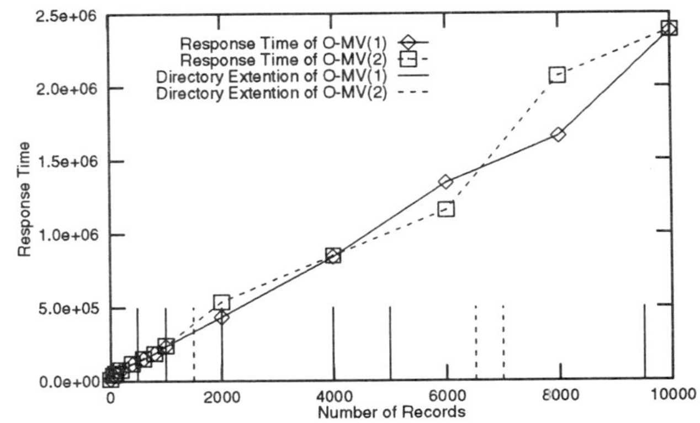

(b) 32 Processors

Figure 10: Effect of Directory Extension

maintenance (P-SV-GD, P-MV-GD), because no transaction can modify a directory entry during the updating of global depth.

Almost the same speedup ratio is obtained for both multi- and single-versioning.

5.2.2 Effect of the number of records

Figure 9 shows the effect of the number of records on the speedup.

When there are few records, few buckets exist. This leads to frequent lock conflicts in buckets and lowers the speedup. The more the records are inserted, the higher the speedup is.

The speedup of an ordinary hashing (O-MV, O-SV), however, saturates when there are more than 2,000 records. This is because the waiting time for locking the directory degrades the performance of an ordinary extendible hashing as described in Section 5.3.

5.3 Effect of Directory Extension

Figure 10 shows the response times of original methods (O-MV, O-SV) and the time when directory extension occurs with two key distributions, and describes the reason the response time and the speedup of ordinary methods fluctuate.

Though the response time with a processor is proportional to the number of records, that with 32 processors suddenly increases near the directory extension during which no directory entry modifications or references are allowed. This means that in an ordinary extendible hashing the waiting time for locking the directory degrades the performance.

5.4 Concurrent Execution of Inserts and Retrievals

Figure 11 is histograms of the response times of transactions retrieving a record, i.e., concurrent execution of 32-insert and 32-retrieval processes using 64 processors, and sequential execution of retrievals after the inserts are finished. The number of records is 1,000.

In multi-versioning (O-MV, P-MV-GD, P-MV-NGD), since the retrieving transactions never have to wait for a reference to a bucket, concurrent execution with inserts increases response time less than in single-versioning (O-SV, P-SV-GD, P-SV-NGD). In the proposed hashing, since the retrieving transactions never have to wait for referring to the directory, concurrent execution with inserts does not increase response time of retrievals at all.

In the improved extendible hashing, the response time without global depth maintenance (P-MV-NGD,

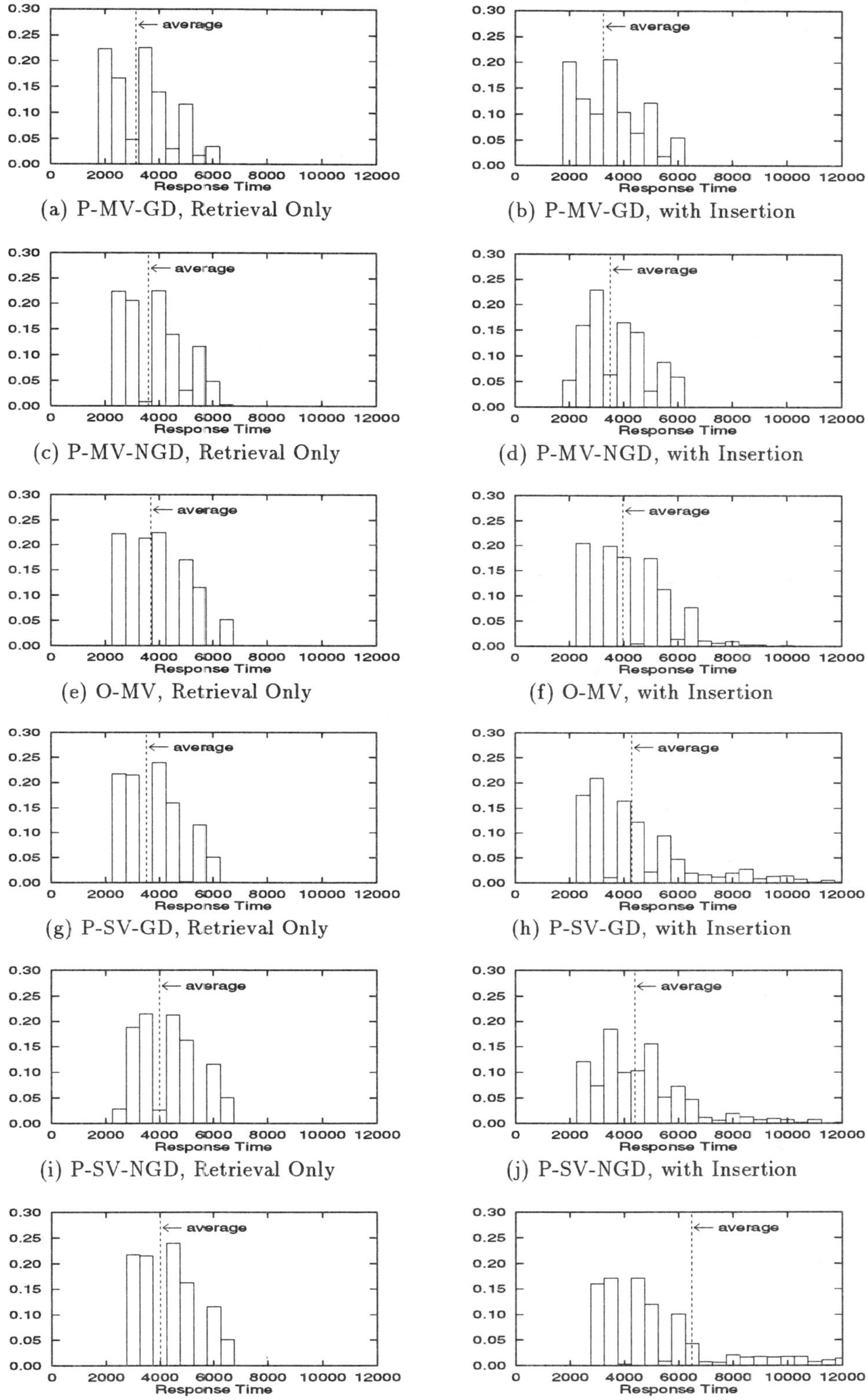

(a) P-MV-GD, Retrieval Only

(b) P-MV-GD, with Insertion

(c) P-MV-NGD, Retrieval Only

(d) P-MV-NGD, with Insertion

(e) O-MV, Retrieval Only

(f) O-MV, with Insertion

(g) P-SV-GD, Retrieval Only

(h) P-SV-GD, with Insertion

(i) P-SV-NGD, Retrieval Only

(j) P-SV-NGD, with Insertion

(k) O-SV, Retrieval Only

(l) O-SV, with Insertion

Figure 11: Histograms of Retrieval Response Time

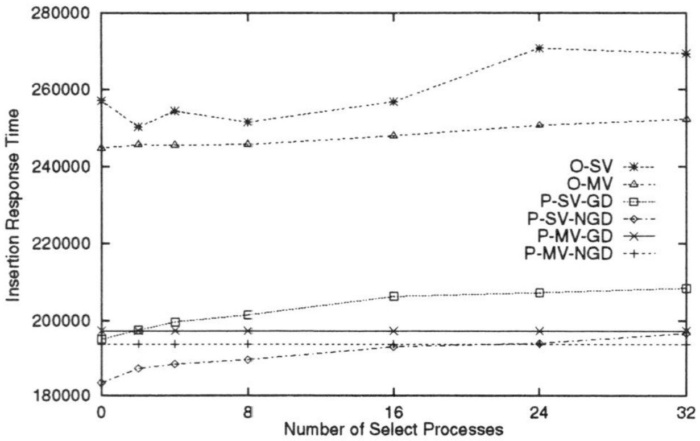

Figure 12: Effect of Retrieval on Insertion

P-SV-NGD) is longer than that with the maintenance (P-MV-GD, P-SV-GD), because of the repeated directory reference.

Figure 12 shows the effect that retrieving transactions have on the response time of inserts. Here, 64 processors employ 32 processes to insert 1,000 records.

The improved extendible hashing and bucket multi-versioning (P-MV-GD, P-MV-NGD) shows a constant response time when varying the number of retrieving processes. Therefore, these two techniques make it possible for insertions and retrievals to run concurrently without affecting each other.

6 Related Work

In [3], a link technique [8] is used to recover from incorrect navigation, i.e., a bucket contains a link to the next bucket as the leaf pages in B+-tree.

This method, however, must maintain all the directory entries as the original extendible hashing. On the other hand, our improved hashing can omit or delay the directory maintenance.

Simulation results showed that modifying the directory entries, especially in the directory extension, reduce the concurrency. Therefore, our improved hashing would provide higher concurrency than that method.

7 Conclusion

This paper proposed an improved extendible hashing that reduces the lock contention on the directory, and a bucket multi-versioning that enables transactions to split and refer to the same bucket simultaneously. The results obtained through simulation studies are also described.

Concurrent access to the extendible hashing requires an atomic treatment of global depth and directory entries. Unfortunately, since many directory entries are modified when a bucket is split, the critical section elongates and the concurrency is reduced.

In the improved extendible hashing, modifications of global depth and directory entries can be asynchronously done, and the number of directory entries that must be modified during bucket splitting is less than in the original extendible hashing.

Due to the splitting of a bucket making it inaccessible to other transactions, concurrency between inserts and retrievals is reduced by the splitting. To solve this problem, we introduced the bucket multi-versioning. This also enhances the concurrency on the directory.

We compared the performances of the improved extendible hashing and the original ones. Simulation results showed that the improved extendible hashing is suitable for inserting records in parallel and provides speedup in proportion to the number of processors. The proposed hashing is superior to a conventional extendible hashing because it reduces the contention on the directory, especially for cases in which there are many records, where the contentions on buckets are a less significant problem.

The simulation results also showed that the improved extendible hashing and bucket multi-versioning enable concurrent insertions and retrievals to be performed without either one affecting the other.

The improved extendible hashing may also provide high performance in distributed environments, because it allows delayed updating of the directory. Applying this hashing to such environments is a subject for further study.

Acknowledgement

We would like to thank Shoichiro Ishigaki of NTT and Ushio Inoue of NTTDATA for their supports of this work. We also thank Ryoji Kataoka of NTT for his help with simulations.

References

[1] D. Bitton , D. J. DeWitt, and C. Turbyfill, "Benchmarking Database Systems - A Systematic Approach," Proc. 9th Conf. on VLDB, pp. 8–19 (Oct. 1983).

[2] R. J. Enbody and H. C. Du, "Dynamic Hashing Schemes," ACM Computing Surveys, Vol. 20, No. 2, pp. 85–113 (1988).

[3] C. S. Ellis, "Extendible Hashing for Concurrent Operations and Distributed Data," ACM SIGMOD, pp. 106–116 (1982).

[4] R. Fagin, J. Nievergelt, N. Pippenger, and H. R. Strong, "Extendible Hashing - A fast access method for dynamic files," ACM Trans. Database Syst., Vol. 4, pp. 315–355 (1979).

[5] W. d. Jonge and A. Schijf, "Concurrent Access to B-trees," Proc. IEEE Parbase-90, pp. 312–320 (1990).

[6] W. Litwin, "Linear Hashing: A New Tool for File and Table Addressing," Proc. 6th VLDB, pp. 212–223 (1980).

[7] W. Litwin, M.-A. Neimat, and D. A. Schneider, "LH* - Linear Hashing for Distributed Files," ACM SIGMOD, pp. 327–336 (1993).

[8] D. Shasha and N. Goodman, "Concurrent Search Structure Algorithms," ACM Trans. on Database Systems, Vol. 13, No. 1, pp. 53–90 (1988).

Trace Analysis with a Relational Database System

Rolf Borgeest, Christian Rödel
Technische Universität München
Lehrstuhl für Rechnertechnik und Rechnerorganisation (LRR-TUM)
Fakultät für Informatik
Arcisstr. 21, D-80290 München
Tel.: +49-89-2105-8489, Fax: +49-89-2105-8232
email: borgeest@informatik.tu-muenchen.de

Abstract

One of the main problems dealing with trace based analysis of parallel systems is the management of the vast amounts of data produced by monitors. This paper describes the experiences made with a database approach for the management of trace data. The system is configurable in terms of trace formats and of metrics defined on this trace format. Performance measurements of the system conclude the paper.

1 Introduction

Trace based monitoring of parallel Systems produces big amounts of data. To analyze the trace data existing tools either read the complete trace into internal data structures for processing [1], or filter through the trace file once to calculate the interesting metrics [2].

The first approach soon reaches the memory limits of the system on which analysis takes place. The second approach makes repeated analysis tedious, since the trace has to be read again and again. What is desirable, is a random access to the trace data, which does not saturate the hardware of the analyzing computer.

A trend exists towards a more integrated approach of design and implementation of parallel systems. The designs are first simulated and simulations are replaced by measurements on the target system in later stages of project development. Simulation can model aspects of the program behavior which cannot be measured on the target system and vice versa. One example for this are contention on communication links. This means the same project produce traces of different formats and different semantical contents and different metrics must be defined. Some metrics are of interest only for one project. Therefore a trace analysis tool must be configurable in respect to the accepted formats and the metrics it can calculate.

The standard way of accessing and processing big amounts of data is the use of a database system. We will show in the remainder of this paper, how to use a standard relational database as base for the management of trace data.

While temporal database languages would have offered some very convenient operations for the analysis of timestamped data, we used a relational database. This was mainly for reasons of availability and maturity.

The objective for this project was to analyze the feasibility and performance of a database based approach for trace analysis, taking into consideration configurability of trace format and metrics.

The next section discusses related work. In the third section the starting point of our implementation, the trace analysis tool TATOO is presented. Section 4 and 5 discuss configurability of trace formats and metrics, their implementation and the limitations of the approach. Section 6 compares the performance of the database solution with a main memory based solution. In the final section we present our conclusions.

2 Related Work

2.1 Relational approach

Snodgrass [3, 4] uses the relational approach as a fiction only that guides the processing and especially guides the decisions what has to be monitored and how the data has to be collected.

Sarukkai and Gannon [5] propose a system with a more or less uniform trace format. The data is analyzed with help of a spreadsheet.

Lei and Zhang [6] actually use a relational database to store and process fixed format traces. The metrics are not configurable.

2.2 Configuration of trace formats and metrics

Most of the available trace analysis tools use fixed trace formats and a fixed set of possible metrics.

1066-6192/96 $5.00 © 1996 IEEE
Proceedings of PDP '96

Two advanced approaches for the definition of trace formats and metrics exist: Pablo [7] with the trace format SDDF [8] and SIMPLE [2] with the trace format TDL [9].

In SDDF the format specification is given in the header of the trace file. In TDL, the description of the trace format is given in a separate file. By this separation the TDL approach allows processing of traces produced from nearly any source.

One drawback of both formats and their associated access functions is, that they cannot cater for implicit information as id to name translation.

To configure a metric, the Pablo system offers a graphical user interface to read, filter and display trace data. The configuration of the metrics consists in creation of a analysis graph. It is not possible to relate different streams of events. Delay measurements rely on the fact, that start time and duration are recorded in the same event record.

In SIMPLE unwanted events can be filtered from the trace. The filtered data is handed over to a number of analyzers, which are configured by means of configuration files. Each analyzer has a different way of presenting the calculated metrics and slightly different configuration languages.

Both formats are free of semantical knowledge of the trace data. In both cases semantics are introduced by the user when metrics are defined. The components for analyzing and displaying the data access the trace data over the names defined in the trace format definitions.

3 Trace Analysis Tool TATOO

Base of our study was the trace analysis tool TATOO [1]. TATOO is developed as part of the HAMLET programming environment [10]. The programming environment is dedicated to the development of industrial applications. It was designed in close cooperation with application programmers in the framework of the ESPRIT-III project HAMLET.

The environment consists of a design entry system (DES) with code generator, a simulation tool, a monitor and the trace analysis tool (see Fig. 1). The tools can be used separately or under a common control interface. For system configuration, compiling and debugging vendor supplied tools are integrated into the environment. The tools run under Motif and SunOS4.1.x on SPARCstations.

The design entry system is a CASE tool used for specification of hardware and software topologies. Its code generating capabilities provide skeleton code and mapping files for hardware and software [11]. The output of the DES is used as input to a simulator and as basis for the target program. The simulator takes user supplied estimates of computing times and computes communication delays in dependency of system communication load [12]. It produces trace files, which are analyzed with TATOO. Trace files can also be produced by monitoring the program execution on a target system.

TATOO reads trace files. Then the user can define measurement queries according to the data read. The measurements are visualized in different sort of displays like multicurve displays, bargraphs and ganttcharts.

For every display a resolution or update interval is chosen. This is the time interval which is covered by every value displayed. All values are averaged over this interval. Resolution is chosen in dependency to the length of the traced time interval and the desired level of granularity.

TATOO supports the user in his task of finding performance bugs by a two dimensional hierarchical approach: The way of defining measurements goes from system to groups of processes or processors to single processes or processes down to function and area level. On the other dimension is the time granularity with which the data is analyzed: from very coarse grain, which covers the complete trace data down to the level of the single event.

The tool is controlled by a time control window, which allows to start, stop and single step the advance in time. The observation time can adjusted randomly to focus analysis around a certain point in time.

The trace format used has fixed format and semantics.

Traced events include scheduling events for nodes and processes, communication, function and area entry and exit points. Since the instrumentation is not under the control of TATOO, information about the target system, like mapping of processes on nodes and names of the different objects, are encoded in the trace file.

Entry to and exit from a state (e.g. a function call) are stored as separate events. This was necessary especially for areas which can be entered on one process and left on another. The presence of source related information and separate events for entry and exit points imposes special boundary conditions on TATOO.

4 Implementation

Goal of our project [13] was to change the modules of TATOO which deal with the reading of trace files, the definition of measurements and the analysis of data in such a way that they use a database system

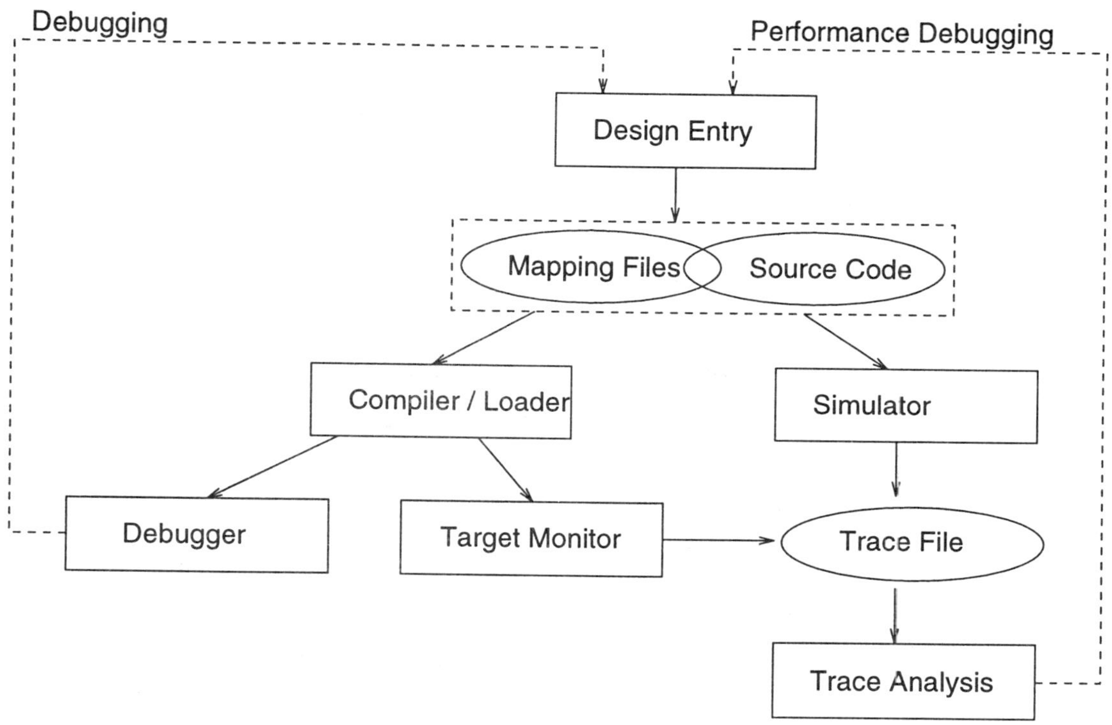

Abbildung 1: The HAMLET programming environment

instead of internal data structures. The user interface had to remain unchanged.

The new trace reading and analysis component has been implemented using TransBase V4.1 with ESQL embedded in C++ code. The offers the same interface as the existing implementation. An additional requirement was to make the new component configurable in regards to the trace format and the possible metrics.

When using a relational database as storing facility, it is reasonable to formulate the configuration as close to the relational model and ESQL as possible. This facilitates programming of the component and leaves as much as possible to the optimization capabilities of the RDBS.

4.1 System Architecture

The system architecture is depicted in Fig. 2. The component has a C++ interface towards the user interface of TATOO and a lower interface connecting to the database system. Inside the component four modules are responsible for initialization of the system database, reading trace files, definition of measurements and for reading of measurements for single time intervals.

The RDBS has to manage the system database and a number of trace databases. The system is designed to accommodate to store event data from different traces. For every trace a separate trace database is created, according to the configuration data associated with the trace format. This allows comparison of test runs.

The system database stores the following informations:

- configuration data
  - trace format description
  - description of metrics
  - object hierarchy of the parallel programming environment
  - schemes for trace databases
- description of the trace databases
  - configuration used
  - general informations about the trace file read

The databases for the trace files contain the following informations:

- event data
- object information (id to name mapping, hierarchical data)

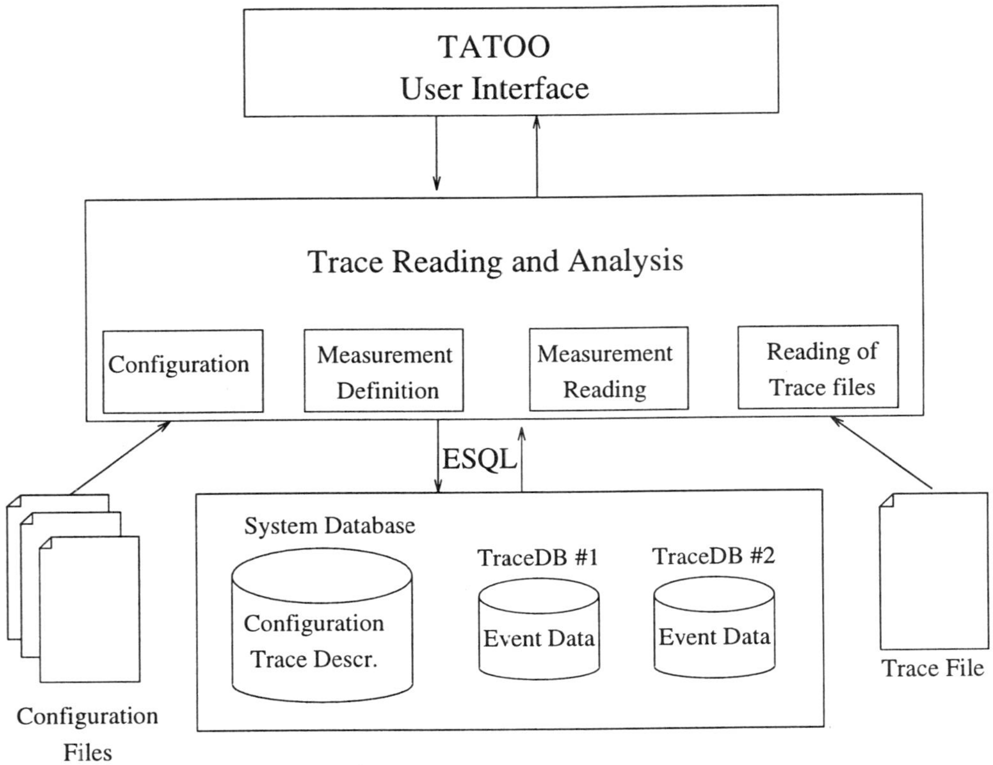

Abbildung 2: System Architecture

Information about the hierarchy of the programming model objects is used to reflect this hierarchy in the measurement definition. E.g. use all processes located on on processor.

4.2 Reading of trace files

Instead of using one of the open formats mentioned in Subsection 2.2, we decided to use a simpler approach, which has the following restrictions:

- the data must be given in ASCII format
- the event identifier is on the first position
- parameters are separated by spaces
- events are separated by line feeds

First a trace database is initialized with help of the configuration information concerning the trace format. The trace file is read line by line. The configured relation `parameter_mapping` (see Table 2) determines how the parameters of an event record are entered into the event relations of trace database.

`TraceDesc` is a special table, which is used for reasons of memory efficiency and simpler definitions of measurements. `TraceDesc` contains those parameters which constitute a key to an event record, i.e. those parameters which map an event to a certain entity of the programming model. The event tuples contain only the changeable data and a reference to the `TraceDesc` relation. Table 1 depicts this connection. In this example the use of the relation `TraceDesc` saves 2 to 4 attributes per event. Null values for `TraceDesc` attributes are given as -3.

Fig. 3 illustrates the reading of trace data. The first value in the line identifies the type of event. This event number selects all tuples in `parameter_mapping`. They determine how the following parameters are to be interpreted and how they are combined into tuples. After the line has been processed, created tuples are inserted in their relations.

4.3 Metrics

Fixed format tools normally offer only a fixed set of metrics. Insight into system behavior is restricted by the metrics. Examples for metrics are: delay in communication calls, differentiated by process, communication medium (e.g. channel), counts in relation to a source code construct, busy times for processes or nodes etc..

Literature proposes many different metrics which

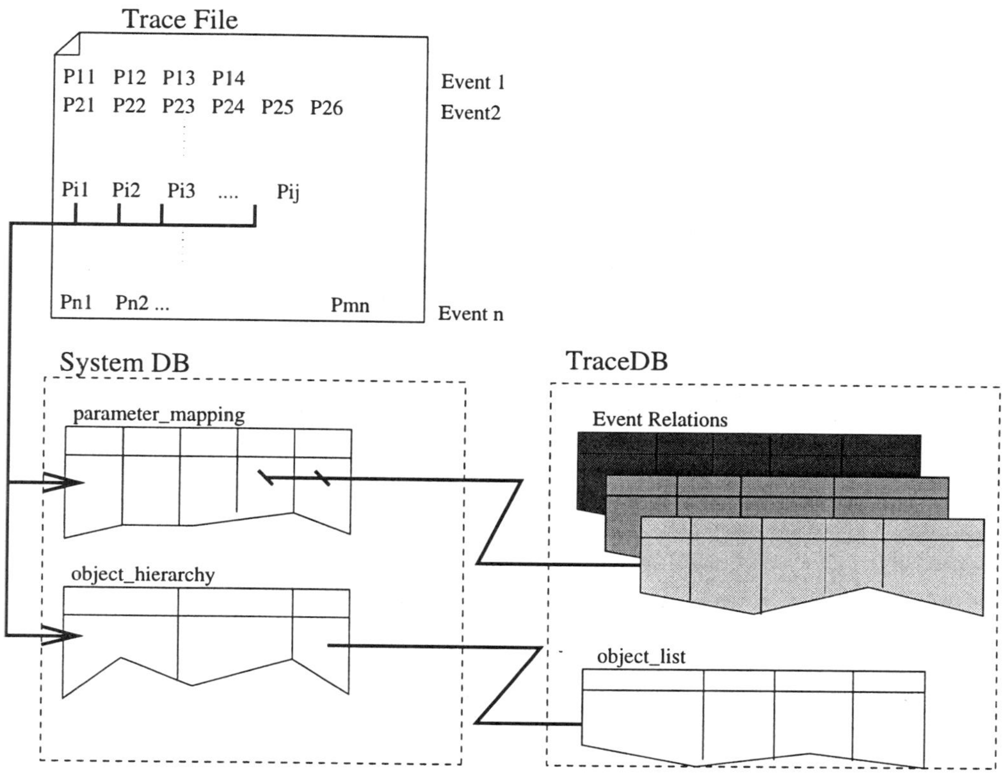

Abbildung 3: Reading of trace data

TraceDesc						
TDId	eventtype	subtype	origin	function	area	partner
1	2	10	7	-3	-3	4
2	2	11	7	-3	-3	4
4	2	10	7	-3	-3	2

ob_ox		
clock	TDId	volume
101	1	4
104	1	4
100	2	8
99	4	7

Tabelle 1: Relation `TraceDesc` and one of the event relations

EventNo	ParamNo	Name	Relation	Attribute
2	2	'subtype'	'TraceDesc'	'subtype'
2	3	'clock'	'ob_ox'	'clock'
2	4	'origin'	'TraceDesc'	'origin'
2	5	'debugID'	'ob_ox'	'debugID'
2	6	'partner'	'TraceDesc'	'partner'
2	7	'volume'	'ob_ox'	'volume'
4	2	'subtype'	'TraceDesc'	'subtype'
4	3	'clock'	'oc_od'	'clock'
4	4	'parent'	'TraceDesc'	'origin'
4	5	'debugID'	'oc_od'	'debugID'
4	6	'child'	'TraceDesc'	'partner'
4	7	'initinfo'	'oc_od'	'initinfo'

Tabelle 2: Part of the relation `parameter_mapping`

should be of use to performance analysts. For example [14] and [2] contain detailed studies which metrics could be of use.

Many questions a developer could ask about the system cannot be foreseen. Examples are delay times for components of the system which are not obviously connected or assertions that two events with certain parameters will always occur alternating. A good analysis tool should give the user possibility to define such metrics.

Traces contain possibly redundant information. For example, the busy time of a process can be given by its scheduling and descheduling events and/or by counters, which integrate the busytime over a time interval. Several possibilities exist to calculate one metric.

Most metrics like utilization, calls per second, delay and data volume in communication can be calculated with some simple operations, which could be in principle executed directly by the database.

Aggregate functions of the DBS like MIN, MAX etc. can be used for measurement evaluation. Normal use would be SUM, but there exist good uses for statistical calculations.

TATOO requests data for random time intervals and it the attributes to be taken into consideration for a metric are configurable. The cutting of time intervals with regards to the events represented in the event relations and the unknown number and type of the attributes made it necessary to use C++ methods to post-process selected data. We have implemented several methods, which were sufficient for our purposes and can easily be augmented. They include methods which take into account either one or two streams of events and can evaluate one attribute apart from the timestamps.

Metrics are configured and defined by entries in `measure_plans`, shown in the Table 3. Attribute `MName` gives the name of the metric. When a metric can be calculated in several ways, several entries with the same `MName` exist. `EventTypes` and `relations` define the relations where the relevant event data is stored. `std_agg` defines with which aggregate function is to be applied normally to the retrieved data before the method `Operation` processes the data. `std_agg` can also be changed in the measurement definition. If `cond_param` is present it defines which attribute has to be evaluated by `Operation`.

4.4 Definition and Reading of Measurements

A measurement is a metric applied to a defined set of objects. The component uses a two-step approach to measurement definitions. In the first step a measurement is defined, in the second the data is retrieved for given time intervals.

The first step prepares the query. The interface of the definition module passes several lists of objects which take part in the measurement. The `measure_plans` relation is used to find the tables with the events needed for the measurement.

A first test is executed, whether the needed data is present for the selected objects. For this the `TraceDesc` relation is used. If no appropriate entry for the given objects and the selected event types can be found, the next `measure_plan` tuple with the same `MName` is selected and the search is repeated. If a entry in `TraceDesc` is found, `TDId` represents a selection criterion for selection of the trace data in the event relations given in `measure_plans`.

MNo	MName	relations	EventTypes	Operation	std_agg	cond_param
1	'busy_time'	'cc'	'20'	'counter'	'SUM'	'value'
2	'busy_time'	'ps_pe'	'10,11'	'pair'	'SUM'	"
5	'delay_receive'	'ob_ox'	'2,3'	'pair'	'SUM'	"
6	'com_volume'	'ob_ox'	'2,3'	'single_val'	'SUM'	'volume'

Tabelle 3: Part of the relation `measure_plans`

If the data needed for the measurement is present in the trace database, a skeleton of the SQL query is created and kept for the second step.

In the second step a time interval is selected and inserted into the prepared SQL statement, which is then executed. The method given in `measure_plans` uses the results of the query to calculate the associated metric.

5 Measurement Results

We compared the performance of the implemented system to the hand-coded version used in the existing version of TATOO. We present performance measurements for reading of trace files and for the reading of two types of measurements.

All measurements were carried out on a SUN Sparc10 under SunOS 4.1.3 with 32 MB of main memory. Trace data and the data bases were on separate but local disks.

The reading of trace file into the data base is done with a rate of about 300 events per second. The same operation in the hand-coded version works with about 3000 events per second. In both cases the user does not have to wait with the analysis until the complete file is read. Analysis can start concurrently. See also Table 4. The handcoded version soon reaches the limits of the available swap space.

Evaluation of measurements is a linearly dependent from the length of the time interval covered in the query. We compare analysis of a 100 MB trace file with about 4.7 mio events. The first measurement concerned average busytime of one processor, the second average busy time of all 16 processors in the system. See Table 5.

As you can see, the hand-coded version is about one order of magnitude slower than the database solution.

6 Conclusion

We presented a trace analysis component based on a relational database. The component is configurable in regard to the accepted trace format and the usable metrics. It overcomes memory restrictions encountered in main memory based solutions. The raw trace data does not have to be read repeatedly and can be accessed by several developers at the same time.

The performance of the component is about one order of magnitude below a hand-coded version. We feel that this is still acceptable, regarding the advantages and restrictions of this approach.

One perspective to boost the performance of the system would be a hybrid approach, which leaves measurement definition in the RDBS and stores the event data in indexed sequential files. This would improve the access time for the trace data by keeping the ordering in time.

Other means like programming on the low level interface of the database system would spoil the advantages of the use of the standard interface SQL.

As soon as temporal databases are available, the approach should be re-evaluated.

Future research will deal with the comparison of trace data from different performance experiments and the integration of performance assessment techniques.

Literatur

[1] Rolf Borgeest, Bernward Dimke, and Olav Hansen. A trace based performance evaluation tool for parallel real time systems. *Parallel Computing*, 21(4):551 – 564, April 1995.

[2] Rainer Klar. *Messung und Modellierung paralleler und verteilter Rechensysteme*. Teubner Stuttgart, Stuttgart, first edition, 1995.

[3] R. Snodgrass. Monitoring in a software development environment: A relational approach. *SIGPLAN Notices*, 19(5):124–131, May 1984.

[4] R. Snodgrass. A relational approach to monitoring complex systems. *ACM Transactions on Computer Systems*, 6(1):157–196, Feb 1988

[5] Sekhar R. Sarukkai and Dennis Gannon. Sieve: A performance debugging environment for parallel programms. *Journal of Parallel and Distributed Computing*, 18:147–168, 1993.

No. of events	Database solution time	events/sec	Hand-coded version time	events/sec
120	12	10	.5	240
958	13	74	1.3	737
5000	18	277	1.5	3333
10.000	26	384	2.6	3846
51.500	83	620	10.2	5049
124.034	322	385	27.6	4494
1.000.000			207	4831
4.702.616	15600	301		

Tabelle 4: reading of trace files

Measurement	Database solution time (sec)	Hand-coded version time (sec)
Busy time (1 processor)	1697	130
Busy time (16 processors)	5865	525

Tabelle 5: Reading of measurements

[6] Sute Lei and Kang Zhang. Performance visualisation of message passing programs using relational approach. In *Proceedings on the 7th International Conference on Parallel and Distributed Computing Systems*, page ?? ISCA, Oct 1994.

[7] Daniel A. Reed. Experimental analysis of parallel systems: Techniques and open problems. In Günter Haring and Gabriele Kotsis, editors, *Computer Performance Evaluation*, volume 794 of *LNCS*, pages 25–51. Springer, 1994.

[8] Ruth A. Aydt. The pablo self-defining data format. User manual, DCS, University of Illionois, Urbana, Ill., July 1994.

[9] B. Mohr. Standardization of Event Traces Considered Harmful or Is an Implementation of Object-Independent Event Trace Monitoring and Analysis Systems Possible? In J.J. Dongarra and B. Tourancheau, editors, *Environments and Tools For Parallel Scientific Computing, Advances in Parallel Computing, Vol. 6 (Proc. of the CNRS-NSF Int'l Workshop, Saint Hilaire du Touvet, September 7-8, 1992)*, pages 103–124. Elsevier, 1993.

[10] J. Irion. High performance computing applications for idustrial embedded systems. In *European Informatics Congress on Computing Systems Architectures EUROARCH 93, Munich*, 1993.

[11] M. van Steen, T. Vogel, and A. ten Dam. Adl: A graphical design language for parallel real time applications. In P. Welch (ed.) J.H. R. Grebe S. Hilton, M. Jane, editor, *Proceedings World Transputer Congress 1993*, pages pp. 365 – 379. IOS Press, 1993.

[12] P. Pouzet, J. Paris, and V. Jorrand. Parallel application design: The simulation approach with HASTE. In W. Gentzsch and U. Harms, editors, *High-Performance Computing and Networking*, volume 797 of *LNCS*, pages 379 – 393. Springer-Verlag, April 1994.

[13] C. Rödel. Eine Datenbank zur Leistungsanalyse von Parallelrechnern. Master's thesis, TU München, Mai 1994.

[14] A. Marconi, M. R. Nazzarelli, S. Sabina, E. N. Houstis, K. N. Pantazopoulos, and M. A. Tsoukarellas. Peps esprit project 6942; monitoring work package wp 4; tasks t4.2.1 - t4.2.2; deliverable d4.2; monitoring and performance analysis tools requirement analysis. Technical report, CEU, Oct. 1994.

❖ Open Forum Session II ❖

Chair

E. Luque

Load Balancing with Internode Precedence Relations: a New Method for Static Allocation of DAGs into Parallel Systems

M.Coli, P.Palazzari
Dipartimento di Ingegneria Elettronica
Università "La Sapienza"
Via Eudossiana 18, 00184 Roma
Ph +39-6-44585345, Fax +39-6-4742647, E-mail coli@die.ing.uniroma1.it

Abstract

In order to execute a parallel program Pp into a parallel machine PM, we must determine an allocation function which assigns Pp operations to PM processors in a way such as the execution time of Pp is minimum. As this problem is known to be NP-complete, a lot of alternative approaches have been proposed in the literature. In this paper we refer to load balancing (LB) approaches, i.e. to mapping algorithms which determine allocation function by uniformly distributing the computational load among PM processors.

Through a simple example we show that internode precedence relations (IPR) cannot be neglected in LB algorithms when we want to achieve high speed up. As far as we know, LB algorithms do not consider IPR, so we present a new LB algorithm which determines an allocation of Pp on PM respecting IPR.

We compare the parallel execution times achievable through the presented algorithm with the ones given by mapping algorithm described in [2]; comparisons, based on actual executions of Pp with diferent sizes and granularities, show that the presented algorithm gives performance improvements varying from 6% to 76%.

Keywords: *Directed Acyclic Graphs, Internode Precedence Relations, Load balancing, Static Allocation, Simulated Annealing.*

1 Introduction

A parallel program Pp is represented through a Directed Acyclic Task Graph G=(**N**,**E**), where

$$\mathbf{N} = \{n_i,\ i=1,2,\ldots,n\}$$

is the node set,

$$\mathbf{E} = \{(n_i,n_j) \mid n_i,n_j \in \mathbf{N},\ n_i \text{ sends a message to } n_j\}$$

is the internode communication set; $e=|\mathbf{E}|$. Then we define a labelling function

$$L_E : \mathbf{E} \rightarrow \mathbf{R}^+;$$

$L_E[(n_i,n_j)]$ is the length of the message sent from n_i to n_j.

If G is cyclic, we suppose that it is transformed into an acyclic graph through the operations described in [9].

A parallel machine can be represented through the graph PM=(**P**,**L**) where

$$\mathbf{P} = \{p_i,\ i=1,2,\ldots,p\}$$

is the processor set,

$$\mathbf{L} = \{(p_i,p_j) \mid p_i \text{ and } p_j \text{ communicate through a link}\}$$

is the communication channel set. As for G, a labelling function

$$L_L : \mathbf{L} \rightarrow \mathbf{R}^+$$

is defined; $L_L[(p_i,p_j)]$ is the bandwidth of the channel connecting p_i with p_j.

We assume the function

$$T_X : \mathbf{N} \times \mathbf{P} \rightarrow \mathbf{R}^+$$

to be known; $T_X(n_i,p_j)$ is the execution time of n_i in processor p_j.

In order to execute Pp on the Parallel Machine (PM), we must determine the allocation function

$$A : \mathbf{N} \rightarrow \mathbf{P}$$

which assigns a processor p_j to each n_i; $A(n_i)=p_j$ means that node n_i is allocated into processor p_j. The allocation function can be expressed through a $(n \times p)$ $X=\{x_{ij}\}$ matrix, being

$$x_{ij} = \begin{cases} 1 & \text{if } n_i \text{ is allocated in processor } p_j \\ 0 & \text{otherwise} \end{cases}.$$

We search for an allocation matrix X^* which minimizes the execution time of Pp ($T_{exe}(Pp,X)$), that is

$$T_{exe}(Pp,X^*) = \min_X\left(T_{exe}(Pp,X)\right). \quad (1)$$

As known, problem (1) is NP-complete. Approaches proposed in the literature make some simplifying assumptions and are based on the application of heuristics [9],[10], 0-1 programming [1], load balancing [11],[2],[14], graph theory [12], clustering [6] and list scheduling [13].

This paper deals with the load balancing approach; algorithms based on load balancing search for an allocation matrix X which makes the computational load to be uniformly distributed among all the processors. The basic idea underlying load balancing is that processor idle time is minimized when computational load is equidistributed. In [4] we showed that execution time of Pp is not minimized if internode precedence relations (IPR) are neglected. In this paper we present a new load balancing approach which takes into account IPR: it is based on a new cost function which is minimized through a Simulated Annealing (SA) [8] algorithm.

The paper is organized as it follows: in the next section we show that IPR cannot be neglected in order to minimize the execution time of Pp; in the third section we introduce a new cost function which will be minimized through SA; in the fourth section we give an efficient SA implementation; in the last section we show some experimental results which demonstrate the effectiveness of the proposed mapping method by comparing the obtained results with those achievable by applying the mapping algorithm given in [2].

2 Relevance of IPR in T_{exe} minimization

As far as we know, load balancing algorithm presented in literature do not take into account IPR. In the following we will refer to the well known and widely used load balancing algorithm presented in [2] by Bultan and Aykanat. They find the allocation matrix X by minimizing the following cost function

$$f_B(X) = \frac{1}{2}\sum_{i=1}^{n}\sum_{j\neq i}\sum_{p=1}^{p}\sum_{k\neq p} c_{ij}x_{ip}x_{jk}d_{pk} + \\ +\frac{r}{2}\sum_{i=1}^{n}\sum_{j\neq i}\sum_{p=1}^{p} x_{ip}x_{jp}w_{ip}w_{jp},$$

where

- c_{ij} is the time spent in the communication from n_i to n_j,
- d_{pk} is the distance between processors p_k and p_p,
- w_{ik} is the execution time of n_i in p_k,
- $r = \dfrac{\sum_{i=1}^{n}\sum_{j\neq i}\sum_{p=1}^{p}\sum_{k\neq p} c_{ij}x_{ip}x_{jk}d_{pk}}{p\times\sum_{i=1}^{n}\sum_{j\neq i}\sum_{p=1}^{p} x_{ip}x_{jp}w_{ip}w_{jp}}$ is a weighting factor initialized on the basis of a randomly chosen X.

In order to illustrate the impact of neglecting precedence relations, we consider the simple graph in figure 1; the number close to each node represents the execution time of the node; the communication time associated to each edge is 1.

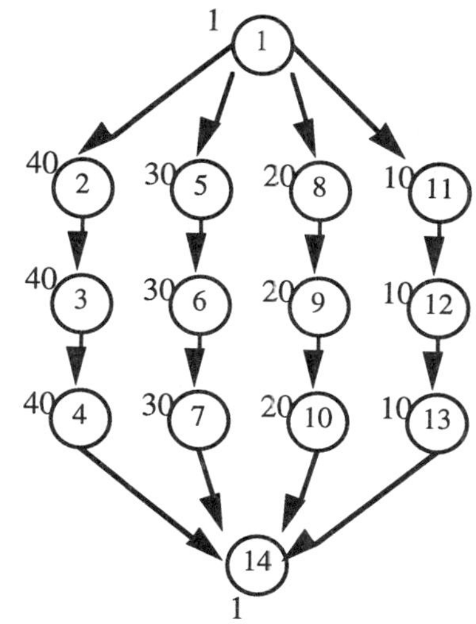

figure 1 : simple graph with 14 nodes

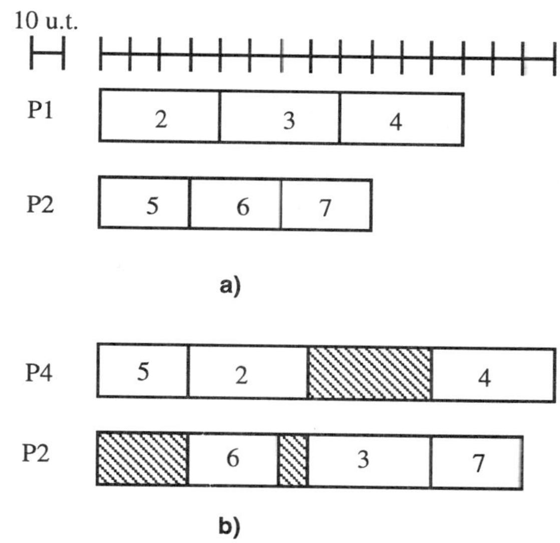

figure 2 Gantt Charts

The best execution time (122 unit of time) in a 4 processor computer is achieved by allocating nodes 1,2,3,4,14 in processor p1, nodes 5,6,7 in processor p2, nodes 8,9,10 in processor p3 and the nodes 11,12,13 in processor p4, i.e. we have $X_{opt} = \begin{cases} p1 = 1,2,3,4,14 \\ p2 = 5,6,7 \\ p3 = 8,9,10 \\ p4 = 11,12,13 \end{cases}$;

$f_B(X)$, initialized with r=1, assigns to this allocation the value $f_B(X_{opt})$=1158. The Gantt Charts corresponding to this allocation for processor p1 and p2 are shown in figure 2.a; the communication costs and the execution times of nodes 1 and 14 are neglected. When $f_B(X)$ is minimized, we found the following allocation X_{min} ($f_B(X_{min})$ = 982):

$$X_{min} = \begin{cases} p1 = 1,11,12,13,14 \\ p2 = 3,6,7 \\ p3 = 8,9,10 \\ p4 = 2,4,5 \end{cases}$$

If we analyze the Gantt Charts (reported for critical processors p4 and p2 in figure 2.b) relative to the best scheduling for X_{min}, we see that the execution time corresponding to X_{min} is greater than the execution time corresponding to X_{opt}. The simple example shows that the minimization of cost functions which do not consider IPR leads to an allocation which does not minimize the execution time of G.

3 The new cost function

The analysis of the previous simple example shows that minimization of $f_B(X)$ returns an allocation which gives an execution time longer than the one achievable with the optimal allocation because sequential nodes (2,3,4 and 5,6,7) are allocated into different processors. We can achieve considerable performance improvements if we introduce into $f_B(X)$ a weighting factor which makes more probable the coallocation of nodes connected by a path. In order to introduce a new cost function derived from $f_B(X)$ by inserting in it an adequate weighting factor, we recall that the transitive closure of a graph G(**N**,**E**) is defined as the graph $G^+(\mathbf{N},\mathbf{E}^+)$ which has an edge between two any nodes n_i and n_j if in G they are connected by a path; the transitive closure of a graph can so be represented by a (nxn) TC={tc_{ij}} matrix, being

$$tc_{ij} = \begin{cases} 1 \text{ if there is a path from } n_i \text{ to } n_j \\ 0 \text{ otherwise} \end{cases}.$$

By analizing $f_B(X)$ we see that its first (contracting) part depends on interpocessor communications, while the second (expanding) part depends on the execution times of the nodes; it seems to be reasonable to assume that the first part of $f_B(X)$ is less important than the second part if communication times in G are smaller than the computing times. On the basis of this intuitive consideration, we weight the summation of the contractive and of the expansive part of the cost function through the granularity [7] g(G) of the graph G, being g(G) defined in the following way:
let father(n_i) be the set of all the fathers of n_i, i.e.

$$\text{fathers}(n_i)=\{n_k|(n_k,n_i)\in \mathbf{E}\}$$

and let son(n_i) be the set of all the sons of n_i, i.e.

$$\text{sons}(n_i)=\{n_k|(n_i,n_k)\in \mathbf{E}\};$$

we define the two functions

$$g(J_i) = \frac{\min_{n_k \in \text{fathers}(n_i)} (w_k)}{\max_{n_k \in \text{fathers}(n_i)} (c_{ki})}$$

and

$$g(F_i) = \frac{\min_{n_k \in \text{sons}(n_i)} (w_k)}{\max_{n_k \in \text{sons}(n_i)} (c_{ik})};$$

granularity of n_i is then defined as

$$g(n_i)=\min(g(J_i),g(F_i))$$

and granularity of the whole graph G is defined as

$$g(G) = \min_{n_i \in \mathbf{N}} (g(n_i)).$$

Now we give the following f_{IPR-LB} cost function:

$$f_{IPR-LB}(X) = \sum_{i=1}^{n} \sum_{j \neq i} \sum_{p=1}^{p} \sum_{k \neq p} c_{ij} x_{ip} x_{jk} d_{pk} + $$
$$+ rg \sum_{i=1}^{n} \sum_{j \neq i} \sum_{p=1}^{p} x_{ip} x_{jp} w_{ip} w_{jp} (1 - tc_{ij} - tc_{ji})$$

being
- r the weighting factor defined in $f_B(X)$,
- g the granularity of G,
- tc_{ij} the elements of the TC matrix.

The (1-tc_{ij}-tc_{ji}) term can assume only the 0 or 1 values: in fact tc_{ij}=tc_{ji}=1 can never result because G is an acyclic graph; as a consequence, the expansive term of f_{IPR-LB} is minimized when nodes connected by a path are coallocated (1-tc_{ij}-tc_{ji}=0) and, as secondary goal, when the computational load is (nearly) balanced. If we allocate the simple graph in fig. 1 by minimizing f_{IPR-LB}, we find that minimum of f_{IPR-LB} corresponds to the optimal allocation X_{opt}.

Once the transitive closure of G has been computed ($O(n^3)$), the evaluation of f_{IPR-LB} has an $O(n^2)$ time complexity.

4 Efficient SA Implementation

In order to minimize $f_{IPR-LB}(X)$ through SA, we must define a new(X) function which returns a new allocation X' which is adjacent to X according to a given adjacency criterion; we define two allocation matrices to be adjacent if the following adjacency condition holds:

adjacency condition AC: two allocation matrices $X=\{x_{ij}\}$ and $X'=\{x'_{ij}\}$ are adjacent if they allocate *n*-1 nodes in the same processors and one node in two different processors. Formally AC is expressed as in the following:

$$\exists((i_0,j_0),(i_0,j_1)):\begin{cases} x_{ij}=x'_{ij} & \forall(i,j)\neq((i_0,j_0),(i_0,j_1)) \\ x_{i_0j_0}\neq x'_{i_0j_0} & \text{and } x_{i_0j_1}\neq x'_{i_0j_1} \end{cases}.$$

According to the previous definition of **AC**, function new(X) generates a new allocation X' by moving *one* node from a processor to another one.

We can now give the following SA minimization algorithm for $f_{IPR-LB}(X)$:

Input
- G=(**N**,**E**) and PM=(**P**,**L**);
- the input parameters Init_Temperature, n_elem, the cooling parameter red<1 and the stopping criterion are chosen as referred in [5];

Output
X^*: $f_{IPR-LB}(X^*)\leq f_{IPR-LB}(X)$ $\forall$ X generated by SA.

```
Begin
   X:=Random;
   (* the starting allocation is randomly selected *)
   fold:=fIPR-LB(X);
   T:=Init_Temperature;
   while not final_condition do
      for i:=1 to n_elem do
         X':=New(X);
         if ΔF=fIPR-LB(X')-fold<0 then
               X:=X';
               fold:=fIPR-LB(X')=fold+ΔF
            else
               q:=Random(0,1); (* q ∈ [0,1) *)
               if 1/(1+exp(-ΔF/T))<q then
                  (*accept with probability q*)
                     X:=X';
                     fold:=fIPR-LB(X')=fold+ΔF
               endif
         endif;
      endfor
      T:=red*T;
   endwhile
end.
```

If the number of iterations of the **while** and the **for** constructs are respectively *nw* and *nf*, SA algorithm has a time complexity $O(n^2\ nw\ nf)$, being $O(n^2)$ the complexity of $f_{IPR-LB}(X')$.

SA algorithm can be more efficiently implemented because only ΔF computation is required at each iteration of SA. As ΔF is given by $f_{IPR-LB}(X')-f_{IPR-LB}(X)$, and X and X' are two adjacent matrices (according to the adjacency criterion AC) which differ because n_l is moved from processor p_q (matrix X) to processor p_p (matrix X'), it is easy to derive for ΔF the following expression:

$$\Delta F = 2rgw_l \sum_{\substack{j=1 \\ j\neq l}}^{n} w_j(1-tc_{lj}-tc_{jl})(x_{jp}-x_{jq}) + \sum_{\substack{n_j\in son(n_l) or \\ n_j\in father(n_l)}} (c_{lj}-c_{jl})\Delta$$

being

- $\Delta = \sum_{\substack{k=1 \\ k\neq p,k\neq p}}^{p} x_{jk}\left(d_{pk}-d_{qk}\right)+(x_{jq}-x_{jp})d_{pq}$
- $son(n_l)=\{n_j|(n_l,n_j)\in \mathbf{E}\}$ the set of all the sons of n_l and
- $father(n_l)=\{n_j|(n_j,n_l)\in \mathbf{E}\}$ the set of all the fathers of n_l.

Computation of ΔF has time complexity O(*n*), so SA algorithm has time complexity $O(nw\ nf\ n)$ and the overall allocation algorithm, which requires the computation of the transitive closure of G, has time complexity $\max(n^3, nw\ nf\ n)$.

5 Experimental Results

In order to evaluate performance improvements achievable by allocating DAGs through the proposed mapping algorithm, we have randomly generated graphs with different sizes and different granularities; we have then allocated them by minimizing either $f_{IPR-LB}(X)$ or $f_B(X)$ and we actually executed them on a mesh connected parallel system with 9 transputers. Execution modality for each graph is the following:
- allocation is the one determined by minimizing $f_{IPR-LB}(X)$ (IPR-LB modality) or $f_B(X)$ (BA modality) through SA;
- routing is performed by adopting the deadlock free routing algorithm described in [3]; communications are overlapped to computing operations;
- nodes are executed according to a data flow modality, i.e. they are executed as soon as all their input data are available; if more nodes are contemporaneously ready for execution in the same processor, they are scheduled according to the time-sharing policy controlled by the internal HW transputer scheduler.

In each transputer OCCAM program is built by collecting through the PAR construct all processes implementing the nodes allocated in it; this parallel process is activated in parallel to the routing processes through a PRI PAR construct so as routing processes are executed at high priority while computing processes are executed at low priority.

Each node is implemented through an OCCAM process like the following:

```
--process implementing ni
SEQ
  -- Rx of all the messages from the
  -- parent nodes
  SEQ j = 0 FOR n_fathers(ni)
    delivery.channel(ni) ? message
  execute operations for Texe(ni) sec
  -- Tx of the result to all the sons
  SEQ j = 0 FOR n_sons(ni)
    injection.channel(ni) ! message
```

We report the results achieved by executing with IPR-LB and BA modalities 9 graphs with different sizes and granularities. The parameters describing the used 9 graphs are the following:

G1: 60 nodes, granularity g=1, sequential execution time t_{seq}=728 ms, execution time (T_{exe}) for the nodes randomly chosen in [10ms-15ms] and communication times (T_c) randomly chosen in [5ms-10ms], max number of sons of each node max_sons= 4;
G2: 60 nodes, g=8, t_{seq}=2850 ms, $T_{exe} \in$ [40ms-60ms], $T_c \in$ [5ms-10ms], max_sons=4;
G3: 60 nodes, g=100, t_{seq}=13171 ms, $T_{exe} \in$ [200ms-250ms], $T_c \in$ [1ms-2ms], max_sons=4;
G4: 80 nodes, g=1, t_{seq}=973 ms, $T_{exe} \in$ [10ms-15ms], $T_c \in$ [5ms-10ms], max_sons=4;
G5: 80 nodes, g=8, t_{seq}=3833 ms, $T_{exe} \in$ [40ms-60ms], $T_c \in$ [5ms-10ms], max_sons=4;
G6: 80 nodes, g=100, t_{seq}=17739 ms, $T_{exe} \in$ [200ms-250ms], $T_c \in$ [1ms-2ms], max_sons=4;
G7: 100 nodes, g=1, t_{seq}=1222 ms, $T_{exe} \in$ [10ms-15ms], $T_c \in$ [5ms-10ms], max_sons=4;
G8: 100 nodes, g=8, t_{seq}=4894 ms, $T_{exe} \in$ [40ms-60ms], $T_c \in$ [5ms-10ms], max_sons=4;
G9: 100 nodes, g=100, t_{seq}=21988ms, $T_{exe} \in$ [200ms-250ms], $T_c \in$ [1ms-2ms], max_sons=4.

In table 1 we show, for each graph, the parallel execution times we obtained when we actually executed the graphs by using the allocations derived from BA algorithm (BA column) or the presented algorithm (IPR-LB column).

	60 nodes	
	BA	IPR-LB
g=1	275	214
g=8	1102	870
g=100	5700	3333

table 1 a)

	80 nodes	
	BA	IPR-LB
g=1	241	266
g=8	1384	753
g=100	5614	3399

table 1 b)

	100 nodes	
	BA	IPR-LB
g=1	539	504
g=8	1679	1240
g=100	8257	4277

table 1 c)

table 1: parallel execution times (in ms) for the graphs G1-G9 when BA and IPR-LB modalities are used.

Figures 1, 2, and 3 show the obtained parallel execution times for graphs with the same dimension and with different granularities.

In order to measure the better performances achievable through the presented mapping algorithm, we introduce the Differential Speed-up Ratio (DSR) between mapping BA and mapping IPR-LB:

$$DSR = \frac{S_{IPR-LB} - S_{BA}}{S_{BA}},$$

being S_{IPR-LB} and S_{BA} the speed-up achieved by using the mapping given by our algorithm or by BA algorithm.

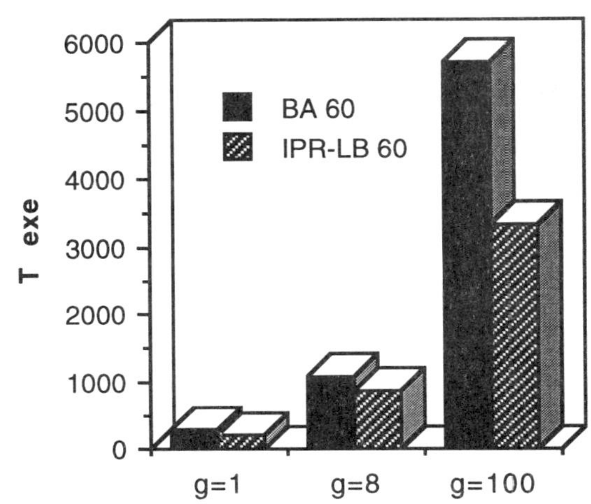

figure 3

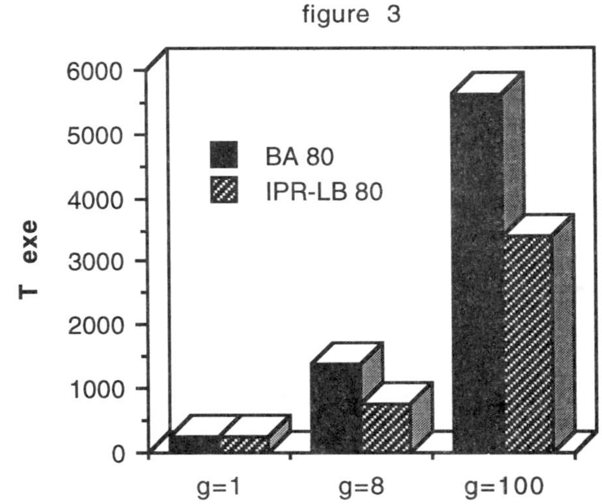

figure 4

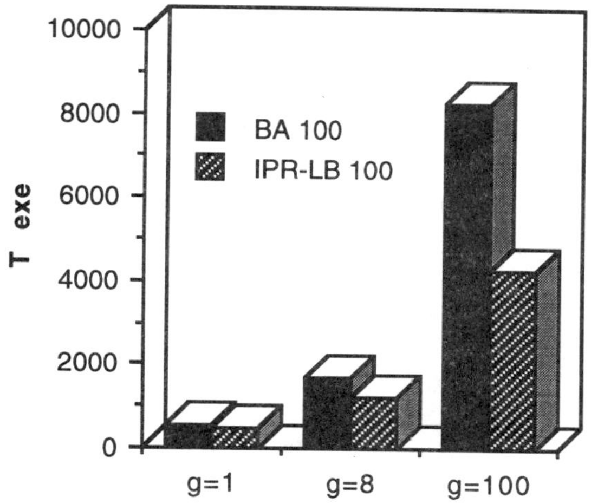

figure 5

By using data of table 1 we can compute the average speed up for a given granularity g by averaging the speed-up obtained for different graphs with the same granularity g. We use data in table 1 in order to evaluate DSR for the granularities g=1, g=8 and g=100; we have:

DSR(g=1) = 0.06
DSR(g=8) = 0.49
DSR(g=100) = 0,76.

Above data show that the bigger is g, the higher is DSR; this happens because at low granularities communications become a dominant factor and they must be explicitly allocated; as our mapping algorithm does not consider the mapping of communications to processor links, we obtain little improvements at low granularities (6%) while large improvements (76%) at high granularities are obtained.

Conclusions

Load balancing of the computational load is a widely used criterion to determine the mapping of a Directed Acyclic Task Graph into a given parallel machine. Usually, the mapping algorithms based on load balancing do not consider Internode Precedence Relations (IPR) when the mapping is determined; through a simple example, we have shown that high speed up cannot be achieved if we neglect IPR. We have presented a new load balancing algorithm which takes into account IPR; it is based on the minimization through Simulated Annealing of a new cost function which, in order to respect IPR, uses the transitive closure of the graph under allocation. An efficient implementation of SA algorithm is given.

We have randomly generated graphs with differents sizes and granularities and we have allocated them by using the presented algorithm and the one described in [2]; then we have actually executed them on a parallel machine by using the obtained allocations. Comparative results show that our algorithm gives performance improvements, with respect to [2], varying from 6% (graphs with small granularity) to 76% (graphs with large granularity).

References

[1] Billionnet,A., Costa,M.C., Sutter,A. : 'An efficient algorithm for a task allocation problem'. Journal of the ACM, vol. 39, N. 3, Jul. 1992.
[2] Bultan,T., Aykanat,C. : 'A new mapping heuristic based on mean field annealing'. Journal of Parallel and Distributed Computing, vol. 16, N. 4, Dec. 1992.
[3] Coli,M., Palazzari,P. : 'An Adaptive Deadlock and Livelock Free Routing Algorithm' Euromicro Workshop on Parallel and Distributed Processing - Sanremo (Italy) January 25-27 1995.
[4] Coli,M., Palazzari,P. : 'Global Execution Time Minimization By Allocating Tasks In Parallel Systems' Euromicro Workshop on Parallel and Distributed Processing - Sanremo (Italy) January 25-27 1995.
[5] Deckers,A., Aarts,E. : 'Global optimization and simulated annealing'. Mathematical programming, 50, 1991.
[6] Gerasoulis,A., Yang,T. : 'A comparison of clustering heuristics for scheduling directed acyclic graphs on multiprocessors'. Journal of Parallel and Distributed Computing, vol. 16, N. 4, Dec.. 1992.
[7] Gerasoulis,A., Yang,T. : 'On the granularity and clustering of directed acyclic task graphs'. IEEE Transactions on Parallel and Distributed Systems, vol. 4, N. 6, Jun. 1993.
[8] Kirkpatrick,S., Gelatt,C.D., Vecchi,M.P. : 'Optimization by simulated annealing'. Science, Vol. 220, N. 4589, 13 May 1983.
[9] Lee,B., Hurson,A.R., Feng,T.Y. : 'A vertically layered allocation scheme for data flow systems'. Journal of Parallel and Distributed Computing, N. 11, Nov. 1991.
[10] Malloy,B.A., Lloyd,E.L., Soffa,M.L. : 'Scheduling DAG's for asynchronous multiprocessor execution'. IEEE Transactions on Parallel and Distributed Systems, vol. 5, N. 5, May. 1994.
[11] Meuwissen,J., Plateau,B., Seredynski,F. : 'Allocation of parallel programs by migrating Boltzman machine'. Proceedings of the International Conference on Parallel Computing and Transputer Applications PACTA 92 - 21:24 Sept 1992 - Barcellona - CIMNE, Barcellona - IOS Press, Amsterdam, Washington.
[12] Shen,C., Tsai,W. : 'A graph matching approach to optimal task assignment in distributed computing systems using a minimax criterion' - IEEE Transactions on Computers, Vol. c. 34, n. 3, Mar. 1985.
[13] Yang,T., Gerasoulis,A. : 'DSC: scheduling parallel tasks on an unbounded number of processors'. IEEE Transactions on Parallel and Distributed Systems, Vol. 5, n. 9, Sept. 1994.
[14] Woodside,C.M., Monforton,G.G. : 'Fast allocation of processes in distributed parallel systems'. IEEE Transactions on Parallel and Distributed Systems, vol. 4, N. 2, Feb. 1993.

Analysis and Evaluation of Sorting on Hypercube-Based Systems

Erich Schikuta and Peter Kirkovits
Inst. f. Applied Computer Science, Dept. of Data Engineering, University of Vienna
Rathausstr. 19/4, A-1010 Vienna, Austria

Abstract

This paper analyzes disk based sorting in parallel database systems. The parallel merge sort and the bitonic sort algorithms are modeled analytically and their performance is estimated. The obtained results are evaluated by and compared with benchmark results of an implementation on a hypercube based system.

Furthermore a novel, concise, but comprehensive analytical model for the evaluation of parallel database operations is presented.

1. Introduction

In the last few years parallel database systems [1] gained an important role in database research. This was connected with the shift from the (actually failed) development of highly specialized database machines to the usage of conventional parallel hardware architectures. Generally parallelism is employed in parallel database systems by operator and/or data parallelism [2]. Operator parallelism is achieved by executing the different operators of a partitioned query execution plan in parallel. Data parallelism is reached by executing the same operation in parallel on the partitioned data set among multiple processor.

Sorting is a extremely demanding operation in a database system. It is one of the most frequently used operators in query execution plans generated by database query optimizers. Therefore its performance influences dramatically the performance of the overall database system [3], [4].

Generally sorting algorithms can be divided into internal (main memory based) and external (disk based) algorithms [5]. An external sorting algorithm is necessary, if the data set is too large to fit into main memory. Obviously this is the common case in database systems. Sorting algorithms are very well analyzed and examined for sequential processors. Also internal sorting algorithms for parallel architectures are investigated (e.g. [6], [7], [8]), but the topic of external sorting for parallel computer architectures has not yet received adequate consideration.

The paper is organized as follows. In section 2 the parallel sorting algorithms in focus, parallel binary merge sort [9] and block bitonic sort [10] are described. The following section presents a framework of the underlying parallel hardware architecture, the model of analysis and its justification. The 4th section gives a comprehensive analytical formulation of the parallel sorting algorithms, followed by the results of the implementation according to varying test parameters, as number of nodes, data set size and page size. In the last section the analytical model is evaluated by comparing the results obtained by the theoretical formulation and the practical implementation. The obtained results are discussed and the algorithms compared.

2. Parallel disk based sorting algorithms

In this paper we concentrate on 2 parallel sorting algorithms, the *parallel binary merge sort* and the *block bitonic sort* algorithm and analyze their performance theoretically and practically. These 2 algorithms are broadly accepted and the algorithms of choice in parallel database systems, because of their clear design and well studied properties. They were theoretically analyzed by Bitton et al. [9] by a rather restricted model with the result that the block bitonic sort generally outperforms the binary sort merge. Variations for declustered data sets were developed and theoretically analyzed in [16].

Due to the size restriction of the paper only a short description of the 2 well known algorithms is given in the following. A more detailed and comprehensive discussion can be found in the cited literature.

2.1 Binary merge sort

Binary Merge-Sort uses several phases, to sort $m*tpp$ tuples, where m is the number of pages containing the data set and tpp denotes the number of tuples per page. We assume, that there are much more pages m than processing nodes p (i.e. $m>>p$) and that the size of the data set is much larger than the available main memory of the nodes.

We assume the very general case that the pages are *not* distributed equally among the mass storage media of the available nodes and that the tuples are *not* presorted according to the sorting criteria in the pages. Therefore the

1066-6192/96 $5.00 © 1996 IEEE
Proceedings of PDP '96

algorithm starts with a prepare phase (see Figure 1), which distributes the pages equally across all p nodes, sorts the tuples inside every page according to the sort criterion and writes the pages back to disk. After the prepare phase *m/p* (respectively *m/p-1*) pages are assigned to each node and the tuples of each page are sorted.

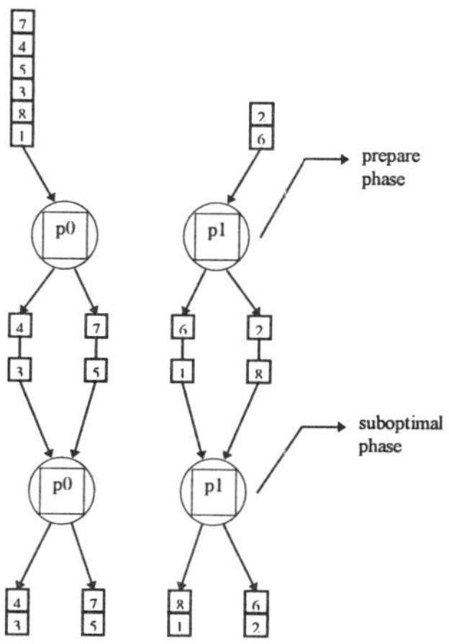

Figure 1: Prepare phase

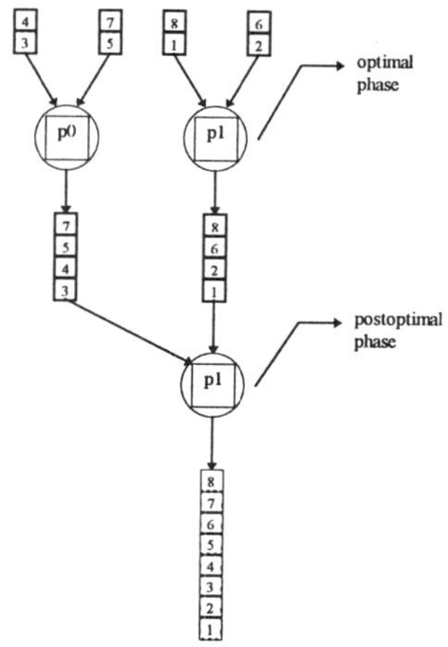

Figure 2: Binary merge sort

The algorithm continues with the suboptimal phase (see Figure 2) by merging pairs of longer and longer runs (i.e. ordered sequences of pages). In every step the length of the runs is twice as large as in the preceding run. At the beginning each processor reads two pages, merges them into a run of 2 pages and writes it back to the disk. This is repeated, until all pages are read and merged into 2-pages-runs. If the number of runs exceeds *2*p*, the suboptimal phase continues with merging two 2-page-runs to a sorted 4-page-run. This continues until all 2-page-runs are merged. The phase ends, when the number of runs is *2*p*. At the end of the suboptimal phase exist on each node 2 sorted files of length *m/(p*2)*. In the suboptimal phase the nodes work in independently parallel. Every node accesses its own data.

During the following optimal phase each processor merges 2 files of length *m/(2*p)* and pipelines the result (file of length *m/p*) to a target node. The number of target nodes is *p/2*. The identification of the target-node is calculated by

$$tar\_node\_nr := \frac{p}{2} + source\_node\_nr$$

for even source-node-numbers, and

$$tar\_node\_nr := \frac{p}{2} + source\_node\_nr + 1$$

for odd source-node-numbers.

In the postoptimal (last) phase the remaining *p/2* runs are merged into the final run of length m. At the beginning of the postoptimal phase, we have *p/2* runs. During this phase one of the p nodes is no longer used. Each of the other nodes is used only once during this phase. Two forms of parallelism are used. First, all nodes of one step work in parallel. Second, the steps of the postoptimal phase overlap. The execution time between two steps consists of merging the first pages, building the first output-page and sending it to the target-node. During the postoptimal phase every node is used only in one step, that means that every node is idle for a certain time.

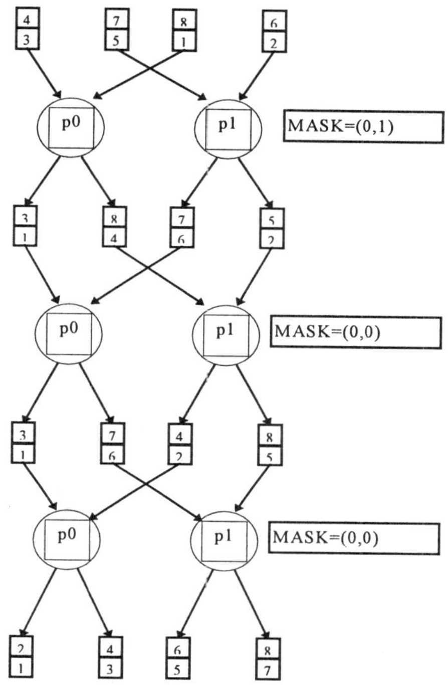

Figure 3: Bitonic sort

2.2 Bitonic-sort

Batcher's bitonic sort algorithm sorts n numbers with n/2 comparator modules in $\frac{1}{2} * \log n * (\log n + 1)$ steps [10]. Each step consist of a comparison-exchange at every comparator module and a transfer to the target-comparator module. The comparator modules are connected by the perfect shuffle [14], [15] (Figure 3). The perfect shuffle uses three types of comparator modules (Figure 4). The comparator module is represented by a node, which merges two pages and distributes the 'lower' page and the 'higher' page to two target-nodes. The target-nodes are defined by using a *mask*-information (i.e. the information for the perfect shuffle).

The algorithm uses three basic operations, which are described below.

1. **circulate**(S)
   From each of the 2*p files the pages are routed to a node through the perfect shuffle interconnection.
   each node p_i creates its MASK(i)
   each node merges its pages and distributes them according to MASK(i) = {0, 1, -1}
2. **shuffle**(mask)
   This operation shuffles the MASK-array from the second *2**p-1* nodes to their target-nodes such that the target-nodes will use the same type o
3. **mask**(j)
   It computes the entries of the MASK-array. Given an integer *j*, an array of length *2**p* is created as follows.
   MASK = -1, -1, -1, ..., -1 if *j = -1*
   MASK = 0, 1, 0, 1, ..., 0, 1 if *j <= p - 1*
   MASK = 0, 0, 0, ...,0, 0 if *j = p*

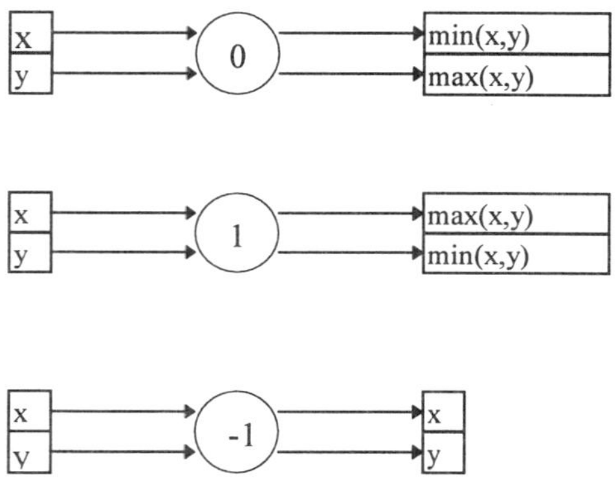

x ... page of first run
y ... page of second run
min(x,y) ... 'lower'page
max(x,y) ... 'higher'page

Figure 4: Three types of the comparator module

It is necessary to build *2*p* equally distributed and sorted runs of length *m/(2*p)*. The prepare-phase and the suboptimal phase (see Section 2.1) produce the *2*p* runs. The algorithm for the perfect shuffle is given below

```
for i=1 to p;
{
    mask(-1);
    for j=1 to (p-i)
    {
        circulate(S);
    }
    mask(i);
    for j = p - i + 1 to p
    {
        circulate(S);
        shuffle(MASK);
    }
}
```

3. Model of analysis

3.1 Differences to other models

It was our goal to define a model, which is as concise as possible, but does not loose completeness. Further we tried to simulate the reality as close as possible.

Our model used in the following analysis differs in a number of important points from other models in the literature, as [6], [12] or [13]. In particular it is more general than the model of Bitton et al. [9], which is the generally accepted reference model in the literature.

The conventional models assume, that the pages are pre-sorted internally. Therefore no time for sorting the pages is taken into account. As we saw in our tests, plenty of time is spent to sort the pages internally. Due to the requirements in relational database systems relations have to be sorted according to different attributes very often. Therefore, the assumption, that the pages of the relation are sorted internally, is NOT realistic.

The conventional metric in the algorithm analysis are large execution (time) units (e.g. the well known C_2^p two-page-units). The differences in the execution times for one page operations depending on the different phases of the algorithms are lost. Therefore the models loose precision and calculate inaccurate results.

One proposition of the conventional models is that the pages are distributed equally. Mostly the algorithms do not consider that pages are distributed on different disks with different access times. It is common that the algorithms assume a hardware-architecture, where all nodes have access to one common secondary storage medium.

Many models are purely disk based, i.e. all temporary results are stored on to disk. This makes the algorithm analysis easier, but neglects the possibility of exploiting the local communication network of the system for a pipelined data flow (the output of one node is the input of another node).

3.2 Architectural framework

The architectural framework of our analysis is very general. The assumed underlying parallel computer architecture consists of 3 describing components,

- a number of processing units (P_1, P_2, ... P_n)
- a number of disks (mass storage system)
- an interconnection network

A set of processing units with their local main memory and/or a set of disks build a computational unit. The connection between these components is via a primary, high-speed bus system (e.g. local bus, a system bus, etc.). A processing unit can be seen as a topological unit< with other words, all components reside on one board.

The parallel system consists of a number of computational units (C_1, C_2, ... C_p) interconnected via a secondary (slower) interconnection network. This model comprises systems, where the components reside on different boards (but occupy one racket) or are spread across a network cluster among different systems.

This very general framework allows to model any thinkable processor-disk architectures. On the one hand it is possible to describe systems, where each processor has its own physical disk, as the IBM SP-1/2 or iPSC-2 hypercube. On the other hand also systems with dedicated data server pools are allowed, as the Intel Paragon. Of course combinations of such systems are feasible too.

3.3 Basics of the model

Our model depends on three describing static Parameters:

Parameters	Description
m	number of pages
p	number of nodes (processors) available for execution
tpp	number of tuples per page

The following derived and system dependent operations are introduced

Operation	Description
CC(tpp)	time, to transfer between the main memories of node i and j, 0<i,j<=p
CI(tpp)	time, to read one page from the disk to the main memory
CO(tpp)	time, to write one page from the disk to the main memory
max(m)	maximum number of pages on a single node

These operations describe the basic dynamic run-time behavior of the underlying system architecture. The effective values for these terms have to be measured in practice by suitable benchmark programs. These terms are generically used as the basic notation for the construction of the model.

A basic assumption in our model is that the relations of the database system are too large to fit into the total main memories of the processing units. Consequently the sorting has to be done externally and the I/O costs are an influencing factor for the system performance.

Due to the fact that in our architectural framework processors are possible, which have access to multiple disks, we assume in our model that each processor has access to just one *logical* disk. The describing access characteristics of this logical disk are chosen as a weighted average of the characteristics of the physical disks.

The following analytical formulation of the 2 sorting algorithms is based on the introduced terms

4. Analytical formulation

4.1 Phases of the algorithms

At the beginning both sorting algorithms employ the same two phases to achieve *p*2* sorted runs, a prepare phase and a suboptimal phase

After that both algorithms use different phases to reach the final state. These phases are:

for **binary merge sort**	for **bitonic sort**
optimal phase	bitonic phase
postoptimal phase	

4.1.1 Prepare phase

We suppose, that the pages are distributed among different disks (and therefore on different nodes, too). Furthermore we suppose, that the number of pages is not the same on every node. Third, the single pages are not presorted internally. The prepare phase includes following operations:

1. **distributing the pages**, such that the number of pages on every node is *m/p*. If *m* could not be divided by *p* without a remainder, the maximum difference of number of pages on the distinct nodes is 1. While distributing the pages, it has to be guaranteed, that a minimum number of pages are moved from the source-nodes to the target nodes.
2. **sorting** the **single page** internally. In our model we assume quadratic execution costs (to be on the secure side), due to the situation that we have on one hand no information of the tuple value distribution and on the other hand strict memory restrictions.
3. **building** *2*p* **files** of (nearly) equal size. The maximum difference of file-size is 1 page (see operation 2).

Distributing the pages. We have to read the pages into main memory. Because of different numbers of pages on every node this operation will require different execution costs on every node. Obviously the maximum amount will require the node with the maximum numbers of pages.

Reading a relation with *m* pages needs

$$read\_R(m, tpp) := m * CI(tpp)$$

Since the relation is distributed among several nodes, it will need

$$read\_R(\max(m), tpp)$$

to read all *m* pages in parallel.

Now these nodes, which have more than *m/p* pages, have to send the remaining pages to those nodes, which have less than *m/p* pages, which is

$$dist\_R(m,p,tpp) := \left(\max(m) - \frac{m}{p}\right) * CC(tpp)$$

Sorting single page. We assume a quadratic runtime behavior of the applied internal sorting algorithm. Therefore we put up the expression

$$sortpage(tpp) := tpp^2 * A + tpp * B + C$$

Building files. To write *m* pages, we need

$$write\_R(m,tpp) := m * CO(tpp)$$

Since we have already distributed the pages equally to all nodes, the effort to write back *m/p* pages back is

$$write\_R(\frac{m}{p}, tpp)$$

Combining all formulas, the whole prepare-phase is

$$\begin{aligned} prepare\_R(m,p,tpp) &:= read\_R(\max(m),tpp) + \\ &+ dist\_R(m,p,tpp) + \frac{m}{p} * sortpage(tpp) + \\ &+ write\_R(\frac{m}{p}, tpp) \end{aligned}$$

4.1.2 Suboptimal phase

Sorting the *2*p* files can be done independently on every node. Because of the prepare phase we can assume that all of the nodes will use nearly the same time to sort their 2 files. The suboptimal phase consists of merging pairs of runs. At the beginning the single pages are sorted internally only. After step 1 we have buckets of 2 sorted pages. After step 2 we have buckets of 4 sorted pages, and so on. It takes *ld(m/2p)* steps to merge all runs iteratively.

To calculate the costs of the whole phase we have to compute the time for merging the tuples of one single page. This is

$$sub\_workpage(tpp) := tpp * (3 * If\_stmt + 9 * Expr\_stmt)$$

where we have to sum up the expenses for each statement type.

During the algorithm, one single action is:

- reading two pages
- merging the tuples of these pages
- writing back the two merged pages

This action costs

$$2 * (CI(tpp) + sub\_workpage(tpp) + CO(tpp))$$

Because every file keeps *m/2p* pages and every node handles two files, a step will need

$$\frac{m}{2*p} * (2 * (CI(tpp) + sub\_workpage(tpp) + CO(tpp)))$$

We have *ld(m/2p)* steps in this phase, which results in the total time of

$$\begin{aligned} subopt\_R(m,p,tpp) &:= ld\left(\frac{m}{2*p}\right) * \frac{m}{p} * \\ &* (CI(tpp) + sub\_workpage(tpp) + CO(tpp)) \end{aligned}$$

4.1.3 Optimal phase

Now we merge 2 runs of the length *m/2p*. We do not write back the sorted file. We use the local communication network to send the sorted pages to the designated node using a pipelined data flow.

To handle one page during the optimal phase needs

$$\begin{aligned} opt\_workpage(tpp) &:= 6 * If\_stmt + 9 * Expr\_stmt + \\ &tpp * (6 * If\_stmt + 12 * Expr\_stmt) \end{aligned}$$

During the optimal phase, we have to

- read *m/p* pages
- merge *m/p* pages
- send *m/p* pages to the target-node

on every node in parallel, therefore

$$\begin{aligned} opt\_R(m,p,tpp) &:= \frac{m}{p} * \\ &* (CI(tpp) + opt\_workpage(tpp) + CC(tpp)) \end{aligned}$$

4.1.4 Suboptimal phase

During the suboptimal phase the designated nodes merge two files. The number of nodes involved decreases every step. It starts with *p/2* nodes and ends with one single node, which produces the final (sorted) file. The first step starts with two runs of the size *m/p*. In every further step the size of the runs is doubled. Consequently the last step (*ld(p)-th* step) sorts two runs of the length *m/2*.

Every single step needs

$$opt\_workpage(tpp) + CC(tpp)$$

Therefore the cost for the first page to reach the last step is

$$\begin{aligned} first\_page\_to\_top(p,tpp) &:= ld(p) * \\ &* (opt\_workpage(tpp) + CC(tpp)) \end{aligned}$$

Now we have to calculate the time for merging 2 runs of size *m/2* at the last node. Handling one page during the last step needs

$$\begin{aligned} sub\_workpage(tpp) &:= 7 * Expr\_stmt + \\ &+ tpp * (2 * If\_stmt + 8 * Expr\_stmt) \end{aligned}$$

The last step takes

$$final\_step(m,tpp) := m * (sub\_workpage(tpp) + CO(tpp))$$

Therefore cost formula for the whole phase is

$$\begin{aligned} postopt\_R(m,p,tpp) &:= first\_page\_to\_top(p,tpp) + \\ &+ final\_step(m,tpp) \end{aligned}$$

4.1.5 Bitonic phase

Bitonic-sort sorts n numbers by *n/2* comparator-modules in *1/2*ld(n)*(ld(n)+1)* steps (see Section 2.2). The size *n* is *2*p*, because we have to shuffle *2*p* files. To merge two pages, we need

$$2*(opt\_workpage(tpp)+CC(tpp))$$

In every step, two files are merged with *m/2p* pages each. Therefore the time for one step is

$$\frac{m}{2*p}*2*(opt\_workpage(tpp)+CC(tpp))$$

Now we have to multiply this formula with the number of steps. Furthermore a single parallel read of the pages at the beginning and a single write at the end of the bitonic-phase have to be added.

$$bitphase\_R(m,p,tpp):=\frac{m}{p}*CI(tpp)+ \\ +\frac{ld(2*p)}{2}*(ld(2*p)+1)*\frac{m}{2*p}* \\ *\left(2*\left(opt\_workpage(tpp)+CC(tpp)\right)\right)+ \\ +\frac{m}{p}*CO(tpp)$$

This formula can be simplified

$$bitphase\_R(m,p,tpp):=\frac{m}{p}* \\ *(CI(tpp)+\frac{ld(2*p)}{2}*(ld(2*p)+1)* \\ *(opt\_workpage(tpp)+CC(tpp))+CO(tpp))$$

4.2 Combined formulas

Now we can calculate the total expenses for the two sorting-algorithms. We combine the formulas of the single phases for each algorithm.

4.2.1 Binary-merge-sort

We get for the binary-sort merge

$$binsort\_R(/m,p,tpp):=prepare\_R(m,p,tpp)+ \\ +subopt\_R(m,p,tpp)+opt\_R(m,p,tpp)+ \\ +postopt\_R(m,p,tpp)$$

4.2.2 Bitonic-sort

Accordingly we calculate for the bitonic-sort

$$bitonic\_R(m,p,tpp):=prepare\_R(m,p,tpp)+ \\ +subopt\_R(m,p,tpp)+ \\ +bitphase\_R(m,p,tpp)$$

5. Evaluation

All tests were performed on an iPSC/2 hypercube system with 8 processing nodes. In contrast to conventional iPSC/2 or iPSC/860 platforms, each processor of the system serves both as a computing and I/O node. Each node is equipped with 8 MB of main memory and a local 650 MB disk. The underlying operating system of the nodes is a UNIX derivative, called NX/2. We bypassed the conventional Concurrent File System (CFS) and accessed the disks directly. As interprocess communication system we used the Intel process communication library.

5.1 Benchmarking the model

The operations *CI(tpp), CC(tpp)* and *CO(tpp)* showed different values when changing the number of tuples per page *(tpp)* (see Table 1). The benchmarks showed, that with increasing *tpp* the three parameters grew linearly (see Figure 5, which gives the runtime behavior of the basic I/O functions).

tuple	100	200	500	1000
CI	5.495	5.816	7.003	10.627
CC	1.168	1.327	1.799	2.706
CO	11.737	14.034	19.887	32.359

Table 1: Execution Times for CI, CO, CC respective to the numbers of tuples (tpp)

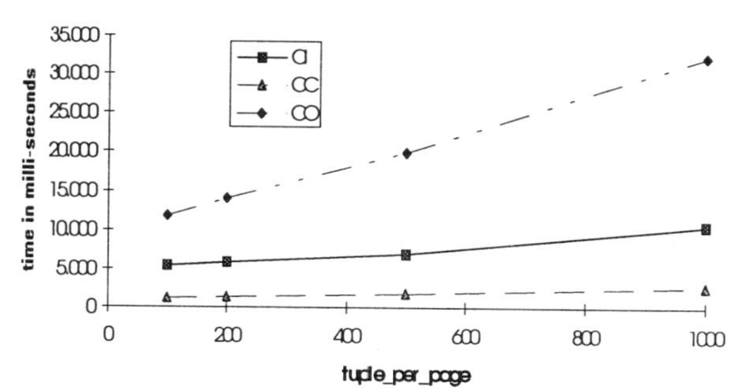

Figure 5: Determining the values for CI, CC, CO

To describe the behavior of the sorting-algorithm, we benchmarked the algorithm in our test environment for different numbers of *m* (100, 500, 1000) and found the formula

$$sortpage(tpp):=tpp^2*0.00117675+tpp*0.012546-0.01$$

5.2 Comparisons and results

We performed the tests varying the three variables of our model as seen in Table 2. Each run was performed several times and the numbers given in the analysis represent average values of the test results.

Variable	Values
number of pages (m)	100,200,500,1000
number of nodes (p)	2,4,8
tuples per page (tpp)	100,200,500,1000

Table 2: Evaluation variables

In the following comparisons, due to space restrictions, we present only subset of the analysis results, which is sufficient for the analysis.

Binary-merge-sort shows one big disadvantage. It does not use all the nodes for the whole time of sorting (see Figure 6, which gives the results for 1000 pages, 100 tuples per page and 8 nodes). While the last node is still processing, all other nodes are idle. One of the nodes is not used in the suboptimal phase at all.

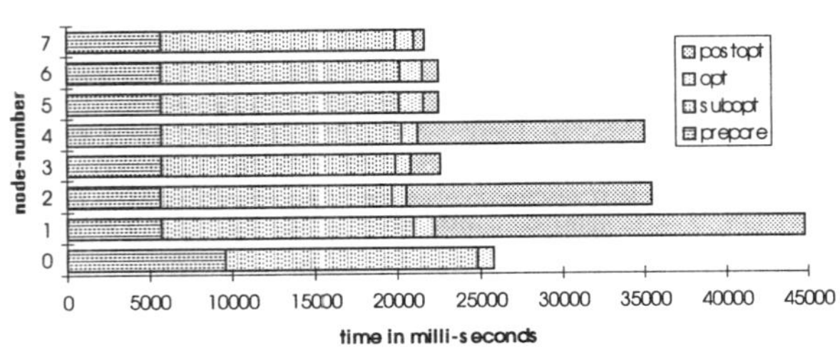

Figure 6: Different phases of binary-merge-sort

Bitonic-sort produces runtime overhead too, but uses all the nodes nearly the same time (see Figure 7 for 1000 pages, 100 tuples per page and 8 nodes). The different lengths of the bitonic phase of several nodes depend on the way of measuring the time. In our tests we started counting with the node waiting for the first page of the bitonic phase. Due to the uneven file distribution one node had to work more in the prepare phase and therefore finished later than the other nodes with the prepare and the suboptimal phase. Thus the other nodes had to wait for its pages. This wait time is concerned belonging to the bitonic phase.

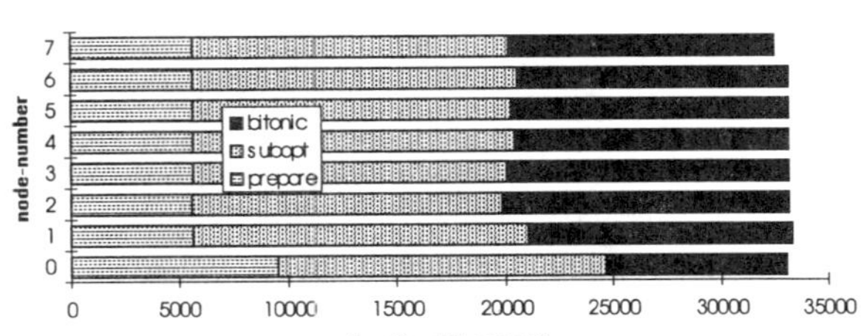

Figure 7: Different phases of bitonic-sort

Varying the number of nodes bitonic sort outperforms binary merge sort in all versions except for two nodes (see Figure 8 for 200 pages and 100 tuples per page).

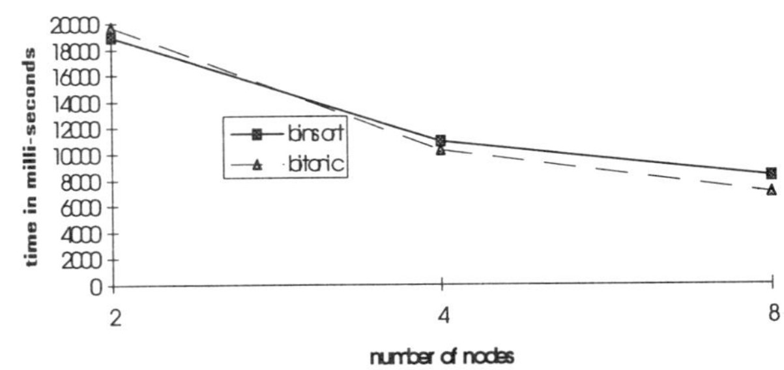

Figure 8: Execution times res. varying numbers of nodes

These practical result conforms with the theoretical analysis of Bitton et al. [9].

As stated by our tests the analytical model resembles the runtime behavior of the two algorithms very well and computes excellent estimations. Figure 9 and Figure 10 show comparisons between the real and estimated runtime costs. Our simulation caught the runtime characteristics of the 2 algorithms.

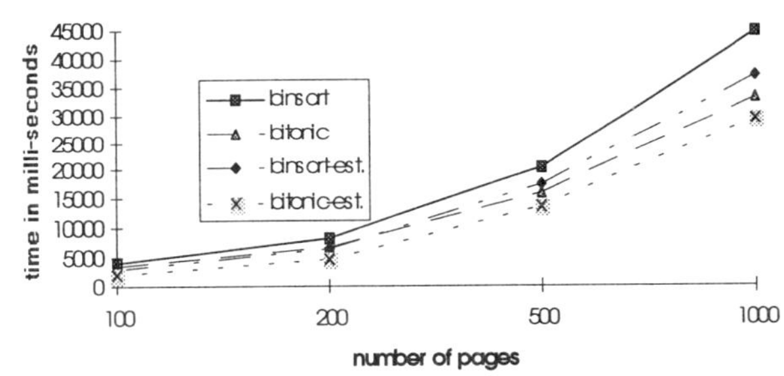

Figure 9: Comparison algorithms, model versus reality, 100 tuples, 8 nodes

Generally we observed that our model underestimated the real values. This is based on the fact that it simulates the pure algorithmic behavior and underestimates system services, as operating system or communication system. This adds in reality to the runtime expenses. Obviously this does not affect the general statement. The system load is directly correlated to the specific operations of the sorting algorithms. It modifies the over-all costs of the algorithms only by a constant factor, but does not change the run-time behavior at all.

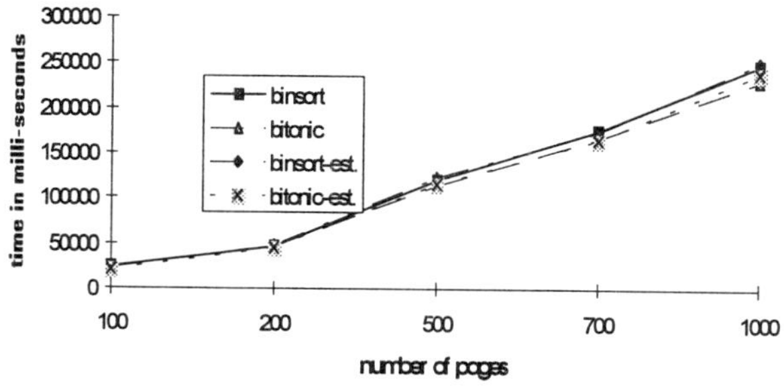

Figure 10: Comparison algorithms, model versus reality, 1000 tuples, 8 nodes

It is noteworthy that with increasing problem size and processor number this 'underestimation' characteristic of our model looses significance and 'disappears' finally (see Figure 10).

6. Conclusions

In this paper the performance of the well-known parallel merge sort and bitonic sort algorithms for parallel database systems was analyzed.

We developed an analytical evaluation model based on a very general parallel hardware architecture and formulated the runtime behavior of the algorithms. It was our aim to define a concise but comprehensive model and tried to avoid 'un-realistic' model restriction, e.g. pre-sorted and/or evenly distributed pages.. Further we implemented the algorithms on a parallel hardware architecture and measured the execution times of the algorithms in practice. The times calculated by the theoretical model were compared with the real values and led to a justification of the simulation.

The analysis showed that the bitonic sort outperforms the merge sort approach for large data set size and processor number.

These are important results for the creation of parallel execution plans for database queries. This work was performed as part of a project, which aims towards the development of a query optimizer for parallel database systems. We try to find a general execution time model for parallel query evaluations. It should give us the basis to create (near) optimal bushy query execution plans, which exploit operator- and data-parallelism.

7. References

[1] D.J. DeWitt, J. Gray, Parallel Database Systems: The Future of Database Processing or a Passing Fad?, SIGMOD record, 19, 4, Dec. 1990

[2] W. Hong, M. Stonebraker, Optimization of Parallel Query Execution Plans in XPRS, Proc. 1st Int. Conf. on Parallel and Distributed Information Systems, 1991

[3] B.R. Iyer, D.M. Dias, Syste, Issues in Parallel Sorting for Database Systems, Proc. Int. Conf. on Data Engineering, pp. 246-255, 1990

[4] M. Jarke, J. Koch, Query Optimization in Database Systems, ACM Computing Surveys 16, 2, pp. 111--152, 1984

[5] D. Bitton, D. DeWitt, D.K. Hsiao, J. Menon, A Taxonomy of Parallel Sorting, ACM Computing Surveys, 16, 3, pp. 287-318, September 1984

[6] G. Baudet, D. Stevenson, Optimal Sorting Algorithms for Parallel Computers, IEEE Transactions on Computers, 27, 1, pp. 84-87, January 1978

[7] K. Sado, Y. Igarashi, Some Parallel Sorts on a Mesh-Connected Processor Array and Their Time Efficiency, Journal of Parallel and Distributed Computing, 3, pp. 398-410, 1986

[8] F. Meyer auf der Heide, A. Wigderson, The Complexity of Parallel Sorting, SIAM Journal of Computing, 16, 1, pp. 100-107, February 1987

[9] D. Bitton, H. Boral, D.J. DeWitt, W.K. Wilkinson, Parallel algorithms for the execution of relational database operations, ACM Trans. Database Systems, 8, 3, 324-353, 1983

[10] K.E. Batcher, Sorting networks and their applications, In Proc. of the 1968 Spring Joint Computer Conference (Atlantic City, NJ, Apr. 30 - May 2), vol. 32, AFIPS Press, Reston, VA, pp. 307-314, 1968

[11] S. Ghandeharizadeh, D.J. DeWitt, W. Qureshi, A performance analysis of alternative multi-attribute declustering strategies, Proc. of SIGMOD 92, 1992

[12] C.D. Thompson, H.T. Kung, Sorting on a mesh-connected parallel computer, Communications of the ACM 20, 4 , pp. 263--271, 1977

[13] H. Boral, D.J. DeWitt, Design Considerations for data-flow Database Machines, Proc. ACM SIGMOD 80, pp 94--104, 1980

[14] S. Akl, Parallel Sorting Algorithms, Academic Press, Inc., 1985

[15] H.S. Stone, Parallel Processing with the Perfect Shuffle, IEEE Trans. Computing, 20, 2, 1971

[16] E. Schikuta, Parallel Relational Database Algorithms Revisited for Range Declustered Data Sets, Proc. Int. Symp. on Parallel Architectures, Algorithms and Networks (ISPAN), IEEE Computer Society Press, Dec. 1994

Achieving Good Performance for Dictionary Machines: a Scalable Distributed Data Balancing Technique*

Thibault Duboux Afonso Ferreira†

Laboratoire de l'Informatique du Parallélisme
URA 1398 du CNRS
Ecole Normale Supérieure de Lyon
69364 Lyon Cedex 07, FRANCE

Abstract

In this paper, we address the problem of how to process utility commands in database applications while the system remains operational and the data remain available for concurrent accesses. In particular, we focus on the on-line reorganization of a dictionary, *a database reduced to its simplest instance, showing its implementation on a multicomputer. As is the case with implementations of dynamic structures on distributed memory architectures, a crucial load balancing problem has to be solved. We propose an elegant solution and prove that it solves this problem. Experimental results are shown and analyzed.*

1 Introduction

The fast development over the last years of high performance multiprocessor machines makes them attractive candidates as the base technology for scalable and performance oriented applications. In order to handle the increasing amount of data, parallelism appears as a very promising research axe since loading or reorganizing a terabyte database can take several days. In the SQL world, typical utilities create indices, add or drop attributes, and physically reorganize the data, changing its clustering. Clearly, parallelism is needed if such utilities are to complete within a reasonable time. Even then, it will be essential that the data be available while the utilities are operating.

One unexplored and difficult problem is how to process database utility commands while the system remains operational and the data remain available for concurrent reads and writes. The fundamental properties of such algorithms is that they must be *online* (operate without making data unavailable), *incremental* (operate on parts of a large database), and *parallel.*

In this paper, we focus on this on-line reorganization applied to a *dictionary,* a database reduced to its simplest instance. The dictionary is an important data structure used in applications such as sorting and searching, symbol-table and index-table implementations. It is a basic data type which provides update and retrieval operations on a set of records. There is a unique search key K from a totally ordered set associated with each record. The standard dictionary operations are INSERT, DELETE and SEARCH. In addition, the EXTRACT-MIN *priority queue* operation may also be provided [1]. Note that some of these operations require a response to be produced.

The dictionary task can be loosely defined as the problem of maintaining a set of key-record pairs (K,R). For simplicity, the record whose associated key is K will be denoted record K. The dictionaries we consider support at least the following set of operations on its entries.

- INSERT(K,R): inserts key-record pair (K,R) in the dictionary;
- DELETE(K): deletes record K from the dictionary;
- SEARCH(K): retrieves record K if currently stored, does nothing otherwise;
- EXTRACT-MIN: returns the current minimum record and deletes it.

Insert and Delete can be *redundant.* An insertion is redundant when the key being inserted already exists in the dictionary; a deletion is redundant when the key being deleted does not exist.

Because of its general and fundamental capabilities, one important problem consists in designing special-purpose multiprocessor systems, called *dictionary machines*, implementing dictionaries of more or less restricted types. In a dictionary machine, a sequence of instructions (i.e., requests to perform dictionary or priority queue operations) is received through an I/O port. The machine executes the corresponding operations in a pipelined fashion, and reports the responses, if any, via the I/O port. Thus, performance of such a machine can be measured in terms of the following parameters.

Response time: The elapsed time between initiation and completion of an instruction.

Pipeline interval: The minimum elapsed time between the initiation of two distinct instructions.

*This work was partially supported by Stratagème project of the french CNRS and the DRET.

†CNRS.

Capacity: The maximum number of records that may be stored in the machine.

Several specially designed parallel architectures have been proposed in the literature for the implementation of dictionary machines on VLSI chips [12]. Almost all proposed designs are based on the complete binary tree structure [9, 14, 10, 6], while few papers report on other topologies, like systolic meshes [15], Cube Connected Cycles (CCC) [16] or hypercubes [3]. The problem of scalability of these VLSI designs has been studied [5].

Since those parallel dictionary machines are primarily intended for implementation in VLSI, one of their main characteristics is complete processor utilization, i.e., there is one data item per processor in the system. Only a few papers proposed dictionary machines where the number of processors is several orders of magnitude smaller than the number of records [7, 13, 2]. Some of them have led to implementations in existing parallel systems as on the Maspar MP1, a SIMD architecture, and on the Volvox i860 [8, 4].

In this paper, we consider the implementation of a dictionary machine on a real parallel computer. Our goals are to show that good performance can be achieved with general purpose parallel machines, and to study the influence of the MIMD approach on the algorithms and the results. We also develop a general technique to dynamically solve the load balancing problem arising in many on-line applications on distributed memory machines.

We present the main features of our design in the following section. We propose an elegant solution to the load balancing problem, and show interesting properties of the chosen strategy. The corresponding implementation is then described and analyzed after a presentation of the target architecture and its characteristics, necessary to understand the choices made during the implementation. Some results of our experiments are shown, and figures comparing different executions are analyzed. We end the paper with some concluding remarks.

2 Design issues

In this section, we present all the points and ideas independent of the target architecture. The ideas of partitions, partial and total sum calculation for balancing were first introduced in [2].

2.1 Partitioning the space of the keys

The idea to get a distributed data structure is to split S, the space of the keys. We sort and make a partition of this space. Each node i will handle a *working domain* D_i, with $\bigcup D_i = S$ and $\bigcap D_i = \emptyset$, such that if $k_i \in D_i$ and $k_j \in D_j$ then $k_i < k_j$ if and only if $i < j$. One can notice that assuming a balanced structure, with the same amount of data on each node, means that the distribution law of the keys is known. Indeed, with this law, it is easy to split S in domains that have the same probability concerning instructions. Saying that processor p_i handles D_i does not mean that p_i can store all the keys belonging to D_i, as the space can be very large and the distribution of the keys very sparse. Therefore, a bad or moving distribution of the keys may cause a memory overflow on a node, even though others are empty.

2.2 Broadcasting a query and getting the response

Let us consider an instruction to be performed on the (global) dictionary machine. It has to be broadcast to the processors, to be executed by one of them. After this broadcast, the response has to be collected on the host. It is important to note here that we take into account the time necessary for input/output, which is not the case in many other suggested machines.

2.3 The local data structure: balanced trees

We have now to define the local data-structure to be stored and maintained on each processor. In the case of sequential algorithms, balanced trees are the most powerful. Several data structures yield such balancing, but just a few can support exact balancing along with logarithmic time operations needed for distributed load balancing, SPLIT and CONCAT (see Section 2.4). We have chosen to work with 2-3-4 trees because of these parameters, and used binary colored trees (*BCT*) where data are stored in the leaves, to implement them ([11]).

A SEARCH is implemented exactly as in a binary search tree. INSERT, DELETE, EXTRACT-MIN instructions all have the same behavior: first, locate the required leaf, then modify this leaf (remove it or duplicate it) and perform rotations (when necessary) in the path from this leaf to the root. Each of these instructions are executed in $O(\log N)$ time, N being the number of elements in the tree.

CONCAT instruction is used to merge two trees. Let H be the height of the first tree and h the height of the second tree. We suppose, w.l.o.g., that $H \geq h$. CONCAT can be described as follows.

1. Selection of the largest node $\mathcal{N}$ belonging to level $H - h - 1$ in the tree of height H.
2. Creation of a new node, whose left child is the right child of $\mathcal{N}$ and its right child is the root of the other tree.
3. Insertion of this new node as right child of $\mathcal{N}$ (with the same rotations in the path as for a standard insertion).

In the same way, SPLIT instruction is used to split a given number of the largest elements from a tree. To perform it in optimal time, we append to the content of each inner node the number of elements in the subtree rooted at that node. This value is updated at each modification in the tree but does not change the order of complexity. SPLIT is described as follows

1. Determine the set of vertices to be split.
2. Remove the inner nodes at the boundary of the two trees (with a depth-first traversal).
3. CONCAT the disconnected branches to their respective trees.

Both of these instructions are executed in $O(\log N)$ time.

2.4 Load balancing the dictionary

So far we have assumed that the distributed data was balanced, i.e., that the distribution law of the keys was known beforehand. However, this is not the case in general, and this assumption does not make sense if the law changes in time. In general, under conditions like real time constraints, the law is not known. It means that no hypothesis can be made *a priori* about the key distribution among the processors. Moreover, the load of a processor (in memory space as well as in work) directly depends on the size of its data structure. In fact, the larger this structure, the larger the time for executing one instruction.

To solve this problem, we propose a simple strategy, based on local data exchanges. The balancing algorithm can be decomposed in two phases. During the first one, each processor p_i computes TS, the size of the whole data structure, and PS_i, the size of the dictionary handled by processors with a number smaller than i (this for $i = 0...P-1$ where P is the total number of processors). Formally, with n_j the size of the local data structure on processor j :

$$TS = \sum_{j=0}^{j<P} n_j \qquad PS_i = \sum_{j=0}^{j<i} n_j$$

From this, each processor can compute where there is an imbalance and decide if data have to be sent to its left, to its right, to both sides or none of them.

The second phase consists of exchanging data with neighbors, according to the previous calculation. It follows the updates of the dictionary, the size, and the bounds of the working domain on each processor. After that, the distributed data structure is balanced.

Theoretically, this strategy was proven to be efficient in [2]. In this paper, we shall show how to take into account the parameters of real machines in order to design a balancing strategy that really works.

Let **Split&Send(**$dict_i$**,size,dest)** be the function that splits the **size** smallest (or largest) data from structure $dict_i$ (on the current processor i) and sends them to processor **dest**. Note that reception is implicit. Let **Concat&Update(**$dict_i$**)** restore a coherent data structure $dict_i$. Let further MIN and MAX be constants, and DR_i and DL_i be the amount of data to be sent to the right and left respectively. If n_i is the size of the local data structure $dict_i$ on processor p_i, the algorithm for balancing can be written as follows:

BALANCE ALGORITHM:
/* Sum Calculation */
for all i **do in parallel**
$TS = \sum_{j=0}^{j<P} n_j$;
$PS_i = \sum_{j=0}^{j<i} n_j$;
$DL_i = \lceil \frac{TS}{P} \times i - PS_i \rceil$;
$DR_i = \lfloor \frac{TS}{P} \times (P-i-1) - (TS - PS_i - n_i) \rfloor$;

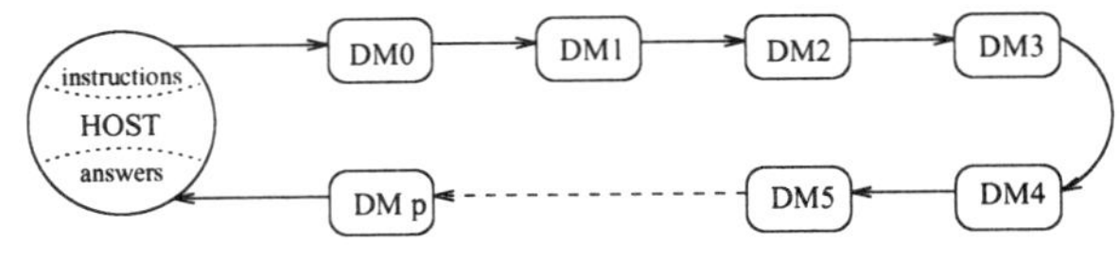

Figure 1: Architecture of the Dictionary Machine.

/* Data Balancing */
for all i **do in parallel**
If $DL_i > MIN$ **Then**
Split&Send($dict_i$, **Min(**MAX, DL_i**)**, p_{i-1}**)**;
If $DR_i > MIN$ **Then**
Split&Send($dict_i$, **Min(**MAX, DR_i**)**, p_{i+1}**)**;
Concat&Update($dict_i$**)**;
$n_i = n_i +$ **Size(Received)** $-$ **Size(Sent)**;
Update($bounds_i$**)**;

The constant MIN corresponds to the minimum number of elements in excess to justify balancing. MAX is the maximum number of elements sent during a balancing.

One can remark that data are exchanged only between neighbors in the ring. Furthermore, if $DR_i < 0$ (or DL_i), processor i only receives data.

Lemma 1 *[4] The following statements are always true:*

1. $DL_0 = 0$
2. $DR_{P-1} = 0$
3. $\forall i \in [0, P-2], DR_i = -DL_{i+1}$

Clearly, a good strategy to use **BALANCE** efficiently depends upon the programming mode of the target architecture. In the following section we shall show how we take it into account in our implementation.

3 Solution in the target architecture

Our target architecture, the Volvox machine, is a distributed memory parallel computer. The implementation we describe below is based on a ring of Dictionary Machines (DM's), as shown in Figure 1. Instructions to be executed are pipelined in this ring. Each DM processes the subset of the instructions belonging to its working domain, and forwards the other instructions to the next DM. Input (respectively, output) is supposed to come from (respectively, go to) users outside the machine, being supported by the host.

Instructions sent by the host are analyzed by the processors in the ring. Once a processor has selected a particular instruction to treat, it will access the local data structure. Algorithms corresponding to dictionary instructions are described in Section 2.3. Just recall that SEARCH, INSERT, DELETE and EXTRACT-MIN algorithms are locally performed in $O(\log n_i)$ time, where n_i corresponds to the size of a local data structure.

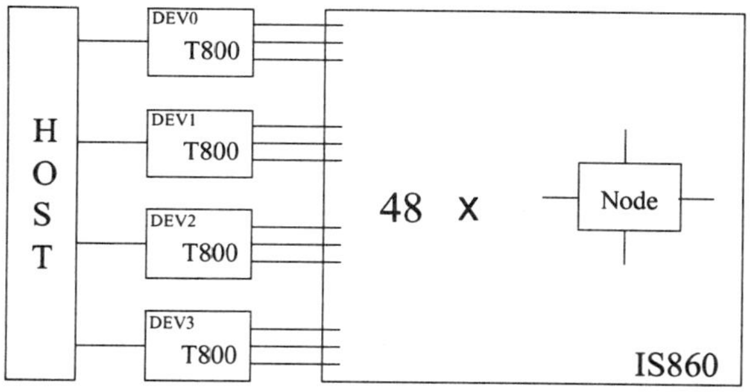

Figure 2: The Volvox IS860 architecture.

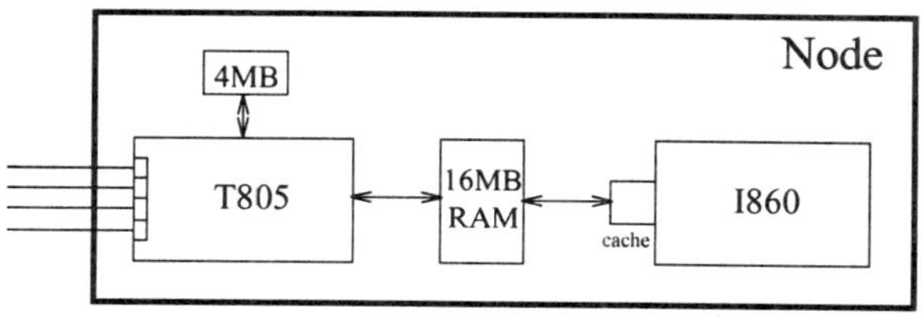

Figure 3: A node of the machine.

3.1 The Volvox IS860: a distributed memory architecture

The test-bed for the implementation of our distributed dictionary machine was a Volvox IS860 from Archipel. The Volvox Supercomputing server (see Figure 2) is a distributed memory architecture implementing the CSP message passing model. It has 48 available nodes, accessed via 4 independent communication boards lying in a Sun workstation (the host). Each communication board is a *Transputer T800* with 1MB of memory. In order to allow the user to define any variable topology, each physical node (see Figure 3) is composed of a Transputer T800 with 4 reconfigurable communication links, as a Communication Processor, and an Intel 860 as an Application Processor. The total memory of a node is formed by 4MBytes of Transputer's private memory plus 16MBytes RAM independently accessed by the two processors via a double port mechanism. The application described in this paper takes into account the extensibility of the machine.

An application is described by a set of communicating tasks. Tasks are mapped onto processors as defined by the user without any limitations except that each i860 can support only one task. Tasks communicate by primitives from Volvox library. Communication can be synchronous (blocking) or asynchronous. Message routing is automatic and implicit.

Communication costs can be modeled by the well-known linear model. Thus, for a message of length L, the time for a communication is: $t = \beta + L\tau$ where β is the startup time and τ the time for a byte to be transmitted. Table 1 summarizes values of β and τ for various cases of communication: between two neighboring Transputers, two neighboring i860 and a T800-i860 communication inside a node. We verify experimentally that β increases with the number of user tasks in the application.

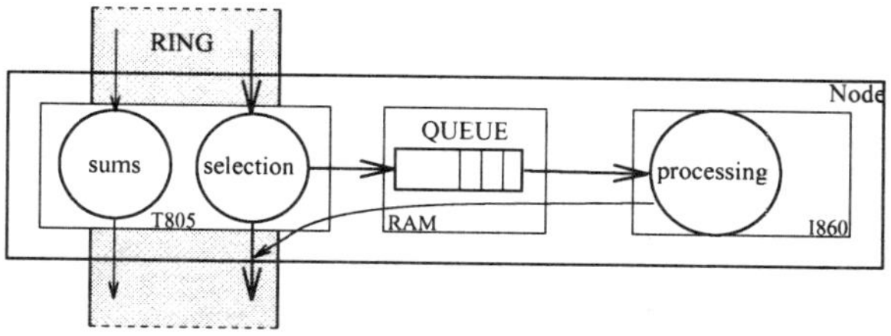

Figure 4: Organization of the processes.

Communication	β	τ
T800-T800 (neighbors)	766.5	1.1
i860-i860 (neighbors)	1305	1.23
T800-i860 (same node)	1040	0.1

Table 1: Costs of communications in μs.

For our application, communications between a T800 and the i860 inside the same node with system primitives is too slow to be used. Indeed, we need to communicate once for each instruction processed, and communication takes at least 1040μs while an elementary instruction manipulating trees on i860 takes at most 130μs (for instance an insertion, see Section 2.3). To avoid this problem, we must implement a low level technique via the double-port shared memory.

It is also interesting to compare T800-T800 communication costs (at least 766μs), with our computing cost (at most 130μs). We will analyze the impact of such values in Section 3.5.

3.2 The parallel dictionary machine

We describe here the global behavior of the proposed dictionary machine. As seen before, each physical node is a dictionary machine by itself, and they are connected in a ring architecture. The instructions circulate on the ring, starting at the host. Because of the internal organization of the nodes of the Volvox parallel computer, we implemented a client/server protocol inside each node (see Figure 4). The Transputer selects instructions within its working domain. It also forwards output messages that arrive from its predecessor in the ring.

The binary colored tree storing the elements of the dictionary is located in the i860 memory, which is used as the actual processing element of the application. The i860 executes the current instruction, modifying the data structure. Eventual output messages are sent by the i860 directly to the next node on the ring.

Communications between the two processors of a single node are performed via the shared memory. It stores a circular queue containing the instructions selected by the *selection* task on the Transputer and waiting to be processed by the i860. The head of the queue is controlled by the *processing* task on the i860, i.e., every time an instruction is to be executed, it is extracted from the queue. Similarly, the *selection* task on the Transputer controls the tail of the same circular queue. Every time an instruction is selected from the instruction flow in the ring, it is inserted into the queue.

The working domain of a node is given by a lower and an upper bound on the key values. Any instruction containing a key in that interval should be treated by that node. As described in Section 2.4, a dynamic updating of the working domains is essential to ensure load balancing. For this reason, we add a task on each Transputer, called *summation* task, to compute total and partial sums. These values are useful for our distributed load balancing technique. First, these sums are globally computed, concurrently with instruction processing, and then, instruction processing is suspended during data balancing. After that, the normal behavior is restored till the next balancing phase.

3.3 Details on dynamic load balancing

During the instruction processing phase, *summation* tasks keep computing total sum and partial sums, as described in Section 2.4. The algorithm for computing these sums uses a simple strategy corresponding to a token circulating two rounds on the ring of nodes. Other strategies were tested (e.g. on a hypercube structure as proposed in [2]) but the simplest one is also the most powerful for synchronization reasons on our machine.

When partial and total sums are available, each *summation* task can evaluate the difference between the size of its local data structure and the average size of the other structures. It can also evaluate which sides show a deficit or an excess (through the values DL_i and DR_i). If the difference is large enough, we enter the data balancing phase.

For a node, this balancing phase consists of using *split* on a part of the local structure to be sent to the side showing a deficit or using *concat* on a set of elements received from the side showing an excess. *Split* and *concat* are done in $O(\log n_i)$ by the corresponding sequential algorithms described in Section 2.3.

3.4 Correctness and Performance Analysis

In this section, we use the following notations:

- L denotes the size in bytes of an element (key, record), and l the size of a key.
- t_i denotes the maximal time for an instruction to be processed locally in a node (tree manipulations).
- t_c corresponds to the time for a neighbor-to-neighbor communication of a message containing an instruction. We assume that $t_c = \beta + L\tau$ where β and τ are machine-dependent values (linear communication model).
- t_s is the time of total and partial sum calculation (during processing phase).
- t_b is the time of a balancing phase.
- Int is the minimum pipeline interval between two instructions sent by the host.
- MIN and MAX are machine dependent constants corresponding to numbers of elements.

Global consistency of this dictionary machine is ensured by its working mode. Here are some details of its behavior during balancing phases. Each time two nodes are involved in a balancing phase, they freeze the instruction flow upstream on the ring, then they process instructions waiting in their queues. Only after that they perform the data balancing between them. In this way, we ensure that every instruction is processed by the node corresponding to the appropriate working domain.

Furthermore, because the only synchronization mechanism used in the machine is this pairwise synchronization, our application is deadlock free. This is true if the *logical capacity* of the nodes is not exceeded.

Definition 1 *The* logical capacity *of a node is* $\frac{N}{P} - MAX$ *elements (N is the global physical capacity of the machine).*

We will see that this logical limit is necessary during balancing phases. Now, we want to prove that our machine maintains a balanced data structure.

Definition 2 *The data structure is said to be* balanced *if and only if* $DR_i \leq MIN$ *for all i (and* $DL_i \leq MIN$ *for all i).*

Lemma 2 *The execution of* $\mathcal{I}$ *instructions can increase the imbalance by at most* $\mathcal{I}$.

Proof: The proof is based on the fact that the execution of a single instruction increases the imbalance by at most one.

As seen previously, the imbalance is defined by $DL_j = \lceil \frac{TS \times j}{P} - PS_j \rceil$ (the case of DR_j is handled analogously). Let us consider DL_j before a given instruction, $Instr$, and after the execution of this instruction. Suppose that $Instr$ is a *delete*. Clearly, TS decreases by one, and PS_j stays constant or decreases by one (depending on j). Hence, DL_j does not change or decreases by one. The case of the instruction *insert* is symmetric, so an insertion increases DL_j by 0 or 1.

Using this result, we can say that $\mathcal{I}$ instructions can modify DL_j by at most $\mathcal{I}$, for all j. □

In the remainder of this section, we suppose that each node handles at least MAX elements at the beginning of balancing phases. This restriction is not severe as it just means that the data structure is not completely empty. However, even if this condition is not true, the balancing strategy can be applied. It can be shown that the resulting structure is not balanced immediately after one balancing phase, but becomes more and more balanced in time. This phenomenon is illustrated in the experimental results by Figure 9. A similar analysis for empty structures can be found in the case of a SIMD implementation [8].

Proposition 1 *If the instruction flow is globally frozen during the balancing phase, then, for fixed values of MIN and MAX, the following relation exists: If just before balancing, we had:*

$$\forall i \in [0..P-1], max_i(DR_i) \leq MAX$$

then, just after the balancing phase, we have:

$$max_i(DR_i) \leq MIN, \forall i \in [0..P-1].$$

Proof: During a data balancing phase, as described in subroutine `balance`:
"`If` DR_i > MIN `Then` `Split&Send`($dict_i$, `Min`(MAX, DR_i), p_{i+1});"

- Thus, if $DR_i > MIN$, each node can send up to MAX data, which is enough to balance every DR_i.
- If $DR_i \leq MIN$, `Send` is not performed, DR_i is unchanged, but the proposition still holds.

Since, according to lemma 1,$DL_i = -DR_i$, we only need to study DR_i. □

Definition 3 *The value $MAX - MIN$ represents the* capacity of balancing *for a node, i.e., the maximum number of elements balanced during one balancing phase.*

Lemma 3 *At most $\frac{t_s}{Int}$ instructions are processed between two successive balancing phases.*

Proof: Our application alternates processing phases (with sum calculations) and balancing phases. The partial and total sum calculations are done simultaneously with the processing phase. The balancing phase starts at the end of this calculation. Therefore, between two successive balancing phases, instructions arrive and are processed, with a pipeline interval Int, during time t_s. □

Hence, there is an imbalance of at most $\frac{t_s}{Int}$ between two successive balancing phases (by Lemma 2). So, our data structure remains balanced whenever:

$$MAX - MIN \geq \frac{t_s}{Int}.$$

Now, we want to relax the hypothesis of Proposition 1 so that dictionary instructions may be processed on some nodes while other nodes are balancing. This is very important in order to use the asynchronous capabilities of the host parallel computer at their best.

To ensure efficiency of our balancing strategy, the *capacity of balancing* has to be greater than the number of instructions potentially processed during a complete cycle (processing phase plus balancing phase):

$$MAX - MIN \geq \frac{t_b + t_s}{Int}.$$

Lemma 4 *The cost of one balancing phase is bounded by:*

$$t_b = 2t_i + \beta + MAX \times (L + l + 10)\tau.$$

Proof: During a balancing phase, each node may execute one *split* (cost: t_i), followed by a send of size up to MAX elements, followed by one *concat* (cost: t_i). Since we need to maintain information from the split tree to ensure a CONCAT in $O(\log n)$ time in the destination node, each element (of size L) is encapsulated in a structure of size $(L + l + 10)$ bytes. Thus, the cost of the send is bounded by $\beta + MAX \times (L + l + 10)\tau$. □

Theorem 1 *Our balancing strategy is correct if we respect the following constraint:*

$$MAX \geq \frac{(\beta + L\tau) \times MIN + 2t_i + \beta + t_s}{\beta - (l + 10)\tau}.$$

Proof: The proof should be found in [4].

Our strategy for partial and total sum calculations needs $2P-1$ communications to complete ($t_s = (2P-1)(\beta+s\tau)$, where s is the size of an integer). As $L \geq s$, at most $2P$ instructions are processed during this time ($\frac{t_s}{Int} \leq 2P$). The constraint to be satisfied is now:

$$MAX \geq \frac{(\beta + L\tau) \times (MIN + 2P) + 2t_i + \beta}{\beta - (l + 10)\tau}.$$

For instance, typical values for a variety of existing machines are: a ring of 32 nodes ($P = 32$), communication rate τ equals to $1\mu s$, the size of an element $L = 40$ with a key of size $l = 4$, the time of one local processing of an instruction $t_i = 130\mu s$, and the constant MIN fixed to 10.

With a communication startup β equals to $767\mu s$ (the actual value on the Volvox), we obtain $MAX > 80$, which is feasible. Even if β was small ($\beta = 50\mu s$), we would obtain $MAX > 193$ which still corresponds to a realistic value.

When P becomes large, it is possible (and even necessary) to implement partial and total sum calculations so that $\frac{t_s}{Int} \leq O(\log P)$, see for example [2].

Now, if available local memory is large enough to allow us a larger MAX, we can introduce a delay between the end of a balancing phase and the beginning of the next sum calculation. Let WAIT be the number of instructions processed during this delay. We have to maintain the new capacity of balancing:

$$MAX - MIN \geq WAIT + \frac{t_b + t_s}{Int},$$

which leads to the following constraint:

$$WAIT \leq MAX - MIN - \frac{t_b + t_s}{Int}.$$

In our machine, with a reasonable value of $MAX = 1000$, we can process 920 instructions during this delay (0.7 seconds). Clearly, we can increase this delay by increasing MAX.

We remark that a finer analysis of the behavior of the queues storing instructions between the two processors inside each node is not necessary. In fact, with an appropriate value of Int, these queues are always empty with the exception of the duration of the balancing phases. Queues are made empty at the beginning of the next processing phase. In our target machine, we fix the value of Int to t_c since $t_c > t_i$. With a better computation/communication ratio, Int has to be greater than $\max(t_c, \frac{t_i}{P})$.

Further, we can easily calculate a lower bound for the response time of the dictionary machine: $(P + 1)t_c + t_i$. This value is close to the average response time experimentally measured.

3.5 Experimental results

Our balancing mechanism has a small cost. To ensure an imbalance of up to 1% ($MAX = 3600$ for a local capacity of 360000), our machine spends 3% of its time in balancing operations.

The following experimental results were obtained with the values: $MIN = 0$, $MAX = 5000$, $L = 4$, $P = 8$, and waiting time $WAIT \times Int = 3.9s$. As the memory of a node is 16 MBytes, the capacity of our dictionary is 360000 elements per node.

We can see in Figure 5 the time to "fill up" the machine. It corresponds to the time spent for the machine to insert a given amount of elements. It is drawn by a line, up to the capacity of the dictionary (2.88 million elements in this configuration).

In Figure 6, obviously, the minimum possible pipeline interval is constant whatever the current population is in the dictionary. The throughput is independent of the amount of data already inside the machine. This is explained by t_c being much greater than t_i in this machine thus $Int = t_c$ that is a constant.

Figure 7 shows that the communication corresponds to the model proposed: the minimum possible value for the pipeline interval increases linearly with the size of the processed elements.

In Figure 8, we can see that the pipeline interval increases slightly with the number of processors involved in the dictionary. We could hope that the number of processors would not change the pipeline interval since, indeed, processors are along the pipeline. But this phenomenon is justified by the machine-dependent remark that β increases abnormally with the number of user tasks running on the Volvox.

Figures 9 and 10 represent the behavior of the machine quantified by the evolution of the current amount of elements in each node during series of insertions processed.

The first one (Figure 9) corresponds to series of insertions of elements with keys that increase continuously. We can verify that, even in that extreme case, after a first period where not enough data were inserted (as explained in the analysis), our dictionary machine becomes and remains balanced.

Finally, the other situation visualized in Figure 10 corresponds to series of insertions performed in a random order for a while (only a small part of these insertions are visualized in the plot), and suddenly changed to an increasing order like in the previous figure. We can see that even when the distribution of the keys inserted changes, the structure stays balanced.

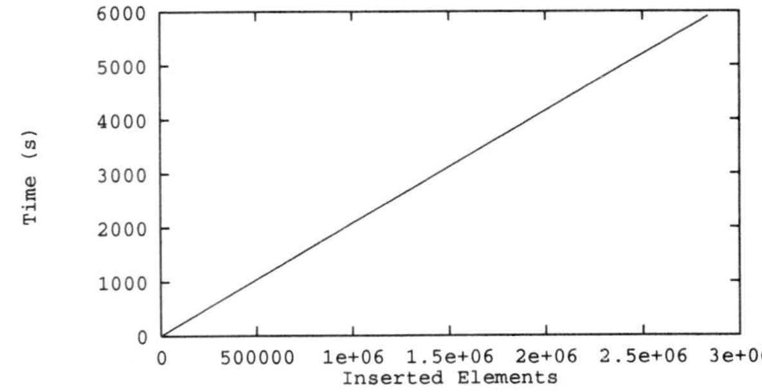

Figure 5: Filling time on 8 nodes.

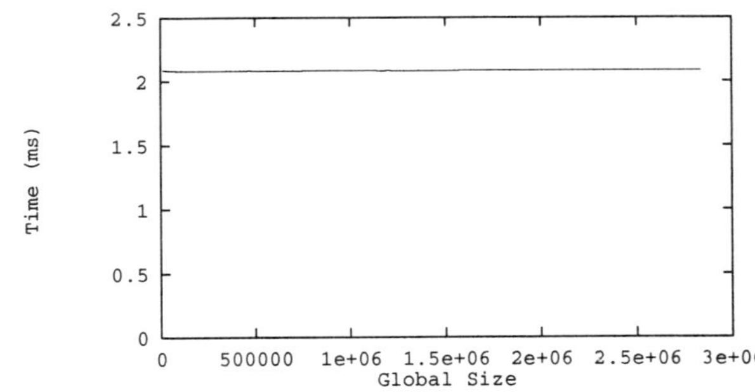

Figure 6: Int versus current population.

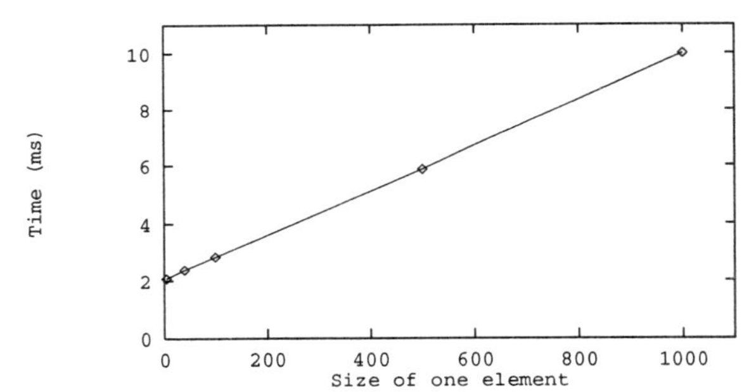

Figure 7: Int vs L.

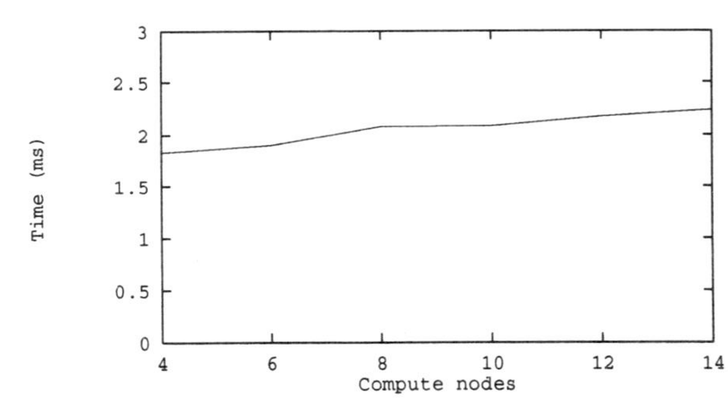

Figure 8: Int vs P.

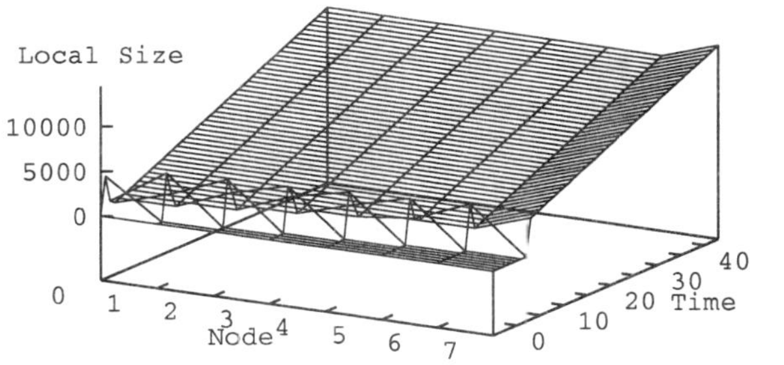

Figure 9: Behavior for key-increasing insertions.

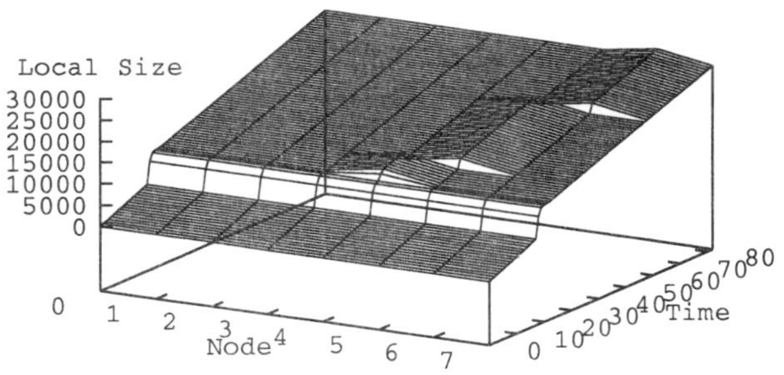

Figure 10: Behavior for random then key-increasing insertions.

4 Conclusion

Multicomputers represent the cutting edge technology for database applications. Unfortunately, implementing dynamic data partitioning seems to be a very challenging problem. In this paper we gave a first step towards its solution, by presenting an implementation of a dictionary machine – a database reduced to its simplest instance –, on a distributed memory architecture. Our goal was to achieve good performance, which required a dynamic balancing scheme. Using this scheme and exploiting the capacities of the target architecture, we have proved that choosing an adapted local data structure, good performance can be attainable for information maintenance and retrieval on a general purpose parallel architecture.

More generally, we have proposed a powerful balancing strategy, and we have proved that it solves the load balancing problem. This strategy induces a very reasonable overhead and can be used with success in many other situations, where a bad dynamic data distribution would lead to weak performance.

In the near future, we hope to implement the techniques shown in this paper into a parallel database application. Interesting applications are evolutionary ones, where the insertions and deletions of data are significant compared to the amount of information retrievals (queries).

Acknowledgments

The authors would like to thank Nashib Qadri whose comments have greatly improved the quality of presentation of the manuscript.

References

[1] A.V. Aho, J.E. Hopcroft, and J.D. Ullman. *Data structure and algorithms.* Addison-Wesley, 1983.

[2] F. Dehne and M. Gastaldo. A note on the load balancing problem for coarse grained hypercube dictionary machines. *Parallel Computing*, 16:75–79, 1990.

[3] F. Dehne and N. Santoro. An optimal VLSI dictionary machine for hypercube architectures. In M. Cosnard, editor, *Parallel and Distributed Algorithms*, pages 137–144. North Holland, 1989.

[4] T. Duboux and A. Ferreira. Towards a dynamic parallel database machine: data balancing techniques and pipeline. Technical Report RR 94-47, LIP, Lyon, France, December 1994. Preliminary version published in CONPAR 92.

[5] T. Duboux, A. Ferreira, and M. Gastaldo. A scalable design for dictionary machines. In *3rd International Workshop on Algorithms and Parallel VLSI Architectures*, Leuven, Belgium, August 1994. Elsevier.

[6] Z. Fan and K.-H. Cheng. A generalized simultaneous access dictionary machine. *IEEE Trans. on Parallel and Distributed Systems*, 2(2):149–158, 1991.

[7] A. Fisher. Dictionary machines with small number of processors. In *Int. Symp. on Computer Architecture*, pages 151–156, June 1984.

[8] M. Gastaldo. Dictionary Machine on SIMD Architectures. Technical Report RR 93-19, LIP ENS-Lyon, July 1993.

[9] C. E. Leiserson. Systolic priority queues. Rep. CMU-CS-79-115, Dept. Comp. Sci., Carnegie-Mellon University, 1979.

[10] H.F. Li and D.K. Probst. Optimal VLSI dictionary machines without compress instructions. *IEEE Trans. on Computers*, 39:332–340, 1990.

[11] K. Mehlhorn. *Data structure and Algorithms I : Sorting and searching.* Springer Verlag, 1984.

[12] T.S. Narayanan. A survey of dictionary machines. Technical Report CSD-86-2, Concordia University, 1986.

[13] A.R. Omondi and J. D. Brock. Implementing a dictionary on hypercube machines. In *Int. Conf. on Parallel Processing*, pages 707–709, 1987.

[14] T. Ottmann, A. Rosenberg, and L. Stockmeyer. A dictionary machine (for VLSI). *IEEE Trans. on Computers*, c-31(9):892–897, September 1982.

[15] H. Schmeck and H. Schroder. Dictionnary machine for different models of VLSI. *IEEE Trans. on Computers*, C-34(5):472–475, May 1985.

[16] A.M. Schwartz and M.C. Loui. Dictionary machines on cube-class networks. *IEEE Trans. on Computers*, 36:100–105, 1987.

Simulating Asynchronous Architectures on Transputer Networks

G. Theodoropoulos J. V. Woods
Department of Computer Science, University of Manchester
Oxford Road, Manchester, M13 9PL, United Kingdom

Abstract

Recently, there has been a resurgence of interest in asynchronous design techniques due to the potential of asynchronous logic for higher performance, power efficiency and immunity from clock-related timing problems. Occam, a CSP-based parallel language provides for the rapid development of asynchronous architectural simulation models which may then be executed on a transputer network to achieve high performance. This paper discusses issues related to the design and execution of such models.

1 Introduction

Conventional synchronous architectures use design techniques based on global clocking, whereby all the functional units operate in lockstep under the control of a central clock. As VLSI technology advances and systems become larger, faster and more complex, timing problems become increasingly severe and account for more and more of the design and debugging expense. Increased clock speeds make on-chip clock skew significant and interchip skew a major problem. One solution to clock-related timing problems is to use asynchronous design techniques without any global synchronization signals to control the rate at which different elements operate [13]. Another potential advantage of asynchronous logic, which recently has led to a resurgence of interest in its use, is lower power consumption.

An asynchronous system may be designed as a set of functional modules each operating at its own rate and cooperating through communication. The communication protocol synchronizes the modules involved in the communication and allows data to be shared between them. There exist many different approaches for designing asynchronous systems. In his influential 1989 Turing Award lecture, Sutherland presented an asynchronous design approach called "Micropipelines" [14]. A micropipeline is a simple data processing pipeline whose stages operate asynchronously. This approach uses bundled data with an event-signaled handshake protocol (figure 1).

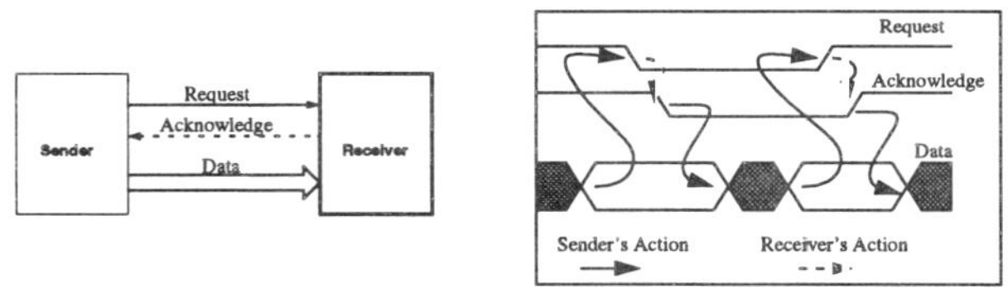

Figure 1: The Bundled Data Interface Protocol

Following Sutherland's approach, the AMULET group at the University of Manchester, U.K., have designed and implemented AMULET1, an asynchronous version of the ARM RISC processor as part of the ESPRIT OMI-MAP project (figure 2) [5].

2 Modelling Asynchronous Architectures with Occam

The recent research activity in the area of asynchronous systems has pointed to the need for suitable techniques for modelling and simulating them. Several notations and techniques have been suggested for this purpose [7]. CSP [6] in particular has attracted the interest of many researchers due to the strong relationship between its semantics (synchronous, unbuffered interprocess communication) and the behaviour of asynchronous systems [10]. To support the design of AMULET1, a methodology for using occam [8], a CSP based, parallel distributed language, for rapidly building executable models of asynchronous architectures at the Register Transfer Level has been developed [15] [16] [17]. Using this methodology, an asynchronous architecture is modelled as a set of concurrent occam processes which communicate by exchanging timestamped messages. The processes are entirely data-driven, and self scheduled. Two channels are used for the synchronization of communicating processes, one for Request/data and one for the Acknowledgement signal. To describe the nondeterministic behaviour of arbiters, the occam ALT statement is used. Following this approach, **occarm** , an occam model of the AMULET1 processor has been developed. **Occarm** consists of a hierarchy of occam processes, has the

1066-6192/96 $5.00 © 1996 IEEE
Proceedings of PDP '96

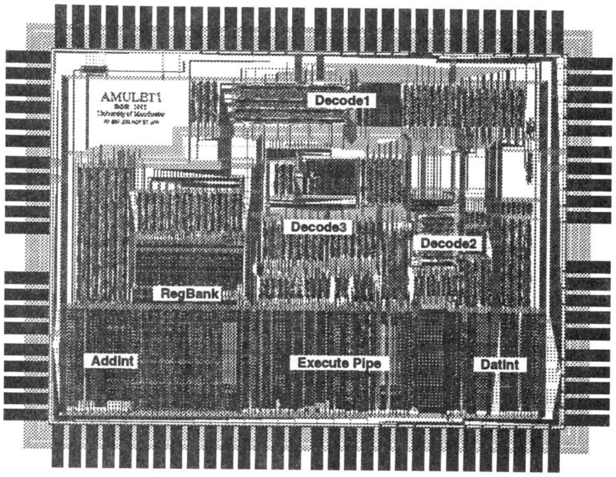

Figure 2: The AMULET1 Processor Physical Layout

same granularity as the processor and executes ARM machine code. Figure 3 shows the top level process graph of the **occarm** model.

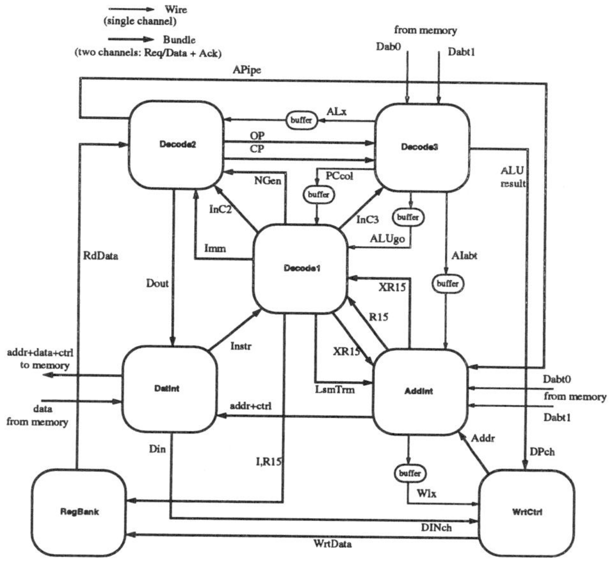

Figure 3: Occarm Top Level Process Graph

3 Simulation Issues

One of the advantages of using occam as a specification language for asynchronous architectures, is the ability to exploit the inherent parallelism of the simulated architecture, and thus to achieve higher performance by executing the occam simulation model on a multi-transputer machine. This execution however is not straightforward. The extra dimension that concurrency introduces to distributed systems complicates the programming activity and imposes a number of issues that need to be addressed before any parallel program may be executed. These issues include monitoring and debugging the processes of the system; for multiprocessor configurations, remote I/O, partitioning, mapping and load balancing issues need also to be addressed. This is particularly true for the development of occam systems since the static nature of occam and the lack of a transputer operating system make the above task the responsibility of the application developer.

This paper discusses how the aforementioned issues have been addressed in connection with the **occarm** simulation model. Two different environments for **occarm** have been developed, one for the execution of the model on a single transputer and one which provides for a multi-transputer implementation.

4 The Host Machine: The ParSiFal T-Rack

The system used to host the simulation model is the ParSifal T-Rack [3], a reconfigurable 64-Transputer machine, which has been developed at the University of Manchester to support the parallel simulation of computer architectures (figure 4). Two of the four links from each transputer of the T-Rack (*link0* and *link1*) are permanently hardwired to form a processor chain known as the *necklace.* The off-necklace links(*link2* and *link3*) may be connected by means of a crossbar switch, into a configuration which is appropriate for the code being executed. The crossbar switch is built using twenty six INMOS C004 switch chips housed on two boards (*S1* and *S2*). The T-Rack is hosted by a Sun 3/160 workstation containing a Tadpole Transputer Board which acts as the "root" node of the transputer network. The existence of the necklace limits the set of processor graphs which may be implemented to those which possess a Hamiltonean Cycle [11]; the route taken by the Hamiltonean Cycle through the network corresponds to the position of the necklace in the switched network implementation.

5 Monitoring

Monitoring the runtime behaviour of the simulation model and collecting information regarding the characteristics of the simulated system is one of the main objectives of the simulation process. Monitoring is essential for the testing and performance evaluation of the simulated system as well as for the debugging of both, the simulated system and the simulation model. The inherent properties of distributed asynchronous systems, such as occam architectural models, make monitoring a difficult and complicated issue for which

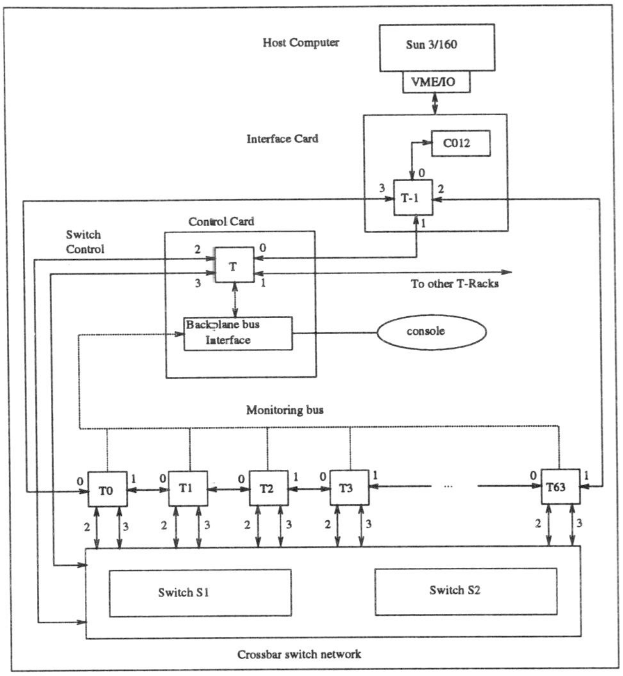

Figure 4: The T-Rack

Process **process_name:** instruction **instruction_type** was executed at time **clock**

a) Execution event trace

Process **process_name:** variable **variable_name** has the value **val** at time **clock**

b) Data event trace

Process **process_name:** sending value **val** to process **proc** on channel **chan** at time **clock**

Process **process_name:** receiving value **val** from process **proc** on channel **chan** at time **clock**

c) Parallelity event traces

Figure 5: Event Traces for Debugging

sequential techniques are insufficient; these properties include the multiple threads of control, the difficulty to get snapshots of the system, the non-deterministic behaviour, the intrusiveness of the monitoring system and the need to cope with a vast amount of monitoring data generated from multiple sources [12].

5.1 Monitoring Occarm

The simulation of an asynchronous architecture has two main objectives, namely the testing and debugging of the architecture, and the evaluation of the architecture's performance.

5.1.1 Debugging

For the debugging of the architecture (as well as the simulation model) it is necessary to monitor both the flow of control and the flow of data in each of the different occam processes in the model; this is achieved by collecting traces regarding the *execution* and *data events* of the processes respectively (figure 5a,b). Furthermore, for the detection of deadlocks, it is essential to know the state of the processes in the system when the deadlock occurred. For this purpose, the *parallelity events* need to be monitored (figure 5c). These will appear in pairs, one for the sending and one for the receiving process. The absence of one parallelity event from a pair in the final trace indicates the occurrence of a deadlock.

In occarm, monitoring is performed by means of a parallel network of occam monitoring processes (known as *reactive processes* [12]), one for each of the top level processes (the *active processes*) of the **occarm** model. Monitoring messages are issued to the reactive processes in an event driven fashion. *Probes*, in the form of a procedure call, have been inserted (manually) in the source occam code of the active processes. Each time the procedure that implements the probe is called, it constructs the corresponding monitoring message and sends it to the monitoring process. Since probes will be invoked in different parallel sections of the active process, several monitoring messages are issued simultaneously. Thus, for the communication between an active and its reactive process a channel array is used (*monitor*, see figure 6). The monitoring process acts as a multiplexor, employing an ALT construct to gather the messages issued by the corresponding active process on the channel array; in order to reduce the effects of the ALT bottleneck, the channel array is buffered in order to decouple the processes involved.

The monitoring data are generated in a copious volume and their transportation can have a significant negative impact on both the computational resources and the communication network of the distributed system. Occam monitoring processes support two *transport strategies*, namely *immediate transport*, in which the monitoring data are transported as soon as they are generated and *store and unload*, whereby the data are stored in a buffer before they are transported. The latter makes use of a circular buffer to store only the recent history of the active process. If no monitoring message arrives for a user-defined time interval (i.e. in the case of deadlock), the monitoring process flushes the contents of the history buffer. The store and unload transport option is particularly useful as in most, if not all, cases the most recent history of the processes is sufficient to identify the cause of errors or deadlocks. Since the monitoring messages do not propagate further into the system, the communication overhead of

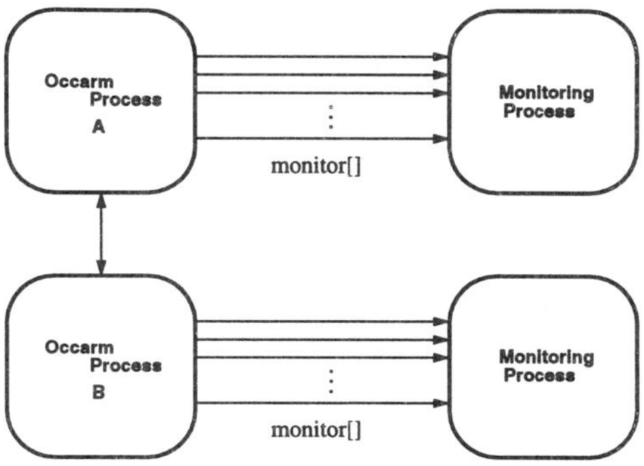

Figure 6: Collecting Event Traces in Occarm

the store and unload policy is minimum (see section 8).

5.1.2 Performance Evaluation

When analysing the performance of asynchronous pipelines, values of special importance and interest are the *occupancy* as well as the *stall* and *idle* periods of the pipeline.

Occupancy. The occupancy of a N stage pipeline is defined as the proportion of time the pipeline has 1, 2, ..., N elements in it. In a synchronous pipeline, the clock frequency defines the period that any element stays in the pipeline; thus for the calculation of the occupancy only the entry (arrival) times of elements are required. In asynchronous micropipelines however, the times that a particular data bundle enters and leaves the pipeline are completely independent. Therefore, the calculation of occupancy in this case requires knowledge of both, the entry and exit times of bundles in the pipeline. The values of the two timestamps required for the calculation of the duration of a message's staying in the pipeline are not directly available, for they are possessed by different occam processes and occam does not support global variables. To overcome this problem a solution has been devised whereby request messages exiting the pipeline carry with them an extra timestamp denoting the time of their entry to it. Using this information, the calculation of the pipeline occupancy by the control process at the output side is straightforward.

Stalls. An asynchronous pipeline will stall if the rate that request events are issued to the pipeline is greater than the rate that events propagate through the pipeline or the rate that events exit the pipeline (i.e. the rate that events are consumed and processed

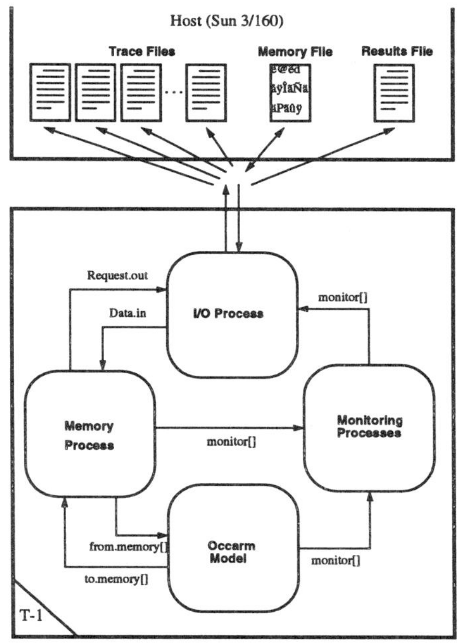

Figure 7: The Single transputer Environment of Occarm

at the output side). Stall situations refer to the input side of the pipeline. They may be detected by examining the delay between the sending of a Request event (R_{in}) to the pipeline and the issuing of the corresponding Acknowledgement signal (Ack_{in}) by the first register of the pipeline: a stall situation has occurred if $timestamp(R_{in}) < timestamp(Ack_{in})$. The duration of the stall is $timestamp(Ack_{in}) - timestamp(R_{in})$; clearly the minimum stall period is equal to the propagation delay of the first register in the pipeline.

Contrary to the debugging traces which are sent immediately to the corresponding monitoring process, the type and quantity of data that concern the performance characteristics of the architecture permit active **occarm** processes to calculate and store them locally; this eliminates the extra communication overhead that their transport would impose. The stored values are unloaded by the **occarm** control processes upon termination of the simulation.

6 The Simulator Environment

The single-transputer simulator environment is depicted in figure 7.

The Memory process models the memory control logic of the processor; the memory itself is implemented as a binary file to achieve compatibility with the existing ARM development environment [2]. The operation of the simulator consists of reading instructions from the memory file, executing them and writing possible results back into it. Within the INMOS occam toolset environment, only one occam process may have access to the host machine's file system. In the **occarm** simulator environment this role is served by the I/O process via which all interaction with the outside world is performed. I/O process employs an occam ALT construct to allow the multiplexing of system and monitoring messages arriving from the Memory and Monitoring processes respectively. Event traces arriving from the monitoring processes are distributed to different trace files according to their "process_name" field (see figure 5); the existence of a separate trace file for each process provides a view of the parallelism of the system and thus facilitates the post-mortem debugging task.

7 Multiprocessor Implementation

The static nature of the occam language requires that the mapping of the occam process graph on the transputer network is specified in advance by the application developer. The mapping scheme should ideally take into account the following considerations[1]:

- The limitations imposed by the four links of the transputer: the degree of each node in the top level process graph should not be greater that four, with an edge in the graph representing a bidirectional link.
- The limitations imposed by the interconnection network of the machine. Typically, transputer networks are not fully connected and therefore process graphs have to be transformed to match the underlying structure.
- The computation and communication load should be evenly balanced over the transputers and the links of the system respectively.

Based on the above considerations, the first step for mapping occarm onto the T-Rack is the modification of the the top level process graph of **occarm** as depicted in figure 3 so that each node has at most four neighbours. To address this issue the *Process Interconnection Table* (*PIT*) depicted in figure 8 has been devised. The number of asterisks in a row of the table represents the number of neighbour processes of that

[1] The T9000 transputer with the message forwarding facilities of the associated C104 link switch device eliminates most of these considerations; however for systems which are based on older generation transputers (this covers the vast majority of existing transputer based machines, including the ParSiFal T-Rack) these considerations have to be taken into account [9].

	Decode1	Decode2	Decode3	DatInt	AddInt	RegBank	WrtCtrl	Memory	I/O.Process
Decode1		*	*	*	*	*			
Decode2	*		*	*	*	*			
Decode3	*	*			*		*	*	
DatInt	*	*			*		*	*	
AddInt	*	*	*	*			*	*	
RegBank	*	*					*		
WrtCtrl			*	*	*	*			
Memory			*	*	*				*
I/O.Process								*	

(shaded oval) : Merge into one link

Figure 8: Occarm Process Connectivity Table

Occarm Process	Node
Decode1 + Decode2	1
AddInt	2
Decode3 + DatInt	3
RegBank	4
WrtCtrl	5
Memory	6
I/O.Process	-1

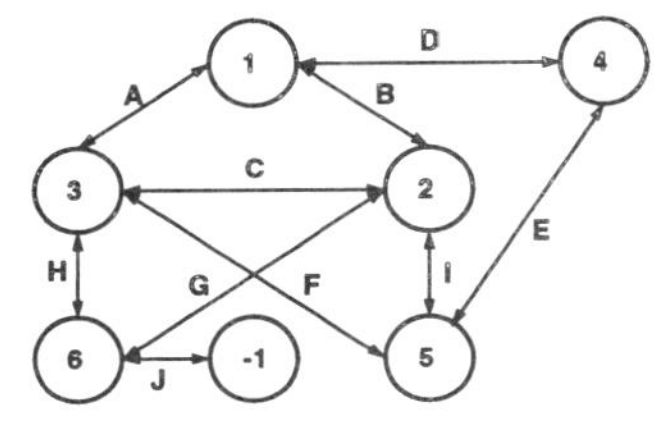

Figure 9: Modified Occarm Top Level Process Graph

particular process. Merging two columns together effectively adds one more level of abstraction to the process hierarchy, assigning the corresponding processes to the same processor and forcing the two channels to share the same link.

7.1 Balancing the Workload

The criterion adopted for the selection of the level of the **occarm** process hierarchy whose each process has at most four neighbours is the maximization of processor utilization; namely, to occupy as many processors as possible.

Following this criterion the merges presented in figure 8 have been applied to occarm, deriving as a result the alternative graph of figure 9; this graph represents the lowest level in the process hierarchy that satisfies the four-link-per-transputer limitation.

7.1.1 Balancing the Communication Load

The new top level **occarm** process graph possesses more than one Hamiltonean cycle, thus allowing an equivalent number of possible mappings on the T-Rack.

For the selection of the appropriate mapping, the criterion which has been followed is to balance the communication load. In the T-Rack the communication performance of a hardwired link is approximately double that of a switched link (1.72 and 0.87 Mbytes per second respectively). Consequently,the objectives of the communication load balancing policy are to use as few switched links as possible, and to place onto

Link	No. of Multiplexed Channels
A	13
B	9
C	4
D	6
E	3
F	6
G	2
H	8
I	3

Table 1: Communication Load on Occarm Links

hardwired links as many (multiplexed) channels as possible.

The communication load on the links of the top level **occarm** process graph is given in table 1. Figure 10 presents alternative mappings of the graph onto the T-Rack; $a \ldots c$ are examples of mappings which are not feasible due to the limited link connectivity of the T-Rack. The remaining $d \ldots h$ illustrate all the different feasible ways to map **occarm** onto the T-Rack: from these mapping h satisfies the communication balancing criteria specified above and therefore has been selected for occarm. Indeed, this mapping uses the minimum possible number of switched links (namely 4) while allocating the maximum total number of channels onto the necklace (namely 36); mapping e makes use of 5 switched links while mappings d, f and g place onto the necklace 30, 28 and 30 channels respectively.

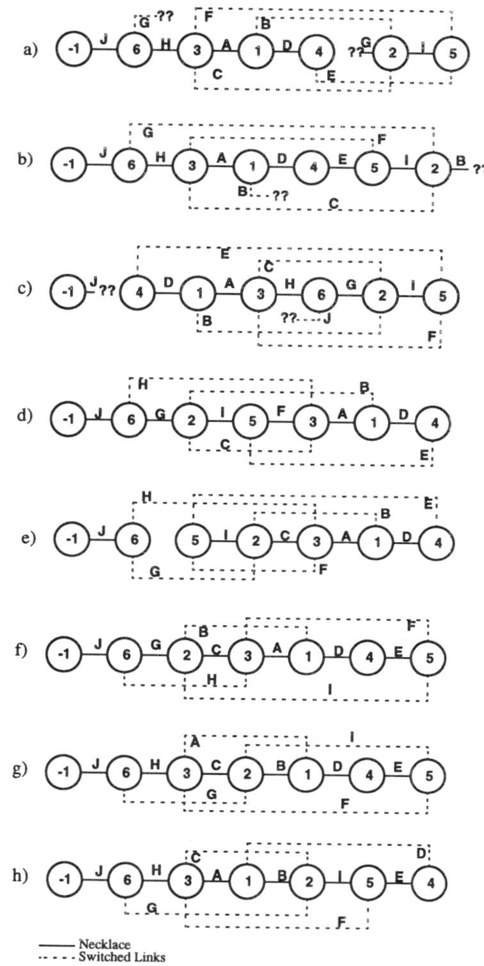

Figure 10: Occarm Graph Mappings

7.1.2 The Monitoring Path

To minimize the communication overhead imposed by the monitoring messages, the characteristics of the T-Rack may be exploited. Since the Tadpole transputer, where the I/O process resides, is connected to both ends of the necklace, the interaction with the Memory process may take place via one end of the necklace, with the monitoring messages following the other direction towards the other end of the necklace. This scheme is depicted in figure 11, where the complete mapping of **occarm** onto the T-Rack is presented; transputers T0-T5 host the simulation model, while transputers T6-T63 are simply used to forward monitoring information.

7.1.3 The Generic Simulator Node

Figure 12 depicts a generic node of the distributed implementation of the simulator. Typically this will include a number of active processes together with the corresponding monitoring modules. Extra multiplexing/demultiplexing processes are included to allow the sharing of the transputer links; to prevent deadlock situations (which for example might occur if one of the transputer links is blocked by a message destined for a particular process, while this process is blocked waiting for a message that may follow the former on the link), extra buffering has been incorporated into the the demultiplexing modules (i.e. the distributor process).

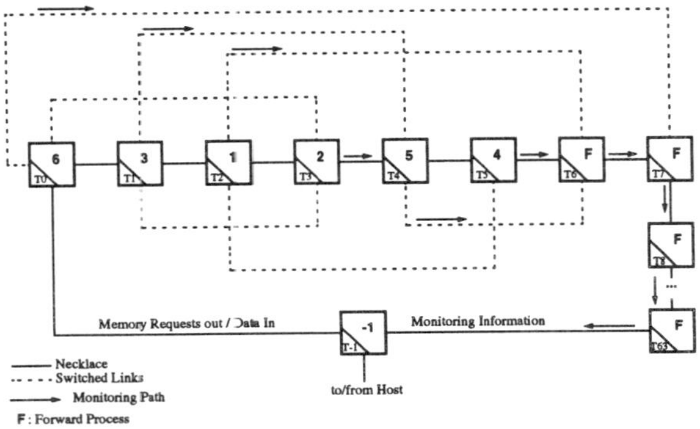

Figure 11: Mapping Occarm onto the T-Rack

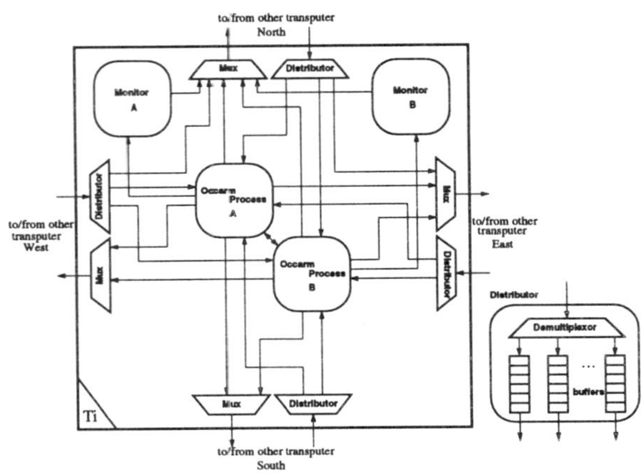

Figure 12: The Generic Simulator Node

Model	Elapsed Time (minutes)
Occarm (Single)	1.72
Asim	1.48

Benchmark: Dhrystone (1 loop)

Table 2: Asim versus Occarm (Single Transputer Implementation)

Transport Policy	Elapsed Time (minutes)	
	Occarm Single	Occarm Multi
Tracing Off	1.72	1.02
Store and Unload	4.22	1.87
Immediate Transport	9.75	7.21

Benchmark: Dhrystone (1 loop)

Table 3: Performance of Occarm

8 Performance

For the verification and evaluation of both the AMULET1 processor and the **occarm** model, the *Dhrystone* synthetic benchmark has been used [18]. Within the single transputer configuration (i.e. on a single 20MHz, T414 transputer), **occarm** requires on average 1.72 minutes to execute one Dhrystone loop when no monitoring traces are generated (table 2); this figure is smaller than that achieved by an equivalent sequential simulator written in ASIM (the ARM's in-house simulation language), by a factor of 1.16, when the latter executes on an IPX Sun workstation. This is a reasonable and expected performance, for the execution of the **occarm** processes on a single transputer is performed not in a parallel but rather in a time sharing fashion and the large number of processes in the model (more than 120) makes the context switching overhead in the transputer significant.

Table 3 presents the performance of **occarm** for both, its single and multiple transputer configurations and for the different policies employed for the transportation of monitoring data. When no monitoring traces are generated, the distribution of **occarm** on to the seven transputers of the T-Rack yields a speedup of 1.69. The "store and unload" transport policy allows a speedup of 2.26 to be achieved since in this mode of operation, the performance of occarm on a single transputer drops by a factor of 2.45 as opposed to 1.83 in the multi transputer implementation. This difference in the performance drop may be attributed to the fact that the activation of the monitoring processes severely increases the frequency and, consequently, the overhead of context switching on the single transputer. The distribution of the monitoring processes onto multiple transputers alleviates this phenomenon as the context switching overhead is also distributed.

When the "immediate transport" policy is employed, the performance of both the single and multiple transputer configurations of **occarm** drops dramatically allowing a speedup of only 1.35. This behaviour may be attributed to the operation of I/O process. I/O process acts as a multiplexor for messages arriving from both the Memory and the Monitoring processes. This introduces a major bottleneck in the system, which imposes the ultimate limit in the performance of the simulator. The large number of monitoring messages generated by the "immediate transport" policy occupy a large proportion of I/O process activity, thus reducing the rate that instructions and data are supplied to the model; as a consequence, the processes of the model remain idle for substantial periods.

The low speedups achieved by the distribution of **occarm** onto the multiple transputers of the T-Rack may be attributed to a number of factors related to the characteristics of both, the simulated architecture and the machine that hosts the simulator.

- Amdahl's law [1] specifies that the maximum possible speedup depends on the inherent parallelism of the executed system which may be potentially exploited. In the case of AMULET1, the requirement for instruction compatibility with the synchronous ARM, has resulted in an asynchronous design with a very complex pipeline structure and, indicatively, very limited parallelism. The performance of AMULET1 itself is only 70% of the performance of the synchronous ARM.
- Asynchronous architectures are communication bound systems and therefore the efficiency of the communication system is crucial. The complex irregular interconnection pattern of AMULET1's functional modules and the extra multiplexing/demultiplexing processes required to cope with the connectivity constrains of the Transputer and the T-Rack introduce major bottlenecks in the system that severely reduce the communication efficiency.

9 Conclusions

Asynchronous logic promises to provide solutions to problems such as clock skew, power efficiency, performance and modularity on VLSI design and is currently experiencing a resurgence of interest. AMULET1, being the first asynchronous implementation of a complex commercial RISC architecture, has demonstrated the feasibility and merits of the asynchronous approach. Occam is particularly suitable for the specification and description of asynchronous systems. Its parallel distributed nature offers the potential for high simulation performance, but introduces a number of design and implementation problems, common in parallel asynchronous programs. This paper has discussed the solutions and techniques developed to address these issues in connection with **occarm**, the occam model of AMULET1.

Acknowledgements

For this work Georgios Theodoropoulos has been supported by the *Mpakalas Foundation*, Athens, Greece, under Grant No. 466/21121992.

References

[1] Amdahl, G. M., "Validity of the Single Processor Approach to Achieving Large Scale Computing Capabilities", Proceedings AFIPS 1967 Sping Joint Computer Conference, Atlantic City, April 1967, pp 483-485.

[2] ARM Ltd, Fulbourn Road, Cherry Hinton, Cambridge, CB1 4JN, England.

[3] Capon, P.C., "ParSiFal: A Parallel Simulation Facility", IEE Colloquium: The Transputer: Applications and Case Studies, IEE Digest, 1986/91.

[4] Brunvand, E. and Sproull, R., "Translating Concurrent Communicating Programs into delay-Insensitive Circuits", Technical Report CMU-CS-89-126, Carnegie Mellon University, April 1989.

[5] Furber, S. B., et al., "A Micropipelined ARM", Proceedings of VLSI '93 (Best Paper Award), September 1993, pp. 5.4.1-5.5.8.

[6] Hoare, C.A.R., "Communicating Sequential Processes", Communications of the ACM, Vol. 21, Number 8, August 1978, pp 666-677.

[7] Hauck, S., "Asynchronous Design Methodologies: An Overview". Technical Report UW-CSE-93-05-07. Department of Computer Science, University of Washington, April 1993.

[8] Inmos Ltd, "Occam Programming Manual", Prentice Hall, 1984.

[9] Inmos Ltd, "Networks Routers and Transputers", IOS Press, 1993.

[10] Martin, A. J., "Compiling Communicating Processes into Delay-Insensitive VLSI Circuits" Distributed Computing, 1, 4, April 1986, pp 226-234.

[11] Murta, A., "Tools for the Automated Configuration of a Transputer Network", MSc Thesis, University of Manchester, October 1987.

[12] Riek, M., Tourancheau, B., Vigouroux, X. F., "Monitoring of Distributed Memory Multicomputer Programs", Technical Report UT-CS-93-204, University of Tenessee, October 1993.

[13] Mead, C. and Conway, L., "Introduction to VLSI Circuits", Addison Wesley, 1980, Chapter 7, pp 218-254.

[14] Sutherland, I., "Micropipelines", Communications of the ACM, Vol. 32, Number 6, June 1989, pp 720-738.

[15] Theodoropoulos, G., Woods J.V., "Building Parallel Distributed Models for Asynchronous Computer Architectures", Proceedings of the World Transputer Congress 1994, Como, September 1994, pp 285-301.

[16] Theodoropoulos, G., Woods J.V., "Distributed Simulation of Asynchronous Computer Architectures: The Program Driven Conservative Approach", Proceedings of the European Simulation Symposium 1994, Istanbul, October 1994, pp 230-234.

[17] Theodoropoulos, G., Woods J.V., "Analysing the Timing Error in Distributed Simulations of Asynchronous Computer Architectures", Eurosim Congress '95, Vienna, Austria, September 1995, to appear.

[18] Weicker, R. P., "Dhrystone, A Synthetic Systems Programming Benchmark", Communications of the ACM, 27, 10, October 1984, pp. 1013-1030.

A Novel Asynchronous ALU for Massively Parallel Architectures

R S Hogg, W I Hughes, D W Lloyd

Sheffield Hallam University, 100 Napier Street, Sheffield S11 8HD, ENGLAND

Abstract

A self-timed asynchronous bit-serial massively parallel architecture is currently being developed to overcome limitations associated with clocked control, namely those of fixed word length, causing performance loss for small magnitude data, clock skew and scalability. This paper introduces the self-timed communication techniques and arithmetic logic unit (ALU) of the adopted research vehicle, the self-timed single instruction systolic array (ST-SISA), highlighting the novel architectures developed for variable length bit-serial logical and arithmetic operations. Two self-timed delay-insensitive techniques have been used to produce both a 2-phase (return-to-zero) and a 4-phase (non-return-to-zero) ALU for means of comparison. The self-timed designs and communication techniques developed are evaluated on a cost and performance basis demonstrating the speed-up potential of the novel self-timed approach.

Keywords: *ALU, Self-timing, Scaleable, Bit-serial, Systolic, Word-length.*

1: Introduction

In most real-time digital signal processing (DSP) applications the dominating properties of most of the algorithms are those of regularity, recursiveness and locality, which are effectual to array processor design. These properties are best exploited by computationally intensive and repetitive pipelined massively parallel architectures, such as the systolic array (SA) [1,2]. One such architecture is called the single instruction systolic array (SISA) [3], where instead of a data as in the conventional SAs, instructions are pumped through the array. Therefore, the size of each processing element (PE) is reduced as there is no need for a control store. In addition, each PE is bit-serial in nature resulting in further circuit area savings. This attractive for our research vehicle [4] because circuit overhead, associated with self-timed design methods, is kept to an absolute minimum.

Like most globally clocked high performance architectures the SISA suffers from problems of fixed word length and worst case processing speed. The fixed word clock cycle causes significant loss of performance in the ALU because data items are encoded using the same worst case number of bits even if the magnitude of the data is small. Also, fast processing functions, such as addition or logical operations, are fixed to the same worst case speed as that of the slowest function, such as the multiplier.

However, these problems can be overcome by adopting self-timed [5-8] asynchronous control techniques. This paper presents the self-timed communication techniques adopted for our research vehicle, the self-timed single instruction systolic array (ST-SISA) [4], and the variable length bit-serial data tagging techniques (section 2) developed to realise variable length data words. Two versions of the ST-SISA arithmetic logic unit (section 3), adopting the data encoding and tagging techniques, are introduced that process variable length words.

2: Self-timed Communication

Two problems need to be solved in order to realise self-timed communication in a bit-serial architecture. Firstly, encoding techniques must be identified that encode bit-serial data in a delay-insensitive manner (section 2.1); so that the arrival of new data can be detected in an environment where we assume unbounded delays. Secondly, because there is no global timing reference in self-timed architectures the end of a bit-serial word cannot be signalled as for the conventional SISA. Therefore, end-of-word (EOW) tagging techniques must be developed in order to signal the end of an asynchronous bit-serial word (section 2.2).

1066-6192/96 $5.00 © 1996 IEEE
Proceedings of PDP '96

2.1: Encoding Techniques

Two dual rail encoding techniques could be used to realise delay-insensitive data communication in a self-timed bit-serial array, namely; return-to-zero (RTZ) [9] and non-return-to-zero (NRTZ) [10]. In the next two sections we will give a brief summary of both encoding techniques.

2.1.1: Return-To-Zero RTZ Signalling

The most frequent approach to self-timing is the return-to-zero 4-phase mechanism where values exist in one of two states, namely empty (no-data) and valid. Valid is data-true or data-false. These values are coded in two bits (F1,F0) as (empty 0,0), (data-true 1,0) and (data_false 0,1), table 1. Data is transmitted by alternating valid and empty states. Thus the arrival of data is determined by detecting an *empty to valid transition;* the removal of a piece of data (e.g. when it is read), by detection of a *valid to empty transition.* The passage of the empty value has the effect of resetting all lines to zero.

Table 1.

F1	F0	STATE
0	1	data-false
1	0	data-true
1	1	Unused
0	0	EMPTY

2.1.2: Non-Return-To-Zero (NRTZ) Signalling

Encoded 2-Phase Dual Rail (LEDR), differs from the The NRTZ method, also referred to as Level-more traditional dual-rail signalling (i.e. RTZ) method by not requiring an empty token between data items. NRTZ can therefore increase throughput by up to 100% as compared to RTZ. Like RTZ, NRTZ uses two wires to encode data values using two states, ODD and EVEN. Each data token in the data stream must have the opposite phase of the data preceding it, table 2. The F1 wire carries the logic state of the data, while the F0 wire is equal to F1 on even phases and the inverse of F1 on odd phases. This encoding technique ensures that exactly one wire changes value for every successive data token.

Table 2.

F1	F0	PHASE	STATE
0	1	ODD	data-false
1	0	ODD	data-true
1	1	EVEN	data-true
0	0	EVEN	data-false

2.2: Self-timed Tagging Techniques

RTZ and NRTZ encoding provide self-timed communication techniques for synchronising bit by bit operations, therefore replacing the function of the global bit clock. However, neither of these approaches provides a facility to signal the end of a bit-serial word. The main use of these above mentioned techniques is in bit-parallel systems. Consequently end-of-word (EOW) tagging techniques are required for both RTZ and NRTZ encoding in order to make the ST-SISA feasible, and are considered in following two sections.

2.2.1: RTZ EOW Tagging

In the RTZ encoding technique valid data is encoded on two lines, using two bit representations for data-true(1,0), data-false (0,1), and the empty state(0,0). This leaves the unused (1,1) state to be utilised as a EOW tag bit (Table 1). This approach is attractive as it inherently allows the (T)ag bit to be placed after any (V)alid bit in the stream, and before the (V)alid bit of the successive word, thus promoting variable length words (e.g. 1.).

e.g. 1.

```
TVEVEVTVEVEVEVEVEV
100101110001000100
110000100100010001
◄– W2–►◄—— W1———►
```

The conventional RTZ register cannot accommodate the illegal (1,1) state, so an alternative FIFO register design must be adopted. An appropriate alternative is the NRTZ register [11], comparable in size to the RTZ register, which can accommodate all dual-rail bit combinations. An advantage of this approach is that the tag can be placed at any position in the bit-serial transmission and so it does not restrict possible word sizes. Also, taking the logical 'AND' of the dual-rail is all that is required to detect the EOW tag.

2.2.2: NRTZ EOW Tagging

Signalling the end of a NRTZ bit-serial word is a much more complex problem than for RTZ, as no spare bit representation can be used (Table 2). As a result the task of finding the end of a NRTZ stream is reduced to a process of counting bits or imposing a second encoding technique such as Huffman encoding [12]. The second technique is unattractive because data would have to be encoded and subsequently decoded at some point resulting in a loss of performance and extra circuitry. Consequently we will concentrate on the first approach. The method we have developed periodically reserves a bit position in the data stream to indicate the EOW. For example, every fourth bit in the data stream in the example below (e.g. 2.) is reserved to indicate the EOW, if it is set to logic true then the EOW (T)ag is indicated, otherwise if logic false then more (D)ata bits for that word are expected. In this approach every fourth bit is simply ignored by arithmetic/logical functions and so the extra decoding circuitry required by the Huffman approach is not needed. In addition, unlike the RTZ method extra registers are not required to store empty states. The disadvantage of this approach is that the word size is a multiple of the tag period.

e.g. 2.

```
TDDDTDDDTDDDTDDDTDDD
11000010101000110000
10010111111101100101
◄— W2 —►◄— W1 —►
```

In a latched pipeline, with at least three latches, it possible to connect the output of the last stage to the input of the first, forming a delay-insensitive ring [13]. Therefore, if the ring is initialised to contain a bit sequence, a series of logic zeros followed by a tag, a simple counter circuit is realised, figure 1. If the length of the ring is matched to the period of the tag position then this ring can be used to detect the end of a word. Hence, for each bit input into the ALU the contents of the ring are rotated and it's output is monitored in order to differentiate between a tag and data bit.

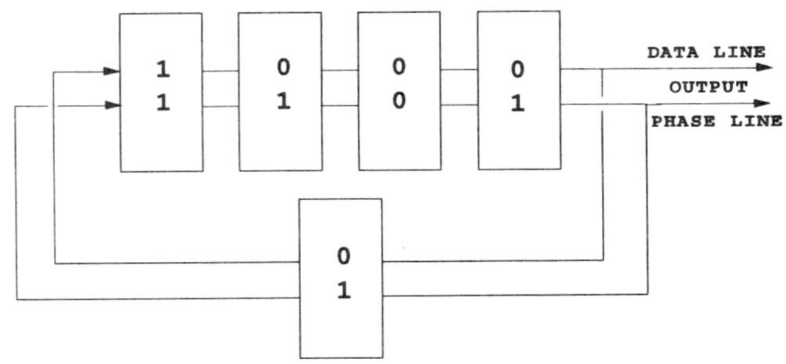

Figure 1. An NRTZ Delay-insensitive ring for Tag Detection

3: EXPERIMENTS

The performance and cost of an ALU is critical to the design of any massively parallel processor. As shown in the previous section the different encoding and tagging techniques have different advantages and disadvantages and the trade-offs between them are not clear. Therefore, the aim of this experiment is to assess performance and area trade-offs for the various designs developed to implement variable length bit-serial logic and arithmetic functions. The vehicle used for this experiment is the ST-SISA ALU which will be introduced in section 3.1. Two functions of the ALU are considered in this paper and are detailed in sub-sections 3.2 and 3.3. Section 3.2 presents the designs developed for both the RTZ and NRTZ bit-serial variable length logical 'AND' function. Section 3.3 introduces the designs created for both the RTZ and NRTZ bit-serial variable length addition function.

3.1: The ST-SISA ALU

The ST-SISA is a programmable architecture supporting a diverse set of word size instructions of varying complexity. These include register assignment, logical operations, addition, subtraction, multiplication and comparison. The instructions of the ST-SISA ALU are performed at a varying rate of computation dependent on the instruction word length, the data word length, the complexity of the instruction executed, and data. Thus providing four levels of possible performance improvement over that of the equivalent synchronous SISA. Bit-serial data words input to the ALU not only vary in length from one instruction cycle to the next, but can vary in length in respect to one another in the same execution cycle. For example, an addition operation can add a word of 4 bits to a word of 12 bits producing a 13-bit result. This is the case for all arithmetic and logic instructions. However, logic or arithmetic functions, such as 'AND' or addition, must receive a state change on all their inputs on every bit cycle in order for their function to be performed. This is clearly not the case, if words vary in length, and will result in the circuit locking up because one of the inputs will cease to receive data bits for that word cycle. Therefore, pseudo dummy bits must be appended to the end of short words to ensure each input receives a state change on every bit cycle. The RTZ and NRTZ architectures of typical logic and arithmetic instructions, such as AND and ADD, that operate on unsigned integers of varying word length, are presented in the following two sections.

3.2: Variable Length Logical 'AND' Architecture

The ST-SISA supports a number of typical logical operations such as OR, AND and EX-OR. Here we present the architectures for a bit-serial variable length RTZ and NRTZ logical 'AND' function.

3.2.1: RTZ Variable Length Bit-Serial 'AND'

The RTZ 'AND' consists of eight major components (Figure 2), namely: two input multiplexors, two input tag converters, an output tag converter, two multiplexor controllers and the 'AND' function itself. Each component, except for the 'AND', operates on the RTZ tagged encoding sequence.

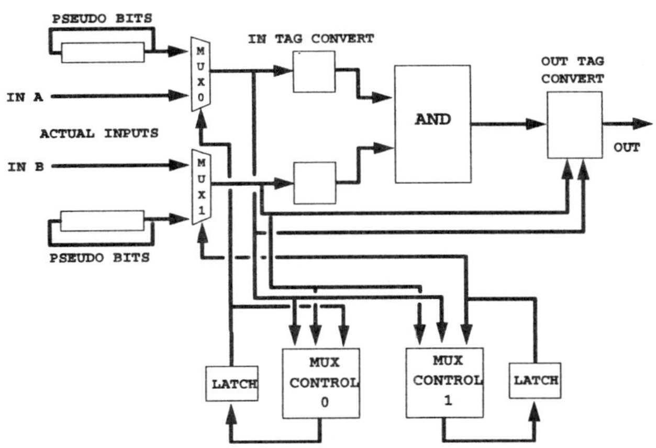

Figure 2. The RTZ variable length bit-serial 'AND' architecture.

The functionality of these components is explained as follows:

Multiplexor: The multiplexor (mux) has two data bit inputs, an actual data input and a pseudo data input, which are under the control of the selector input, which is fed by the mux controller. For every state change on the select input either an actual bit or a pseudo bit is passed to the data output, depending on the select logic value. The pseudo input is fed by a FIFO ring buffer such that dummy bits can be appended to the end of short words.

Multiplexor Controller: The controller monitors the output bits from the two multiplexors, for each bit cycle, which are termed the primary multiplexor, the controlled device, and the secondary multiplexor, which is simply monitored. Also, the previous state of the controller is latched and fed back as input. The controller behaves as follows. When the secondary bit (SB) is a tag and the primary bit (PB) is an spacer token (i.e. the secondary word is shorter than the primary word), or both the SB and PB are tag bits, then mux controller selects the actual input on the next bit cycle. When the PB is a tag and the SB is a spacer (i.e. the primary word is shorter than the secondary word) the multiplexor's pseudo input is selected in order to attach a dummy bit to the end of the word. The pseudo input will continue to be selected on each bit cycle until the SB is a tag.

Input Tag Converter: Whenever a tag is input this circuit converts it to an empty state. All other states are left unchanged.

Output Tag Converter: Converts an empty state, output from the 'AND' function, into a tag state whenever the two input bits to the 'AND' are tags.

The 'AND' Gate: This is a conventional RTZ logical 'AND' circuit.

3.2.2: NRTZ Bit-serial Variable Length 'AND'

The functionality of the NRTZ 'AND' architecture is similar to that of the RTZ, except that it operates on the NRTZ data encoding scheme. Consequently, a counting mechanism, realised by the ring buffer presented in section 2.2.2, is necessary to differentiate between the tag and data bits in the bit-serial stream. This ring buffer feeds the multiplexor controllers, shown in figure 3. The NRTZ mux controller operates in a similar manner to the previously explained RTZ mux controller. In the event of a tag bit on the bit count input, the mux control selects the actual input if the primary input tag bit is low (0,0) and the secondary tag bit is low, or high (1,1), or if both tag bits are high. However, if the primary input tag bit is high and the secondary input tag bit is low the pseudo input is selected in order to append dummy bits on to the end of the word.

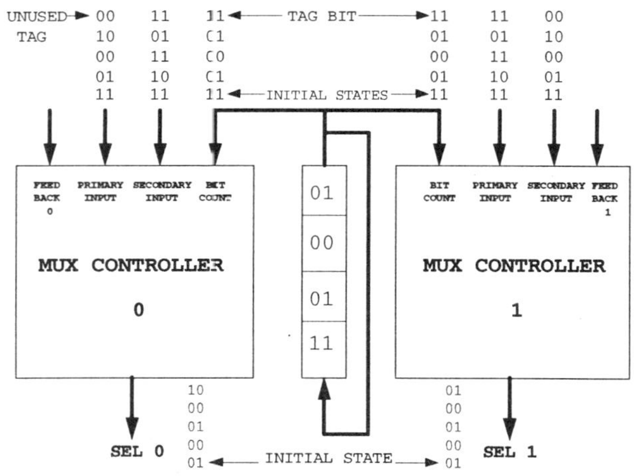

Figure 3. The NRTZ multiplexor control modules with ring buffer bit count.

3.3: Variable Length Adder Architecture

The RTZ and NRTZ adders presented here perform their operation upon unsigned integers of no maximum word length. The major difference between a variable length bit-serial arithmetic function and a bit-serial logical function is that the word size in the former may increase as a result of carry propagation or overflow. This can be catered for, in the event of overflow, by simply appending pseudo bits to the end of the word in order to propagate the carry to the sum output, thus increasing the length of the word.

3.3.1: RTZ Variable Length Bit-Serial Adder

The RTZ adder (Figure 4) is essentially the same as the RTZ 'AND' except for changes to the mux controller, output tag converter and of course the substitution of the 'AND' with the RTZ Full Adder.

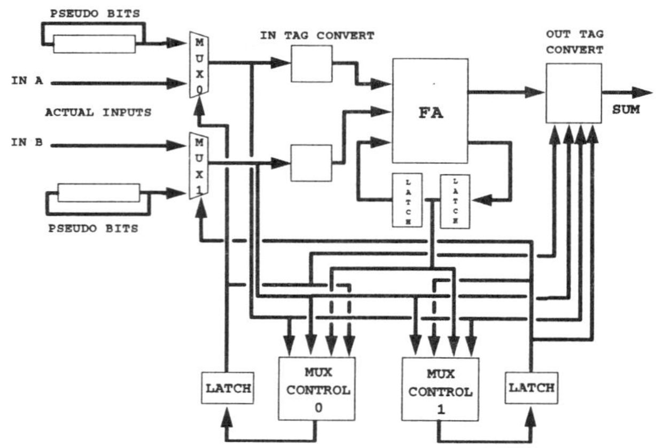

Figure 4. The RTZ bit-serial variable length adder architecture

These changes are explained as follows:

Multiplexor Controller: The operation of the add RTZ mux controller is the same as that used for the 'AND' circuit, except it monitors the carry-out bit produced by the full adder. Consequently, if the previous addition produces a carry and the present input operands bits are tags the pseudo input is selected in the next bit cycle thus appending a logic '0' and a tag bit, in consecutive bit cycles, to the end of the operand.

Output Tag Converter: This function converts an empty state to a tag state only when both inputs are tags and both mux controller outputs are selecting the next actual data input. This indicates that either there is no overflow or the overflow has been previously handled.

Full Adder: This is a conventional RTZ full adder.

3.3.2: NRTZ Variable Length Bit-Serial Adder

The NRTZ adder incorporates the functions used for the logical 'AND' with small modifications to the multiplexor controller in order to cater for overflow. However, carry feedback in the NRTZ full adder introduces two problems. These problems are explained and their solutions presented as follows.

For both encoding techniques successive data bits alternate in phase. To ensure the phase of the present carry, which is fed back as input to the full adder, matches the phase of the succeeding input data bits, phase conversion must be performed on the fed back carry bit. For example, a carry output of EVEN phase data will be out of phase with the succeeding ODD data input bits. This is clearly undesirable and will result in the full adder locking up. However, this can be easily overcome by inserting an invertor gate in the phase wire of the carry output from the full adder (figure 5). This ensures the phase of the carry toggles without it affecting it's logic level.

The second point of interest is concerned with the propagation of the carry bit from the addition preceding the input of tag bits, which are always logic false due to the input phase conversion, to the addition of the data bits succeeding the unused tag bits. In other words, we must ensure that the tag bits, whether set or not, are added together producing a sum of logic '0', in conjunction with passing the carry of the previous addition through the full adder in readiness for the next data bit addition. This can be achieved by adding one of the tag bits to two copies of the previous carry bit, such that the carry is input instead of one of the tag bits. Therefore, if the carry input is logic '1' the sum is '0' and the carry produced is '1', otherwise, if the carry input is '0' both the sum and carry outputs are '0'. This functionality is implemented by making use of an NRTZ symmetric switch which is based on the RTZ asymmetric switch introduced by Staunstrup[13].

The functionality of the NRTZ symmetric switch, as depicted in figure 5, is as follows. The switch has two data inputs, two data outputs and a control input. Whenever the logic level of the control input is logic '0' (i.e. '00' or '01') the inputs are passed to their respective outputs. However, when the control input is logic '1' (i.e. '11' - Tag) the inputs are passed to each others respective output, in other words they are crossed over. In context with the above mentioned NRTZ adder functionality, the device under normal operation passes the operand bit to the full adder, and the carry bit to a null circuit that simply acknowledges it's receipt without actually performing any function upon it. In the event of tag detection the carry is fed to the full adder and the tag is passed to the null circuit, thus implementing the functionality as outlined above.

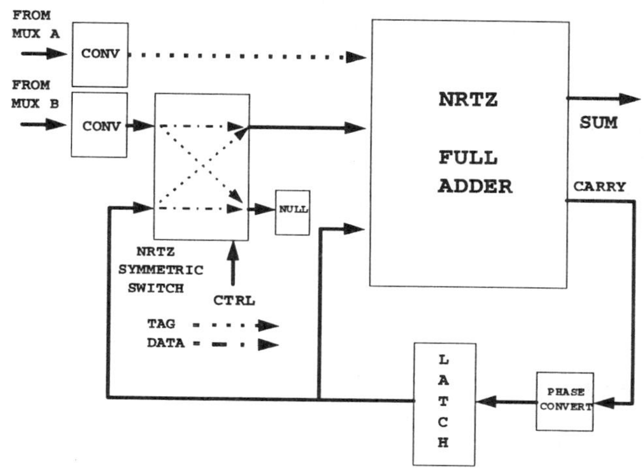

Figure 5. The NRTZ full adder.

4: Results

This section aims to evaluate the encoding and tagging techniques introduced in this paper on a cost/performance basis for both the RTZ and NRTZ 'AND' and Full Adder architectures. All results are generated using gate primitives from the MCE 5-micron Cell Library[14]. The units used for evaluation are the operation delay and the circuit area.

4.1: Logical 'AND' Function

Figure 6 compares the functional delay (µs) for varying word lengths, up to a maximum of 64 bits, for both the RTZ and NRTZ 'AND' functions.

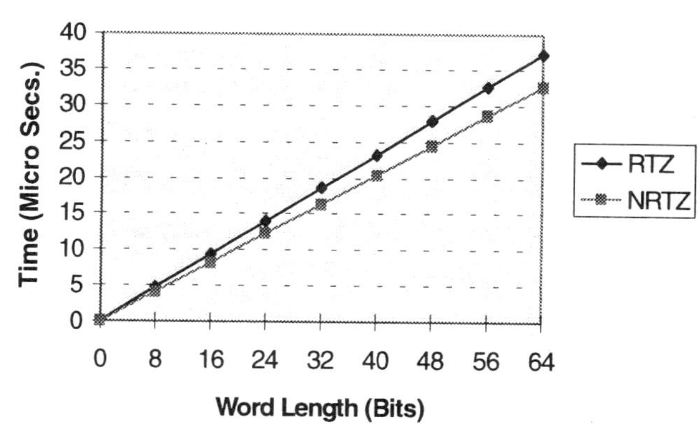

Figure 6. Performance results for the RTZ and NRTZ 'AND' function.

4.2: Full Adder Function

Figure 7 compares the functional delay (μs) for varying word length, up to a maximum of 64 bits, for both the RTZ and NRTZ Full Adder functions.

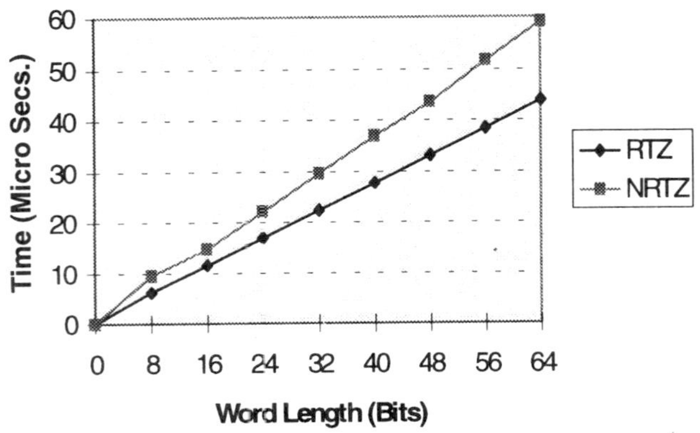

Figure 7. Performance results for the RTZ and NRTZ Full Adder.

5: Discussion

Figure 6 indicates that the NRTZ 'AND' logical operation is faster than the RTZ equivalent. However, figure 7 shows that the RTZ Full Adder arithmetic operation is faster than the RTZ. Both figures show the significant performance increase available for small magnitude data using the variable word methods as compared to the same data in a large fixed word. In terms of circuit area, we have discovered that the NRTZ 'AND' is 4 times bigger that the RTZ equivalent. Whereas the NRTZ Full Adder is 3 times bigger the RTZ equivalent. These results can be attributed to the increased complexity of the NRTZ mux controller, and as an effect of the extra expense of NRTZ circuits as the number of inputs is incrementally increased.

For implementations where circuit area is limited the results show that we must use the RTZ approach. To obtain high performance, however, the choice between the NRTZ and the RTZ approach is determined by the relative frequency of occurrence between arithmetic and logical operations for the chosen processor workload.

6: Conclusion

This paper has shown the feasibility of realising an ALU which supports variable length words for two distinct self-timed design techniques. Two different tagging methods have been introduced that augment existing RTZ and NRTZ encoding techniques such that they can implement variable length words. In addition, we have developed novel logical and arithmetic architectures to operate upon these tagged words. Results demonstrate the removal of the requirement for fixed word length leads to substantial performance increases for small magnitude data which would normally be fixed to the worst case word length.

Future work will compare the variable word length self-timed designs against synchronous designs which enforce a fixed word length on both data and instructions.

References

[1] H. T. Kung, "Why Systolic Architectures?" Computer, Vol. 15, No. 1, Jan. 1982, pp. 37-46.

[2] K. T. Johnson. et al, "General-Purpose Systolic Arrays", Computer, Nov. 1993, pp. 20-31.

[3] H. W. Lang, "ISA and SISA: Two variants of a general purpose array structure", Proc. Second International Conference on Supercomputing, Vol. 1, pp. 460-467, 1987.

[4] R. S. Hogg. et al, "Communication Techniques for a Self-Timed Massively Parallel Architecture", Proc. First International Conference on Massively Parallel Computing Systems", May 2-6 1994, Ischia, Italy, IEEE Computer Society Press, pp. 55-61.

[5] D. W. Lloyd, "Self-Timed Fine Grained Parallel Processing Array Design", The Workshop on High Performance Special Purpose Architectures, International Symposium on Computer Architecture, Hamilton Island, Australia, 23 May 1992.

[6] T. H. Meng, "Synchronization Design For Digital Systems", Kluwer Academic Publishers 1991.

[7] C. D. Neilsen, et al, "Potential Performance Advantages of Delay-Insensitivity", Proceedings of the IFIP WG 10.5 Workshop, St. Paul-de-Vence, France, 28-30 Nov 1990, pp. 271 - 82.

[8] C. L. Seitz, "System Timing," in C. Mead and L. Conway, Introduction to VLSI systems, Addison-Wesley, 1980, pp. 218-262.

[9] I. David, et al, "An efficient Implementation of Boolean Functions and Finite State Machines as Self-Timed Circuits", COMPEURO 90, Proceedings of the 1990 IEEE International Conference on Computer Systems and Software Engineering, IEEE Computer Society Press, pp . 148 - 55

[10] M. E. Dean, "Efficient Self-Timing with Level-Encoded 2-Phase Dual-Rail (LEDR)", MIT Conference on Advanced Research in VLSI, March 1991.

[11] D. W. Lloyd, "Design Methods for Asynchronous Circuits", PhD Thesis, Dept. of Electrical and Electronic Engineering, University of Nottingham, England, May 1995.

[12] L. Sham, "The Evolution of Data Compression Techniques", Proceedings of the International Society For Computers and Their Applications Conference, Long Beach, California, U.S.A. March 17-19, 1994, pp. 135-139.

[13] J. Staunstrup, et al, "Design of Delay-insensitive circuits using multi-ring structures", In the Proceedings of EURO-DAC, European Design Automation Conference, EURO-VHDL 1992, pp. 15 - 20.

[14] MCE Array Design Manual and Cell Library 5-Micron Array.

Design and Implementation of the Control Structure of the PAPRICA-3 Processor

F. Gregoretti, F. Intini, L. Lavagno, R. Passerone, L. M. Reyneri

Dipartimento di Elettronica
Politecnico di Torino
Torino, ITALY, 10129

Abstract

This paper describes the pipeline architecture designed to control the execution of instructions on the linear array processor PAPRICA-3, which is being developed at the Politecnico di Torino. The main applications of the array processor lay in the area of image processing, image recognition, embedded systems for guidance assistance and the like. Exploitation of this architecture is currently investigated in the area of real-time image processing, a very demanding task in terms of overall performance. Our design is aimed at improving the algorithmic efficiency by taking advantage of a multi-path queue structure which allows different instructions to run simultaneously, and by optimizing particular patterns of instructions which often appear in envisaged application programs.

1 Introduction

Real-time systems for image processing may benefit from Application-Specific Instruction Processors (ASIPs [6]). Such processors play an intermediate role between general-purpose programmable processors, which may not have enough processing power or memory access bandwidth for the application, and Application Specific Integrated Circuits, which may be too expensive and too rigid for rapidly evolving application needs. In this scenario, a processor is designed for a *class* of applications, and its instruction set and architecture are specifically tuned for that class. This allows to simultaneously achieve the required performance, as well as the required degree of programmability. The PAPRICA-3 system [2, 3] is a SIMD massively parallel processor designed for real time image processing applications. The system is composed of multiple instances of the same basic Processor Element (PE) which execute in parallel the same instructions on different pixels. This approach exploits the parallelism intrinsic to the data structure to boost the overall performance. The paper describes the implementation of the control of the processing array and is organized as follows. Section 2 provides a condensed description of the general architecture and Section 3 describes the instruction set. Section 4 and 5 present in detail the pipeline structure and section 6 analyzes its performance. Finally section 7 presents some conclusions.

2 General description

As shown in figure 1, the kernel of the PAPRICA-3 system is based on a linear array of Q identical 1-bit PEs connected to an image memory via a bidirectional Q-bit wise bus. The image memory is organized in

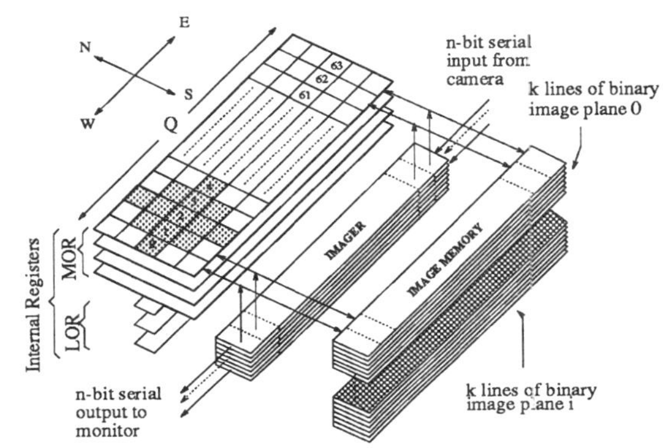

Figure 1: **Block diagram of the processor Array**

addressable words whose length matches that of the processor array; each word contains data relative to one binary pixel plane (also called *layer*) of one line of an image, and a single operation is needed to load an entire line of data into the PE's internal registers. The rationale behind this system is that the size of the PE array equals (or is larger than) the height (or width) of the input image. This solution reduces the PE virtualization mechanism problem, which has been proven to be a critical design issue in bi-dimensional arrays [2].

Data are transferred into internal registers of each PE, processed and explicitly stored back into memory according to a RISC-like processing paradigm. The external memory can therefore be seen as a set of individually addressable Q bit wide lines. We will refer to the address of each line as an *absolute line address.*

Each PE processes one pixel of each line and is composed of a Register File and a 1-bit Execution Unit. The instruction set core is based on morphological operators [1]. The result of an operation depends, for each processor, on the values of pixels in a given neigh-

1066-6192/96 $5.00 © 1996 IEEE
Proceedings of PDP '96

borhood (reduced 5 × 5, as shown in figure 1). Data from EAST and WEST directions may be obtained by direct connection with neighboring PEs while all other directions correspond to data of lines which have been previously processed (N, NE, NW) or which will be processed in the future (S, SE, SW). For this reason a number of processor registers have a structure which is more complex than that of a simple memory cell, and are actually composed of five 1-bit cells with a S→N shift register connection. When a load operation is performed, all data are shifted north by one position and the south-most position is taken by the new line from memory. In this way, data from a 5×5 neighborhood are available inside the array for each PE. This type of registers will be referred to in the following as *Morphological Registers (MOR)*. A second part of the instruction set comprises logical and algebraic operations which may be performed between the central pixels of MOR registers of the same PE, or between a number of single bit *Logical Registers (LOR)* which may be used for intermediate storage. The Execution Unit is responsible for applying morphological operators and for all the logical and algebraic operations. An Accumulator Register is used when a ternary algebraic operation, such as addition or subtraction, is executed to hold the value of the carry.

Two logical inter-processor communication mechanisms are available to exchange information among PEs which are not directly connected. The first one is the Status Evaluation Network (SEN) to which each processor sends the content of one of its registers under program control. The SEN provides two global flags, named SET and RESET, which are true when the specified register content is either all 1s or all 0s, and a status word which is set to the number of 1s in the specified register. This global information may be used to conditionally modify the program flow.

The second one is the Inter-processor Communication Network which allows global and multiple communication among components of different subsets of the PA (clusters of PEs). The topology of the communication network may be varied during program execution. In fact, each PE drives a switch that enables or disables the connection between it and the adjacent one. The PEs may thus be dynamically grouped into clusters, in which each PE can broadcast a register bit value to the whole cluster within a single instruction. This feature can be extremely useful in algorithms involving *seed-propagation* techniques, and in the emulation of pyramidal (hierarchical) processing.

An important characteristic of the system is the integration of a Serial-to-Parallel I/O Device, called *Video Interface* (VIF), which can be connected to a conventional imaging device (camera, linear CCD, etc). While a line is processed, the VIF automatically loads the following image line from the camera. At the end of this processing, the PA stores the results back into the VIF (on different bit-planes) and loads in parallel the following image line. During the data acquisition process, the VIF behaves like a shift-register, loading raw data serially from a camera, and outputting processed data serially to a display.

The system is designed to fit into a single integrated circuit, hence the control of all the processing elements is centralized at the chip level. Its design has been driven by two main considerations.

First many image analysis algorithms consist of sequences of low level steps, such as filters, convolutions, etc., to be performed over the whole image. Instruction fetching from an external memory is an important source of overhead. Hence we chose to pre-load each block of instructions (to be repeated for the whole image) into an internal memory, named Writable Control Store (WCS), and to fetch the instructions from there. In such a way it is possible to obtain the performance of a fast cache with a hit ratio close to 1, at a fraction of the cost and complexity.

The second consideration has been to avoid performance bottlenecks by matching the performance of the control section to that of the processing elements. To achieve this result, a sophisticated pipeline scheme has been developed which is expected to sustain an instruction execution flow of 100 Mops/s.

3 Instruction set

PAPRICA's instruction set has been designed to efficiently implement image processing algorithms. A dedicated hardware structure, named Image Descriptor, stores the base memory address of the image, the index of the line being processed at any time, and some other information regarding the way in which the image should be processed. This allows, for example, indirect memory access. To increase the flexibility of the processor, memory references may also be indexed using the contents of some special purpose counter registers, which are used as indices in loops. In addition to that, two instructions provide full synchronization and transfer capability to directly acquire data from a camera and send it after processing to a display. The instruction set fully supports the Mathematical Morphology approach to image processing, exploiting matching operations and logical operations. Bit-serial addition and subtraction with carry are also implemented. A branch instruction allows the programmer to take decisions on the flow of operations: considering the SIMD architecture, conditions must be set up on the base of global information, for which specific evaluation and accumulation instructions are provided.

PAPRICA's assembly language comprises the following classes of instructions:

- **General** and **Initialization** Instructions:

  NOP performs no operation.

  STOP performs soft and hard program stops.

  CONFIG configures neighborhood connection for sidemost processors.

  BASE, SKIP, RESET initialize image descriptor contents.

- **Memory Transfer** Instructions:

  LD loads data from memory into an internal register.

  ST stores data from an internal register to memory.

LDC loads data from the camera interface into internal registers.

STV stores data from internal registers to the camera interface.

ADD updates the memory address information of a specified image descriptor.

COMMOUT transfers internal register data among processor elements.

- **Morphological** Instructions:

LOP performs a logical or algebraic operation between two internal registers. Stores the result into an internal register.

MOP performs a match operation between an internal register (and its neighborhood) and the last set template. The result is then treated as the first operand of a logical or algebraic operation.

TEMPLATE sets the match template.

- **Status Evaluation** and **Flow Control** Instructions:

INIT initializes the status evaluation hardware.

EVAL performs status evaluation.

ACCUM accumulates status data on the dedicated status registers.

SET, INC initializes and increment counter register contents.

FOR repeats a block of instructions for a prespecified number of times. Enables indexed addressing.

ON sets up and evaluates a condition that influences the execution of the following instruction.

BRC unconditionally branches to a specified program memory address.

4 Pipeline description

In order to devise an efficient pipeline structure, instructions must be first divided into classes sharing the same kind of operations. For this purpose, only a coarse division of the instruction execution process is necessary. In our case the classical five phase pipeline [5] may be used:

IF Instruction fetch

ID Instruction decode

OR Operand read

EX Execution

OW Operand write back

Instructions	IF	ID	OR	EX	OW
NOP	x	x	-	x	-
STOP	x	x	-	x	-
CONFIG	x	x	-	x	-
BASE	x	x	-	x	-
SKIP	x	x	-	x	-
RESET	x	x	-	x	-
ADD	x	x	-	x	-
TEMPLATE	x	x	-	x	-
INIT	x	x	-	x	-
ACCUM	x	x	-	x	-
FOR	x	x	-	x	-
BRC	x	x	-	x	-
ST	x	x	x	x	mem
LD	x	x	mem	x	x
LDC	x	x	vif	x	x
STV	x	x	x	x	vif
COMMOUT	x	x	x	x	x
MOP	x	x	x	x	x
LOP	x	x	x	x	x
EVAL	x	x	x	x	x

Table 1: **Instruction phase requirements**

Only the IF, ID and EX phases must be present in all instructions. We can thus partition the instruction set on the basis of the required phases, as shown in table 4. The simplest pipeline structure would then comprise five stages corresponding to the five basic phases. This scheme, known in the literature as *mono-functional* ([5]), forces even unrelated instructions to wait if the preceding ones stall due to conflicts, thus degrading the overall performance. To avoid this effect, a multi-functional pipeline has been designed, which allows multiple instructions to be routed on different paths and execute simultaneously. The design objective was to reach peak performance for those patterns of instructions that most often are exploited in image processing: these comprise sequences of morphological instructions, loops, load-process-store, bit-serial computations. A particular attention has been dedicated to allowing potentially long instructions to run in parallel with shorter ones, by providing different paths for some of them. For example, flag evaluation, inter-processor communication, memory access and synchronization all share a wait mechanism that lets them "run in the background".

A comprehensive block-diagram of the proposed architecture is depicted in figure 2. A brief description of the functionality associated with each block follows:

IF Instruction Fetch. Updates the program counter content. Checks for active loops and handles their data management.

ID Instruction Decode. Decodes and routes instructions. Those which need operand read or write are routed to the conflict detection stage, after effective address calculation has been performed. The others are immediately executed. Branch instructions are executed at this stage, and require that IF be flushed to discard unwanted data. Flow control conflict detection and address evaluation are performed by this block. Due to the complexity associated to this stage, ID may be replicated many times in the implementation to meet the timing constraint.

CD Conflict Detection. Checks for data conflicts and handles the *booking table* for internal registers. Routes instructions to the proper block for execution.

OR Operand Read. Reads operands from internal registers. Checks for operand availability before execution. Routes instructions to the proper block for execution.

BP Bit Propagation. Delays MOP instruction execution for one cycle, to allow data propagation between neighboring processors.

EX Execution. Executes matching, logical and algebraic operators.

FE Flag Evaluation. Performs status evaluation and waits for completion. Stores the result in the status register.

CO Communication Out. Sends data to the communication network and waits for completion. Stores the result in the dedicated internal register.

MU Memory Unit. Manages all accesses to the image memory and waits for completion. Redirects instructions to the correct stage for operand write back (OW2 for logical registers, SM for morphological registers to perform the shift operation).

SY Synchronize. Waits for synchronization with the external camera and display.

OW1 Operand Write 1. Stores results back into internal registers. Checks for availability of the resource.

OW2 Operand Write 2. Stores results back into internal registers. Releases register occupancy flags and notifies the CD stage.

SM Shift MOR. Stores incoming data from image memory into internal morphological registers and shifts their content one line up. Releases the register's occupancy and notifies the CD stage.

SV Shift VIF. For LDC: load data from the camera interface into the internal morphological registers and shifts their content one line up. For STV: stores data from internal registers to the camera interface. Releases the register's occupancy and notifies the CD stage.

Instructions stall either when the desired operation cannot be executed because of resource contention, or when the block where the instruction must be issued

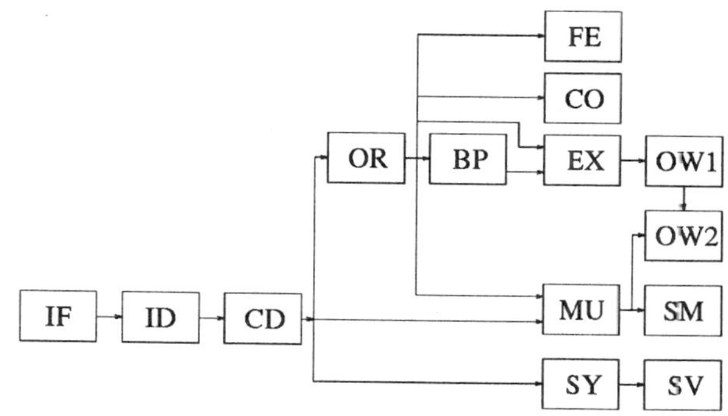

Figure 2: **Pipeline block-diagram**

is already occupied. The latter circumstance is minimized when different instructions are allowed to take different paths. This condition can be accomplished, as in our design, by multiple instances of the execution stage. On the other hand, this approach requires a more complex design of the conflict detection mechanism.

5 Conflict management

The concurrent execution of instructions in a pipeline structure causes contention conditions which must be detected and resolved in the most effective way. These conflicts between instructions may be classified as follows: ***structural conflicts*** which arise from the request of the same resource by two different instructions at the same time, ***data conflicts*** which arise because a pipeline structure allows the sequence of data accesses to be altered, and ***control conflicts*** which occur when the normal flow of operation is changed [5].

5.1 Structural conflicts

Given the structure of the pipeline, these conflicts are regarded as potential conflicts, since they occur only for particular sequences of instructions. Different structures are present in PAPRICA's hardware to perform different tasks:

- Register File read ports.
- Register File write port.
- Morphological Register shift.
- Video InterFace load/store.
- Execution unit (match, logical and algebraic).
- Flag Evaluation unit.
- Inter-processor Communication Network.
- Memory read/write access.

Each of these functional units corresponds to a different block in the pipeline block diagram, thus structural conflicts related to simultaneous requests of the same resource by two different blocks cannot occur. A conflict arises only when two instructions originating in the *execution* and *memory* units request for an operand write back. As seen in figure 2, block OW has been duplicated into two instances named OW1 and OW2. OW1 executes the write operation only when OW2 is empty, otherwise it behaves as a buffer booking OW2 for the following cycle and trasferring to it its content. In this way, while memory instructions may stall until a MOP/LOP sequence ends, only the latency of morphological instructions is increased without losing steady-state performance.

A conflict arises when a pipeline block may be accessed by different stages. This problem is caused by the MU and EX blocks:

- The MU stage may be accessed both by an LD in CD and by an ST in OR: in this case, the LD is stalled and the ST proceeds first, as in the natural order.
- The EX stage may be accessed by both a MOP in BP and a LOP in OR. Instead of stalling the LOP instruction in the operand read stage, the LOP is issued to the BP stage, which does nothing but delays it for one cycle. As for the OW stage, only latency is increased with no performance loss (in this case stalling is completely avoided).

5.2 Data conflicts

These conflicts occur when two instructions refer to the same data. The most common problem arises when the second instruction tries to read the data *before* the first one has changed it. To avoid this error, the second instruction must be stalled until the first has completed.

Different policies are implemented to avoid data conflicts for the different hardware structures.

- Image Memory data. This conflict never occurs because memory references are always performed by the same block (MU) *in order*.
- Status Registers data. This conflict occurs when an accumulation instruction is issued before the status evaluation from the previous one has completed. A dedicated flag in the pipeline informs the ID stage that an evaluation is in progress, stopping the accumulation until the evaluation completes.
- Internal Register data. This conflict originates from instructions which refer to the internal registers. They are: LD, ST, LDC, STV, MOP, LOP, COMMOUT, EVAL. Complexity arises from the different possible paths that these instructions may take, forcing the use of a sophisticated mechanism to detect contention. For each register in the Register File, a busy bit indicates whether a write operation for that register is in progress. The CD, OR and write back stages are in charge of handling such bits through the following procedure:

  1. For any instruction willing to write into an internal register, the register availability is checked in the CD stage against the state of the corresponding busy bit. If the busy bit is already set, the instruction waits in the CD stage until the register is released by one of the write back stages. Otherwise, if the busy bit is not set, the register is occupied by the instruction and control passes to one of the following stages. Only in the case of an STV, registers are booked as for a write operation, even though only a read operation will take place. This is necessary to avoid data being changed by other instructions during the VIF synchronization phase, which may take an unpredictable number of cycles.
  2. In the OR stage the source operands' busy bit is checked and the instruction is stalled if a write operation on such registers is in progress. Instructions referring to the same register as both the source and the destination operand do not execute the check phase (which had already been performed in the CD stage) to avoid deadlock.
  3. The write phases (OW1, OW2, SM, SV) inform the CD stage of the completion of their operation, and release the occupation of the internal register, making it available to the following instructions.

Correct operation is ensured by the CD stage, through which every instruction referring to internal registers must pass.

The CD stage handles such conflicts as *Write after Write* and *Write after Read*, while the *Read after Write* is managed by the OR stage. The *bypass* technique is often used in many pipeline structures to avoid stalling an instruction for a *Read after Write* conflict. This technique basically feeds the result of the execution stage back to the operand read stage, to make it immediately available. This technique is not applicable to our case, because:

- results are produced by both the EX and the MU stage, so a decision must be taken to get the data from the proper place.
- source operands come from different PEs, so a bit propagation delay must be taken into account before data are available to the OR stage.
- logical and morphological instructions may accumulate their result in AND or OR with the previous value stored in the destination register, so that the new value may not correspond to that computed by the execution stage.

However, this technique is applicable to the accumulator used for bit-serial computations, since its value is immediately available for the following instructions which need not be stalled.

Note that data stored in the image descriptors may be changed before an LD or ST completes: this does not matter because address calculation is performed immediately in the ID stage and the effective address in then delivered to the MU stage. On the other hand, the register which holds the template value must be preserved until every morphological instruction has terminated: for this reason, a TEMPLATE instruction waits in the ID stage if a MOP is still running in the pipeline.

5.3 Control conflicts

The program flow may be changed by the compound statements ON–BRC, which are executed in the ID stage. The first instruction is used to evaluate the condition, and the second to decide whether the jump must be taken or not. Since the ID stage is not released by the ON–BRC, only one other instruction is fetched before any decision is taken. Hence only the first stage of the pipeline need be flushed. Moreover, at least two more cycles are lost in the condition evaluation and branch execution. To avoid this loss of performance, a dedicated instruction has been introduced to handle fixed loops, which are a very common occurrence in the sort of application programs that we are targeting. The FOR instruction is executed in the ID stage, and simply sets some registers used by the IF stage to determine the value of the next program address. Since the number of instructions within the loop and the number of iterations are known *a-priori*, the IF stage always fetches the correct instruction and no cycles are lost for evaluating the end of the loop. Thanks to the indexed addressing mode, this mechanism highly increases performance and saves precious space in the program memory cache (WCS).

6 Performance evaluation

In this section, a few examples are examined based on the simulation of a behavioral model written in the Verilog Hardware Description Language [7]. A state diagram shows the instruction queue in the pipeline for a sequence of clock cycles.

The first example is shown in figure 3 and consists of a two-instruction loop (one morphological and one logical) *without* data dependency, and repeated 3 times. One instruction is issued for each cycle with no delay. Note how LOPs are routed to the BP stage to wait for a MOP bit propagation and leave space to the following instruction. Not considering the first (FOR) and the last (STOP) instruction, and assuming an infinite number of iterations, the performance gain over a non-pipelined solution is 5.5 (in real cases it is expected to be between 3.5 and 4.5).

The second example is shown in figure 4, and consists of a sequence of a MOP and a LOP instructions *with* data dependency. The second instruction waits in the OR stage for the MOP completion, and is then directly issued to the EX stage with no bit propagation. Note that the CD stage is free to manage other instructions to be delivered to different blocks. Peak speed up is 1.57 (in real cases it is expected to be between 1.3 and 1.45).

The last example is shown in figure 5 and consists of an LD and a MOP *without* data dependency. In this

FOR cycle : body of 2 instructions without data dependencies repeated 3 times
FOR 0 TO 2 DO 2
MOP
LOP
STOP

cycle no.	IF	ID	CD	OR	BP	EX	OW1
0	FOR						
1	MOP0	FOR					
2	LOP0	MOP0					
3	MOP1	LOP0	MOP0				
4	LOP1	MOP1	LOP0	MOP0			
5	MOP2	LOP1	MOP1	LOP0	MOP0		
6	LOP2	MOP2	LOP1	MOP1	LOP0	MOP0	
7	STOP	LOP2	MOP2	LOP1	MOP1	LOP0	MOP0
8		STOP (s)	LOP2	MOP2	LOP1	MOP1	LOP0
9		STOP (s)		LOP2	MOP2	LOP1	MOP1
10		STOP (s)			LOP2	MOP2	LOP1
11		STOP (s)				LOP2	MOP2
12		STOP (s)					LOP2
13		STOP					

Legend:
(s) - stall cycle

Figure 3: **For cycle: 2 instructions, 3 times, no data dependency**

LOP instruction waits for operand release by a previous MOP
Note that BP Stage free lets to bypass it by a LOP instruction
R4 = MOP R1 LOP R2; // this MOP locks R4
R12 = R4 LOP R3; // this LOP needs R4 as read operand
STOP

cycle no.	IF	ID	CD	OR	BP	EX	OW1
0	MOP						
1	LOP	MOP					
2	STOP	LOP	MOP				
3		STOP (s)	LOP	MOP			
4		STOP (s)		LOP (s)	MOP		
5		STOP (s)		LOP (s)		MOP	
6		STOP (s)		LOP (s)			MOP
7		STOP (s)		LOP			
8		STOP (s)				LOP	
9		STOP (s)					LOP
10		STOP					

Legend:
(s) - stall cycle

Figure 4: **MOP - LOP sequence with data dependency**

MOP instruction bypasses LD instruction waiting for memory read completion
No data dependencies
LD
MOP
STOP

cycle no.	IF	ID	CD	MU	SM	OR	BP	EX	OW1
0	LD								
1	MOP	LD							
2	STOP	MOP	LD						
3		STOP (s)	MOP	LD (w)					
4		STOP (s)		LD (w)		MOP			
5		STOP (s)		LD (w)			MOP		
6		STOP (s)		LD (w)				MOP	
7		STOP (s)		LD (w)					MOP
8		STOP (s)			LD				
9		STOP							

Legend:
(s) - stall cycle
(w) - wait cycle

Figure 5: **MOP overtakes a waiting LD**

case, a slow memory access time is assumed, so that the LD waits for 5 cycles in the MU stage. The MOP is free to overtake the waiting LD, and to complete its execution.

Obviously, it is not possible to evaluate exactly the speed up which may be obtained by a pipeline structure in the general case, because it essentially depends on the application program. Effective instruction scheduling by the programmer or by the compiler, aimed at avoiding data dependencies and at taking advantage of instruction concurrency may, in the best case, allow an overall speedup of 6 over the non-pipelined case. However, in the worst case only IF, ID and CD overlap giving a total speedup of 1.2. It has therefore been our goal to design a structure that would easily be exploited by image processing algorithms. An estimation of the number of 10ns cycles needed to filter one line of an 8-bit grey level image using a 100ns external memory and a 10ns internal memory is shown in the following table:

mem. cycle	no pipe	pipe	speed up
100ns mem.	554	241	2.3
10ns mem.	410	97	4.2
		imp. sch.	speed up
100ns mem.	554	131	4.2

The *no pipe* column refers to the number of cycles needed by a conventional sequential controller, while the *pipe* column refers to the pipelined case. The *speed up* colums reports the speed up achieved. The *imp. sch.* column refers to the case in which many cycles may be saved because part of the operation on the old line can be executed while loading the new data. Obviously, this possibility depends on the implementation of the algorithm.

7 Conclusions

A pipelined controller has been designed to execute instructions on a massively parallel processor. The main design objective was to boost performance for image analysis algorithms in order to be able to use the system in hard real time applications. Simulation shows that for a system comprising an internal fast image memory, the achieved speed up may reach a factor of 4-5 when little data dependency is involved. When using an external memory whose access time dominates the total processing time, intelligent instruction scheduling and concurrency exploitation are effective tools to gain further advantages. The design is currently being implemented using a mixed Macro module-based and Standard Cell-based methodology which relies on synthesis tools.

Acknowledgements

This work has been partially supported by Progetto Finalizzato Trasporti under contract number 94.01376.PF74, Progetto Speciale on VLSI Architecture for HDTV, and by MURST 40% on VLSI Architectures.

References

[1] J. Serra, "Image Analysis and Mathematical Morphology," *Academic Press*, London, 1982.

[2] F. Gregoretti, L. M. Reyneri, C. Sansoè, A. Broggi, and G. Conte, "The PAPRICA SIMD Array: Critical Reviews and Perspectives," *Proceedings ASAP'93 - IEEE Computer Society International Conference on Application Specific Array Processors*, Venezia, Italy, October 25 - 27 1993. IEEE Computer Society.

[3] A. Broggi, G. Conte, F. Gregoretti, L. Lavagno, L.M. Reyneri, C. Sansoè, G. Burzio, "PAPRICA-3 A Real Time Morphological Image Processor," *Proceedings of the 1st IEEE International Conference on Image Processing*, Austin, USA, November 1994.

[4] Yamashita et al, "A 3.84 GIPS Integrated Memory Array Processor with 64 Processing Elements and a 2-Mb SRAM," *IEEE Journal of Solid-State Circuits*, Vol. 29, No. 11, pp. 1336-1343, November 1994.

[5] D. A. Patterson, J. L. Hennessy, "Computer Architecture: a Quantitative Approach," *San Mateo: kaufmann*, 1990.

[6] P.G. Paulin, C. Liem, T.C. May, S. Sutarwala, "DSP Design Tool Requirements for Embedded Systems: a Telecommunications Industrial Perspective," *Journal of VLSI Signal Processing*, Vol. 9, No. 1-2, pp. 23-47, January 1995.

[7] D. E. Thomas, P. Moorby, "The Verilog Hardware Description Language," *Kluwer Academic Publishers*, 1991.

MANNA: Prototype of a Distributed Memory Architecture With Maximized Sustained Performance

W.K. Giloi, U. Bruening, W. Schroeder-Preikschat

* GMD Institute for Computer Architecture and Software Technology, Rudower Chaussee 5, 12489 Berlin, Germany,
e-mail: giloi(a)computer.org, ulrich@first.gmd.de, wosch@first.gmd.de

Abstract

The sustained performance of superscalar microprocessors amounts to only a fraction of their peak performance rating. In parallel computers realized with them this discrepancy is even more dramatic. Reaching a satisfactory sustained performance for the single processor is mainly a compiler problem. The sustained performance of parallel computers depends also on other components of the architecture such as the interconnect and the operating system. In the paper it is shown how through a combination of innovative architectural solutions the sustained performance of a distributed memory parallel computer can be significantly improved. The key to effective latency hiding by overlapping communication and computation is the operating system. The programmability of such architectures can be enhanced by providing the programmer with parallelizing compilers and/or a global address space provided by virtual shared memory. All these measures have been incorporated in the MANNA computer described in this paper. Benchmark performance figures obtained with it are reported.

1. Introduction: Rationale for MANNA

1.1 Goals of the MANNA Development

Until 1990, the only way to achieve a sizable node performance of a parallel computer was to add a vector processor to the node CPU [1]. The advent of the superscalar processor in 1990 suddenly raised the prospect of obtaining some 10 megaFLOPS with a single-chip microprocessor. From then on it was understood that future parallel computer design had to be based upon off-the-shelf superscalar processors. Though a custom-designed node hardware might allow for a more unconventional node architecture, it will hardly lead to a competitive product for the reason that stock processors not only are less expensive but also automatically on the future upgrade path of the device.

The MANNA development began in 1990, just at the time when Intel announced the i860, the first superscalar processor. Novel features of the i860 were: (i) an envisioned peak performance of 50 MIPS and 50 MFLOPS d.p., respectively (i860XP, 50 Mhz version, true theoretical peak); (ii) fast, on-chip snooping logic for the data cache; (iii) pipelined memory access in burst mode.

The MANNA node design began actually a year before the first silicon became available. This was possible because of the availability of a bus-functional simulation model of the processor. This allowed us to simulate and verify the complete 2-processor node during the time we waited for the first samples.

1.2 Programming Models Supported

The natural programming paradigm for distributed memory architectures is the message-passing model. This model, however, is considered difficult by most users, since it requires the programmer to explicitly take care of data distribution and inter process communication through the insertion of send and receive constructs into the code at the proper places.

In contrast, the shared-memory programming model avoids—at least in principle—the difficulties of the message-passing paradigm. Since data are globally accessible, no specific data distribution is mandated, and since communication happens through shared variables, no message-passing constructs are needed. However, only the distributed memory architectures are widely scalable.

One can try to obtain the best of both worlds by realizing a global address space on a distributed memory machine through either virtual shared memory (VSM) or distributed shared memory (DSM). VSM costs software overhead but no additional hardware. DSM requires in each node a sufficiently large secondary cache and a directory to maintain cache coherence, driving up thereby the hardware cost. Thus, in both cases is cost-effectiveness traded for the convenience of the shared memory programming model. Therefore, we ruled out the DSM approach but decided to rather build a pure message-passing machine with the highest possible performance and cost-effectiveness and find better ways of simplifying parallel programming.

We see the ultimate solution to the parallel programming problem in parallelizing compilers that allow the user to formulate applications at a high level of abstraction, without having to be concerned with specific parallel computing aspects such as program decomposition, data distribution, data access synchronization, and inter process communication/coordination. High Performance Fortran [2] is a first step in that direction. In cases where the data type *pointer* is needed, e.g., in non-numerical applications programmed in AI languages like Lisp, the programmer may optionally be provided with a global address space created through an efficient VSM mechanism. The MANNA architecture is based on that rationale.

1.3 Sustained vs. Peak Performance

Parallel computers are usually rated by a *peak performance* computed as the sum of the peak performances of all the node processors. For the user, peak performance is a useless figure. In the peak performance rating, different parallel computers using the same node processor are rated the same, yet they may differ significantly in terms of sustained performance. The purpose of the MANNA design was to maximize sustained performance, by analyzing the reasons for the poor sustained-to-peak performance ratio of message-passing machines and devising measures to avoid performance degradation wherever possible.

1.4 The Week Points of Distributed Memory Architectures

Potential drawbacks of distributed memory architectures are:

- poor utilization of the superscalar node processor by the compiler;
- communication latencies;
- inadequate interconnection topologies;
- inefficient implementation of the VSM mechanism.

The utilization of the superscalar node processor depends on the degree of optimization the compiler can do in order to fill the instruction execution pipeline(s) of the processor with useful operations rather than bubbles. At the present state-of-the art, this still leaves much to desire. More research and, thus, time is needed to improve the compilers. A promising approach is the multi-threading compiler [3].

Communication latency usually is the largest performance-limiting factor in message-passing machines. The latency of a message transfer activity such as *send* or *receive* is given as the sum of the message start-up time and the transmission time. In principle, a message transfer may be performed by one of the following instances (which decreasing start-up time): (i) operating system, (ii) compiler, (iii) dedicated hardware. For a general-purpose machine the communication primitives should be provided as operating system services. In this case, the start-up time is typically in the range of some 10 to some 100 microseconds; thus, the fastest interconnect of the world could not eliminate the communiation latency. On the other hand, if the entire inter process communication is handled strictly by hardware, one can get the start-up time down to a range of some 100 nanoseconds to some microseconds. In this case, the message transmission time becomes the dominating factor. However, a machine without any operating system support would be hard to program.

There are two possible ways to minimize comunication latency (which may be combined):

- *latency minimization*—making the node hardware, the operating system, and the interconnect very fast;
- *latency hiding*—avoiding idle times caused by waiting for communication.

The remainder of this paper deals with the measures taken in MANNA to maximize the sustained performance of the system by minimizing communication latency by an appropriate operating system (Chapters 2 and 3) and node architecture (Chapter 4) and by devising an innovative interconnection topology with minimal cost and maximum performance (Chapter 5). Chapter 6 gives performance figures. Chapter 7 discusses the mechanisms for an efficient implementation of virtual shared memory. Chapter 8 mentiones some uses of the system.

2 Start-up Latency Minimization

2.1 OS Functionality and Start-up Time

In order to be universally applicable and programmable, a parallel computer must provide the appropriate operating system (OS) services. If this includes inter process communication, the message start-up latency depends strongly on the functionality of the OS *kernel*.

The simplest case is the single-user, single-tasking operation with one thread of control or several concurrent, unscheduled threads (lightweight processes). Here the *single address space mode* is appropriate, in which the entire node software—application as well as OS functions—runs without protection in one address space. Communication is usually provided not by an OS process but by run time library routines.

However, there may be cases where the operating system should provide a *multi-processing environment* by adding pre-emptive scheduling and process environment separation. In a single-processor node, each communication activity leads now to an OS kernel trap and, consequently, an environment switch. Even when the user needs only a dedicated machine, the overhead for the potential multi-processing operation must be paid. The highest overhead is encountered when the system is designed for multi-user operation by adding user task isolation.

2.2 The PEACE Family of OS Kernels

The MANNA operating system PEACE (Program Execution And Communication Environment) is based on the novel concept of the *OS kernels family* [4] which allows any desired OS functionality to be provided with minimal overhead by applying the following construction principles [5].

- The variety of kernels tuned to optimally support specific user demands and operating modes [5] is obtained by a common communication nucleus augmented for the specific use by minimal function extensions as indicated in Figure 1. The nucleus runs in supervisor mode, while all functional extensions are lightweight processes running in user mode.
- Since the family members typically differ only in a few components that concern the user interface or the run time behavior, object-orientation is the natural approach toward implementing the kernel family. That is, new family members are derived from existing ones through inheritance, and type and function polymorphism is used to tailor OS abstractions to specific user demands.

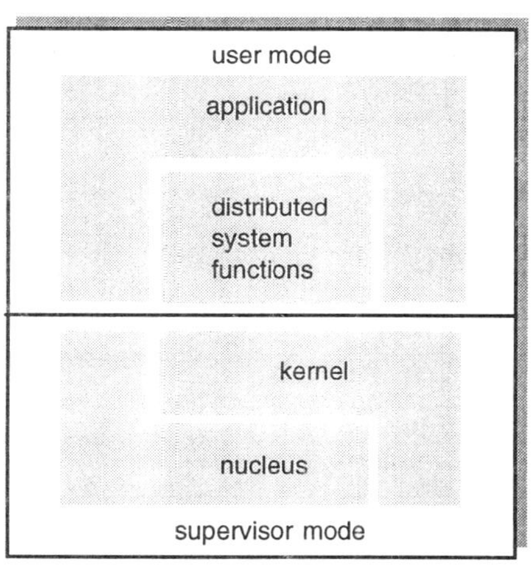

Figure 1 Architecture of the MANNA operating system

2.3 Performance Figures

Table 1 lists the latency for a single communication activity (*send* or *receive*) of a number of commercial computers including MANNA [6]. OSF/1 (Mach 3.0) is a UNIX look-alike. PUMA, NX, and CMOST are typical microkernel operating systems. "Active Messages" is an experimental OS based on the active message concept [7]. Compared to the microkernel OSs and by virtue of the family concept, PEACE is approximately a factor of 2 faster. This stems from the fact that the overhead of any member of the PEACE family of kernels is only what is absolutely needed for the functionality provided, so that the user newer pays for something (s)he doesn't need nor want.

Machine	Operating System	Latency [μs]
Paragon XP/S	OSF/1 (Mach 3.0)	240
nCUBE/2	PUMA	110
iPSC 860	NX	100
CM-5	CM OST	65
Paragon*	PUMA	50
nCUBE/2	Active Mesages	32
Paragon**	PUMA	30
MANNA*	PEACE	23
MANNA**	PEACE	≤ 4

* single processor operation ** double processor operation

Table 1: Message-passing latency of parallel computers

If the multiprocessing kernel of PEACE is invoked on MANNA, the start-up time becomes about 80 microseconds. Over one third of that time must be attributed to the *kernel* trap that becomes part of each communication.

2.3 Additional Kernel Functionality

As discussed below, there are other optional functionalities of the MANNA architecture that require specific OS support. Therefore, specific kernel family members are provided for:

- *AP-AP Operation:* the use of both processors in the node as *application processor* (AP);
- *AP-CP Operation:* the use of one of the node processors as dedicated *communication processor* (CP);
- *VSM Operation:* a variant of the AP-CP operation which provides a global address space through *virtual shared memory* (VSM).

3. Latency Hiding in MANNA

3.1 Latency Hiding

The effect of communication latency can be drastically reduced by equipping the node with a dedicated *communication processor* (CP) in addition to the *application processor* (AP) [8]. In this symbiosis the task of the AP is to uninterruptedly *produce megaflops*, while the CP executes the communication tasks of the OS *kernel*. Both processor work in parallel; consequently, the communication start-up time occurs in the CP but is hidden from the AP. The AP sees only the latency of sending a communication request to the CP.

The concept of overlapping communication with computation is about 15 years old. The first system ever built with a dedicated communication processor was UPPER [9], an early distributed memory parallel architecture completed in 1981. The result was disappointing: the gain in communication speed was only marginal, for the communication latency between AP and CP of 1...2 millisecond used up most of what we had hoped to gain.

3.2 Efficient Latency Hiding

The prerequisite for efficient latency hiding in message-passing machines through the use of two processor is an appropriate OS architecture. In that respect, all commercial parallel computers that have also a two-processor node fail to utilize it to its full potential because of the communication overhead of their microkernel operating systems.

The unique kernel family concept of PEACE leads not only to extremely lightweight OS kernels but also to their modularization—in contrast to the monolithic microkernel. The PEACE kernel consists of 3 layers [5]: NICE (Network Independent Communication Environment), COSY (COmmunication SYstem), and POD (POrt Drivers). NICE takes care of the inter-thread communication policies, COSY handles the communication protocols, and POD is the glue between the OS nucleus and the communication hardware (the network). This modularization allows for an optimal distribution of OS functions over the two processors of the MANNA node as shown in Figure 2 [6].

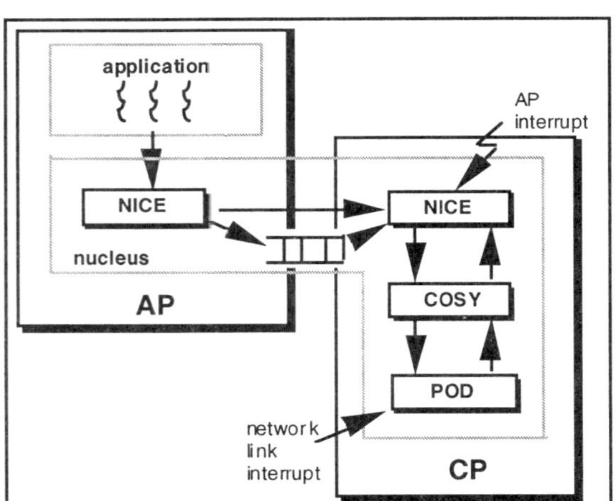

Figure 2 Distribution of kernel functions over AP and CP

The application processor (AP) executes solely NICE functions, while the complete NICE-COSY-POD suite is executed only on the communication processor (CP). On the CP this may take 23 microseconds, yet the AP "sees" only the couple of microseconds needed to put a communication request to the CP. With the latency hiding mechanisms provided by the MANNA two-processor node architecture and PEACE, the effective latency is at most 4 microseconds.

The overall advantages of the innovative PEACE concepts are:

- an order of magnitude lesser code for the kernel implementation;
- an order of magnitude lesser communication latency;
- extremely efficient latency hiding (start-up time as with naked hardware).

4. The 2-Processor MANNA NODE

Figure 3 depicts the block diagram of the 2-processor MANNA node.

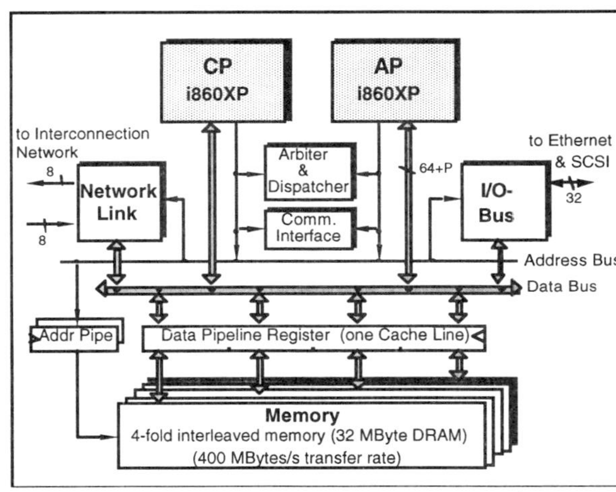

Figure 3 Block diagram of the MANNA node

The node is symmetric in the two processors which both are superscalar processors i860XP. Thus, both processors have the same memory management and can snoop on each other's caches. They communicate through the shared 32-Mbyte DRAM node memory. The elaborate memory design features burst transfer support from 4 interleaved memory banks in page mode via a three-stage pipeline; that is, the memory access latency of 7 clock ticks is overlapped with the previous access cycle. This gives the memory a 7-1-1-1 cycle access pattern and a resulting access bandwidth of 400 Mbytes per second once the pipeline is filled and the accesses are to the same page. Hence, the DRAM node memory has almost the behavior of a secondary cache. A bi-directional communication link with a data rate of 2x50 Mbytes/second connects the node with the interconnection network, a hierarchy of crossbars (see Chapter 5).

Since the node is symmetric, it does not matter which processor is AP and which is CP. For applications that have a relatively low message traffic, the dedicated CP may not be sufficiently utilized. In this case, it is a better approach to use both processors as APs. PEACE provides specific kernels for both operations.

5. MANNA Interconnection Networks

The desired general applicability of MANNA would be in conflict with an interconnect that penalizes non-local communication. This rules out topologies that work satisfactorily only for strongly local access patterns, e.g., the 2D or 3D mesh. Another MANNA invention, the *hierarchy of crossbar interconnect* [10], provides "the best of all worlds" by satisfying the requirements of

- high global connectivity (no penalty for non-locality);
- low blocking probability;
- minimal hardware cost.

The basic building block of this unique, scalable network topology is a byte-wide, bi-directional 16x16 crossbar switch realized as a mask-programmed gate array on one chip. The transmission rate is the same as that of the link, both are clocked by the bus clock of the processor. Groups of 10 nodes are interconnected via the 16x16 crossbar to form *clusters*, each cluster thus having 10 processors. This leaves 6 uncommitted links of the cluster crossbar for interconnecting the cluster with other clusters. Up to 4 clusters, i.e., 40 nodes, can be directly interconnected through a single back plane with 4 crossbar chips on it. Larger systems require an additional central crossbar switching facility, to interconnect the clusters. Figures 4 shows an example of a 40 node configuration. Systems with more than 16 clusters, practically of any arbitrary size, could be built by applying the hierarchical crossbar topology recursively, i.e., have clusters of clusters of clusters, and so on.

Simulations proved that the hierarchy of crossbar topology of MANNA has the same low blocking probability as the hypercube [11]. However, whereas the hypercube requires for each node (log N) links into the interconnect and, thus, is not affordable in massively parallel systems, the MANNA topology requires only one link per node. Hence, the hierarchy of crossbars combines excellent connectivity (low blocking probability, minimum number of hops) with utmost economy. In fact, it is significantly less expensive than the 2D-mesh (which has a poor blocking behavior).

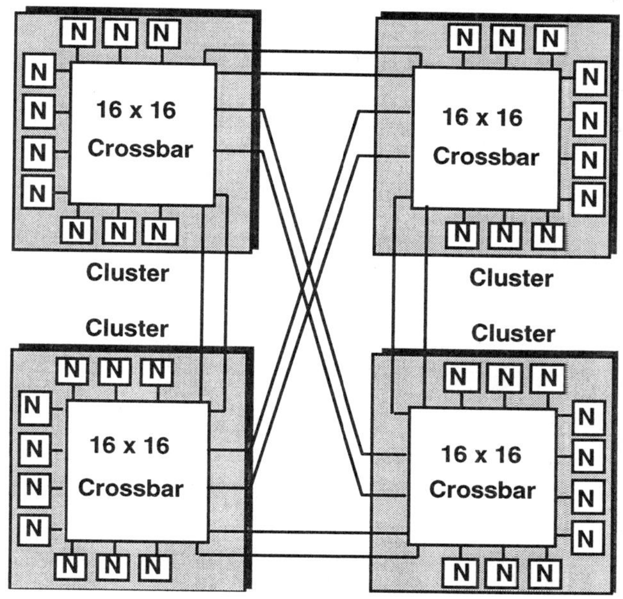

Figure 4 MANNA computer with 40 nodes

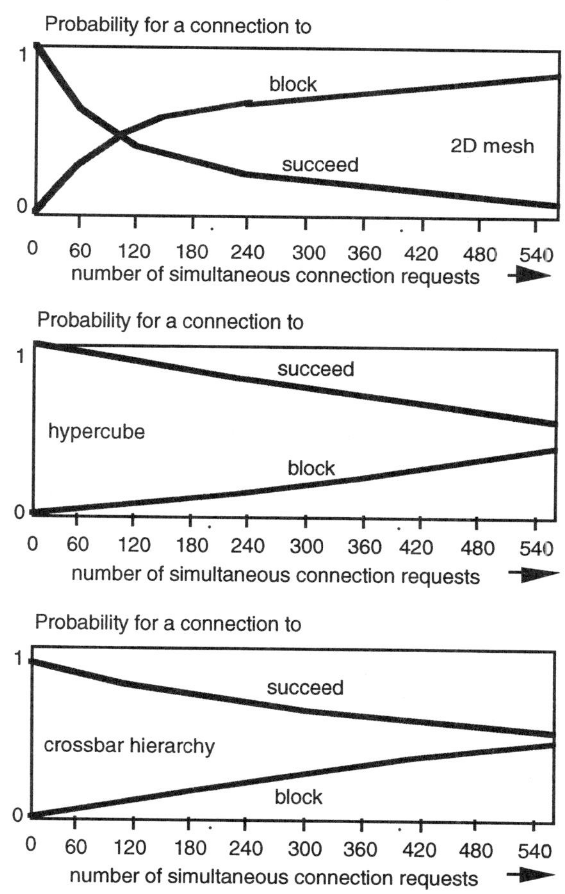

Figure 7 Blocking behavior of mesh, hypercube, and crossbar hierarchy

Figure 5 shows the blocking probability for three types of 1024x1024 interconnects as function of the number of simultaneous connection requests. As the figure demonstrates, the blocking behavior of the crossbar hierarchy is almost as good as that of the hypercube, and both behave much better than the 2D-mesh. The crossbar is a dynamic topology with a high switching complexity of $O(n^2)$; however, this costs only silicon but not cables and connectors.

6. Performance Figures

It should be expected that the high memory bandwidth of MANNA and the high connectivity and transmission bandwidth of its interconnect results in an excellent performance. The 1000x1000 Linpack performance of the 1-processor MANNA node, obtained with the *Portland Group* Fortran compiler and PVM, is 18 MFLOPS. However, this tells only something about the processor and the compiler. A better indicator for the performance of the overall *architecture* is the speed-up with the number of processors. This measurement is shown in Table 3 in comparison to the Intel iPSC860 and the Meiko CS-2.

# of nodes	iPS860	CS-2	MANNA
2	1.68	1.88	1.96
4	2.42	3.20	3.70
8	3.31	4.79	6.72
16	4.22	6.12	11.35

Table 3 Linpack speed-up (1000x1000 elements)

For the inner product of two matrices with 100x100 elements the sustained performance of the 2-processor node is 68 MFLOPS d.p., at a theoretical peak performance of 100 MFLOPS, respectively. The 2-processor node performance in ray tracing amounts to 700 000 polygons per second.

7. Virtual Shared Memory

7.1 Adaptive Consistency

Another major goal of the project concerned the development of a highly efficient virtual shared memory (VSM) realization. The goal was to achieve acceptable performance by appropriate hardware and OS support, to make VSM practically viable. MANNA utilizes the usual mechanism where pages of a virtual memory migrate to those nodes where they are needed [12].

The following concepts enhance the efficiency of VSM on MANNA:

- the adaptive consistency model [13], allowing for multiple writes during the computation phases of data parallel algorithms without the danger of semantics violations;
- the support of the VSM mechanism by a specific VSM kernel of PEACE;
- the strong support of the VSM-related OS functions by the 2-processor node architecture.

Adaptive consistency is a variant of *release consistency* [14] which works particularly well in connection with the common SPMD mode of execution. During the computation phases, the nodes work without observing states of objects in other nodes. Therefore, the system may work in the MRMW (Multiple Readers — Multiple Writers) mode, as long the system merges the diverging copies into one consistent object before entering a communication phase. During a communication phase the system works in the MRSW (Multiple Reader — Single Writer) mode.

The programmer can make the following use of the adaptive consistency mechanism. By a specific system function a thread is given the unconditioned write capability for its local copy. The write access to the copy is confined to the node, i.e., does not affect the copies of the same object in other nodes. Thus, threads in different nodes may write into the same page, each one into its local copy. The only restriction is that the threads are not allowed to write into the same location in the page, i.e., the write addresses must be mutually exclusive. For example, in array processing each writer may contribute a row or a column to a result matrix. This mechanism avoids the page thrashing problem [12].

At the end of the write phase, one of the writers—it does not matter which one—executes a system function to the effect that (i) the system unifies the local copies into a single global object whose content is the union of the local changes, while all local copies are invalidated, and (ii) the thread that executes that function becomes the new owner of the unified copy. The unification is performed by a fast hardware algorithm [13]. The order in which the copies are merged is arbitrary. The merging procedure can be pipelined or executed in parallel. This mechanism is provided by OS functions executed on the CP [13]. Consequently, its overhead is hidden from the application.

7.2 Consistency Manager

In VSM the nodes must know the owners of the shared objects; and the owner of an object (the writer) must know who else has a copy of it. This information is furnished by a compiler-generated *access list* containing the identifiers of all the sharers. In the VSM kernel of PEACE, access lists are maintained by a service called *consistency manager* [15]. Under normal conditions a consistency manager never changes its location; therefore, the page tables need not be updated after a change of ownership. Since the consistency manager has a copy of the object, it can directly satisfy requests for copies, without having first to go to the owner. This saves a significant amount of message traffic, and it allows the system to destroy obsolete processes without destroying the shared objects they own.

8. Programming MANNA

A programming enviroment for application software production is provided on MANNA by the *Portland Group* Compilers for C and Fortran, enhanced by parallelization tools such as PVM and MPI. The elaborate environmental control simulation systems running on MANNA were programmed in that environment. In addition, there exist several research-grade programming systems for automatic or interactive parallelization by compiler. These are:

- PROMOTER: compiler and runtime system for a high-level, object-parallel programming model [16]
- parLisp: interactive commonLisp parallelization tool set [17].

9. Conclusion, Future Work

Through a host of innovative architectural concepts, the scalable distributed memory MANNA architecture excels other, comparable machines significantly in performance. Easiness of programming is not bought with sacrifices in cost-effectiveness and/or performance but is provided through appropriate parallel programming languages and parallelizing compilers such as HPF and PROMOTER. An exception is the global address space programming paradigm provided through VSM which, of course, carries some (minimized) performance penalty.

A number of MANNA computers with a total of 160 nodes were built. MANNA has become the main "work horse" at GMD FIRST for "grand challenge" applications such as the simulation of summer smog or other air pollution control tasks. MANNA is also the development platform for the high-level PROMOTER programming system, a project of the Real World Computer Program. Last but not least, a couple of MANNA computers have been installed at the site of major cooperation partners of FIRST, e.g., at the Fraunhofer Institute for Graphical Information Processing at Darmstadt, Germany (where it has become their most powerful tool for virtual reality applications) and at McGill University at Montreal, Canada (where it is used as the development platform for multi-threaded architecture concepts and software, see http://www-acaps.cs.mcgill.ca/info/EARTH/).

A major step towards the further improvement of the MANNA is the development of *powerMANNA* currently conducted at FIRST. The powerMANNA architecture is the one described in this paper, with the Intel processor i860 being replaced by the Motorola/IBM powerPC 620. The bandwidth of the node memory and the interconnect will be adequately increased to 720 Mbytes per second.

References

[1] Giloi W.K.: Giloi W.K.: The SUPRENUM Supercomputer — Concepts, Achievements, and Lessons Learned, Parallel Computing, October 1994

[2] High Performance Fortran Forum: High Performance Fortran — Language Specification (DRAFT), Version 0.4, November 1992

[3] Hendren L.J., Donawa C., Emami M., Gao G.R., Justiniani, Sridharan B: Designing the McCAT compiler based on a family of structured intermediate representations; in: Conference Record of Fifth International Workshop on Languages and Compilers for Parallel Computing, 1992, LNCS 757, Springer Verlag, 1993.

[4] Schroeder-Preikschat W.: Overcoming the Startup Time Problem in Distributed Memory Architectures, in Milutiniovic V., Shriver B.(eds.): *Proc. 24th Hawaii Internat. Conf. on System Sciences, vol.1*, IEEE Society Press 1991, IEEE catalog no. 91TH0350-9, 551-559

[5] Schroeder-Preikschat W.: *Logic Design of Parallel Operating Systems* , Prentice-Hall, Englewood Cliffs NJ 1994

[6] Bruening U., Giloi W.K., Schroeder-Preikschat W.: Latency Hiding in Message-Passing Architectures, *Proc. IPPS '94*, IEEE-CS Press 1994

[7] von Eicken T., Culler D.E., Goldstein S.C., Schuster K.E.: Active Messages : A Mechanism for Integrated Communication and Computation, Tech. Report UCB/CSD 92/675, University of California at Berkeley 1992

[8] Giloi W.K., Schroeder W.: Very High-Speed Communication in Large MIMD Supercomputers, *Proc. ICS '89*, ACM Order No. 415891, 313-321

[9] Giloi W.K., Behr P.: An IPC Protocol and Its Hardware Realization For High-Speed Distributed Multi-computer System, *Proc. 8th Internat. Sympos. on Computer Architecture*, IEEE Catalog No. 81CH1593-3, 481-494

[10] Giloi. W.K., Montenegro S.: Choosing the Interconnect of Distributed Memory Systems by Cost and Blocking Behavior, Proc. 5th Internat. Parallel Processing Symposium, IEEE Catalog no. 91TH0363-02 (1991), 438-444

[11] Montenegro S.: Kommunikationsstrukturen für verteilte Rechnersysteme, PhD thesis, Tech. University of Berlin 1989

[12] Li K.: Shared Virtual Memory on Loosely Coupled Multiprocessors, PhD thesis, Yale University 1986

[13] Giloi W.K., Hastedt C., Schoen F., Schroeder-Preikschat W.: A Distributed Implementation of Shared Virtual Memory with Strong and Weak Coherence, in Bode A.(ed.): *Distributed Memory Computing*, Proc. EDMCC2, LNCS 487, Springer-Verlag 1991, 23-31

[14] Gharachorloo K., Lenoski D., Laudon J., Gibbons P., Gupta A., Hennessey J.: Memory Consistency and Event Ordering in Scalable Shared-Memory Mulriprocessors, *Proc. 17th Annual Sympos. on Computer Architecture*, IEEE catalog no. CH2887-90, 15-26

[15] Cordsen J.: Basing Virtually Shared Memory on a Family of Consistency Models, Proc. 1st Internat. Workshop on Scalable Shared Memory Systems, 1994

[16] Giloi W.K., Kessler M., Schramm A.: PROMOTER: A Programming System for High-Level Massively Parallel Programming With Arbitrary Application Topologies, Proc. RWC Symposium 1995, RWC Partnership, Tokyo, June 1995

[17] Sodan A.: Mapping Symbolic Problems with Dynamic Tree Structures to Parallel Machines, Ph.D. thesis, Technical University of Berlin 1995

System-Diagnosis of Cluster-Based Parallel Architectures

O. Benkahla, C. Aktouf & C. Robach

LGI - IMAG - 46, avenue Félix Viallet - 38031 Grenoble Cedex 1- FRANCE

Abstract

This paper explores the diagnosis of cluster-based parallel architectures. A hierarchical strategy which well suits to such architectures is proposed. This strategy avoids a costly full distributed diagnosis of the network by running an adaptive diagnosis algorithm into each cluster and collecting all the test results at the host level. Key results of the paper include realistic fault and architecture models, an adaptive cluster diagnosis algorithm and a global diagnosis strategy of cluster-based parallel machines.

1: Introduction

Massively parallel machines become vital for a wide range of applications due to their high computational power. However, a fault on a processor or a link may seriously compromize the whole machine performances. Consequently, fault-tolerant mechanisms must be implemented to improve the reliability of parallel architectures. One such technique is to use inter-processor tests that are scheduled with user applications, in order to detect and locate faulty components (i. e. processors or links) in the system. This distributed testing takes advantage of the inherent parallelism of message-passing architectures and is known as *system-level diagnosis*.

Preparata, Metz and Chien [1] have introduced a fundamental fault model for system level diagnosis and many authors have worked on the problem of choosing a set of testing links, and analyzing the test results to identify the faulty units [2-13]. System-level diagnosis has evolved from centralized diagnosis [2-5] to distributed diagnosis [6-13]. In centralized diagnosis, it is assumed that a central reliable device monitors the tests execution and computes the system state on the basis of tests results. Distributed diagnosis algorithms assume no central device and make each processor aware of the whole system state. So they are called *self-diagnosis* algorithms. Depending on the way tests are assigned, distributed diagnosis algorithms can be *static* or *adaptive*. Static algorithms are studied in [6-9] whereas adaptive ones are proposed in [10-13]. In the static approach, test assignments are fixed ahead of time and due to the t-diagnosability condition [7], each processor has to be tested by at least t other ones. As a result, this approach generates too much unnecessary testing overhead. In fact, it is sufficient to test every unit by exactly one fault-free unit that will correctly report its state. The adaptive testing strategy overcomes this drawback by making the tests evolve according to the network state.

In all the proposed algorithms, the main goal is to ensure the self-diagnosability of the system, i. e. to make every fault-free processor aware of the whole system state. Applying such algorithms to massively parallel architectures with thousands of processors leads to a great amount of communication and storage overhead that will certainly decrease the system performance. However, by partitioning the system and executing the diagnosis algorithm in every partition, diagnosis overhead can be dramatically decreased [14]. This paper presents a partition-based diagnosis strategy that is suited for large cluster-based parallel systems. A hierarchical control, performed by *Control Processors* (CPs) associated to each cluster, is used to allow state information gathering at the host level and then the exchange of these information between clusters. Furthermore, a functional fault-model that separates communication tests and processor ones is introduced. Such a model is motivated by the architectural characteristics of parallel machines. Based on this model, an adaptive distributed diagnosis algorithm is proposed and executed at each partition level.

This paper is organized as follows : in the next section, basic assumptions related to the fault and architecture models are presented. Section 3 deals with the hierarchical diagnosis strategy. Section 4 presents the diagnosis algorithm executed at each partition and preliminary performance evaluation results. Conclusions are presented in section 5.

2: Preliminaries and basic assumptions

2.1: Basic definitions

In system-level diagnosis, two graphs are associated with a system S : The *system graph* and the *testing graph*. The system graph $G_S(V, E)$ shows the physical interconnection structure of the system S. It is an undirected graph with vertices set V and edges set E that represent respectively the processors and the physical communication links of the system S. The testing graph is a digraph $T_S(V, A)$ where A is the set of test relations in S. A directed edge $(u_i \rightarrow u_j)$ indicates that unit u_i is assigned to test unit u_j. The label a_{ij} associated with an edge $(u_i \rightarrow u_j)$ on the testing graph indicates the test result that can be either 0 (the tested unit u_j is supposed to be fault-free by the testing unit u_i) or 1 (u_j is supposed to be faulty by u_i). The set of all test results is called *syndrome*.

1066-6192/96 $5.00 © 1996 IEEE
Proceedings of PDP '96

2. 2: Fault model

In most current message-passing machines, the communication task is performed by a communication device called *router* which can be seen as the wired solution for the processor communications. Hence, each node or unit u_i is seen as divided into a processor p_i which computes user tasks and a router r_i which manages the incoming and outgoing messages : $u_i=(p_i, r_i)$. This is taken into account in this work by the use of the fault-model detailed below. Let $(u_i \rightarrow u_j) \in A$. $(u_i \rightarrow u_j)$ includes the two routers r_i and r_j and the link which joins them. Hence, for a set of faults $F = F^p \cup F^l$ (F^p is the set of faulty processors, and F^l the set of faulty routers and/or communication links), a_{ij} is defined as follows :

- if $p_i \notin F^p$ and $(u_i \rightarrow u_j) \notin F^l$ then $a_{ij} = 0$ if $p_j \notin F^p$ and $a_{ij} = 1$ if $p_j \in F^p$,
- if $p_i \notin F^p$ and $(u_i \rightarrow u_j) \in F^l$ then $a_{ij} = 1$ ($\forall$ the state of p_j),
- if $p_i \in F^p$ then $a_{ij} = x$. x corresponds to an unknown or an unpredictable test result ($x \in \{0,1\}$).

2. 3: Architecture model

In recent years, many cluster-based parallel systems have been proposed. This trend is especially motivated by the easy scalability of these systems without generating a great control or monitoring overhead. This is due to the fact that a Control Processor (CP) is generally associated with each cluster of processors. Thus control and monitoring functions related to a cluster are centralized on the corresponding CP while productive tasks are conducted by the remaining processors. Examples of these architectures are the Parsytec GC [15], the Supernode family [16] and the IBM SP1 [17]. In this paper, we suppose that CPs communicate with a host computer that is fault-free. Figure 1 depicts the general scheme of cluster-based architectures considered in this paper.

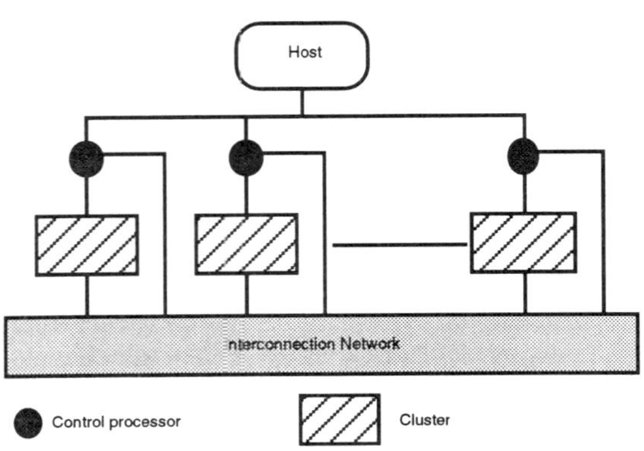

Figure 1. General scheme of cluster-based architectures

3: Hierarchical diagnosis strategy

A previous work on hierarchical diagnosis of parallel architectures has been proposed by Altmann et al. [18] and applied to the Parsytec GC. In this work, detection of faults is based on the use of periodic and timely "I am alive" messages. These messages are exchanged between a cluster processor and the associated CP on one hand, and between a CP and its neighboring CPs on the other hand. No distributed testing is used between the processors of a given cluster. The strategy proposed in this paper combines distributed inter-processor testing with centralized diagnosis. Distributed inter-processor tests are performed between the processors of the same cluster in an adaptive manner using the Cluster Diagnosis Algorithm presented below. Centralized diagnosis of a given cluster is performed by the associated CP that collects diagnosis information generated by the cluster diagnosis algorithm. All diagnosis information synthesized at a CP level are transmitted to the host that stores them in a global data base. For each cluster, the host keeps the number of reported faults. This information is useful when reconfiguration has to be undertaken. The host computer tests periodically all the CPs to request new diagnosis information from the correct ones. If the host detects a fault at a CP, a reconfiguration process is started. This process consists of partitioning the known fault-free processors of the considered cluster among neighboring clusters which CPs are still fault-free and which diagnosability has not been reached yet. Figure 2 presents the most important modules that implement the proposed diagnosis strategy.

The remaining part of this paper is devoted to the presentation of the Cluster Diagnosis Algorithm (CDA) and some performance evaluation results.

4: The Cluster Diagnosis Algorithm (CDA)

4. 1: Overview of CDA

As processors in a parallel system are mainly intended to execute highly computational tasks, overhead induced by the execution of a diagnosis algorithm has to be as low as possible in order to lessen the effect of testing and diagnosis operations on the system performances. To this end, processors in a cluster are mainly concerned by testing each others and reporting tests results. Diagnosis operations that determine the actual state of each processor and link in the cluster are centralized at the CP level. As a result, CDA doesn't perform a classical self-diagnosis which would necessitate much more testing and communication overhead. In this work, we assume that tests and user tasks that share the same cluster's resources are effectively scheduled. CDA is performed periodically during the system operational state. A round of testing of CDA starts at the CP which tests its neighbors and allows fault-free ones to test other processors in the same cluster. This process goes on until all the cluster processors are tested. While tests are being performed, tests results are routed towards the CP through reliable paths, i. e. fault-free nodes and links. The same idea for detecting and locating link faults as in SELF algorithms is used [7].

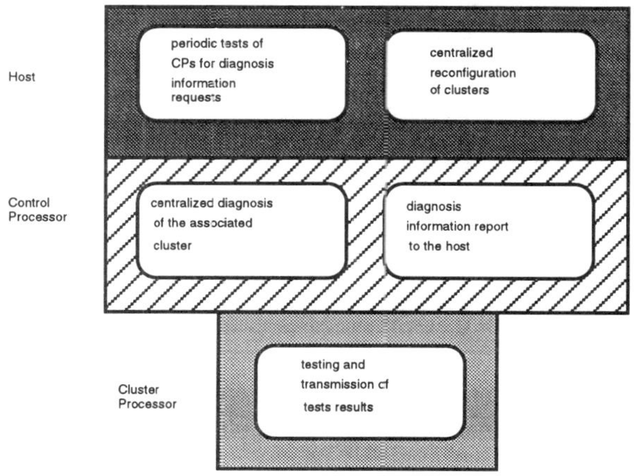

Figure 2. Hierarchical diagnosis strategy

However, an important feature of CDA algorithm stands in a functional fault testing based on the functional fault model introduced in section 2. In fact, the test of a unit u_j by a unit u_i concerns both the processor p_j and the link $(u_i \rightarrow u_j)$. During a testing round of CDA, p_j is tested only once, but CDA evaluates all u_i possible communications with other units including the remote ones. In message-passing machines, the router is a complex device which could simultaneously have faulty and fault-free parts. Hence, faults may corrupt a subset of the router functionalities while the others remain correct. The functional test proposed thus minimizes the cost related to tests generation as well as the cost of routers tests. As shown in the example of Figure 3, suppose that the router r_k is partially faulty, so that the test performed by u_i to evaluate the communication between u_i and u_k fails. Consequently, u_i concludes that the link $(u_i \rightarrow u_k)$ is faulty. However, u_i cannot make any conclusion concerning the communication path between u_i and u_z even if the link $(u_i \rightarrow u_k)$ is a part of this path, as the router functionalities involved in both communications are different. So a test concerning the communication between u_i and u_z is necessary and this is taken into account by CDA , by assigning to a given unit to test its communication with not only its direct neighbors but the remote ones as well. Such a functional testing ensures that all fault-free available resources in the system are exploited.

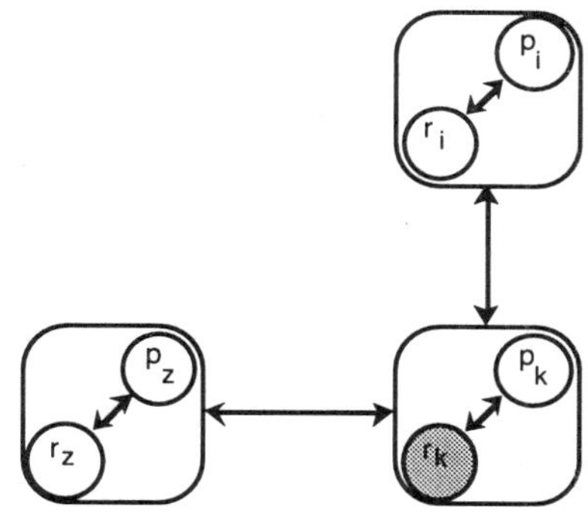

Figure 3. Remote communication test

4. 2: CDA outline

Two main procedures constitute the gist of CDA : procedure *TEST* and procedure *TESTED_BY*. These procedures correspond respectively to the two only states of a unit with respect to the execution of CDA : the "*testing*" state in which a unit tests other ones and the "*being tested*" state in which the unit executes the test programs and sends the result to its tester unit. These two procedures use the following messages and data structures :

- [REQUEST_TO_TEST $<u_j,u_i>$] is the message sent by u_j to u_i for a test request,
- [ACCEPTATION_TO_BE_TESTED $<u_i,u_j>$] is the message sent by u_i to u_j informing u_j that u_i accepts to be tested,
- [LINK_TO_PROCESSOR $<u_j,u_i>$] is the authorization received by u_i from u_j in order to pass from a communication test to a processor test,
- [CONTINUATION $<u_j,u_i>$] corresponds to the authorization that u_j sends to u_i in order to make u_i able to perform tests of other units,
- [FAULT_FREE $<u_j,u_i>$] indicates that the node u_i tested by u_j is evaluated as fault-free. It means that u_i has successfully passed the two tests T_p (processor test) and T_c (communication test), i.e. $p_i \notin F^p$ and $(u_j \rightarrow u_i) \notin F^l$,
- [SUSPECT $<u_j,u_i>$] corresponds to the fact that the node u_i tested by u_j or the link $(u_j \rightarrow u_i)$ or both are faulty. Indeed, with an unsuccessful test, if the node u_j encounters difficulties in communicating with its neighbour u_i, it can not determine whether it is the communication link $(u_j \rightarrow u_i)$ or u_i that has failed,
- [FAULTY $<u_j,u_i>$] indicates that the node u_i is evaluated by u_j as faulty (this is possible if the communication test has passed),
- [FAULT_FREE $<u_j, u_i>$ link]/[FAULTY $<u_j, u_i>$ link] indicates that the link joining u_j to u_i is respectively fault-free/faulty,
- LIST_TO_BE_TESTED$_i$ is the set of nodes which u_i should test. This list is composed by u_i based on the procedure COMPOSE_LIST_TO_TEST (u_i),

- The set FAULT_FREE_NODES$_i$ / FAULTY_NODES$_i$ stored at the unit level u_i corresponds to the nodes u_x known by u_i to be respectively fault-free/faulty,

- The set SUSPECTED_NODES$_i$ contains the nodes suspected to be faulty and which u_i knows.

- The set FAULT_FREE_LINKS$_i$, also stored at each unit level and which indicates the links known as fault-free.

These sets are composed and updated according to the diagnostic messages received by u_i (i.e. [FAULT_FREE <u_y,u_x>], [SUSPECT <u_y,u_x>], [FAULTY <u_y,u_x>] and [FAULT_FREE (u_x-->u_y link)]). The CP associated to the cluster keeps two additional sets of data, the FAULTY_NODES and the FAULTY_LINKS sets to synthesize the accurate state of the cluster.

The outlines of procedures TEST and TESTED_BY are depicted below. Test_C and Test_P indicate a communication test and a processor test respectively.

```
Procedure TEST(u_k):
BEGIN
    Send_message (REQUEST_TO_TEST <u_i,u_k>)
    IF (ACCEPTATION_TO_BE_TESTED <u_k,u_i>) is
        received THEN
    BEGIN
        Receive the result of TEST_C from u_k
        IF TEST_C passes THEN
            IF (Test_P_EXECUTED) is received THEN
                Fault-Free_link(u_i,u_k)
            ELSE
                BEGIN
                Send_message (LINK_TO_PROCESSOR
                                  <u_i,u_k>)
                IF TEST_P passes THEN
                    BEGIN
                        Fault_free_node (u_i,u_k)
                        Continuation (u_i,u_k)
                    END
                ELSE
                    Faulty_node (u_i,u_k)
                END
        ELSE
            IF u_k ∉ FAULT_FREE_NODES_i THEN
                Suspect_node (u_i,u_k)
            ELSE
                Faulty_link(u_i,u_k)
    END
    ELSE
        IF u_k ∉ FAULT_FREE_NODES_i THEN
            Suspect_node (u_i,u_k)
        ELSE
            Faulty_link(u_i,u_k)
END;
```

```
Procedure TESTED_BY(u_z);
BEGIN
    On the receipt of a REQUEST_TO_TEST<u_z,u_i>
    IF u_z ∈ TESTERS_OF (u_i) DO
        BEGIN
            Execute Test_C and send result to u_z
            IF Test_P has been executed THEN
                Send_message (Test_P_EXECUTED)
            ELSE
                IF (LINK_TO_PROCESSOR <u_z,u_i>) is
                received THEN
                BEGIN
                    Execute Test_P and send the result to u_z
                    IF (CONTINUATION <u_z,u_i>) is received
                    THEN
                    Receive sets SUSPECT_NODES_z,
                    FAULT_FREE_NODES_z,
                    FAULTY_NODES_z, FAULT_FREE_LINKS_z
                    and FAULTY_LINKS_z
                    SUSPECT_NODES_i <--SUSPECT_NODES_z
                    FAULT_FREE_NODES_i <--
                                 FAULT_FREE_NODES_z
                    FAULTY_NODES_i <-- FAULTY_NODES_z
                    FAULT_FREE_LINKS_i <--
                                 FAULT_FREE_LINKS_z
                    FAULTY_LINKS_i <-- FAULTY_LINKS_z
                    COMPOSE_LIST_TO_TEST(U_i)
                END
            TESTERS_OF (u_i) <- TESTERS_OF (u_i) - {u_z}
        END
END;
```

The execution of algorithm CDA on a cluster of N nodes necessitates $O(N^2)$ tests and the transmission of $O(N^3)$ messages. The testing latency i. e. the time necessary for a CP to get the accurate state of the corresponding cluster has been obtained by experimental results presented in the next section.

4. 3: Performance evaluation of CDA

Preliminary evaluation results are obtained with respect to the behavior of CDA algorithm in one cluster. Generalization to several clusters is being conducted and related results will be presented in future work.

To evaluate CDA, a 2D grid topology cluster containing 16 nodes has been modelled using a queueing network model and a discrete event simulation [19][20]. These results suppose that all faults occur before the current testing round and evaluate the diagnosis latency, i. e. the time duration for the CP to get the actual state of the cluster. Such a result is useful to determine the most suitable diagnosis round, which affects both diagnosis efficiency and user tasks performances. Presented results are obtained with service times (transmission times, elementary operations times, ...) equalling the IMS T425 transputer ones [21].

From Figure 5, we notice a slow increase of the diagnosis latency as the test duration grows up, particularly when we deal with more faults. We also remark that the diagnosis latency decreases given increasing numbers of faults. This is an interesting feature for multiprocessor systems prone to several faults, as a test is time-costly. Such a behaviour can be explained by the fact that less units are involved in the testing process when the cluster contains more faulty units.

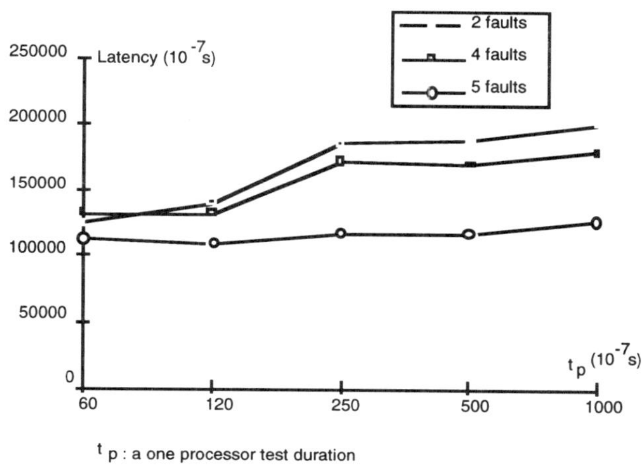

Figure 5. Diagnosis latency in terms of the test duration for different number of faults

5: Conclusion

We have presented a hierarchical diagnosis strategy for cluster-based parallel architectures. Other key results of this paper are the functional fault communication model and the cluster diagnosis algorithm CDA. Preliminary evaluation results of CDA behavior were presented. Future results concern the determination of the effect of testing on the system performances as well as the generalization of the performances results to many simulated clusters. Based on the obtained results, real applications will be conducted on available cluster-based architectures.

6: References

[1] F. P. Preparata, G. Metz and T. Chien, "On the connection assignment problem of diagnosable system", IEEE Trans. Comp., Vol. EC-16, N° 6, Dec 1967, pp. 848-854.

[2] T. Kameda, S. Toida and F. Allan, "A diagnosing algorithm for networks", Inf. Contr. 29, 1975, pp. 141-148.

[3] P. Ciompi, F. Grandoni and L. Simoncini, "Distributed Diagnosis in multiprocessor systems: the MU-TEAM approach", in Proc. 11th International Symposium on Fault Tolerant Computing, Jun. 1981, pp. 25-29.

[4] A. Dahbura and G. Masson, "An $O(n^{2.5})$ fault identification algorithm for diagnosable systems", IEEE Trans. Comp., Vol. C-33, N° 6, Jun. 1984, pp. 486-492.

[5] G. Sullivan, "An $O(t^3+|E|)$ fault identification algorithm for diagnosable systems", IEEE Trans. Comp., Vol. 37, N° 4, Apr. 1988, pp. 388-397.

[6] J. Kuhl and S. Reddy, "Distributed Fault-tolerance for large multiprocessor systems", in proceeding of the 7th Annual Symposium on Computer Architecture, May 1980, pp. 22-30.

[7] J. G. Kuhl, S. M. Reddy, "Fault-Diagnosis in Fully Distributed Systems", 11th IEEE Symposium on Fault-Tolerant Computing, 1981, pp. 100-105.

[8] S. H. Hosseini, J. G. Kuhl, S. M. Reddy, "A Diagnosis Algorithm for Distributed Computing Systems with Dynamic Failure and Repair", IEEE Transactions on Computers, Vol. c-33, N°3, March 1984, pp. 223-233.

[9] R. Bianchini, K. Goodwin, D. Nydick, "Practical Application and Implementation of Distributed System-level Diagnosis Theory", Proc. 20th Intl. Symp. Fault-Tolerant Comput. , IEEE, New York, 1990, pp. 332-339.

[10] R.Bianchini, R.Buskens, "An adaptive Distributed system-level diagnosis algorithm and its implementation", 21st IEEE Symposium on Fault-Tolerant Computing, pp. 222-229.

[11] A. Bagchi, S. Hakimi, "An optimal algorithm for distributed system level diagnosis", 21st IEEE Symposium on Fault-Tolerant Computing, pp. 214-221.

[12] F. J. Meyer and D. K. Pradhan, "Dynamic Testing Strategy for Distributed Systems", IEEE Transactions on Computers, vol. 38, N°3, March 1989, pp. 356-365.

[13] S. H. Hosseini and N. Jamal, "Efficient Distributed Algorithms for Self Testing of Multiple Processor Systems", IEEE Transactions on Computers, vol. 41, N°11, November 1992, pp. 1397-1409.

[14] M. Barborakand M. Malek, "Partitioning for Efficient Consensus", Proc. 26th Hawaii International Confernece on System Sciences, Vol. II, Jan. 1993, pp. 438-446.

[15] Parsytec Computer GmbH, The Parsytec GC Technical Summary, Ver. 1.0, Aachen (Germany), 1991.

[16] T. Muntean and P. Waille, "L'architecture des machines Supernode", La Lettre du Transputer et des Calculateurs Distribués, Sep. 1990, pp. 11-40.

[17] Presentation de l'IBM 9076 Scalable POWERparallel 1, IBM 1993.

[18] J. Altmann, F. Balbach and A. Hein, "An Approach for Hierarchical System Level Diagnosis of Massively Parallel Computers Combined with a Simulation-Based Method for Dependability Analysis", First European Dependable Computing Conference, Oct. 1994, Berlin, pp. 371-385.

[19] C. Aktouf, O. Benkahla and C. Robach, "Distributed Validation of Massively Parallel Machines", International IEEE Symposium on Parallel Architectures, Algorithms and Networks (ISPAN'94), Dec. 1994, Japan.

[20] C. Aktouf, O. Benkahla and C. Robach, "Functional Testing of Parallel Message-Passing Machines", Euromicro, Sep. 1995, Italy, pp.413-420.

[21] INMOS, The Transputer Databouk, Third Edition 1992.

Application-Dependent Performability Evaluation of Fault-Tolerant Multiprocessors

S. Dalibor, A. Hein, W. Hohl

Universität Erlangen-Nürnberg
IMMD III, Martensstraße 3, 91058 Erlangen, FRG
hohl@informatik.uni-erlangen.de

Abstract

A case study of performance and dependability evaluation of fault-tolerant multiprocessors is presented. Two specific architectures are analyzed taking into account system functionality, actual workloads, failures of system components as well as the inter-component dependencies. Since the evaluation of such complex systems has to be performed already during the design phase, simulation models are developed and used to provide insight into the system behavior and to uncover weak points and bottlenecks. Object-oriented software design and process-oriented simulation techniques are used for model construction allowing sophisticated performance and dependability analysis of massively parallel systems.

Keywords: performability analysis, reconfiguration policies, workload modeling, simulated fault injection

1. Introduction

Multiprocessors become more and more important to solve computationally extensive and time-consuming problems in science, industry, and engineering. Since failure probability increases with rising number of components, fault tolerance is an essential characteristic of massively parallel systems; they have to provide redundancy and mechanisms to detect and localize errors as well as to reconfigure the system and to recover from error states. These fault tolerance mechanisms are typical features of the so-called *gracefully degrading systems* that continue working with deteriorated performance if components fail.

Computer systems have to be evaluated as early as possible in order to compare alternative design approaches and to facilitate the change of a current design, i.e., methods are needed to analyze the target systems already during the early design phase. Since the real system is not available for benchmarking or monitoring in this stage, the system designer has to rely on theoretical methods such as analytical and simulation models.

To reflect the important features of multiprocessors we have developed simulation-based models of the target systems including their essential functionalities (e.g. the scheduling and routing mechanisms), actual workload, and fault tolerance mechanisms. Number-crunching algorithms solving scientific problems represent typical workload for the target systems. Additionally, fault tolerance mechanisms developed for the real multiprocessors are implemented and tested via the simulation models.

We want to emphasize the fact that performance and dependability are not analyzed separately, but a performability analysis - a combined performance and dependability analysis - of the overall system is conducted (Fig. 1). In Chapter 2. the modeling approach is discussed. The target systems and their simulation models are presented in Chapter 3. The systems are analyzed in Chapter 4. and a summary including an outlook is given in Chapter 5.

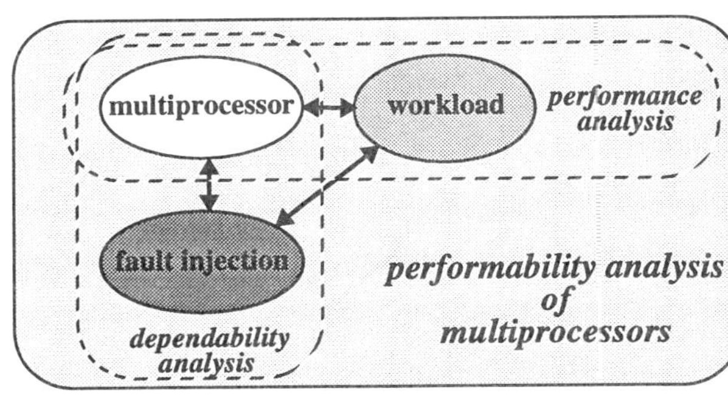

Fig. 1 Performability Analysis

2. The Modeling Approach

Simulation models of the target architecture are powerful means delivering accurate results and avoiding some constraints of *analytical modeling* such as state-space explosion and unrealistic simplifying assumptions, for instance the 'memoryless' property in Markovian models. In comparison to *Petri net*- and *Markov*-based analytical models, simulation-based models offer greater accuracy

1066-6192/96 $5.00 © 1996 IEEE
Proceedings of PDP '96

and flexibility. Surveys of different modeling techniques and various tools can be found in [6], [11].

In order to perform a sophisticated analysis of fault tolerant multiprocessors the system-level simulator *SimPar* has been developed for performance and dependability evaluation [5]. To implement *SimPar* the *Depend* tool [3] is taken as the underlying simulation engine which provides basic components such as simulation classes for fault-tolerant servers and link connections. It has successfully been used for the analysis of a TMR-based system and for the simulation of software behavior under hardware faults [4]. *SimPar* provides new enhancements to facilitate the model development and the performance and dependability analysis of massively parallel fault tolerant systems.

The main characteristics of the modeling approach are *process-oriented simulation* and *object-oriented software design*. Another essential feature is the *fault injection* into components of the simulation model in order to interrupt and disturb their regular and predefined behavior.

The behavior of the system is modeled by light-weight processes. The *process-oriented approach* provides an intuitive model development in depicting the system from the point of view of a participating entity. Therefore, it is well-suited for the design of large-scale models and for the modeling of complex inter-component dependencies. A comprehensible introduction into the technique of *process-oriented simulation* can be found in [10]. The overall system behavior is described by a collection of asynchronously interacting processes. Processes depict the functionalities of the system components such as processors and switches. Besides, the process-oriented simulation environment allows actual user-defined distributed programs (written in C or C++) to be executed within the simulation model to perform detailed analysis and to test the efficiency of implemented fault tolerance algorithms. These programs represent user-defined workload such as distributed numerical algorithms as well as system software for routing and reconfiguration tasks.

Object-oriented design is the construction of a software system as a structured collection of abstract data type implementations [8]. Data abstraction and inheritance are central features of the object-oriented software design of large-scale models representing massively parallel systems [7]. Reusability and scalability of the models are supported by the possibility of inheritance and derivation. In several phases of inheritance and derivation, very powerful and specialized classes can be provided by keeping an hierachical and clear model design without reimplementing every class from scratch. Additionally, the class hierarchy facilitates the reusability and maintainability of complex simulation models by hierarchical model construction and step-by-step refinement.

In accordance with the *object-oriented software design* [8] classes are implemented in the object-oriented language C++ encapsulating the functionalities of the processors, switches, and links. Objects of the simple classes are combined to the highly complex structures of multiprocessors. When the model of the target multiprocessor is initialized, objects of these classes are instantiated and dependencies between the objects are defined depicting the characteristics of the real system. The physical connections between the processors, switches, and links are simulated via logical dependencies between corresponding objects. The model can easily be modified, for example, by replacing the current class of the processor by another class, simulating the real processor in more detail or representing a completely different type of processor.

Faults can be injected in objects of every basic class, disturbing and interrupting the predefined fault-free behavior in order to examine the influence of faults on the overall system. The model designer can define his or her own fault model by assigning functions to the basic classes which are called as soon as faults are injected; if no such fault function is defined, the implemented default fault model is assumed which is outlined in Section 3.3.

3. The Target Architectures and their Model Representation

In this chapter we describe the architectures of two multiprocessors as well as the respective simulation models.

3.1 Distributed Shared-Memory Architecture

MEMSY (Modular Expandable Multiprocessor System) is a massively parallel multiprocessor architecture developed at the University of Erlangen-Nürnberg for large-scale scientific and technical computations, based on the concept of distributed shared communication memory [1], [2]. Its principal design goal is to enhance the shared memory paradigm with the possibility of unlimited scalability; this is achieved by the arrangement of processing nodes in an easily extensible, regular structure. Only the communication memory and the interconnection network for accessing the shared memory modules consist of specialized hardware. The processing nodes are built from state-of-the-art microprocessors.

The processing nodes form a topology with constant local interconnection complexity: Toroidal grids of tightly coupled nodes are stacked so that each node of an upper level has access to the communication memories of the four nodes directly below. As the number of nodes of each level is four times smaller than the number in the grid below, the global structure resembles a pyramid. Scalability

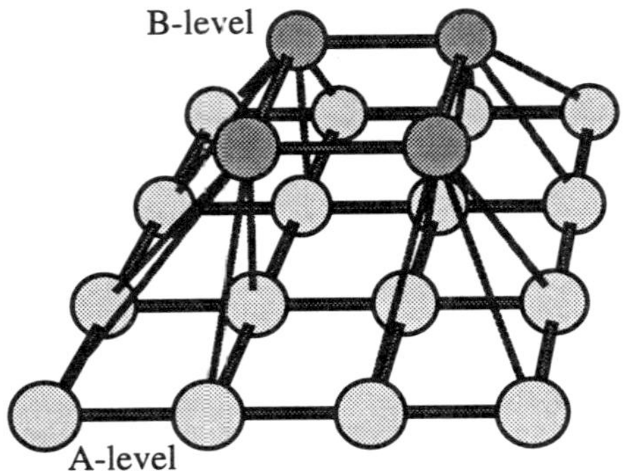

Fig. 2 MEMSY Topology

is possible due to the constant local connectivity: The structure can be extended by adding more levels of grids or by enlarging the number of nodes per grid. An experimental prototype of MEMSY is currently operating; it contains 20 (4+16) nodes in two levels (see Fig. 2; the toroidal connections are not shown). Each processing node consists of a standard Motorola MVME188 board system (with four MC88100 RISC CPUs) plus additional hardware for the memory interconnection.

The fact that each MEMSY-node is a full-fledged parallel computer is also reflected by the operating system MEMSOS: Per node a standard UNIX System V kernel is running with symmetric multiprocessing capabilities (referring to the four CPUs) as well as extensions for access to the communication memory, inter-node-interrupts, and management of applications with processes distributed over various nodes. Because the nodes are running a multiuser, multi-tasking operating system, and are accessible through standard network services like Telnet and Remote Login, it is not unusual that some or all nodes are shared between several distributed applications and other user-oriented processes like editors or compiler jobs. In general, this is not a problem because four CPUs are available per node. However, from the viewpoint of an application it is possible that one or more nodes participating in computing are slowed down due to heavy load and the fact that application processes have no special priority compared to other UNIX-processes running on a node. The impact of such performance degradation of the nodes involved in an application is investigated in Section 4.1.

3.2 Message-Passing Architecture

The target message-passing architecture is a Parsytec GC multiprocessor [9]. This massively parallel machine is designed for scientific and technical applications requiring huge computing power. High performance is achieved by

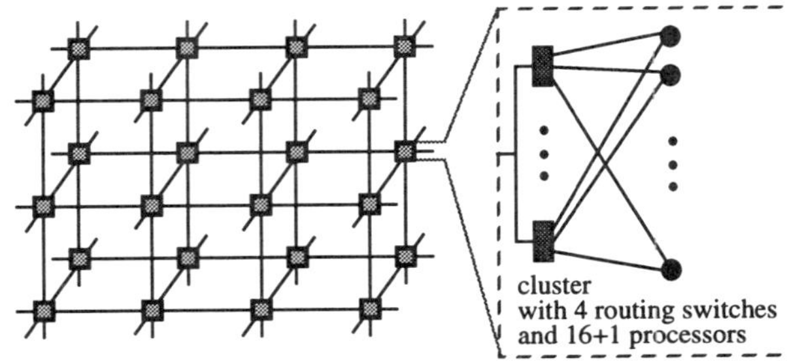

Fig. 3 Data Network of the Parsytec GC

the large number of processing elements and their interprocessor connections providing high bandwidth. In addition, this system takes into account the increasing probability of a failure of system components: Redundant processors may replace faulty ones and the communication paths are redundant to reduce communication delays as well as to tolerate failures of links and switches. The architecture consists of a *data network* forming a three-dimensional grid on which the user application runs. The nodes are connected to every neighbouring node via 8 communication links. Each of the nodes corresponds to a cluster containing 17 INMOS T9000 processors which are redundantly connected via four crossbar-like INMOS C104 routing switches (Fig. 3). Only 16 out of the 17 processors of a cluster are used for application programs; the 17th processor serves as spare component. Besides, an additional network - the so-called *control network* which is not shown in the figure - supervises and controls the components of the data network.

3.3 Simulation Models

The following three model components are the basic constituents of the overall simulation model providing the essential functionalities of the target components as well as default fault models. The model designer can define another fault model for all the basic objects by simply writing functions which are called when a fault is injected:

- The *processor object* P is supposed to perform processes, to schedule them, and it has to receive and send messages. If the model designer does not provide another fault model, P ejects any jobs in progress and stops handling messages as soon as a fault is injected.
- The *routing switch object* R receives and forwards messages in accordance with a predefined routing scheme. A faulty switch no longer communicates with its links, and all messages buffered in the switch are lost.
- The *link object* receives messages at a port and forwards them to another port. When a link object is injected by a fault, it stops forwarding messages from the incoming to the outgoing port or the messages are corrupted.

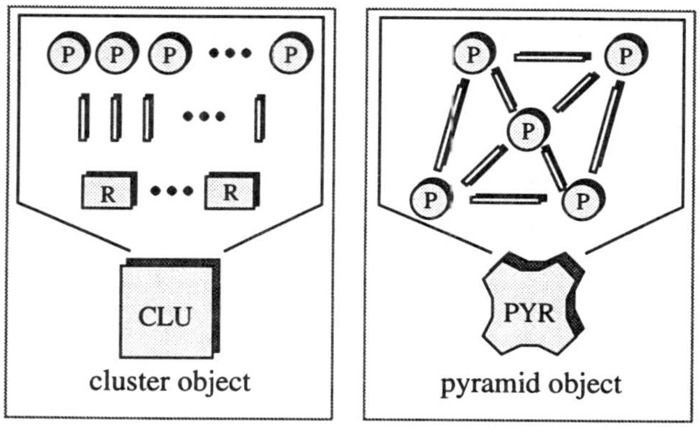

Fig. 4 Basic Objects of the Simulation Models

The relationships and dependencies among the basic components of the simulation environment represent the topology and functionality of the target system. Based on the three basic components more complex objects are created which model parts of the multiprocessor such as the clusters of the Parsytec GC consisting of 17 processor objects and 4 routing switch objects connected by link objects (object CLU in Fig. 4 and Fig. 5).

Similarly, 5 processor objects and several link objects are combined in an object representing the smallest unit of the MEMSY topology (object PYR in Fig. 4 and Fig. 6).

After the user has defined the number of clusters in the

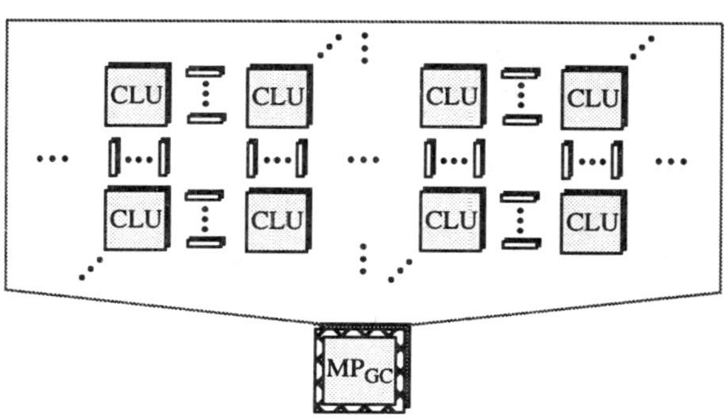

Fig. 5 Object MP_{GC}: Model of the Parsytec GC
(only two of the three dimensions are sketched)

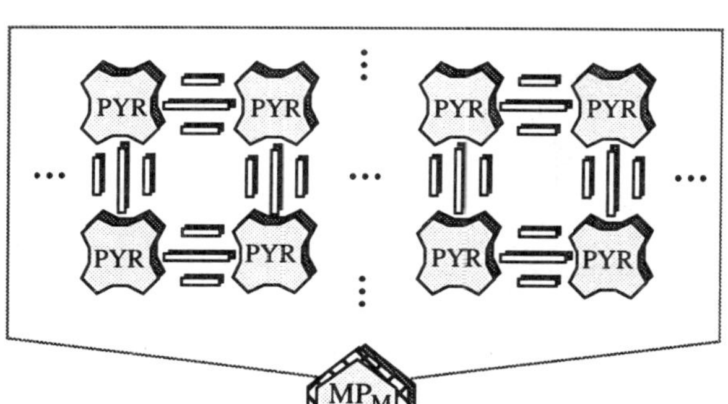

Fig. 6 Object MP_M: Model of MEMSY

three spatial dimensions of the data network, the required set of cluster objects CLU is initialized and the topology of the Parsytec GC is automatically modeled by defining the communication paths between the clusters. The model of MEMSY is initialized in a similar way; the user inputs the number of basic pyramids in the two dimensions, and the according pyramid objects PYR are initialized and put together. The final objects MP_{GC} and MP_M are models of the overall target multiprocessors (Fig. 5 and Fig. 6).

The multiprocessor objects MP_{GC} and MP_M are totally scalable by varying the number of clusters and pyramids in the three respectively two dimensions of the networks. These objects are the interfaces to the user-written control program, i.e., the user has to call methods of these objects to load user-defined processes on the processors. These processes can be real distributed application programs as well as operating system routines. Besides, programs to perform fault diagnosis and reconfiguration of the simulated multiprocessor can run concurrently to distributed number crunching algorithms modeling realistic workload. In the Parsytec GC model MP_{GC} messages are sent from the sending processor object through the intermediate link and switch objects of the network to the receiving processor object. As in the target system, successfully received messages are acknowledged.

Additionally, the MP_{GC} and MP_M objects provide methods to define the fault injection, to get information about the current system state, and to output fault reports. The system analyser defines and controls the experiments by simply calling methods of these objects.

4. Results

In this section we present the two specific analyses of our target multiprocessor architectures performed by using the *SimPar* simulation models.

4.1 Impact of Node Performance Degradation on Execution Times on MEMSY

Each MEMSY-node consists of four CPUs - but from the viewpoint of the application programmer they are considered as one computational resource. A MEMSY application takes full advantage of the computing power of a node by creating several UNIX-processes per node; as long as no other jobs are started on the node, up to 4 processes are running completely parallel. Because accesses to the communication memory are satisfied directly by the hardware (i.e. the memory management units and the system bus), the load generated by the operating system is negligible after an initialization phase. If however more than four processes per node have to be scheduled, the operating system distributes the CPUs in a time sharing manner among the processes. With regard to a single application, this can be considered as *performance degradation* of the node: For each additional process started, the computing power available for one specific application is diminished.

In order to investigate the impact of the performance degradation of one or more nodes due to application-external load under controlled conditions, a typical distributed algorithm solving the many-body-problem has been executed on the MEMSY simulation model. This algorithm requires a complete information exchange between all nodes after every computing phase; taking into account the distributed memory structure of MEMSY, this is realized as distributed broadcast exploiting the toroidal connection within the grid-level. Between the computing phases, the processes exchange data packets of varying size with neighboring nodes via their communication memories by performing ring-shifts in horizontal and vertical direction until the information from all the other nodes is available at each node of the grid.

The influence of application-external load was simulated by decreasing the number of CPUs working for the application; the following cases were taken into account:

- *exp_0*: no external load, all CPUs working for the application.
- *exp_1*: 1 CPU on 1 node was taken from the application.
- *exp_2a*: 2 CPUs on 2 different nodes were taken from the application.
- *exp_2b*: 1 node was working for the application with only 2 CPUs.
- *exp_3a*: 3 CPUs in 3 different nodes were withdrawn from the application.
- *exp_3b*: 2 CPUs in 1 node and 1 CPU in another node were unavailable for the application.
- *exp_3c*: in 1 node, only 1 out of the 4 CPUs was working for the application.

The experiments have been conducted with two different message sizes on a system with four basic pyramids; the results are shown in Table 1. In the experiment with larger message size, the total run time is less increased - this can be explained by the fact that the nodes are exchanging messages for the most part of the time and the reduced node performance has no significant impact on the overall run time. The experiments have shown clearly that the overall run time of the application depends to a high degree on the slowest node involved in the computation - it is for example considerably worse to have only 2 CPUs in 1 node (*exp_2b*) participating in the application than 3 CPUs in 3 different nodes (*exp_3a*). Besides, the impact of the application-external load is not at all negligible: Deterioration of the total run time of more than 30% if only 1 node of the A-level contributes to the application with 3 instead of 4 CPUs indicates that measures should be taken to compensate for the additional load or to restrict the number of the additional processes (see Table 1).

	small messages		large messages	
run time	absolute	relative	absolute	relative
exp_0	22.2286	1.0	264.158	1.0
exp_1	30.2822	1.3623	265.158	1.0038
exp_2a	31.1584	1.4017	265.958	1.0068
exp_2b	38.7822	1.7402	267.283	1.0118
exp_3a	31.5528	1.4195	266.587	1.0092
exp_3b	38.7822	1.7447	268.083	1.0149
exp_3c	63.7822	2.8694	276.742	1.0476

Table 1 Results of the Simulation Experiments

Referring to the operating system MEMSOS, a special run-queue with increased priority for the processes involved in distributed applications could be a possibility to avoid exaggerated slowdown of computations. Another method currently under investigation is the utilization of the B-level-nodes as 'spare-processors' - if one of the A-level-nodes gets overloaded to an intolerable extent, the belonging B-level-node could either 'lend' one or more of its CPUs or take over the task of the loaded node completely. The integration of adaptive load-balancing into the operating system seems to be desirable - future experiments with the MEMSY simulation model MP_M will be useful to investigate possible strategies.

4.2 Evaluation of Reconfiguration Policies in a Message-Passing Architecture

The Parsytec GC system is analyzed by injecting faults into the processors of the *SimPar* model. After error detection and localization of the faulty component, the system has to be reconfigured, i.e., spare processors replace faulty processors and continue their tasks. Each of the clusters contains a 17th processor as spare (cf. Fig. 3). As the user is shielded from the actual network topology and the system is reconfigured automatically, a reconfiguration policy has to be specified and implemented in order to determine the spare processor to replace the faulty processor dependent on the state of the overall system.

Loss of performance in terms of longer execution time can be caused by the following reason: Processes running on physically neighboring processors exchange messages relatively fast. After a reconfiguration these processes are possibly assigned to not-neighboring processors, i.e., they belong to different clusters of the multiprocessor; communication between processes assigned to different clusters cause time-consuming intercluster data exchanges increasing the overall run time of the application program.

Different reconfiguration policies are considered and compared with regard to application programs with various communication patterns. Identification numbers are assigned to the clusters ranging from *0* to *number_of_ clusters-1*. We assume that a processor fails in cluster *fcl* and a spare processor is selected in cluster *scl*; fcl_x, fcl_y, and fcl_z are the grid coordinates of cluster *fcl*. The distance *d* between two processors corresponds to the distance of the clusters the processors belong to; *d* is defined as:

$$d = |fcl_x - scl_x| + |fcl_y - scl_y| + |fcl_z - scl_z|$$

The following six reconfiguration policies are evaluated in the experiments described in this chapter:

- *rec_a*: The spare processor is chosen according to the *internal order* of the clusters. If the spare processor of cluster 0 is intact and free, it replaces the faulty processor; otherwise, if the spare processor of cluster 1 is still intact and free, it is selected; otherwise the spare processor of cluster 2 is checked, etc.
- *rec_b*: The spare processor of cluster *fcl* takes over the processes of the faulty processor, if it is fault-free and unused. Otherwise, the clusters *fcl+1, fcl+2, fcl+3,etc.* are searched for an available spare processor.
- *rec_c*: The cluster is *randomly* chosen until a cluster *scl* with an unused and intact spare processor is found to replace the faulty one.
- *rec_d*: The spare processor of cluster *fcl* replaces the faulty processor (*scl* = *fcl*), if it is fault-free and unused. Otherwise, a spare processor is selected in the cluster *scl* with *minimal distance d* to cluster *fcl*.
- *rec_e*: Policy *rec_e* is a variant on *rec_c*: Again, the spare processor of cluster *fcl* replaces the faulty (*scl* = *fcl*), if it is fault-free and unused. Otherwise, another cluster is *randomly* chosen which still contains a spare processor.
- *rec_f*: This policy is the contrary of *rec_d* and is used for comparison purposes. After the failure of a non-spare processor of cluster *fcl*, *rec_f* determines a cluster *scl* which contains a spare and has *maximum distance d* to cluster *fcl*, i.e., the communication paths become as long as possible.

Simulating a system with 8 clusters, the processes are mapped on the processors and the applications are running on the 128 processing nodes. First, we have measured the mean run time T_0 of the distributed application without processor failures; this times are compared with mean run times T_k after *k* processors have failed, and after fault diagnosis, reconfiguration, and recovery have been carried out. The results presented are given in *ratio of mean run time* $R_k = T_k/T_0$. In the optimal case, at most one processor per cluster fails and is replaced by the spare processor of the same cluster keeping short communication distances. A primitive reconfiguration algorithm not considering this issue of close or long communication distances increases the communication overhead. Additionally, if more than one processor per cluster fails, spare processors of other clusters, which are selected in accordance with the predefined reconfiguration policy, have to take over the processes.

Most of the numerical algorithms implemented on multiprocessors can be characterized by a loop containing a computation phase and a communication phase for data exchange:

```
while (result accuracy is not sufficient) {
  compute();
  /* phase I: compute on private data */

  communicate();
  /* phase II: exchange data */
}
```

Phase II is responsible for the communication overhead and can have a large impact on the overall execution time dependent on the message handling, the topology of the multiprocessor, the size and the frequency of the messages. We started algorithms with typical communication patterns on the simulator MP_{GC} and analyzed the impact of the reconfiguration policies on the execution times.

4.2.1. Linear Array Communication

A numerical algorithm is started on the simulated multiprocessor, whose communication pattern is a linear array, i.e., process *i* exchanges data with process *i+1* and process *i-1*. This pattern is very common in parallel computation of partially differential equations; the data is partitioned among the processes and the border areas of the data have to be exchanged between logically neighboring processes. For this communication pattern it is straightforward to construct an optimal mapping scheme allowing shortest communication time and therefore shortest run time of the distributed algorithm (Fig. 7a). As soon as a processor fails and the failure is detected, the system is reconfigured, the processes are re-mapped following the predefined reconfiguration policy, and the distributed application is restarted. A faulty processor is replaced by a spare processor as long as spare components are available. A possible communication pattern after reconfiguration is shown in Fig. 7b.

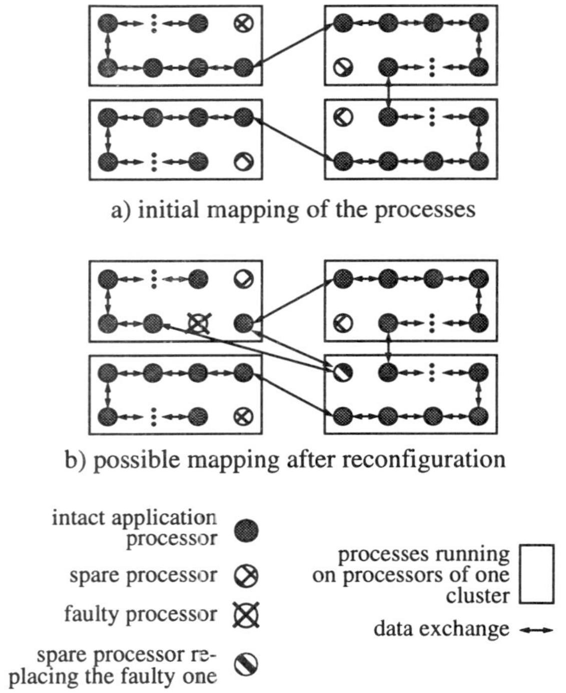

Fig. 7 Linear Array Communication

A single processor failure has no impact on the run time of the algorithm if reconfiguration policy *rec_b*, *rec_d*, or *rec_e* is selected (Fig. 8). This is due to the facts that the spare processor belongs to the same cluster as the faulty processor and within a cluster the interprocessor connections are symmetric and redundant (cf. Fig. 3), i.e., there is no additional communication overhead caused by the reconfiguration. The mean run time of strategies *rec_b, rec_d,* and *rec_e* are clearly shorter than the mean run times of *rec_a* and *rec_c* which show only minor differences for any number of processor failures. *rec_d* requires the largest administration overhead in determining the cluster with smallest distance containing a spare processor but results in the shortest run time. If 8 processors fail in the system with 8 clusters the mean run time deterioration is about 2.2 percent if using the *rec_d* reconfiguration policy and about 3.9 percent for police *rec_a*, which is even worse than the random selection of the spare processor (*rec_c*).

Comparing the ratios of the mean run times of policies *rec_c* and *rec_e* we see the positive impact of the very simple policy in looking for a spare processor in the same cluster. The policy *rec_e* selects a spare processor at random if no spare is available in the cluster of the faulty processor; this strategy shows even better results than the policy to select a spare processor following the internal order of the clusters (*rec_b*). Policy *rec_f* represents the worst case by looking for a spare processor with maximum distance to the faulty processor. Even in the case of a single processor failure, the mean run time is decreased by 3.3 percent, which shows a larger mean communication overhead than in a system with 8 processor failures and reconfiguration policy *rec_b*, *rec_d* or *rec_e*.

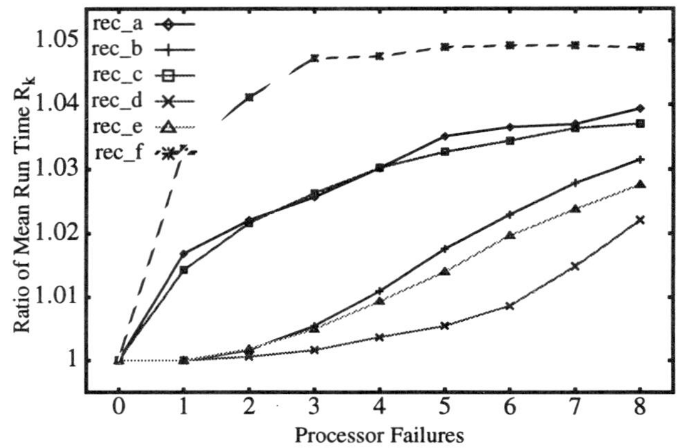

Fig. 8 Linear Array Communication (8 Clusters)

4.2.2. Cluster Internal Communication

This communication pattern takes into consideration the cluster structure of the multiprocessor. A typical scenario is the assignment of only a single cluster to every user, i.e., a distributed application can be started on the processing nodes of a single cluster but several clusters cannot be allocated by the same user at a time and data exchange between processes initially assigned to different clusters is prohibited.

After every computing phase a cluster internal data exchange takes place. Every process exchanges data with every other of the 16 processes running on processors of the same cluster. Initially, there is no data exchange between processes of different clusters and processes of different clusters can be considered to be independent (Fig. 9a). However, after reconfiguration processes can be mapped on processors of other clusters resulting in intercluster communications (Fig. 9b).

The analyses for *rec_a* and *rec_c* show only minor differences and cause longer mean run times than for the policies *rec_b*, *rec_d,* and *rec_e* (Fig. 10). Already in the case of a single processor failure in a system of 8 clusters these policies result in an average deterioration of more than 6.3 percent. The mean run times of policy *rec_b* are slightly larger than the ones of policy *rec_e* for 3 to 8 processor failures. Policy *rec_f* causes an increase of the mean run time of 15.4 percent if only a single processor fails; this value is even worse than the mean run times of all the other policies if 8 processors fail. The maximum relative loss of performance - in the case of 8 processor failures - is in the range of 8.8 percent (*rec_d*) and 18.2 percent (*rec_f*).

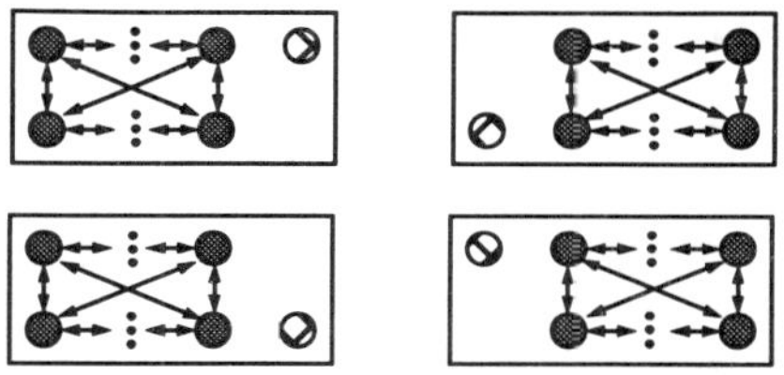

a) initial mapping of the processes

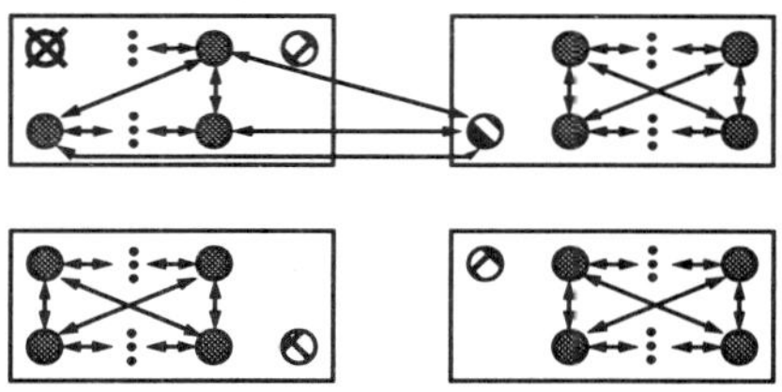

b) possible mapping after reconfiguration

Fig. 9 Cluster Internal Communication

The ratios of mean run times measured in this cluster internal communication pattern are clearly larger than in the previous example (Subsection 4.2.1.). The communication requirements are more intensive; every process exchanges messages with 15 other processes. If a faulty processor is replaced by a spare processor of another cluster, a lot of time-consuming intercluster communications has to be executed causing large deterioration of the overall run time.

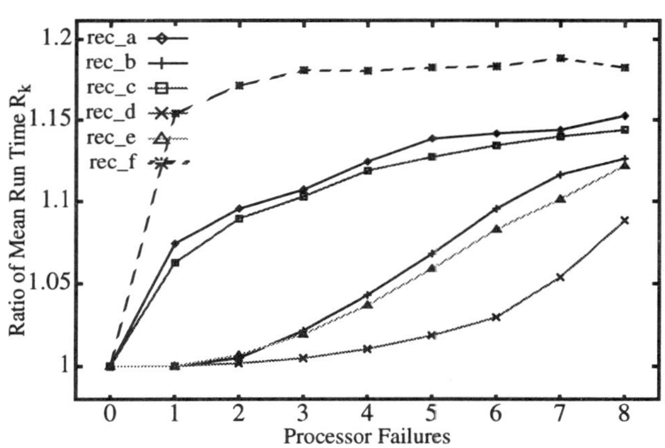

Fig. 10 Cluster Internal Communication (8 Clusters)

4.2.3. Cluster Oriented Communication

The cluster structure of the target system is considered by this communication pattern in order to reduce intercluster communications in the initial fault-free state.

A central process *p_0* broadcasts the initial data to the other application processes in a tree like manner. In order to reduce intercluster communication, data are sent to one specific process *p_i* per cluster which broadcasts the data

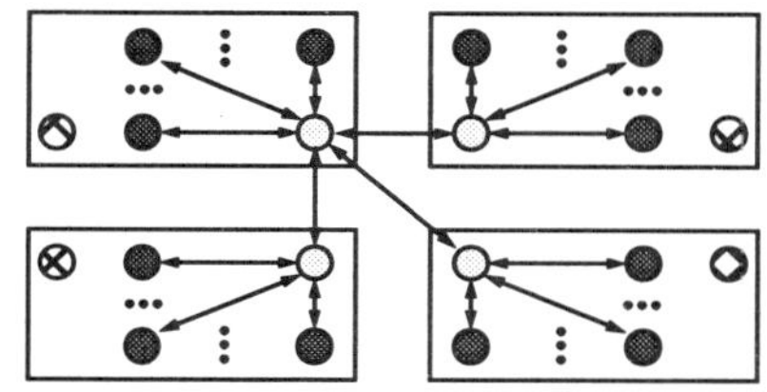

a) initial mapping of the processes

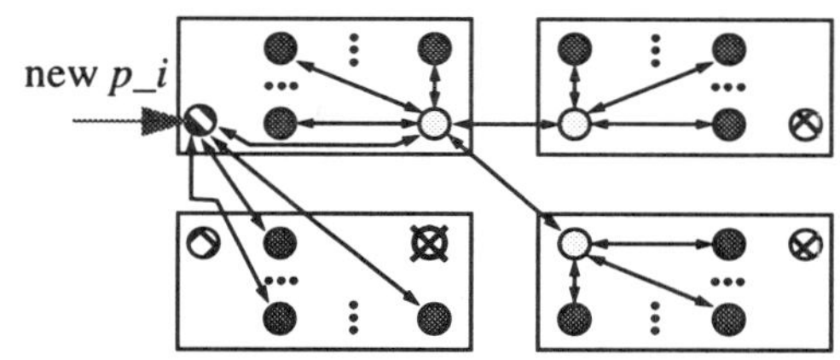

b) possible mapping after reconfiguration

Fig. 11 Cluster Oriented Communication

within the cluster. After the computation phase, *p_i* gathers the data of the other 15 processes of the same cluster and sends a message to the central process *p_0* (Fig. 11a). Several computation and message exchange phases are executed. After a reconfiguration of the system this cluster oriented communication pattern is possibly destroyed (Fig. 11b). If a faulty processor is replaced by a spare processor of another cluster the number of intercluster communications is increased.

When running the application program with a cluster oriented communication pattern, we obtain results similar to the previous communication patterns, i.e., the differences between the ratios of the mean run times of the reconfiguration policies *rec_a* or *rec_c* on the one side, and *rec_b* or *rec_d* on the other side are obvious (Fig. 12). Simulating a system of 8 clusters and assuming 8 processor failures, the mean run time is prolonged by a factor between 1.3 percent (*rec_d*) and 4.75 percent (*rec_f*). It is worth mentioning that reconfiguration policy *rec_d* exerts almost no influence on the mean run time if at most 6 processors fail (deterioration of less than 0.23 percent). Furthermore, policy *rec_e* results in slightly shorter mean run times than policy *rec_d* for 7 and 8 processor failures and delivers better results than policy *rec_b* at any rate.
The results of policy *rec_f* are very different from the previous results of this policy. In this cluster oriented communication pattern the ratios of mean run times increase approximately linearly with the number of processor failures. In the previous examples the mean run time has grown very fast even if only one processor failed and did not increase so clearly if further processors failed.

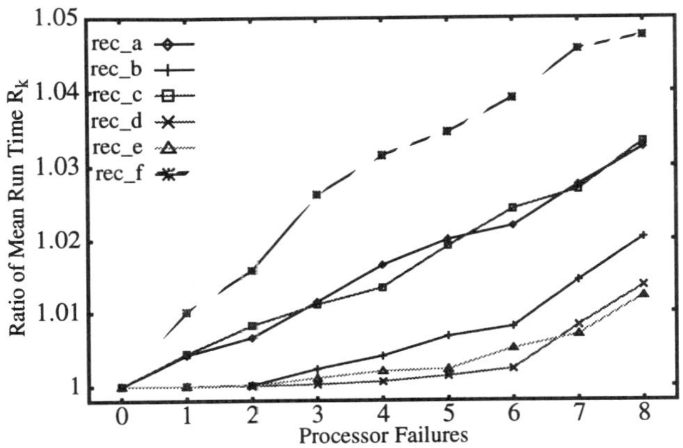

Fig. 12 Cluster Oriented Communication (8 Clusters)

4.2.4. Experiment Summary

The results of the presented simulation experiments considering three different communication patterns and six reconfiguration policies differ in terms of absolute values. The mean deterioration of run times is more obvious in the application with heavy cluster internal communication (Subsection 4.2.2.) than in the other cases. Nevertheless, in all of the considered examples it has been proven that an intelligent reconfiguration policy, which takes into account the hardware architecture of the underlying multiprocessor as well as the communication paths between processors, results in clearly shorter run times for distributed application programs.

5. Summary

Two case studies of combined performance and dependability analysis of fault-tolerant multiprocessors have been carried out. The presented simulation technique has successfully been used allowing detailed evaluation of the target systems including the underlying architecture, fault-tolerance mechanisms, and actual workload. Intensive research is going on to extend the simulation environment and to run more detailed evaluation experiments taking into account various types of multiprocessors, other typical communication patterns and message sizes, different fault-tolerance mechanisms such as fault diagnosis algorithms as well as various workload scenarios. Currently, the components of the MEMSY model MP_M are being refined in order to reflect the internal structure and the communication protocols in more detail. Furthermore, simulation components of I/O subsystems are being added to *SimPar* in order to examine I/O behavior of parallel systems and methods are implemented facilitating easy hierarchical model development of multiprocessor architectures.

Acknowledgments

The authors want to thank the Deutsche Forschungsgemeinschaft (DFG) for supporting the development of MEMSY as part of the Collaborative Research Center SFB 182 and the European Union (EU) for supporting the investigations on the GC architecture in the frame of the ESPRIT project 6731 FTMPS.

References

[1] Dal Cin, M., W. Hohl, J. Hönig and A. Pataricza. *MEMSY - A Modular Expandable Multiprocessor System with Fault Tolerance.* Proc. Parallel Systems Fair of the 8th Intl. Parallel Processing Symposium, Cancun, April 26-29, 1994, IPDS'94 Publication 1994, pp. 21-28.

[2] Dal Cin, M., W. Hohl et al. *Architecture and Realization of the Modular Expandable Multiprocessor System MEMSY.* Proc. First Intl. Conf. on Massively Parallel Computing Systems (MPCS'94), Ischia, May 2-6, 1994, IEEE CS Press, 1994, pp 7-15.

[3] Goswami, Kumar K. and Ravi K. Iyer. *DEPEND: A Simulation-Based Environment for System-Level Dependability Analysis.* Center for Reliable and High-Performance Computing (CRHC), Univ. of Illinois at Urbana-Champaign, 1992.

[4] Goswami, Kumar K. *Design for Dependability: A Simulation-Based Approach.* Ph.D. Thesis, Center for Reliable and High-Performance Computing (CRHC), Univ. of Illinois at Urbana-Champaign, 1993.

[5] Hein, Axel. *$SimPar_{GC}$ - Ein Simulator zur Leistungs- und Zuverlässigkeits-Analyse des Multiprozessorsystems Parsytec GC, Version 1.0.* Internal Report 2/94, IMMD III, Univ. of Erlangen-Nürnberg, 1994.

[6] Hein, Axel. *Evaluation Report on Modelling Tools.* FT-MPS, Esprit Project 6731, Report R 4.2.1; Internal Report 3/94, IMMD III, Univ. of Erlangen-Nürnberg, 1994.

[7] Kreutzer, Wolfgang. *Object Oriented Modelling & Simulation Towards Reusable Frameworks for Simulator Design.* Proc. European Simulation Symposium ESS 94, Istanbul, Turkey, October 9 - 12, 1994.

[8] Meyer, Bertrand. *Object-Oriented Software Construction.* New York [et. al.]: Prentice Hall Internat., 1988.

[9] Parsytec Computer GmbH. *The Parsytec GC Technical Summary*, Version 1.0. Aachen (Germany), 1991.

[10] Schwetman, Herb. *CSIM: A C-Based, Process-Oriented Simulation Language.* Proc. 1986 Winter Simulation Conference (WSC' 86), Washington, D.C., 1986.

[11] Trivedi, Kishor S. and Manish Malhotra. *Reliability and Performability Techniques and Tools: A Survey.* in B. Walke and O. Spaniol (eds), *Messung, Modellierung und Bewertung von Rechen- und Kommunikationssystemen*, 7. ITG/GI Fachtagung, Aachen, September 1993. Berlin, Heidelberg: Springer-Verlag, 1993.

Cyclo-Dynamic Dataflow

Piet Wauters, Marc Engels, Rudy Lauwereins, J.A. Peperstraete
Katholieke Universiteit Leuven, ESAT Department
Kard. Mercierlaan 94, B-3001 Heverlee, Belgium
Tel. +32-16-32 11 42, Fax. +32-16- 32 19 86
email: Piet.Wauters@esat.kuleuven.ac.be

Abstract

In this paper we present cyclo-dynamic data flow (CDDF), a new data flow model for real time digital signal processing (DSP) applications. CDDF is an extension of cyclo-static dataflow (CSDF) [1,2] that keeps the interesting properties like analyzability and efficient compile time scheduling, while introducing data dependent control flow to improve the expressivity. The semantics are constructed such that extra knowledge about the internals of the actors, which is known to the programmer, can be expressed both in a natural way, and in a syntax that can be analyzed by automatic tools. In this paper we describe the proposed model in the context of already existing data flow languages, demonstrate its schedulability and its improved analyzability as compared to the Boolean data flow model [3].

1. Introduction

The programming model presented in this paper is mainly targeted at *real-time* DSP applications. DSP systems typically consist of large parts of stream processing at high sampling rates - hundreds of kilo Hertz or even Mega Hertz are no exception. Because of the vast computation power needed, an *efficient* implementation on a *multiprocessor* is often required. We propose a *data flow* programming model because it is one of the most natural models to program DSP applications. Moreover data flow makes the inherent *parallelism* of a program explicit, which makes it especially well suited for implementation on a multi-processor. To obtain the high sample rates, it is important that the program can be *analyzed* and optimized *at compile time* to reduce the *runtime* overhead.

A data flow graph consists of *nodes* interconnected by *directed edges*. The nodes represent actors that transform input data streams into output streams. The directed edges between the nodes represent channels which carry streams of data. An atomic data object is called a token. In this paper all channels are considered to be First-In-First-Out (FIFO) queues, theoretically of unbounded capacity. When an actor executes it *consumes* a certain number of tokens from its *inputs* and it *produces* a number of tokens to its *outputs*. To avoid the cumbersome expression "consumption from an input and production to an output " we use in this text: "*transfer* over a terminal", where a terminal stands for either an input or an output of an actor. The program flow is *data driven* in the following way: an actor is *executable* as soon as its *firing rule* evaluates "true". A firing rule is a Boolean expression in the number and/or the value of tokens present in the FIFOs. Depending on how the consumption and production together with the firing rules are specified, we can divide graphs or subgraphs into different classes, ranging from synchronous data flow (SDF) [4]and cyclostatic data flow (CSDF) [1,2] over Boolean and integer controlled dataflow (BDF [3], IDF[5]) to dynamic data flow (DDF). In a single graph any combination of these types can occur. In the following sections we briefly describe these different dataflow models based on the token transfers and the firing rule.

Synchronous data flow:

In SDF [4] token transfers are constant integers x_v^u, known at compile time where v is the transferring actor and u the edge over which the tokens are transferred. The firing rule of an actor becomes "true" if and only if each input FIFO contains at least x_v^u tokens. If all token transfers equal one, we speak of *single-rate* SDF; otherwise we have *multi-rate* SDF.

Cyclo-static data flow:

In cyclo-static data flow (CSDF) [1,2] an actor v executes as a sequence of phases $\varphi_1, \varphi_2, \ldots, \varphi_{l_v}$. The length of the sequence is l_v. This phase-firing sequence is repeated in time: the kth time an actor fires, it executes the code of phase φ_i where $i = k \bmod l_v$. During each phase a specific code segment is executed. A code

1066-6192/96 $5.00 © 1996 IEEE
Proceedings of PDP '96

segment can be seen as a way to split a non-preemptable chunk of code into different smaller pieces which are bounded by pre-emption points. Each phase φ_i has its own set of token transfers $x_v^u(i)$ for each terminal of the actor, similar to SDF. The firing rule of phase φ_i of a cyclostatic actor evaluates as "true" for the kth firing of the actor if and only if all input FIFOs contain at least $x_v^u(i)$ tokens where $i = k \bmod l_v$. In CSDF a code segment is considered to be an atomic program entity: no precedence relations are imposed between the individual token transfers.

Using CSDF, multi-rate SDF graphs can be modeled more efficiently, requiring less memory and resulting in shorter input-output delays. This can be seen in the example of Figure 1. It is a simple mux/demux example. The demultiplexer always reads one token from its input, and produces one token on the first output during the first phase, and no tokens during the second phase, and vice versa for the second output. The multiplexer performs the opposite action. The actors in and out represent I/O tasks. A and B are downsampling actors: the output produces half as much tokens than consumed at the input. Actor B is a SDF actor whereas A is a CSDF actor with two phase A1 and A2. Actor A only needs one input token before it can produce an output. Actor B needs two input tokens before it can produce one output. These *two* tokens have to be stored in the queue, wheras for actor A only *one* token has to be stored.

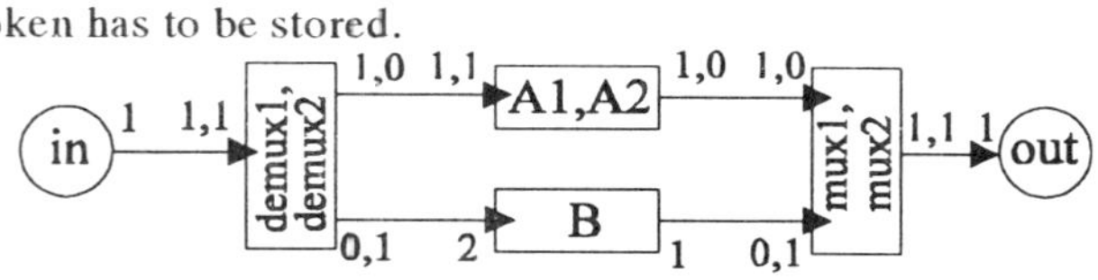

Figure 1: CSDF multiplexer/demultiplexer

Boolean data flow:

In Boolean data flow [6] a token transfer is either a constant x_v^u as in SDF or a two valued function $x_v^u(b)$ of the Boolean value b of a token present at an other terminal of the same actor. Such a Boolean token is called a control token. A terminal of which the token transfer is controlled by a Boolean token is called a conditional terminal. The terminal that transfers the Boolean control token is called the controlling terminal. A controlling input is never conditional. A BDF actor is fireable if on each *unconditional* input there are at least x_v^u tokens present. For each *conditional* input, there must be at least $x_v^u(b)$ tokens present, where $x_v^u(b)$ is one of two values depending on the *value* of the control token. Typical examples are the switch and the select actors shown in Figure 2 where they are combined in an if-then-else construct. The small squares on the splitting of two edges represent an implicit copy: the first stream is transformed into two identical streams.

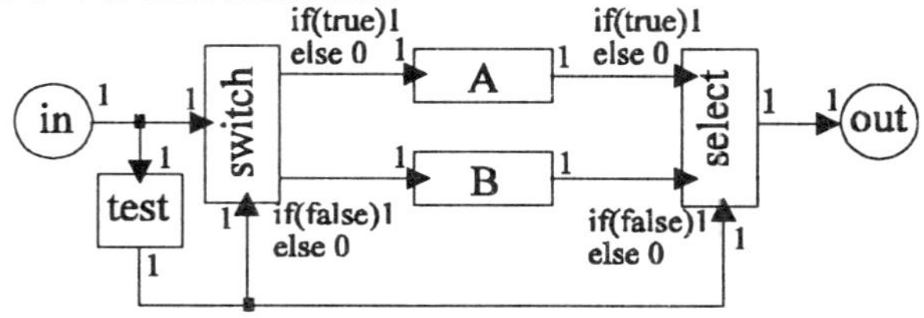

Figure 2 if-then-else construction in BDF

Integer controlled data flow:

Buck extends the BDF model in [5] as follows: the value of the control tokens can be an integer instead of a Boolean. The token transfer of a conditional terminal is now either zero or a constant, depending on whether the value of the control token is a member of some set. The token transfer can also be a constant multiple of the integer control token. Buck also allowes a multi-rate actor to be executed in different phases, although no rigorous definition is given.

Dynamic data flow:

In DDF the firing rule can be any Boolean expression. For instance in Figure 3 the actor can fire if only one of its inputs has at least one token. Which input is not important. In this way an Alt-construct can be specified: the first token that arrives on one of either inputs is transferred to the output. In DDF the consumption and production can be left undefined (unknown at compile time). Often the program can give some unprecise specification of production and consumption, e.g. minimum and maximum numbers. Because of this partial knowledge at compile time, DDF needs a run time scheduling mechanism to determine when an actor becomes executable. It is clear that graphs specified in DDF can sometimes behave in a non-deterministic way.

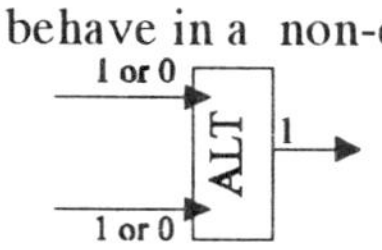

Figure 3: A DDF ALT-construct

If a data flow graph must be executed on a real architecture, it is essential to know the answer to the following questions:

- *periodicity*: do sequences of actor firings exist which return the graph into its original state? If such a sequence exists, it is called a *cycle*, and then the graph can be executed repeatedly.
- can these cycles be executed in *bounded time*? This is an important issue for hard real-time applications like DSP systems.

- can the graph be executed using *bounded memory*? If the graph can be scheduled in bounded time, it can also be scheduled using bounded memory, although the opposite is not always true.
- *liveness*: does the graph *deadlock*?

The most important advantage of CSDF and SDF graphs is that all these questions can be answered at compile time, resulting in a predictable run time behavior. Moreover the timing and storage requirements can be verified, resulting in a very efficient implementation (e.g. there is no need for dynamic buffer allocation). However the *expressivity* of CSDF and SDF is too limited because only stream processing with no *data dependent decisions* is possible. For instance data dependent iteration and conditional execution are not covered by the model. Therefore Buck and Lee extend their SDF model to BDF. Buck proves in [3] that BDF is Turing equivalent. Thus the BDF programming model is in a sense complete: each algorithm that can be programmed in some model, can be programmed in BDF. However it turns out that automatic tools are often not able to answer the above questions, because they can base their analysis only on the limited *topological* information of the graph, and not on the *internal functional* behavior of the actors. For instance, if a for-loop is programmed in BDF, it is not possible to determine that the graph can be scheduled in bounded time, although the programmer perfectly knows that this time is bounded by the maximum number of iterations. Thus often the analysis fails to determine the properties of a BDF graph because some essential information, known to the programmer, cannot be explicitly specified by the limited semantics.

The goal of CDDF is to extend CSDF to give it the expressivity of BDF while improving the analyzability compared to BDF. Therefore CDDF is constructed such that the extra knowledge about the internals of the actors known to the programmer, can be expressed both in a natural way, and in a syntax that can be automatically analyzed. How this is achieved will be explained throughout the rest of the paper.

In the next section we define the CDDF model. In section 3 we clarify the model with some examples followed by a section in which we demonstrate the schedulability. In section 5 we demonstrate the improved analyzability of CDDF compared to BDF. We end with some reflections on our current work and a conclusion.

2. Cyclo-dynamic dataflow

In CDDF, as in CSDF, an actor executes as a sequence of phases. The behaviour of a CDDF actor is dynamic in three ways:

- the code segment corresponding to a given phase can vary at run time.
- the token transfer for a given code segment can vary at run time.
- the length of the phase firing sequence can vary at run time.

In the next section we define the behaviour of CDDF actors and the restrictions imposed on some dynamical aspects. In section 3 these definitions are clarified with some examples.

Definition 1: An actor fires as a *sequence* of *phases.* The actual code segment that is executed during a specific phase is a function of the *sequence index* and of the *value* of some *input token(s)*.

A token of which the *value* is used to control the dynamical behavior of an actor is called a *control token.* Similarly an edge which transfers control tokens is called a *control edge.* Note however that a control edge can carry normal data and is therefore not a special edge. The word control edge is only used to simplify explanations.

Definition 2: The sequence index of an actor is a variable representing the current position in the phase firing sequence.

Suppose a sequence Φ is specified symbolically as $\Phi = \varphi_1, \varphi_2, \ldots, \varphi_i, \ldots, \varphi_n$ then i is the sequence index, ranging from 1 to n. Each of the code segments has its own token transfer behavior. A sequence of phases thus results in sequences of token transfers over the different terminals of the actor:

Definition 3: The *token transfer* of a terminal is a *sequence* of *non-negative integers* which may be function of the *sequence index* or of the *value* of some *input token(s)* of the same actor. The token *production* can also be function of the *value* of some *symbolical variable(s)*.

The length of the phase firing sequences can be data dependent.

Definition 4: The *length* of a *sequence* may be function of the *value* of some *input token(s)* or of the value of *symbolical variable(s)*.

Definition 5: A *symbolical variable* is a symbol, local to one specific actor, that reflects some relevant property of the internal functional behavior of an actor. Note however that the value of a symbolical variable has no active influence on the behavior of the actor.

This property can be used in the analysis of the graph. For instance in the example of Figure 11, n is a symbolical variable that represents the number of times the actor has fired before the first output token is produced. Although not mandatory, the value of a symbolical variable is often produced by the actor as an output token. In this way, the local information of the actor can be passed to other actors. The value of the symbolical variable can be function of the value of some input tokens and some other symbolical variables. A programmer can specify this function explicitly.

To be able to schedule and analyze CDDF graphs we have to make some restrictions to the above definitions. In this paper we assume that actors don't posses state. All information of a previous actor execution that is needed in a subsequent execution, must be communicated explicitly through a feed-back edge. Therefore we have to make the following restriction:

Restriction 1: A control token *must* be read (and thus be present) in the *same phase* in which it is used to control the token transfer or the actual code segment to be executed.

The reader might argue that the sequence index is a kind of state. However this sequence index is only used by the scheduler to determine which code segment must be fired. Therefore it is not a state of the actor, but merely a state of the scheduler.

Restriction 2: The *actual code segment* to be executed and the *consumption* should not depend on a *symbolical variable*, neither directly nor indirectly (e.g. via the sequence index).

This limitation is required for causality: it is not possible that the code segment that must be fired depends on a symbolical variable since this variable is produced during the execution of that code segment.

Restriction 3: The *value* of a control token must be member of a *finite set.* e.g. a Boolean value.

CDDF is constructed such that all firing rules are derivable from the consumption. Thus we have *implicit* firing rules which cannot conflict with token transfer. A firing rule evaluates as "true" if and only if on each input there are enough tokens present to satisfy all consumption. We do not introduce special actors like switch and select. It is possible to derive the type of an actor from its token transfer and phase firing sequences.

3. Examples

In this section we clarify these definitions with some examples. We use the following notations: sequences of numbers placed near a terminal are the token transfer sequences. If the length of a sequence is variable we use an abbreviation like $n*(1,0,1)$, which means that we have a sequence of length $3*n$ where the subsequence (1,0,1) is repeated n times. The phase firing sequences are placed inside the actors. A symbol between square brackets after a token transfer number is a placeholder for the actual value of the token that will be transferred.

Conditional phase execution:

In the example of Figure 4 the phase-firing sequence is of (constant) length one. Which code segment will be fired only depends on the ***value*** of a Boolean ***input token.***

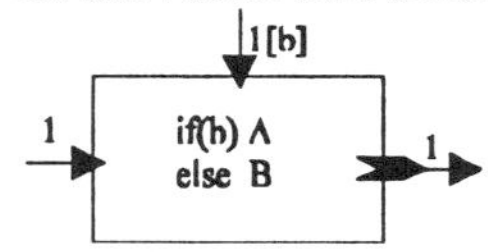

Figure 4: Conditional phase execution

If the value of the control token is "true" then segment A executes, else segment B fires. This is typically an if-then-else construct, where the internal (hierarchical) behavior is partially hidden. Thus in this example the sequence length is one, there are two code segments which have both the same token transfer behavior.

Input controlled token transfer:

In Figure 5 one token (with values *n*, respectively *m*) is read from each input and *x* tokens are placed on the output, where *x= f(n,m)* and *f()* can be an arbitrary function of *n* and *m*. Thus, the phase firing sequence has constant length one, there is only one code segment. Only the token transfer behavior varies at run time.

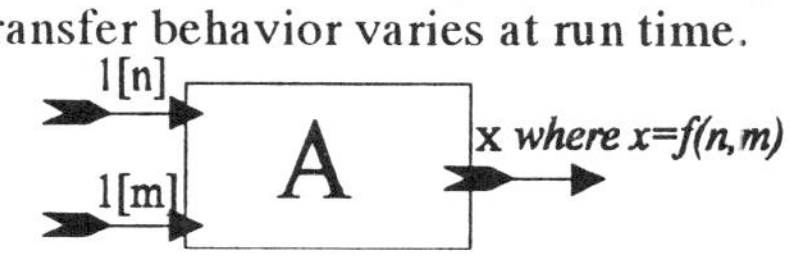

Figure 5: Input controlled token transfer

State Problem:

A possible problem which has to do with state can be seen in Figure 6: The token of which the value *n* is used to determine the number of tokens that will be consumed in the next phase is consumed before it is used to compute the consumption number. Thus *n* should be stored somewhere such that it can be used in the second phase. This is a kind of state! Since we don't allow actors to have state, the example must be rewritten as in Figure 7.

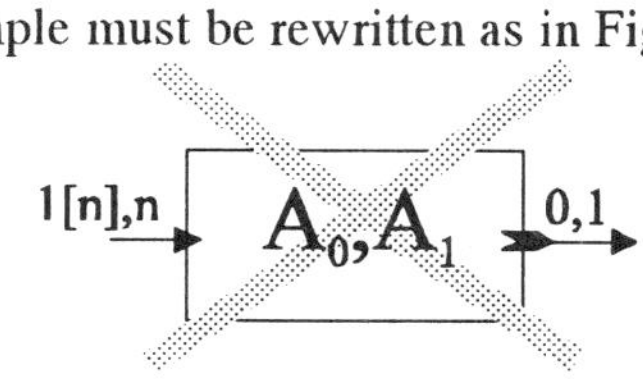

Figure 6

Thus the control token is read in the same phase as in which it used to control the transfer over the input terminal. It is important to see that it can be shown at compile time that the behavior of Figure 7. corresponds exactly to the desired one. The number of tokens consumed in the second phase equals the value of the token consumed in the first phase.

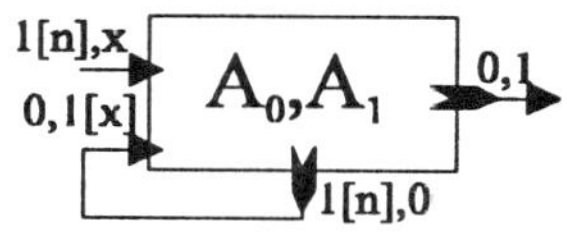

Figure 7: State problem

Production function of a symb. var:

Until now we examined examples where the token transfer depends only on the value of an *input* token. A syntactically similar, but semantically totally different case is the example of Figure 8. Indeed the number of tokens produced on the first output seems to be function of the value of the second output. However this should be interpreted as follows: both the value produced on the second output as well as the number of tokens produced on the first one are function of the internal behavior of the actor, and are as such related with each other. However, they have no ***active*** influence whatsoever on each other. This - possibly complex -relationship is in this case reflected by the use of the same ***variable*** *n*, both as a production ***value*** and as a production ***amount.*** Semantically the internal algorithm guarantees the relations between output values and production numbers. This behavior is not guaranteed by the scheduler. However this extra knowledge can be used by the tools to obtain better performance. In this example we say that the production of tokens is function of the *symbolical variable n*.

Figure 8: Production function of a symb. var

This actor has a phase firing sequence of constant length one, one code segment. Only the output token transfer is function of a symbolical variable.

Downsampling by a variable factor:

In the example of Figure 9, the first time the actor fires, one token is consumed from the control input. The value of this token *(n)* corresponds to the length of the sequence. Thus the n-1 next firings of the actor no tokens are consumed from the control terminal. For other terminals the token transfer sequence is function of the value of the first token read from the control-edge. This actor has a phase firing sequence of variable length *n*, there are three code segments, each of them with constant token transfer.

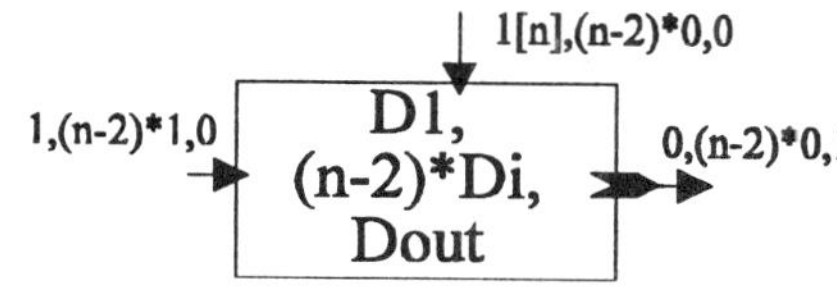

Figure 9: Downsampling by a variable factor

Frame consisting of header followed by variable number of data packets:

In the example of Figure 10 data enters the actor as a sequence of 1 header packet, followed by a variable number (encoded in the header) of data packets. The first phase decodes the header and determines the number *(c)* of data packets that will follow. During the *c* next phases the data is simply passed through the actor. Thus the length of the sequence depends on the value of an input control token. Note however that it is not necessary as in IDF that the control token is present at the start of the sequence.

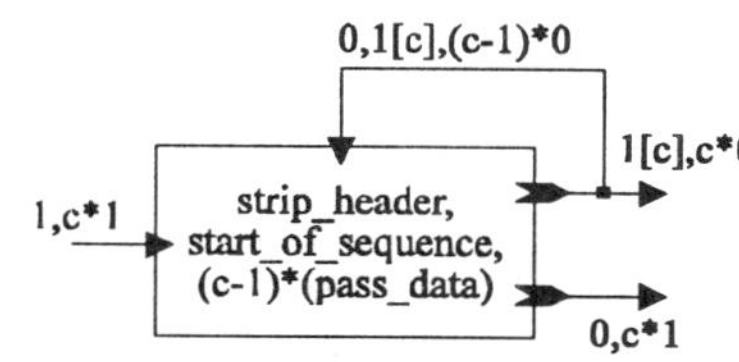

Figure 10: Frame consisting of header followed by variable number of data packets

Runlength encoder:

Another example is the run-length-encoder of Figure 11 an input bit stream is converted into a stream of integers n. Each n represents the length of a sequence of identical bits. e.g. the stream [1,1,1,1,0,0,1,1,0,1,...] would be converted into [4,2,2,1,1,...]. An output token is produced each time a sequence of consecutive 1's or 0's ends. The value of the token is the length of the sequence. The state of the actor, the value of the previous input bit, and the current number of consecutive bits, is made explicit in the feedback loop.

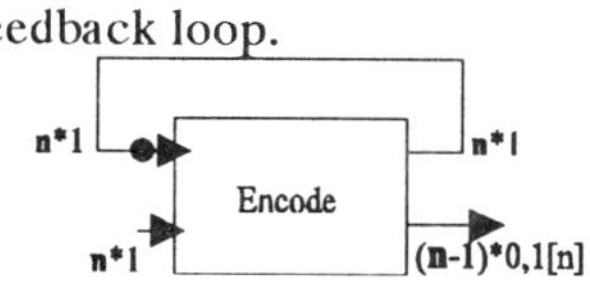

Figure 11: Runlength encoder

We see that the length of the phase firing sequence depends on the symbolical variable *n*. The value of *n* is produced once during the data dependent sequence. In this way we are able to analyze the relationship between this actor and its successors.

4. Schedulability of CDDF

To execute a data flow graph, it must be possible to determine a correct execution order for the different actors. In SDF and BDF the actor execution order only depends on the availability of tokens. Thus a correct execution order is determined completely by the firing rules of the actors. If the token transfer is data dependent, as in BDF, the firing rule is also data dependent and a runtime scheduler is needed.

In CSDF and CDDF actors execute as different phases, with their own firing rule. Therefore, for each actor execution, a scheduler must first determine which phase must be executed before the corresponding code segment can be determined and its firing rule can be evaluated. The phase that must be executed at a given moment depends on the number of times the actor has already been fired. Therefore the *scheduler* needs, conceptually, a state variable to keep track of the current position in a sequence. Each time an actor executes, this sequence index is incremented. When the last phase of a sequence executes, the sequence index is reset. Note that the actor itself has no knowledge of this sequence index.

In CSDF graphs the phase firing sequence is constant. The value of the state variable is reflected in the number of times the actor has already occurred in the schedule. As a consequence, the state variable is implicitly present in the schedule and must not be updated at run-time. In the example of *Figure 1*, for instance, *in* can be executed immediately. After this execution, the first phase of the actor *demux*, i.e. *demux1*, must be considered. Like in SDF, the firing rule can be evaluated at compile-time. For the next execution of the actor *demux*, *demux2* must be used. A similar reasoning can be applied to all actors in the graph.

In CDDF graphs, the code segment to be executed can be function of some control tokens. In this case, the scheduler must be able to read the values of these control tokens to determine the actual phase of the actor. To guarantee this, the model was restricted in section 3 as follows: the actual phase that will be invoked by the scheduler must not depend on a symbolical variable; in addition, control tokens must be present at the moment that the actual phase is determined. In the example of Figure 4, for instance, the scheduler has to read the value of *b* to determine the next phase. As a consequence, this must be done at run time.

Also the length of a phase firing sequence can be data dependent in CDDF, in function of some control tokens or symbolical variables. For the symbolical variables no provisions must be made in the scheduler, because the model of section 3 guarantees that they have no influence on the actual phase or firing rule. For the control tokens, the scheduler must once again be able to read them. By storing them in its internal state, he can use them for the determination of the actual phase of the actor. In the example of Figure 10, for instance, a possible schedule takes the form of: execute phase0: Strip_header, read c, for(i = 1 to c) pass_data.

The evaluation of the firing rule for CDDF graphs is similar to that for BDF graphs. To be able to evaluate the firing rule for a given phase the model was restricted as follows: for *input* terminals the consumption numbers must not depend on a symbolical variable.

5. Analysis of dataflow graphs

In this section we demonstrate the improved analyzability of CDDF compared to BDF. To do this, we use one aspect of the general analysis method described in [3]: the *consistency* check of data flow graphs. Consistency is a necessary condition for a graph to be schedulable cyclically. Basically it states that the number of tokens produced on each edge equals the number of tokens consumed from the same edge during one cycle[7,8]. Let r_v and r_w represent the number of invocations, respectively of actor v and actor w, during a cycle. Γ_{uv} is the number of tokens actor v produces on link u during one sequence, whereas $-\Gamma_{uw}$ is the number of tokens actor w consumes from link u. The equality of production and consumption can then be expressed as a *balance equation*: $\Gamma_{uv}.r_u = \Gamma_{uw}.r_w$. The set of balance equations for each link can be represented in a matrix representation $\Gamma.\vec{r} = \vec{0}$. Γ is called the topology matrix and $\vec{r}$ is the sequence repetition vector. Each element r_j from $\vec{r}$ represents the number of sequence invocations of *actor* j during a cycle. For CSDF the topology matrix must be constructed as:

$$\Gamma_{ij} = \begin{cases} \sum_{k=1}^{l_j} x_j^i(k) \text{ if task j produces data to edge i} \\ -\sum_{k=1}^{l_j} x_j^i(k) \text{ if task j consumes data from edge i} \\ 0 \text{ otherwise} \end{cases}$$

The r_j*'s* must be multiplied by the sequence length l_j of the actor to know the number of *phase* invocations $q_j = r_j * l_j$ during one cycle.

For the example of Figure 1 the balance equations become:

$$\Gamma.\vec{r} = \vec{0} \text{ where } \Gamma = \begin{bmatrix} 1 & -1 & 0 & 0 & 0 & 0 \\ 0 & 1 & -2 & 0 & 0 & 0 \\ 0 & 0 & 1 & 0 & -1 & 0 \\ 0 & 1 & 0 & -2 & 0 & 0 \\ 0 & 0 & 0 & 1 & -1 & 0 \\ 0 & 0 & 0 & 0 & 2 & -1 \end{bmatrix}$$

A possible solution for r is : $\vec{r} = [4 \quad 2 \quad 1 \quad 1 \quad 1 \quad 2]^T$; $q_{in} = 4$; $q_{demux} = 2*2 = 4$; $q_A = 2*1 = 2$; $q_B = 1$; $q_{mux} = 2*1 = 2$; $q_{out} = 2$;

In BDF a similar analysis can be performed [6]. However, because the exact number of token transfers $x_j^i(b)$ over the conditional terminals is not known at compile time, the method has to be modified: for each controlling edge c a symbol n_c is introduced. This n_c is the number of control tokens that have value "true", during a cycle. If the actor executes r_j times during a cycle, then the number of tokens that had value "false" equals $r_j - n_c$. The topology matrix Γ is no longer constant, but a function of all n_c's and also of the r_j's of actors with conditional token transfer: $\Gamma_{ij} = (n_c.x_j^i(true) + (r_j - n_c)x_j^i(false)) / r_j$. This is a weighted average of the token transfer for all possible values of the controlling tokens. In [3] Buck substitutes n_c / r_j by p_j. The balance equations must now be solved symbolically.

Consider the example of Figure 2. The topology matrix now becomes a function of p_1 and p_2.

$$\Gamma(\vec{p}) = \begin{bmatrix} 1 & 0 & -1 & 0 & 0 & 0 & 0 \\ 0 & 1 & -1 & 0 & 0 & 0 & 0 \\ 0 & 0 & p_1 & -1 & 0 & 0 & 0 \\ 0 & 0 & 0 & 1 & 0 & -p_2 & 0 \\ 0 & 0 & 1-p_1 & 0 & -1 & 0 & 0 \\ 0 & 0 & 0 & 0 & 1 & p_2-1 & 0 \\ 0 & 1 & 0 & 0 & 0 & -1 & 0 \\ 0 & 0 & 0 & 0 & 0 & 1 & -1 \end{bmatrix}$$

From the graph it can be analyzed that $n_1 = n_2 = n$ since the two streams are a copy of each other. In this example there always exists a solution, independent of the value of n: $\vec{r} = k.[1 \quad 1 \quad 1 \quad p \quad (1-p) \quad 1 \quad 1]^T$, where $p = n / r_{sw} = n / r_{sel}$.

If a non trivial solution for the balance equations exists, independent of n, the graph is said to be strongly consistent. If solutions only exist for particular values of n, the graph is called weakly consistent. Because only topological information about the graph, and not about the functionality of the actors can be used in BDF, it is sometimes impossible to prove automatically either consistency or inconsistency. For instance it would have been impossible to determine the consistency of the above example if the implicit stream duplication had been replaced by an explicit copy actor. In this case we would have needed extra information about the internals of the copy actor to prove that $n_1 = n_2 = n$. An other example is given in Figure 12: a runlength encoder/decoder it is impossible to decide that the graph is either consistent or inconsistent. The first part of Figure 12 is a runlength encoder, which was already described in CDDF in Figure 11. The second part decodes the encoded datastream back into the original one. If we apply Buck's method to this example, we would have to prove that the number of "true" tokens produced during a cycle is equal for all control streams. This is however impossible without the knowledge of the functional behavior of the actors.

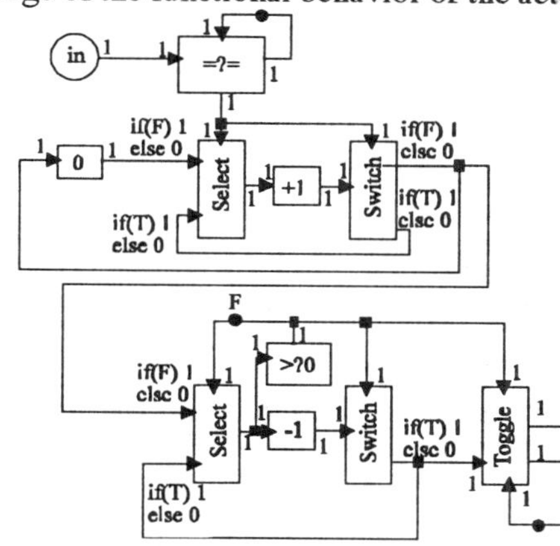

Figure 12:Runlength encoder-decoder

Although it was not possible to decide whether or not the graph is consistent, the programmer *knows* it is: the graph is constructed as a while loop followed by a for loop with exactly the same number of iterations.

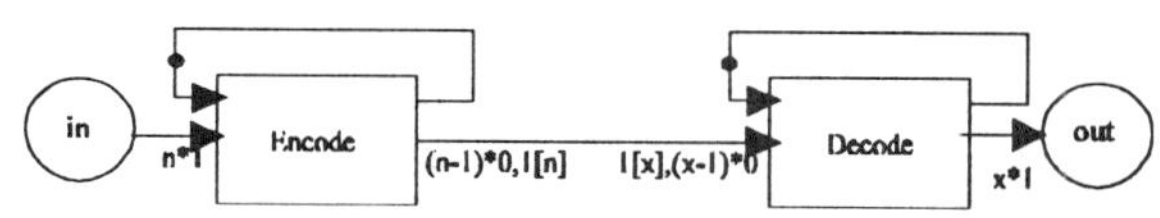

Figure 13: runlength coder specified in CDDF

CDDF allows to specify this extra information explicitly. Therefore the following mechanisms were introduced:

- a symbol can be associated with an input. This symbol is a placeholder for the value of the token that will be consumed at run time.
- a number of symbolical variables can be associated with each actor. A symbolical variable makes some relevant property of the internal behavior of the actor explicit.
- a function of the input symbols and the symbolical variables can be associated with the value of an output.

these values can be passed to other actor to make some information, local to one actor, accessible by other actors via an edge. If two terminals are connected by an edge, this means that the value of the input token equals the value of the output token. We call this the *assignment* of an output value to an input value.

If we apply these principles to the runlength encoder/decoder example we obtain a CDDF specification as in Figure 13. Here we see that the number of times the encode actor has been executed before it produces the first token is given by the symbolical variable n. The value of n is passed to the decode actor by the assignment of n to x. The decode actor executes in $x=n$ phases.

For the consistency analysis of a CDDF graph we combine the method of Bilsen and Buck as follows: the token transfer $x_j^i(k)$ of the kth phase can be function of some input values and of some symbolical variables. We denote this by $x_j^i(k, c_1, c_2, c_3, \ldots)$, where $c_1, c_2, c_3, \ldots$ are the input values or the symbolical variables that control the token transfer. This is abbreviated by $x_j^i(k, \vec{c})$. As in BDF, $x_j^i(k, \vec{c})$ must be replaced by a weighted average $\overline{x}_j^i(k, \vec{c})$ for all possible combinations of $\vec{c}$. Let $\vec{c}_p$ denote the pth combination of control values out of P possible combinations, then $\overline{x}_j^i(k, \vec{c}) = \frac{1}{r_j} \sum_{p=1}^{P} n_{\vec{c}_p} . x_j^i(k, \vec{c}_p)$, where $n_{\vec{c}_p}$ is the number of times combination $\vec{c}_p$ occurred during the cycle. Since also the length of the sequences $l(\vec{c})$ can be data dependent, an analogous weighted average must be made for the sequence lengths. Thus the total token transfer of an actor over an edge becomes: $\Gamma_{ij} = \frac{1}{r_j} \sum_{p=1}^{P} n_{c_p} . (\sum_{k=1}^{l(\vec{c}_p)} x_j^i(k, \vec{c}_p))$

Let us apply the above to the runlength encoder/decoder example of Figure 13. For the edge between the input and the encoder, the balance equation can be obtained as follows: actor *in* has only one phase and produces always 1 token to the edge. Actor *encode* has n phases, and during each phase it consumes one token from the edge. Thus the weighted average, denoted as $\overline{n}$ becomes: $\overline{n} = (n_1.1 + n_1.1 + \ldots + n_i.1 + \ldots + n_{\max}.1) / r_{encode}$, where n_i stands for the number of times n had value i during a cycle, and n_{max} is the maximum value of n. The topology matrix becomes:

$$\begin{bmatrix} 1 & -\overline{n} & 0 & 0 \\ 0 & 1 & -1 & 0 \\ 0 & 0 & \overline{n} & -1 \end{bmatrix} . \vec{r}(\overline{n}) = \vec{o} \, ;$$

A solution clearly is $\vec{r}(\overline{n}) = k.[\overline{n}, 1, 1, \overline{n}]^T$; There always exists a solution, independent of the value of $\overline{n}$. In this example the knowledge of the programmer could be directly translated into a description of which the consistency can be checked.

6. Conclusions and current Work

In this paper we presented CDDF, a dynamic data flow model, which is an extension of CSDF to obtain the expressivity of BDF. Instead of introducing new types of actors or edges a unified semantics was proposed: all CSDF and BDF actors can be expressed in CDDF semantics. It was shown how CSDF is extended to give it the expressivity of BDF. The schedulability of the model was demonstrated. The mechanisms used to improve the analyzability as compared to BDF were explained and the effectiveness was demonstrated with a runlength encoder/decoder example. Currently our research focuses on the real time scheduling of CDDF graphs on multi processors.

7. Acknowledgments

Rudy Lauwereins is a senior research associate and Marc Engels a senior research assistant of the Belgian National Fund for Scientific Research. The work presented in this paper is partly supported by the Belgian Interuniversity Pole of Attraction IUAP-50, by the Belgian Concerted Research Action on Applicable Neural Networks and by the European Community Esprit-III project 6800 Real-Time DSP Emulation System. K.U.Leuven-ESAT is a member of the DSP Valley™ Network.

8. References

[1] Greet Bilsen, Marc Engels, Rudy Lauwereins, J.A. Peperstraete, "Cyclo-Static Dataflow", *submitted for IEEE Transactions on Signal Processing.*

[2] M. Engels, G. Bilsen, R. Lauwereins, J. Peperstraete, "Cyclo-Static Dataflow: Model and Implementation", *(invited) 28th Annual Asilomar Conference on Signals, Systems, and Computers*, Asilomar Hotel & Conference Grounds, Pacific Grove, California, USA, October 31 - November 2, 1994, pp. 503-507.

[3] J.T. Buck, "scheduling Dynamic Dataflow Graphs With Bounded Memory Using the Token Flow Model",Memorandum No. UCB/ERL M93/69 (Ph.D. Thesis), EECS Dept., University of California, Berkeley, September 1993.

[4] E.A. Lee, D.G. Messerschmitt, "Synchronous Dataflow",Proceedings of the IEEE, September 1987.

[5] J.T. Buck, "Static Scheduling and Code Generation from Dynamic Dataflow Graphs With Integer- Valued Control Streams", *28th Annual Asilomar Conference on Signals, Systems, and Computers*, Asilomar Hotel & Conference Grounds, Pacific Grove, California, USA, October 31 - November 2, 1994.

[6] J.T Buck, E.A. Lee, "Scheduling Dynamic Dataflow Graphs With Bounded Memory Using the Token Flow Model", Proc.of ICASSP '93, 1993.

[7] E.A. Lee,"Consistency in Dataflow Graphs", *IEEE Transactions on Parallel and Distributed Systems*, Vol. 2, No. 2, April 1991.

[8] Greet Bilsen, Static Scheduling of Multi-Rate and Cyclo-Static DSP applications", *Proc. IEEE Workshop on VLSI Signal Processing*, 1994, pp.137-146

Symbolic Executions of Symmetrical Parallel Programs

Isabelle Vernier
Laboratoire IBP-MASI
Université Paris 6
4 place Jussieu, 75252 Paris - Cedex 05, France
email: isabelle.vernier@masi.ibp.fr
tel: (33 1) 44 27 71 04, fax: (33 1) 44 27 62 86

Abstract

We propose an algorithm to execute symbolically parallel programs with an unknown number of processes. Usually one instantiates the programs before their execution, i.e., one fixes the number of processes. We exploit the symmetrical behaviors of the processes to execute simultaneously all the instantiated programs. We define symbolic states that represent sets of states of an infinite number of instantiated programs. We compute simultaneously all the successors of states represented by a symbolic one. After an exhaustive execution, we build a graph that represents all the reachable states and possible executions of the instantiated programs. We can explore this symbolic graph to verify properties expressed with temporal logic formulas.

I. Introduction

Many parallel programs are described with a parameter, the number of processes, and are instantiated, i.e., the number of processes is fixed, to be executed. It is usually impossible to extend to all the instantiated programs the results of the analyze of a particular one. It is prohibitive to analyze again a program for multiple values of the parameter. A way to overcome this drawback is to analyze a program independently of the value of the parameter. We present such a method.

Formal methods exist to verify properties of parameterized programs even if the number of processes is unknown. They all work on symmetrical parallel programs. Processes have symmetrical behaviors if they have the same possible executions that are independent of their identity [2]. Symmetric algorithms as termination detection [7], mutual exclusion [6, 10] or reaching agreement algorithms [11], compose an important subclass of the parallel algorithms. They may be categorized according to two criteria [12]: the knowledge that a process has of its environment and the influence of a process on the behavior of the others. In our work, we consider that processes do not know about their identity and the number of other processes. They still are aware of the presence of the other processes. Processes communicate through shared variables or directly with other ones. All the works on parameterized programs assume the same hypothesis.

As the general problem is undecidable, methods concern only part of it. The principle common to the methods is to find an abstraction of the instantiated programs, independent of the number of processes, that preserves a given set of properties. The abstraction verifies a property of the set if and only if all the instantiated programs do so. Once the abstraction is defined, one builds its state graph and checks properties expressed with temporal logic formulas. All the methods give a solution only if the instantiated programs verify the same properties for all the number of processes greater than a bound. The programs instantiated with fewer processes may have a particular behavior. The problem is to find the abstraction. One cannot always decide the existence of an abstraction. It depends on the set of possible abstractions we consider. In [15] the set is finite therefore the method fails if it does not find one abstraction in the set. In [1, 4, 9, 14, 19], the set of possible abstractions is not limited. The methods that are described in [4, 9, 19] are not fully automated. In [8], only properties that refer to the behavior of a single process can be verified.

All these methods do not allow to represent reachable states and execution sequences of the instantiated programs. They give no intermediate results if it is impossible to build the state graph of the abstraction. The size of the state graph may be too big or infinite. We propose a method to execute symbolically parameterized parallel programs. We can build a symbolic graph and explore it to verify properties expressed with temporal logic formulas when we have computed all the possible executions and reachable states. In [18] we present the verification algorithm. Our method allows us to compute the bound that separates the instantiated programs with a particular behavior from the others.

The main point is to represent, with a symbolic state, set of states of instantiated programs. We bring states together according to the actions they enable and the states where the processes and resources are. For each action we compute the successor symbolic states of another one at the same time. When it is not possible to represent with a finite number of symbolic states all the states of the

1066-6192/96 $5.00 © 1996 IEEE
Proceedings of PDP '96

instantiated programs, the method fails. Otherwise, the finite symbolic graph represents exactly all the reachable states and executions of all the instantiated programs. We give the proofs of both properties and theorems in [17].

Section 2 presents the programs we study and the model we use. We choose extended Petri nets to model the programs because of their well-known expressive power [13]. The symbolic states are symbolic markings of the Petri nets. Section 3 defines the symbolic markings. Section 4 gives the rule to execute the Petri net and conditions to have an exhaustive execution. In Section 5 we conclude and present possible extensions of our work.

II. Symmetrical parallel programs and formal model

Two parts including a parameterized one compose the programs we consider. The parameterized part represents the behavior of *n* identical processes that communicate through shared variables or by synchronization. The other part, the control net, concerns the processes in given number and resources. It is an optional part. The control net manages the accesses to the resources. The conditions that govern the execution of each action are independent of the identity of the processes.

II.1. Petri nets

We model parallel programs by means of Petri nets. A Petri net is a bipartite graph. The vertices are the places and the transitions. The places and the transitions represent respectively the states or values and the actions. A token represents a process or a variable. The place that contains the token associated with a process (or a variable) gives its state (or its value). The marking of a place is the number of tokens it contains. The marking of a net is a vector. It associates with each place its marking. The initial marking represents the initial state of the program. The firing of a transition corresponds to the execution of an action.

An arc weighted by *n*, that links a place *p* to a transition *t*, *p* is an input place of *t*, means that *n* tokens in *p* are necessary for the firing of *t*. An arc, weighted by *n*, that links a transition *t* to a place *p*, *p* is an output place of *t*, means that *n* processes reach *p* after the firing of *t*.

Graphically, circles, rectangles and arcs with an arrow represent respectively the places, the transitions and the arcs. We represent the weight of an arc only if it is different from one. We do not represent the arcs with a weight that equals zero.

Definition 1 Petri net and marking

A Petri net is noted <P, T, Pre, Post> where:

- P is a set of places, T is a set of transitions, $T \cap P = \{\}$, $T \cup P \neq \{\}$,
- Pre, an application from $P \times T$ to $\mathbb{N}$, represents the weight of the arcs linking the places to the transitions,
- Post, an application from $P \times T$ to $\mathbb{N}$, represents the weight of the arcs linking the transitions to the places,
- a marking m is an application from P to $\mathbb{N}$.

To test the enabling of a transition, we compare for each place, the values of both the marking and the application Pre.

Definition 2 Enabling of a transition

Let P = <P, T, Pre, Post> be a Petri net, m a marking and t a transition that belongs to T. The marking m enables t, m[t>, if and only if:

$\forall P \in P, m(p) \geq Pre(p,t)$.

The decrease (respectively increase) of the marking of the input (respectively output) places gives the marking reached after the firing of a transition. The value of the decrease equals the weight of the arc that connects the place to the transition. The value of the increase equals the weight of the arc that connects the transition to the place. This firing rule allows one to compute the reachable markings of the Petri net.

Definition 3 Firing rule

Let P = <P, T, Pre, Post> be a Petri net, m a marking and t a transition enabled from m. The marking m' reached after the firing of t, m[t>m', is computed as follows:

$\forall p \in P, m'(p) = m(p) - Pre(p,t) + Post(p,t)$.

A state machine is a Petri net. Each of its transitions has exactly one input place and one output place. The weight of all the arcs is one. A transition represents an action executed by one process. The input (respectively output) place is the state of the process before (respectively after) the execution. An extended state machine allows one to model synchronization between several processes. A fixed number of processes can cooperate to execute a common action. An action does not create or kill a process.

Definition 4 Extended state machine

An extended state machine is noted <P, T, Pre, Post> where:

- <P, T, Pre, Post> is a Petri net,
- $\forall t \in T, \sum_{p \in P} Post(p,t) = \sum_{p \in P} Pre(p,t)$.

II.2. Programs

An extended state machine models the behavior of the identical processes. A Petri net models the behavior of the control net. P (respectively T) denotes the set of places (respectively transitions) of the whole Petri net. P_c (respectively P_p) is the set of places of the control net (respectively the extended state machine). The actions of synchronization are of two kinds: between several identical processes or between process(es) and the control manager.

Transitions common to the two nets represent synchronization actions.

Example 1 Rooms and users

Let us consider a problem of access to rooms. Several users cannot access simultaneously to the same room. All the keys open all the rooms. Petri net of Figure 1 models the system. Each user is in state idle since he decides to work. Then he is waiting for one key. Once he holds one key and if one room is free he enters it and gives the key back. To leave the room he must have a key to lock the door. He gives the key back at the same time as he leaves the room. The users are the processes.

The places of the control net are: keys and rooms. All the transitions, apart from the transition want-to-work, are synchronization transitions between the control net and one process. We fix the number of rooms and keys before computing the reachable states of the program.

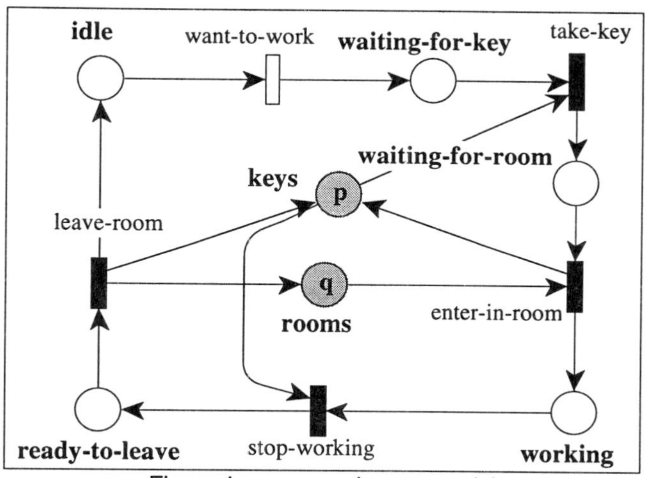

Figure 1: rooms and users model

III. Symbolic markings

Markings associate with each place an integer that represents the number of tokens it contains. They are not suitable to consider states of parameterized programs since the number of identical processes is unknown. For some places, we only know the minimum number of tokens they contain. To this purpose we define symbolic markings. They represent infinite sets of markings of instantiated programs. A symbolic marking represents markings that enable the same transitions.

III.1. Symbolic markings

The key point of the representation of a symbolic marking is to associate an integer and a relational operator "=" or "≥" with each place. The intended meaning is:

- if "= x" is associated with a place, then exactly x processes are in this place,
- if "≥ x" is associated with a place, then at least x processes are in this place.

To ensure that a symbolic marking represents only markings that enable the same transitions, we define a function Limit. It associates with each place the maximum number of tokens necessary for the firing of all the transitions. This function computes the maximum value to which we may have to compare the marking of each place.

Definition 5 Limit function

$\forall p \in P$, Limit(p) = MAX(Pre(p,t)), $t \in T$.

We use the function Limit to define symbolic markings. If we do not know the exact number of tokens in a place p the integer associated with this place must be greater or equal to Limit(p). We will explain in Section III.2 why this condition is sufficient to ensure that a symbolic marking represents only markings that enable the same transitions. As the control process is not parameterized, we associate the operator "=" with each of its places.

Definition 6 Symbolic marking

sm = <OP, M> is a symbolic marking with:

- OP is an application from P to {"=", "≥"}
- M is an application from P to $\mathbb{N}$,
- $\forall p \in P_C$, sm.OP(p) = "=",
- $\forall p \in P$, (1)
  if sm.M(p) < Limit(p) then sm.OP(p) = "=".

Notation

{p sm.OP(p) sm.M(p) / $p \in P$} denotes a symbolic marking sm. We omit the places such that sm.M(p) = 0 and sm.OP(p) = "=".

We note set[sm] the set of markings represented by sm.

Definition 7 Set of markings

A symbolic marking sm represents a marking m if an only if m fulfills the relations expressed by the functions sm.OP and sm.M. A symbolic marking sm contains a marking m, m ∈ set[sm], if and only if:

$\forall p \in P$, if sm.OP(p) = "=" then m(p) = sm.M(p)
else m(p) ≥ sm.M(p).

A symbolic marking represents markings of an instantiated program only if the number of identical processes is greater than a bound. This bound corresponds to the minimum number of processes necessary to respect the conditions expressed by the symbolic markings.

Definition 8 Bound associated with a symbolic marking

Let sm be a symbolic marking then $B(sm) = \sum_{p \in P_p} sm.M(p)$

Property 1

Let PP be a program instantiated with n, M the set of possible markings of PP and sm a symbolic marking, set[sm] ∩ M ≠ Ø if and only if $n \geq B(sm)$.

Example 2 Symbolic markings

The symbolic marking {idle ≥ 1, waiting-for-key ≥ 1, keys = p, rooms = q} represents markings of programs with at least two processes. If the program is instantiated with one process, this process cannot be in state idle and waiting-for-key simultaneously.

To symbolically execute parallel programs, it is essential to be able to compare two symbolic markings. The two relations we define, inclusion and inferiority, are partial relations. They both apply to the sets of markings represented by the symbolic markings.

Definition 9 Inclusion

Let sm and sm' be two symbolic markings, sm is included in sm', sm ⊆ sm', iff:

- ∀m ∈ set[sm], m ∈ set[sm'].

Definition 10 Superiority

Let sm and sm' be two symbolic markings, sm is greater than sm', sm ≥ sm', iff:

- ∀m ∈ set[sm], ∃m' ∈ set[sm'], m ≥ m',
- ∀m' ∈ set[sm'], ∃m ∈ set[sm], m ≥ m'.

The algorithms to test the two relations compare the operators and integers associated with each place. We present them in [17].

III.2. Enabled transitions

We now define the enabling of a transition and we prove that a symbolic marking enables the same transition as all the markings it represents.

Definition 11 Enabling of a transition

Let sm be a symbolic marking and t a transition, sm enables t, sm[t>, iff:

∀p ∈ P, sm.M(p) ≥ Pre(p,t) or sm.OP(p) = "≥".

The definition of a symbolic marking ensures that if sm.M(p) < Pre(p,t) then sm.OP(p) = "=". Therefore, if sm.OP(p) = "≥", we are sure that sm.M(p) ≥ Pre(p,t) for each t. As each marking m represented by sm is such that m(p) ≥ sm.M(p), we obtain m(p) ≥ Pre(p,t). This condition ensures that a symbolic marking enables a transition only if all the markings it represents enable the transition. If sm represents a marking such that m(p) < Pre(p,t), we are sure that sm.M(p) = m(p) and sm.OP(p) = "=". Each marking m represented by sm is such that m(p) = sm.M(p). This condition ensures that if a marking represented by a symbolic one does not enable a transition, all the markings represented by the symbolic one do so.

Property 2

Let sm be a symbolic marking and t a transition:

- if ∃m ∈ set[sm] and m[t> then sm[t>,
- if ∃m ∈ set[sm] and m does not enable t then sm does not enable t.

IV. Symbolic execution

As all the markings represented by the same symbolic markings enable the same transitions, it is interesting to be able to study simultaneously their evolution. This is what we call symbolic execution. We do not represent the execution from a marking but from a set of markings.

IV.1. General symbolic markings

We introduce the notion of general symbolic markings to simplify the symbolic firing rule. The firing of a transition may lead to a general symbolic marking. They are less restrictive than symbolic markings. General symbolic markings gather markings regarding the places where the tokens are. They do not take into account the enabling of transitions. There is no relation between the Limit function and the operator associated with a place. We suppress the condition (1) of definition 6. We can split each symbolic marking into a finite number of disjoint symbolic markings.

Definition 12 Splitting up

Let gsm be a general symbolic marking and p a place such that gsm.M(p) < Limit(p) and gsm.OP(p) = "≥". We split up gsm into gsm_0, ..., gsm_n (n = Limit(p)-gsm.M(p)) where:

- ∀p' ≠ p, ∀i, 0 ≤ i ≤ n, gsm_i.M(p') = gsm.M(p') and gsm_i.OP(p') = gsm.OP(p'),
- ∀i, 0 ≤ i < n, gsm_i.M(p) = gsm.M(p) + i and gsm_i.OP(p) = "=", (the number of processes in place p is less than Limit(p)),
- gsm_n.M(p) = Limit(p), gsm_n.OP(p) = "≥" (the number of processes in place p is greater than Limit(p)).

We apply the same procedure to the gsm_i until we compute only symbolic markings.

Property 3

- The result of the splitting up of a general symbolic marking is unique.
- At each step of the splitting up, we compute only disjoint sets of markings.
- A general symbolic marking represents the same set of markings as the union of the sets represented by the symbolic markings obtained after the splitting up.

Example 3 Splitting up of a general symbolic marking

Let gsm = {p ≥ 1, q ≥ 1, r = 2}, Limit(p) = 2 and Limit(q) = 1. gsm.M(p) < Limit(p) and gsm.OP(p) = "≥". We split up gsm into the two following symbolic markings:

sm_0 = {p = 1, q ≥ 1, r = 2}, sm_1 = {p ≥ 2, q ≥ 1, r = 2}.

IV.2. Symbolic firing rule

The symbolic firing rule is similar to the firing rule of Petri nets. We apply the modifications to the integers associated with the places. It may lead to a general symbolic marking.

Definition 13 Symbolic firing rule

Let sm be a symbolic marking and t a transition, sm enables t and the reached set of markings gsm', sm[t>gsm' is computed as follows:

- $\forall p \in P$,
  gsm'.M(p) = sm.M(p) - Pre(p,t) + Post(p,t),
  gsm'.OP(p) = sm.OP(p),
- gsm' is split up.

The general symbolic marking gsm' represents exactly the markings reachable from sm. The symbolic markings $sm'_0 \ldots sm'_n$ are the result of the splitting up of gsm'. The markings m belonging to set[sm] that lead to a marking of set[sm'_i] are such that: if $sm'_i.OP(p)$ = "=" then $m(p) = sm'_i.M(p) + Pre(p,t) - Post(p,t)$ else $m(p) \geq sm'_i.M(p) + Pre(p,t) - Post(p,t)+1$.

Property 4

Let sm be a symbolic marking, gsm a general symbolic marking and t a transition. gsm is split up into $sm_0, \ldots, sm_n$. If sm[t>gsm then:

- $\forall m \in$ set[sm], $\exists m'$, m[t>m' and $\exists i$, $0 \leq i \leq n$, $m' \in$ set[gsm_i],
- $\forall i$, $0 \leq i \leq n$, $\forall m' \in$ set[gsm_i], $\exists m \in$ set[sm], m[t>m'.

Example 4 Reachable symbolic markings

We consider the Petri net of Figure 1 and the symbolic marking {idle ≥ 1, waiting-for-key ≥ 1, keys = p, rooms = q}. The firing of transition want-to-work leads to the general symbolic marking {idle ≥ 0, waiting-for-key ≥ 1, keys = p, rooms = q}. It is split up into two symbolic markings represented by Figure 2. On the transitions we represent the conditions verified by the markings that lead to each component of the splitting up.

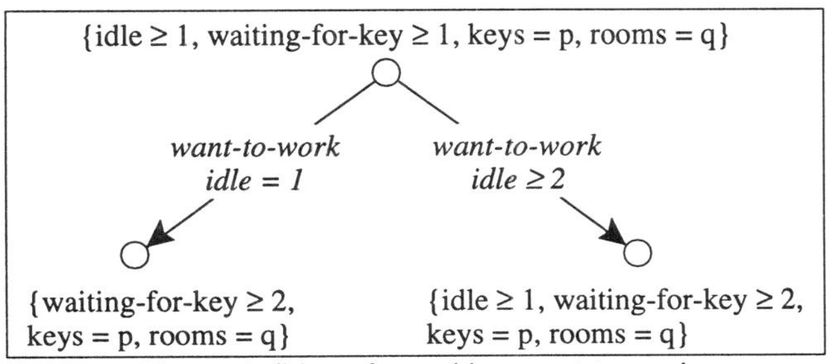

Figure 2: firing of transition want-to-work

The symbolic marking {waiting-for-key ≥ 2, keys = p, rooms = q} represents all the markings reached after the firing of transition want-to-work when one process is in place idle and at least one process is in place waiting-for-key. The symbolic marking {idle ≥ 1, waiting-for-key ≥ 2, keys = p, rooms = q} represents the states reached after the firing of transition want-to-work when the place idle holds at least two processes. This last execution represents an execution of programs instantiated by at least three processes.

IV.3. Exhaustive executions

During an exhaustive execution, we compute all the reachable markings. An execution may be exhaustive only if the set of reachable markings is finite. Some infinite executions are inherent in the program. The symbolic firing rule introduces some others.

Usually, the marking computed with a firing rule represents the state changes of processes and resources. With the symbolic firing rule the decrease of processes in some places may not be represented. This may introduce infinite sequences of symbolic markings. We may avoid these infinite sequences if we are able to represent it with a finite number of symbolic markings. This possibility depends on features of the sequence of transitions. We present here such sequences, the "state change for one process" sequences.

Example 5 Infinite sequence

From the symbolic marking {idle ≥ 1, keys = p, rooms = q} the firing of transition want-to-work leads to two symbolic markings including {idle ≥ 1, waiting-for-key = 1, keys = p, rooms = q}. It is greater than its predecessor. If we iterate the sequence we obtain the symbolic markings of Figure 3.

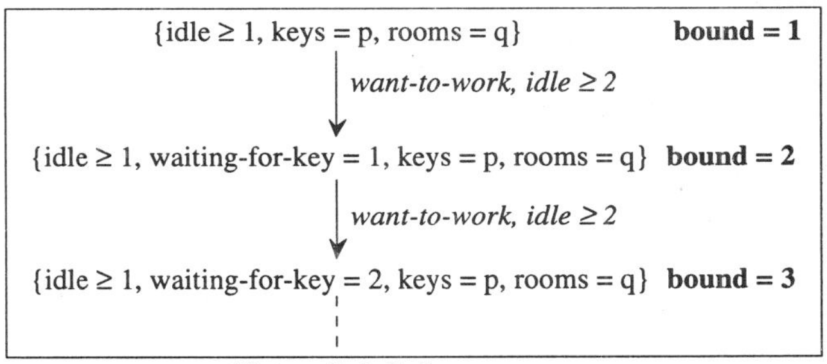

Figure 3: infinite sequence

The reached symbolic markings do not represent that after the execution of action want-to-work there is one process less in place idle. The only trace of this fact is the increase of the bound. A single symbolic marking can represent all the symbolic markings reached after the iteration of sequence want-to-work:

{idle ≥ 1, waiting-for-key ≥ 1, keys = p, rooms = q}.

A "state change for one process" sequence has the characteristic that after its execution only one process has moved from a source place to a target place. All the other processes and resources return to or stay in the same state as before the execution. If the execution of the program does not represent the decrease of the number of processes in the source state, we may have an infinite sequence of symbolic markings. Each of them differs from its predecessor in the number of processes in the target place. It is increased by one. All these symbolic markings can be represented by a single one that represents all the possible distributions of the processes initially in the source place between the source and the target places.

We now give the formal definition of a "state change for one process" sequence.

Notation We extend the applications Pre and Post to sequences of transitions. Let p be a place, $s = t_1 \ldots t_m$ a sequence of transitions.

$$Pre(p,s) = \sum_{i=1}^{m} Pre(p,t_i),\ Post(p,s) = \sum_{i=1}^{m} Post(p,t_i).$$

Definition 14 "State change for one process" sequence

Let $s = t_1 \ldots t_m$ be a sequence of transitions, s is a "state change for one process sequence" iff:

- $\exists p_{source} \in P_p$, $Post(p_{source},s) - Pre(p_{source},s) = -1$,
- $\exists p_{target} \in P_p$, $Post(p_{target},s) - Pre(p_{target},s) = 1$,
- $\forall p \neq p_{source}, p_{target}$, $p \in P$, $Post(p,s) - Pre(p,s) = 0$,
- $\forall i \leq m$, $\forall p \in P_p$,

$$\sum_{j=1}^{i} Post(p,t_j) - \sum_{j=1}^{i} Pre(p,t_j) \geq -1.$$

To execute symbolically a model, we apply the following procedure. We denote S the set of symbolic markings whose successors must be computed.

```
S = {initial symbolic marking}
While S is not empty do
    sm is an element of S,
    S = S - {sm},
    If sm is not included in one of its ancestors
    then
        If sm is greater than one of its ancestors
        then
            We examine the sequence that links sm to
            its ancestor.
            If it is not a "state change for one process"
            sequence
            then
                We inform the user that the execution
                will be infinite
            else
                If the integer associated with the place
                ptarget is less than Limit(ptarget)
                then
                    We continue
                else
                    We modify the symbolic marking by
                    changing to "≥" the operator
                    associated with the target place.
        We compute the successor symbolic markings
        of sm and we add them to S.
    else
        The execution from sm will give no new
        information.
```

When we have no new symbolic marking to examine, we have performed an exhaustive execution. The symbolic markings that represent the reachable markings and executions of the instantiated programs are in finite number.

The following theorem ensures that the symbolic execution is correct. We give the proof in [17].

Theorem

- A symbolic marking, modified because of the execution of a "state change for one process" sequence, represents exactly all the markings, with at least $Limit(p_{source})$ processes in the source state, reachable by the iteration of the "state change for one process" sequence.
- If the symbolic execution is finite, we compute exactly all the reachable states and sequences of the instantiated programs.

Example 6 Part of a symbolic execution

The following tree represents a part of the symbolic execution of the model of Figure 1 when there are 2 keys and 3 rooms and all the processes are initially in state idle. We only consider transitions want-to-work and take-key.

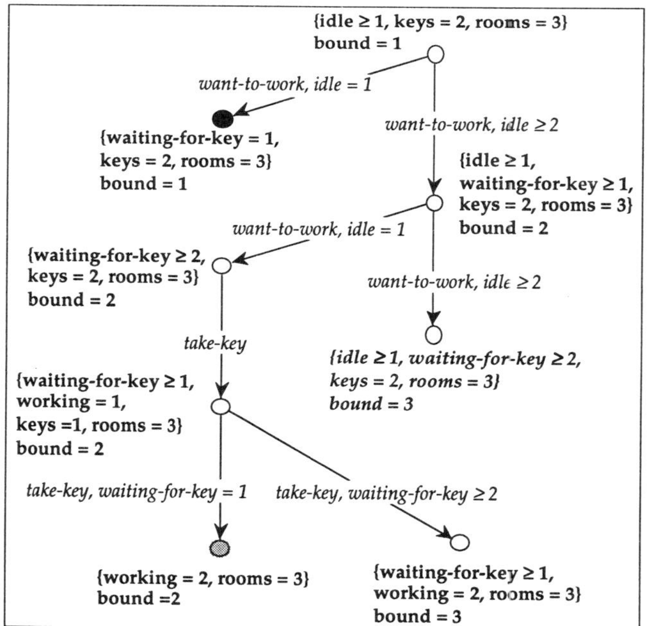

Figure 4: part of the symbolic execution

As the number of processes in each state is known, the executions from the black (respectively gray) node are executions of the programs with exactly one (respectively two) process(es). The two successors of the initial node result from the splitting up of a general symbolic marking and from the execution of a "state change for one process" sequence. The symbolic marking {idle ≥ 1, waiting-for-key ≥ 2, keys = 2, rooms = 3} is included in its predecessor. Its study will give no new results. As the bound associated with the symbolic marking {waiting-for-key ≥ 1, working = 2, rooms = 3} is 3, the symbolic executions from it will represent executions of programs instantiated with at least three processes. To study the programs with one or two processes, we have to compute the markings reachable from the black and gray nodes.

The symbolic execution of the model gives an exhaustive one. The whole graph gives the following information:

- programs with less than 7 processes have particular behaviors.
- with more than 4 processes the program deadlocks when 3 processes are working, 2 are waiting for a room and all the others, if any, are waiting for a key. The programs with fewer processes have no deadlock.

The whole symbolic graph has 80 states and 140 edges. The graph of the program with 7 processes has 110 states and 227 edges. To detect that a deadlock appears when the number of processes is greater than 4, if no symbolic method is used, it is necessary to build the reachability graphs of the programs with 1 to 5 processes. This will not assure that a deadlock exists for all programs with more than 7 processes. The five graphs represent 171 nodes and 373 edges.

V. Conclusion

We propose an algorithm to symbolically execute parallel programs with a finite but undefined number of processes. This algorithm allows us to execute, at the same time and by the same computations, an infinite number of instantiations of a parallel program. We have exhibit conditions that ensure that an exhaustive execution is possible. In this case, we can build a graph used for the verification of temporal logic formulas [18]. The number of computed symbolic markings is limited by the size of the memory. It will be interesting to see how to reduce the space used in particular with the BDDs and its extensions [3]. We have implemented and integrated the execution algorithm in the AMI framework [5]. The Petri nets are described through the user interface Macao.

We have identified a type of sequences that allow us to aggregate the information of the executions. Further works will deal with the definition of other types of sequences.

As an integer represents the minimum number of tokens in a place, we cannot study all the programs with the symbolic markings we have defined. For some parallel programs, the aggregation of the information requires the definition of new symbolic markings. This is the case when the possible executions depend on the parity of the number of processes or on relations between the number of processes and the number of resources. An advantage of our restriction is that the operations on the symbolic markings are easy and fully automated.

Another extension of our work will be the consideration of more complex programs. In [16] we have presented a model that allows one to distinguish dynamically the behavior of one process. We describe in [17] the adaptation of the symbolic execution algorithm.

It will be important to study the effects of the extensions of the exhaustive execution algorithms on the possibility to verify temporal logic formulas.

References

1. Balarin F., Sangiovanni-Vincentelli A.L., "*On the Automatic Computation of Network Invariants*", proceedings of Computer Aided Verification: 6th International Conference, CAV'94, Stanford, CA, David L. Dill (Eds.), LNCS 818, Springer-Verlag, pp 234-246, 1994.
2. Bougé L., "*On the Existence of Symmetric Algorithms to Find Leaders in Networks of Communicating Sequential Processes*", Acta Informatica, vol. 25, pp 179-201, 1988.
3. Bryant R.E., "*Symbolic Boolean Manipulation with Ordered Binary Decision Diagrams*", ACM Computing Surveys, vol. 24, n°3, pp 293-318, September, 1992.
4. Clarke E.M., Grumberg O., "*Avoiding The State Explosion Problem in Temporal Logic Model Checking Algorithms*", Proceedings of the 6th ACM Symposium on Principles of Distributed, Vancouver, British Columbia, pp 244-303, 1987.
5. CPN-AMI, "*Reference manual, 1.2 version*"1994.
6. Dijkstra E.W., "*Solution of a Problem in Concurrent Programming Control*", Communications of the ACM, vol. 8:9, September, pp 569, 1965.
7. Dijkstra E.W., Scholten C.S., "*Termination Detection for Diffusing Computations*", Information Processing Letters, vol. 11:1, August, pp 1-4, 1980.
8. German S., Sistla A.P., "*Reasoning about Systems with Many Processes*", JACM, vol. 39, pp 675-735, 1992.
9. Kurshan R.P., McMillan K., "*A Structural Induction Theorem for Processes*", Proceedings of the Eighth Annual ACM Symposium on Principles of Distributed Computing, Alberta, Canada, pp 239-247, 1989.
10. Lamport L., "*A new Solution of Dijkstra's Coucurrent Programming Problem*", Commications of ACM, vol. 17, n°8, pp 453-455, August, 1974.
11. Pease M., Shostak R., Lamport L., "*Reaching Agreement in the Presence of Faults*", Journal of ACM, vol. 27,n°2, pp 228-234, April, 1980.
12. Raynal M., "*Algorithms for Mutual Exclusion*", *Ed.* North Oxford Academic Publishers Ltd, 1986.
13. Reisig W., "*EATCS Monographs on Theoretical Computer*", *Ed.* Science, Springer Publ. Company, 1985.
14. Rho J.K., Somenzi F., "*Automatic generation of networks invariants for the verification of iterative sequential systems*", Proceedings of the 5th International Conference, CAV'93, LNCS 697, Elounda, Greece, pp 123-137, 1993.

15. Shtadler Z., Grumberg O., "*Network Grammars, Communication Behaviors and Automatic Verification*", Proceedings of the International Workshop on Automatic Verification Methods for Finite State Systems, LNCS 407, Grenoble, France, pp 152-165, 1989.
16. Vernier I., "*Specification And Verification of Parametrized Parallel Programs*", Proceedings of the 8th International Symposium on Computer and Information Sciences, Istanbul, Turkey, pp 622-625, 1993.
17. Vernier I., "*Graphe symbolique paramétré de réseaux de Petri et Logique temporelle*", thèse de Université Paris 6, 1994.
18. Vernier I., "*Symbolic Verification of Parallel Programs*", IBP - MASI report, n° 95/03, 1995.
19. Wolper P., Lovinfosse V., "*Verifying Properties of Large Sets of Processes with Network Invariants*", Proceedings of the Proc.International Workshop on Automatic Verification Methods for Finite State Systems, LNCS 407, Grenoble, France, pp 68-80, 1989.

❖ **SESSION 7** ❖

Object-Oriented Programming

Chair

P. Kacksuk

DO-OPEN: a Distributed Object-Oriented Programming ENvironment★

Andrea Omodeo [1], Matteo Pugassi [2], Nello Scarabottolo [3]

1 ENEL, Centro Ricerca di Automatica — via Volta 1, I20093 Cologno Monzese (MI), ITALY
ph.: +39-2-7224.5760, fax: +39-2-7224.5525, e-mail: omodeo@cra.enel.it

2 Dipartimento di Elettronica e Informazione, Politecnico di Milano — piazza L. da Vinci 32, I20133 Milano, ITALY
ph.: +39-2-2399.3400, fax: +39-2-2399.3411, e-mail: pugassi@elet.polimi.it

3 Dipartimento di Scienze dell'Ingegneria, Università degli Studi di Modena — via Campi 213, I41100 Modena, ITALY
ph.: +39-59-378519, fax: +39-59-370040, e-mail: scarabot@dsi.unimo.it

Abstract

This paper discusses the key aspects and presents the preliminary version of an Object-Oriented programming environment, designed to support distributed applications in heterogeneous, networked UNIX systems.
Main characteristics of this environment are:

- *usage of UNIX-based industry-standard software tools and components;*
- *definition of a simple, C++-like syntax, to facilitate usability and readability of the distributed code;*
- *implementation of a light-weight run-time support, adopting PVM as the base engine.*

The paper outlines the rationale behind the design of such a programming environment, and discusses in details the solution adopted to remotise interacting objects. In particular, a simple solution for allowing parallel execution of remotised objects is presented.
Performance evaluations are currently being carried on.

1. Introduction

In the recent past, distributed computing started attracting an ever increasing interest from the computer scientists and technicians community, as shown by the number of research and development activities presented in literature. Among the main driving forces of this phenomenon, it is easy to identify the following ones.

1. The distribution of computing power associated with the success of personal computers and workstations: the favorable cost/performance ratio of small but powerful computers suggests to increase their involvement in the global computation activities.
2. The widespreading of high-performance computer networks: their presence in almost all sites where personal computing has been adopted allows to design and to effectively implement computer programming models — like the well known *client-server* computing — where a global activity is made by several programs, running on different machines and (even heavily) interacting among each other through the network.
3. The presence of a huge amount of "wasted" computing power: today's personal computers and workstations are able to sustain hundreds of MIPS and MFLOPS, very seldom used during daily activities (e.g., word processing, program coding and debugging, ...thinking!) of their users; this suggested to define techniques and supports for programming a distributed, networked system as a distributed-memory parallel machine, where a given computation is partitioned among several processing elements and carried on in parallel, and where data exchanges among these partitions are allowed by messages, delivered to the various processing elements by the interconnection structure.

The work described in this paper addresses in particular this last point. Its main goal is — in fact — the definition of a programming environment, supporting the production and the maintenance of high-quality industrial software for distributed systems, with particular attention to compute-intensive applications (like simulation of electric power generation and distribution plants [18], emulation of large neural networks, etc.).

To be more precise, the rationale behind the research and development activities here described is constituted by the following considerations:

- as already outlined, distributed computing is becoming also in industrial environments a challenging opportunity for enhancing computing performances without large hardware investments;

★ This work has been supported by ENEL, the Italian Power Company, under research contract CRA 71/94.

- the *client-server* programming model — even very interesting — is not enough flexible to deal with the addressed application environments, mainly due to its intrinsic point-to-point, star-shaped structure, where several independent users are expected to ask a central point to provide some form of service;
- the management (i.e., the design, the implementation and especially the maintenance) of large computing programs requires the adoption of methodologies and techniques capable of supporting team work, thus enforcing problem partitioning, information hiding, modular programming, clear identification of interfaces; in this perspective, the Object-Oriented (from here on, O-O) approach is nowadays a "must", since objects constitute one of the best ways for modularizing a program, and object interactions can be spontaneously mapped upon message exchanges;
- the "vitality" of programs, whose expected lifetime spans over several years, imposes the largest possible adoption of *de jure* and *de facto* standards in terms of design paradigms, programming languages, run-time supports, in order to avoid obsolescence; this requires in particular to carefully consider the maintenance needs and the portability characteristics of the software development environment itself, for its impact on both the programs and the programmers.

The paper is organized as follows:

- section 2 locates the present work in the panorama of O-O development environments for distributed computing systems, present in the literature;
- section 3 defines the objectives of the approach here proposed, and highlights the main characteristics of the adopted tools and supports;
- section 4 discusses the design criteria of DO-OPEN, detailing through code examples its usage and its behavior;
- section 5 reports some considerations about the limits of the present version of DO-OPEN, showing the most important developments being undertaken.

2. Analysis of related works

Following the considerations made above, a first step we activated has been an analysis of the most widely known O-O programming environments for distributed systems, presented in the literature and possibly available as public domain software.

2.1 Arjuna

A first environment we considered is the Arjuna system [4][5], a Distributed Object programming environment developed at the University of Newcastle. Arjuna objects are declared in a text file following a syntax very close to C++, and are then translated to C++ code by a preprocessor.

A first characteristic of the Arjuna system is its client/server programming paradigm: in fact, each class declaration generates multiple C++ files: some to be linked with the user code at the client side and some to produce the remote object server program.

The system gives great importance to data integrity, assuming that the "real" object state is always the one recorded on persistent storage: the in-memory copy is seen only as a temporary value [6][7]. This could impose a great speed penalty on systems where data integrity is not so necessary.

Moreover, Arjuna provides data distribution and remote execution of methods, but not parallel execution: the caller of a method is suspended until the remote process finishes the invoked job.

Finally, Arjuna is — up to now — available only on a limited set of UNIX architectures, mainly because it adopts a custom communication layer.

2.2 Mentat

A second environment we studied is the Mentat system [8][9][10][11], the result of a parallel computing project at the University of Virginia.

In a way very similar to Arjuna, Mentat uses a C++-like syntax to define distributed objects. One significant distinction of Mentat is its automatic parallelization: the caller of a method can continue its execution until it reaches a statement whose execution requires the method return value.

From our point of view, one of the limits of Mentat is that its preprocessor directly invokes the C++ compiler on the intermediate code, which is not supposed to be user-inspectable (in fact, even for very simple programs, the intermediate code is huge and difficult to understand/maintain).

We judge this a great drawback because the C++ syntax is still evolving, causing the non-complete compatibility of the currently available C++ compilers. On a heterogeneous computer network, a programmer is forced to rely on heterogeneous C++ compilers, or to use freely available multiplatform compilers like the GNU g++. Unfortunately, the g++ version supported by Mentat is very old and the Mentat team plans to stop supporting it in the future.

Moreover, as for Arjuna, the Mentat system adopts a custom communication layer.

2.3 PO

The third environment we deeply analyzed is the PO system [12][13], an experimental programming environment developed at the Università di Bologna and operating on the Transputer-based Meiko Computing Surface machine.

PO defines a new language to give O-O properties to user-defined methods written in C. Like in Mentat, parallel execution is granted by delaying the synchronization between a method and its caller. Differently from Mentat, this synchronization is explicitly defined by a programming construct named "future variable": this means that no automatic parallelization is performed by the compiler, and the programmer has all duties and visibility upon the interactions among parallel objects. Of the three systems, only PO allows concurrent execution of two methods on the same object, as long as they respect a set of user-defined constraints.

The problems of the PO approach are the definition of a non-standard language and the complete change in programming style imposed by the use of active objects. In a PO program, each object method is written in standard C but the corresponding method invocation requires a special syntax.

All PO objects are active (i. e. capable of running in parallel with other objects) and this makes a great difference with respect to the conventional O-O languages where execution is strictly sequential. This implies a rethinking of all the internal organization of an application before porting it to PO in order to obtain proper execution.

The porting of the PO environment to PVM is under development at the Università di Modena, and preliminary results are discussed in [14].

2.4 Do-PVM

Do-PVM[15] was an experimental extension to PVM, written by one of the authors of the PVM environment.

We have not considered this system for our needs, because it provides a passive-object programming environment, consisting only in the capability of transparently sharing the internal state of the object.

It is impossible for a Do-PVM task to activate a new computing thread by using this mechanism.

3. Problem Statement

As already said, the main goal of DO-OPEN (Distributed Object-Oriented Programming ENvironment) is to provide a development system for distributed applications, adopting the O-O programming model and designed to emphasize the usage of standard platforms and tools, in order to maximize the portability, the usability and the "vitality" of the DO-OPEN environment itself. The above goal led to the following three main choices.

First, at the programming language level, we consider fundamental to adhere to a *de facto* standard, in order to guarantee a significant lifetime to the environment and — even more important — to plan a gradual, spontaneous conversion of skills of the programmers. We decided to adopt C++ as *the* DO-OPEN programming language for the following reasons:

1. UNIX is the operating system most widely available on distributed computing systems;
2. C is by far the most widely adopted programming language by UNIX users;
3. C++ [16] is — as well known — the O-O version of C, where a C-like programming style is still possible (thus allowing a gradual conversion to its O-O features).

A significant support to this decision comes from the ANSI activities, currently undergoing for the standardization of the C++ language [17] in the same way already used for C.

For similar reasons (namely, diffusion on UNIX environments and international resonance) the PVM (Parallel Virtual Machine: see [1][2][3]) message passing support for parallel programming in distributed processing environments has been adopted. In fact, its simplicity and its availability have imposed PVM as a *de facto* standard for parallel programming on distributed systems as well as on MIMD massively parallel computers.

Finally, it has been decided to adopt a C++-like syntax for defining the basic DO-OPEN statements, and to design a very simple translator for converting a DO-OPEN source program into a C++ compilable file. This decision has the twofold effect of facilitating the usage of the DO-OPEN statements and of minimizing the amount of code which may require to be partially rewritten in case of major changes in the programming language and/or run-time support.

3.1 C++ and Object-Oriented Programming

O-O programming has now evolved into a practical way of structuring software projects as a collection of interacting objects. The well known key features of O-O systems are:

- **encapsulation:** is the feature stating that users of a class are allowed to use only its published interface. Encapsulation is the O-O name for *information hiding* and is the mean for formally specifying the boundaries among program modules. As a result, the implementor of a class is allowed to change the internal working of the class without affecting the external class behavior (thus, the remaining part of the application code depending on such a class). The user interface of a class is in the form of public callable procedures named *methods*;
- **inheritance:** is the capability of defining a new class

based on the features of an already existing class. The resulting (derived) class can then specialize the base class behavior to adapt it to a special case. Given a set of required class definitions, a programmer can implement the common features in a base class (e.g. class `container`) and then derive from this base class the specialized ones (e.g. class `list` or class `binary_tree`). Inheritance is a key feature for code reuse: if a suitable base class is available, the programmer can derive from it all the needed features and enhance (or even delete) part of the existing interface to get a new class definition;
- **polymorphism:** an object belonging to a derived class is also an object of the base class (e.g. a `binary_tree` is still a `container`). This feature is very important when some parts of the user code are aware of the behavior of the base class only, but they are actually working on objects of the derived class (e.g. a call to `a->print()` translates to printing a `container` or a `binary_tree` depending on the run-time value of `a`).

O-O programming has been based in DO-OPEN upon the C++ language, mainly due to its availability on UNIX platforms. As it is well known, the C++ programming language is an extension (or a superset) of C, allowing the declaration of classes and methods while remaining source-code and object-code compatible with C.

Object-code compatibility allows to use existing C libraries also in C++ programs. Source-code compatibility has the advantage of allowing C programmers to learn the new language gradually and to convert their programs at the same pace. Even better, they can convert only parts of existing programs, since C and C++ statements are intermixable.

As a proof of the above consideration, it must be noticed that, even if PVM is written in C, we have been able to use it in C++ without modification, and this is true for every other library written for C.

However, source-code compatibility is also the reason of many criticism to the language, because C++ programs are given the chance of using C constructs and avoiding the stricter O-O rules. At this proposal, DO-OPEN uses only a subset of the functionality of C++ to define PVM tasks in terms of objects, ensuring that the method invocations are cross-checked during compilation in order to avoid programming errors or lost messages.

4. Distributed programming with PVM

PVM is one of the most widely used environments for writing message-passing distributed programs in a networked environment. It is the main result of an ongoing research project on Heterogeneous Network Computing, sponsored by Oak Ridge National Laboratory, the University of Tennessee, Emory University and Carnegie Mellon University [1] [2] [3].

PVM is a message passing tool, meaning that programmers must think of interprocess communications as a series of messages exchanged among active processes. PVM processes can reside on UNIX hosts, communicating via the standard TCP/IP network facilities, or on dedicated processors of a MIMD multiprocessor machine, where they use the native communication layer. The PVM runtime support takes care of delivering and queuing of messages, as well as of any conversion required if the involved hosts use incompatible binary representations of data.

Other PVM features include the capability of dynamically starting slave tasks on remote hosts, with a minimal (but user-extensible) support for static load balancing.

It should be noticed that the only aspect guaranteed by PVM is the ordered delivery of messages exchanged among tasks distributed in the network. In fact, it is left to the programmer to deal with the correctness of exchanged messages: the coordination of send and receive actions can then be very difficult when dealing with large projects involving a huge quantity of different messages.

Also, PVM does not enforce any form of type checking on data exchanged by messages: for instance it is possible to send an integer variable and try to receive it as a float without compile-time error detection.

The need for formal specification of inter-task communication interfaces can be solved if we base our module definitions on the O-O programming paradigm.

4.1 An introduction to DO-OPEN

The aim of the DO-OPEN environment is to make available to distributed programmers a formal tool for defining task interfaces. DO-OPEN tasks are defined as instances of classes written in a custom syntax similar to C++.

It must be noticed that this custom syntax is due to the availability for the first DO-OPEN prototype of a simple LL(1)-based parser.

These class definitions are used to generate all the communication interfaces among tasks, ensuring that they are fully coherent. Obviously, the programmer must provide the proper implementation methods for the object, as well as the client code for invoking these methods. DO-OPEN-enabled programs still have a C++ programming syntax, so it is possible to compile and test DO-OPEN classes with a common C++ compiler and then enable parallelism on these classes.

5. DO-OPEN implementation

A transparent remotisation of a user class across a parallel machine (i. e., allowing objects of this class to be instantiated on remote hosts) requires definition of the following two agents:

1. a "mirror" class (from here on called *stub* class) reproducing on the local host the same interface of the original one;
2. a "wrapper" task, embedding each remote instantiation of the original, real class and dealing with all messages exchanges required to properly handle method invocations.

Each local stub object receives all the object methods invocations and must react like the real object in order to present the same programming interface. Then, it has to transmit each request to the remote object wrapper.

The wrapper is the receiver of the stub messages: it must decode them and then call the methods of its embedded object. Then it packs the results and sends them back to the stub object, that will deliver the results themselves to the user code. Note that it is possible to share the same object instance among several client tasks: this implies that a single wrapper can serve several stubs, by serializing their requests.

With the agents defined above at the two sides of the network, it is not difficult to obtain a real transparent distribution of many objects around the network without user intervention. In order to obtain this result, we have defined a simple C++-like language able to describe public methods, private methods and the private data of the to-be-remotised class. The user must provide only the real class code and the class description: with this minimal information our translator builds automatically all the necessary files.

Due to the C++-likeness of the specification language, it is not difficult for the user to remotise a known working class by only editing the existing C++ class definition. The main advantages of this approach are the following:

- this grammar contains only the class definition part of C++, so the translation phase is very fast, allowing for a reduced development cycle time;
- due to the simple grammar we defined (only class definition statements, with restrictions on accepted data types), coding errors are very difficult, thus enhancing correct coding of distributed applications.

Particular care has been paid to deal with the fact that C++ allows to access the private memory of an object from outside, as well as to pass between objects references to common memory areas. In order to enforce the O-O programming approach and to avoid dealing with common memory accesses in a distributed environment, we decided to forbid in DO-OPEN passing data by reference.

5.1 Implementation details

The creation of the stub object and the remote wrapper involves the generation of the following four files:

1. the local stub object definition: a C++ header file describing the stub class;
2. the local stub object implementation: the C++ code that implements the stub class;
3. the remote message wrapper: the C++ code that receives stub messages and calls the real remote methods;
4. the real class definition: a C++ header file that is used during the real class compilation in order to verify the consistency between stub and remote classes.

As an example of DO-OPEN usage, we present a simple C++ class, implementing a stack, and we show how it can be converted to a remotely accessible class.

This class implements a simple integer stack that presents `push()`, `pop()` and `is_empty()` methods and has an internal buffer area and a stack index as private variables. A possible C++ definition of this stack class is the following:

```
class stack
{
   // class interface methods
public:
   // constructor to initialize an instance
   stack();
   // insert an int: return true if succesful
   bool push( int );
   // pop an integer
   int pop( void );
   // true if stack empty
   bool is_empty( void );
private:
   // private data declaration
   int data[10];                  // stack area
   int index;                     // stack index
};
```

To remotise the above class, the programmer must modify the class definition by inserting the suitable DO-OPEN keywords, necessary for the DO-OPEN translator to produce the four files listed above. The result of such a modification is listed here, with DO-OPEN keywords in boldface (note that — since the constructor will be automatically declared by the DO-OPEN translator — it has to be dropped from the class definition):

```
class stack
{
public_methods:
    // public methods declaration:
    // due to automatic void constructor declaration,
    // declaring class constructors is not allowed here
    bool push( int );
    int pop( void );
    bool is_empty( void );
private_variables:
    int data[10];
    int index;
};
```

This definition is the only thing the user must provide to remotise his/her class because the remotisation is independent from the real class implementation and depends only from the method parameters type. The C++ stub declaration required to remotise the previous example (i.e., the first file produced by the DO-OPEN translator) has the following aspect:

```
class stack
{
public:
    // constructor of the stub
    stack( void );
    // destructor of the stub
    ~stack( void );
    // method to connect the stub to the wrapper
    void connect( char * );
private:
    // PVM address of the wrapper
    int child_tid;
public:
    // original methods with modified return type
    token<bool> push( int );
    token<int> pop( void );
    token<bool> is_empty( void );
};
```

It must be noticed that — in the last code — the return types of the methods have been changed by using the DO-OPEN `token<>` types. As it will be discussed in section 5.2, this allows — in conjunction with the `future<>` data types — to parallelize execution of caller and called objects.

The second file produced by the DO-OPEN translator is the actual code implementing the stub. Using the DO-OPEN approach, the invocation of a remote method requires the following four steps:

a) creation of a unique ID to avoid erroneous receptions;
b) insertion of the parameters in the PVM buffer;
c) delivery of the PVM buffer to the object wrapper;
d) return the message handle to the caller.

For instance, the `push` method must become:

```
token<bool> stack::push( int do__param00 )
{
    int mesgid = MSG_METHOD(1)+ k_id;   // step a)
    pvm_initsend( PvmDataDefault );     // step b)
    DO_PACK( do__param00 );
    pvm_send( child_tid, mesgid );      // step c)
    return token<bool>( mesgid );       // step d)
}
```

and similarly for the `pop()` and `is_empty()` methods.

The DO_PACK functions are a set of functions able to insert a data type in the PVM buffer; in the present DO-OPEN version the system provides function implementations only for the simple data types (int, float, ...) but the user can provide functions for each structured data type, enabling their usage as arguments and return values of remote class methods invocation.

The remote class definition (i.e., the third file produced by the DO-OPEN translator) reproduces the original C++ class but it is based on the DO-OPEN syntax to enforce consistency verification:

```
class do_stack
{
public:
    // class interface methods
    // constructor of the remote instance
    do_stack();
    // destructor of the remote instance
    ~do_stack();
    // real implementation of "push" method
    bool push( int );
    // real implementation of "pop" method
    int pop( void );
    // real implementation of "is_empty" method
    bool is_empty( void );
    // private data declaration
private:
    int data[10];          // stack area
    int index;             // stack index
};
```

The fourth file generated by the DO-OPEN translator is the remote object wrapper implementation; it performs an infinite loop waiting for messages coming from the existing class stubs. The general structure of this file is listed here (for the sake of simplicity, the reception and the decoding of the incoming messages have been summarized as *`receive( requested_method )`*):

```
while ( true )
{
  receive( requested_method )
  // message calling a method
  switch ( requested_method )
  {
  case PUSH:
    // method parameter(s)
    int do_param00;
    // return value
    bool result;
    // receive parameter(s)
    DO_UNPACK( do_param00);
    // invoke method on embedded obj.
    result = object->push( do_param00 );
    // pack and send back the result.
    DO_PACK( result );
    pvm_send( stub, mesg_id );
    break;
  case POP:                    .....
  case IS_EMPTY:               .....
  }
}
```

5.2 Using a DO-OPEN class

In the following example, the remotised stack discussed in the previous section is used by an application code (again, modifications required to use remotised objects are listed in boldface):

```
void main()
{
  // declare the stub object
  stack s0;
  bool b;
  // connect to a remote stack named stack_instance_00
  s0.connect( "stack_instance_00" );
  cout << "Stack testing program\n";
  cout << "Stack is ";
  // test remote stack state
  if (s0.isempty()) cout << "empty\n";
  else cout << "not empty\n";
  // push a value in remote stack
  b = s0.push( 3 );
  cout << "Extracting value:\n";
  // pop a value from remote stack
  cout << s0.pop() << "\n";
}
```

It is worth noting that this program is identical to the one that would be used with the original class definition: the only added line is the invocation of the `connect()` method, which connects to (and eventually starts) a remote named object.

In the previous example, remotisation only (i. e., no parallelization) of an object has been achieved. In fact, without the declaration of `future<>` variables, the execution is strictly sequential because, after each method invocation, the caller is suspended waiting for the result. To enable parallel execution of remote methods it is necessary to modify the caller's code as follows:

```
void main()
{
  stack s0; // declare the stub object
  bool b;
  // declare a future int variable
  future<int> fi;
  // connect to a remote stack
  // named stack_instance_00
  s0.connect( "stack_instance_00" );
  cout << "Stack testing program\n";
  cout << "Stack is ";
  // test remote stack state
  if (s0.isempty())
    cout << "empty\n";
  else
    cout << "not empty\n";
  // push a value in remote stack
  b = s0.push( 3 );
  // get only a reference to result
  fi = s0.pop();
  ... // do something else while running in parallel
  ... // with the remote object
  // ask for the real result and wait until it arrives
  cout << fi << "\n";
}
```

Again, it is worth noting that, with only these few changes, a strictly synchronous program can be easily parallelized using only the normal C++ syntax, a simple class definition file and a light-weight library containing the run-time support routines. The concurrent execution is controlled by waiting or not waiting method results, because each remote method invocation which is not waited for activates a concurrent task running on PVM.

Using the value referred by a `future<>` variable produces the blocking reception of the expected value, synchronizing the receiver with the remote object.

6. Future developments

In the present version of DO-OPEN, the most used O-O feature is encapsulation, as a mean for formally representing inter-task communication. It is important to remember that the other features of O-O systems, namely inheritance and polymorphism, can be very useful in a system like DO-OPEN.

We are currently working on the language and runtime extensions to be defined and implemented for single inheritance support between DO-OPEN classes. Implementation of multiple inheritance could in fact cause problems to the current DO-OPEN structure and it is unlikely it will be added in the near future. By the way, there is no general consensus about the real usefulness of multiple inheritance in O-O languages like C++.

Polymorphism in the DO-OPEN environment means being able to instantiate a server object of a "descendant" class and to invoke its methods through a stub object of the "ancestor" class. A DO-OPEN extension supporting inheritance could also implement polymorphism without great effort.

6.1 Libraries supporting program decomposition

After enabling single inheritance in DO-OPEN, it will be easier to write DO-OPEN libraries.

For instance, many parallel programs rely on few well-known task configurations (processor farm, pipeline,...). With inheritance it will be possible to define "container" configurations like a pipeline made up of objects that do nothing apart exchanging messages. Using inheritance, it will be possible to extend the behavior of these objects in order to get a user-defined work done before the results are passed down the pipeline.

6.2 Support for persistent objects

Some distributed O-O environments (like Arjuna) require every object to be persistent and continuously mirrored to disk storage. This imposes a penalty in systems were data integrity is not so critical and many objects are used only during temporary computations.

By the way, persistence is a key feature of some classes in specific applications (e.g. distributed O-O databases). We assume it is both simpler and more efficient to consider persistency as an implementation issue to be included by the programmer on a per-class basis. DO-OPEN extensions aimed at supporting this feature can be limited to providing an optional parameter to the user-defined remote class constructor, to be used as an handle (e.g. a file name) for retrieving object state.

7. Acknowledgments

Thanks are due to Dario Lucarella from the Information Technology Department of ENEL, for having promoted and advised the DO-OPEN research project.

8. References

[1] V. S. Sunderam "PVM: a Framework for Distributed Computing", *Concurrency: Practice and Experience*, Vol.2, n.4, Dec.1990.

[2] A. Geist, A. Beguelin, J. Dongarra, W. Jiang, R. Mancheck, V. Sunderam: "PVM — A Users' Guide and Tutorial for Networked Parallel Computing", *MIT Press*, 1994.

[3] A. Beguelin, J. Dongarra, A. Geist, R. Mancheck, V. Sunderam: "Recent Enhancements to PVM", 1994, available via anonymous ftp from netlib2.cs.utk.edu in /pvm3.

[4] S. K. Shrivastava, G. N. Dixon and G. D. Parrington: "An Overview of Arjuna: a Programming System for Reliable Distributed Computing", *IEEE Software*, Vol.8, n.1, Jan.1991.

[5] S. J. Caughey and S. K. Shrivastava: "Implementing Fault-Tolerant Object Systems on Distributed Memory Multiprocessors", *Proc. of the 2nd IEEE International Workshop on Object Orientation in Operating Systems*, Sep.1992.

[6] G. D. Parrington: "Reliable Distributed Programming in C++: the Arjuna Approach", *2nd USENIX C++ Conference*, Apr.1990.

[7] M. C. Little and D. L. McCue: "The Replica Management System: a Scheme for Flexible and Dynamic Replication", *Proc. of the 2nd International Workshop on Configurable Distributed Systems*, Pittsburgh, Mar.1994.

[8] A. S. Grimshaw: "An Introduction to Parallel Object-Oriented Programming with Mentat", *University of Virginia, Computer Science TR. 91-07*, Apr.1991.

[9] A. S. Grimshaw: "The Mentat Run-Time System: Support for Medium Grain Parallel Computation", *Proc. of the 5th Distributed Memory Computing Conference*, Apr.1990.

[10] A. S. Grimshaw: "Easy to use Object-Oriented Parallel Programming with Mentat", *IEEE Computer*, May 1993.

[11] A. S. Grimshaw: "Mentat Programming Language (MPL) Reference Manual", *University of Virginia, Computer Science TR. 91-32*, 1991.

[12] A. Corradi, L. Leonardi: "Parallelism in Object-Oriented Programming Languages", *Proc. of the IEEE Intl. Conference on Computer Languages,* Mar.1990.

[13] A. Corradi, L. Leonardi: "PO Constraints as Tools to Synchronize Active Objects", *The Journal of Object Oriented Programming*, Vol.4, n.6, Oct.1991.

[14] M. Pugassi, F. Zambonelli, L. Leonardi, N. Scarabottolo: "Experiences on Porting the PO (Parallel Objects) environment from a Transputer Network to a PVM-based Distributed System", *Proc. of the 4th EUROMICRO Workshop on Parallel and Distributed Processing*, Braga (P), Jan. 1996.

[15] C. L. Hartley, V. S. Sunderam: "Concurrent Programming with Shared Objects in Networked Environments", Emory University Technical Report.

[16] B. Stroustrup: "The C++ Programming Language", 2nd ed., *Addison-Wesley*, 1991.

[17] ANSI Committee X3J16: "Working Paper for Draft Proposed International Standard for Information Systems — Programming Language C++", Apr.1995.

[18] A. Femminella, A. Omodeo: "PVM-based parallel computing: a case study on power plant simulation", *Proc. of the 20th EUROMICRO Conference*, Liverpool, Sep.1994.

Visual Parallel Programming in Monads-DPV*

Péter Kacsuk[1] Günter Haring[2],
Szabolcs Ferenczi[1], Georg Pigel[2], Gábor Dózsa[1], Tibor Fadgyas[1]

[1]KFKI-MSzKI Research Institute
of the Hungarian Academy of Sci.
P.O.Box 49, H-1525 Budapest, Hungary

[2]Inst. of Appl. Comp. Sci. and Inf. Syst.
University of Vienna
Lenaugasse 2/8, A-1080 Vienna, Austria

Abstract

A layered visual parallel programming approach based on object-oriented model is presented in the paper together with the methodology how to construct very high level parallel programs for massively parallel processors. After a concise description of the basic principles and the main features of the language, two examples are elaborated as case studies to demonstrate the feasibility and benefits of the proposed methodology and graphical notation.

Introduction

For programming Massively Parallel Processors (MPPs) a visual programming language, called MONADS-DP VISUAL (MONADS-DPV)[1] [11, 10, 14], is developed. MONADS-DPV encourages programming parallel parts of the algorithm by graphical symbols applying object-oriented parallel programming technology.

In our parallel programming experience, some kind of drawing had to be always made before actual program coding could begin. We hold that for human beings a good picture of the problem is necessary to think about any parallel algorithms. The purpose of our graphical notation called MONADS-DPV is to make use of the drawings made in the planning phase. While it is quite natural to make drawings about the overall parallel arrangement, it seems to be somewhat artificial for very low level details and especially for sequential parts.

For developing parallel programs in MONADS-DPV, two fully worked out parallel programming examples are presented for scientific computations in MONADS-DPV: cellular automata and the Poisson Problem.

The outline of this paper is the following: Some methodological points in connection with our proposed graphical programming notation are introduced in the next section. In Sect. 2, the graphical notation is briefly described. The main part of the paper is Sect. 3 where two programs for scientific computations are developed using the graphical notation. Two different programming styles are applied in the two programs intentionally to show different programming solutions for similar problems.

1 Monads-DPV as a Hybrid Language

MONADS-DPV does not attempt to do everything visually. Visual representation takes much screen space and, therefore, it does not seem to be suitable to represent the very detailed information which is needed not only when designing software but actually when implementing it. This has been done successfully in textual form and it is also done textually in MONADS-DPV. The visual features of MONADS-DPV aids the developer in coping with additional complexity that comes into play when dealing with parallel programs.[2] It also proves to be as a useful representation when the execution of a parallel program has to be visualized, i.e. in the debugging and testing phases. Using a visual tool for programming algorithms during the software development, some support for debugging and testing can also be integrated into the tool-set without having to change the representation.

The use of graphics and visual environments during the process of parallel software development is demanded by many experts [17, 12].[3] Nevertheless, it is often neglected that graphics and cute pictures are no *panacea* for all problems in computer science, especially when dealing with complex systems. A visual tool for parallel programming must also offer concepts, principles and methodologies to aid the user more than just in producing pictures.

The concept behind MONADS-DPV is based on the simple observation that most parallel programs contain two logical levels of parallelism: (1) coarse grain parallelism and (2) fine grain parallelism.

*This work was funded by the Austrian-Hungarian Inter-Governmental Research Agreement under project number A.9 (1993–1994)

[1] The system is named after the basic building blocks in the Monadology of GOTTFRIED WILHELM LEIBNIZ. The DP suffix comes from Distributed Processes [1].

[2] "[In a parallel world] we have many more dimensions that affect performance of algorithms than we were accustomed to in the sequential world." [17], p. 56

[3] "... the group [Industry Advisory Board (IAB)] agreed that high-performance computing users are having trouble with the current text-oriented tools,and that effective graphical techniques could alleviate many of their problems." [17], p. 58

1.1 Coarse Grain Parallelism

The overall structure of the application is interactively and visually designed with the MONADS-DPV tool-set. This is the job of the application programmer because every application is different. But even here MONADS-DPV can ease the developer's job: Although the applications are basically all different, they often have similar structures [2]. It is especially valid for the strategies of parallelization like master-worker and pipeline. Therefore, the tool can provide such "algorithmic skeletons" [6] or templates as they are called in MONADS-DPV. These templates have the advantage that the application developer can simply fill the application specific code into pre-built structures which were developed and tested by experts instead of having to be developed from scratch for each application. The use of templates also have the advantage that they can be specified to be scalable. Hence, the user can try out the program in a small size, check whether it works and, afterwards, scale it up to a realistic program size with hundreds or even thousands of processors, which would be impossible to be specified manually. Besides the interactive visual facilities offered by MONADS-DPV, its templates are key factors in the faster production of better software.

1.2 Fine Grain Parallelism

The tasks dealt with in the coarse grain parallel program design can often be themselves parallelized at a finer level. But this fine grain parallelization is a job for very experienced programmers if it is required to be efficient. Therefore, these fine grain parts are to be implemented by experts and included into libraries. They do not need to be specified graphically but can also be implemented in a textual language, e.g. C or FORTRAN. Thus, existing parallel code can be reused. This way the application programmer can gain profit from the results of other experts (so also non parallel programming experts can create parallel programs by – metaphorically expressed – "standing on the shoulders of others"). Therefore, the application programmer does not need to have a parallel programming experiment to create parallel programs himself.

2 Outline of the Main Features of Monads-DPV

MONADS-DP VISUAL (MONADS-DPV) is a visual language for parallel programming. It supports building the parallel parts of an algorithm by graphical symbols but sequential program parts can be inserted wherever it is more convenient to use. MONADS-DPV is built onto an object-oriented concurrent programming model called MONADS-DP [7, 8]. The core of the MONADS-DP execution model is the concept of Distributed Processes [1]. Elements of the MONADS-DPV language are described in [11, 10, 14]. The interested reader should refer to these publications. However, to help understanding the example programs, the basic graphical symbols of MONADS-DPV are explained in this section.

The "keywords" of a visual programming language are graphical symbols. The basic graphical symbols

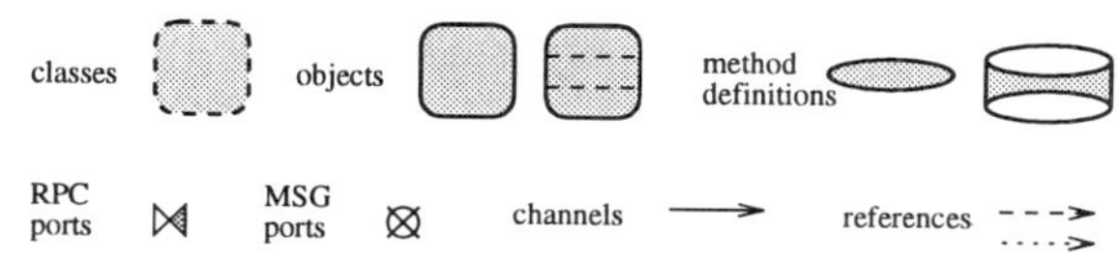

Figure 1: The basic graphical symbols

for the MONADS-DPV are given in Fig. 1.

Most of the graphical symbols can have an attached label which identifies that particular instance of the symbol. The scopes of the labeled symbols are naturally denoted by the border-lines of the encapsulating symbols.

Object symbols are rounded boxes. If the box is divided into three parts by dashed lines, the upper part contains the attributes, the middle part is the body of the object containing valid methods, and the lower part is the initial part which contains statements to be executed at object initialization time as the first local process in the object (see also DP [1]).

All objects in MONADS-DPV belong to classes which are represented by dashed rounded boxes. The form of class symbols is similar to that of the objects because classes are possible objects. However, classes themselves are not objects existentially.

Methods are represented by oval symbols and labeled by a name. The condensed representation contains the name and possibly the parameters of the method declaration only. The detailed representation of a method is a tube closed by oval symbols at both ends (see for example 6). The body of the tube may contain the details of the method by either graphical block symbols or textually. The block symbols are described in detail elsewhere [11, 10, 14].

Communication is done through ports which are connected by synchronous communication channels. There are two kinds of ports in MONADS-DPV: ports for Remote Procedure Calls (RPCs) which correspond to object messages; and ports for messages between processes (MSG ports). Ports can be placed onto the border-lines of either object or method symbols. It means that the object or method may communicate through those ports. An arrow (channel), pointing directly from an RPC port symbol on the border-line of an object to a method symbol inside the object symbol, means that a message arriving at that port will provoke the execution of that method inside the object (as a local process or thread of execution).

Reference arrows might appear among graphical symbols representing several kinds of relations. For instance, class symbols might be connected to instances by dashed arrows. However, dashed lines can be freely used as graphical comments.

2.1 Concurrent and Parallel Layers in Monads-DPV

MONADS-DPV supports both concurrent and parallel programming (i.e. functional parallelism and data parallelism, respectively).

Concurrency comes from the fact that parallel activities can be initiated by parallel blocks which correspond to structured parallel statements in textual lan-

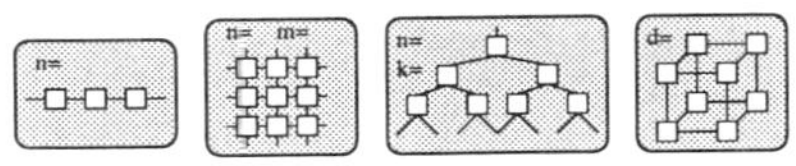

Figure 2: Some predefined topologies

guages. Thus, there are simultaneous ongoing activities around in a MONADS-DPV program. RPC messages arriving to objects provoke an execution thread of a corresponding method. Since multiple messages may arrive to an object and, thus, multiple execution threads may be active simultaneously, concurrency arises among the threads in using the encapsulated data space of the object which plays the role of a shared resource. As a rule to be checked by the compiler, the encapsulated variables of an object can only be accessed from the methods inside critical regions. An adapted form of the Conditional Critical Region (CCR) is used in MONADS-DP for concurrency control. The CCR construction used in MONADS-DPV is derived from HOARE's proposal [15]. The `with` clause is omitted in MONADS-DPV since the critical resource referenced by the CCR construction is the encapsulated variable space of an object in which the CCR construction occurs.

For data parallel programs MONADS-DPV provides some regular arrangements of homogeneous object spaces as templates. In data parallel programs objects are associated with processes which communicate with each other through MSG ports. Some template arrangements are shown in Fig. 2.

Ports appearing at the boundary of template topologies represent many-to-one communications. All the element objects of a template can communicate through this kind of port. On the other hand, message sent to a port on the border of a template is broadcasted among member objects.

3 Examples

Two example programs for scientific computation are presented (for illustrative purposes only): cellular automata and the Poisson problem. To show the twofold capabilities of MONADS-DPV, the two programs are developed in different styles, although, they have many common features. The cellular automata is developed in an object-oriented style using RPC messages while process-based techniques and MSG messages are applied in the solution of the Poisson problem. Our intention is to show the two programming styles.

3.1 Cellular Automata

The model program for cellular automata is inspired by that published in [3]. However, the solution presented here differs from the one in [3]. The latter is programmed in programming language SuperPascal [5, 4], a block structured parallel programming language for teaching parallel programming and publishing parallel algorithms. One of the main differences between the SuperPascal and the MONADS-DPV versions of the cellular automata is that while the former is intentionally a block structured but un-modular

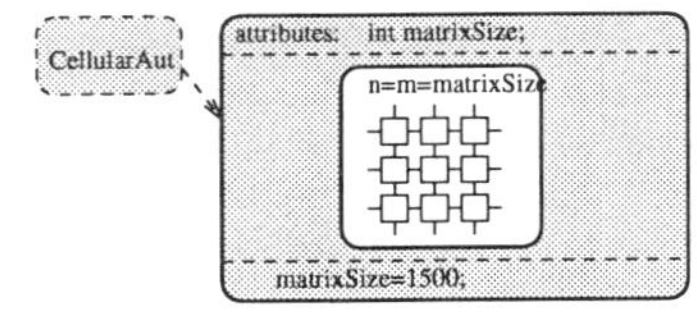

Figure 3: Cellular automaton

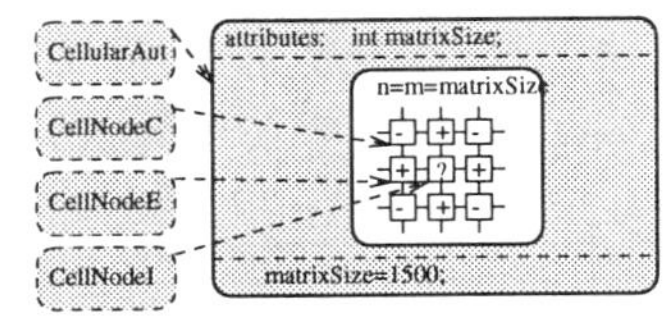

Figure 4: Cellular automaton with object groups

program, the latter is a modular one. Another difference is that the MONADS-DPV program in this paper is a fine grain solution.

The outermost module of a program is represented by an object as depicted in Fig. 3. The object will contain a single variable as its sole attribute. This attribute is initialized to some value (e.g. 1500) in the initialization part of the object at object creation time. The initialization part of the main object is finished after the initialization of the attribute but the object remains valid together with its sub-object structure. The outermost object will belong to the class of `cellularAuts` as indicated in Fig. 3.

There are at least two possibilities for further refining the algorithm:

1. One of the possibilities is to regard each element of the homogeneous object space identical, belonging to the same class and a single algorithm is to be developed for them. In the algorithm the cells of different positions are differentiated by `if` statements when it is necessary. This alternative is taken by BRINCH HANSEN in [3].

2. The other possibility is to group the objects in the homogeneous object space into subgroups according to their positions. Then, different algorithms should be given for each group. This approach is taken by the matrix multiplication example of HOARE in [16]. This approach will be taken in this paper as well since it can be easily specified by a graphical notation where a programmer can visually distinguish between the different groups (Fig. 4). Another reason is that since MONADS-DPV is an object-oriented language, common parts of the algorithms can easily be abstracted into classes.

The sub-object structure of the main object is chosen from a predefined set of templates which is provided by the MONADS-DPV system (Sect. 2.1). This set of templates is given to define homogeneous object spaces of any size. Each template has some parameters that must be set when instantiating from the template. In our example both dimensions of the square matrix will be 1500. The template in Fig. 3 indicates that all of the cells have four ports for interactions. It is a design decision point whether the ports should be RPC or message (MSG) ones.

1. Choosing RPC ports means that remote procedure calls will serve as communication for the exchange of the states.

2. Choosing MSG ports means that processes will exchange messages explicitly.

The main difference between the two mechanisms are as follows: Remote procedure calls are sent by processes but accepted by objects. Process messages are both sent and accepted by processes. In the case of MSG ports the assumption is that each object holds an internal housekeeper process while it is not necessary in the case of RPC messages.[4]

According to the naive solution, each sub-object will represent a cell from the cellular automata. It results in a fine grain parallelism which is not expected on todays MIMD computers. We are going to make the program general enough to be efficient in case of coarse grain parallelism. Although, all the cells are arranged in a single square matrix, groups of cells can be distinguished in the pattern according to their positions. These different kinds are represented in the figure with different labels. There will be middle cells (?), edge cells of four type (+) and corner cells (-). Since these cells belong to different categories, it follows that they will belong to different classes, accordingly.

The solution by RPC messages corresponds to the object-oriented style. Before the classes of the specialized cells would be introduced, we are going to define the class of some abstract cells with the features common to any of the cells. It is a common feature of the cells that each of them contains one distinct piece of the data space of the whole cellular automaton. An object representing a single cell provides the basic operations that can be made on a cell in the form of methods. These operations basically return the current state of the cell (`cellState()`) and do the state transition (`next()`) as shown in Fig. 5. Method `next()` is depicted by dashed lines indicating that it is a virtual method which will be bound to some body later. The initialization of this kind of cells is supposed to be terminated without creating any local processes. Thus, the object becomes passive: it can respond to messages `cellState` and `next`.

Methods of class `cellAbstract` are given textually since it would be no help to use the graphics for the further details. If you work with a suitable programming environment, pointing to the method symbol in the figure, a window is opened in which you can put the relevant piece of program text. In a paper like this we just put the text here:

[4]If the object from which a process issues an RPC message and the object that absorbs the RPC message is located on the same processing element, no receiving process is necessary but the RPC will be reduced to normal procedure call.

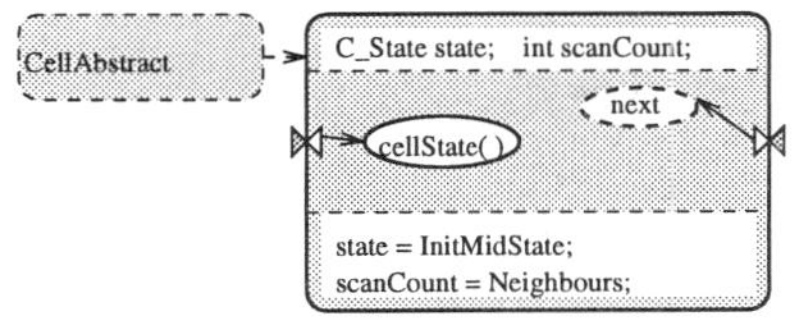

Figure 5: The structure of the abstract cell

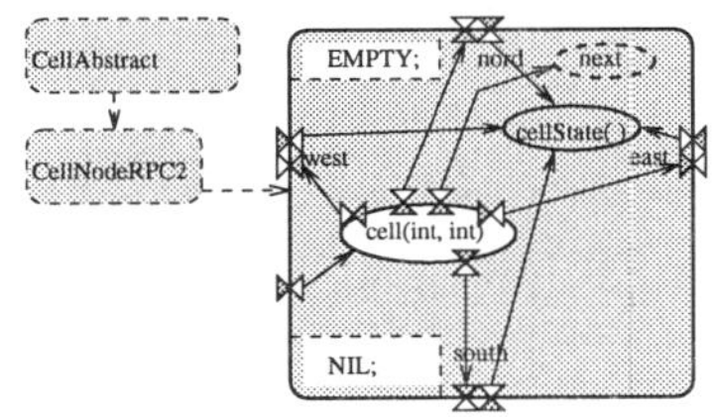

Figure 6: The structure of cells with RPC ports

```
method cellState(C_State s)
{ s = state;
  if (scanCount > 0)
    CCR (true)
      scanCount--;
}
virtual method next(C_State current,
                    C_State east, C_State west,
                    C_State nord, C_State south);
```

The `CCR(){}` construction in the code fragment above means a critical region made from CCR construction by putting `true` into the condition part. The use of the critical region is necessary to prevent interference in the manipulation of variable `scanCount`.[5] Variable `scanCount` always shows how many neighbours has not scanned the state yet. Initially, its value equals to the number of neighbours which is given by the constant `Neighbours`. Another constant `InitMidState` gives the initial state of the interior cells.

Constants `N` and `M` are automatically valid in the class because the objects from the class are members in a template topology. The names of the constants are always derived from the variable parameters of the templates and the constants determine the current positions of the instance in the topology.

The class `cellAbstract` can be used to make a specialized version of the cell objects. It is done by making a sub-class of class `CellAbstract`. Note that the methods defined in class `CellAbstract` are merged with the newly created methods due to the inheritance mechanism (Fig. 6). As a representational sugar, the inherited methods are shaded as the background and the newly created one is highlighted.

The state space is not extended, rather, both the state space and the initialization part are empty at this level. However, the new class of objects is extended by some RPC ports. All the four input RPC ports are

[5]In computer architectures where integer variable decrement is an atomic operation, the compiler can omit the critical region.

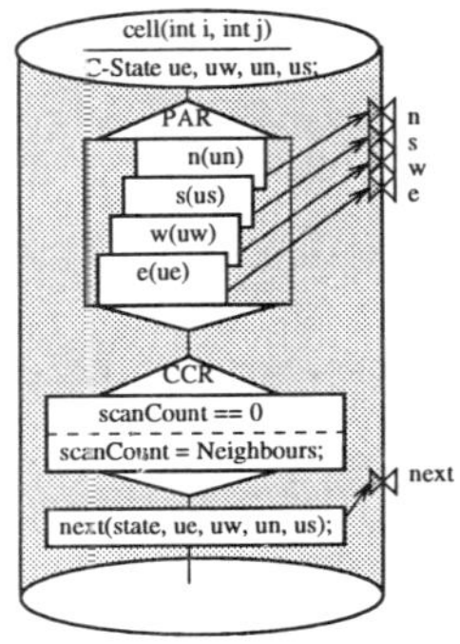

Figure 7: The methods of the nodes with RPC

directed to the inherited method `cellState()`, thus, this method will work for any call of the four RPC ports. The four output RPC ports are used by the new method.

What remains is to give the details for method `cell()` (Fig. 7). The `cell()` method implements additional functionality of an interior cell. The method body of `cell()`, regarded equivalent to the graphical notation in Fig. 7, could be given textually as follows:

```
method cell(int i, int j, RPC_port next,
            RPC_port n, RPC_port s,
            RPC_port e, RPC_port w)
{  C_State ue, uw, un, us;
   PAR{ n(un);
        s(us);
        e(ue);
        w(uw);  };
    CCR (scanCount==0) {
      scanCount = Neighbours; };
    next(state, ue, uw, un, us);
}
```

The cell, which is a method of interior cells having four neighbours, works as follows: If the method `cell()` is called, the cell scans the current state of the four neighbours in parallel. Then, it calculates its own next state only when the previous one is already scanned by the four neighbours (see the Conditional Critical Region construction).

So far the data structure is described for a cellular automata but it is not yet specified how many processes will execute the various parts of the program simultaneously. It would be a natural solution to assign a process to every cell as shown in Fig. 8 but it results in a very fine grain parallel program that would not be efficient on today's Massively Parallel Processors. Since our goal is not to develop sophisticated programs but to show how the graphical elements can be used to "write" or better to draw a program, we accept this solution.

The code of the method `cellProcess()` is as follows:

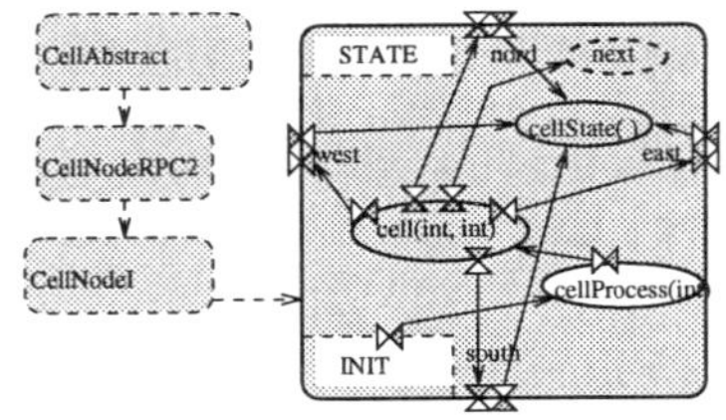

Figure 8: Each cell is driven by its own process

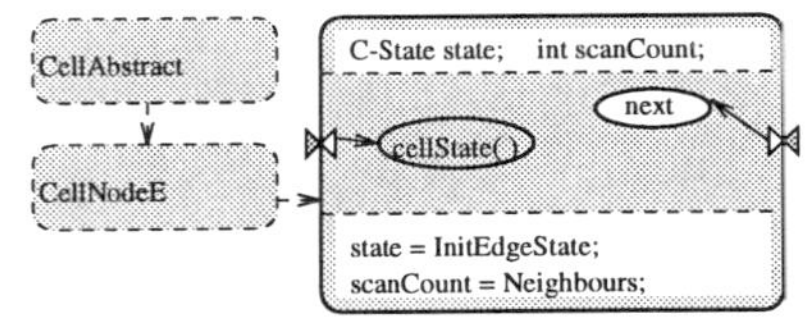

Figure 9: The class of edge cells derived from abstract cells

```
method cellProcess(int cycle, RPC_port cell)
{  int count=0;
   while (count < cycle) {
      cell(i, j, next, n, s, e, w);
      count++;  }
}
```

The initialization part labeled `INIT` consists of one procedure call:

```
INIT:: cellProcess(STEPS, cell());
```

Thus, the class of interior nodes (see class `cellNodeI` in Fig. 4) has been developed. The class of the edge cells can also be derived from the abstract cell class (Fig. 9).

Cell objects at the edge differ from the general cells only in the fact that their state is initialized to `InitEdgeState` and virtual method `next()` is bound to an empty body:

```
method next(C_State current,
            C_State east, C_State west,
            C_State nord, C_State south)
{ skip; }
```

Edge cells do not change states and, therefore, they do not need specialized methods. Furthermore, method `next()` will be never called.

The program developed above is a general one. Class `cellNodeI` is to be further refined for a specific application of a cellular automata by bounding virtual method `next()` to a specific computation as described in [3].

3.2 The 2-D Poisson Problem

The Poisson problem is a simple partial differential equation (PDE) that is at the core of many applications. The description of the problem and the textual program code of the parallel algorithm we present here can be found in [13]. To simplify the discussion, we

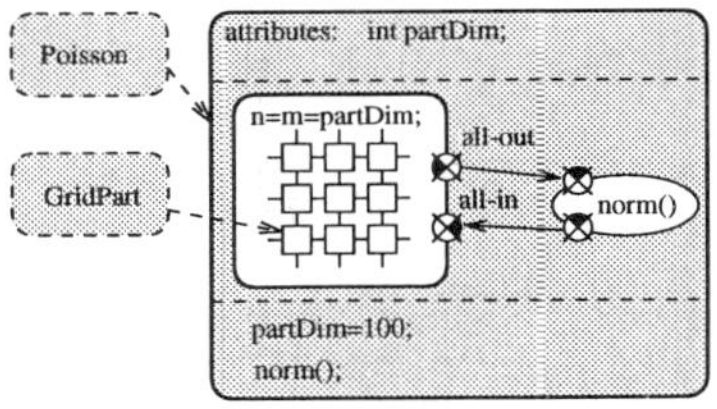

Figure 10: 2-D Poisson Problem

use the unit square as the domain. We define a square mesh (also called a grid), and we will find an approximate solution to the problem at the points of the grid only. We will denote the points of the grid with $u(i,j)(0 \le i \le n+1, 0 \le j \le n+1)$. The method we use is the so called Jacobi iteration, where in each step the following formula is applied on every grid points:

$$u(i,j)^{k+1} = \frac{1}{4}\left(u(i-1,j)^k + u(i,j+1)^k + u(i,j-1)^k + u(i+1,j)^k - h^2 \cdot f(i,j)\right)$$

where $h = \frac{1}{n+1}$ and $f(i,j)$ are predefined values $(0 \le i \le n+1, 0 \le j \le n+1)$.

So the new value of any grid point depends on the neighbours' current values. This step is repeated until the solution is reached, more precisely, until the difference between the new and the previous values of the grid points becomes small enough.

To parallelize this algorithm we must distribute the data across processes. We will use the two-dimensional decomposition of the square mesh. Each process will be responsible only for a part in size $k \times k$ of the whole grid, where $1 \le k \le n+2$ and $(\bmod\ k, n+2) = 0$.

3.2.1 Poisson class.

Fig. 10 depicts the definition of `Poisson` class which contains the whole application.

1. **Attributes:** `partDim`: size of the subobjects mesh
2. **Subobjects:** Subobjects represent the appropriate parts of the grids, so they belong to the `GridPart` class and they are arranged into mesh topology. Subobjects have a common input message port called `all-in` and a common output message port called `all-out`.
3. **Init:** The `partDim` variable is set here first, then the `norm()` method (process) is started.
4. **Method:** `norm()`: This method is used to synchronize the iteration steps of the subobjects and to check whether the difference among the new and old grid values is small enough to finish the iteration.

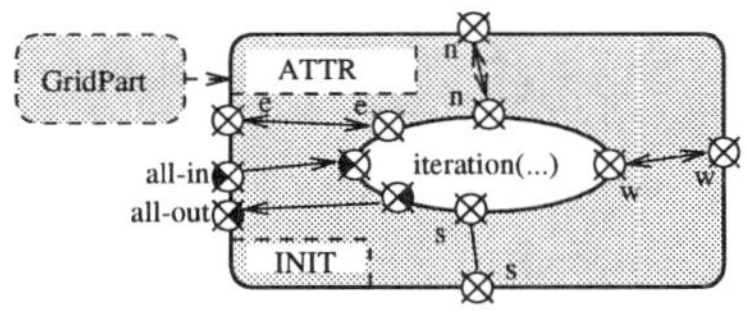

Figure 11: The gridPart Class Definition

3.2.2 GridPart class (Fig. 11)

1. Attributes (Label `ATTR`)

```
ATTR :: int gridSize = 1000, partSize = 100;
        double a[partSize+2][partSize+2],
               b[partSize+2][partSize+2],
               f[partSize][partSize];
```

- `gridSize`: size of the whole square mesh (grid)
- `partSize`: size of that part of the grid which belongs to this object
- `a[][],b[][]`: 2-D buffers (matrices) to store the appropriate part of the grid. The part of the grid is extended with the so called ghost points on each edge. Ghost points contain values which are calculated by the neighbour objects and are necessary to determine the values of the local part of the grid. During the iteration one of these buffers contains the old values while the other one contains the new values.
- `f[][]`: buffer to store the values of the 'f' function

2. Methods : `iteration()`: this method accomplishes actually the iteration regarding to the local part of the grid.
3. Init (Label `INIT`): The `iteration()` method (process) is started.
INIT :: iteration();

3.2.3 The `norm()` method.

This method belongs to the `Poisson` class. It has two message ports which are connected to the common input and output message port of the mesh (called `all-in` and `all-out` respectively). The method starts when the `Poisson` object is created and remains active during the iteration process. In every iteration step `norm()` receives the difference between the new and the old values of the local part of the grid from every `PartGrid` object via the `all-out` port. It adds the local differences to get the global difference with respect to the whole grid. If the global difference stored in the variable '`d`' is not smaller than the predefined value '`epsilon`' then one more iteration step is necessary; otherwise, the iteration process has to terminate. After the norm method determines the global difference, it must send this value back to every `PartGrid` objects

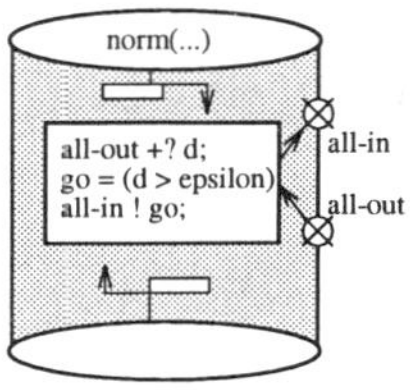

Figure 12: The norm() Method

via the all-in port so as they can decide whether they have to continue the iteration or can finish their work. The graphical representation of the norm() method is depicted in Fig. 12 while its textual code is given as follows:

```
void norm(void)
{ bool go = TRUE;
  double d;
  while ( go ) {
      d = 0;
      all-out +? d;
      go = (d >= EPSILON);
      all-in ! go;
  }
}
```

The operation '+?' means that the port 'all-out' belongs to more than one objects and the values received from these objects are summed up in variable 'd'.

3.2.4 The iteration method.

This method belongs to the GridPart class and actually performs the iteration with respect to the local part of the grid. It starts when the GridPart object is created and repeats the iteration steps inside a cycle. (First of all it calls the init() routine to give starting values for the local buffers but this step is not relevant here.) The condition of the cycle is the same as in the case of the norm() method since at the end of each iteration step this method receives the value of the 'go' variable from the norm() method. One iteration step consists of calling the exchng() and then the sweep() routine. The graphical representation of the method is depicted in Fig. 13.

The exchng() has only one argument, one of the two buffers (matrices) containing the values of the local part of the grid ('a[][]' or 'b[][]'). The routine receives the values of the ghost points of the buffer (i.e. the edges of the 2-D buffer, values which are calculated by the neighbour objects), and sends the local values of the grid which are necessary for the neighbour objects (which are the values of the ghost points of the neigbours' buffers).

The sweep() routine performs the calculation of the new values of the local part of the grid. It has two arguments, the two 2-D buffers ('a[][]' and 'b[][]'). The first one contains the old values, the second one contains the new values.

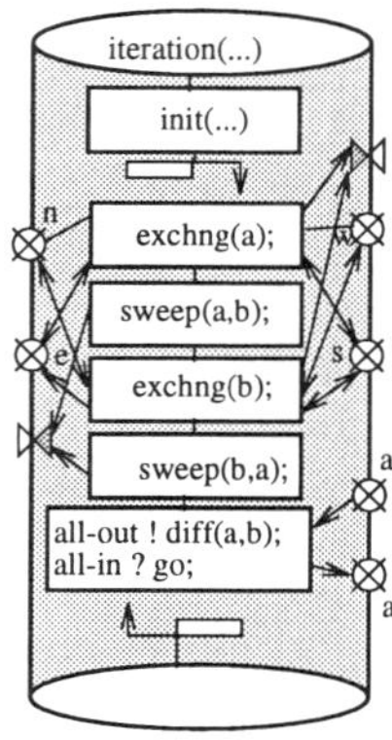

Figure 13: The iteration() Method

Inside the cycle, the method performs two iteration steps in succession. After that, it calls the diff() to get the difference between the new and old values of the local part of the grid and sends this value to the norm() method via the all-out port. Then it waits for the value of the 'go' variable (the cycle condition) sent by the norm() method. If that value is 'TRUE' then iteration() method continues its work, or else it terminates.

The textual code of the iteration() method is:

```
void iteration(void)
{ bool go = TRUE;
  init();
  while ( go ) {
       exchng(a);
       sweep(a,b);
       exchng(b);
       sweep(b,a);
       all-out ! diff(a,b);
       all-in ? go;
  }
}
```

Since the sweep() routine represents a pure sequential code fragment, we define it only in textual way:

```
void sweep(double a[][], double b[][])
{ static double h = 1.0 / ( 1.0 + (double)gridSize );
  int i,j;
  for (i=1; i<=k; i++)
    for(j=1; j<=k; j++)
      b[i,j] = 0.25*(a[i-1,j]+a[i,j+1]+a[i,j-1]+
                a[i+1,j])-h*h*f[i-1,j-1];
}
```

3.2.5 The exchng() method.

It belongs to the iteration() method (i.e. it is a local routine of the iteration() method). Its functionality is described above. The method contains a simple PAR construction, in which it exchanges the appropriate

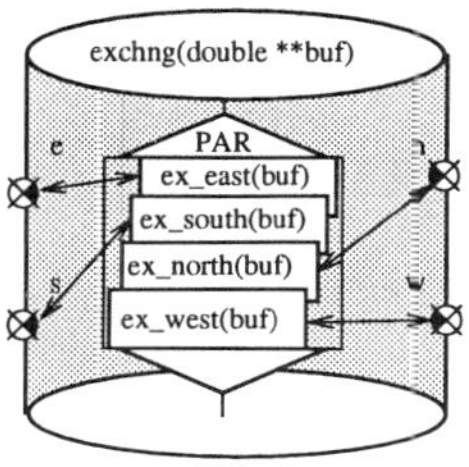

Figure 14: The exchng() Method

ghost point values with all possible neighbours in a parallel manner (Fig. 14).

The textual code of the `exchng()` method is:

```
void exchng(double buf[][])
{
  PAR{ ex_north(buf);
       ex_east( buf);
       ex_south(buf);
       ex_west( buf);  }
}
```

3.2.6 Auxiliary procedures.

The routines `ex_north()`, `ex_east()`, `ex_south()` and `ex_west()` have a kind of inner structure which better fits to be described in a textual way without any graphics. Due to lack of space, the textual code is omitted here.

Conclusions

While a textual program can be written by paper and pencil, it is no more a way in visual programming. Rather the programmer is expected to develop a parallel algorithm interactively on the computer screen by making drawings about the program. A suitable programming environment can give enormous support during the development phase. A graphical development environment is under investigation to promote developing parallel programs in MONADS-DP VISUAL.

Efforts will be spent in the future to avoid large number of arcs in graphs describing parallel programs.

References

[1] P. Brinch Hansen. Distributed Processes: A Concurrent Programming Concept. *Commun. ACM*, 21(11):932–941, Nov. 1978.

[2] P. Brinch Hansen. Model programs for computational science: A programming metholology for multicomputers. *Concurrency: Practice & Experience*, 5(5):407–423, Aug. 1993.

[3] P. Brinch Hansen. Parallel cellular automata: A model program for computational science. *Concurrency: Practice & Experience*, 5(5):425–448, Aug. 1993.

[4] P. Brinch Hansen. SuperPascal—a publication language for parallel scientific computing. *Concurrency: Practice & Experience*, 6(5):461–483, Aug. 1994.

[5] P. Brinch Hansen. The Programming Language SuperPascal. *Software—Practice & Experience*, 24(5):467–483, May 1994.

[6] M. Cole. *Algorithmic Skeletons: Structured Management of Parallel Computation.* Research Monographs in Parallel and Distributed Computing. Pitman Publishing (The MIT Press), 1989.

[7] Sz. Ferenczi. Concurrent Objects with Inherited Synchronizations. In M. Mango Furnari, editor, *Proceedings of the 2nd International Workshop on Massive Parallelism: Hardware Software and Applications*, pages 80–89, Capri, Italy, Oct. 3–7, 1994. World Scientific Publishing Co. Also available from the WWW, http://www.kfki.hu/~ferenczi/MP94.html

[8] Sz. Ferenczi. MONADS-DP: Outline of an Object-Oriented Concurrent Programming Model for Multiprocessor Systems. In Ferenczi and Kacsuk [9]. Also available from the WWW, http://www.kfki.hu/~ferenczi/AH-WS-MonDP.html

[9] Sz. Ferenczi and P. Kacsuk, editors. *Proceedings of the 2nd Austrian-Hungarian Workshop on Transputer Applications*, Budapest, Hungary, September 29–October 1, 1994. ACPC & NJSZT-HTUG.

[10] Sz. Ferenczi, G. Pigel, G. Dózsa, T. Fadgyas, G. Haring, and P. Kacsuk. Monads-DPV: An Object-Oriented Graphical Support for Developing Supercomputer Software System. Technical report, KFKI-MSzKI, Budapest, 1994.

[11] Sz. Ferenczi, G. Pigel, P. Kacsuk, G. Haring, and G. Dózsa. Graphical Support for Parallel Program Design. In Ferenczi and Kacsuk [9].

[12] E. P. Glinert. Introduction and Tutorial Overview. In E. P. Glinert, editor, *Visual Programming Environments: Applications and Issues.* IEEE Computer Society Press, 1990.

[13] W. Gropp, E. Lusk, and A. Skjellum. *Using MPI. Portable Parallel Programming with the Message-Passing Interface.* The MIT Press, Cambridge, Massachusetts, London, England, 1994.

[14] G. Haring, P. Kacsuk, G. Dózsa, T. Fadgyas, Sz. Ferenczi, and G. Pigel. Computer Aided Parallel Processing Software Technology—Final Report. Technical report, KFKI-MSzKI/UW, Budapest/Vienna, 1994.

[15] C. A. R. Hoare. Towards a Theory of Parallel Programming. In C. A. R. Hoare and R. H. Perrott, editors, *Operating Systems Techniques*, pages 61–71. Academic Press, New York, 1972.

[16] C. A. R. Hoare. Communicating Sequential Processes. *Commun. ACM*, 21(8):666–677, Aug. 1978.

[17] C. M. Pancake. Software Support for Parallel Computing: Where Are We Headed? *Communications of the ACM*, 34(11):53–64, November 1991.

Modelling Dynamic Distributed System Structures in PARSE

A. Liu, and I. Gorton
CaST Lab, School of Computer Science and Engineering,
University of New South Wales, Kensington 2033, Australia

Abstract

*With the increasing availability of parallel and networked computers, applications based on distributed systems are gradually becoming commonplace. It is therefore important for software professionals to practice sound parallel software engineering methods. PARSE (**Par**allel **S**oftware **E**ngineering) is an object-based software engineering methodology to facilitate the design of reliable and reusable parallel systems. Systems designed using PARSE are represented using a graphical notation known as process graphs, which enable process structures and their precise interactions to be hierarchically constructed. However, the current PARSE graphical notation cannot adequately handle the design of concurrent systems which incorporate dynamic features. This paper describes extensions to the present PARSE process graph notations to support the design of well-engineered distributed systems. Example designs are given to illustrate the utility of the approach, and a mapping to the Windows NT WIN32 Application Programming Interface is given.*

1. Introduction

Parallel programming is a natural way to model the real world. With the availability of parallel and networked computers, there is an increasing need for writing effective, reliable and verifiable parallel and distributed software. It is also essential that large, distributed systems are constructed using sound software engineering practice. Ideally, this software design methodology should be easy for software engineers to learn and use; it should also provide formal verification to validate the software's correctness; and facilitate automatic program generation from the system design. [1]

PARSE (**Par**allel **S**oftware **E**ngineering) [2] is an object-based software engineering methodology to facilitate the design of reliable and reusable parallel and distributed systems. This methodology has the following features:

- Systems are composed using a graphical design notation, which enables process structures and their precise interactions to be hierarchically constructed.
- PARSE designs are language, architecture independent.
- PARSE designs can be transformed into formalisms such as Petri nets or CSP to provide for design verification. [3]

However, the PARSE process graph notation cannot adequately handle the design of concurrent systems which incorporate the dynamic creation and deletion of processes and of communication paths. Similarly, the dynamic reconfiguration of systems can not easily be captured in the design. In many distributed systems such as retail banking systems, factory automation, and telecommunication, the provision of these facilities is important.

Furthermore, common desktop operating systems such as Windows NT and Solaris provide a rich set of facilities to enable applications to exploit multiple processors. With the availability of symmetric multi-processing machines in the personal computer market, future applications should be developed to utilise this increased processing power. These applications will be inherently distributed, using spare resources located at different locations within the network [4]. Applications built using the *multithreaded* approach will benefit from improved performance, lower cost, and higher reliability. Hence, it is important to explore the design issues involved in developing multithreaded applications.

This paper presents a suitable graphical notation to support the design of well-engineered distributed systems. So far, the focus of the work with PARSE has been upon tightly-coupled, high-performance parallel software systems which are implemented in parallel programming languages such as Occam, Ada or Parallel C. This project attempts to extend the current work to cater for the design of loosely-coupled distributed applications. Typically, such applications are written in conventional programming languages such as C or C++, with concurrency and inter-process communication facilities provided by an underlying distributed operating system, such as Windows NT or UNIX.

2. Ext-PARSE Process Graph Components

The Extended-PARSE (Ext-PARSE) process graph notation (Fig.2) is designed to supplement the current PARSE process graph notation (Fig.1). The resulting extended notation enables the design of distributed and parallel systems incorporating dynamic features. Many usage rules present in the current PARSE methodology are also applicable in the new set of notations. The machine and language independent property is also maintained in the new graph notation.

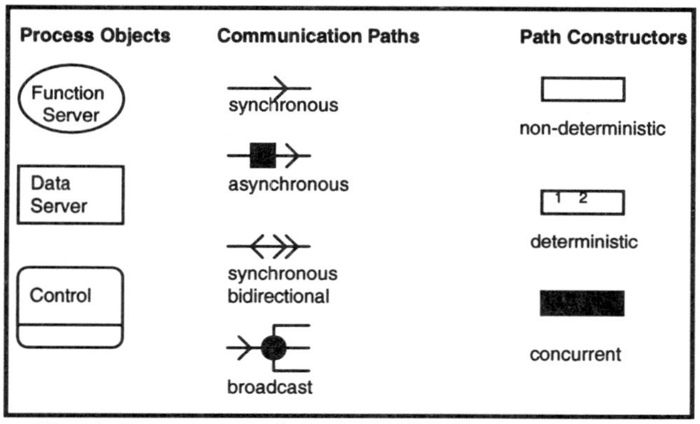

Fig.1. Summary of the PARSE Process Graph Notation

Dynamically Created Process Objects: function server, data server, and control processes all may be created and deleted dynamically. The existing behavioural and functional rules applying to their static counterparts also apply to them (Fig.2). In addition to the *inherited* functionality of their static counterparts, these dynamic process objects may enter/exit the system at run time. This should not affect the execution of other processes. Also, communication paths going into and or coming out from dynamic process objects are also dynamic in nature. These communication paths are set up when the associated process objects are created, and are destroyed when process objects terminate.

Dynamic process objects are often replicated. Each replicated instance has the same process-internal. However, not all instances of the process are created right at the beginning. Different instances may be created and terminated at different times. The series of numbers enclosed by square brackets [0..n] denotes the range of the number of instances of the object that may be present in the system at any one time. The symbol 'n' may be replaced by a constant integer, or by default, is the maximum number of thread instances a process may have as defined by the underlying system. When expanded, each instance has an associated subscript. This provides a way to uniquely identify each instance of the process.

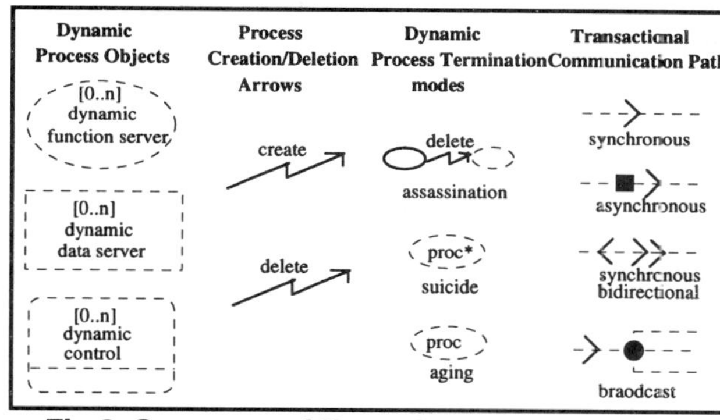

Fig.2. Summary of Extended-PARSE Process Graph Notation

Creation/Deletion of Dynamic Process Objects: Function servers and control process objects may create and delete dynamic process objects by 'invoking' create and or delete signals. They are shown via the 'twisted arrow' notation. There are two rules of usage:

Rule 1: the process object at the **invoked** end of a creation/deletion arrow must be of *dynamic* type.

Rule 2: the process object at the **invoking** end of a creation/deletion arrow must be an *active* process object. (this means data server is excluded).

Termination Modes of Dynamic Process Objects: There are three ways that dynamic process objects may exit from the system: **assassination**, **suicide**, and **aging**.

Assassination - Any active process can kill a dynamic process. This ensures that Ext-PARSE designs are machine and language independent. In different distributed operating systems, there are limitations imposed on deletion of processes by other processes. For examples, in some operating systems, only parent processes may kill their own children processes. In others, as long as the process id is known, any process may kill it [5].

Suicide - A thread may terminate its own execution. For example, threads in Windows NT may terminate themselves by calling the Win32 function: *ExitThread.*

Aging - This is the default termination mode. The created thread dies from aging when it completes its work. This occurs naturally, hence the term *aging*.

The notation caters for all three possible ways of termination, and leaves the design decision for the software engineer.

Dynamically Created Communication Path: The four types of communication paths can be used to connect to dynamic process objects. All existing PARSE design rules apply here. In figure 3, the communication path *data* is not valid at all times. It is valid when both the sending process, and the receiving process are present in the system. Hence, in this case, the *data* path is set up only after the creation of *sender* by *control*, and the creation of *receiver* by an *external entity*[1]. Note that Ext-PARSE does not require the designer to specify which process creates the *data* path, this should be left as an implementation decision.

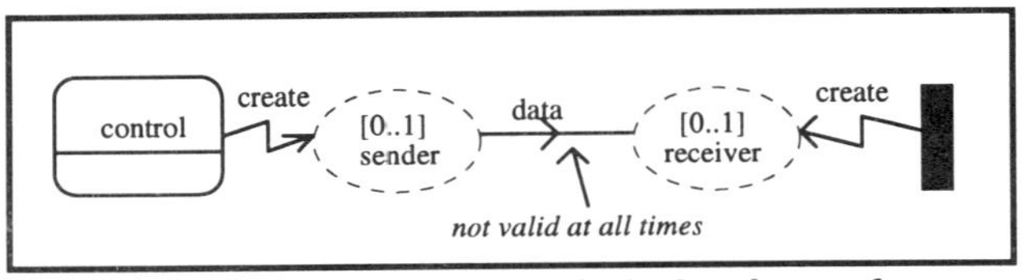

Fig.3. Implicit dynamic behaviour of communication paths

In the above example (Fig.3), there is (at any time) a maximum of one communication path between the two dynamic process objects. However, this is not always the case. By default, a communication path going into or coming out from a dynamic process object is replicated if there are multiple instances of the process.

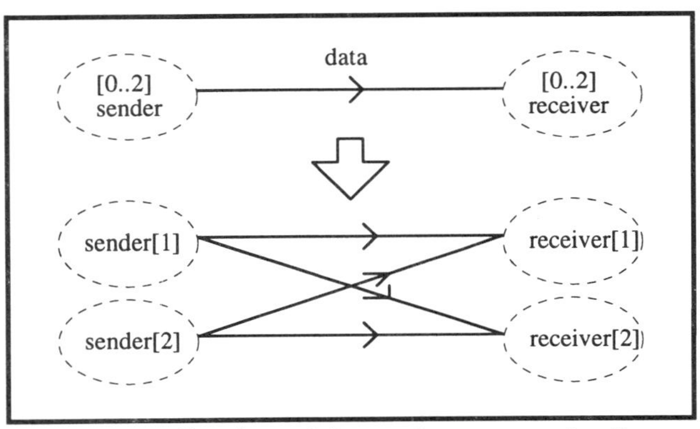

Fig.4. Replication of dynamic communication path

The existing replication rules and notations in PARSE also apply to dynamic processes in Ext-PARSE [6]. That is, by default, all associated processes are fully connected by communication paths, even though the paths are dynamic in nature in Ext-PARSE (see Fig.4). Path restriction can also be used here to overwrite default behaviours (see Fig.5).

Transactional communication path: Software designers can explicitly show that the communication between two processes is of a transactional type by using dotted arcs (see Fig.6). These are different to the ordinary communication paths in the sense that they are set up only when they are needed to transfer messages. As soon as the transfer is complete, the path is no longer valid. Hence, the life span of a communication path is not dependent on the life spans of the processes using it, but is dictated by the activity of transferring the message. In a database system, a typical example would be a *transactional update* to a data store.

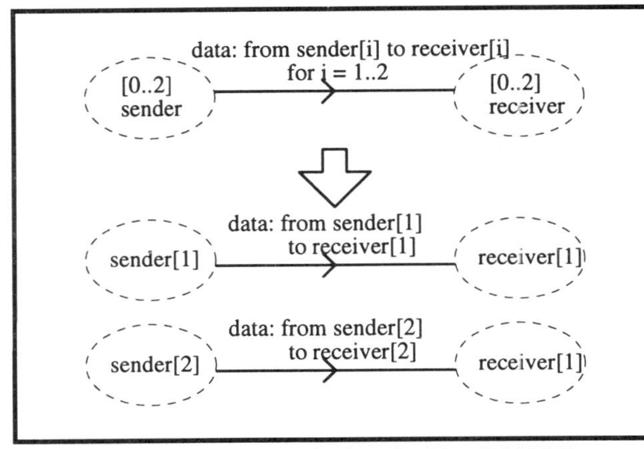

Fig.5. Path restriction in Ext-PARSE

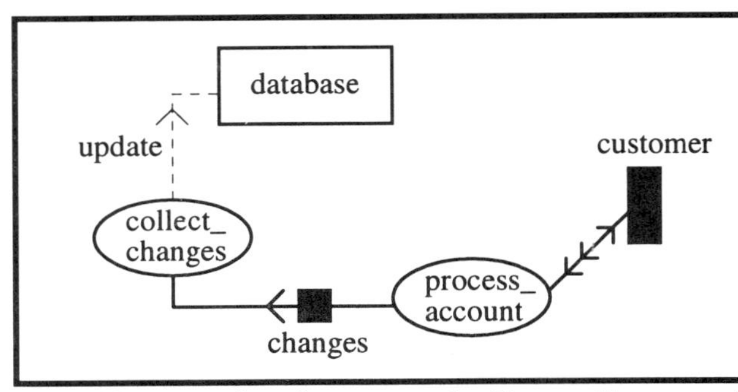

Fig.6. Transactional communication path example

The period of validity of the communication path depends on the associated process internals. This can be explicitly defined using BSL [6].

Communication Path Constructors: Not all four types of path constructors may be applied when dynamic process objects are associated. Consider the example in figure 7: the *updates* communication paths may be replicated depending on the number of worker processes present in the system. Hence, there may be multiple paths going into the data store, which needs to be handled non-deterministically. The data server receives update messages from workers randomly.

Concurrent and deterministic input handling can not be used here as explained in the following: concurrent input handling implies there is concurrency within the process, that is, the process may be further decomposed. This cannot be used here since the data store is primitive. With deterministic input handling, the receiving process selects between ready paths according to path labels. However, when the paths are coming from instances of the same dynamic process, the priority cannot be specified since there is no guarantee that a particular instance of the process is present at a point in time. Hence, deterministic

[1] the solid bar represents an 'external entity' in the PARSE notation [6].

input handling cannot be used here.

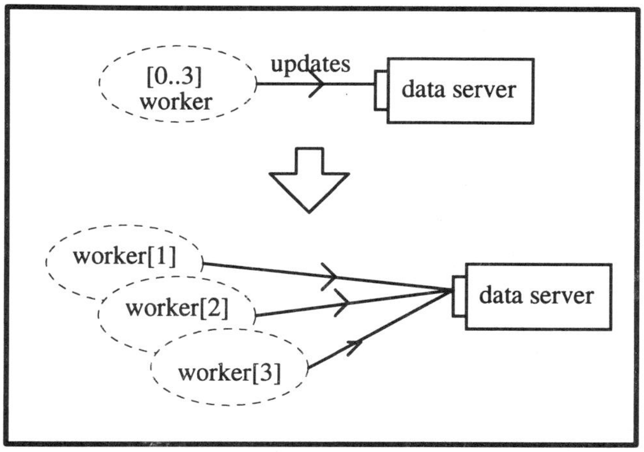

Fig.7. Dynamic updates to data store requiring non-deterministic constructor

Multithreaded Object: The ability to handle large designs using hierarchical decomposition is a powerful feature of PARSE. Further, in many parallel and distributed software systems, it is often desirable for processes to spawn new helper processes to service multiple clients' requests. **Multithreaded object** provides abstraction for the low level process creation/deletion activities.

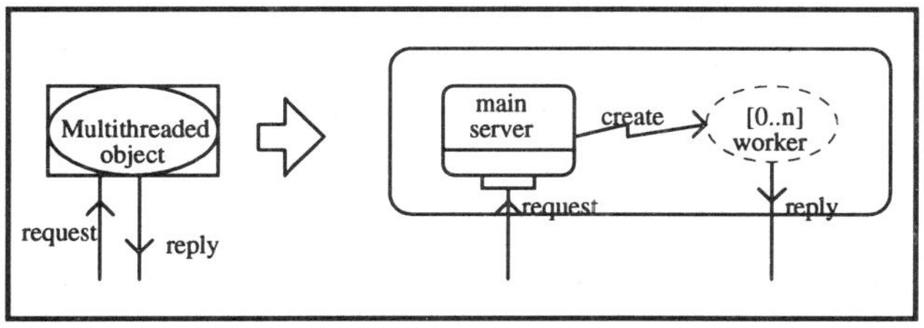

Fig.8. Default behaviour of a Multithreaded Object

A multithreaded object is represented by an ellipse enclosed by a rectangle. It receives requests from multiple clients. Its default structure (expressed within the roundangle) is as shown in figure 8. The following is a list of its behavioural characteristics:

- A control process receives requests from clients non-deterministically, and creates processes to service those requests.
- The control process is static.
- Unlimited numbers of dynamic processes can be created. This is only limited by the underlying operating system.
- Worker processes die from aging. That is, the worker processes leave the system once their work is complete, and reply directly back to client.
- The *request* path may be replicated depending on number of clients present.
- The number of *reply* paths depends on the number of worker processes. There is one reply path coming out from each instance of the worker process.

A designer may override this default structure and or behaviour by providing the decomposition of the multithreaded object. If this is the case, the multithreaded object simply provides an abstraction at the higher level of design, and frees the designer from being too concerned about using multithreaded processes to exploit parallelism at early stages of software development.

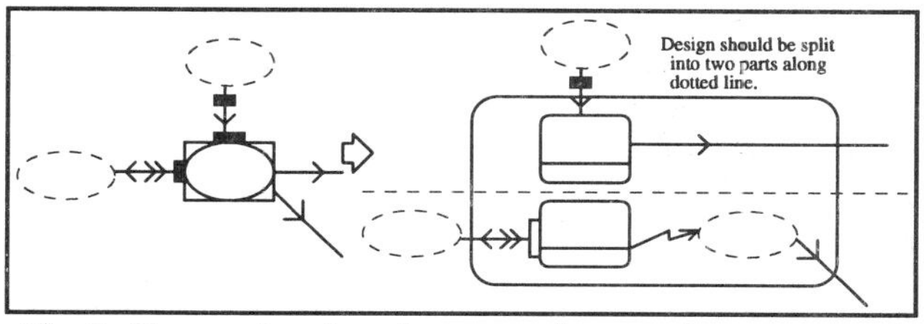

Fig.9. Example of an incorrect use of concurrent path constructor on a multithreaded object

Designers should find that there is no need to use path constructors with multithreaded objects. Input handling can be conveniently left as *unspecified.* In this case, if there are multiple input paths going into the multithreaded object, then, they are handled non-deterministically by default. If deterministic input handling is desired (in the case of static clients), this should be specified at the decomposed level. Concurrent input handling should never be applied to multithreaded objects. If the need to do this arises, designer should have decomposed the parallel processes at a higher level (Fig.9).

The process and path names in figure 9 have been left out deliberately. The functionality and behaviour of the various process objects should be clear even without the labelling.

3. Sample Designs

3.1. Client-Server Paradigm

Client-server computing exploits all the strong points of a distributed system, such as fault tolerance and application portability. Developing software using the client-server paradigm encourages code reuse. In a networking environment, a server often serves multiple clients [7] [8]. In order to exploit the hardware parallelism, the *main server* often creates multiple *workers* to provide services to all clients (see Fig.10b).

In the top-level diagram, *client* is modelled to be a dynamic process. This means there may be multiple clients at any one time, or no clients at all. An external object called *client_generator* is used to create clients in the system. In real world applications, the client request may come from the user keying request through the keyboard, or may simply be a part of an application program needing certain computation carried out by another program.

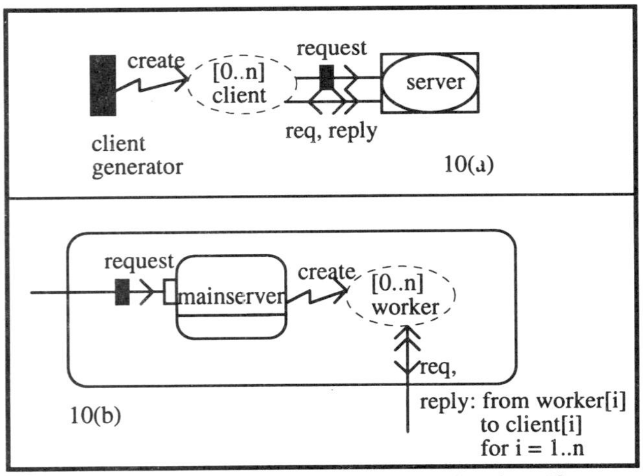

Fig.10(a). Top level process graph of a client-server system
Fig.10(b). Decomposition of the server process

There are two communication paths between a *client* and the *server*. There is a non-blocking send from the client to *request* service to be done with a blocking receive at the server's end. Then, a bi-directional communication path is set up, for the actual *request* message and *reply* to be transferred.

The *server* process here is modelled as a multithreaded process. Its decomposed structure is as shown in Fig.10(b) enclosed by the module symbol *roundangle*. Its function is to receive requests from clients, create instances of workers to perform the necessary work or computation, and upon completion, send the required result back to clients. Notice that the work request and reply messages are passed between clients and the worker processes without the supervision of the main server process. Upon work completion, instances of the worker process objects exit the system. Hence the default termination behaviour: aging.

3.2. Primes Sieve of Erastosthenes

The problem of generating prime numbers using multiple processes is described in [9]. The aim is to compute all the prime numbers up to a certain positive integer *limit*.

To achieve this, we require a process that generates a stream of odd numbers, a set of processes that filters out non-primes, and an output process that returns prime numbers. However, we do not know in advance how many *filtering* processes are required since we do not even know how many prime numbers to compute. Ext-PARSE allows the design of this type of program, where the structure cannot be determined statically.

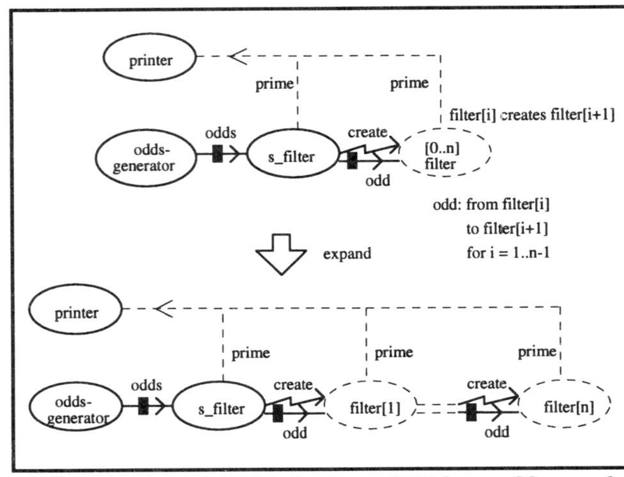

Fig.11. Ext-PARSE design of 'Primes Sieve of Erastosthenes'

The process graph in Fig.11 computes prime numbers. The process *odds_generator* generates a stream of odd numbers which are fed into a pipeline of processes. Each *filter* process sends the first number it receives to a *printer* process and subsequently filters out multiples of that number from the stream of odd numbers. It also creates a new filter process when it detects a new prime. The program terminates when a filter sends a prime to the printer process which is greater than *limit*.

For example, *odds_generator* generates '3' as the first number, and passes it to the first *filter* process. This *filter* process passes '3' as a prime number to the *printer* process, and the *printer* process subsequently prints '3'. The next number generated is '5', since '5' is not a multiple of '3', the first *filter* process creates a second *filter* process, and passes '5' to it. Upon receiving the number '5', the second *filter* process sends '5' to the *printer* process for printing. This process is continued for number '7', hence a third *filter* process is created. When '9' has been generated, it however does not bypass the first *filter* process. Since '9' is a multiple of '3', it is discarded. We can see from this process, a sequence of prime numbers is generated: 3, 5, 7, 11, 13, ... and so on, with each prime number received by the last *filter* in the pipeline at all times.

The following is a set of design features:

- The *s_filter* process is static. It is created when the system begins execution.
- Value of n depends on *limit*. It is determined at run time. This is consistent with *filter* processes being

created at run time.

- The creation of *filter* processes in the *growing* pipeline is ordered. Each *filter* process is created by the process that was most recently created. The unique numbering of *filter* process instances can be used to define the ordering here: *filter[2]* is created after *filter[1]*, *filter[3]* is created after *filter[2]*, and so on. Hence, for example, *filter[4]* does not exist in the system if *filter[i] for i = 1,2, and 3* are not present in the system.
- Once an instance of the *filter* process has been created, it stays in the system until the termination of the entire program itself. That is, when all prime numbers up to *limit* have been computed.
- The paths named *prime* going into the printer process are *dotted*. There is always just one prime number coming from the last filter in the pipeline. As soon as a particular filter instance has used its *prime* path to send a number to printer, that path is no longer needed. Hence the *transactional* nature of this communication path.
- The printer process may be modelled as a control process if it controls the termination of the program. Whenever the printer process receives a prime number from an instance of the filter process, it checks to see if it is greater than *limit*. If it is, then the program is terminated.
- The pipeline may grow forever. If *limit* is specified as *unlimited* or not specified at all, then the printer process accepts all numbers coming from the *prime* communication path, and new *filter* processes are generated all the time (although becoming less frequent!).

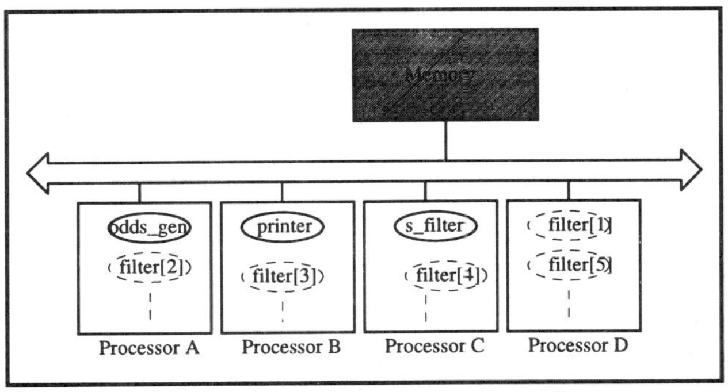

Fig.12. Process distribution on a multi-processor machine

The solution to this problem is a perfect example of an application program that can fully exploit the processing power of symmetric multi-processing machines. Each time a *filter* process is created, the underlying system would dispatch it to a processor with the smallest load. So, basically, all *filter* processes could be more or less evenly distributed around different processors.

3.3. A Lift Controller

This example shows how a program structure changes according to client requests. It is a simplified version of the *Ubiquitous Elevator Problem* discussed in [10].

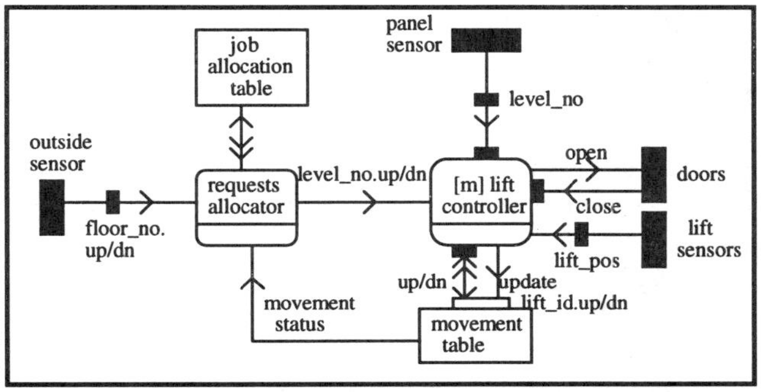

Fig.13. Top level process graph of the 'Lift Problem'

The requirement is to design software which controls passenger elevators. Elevators can be called via *up* or *down* buttons on each floor. Inside an elevator, passengers may select destination floors by pressing buttons on a panel. However, while the elevator is in motion, only requests to go to floors in the same direction are accepted by the controller.

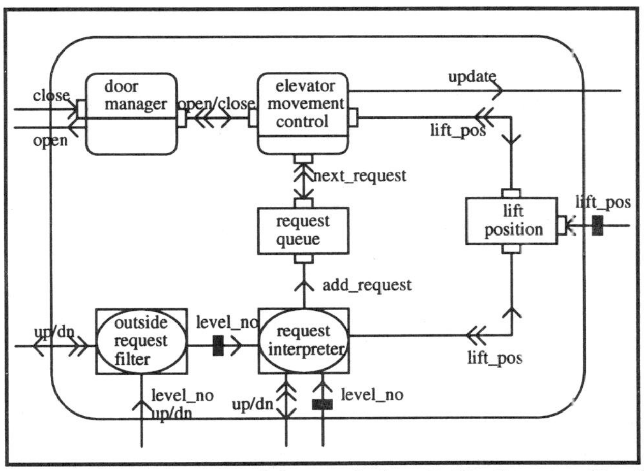

Fig.14. Decomposition of the 'Lift Controller' process

For a set of 'm' lifts, there are 'm' lift controller processes, each controls their own lifts (see Fig.14). There is also a process *requests allocator*, which delegates tasks to different lifts upon the receipt of requests from outside sensors. Notice there is only one path being used at any time between *requests allocator* and *lift controller*. There is always only one lift allocated the job to service a request. The *request allocator* chooses a lift by reading the *movement status* of all lifts, as well as the *job allocation table*. Thus ensuring all lifts have approximately equal number of requests to serve, and at the same time minimises overhead movement of lifts in order to service requests. Lastly, the external entities: *doors* and *lift_sensors* provide status information to the corresponding lift controller.

The process objects inside a *lift controller process* are:

- Data server **lift position** accepts input from the external entity *lift sensor*. Whenever requested, it provides the lift position information to the control process *elevator movement control*, and a multithreaded object *request interpreter*.
- **Outside request filter** is modelled as a multithreaded object. Its main function is to receive requests from the *request allocator* and obtains movement information from the *movement table*. It subsequently sends processed requests to *request interpreter*.
- **Request interpreter** is also a multithreaded object. It receives requests to go to particular levels from two sources: the *outside request filter* - requests from outside the lift, and *panel sensors* - request from inside the lift. *Request interpreter* obtains current lift position information and determines which requests to be placed onto the *request queue*.
- **Request queue** stores requested level numbers.
- **Elevator movement control** obtains the next request to service from the *request queue*. It determines the movement direction of the lift. If a change in direction is required, it sends an *update* message to the *movement table*. This control process also tells the *door manager* when the requested level has been reached or not. It does this by comparing the requested level with the current lift position.
- **Door manager** controls the opening and closing of the lift door.

The decomposition of the two processes: *outside request filter* and *request interpreter* are shown in Fig.15.

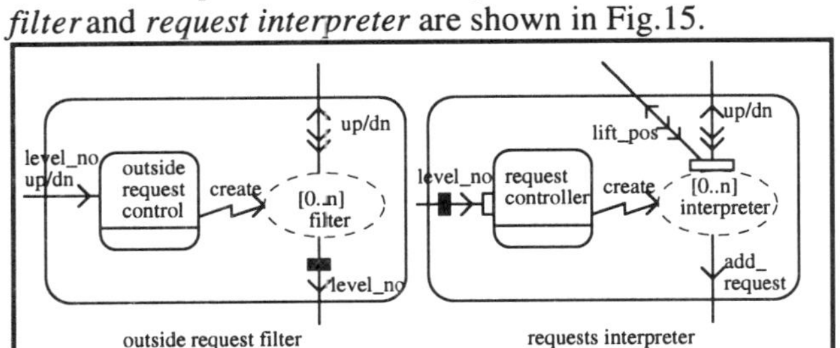

Fig.15. Decompositions of 'Outside Request Filter' and 'Requests Interpreter'

In both multithreaded processes, the level numbers (and up or down signals in the case of *outside request filter*) are received by the control processes, which then create dynamic worker processes to carry out the work. The information such as *level numbers* and *up* or *down* signals are passed to corresponding instances of dynamic worker processes upon creation.

The *filter* process inside the process *outside request filter* simply checks whether the request is going up or down. It also obtains current movement from the movement table. If the request is in the same direction as the *lift movement*, then the request is sent to *request interpreter* which subsequently places the request onto the queue. If however, the request is in the other direction, the filter process waits till the lift movement has changed before sending request to the *interpreter*.

Within the process *request controller*, each instance of the interpreter checks current *lift movement* and *position* in order to decide if the request can be serviced without changing lift movement direction. Thus adding the request to the *request queue*. Both requests from outside and inside the lift are serviced.

Both *filter* and *interpreter* processes die from *aging*.

4. Implementation Support - Win32

Several Ext-PARSE designs have been successfully enacted using Win32 API running on Windows NT. The Application Programming Interface Win32 API provides a rich set of function calls that enables the development of distributed systems [11] [12]. Table 1 gives a summary of Win32 API calls that supports the implementation of any Ext-PARSE designs:

Note: actual Win32 function calls are in *italic*.

5. Summary and Further Work

In this paper, an extension to the PARSE methodology was introduced. This new set of graphical notations caters for the design of distributed applications with dynamic properties. We have demonstrated the expressiveness of Ext-PARSE by presenting a wide variety of examples.

These examples vary from typical client-server applications, programs with regular structures, to large scale software systems. Ext-PARSE designs have been implemented using the Win32 API, and the mapping rules used have been presented. It should also be possible to derive mapping rules for other distributed operating system APIs. While few implementation environments support all the abstract process graph features, it is possible to simulate them using a combination of primitives. The development of distributed and multithreaded programs is crucial in exploiting the networking and multi-processor architecture in many common computer systems. Already, desktop operating systems like Windows NT are providing a rich set of Application Programming Interface. In support, Ext-PARSE exhibits many desirable features such

Ext-PARSE process graph feature	Win NT/Win32 API Equivalent
Dynamic process objects • create dynamic process objects • delete dynamic process objects: - aging - assassination - suicide • data server objects	Processes, threads • *CreateThread, CreateProcess, CreateRemoteThread* • thread termination: - return from function - *TerminateThread* - *ExitThread* • thread: Thread-Local Storage, shared memory: synchronisation objects
Communication Paths • creation • synchronous • asynchronous • bi-directional synchronous • broadcast	NamedPipes • *CreateNamedPipe* (an instance of a named pipe is always deleted when the last handle to the instance of the named pipe is closed) • blocking send, blocking receive, overlapped mode not enabled, *pipe-specific mode = PIPE WAIT* • non-blocking send, blocking receive, *pipe open mode = overlapped, pipe-specific mode = PIPE WAIT* • blocking send, blocking receive, *pipe open mode = PIPE ACCESS DUPLEX* • multiple instances of named pipes, or mailslots
Path Constructors • unspecified (not used in primitive processes) • concurrent • non-deterministic • deterministic	Input selection methods • no need to consider this in Win NT • independent threads carrying out work separately • NamedPipes non-deterministic by default • *WaitNamedPipe*

Table 1: Mapping between Ext-PARSE and Win32

as: architecture and language independence, and hierarchical process object structuring promoting high level of design abstraction. The graphical approach also provides an intuitive method for software design.

The next step in developing Ext-PARSE for the engineering of reliable distributed systems is design verification. PARSE designs currently can be verified using Petri Nets. For Ext-PARSE to be a versatile distributed systems design methodology, design verification is an important stage. It is believed that the work on π-calculus by Milner[13] offers a possible answer.

References

1. Ian Gorton, Innes Jelly, and Jonathan Gray, *"Parallel Software Engineering with PARSE"*, in Proceedings of COMPSAC-17, IEEE Int. Computer Software and Applications Conference, Nov. 1993, Phoenix, Arizona, USA, IEEE (1993).
2. Ian Gorton, Jonathan Gray, and Innes Jelly, *"Object-based Modelling Of Parallel Programs"*, IEEE Parallel and Distributed Technology, Summer edition, 1995, pp52-63.
3. Ian Gorton, Toong Shoon Chan and Innes Jelly, *"Engineering High Quality Parallel Software Using PARSE"*, Parallel Processing: CONPAR 94 - VAPP VI, pp.381-392.
4. Ian Gorton, Innes Jelly, Peter Croll and Patrick Nixon, *"Directions in Software Engineering for Parallel Systems"*, Proceedings of 28th Hawaii International Conference on System Sciences, Software Technology Track, Jan 3-6, 1995, IEEE.
5. Silberchatz, J. Peterson, and P.Galvin, *"Operating System Concepts"*, 3rd ed., Addison-Wesley, 1991.
6. Jonathan Gray, *"Definition of the PARSE Process Graph Notation, version 2 (PGN/2)"*, Technical Report PARSE-TR-2b, March 1994.
7. Richard Comerford, *"Engineering Workstations and PCs"*, IEEE Spectrum, April 1994, pp 45-46.
8. Judy Larocque, *"Client-Server Trend"*, IEEE Spectrum, April 1994, pp 48-50.
9. Jeff Kramer and Jeff Magee, *"Dynamic Configuration for Distributed Systems"*, IEEE Transactions on Software Engineering, vol. SE-11, no. 4, April 1985, pp 424-435.
10. Kyle Howland-Rose, Ury Szewcow, *"Exposing Concurrency, an Object Oriented Approach - Objects to Occam"*.
11. Jeffrey Richter, *"Advanced Windows NT, The Developer's Guide to the Win32 Application Programming Interface"*, Microsoft Press, 1994.
12. Helen Custer, *"Inside Windows NT"*, Microsoft Press, 1993.
13. Robin Milner, *"The Polyadic π-Calculus: a Tutorial"*, University of Edinburgh, Oct. 1991.

Behaviour Equation as Solution of Inheritance Anomaly in Concurrent Object-Oriented Programming Languages

Barry C.L. Leung and Peter P. K. Chiu

Department of Electronic Engineering
The Hong Kong Polytechnic University, Hong Kong

Abstract

In this paper, we propose a new model called Behaviour Description Equation which solves the problem of inheritance anomaly [3] found in concurrent object-oriented programmming languages and provides a means for the reuse of synchronisation code. The fundamental reason why inheritance anomaly occurs is that for a concurrent object, when synchronisation code is not properly separated from the method code, the extension of code to produce a derived class may force the change of both the synchronisation code and method code in the super class. We believe that both synchronisation code and method code should be treated in a separated manner as two different inheritance systems so that the interference between inheritance and object-based concurrency is avoided.

1. Introduction

In the last decade, people have been very interested to incorporate the concepts of object-oriented[1] design in the development of concurrent programs. There are two ways of achieving it. The first way is to extend the traditional object-oriented sequential programs with the concurrent features as reported in [6, 7, 8, 12 and 22]. The second way is to incorporate object-oriented concepts in concurrent programs. Examples include Actors [1], POOL [3, 4], Maude [15] and ABCL [23]. Some progress has been made. However, some fundamental problems still remain open, such as inheritance anomaly [3]. In this paper, we propose a simple but effective solution to such a problem.

The avoidance of inheritance anomaly has been identified to be one of the most difficult problems in concurrent object-oriented programming languages (COOPL). Inheritance anomaly is due to the conflict or interference between synchronisation and inheritance of concurrent object as pointed out in [2, 3, 5, 11, 13, 18 and 20]. Many methods have been proposed to reduce the interference between them. These proposals can be categorised into two different types of approaches. One type of approaches make use of the method guard concept [14], and the other type of approaches make use of the accept-set concept [20]. A method guard assigns a predicate to each method, and a message is accepted if it satisfies the predicate. But for an accept-set approach, the next set of messages to be accepted within a method code is specified in it. The results are not satisfactory because they usually cause the breaking of the encapsulation, the most important feature in object-oriented design.

Recently, several proposals have been made for minimising the effect of inheritance anomaly and improving the re-use of code in object-oriented programs [9, 14, 15 and 19]. Their point of view is similar to the accepted-set approach. They show that inheritance anomaly can be solved under some circumstances. The principal idea is that an object is made up of method code and synchronisation code. As described in [14], inheritance anomaly occurs under any one of the following conditions:-

1. partitioning of acceptable states,
2. history-only sensitiveness of acceptable states,
3. modification of acceptable states.

That is to say, if under each of these three conditions, the inheritance of code does not require any re-definition of the method code and at the same time, encapsulation is ensured, the concurrent object-oriented programming language is free from inheritance anomaly in most of the practical cases. This forms the criteria to test whether a method ensures a concurrent object-oriented programming languages free from inheritance anomaly.

In this paper, we propose the model of Behaviour Description Equation and show how this model provides a simple solution to the inheritance anomaly problem. To illustrate various concepts about inheritance anomaly,

[1] The terms on Object-Oriented Design we use in this paper are in the sense of [21].

1066-6192/96 $5.00 © 1996 IEEE
Proceedings of PDP '96

consider the example of a bounded buffer. The bounded buffer consists of two methods, *get()* and *put()*, and one instance variable, *number*. The *put()* method places an item into the *buffer* whereas the *get()* method removes an item from the buffer. For a *get_2_buffer*, it has three methods, i.e. *get()*, *put()* and *get_2()*, and an instance variable, *number* where the methods, *put()* and *get()*, and the instance variable, *number*, inherit from the super class, *buffer* and the method *get_2()* is defined as follows. The behaviour of this *get_2()* method is similar to that of the method *get()* except that it removes two consecutive items in the *get_2_buffer*. Of course, for invoking such method, the buffer must have at least two items inside. In a inheritance anomaly free concurrent program, the methods from the super class should work without any re-definitions. However, the following pseudo code using the concept of the behaviour abstraction [11] shows that the inherited methods need to be re-defined in the derived class. If we compare the definition of the method *put* in the two classes *buffer* and *get_2_buffer*, we find that for the method *get_2*, we need one more state and thus one more *become* statement. That is to say encapsulation has been broken.

```
// Behaviour Abstraction

Class buffer: {
  int    number = 0, SIZE;
Behaviour:
  Initial_State   = {empty};
  empty           = {put};
  partial         = {put, get};
  full            = {get};
Members:
  void   put() {
    number += 1;
    ...;
    if [number = SIZE]     Become full
    else                   Become partial;
  }
  void   get() {
    number -= 1;
    ...;
    if [number = 0]        Become empty
    else                   Become partial;
  }

Class get_2_buffer: buffer {
Behaviour:
  Initial_State  = Super(Initial_State);
  empty          = Super(empty);
  one            = Super(partial);
  partial        = Super(partial) + {get_2};
  full           = Super(full)    + {get_2};
Members:
  void   get_2() {
    number = number -2;
    ...;
    if [number = 0]        Become empty
    elseif [number = 1]    Become one
    else                   Become partial;
  }
  void   put() {
    number += 1;
    ...;
    if [number = SIZE]              Become full
    elseif [1 < number < SIZE]      Become partial
    else                            Become one;
  }
  void   get() {
    number -= 1;
    ...;
    if [number = 0]              Become empty
    elseif [number = 1]          Become one
    else                         Become partial;
  }
}
```

2. Object Models

2.1 The Traditional Object Model

In a concurrent object-oriented programming language, the object model from sequential program is extended to characterise the concurrent nature of the object. Special attention has been paid on determinism of the execution and communication. Otherwise, deadlock may result during execution, or data may become inconsistent after execution. As suggested by Kafura, the extra code needed for concurrent object in is the interface controller [11]. As shown in Figure 1, the interface controller decides whether the input message in the message queue can be forwarded to the object for further processing. In [11, 14 and 20], the interface controller uses the input message and considers the set of allowable methods for this state to decide whether a method is invoked. After starting the method execution, it is no longer synchronised by the interface controller. Having completed the method execution, the next message arrived in the message queue is processed by the interface controller. The interface controller can synchronise the operation inside the object again. Therefore, the decision of the concurrency and synchronisation control depends on the current message in the message queue and the current state of the interface controller, i.e. the state of the object.

The problem of synchronisation mechanisms based on the interface controller and the interface control space is that a new method defined in a derived class may cause the re-definition of the methods in the super class [11]. This sort of synchronisation mechanism in COOPL still suffers from the interference between method code and the synchronisation code of an object, even though the problem of inheritance anomaly can be solved in some situations.

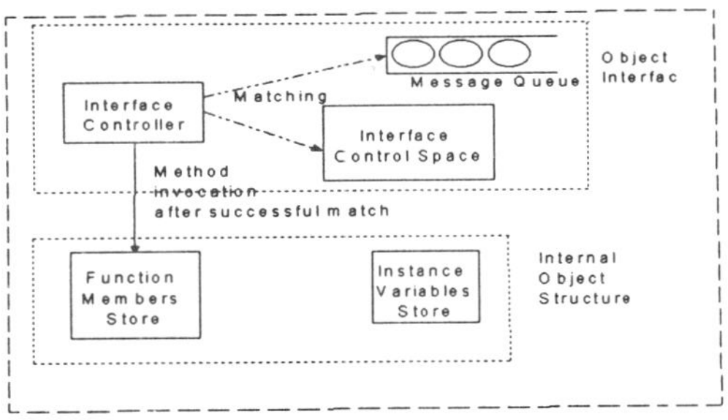

Figure 1. Kafura's Object Model.

2.2 Our Model

The main reason why the traditional object model fails is that the model is based on the exclusive working of the concurrency interface controller on the interface control space and the method code on the instance variables of the object. The complete separation of the dependence between these two parts can provide a methodology with reduced design complexity. However, in the previous model [11], these two parts of an object are not totally orthogonal. As a result, this model cannot manage all the possible situations of inheritance anomaly. In the our model, the minimum dependence of the relationship between the synchronisation code and object members code is maintained.

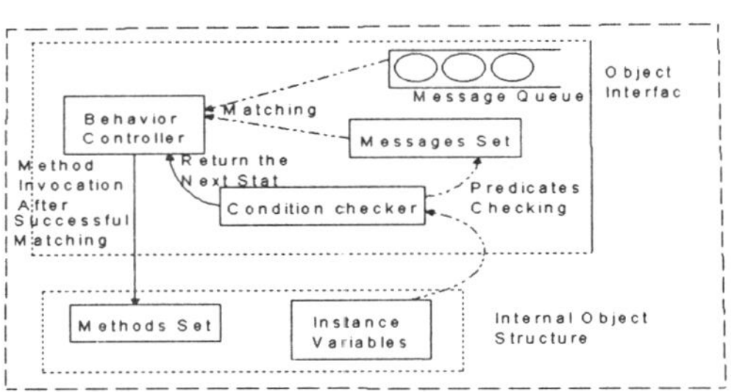

Figure 2. Object Model Based on Behaviour Equation.

Figure 2 shows the details of the relationship between the synchronisation code and object members code. Any incoming message is queued in the message queue. The description of our model can be divided into two parts:-

a. An object creation and initialisation: When an object is created it is in its initial state, and a message set will be enabled which corresponds to this initial state of the object. The state information of an object is stored in the condition checker.

b. The internal operation of an object: After the execution of the methods, the instance variables will be updated. The next state of an object is obtained by the updated value of the instance variables in the conditional checker. Based on the information of the current state and the value of the instance variables, the next enabled-set is obtained. Meanwhile, the conditional checker will inform the message set which enabled-set should be used in the next. Finally, the behaviour controller will gather the information of the next state from conditional checker, the enabled-set from the message set, and the next message key from the message queue so as to determine which method should be invoked.

Figure 2 shows the details of the relationship between the synchronisation code and object members code. When an object is created, it is in its initial state, and a message set will be enabled which corresponds to its initial state of an object. The responsibility of the behaviour controller is used to decide the future behaviour of the object. Before it invokes the corresponding method, the behaviour controller reads an input message from the message queue. This input message will be checked whether it is included in the message set just enabled. If the input message is valid, a corresponding method is invoked. If the input message is invalid, an exception handler is invoked. After execution of the method, the object's instance variables may be changed. The condition checker will then take the responsibility to find out the next state of the object depending on the previous input message and the predicate. Finally, the condition checker will inform the behaviour controller what the next state of an object will be.

3. Behaviour Equation

In this section, some examples will be presented to illustrate the concepts and the model of Behaviour Description Equation. Firstly, we explain the details of various types of bounded buffers. They are chosen because they have been used extensively by many research workers to illustrate the problem of inheritance anomaly and their solutions to such problem. The problems of their solutions will be discussed and we also show how the Behaviour Equation solves various cases of inheritance anomaly as described in Section 1. Furthermore, we will also discuss the inheritance anomaly in the case multiple inheritance and how we apply the model of the Behaviour Description Equation to handle it.

3.1 The Syntax of the Behaviour Equation

Some ideas of the Behaviour Description Equation are from the CCS model of Milner [16]. Emphasis of the model is put on the characterisation of the concurrent nature of an object. The concept of "state" is very important for this model. The syntax used in the Behaviour Equation is described as follows.

STATE = TERM + TERM + ... (1)
TERM = A_ACT{[PRED][PRED]...}.OBJ_STATE; (2)
STATE = Based(CLASS.STATE + CLASS.STATE + ...)/
{-([TERM]), +([TERM])}; (3)

Equation (1) is a behaviour equation which is used to represent the object behaviour when the object is in a particular state. Equation (2) denotes the composition of the object behaviour. The word *TERM* in this equation is called the behavioural term because it shows the object behaviour. After the execution of a given method, or atomic action, the predicate *[PRED]* will be checked. If the *[PRED]* is true, the *[OBJ_STATE]* will be the next state. In some cases, the predicate may be always true. In this case, this item may be omitted for brevity.

Equation (3) only appears in the derived class definition only. The word, *Based*, is a keyword, which means all the behavioural terms of the indicated super class after the word, *Based()*, will be inherited to the derived class. Note that in the case of multiple inheritance, more than one super class can be specified. The term *-([TERM])* means that some behavioural terms belonging to the given state that are inherited from the super class will be discarded. On the other hand, the term *+([TERM])* means that some new behavioural terms belonging to the given state are introduced.

3.2 The Bounded Buffer

Bounded buffer denoted as *buffer* as described in Section 1 is modelled by the following Behaviour Equation which show all the possible next-state behaviour of an object:-

```
EMPTY     = put.PARTIAL                              (4)
PARTIAL   = put[0 < number < SIZE].PARTIAL   +
              put[number = SIZE].FULL          +
              get[0 < number < SIZE].PARTIAL   +
              get[number =0].EMPTY                   (5)
FULL      = get.PARTIAL                              (6)
```

Equation (4) shows that if the current state of an object is *EMPTY* and the input message is "*put*", its next state will be *ONE*. For implementation, the *buffer* may be described using the C++ like syntax as follows.

```
CLASS   buffer {
  int  SIZE,   number = 0;
BEHAVIOR_CONTROLLER:
  EMPTY     = put.PARTIAL;
  PARTIAL   = put[0 < number < SIZE].PARTIAL   +
              put[number = SIZE].FULL          +
              get[0 < number < SIZE].PARTIAL   +
              get[number = 0].EMPTY;
  FULL      = get.PARTIAL;
MEMBERS;
  void   put(int item)
    {number ++; ...};    // Put an item into the bounded buffer.
  int  get()
    {number --; ...};    // Remove an item from the bounded
                         // buffer.
}
```

The pseudo code of the bounded buffer includes two main parts, the *BEHAVIOR_CONTROLLER* and the *MEMBERS*. These two parts correspond to the synchronisation code and the method code respectively. The local variable, *SIZE*, defines the bounded buffer size.

3.3 The Bounded Buffer with the *get_2* Method

In this section, the *get_2_buffer* is introduced. As compared with *buffer*, there is an additional method called *get_2()* which is used to get two items each time. For the rest of its behaviour, it is indistinguishable from that of the *buffer*. That is why we say that the *get_2_buffer* inherits from *buffer*. However, we may need additional state to handle the case that the buffer has only one item. Under such state, the invocation of the *get_2()* method is not allowed. The *get_2_buffer* is described by the following set of behaviour description equations.

```
EMPTY     = put.ONE                                     (7)
ONE       = put.PARTIAL + get.EMPTY                     (8)
PARTIAL   = put[0 < number < SIZE].PARTIAL    +
            put[number = SIZE].FULL           +
            get[0 < number < SIZE].PARTIAL    +
            get[number = 1].ONE               +
            get_2[number = 0].EMPTY           +
            get_2[number = 1].ON              +
            get_2[0 < number < SIZE].PARTIAL            (9)
FULL      = get.PARTIAL  + get_2.PARTIAL                (10)
```

Note that the Equation (8) which involves state *ONE* is a new behaviour equation in class *get_2_buffer*. This equation and state do not appear in the class *buffer*. As a result, the inheritance of any behaviour related to the Equation (8) from the class *buffer* to the *get_2_buffer* is impossible.

The pseudo code of the *get_2_buffer* written in C++ syntax like format is shown as follows.

```
CLASS   get_2_buffer: buffer {
BEHAVIOR_CONTROLLER:
  EMPTY  = Based(EMPTY)/{-(put.PARTIAL), (put.ONE)};
  ONE    = put.PARTIAL    + get.EMPTY;
  PARTIAL= Based(PARTIAL)/{-(get[number = 0].EMPTY),
                           +(get[number = 1].ONE)};
  FULL   = Based(FULL);
MEMBERS:
  int  get_2()
    {number += 1; ...}  // get_2() will remove two consecutive
                        // items in the get_2_buffer
}
```

Comparing the behaviour equation for state *EMPTY* of *buffer* (i.e. Equation (4)) and that of *get_2_buffer* (i.e. Equation (7)), the behavioural terms in Equation (7) are behavioural terms in Equation (4) except the behavioural term "*put.PARTIAL*". Therefore, the *PARTIAL* state of *get_2_buffer* is based on the *PARTIAL* state of *buffer* and the different behavioural term must be discarded. Besides, the behavioural term "*put.ONE*" is added to the behaviour equation (4) to obtain that for *get_2_buffer*. As a result, the new behaviour equation *EMPTY* of the *get_2_buffer* is introduced. The others are obtained in the similar way.

According to the above code, no method re-definition is needed. That is to say, method code can be inherited completely from its super class. Furthermore, using the Behaviour Equation, re-use of the synchronisation code is also possible. For other models, the reason why the synchronisation code cannot be inherited completely from its super class, like the method code, is that the synchronisation code used in the other models do not exactly represents the behaviour of an object. That is the reason why these models will fail in some cases. In our point of view, if two objects with the same synchronisation code, these two objects will be said having the same observable external behaviours. Any difference in observable external behaviour of the objects may conclude that their synchronisation code must be different where this synchronisation code different depends on the degree of the behaviour different of the objects.

3.4 The Bounded Buffer with the *naget()* Method

In this section, we will show that how Behaviour Equation is used to solved the inheritance anomaly of the history sensitiveness of acceptable states problem. We introduce a new concurrent object called *naget_buffer*. For this object, a new method called *naget()* is introduced to the *buffer*. The behaviour of the method, *naget()*, is similar to that of *get()*, with the exception is that it cannot be accepted immediately after the invocation of the method *get()*. The behaviour description equation that model the behaviour of the *naget_buffer* are shown as follows.

```
EMPTY   = put.PARTIAL                                  (11)
PARTIAL = put[0 < number < SIZE].PARTIAL      +
          put[number = SIZE].FULL             +
          naget[0 < number < SIZE].PARTIAL    +
          naget[number = 0].EMPTY  +  get.GET          (12)
FULL    = get.GET  +  naget.PARTIAL                    (13)
GET     = get[number = 0].EMPTY  +
          get[number < SIZE].GET  +  put.PARTIAL       (14)
```

The pseudo code of the *naget_buffer* where the class buffer is its super class. Note that the Equation (14) and state *GET* are new.

```
CLASS   naget_buffer: buffer {
BEHAVIOR_CONTROLLER:
  EMPTY    = Based(EMPTY);
  PARTIAL  =Based(PARTIAL)/{
              -(get.[number = 0].EMPTY,
                get[0 < number < SIZE].PARTIAL),
              +(get.GET, naget[number = 0].EMPTY,
                naget[0 < number < SIZE].PARTIAL)};
  FULL     = Based(FULL)/{-(get.PARTIAL), +(get.GET)};
  GET      = put.PARTIAL + get[0 < number < SIZE].GET +
             get[number = 0].EMPTY;
MEMBERS:
  int  naget()
     {number ++; ...}     // naget() will get an item excepted that
                          // it cannot be
          // accepted immediately after the invocation of the
          // method get().
}
```

We can see that the inheritance anomaly in the method code and the synchronisation code do not occur. None of the inherited methods need to be re-defined. In the synchronisation code, we need to subtract more behavioural terms and introduce some behavioural terms. It is because it has few changes of the behaviour of the *naget_buffer* from that of *buffer*. However, large portions of the synchronisation code, and around half of the class *buffer* code can be reused. Additionally, it provides a unique and a systematic code re-use way for the users.

3.5 The Bounded Buffer with *Lock()* and *Unlock()* Methods

In this section, we introduce the class *lock_buffer*, which involves the modification of the acceptable states. For such a buffer, the instance variable *no_lock* is used to count how many times of an object being locked so that it provides a multi-level locks of an object. The method *lock()* will lock the object and increases the counter *no_lock* by one. The method *unlock()* will unlock the object and decreases the counter *no_lock* by one. The behaviour description equations associated with the class *lock* are shown as follows..

```
LOCK = lock.LOCK  + unlock[no_lock = 0].UNLOCK +
          unlock[no_lock > 0].LOCK                     (15)
UNLOCK  = lock.LOCK                                    (16)
```

The pseudo code of the class *lock* is shown as follows.

```
CLASS   lock {
  int  no_lock = 0;
BEHAVIOR_CONTROLLER:
  LOCK     = lock.LOCK  +  unlock[no_lock = 0].UNLOCK  +
               unlock[no_lock > 0].LOCK;
  UNLOCK   = lock.LOCK;
MEMBERS:
  void lock()
     {no_lock += 1; ...}  // locking the object and increasing the
                          // lock counter, no_lock, by one.
  void unlock()
     {no_lock -= 1; ...}  // unlocking the object and decreasing
                          // the lock counter, no_lock, by one.
}
```

We will show how to reuse the synchronisation code from both classes *lock* and *buffer* for the new class *lock_buffer*. This is a special kind of multiple inheritance with no method duplication appeared in the derived class.

Multiple inheritance with ambiguities of the method duplication in the derived class will be introduced in the next section.

The behaviour description Equation of the class lock_buffer are shown as follows.

```
EMPTY     = put.PARTIAL + lock.LOCK                        (17)
PARTIAL   = lock.LOCK                                      +
            put[0 < number < SIZE].PARTIAL                 +
            put[number = SIZE].FULL                        +
            get[0 < number < SIZE].PARTIAL                 +
            get[number = 0].EMPTY                          (18)

FULL      = get.PARTIAL     + lock.LOCK                    (19)
LOCK      = lock.LOCK    +
        unlock[number = 0][no_lock = 0].EMPTY              +
        unlock[0 < number < SIZE][no_lock = 0].PARTIAL     +
        unlock[number = SIZE][no_lock = 0].FULL            +
        unlock[no_lock > 0].LOCK                           (20)
```

The pseudo code of the class *lock_buffer* is shown as follows where *buffer* and *lock* are the super classes.

```
CLASS lock_buffer: buffer, lock {
STATE_CONTROLLER:
   EMPTY     = Based(buffer.EMPTY + lock.UNLOCK);
   PARTIAL   = Based(buffer.PARTIAL + lock.UNLOCK);
   FULL      = Based(buffer.FULL + lock.UNLOCK);
   LOCK      = Based(lock.LOCK)/
        {+(unlock[number = 0][no_lock = 0].EMPTY,
           unlock[0 < number < SIZE][no_lock = 0].PARTIAL,
           unlock[number = SIZE][no_lock = 0].FULL,
           unlock[no_lock > 0].LOCK)};
MEMBERS:
}
```

According to the above pseudo code, we observe that all the behavioural terms in the class buffer and the class lock can be reused, all of the behavioural terms of the super classes are reusable. We can conclude that our behaviour-oriented object-oriented language solves the problem of inheritance anomaly.

3.6 Multiple Inheritance

In this section, we will discuss the use of the Behaviour Equation in COOP with multiple inheritance. In the class, *new_buffer*, all methods are inherited from its super classes, *get_2_buffer* and *naget_buffer*. Obviously, the methods *put()* and *get()* appear twice in the super class of the class *new_buffer*. So, some criteria for method selection from the super classes should determined, so as to avoid the ambiguities of the method code in the class *naget_buffer*.

The behaviour description equations for the class *new_buffer* are shown as follows. Note that for Equation (23), a new state *TWO* is added, i.e. no behavioural terms can be inherited from its super classes.

```
EMPTY   = put.ONE                                          (21)
ONE     = put.TWO + get.EMPTY + naget.EMPTY                (22)
TWO     = put.PARTIAL + get.GET + naget.ONE +
          get_2.EMPTY                                      (23)
PARTIAL = get.GET + put[0 < number < SIZE].PARTIAL   +
             put[number = SIZE].FULL                 +
             naget[2 < number < SIZE]. PARTIAL       +
             naget[number = 2].TWO                   +
             get_2[number = 0].EMPTY                 +
             get_2[number = 1].ONE                   +
             get_2[2 < number < SIZE].PARTIAL        +
             get_2[number = 2].TWO                         (24)
FULL    = get.GET + get_2.PARTIAL + naget.PARTIAL          (25)
GET   = put[2 < number < SIZE].PARTIAL          +
          put[number = 2].TWO         +
          get[number = 0].EMPTY       +
          get[number < SIZE].GET                           (26)
```

The pseudo code of the class *new_buffer* is shown as follows.

```
CLASS new_buffer: get_2_buffer, naget_buffer {
BEHAVIOR_CONTROLLER:
   EMPTY   = Based(get_2_buffer.EMPTY);
   ONE     = Based(ONE)/{-(put.PARTIAL), +
                         (put.TWO, naget.EMPTY)};
   TWO     = put.PARTIAL + get.GET + naget.ONE +
             get_2.EMPTY;
   PARTIAL  = Based(get_2_buffer.FULL +
             naget_buffer.FULL)/
                 {-(get_2[0 < number < SIZE].PARTIAL,
                    get[number = 1].ONE,
                    get[0 < number < SIZE].PARTIAL,
                    naget[number = 0].EMPTY,
                    naget[0 < number < SIZE].PARTIAL),
                  +(get_2[number = 2].TWO,
                    get_2[2 < number < SIZE].PARTIAL,
                    naget[number = 2].TWO,
                    naget[2 < number < SIZE].PARTIAL)};
   FULL  = Based(get_2_buffer.FULL + naget_buffer.FULL)/
                 {-(get.PARTIAL)};
   GET   = Based(GET)/
            {-(put.PARTIAL),
             +(put[number = 2].TWO,
               put[2 < number < SIZE].PARTIAL)};
MEMBERS:
}
```

In Equation (21), *EMPTY* means that the behavioural terms of it is inherited from its super class *get_2_buffer*, not from the class *naget_buffer*. Because we find that, by comparison, the behaviour equation *EMPTY* of the class *get_2_buffer* is the same as that of the class *new_buffer*. The others are obtained in the similar way. In the above pseudo code, no method need to be redefined. This satisfies the criteria for the inheritance anomaly free as stated in Section 1. Moreover, nearly 70% of the behavioural terms can be re-used. The result is inspirational and promising. Together with the various cases as described before, this shows that Behaviour

Equation does solve the problem of inheritance anomaly in various cases as described in [14].

4. Conclusion and Future Work

In this paper, we have described the Behaviour Equation and demonstrate that it provides a solution for the problem of the interference between the method code and the synchronisation code. All the conditions under which inheritance anomaly occurs as described in [14] have been handled successfully. Not only all of the method code can be reused and in some cases all of the synchronisation code as well. This model provides a systematic approach to analysis this problem, and results in inheritance anomaly free concurrent object-oriented programs.

Despite this model provides a way to avoid the inheritance anomaly in COOP, further improvements are possible. For instance, a little change of a predicate of a behavioural term always causes the replacement of the whole behavioural term. Possible improvement may be made on the separating the dependencies between the predicates with the remaining parts of the behavioural terms, such that the new behavioural terms are orthogonal to the predicates. This facilities the re-use of the synchronisation code and the design considerations of an object. To further enhance our model, we are now working on the study on the application of CSP [10], CCS [16], or π-Calculus [17] to our work.

Acknowledgement:

We are grateful to the Research Committee, The Hong Kong Polytechnic University for their support to this project under the account 340/535.

References:

[1] Gul Agha, Actors: A Model of Concurrent Computation in Distributed Systems, The MIT Press 1986.

[2] Mehmet Aksit, Anand Tripathi, "Data Abstraction and Mechanism in Sina/St," in Proceedings of OOPSLA '88, ACM SIGPLAN Notices, vol. 23, 9/1988, pp. 267-275.

[3] Pierra America, "Inheritance and Subtyping in a Parallel Object-Oriented Language," in Proceedings of OOPSLA '88, LNCS 276, Springer-Verlag, 1987, pp. 234-242.

[4] Pierra America, "A Parallel Object-Oriented Language with Inheritance and Subtyping," in Proceeding of OOPSLA '90, ACM SIGPLAN Notices, vol. 25, 10/1990, pp. 161-168.

[5] Jean-Pierre Briot, Akinori Yonezawa, "Inheritance and Synchronisation in Concurrent OOP," in Proceedings of ECOOP '87, LNCS 276, Springer-Verlag, 1987, pp. 33-40.

[6] Denis Caromel, "A General Model for Concurrent and Distributed Object-Oriented Programming," in Proceedings of the 1988 ACM SIGPLAN Workshop on Object-Based Concurrent Programming, ACM SIGPLAN Notices, vol. 24, 1989, pp. 102-104.

[7] Denis Caromel, "Concurrency and Reusability: From Sequential to Parallel," Journal of Object-Oriented Programming, 9-10/1990, pp. 34-42.

[8] D. Decouchant, P. Le Dot, M. Riveill, C. Roisin, X. Rousset de Pina, "A Synchronisation Mechanism for an Object Oriented Distributed System," ACM SIGPLAN Workshop on Concurrent Object-Based Language Design, Special Issue of SIGPLAN Notices 24(4), 4/1989, pp. 105-107.

[9] Svend Frolund, "Inheritance of Synchronisation Constraints in Concurrent Object-Oriented Programming Languages," in Proceedings of ECOOP '92, 1992.

[10] C. A. R. Hoare, "Communicating Sequential Processes," CACM , 21(8), 1978, pp. 666-677.

[11] Dennis G. Kafura, Keung Hae Lee, "Inheritance in Actor Based Concurrent Object-Oriented Languages," in Proceedings of ECOOP '89, 1989, pp. 131-145.

[12] Klaus-Peter Lohr, "Concurrency Annotations," in Proceeding of OOPSLA '92, 1992, pp. 327-340.

[13] Satoshi Matsuoka, Ken Wakita, Akinori Yonezawa, "Synchronisation Constraints With Inheritance: What Is Not Possible- So What Is?" Technical Report 90-010, Department of Information Science, University of Tokyo, 1990.

[14] Satoshi Matsuoka, Akinori Yonezawa, "Analysis of Inheritance Anomaly in Object-Oriented Concurrent Programming Languages," in Gul Agha, Akinori Yonezawa, Peter Wegner, Editors, Research Directions in Concurrent Object-Oriented Programming, MIT Press, 1993.

[15] Jose Meseguer, "Solving the Inheritance Anomaly in Concurrent Object-Oriented Programming," in Proceedings of ECOOP '93, 1993, pp. 220-246.

[16] R. Milner, A Calculus of Communicating Systems, LNCS 92, Springer-Verlag, New York, 1980.

[17] Robin Milner, "The Polyadic Pi-Calculus: A Tutorial," ECS-LFCS-91-180, Department of Computer Science, University of Edinburgh, 1991.

[18] Christian Neusius, "Synchronising Actions," in Proceedings of ECOOP '91, LNCS 512, Springer-Verlag 1991, pp. 118-132.

[19] Etsuya Shibayama, "Reuse of Concurrent Object Descriptions," in Proceedings of TOOLS3, Sydney, 11/1990, pp. 254-266.

[20] Chris Tomlinson, Vineet Singh, "Inheritance and Synchronisation with Enabled-Sets," in Proceedings of OOPSLA '89, ACM SIGPLAN Notices, vol. 24, 10/1989, pp. 103-112

[21] Peter Wegner, "The Dimensions of Object-Based Language Design," in Proceedings of OOPSLA '87, ACM SIGPLAN Notices, vol. 22, 12/1987, pp. 168-182.

[22] Y. Yokote, M. Tokoro, "The Design and Implementation of Concurrent Smalltalk," in Proceedings of OOPSLA '86, ACM SIGPLAN Notices, vol. 21, 11/86.

[23] Akinori Yonezawa, ABCL: An Object-Oriented Concurrent System, The MIT Press 1990

Experiences on Porting a Parallel Objects Environment from a Transputer Network to a PVM-Based System

Franco Zambonelli

Dipartimento di Elettronica Informatica e Sistemistica - Università di Bologna
Viale Risorgimento 2 - 40136 Bologna - ITALY
E-mail: fzambonelli@deis.unibo.it

Matteo Pugassi

Dipartimento di Elettronica e Informazione
Politecnico di Milano
Piazza L. da Vinci 32 - 20133 Milano - ITALY
E-mail: pugassi@elet.polimi.it

Letizia Leonardi

Nello Scarabottolo

Dipartimento di Scienze dell'Ingegneria - Università di Modena
214, Via Campi - 41100 Modena - ITALY
E-mail: {leonardi, scarabot}@dsi.unimo.it

Abstract

Parallel Objects is a powerful model for distributed/parallel Object-Oriented program-ming. Goal of this paper is to present the approach adopted in porting the support of the Parallel Objects environment, originally implemented for a massively parallel architecture, onto the PVM environment, which is nowadays a de-facto standard in the design of distributed applications on heterogeneous networks of computers.

1. Introduction

Heterogeneous computer networks are rapidly growing as the preferred target architectures for the development of parallel and distributed applications, for several reasons:

- high availability;
- low costs;
- ease of scaling.

The lack of standards has seriously compromised for many years the diffusion of general purpose environments for the development of large and portable applications. In the last few years, several proposals have been issued, with the aim of defining a stable and portable interface to the applications. Among the others, the PVM environment [1, 2], has become a de-facto standard in the design of distributed applications because PVM is now available for a wide range of architectures, from workstations to massively parallel architectures.

The PVM environment defines a message passing abstract architecture, by means of a set of primitives with a simple and clearly specified interface. However, the outlined model is still low-level and forces users to explicitly deal with process creation and inter-process communication directives.

A higher level of abstraction is needed to make parallel programming widely accepted. A promising field is given by object-oriented programming.

The above considerations have driven our work toward the implementation of the support for a parallel Object-Oriented programming environ-ment on the top of the PVM architecture, in order to offer a high-level programming interface to PVM users.

The paper presents the Parallel Objects (PO for short) programming environment [3], based on the object-oriented paradigm [4] and enriching it with parallelism. PO applications were originally conceived for massively parallel architectures, in particular for a transputer-based Meiko Computing Surface - 1 (from now on, MCS) [5].

1066-6192/96 $5.00 © 1996 IEEE
Proceedings of PDP '96

The peculiar characteristics of the MCS architecture have influenced the implementation of the support. Thus, the porting of the support onto the PVM had to deal with several problems, mainly due to the different computational model defined by the Meiko concrete architecture and the PVM abstract one.

Goal of the paper is to present our experience on the porting and to describe the implementation of the PVM support.

The paper is organized as follows. Section 2 describes the Parallel Objects model. Section 3 discusses the MCS support of PO. The need for moving toward distributed systems and the choice of the PVM system are motivated in section 4. The experience and the problems encountered in porting the PO environment from the MCS architecture to PVM are analyzed in section 5. Finally, section 6 briefly describes the PVM-based support to PO.

2. Parallel Objects

PO is an Object-Oriented parallel environment based on the **active objects** model [6].

PO can express parallelism with two dimensions of concurrency: by associating independent execution capacity with objects and by allowing multiple threads of execution within the same object. We distinguish then between **inter-object** and **intra-object parallelism** [3].

In parallel object languages, computation results from message passing between objects. When one object requires an external service, it sends a message to another object: the message specifies the service the sender needs. The receiving object verifies whether the operation is correct or not, then executes the requested operation. In PO both synchronous, asynchronous and future communication modes are available. Asynchronous communication modes enforce real inter-object parallelism: both the sender and the receiver objects can execute at the same time.

The second form of parallelism, the intra-object one, arises because of **multiple activities** within the same object. Since a parallel object can receive more than one request, each parallel object can execute several internal activities, one for each service request. Activities are created on request and terminated when the service is completed. The PO model does not constrain the number of internal activities that may run within the same object.

Incoming service requests are issued to execution on the basis of internal **synchronization constraints** against the already executing activities [7]. When it is the case, a request is served by creating an activity to execute the specified operation.

PO objects are always instances of a given class. PO **classes** describe both the non-parallel and the parallel part of an object. In particular, a class describes the interface (i.e. all the operations that can be requested to its instances), the state variables of its instances and the synchronization constraints. PO classes can be incrementally defined by means of a multiple inheritance mechanism.

3. The MCS Support to PO

This section describes the PO support for the MCS transputer-based architecture [5] and analyzes the characteristics of the MCS architecture that deeply influenced its implementation.

3.1. The PO Preprocessor

PO introduces a high-level language for defining classes and for developing application by using them: for further details see [3]. Starting from the PO language, a **preprocessor** parses the code of PO classes in order to solve the inheritance relationships and to translate the PO code into C code with calls to the support library.

Main tasks of the preprocessor are:

- to check the syntax of the PO sources in order to detect syntax errors or invalid semantic;
- to handle class inheritance;
- to translate the class implementation into C code, enriched with calls to the primitives of the PO support.

With regard to the last point, PO primitives are defined for:

- dynamic object creation and deletion;
- object naming;
- requesting services in asynchronous, synchronous and future mode;
- accessing the object state.

In addition, primitives for dealing with explicit object allocation are under implementation.

PO primitives encapsulate any architectural dependency: in particular, their interface has been conceived to be as general as possible to guarantee the portability of both the preprocessor and the run-time support, below described.

3.2. The Run-Time Support

The MCS support implementation consists of two levels: a support for the intra-object parallelism, replicated in each object, and a support for inter-object parallelism.

The intra-object support is composed by a set of threads (see Figure 1) that realize the execution management for each PO object [8]: they are the **Object Manager** (OM for short) and one or more **State Managers** (SM).

The OM represents the identity of the object itself: it is in charge of receiving the service requests from other objects. Moreover, it is the only entity authorized to access and modify the so called object **execution state** (represented by the state of the pending requests and of the executing activities). When it is the case the OM is in charge of creating a new activity, on the basis of the given intra-object scheduling policy, and to pass it the reference to the state.

Activities of a PO object that reside on the same node of the OM have access to the state with direct memory reference. However, the state of any PO object can be split in several partitions: one SM is associated with each partition. When the activities of an object are distributed onto different nodes, the SMs allow activities to remotely access the managed part of the state. An access to a non-local state partition is transparently translated into a message for the corresponding SM.

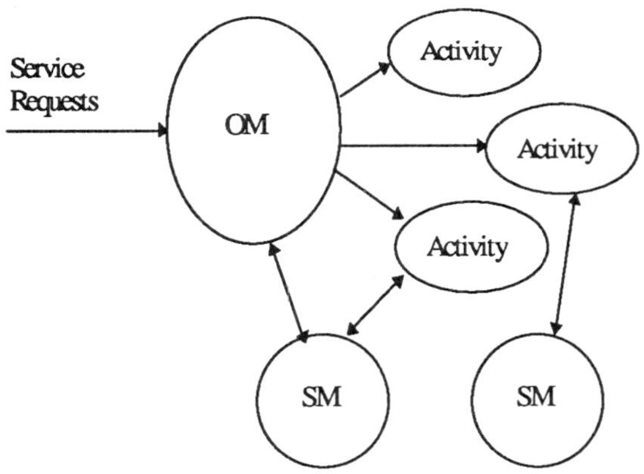

Figure 1. A MCS PO Object

The PO support for inter-object management is constituted by a set of entities - replicated on each node and composed by one or more threads - and called **system managers** [9].

The *monitoring manager* periodically measures the application behavior to detect its evolution. The *allocation manager* is in charge of deciding the allocation of newly created objects [10]. The *creation manager* implements the decision taken by the allocation manager: it receives the command to create each new objects in its node. The *router manager* is in charge of delivering all messages that flow between application objects (both inter-object and intra-object communications) and between the managers of non physically connected nodes.

3.3. MCS Issues in the Support Design

Even having designed the PO environment with the aim of portability, the peculiar characteristics of the MCS architecture have influenced the implementation of both the support and the environment itself. In particular:

1. the **threaded scenario** with a globally shared and unprotected memory space: all processes on a node have access to the whole local memory;
2. the presence of a **high speed** and point to point communication **network**, having (or pretending to have!) communication times comparable to the local memory access times;
3. the single application **partition-based scheduling** policy of the system, allowing only one application at a time to be in execution within a partition of the system;
4. the difficulty of accessing **external resources**, in particular mass storage devices.

Point 1 has facilitated the implementation of the MCS support for intra-object parallelism. The parallel activities within a single PO object must share the state of the object itself. Because parallel activities, in the MCS, are threads, they share the whole local address space. Thus, holding a pointer to the state is all what is needed to access it. Any unsafe or non consistent access to the shared state is prevented by the a priori synchronization policy.

Again with regard to the access to the state, point 2 has allowed objects to be capable of inter-node distribution. In fact, if the costs of accessing the network are comparable with the memory accesses costs, objects can profit of internal distribution and remote access to the state, by means of the SMs, in order to make the intra-objects concurrency real parallelism.

As a consequence of the single application scenario (point 3), the unprotected approach does not have to deal with any protection /authentication problem: no resources are shared among different users.

Finally, referring to point 4, it must be noticed that, since the support to the MCS architecture does not provide any way to load new parts of code during execution, all the code of an application has to be loaded onto the transputer nodes before starting the execution of the application itself: that results in an excessive utilization of the local memory for each node of the system.

An important characteristic that has to be analyzed in an Object-Oriented environment is the class-instances relationship. In the PO support, both the creation manager and each OM need to have access to class data structures. The former to handle object creation correctly, the latters to handle the creation of new activities.

Thanks to the capability of sharing memory, the preprocessor builds the class lattice as a global data structure to be maintained in the local memory of each node during the whole application execution. Since this structure is globally accessible from any thread within a node[1], classes and instances share the same description. This makes it also possible to dynamically solve any inheritance related bounding, such as the reference to a method or to an instance variable.

4. Moving to Distributed Systems

4.1. Motivations

The diffusion of massively-parallel systems for general-purpose computing have been limited for different reasons:

- on the one hand, non standard environments and/or system libraries give no guarantee on software porting and reuse;
- on the other hand, the widely claimed power scalability of this kind of architectures cannot be appreciated: scaling up a parallel system by replicating its components does not outweigh the technological obsolescence of each single component.

In addition, the lack of any general-purpose solution to the typical problems regarding the efficiency of massively parallel architectures, such as load balancing [11] and routing [12], makes it often necessary to solve them by scratch.

All these reasons have limited the diffusion of massively parallel architectures to special-purpose applications, where their intrinsic characteristics are welcome and porting and/or economic aspects are not so important.

In the last few years, the idea of considering clusters of connected workstations as the preferred target architecture for general-purpose parallel computing has been come out. Networked workstations, because they are already present in every computing center, show a lower cost/performance ratio with respect to massively parallel architectures. In addition, scalability is guaranteed by:

- the capability of frequently updating the hardware at the level of single workstations;
- the possibility of enlarging a system by simply adding new workstations.

Not only hardware factors make the use of those systems as virtual parallel machines increase, but also software ones:

- the standardization of the many UNIX versions and the high level of connectivity reached among different computer manufacturers;
- the multi-user scheduling capabilities, making the system always available for execution;
- the fact that only simple (and often low cost) software add-ons allow to turn networked computers in a ready-to-use message-passing parallel architecture.

One of the key points that could make parallel programming on a network of workstations a widely diffused technology, is standardization: one must guarantee software investments by providing parallel libraries with and a defined and long-lived interface and made them available for most of the commercial systems. In addition, to provide hardware transparency (heterogeneous nodes within a network may have different internal data representation) translation data protocols are needed.

Currently many development environments are available that try to step over these problems. However, the programming level defined by those libraries is usually low level, making the user in charge of dealing with explicit message-passing and process creation: we believe that higher level parallel programming environments are needed. For this reasons, we decided to implement the support of the PO programming environment upon the library that, as far as we think, is growing as a standard.

4.2 PVM

Presently, one of the most widely diffused libraries for parallel programming on networks of workstations is the Parallel Virtual Machine, **PVM** [1, 2]. Developed by the Oak Ridge University, it is a well known and supported system for message-passing programming and remote tasks execution management over a network of TCP/IP connected heterogeneous machines. Its availability as a public domain software, its frequent updates, the wide and growing number of supported systems, its simplicity, have made PVM the “de facto” standard for parallel virtual machines management and programming.

Main features of PVM are:

[1] The distribution of the replicas of the class lattice does not cause any consistency problem: up to now, PO classes cannot change at run-time.

- **message-passing** communication protocol in order to use distributed memory machines;
- **non-blocking communications** in order to enhance concurrent execution;
- **automatic data format translation** to maintain data integrity during heterogeneous inter-node communications;
- **processes** that can access all the external resources of the node where they are running;
- **unique process ID** across all the virtual machines to allow global referencing;
- **dynamic process creation** with some limited, but user modifiable, load balancing capabilities;
- use of the **standard C** and **Fortran** compilers and libraries available on the nodes;
- availability of **graphics tools** for helping users during the development and testing phases.

Providing only simple message-passing primitives, PVM can be used as a basis for more elaborated and powerful programming environments, using it like a lower level abstraction layer that hides all the implementation details of the underlying operating systems and hardware architectures.

5. From MCS to PVM: Porting Issues

To provide the same PO programming paradigm on top of PVM, a different design is required for the support system due to the architectural differences of virtual machines with respect to massively parallel ones. In particular, with reference to the key points analyzed in section 3.3, the implementation of the PO support onto a network of PVM workstations has to deal with a different scenario:

1. **PO processes** are mapped into UNIX processes: this implies that memory protection mechanisms do not support memory sharing among them;
2. the **slow** (if compared with the time needed to access the local memory) **non-dedicated communication network** forbids state distribution among nodes;
3. the available **physical resources** are shared among several users and several applications;
4. there is the capability of dynamically accessing the **file system** for loading new code on need.

Let us analyze how these characteristics have influenced the porting of the PO support.

5.1. The Problem of the State

The lack of any shared memory among processes has posed the problem of implementing the **objects state**: the state of an object, in fact, must be shared among the concurrent activities within it. Since any PVM process is a closed entity, providing this capability is not trivial.

Possible solutions are:

- to create a PVM process, that manages the state the same way State Manager does in the MCS support;
- to overcome the PVM model by using threads, such as Sun light-weighted processes [13] or DCE threads [14].

All these solutions present some drawbacks. The former makes accesses to the state costly, since any access is translated into a slow request sent to the State Manager. The latter makes the implementation of the support non standard. We have chosen to overcome these problems by adopting the UNIX **shared memory library** within a PVM process [13]. This makes the support portable, since this library is available on most of the UNIX based systems. However, we claim that any access to the state is translated by the preprocessor into a primitive of the support (see section 2.2). Thus, it is not needed to know how the shared state is implemented by the support: any change in the implementation of the access to the state would not mine the portability of PO applications. Our hope is that the urge for light-weighted processes to achieve greater flexibility in the area of distributed environments, emerged from our experience too, will produce a feedback in future PVM releases.

5.2. Concentrated vs. Distributed Objects

With regard to the access to the object state problem, one can criticize that even in the MCS implementation the access to the object state is granted by the State Manager processes. However, an important difference arises: in the transputer implementation State Managers were introduced only to provide remote state access capabilities (that thank to the high speed network, can be effectively granted). In a distributed implementation, the cost of accessing the network is higher and unpredictable. Thus, we have chosen not to allow, as a general rule, an object to be distributed onto more than one node. In particular, any activity within an object that needs to access the state is not allowed to execute on a node different from the one where the state resides, i.e., the Object Manager node. Without this limitation, the cost of accessing such a state would become too high, degrading the execution time. Only activities that can execute independently without accessing the state - or activities that belong to an object with no state at all - can be allocated everywhere in the system. Because of this choice, no support for remotely accessing the object state was provided.

5.3. Structuring Application Code

A distributed architecture, composed of a set of networked workstations, has the capability of making resources shared among several users and/or several applications. This means that, in general, protection and authentication mechanisms have to be added to the system to guarantee execution among unauthorized accesses.

Using only the TCP/IP communication protocol and the normal UNIX libraries PVM builds the virtual machine in the user space, thus allowing many non intersecting virtual machines running on the same nodes from different users.

Running in the user space PVM inherits the standard UNIX access controls, because only an authorized user can start PVM processes and only acknowledged machines can become PVM nodes.

5.4. Dynamic Code Loading

In the MCS support, no code can be executed by a process if not loaded at the application booting time. In the PVM system, instead, the creation of a new process is associated with the file name that contains its executable code. Thanks to this capability, code can be loaded on need onto the system nodes and, thus, memory usage can be improved. However, to provide this characteristic to the support, the preprocessor and the way it builds the inheritance lattice and the enriched PO code have to change. In particular, all the class inheritances must be resolved at compile time.

5.5. The Preprocessor

The PO preprocessor is in charge of parsing the PO code and translating it into C code enriched with the PO primitives. However, it is also in charge of solving the inheritance and building the class hierarchy. In the MCS support, the globally shared memory makes it possible to provide the inheritance lattice as a global data structure. In a PVM system, like in all non-threaded operating systems, there is no way of accessing other tasks memory to execute code, thus, whenever an object or an activity within an object have to be created, the associated code must be loaded from the file system. To provide a global view of the inheritance hierarchy, one could build a global file containing the whole application hierarchy and made objects and activities execute the various parts of this file. However, it is clear that such a choice is neither feasible nor convenient because loading a file from the storage memory is a very expensive task.

For this reasons, the way the preprocessor acts on the PO code to produce C code has to be changed: each class implementation requires a copy of all the inherited methods code in self-contained C files. More in detail, the translation phase breaks each class implementation in two different files:

- a class description file, that maintains a description of the state instance variables, of the interface provided by the objects of its class and of the class scheduling policy;
- a file containing all class methods implementation.

As a consequence, the global produced code has larger dimensions that the MCS one. Moreover, dynamic binding is no more allowed.

6. The PO-PVM Support

6.1. Intra-Object Management

In the PVM implementation, for each class, the Object Manager code is executed from the class description file. As soon as a new object is created, the OM is in charge of:

- initializing the internal state by allocating it in a shared memory area and setting it to the proper values before activity start-up;
- connecting itself to the PVM communication sub-system in order to provide a gateway for incoming method invocations.

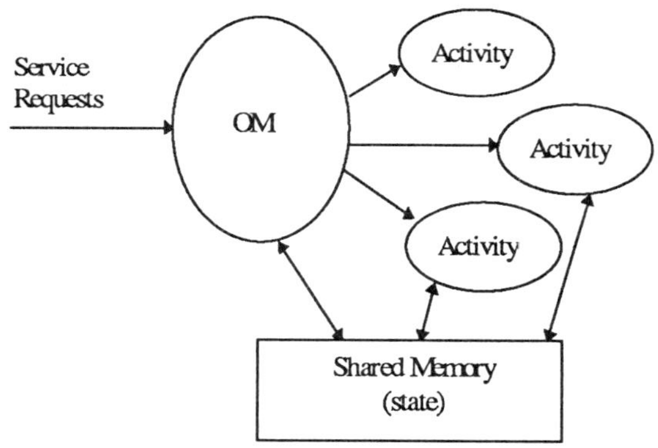

Figure 2. A PVM PO Object

A PO object, in fact, is a complex autonomous entity capable of reacting to asynchronous events. Then, after the initialization phase, the Object Manager waits on the PVM port for a message. In particular, there are two possible message types corresponding to different events:

- external messages, sent by other objects requesting methods execution;
- internal messages, sent by the object activities for signaling a change on their execution state.

Whenever an external message is received the OM:

- verifies its correctness with respect to the provided interface;
- checks the possibility of activating the operation with respect to already executing activities. If the object internal scheduling policy allowed activation, the OM starts a new PVM task from the method implementation file and sends it the requested method name together with the parameters, otherwise the request is enqueued in the internal waiting-to-start task list.

To maintain efficiency, each activity within an object is an autonomous entity: it is capable of sending the reply directly to the client that requested it, bypassing the Object Manager and thus avoiding unnecessary multiple slow PVM calls.

Once accomplished its task, each activity sends an internal message to the OM, allowing the OM itself to test the activation of enqueued requests with respect to the synchronization constraints and, if it is the case, to activate them.

The OM is also responsible for object shutdown, required by an explicit termination message to objects that are not used anymore.

6.2. Inter-Object Management

Currently, the inter-object support level is limited to the presence of a single entity - we call it the **PO spawner**, in analogy with the PVM terminology - replicated onto each system node (see figure 3). The PO spawner is in charge of:

- activating new objects;
- terminating running ones;
- providing name service facilities for public objects.

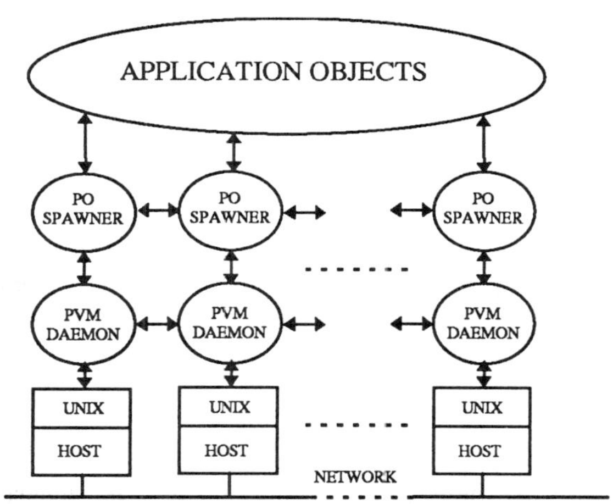

Figure 3. The PO-PVM Support

The creation of a new object is explicitly commanded by means of a message sent to the PO spawner. The allocation of the new objects can be either decided by the PO spawner, on the basis of an integrated policy, or by the PVM system itself on the basis of its internal, cyclic, allocation policy.

In PO there are two types of objects:

- the private ones, owned by their creator and not accessible in a public manner;
- the public ones, that are created with a public name that can be used by other objects that need their services.

Public names require some checking in order to avoid duplications and/or bad name resolution.

A simple solution to this problem is charging a single PO spawner of providing name services. This is possible, and is currently used in our implementation, but produces network traffic towards the node of the PO spawner in charge of the naming service. To avoid this problem, a distributed implementation of the name server will be adopted in the future.

7. Conclusions and future works

The paper presented the Parallel Objects environment and reported our experience in porting it from a massively parallel architecture to the PVM system.

The work was motivated from the clear advantages of having a standard parallel programming library over a networked computer system to be used as the target architecture for the development of parallel and distributed applications.

The PO environment was originally conceived for massively parallel architectures, in particular transputer-based ones: the scenario of the PVM system obliged us to several design rethinkings In particular, the main topics that we had to deal with are:

- the different memory model;
- the different network model;
- the different system scheduling policy;
- the different resources the system nodes can access.

First experimental results show that the advantages of a high-level programming environment do not have to pay too much in performance, i.e., the overhead of the support is limited with respect to the one imposed by the PVM system.

Future works will deal with extending the support in order to allow object migration and persistency.

References

1. G. A. Geist, V. S. Sunderam, "Network-Based Concurrent Computing on the PVM System",

Concurrency Practice and Experience, Vol. 4, No. 4, June 1992.
2. A. Beguelin et al., "Recent Advances to PVM", 1994, available via ftp at: netlib2.cs.ukt.edu:/pvm3.
3. M. Boari et al., "A Programming Environment Based on Parallel Objects for Transputer Architectures", Models and Tools for Massively Parallel Architectures, Napoli (I), June 1993.
4. Wegner, "Concepts and Paradigms of Object Oriented Programming", ACM OOPS Messenger, Vol. 1, No. 1, Aug. 1990.
5. Meiko Ltd., "Computing Surface Reference Manual", Meiko Ltd.,1989.
6. Chin, S.T. Chanson, "Distributed Object-Based Programming Systems", ACM Computing Surveys, Vol. 23, No. 1, March 1991.
7. Corradi, L. Leonardi, "PO Constraints as Tools to Synchronize Active Objects", The Journal of Object-Oriented Programming, Vol. 4, No. 6, Oct. 1991.
8. Ciampolini, A. Corradi, L. Leonardi, "The Support for a Dynamic Parallel Object Model on a Transputer Based Architectures", IEEE Int. Phoenix Conf. on Computers and Communications, March 1991.
9. A. Ciampolini, A. Corradi, L. Leonardi, F. Zambonelli, "The Benefits of Migration in a Parallel Objectsd Environment", EUROMICRO Workshop on Parallel and Distributed Processing, Malaga (E), Jan. 1994.
10. Corradi, L. Leonardi, F. Zambonelli, "Load Balancing Strategies for Massively Parallel Architectures", Parallel Processing Letters, Vol. 3, No. 2&3, Sept. 1992.
11. M. Shivaratri, P. Krueger, M. Singhal, "Load Distributing for Locally Distributed System", IEEE Computer, Vol. 25, No. 12, Dec. 1992.
12. M. Boari et al., "Adaptive Routing for Dynamic Applications in Massively Parallel Architectures", IEEE Parallel and Distributed Technology, Vol. 3, No. 1, Spring 1995.
13. Sun Ltd., "SunOS Reference Manual", N- 800-3827-10, 1990.
14. Open Software Foundation, "Introduction to OSF DCE", Prentice Hall, N.J., 1992.

❖ KEYNOTE SESSION II ❖

"HPCN in Portugal"

Speaker

H. Pina

❖ SESSION 8 ❖

Numerical Algorithms II

Chair

E. Pissaloux

Exploiting the Symmetry on the Jacobi Method on a Mesh of Processors

D. Giménez
Departamento de Informática y Sistemas
Universidad de Murcia
Aptdo 4021. 30001 Murcia. Spain
domingo@dif.um.es

R. van de Geijn
Department of Computer Sciences
University of Texas at Austin
Austin, Texas, 78712
rvdg@cs.utexas.edu

V. Hernández* A. M. Vidal*
Departamento de Sistemas Informáticos y Computación
Universidad Politécnica de Valencia
Aptdo 22012. 46071 Valencia. Spain
{cpvhg,cpavm}@dsic.upv.es

Abstract

In this paper, we study the parallelization of the Jacobi method to solve the symmetric eigenvalue problem on a mesh of processors. To solve this problem obtaining a theoretical efficiency of 100% it is necessary to exploit the symmetry of the matrix. The only previous algorithm we know exploiting the symmetry on multicomputers is that in [1], but that algorithm uses a storage scheme adequate for a logical ring of processors, so having a low scalability. In this paper we show how matrix' symmetry can be exploited on a logical mesh of processors obtaining a higher scalability than that obtained with the algorithm in [1]. In addition, we show how the storage scheme exploiting the symmetry can be combined with a scheme by blocks to obtain a highly efficient and scalable Jacobi method for solving the symmetric eigenvalue problem for distributed memory parallel computers. We report performance results from the Intel Touchstone DELTA.

Keywords: Jacobi methods, symmetric eigenvalue problem, algorithms by blocks, multicomputers, mesh topology.

1 Introduction

Many different methods exist for computing the eigenvalues of a symmetric matrix, including bisection methods, the QR algorithm, divide and conquer (Cuppen's algorithm), and Jacobi's method. For a complete survey and references, we suggest the reader turn to [2, 3].

Jacobi's method is the oldest, dating back to the mid-1800's. It has fallen out of favor and been resurrected on many occasions. Its most recent resurgence is mainly due to better stability properties [4] and straight-forward parallelization [5, 6].

The primary purpose of this paper is to show how to obtain highly efficient parallel Jacobi algorithms. To achieve this goal we have used the very well known techniques of reformulating dense linear algebra algorithms to operate on blocks (submatrices) to obtain algorithms rich in matrix-matrix operations [7]. We combine this improvement in the sequential implementation with an assignment of data and work to the processors of a multicomputer to yield a parallel implementation that is both efficient and scalable.

The symmetric eigenvalue problem appears in many applications. In some applications in computational chemistry [8] it is necessary to solve the eigenvalue problem obtaining all the eigenvalues of a symmetric, dense and real matrix of size of some hundred or a few thousand. In this case it could be interesting to solve the problem by efficient Jacobi methods on Multicomputers.

In Section 2, we review some of the bases of Jacobi's method. In Section 3, a sequential Jacobi algorithm by blocks is given. In Section 4, the storage scheme that allows us to exploit the symmetry of the matrix on a logical mesh of processors is studied. In Section 5 the experimental results obtained on the Intel Touchstone DELTA are presented and analyzed. And in Section 6 the conclusions are given.

2 Jacobi's method

The basic idea behind Jacobi-like methods is to construct a matrix sequence $\{A_l\}$ by means of

$$A_{l+1} = Q_l A_l Q_l^t \ , \ l = 1, 2, \ldots \tag{1}$$

where $A_1 = A$, and Q_l is a plane-rotation (Jacobi rotation) in the (p, q) plane with $1 \leq p, q \leq n$. Under

*Partially supported by ESPRIT III Basic Research Program of the EC under contract No.9072 (Project GEPPCOM) and partially supported by Generalitat Valenciana Project GV-1076/93

1066-6192/96 $5.00 © 1996 IEEE
Proceedings of PDP '96

certain conditions [9], sequence $\{A_l\}$ converges to a diagonal matrix D,

$$D = Q_k Q_{k-1} \cdots Q_2 Q_1 A Q_1^t Q_2^t \cdots Q_{k-1}^t Q_k^t \quad (2)$$

whose diagonal elements are the eigenvalues of A.

Each product $Q_l A_l Q_l^t$ represents a similarity transformation that annihilates a pair of nondiagonal elements, a_{ij} and a_{ji}, of matrix A_l. Matrix Q_l coincides with the identity matrix except in elements $q_{ii} = c$, $q_{ij} = s$, $q_{ji} = -s$, and $q_{jj} = c$, where $c = \cos\,\theta$, $s = \sin\,\theta$, and [3]

$$\tan\, 2\theta = \frac{2a_{ij}}{a_{ii} - a_{jj}} \; . \quad (3)$$

This transformation only affects rows i and j when applied from the left, and columns i and j when applied from the right. The different ways of choosing pairs (i, j) have given rise to different versions of the Jacobi method. In the cyclic-by-row method the pairs are taken in the order

$$(1,2),(1,3),\ldots,(1,n),(2,3),(2,4),\ldots,\\ (2,n),\ldots,(n-1,n) \; . \quad (4)$$

A cyclic Jacobi method works by making successive sweeps until some convergence criterion is fulfilled, normally until $\mathrm{off}(A) < \mathit{bound}$, where $\mathrm{off}(A) = \sqrt{\sum_{j=1,j\neq i}^{n} \sum_{i=1}^{n} a_{ij}^2}$. A sweep consists of successively nullifying the $n(n-1)/2$ nondiagonal elements in the lower triangular part of the matrix. The convergence of the cyclic-by-row method is analyzed in [9]. More recently, [10, 11] demonstrate that the Jacobi method converges with other ordering schemes when the cyclic-by-row method is convergent.

In this paper the odd-even order will be used [6]. This order was intended to allow parallelization of the method, but, as we shall see, it also simplifies a block based implementation of the sequential algorithm. We will demonstrate this ordering by examining the case where $n = 8$. Numbering indices from 1 to 8, and initially grouping the indices in pairs $\{(1,2),(3,4),(5,6),(7,8)\}$, the sets of pairs of indices are obtained as follows:

$$\begin{array}{ll} k=1 & \{(1,2),(3,4),(5,6),(7,8)\} \\ k=2 & \{2,(1,4),(3,6),(5,8),7\} \\ k=3 & \{(2,4),(1,6),(3,8),(5,7)\} \\ k=4 & \{4,(2,6),(1,8),(3,7),5\} \\ k=5 & \{(4,6),(2,8),(1,7),(3,5)\} \\ k=6 & \{6,(4,8),(2,7),(1,5),3\} \\ k=7 & \{(6,8),(4,7),(2,5),(1,3)\} \\ k=8 & \{8,(6,7),(4,5),(2,3),1\} \end{array} \quad (5)$$

where odd sets have four pairs of indices and even sets have three pairs of indices, so n iterations are needed to obtain the $n(n-1)/2$ pairs of indices.

3 A Jacobi algorithm by blocks

The underlying idea behind blocked algorithms is that traditional implementations of dense linear algebra algorithms encounter a bottleneck in modern architectures due to limited bandwidth between the CPU and main memory. The data and computation requirements of matrix-matrix operations can be arranged so that more computation is performed between memory accesses. As a result, these operations can take advantage of hierarchical memories. A suite of such matrix-matrix operations are part of the Basic Linear Algebra Subprograms (BLAS) [12]. In this section, we show how blocking can be used for Jacobi's method.

3.1 The Level-1 BLAS implementation

We start by giving in figure 1 a pseudo-code for a Jacobi's method implementation which is rich in vector-vector operations. In this figure, the operation **update matrix** consists of applying rotation to rows and columns i and j of A, which can be done using the level-1 BLAS routine drot. When taking advantage of symmetry, three calls to drot are required, rotating row and column pieces labeled by 1, 2 and 3 in figure 2. For each sweep, update matrix is executed $n(n-1)/2$ times at a cost of $6n$ floating point operations (flops) per execution. Thus the total cost per sweep is $3n^3$ flops.

```
WHILE convergence not reached DO
        FOR every pair (i,j) of indices in a sweep DO
                compute parameters c and s
                update matrix
        ENDFOR
ENDWHILE
```

Figure 1: **Basic Jacobi iteration.**

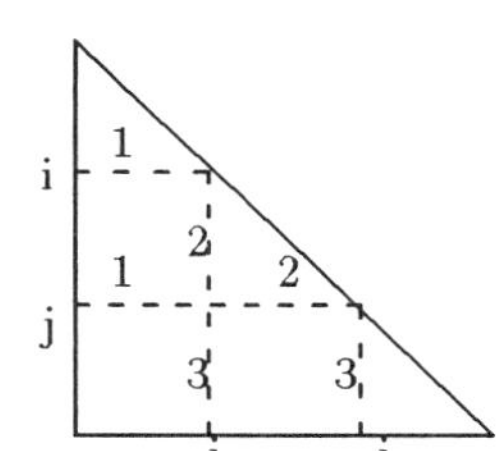

Figure 2: **Applying a single Jacobi transformation to matrix A using BLAS 1.**

In general, vector-vector operations like drot are memory intensive, and hence inefficient. Moreover, while applying a rotation from the left, the vectors require a stride through memory (when column-major storage is used), which is further added to the inefficiencies due to memory accesses.

3.2 The use of level-3 BLAS

In this subsection we show how to obtain a Jacobi algorithm by blocks. The method is similar to this used by Bischof for the SVD problem [13].

If matrix A is divided into columns and rows of square blocks of size s, it is possible to make a sweep over these blocks using some Jacobi order, *treating blocks as units.* For reasons that will become apparent later, we will use the odd-even order. So, with $n = 8s$, blocks are treated in the order indicated by the numbers in figure 3. In each block the algorithm works by making a sweep over the elements in the block. In our case, a cyclic-by-rows order has been used. Notice that some nondiagonal elements of the matrix are not covered by this method. In particular, the subdiagonal elements belonging to diagonal blocks in figure 3 will not be zeroed. To correct this, blocks 1, 2, 3 and 4 in figure 3 are considered to have size $2s \times 2s$, adding to each block the two adjacent diagonal blocks and the symmetrical block (figure 4.a). A sweep can now be performed covering all elements in these newly created blocks. Now the algorithm works on the blocks in the order $1, 2, 3, 4, \ldots$ until a sweep is completed, making successive sweeps until convergence is reached.

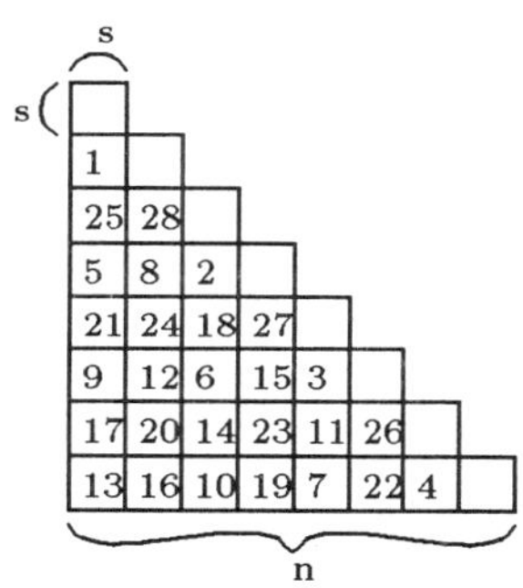

Figure 3: **Odd-even order by blocks.**

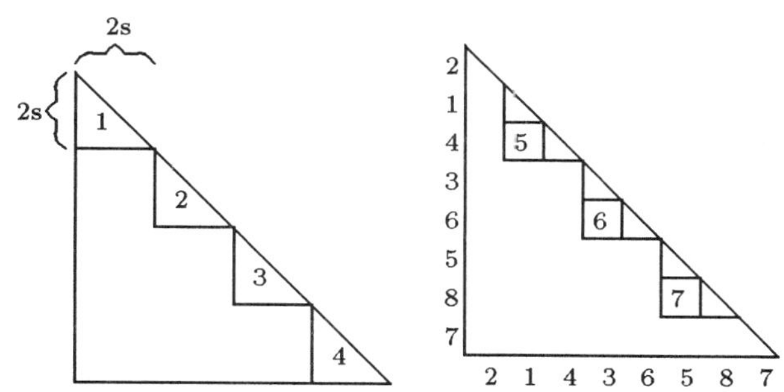

Figure 4: **a) Work on triangular blocks, b) Work on square blocks.**

We have now set the stage for an algorithm rich in level-3 BLAS operations (in this case matrix-matrix multiplications): Sweep over block 1 exploiting the symmetry of the matrix and using level-1 BLAS. In the process, the corresponding rotations are accumulated to form a matrix Q of size $2s \times 2s$. Finally, the first column of blocks of size $2s \times 2s$ is postmultiplied by this Q (except the $2s \times 2s$ block 1, obviously). This matrix-matrix multiplication can be done using level-3 BLAS. The work on blocks 2, 3 and 4 is done similarly.

After completing this first set of blocked rotations, a swap of column and row blocks is performed, using the odd-even order. This brings the next blocks of size $2s \times 2s$ to be zeroed to the diagonal, and the process continues similarly to operations performed on blocks 1, 2, 3 and 4. However, in this case the elements to be nullified are in square blocks of size $s \times s$ inside diagonal blocks of size $2s \times 2s$.

So, if initially the pairs of block indices are $\{(1,2),(3,4),(5,6),(7,8)\}$, after swapping indices a new set of pairs is obtained $\{(1,4),(3,6),(5,8)\}$. This requires swapping row and column blocks, yielding a new distribution (figure 4.b). Now the work is done on the diagonal blocks of size $2s \times 2s$ marked in figure 4.b, zeroing only elements in blocks 5, 6 and 7. After this the algorithm continues similarly until a sweep is completed. The Jacobi algorithm using this ordering by blocks converges, as can be easily proved using results in [11].

The swapping of row and column blocks is illustrated in figure 5. In this figure a bidirectional arrow $\longleftrightarrow$ represents a swap and a unidirectional arrow $\longrightarrow$ a copy. One way to view such data movement is to recognize that it is equivalent to pre- or post-multiplying by a permutation matrix

$$P = \begin{pmatrix} \hat{P} & 0 & \cdots & 0 \\ 0 & \hat{P} & \cdots & 0 \\ \vdots & \vdots & \ddots & \vdots \\ 0 & 0 & \cdots & \hat{P} \end{pmatrix} ,$$

where $\hat{P}$ is the matrix of size $2s \times 2s$

$$\hat{P} = \begin{pmatrix} 0 & I \\ I & 0 \end{pmatrix} .$$

Next, since the updates of blocks involves an operation like $A = QAQ^t$, the permutation can be incorporated into Q, updating $A = (PQ)A(PQ)^t$ instead. Regardless, for the blocked algorithm, swapping represents a lower order operation.

3.3 Theoretical cost

To study the cost of the algorithm it suffices to consider only the number of flops. The additional time due to the data movement is inconsequential.

The number of blocks of size $s \times s$ is

$$\frac{\frac{n}{s}\left(\frac{n}{s}-1\right)}{2} = \frac{q\,(q-1)}{2}. \qquad (6)$$

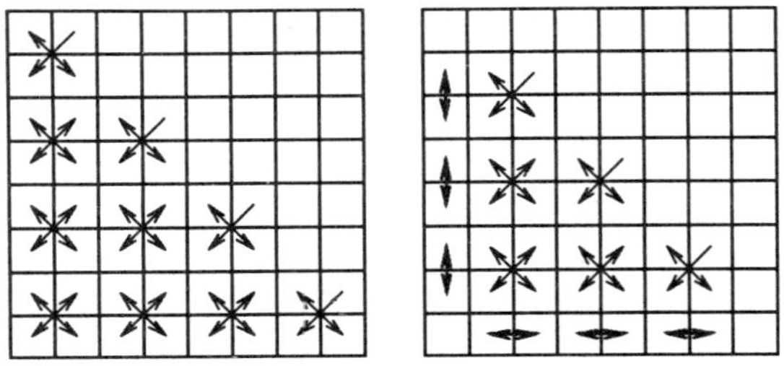

a) b)

Figure 5: **Movement of blocks. a) Odd step, b) Even step.**

The first $q/2$ blocks are considered triangular blocks of size $2s \times 2s$, each requiring $3(2s)^3$ flops to make a sweep over the offdiagonal elements of the block and $3(2s)^3$ flops to accumulate the rotations, for a total of $6(2s)^3$ flops. In the rest of the blocks only s^2 elements are zeroed, thus needing $24s^3$ flops per block. So, the total number of flops to make the local sweeps over all blocks is:

$$\frac{q}{2}6(2s)^3 + \left(\frac{q^2}{2} - q\right) 24s^3 = 12n^2 s \text{ flops.} \quad (7)$$

The rest of the work in the algorithm is the updating of rows and columns of blocks. After a sweep over one of the blocks of size $2s \times 2s$, matrices of sizes $2s \times (n - 2s - i)$ and $2s \times i$ are updated (where i takes values $0, s, 2s, \ldots, n - 2s$), and these updates are done by premultiplying or postmultiplying by matrices of size $2s \times 2s$, thus needing $2(2s)^2(n - 2s) = 8s^2(n - 2s)$ flops. Because the number of $s \times s$ blocks is $q(q - 1)/2$, the total cost of "update matrix" is:

$$\frac{q(q-1)}{2} 8s^2 (n - 2s) = 4n^3 - 12n^2 s + 8ns^2 \text{ flops.} \quad (8)$$

So, adding (7) and (8) the cost of the algorithm is approximately $4n^3$ for $s << n$. Comparing this to the cost of the level-1 implementation, $3n^3$, we could conclude that blocking is a bad idea. However, it should be noted that for the blocked algorithm almost all of the cost is in matrix-matrix multiplication, which can be expected to be performed at a faster rate than the vector-vector operations of the level-1 implementation. Letting the time required for a floating point operation be k_1 and k_3 for a level-1 and level-3 BLAS based implementation, respectively, the expected speedup by using the blocked method becomes

$$\frac{3}{4}\frac{k_1}{k_3}. \quad (9)$$

4 A Jacobi algorithm by blocks on a mesh of processors

We now present a parallel implementation of the blocked algorithm for a logical mesh of processors. The assignment of elements of the matrix (storage scheme) we will use is obtained by dividing matrix A into four square submatrices of size $\frac{n}{2} \times \frac{n}{2}$ (figure 6.a). These four submatrices will be called A_{NW}, A_{NE}, A_{SW} and A_{SE}, where the subindices indicate the relative position of each submatrix in matrix A, and N, S, E, and W stand for north, south, east, and west, respectively. The matrix is symmetric, and so, it is necessary to work only with submatrix A_{SW} and the lower triangular parts of submatrices A_{NW} and A_{SE}.

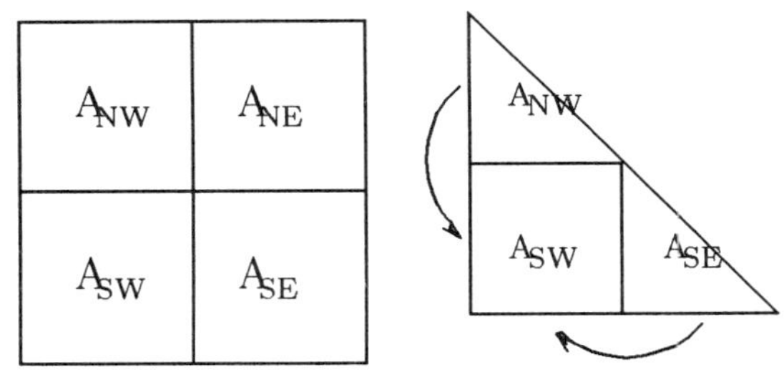

a) b)

Figure 6: **a) Partition of the matrix by blocks, b) Folding.**

If we employ a square mesh with $p = r^2$ processors we divide submatrix A_{SW} into p square submatrices of size $\frac{n}{2r} \times \frac{n}{2r}$:

$$\begin{matrix} A_{SW_{0,0}} & A_{SW_{0,1}} & \cdots & A_{SW_{0,r-1}} \\ \cdots & \cdots & \cdots & \cdots \\ A_{SW_{r-1,0}} & A_{SW_{r-1,1}} & \cdots & A_{SW_{r-1,r-1}} \end{matrix} \quad (10)$$

and assign submatrix $A_{SW_{i,j}}$ to processor $P_{i,j}$. To assign the lower-triangular parts of A_{NW} and A_{SE} to the processors, they are folded over A_{SW} (figure 6.b). So, if we consider matrices A_{NW} and A_{SE} divided into submatrices of size $\frac{n}{2r} \times \frac{n}{2r}$, $A_{NW_{i,j}}$ and $A_{SE_{i,j}}$, with $i = 0, \ldots, r-1$ and $j = 0, \ldots, i$, these submatrices will be assigned to the processors in the following way: $A_{NW_{r-1-i,j}}$ is assigned to $P_{i,j}$, $i = 0, \ldots, r-1$; $j = 0, \ldots, i$, and submatrix $A_{SE_{i,r-1-j}}$ is assigned to $P_{i,j}$, $i = 0, \ldots, r-1$; $j = r-1-i, \ldots, r-1$.

For simplicity we have assumed that $n = 2rk$, where k is the size of the submatrices being assigned to processors. To combine this method with the sequential blocked scheme, we will further assume that k is a multiple of $2s$. Naturally, an approximate decomposition can be used to overcome this restriction.

Thus, to combine this Storage Scheme with the design of an algorithm rich in matrix-matrix multiplications, it is necessary to divide each submatrix $A_{SW_{i,j}}$, $A_{NW_{i,j}}$ and $A_{SE_{i,j}}$ into submatrices of size $s \times s$ that we will call $A_{SW^{l,m}_{i,j}}$, $A_{NW^{l,m}_{i,j}}$ and $A_{SE^{l,m}_{i,j}}$, with $l = 0, \ldots, t-1$, $m = 0, \ldots, t-1$, where $t = \frac{n}{2rs}$.

The basic parallel algorithm is given by figure 7. We will explain briefly how each step in the parallel scheme works.

```
In parallel for each P_{i,j} i = 0,...,r-1; j = 0,...,r-1:
    WHILE off(A) > bound DO
        FOR k = 1 TO n/s
            IF i = r - 1 - j
                Compute rotations
            ENDIF
            Broadcast Rotations
            Update matrix
            Transfer data
        ENDFOR
    ENDWHILE
```

Figure 7: **Parallel Jacobi iteration.**

4.1 Compute rotations

For the design of the algorithm we have used the odd-even ordering. With this ordering different nullification schemes are obtained on odd and even steps. On odd steps every antidiagonal processor will compute the same number of rotations, but on even steps one processor computes rotations for one pair less than the other antidiagonal processors (processor $P_{r-1,0}$).

We will show how blocks are stored in memory with an example with $p = 4$ and $\frac{n}{4s} = 4$, on odd (figure 8) and even (figure 9) steps. In these figures there are blocks of memory containing blocks of matrices (marked with X) and other additional memory blocks used in some parts of the program. Some blocks of size $2s \times 2s$ have been marked. The subsweeps are done over these blocks, and so, it is necessary to accumulate rotations corresponding to each one of these blocks and then to broadcast the resulting matrices.

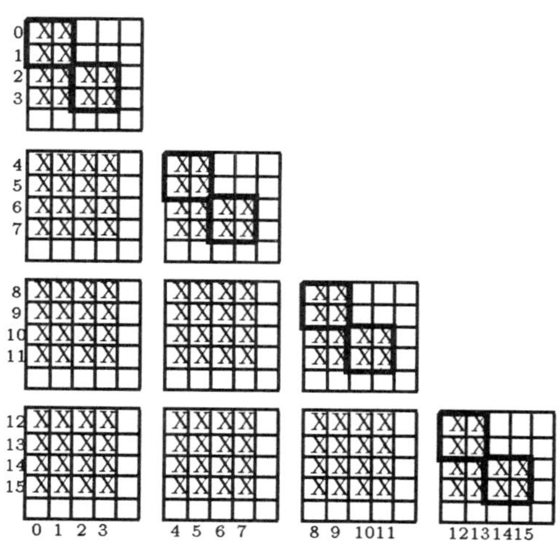

Figure 8: **Computing rotations. Odd step.**

The procession from figure 8 to figure 9 and from figure 9 to figure 8 will be explained when we study how the data transference is performed.

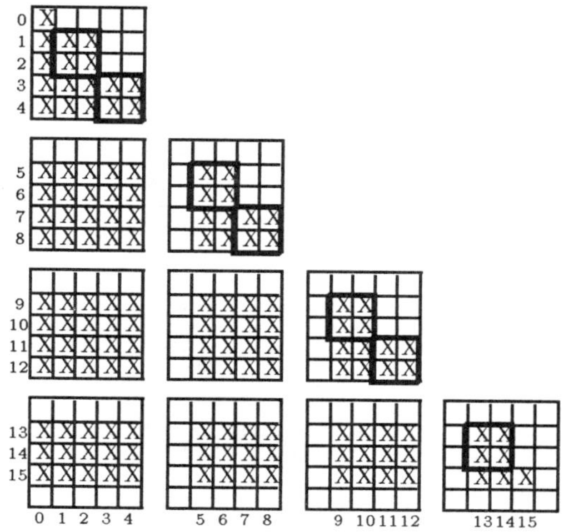

Figure 9: **Computing rotations. Even step.**

4.2 Broadcast rotations

The broadcast of rotations is done in the same way on each step.

To update a $2s \times 2s$ block it is necessary to know the matrices where the rotations modifying the diagonal blocks in the same row or column as the block to be updated have been accumulated. So, the matrices where rotations have been accumulated are sent to processors containing blocks in the same row or column, that is, to the processors on the same row or column of processors where the diagonal matrices are. But it isn't necessary to send all the matrices of rotations because we work only with the lower triangular part of the matrix. It is therefore necessary to send these parameters to the south and the west of the matrix. In the mesh, the rotation matrices computed in A_{NW} are sent west, south and north, and the matrices computed in A_{SE} are sent west, east and south (figure 10).

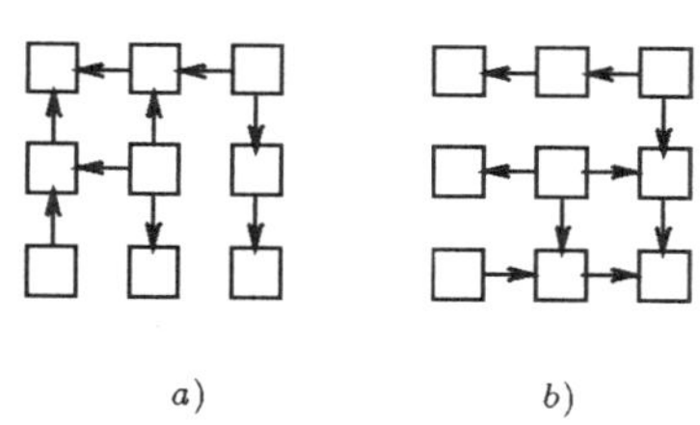

Figure 10: **Broadcast rotations. a) rotations computed in A_{NW}. b) rotations computed in A_{SE}.**

The matrices generated by rotations corresponding

to A_{NW} and A_{SE} are sent together to the adjacent processors, and are sent in the order:

processor $P_{0,r-1}$ to $P_{0,r-2}$ and $P_{1,r-1}$

processor $P_{r-1,0}$ to $P_{r-2,0}$ and $P_{r-1,1}$

processor $P_{i,r-1-i}$ with $i = 1, \ldots, \lfloor \frac{r-1}{2} \rfloor$, to $P_{i,r-2-i}$, $P_{i+1,r-1-i}$, $P_{i,r-i}$ and $P_{i-1,r-1-i}$

and processor $P_{i,r-1-i}$ with $i = \lfloor \frac{r-1}{2} \rfloor + 1, \ldots, r-2$, to $P_{i,r-i}$, $P_{i-1,r-1-i}$, $P_{i,r-2-i}$ and $P_{i+1,r-1-i}$.

This order of broadcasting is in figure 11, where the numbers by the rows indicate the order in which the corresponding messages are sent. Processors not in the main antidiagonal merely pass the rotation matrices they receive.

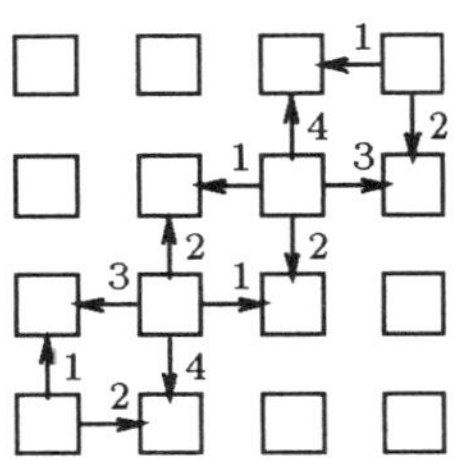

Figure 11: **Order in which rotation matrices are sent.**

4.3 Update matrix

Once the rotation matrices have been broadcasted, updating of matrix A proceeds as in the sequential algorithm, except that rows and columns of blocks are now distributed among processors.

4.4 Data transference

Data exchange between processors in even and odd steps is shown in figures 12 and 13.

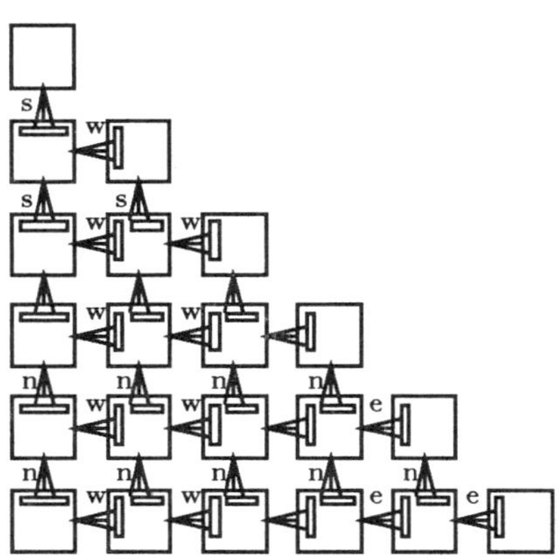

Figure 12: **Data transference. Odd step.**

After each step, data movement consists of columns being communicated to the east and west, and rows to the north and south in the matrix (what causes in the mesh the data movement shown in figures 12 and 13). In addition, after the exchange of data an internal movement of data is needed to obtain the new grouping of blocks, and this movement can be incorporated into the rotation matrices by appropriate permutation, as in the sequential algorithm.

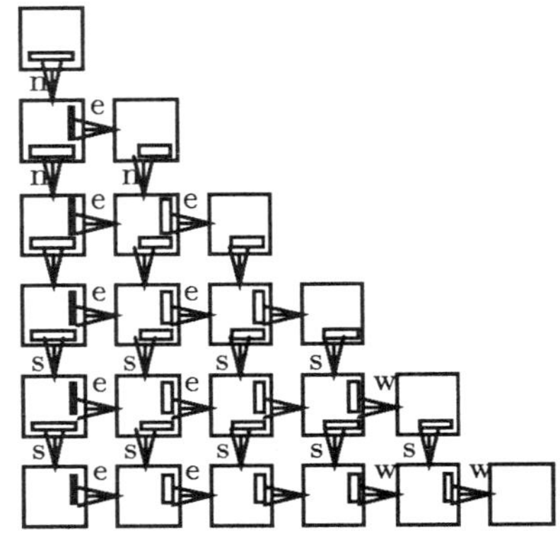

Figure 13: **Data transference. Even step.**

4.5 Theoretical cost

During each step, antidiagonal processors compute $\frac{n}{2s}$ or $\frac{n}{2s} - 1$ rotation matrices on a subsweep, computing on each antidiagonal processor $\frac{n}{2rs} = t$ or $\frac{n}{2rs} - 1 = t - 1$ rotation matrices. So, the cost of this operation for each subsweep is:

$$t48s^3 = \frac{24ns^2}{r} \quad \text{flops} \tag{11}$$

in the first step, and:

$$t24s^3 = \frac{12ns^2}{r} \quad \text{flops} \tag{12}$$

in successive steps.

So, the total cost of "compute rotations" per sweep is:

$$\frac{24ns^2}{r} + \left(\frac{n}{s} - 1\right)\frac{12ns^2}{r} = \frac{12n^2s}{r} + \frac{12ns^2}{r} \text{ flops.} \tag{13}$$

The most expensive communication associated with broadcasting rotation matrices is the one from processor $P_{0,r-1}$, since those matrices need to pass through $r-1$ links.

Each processor on the main antidiagonal computes $\frac{t}{2}$ rotation matrices of size $2s \times 2s$ from matrix A_{NW} and also $\frac{t}{2}$ from matrix A_{SE}. Hence, on each dispatch, processor $P_{0,r-1}$ sends $4ts^2 = \frac{2ns}{r}$ elements, sending first on link 1 and then on link 2 (figure 11). Thus, the cost of broadcasting rotations is:

$$r\alpha + 2ns\beta, \tag{14}$$

and the cost per sweep is:

$$\frac{n}{s}\left(r\alpha + 2ns\beta\right) = \frac{nr}{s}\alpha + 2n^2\beta, \qquad (15)$$

where α is the start-up time and β is the word sending time.

While updating the matrix, during even steps each processor not on the main antidiagonal has the same amount of work, and updates a total of $\frac{n^2}{2p}$ elements, requiring $\frac{4n^2s}{p}$ flops. During odd steps, processors on column 0 must also update $2s\frac{n}{2r}$ elements, which is done in $\frac{4s^2n}{r}$ flops. Hence $\frac{4n^2s}{p} + \frac{4s^2n}{r}$ flops per sweep are required to update the matrix on odd steps. Thus the cost per sweep of "update matrix" is:

$$\frac{n}{2s}\frac{4n^2s}{p} + \frac{n}{2s}\left(\frac{4n^2s}{p} + \frac{4s^2n}{r}\right) = \frac{4n^3}{p} + \frac{2sn^2}{r} \text{ flops.} \qquad (16)$$

During odd steps some processors send $\frac{n}{r}s$ elements to the west and $\frac{n}{2r}s$ to the east, $\frac{n}{r}s$ to the north and $\frac{n}{2r}s$ to the south. The cost is $4\alpha + \frac{3ns}{r}\beta$. During even steps some processors send $\frac{n}{2r}s$ elements to the north, $\frac{n}{r}s$ to the south, $\frac{n}{r}s$ to the east and $\frac{n}{2r}s$ to the west. And the cost is $4\alpha + \frac{3ns}{r}\beta$. Thus, the cost per sweep of exchanging data is:

$$\frac{n}{2s}\left(8\alpha + \frac{6ns}{r}\beta\right) = \frac{4n}{s}\alpha + \frac{3n^2}{r}\beta. \qquad (17)$$

The total arithmetic cost per sweep, given by adding (13) and (16) is

$$4k_3\frac{n^3}{p} + (2k_3 + 12k_1)\frac{n^2s}{r} + 12k_1\frac{ns^2}{r} \text{ flops,} \qquad (18)$$

where k_3 and k_1 are the constants affecting the execution times obtained using BLAS 3 and BLAS 1, respectively. The communication cost per sweep, given by adding (15) and (17), is

$$(4 + r)\frac{n}{s}\alpha + \left(2 + \frac{3}{r}\right)n^2\beta. \qquad (19)$$

Since the overhead related with the communication and load imbalance is of lower order, 100% efficiency can be approached by this algorithm when the matrix size is large enough.

5 Experimental results

The results presented here have been obtained on the Touchstone DELTA. This multicomputer consists of 512 i860 processors connected by a mesh network of dimension 16 × 32. The codes were written in C, using double precision arithmetic. Test matrices were generated by taking elements with values uniformly distributed between -10 and 10. The number of sweeps to reach the convergence is similar to those obtained by cyclic methods and is approximately $log_2\ n$. This allows us to report only times per sweep.

5.1 Sequential algorithm

Table 1 shows the execution time per sweep in seconds when only eigenvalues are computed on an i860 processor. This table reports a comparison of the algorithms that use BLAS 1 and 3, respectively. The optimal value of block size increases with the matrix size, and for the test matrices was between 16 and 32.

size	B1	B3. 4	B3. 8	B3. 16	B3. 32	B3. 64
256	9.2	8.8	5.7	**4.9**	5.4	7.6
512	88.5	68.0	40.1	**30.8**	31.8	43.6
768	306.2	220.1	126.7	94.1	**92.3**	117.4
1024	738.1	510.5	291.6	211.1	**207.1**	244.3

Table 1: **Execution times of sequential algorithms using BLAS 1 and BLAS 3 with different block sizes.**

Table 2 shows the Mflops obtained with the algorithm using BLAS 3 with optimal block size, when only eigenvalues are computed and when eigenvalues and eigenvectors are computed. When eigenvalues and eigenvectors are computed, a better performance is obtained, due to the fact that the amount of computation is greater when eigenvalues and eigenvectors are computed and hence using level-3 BLAS becomes beneficial sooner.

size	256	384	512	640	768	896	1024
values	13.6	15.9	17.4	18.3	19.6	20.3	20.7
vectors	18.1	20.6	22.6	22.9			

Table 2: **Mflops obtained using the sequential algorithm with BLAS 3 and optimal block sizes.**

5.2 Parallel algorithm

In table 3 the execution times obtained on the Touchstone DELTA are shown, with different mesh and matrix sizes, and with block sizes 16 and 32. The optimal block size is always 16, but when the matrix size increases the difference between times obtained with block sizes 16 and 32 decreases as in the sequential algorithm. In the parallel case the pre- and post-multiplication of rows and columns of blocks by a rotation matrix is performed by rows and columns of processors, each processor working thus with smaller matrices and obtaining less benefit from the work with BLAS 3.

	processors					
	4		16		64	
	block size					
	16	32	16	32	16	32
512	**10.8**	13.3	**4.5**	5.9	**2.0**	
1024	**66.3**	71.1	**23.5**	27.9	**9.1**	12.2
1536	**202.7**	203.0	**64.8**	72.5	**23.6**	
2048			**138.0**	147.4	**47.7**	56.8

Table 3: **Execution time per sweep of the parallel algorithm on the Touchstone DELTA.**

To analyze experimentally the scalability of the algorithm the Mflops/node obtained with meshes of different sizes when using the same memory per node are shown in table 4. Also the matrix size used are shown in the table. We consider the obtained results satisfactory, showing good scalability (approximately 3.5 Gflops have been obtained using 256 processors with matrices of size 6144).

processors	1	16	25	36	64	256
Mflops/node	15.2	13.8	13.5	13.7	13.6	13.5
matrix size	384	1530	1920	2302	3072	6144

Table 4: **Mflops per node obtained by the parallel algorithm on the Touschtone DELTA.**

6 Conclusions

The use of BLAS 3 to solve the symmetric eigenvalue problem by Jacobi methods can produce efficient algorithms. A small block size (between 16 and 32) gives good results. The optimal block size increases with the matrix size. When eigenvalues and eigenvectors are computed a bigger optimal block size is obtained. This is due to a higher amount of computations, which produces a better utilization of BLAS 3.

This sequential algorithm can be combined with an appropriate Storage Scheme (folding) to obtain an algorithm by blocks on a mesh of processors that presents good scalability properties.

Acknowledgments

This work was performed in part using the Intel Touchstone Delta System operated by the California Institute of Technology on behalf of the Concurrent Supercomputing Consortium. Access to this facility was provided by Intel Supercomputer Systems Division and the California Institute of Technology. In addition, this work was performed in part on the 32 node Intel iPSC/860 operated by the University of Texas Center of High Performance Computing.

References

[1] R. A. van de Geijn. Storage schemes for Parallel Eigenvalue Algorithms. In G. H. Golub and P. Van Dooren, editor, *Numerical Linear Algebra. Digital Signal Processing and Parallel Algorithms*, volume 70 of *NATO ASI Series*. Springer-Verlag, 1991.

[2] K. A. Gallivan, R. J. Plemmons and A. H. Sameh. Parallel algorithms for dense linear algebra computations. *SIAM Review*, 32(1):54–135, 1990.

[3] G. H. Golub and C. F. Van Loan. *Matrix Computations*. The Johns Hopkins University Press, 1989.

[4] J. Demmel and K. Veselić. Jacobi's method is more accurate than QR. *SIAM Journal on Matrix Analysis and Applications*, 13:1204–1245, (1992).

[5] R. P. Brent and F. T. Luk. The solution of singular-value and symmetric eigenvalue problems on multiprocessor arrays. *SIAM Journal on Scientific and Statistic Computation*, 6(1):69–84, (1985).

[6] G. W. Stewart. A Jacobi-like algorithm for computing the Schur decomposition of a nonhermitian matrix. *SIAM Journal on Scientific and Statistic Computation*, 4:853–864, (1985).

[7] E. Anderson, Z. Bai, C. Bischof, J. Demmel, J. Dongarra, J. Du Croz, A. Greenbaum, S. Hammarling, A. McKenney, S. Ostrouchov and D. Sorensen. *LAPACK Users' Guide*. SIAM, 1992.

[8] A. Edelman. Large dense linear algebra in 1993: The parallel computing influence. *The International Journal of Supercomputer Applications*, 7(2):113–128, 1993.

[9] G. E. Forsythe and P. Henrici. The cyclic Jacobi method for computing the principal values of a complex matrix. *Transactions of American Mathematical Society*, 94:1–23, (1960).

[10] F. T. Luk and H. Park. A proof of convergence for two parallel Jacobi SVD algorithms. *IEEE Transactions on Computers*, 28(6):806–811, (1989).

[11] G. Schroff and R. Schreiber. On the convergence of the cyclic Jacobi method for parallel block orderings. *SIAM Journal on Matrix Analysis and Applications*, 10(3):326–346, (1989).

[12] J. J. Dongarra, J. Du Croz, S. Hammarling and I. Duff. A set of Level 3 Basic Linear Algebra Subprograms. *ACM Trans. on Math. Soft.*, 16(1):1–17, (1990).

[13] C. H. Bischof. Computing the singular value decomposition on a distributed system of vector processors. *Parallel Computing*, 11:171–186, 1989.

Vector and Parallel Interpolation by Natural Cubic Splines and B-Splines

Josep-L. Larriba-Pey†, Juan J. Navarro† and Angel Jorba‡
Universitat Politècnica de Catalunya
† Departament d'Arquitectura de Computadors
‡ Departament de Matemàtica Aplicada I
Barcelona, e-mail: larri@ac.upc.es

Abstract

In this paper we deal with the solution of the almost Toeplitz tridiagonal systems that arise from the problem of curve fitting by Natural Cubic Splines and B-Splines. We propose the TJ decomposition that gives rise to a method which is more accurate and faster than other previously proposed methods as we prove along the work. For the solution of the recurrences that arise from the TJ decomposition, we propose a specialization of the Overlapped Partitions Method (OPM). We show that OPM compares favourably in the context of the problem to the classic Divide and Conquer and R-Cyclic Reduction on the Convex C-3480 supercomputer.

1: Introduction

Curve fitting is used in many applications. In the context of graphic animation, curve fitting is used in the process of inbetweening images [1]. In the context of CAD, curve fitting is used to define the shape of the surfaces that form the objects being designed [11]. Also, in the context of graphic representation, curve fitting is used in the modelization of data obtained from different phenomena, i.e. medical information [1].

The process of curve fitting is performed upon a set of given points. There are different techniques to obtain a mathematical curve model of a given set of digitized points. Among these techniques we can remark Hermite, Natural Cubic Spline and B-Spline interpolation.

The solution of almost Toeplitz tridiagonal systems arises during the computation of Natural Cubic Splines and B-Splines and is the object of analysis of this paper. For the case of normalized splines those systems are of the type

$$\begin{bmatrix} c & 1 & & & \\ 1 & 4 & 1 & & \\ & & \cdots & & \\ & & 1 & 4 & 1 \\ & & & 1 & c \end{bmatrix} \cdot \begin{bmatrix} t_{[1]} \\ t_{[2]} \\ \cdots \\ t_{[N]} \end{bmatrix} = \phi \cdot \begin{bmatrix} b_{[1]} \\ b_{[2]} \\ \cdots \\ b_{[N]} \end{bmatrix} \leftrightarrow At = \phi b \qquad (1)$$

where the value of c depends on the imposed boundary conditions and the value of ϕ depends on the type of spline being used. In particular, for the case of Natural Cubic Splines, these values are 2 and 3 respectively [1] and for the case of B-Splines when the boundary points are doubled, these values are 5 and 6 respectively [2]. The solution of (1) has to be performed for each of the coordinates of the points to be fitted. For more details on curve fitting and the specific problems of Natural Cubic Splines and B-splines, one can read [1] and [11].

The combined use of the *TJ* decomposition and OPM is compared to the combined use of our decomposition with the fastest vector methods for the solution of recurrences on a Convex C-3480. Those methods are the Divide and Conquer algorithm (DC) which was proposed by Sameh and Kuck [12] and the *R*-Cyclic Reduction family of methods (*R*-CR) that has its origins in the classic Cyclic Reduction and the generalized Cyclic Reduction [6, 14].

The paper is structured as follows. In section 2, we describe the *TJ* decomposition. Then, in section 3, we describe the decomposition proposed in [2] and compare its accuracy to that of the *TJ* decomposition. In section 4, we describe the Overlapped Partitions Method and give formulae for the accuracy of its solution. In section 5 we overview the Divide and Conquer and *R*-Cyclic Reduction methods. In section 6 we compare the implementation of the *TJ* decomposition using OPM and using DC and *R*-CR on the Convex C-3480. Also, in section 6 we compare the execution time of our method with the method arising from the decomposition described in section 3. Finally, in section 7 we draw some conclusions.

2: The *TJ* decomposition

The *TJ* decomposition is a variation of the decompositions proposed in [4] and [15] for almost Toeplitz systems. We describe the *TJ* decomposition below and show how to solve $At = \phi b$ with the decomposition in section 2.1. In section 2.2 we make some remarks on how to reduce of the work to solve $At = \phi b$ with the *TJ* decomposition given the strict diagonal dominance of A.

1066-6192/96 $5.00 © 1996 IEEE
Proceedings of PDP '96

For the matrix of the problem described above, it is possible to find a decomposition of the type

$$\begin{bmatrix} c & a & & & \\ a & d & a & & \\ & & \dots & & \\ & & a & d & a \\ & & & a & c \end{bmatrix}_{N \times N} = \alpha T J =$$

$$= \alpha \begin{bmatrix} \rho & 1 & & & \\ & \beta & 1 & & \\ & & \dots & & \\ & & & \beta & 1 \\ & & & & \beta \quad \sigma \end{bmatrix}_{N \times (N+1)} \begin{bmatrix} \gamma & & & & \\ 1 & \gamma & & & \\ & & \dots & & \\ & & 1 & \gamma & \\ & & & 1 & \gamma \\ & & & & 1 \end{bmatrix}_{(N+1) \times n}$$

where the values of α, β, γ, ρ and σ are

$$\alpha = \frac{d \pm \sqrt{d^2 - 4a^2}}{2} \qquad \beta = \gamma = \frac{a}{\alpha}$$

$$\rho = \left(\frac{c}{\alpha} - 1\right)\frac{\alpha}{a} \qquad \sigma = \frac{c}{\alpha} - \frac{a^2}{\alpha^2}$$

For example, for the specific case of B-Splines where $a = 1, \ d = 4, \ c = 5$, we have that

$$\alpha = 2 + \sqrt{3}, \qquad \beta = \gamma = (2 + \sqrt{3})^{-1},$$
$$\rho = \sigma = 3 - \sqrt{3}$$

α, β and γ are the same for the case of Natural Cubic Splines.

The number of arithmetic operations and the amount of storage required for this decomposition is $O(1)$.

2.1: Solution of the system

The solution of (1) can be found by solving $At = \alpha TJt = \phi b$ in the following steps

1. Solve $Ty = \phi b/\alpha$. This is performed by scaling b by ϕ/α $(b' = \phi b/\alpha)$ and finding the solution of $Ty = b'$ assuming that y is an order $N+1$ vector, $y = \begin{bmatrix} y_{[0]} & y_{[1]} & \dots & y_{[N-1]} & y_{[N]} \end{bmatrix}^{\mathrm{T}}$. Given that the system is underdetermined, variable y_0 is considered a parameter. Thus, the system can be transformed into $T'y' = b' - y_{[0]}f$ where

$$T' = \begin{bmatrix} 1 & & & \\ \beta & 1 & & \\ & \dots & & \\ & & \beta & 1 \\ & & & \beta \quad \sigma \end{bmatrix}_{N \times N}, \quad y' = \begin{bmatrix} y_{[1]} \\ \dots \\ y_{[N-1]} \\ y_{[N]} \end{bmatrix}, \quad f = \begin{bmatrix} \rho \\ 0 \\ \\ \\ 0 \end{bmatrix}$$

The solution of this new system can be found by solving two bidiagonal systems $T'g = b'$ and $T'h = f$. Note that, in order to find the solution of $g_{[N]}$ and $h_{[N]}$, it is necessary to divide the respective right hand side elements in position N by σ at the end of this step.

Now, y' is a linear combination of the two solutions $y' = g - y_{[0]}h$.

2. Solve $Jt = y$. With the value of y' it is possible to see that $Jt = y = \begin{bmatrix} y_0 \\ y' \end{bmatrix} = \begin{bmatrix} 0 \\ g \end{bmatrix} - y_{[0]} \begin{bmatrix} -1 \\ h \end{bmatrix}$.

Assuming that $t = t1 - y_{[0]}t2$, solve the following systems $J't1 = g$ and $J't2 = h$ where

$$J' = \begin{bmatrix} 1 & \gamma & & \\ & \dots & \dots & \\ & & 1 & \gamma \\ & & & 1 \end{bmatrix}_{N \times N}$$

Now, it is necessary to find the value of y_0. We know that $y_{[0]} = \gamma \ t_{[1]}$. We also know that $t_{[1]} = t1_{[1]} - y_{[0]}t2_{[1]}$. With these two equations we have that $y_{[0]} = \gamma \dfrac{t1_{[1]}}{1 + \gamma \ t2_{[1]}}$.

Finally, the solution of the system can be found by solving $t = t1 - y_{[0]}t2$.

2.2: Remarks to the solution of $At = \alpha TJt = \phi b$

Remark 1) From the method described above, it is easy to see that four recurrences have to be solved $T'g = b'$, $T'h = f$, $J't1 = g$ and $J't2 = h$. Those recurrences are Toeplitz (the case of T' is almost Toeplitz but can be solved as a Toeplitz system as we said before).

Remark 2) $T'g = b'$, $T'h = f$, $J't1 = g$ and $J't2 = h$ are strictly diagonal dominant with $\delta = 2 + \sqrt{3}$. The original diagonal dominance $\delta = 2$ has grown with the *TJ* decomposition.

Remark 3) $T'h = f$ has only one element on top of its right hand side. For the case of strictly diagonal dominant systems, the value of element $h_{[i]}$ of the solution decreases in absolute value to zero as i grows to N. The absolute value of $h_{[i]}$ can be quantified by $\left|h_{[i]}\right| \le |\rho|\delta^{-i+1}$ which is proved [9]. From this equation it is easy to see that the number of elements of the solution vector that are larger in absolute value than a certain value ε are

$$u = \left\lceil \frac{\log(\varepsilon/|\rho|)}{\log \delta^{-1}} \right\rceil.$$

So, only the first u variables of $T'h = f$ have to be solved if we want an error larger or equal than ε. Also, only equations u through 1 have to be solved in $J't2 = h$ because the N - u last equations have a 0 in their right hand side. As a consequence, for the case of the axpy type operation $t = t1 - y_{[0]}t2$ only elements 1 through u have to be modified.

Remark 4) The solution of $T'h = f$ and $J't2 = h$ can be performed once for all in an inicialization phase because those systems do not depend on the right hand side of $At = \alpha TJt = \phi b$.

Remark 5) If the maximum error allowed to the solution of (1) is $\varepsilon = 10^{-7}$ then $u = 14$ and if the error allowed is $\varepsilon = 10^{-16}$ then $u = 30$.

Remark 6) For the implementation of the method on vector supercomputers, $b' = \phi b/\alpha$ can be performed by means of 1 scalar divide and 1 vector multiply. $t = t1 - y_{[0]}t2$ can be performed in vector form. Also, specialized vector solvers have to be found for $T'g = b'$ and $J't1 = g$.

Remark 7) In terms of the implementation of the method on parallel computers, the scaling $b' = \phi b/\alpha$ can be fully parallelized. The solution of $t = t1 - y_{[0]}t2$ can be performed on a single processor without incrementing the sequential fraction of the problem significatively. Specialized parallel solvers have to be found for $T'g = b'$ and $J't1 = g$.

3: A different decomposition for the problem

In this section we give a brief description of the decomposition proposed by Chung and Shen in [2] and we compare its accuracy to the *TJ* decomposition. For more details about this method we suggest the reading of the referenced paper. We will call this decomposition $L'D'U'$.

Let us suppose that we approximate the matrix of the problem A by the following matrix

$$A' = \begin{bmatrix} 2+\sqrt{3} & 1 & & & \\ 1 & 4 & 1 & & \\ & & \cdots & & \\ & & 1 & 4 & 1 \\ & & & 1 & 4 \end{bmatrix}$$

One can find an $L'D'U'$ decomposition of A' such that

$$\begin{bmatrix} 1 & & \\ 2-\sqrt{3} & 1 & \\ \cdots & \cdots & \\ & 2-\sqrt{3} & 1 \end{bmatrix} \begin{bmatrix} 2+\sqrt{3} & & \\ & \cdots & \\ & & 2+\sqrt{3} \end{bmatrix} \begin{bmatrix} 1 & 2-\sqrt{3} & \\ \cdots & \cdots & \\ & 1 & 2-\sqrt{3} \\ & & 1 \end{bmatrix}$$

Given that matrix A is approximated by matrix A' the solutions to the first equations of $A't = \phi b$ are incorrect. A perturbation analysis that we have made shows that, the first v solutions to the system are incorrect. For the case of $c = 5$, the value of v is

$$v = \left\lceil -\log_2 \frac{12 \cdot \varepsilon}{\phi \cdot \max_j b_{[j]}} \right\rceil$$

where ε is the maximum error allowed. Thus the interpolation given by this method is not correct in the first $v = 22$ elements of the solution if the maximum error allowed is $\varepsilon = 10^{-7}$ and $v = 52$ if the maximum error allowed is $\varepsilon = 10^{-16}$ for $\phi = 3$ and $\max_j b_{[j]} = 1$.

Note that the *TJ* decomposition is accurate while this decomposition is not.

4: The Overlapped Partitions Method

The Overlapped Partitions Method is a new parallel method specialized for narrow banded strictly diagonal dominant systems proposed in [8]. In this section we describe the method and comment on its special features for the solution of recurrences $T'h = f$ and $J't2 = h$ that arise from the *TJ* decomposition.

For the decription of OPM we start assumming the partitioning of matrix A and the notation shown in Figure 1. Note that the indices of elements of vectors and matrices are between brackets while the indices of subvectors or submatrices are not. We assume $\delta > 1$ and N to be divisible by an arbitrary number R for simplicity.

As an initial approach to OPM, we start solving the independent systems $D_p q_p = s_p$ for $1 \le p \le P$, and then we gather their solutions. With this, we form $\tilde{t} = (q_1, \ldots, q_p, \ldots, q_P)$. Vector $\tilde{t}$ is an approximation to the solution t. This approximation $\tilde{t}$ is not correct as the information contained in vectors l_p has been omitted. This is shown in figure 2. So, each of the independent solutions q_p incurs in a certain amount of error (figure 2.b). Depending on the diagonal dominance δ of the system and the order of the partitions R, this error can be very small for the elements that are near the lower boundary of q_p and larger as the elements approach the upper boundary of q_p.

$$At = \begin{bmatrix} 1 & & 0 \\ a_{[2]} & 1 & \\ & \dots & \dots \\ 0 & a_{[N]} & 1 \end{bmatrix} t = \begin{bmatrix} D_1 & & 0 \\ L_2 & D_2 & \\ & \dots & \dots \\ 0 & L_P & D_P \end{bmatrix} \begin{bmatrix} t_1 \\ t_2 \\ \dots \\ t_P \end{bmatrix} = \phi \begin{bmatrix} b_1 \\ b_2 \\ \dots \\ b_P \end{bmatrix} = s$$

$$l_p = L_{p\,[j,R]} = \begin{bmatrix} a_{[i+1]} \\ 0 \\ \dots \\ 0 \end{bmatrix}, \forall j$$

Figure 1. Notation used for the description of OPM.

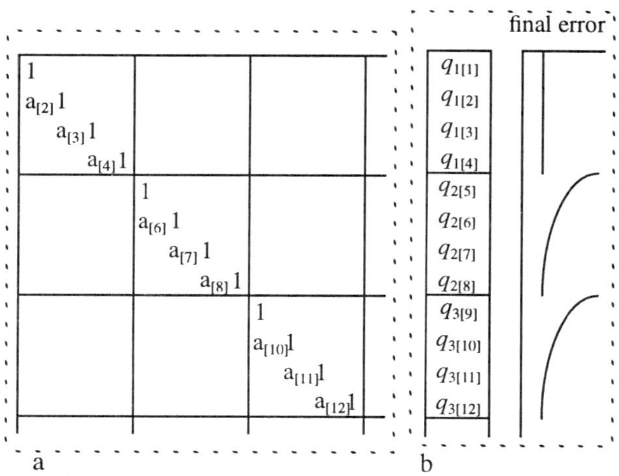

Figure 2. Solution and error of $D_p q_p = s_p$. a) Partitioning of $Ax = b$. b) Error of the solutions.

A possible way to reduce this error is to add m equations at the beginning of each partition except for the first partition. The new blocks $D'_p q'_p = s'_p$ overlap as shown in figure 3.a for $R = 4$ and $m = 2$. So, the Overlapped Partitions Method consists in solving $D'_p q'_p = s'_p$. From the solutions to the independent partitions q'_p we take the following elements: the R elements of the first solution vector q'_1 and the R last elements of the rest of the solution vectors q'_p (for $2 \le p \le P$). With those elements, we form t' which is an approximation to the N elements of the solution vector t (see figures 3.b and 3.c). An adequate choice of the overlapping m reduces the error (see figure 3.c). $D'_p q'_p = s'_p$ can be solved with Gaussian Elimination although any parallel method could be used.

OPM leads to inexact solutions that can be controlled with the amount of overlapping m

$$m \ge \left\lceil \frac{\log \frac{\varepsilon\left(1-\delta^{-1}\right)}{\|s\|_\infty}}{\log \delta^{-1}} \right\rceil \qquad (2)$$

This formula is proved in [9]. For the particular case studied here, $m = 13$ for $\varepsilon = 10^{-7}$ and $m = 29$ for $\varepsilon = 10^{-16}$.

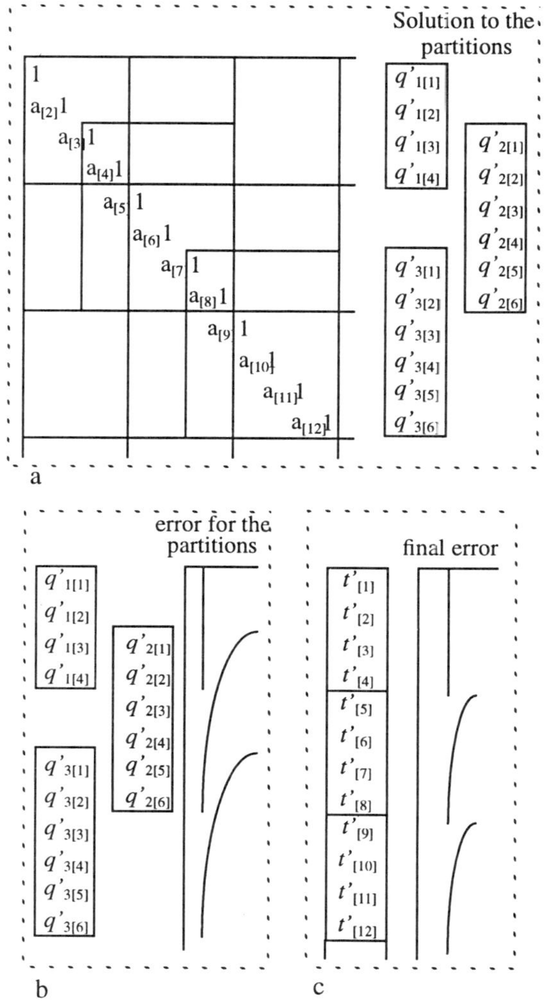

Figure 3. The Overlapped Partitions Method. a) Overlapping for OPM and solutions to each partition. b) Solution and error of the different partitions. c) Final solution and error for OPM.

5: Other parallel recurrence solvers

The classic methods for the parallel and vector solution of recurrences are R-Cyclic Reduction and Divide and Conquer. Also, Recursive Doubling [13] can be used for such problems but we discard it as it is not competitive with the methods studied [7].

5.1: Divide and Conquer and *R*-Cyclic Reduction

DC and *R*-CR have been analyzed for the solution of recurrences in [5], [10] and [16]. Here, we describe the two algorithms from the unified point of view proposed in [9]. We start with the description of *R*-CR to deduce that DC is a particular case of the unification.

The algorithms start with a partitioning of the system as shown in figure 4.a. The size of each partition is *R* (in the example, $R = 4$). The algorithm is based on two different stages called forward and backward. Each of these stages can be divided into different steps. During the first step of the forward stage of the algorithm, the subdiagonal elements of matrix *A* are zeroed with Gaussian Elimination within each partition. During this step, the right hand side of the system is modified and some fill-in appears in matrix *A*.

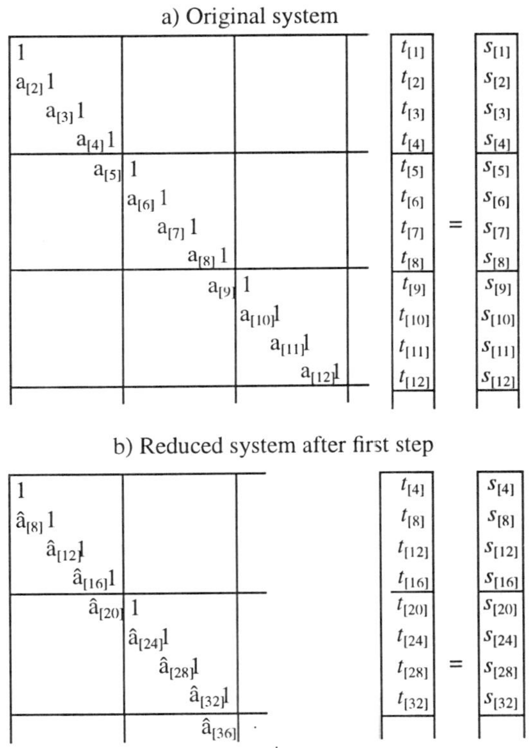

Figure 4. Steps for Divide and Conquer and *R*-Cyclic Reduction. â stands for modified value of a in the original system.

After the first step, the system has been decoupled. Only equations in positions $k*R$ still depend on each other (for the example, equations in positions 4, 8, 12, etc.). Equations in positions $k*R + 1, ..., (k+1)*R - 1$ depend only on equation $k*R$ (for the example, equations 5, 6 and 7 depend only on equation 4, etc.). With equations in positions $k*R$, a new smaller system can be formed as shown in figure 4.b. This system is bidiagonal and preserves all the characteristics of the predecessor system (it is Toeplitz and diagonal dominant). A partitioning similar to that shown in figure 4.a can be applied to this reduced system. The same strategy can be applied again and a new reduced system appears. After $\lfloor \log_R N \rfloor$ recursive applications of this strategy, only one equation remains and does not depend on any other equation. The trivial solution of this equation is used as a seed to find the solutions of the unsolved equations during the backward stage in $\lfloor \log_R N \rfloor$ steps. With this backward process, the final solution of the equations is found.

This recursive process is known as *R*-Cyclic Reduction. For example, the classic Cyclic Reduction is a particular case of this process with $R = 2$. For the Cyclic Reduction algorithm, the number of steps for the forward and backward stages is $\lfloor \log_2 N \rfloor$.

The Divide and Conquer algorithm is a particular case of this recursive process in which only one step is performed. The reduced system obtained after the first stage is solved with a strategy like Gaussian elimination. After the solution of the reduced system the backward step is performed. For the case of DC, the size of the partitions is usually larger than for *R*-CR.

For the specific case of Toeplitz systems, the fill-ins of the different partitions during a certain step have the same value in equivalent positions (for the example $\hat{a}_{[8]} = \hat{a}_{[12]} = \ldots$ and $\bar{a}_{[32]} = \bar{a}_{[48]} = \ldots$). Thus some work can be saved if the spikes are computed only once.

5.2: Early termination of the methods

When $\delta > 1$, the diagonal dominance of the reduced systems formed during the forward stage grows at each step of *R*-CR. Thus, at a certain step this diagonal dominance may be so large that an approximation of the reduced system matrix by the identity matrix may be valid for a given maximum error allowed ε. So, some steps can be saved to *R*-CR. For the case of DC, the value of the elements of the fill-in decreases to a point that they can start to be considered zero. With this, the solution of the reduced system can be avoided by DC. The saving of some work to *R*-CR and DC is called early termination. With this, the methods are solved with some controllable error.

A large amount of the work of *R*-CR is performed during its first steps. Also, for our problem ($\delta = 2 + \sqrt{3}$), we need more than 2 steps to achieve accuracies larger than $\varepsilon = 10^{-4}$ [9]. In this case, it makes no sense to terminate *R*-CR early because less than a 5% of the work is saved [9].

For DC, the minimum size of the partition *k* to avoid the

solution of the reduced system is

$$k \geq \left\lceil \frac{\log \frac{\varepsilon\left(1-\delta^{-1}\right)}{\|s\|_{\infty}}}{\log \delta^{-1}} \right\rceil \quad (3)$$

where ε is the accuracy required, δ is the diagonal dominance and s is the right hand side vector. This formula, which is equal to (2), is proved in [9]. If the size of the partitions is chosen to be larger than k, some more work can be eliminated appart from avoiding the solution of the reduced system [9].

6: Vector implementation and results

OPM, DC and R-CR can be easily implemented on vector computers. In all the cases, vectorization can be obtained by performing the same operation to the same equation of different partitions. We call this, vectorization accross partitions. Nevertheless, during the backward stage of DC, vectorization can also be applied within partitions [16]. Thus the stride of the accesses to memory is determined by R^i (being i the number of step) except for the backward step of DC in which it can also be 1 if we vectorize within partitions. For the present paper we consider the case of vectorization within partitions for the backward stage of DC.

In order to avoid conflictive strides on the interleaved memories of vector computers, it is advisable to use odd strides. So, we choose odd values of R for all the methods implemented here.

Strip mining may have to be performed if the length of the vectors (number of partitions for a given step) is larger than the maximum vector length. The implementation of R-CR in this paper assumes that strip mining may be necessary. Nevertheless, for OPM and DC we restrict the number of partitions to be smaller than the maximum vector length.

6.1: Optimization of the vector implementations

The optimum vector implementation of OPM and the early terminated DC and R-CR has been studied in [9]. This vector implementation can be optimized by means of several techniques that we do not explain here in detail. Nevertheless, an important issue is to find the optimum size of the partition R for each method.

The optimum value of R for R-CR can be found by interchanging and unrolling the loops involved in the algorithm. With these transformations, it is possible to save a considerable amount of traffic with memory. Nevertheless, the traffic saved decreases assimptotically for growing values of R. For the Toeplitz systems analyzed here on the C-3480, the optimum value of R is 5.

The optimum value of R for OPM and DC can be found in a more complex way. In this case, it is also possible to perform loop transformations to reduce the amount of traffic with memory. Also, the minimization of the time models of OPM and DC help to find the optimum value of R. Those execution time models are

$$\begin{aligned} T_{OPM} &= K_1\frac{N}{P} + K_2N + K_3m + K_4mpP + K_5 \\ T_{DC} &= K_6\frac{N}{P} + K_7N + K_8P + K_9k + K_{10}kP + K_{11} \end{aligned} \quad (4)$$

where, $P = N/R$ is the number of partitions and the constants stand for the amount of work performed depending on each variable for a certain computer. It is easy to see that the minimum execution times are determined by

$$\text{OPM} \rightarrow P = \sqrt{\frac{K_1N}{K_4m}} \qquad \text{DC} \rightarrow P = \sqrt{\frac{K_6N}{K_8 + K_{10}k}}$$

For the optimum value of P for the algorithms tested here, the values of the constants in (4) have to be fitted to different executions varying parameters N, P, k and m.

For the cases with a value of k larger than the size of the partition, DC has been fully terminated (the reduced system has been solved). For the cases with a value of m larger than the size of the partition, the number of partitions for OPM has been changed into $P = \lfloor N/(m+1) \rfloor$.

6.2: Results

In this section we compare the variants of the method arising from the TJ decomposition and the method proposed in [2]. For the solution of the recurrences arising from the TJ decomposition four algorithms have been executed, namely, Gaussian Elimination, Divide and Conquer, 5-Cyclic Reduction and the Overlapped Partitions Method. For the implementation of the method arising from the $L'D'U'$ decomposition, we have executed the exact copy of the algorithm in [2] which implements the Recursive Doubling method for the solution of the recurrences.

The methods have been programmed in Fortran on one processor of the Convex C-3480 [3]. They have been run in multiple user mode and taking the smallest execution time out of 100 executions for each size of matrix. The assembly code generated by the compiler has been modified in order to optimize the execution time of the bidiagonal solvers. For the case of the method based on the $L'D'U'$ decomposition, the vector directives of the Cray Fortran have been changed into directives of the Convex Fortran. No assembly modifications have been made to this algorithm.

For the practical executions, double precision arithmetic

has been used for all the methods although two different maximum errors allowed have been tested for the method proposed here, this is $\varepsilon = 10^{-7}$ and $\varepsilon = 10^{-16}$. Note that for the method based on the $L'D'U'$ decomposition there is no choice for the accuracy required and the error is larger than for the method proposed here.

The models shown above for OPM and DC have been fitted for the the Convex C-3480, and the values of the constants in the expressions for the optimum number of partitions P are

$$K_1 = 2.5 \cdot 10^{-6} \quad K_4 = 7.8 \cdot 10^{-8} \quad K_6 = 2.5 \cdot 10^{-6}$$

$$K_8 = 3.5 \cdot 10^{-6} \quad K_{10} = 9.6 \cdot 10^{-8}$$

Figures 4 and 5 show plots of the execution times of the methods for the case where a maximum error $\varepsilon = 10^{-7}$ is allowed. Figure 4 shows plots for systems ranging from 50 to 4000 and figure 5 shows a zoom of figure 4 for matrices of size 50 to 1000. There, we can see that the *TJ* decomposition using Gaussian Elimination is faster than the other methods for matrices smaller than approximately 180. In the rest of the cases,the *TJ* decomposition using the Overlapped Partitions Method is clearly faster than the other methods.

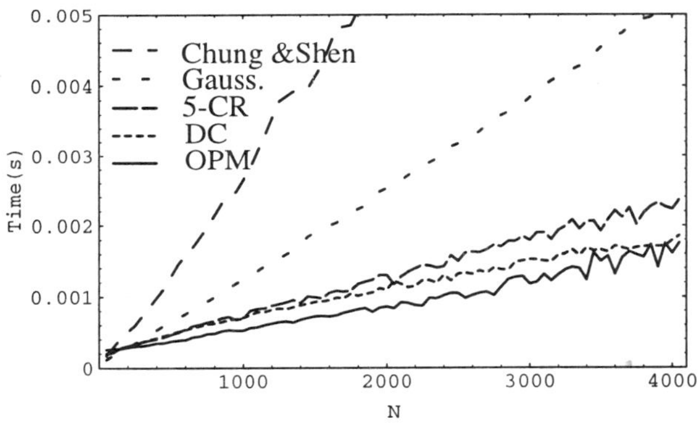

Figure 4. Execution time of the methods compared for $\varepsilon = 10^{-7}$ and n ranging from 50 to 4000.

Figures 6 and 7 show plots of the execution times of the methods for the case where a maximum error $\varepsilon = 10^{-16}$ is allowed. Figure 6 shows plots for systems ranging from 50 to 4000 and figure 7 shows a zoom of figure 6 for matrices of size 50 to 1000. In figure 7, we can see that the *TJ* decomposition using Gaussian Elimination is faster than the other methods for matrices smaller than approximately 220. For the case of matrices in the range between 220 and 650, the *TJ* decomposition using 5-CR is the fastest algorithm. For matrices larger than 650, the *TJ* decomposition using the Overlapped Partitions Method is the fastest.

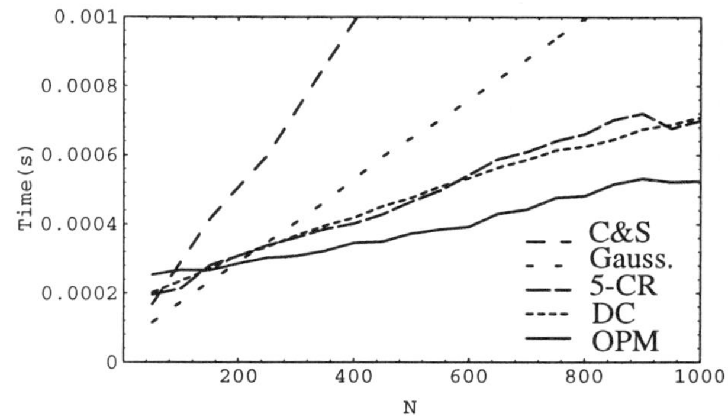

Figure 5. Execution time of the methods compared for $\varepsilon = 10^{-7}$ and n ranging from 50 to 1000.

As it can be noticed in figures 4 through 7, the *TJ* decomposition using the Overlapped Partitions Method is the fastest for moderate to large systems of equations.

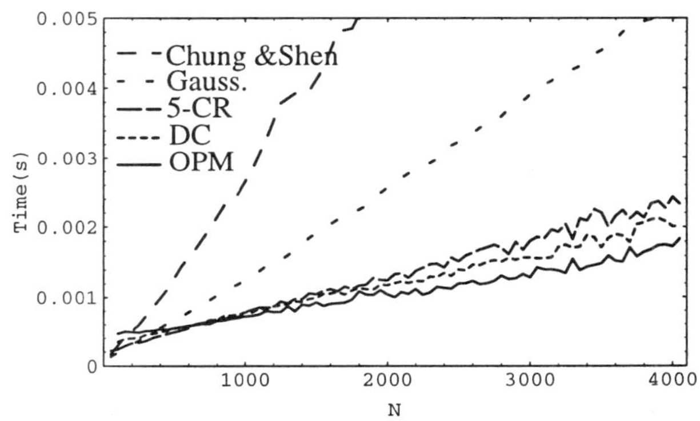

Figure 6. Execution time of the methods compared for $\varepsilon = 10^{-16}$ and n ranging from 50 to 4000.

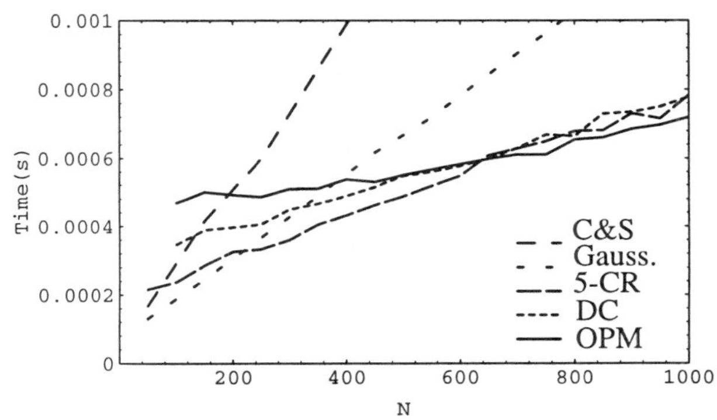

Figure 7. Execution time of the methods compared for $\varepsilon = 10^{-16}$ and n ranging from 50 to 1000.

Note that the method the method based on the $L'D'U'$ decomposition is slower than the method based on the *TJ* decomposition because it makes use of the Recursive Doubling algorithm to solve the recurrences. If that method used OPM, DC or R-CR would be competitive with the method we propose in terms of the execution time. Nevertheless, the method based on the $L'D'U'$ decomposition has the disadvantage that it incurs in a significative error in the upper boundary of the solution vector.

7: Conclusions

In this paper we have proposed the *TJ* decomposition for the solution of tridiagonal systems arising from curve fitting by Natural Cubic Splines and B-Splines. This decomposition is based on the idea behind the reversed triangular factorization by Evans in [4] and the *LU*-like decomposition proposed by Taha and Liaw in [15]. Nevertheless, the *TJ* decomposition reduces the amount of computation of those decompositions and also proves to be accurate while other previously proposed decompositions were not [2].

For the solution of the recurrences arising from the *TJ* decomposition, we propose the use of the Overlapped Partitions Method. OPM offers a large amount of inherent parallelism at the cost of introducing some controllable error in the solutions.

The *TJ* decomposition and the use of OPM have been compared to the fastest existing solvers on a vector supercomputer. The methods compared to OPM in the context of the *TJ* decomposition are Gaussian Elimination, Divide and Conquer and *R*-Cyclic Reduction. Also, the method arising from the decomposition proposed in [2] has been compared. The method in [2] uses the Recursive Doubling algorithm for the solution of the recurrences.

The *TJ* decomposition that uses Gaussian Elimination to solve the recurrences is the fastest for systems smaller than $n = 180$ for $\varepsilon = 10^{-7}$ and for systems smaller than n=220 for $\varepsilon = 10^{-16}$. On the other hand, the *TJ* decomposition that uses 5-Cyclic Reduction shows to be the fastest method for medium sized systems ($220 < n < 650$) for the case of double precision $\varepsilon = 10^{-16}$. Finally, the use of the Overlapped Partitions Method is the fastest approach for systems larger than $n = 180$ for $\varepsilon = 10^{-7}$ and $n = 650$ for $\varepsilon = 10^{-16}$.

Acknowledgements

The authors want to thank the Ministry of Education and Science of Spain for grant CICYT TIC-880/92, the EC for granting ESPRIT Project APPARC 6634 and to CEPBA for its support to basic research.

The authors want to thank Oriol Roig i Mansilla for programming the 5-CR algorithm used in this paper.

References

[1] R. Bartels, J. Beatty and B. Barsky. An introduction to Splines for use in computer graphics and geometric modeling, Morgan Kaufmann Publishers, inc., Los Altos (CA) 1986.

[2] K. Chung and L. Shen. Vectorized Algorithm for B-Spline curve Fitting on Cray X-MP EA/16se. Proceedings of the Supercomputing'92 conference. pp. 166-169.

[3] Convex Computer Corp. Convex C-3400 Supercomputer System Overview. Richardson, Texas, 1991.

[4] D. J. Evans. An algorithm for the solution of certain tridiagonal systems of linear equations. The Comp. Journal, Vol. 15, No. 4, 1972, pp. 356-359

[5] H. Häfner, W. Schönauer. Investigation of different algorithms for the first order recurrence, Supercomputer, 40 (1990), pp. 34-41.

[6] R. W. Hockney. A Fast Direct Solution of Poisson's Equation Using Fourier Analysis. J ACM, Vol. 12, No.1 (1965) pp 95-113.

[7] J. J. Lambiotte and R. G. Voigt. The solution of tridiagonal linear systems on the CDC STAR-100 computer, ACM TOMS, 1 (1975), pp. 308-329.

[8]J.-L. Larriba-Pey, A. Jorba and J. Navarro. A Parallel Tridiagonal Solver for Vector Uniprocessors. SIAM Int. Conf. on Par. Proc. for Sci. Comp.. March 1993. Norfolk, VA. 22nd-24th March 1993. pp. 590-597.

[9] Josep-L. Larriba-Pey. Design and Evaluation of Tridiagonal Solvers for Vector and Parallel Computers. PhD dissertation (preprint). Departament d'Arquitectura de Computadors. UPC, January 1995.

[10] Josep-L. Larriba-Pey, Juan J. Navarro, O. Roig and Àngel Jorba. A generalized vision of some parallel bidiagonal systems solvers. Proc. of the Intl. Conf. on Supercomputing 1994, ACM Press, pp. 404-411.

[11] D.F. Rogers and J.A. Adams. Mathematical Elements for Computer Graphics, McGraw- Hill, New York, 1990.

[12] A. Sameh and D. Kuck. On Stable Parallel Linear System Solvers, J. ACM, 25 (1978), pp. 81-91.

[13] H. S. Stone. An efficient parallel algorithm for the solutionof a tridiagonal linear system of equations. J. ACM, Vol. 20, No. 1, pp. 27-38, 1973.

[14]] R. Sweet. A generalized Cyclic Reduction algorithm. SIAM J. Num. Anal, Vol. 11 No 3, June 1974, pp. 506-520.

[15] T. Taha and J. Liaw. An Algorithm for solving a 4-Diagonal Toeplitz Linear System of Equations on Vector Computers. Proceedings of the Sixth SIAM Conf. on Parall. Process. for Scientific Computing. pp. 510-514. Norfolk, Va.

[16] H. A. Van der Vorst and K. Dekker. Vectorization of linear recurrence relations, SIAM J. Sci. Stat. Comput., 10 (1989), pp. 27-35.

Fast Parallel Algorithm for Finding Centers and Medians of Graphs

P. Chaudhuri

[*This paper not received in time for publication*]

Divide and Conquer for the Solution of Banded Linear Systems of Equations

M. Hegland
Computer Sciences Laboratory
Australian National University
Canberra, ACT, 0200

Abstract

An algorithm for the solution of banded linear systems is presented and discussed which combines stability with scalability. This is achieved by implementing divide and conquer for Gaussian elimination with partial pivoting. Earlier divide and conquer algorithms for Gaussian elimination have problems with instabilities and can even break down as they implement a more restricted form of pivoting.

The key observation used for the implementation is the invariance of LU factorization with partial pivoting under permutations. Theoretical analysis shows that the algorithm has low redundancy, a high degree of parallelism and relatively low communication.

1 Introduction

One of the difficulties in the development of parallel numerical algorithms is to maintain the precision of the sequential algorithm while achieving speedup through parallelism. An example of this is the solution of banded linear systems

$$Ax = b \tag{1}$$

with small bandwidths. Whereas sequential methods implement Gaussian elimination with partial pivoting, the suggested parallel methods so far only use restricted forms of pivoting or do not do any pivoting for stability at all [1, 2]. This contrasts with the case of dense linear systems (which are used in the standard LINPACK benchmarks [3]). For dense linear systems partial pivoting is used routinely as the other schemes can lead to poor accuracy and can even break down [4].

Current parallel solvers partition A into blocks. They break down if the diagonal blocks are singular. An example is

$$A = \begin{bmatrix} -1 & 1 & & \\ 1 & -1 & 1 & \\ & 1 & -1 & 1 \\ & & 1 & -1 \end{bmatrix}$$

which is regular but the diagonal 2x2 blocks

$$A_{1,2} = \begin{bmatrix} -1 & 1 \\ 1 & -1 \end{bmatrix}$$

are singular.

Near break-down where the diagonal blocks are ill-conditioned while the full matrix is well-conditioned occur frequently in practice. This ill-conditioning of the diagonal blocks has a severe impact on the precision of the current parallel solvers. In the case of

$$A = \begin{bmatrix} q & 1 & & & & \\ 1 & q & 1 & & & \\ & 1 & q & 1 & & \\ & & 1 & q & 1 & \\ & & & 1 & q & 1 \\ & & & & 1 & q \end{bmatrix}$$

with $q = 1.4142$ the rounding error of Gaussian elimination was found to be 10'000 times larger for a typical current parallel method than for the new method suggested here. These situations are very likely to occur in practice for larger matrices. Examples are encountered in the solution of eigenvalue problems by inverse iteration. Thus the method suggested here is certainly competitive as the earlier methods are often incapable of solving the problem.

This deficiency of current parallel banded solvers is addressed in the following and a new approach is suggested which allows the efficient parallel implementation of Gaussian elimination with partial pivoting for banded linear systems. A different approach, although only for the vectorized solution of tridiagonal systems was suggested by Hegland [5]. A disadvantage of the earlier method was the difficulty of the implementation. With the new approach this disadvantage disappears and the implementation compares well with the other divide and conquer methods based on Gaussian elimination.

Basically, the new algorithm has two parts: First the original problem is reformulated. Then a divide

1066-6192/96 $5.00 © 1996 IEEE
Proceedings of PDP '96

and conquer algorithm is used to solve the reformulated problem. Of course the reformulation has to be such that the precision achievable for the original problem is not compromised. This "stable" reformulation is what distinguishes the new algorithm from earlier attempts.

The computations in the reformulated problem turn out to be exactly the same as they would have been for the original problem but the data locates in different places. In fact, the reformulated problem is obtained from Equation 1 by permutation and is $PAx = Pb$ for an appropriate permutation matrix P. It will be seen that Gaussian elimination with partial pivoting (and a tie breaking strategy) is computationally invariant under permutations. The permutation used here is referred to as reformulation as no data movement is involved, the permutation is purely "virtual".

The reformulated problem is a block bidiagonal system and the diagonal blocks are lower triangular and banded with (lower) bandwidths equal to the sum of the upper and lower bandwidth of the original problem. The number of block-rows of the system is equal to the number of processors and each processor contains one block-row. The divide and conquer method to solve the block bidiagonal system consists of two stages: In the first "concurrent" stage all the independent elimination is done and a block-bidiagonal system with the same number of blocks as the first block-bidiagonal system but with much smaller block sizes is obtained. The second stage consists of a cyclic reduction method to solve the "reduced" block bidiagonal system.

The solution of a linear system of equations usually consists of three stages: First, in the elimination stage the matrix A is factorized, then, using this factorization, the system is solved with forward-elimination and back-substitution [4]. In the following only the elimination stage, i.e., the factorization of the matrix A is discussed. However, the discussion easily extends to the forward-elimination and back-substitution stages as well. The algorithm discussed here also extends to QR factorization, see [6] for a related algorithm for QR factorization on vector processors.

2 Reformulation and shift invariance

This section has two aims: First, to introduce the class of cyclically banded matrices. This class is a superset of the class of banded matrices and has some essential invariance properties under shift permutations which are fundamental to the new algorithms. The second aim of this section is to show that Gaussian elimination with partial pivoting is invariant under shifts.

Definition 1 *A matrix $A = [\alpha_{i,j=1,\ldots,n}]$ is* cyclically banded *with lower bandwidth k_l and upper bandwidth k_u if*

$$\alpha_{i,j} = 0 \quad if \begin{cases} \operatorname{mod}(n+j-i, n) > k_u \\ and \\ \operatorname{mod}(n+i-j, n) > k_l \end{cases}$$

The set of cyclically banded matrices with lower bandwidth k_l and upper bandwidth k_u is denoted by $\mathcal{B}^n_{k_l,k_u}$ and, for short, $\mathcal{B}^n_k = \mathcal{B}^n_{k,0}$.

Cyclically banded matrices arise, e.g., from discretized boundary value problems with periodic boundary conditions or periodic splines [7]. If $k_u + k_l \geq n$ then $\mathcal{B}^n_{k_l,k_u}$ coincides with $\mathbb{R}^{n,n}$, the set of all $n \times n$ matrices. As an example, the nonzero structure of the matrices in $\mathcal{B}^6_{2,1}$ is:

$$\begin{bmatrix} x & x & & & x & x \\ x & x & x & & & x \\ x & x & x & x & & \\ & x & x & x & x & \\ & & x & x & x & x \\ x & & & x & x & x \end{bmatrix}$$

Banded matrices are examples of cyclically banded matrices. Thus any algorithms for cyclically banded matrices also apply to banded matrices. While there is usually a tradeoff in complexity for the larger generality this is not the case for parallel algorithms (which have the same complexity for banded and cyclically banded matrices).

The bipartite graphs of cyclically banded matrices are rotationally symmetric. This is formulated more concisely using shift matrices. Let S denote the *shift matrix* where $Sx = (\xi_n, \xi_1, \ldots, \xi_{n-1})^T$ for every $x = (\xi_1, \ldots, \xi_n)^T \in \mathbb{R}^n$. Then cyclically banded matrices are invariant under shifts.

Proposition 2 *If $A \in \mathcal{B}^n_{k_l,k_u}$ and S is the shift matrix then*

(a) $SAS^T \in \mathcal{B}^n_{k_l,k_u}$

(b) if $k_u \geq 1$ then $SA \in \mathcal{B}^n_{k_l+1,k_u-1}$

(c) $S^{k_u}A \in \mathcal{B}^n_{k_l+k_u}$

Proof: The proof of this proposition is obtained by applying the definitions of S and $\mathcal{B}^n_{k_l,k_u}$. ∎

The last statement in Proposition 2 gives rise to the reformulation of the problem. It says that with an appropriate shift any cyclically banded matrix, and, in particular any banded matrix, can be mapped into a cyclically banded matrix with upper bandwidth

$k_u = 0$. In contrast, simple bandedness is not preserved. As a consequence, algorithms for cyclically banded matrices with upper bandwidth 0 can be used to solve systems with cyclically banded matrices with arbitrary bandwidths, including the ordinary banded matrices and this is done by premultiplying the system with a permutation. For example, $\mathcal{B}^6_{1,2}$ is mapped onto $\mathcal{B}^6_{3,0}$ which consists of matrices with the following nonzero structure:

$$\begin{bmatrix} x & & & x & x & x \\ x & x & & & x & x \\ x & x & x & & & x \\ x & x & x & x & & \\ & x & x & x & x & \\ & & x & x & x & x \end{bmatrix}$$

Note that this matrix has no nonzeros in the lower left corner and the only nonzeros in the upper half are in the upper right corner. In the remaining sections parallel algorithms for such matrices will be developed. Before that, it will be demonstrated that permuting the system does not introduce any new numerical errors.

Gaussian elimination [4] is defined as a sequence of elimination steps acting on a sequence of matrices of diminishing size. Each of these steps consists of two stages: In a first stage the pivot row is determined and interchanged with the first row. It is assumed that the choice of the pivot row depends only on the components of the row and not on the row index and is unique. Thus if two potential pivots are of the same size a tie braking strategy is used which depends not on the position of the pivot but only on the matrix entries. The second stage of the elimination process is the actual elimination which mainly consists of the formation of the Schur complement of the pivot. The two stages of a first elimination step are summarized by the factorization

$$\begin{aligned} \hat{P}A &= \begin{bmatrix} \alpha & w^T \\ v & C \end{bmatrix} \qquad (2) \\ &= \begin{bmatrix} 1 & 0 \\ v/\alpha & I_{n-1} \end{bmatrix} \begin{bmatrix} \alpha & w^T \\ 0 & C - vw^T/\alpha \end{bmatrix}. \end{aligned}$$

The factorization then continues by recursively applying this idea until $P_1(C - vw^T/\alpha) = L_1U_1$ is obtained. From this factorization one gets the factorization $PA = LU$ [4] defined by Gaussian elimination with partial pivoting with

$$L = \begin{bmatrix} 1 & 0 \\ P_1^T v/\alpha & L_1 \end{bmatrix} \quad \text{and} \quad U = \begin{bmatrix} \alpha & w^T \\ 0 & U_1 \end{bmatrix}$$

and $P = \begin{bmatrix} 1 & \\ & P_1 \end{bmatrix} \hat{P}$.

If Gaussian elimination with partial pivoting has the properties just described it is invariant under permutations in the following sense.

Proposition 3 *Let $A' = QA$ for a permutation Q, $PA = LU$ and $P'A' = L'U'$ defined by the LU factorization with partial pivoting. Then $L = L'$, $U = U'$ and $P = P'Q$.*

Proof: The first pivot row has to be the same for A and A' as the rows have only changed in their order by the permutation. Thus the first row of U is the same as the first row of U'. The rest follows by induction. ■

The invariance of Gaussian elimination under permutations can also be used to get distribution-independent algorithms [8].

In view of Propositions 2 and 3 the algorithm to factorize (cyclically) banded matrices $A \in \mathcal{B}^n_{k_l,k_u}$ is

1. Permute A to $B := S^{k_u}A$.

2. Factorize B such that $P_B B = LU$

As a consequence the factorization defined by Gaussian elimination with partial pivoting is obtained as $PA = LU$ with $P = P_B S^{k_u}$. The reformulation step or permutation is done by reinterpreting the meaning of the data in the memory and thus does not require any data movements.

3 Concurrent stage

Divide-and-conquer methods usually have two stages [9]: In the first, concurrent stage independent subproblems are solved without the need for communication. The second stage consists of the combination of solutions of the subproblems to produce the solution to the overall problem. In case of linear equation solvers the subproblems correspond to a representation of the matrix A as a block matrix.

Proposition 4 *Let $n = pq$, $q > k$, $p > 1$ and $A \in \mathcal{B}^n_k$. Then A is block-bidiagonal,*

$$A = \begin{bmatrix} A_1 & & & B_1 \\ B_2 & A_2 & & \\ & \ddots & \ddots & \\ & & B_p & A_p \end{bmatrix} \qquad (3)$$

and the blocks $A_r = [\alpha^r_{i,j}]$ are banded lower triangular matrices with (lower) bandwidth k, i.e., $\alpha^r_{i,j} = 0$ if $j > i$ or if $i > j + k$, and $B_r = [\beta^r_{i,j}]$ where $\beta^r_{i,j} = 0$ if $j < q - k + i$.

The blocking is connected with the data distribution and it will be assumed that blocks A_r and B_r will reside on processor r for $r = 1, \ldots, p$.

For example, if $k = 2$ and $q = 6$ then the nonzero structure of the blocks is

$$A_r = \begin{bmatrix} x & & & & & \\ x & x & & & & \\ x & x & x & & & \\ & x & x & x & & \\ & & x & x & x & \\ & & & x & x & x \end{bmatrix}$$

and

$$B_r = \begin{bmatrix} & & & & x & x \\ & & & & & x \\ & & & & & \\ & & & & & \\ & & & & & \\ & & & & & \end{bmatrix}.$$

The case $p = 1$ is different as here $A = A_1 + B_1$ where the A_1 and B_1 have the structure defined above.

Now, in order to eliminate the first unknown from the system, a pivot has to be chosen from the first column of A. As the first column of B_2 is zero the pivot must be an entry in A_1, and the subsequent row interchange and even the elimination step does not affect other blocks than A_1 and B_1 and, in particular, can be done on Processor 1 without any consultations with the other processors.

With the same reasoning, the $q+1$st unknown can be eliminated independently on Processor 2 and the same holds for the $2q+1$st unknown on Processor 3 etc. Furthermore, all these elimination steps can be done concurrently. After one concurrent elimination step eliminating one unknown on each processor the remaining Schur complement is of order $n - p = p(q-1)$. If $q = k+1$ the concurrent part of the algorithm is then completed. In the case $q > k+1$ the concurrent step has to be repeated $q-k-1$ times. After conclusion of the concurrent part, the cyclic reduction part, which is described in the next section, can start.

The matrix factorization which summarizes the operations done on processor r during the concurrent elimination of the unknowns $1, q+1, 2q+1, \ldots$ is

$$\begin{aligned} \hat{P}_r A_r &= \begin{bmatrix} \alpha_r & w_r^T \\ v_r & C_r \end{bmatrix} \\ &= \begin{bmatrix} 1 & 0 \\ v_r/\alpha_r & I_{q-1} \end{bmatrix} \begin{bmatrix} \alpha_r & w_r^T \\ 0 & C_r - v_r w_r^T/\alpha_r \end{bmatrix} \end{aligned} \tag{4}$$

and

$$\begin{aligned} \hat{P}_r B_r &= \begin{bmatrix} u_r^T \\ D_r \end{bmatrix} \\ &= \begin{bmatrix} 1 & 0 \\ v_r/\alpha_r & I_{q-1} \end{bmatrix} \begin{bmatrix} u_r^T \\ D_r - v_r u_r^T/\alpha_r \end{bmatrix}. \end{aligned} \tag{5}$$

The Schur complement does not have the original nonzero structure anymore. A little wave can appear in A_r and the nonzero block of B_r becomes rectangular. The following defines this structure more concisely and it is suggested to call this a wave matrix. Wave matrices are invariant under concurrent Schur complements.

Definition 5 *A matrix A is a* wave matrix *with bandwidth k and p waves if it is block bidiagonal,*

$$A = \begin{bmatrix} A_1 & & & B_1 \\ B_2 & A_2 & & \\ & \ddots & \ddots & \\ & & B_p & A_p \end{bmatrix}$$

and if $A_r = [\alpha_{ij}]$, $B_r = [\beta_{ij}^r]$ and $\alpha_{ij}^r = 0$ if $i > j + k$ or $j > \max(i,k)$ and $\beta_{ij}^r = 0$ if $k < \max(i, q-j)$. The set of wave matrices is denoted by $\mathcal{W}_k^{n,p}$.

For example, if $n = pq$ and $q = 6$, $k = 2$ then the diagonal blocks A_r have the structure

$$\begin{bmatrix} x & x & & & & \\ x & x & & & & \\ x & x & x & & & \\ & x & x & x & & \\ & & x & x & x & \\ & & & x & x & x \end{bmatrix}$$

and the offdiagonal blocks B_r have the structure

$$\begin{bmatrix} & & & & x & x \\ & & & & x & x \\ & & & & & \\ & & & & & \\ & & & & & \\ & & & & & \end{bmatrix}.$$

Proposition 6 *Let $A \in \mathcal{W}_k^{n,p}$ be a wave matrix and let*

$$A' = \begin{bmatrix} A_1' & & & B_1' \\ B_2' & A_2' & & \\ & \ddots & \ddots & \\ & & B_p' & A_p' \end{bmatrix}$$

be the reduced system after one concurrent elimination step, i.e.,

$$A_r' = C_r - v_r w_r^T/\alpha_r, \quad B_r' = D_r - v_r u_r^T/\alpha_r$$

where C_r, D_r, u_r, v_r, w_r and α_r are defined in Equations (4) and (5). Then A' is a wave matrix, in particular $A' \in \mathcal{W}_k^{n-p,p}$.

The number of floating point operations does depend on the choice of the pivot. Two cases can occur: Either the pivot resides in rows 1 to k. In this case the row interchange does not change the nonzero structure of A_r or B_r. In this case the computation of the Schur complement requires $2k(k-1)$ floating point operations for A'_r, $2(k-1)k+k$ floating point operations for B'_r plus k divisions for v_r/α_r. This gives a total of $2k(2k-1)$ floating point operations for the first case.

In the second case the pivot row is the row $k+1$. After an interchange with the first row the nonzero structure is modified. In this case the forming of A'_r requires $2k(k-1)-k$ floating point operations, B'_r requires 0 floating point operations and again k divisions are required for v_r/α_r. This gives a total of $2k^2$ floating point operations.

Note that actually the "worst case" where the row $k+1$ is chosen as pivot requires less floating point operations than the others! For an estimate the maximum has to be taken which is $2k(2k-1)$. In total, each processor has to do $q-k$ steps such that the number of floating point operations required per processor is

$$fl/p = (q-k)2k(2k-1)$$

or summed over all p processors

$$fl = p(q-k)2k(2k-1) = (n-pk)2k(2k-1).$$

This floating point operation count is an upper bound and with careful coding it could be decreased substantially for special cases, for example, the matrix B_r can slowly disappear during the elimination process if the original matrix is large enough and diagonally dominant enough (see [5] for a method which takes this into account for tridiagonal matrices). Diagonal dominance has also been used to generate early terminating cyclic reduction, see [10]. A new parallel solver using diagonal dominance is the overlapped partitions method (OPM) [11, 12].

The effects of early termination or incomplete factorization still remain to be analyzed in detail for the method suggested here. In addition, overlapped partitioning might lead to very fast and stable method if combined with the algorithm presented here. Another open question is to how the "wave" is represented and how the case of no wave is treated. It is suggested that sparse matrix methods could be applied.

4 Cyclic reduction

After completing the concurrent steps one is left with a block bidiagonal matrix A':

$$A' = \begin{bmatrix} A'_1 & & & B'_1 \\ B'_2 & A'_2 & & \\ & \ddots & \ddots & \\ & & B'_p & A'_p \end{bmatrix}$$

Processor i contains one diagonal block A'_i and the corresponding offdiagonal block B'_i in its local memory. All the blocks are dense k by k matrices. This system is then solved by a variant of cyclic reduction. Assume for simplicity that the number of processors is a power of 2. Then $\log_2(p)$ reduction steps are required to complete the factorization.

Each reduction step has two phases: A communication phase and a computation phase. In the *communication phase* half of the processors send their blocks to the other half of the processors. More precisely, processor $2i-1$ either sends its blocks A_{2i-1} and B_{2i-1} to the corresponding even numbered processor $2i$ or receives the blocks A_{2i}, B_{2i} from processor $2i$ where $i=1,\ldots,p/2$. Choosing sender and receiver can be done such as to increase the amount of local communication and decrease non-local communication in hierarchical networks.

Mathematically, the communication phase corresponds to a re-blocking of the matrix:

$$A' = \begin{bmatrix} \tilde{A}'_1 & & & \tilde{B}'_1 \\ \tilde{B}'_2 & \tilde{A}'_2 & & \\ & \ddots & \ddots & \\ & & \tilde{B}'_{p/2} & \tilde{A}'_{p/2} \end{bmatrix}$$

where

$$\tilde{A}'_i = \begin{bmatrix} A'_{2i-1} & 0 \\ B'_{2i} & A'_{2i} \end{bmatrix}$$

and

$$\tilde{B}'_i = \begin{bmatrix} 0 & B'_{2i-1} \\ 0 & 0 \end{bmatrix}, \quad i = 1, \ldots, p/2.$$

In the *computational stage* a concurrent elimination of the first k unknowns corresponding to each $\tilde{A}_i$ can be done. This stage has some similarity with the earlier concurrent elimination stage, however, the structure of the blocks is slightly different.

After the concurrent elimination stage another communication stage of the next reduction step redistributes the matrix to $p/4$ processors and a concurrent elimination again halves the number of unknowns and so on until only one processor has a dense system of order $2k$ which is then factorized. A characteristic feature of this type of reduction algorithm is that the degree of parallelism [9] is halved at every step.

At each step $2k^2$ numbers are communicated between sender and receiver. The number of floating point operations is

$$fl = \sum_{j=1}^{k} 2(2k-j)^2 + (2k-j) = \frac{14}{3}k^3 - \frac{3}{2}k^2 - \frac{1}{6}k.$$

At the end a $2k$ by $2k$ system has to be solved. This requires

$$fl = \sum_{j=1}^{2k-1} 2j^2 + j = \frac{16}{3}k^3 - 2k^2 - \frac{1}{3}k$$

floating point operations.

5 Scalability

The scalability of parallel algorithms is limited by various factors including redundancy, degree of parallelism and communication overhead. These factors shall now be discussed for the new algorithm.

The number of floating point operations is clearly dependent on the algorithm. Sequential algorithms usually have been optimized to minimize operation counts. These optimized algorithms often do not parallelize well and other algorithms with more floating point operations have to be chosen for parallel execution. This is also the case for the algorithm studied here which is not optimal with respect to the floating point operation count. The ratio of floating point operations required for the algorithm used for p processors and the one used on 1 processor is called *redundancy* [9]. For Gaussian elimination with pivoting the floating point operation count can depend heavily on the numerical values. In the following, the floating point operation count is understood to be the best upper bound on floating point operations which can be obtained if nothing about the numerical values of the nonzero matrix entries is known.

By summing up the floating point operation counts obtained in the previous sections on gets that the total floating point operation count of the new algorithm for $A \in \mathcal{M}_k^{n,p}$ on p processors:

$$fl_p = 2k(2k-1)n + \frac{k}{6}(4k-1)(k+1)p - k^2(4k-1).$$

In a similar way one gets the floating point operation count for $A \in \mathcal{M}_k^{n,1}$ on one processor:

$$fl_1 = 2k(2k-1)n - \frac{k}{3}(4k-1)(2k-1).$$

The redundancy is then approximately in the case of very small bandwidths, i.e., $k^3 \ll n$:

$$r_{p,n,k} = fl_p / fl_1 = 1 + \frac{k(4k-1)(k+1)}{12k(2k-1)} \frac{p}{n}.$$

In particular, $r_{p,n,2} = 1 + 0.58\frac{p}{n}$ and $r_{p,n,4} = 1 + 0.9\frac{p}{n}$. Asymptotically in n there is thus no redundancy for fixed p and small k. Thus the algorithm is very scalable from this point of view.

The picture is different if the algorithm is to be used to solve ordinary banded linear systems. For a banded linear system with lower bandwidth k_l and upper bandwidth k_u the floating point operation count is [1] approximately for small k_u and k_l:

$$fl_1 = (2k_l + 2k_u + 1)k_l\, n.$$

The approximate floating point operation count for the new parallel algorithm is obtained by substituting $k = k_u + k_l$:

$$\begin{aligned} fl_p &= 2(k_l+k_u)(2k_l+2k_u-1)\,n \\ &+ \frac{k_l+k_u}{6}(4k_l+4k_u-1)(k_l+k_u+1)\,p. \end{aligned}$$

In this case the redundancy is for small bandwidths:

$$\begin{aligned} r_{p,n,k_u,k_l} &= \frac{2(k_l+k_u)(2k_l+2k_u-1)}{(2k_l+2k_u+1)k_l} \\ &+ \frac{(k_l+k_u)(4k_l+4k_u-1)(k_l+k_u+1)}{6(2k_l+2k_u+1)k_l}\frac{p}{n}. \end{aligned}$$

Asymptotically for large n one gets

$$r_{p,\infty,k_u,k_l} = \frac{2(k_l+k_u)(2k_l+2k_u-1)}{(2k_l+2k_u+1)k_l}.$$

This is bounded from above by $2 + 2\frac{k_u}{k_l}$ so for banded matrices with $k_u = k_l$ the upper bound of the redundancy is 4. For tridiagonal and pentadiagonal matrices one has $r_{p,\infty,1,1} = 2.4$ and $r_{p,\infty,2,2} = 3.1$. These asymptotic ratios compare well to the redundancies for Gaussian elimination without pivoting or Cholesky factorization which can be found in [1, 13].

Another determining factor for the scalability of an algorithm is the *average degree of parallelism*. It is seen to be [9]

$$a_{p,n,k} = \frac{fl_p}{\sum_{j=1}^{p} \frac{fl_p^{(j)}}{j}}$$

where fl_p is the total amount of floating point operations and $fl_p^{(j)}$ is the amount of floating point operations which are done concurrently on j processors.

For the algorithm discussed one gets from the previous sections

$$fl_p^{(j)} = \begin{cases} \frac{16}{3}k^3 - 2k^2 - \frac{1}{3}k, & \text{for } j = 1 \\ \frac{14}{3}k^3 - \frac{3}{2}k^2 - \frac{1}{6}k, & \text{for } j = 2, 4, \ldots, \frac{p}{2} \\ 2k(2k-1)(n/p - k) & \text{for } j = p \\ 0 & \text{else.} \end{cases}$$

If n/p is large most of the time is spent concurrently on all p processors. The average degree of parallelism is for small bandwidth and large numbers of processors p:

$$a_{p,n,k} = \left(\frac{1 + \frac{(4k-1)(k+1)}{12(2k-1)} \frac{p}{n}}{1 + \left(\frac{28k^2 - 9k - 1}{12(2k-1)} \log_2(p) - 3k/2 \right) \frac{p}{n}} \right) p.$$

This is for tridiagonal systems:

$$a_{p,n,2} = \frac{1 + 0.58p/n}{1 + (2.6 \log_2(p) - 3)p/n} p.$$

This shows that the algorithm is well balanced for large problem sizes, e.g., $a_{10^3,10^6,2} = 980$. For pentadiagonal systems $k = 4$ and so

$$a_{p,n,4} = \frac{1 + 0.9p/n}{1 + (5 \log_2(p) - 6)p/n} p,$$

for example, $a_{10^3,10^6,2} = 950$.

Even an algorithm which has low redundancy and a high average degree of parallelism can still perform very poorly on a distributed memory computer if it requires a high amount of *communication*. This is quite often the real bottleneck of many algorithms including the one discussed here. The reason for this is that communication speeds are often orders of magnitudes lower than computation speeds.

Communication is needed in the cyclic reduction phase of the elimination algorithm. This is done in $\log_2(p) - 1$ steps where $2k^2$ floating point numbers are communicated per sender. A simple model for the time required to send m floating point numbers from any processor to any other is

$$t_{\text{comm}} = \alpha + \beta m$$

where α is the latency and β is the communication throughput. With this the ratio of communication time to computation time is modelled as

$$\kappa = \frac{6(\log_2(p) - 1)\frac{\alpha}{k\rho} + 12k(\log_2(p) - 1)\frac{\beta}{\rho}}{6(2k-1)(2\frac{n}{p} - 3k) + \log_2(p)(28k^2 - 9k - 1)}$$

It is seen that for large enough n this can be made arbitrarily small but for practical cases this might be extremely large. As the data is sent in relatively small packets the communication latency is usually the determining part, especially for very small bandwidths.

6 Conclusions

By reformulating banded linear systems as cyclically banded linear systems with zero upper bandwidth a parallel algorithm is developed which includes partial pivoting. Redundancy is no higher than for comparable algorithms which do not use pivoting and the algorithm shows good scalability properties. The redundancy is partly due to "fill-in" in the nonzero structure of the matrix and further investigations will show how incomplete factorizations can reduce this fill-in and with that reduce redundancy. At the moment this algorithm is implemented on the Fujitsu AP 1000 [14]. The numerical computations are identical to the computations done to do an LU factorization with partial pivoting of a wrapped-around matrix but the data storage and movement has been chosen such that the algorithm is easily implemented. The algorithm can be described as a multi-frontal algorithm [15] for the parallel solution of banded linear systems.

Acknowledgements

The author would like to thank M. Osborne, ANU, who suggested to study block-bidiagonal systems for the solution of banded linear systems. Furthermore, P. Arbenz, ETH Zürich, and A. Cleary, University of Tennessee, assisted by carefully reading the manuscript and suggesting several improvements. The research was partially supported by the "Advanced Computational Systems" CRC.

References

[1] P. Arbenz and W. Gander, "A survey of direct parallel algorithms for banded linear systems", Tech. Rep. 221, Departement Informatik, ETH Zürich, 1994.

[2] J.M. Ortega, *Introduction to Parallel and Vector Solution of Linear Systems*, Plenum Press, New York, 1988.

[3] J.J. Dongarra, "Performance of various computers using standard linear equation software", Tech. Rep., CS Dept., University of Tennessee, 1992.

[4] G.H. Golub and C.F. Van Loan, *Matrix Computations*, The Johns Hopkins University Press, 2nd edition, 1989.

[5] M. Hegland, "On the parallel solution of tridiagonal systems by wrap-around partitioning and incomplete LU factorization", *Numerische Mathematik*, vol. 59, no. 5, pp. 453–472, 1991.

[6] D. Dun, M. Hegland, and M. Osborne, "Parallel stable solution methods for banded linear systems of equations", Tech. Rep., Centre Math. Appl. and Comp. Sci. Lab., Australian National University, 1995.

[7] C. de Boor, *A Practical Guide to Splines*, Springer, 1978.

[8] M. Hegland, "A distribution independent algorithm for the reduction to tridiagonal form using one-sided rotations", in *Proceedings of the IEEE First International Conference on Algorithms And Architectures for Parallel Processing*, 1995, vol. 1, pp. 286–289.

[9] K. Hwang, *Advanced Computer Architecture*, McGraw Hill, 1993.

[10] D. Heller, "Some aspects of the cyclic reduction algorithm for block tridiagonal linear systems", *SIAM J. Numer. Anal.*, vol. 13, no. 4, pp. 484–496, 1976.

[11] J.-L. Larriba-Pey, A. Jorba, and J.J. Navarro, "OPM: a parallel method to solve banded systems of equations", Tech. Rep. UPC-CEPBA-92-09, Universitat Politècnica de Catalunya, 1992.

[12] J.-L. Larriba-Pey, A. Jorba, and J.J. Navarro, "Solution of strictly diagonal dominant tridiagonal on vector computers", Tech. Rep. UPC-DAC-93-18, Universitat Politècnica de Catalunya, 1993.

[13] A.J. Cleary, "Parallelism and fill-in in the Cholesky factorization of reordered banded matrices", Tech. Rep. SAND-90-2727, Sandia National Laboratories, Albuquerque, New Mexico, 1990.

[14] H. Ishihata, T. Horie, S. Inano, T. Shimizu, and S. Kato, "Cap-ii architecture", in *First Fujitsu-ANU CAP Workshop*, 1990.

[15] I.S. Duff, A.M. Erisman, and J.K. Reid, *Direct Methods for Sparse Matrices*, Clarendon Press Oxford, 1986.

Computing the nth Roots of Matrices on PVM

M. Inceoglu and S. Yilmaz

[*This paper not received in time for publication*]

❖ SESSION 9 ❖

Load Balancing and Loop Parallelization

Chair

L. Richter

Classification of Load Distribution Algorithms

Reinhard Riedl and Lutz Richter
Department of Computer Science
University of Zürich
Zürich, Switzerland, CH-8057

Abstract

The allocation of workload in distributed systems has almost as many views as one would like. The attempt to find suitable structures to classify the different ways of solving this task can therefore reflect the underlying model only. In the following paper a three models is developed. The load model is used to describe the workload and its current distribution within the system. The action model defines for a given algorithm at any instant of time the eligible next step(s). And finally, the solution model shows the formal context for obtaining and evaluating the load distribution decisions. All three models and their interrelationship are illustrated by selected examples of existing load distribution approaches. The result of the following investigation is the recommendation that load distribution algorithms can be classified according the five criteria: objectives, type and amount of used information, the source of the distribution, the parameter time, and the initiating instance.

1 Introduction

Aim and ambition of the following lines is to discuss different *adaptive load distribution algorithms for sequential execution of work in distributed systems* by way of a *specification and classification.* In the past there has been published an enormous amount of literature on such algorithms. Most of them were shown to work well in the environments and for the test cases presented by their authors. Little work, however, has been done to compare the qualities of different algorithms.

Therefore, we propose and discuss various criteria for the classification of adaptive load distribution algorithms, since we believe that detailed descriptions of existing algorithms according to these classification schemes will make such comparisons considerably easier. We believe that this is especially of importance to the customer who has to decide on the choice of the load distribution procedures. In particular, we suggest that future publications of new algorithms ought to be accompanied by their classification according to the main schemes discussed in the following.

Most load distribution algorithms presented in literature are only partial load distribution mechanisms, as they deal with particular aspects of load distribution and lack complete implementation in real life systems. Therefore, a main point of any classification ought to be a specification of the part of load distribution, which is covered by the algorithm, since this makes simulation results and analytic performance evaluations more transparent and their comparison easier.

In the following, we shall only deal with explicit load distribution activities of the distributed system. We shall ignore implicit load distribution, as e.g. data moving or system component performance control, system administrator activities and input control activities. Little work has been done on that so far. Moreover, we shall not deal with specific real time computing aspects either. For other classifications see e.g. [3] and [9].

2 Models and heuristics

There is nothing like a general model for distributed systems, which could yield analytic algorithms for load allocation. Even if there were such a general model available it would necessarily be too complicated for algorithmic treatment in run-time. Therefore, *heuristics* have to be used by any load allocation algorithm, in particular for the choice of the used formal models.

There is a hierachy of **formal models** involved in load distribution. Any load distribution mechanism relies on an architecture model which specifies the functions of the various system components. We shall not discuss this model here explicitely, but put emphasis on its reflection in the specific models affiliated with load distribution.

In that respect, first there is the model of the dynamic components of the distributed system considered by load distribution, which we shall call **load**

1066-6192/96 $5.00 © 1996 IEEE
Proceedings of PDP '96

model. It describes the *workload* the system has to deal with, comprises a formal description of runtime *system states* as they are considered by the load distribution mechanisms, and it describes the *information* about these states available at runtime. The description of the workload has to contain, among others, the definition of load units, relations among them, and their processing needs, and it has to contain the description of data units and their relations, accessed by the load units. The description of the system states and the description of available information may concern the state of system resources, the distribution of load units in the system, and the distribution of data with respect to load units – the latter usually in an implicit way due to the complex nature of that issue.

Seen from another point of view, the load model consists of the following three parts: a model of physical reality, a model of observations, and a model of relations among observations and reality (which describes how one can derive conclusions on load states from observations). For an algorithm which puts emphasis on the latter see e.g. [13]. In most cases the load model, which represents the *knowledge* of the load distribution and thus relies on heuristic choices of its designers, cannot completely be determined from the knowledge of the load distribution algorithm, if it is not explicitely supplied by its designers.

Then there is a model which defines the actions allowed in which situations to be taken by which component of the distributed system – due to hardware and software availabilities and possibly a heuristic choice of restrictions. We shall call that model **action model**. It deals with distribution actions *and* collecting information – and thus represents the *physical activities* of the load distribution – and it describes the *initiation* of any kind of decision making involved.

Thirdly, for that decision making, there is the model which sets the algorithmic formal context for the load distribution decisions as well as the decisions for information collecting. We shall call that model **solution model**. It primarily reflects the *objectives* which the load distribution algorithm is supposed to pursue, the *strategy* it is supposed to use for their pursuit, and the heuristic knowledge of the computing context and its relevant factors for system performance.

Note that so-called heuristic algorithms typically restrict their intuitive reasoning to the choice of a simple solution model (or even a trivial solution model in case the algorithm is completely determined by the action model). On the contrary, so-called analytic load distribution algorithm, impose heuristic assumptions at many different places. (For this reason, we shall not use an 'analytic versus heuristic' classification, which may often be found in the classification literature.)

In order to use the solution model for load distribution activities system state information has to be supplied. In some cases this supply is again subject to decisions based on runtime evaluation of a component of the solution model.

Only after the load model, the action model and the solution model have been fixed, there appear nonheuristic analytic solutions in the strict sense of the word. In order to distinguish between the solution model and the solutions obtained by the implementation of the algorithm in the context of the solution model we shall address the actual problem solving by the algorithm as the **solution making procedure**. Implementations may apply various heuristics for approximate solution of the formal problems set up by the solution model in order to save overhead, or the nature of the problem may exclude exact solutions. Thus the solution making procedure may determine the performance in a characteristic way. For example in [6] Newton's approximation method is used for the solution of the adaptive optimization problem of the solution model.

In principal there are three different tactics to make load distribution decisions, when objectives, strategies and heuristic system performance models are given by a load model – which might then indeed be used for classification: solving the formal problem analytically, either exactly or approximately, solving a simplified problem, or guessing the solution according to some heuristics, respectively. The solution of the formal problem in the context of the solution model may thus take very different forms, but these are only a secondary issue for our purposes compared with the load model, the action model and the solution model.

It follows from the above that there are overlaps between the three models quoted above, and there are logical and physical implications among them. Objectives both influence the choice of the action model and the solution model (and to some extent the choice of the load model, too). The action model relates to the load descriptions of the load model. The load model model both supplies static load characterizations and the formalism for dynamic system state descriptions to the solution model. And the solution model only considers actions defined by the load model.

Various heuristics identical in nature may appear at different stages of the load allocation procedure yielding different views and results. The analysis of algorithms with respect to the application of heuristics may help to clarify algorithmic results and to avoid misunderstandings. We suggest that future presentation of new algorithms should be accompanied by an informal, but detailed description of which heuristics are applied in which model, in order to make the comparison of algorithmic qualities easier and research results more transparent.

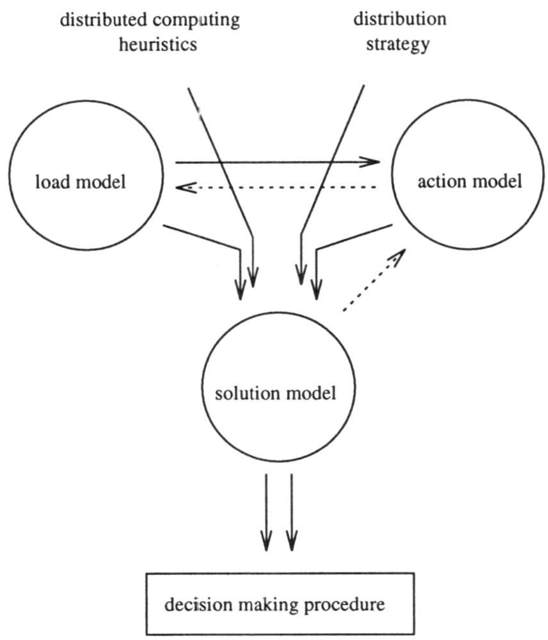

Figure 1

Figure 1 represents the various 'control flows' among the three models and the solution making procedure. The choice of the load model essentially restricts the possibilities for the choice of the solution model, as all objects subject to distribution appear in the solution model. (This does not relate to the process of the development of the load distribution algorithm, but only to the a-posteriori logical implications.) Therefore, there are also some implications in the opposite direction. The solution model makes use of the load model and the action model, and it reflects performance measurements of distributed computing in the system under consideration as well as the distribution strategy chosen by the designer. (Again, this only relates to the logical a-posteriori implications.) In the opposite direction, the solution model suggests the choice of the action model. Finally, the decision making procedure results from the implementation of all three models. It is the realization of the solution model.

2.1 Examples

As an example let us look at the algorithms discussed in [14]: They are based on the well known four-rules model, or equivalently four-policies model, with *information rule, transfer rule, location rule,* and *selection rule.* That model is concerned with fully distributed load-distribution, where nodes may either fetch load units from remote nodes or deliver them to remote nodes.

The load model underlying [14] assumes that all load units are undistinguishable, enter the system at any one of the nodes, and leave it after execution. Each load unit remembers the number of transfers it has experienced so far. Moreover, the mean service times for load units at each particular node are known, too. Further stochastic assumption on the input and the load execution, which are made to describe the simulation model, do not concern the algorithm itself.

A system state at runtime (of the N-nodes system) is represented as an (N+1)-dimensional vector, whose first N entries are the numbers of load units residing at each node, and whose last entry is the number of load units in the communication system. There is only local knowledge of the local entry to this vector available for load distribution plus – in one version of the algorithm – additional knowledge of the loads units having been transfered from a remote node in the recently past time interval of some fixed length. For that version the system state is described by the above N-dimensional vector plus a record of all transfers of load units in the time window.

The action model contains only fully distributed (i.e. local) activities: local-remote (one-way) transfer of load units, local-remote (both ways) communication for the collection of information, local decision making and a local triggering of decision making. Transfer is restricted to that load unit which arrived most recently, but more than one transfer per unit is allowed. The arrival of a load unit triggers, in that order, decision making according to the transfer rule, the information rule and the location rule (where the latter two are only used in case that an attempt to transfer a load unit was decided).

In a general four-rules model, the information rule describes, when and how to collect and where to store information used in decision making. Its activities are described by that part of the action model concerned with the collection of information, while the information rule itself is that component of the solution model concerned with information collection. Moreover, the triggering of decision making with respect to the collection of information, as it is described in the action model, is defined by the information rule, too.

In [14] three distinct information rules are evaluated, each of which assumes that the collection of information takes place at each node separately triggered by the decision to attempt to transfer a load unit and that it is performed only at instances when a node has decided locally to transfer one of its tasks. Additionally, one of the three algorithms, LBT, keeps track of the tasks which it has received from other nodes. The part of the solution model concerned with the collection of information either demands information from all remote nodes, or, in the other two versions, from a fixed number of remote nodes. In the latter case it considers all nodes as equally eligible for a load transfer, except for the LBT–version, which restricts attention to nodes, which did not send a task to the local node in the recent past, and it chooses the nodes by random choice – i.e. the final decision making is performed as random polling from a set of nodes specified by the solution model.

In general the transfer rule describes when to initiate an attempt to transfer a load unit, and whether or not to perform it, finally. It is affiliated to that component of the action model concerned with the triggering of decision making and to that component of the solution model, which deals with distribution decisions. Used in that four-rules approach, it implies that the set of load distribution activities defined in the action model contains only local-remote load unit transfers.

In [14] the transfer rule defines the initiation of decision making by the arrival of a new task. Decisions (on whether or not to attempt a load transfer) are made by the comparison of the local load state with a fixed local threshold value (depending on the assumed mean local servive time and a general choice of the system administrator).

In general, the location rule defines how to choose the partner for the load transfer. It is thus affiliated with the solution model.

In [14], first the node with the lowest virtual load (among those nodes which the local node communicated with about their load state) is calculated. Then the difference δ of its virtual load with the local virtual node is calculated. Finally that δ is compared with the number of times the 'triggering load unit' has been transfered so far, and a decision is taken. Decision making affiliated with location policy is thus completely deterministic. In general, the selection rule is used to select a task for the transfer. It is thus affiliated with the solution model.

In [14] the selection rule is already fixed by the restriction of the action model to transfer only the 'triggering units'.

As another example, let us consider the algorithm presented in [10], which involves a stochastic learning automaton. The load units in its load model are again all undistinguishable. The system state (of the N-nodes system) is described by a an (N+1)-dimensional vector, whose first N entries take the values *underloaded / overloaded*, while the last entry is itself an N-dimensional vector, whose entries define the locally (at each node) observed global system load state, taking values in $\{0, 1, ..., N-1\}$. System information for load distribution is only locally available as a 2-dimensional vector whose first entry is the local load state and whose second entry is the locally observed global system state. The latter information is considered to differ from reality, which is the basis for the usage of a stochastic learning automaton – otherwise the whole concept would fail. At regular instances node to node communication exchanges the first component of the local load vector, and the recalculation of the second entry of the local load vector takes place at each node independently, after the node has obtained information from all other nodes.

Thus the action model contains node to node communication about load states at regular instances, and the local triggering of the computation of the system wide load state. Moreover, it contains the local triggering of the local decision making when a new load unit arrives, and local-remote transfer of load units. The resulting load distribution is fully distributed and sender-initiated.

The solution model is made up of two parts: the one described above concerned with the local calculation of the global system state, and the one which is concerned with the decision where to execute a load unit. The latter is a stochastic learning automaton, which calculates load distribution matrices using feedback about the success or failure of a transfer to a remote node (dependent on whether the chosen remote node was underloaded or overloaded). It consists itself of two parts: distribution according to a probability law and the following update of the probability law upon feedback.

The decision making involves three procedures: straightforward calculations of locally observed global load states, throwing the coin according to a probability distribution in order to decide where to execute a load unit, and a straightforward calculation of the update of the probability vector using remote feedback information.

So far, we have not yet specified the meaning of overloaded, respectively underloaded load states, and we shall revisit the algorithm for that pupose in the following. There is one ambiguity in the specification of the algorithm with respect to the load model, the action model and the solution model. Information is passed from one decision making procedure to the next as distribution matrix, whose rows correspond to system wide load states. Thus, more precisely, the information about the system state available for load distribution consists of the 2-dimensional vector described above plus the local distribution matrix, and consequently, the global load state is described by the above (N+1)-dimensional vector plus an N-dimensional, whose entries are distribution matrices.

The choice of the two examples above does not imply any statement whatsoever about the quality, importance or originality of the cited papers. Both load distribution mechanisms have been discussed in the literature various times. We chose them as they enabled us to demonstrate various different features of our models.

Finally, we would like to emphasize that although there are no purely analytic algorithms, load distribution cannot successfully be based on purely heuristic reasoning only. Quite to the contrary, since the choice of models and heuristics more or less determines success and failure of load distribution, that choice ought to be based on analytic reasoning.

In the following chapters we shall discuss various choices of load, action and solution models and the resulting classifications, some of which have been indicated in the examples above. For comparisons of various different distribution algorithms see e.g. [15].

3 Objectives

Objectives are an important issue for classification of algorithms. There are two ways, how objectives may appear in the solution model (and we shall only consider objectives, which appear explicitely in the solution model): as *cost functions* and as *input variables to the solution model.*

As cost functions are necessarily heuristics only, objectives related to them cannot always realized with certainty. Obviously, in general it is impossible to attribute a unique objective to a cost function, as various different objectives considered by load distribution algorithms are positively correlated. Moreover, the attributes may depend on load state and other variables as well. Analysis in the language of fuzziness might therefore help in the future to demonstrate implicit correlations among different objectives and different cost functions. Results of the analysis of correlations in turn may be used for the design of fuzzy decision machines, which are extensions of decision machines as presented in [13], and make use of load dependent performance of algorithms with respect to objectives on the one hand, and fulfil sensible users' needs on the other hand.

Another natural way how objectives determine the performance of load distribution algorithms are input variables to the solution model (cf. [10]). This is characteristic of models without explicitely formulated cost functions, where control of quantities to be optimized takes place.

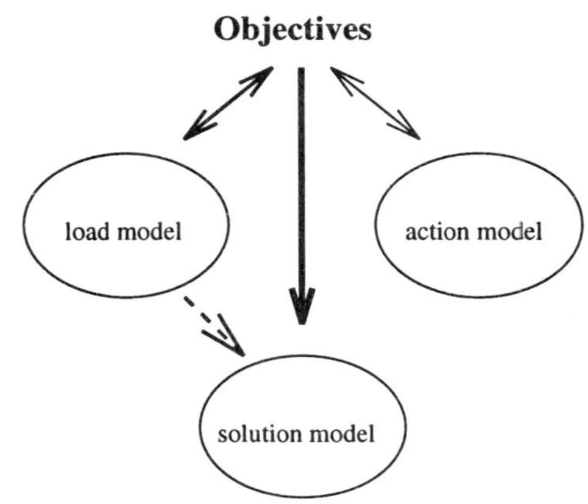

Figure 2

Primary objectives are

- 'good' service performance, as observed by tasks:
  - high performance in terms of
    - short waiting times
    - short service times
    - short elapsed (response) times
  - predictability of elapsed (response) times
  - availability of services
  - reliability of the system
- small (physical) distances between tasks and data, i.e. 'high' affinity
- 'good' service performance, as observed by resources of the system:
  - high global performance, in particular high throughput

- high local performance, for example in the view of few cache misses or short communication times

- balanced situations, in particular
  - equallized distribution of load
  - adjusted usage of available resources
- 'good' utilization of resources:
  - small idle times of resources, or to the contrary
  - little usage of resources, e.g. little traffic

Fairness or *preferential treatment of special task classes* are secondary objectives of load allocation (which may be defined as a boundary condition or as a weighting factor in a cost function). Some of the above objectives are negatively correlated for special load situations. Others are only weakly positively correlated as they deal with different functions of the same quantity: e.g. availability and throughput. Evaluation of algorithms may reveal orientation towards some quantitative load situations or some qualitative load situations with respect to data access patterns of the load, which in turn might be used for classification too.

Figure 2 indicates how objectives are related with the choice of the three models. As we have explained above they may appear in the solution model explicitely via cost functions and implicitely via observables defined in the load model. Moreover, the choice of the action model is somewhat influenced by the objectives. On the contrary, the load model and the action model set boundary conditions for the pursuit of the objectives.

On the one hand any objective may be formulated in terms of a (non-unique) cost function. On the other hand, most algorithms which do not make use of a cost function explicitely, may be reformulated in terms of cost functions – for the price of leaving the (local) context of the solution model as it was set by the load model (and allowing solutions to be taken only from a small set).

As an example for the latter case let us consider the algorithms in [10]: There the costs for a distribution decision at node k are the sum of the entries of an N-dimensional cost vector. Its i-th entry is the product of the i-th entry of the global system state vector and the i-th entry in the row of the decision making matrix with the number found as the k-th entry of the N+1st coordinate of the global system state vector. Consequently, the decision making is the update of one row of the system matrix in order to reduce the costs. Hereby only updating operations are allowed, which add a reward vector whose entries are functions of the corresponding entry in the row to be updated and the cooresponding entry in the global system state vector.

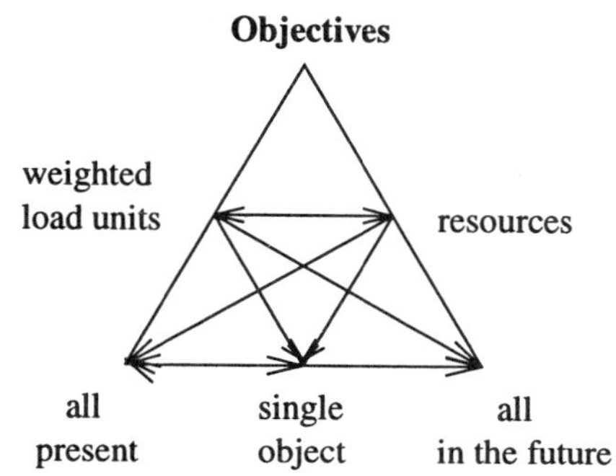

Figure 3

The pursuit of objectives may depend dynamically on load states. We distinguish between algorithms with

- various different strategies,
- a single strategy algorithms but dynamic parameter tuning
- a static single strategy

For the second case see e.g. [1]. Case 1 may be realized with the usage of (fuzzy) decision machines. (It appears to some extent in [10], where load distribution depends on observed load states.) The cost function in the solution model may either consider *local or global performance* of tasks or resources as it is depicted in Figure 3. In the latter case, this may be done with or without inclusion of *future workload*, and tasks may be attributed weights. The comparison of different algorithms ought to contain their detailed specifation in that respect. For example, these weights may be positively or negatively correlated to the complexity of the tasks. (FCFS-disciplines correspond to a weighting according to which each task is worth its execution time.)

4 Information usage

4.1 Suppliers and users of information

Part of the load model is the definition of

- which source supplies information in runtime and
- what kind of information is supplied (in runtime), while part of the solution model is the definition of

- which component exploits the supplied information, i.e. which component carries out the decision making procedure.

There are two distinct ways how information about the system's load state may be obtained:

1. it is taken from measurement communicated to the load distribution source
2. it is obtained from conjectures differing from the communicated information, either because available information is incomplete, or it is assumed to differ from physical reality.

In [13] Bayesian analysis is applied in order to calculate the expectation of performance as a function of the observed system state (assuming that observation and physical reality are correlated but differ in general). A so-called decision machine is used for that purpose, which makes use of a formal load model listing the possible states together with their probabilities and the possible observations together with the conditional probabilities of states with respect to observations, a formal action model listing the possible actions, and a formal solution model containing an utility function as cost function. However, it is important to observe that the corresponding load model, action model and solution model of the algorithm discussed in [13] *differ* from the models of the decision machine (but contain them as *submodels*). In particular monitor nodes are involved for regular updates of the conditional probabilities, which moreover vary from node to node. In [12] regression-based algorithms are discussed, which rely on the idea that looking at the past enables one to predict the future.

This leads us to the distinction between solution models which use past decisions of the same decision making instance as input and those who do not. [10] is another example of the first ones, [14] is an example of the latter ones. As we have shown above, in the first case the runtime system state description is increased by the corresponding description of that information. *LBT* in [14] is a special case, though not a rare case: there information about load distribution decisions at other places in the system is used as input for the decision making procedure – in form of some version of vector time stamps; cf. [11].

There is information used about current states and past performance of resources, about distribution of tasks in the system and past performance of tasks the system, and about distribution of data throughout the system. The influence of the type of information used on the performance of the algorithm has been investigated in [10]. There the load model describes the system state with the terms overloaded and underloaded. The author compared algorithms which used different interpretations of these terms, all of which were resource oriented: waiting queue lengths, size of free available memory, CPU usage, combinations of these, etc. As the author indicates, the algorithm itself was designed with task oriented intentions, namely reduction of response times. However, as response times does not appear explicitely in the solution model, it is not one of the objectives according to our definition..

Locality of data accesses plays a major part in load distribution. That phenomenon is usually addressed by the term *affinity*. More generally, affinity addresses the fact that certain tasks have preferences for special executing nodes, or may even be executed exclusively at special nodes, due to the distribution of data and tools. See e.g. [7].

Algorithms may use information both explicitely and implicitely. A special case of implicit usage is *feedback* of a posteriori judgement of decisions for the purpose of adaption of decision strategies, namely *'primitive learning'* algorithms, as for example the algorithm in [10].

Classification of algorithms with respect to their information usage may be based on distinction between usage of global and usage of local information, on distinction between algorithms with automatic supply of information as input data for the solution model, algorithms with separated solution models for information supply and solution models which jointly consider information supply and load distribution, and on distinction of algorithms with explicit and with implicit information usage. However, there are also algorithms which comprise, in the one or other respect, both alternatives. The various possibilities are depicted in Figure 4.

4.2 Static versus dynamic approaches

The easiest load models, as the corresponding solution models, do not consider any information about the current workload state of the system. We shall call such algorithms

- static distribution algorithms, contrary to
- dynamic algorithms.

Naturally, there are various intermediate forms between completely static and completely dynamic algorithms: e.g. static algorithms which are initialized by some dynamic device reacting to changes in the workload state, or combinations of static and dynamic components.

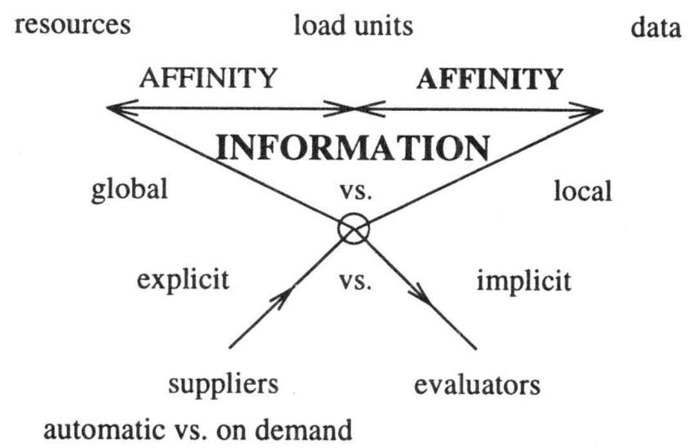

Figure 4

4.3 Affinity scheduling

Differences of data access times essentially determine the performance of distributed computing. This may be considered for the distribution of both tasks and resources.

In order to deal with the problem of data accesses, affinity scheduling is applied. This is already reflected on the level of the load model by an affiliation of a vector to each load unit which describes the execution costs at each of the nodes, mainly reflecting the need for data accesses. On the level of the solution model affinity appears in terms of cost functions, which result from the affinities stated in the load model.

There are various physical factors which set up physical affinity:

- the distribution of data and resource needs for the various task classes
- the degree of static activity initialized by a task
- data and task migration times
- the actual current cache consistencies created by the load distribution algorithms

Only in rare cases, there is no affinity assumed by the load and the solution model. By its very nature physical affinity can only be observed partially, implicitely and with some observation delay. A rough but useful classification of algorithms is the distinction into those, whose load models describe task-data relations, and those which do not. Obviously, affinity scheduling relying on task-data affinities presupposes an appropriate workload analysis. If preprocessing is too expensive, it requires the characterization of load units by a-priori observables which preferably take only values from a small set, and which are strongly positively related with the data accesses of the load unit. For a discussion of workload characterization and further literature see [2] or [5].

5 The action model: initiators, source of distribution and time

A primary classification of load distribution may be based on the *objects of distribution*, and a corresponding secondary classification on the *granularity* of these objects. Algorithms may distribute *tasks, resources* and *data* in various granulations. Two essential properties of the action model are the definition of

- which source initiates load distribution and when it is performed, and
- where it is performed: i.e.
  - which component is in charge of it
  - which sources supply (partial) services;

Another way to classify load distribution algorithms is to distinguish between algorithms with or without (time or event driven) redistribution. (This is of particular importance with respect to thrashing phenomena.)

5.1 Central versus distributed load distribution

As with respect to the source of distribution there are two different approaches: *central load distribution* versus *distributed load distribution.* There is also an intermediary concept: *semicentral load distribution* by a small subset of nodes, each of which is responsible for some rayon.

When discussing and comparing these concepts, distinction has to be made between *logical* and *physical* concepts. In most but not all cases, logical concepts agree with physical concepts. Naturally, physically central algorithms are also logically central, the inverse, however, must not necessarily hold. LINDA, [4], is an example of a logically central service which is implemented in a physically distributed way.

Moreover, one has to distinguish between the mechanism in charge of load distribution, and the services used for load distribution.

Naturally, there are various types of combinations of central, semicentral and distributed mechanisms. Distributed distribution may further be specified according to the range of load exchange partners for each node.

5.2 Sender Initiated versus Receiver Initiated Load Distribution

A classical criterion for the classification of load distributiom algorithms on the level of the action model is their partition into *sender-initiated* and *receiver-initiated* load distribution algorithms. However, it is hard to define a sharp distinction between both concepts, since in most cases sender-initiated mechanisms cooperate with receiver-initiated mechanisms, or sender data are taken into consideration by receiver-initiated mechanisms, and vice versa. In order to be more precise, we distinguish between algorithms which are (essentially)

1. central sender-initiated
2. distributed sender-initiated or receiver-initiated and fully distributed
3. receiver-initiated with a central source of load units

Here, the two cases in 2 exhibit rather similar behaviour. From an analytic point of view, the essential difference between central sender-initiated and distributed receiver-initiated load distribution algorithms which deal with a central input source is the time when distribution takes place. Resulting performance deficits for sender-initiated algorithms are an open mathematical question. The following two subdivisions are related with that time difference: sender-initiated upon-arrival distribution versus sender-initiated distribution with (load state dependent) time delay, and work-conserving versus not work conserving receiver-initiated load distribution. Here work-conserving means that no node will decide to stay idle in case that there are load units in the system without server. Algorithms, which are not work-conserving, are a special form of affinity scheduling. Little work has been done so far on that subject, but somewhat related results exist in the literature on anomalies in task scheduling.

Both sender-initiated and receiver-initiated algorithms do not necessarily use system state information. An example of a central sender-initiated algorithm is *static random load distribution* according to a probability law which only reflects the computing power of each node, see e.g. [8], where steady state optimization is discussed. Receiver-initiated algorithms are necessarily logically distributed, but they may use central services, which may in turn be implemented either at a central place or in a distributed manner, as was indicated above.

On the level of the load model one may classify algorithms with respect to the information about senders and receivers they use. (It is possible to implement a central sender-initiated algorithm which only uses information about receivers: e.g. a central job dispatcher which regularly checks soiurce states.)

6 Probabilistic concepts

Probabilistic concepts play an essential role in load distribution. They may enter as characteristic properties of the load model or of the solution model. Various different quantities may be considered as stochastic processes or variables: e.g. the workload, the current or future states of resources, the knowledge of the current physical state or the future input, or the behaviour of load distributors distinct from the local ones. In the decision making procedure stochastic reasoning may be used to filter rare cases out and to speed up some algorithms. Uncertainty of knowledge about the system's state may be treated by Bayesian analysis. Randomization is used to avoid unpleasant superposition and interference of load patterns.

Algorithms which are based on stochastic workload models do not necessarily apply stochastic solution models and vice versa. The specification and classification of algorithms may thus be based on the place where probabilistic reasoning enters (cf. Figure 5). In particular we distinguish between

- workload models with or without stochastic assumptions on the future
- stochastic and deterministic system state models
- algorithms using deterministic decisions and those applying probability distributions for random decision

These types of classification may substantially improve the understanding of an algorithm. In [6], the solution model suggests random distribution according to a distribution variable, whose value results from a deterministic solution problem, while the implemented solution making procedure approximates that value by a choice from the set $\{0,1\}$, leading to deterministic load distribution. A feedback of this simplification in the decision making procedure into the solution model would lead to a simplified solution model and in turn a simplified solution making procedure (which may be also be derived from formula (5) there).

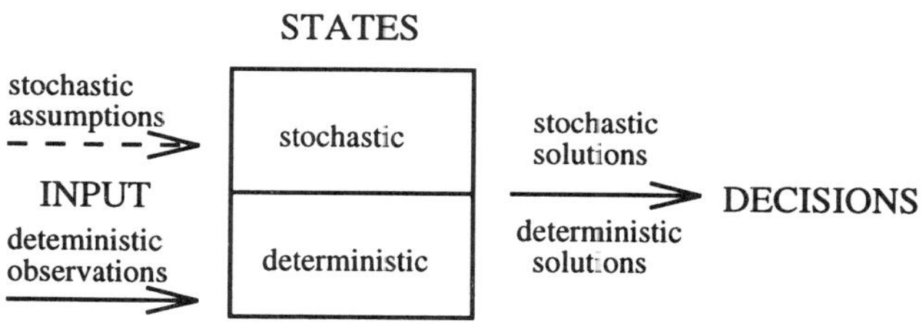

Figure 5

7 Concluding remarks

A primary classification of load allocation algorithms ought to be concerned with the following five issues: *objectives, information usage, source(s) of distribution, time,* and *initiators.*

It results from the above discussion that load distribution algorithms may be specified according to the introduced three models: the load model, the action model and the solution model together with the implemented decision making procedure. There are two major classification lines with a wide range of applicability: *usage of heuristics* and *application of affinity scheduling,* whereby affinity is understood in the most general sense and all kinds of affinities between tasks, data resources and processing resources are considered.

We believe that future work ought to be done on the relations between the three models presented above. In particular a detailed specification of cost functions and an analysis of their nature might prove to be helpful for the understanding of the load distribution issue in distributed computing.

References

[1] Avritzer A. et al.: The Advantage of Dynamic Tuning in Distributed Asymmetric Systems, Proc. Infocom '90, pp. 811 – 818, (1990)

[2] Born E., Delica T., Richter L., Riedl R.: Characterization of Workload for Distributed Processing – Methodology and Guide, Deliverable WP.2/T2.1 ESPRIT III P8144 (1995);

[3] Casavant T.L., Kuhl J.G.: A Taxonomy of Scheduling in General-Purpose Distributed Computing Sustems, IEEE Trans. Softw. Eng. 14, pp. 141 – 154, (1988)

[4] Carriero N., Gelernter D., and Ahuija S., Linda and Friends, IEEE Computer, 19(8), pp. 26 – 34, (1986)

[5] Calzarossa M., Serazzi G.: Workload characterization: a survey, Proc. IEEE, Vol. 81(8), pp. 1136 – 1150, (1993)

[6] Gelenbe E., Kushwaha R., Dynamic Load Balancing in Distributed Systems, Mascots '94, IEEE Computer Society Press, pp. 245 – 249, (1994)

[7] Haldar S., Subramanian D.K.: An affinity-based dynamic load balancing protocol for distributed transaction processing systems, Performance Evaluation 17(1), pp. 53 – 71, (1993)

[8] Kim C., Kameda H.: An Algorithm for Optimal Static Load Balancing in Distributed Computer Systems, IEEE Trans. Comp., Vol. 41(3), pp. 381 – 384, (1992)

[9] Kremien O., Kramer J.: Methodical Analysis of Adaptive Load Sharing Algorithms, IEEE Trans. Par. Distr. Syst. 3, pp. 747 – 760, (1992)

[10] Kunz T.: The Influence of Different Workload Descriptions on a Heuristic Load Balancing Scheme' IEEE Trans. Softw. Eng. 17, pp. 725 – 730, (1991)

[11] Lamport L.: Time, Clocks, and the Ordering of Events in a Distributed System, Communications ACM, Vol 21(7), pp. 558 – 556, (1978)

[12] Leff A., Yu P.S.: A Performance Study of Robust Distributed Load Sharing Strategies, IEEE Trans. Parall. Distrib. Systems, Vol. 5(12), pp. 1286 – 1301, (1994)

[13] Stankovic J.A.: An Application of Bayesian Decision Theory to Decentralized Control of Job Scheduling, Trans. Comp. C-34, pp. 117 – 130, (1985)

[14] Zhang Y., Kameda H., Shimizu K.,: Adaptive bidding load balancing algorithms in heterogeneous distributed systems, Mascots '94, IEEE Computer Society Press, pp. 250 – 262, (1994)

[15] Zhou S.: A Trace-Driven Simulation Study of Dynamic Load Balancing, IEEE Trans. Softw. Eng. 14, pp. 1327 – 1341, (1988)

Dynamic Load Balancing in a Heterogeneous Environment under PVM

J. C. FABERO, I. MARTÍN, A. BAUTISTA, S. MOLINA
Departamento de Informática y Automática
Facultad de Ciencias Físicas
Universidad Complutense. 28040 Madrid. Spain.
E-mail: fabero@fis.ucm.es

Abstract.

An algorithm for dynamic load balancing in an heterogeneous workstations net is presented in this paper. Workstations are not usually a private resource, but a shared one. So, the computational load, and thus, the computational speed, of each workstation in the net is not predictable. Moreover, for some problems the generated load could be variable in execution time. If former conditions appear, static load balancing is not a good approach. The method described in this paper is able to maintain a very good efficiency when the load in the workstations varies on time, or when the computational requirements of the problem are not constants.

1.- Introduction.

PVM [1] has become a standard parallel programming environment. It is used by many users to perform parallel computations on a workstations net. Also, it is the "assemble language" on computers such as Cray T3D [2] or Convex SPP-1000.

Among PVM virtues we could highlight that it is wide-extended (so it ensures program portability), it is easy to learn and to use, and it is public domain.

However, using PVM on a non isolated workstations net has many inconveniences. One of them is the communication cost: workstations are usually communicated by Ethernet. This implies a low bandwidth (less than 10 Mb/s) and, what is more important, that the communications are serialised over the bus. Another problem is that the workstations are shared resources. Usually, they are not fully available all the time we need them for our computations. Other users can run their own programs and, thus, the computational power of our parallel virtual machine can dramatically decay. Static load balancing based on the theoretical speed of each machine cannot improve global performance when a workstation is overloaded. So, dynamic load balancing (DLB) is preferable.

We are studying a Cellular Automaton (CA) to modelize the behaviour of a sheet yielded to strain [3]. In this model, the computational requirements varies with the number of failed cells (that is, the number of elements which have been broken due to stress) in each data domain. When an element has failed, it does not require computation any more. Due to this, if a processor has many failed cells in its data domain, this processor becomes underloaded. So, even in a perfect homogeneous computer (such as T3D), DLB is needed in order to reach the maximum performance.

DLB is usually undertaken by two different approaches: tasks migration and data redistribution [4].

Tasks migration methods are the most general ones, because they are useful with both sequential and parallel applications. However, migration cost is high. Moreover, when a parallel application is involved in task migration, special care must be taken in order to keep data dependencies among processes. Many different tasks migration methods have been proposed in literature, such as Condor [5], DPVM [6], MPVM [7], DASUD [8], etc.

Data redistribution methods are only applicable with SPMD paradigm. Redistribution cost is lower than migration cost. Besides, data redistribution can easily involve heterogeneous workstations nets.

Proceedings of PDP '96

Because we are studying a SPMD problem, we will focus on data redistribution methods, mainly on those based on diffusion paradigm.

Diffusion methods described in literature can be classified into two main groups: centralised and distributed. Centralised methods are more accurate, but they increase communications cost. Distributed methods are less accurate, as they may incur in globally unbalanced solutions since rebalancing decision depends on partial information. However, these methods allow to maintain communications locality, and so they improve its scalability.

This paper describes a distributed diffusion algorithm for DLB under PVM applicable to cellular automata problems. The physic problem which is intended to simulate is introduced in section 2. The algorithm used to perform DLB under PVM is presented in section 3. Finally, some measurements and results are presented in section 4.

2.- Cellular Automata to simulate Rock Fracturing.

As it has said before, the problem to be resolved is the simulation of the behaviour of a bidimensional sheet yielded to strain forces. This problem is usually treated with finite elements methods. A very interesting approach is to solve it with Cellular Automata. CA usually has a few number of states, which can be represented by integer numbers. So, in many cases computation does not involve float or double numbers. The neighbouring, typical on CA, provide local communications requirements. Moreover, the almost microscopic description of the physic problem allows to incorporate more complex phenomena that are not easily expressed with differential equations [9].

Basically, the automaton consists of a regular square grid of cells. Each cell has its own strength. A remote stress is applied to the entire grid. Then, each element computes its effective strength as a function of the original strength and the number of neighbour cells that have failed (a cell has 8 neighbours). If the stress exceeds the element effective strength, that element fails.

The stress function is chosen in a manner that when the number of failed neighbours is small the local stress is lower than the remote stress due to local reliving (negative feedback). When the number of failed neighbours is great, the local stress is higher than the remote stress (positive feedback). So, in each iteration step each cell must know the state of its adjacent cells (that is, if they have failed or not), and the remote stress.

The state of the cell (i,j) in the next iteration, $s_{i,j}$, is a function of the state of its eight neighbours cells, the local strength, and the remote stress:

$$\textit{if } R_S \geq S \cdot f\,(s_{i+1,j+1} + s_{i+1,j} + s_{i+1,j-1} + s_{i,j+1} + s_{i,j-1} + s_{i-1,j+1} + s_{i-1,j} + s_{i-1,j-1})$$

$$\textit{then } s_{i,j} = 1$$

$$\textit{else } s_{i,j} = 0$$

where S is the cell strength, R_s is the remote stress applied to the entire sheet, and f is the stress function. If $R_s \geq S \cdot f$, then $s_{i,j}$ is fixed to 1, to indicate that this cell has failed. Otherwise, it is fixed to 0. Although the stress function can be chosen to be continuous, only eight discrete values (those corresponding to the eight possible failed neighbour cells) are needed.

A more complete description of the problem can be found in [3].

To implement the automaton under PVM in a workstations net, a regular data distribution has been chosen, as it is shown in Figure 1. A circle represents a cell in the CA. Links represent neighbour dependencies among the cells. Links between cells in different processors, require message passing at each iteration step to allow the cells in the boundaries to know the state of its neighbours.

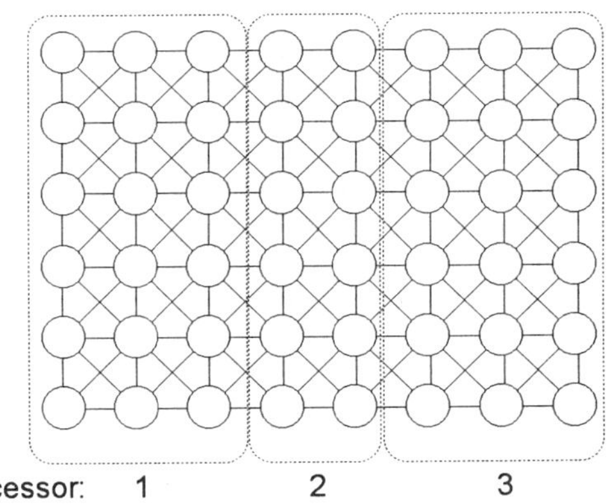

Figure 1: Data distribution for CA cells.

The processors in the virtual machine are connected in a linear ring. This distribution is preferred instead of the two dimensional mesh in order to minimise the number of messages over the network. As it has said before, the communications over an Ethernet are serialised. At each iteration step, a processor needs to know the value of the boundary elements, which belong to some others processors. So, a message must be received from each neighbour processor. When the virtual machine consist of a linear ring of processors, the number of messages needed for each update step is $M = 2 \cdot (N - 1)$ (*N* being the number of processors). On the other hand, when the mesh is a two dimensional mesh, the number of messages needed is $M = 2 \cdot (4 \cdot N - 3 \cdot (W + H) + 2)$, being *W* and *H* the dimensions of the mesh. For example, if $N = 4$ processors, $M = 6$ is the number of messages interchanged per iteration step in the linear ring, and $M = 12$ is the number of messages interchanged in the 2×2 mesh (Figure 2).

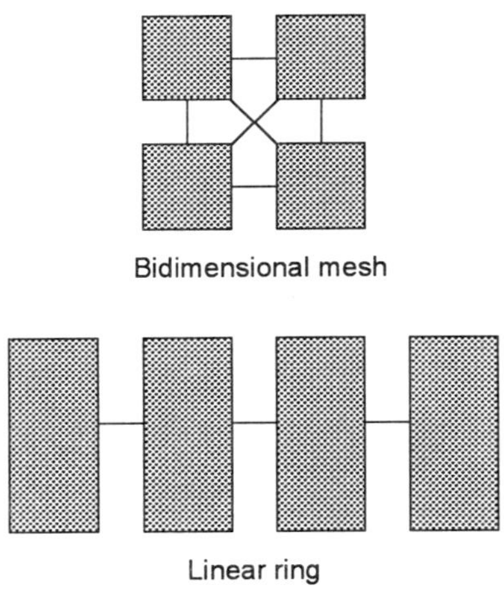

Figure 2: Logical topologies for 4 processors.

As a general rule for PVM over workstations with Ethernet, the fewer messages passing, the best efficiency.

However, this is not generally true for any parallel machine. For example, in a T3D it is preferable the two dimensional distribution because in this way it is taken advantage of the high communication bandwidth of the machine.

3.- Dynamic Load Balancing (DLB).

In this section we will describe the algorithm employed to perform dynamic load balancing in an Heterogeneous Workstation Network (HWN) under PVM.

Let us see the simplest case. Only two virtual processors, **a** and **b**, each of them loaded with $\mathbf{n_a}$ and $\mathbf{n_b}$ data columns respectively. The total process time per iteration for each processor is $\mathbf{t_a}$ and $\mathbf{t_b}$ respectively.

Let us define the column process time as $\tau_i = \frac{t_i}{n_i}$.

Let call n'_i the number of columns of processor *i* after applying rebalancing. Then, the estimated process time for the next iteration will be $t'_i = \tau_i \cdot n'_i$. Our aim is to get $t'_a = t'_b$ so that neither processor will be waiting for any other.

Let be the disposition among processors shown in Figure 3.

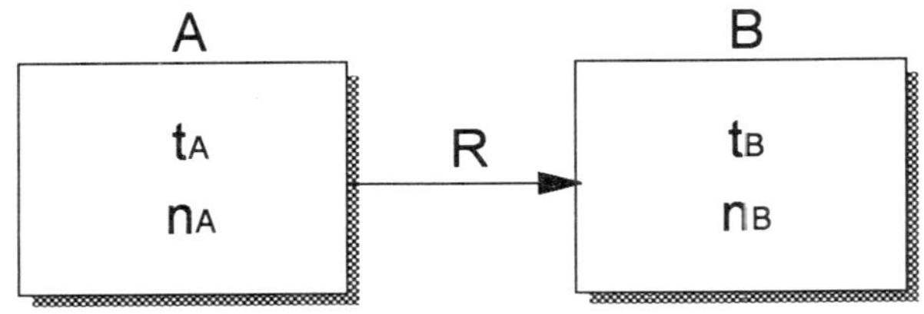

Figure 3: Data redistribution among 2 processors.

By applying rebalancing, if $t_a > t_b$, processor **a** will send a number of columns, say **R**, to the processor **b**. This one will accept the same number of columns from processor **a**.

Knowing that $n'_a = n_a - R$ and $n'_b = n_b + R$, then:

$$t'_a = t'_b \Rightarrow \tau_a \cdot n'_a = \tau_b \cdot n'_b$$
$$\tau_a \cdot (n_a - R) = \tau_b \cdot (n_b + R)$$
$$t_a - \tau_a \cdot R = t_b + \tau_b \cdot R \Rightarrow$$
$$R = \frac{t_a - t_b}{\tau_a + \tau_b}$$

In this way, each processor can compute the number of columns it must send to or receive from its neighbours, knowing its own process time and the process time for its neighbours, and the number of columns held by each one.

The information needed to perform load balancing is appended in the same messages for updating boundary cells. So, the number of messages over the network is not increased in order to include this information. Only when rebalancing is required the traffic over the net is increased.

We have experimented three models to perform DLB: synchronous, asynchronous and mixed model.

In the synchronous model, after a fixed number of iterations, defined by the parameter *INTERREBAL*, each processor applies the rebalancing algorithm and it decides if it must send a number of columns to one or both neighbours, or if it must wait for receiving load from them. *INTERREBAL* must be chosen considering the load balancing cost and the difference on execution times between processors. Choosing this parameter too low (say 1 or 2 iterations) load balancing is intended too often, and overhead grows. On the other hand, choosing it too high, make the system unable to adapt to changing load conditions quickly. In the laboratory, this parameter was fixed to a value of 5 iterations.

In the asynchronous model, when the difference in computation times between two processors is greater than a parameter *DIFMAX*, both processors will rebalance independently from the others. The parameter *DIFMAX* will be chosen taking into account the overhead cost for rebalancing, mainly the time for passing the message through the network, and for packing-unpacking operations. This model is able to adapt quickly when a machine becomes overloaded. However, if *DIFMAX* is great, the execution time can differ so much between two processors, leading to a bad load balancing. If it is small, the overhead is unaffordable.

To keep the advantages of both models, it was experimented the third model.

The third model is a mixed one between the synchronous and the asynchronous. There are three parameters defined in this model: *DIFMIN*, *DIFMAX* and *INTERREBAL*. When the difference on time is less than *DIFMIN*, no rebalancing is done, so overhead is constrained. If the difference is more than *DIFMIN* but less than *DIFMAX*, rebalancing is performed after *INTERREBAL* iterations (that is, in a synchronous way) to allow a fine tune of load balancing. When difference is over *DIFMAX*, load balancing is performed asynchronously in order to reequilibrate the load quickly. This model of DLB is the most flexible one. However, the three parameters must be fixed by the user empirically.

In order to avoid that a processor becomes empty, an additional parameter *CMIN* is introduced to indicate the minimum number of columns that a processor must own. This is done because if a processor is emptied, that processor must be removed from the virtual machine (VM). Then, its neighbours must be signalled about the change in communication routes.

Due to this, when moving data, only the sender knows the actual number of columns being moved. One processor **a** can expect a number of columns greater than the actual number of columns on **b**. In this case, processor **b** will not send all the columns to processor **a**, but only the difference between its present number of columns and the parameter *CMIN*. So, the real number of columns that are being moved in a rebalancing step is included in the message.

When there are three of more processor in the net, the algorithm becomes not optimal. Let be the processors net shown in Figure 4.

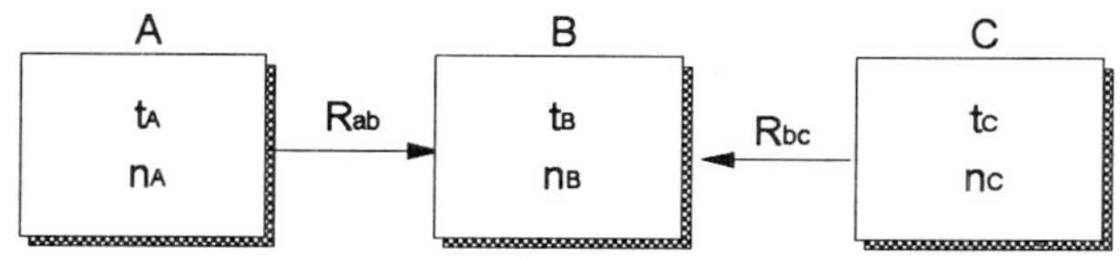

Figure 4: Data redistribution among 3 processors.

Let suppose that $t_a > t_b$ and $t_b < t_c$ (then **b** is the fastest processor). The algorithm will be applied independently to the processor pairs: (**a**,**b**), (**b**,**c**). It will probably assign to **b** an excess of columns, and then it will occur that $t'_a < t'_b$ and $t'_b > t'_c$. In the next iteration, processor **b** will diffuse its overload between processors **a** and **c**. As a result, the behaviour of the algorithm will be as a 3rd order system, with such a transient.

However, this transient is quickly softened and its influence in performance is less important than the increment of messages being passed between all the processors in the VM necessary to perform a global rebalancing when the number of processors is high..

In Figure 5 it is shown the data distribution among 3 processors for a 1000x1000 cells CA simulation. In the vertical axis it can be seen the number of the last column stored into each processor. When the workstation Sparc1 is suddenly overloaded, its data are partially moved to Sparc2. To avoid overloading Sparc2, it transfers some columns to AlphaAXP. Global rebalancing is performed by means of local ones.

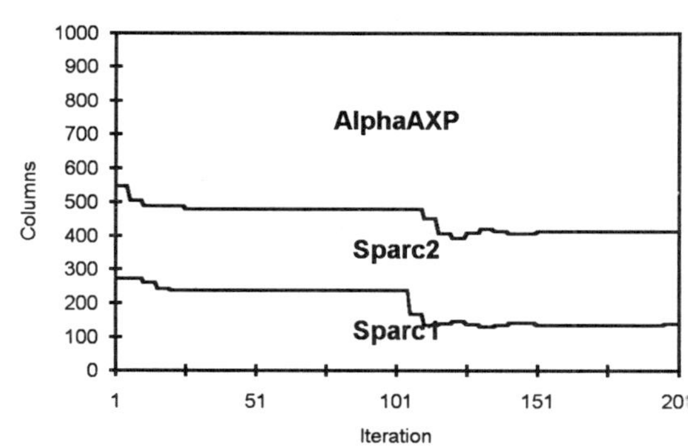

Figure 5: Data subdomains among processors.

4.- Results

Our CA simulation is being performed in an heterogeneous workstations network (HWN). This means that each computer has its own computational speed. Before defining efficiency on a HWN, let us define the canonical computational speed of each machine as the computational speed of the machine when nobody else is using it, and for a fixed problem size.

The theoretical speed of the Virtual Machine (VM) is the summation of the canonical speeds of all the machines working in the problem. Taking into account the communication time, the real execution time for the VM will be greater than the theoretical one. Moreover, if the computational requirements of the problem varies on time, efficiency will drop drastically unless the dynamic load balancing algorithm would be operating.

Let v_p be the computational speed of the VM (empirical), and v_{si} the sequential computational speed of the machine i; then efficiency is defined as:

$$e = \frac{v_p}{\sum v_{s_i}}$$

Figure 6 shows the efficiency when the number of machines in VM varies from 1 to 4, with and without dynamic load balancing. To get these measures, the machines are kept without external load. So, the worse efficiency when there is no rebalancing is due to the variation on computational requirements of the problem and to the static load balancing not being accurate enough.

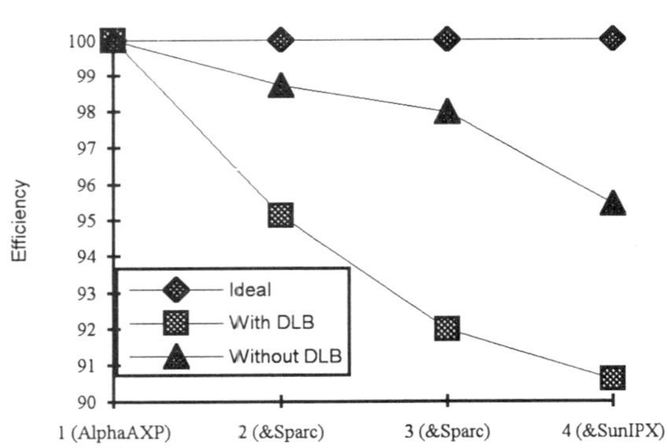

Figure 6: Efficiency.

The efficiency decays as the number of machines increases due to the cost of communications.

Figure 7 shows the expected computational speed when new machines are added to the VM. The ideal is not linear because the machines involved are heterogeneous. The first one is a DEC AlphaAXP, with a sequential computational speed of 105 cols./s, the next are two SUN SparcStation with 55 cols./s each, and the last is a SUNIPX with a speed of 25 cols./s. Each column has 1000 cells.

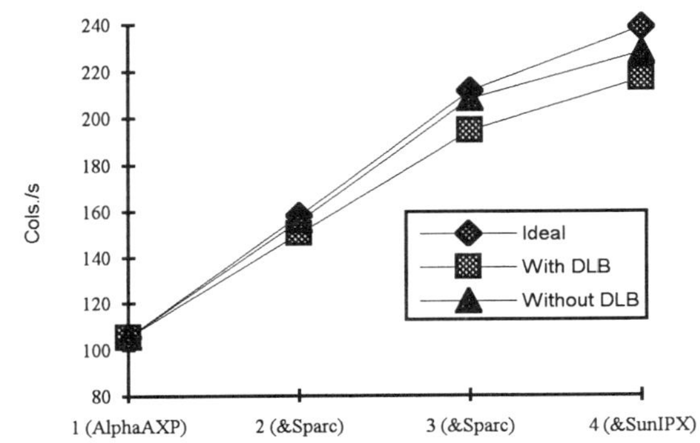

Figure 7: Computational speed of Virtual Machine.

Figure 8 shows the execution time for a VM consisting of three machines, one DEC AlphaAXP and two SUN SparcStations. When there is no rebalancing, the average time per iteration is initially around 7 seconds, for a CA of 1000x1000 cells. By applying rebalancing, the average time is less than 6.5 seconds. As the total execution time for a number of iterations is the integral of the time, that is the horizontal area, the improvement in speed is the area between both plots. For example, when the total number of iterations is of, say, 2000, this represent 1000 seconds less on execution time (more than 15 minutes).

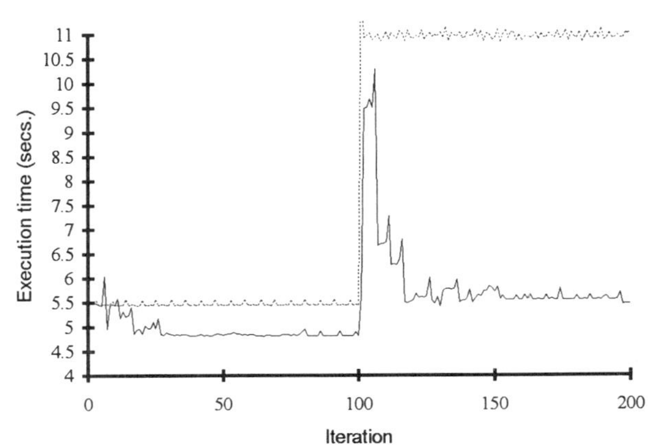

Figure 8: Execution time per iteration for 3 processors. After iteration number 100, one of the processors becomes overloaded.

When the machines are under normal use, the need of dynamic load balancing is evident. The same Figure 8 shows what happens when one of the machines becomes overloaded after iteration number 100. With static load balancing the execution time is the time spent in the slowest machine, so the performance is very poor. If DLB is applied, the VM recover itself and it is able to obtain the maximum available computational power. In this example the execution time per iteration is reduced in almost 53% when applying DLB.

5.- Future Work

This algorithm is a first approach to dynamic load balancing. It takes into account only the wall-time on each processor to carry out rebalancig. Although in this CA problem it has been able to override the communication latencies, it is not always possible. So, a method for evaluating this parameter must be provided. For example, the algorithm would have to be able to take into account the real topology of the HWN (the presence of routers and gateways).

Monitoring the traffic over the network can help to rebalance by looking at the messages passing between processors. That is, the parameters that control the cost of rebalancing can be dynamically adapted to the actual network conditions.

Another idea to be researched is that since the algorithm behaves like a third order system, control technics could be applied to fit the transient to the user requirements.

Another question is the appearance of "thrashing" [10]. When studying PVM over HWN, this phenomenon is less important than the stochastic variations in workload. However, for PVM on multicomputers, a mechanism to detect and avoid thrashing among two processors must be provided.

When considering different workload for each column of cells, thrashing may appear. Moreover, the calculation of R (see section 3) should have to take into account the different computational requirements of the columns being moved in this case.

In order to detect and avoid thrashing, the following definitions are assumed:

Let $\overline{\tau}_A, \overline{\tau}_B$ be the average computation time per column in the sets of columns owned by processor A and B, respectively. Let $\overline{\tau}_R$ be the average computation time per column in the set of data that is currently being moved from processor A to processor B. Then, thrashing will occur if it is verified that $\overline{\tau}_R \geq \overline{\tau}_A + \overline{\tau}_B$. So, when this condition is met, no rebalancing should be performed among processors A and B.

References.

[1] A. Geist, A. Beguelin, J. Dongarra, W. Jiang, R. Manchek, V. Sunderam., "PVM3 User's Guide and Reference Manual", Tech. Report ORNL/TM-12187, Oak Ridge National Laboratory, 1994.

[2] R. K. Koeninger, M. Furtney, M. Walker, "A Shared Memory MPP from Cray Research", Digital Technical Journal, vol. 6, no. 2, 1994.

[3] C. MacLean. "A Simulation of Rock Fracturing on the Connection Machine". Internal Report EPCC-SS92-17. Edinburgh Parallel Computing Center, 1992.

[4] J. Keyser, D. Roose. "Load balancing data parallel programs on distributed memory computers". Parallel Computing, 19 (1993) 1199-1219.

[5] M. J. Liztkow, M. Livny, M. W. Mutka. "Condor- A hunter of the idle workstations". Proc. 8th Int. Conf Distrib. Comput. Syst., 1988, pp. 104-111.

[6] L. Dikken, F. Van der Linden, J. Vesseur, P. Sloot. "DynamicPVM: Dynamic Load Balancing on Parallel Systems". Proc. High-Performance Computing and Networking, vol. 797, pp.273-277, 1994.

[7] J. Casas, D. Clark, R. Konuru, S. W. Otto, R. Prouty, J. Walpole. "MPVM: A Migration Trasparent Version of PVM". Tech. Report CSE-95-002. Oregon Graduate Institute of Science and Technology. February 1995.

[8] E. Luque, A. Ripoll, A. Cortés, T. Margalef. "A Distributed Diffusion Method for Dynamic Load Balancing on Parallel Computers". Proc. Euromicro Workshop on Parallel and Distributed Processing. San Remo, 1995.

[9] M. A. Smith, "Cellular Automata Methods in Mathematical Physics", PhD Thesis, Massachusetts Institute of Technology, 1994.

[10] F. Stangberg. "Recognising and Avoiding Thrashing in Dynamic Load Balancing". Internal Report EPCC-SS94-04. Edinburgh Parallel Computer Center, 1994.

Loop Parallelization: Revisiting Framework of Unimodular Transformations

Jordi Torres, Eduard Ayguadé, Jesus Labarta and Mateo Valero
Computer Architecture Department, Universitat Politècnica de Catalunya
Gran Capità s/n, Mòdul D6, 08034 - Barcelona, Spain
{torres | eduard | jesus | mateo}@ac.upc.es

Abstract

This paper extends the framework of linear loop transformations adding a new non-lineal step at the transformation process. The current framework of linear loop transformation cannot identify a significant fraction of parallelism. For this reason, we present a method to complement it with some basic transformations in order to extract the maximum loop parallelism in perfect nested loops with tight recurrences in the dependence graph. The parallelizing algorithm solves the important problem of deciding the set of transformations to apply in order to maximize the degree of parallelism, the number of parallel loops, within a loop nest, and presents a way of generating efficient transformed code that exploits coarse-grain parallelism on a MIMD system.

1: Introduction

Loop transformations have been recognized as one of the most important components of the parallelizing and vectorizing technology for current supercomputers. The aim is to transform nested-loop structures from the source program into semantically equivalent versions with more opportunities to parallelize them and to generate code that exploit efficiently the hardware resources of the architecture [10,20, 5].

Most of the existing compilers apply a set of basic loop transformations one at a time. At each step, it has to be decided whether the application of a transformation is legal and beneficial. Other approaches have been used, such as deciding a priory the composition of basic transformations or exploring the different compositions of them. These solutions are in general time consuming in obtaining the transformed code and analyzing their effects is also difficult.

An alternative solution to the problem is the use of linear transformations to specify a wide range of basic loop transformations (including loop interchange, loop reversal, loop skewing [4] and loop scaling [9]). In fact, any linear transformation modelled with a non-singular transformation matrix can be seen as a composition or product of these four basic transformations. The problem can be stated as finding a linear transformation that maximizes an objective function, such as degree of parallelism that can be obtained out of the loop [19]. The extend of application is restricted to perfectly nested loops.

From the specification of the source loop and the transformation matrix, a target loop has to be generated. This step has been solved in [4,19] when unimodular matrices are used. Additional problems appear when non-unimodular matrices are considered. The key point in the solutions proposed [9,7,22] is the use of the Fourier-Motzkin elimination method and the Hermite Normal Form decomposition.

Traditionally such a transformation applies to the whole loop. Recently, it has been argued that it can be profitable to apply different transformations to different statements in a loop [2, 16, 6, 8].

In [2] the inclusion of the statement dimension as a new component in the framework of loop transformations was proposed. It can be seen as an alignment before the transformation. In this paper we propose how to include a new step between the alignment and the linear transformation in order to exploit coarse-grain parallelism on a MIMD system. This new step is based on the ideas proposed by Banerjee with the Remainder Transformation [5]. We obtain automatically the transformation from the dependence graph that extracts the maximum loop parallelism. This work can be extended by applying a different unimodular transformation and alignment to each statement in the loop body [8].

The rest of the paper is organized as follows. In section 2 we present the terminology and assumptions used with this paper. In section 3 we show the framework of the method. In section 4 we explain the motivation for this new transformation by showing the limitations of the framework of linear loop transformation. In section 5 we formalize the method proposed. Finally, in section 6 we briefly discuss the results obtained for the working example and present the conclusions and future work.

1066-6192/96 $5.00 © 1996 IEEE
Proceedings of PDP '96

2: Terminology and assumptions

Through out this paper we consider perfectly nested loops $\{L_1, ..., L_n\}$ where the lower and upper bounds (l_k and u_k, respectively) for any loop L_k ($1 \le k \le n$) are affine functions of indices of its outer loops $L_1, ..., L_{k-1}$, that is,

$$i_k \ge a_{k,0} + a_{k,1} \cdot i_1 + ... + a_{k,(k-1)} \cdot i_{k-1} = l_k$$

$$i_k \le b_{k,0} + b_{k,1} \cdot i_1 + ... + b_{k,(k-1)} \cdot i_{k-1} = u_k$$

The iteration space for this loop nest is defined as

$$IS = \{(i_1, ..., i_n) \in Z^n, l_k \le i_k \le u_k, 1 \le k \le n\}$$

and can be written following a matrix notation

$$\alpha \cdot I \le \beta$$

where

$$\alpha = \begin{bmatrix} L - ID \\ ID - U \end{bmatrix} \qquad \beta = \begin{bmatrix} -l \\ u \end{bmatrix}$$

L is constructed from the coefficients $a_{k,i}$ ($1 \le k \le n$, $1 \le i \le k-1$) of the loop indices in the lower bound expressions, U is constructed from the coefficients $b_{k,i}$ ($1 \le k \le n$, $1 \le i \le k-1$) of the loop indices in the upper bound expressions, ID is the identity matrix, and l and u are constructed from the independent coefficients $a_{k,0}$ and $b_{k,0}$ ($1 \le k \le n$) of the lower and upper bounds respectively.

For example, for the loop nest in 1.a, the IS of the loop can be expressed in the following way

$$\begin{bmatrix} -1 & 0 \\ 0 & -1 \\ 1 & 0 \\ 0 & 1 \end{bmatrix} \cdot \begin{bmatrix} i_1 \\ i_2 \end{bmatrix} \le \begin{bmatrix} 0 \\ 0 \\ 9 \\ 9 \end{bmatrix}$$

Figure 1.b shows the aspect of the IS for this loop. Each point represents the execution of one iteration of the inner loop body.

In the scope of this paper we consider dense iteration spaces, i.e., spaces where all points correspond to iterations of the loop.

The loop body is composed of multiple assignment statements $\{S_1, ..., S_m\}$ that reference array variables whose subscripts are affine functions of loop indices $i_1, ..., i_n$. Let V be the set of statements in the loop body. The *Statement per Iteration Space* SIS of a loop nest is defined as the cartesian product

$$SIS = IS \times V$$

Each point in the SIS represents the execution of an iteration of a statement of the loop body. Dependence relations between a pair of statements S_i and S_j appear when there is an execution ordering between them [3]. We do not distinguish between the different kinds of data dependences because they all impose ordering constraints in the same way. When dependence relations are uniform (i.e., invariant through the SIS), they can be characterized by distance vectors $\overline{d} = \langle d^1, ..., d^n \rangle$ expressing the number of iterations that the dependence extends across in each loop dimension. In a sequential loop nest, the iterations are executed in lexicographic order; thus, dependences extracted from such a source program can always be represented as a set of lexicographically positive vectors. A vector $\overline{d}$ is lexicographically positive, written $\overline{d} > \overline{0}$, if $\exists i$:($d^i > 0$ and $\forall$ $j<i$: $d^j \ge 0$).

```
DO i1= 0,9
 DO i2= 0,9
  A[i1,i2]= A[i1-2,i2-2]* 2
 ENDO
ENDO
```

(a)

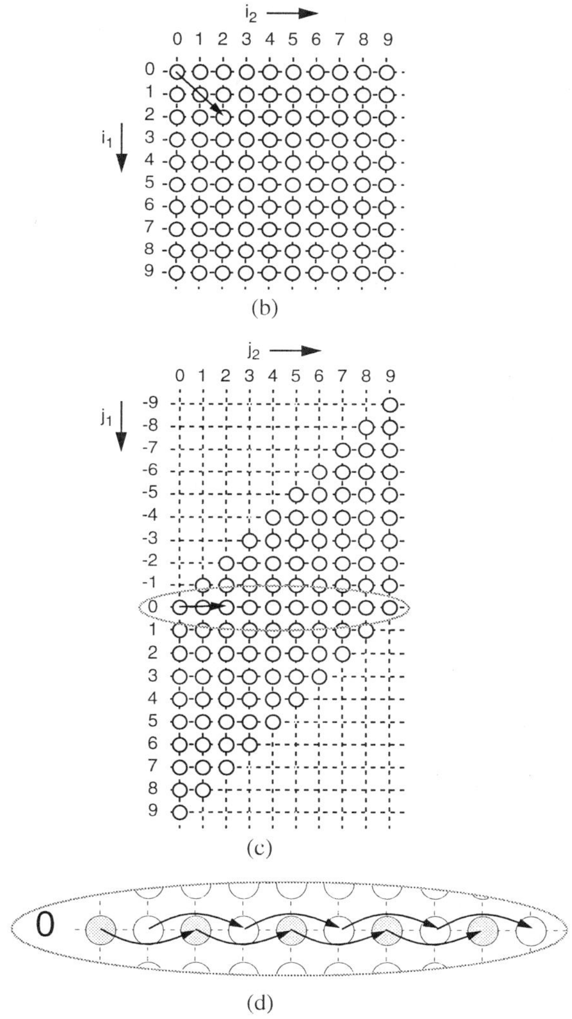

Figure 1: (a) Code of the working example, (b) representation of the original IS and (c) representation of the target IS after transformation and (d) detail of row 0.

Let E be the set of dependence relations in the loop. When uniform dependences are considered, the dependence graph G(V, E) is used to summarize all the dependence information. In this graph, vertices represent statements of the loop body and edges represent dependence relations between them. In this paper, all dependences are assumed to be uniform. We denote the dependence relations between any pair of statements S_i and S_j with $\bar{d}_{ij}$.

A *chain* C_{ij} is an ordered set of arcs $C_{ij} = \{\bar{d}_{ik}, \bar{d}_{kl}, ..., \bar{d}_{mj}\}$ between two statements S_i and S_j such that each node in the chain is visited only once. Given a chain C_{ij}, we define its *weight* w_{ij} as

$$w_{ij} = \sum_{d_{lm} \in C_{ij}} d_{lm}$$

This weight w_{ij} represents the number of iterations between any pair of instances of statements S_i and S_j depend from each other through chain C_{ij}.

A *recurrence* R is a cycle or closed chain in the dependence graph. A *hamiltonian recurrence* is a recurrence going through all nodes in the dependence graph.

Let $B = \{ R_1, R_2, ..., R_r \}$ be the set of recurrences in a given dependence graph G. This graph G is an *acyclic dependence graph* when $B=\emptyset$ and it is a *cyclic dependence graph* when $|B| \geq 1$. When at least one recurrence of B is hamiltonian, the graph is called *hamiltonian graph.*

3: Framework

In this section we briefly review the framework of linear loop transformation where our proposal is developed. A loop transformation is a mapping between two iteration spaces (named original and target IS). In this paper we consider linear transformations modelled by unimodular matrices (i.e., matrices whose determinant is ±1). These transformations can be used to model some basic transformations such as permutations, skewing and reversal [4,19].

Let I be a point of the original IS, J a point of the target IS and T the transformation matrix. The relationship between them is

$$J = T \cdot I$$

Let $\bar{d}$ be a distance vector in the original IS. Since T is a linear transformation, $T \cdot \bar{d}$ is the transformed distance vector in the target IS. A transformation T is legal if

$$T \cdot \bar{d} > \bar{0}$$

for all dependence relations $\bar{d}$ in the dependence graph G(V, E). This means that each transformed dependence has to be lexicographically positive in the target IS.

This basic loop transformation can be extended including the statement dimension as a new component. In [2] it has been shown how different displacements for each statement can be used to break dependences. In [16] this technique has been applied to eliminate non-local references. Figure 2.b summarizes the procedure when the alignment step is included in the transformation process.

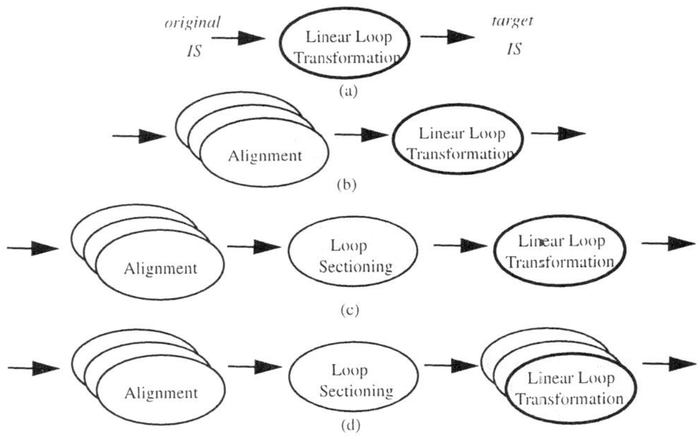

Figure 2: Transforming a IS using a different approaches: (a) [4, 19], (b) [2,16], (c) this proposal, and (d) [8].

But as we will show in this paper, this transformation is not enough to identify a significant fraction of parallelism in a loop. We propose a way to solve this problem by adding a new non-lineal step at the transformation process based on the Remainder Transformation introduced by Banerjee [5]. This step called *loop sectionning* is introduced between the alignment and the linear transformation steps as shown in Figure 2.c.

Finally, it can be profitable to apply different unimodular transformations to different statements in the loop body. This transformation is named *multi-transformation.* In [8] this step is adressed and show how to avoid generating guards in most of the cases. Figure 2.d summarizes how multi-transformations can be combined with the previous steps. Hence we concentrate on the loop sectionning step in this paper.

4: Motivation for a new transformation

Linear loop transformations are a successful solution to the loop transformation problem, but they are not enough as we illustrate by the simple example shown in Figure 1.a (taken from [14]). Figure 1.b shows the original IS and Figure 1.c shows the target IS when the following transformation matrix is used

$$T = \begin{bmatrix} 1 & -1 \\ 0 & 1 \end{bmatrix}$$

This nested loop contains only one dependence vector d=<2,2>. This dependence in the target space is transformed into d'=T·d=<0,2> as shown in the target space of Figure 1.c. This dependence is now carried by the innermost loop and thus the outer loop can be parallelized.

The code that scans the target IS is shown in Figure 3. If the outer loop is executed in parallel, the number of parallel tasks obtained is 19. However, if we carefully analyze each row in Figure 1.c, we can distinguish two independent subsets of iterations. Figure 1.d details the row corresponding to iteration j_1=0. Dependences reveal two independent subset of iterations. Thus we can conclude that linear transformations are not enough if this parallelism has to be exploited.

```
DO j1= -9,9
 DO j2= max(0,-j1),min(9,9-j1)
  A[j1+j2,j2]= A[j1+j2-2,j2-2]* 2
 ENDO
ENDO
```

Figure 3: Target code of the working example.

In this paper we propose a way of extracting this parallelism by adding a new non-linear step at the framework of lineal transformations based on the Remainder Transformations introduced by Banerjee [5]. Basically it consists in creating a new auxiliary space from the original IS where it is more easy to identify this parallelism and where it is possible to extract the maximum parallelism by a linear transformation. In the case of our working example, this auxiliary space can be obtained sectioning the innermost loop with strips of size 2 and then piling the sections as shown in Figure 4.b.

Since the remainder transformation adds an extra loop, it has an effect on the data dependence relations in the target loop. It adds a component to the distance vector. In this working example the new dependence vector becomes d=<2,0,1>. The code that scans this auxiliar iteration space is shown in Figure 5.

Thus, if we use the transformation matrix

$$T = \begin{bmatrix} 1 & 0 & -2 \\ 0 & 1 & 0 \\ 0 & 0 & 1 \end{bmatrix}$$

to transform this auxiliar IS, we obtain the code shown in Figure 6.a where the 2 outermost loops can be parallelized because after the transformation the dependence becomes d=<0,0,1> and it is carried out by the innermost loop as one can see in the Figure 6.b

With this simple example we have tried to show that the linear loop transformation is not sufficient to extract full parallelism out of loops. In the following section we present our approach in order to exploit coarse-grain parallelism for nested loops on MIMD systems.

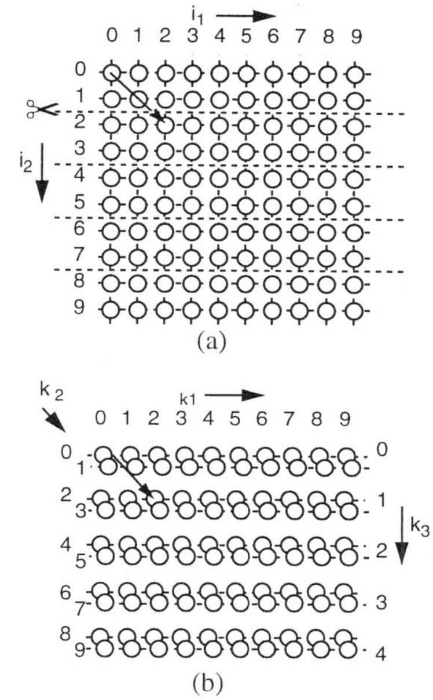

Figure 4: (a) original IS and (b) auxiliary IS of the working example.

```
DO k1= 0,9
  DO k2= 0,1
    DO k3= 0,4
      A[k1,k2+2·k3]= A[k1-2,k2+2·k3-2]* 2
    ENDO
  ENDO
ENDO
```

Figure 5: Code of the auxiliar IS.

```
DO j1= -8,9
  DO j2= 0,1
    DO j3= max(⌈-j1/2⌉, 0),min(⌊(9-j1)/2⌋, 4)
     A[j1+2·j3,j2+2·j3]= A[j1+2·j3-2,j2+2 j3-2
    ENDO
  ENDO
ENDO
```

(a)

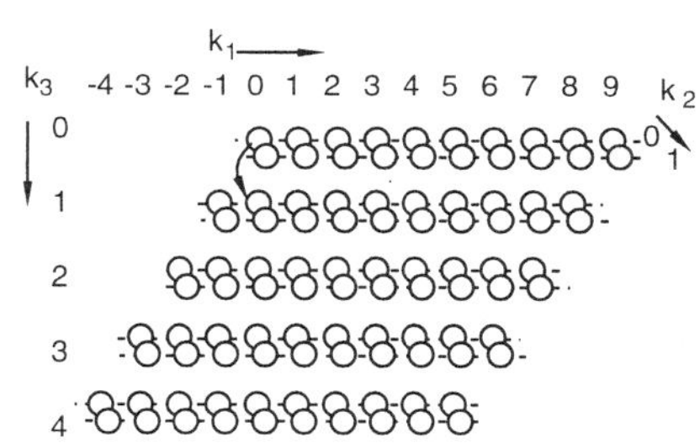

(b)

Figure 6: (a) Target code obtained and (b) target IS of working example.

5: Loop Sectioning

The work presented in this section focuses in loops that present tight recurrences in its dependence graph. In general, loops whose statements are involved in a dependence cycle are considered to be serial. However, techniques such as cycle shrinking [11] can be used to extract parallelism that may be present in the loop. In order to present the methodology proposed in this paper, consider the example of Figure 7.a slightly modified from [11] that has been used by several authors [12,15] in order to show their improvements with respect to the original cycle shrinking method.

```
    DO i1= 0,N1
     DO i2= 0,N2
S1:     A[i1,i2]= B[i1-3,i2-5]
S2:     B[i1,i2]= A[i1-2,i2-4]
     ENDO
    ENDO
```

(a)

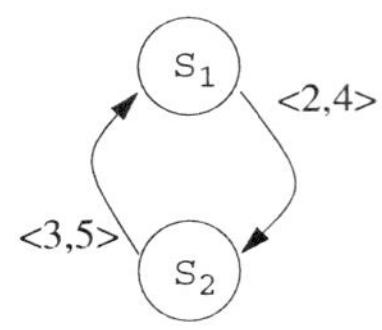

(b)

Figure 7: (a) Nested Loops and (b) its dependence graph.

In this example, variable $A[i_1,i_2]$ is produced in statement $S_1(i_1,i_2)$ and consumed in statement $S_2(i_1+2,i_2+4)$ so there is a dependence between S_1 and S_2 with distance <2,4>. Similarly, there is a dependence between S_2 and S_1 with distance <3,5>. Both dependences are uniform. Figure 7.b shows a graphical representation of the dependence graph. In this example, there is a hamiltonian recurrence than involves all the statements of the loop body.

5.1: Loop Alignment

The basic idea of the alignment component that is added to each statement is to reduce the number of cross-iteration dependences. Figure 8 is intended to visually demonstrate our parallelizing algorithm. Consider that each statement is represented with a hyperplane in the SIS (as shown in Figure 8.a) and then we apply a different transformation to each statement of the loop in Figure 7.a in such a way that the resulting target IS is the one shown in Figure 8.c. We apply a shift of <2,4> to the hyperplane associated to statement S_1 and a null shift to the hyperplane associated to S_2. Different kinds of shades are used to identify the different hyperplanes. Notice that dependence <2,4> is now embedded in the sequential execution of each iteration because the hyperplanes of the statements have been shifted in order to make two dependent points be executed in the same iteration. Now the IS for S_1 is $[0..N_1:0..N_2]$ while for S_2 $[2..N_1+2,4..N_2+4]$. As a consequence, most of the iterations in the target loop execute both statements but others just execute one of them. The new bounds of the target loop nest have to be the union of the bounds for each statement: $[0..N_1+2, 0..N_2+4]$.

Let I be a point of the original hyperplane x corresponding to the statement S_x and J a point of the target hyperplane x after the alignment. The coordinates of each point $J=(j_1,...,j_m,...,j_n)$ can be obtained as

$$j_m = i_m + w^m_{xs}$$

where w^m_{xs} represent the weight of the hamiltonian recurrence from the statement S_x to the last statement S_s of the loop body in dimension m

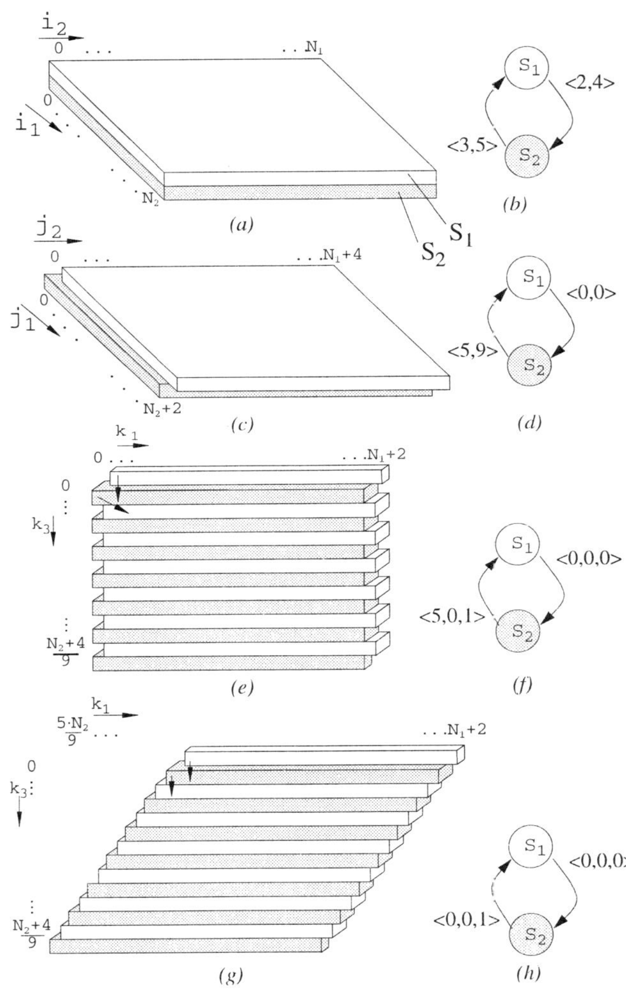

Figure 8: (a) Original SIS for the example of Figure 7, (b) original dependence graph, (c) auxiliar aligned SIS and (d) aligned dependence graph, (e) SIS after sectioning, (f) the resulting dependence graph, (g) SIS after transformation using matrix T and (h) the resulting dependence graph in the transformed space.

5.2: Loop Sectioning

Next we present a new step in the transformation process that is based on the Remainder Transformation introduced by Banerjee [5]. The IS defined by the original loop nest is divided into strips of some maximum size. Graphically it can be seen as if we section the first dimension i_1 of the iteration space in Figure 8.c in strips of size 9 and then pile them. The size of the strip that we propose is the weight of the hamiltonian recurrence in the dimension corresponding to the sectioned loop.

Loop sectioning is always legal; however it affects the data dependence relations in the loop. As we showed in the previous section, loop sectioning adds a new loop in the nest, and an element to the distance vectors. When a loop L_k is sectioned in two loops L_k and L_{k+1}, a dependence relation with a component d^k in the distance vector (corresponding to L_k), produces one or two dependence relations. If d^k is a multiple of the strip size ss, then the elements $d^k=0$ and $d^{k+1}=d^k/ss$ [21]. If d^k is not a multiple of ss, then the distance vector is transformed into two dependence relations, with the elements $<d^k,d^{k+1}>$ of the distance vectors set to $<-d^k \bmod ss, \lceil d^k/ss \rceil>$ and $<d^k \bmod ss, \lfloor d^k/ss \rfloor>$.

In our example the strip size is equal to the corresponding component in the distance vector. That means that the component d^k of the distance vector corresponding to the loop sectioned become equal 0 and the new component d^{k+1} becomes 1 ($d^k=9$, ss=9). This can be reflected in the dependence graph. Figure 8.f represents the dependence graph for the working example where the dependence <5,9> is transformed to <5,0,1>.

Let I be a point of the original space and J a point of the target space after loop sectioning. The coordinates of each point $J=(j_1,...,j_m,...,j_{n+1})$ can be obtained as

$$j_m = \begin{cases} i_m & m<k \\ i_m \bmod ss & m=k \\ \left\lfloor \dfrac{i_k}{ss} \right\rfloor & m=k+1 \\ i_{m+1} & m>k+1 \end{cases}$$

being k the sectioned loop and ss the value of the strip. Sectioning can be applied to any dimension of the original IS; however, [18] shows criteria to select the appropriate dimension. The value of ss is set to the weight of the recurrence in the component k corresponding to the sectioned loop. We denote this strip component with w_R^k.

5.3: Linear Loop transformation

Now we have an iteration space with a cross-iteration dependence with distance equal to <5,0,1>. This dependence is carried by the outermost loop. If we could transform this dependence into <0,0,1>, this dependence would be carried by the innermost loop and the two outermost loops would become parallel. This is what we can achieve with a linear loop transformation using the transformation matrix

$$T = \begin{bmatrix} 1 & 0 & -5 \\ 0 & 1 & 0 \\ 0 & 0 & 1 \end{bmatrix}$$

applied to the auxiliary iteration space of Figure 8.e.

Graphically this transformation is represented in Figure 8.g. The arrows represent the two dependences in the graph of Figure 8.h. Figure 8.g shows the target space after apply the transformation. Observe that in this new space the dependence from S_2 to S_1 is transformed into <0,0,1> as shown in the dependence graph of Figure 8.h. Now in this target space, the iterations of the two outermost loops can be executed fully in parallel because one dependence (d_{12}=<0,0,0>) is internal to a iteration, and the other (d_{21}=<0,0,1>) is carried by the innermost loop.

This transformation can be expressed as a matrix and also as

$$j_m = \begin{cases} i_k & m=k \\ i_{k+1} & m=k+1 \\ i_m - i_{k+1} \times w_R^m & m \neq k \text{ and } m \neq k+1 \end{cases}$$

where we consider again that I represents a point of the original space and J a point of the transformed space.

5.4: Full Transformation

The framework presented in this paper decides which transformation to apply from the dependence graph.The transformation that we propose is obtained from the composition of the three previous transformations. Let I be a point of the original hyperplane x corresponding to the statement S_x and J a point of the target hyperplane x after the whole transformation. The coordinates of each point $J=(j_1,...,j_m,...,j_{n+1})$ can be obtained as

$$j_m = \begin{cases} i_m + w_{xs}^m - \left\lfloor \dfrac{i_k + w_{xs}^k}{w_R^k} \right\rfloor \times w_R^m & m<k \\ \left(i_k + w_{xs}^k\right) \bmod w_R^k & m=k \\ \left\lfloor \dfrac{i_k + w_{xs}^k}{w_R^k} \right\rfloor & m=k+1 \\ i_{m+1} + w_{xs}^{m+1} - \left\lfloor \dfrac{i_k + w_{xs}^k}{w_R^k} \right\rfloor \times w_R^{m+1} & m>k+1 \end{cases}$$

being k the sectioned loop. But the component j_k can be expressed in a different way. From the equality

$$\left(i_k + w_{js}^k\right) \bmod w_R^k = i_k + w_{js}^k - \left\lfloor \frac{i_k + w_{js}^k}{w_R^k} \right\rfloor \times w_R^k$$

the previous expression can be rewritten as follows

$$j_m = \begin{cases} i_m + w_{xs}^m - \left\lfloor \dfrac{i_k + w_{xs}^k}{w_R^k} \right\rfloor \times w_R^m & m < k+1 \\ \left\lfloor \dfrac{i_k + w_{xs}^k}{w_R^k} \right\rfloor & m = k+1 \\ i_{m+1} + w_{xs}^{m+1} - \left\lfloor \dfrac{i_k + w_{xs}^k}{w_R^k} \right\rfloor \times w_R^{m+1} & m > k+1 \end{cases}$$

In [18] we stated and proof several theorems that show the property of achieving the maximum parallelism that we have been referred along the previous section about the transformation proposed. In particular, it is important to remark that all the dependences used for the alignment components and strip component will be embedded in the sequential execution of the innermost loop, leading to fully parallel outermost loops.

The bounds of the transformed space are obtained from the union of the bounds of the original IS of each statement. In [17] we show how the bounds for each statement can be obtained. In general there are points of this transformed space where not all the statements of the loop body are executed. This can be controlled by guard conditionals. Unfortunately this code can be very expensive in terms of run-time overhead. In order to make this code less run-time expensive we define the core part as the part of the transformed space where all the statements of the loop body are executed. This core part can be executed without guard conditionals at the statement level, reducing the run-time overhead introduced by them. The code obtained has three parts, namely prolog, core and epilog parts. We have to include guards conditionals in the prolog and epilog parts in order to control the execution of each statement. The code that is obtained for the example is shown in Figure 9.

We assumed that there was only one recurrence. If more than one recurrence appears in the graph, it is necessary to use synchronization mechanisms that explicitly synchronize dependences not preserved when the parallel code obtained is executed. Explicit synchronization must be introduced for any edge not included in the hamiltonian recurrence in the graph going from node S_i to node S_j. Many mechanisms can be used to perform this synchronization. We will use counting semaphores as synchronization objects. As coupling between tasks will be very tight, we need a fast implementation of primitives on semaphores. The statement S_i source of the dependence will signal the end of its execution to the statement S_j sink of the same dependence, in order to allow its execution. During the code generation phase it is necessary to know the relationship of the parallel iterations related by a dependence d_{ij} in order to parametrize the semaphores. The reader can refer to [18] in order to find how to insert syncronization primitives.

```
DOALL j1 = min(⌈2-(N2+4)·5/9⌉,⌈-N2·5/9⌉),N1+2
   DOALL j2 = max(⌈4+(j1-N1-2)·9/5⌉,⌈(j1-N1)·9/5⌉,0),
              min(⌊N2+4+(j1-2)·9/5⌋,⌊N2+9·j1/5⌋,8)

   lower^1=max(⌈(2-j1)/5⌉, ⌈(4-j2)/9⌉)
   lower^2=max(⌈-j1/5⌉, ⌈-j2/9⌉)
   lower^core=max(lower^1,lower^2)
   lower^cover=min(lower^1,lower^2)
   upper^1=min(⌊(N1+2-j1)/5⌋, ⌊(N2+4-j2)/9⌋
   upper^2=min(⌊(N1-j1)/5⌋, ⌊(N2-j2)/9⌋)
   upper^core=min(upper^1,upper^2)
   upper^cover=max(upper^1,upper^2)                PROLOG

   if (lower^2≤ upper^core-1) and (lower^2≤ upper^2) then
      B[j1+5·lower^2 ,j2+9·lower^2 ]=A[j1+5·lower^2 -2
                                      ,j2+9·lower^2 -4]
                                                    CORE
   if (lower^core≤ upper^core)
      DO j3 = lower^core,upper^core
         A[j1+5·j3-2,j2+9·j3-4]=B[j1+5·j3-5,j2+9·j3-9]
         B[j1+5·j3,j2+9·j3]=A[j1+5·j3-2,j2+9·j3-4]
      ENDO
      LOWER=upper^core+1
   else LOWER=lower^core
                                                    EPILOG
   if (LOWER≤ upper^1)  then
      A[j1+5·upper^1-2,j2+9·upper^1-4]=B[j1+5·upper^1-5
                                        ,j2+9·upper^1-9]

   ENDOALL
ENDOALL
```

Figure 9: Transformed code obtained for the example of Figure 7.

6: Conclusions and Future Work

Program transformations are a powerful tool for studying and exploiting parallelism, specially for nested loop structures that offer the most fruitful source of parallelism in serial programs. But in general, loops whose statements are involved in a dependence cycle are considered to be serial. However in this paper we present how the framework of linear loop transformations can be extended in different ways. The framework presented solves the fundamental problem of deciding which transformation to apply. We focused this paper on the problem of extracting all the parallelism that may be present in a loop. The technique presented in this paper is applicable to codes whose full potential parallelism can not be exploited using linear transformations.

We have shown from a classical example taken from [11], which has been used by several authors [15,12], how our proposed method can be applied. For this example the authors referred present methods based on the technique named "Cycle Shrinking". Basically, they group the index points into packets. These packets are executed sequentially and all the index points within a packet are executed concurrently. They obtain a code with an outermost sequential loop that has about N/4 iterations. Our method presents important improvements: (a) The sequential loop has about N/9 iterations, as a consequence more iterations are executed in parallel. (b) In our method, the sequential loop becomes the innermost loop, this causes the code to be completely parallel. Another important effect is that the method can eliminate the barrier synchronization that is required using the Cycle Shrinking method.

In this particular case, the method proposed does not balance the load assigned to the processors if as many processors as parallel iterations are allocated. The number of tasks generated is greater than the parallelism evaluated [1] and tasks take different time to complete their execution. In [18] this scheme is extended to improve load balancing among processors, reducing the number of parallel tasks without increasing the execution time of the parallel loop.

Next we briefly comment some open questions left by the work presented in this paper. The partitioning method presented assumes the existence of a hamiltonian recurrence in the graph. This is not the common case, so the problem must be taken into consideration and heuristics to find a good solution proposed. Loop distribution can also be used when a hamiltonian recurrence is not present in the graph.

Acknowledgments

This work has been partially supported by the Ministry of Education of Spain under contracts TIC 880/92 and TIC429/95, Esprit BRA APPARC under grant no. 6634 and by the CEPBA (European Center for Parallelism of Barcelona).

References

[1] Ayguadé E., Labarta J., Torres J., Llabería J.M. and Valero M., Parallelism Evaluation and Partitioning of Nested Loops for Shared Memory Multiprocessors, chapter 11 of *Advances in Languages and Compilers for Parallel Processing*, The MIT Press, 1991.

[2] Ayguadé E. and Torres J., Partitioning the Statement per Iteration Space Using Non-singular Matrices, in *Proceedings of the 1993 ACM International Conference on Supercomputing*, July 1993.

[3] Banerjee U., *Dependence Analysis for Supercomputing*, Kluwer Academic Publishers, 1988.

[4] Banerjee U., Unimodular Transformations of Double Loops, chapter 10 of *Advances in Languages and Compilers for Parallel Processing*, The MIT Press, 1991.

[5] Banerjee U., *Loop Parallelization.* A book series on Loop Transformations for Restructuring Compilers Klumer Academic Publishers, Norwell, Massachussetts. 1994.

[6] Darte A., Risset T., Robert Y. Loop Nest Scheduling and Transformations. In J.J. Dongarra and B. Tourancheau, editors, Environment and Tools for Parallel Scientific Computing, volume 6 of *Advances in Parallel Computing*, North Holland, 1993.

[7] Fernández A., Llabería J.M. and Valero-García M., Loop Transformation using non-unimodular matrices, to be published in *IEEE Transactions on Parallel and Distributed Systems*.

[8] Knijnenburg P. M. W., Ayguadé E. and Torres J., Multitransformations: Code Generation and Validity. Technical Report 95-12, Dept. of Computer Science, Leiden University, 1995.

[9] Li W. and Pingali K., A Singular Loop Transformation Framework Based on Non-Singular Matrices, in *Proceedings of the Fifth Workshop on Languages and Compilers for Parallel Computers*, New Heaven (CN), August 1992.

[10] Polychronopoulos C., *Parallel Programming and Compilers*, Kluwer Academic Publishers, 1988.

[11] Polychronopoulos C. P., Compiler Optimization for Enhancing Parallelism and Their Impact on Architecture Design, *IEEE Transactrions on Computers* 37(8) (Aug. 1988) 991-1004.

[12] Robert Y. and Song S., Revisiting cycle shrinking, Parallel Computing 18 (1992), North-Holland, 481-496.

[13] Schrijver A., *Theory of Linear and Integer Programming*, John Wiley and Sons, 1986.

[14] Shang W. and Fortes J., Independendent Partitioning of Algorithms with Uniform Dependencies,

[15] Shang W. , O'Keefe M. and Fortes J. A., On Loop Transformations for Generalized Cycle Shrinking, *IEEE Transaction on Parallel and Distributed Systems*, Vol. 5, No. 2, February 1994, 193-204.

[16] Torres J., Ayguadé E., Labarta J. and Valero M., Align and Distribute-based Linear Loop Transformations, *Languages and Compilers for Parallel Processing*, 6th International Workshop, Portland Oregon, Lectures Notes in Computer Science 768, Springer-Verlag, 1993

[17] Torres J., Ayguadé E., Labarta J. and Valero M., Revisiting Framework of Linear Loop Transformations to Extract Full Loop Parallelism, Department of Computer Architecture, Polytechnic University of Catalunya, April 1995, CEPBA Research Report RR-95/09

[18] Torres J., Automatic Parallelization of Sequential Loops with Recurrences , Ph.D. Thesis, Department of Computer Architecture, Polytechnic University of Catalunya, November 1993, CEPBA Research Report RR-94/01

[19] Wolf M.E. and Lam M.S., A Loop Transformation Theory and an Algorithm to Maximize Parallelism, *IEEE Transactions on Parallel and Distributed Systems*, vol. 2, no. 4, October 1991.

[20] Wolfe M., *Optimizing Supercompilers for Supercomputers*, The MIT Press, 1989.

[21] Wolfe M., More Iteration Space Tiling, *Proceedings of the Supercomputing'89*, 1989.

[22] Xue J., Automating non-unimodular loop transformations for massive parallelism, Parallel Computing 20 (1994), North-Holland, 711-728.

❖ Open Forum Session III ❖

Chair

R. Beivide

A Paralation Model implementation based on a Concurrent Lisp Interpreter Community

Claudia Di Napoli   Maurizio Giordano   Mario Mango Furnari

Istituto di Cibernetica, C.N.R.
Via Toiano, 6 I-80072 Arco Felice, Naples, Italy

Abstract

In this paper we describe the approach we are pursuing on coping with parallelism in symbolic applications. Our purpose is to build a unified and user friendly parallel symbolic programming environment suited to Distributed Memory Parallel Systems (DMPS). This system is based on the Sabot's Paralation model (in particular its LISP *implementation,* PARALATION LISP*), whose main feature is to clearly differentiate the computational aspect from the communication one. In our opinion this distinction allows a clearer and cleaner exploitation of the opportunities of parallelism in symbolic applications. The simple semantics of the Paralation model parallel constructs seems to us well suited to run on a set of* LISP *interpreters. We chose to implement the Paralation model extensions on top of the Parallel Virtual Machine (*PVM*) package because this tool allows to easily use a set of* LAN *interconnected powerful workstations as a general purpose parallel computational resource.*

1 Introduction

Parallel and distributed processing is increasingly being used for providing high levels of performance for numerous applications. In fact significant advances in designing parallel algorithms and architectures have demonstrated the potential for applying concurrent computation techniques to a wide variety of problems. Today parallel processing is being accepted essentially for high–performance scientific computing, whereas a parallel approach to symbolic computations seems to be a more difficult area. In fact symbolic applications generally offer several opportunities of small grain parallelism that are extremely irregular to be "easily" managed by parallel systems. However, an increasing number of symbolic applications suited to be parallelized are emerging every day, like the *natural language systems, expert systems, theorem provers, vision systems.*

The goal of our project is the implementation of a parallel symbolic programming environment suitable for *Distributed Memory Parallel Systems* (*DMPS*), that can manage symbolic applications characterized by coarse grain parallelism. This environment is based on the Sabot's Paralation model[16] (in particular its LISP implementation, PARALATION LISP[17]).

The notion of *global namespace* in LISP is responsible for the intensive work done in implementing parallel extensions of this language on shared memory parallel architectures[12, 4]. Only few extensions have been done for distributed memory parallel architectures, but they seem to keep on using an approach based on a "virtually" shared memory. Furthermore they usually rely on new computational mechanisms to manage synchronization problems concerning the access to shared data structures[6, 14]. We think the features of PARALATION LISP are suitable to be implemented on distributed memory architectures without affecting the semantics of the basic LISP primitives[13].

In the following of the paper we describe the current status of work in implementing the PARALATION LISP on *DMPS*. We start giving an outline of Paralation model, pointing out its main characteristics and describing its parallel constructs. Next, we describe the architectural model we refer to, and the implementation of the PARALATION LISP constructs. Then some implementation experiences together with performance results are reported. Finally some considerations are included.

2 The Paralation Model

The Paralation model is a parallel computational model developed by Gary Sabot[16, 17]. It is independent of the hardware architecture, both for system interconnections, and processor types. The central idea is the clear distinction between *computation* and *communication*.

The basic entity is the new data structure, named *paralation*, which represents a set of virtual processors, or *sites* (see figure 1). A paralation instance is called *field*, that is a collection of values, one for each site. In other words, the paralation may be viewed as a collection of fields, all with the same size. All the fields belonging to the same paralation are aligned in the sense that the i–th elements of them are stored in the same site. This property is called the *intrasite locality*. A paralation has at least one associated field, named the *index field*, that enumerates the paralation elements.

Paralation sites with nearby indices aren't necessarily near each other. The "nearness" is based upon the concept of paralation *shape* (*intersite locality*) that captures the communication costs. Paralation of any

1066-6192/96 $5.00 © 1996 IEEE
Proceedings of PDP '96

shape may be constructed. Thus, the sites of a particular paralation might be arranged in the form of a three-dimensional grid, a ring, a butterfly, a pyramid, or even a double elix. By default, a paralation has not an inherent shape. Shape locality must be explicitly described by the user.

A third kind of locality is the *interparalation locality*: sites and values in different, unrelated paralations are not necessarily near each other, regardless of their indices.

```
(setq p (make-paralation 5))          ;; creates a paralation and
=> #F(0 1 2 3 4)                      ;; returns its index field

(elwise (p) (* p 2))                  ;; computes multiplication in parallel
=> #F(0 2 4 6 8)                      ;; and returns the elwise result field

(elwise (p)                                    ;; assigns list elements
  (elt '(orange apple pear grape tomato) p)))  ;; in parallel to the
=> #F(ORANGE APPLE PEAR GRAPE TOMATO)          ;; elwise result field
```

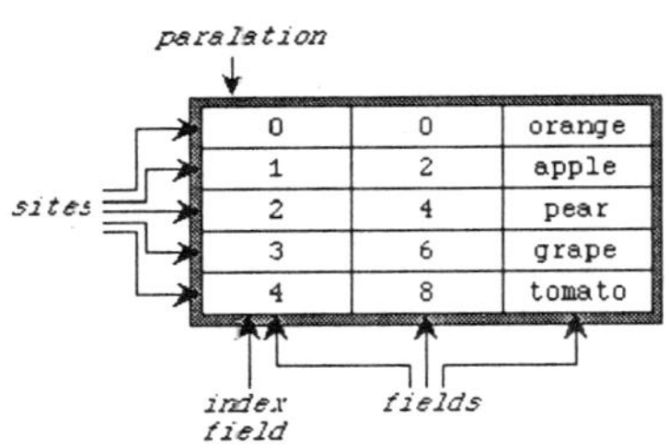

Figure 1: Paralation and **elwise** examples

The paralation itself is never directly accessible, but only fields can be handled. Two special kinds of operators, associated to this new structure, operate upon the paralation fields. The first one is the **elwise** construct for carrying out parallel computations (see figure 1); the other ones are the **match** and <- ("move") constructs for communications (see figure 2). The syntax of the parallel **elwise** construct is:

```
(elwise (<var-list>) <body>)
```

where **<var-list>** is a list of symbols, which will be bound to fields given as arguments and belonging to the same paralation, while **<body>** is the code that will be executed in parallel at each paralation site. The returned value is a new field in the same paralation (see figure 1). The Paralation model assumes a simple synchronization condition:

> *the* **elwise** *function will return only after all computations, carried out each in one site, have finished.*

There are no restrictions on the **<body>** code. This means that the program executed in parallel at each paralation site allows side-effects also on the site's values. Nevertheless there exists a restriction on the side-effects type:

> *since the* **elwise** *does not introduce any synchronization during the site's concurrent computations, having side-effects conflicting is considered as an erroneous behaviour.*

Side-effects may conflict if two or more sites simultaneously read and write the same memory location.

```
(setq map (match f2 f1))                  ;; computes and returns
=> #S(MAPPING                             ;; a mapping between
     :TO-KEY-FIELD   #F(0 1 2 NIL 3 2)    ;; two fields
     :FROM-KEY-FIELD #F(NIL 0 2 3 NIL 0 1))
```

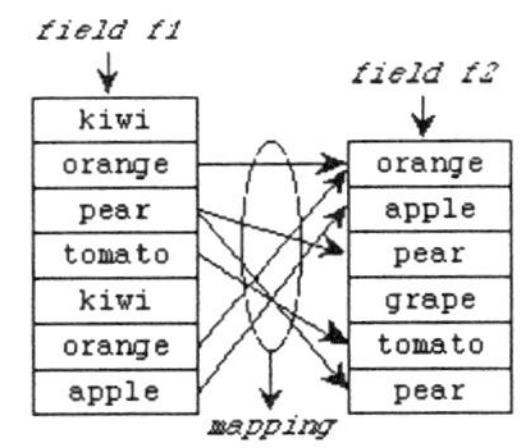


```
(setq def-field (elwise (f2) 'no-value))  ;; computes default field
=> #F(NO-VALUE ... NO-VALUE)              ;; for moving operation

(<- (index f1) :by map                    ;; moves data from source to
               :with '+                   ;; destination field according
               :default def-field)        ;; to the previous mapping and a
=> #F(6 6 2 NO-VALUE 3 2)                 ;; plus combining function
```

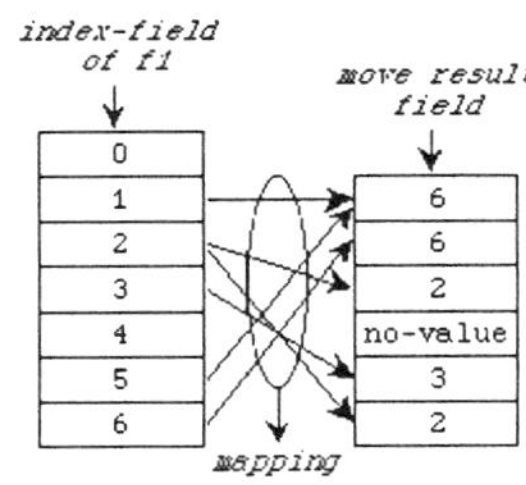

Figure 2: **match** and <- examples

The **match** and <- operators allow communication between the sites of paralations (see figure 2). The **match** operator accepts two key fields (destination and source) and an optional equality predicate as its arguments; it computes and returns a new object, called *mapping*, that encapsulates a communication pattern between two paralations by connecting the source paralation sites to the destination paralation sites if their key values are the same. The <- operator moves field values between paralations according to a mapping given as argument, and returns a new field containing the transferred data. If it is necessary to move more than one field value into the same site, a *combining function* is used to avoid conflicts reducing the multiple values into a single one.

3 The proposed architecture

The architectural model we refer to is a distributed memory parallel system (*DMPS*).

The *DMPS* offer some advantages with respect to shared memory parallel architectures in terms of cost and scalability. Furthermore the new *communication network* hardware and software technologies, such as the optical fiber network interfaces, are increasing the communication speed among processing elements of *DMPS* making their use even more attractive. Our *DMPS* is essentially composed by a set of independent *Processing Elements*, interconnected through a high speed communication network, and a *host* that performs all the I/O operations. Each *PE* has a local memory, i.e. a memory private to the *PE* and invisible to the others, and it communicates with the others via a message–passing mechanism (see figure 3).

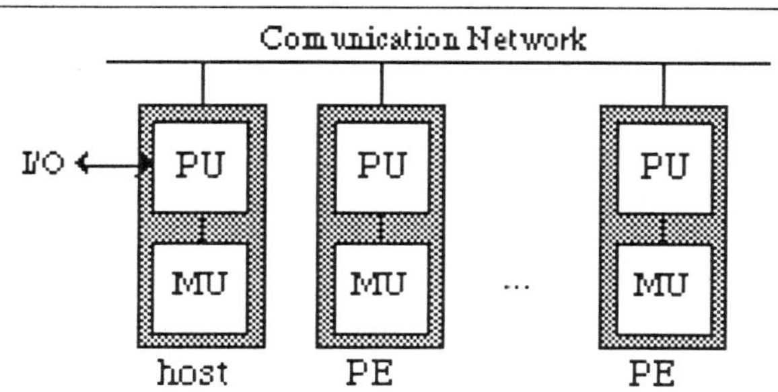

Figure 3: The architectural model

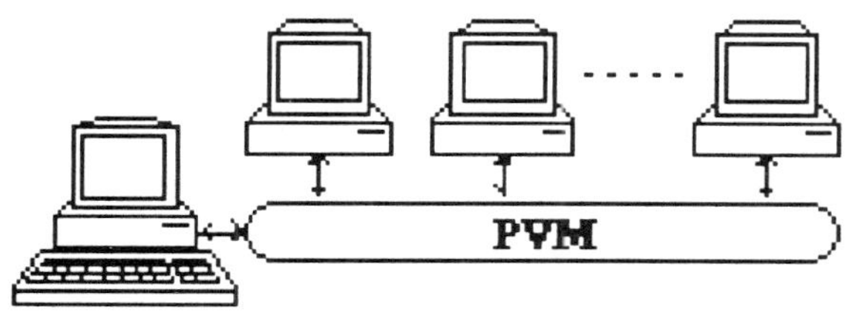

Figure 4: The hardware support

To make available this kind of architecture by simply using a set of LAN interconnected workstations (see figure 4) we chose to use the *Parallel Virtual Machine* package developed at the Oak Ridge National Laboratory[8, 9].

It is an attempt to provide a unified framework within which large parallel systems can be developed in a relatively simple way. It is a general and flexible parallel computing resource that supports shared memory, message–passing, and hybrid models of computations. The main feature of PVM is to allow a heterogeneous collection of workstations and supercomputers to function as a single high–performance parallel machine. PVM is portable and runs on a wide variety of modern platforms. It supports a straightforward but functionally complete message–passing model.

Several design features differentiate PVM from other similar systems. Among these there are the combination of heterogeneity, scalability, multilanguage support, provisions for fault tolerance, the use of multiprocessors and scalar machines, an interactive graphical front end, and support for profiling, tracing, and visual analysis[1].

4 Implementation strategy

The simple semantics of the Paralation model parallel constructs seems to us well suited to run on a *Concurrent Lisp Interpreter Community* (*CLIC*).

We designed the implementation of Paralation Lisp constructs as a library of Lisp functions and macros built on top of the *Concurrent Lisp Interpreter Community*, i.e. a library loaded as an initialization file when the *CLIC* programming environment starts.

So we first implemented a system composed of a set of Lisp interpreters (in particular we used XLisp interpreters, where XLisp is a portable implementation of a Lisp dialect[2]), which can cooperate and run concurrently. The community is organized in the way shown in figure 5. Each interpreter runs on a single *PE* and only one interpreter, called the ***master*** and running on the *host*, communicates with the user and performs all the I/O operations. The communication among interpreters relies on a message–passing paradigm. In the system initialization phase, the master interpreter activates all the others, called the ***slave*** interpreters.

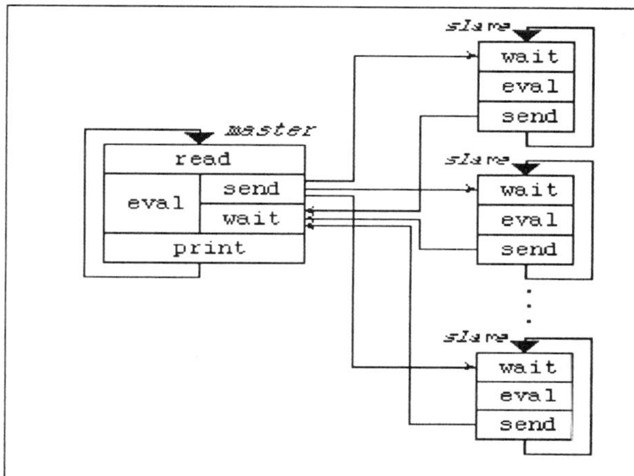

Figure 5: Concurrent Lisp Interpreter Community

The standard `read-eval-print` loop of master interpreter is unchanged, unless when it has to distribute a computation among slaves; in such a case, after the `read` phase, the master sends the slaves messages containing the expressions to be remotely evaluated. Once all slaves have evaluated this expression, they send back messages containing their partial results to the master; the latter continues its computation, previously stopped, composing the slave partial results and printing the final output.

According to this scheme, the standard `read-eval-print` top–level loop of the slave interpreters has been modified in a `wait-eval-send` loop. In fact, the slave interpreters wait for a message from the master, then evaluate this message applying the standard evaluation routine, and, finally, assemble the result in a new message which is sent back to the master. It prints the result only when all slaves have computed their partial results.

It should be noticed that in our implementation only the master interpreter is in charge of evaluating the Paralation Lisp constructs. With this choice, we forbad the possibility to nest the `elwise` parallel construct. Now we are planning to make the roles of master and slave programs symmetric, so that all of them will be able to evaluate the Paralation Lisp constructs, even though only one interpreter will manage the I/O operations.

In developing the *CLIC* programming environment we aimed to attain an easy portable and scalable system.

The LISP interpreters have been interfaced with PVM package, i.e. their source code has been extended with few modules which handle all actual communication among them by using PVM library primitives. These few modules can be easily reimplemented (without using PVM libraries) according to the communication primitives available on different underlying parallel architectures, and in this way the system can be easily ported. At programming level these extensions appear like new LISP primitives which allow remote and concurrent evaluations. The programmer uses these primitives without being aware of the underlying PVM code.

It should be noticed that in the *CLIC* programming environment the distributed computations don't depend on the number of nodes in the parallel machine. Once the programmer has settled the machine configuration in the initialization phase, he/she does not need to use this information any more during a current LISP session. In this way the system is easily scalable.

4.1 The data structure

The implementation strategy for the paralation data structure on *DMPS* is to store the paralation sites on different processors (or nodes), where the number of sites located on the same processor depends upon the number of available processors. In fact, it should be noted that the concepts of site and node are not necessarily synonymous, as more than one site in a paralation could be assigned to only one node; the paralation is only a virtual processor set.

The paralation data structure has been implemented in such a way that the master interpreter keeps a paralation descriptor as a global data structure, while the paralation data values are distributed among the processors' memories. The paralation descriptor has three slots:

- *length*, the total number of sites in the paralation;
- *shape*, the data access topology for the paralation elements, that may be mapped on the *DMPS* processor network;
- *index*, a reference to the paralation index field descriptor.

Descriptions of paralation fields are also located on the master interpreter. They consist of four slots:

- *paralation*, a reference to the paralation descriptor;
- *tids*, *ranges*, and *keys*, three vectors of the same size equal to the number of available processors. These vectors contain, at each position corresponding to a slave program, respectively: a slave interpreter identifier where the paralation sites are stored; the first index and the number of sites stored on that interpreter; the memory reference where field values are stored.

This allocation strategy is sketched in figure 6.

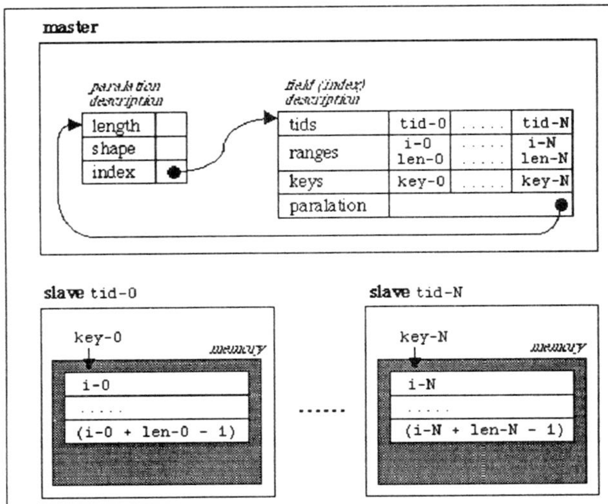

Figure 6: Paralation allocation strategy

When the master interpreter allocates a paralation data structure it calls a *partition* procedure which computes a site partition among the slave interpreters.

The data allocation problem entails the *data partitioning* and *data alignment* problems. At the moment we do not deal with the site allocation strategy problem, that we plan to approach in a near future, but we assume a uniform and static partitioning strategy based only on the number of available processors in the initialization phase.

In a near future we plan to adopt other strategies based on a slave dynamic configuration which can take into account the processor availability, speed, load, and interconnection topology during the computation. At this end, it will not be necessary to change the actual implementation code of the PARALATION LISP constructs, but only the *partition* procedure with a more complex one which manages more information about machine architecture and paralation shape.

According to the paralation partition settled by the *partition* function, the master program builds the *tids*, *ranges* and *keys* vectors of the index field descriptor. Then it sends messages to the slave programs instructing them to store the parts of the paralation index field under the corresponding keys settled before. After the slaves have signalled the end of their jobs, the master links the *paralation* slot of the field descriptor to the paralation which the field belongs to.

4.2 The computation construct

The `elwise` construct has been implemented according to the *Single Program Multiple Data* paradigm.

From the computational point of view, the constraint on side-effects during an `elwise` computation guarantees that there will be no cross dependencies among site evaluations. This condition, together with a data partition along the index field, suggests to distribute the **elwise** computations according to the data partitioning pattern.

Let us describe the **elwise** implementation strategy. What it happens during the **elwise** evaluation has been summarized in figure 7. Here we describe the paralation structure before and after the **elwise** execution in the master node. Moreover, the messages exchanged between master and slave programs have been described together with the information needed for computation.

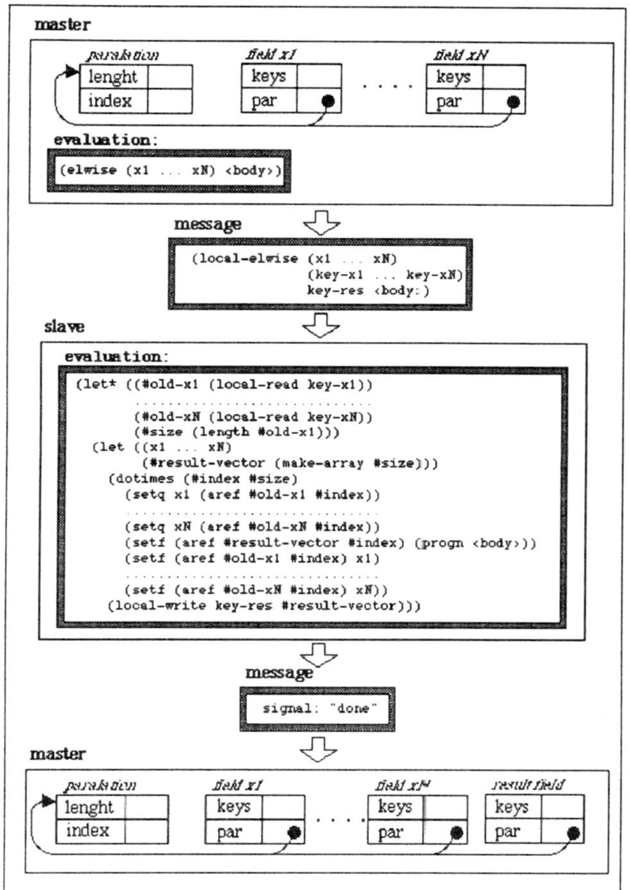

Figure 7: Parallel implementation for **elwise**

First of all, the master program extracts the *tids* information to identify where to send messages. Then it assembles messages with this form:

```
(local-elwise (x1 ...  xN) (key-x1 ...
        key-xN) key-res <body>)
```

where **key-x1 ... key-xN** are references, private to each slave, to memory locations, where each location contains the subset of values of each field given as argument. Similarly, **key-res** is the reference to the memory location where the subset of field values resulting from the slave **<body>** evaluation will be stored. All slave interpreters evaluate concurrently the function call contained in the message, i.e. they execute the code shown in figure 7.

Memory references to the field subsets on each remote node are crucial information. In fact, each node must know where read (by using **key-x1 ... key-xN** references) and write (by using **key-res** reference) the subsets of field values on its local memory.

Each slave interpreter saves the argument field values into local variables (**old-x1 ... old-xN**) initializes a vector (**result-vector**) representing the result field subset, and then executes a loop through the indices of this vector. At each iteration the **elwise** variables (**x1 ... xN**) are bound to the local argument field values, then the **<body>** is executed and the result is stored into each position of the result field vector; finally, the local argument field values are updated for side–effects. After the loop is finished, the reference **key-res** points to the result field subset.

After the **local-elwise** execution, each slave interpreter sends the master a message signalling the end of its job. The master builds a new field descriptor for the **elwise** result, assigns the appropriate values to its slots, and links this descriptor to the same one of the **elwise** argument fields. According to the **elwise** synchronization rule, the master terminates the **elwise** computation only when all the slaves have sent back their results. At the bottom of the figure 7 there is the paralation descriptor on the master node after the **elwise** execution. Now a new result field has been adjoined to the former representation, as it is necessary to store here the vector containing the references to the remote node memory locations where the parallel computation results have been stored.

4.3 The communication constructs

Regarding the **match** and **<-** communication constructs, we followed the same implementation strategy.

The **elwise** construct is defined as a macro function (as in the Sabot's PARALATION LISP), whereas the **match** and **<-** constructs are standard functions. In fact the master interpreter, before sending the slaves the messages containing the expression to be remotely evaluated, has to evaluate the arguments in its local environment.

When the master evaluates the **match** construct, it sends a message to each slave requesting the remote evaluation of a local version of **match** function. This function takes as arguments the whole source field and the destination field subset which has been here previously locally stored. It takes also the keys where the partial mappings, to be concurrently computed by the slaves, have to be stored, and the keys where the local destination field subsets have been previously stored. The messages are addressed to the appropriate slaves using the *tids* identifiers. The partial mapping structures are locally stored like the field subsets. After all slaves have signalled the end of their jobs, the master builds a global data structure with references to the remotely allocated partial mappings.

The <- construct implementation is similar to the `match` one. After having evaluated the <- arguments, the master interpreter assembles messages which instruct the slaves to evaluate a local version of the <- function whose arguments are: the whole source field to be moved, the key where the partial mapping has been previously stored on the slave memory, and the key where the new field subset obtained by moving data has to be stored. Once the slave interpreters receive the messages, they concurrently compute a partial moving according to the local partial mapping, by transferring all the values of source data field into a new field subset which is locally stored. As before, the master builds a global field descriptor with appropriate references, after all slave computations have finished.

Since the source field is entirely available on each slave during the local **move** computation, each slave is able to locally resolve conflicts which may raise when two or more data have to be moved into the same site by using a combining function given as argument.

5 Some experiences

To test the adequacy of the strategies used on designing the implementation of this environment, we ran some simple applications on different machine configurations.

In our implementation the minimal configuration for the system is composed of two interpreters, one playing the master role and the other the slave role, each one running on a single *PE*. For this reason, we defined the speed–up as follows:

$$S(P) = \frac{T_1}{T_P}$$

where T_1 is the program execution time obtained with the minimal configuration, and T_P is the program execution time obtained with P slaves running on P different *PE*.

We decided to test our system by implementing in PARALATION LISP two simple algorithms whose main difference is the amount of communication among processes concurrently executed.

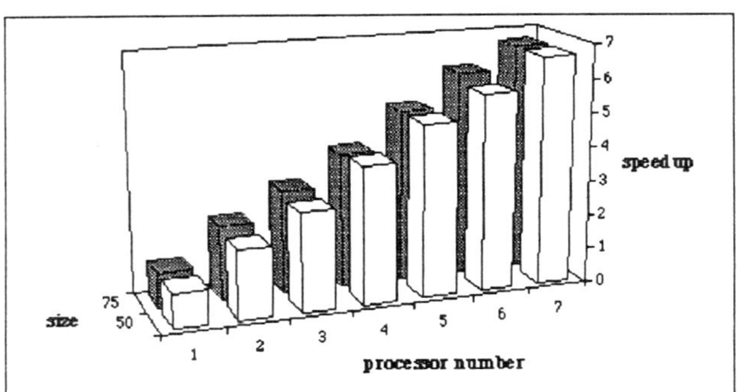

Figure 8: The pattern matcher benchmark

The first algorithm is a simple pattern matcher that uses the form of a symbol to determine its role within a pattern. The basic operations of the benchmark is to search a data base of objects, identifying all of those that satisfy some predicate. The objects contain descriptors which are patterns. The predicate is that a set of search patterns matches the descriptors. The match is done exhaustively, i.e. all search patterns are matched against all descriptors regardless of the outcome of any of the individual matches[7]. The program is intended to perform many of the operations that a simple expert system might perform.

As shown in figure 8 we obtained a linear speed–up which is, at each point, almost equal to the number of the involved slaves. This result confirmed the "soundness" of our system for applications characterized by loose coupling among concurrent computations.

We think many real–world *AI* applications fall in this class. In fact in this domain the solution to a particular problem is often obtained composing or comparing different partial solutions. Theorem provers are typical examples because they exploit several methods when searching for a solution[3].

The second algorithm is the life automaton one which simulates the development of a population of organisms, under the effect of counteracting propagation and extinction tendencies[18]. The automaton is represented by a grid–shaped paralation data structure. During the life automaton computation each cell, represented by a site, interacts with its 8–neighbourhood. So the communications take place between a site and its 8–neighbourhood. We used a block distribution strategy for the paralation data structure. In order to minimize communications among different processors we allocated on each processor memory, other than the sites where the **elwise** computation takes place (*local sites*), also copies of the border sites allocated on the other neighbour processors (*overlapped sites*). This strategy avoids the communication during the **elwise** computation to retrieve the remotely stored data, and introduces the communication only to update the duplicated data after each **elwise** computation.

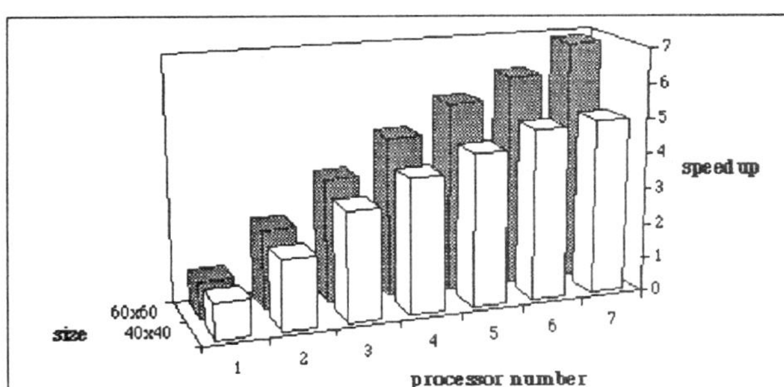

Figure 9: The life automaton benchmark

We ran the life automaton program by incrementing the size of the automaton data structure. As shown in figure 9, we obtained a better speed–up by increasing the automaton size. This result is related to the granularity of the tasks concurrently executed on each processor. In fact when the task granularity increases, the costs due to the data exchange at each new automaton state computation, do not effect the global execution time in a relevant way.

6 Discussion

We investigated the Paralation model as programming language for vision applications by implementing a set of functions which extends the basic Sabot's environment toward vision[10]. This programming environment has been simulated by simply implementing the Paralation model constructs on a sequential standard LISP interpreter. This experience suggested us that the Paralation model is a viable approach to cope with coarse grain parallel symbolic computations and its features look like to be suitable to a distributed implementation.

In this paper we described our current implementation of the Paralation model on *DMPS*.

The choice to adopt a LISP interpreter community to implement our system, allowed us to limit the number of new parallel primitives and to maintain the semantics of the standard LISP primitives. Furthermore in our system the same PARALATION LISP program can run on machine configurations with different number of processors. So, to scale the system it is necessary only to change the set of available nodes at the system initialisation phase.

We implemented our system on the top of PVM package. The main reason of this choice was that it allows us to use a set of LAN interconnected workstations to build a cheap *DMPS*. We think that is very interesting to experiment with tools that allow to have a parallel resource without demanding a large money investment. Furthermore, many computer companies have chosen PVM as *lingua franca* to develop massive parallel applications on the new *DMPS*, for example CRAY *Mpp*, CONVEX, and IBM.

This tool gained a wide spread for numerical applications, so another goal of our experience is to assess its adequacy to support also the development of parallel symbolic applications.

The experimental results we obtained, showed the suitability of the system to run distributed application characterized by coarse grain parallelism. In fact only by increasing the task granularity we are able to overcome the communication costs due to the use of the `match` and `<-` constructs. In our implementation these constructs involve the transfer of an entire paralation field (the source field) to each slave, because each slave during matching and moving data needs to work not only on its local data.

This behaviour cannot be improved using interpreters because it is impossible to restructure the program on fly. For this reason, when paralation data structures are large, and the number of slaves increases, the communication costs become more relevant in comparison with the gain obtained by distributing the computation. So we plan to exploit a compiling approach which allows more information on access patterns to be gathered in order to adopt more efficient strategies of data partitioning and alignment. This approach is crucial when we cope with parallel computations on distributed memory systems.

Furthermore we plan to use in a compiling approach also the information given by the shape notion of paralation model to produce more efficient data-to-processor mappings. In fact the paralation *shape* is useful when a paralation is modeling a problem in which locality between data values is important.

References

[1] A. Beguelin, J. Dongarra, G. A. Geist, R. Mancheck and V. S. Sunderam. *Pvm and Hence traversing the parallel environment*, Cray Channels, pp. 22-25, 1992.

[2] D. M. Betz, T. Almy et al. *Xlisp-plus: Another Object-oriented Lisp - Version 2.1*, 1992.

[3] M. Bigliardo, C. Di Napoli and M. Mango Furnari. "A Distributed Symbolic System for AI applications", *Proceedings of Euromicro Workshop on Parallel and Distributed Processing*, IEEE Computer Society Press, pp. 544-549, 1993.

[4] R. H. Halstead. "Implementation of MultiLisp: Lisp on a multiprocessor", *Conference Record of the 1984 ACM Symposium on Lisp and Functional Programming*, pp. 9-17, 1984.

[5] R. H. Halstead. "New Ideas in Parallel Lisp: Language design, Implementation, and Programming Tools", *Parallel Lisp Languages and Systems*, ed. R. H. Halstead, LNCS 441, Springer-Verlag, pp. 200-234, 1991.

[6] R. R. Kessler and W. R. Swanson. "Concurrent Scheme", *Lectures Notes in Computer Science*, 441, Springer-Verlag, 1989.

[7] R. P. Gabriel. *Performance and Evaluation of Lisp Systems*, MIT Press, pp. 136-146, 1986.

[8] G. A. Geist, A, Beguelin, J. Dongarra et al. *PVM: Parallel Virtual Machine*, MIT Press, Cambridge, U.S.A., 1994.

[9] G. A. Geist, A. Beguelin et al. "Pvm 3.0 User's Guide and Reference Manual", Mathematical Science Section, Oak Ridge National Laboratory, Oak Ridge, TM-12187.

[10] M. Giordano and M. Mango Furnari. "A Paralation Lisp Environment for the Vision: A guide", TR-4/58, 1992.

[11] R. Goldman and R. P. Gabriel. "QLisp: Experience and New Directions", *ACM Symposium on Parallel Programming: Experience and Applications, Language and Systems*, pp. 111-123, 1988.

[12] S. L. Gray. *Using future to Exploit Parallelism in Lisp*, M.S. Thesis, Dept. of Electrical Engineering and Computer Science, MIT, Cambridge, Mass. USA, 1986.

[13] J. M. Piquer. "Sharing Data Structures in a Distributed Lisp", *High Performance and Parallel Computing in Lisp*, Twickenham, London (UK), EUROPAL workshop, 1990.

[14] G. L. Steele and W. D. Hillis. "Connection Machine Lisp: Fine-Grained Parallel Symbolic Processing", *ACM Conference on LISP and Functional Programming*, pp. 279-297, 1986.

[15] G. W. Sabot. *The Paralation Model: Architecture Independent Parallel Programming*, MIT Press, Cambridge, U.S.A., 1988.

[16] G. W. Sabot. *Introduction to Paralation Lisp*, MIT Press, Cambridge, U.S.A., 1987.

[17] T. Toffoli and N. Margolus. *Cellular Automata Machines: A New Environment for Modelling*, MIT Press, 1987.

Parallelism Extraction in Acyclic Code *

João Paulo Luís
jpsl@inesc.pt

Carlos Gonçalves Carvalho
cgc@inesc.pt

José Carlos Delgado
jcd@inesc.pt

Parallel Architectures Group
INESC
Lisboa, Portugal

Abstract

In this article we describe a framework for parallelism extraction and partitioning in acyclic code regions. This framework is an extension of Milind Girkar's work on functional parallelism, using a Petri net model to represent parallel code, and applying modified optimization techniques to minimize the overheads of explicit synchronization. The modifications introduced are directed towards the generation of efficient multi-threaded code. We also describe a simple partitioning technique that can be used to artificially increase the granularity of the extracted parallelism up to a desired level.

1 Introduction

Most research in parallelizing compilers is directed towards loop parallelisation ([2]), however, non-loop parallelism (sometimes called *functional parallelism*) can be worthy of exploration in some applications ([8]). As this kind of parallelism is usually fine-grained, most work done in this area considers low level mechanisms for efficient scheduling ([12]).

As more operating systems start to support multi-threaded programming models at the application level promising to take advantage of parallel hardware when available (usually when hardware supports symmetric multiprocessing), we have tried to develop a set of algorithms that would allow parallelism extracted from acyclic code regions to be exploited on these systems with adequate granularity.

The framework described here is essentially based on Girkar's work on functional parallelism ([6],[7]). We use a Petri net model to represent parallel code with different optimization techniques to minimize the use of explicit synchronization mechanisms directed towards producing efficient multi-threaded code. The techniques described here can be viewed as separate stages of a larger algorithm for parallelism extraction and partitioning in acyclic code regions.

We introduce the basics of our framework in sections 2 through 4. Section 5 introduces a "code sequencing" optimization technique which is performed before the application of Girkar's algorithm for determining essential data dependences, as described in section 6. Section 7 describes the mechanism used to implement explicit synchronization, and finally, in section 8 we introduce a partitioning algorithm that takes advantage of this framework.

An actual implementation of this algorithm is being used on a paralleliser (see [10] and [3]) for the ANDF (Architecture Neutral Distribution Format) program distribution format (see [11]).

2 Input Data

We extract implicit parallelism from an acyclic code region characterized by a *Control Flow Graph* (CFG) and a *Data Dependence Graph* (DDG). We shall explain some details of the algorithm through the use of an example. Figure 1(a) and 1(b) show the CFG and DDG used in this example.

2.1 Control Flow Graph

The CFG of an acyclic code region is an acyclic directed graph defined by a set of vertices V_{CFG} and a set of directed edges E_{CFG}. There are two unique vertices $Entry, eXit \in V_{CFG}$ such that all vertices are *reachable* from $Entry$ and $eXit$ is reachable from all vertices. We say that a vertex j is *reachable* from a vertex i if there is a non-null path from i to j or if $i = j$.

$$CFG = \langle V_{CFG}, E_{CFG} \rangle$$

$$V_{CFG} = \{Entry, 1, 2, 3, ..., n, eXit\}$$

$$E_{CFG} = \{\langle i, j \rangle \mid \text{there is an edge from } i \text{ to} j\}$$

We identify each vertex by an integer number. The numbering order is calculated such that for any pair of vertices $\langle i, j \rangle$, if $i < j$ (where "<" is the usual total ordering *less-than* relation) then the execution of i always precedes the execution of j for all possible sequential executions of the CFG where both i and j are executed. Note that there may be more then one possible numbering order that will satisfy this condition.

2.2 Data Dependence Graph

The DDG is also an acyclic directed graph defined as follows:

$$DDG = \langle V_{DDG}, E_{DDG} \rangle$$

$$V_{DDG} = V_{CFG}$$

*This work was partially supported by ESPRIT Project OMI/GLUE 6062.

1066-6192/96 $5.00 © 1996 IEEE
Proceedings of PDP '96

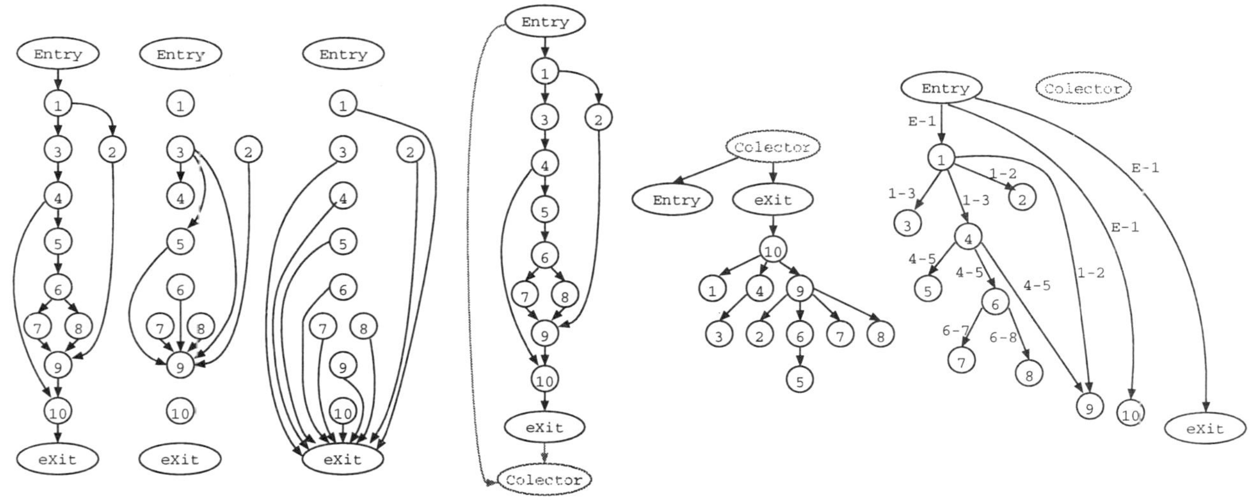

(a) CFG (b) DDG (c) Artificial data dependences to add to the DDG (d) CFG modified for building the CDG (e) Post-Dominance Tree (f) CDG

Figure 1: Graphs used by the algorithm

$$E_{DDG} = \{\langle i, j\rangle \mid i\,\delta_d\, j\}$$

We write $i\,\delta_d\,j$ to say that vertex j is data dependent on vertex i. In this framework, $i\,\delta_d\,j$ only exists if $i \neq j$, j is reachable from i, and the code represented by these vertices has a memory conflict. A memory conflict occurs when two blocks of code access a common memory location with at least one access modifying it.[1] Note that if j is not reachable from i (on the CFG) then there **must not** be any edge from i to j on the DDG. Any memory conflicts will not matter as i and j will never be executed together.

2.3 Artificial Data Dependences

The *Entry* and *eXit* vertices have the particular role of delimiting the parallel execution of this block of code. This is useful when decomposing a parallel program into hierarchical code regions, so that each code region can have a single entry and a single exit point for control flow.

This stage will introduce an artificial set of dependences to force the algorithm to produce a parallel solution where the *eXit* vertex will be the last one to be executed (after all other vertices have finished execution). If this is not needed, then this preprocessing step can be dropped.

The *eXit* vertex is artificially considered data dependent on all other vertices (with the exception of *Entry* and itself). Figure 1(c) represents these artificial dependences.

$$\forall x \in (V_{DDG} \setminus \{Entry, eXit\}),\; x\,\delta_d\, eXit$$

[1] Other algorithms (such as memory renaming) can be applied to minimize memory conflicts before extracting parallelism.

3 Control Dependence

We say that j *post-dominates* i if every path on the CFG from i to $eXit$ (not including i) contains j. Note that a vertex does not post-dominates itself. The *post-dominance* relation can be represented by a tree where an edge from the parent vertex j to a child vertex i indicates that j post-dominates i and there is no other vertex that post-dominates i that doesn't post-dominates j also (j is called the *immediate post-dominator* of i). Figure 1(e) shows the *post-dominance tree* for the modified CFG of figure 1(d) in this example.[2]

We say that a vertex j is control dependent on a vertex i with label $i-k$ if j does not post-dominates i and there is a non-null path from i to j such that j post-dominates all the vertices on that path excluding i and j.

We will represent the control dependence relation using a *Control Dependence Graph* (CDG). We write $j\,\delta_c\,i$ with label $i-k$ to indicate that j is control dependent on i with label $i-k$:

$$CDG = \langle V_{CDG}, E_{CDG}\rangle$$

$$V_{CDG} = V_{CFG}$$

$$E_{CDG} = \{\langle i, j\rangle \mid j\,\delta_c\, i\}$$

We use the algorithm of figure 2 to build the CDG.

Before building the post-dominance tree and the CDG, a temporary modification is made to the CFG. The *Colector* vertex and the edge $\langle Entry, Colector\rangle$

[2] An efficient algorithm for building a *dominance tree* from a CFG is presented in [9]. The post-dominance tree can be obtained using the same algorithm by reversing the edges of the CFG and exchanging the roles of the *Entry* and *eXit* vertices.

```
1 FORALL edges in the CFG, ⟨i,j⟩ ∈ E_CFG DO:
2   IF j is an ancestor of i in the post-dominance
    tree THEN
3     this edge of the CFG does not introduce any
      control dependences.
4   ELSE
3     all vertices in the only possible path on the
      post-dominance tree from the parent of i to
      j are control dependent on i (including j and
      excluding i itself) with label i − j.
```

Figure 2: Algorithm used to build the labelled *CDG*

are artificially added to the *CFG* (as shown in figure 1(d)) so that the *CDG* will have all vertices (excluding *Colector*) transitively control dependent on *Entry*. Assuring that all vertices are transitively control dependent on the *Entry* vertex will assure that the execution of *Entry* will precede the execution of the other vertices. This artificial vertex and edge **will be ignored** for all purposes other than the building of the *CDG*.

Figure 1(d), 1(e) and 1(f) show the modified *CFG*, the post-dominance tree, and the *CDG* for this example.

3.1 Upper Limit for Parallelism

The *CDG* is used as the basis for parallelism extraction. In the absence of data dependences, the information contained in the *CDG* can be used for scheduling the code in a parallel execution using the scheduling algorithm described in figure 3.

```
1 Every vertex that is not control dependent on
  another vertex begins execution.
2 DO FOREVER:
3   When a vertex finishes execution, all vertices
    control dependent on that vertex with the la-
    bel corresponding to the branch that would
    have been taken in the CFG begin execution.
```

Figure 3: Scheduling code for parallel execution based on the *CDG*

In this example, step 1 of this scheduling algorithm will start the execution only of the *Entry* vertex (due to the use of the artificial edge $\langle Entry, Colector\rangle$ when building the *CDG*). When *Entry* finishes executing, vertex 1 and 10 start executing. When vertex 1 finishes execution, if the branch 1→2 is taken, then the vertices 2 and 9 begin executing in parallel, otherwise if the branch 1→3 is taken, then vertices 3 and 4 begin executing in parallel and so on...

The algorithm described in this section executes the same vertices that would have been executed on an equivalent sequential execution of the *CFG*. This is demonstrated in [6].

4 Petri Net Representation

Formally, the Petri net (which we call R) is composed of a set of places P, a set of transitions T, an input function I and an output function O:

$$R = \langle P, T, I, O\rangle$$

The set of places P is in direct correspondence with the set of vertices and the set of transitions T is in direct correspondence with the set of edges in the *CFG*. For this example we have:[3]:

$$\begin{aligned} P &= \{p_E, p_1, p_2, p_3, p_4, p_5, p_6, p_7, p_8, p_9, p_{10}, p_X\} \\ T &= \{t_{E-1}, t_{1-2}, t_{1-3}, t_{2-9}, t_{3-4}, t_{4-5}, t_{4-10}, \\ &\quad t_{5-6}, t_{6-7}, t_{6-8}, t_{7-9}, t_{8-9}, t_{9-10}, t_{10-X}\} \end{aligned}$$

The topology of the net is defined by the input and output functions (I and O respectively).

4.1 Initial Net Topology

Initially the Petri net topology is built to model the parallel execution of the code as described previously in section 3.1.

The function O maps every place p_i on to the set of its output transitions, $O : P \rightarrow T$. Its initial mapping is obtained from set of transitions corresponding to the outgoing edges of vertex i in the *CFG*.

$$O(p_i) = \{t_{i-j} \mid \langle i,j\rangle \in E_{GFC}\}$$

The function O also maps every transition t_{i-j} on to the set of its output places, $O : T \rightarrow P$. Initially, this is the set of of places that correspond to the vertices that have at least one incoming edge in the *CDG* labelled with the branch $i - j$.

$$O(t_{i-j}) = \{p_k \mid \langle i,k\rangle \in E_{CDG} \text{ with label } i - j\}$$

The function I maps every place on to the set of its input transitions, $I : P \rightarrow T$, and every transition on to the set of its input places, $I : T \rightarrow P$. As the function I provides redundant information, we will just define it using function O.

$$I(p_i) = \{t_{j-k} \mid p_i \in O(t_{j-k})\}$$

$$I(t_{i-j}) = \{p_k \mid t_{i-j} \in O(p_k)\}$$

For this example, the initial net topology can be defined by table 1. The net can be represented graphically as shown in figure 4.

4.2 Marking and Evolution

The parallel execution in the Petri net model is initiated by depositing a mark in the p_E place. At any time, to say that a place is marked is equivalent to say that the correspondent block of code is being executed. We say for short that the place is being executed. When a place finishes execution, only one output transition of that place will fire depending on which control flow path is chosen. For example, after the execution of p_1, transition t_{1-2} fires if the branch 1→2 is taken in an equivalent sequential execution of

[3]We have abbreviated the *Entry* and *eXit* vertex names to E and X respectively when talking about Petri net places, so p_E is the place that corresponds to the *Entry* vertex and p_X is the place that corresponds to the *eXit* vertex.

p_i	$O(p_i)$	$I(p_i)$
p_E	$\{t_{E-1}\}$	$\{\}$
p_1	$\{t_{1-2}, t_{1-3}\}$	$\{t_{E-1}\}$
p_2	$\{t_{2-9}\}$	$\{t_{1-2}\}$
p_3	$\{t_{3-4}\}$	$\{t_{1-3}\}$
p_4	$\{t_{4-5}, t_{4-10}\}$	$\{t_{1-3}\}$
p_5	$\{t_{5-6}\}$	$\{t_{4-5}\}$
p_6	$\{t_{6-7}, t_{6-8}\}$	$\{t_{4-5}\}$
p_7	$\{t_{7-9}\}$	$\{t_{6-7}\}$
p_8	$\{t_{8-9}\}$	$\{t_{6-8}\}$
p_9	$\{t_{9-10}\}$	$\{t_{1-2}, t_{4-5}\}$
p_{10}	$\{t_{10-X}\}$	$\{t_{E-1}\}$
p_X	$\{\}$	$\{t_{E-1}\}$

(a)

t_{i-j}	$O(t_{i-j})$	$I(t_{i-j})$
t_{E-1}	$\{p_1, p_{10}, p_X\}$	$\{p_E\}$
t_{1-2}	$\{p_2, p_9\}$	$\{p_1\}$
t_{1-3}	$\{p_3, p_4\}$	$\{p_1\}$
t_{2-9}	$\{\}$	$\{p_2\}$
t_{3-4}	$\{\}$	$\{p_3\}$
t_{4-5}	$\{p_5, p_6, p_9\}$	$\{p_4\}$
t_{4-10}	$\{\}$	$\{p_4\}$
t_{5-6}	$\{\}$	$\{p_5\}$
t_{6-7}	$\{p_7\}$	$\{p_6\}$
t_{6-8}	$\{p_8\}$	$\{p_6\}$
t_{7-9}	$\{\}$	$\{p_7\}$
t_{8-9}	$\{\}$	$\{p_8\}$
t_{9-10}	$\{\}$	$\{p_9\}$
t_{10-X}	$\{\}$	$\{p_{10}\}$

(b)

Table 1: Net topology

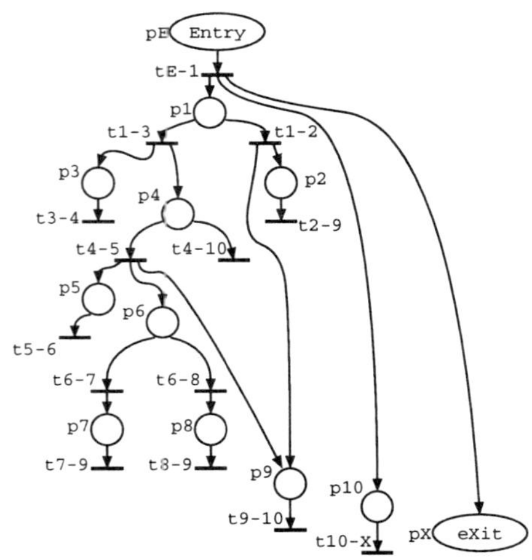

Figure 4: The Petri net R represented graphically

the CFG. When a transition fires, a mark is removed from each one of its input places, and a mark is deposited in each one of its output places.

Given that the Petri net models the parallel execution of the acyclic code based on control dependences and due to the properties of acyclic CFGs and derived CDGs (see [4] and [6]), the Petri nets used by this algorithm present a number of properties. The net is 1-safe (ie. there will be at most one mark on any place in the net at any time). During a parallel execution every transition fires at most once, every place will not be executed more than once and the parallel execution always finishes with a single mark deposited in p_X which has no output transitions (as the sequential execution always finishes in the *eXit* vertex). The Petri net doesn't have any transitions with multiple input places (ie. it doesn't contain any `joins`, just **`forks`**). There are no arcs in the net with multiplicity greater than 1 (ie. for any pair $\langle$transition, place$\rangle$ or $\langle$place, transition$\rangle$ there is at most one arc connecting them, which is enforced by the definition of the O function as a *set* and not as a *collection* as usual).

Care is taken to ensure that these properties will be preserved during the optimization stages, where the net topology will be changed.

4.3 Topological Information

The *reachability* notion that we have defined for directed graphs in section 2.1 cannot be extended in general for Petri nets, but given the specific properties of the net used by this algorithm, specifically the one that states that every transition in the net has no more than one incoming arc (only `forks`, no `joins`), we can provide a recursive definition for a function that we call $REACH_p$ based on the net topology:

$$REACH_p : P \cup T \rightarrow 2^P$$

$$REACH_p(p_i) = \{p_i\} \cup \left(\bigcup_{t_{i-j} \in O(p_i)} REACH_p(t_{i-j})\right)$$
$$REACH_p(t_{i-j}) = \bigcup_{p_k \in O(t_{i-j})} REACH_p(p_k)$$

For the initial net topology in this example, this function would perform the mapping defined in table 2. Note that (for this initial net topology), $REACH_p(p_i)$ gives the set of places that represent the vertices on the CDG reachable from vertex i, and $REACH_p(t_{i-j})$ gives the set of places that represent the vertices reachable on the CDG from the edge with label $i-j$.

Examining the CFG we find that (for all possible sequential executions) when some branches are taken, there are some vertices that definitely won't be executed. For example, when branch $1 \rightarrow 2$ is taken we know that vertex 3 won't get to be executed. Adapting this concept to the Petri net (for all possible parallel executions), we define the NEG_p function to map every place p_i in the net to the set of transitions that when fired avoid the execution of p_i definitely.

$$NEG_p : P \rightarrow 2^T$$

$$NEG_p(p_i) = \{t_{j-k} \mid \; p_i \neq p_j \wedge p_i \in REACH_p(p_j) \wedge p_i \notin REACH_p(t_{j-k})\}$$

p_i	$REACH_p(p_i)$
p_E	$\{p_E, p_1, p_2, p_3, p_4, p_5, p_6, p_7, p_8, p_9, p_{10}, p_X\}$
p_1	$\{p_1, p_2, p_3, p_4, p_5, p_6, p_7, p_8, p_9\}$
p_2	$\{p_2\}$
p_3	$\{p_3\}$
p_4	$\{p_4, p_5, p_6, p_7, p_8, p_9\}$
p_5	$\{p_5\}$
p_6	$\{p_6, p_7, p_8\}$
p_7	$\{p_7\}$
p_8	$\{p_8\}$
p_9	$\{p_9\}$
p_{10}	$\{p_{10}\}$
p_X	$\{p_X\}$

(a)

t_{i-j}	$REACH_p(t_{i-j})$
t_{E-1}	$\{p_1, p_2, p_3, p_4, p_5, p_6, p_7, p_8, p_9, p_{10}, p_X\}$
t_{1-2}	$\{p_2, p_9\}$
t_{1-3}	$\{p_3, p_4, p_5, p_6, p_7, p_8, p_9\}$
t_{2-9}	$\{\}$
t_{3-4}	$\{\}$
t_{4-5}	$\{p_5, p_6, p_7, p_8, p_9\}$
t_{4-10}	$\{\}$
t_{5-6}	$\{\}$
t_{6-7}	$\{p_7\}$
t_{6-8}	$\{p_8\}$
t_{7-9}	$\{\}$
t_{8-9}	$\{\}$
t_{9-10}	$\{\}$
t_{10-X}	$\{\}$

(b)

Table 2: $REACH_p$ for the initial net topology

(Note that t_{j-k} is an output transition from p_j). Table 3 shows the NEG_p function for this example.

This means that during any parallel execution if p_i is not to be executed, there will be one (and just one) transition in $NEG_p(p_i)$ that fires. Otherwise p_i is executed and no transition in $NEG(p_i)$ fires:[4]

$$\forall p_i \in P,$$
$$(\exists^1 t_{j-k} \in NEG_p(p_i) \mid t_{j-k} \text{ fires}) \dot{\vee} (p_i \text{ is executed})$$

This property is demonstrated in [6] for Girkar's framework based on the CFG and CDG properties for acyclic code. This demonstration is valid in this framework for the Petri net built from the CDG as described in section 4.1. As the topology of the net will be changed during the optimization stage, care has been taken in order to preserve this property.

4.4 Execution Precedence

Let i and j be any two vertices in the CFG, which are in direct correspondence with places p_i and p_j on the net. We use $j \prec i$ to denote that p_j finishes execution before p_i begins, in all possible parallel executions

[4] Note that the "$\dot{\vee}$" denotes the logical *exclusive-or* operation, and "$\exists^1$" means "exists one and just one".

p_i	$NEG_p(p_i)$
p_E	$\{\}$
p_1	$\{\}$
p_2	$\{t_{1-3}\}$
p_3	$\{t_{1-2}\}$
p_4	$\{t_{1-2}\}$
p_5	$\{t_{1-2}, t_{4-10}\}$
p_6	$\{t_{1-2}, t_{4-10}\}$
p_7	$\{t_{1-2}, t_{4-10}, t_{6-8}\}$
p_8	$\{t_{1-2}, t_{4-10}, t_{6-7}\}$
p_9	$\{t_{4-10}\}$
p_{10}	$\{\}$
p_X	$\{\}$

Table 3: NEG_p

in which both places p_j and p_i are executed. The function $PREC$ will be used to map a place p_i onto the set of places that are *known* to precede the execution p_i:

$$PREC : P \rightarrow 2^P$$

$$p_j \in PREC(p_i) \Rightarrow \text{we know that } j \prec i$$

Given the algorithm for parallel execution of the CDG as modeled by the Petri net, it can be demonstrated that[5]:

$$p_i \in REACH_p(p_j) \Rightarrow j \preceq i$$

This equivalence can be used to build the $PREC$ table as:

$$PREC(p_i) = \{p_j \mid p_i \in REACH_p(p_j) \wedge p_i \neq p_j\}$$

Table 4 shows the $PREC$ function resulting from the net in figure 4. This precedence relationship satisfies control dependence constraints only.

p_i	$PREC(p_i)$
p_E	$\{\}$
p_1	$\{p_E\}$
p_2	$\{p_E, p_1\}$
p_3	$\{p_E, p_1\}$
p_4	$\{p_E, p_1\}$
p_5	$\{p_E, p_1, p_4\}$
p_6	$\{p_E, p_1, p_4\}$
p_7	$\{p_E, p_1, p_4, p_6\}$
p_8	$\{p_E, p_1, p_4, p_6\}$
p_9	$\{p_E, p_1, p_4\}$
p_{10}	$\{p_E\}$
p_X	$\{p_E\}$

Table 4: Initial precedence "$\prec$" relationship

5 Sequencing Code

The existing net executes code satisfying control dependence constraints (ie, only the places that would be executed in an equivalent sequential execution of

[5] $i \preceq j$ if $i \prec j \vee i = j$

the CFG are executed). Additionally, every data dependence $y \, \delta_d \, x$ constraints the execution of p_x to start only after the execution of p_y (if p_y is executed).

In this stage, an optimization algorithm will attempt to sequence code without loss of implicit parallelism to satisfy data dependences (and thus avoiding the use of explicit synchronization mechanisms whenever possible). The precedence relationship table will be used to check if a given data dependence is already enforced by the net topology or if it needs to be enforced in some other way.

The optimization algorithm is shown in figure 5. Figure 6 illustrates the incremental changes that the algorithm performs on the net as it handles data dependences on DDG. (Dashed arcs represent annotated data dependences that might have to be enforced by explicit synchronization.) Table 5 shows the precedence relationship that results from this optimization.

p_i	$PREC(p_i)$
p_E	$\{\}$
p_1	$\{p_E\}$
p_2	$\{p_E, p_1\}$
p_3	$\{p_E, p_1\}$
p_4	$\{p_E, p_1, p_3\}$
p_5	$\{p_E, p_1, p_3, p_4\}$
p_6	$\{p_E, p_1, p_3, p_4\}$
p_7	$\{p_E, p_1, p_3, p_4, p_6\}$
p_8	$\{p_E, p_1, p_3, p_4, p_6\}$
p_9	$\{p_E, p_1, p_2, p_3, p_4, p_6, p_7, p_8\}$
p_{10}	$\{p_E\}$
p_X	$\{p_E, p_{10}\}$

Table 5: $PREC$ table after code sequencing

6 Determining Essential Dependences

After sequencing code, unsatisfied data dependences will have to be enforced by explicit synchronization, but by doing so for some data dependences, other data dependences may be indirectly satisfied (thus avoiding the need for more explicit synchronization mechanisms).

Figure 7 presents Girkar's algorithm (modified to suit our framework) for determining which dependences are to be satisfied by explicit synchronization (called "essential dependences"). We annotate the *essential dependences* found by this algorithm in the $SYNCH$ set:

$$SYNCH = \{\langle p_j, p_i \rangle \mid j \, \delta_d \, i \text{ is essential}\}$$

Girkar's algorithm steps through all pairs of places in the net that can be both executed in a parallel execution, determining the actual enforced precedence relationships, and adding all unsatisfied data dependences to the $SYNCH$ set.

Figure 8(a) shows the final annotated net, while table 6 shows the final precedence relationship.

7 Explicit Synchronization Mechanism

Considering any data dependence $i \, \delta_d \, j$ (j is data dependent on i) the execution of p_i must finish before

p_i	$PREC(p_i)$
p_E	$\{\}$
p_1	$\{p_E\}$
p_2	$\{p_E, p_1\}$
p_3	$\{p_E, p_1\}$
p_4	$\{p_E, p_1, p_3\}$
p_5	$\{p_E, p_1, p_3, p_4\}$
p_6	$\{p_E, p_1, p_3, p_4\}$
p_7	$\{p_E, p_1, p_3, p_4, p_6\}$
p_8	$\{p_E, p_1, p_3, p_4, p_6\}$
p_9	$\{p_E, p_1, p_2, p_3, p_4, p_5, p_6, p_7, p_8\}$
p_{10}	$\{p_E\}$
p_X	$\{p_E, p_1, p_2, p_3, p_4, p_5, p_6, p_7, p_8, p_9, p_{10}\}$

Table 6: Final $PREC$ table

p_j begins to execute in order to satisfy the dependence. If only data dependences were to be considered and if it was assumed that both p_i and p_j would always be both executed, it would suffice to have p_j to wait for p_i to finish executing. As control dependences are also considered, every time that p_j is going to be executed this wait must terminate if it is known that p_i will not be executed.

When any of the output transitions of p_i fires, we know that p_i has finished executing. When any of the transitions of $NEG_p(p_i)$ fires, we know that p_i will not be executed. Given this, we can define a function DDC that maps every place p_i on to a set of transitions that, when any one of them fires it is known that p_i has finished execution or that p_i will not be executed:

$$DDC : P \rightarrow 2^T$$

$$DDC(p_i) = O(p_i) \bigcup NEG_p(p_i)$$

Table 7 defines DDC for the current example.

p_i	$DDC_p(p_i)$
p_E	$\{t_{E-1}\}$
p_1	$\{t_{1-3}, t_{1-2}\}$
p_2	$\{t_{2-9}, t_{1-3}\}$
p_3	$\{t_{3-4}, t_{1-2}\}$
p_4	$\{t_{4-5}, t_{4-10}, t_{1-2}\}$
p_5	$\{t_{5-6}, t_{1-2}, t_{4-10}\}$
p_6	$\{t_{6-7}, t_{6-8}, t_{1-2}, t_{4-10}\}$
p_7	$\{t_{7-9}, t_{1-2}, t_{4-10}, t_{6-8}\}$
p_8	$\{t_{8-9}, t_{1-2}, t_{4-10}, t_{6-7}\}$
p_9	$\{t_{9-10}, t_{4-10}\}$
p_{10}	$\{\}$
p_X	$\{\}$

Table 7: DDC function tabled for the current example

For every place p_i such that there is at least one annotation $\langle p_j, p_i \rangle \in SYNCH$ we use Girkar's method to determine a boolean expression that evaluates to *true* when all conditions are met for p_i to start execution:[6]

[6]In this boolean expression, net transitions are treated as boolean variables that become *true* after firing.

```
FOR x = Entry, 1, 2, ..., eXit DO:
  FOR y = x − 1, x − 2, ..., Entry DO:
    IF y δ_d x THEN
      /* this dependence will fall within one of the following three possibilities: */
      IF p_x ∈ REACH_p(p_y) THEN
        /* This data dependence is already satisfied due to control dependences or to previous code sequencing. Do nothing. */
      ELSE IF ∃t_{i-j} | t_{i-j} ∈ I(p_x) ∧ p_y ∈ REACH_p(t_{i-j}) THEN
        /* it is possible to solve this dependence by sequencing code. */
        FORALL t_{i-j} | t_{i-j} ∈ I(p_x) ∧ p_y ∈ REACH_p(t_{i-j}) DO:
          CALL Delay(t_{i-j})
      ELSE
        /* This data dependence might have to be satisfied by explicit synchronization. Leave it for the next stage. */
```

```
PROCEDURE Delay(t_{i-j})
  IF t_{i-j} ∉ NEG_p(p_y) THEN
    Remove the arc connecting t_{i-j} to p_x.
    /* There exists one (and just one) exit place from t_{i-j} (let it be called p_z) from where p_y is reachable. Find that unique p_z. */
    ∃¹p_z | p_z ∈ O(t_{i-j}) ∧ p_y ∈ REACH_p(p_z)
    FORALL t_{z-k} | t_{z-k} ∈ O(p_z) DO:
      IF t_{z-k} is not yet connected to p_x THEN
        Connect t_{z-k} to p_x.
    IF p_z ≠ p_y THEN
      FORALL t_{z-k} | t_{z-k} ∈ O(p_z) DO:
        CALL Delay(t_{z-k})
```

Figure 5: Algorithm for sequencing code

$$\left(\bigvee_{t_{k-l}\in I(p_i)} t_{k-l}\right) \wedge \left[\bigwedge_{\langle p_j,p_i\rangle\in SYNCH} \left(\bigvee_{t_{m-n}\in(DDC(p_j)\setminus NEG_p(p_i))} t_{m-n}\right)\right]$$

For this example, the $SYNCH$ set is:

$$SYNCH = \{\langle p_5, p_9\rangle, \langle p_9, p_X\rangle\}$$

The resulting expressions for p_9 and p_X are shown in table 8.

p_i	Execution conditions for p_i
p_9	$(t_{2-9} \vee t_{7-9} \vee t_{8-9}) \wedge [(t_{5-6} \vee t_{1-2})]$
p_X	$(t_{10-X}) \wedge [(t_{9-10} \vee t_{4-10})]$

Table 8: Execution conditions for places dependent on explicit synchronization

An explicit synchronization mechanism like the one illustrated in figure 9 can be used to implement the necessary synchronization for dependent places. The resulting net (from replacing the input arcs of the dependent places by the explicit synchronization mechanism) is shown in figure 8(b). We designate the explicit synchronization mechanisms by *synchronization variables*, and we refer to them as s_9 and s_X in this example.

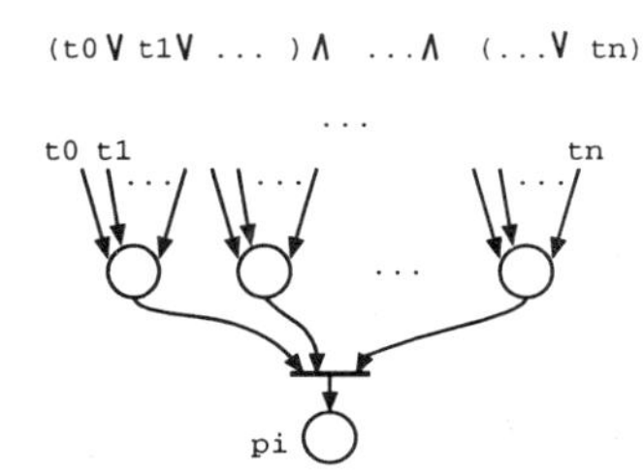

Figure 9: An explicit synchronization mechanism with its associated boolean expression.

Note that after placing the synchronization variables on the net, the conditions for the definition of the function $REACH_p$ (and any other function defined in terms of $REACH_p$) will **no longer be valid**. For this reason, its placement on the net is delayed until the optimizations based on such functions are finished.

In the code generated, we have implemented a synchronization variable as a counter that is initialized to zero and is incremented by one every time a mark is deposited in any place inside the variable. When the counter reaches the number of places inside that variable, the place dependent on it begins execution.

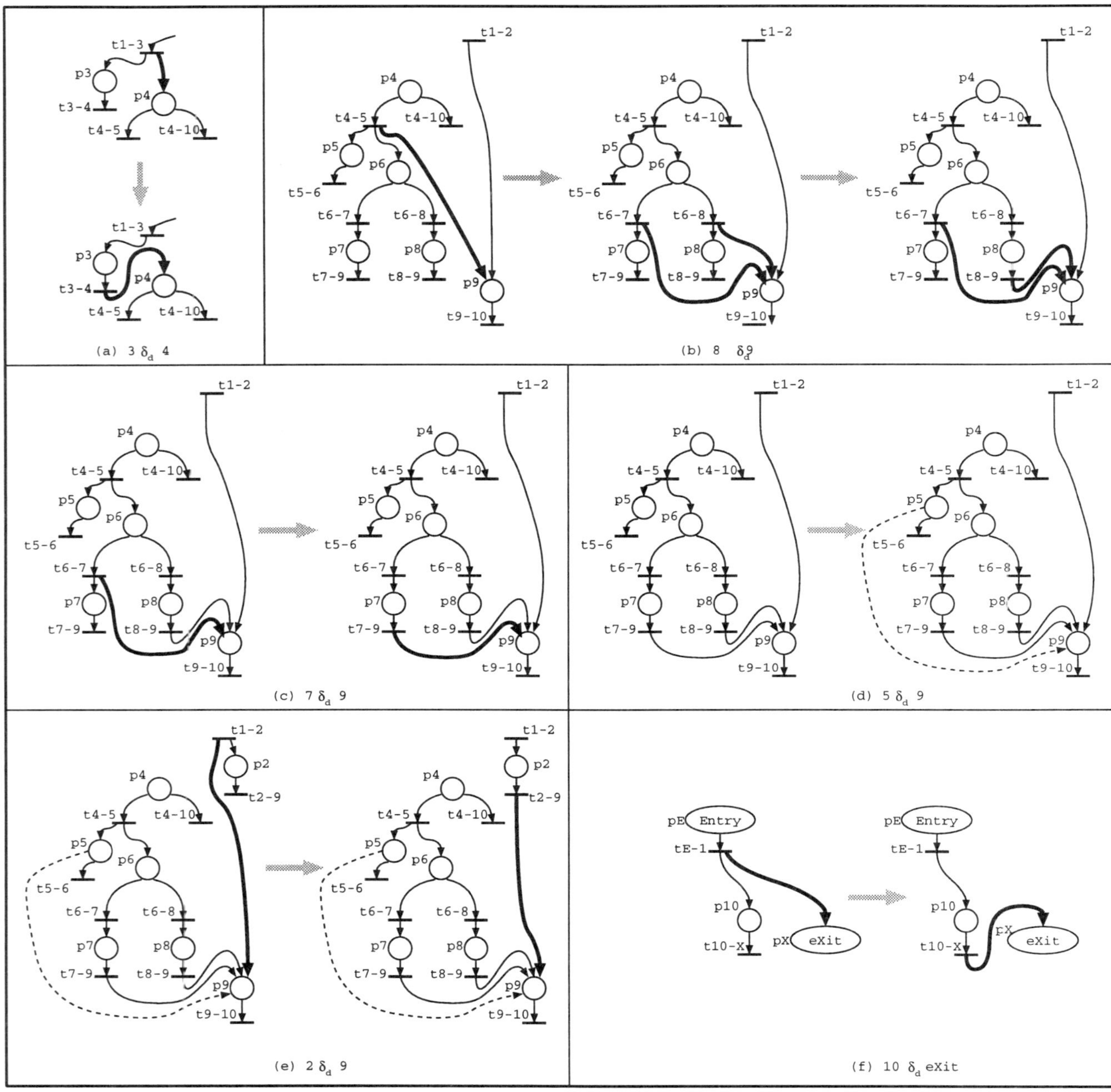

Figure 6: Minimizing the need for explicit synchronization by sequencing code

$SYNCH = \{\}$
FOR $x = Entry, 1, 2, ..., eXit$ **DO:**
  FOR $y = x-1, x-2, ..., Entry$ **DO:**
    IF x is reachable from y in the CFG **THEN**
      IF NOT cont_path(p_y, p_y, p_x) **THEN**
        /* All paths from y to x on the CFG have at least one vertex z such that $p_y \in PREC(p_z) \wedge p_z \in PREC(p_x)$. This assures us that p_y precedes p_x. */
        FORALL $p_t \mid p_x \in REACH_p(p_t)$ **DO:**
          Add p_t to $PREC(p_x)$
      IF $y\, \delta_d\, x \wedge p_y \notin PREC(p_x)$ **THEN**
        /* $y\, \delta_d\, x$ is an essential dependence that must be enforced by the use of explicit synchronization */
        Add $\langle p_y, p_x \rangle$ to $SYNCH$
        FORALL $p_t \mid p_x \in REACH_p(p_t)$ **DO:**
          Add p_t to $PREC(p_x)$

FUNCTION cont_path (z)
/* There is a path from y tc z on the CFG. Returns True if there is at least one path from z to x on the CFG such that there is no vertex s on that path for which $p_y \in PREC(p_s) \wedge p_s \in PREC(p_x)$ */
IF p_z has been visited before for the current $\langle y, x \rangle$ pair **THEN RETURN** False
IF $p_y \in PREC(p_z) \wedge p_z \in PRECENDENTS(p_x)$ **THEN RETURN** False
IF $p_z = p_x$ **THEN RETURN** True
FORALL $p_t \mid \langle z, t \rangle \in E_{CFG}$ **DO:**
  IF cont_path(p_y, p_t, p_x) **THEN RETURN** True
RETURN False

Figure 7: Girkar's Algorithm for detecting essential dependences

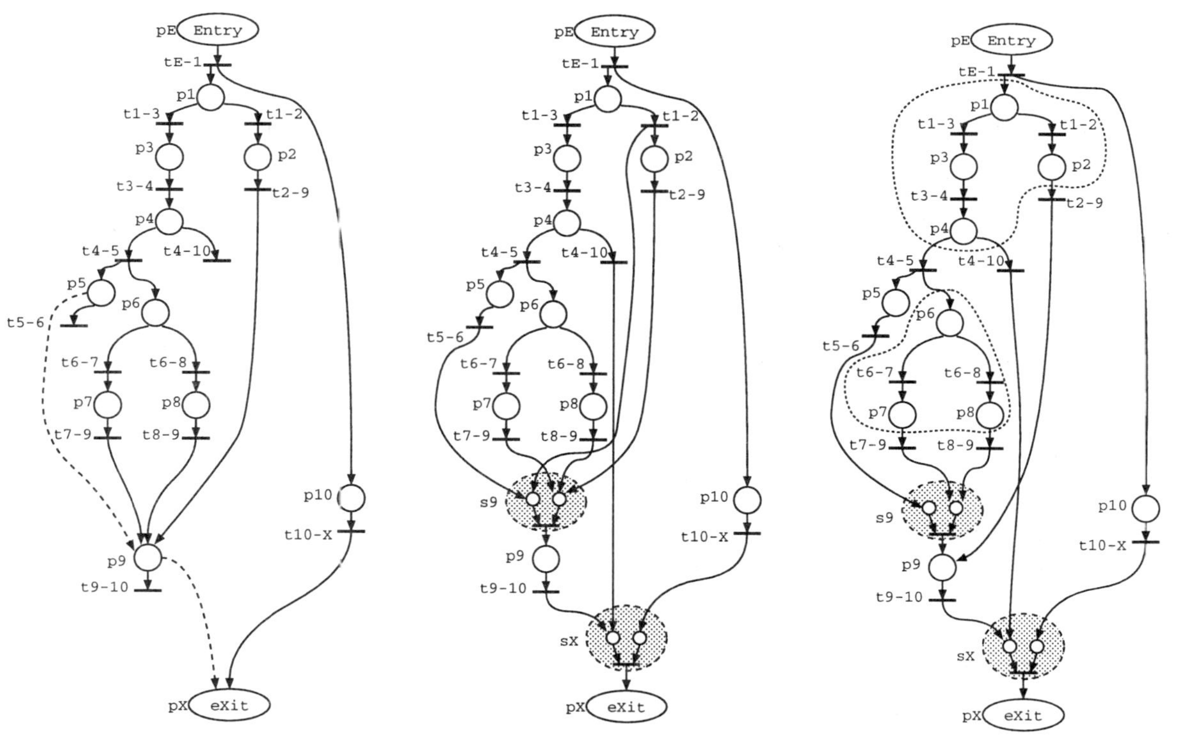

(a) Final annotated net

(b) Explicit snychronization variables added to the net

(c) Optimized for multi-threaded code generation

Figure 8: Output net

This approach is also described in [5].[7] The necessary code to atomically increment and test, and start the execution of the dependent place if necessary, is generated for every transition in the net that is linked to a synchronization variable.

To minimize updates to synchronization variables we define the IMP_t function for the annotated net (as in figure 8(a)) recursively as follows:

$$IMP_t : P \cup T \rightarrow 2^T$$

$$IMP_t(p_i) = \bigcap_{t_{i-j} \in O(p_i)} IMP_t(t_{i-j})$$
$$IMP_t(t_{i-j}) = \{t_{i-j}\} \cup \left(\bigcup_{p_k \in O(t_{i-j})} IMP_t(p_k)\right)$$

$IMP_p(p_i)$ gives the set of transitions that will surely fire after p_i is executed. $IMP_p(t_{i-j})$ gives the set of transitions that will surely fire after t_{i-j} fires (including t_{i-j} itself). Table 9 shows the IMP_t function for this example.

p_i	$IMP_t(p_i)$
p_E	$\{t_{E-1}, t_{10-X}\}$
p_1	$\{\}$
p_2	$\{t_{2-9}, t_{9-10}\}$
p_3	$\{t_{3-4}\}$
p_4	$\{\}$
p_5	$\{t_{5-6}\}$
p_6	$\{t_{9-10}\}$
p_7	$\{t_{7-9}, t_{9-10}\}$
p_8	$\{t_{8-9}, t_{9-10}\}$
p_9	$\{t_{9-10}\}$
p_{10}	$\{t_{10-X}\}$
p_X	$\{\}$

t_{i-j}	$IMP_t(t_{i-j})$
t_{E-1}	$\{t_{E-1}, t_{10-X}\}$
t_{1-2}	$\{t_{1-2}, t_{2-9}, t_{9-10}\}$
t_{1-3}	$\{t_{1-3}, t_{3-4}\}$
t_{2-9}	$\{t_{2-9}, t_{9-10}\}$
t_{3-4}	$\{t_{3-4}\}$
t_{4-5}	$\{t_{4-5}, t_{5-6}, t_{9-10}\}$
t_{4-10}	$\{t_{4-10}\}$
t_{5-6}	$\{t_{5-6}\}$
t_{6-7}	$\{t_{6-7}, t_{7-9}, t_{9-10}\}$
t_{6-8}	$\{t_{6-8}, t_{8-9}, t_{9-10}\}$
t_{7-9}	$\{t_{7-9}, t_{9-10}\}$
t_{8-9}	$\{t_{8-9}, t_{9-10}\}$
t_{9-10}	$\{t_{9-10}\}$
t_{10-X}	$\{t_{10-X}\}$

Table 9: IMP_t function tabled for the current example

With this information, when calculating the expression of explicit synchronization for a place p_i from the set of its annotated data dependences we can substitute any transition t_{m-n} from $(DDC(p_j) \backslash NEG_p(p_i))$ by a transition from $IMP_t(t_{m-n})$ whenever this allows any simplification.

In this example, when calculating the synchronization expression for p_9 we know that t_{1-2} from $(DDC(p_5) \setminus NEG_p(p_9))$ can be substituted by t_{2-9}. This allows the application of usual algebraic simplification rules to simplify the expression from:

$$(t_{2-9} \vee t_{7-9} \vee t_{8-9}) \wedge [(t_{5-6} \vee t_{1-2})]$$

to:

$$t_{2-9} \vee [(t_{7-9} \vee t_{8-9}) \wedge [(t_{5-6})]]$$

Figure 8(c) illustrates the net with synchronization variables placed after this optimization.

[7] Other approaches are also described in [12], but are, in our opinion, less efficient for implementation on conventional multithreaded systems.

8 Partitioning

The first step in partitioning consists in identifying sequential code in the net. This can be done by a trivial algorithm (such as one described in [10]) that gathers places into sequential regions. The net in figure 8(c) identifies sequential regions composed of more than one place by delimiting them with a dashed line. These regions can be replaced on the net by a single equivalent place.

Typically, as more data dependences are present in the input data, larger regions of sequential code are produced. By observing this property the following empiric partitioning algorithm was designed for use when the execution time of a sequential region (including the execution time of its output transitions) can be estimated relatively to the cost of thread management operations: The partitioning algorithm tries to find sequential regions that have an estimated execution time too small to justify its parallel execution. If such regions are found, artificial data dependences are introduced between those regions and other regions that are started in parallel with them. The parallelism extraction and optimization stages are then re-executed to produce a new solution with less parallel code.

In this example, if we consider that the sequential region $\{p_5\}$ has an estimated execution time that is too small to justify the cost of having t_{4-5} creating a new thread for executing $\{p_5\}$ or $\{p_6, p_7, p_8\}$, then the partitioning algorithm introduces artificial data dependences between $\{p_5\}$ and other regions potentially started by t_{4-5} ($\{p_6, p_7, p_8\}$ in this example, and always respecting that a data dependence $i\, \delta_d\, j$ is only meaningful if j is reachable from i on the CFG) and re-executes the parallelism extraction stages. Figure 10(a) illustrates the artificially introduced data dependences while figure 10(b) shows the resulting net.

9 Conclusion

In this paper we presented a framework for determining useful parallelism in acyclic code regions. We showed, through the use of an example, the application of techniques for parallelism extraction with optimizations directed towards multi-threaded code generation.

By attempting to sequence code to satisfy data dependences while preserving program correctness based on information extracted from the net topology, combined with Girkar's algorithm for determining essential data dependences, we are able to eliminate the need for use of explicit synchronization to satisfy most data dependences, achieving better results.

The behavior of this optimization technique allows it to be used in a simple partitioning scheme to artificially increase the granularity of the parallelism extracted up to a desired level, which is essential when using multi-threaded systems with high overheads in thread management operations.

10 Acknowledgment

The authors would like to thanks Paulo Reis for his useful suggestions in improving the readability of this paper.

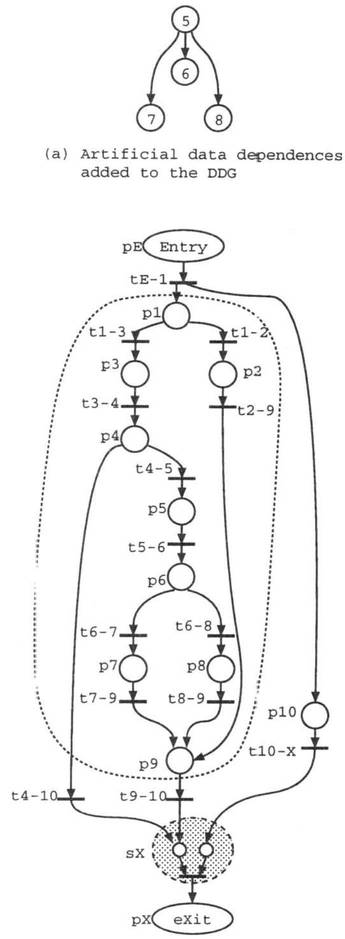

(a) Artificial data dependences added to the DDG

(b) Resulting optimized net

Figure 10: Partitioning (artificially sequencing $\{p_5\}$)

This work was partially supported by ESPRIT Project OMI/GLUE 6062.

References

[1] F. Allen, M. Burke, R. Cytron, J. Ferrante, W. Hsieh and V. Sarkar, "A Framework for Determining Useful Parallelism", *International Conference on Supercomputing*, St. Male, France, July 1988.

[2] U. Barnjee, R. Eigenmann, A. Nicolau, "Automatic Program Parallelization", *Proceedings of the IEEE*, 81(2), February 1993.

[3] C. Carvalho, J. Luís, J. Delgado, "Design of the Paralleliser for a Shared Memory Target", INESC, December 1993.

[4] R. Cytron, J. Ferrante, V. Sarkar, "Experiences using control dependence in PTRAN", *Languages and Compilers for Parallel Computing*, D.Gelertner, A. Nicolau, and D.A. Padua, Eds. Cambridge, MA: MIT Press, 1990.

[5] M. Furnari, "Managing Parallelism in Lisp: Problems and Perspectives", *Parallel Computing From Theory to Sound Practice*, IOS Press, 1992.

[6] M. Girkar, "Functional Parallelism, Theoretical Foundations and Implementations", CSRD Report 1182, Ph.D thesis, Center for Supercomputing Research and Development, University of Illinois at Urbana-Champaign, December 1991.

[7] M. Girkar and C. Polycronopoulos, "Automatic Extraction of Functional Parallelism from Ordinary Programs", *IEEE Transactions on Parallel and Distributed Systems*, vol.3, no. 2, March 1992

[8] M. Lam, R. Wilson, "Limits of Control Flow on Parallelism", *Proceedings of the 19th Annual International Symposium on Computer Architecture*, Gold Cost, Australia, May 1992.

[9] T. Lengauer, R. Tarjan, "A Fast Algorithm for Finding Dominators in a Flowgraph", *ACM Transactions on Programming Languages*, vol. 1, no. 1, July 1979.

[10] J. Luís, "Paralelização Automática de ANDF/TDF" ("Automatic parallelisation of ANDF/TDF" in Portuguese), M.S. thesis, Instituto Superior Técnico, Universidade Técnica de Lisboa, October 1994.

[11] S. Macrakis, "Virtual Binary: An Enabling Technology for Software and Hardware Innovation", *ANDF Technology Collected Papers*, vol. 4, OSF Research Institute, December 1993.

[12] J. Moreira, C. Polychronopoulos, "On the Implementation and Effectiveness of Autoscheduling", CSRD Report No. 1372, Technical Report, Center for Supercomputing Research and Development, University of Illinois at Urbana-Champaign, May 1994.

Parallel Graph Reduction with the PACE Architecture

M.E.Waite, T.J.Reynolds and F.Z.Ieromnimon
Department of Computer Science, University of Essex, UK
email: [waitm, reynt]@essex.ac.uk

Abstract

The PACE architecture is an extensible, distributed memory, multiprocessor that is designed specifically to support the graph reduction model of computation. PACE differs from most other research projects in this area in that it advocates the use of a specially designed processor, rather than currently available devices, as the basic replicable node. In this paper we present the design of a prototype version of the new processor, together with the latest results obtained by simulating the parallel execution of example programs on both a detailed Verilog description of the hardware and a much faster C-simulator (arrays of up to 200 processors are simulated).

1: Introduction

Parallel processing has made considerable advances on platforms consisting of collections of conventional processors. Multiple programs arising from one or many users are easily run concurrently. Languages like Occam, where parallelism is explicitly managed by the user, are directly accomodated. A single process may be run in parallel when task allocation is statically determinable from the program. This latter approach has been successful for many scientific applications, particularily where data-parallelism is present.

The PACE architecture is aimed at applications where none of the above is applicable. Our typical application writer has no desire or ability to think about architectural details, and anyway would like to move the application code unchanged between architectures. Our typical application also demands machine resources in a way which is highly dynamic and input data dependent. Satisfying the needs of such applications is difficult and the principal problem is grain-size. When the size of any task is impossible to predict, tasks may become very small and it becomes imperative that the burden of starting/finishing a task is minimal. It also becomes necessary to break up large tasks. The only satisfactory solution is to go for a fine-grained computational model. Tasks must also be highly mobile between processors to utilise processors well. Furthermore dynamic use of memory requires distributed garbage collection. Conventional processors are so poor at context switching, load balancing, interprocessor communication and garbage collection that they are hopelessly inefficient for our target applications. We conclude that specially designed hardware is required. We must also adopt a computational model which can generate large numbers of independent tasks which require minimal context to process and minimal effort to distribute.

Our architecture combines elements of dataflow [1-4] and combinator graph reduction. We choose a small fixed set of combinators in order to allow our processor to directly implement the combinator rewrites. Our initial choice is Turner's SK set [5][6]. Early successful serial SK-combinator graph reduction machines [7][8] were superceded using better compilation technology on conventional processors. This history has cast doubt on the use of SK-combinators for the *sequential* implementation of functional languages and supercombinator approaches became more favoured. Over the last ten years systems have been built to perform parallel graph reduction [9][10], but typically stock hardware was incorporated to do the actual rewriting. Such stock hardware cannot execute graph manipulations directly as its native instruction set, but rather executes sequences of its own code which implement the graph manipulation. This extra layer of implementation is very damaging. What is worse is that these processors were not designed to perform the other tasks involved in a *parallel* graph rewriting model. Our results show that SK combinators are not necessarily inefficient, indeed, because they are simple we can do them fast. Only a few projects are pursuing our approach, of which we can mention the MaRS project [11].

2: The PACE evaluation model

Dataflow has the potential to use fine-grained multi-tasking to hide network communication latency. In PACE we combine this potential with the synchronisation properties of graph reduction. We treat the combinator graph as a dynamic dataflow graph, and then introduce a demand element to preserve the desirable aspects of lazy evaluation.

In dataflow architectures input data tokens are matched with process templates to form packets which are queued at processors for action. Since each packet contains all the

1066-6192/96 $5.00 © 1996 IEEE
Proceedings of PDP '96

necessary information to complete the task, the processor is able to perform completely independent tasks in rapid succession. In order to reproduce this situation in a combinator graph, we require that the processor is capable of performing a complete combinator rewrite as an atomic action. This is possible with the SK set as the rewrite rules associated with these combinators are very straightforward, usually involving simple rearrangements of their arguments. It is also necessary to present complete redexes to the processor so that it can perform the rewrite without the need to access memory. This is made possible by adopting a representation involving application sequences, rather than the simple binary applications used in Turner's original scheme. (A maximum sequence length of 5 can accommodate the long-reach combinators introduced in [6]). For example, if we take the following program:

*DEF fac n = (n=1) -> 1; n * fac(n-1) ?*
fac 5 ?

then the definition of the function fac compiles into the following combinator expression:

*S (C' COND (C =1) 1) (S * (B fac (C - 1)))*

and this is represented by the following set of sequences:

#L2: < S #L3 #L5>
#L3: < C' COND #L4 1>
#L4: < C = 1>
#L5: < S * #L6 >
#L6: < B fac #L7 >
#L7: < C - 1 >

The expression to be evaluated, fac 5, is represented by #L1: < #L2 5 >

Sequences can be classified as being one of three types:

A *redex* is defined to be a sequence that consists of an operator (combinator or built-in primitive) followed by at least the required number of arguments. In the case of strict operators, the relevant arguments must be fully evaluated.

A *head-normal form* (HNF) can consist of a single data item, a constructed pair, or a combinator followed by fewer arguments than it requires.

An *intermediate sequence* (IS) cannot be classified as either redex or HNF. It can be a sequence representing an application of a strict operator to unevaluated arguments, or a function application where the function part is a reference, or just a simple indirection.

The classification of an active sequence determines the operation that can be applied to it. There are just two basic operations, reduction and dereference.

Reduction is applied to redex sequences according to the leading combinator's rewrite rule, e g

#Li:<S a b c> => #Li:<a c #Lj> + #Lj:<b c>

Dereference associates the leftmost label in an IS (which we have called the target), with the HNF of the sequence bearing that label, and then replaces the label with the HNF.

The dereference operation not only supplies arguments to strict operators, e.g.

#Li:< + 2 #Lj > + #Lj:< 4 > => #Li:< + 2 4 >

but also supplies relevant parts of the compiled function definition code to the expressions undergoing evaluation. For example, the first step in the evaluation of our example expression, fac 5, is to dereference the leftmost label of the sequence, thereby producing a redex sequence.

#L1:<#L2 5> + #L2:<S #L3 #L5> => #L1:<S #L3 #L5 5>

2.1: Representation

Sequences which need to be stored in memory have the following format:

<STATUS SEQUENCE RETLINK SHARELINK>

where the status of a sequence may be:

DORMANT	not yet been demanded
ACTIVE	undergoing evaluation
SUSPENDED	stored awaiting an HNF
REDUCED	is in HNF

The two link fields provide the means by which ISs can be associated with the HNFs they require. The return link indicates the IS that requires the value of this sequence when it achieves HNF. The sharers field is used to connect ISs which are waiting for the same HNF.

2.2: The dereference algorithm

If the target sequence is DORMANT then we activate the target and store the IS. Also if the target is ACTIVE or SUSPENDED then the IS is stored. Activating the target involves setting the target sequence's status to ACTIVE, and placing it in the active sequence queue. Storing an IS involves moving the content of the target's return link into the IS's sharers link, placing the IS's label in the target's return link, and then storing the IS in the slot corresponding to its own label. The list of target sharers is thus a simple pushdown stack. When an input sequence is discovered to be in HNF its slot is accessed and the links used to associate it with the one or more ISs which require its value.

If a dereference produces a sequence of more than 5 items it is decomposed. For example, if the result of a dereference is of the form #Li:<a b c d e f>, then a new sequence #Ln:<a b c d e> is generated and made active, with its return link set to #Li. The sequence labelled #Li is rewritten as #Li:<#Ln f> and stored to await the evaluation of #Ln.

We need to be able to deal with foreign labels. All labels are taken from one global address space of which each PACE processor owns a segment. This allows us to determine the home processor of any label. If the input sequence bears a foreign label, and is in HNF, then it is sent back to the processor from which it originated. If it is an IS, then we proceed exactly as in the local case, i.e. we perform the substitution if the target is in HNF, otherwise store it. In order to store a foreign IS, we first have to give it a local alias. For example, if we wish to store the IS #Lf:<..#Lt..>, where #Lt is the target of the IS, then we give it a new label, #Ln, and store the sequence #Ln:<..#Lt..>. The return link for #Ln is set to be #Lf and the return link for #Lt is set to be #Ln. When #Ln finally achieves HNF, its return link, #Lf, is recognised as foreign. The sequence is then relabelled with #Lf, and returned home.

If an incoming IS has a foreign target, then an indirection has to be formed. For example, given the input sequence #Li:<..#Lf..>, where #Lf is the target of the IS, it is rewritten as #Li:<..#Ln..>, where #Ln is a new label, and a new sequence #Ln:<#Lf> is directed to the processor where #Lf originated. The sequence #Li is stored, and the return link of #Ln is set to #Li. Eventually the sequence #Ln will return as an HNF, and be dereferenced into the waiting sequence sequence #Li in the normal way.

It may be necessary to perform some combination of the preceding actions and in all there are 14 dereference situations. These not only provide the means for preparing redexes, but also account for all the inter-processor communications required. The automatic return of foreign HNFs to the processor where they originated is a sufficient mechanism for returning the values of exported tasks to the tasks that demanded their evaluation. The forming of indirections for foreign targets provides the method for demanding and receiving remote values. The sequences that are passed between processors have exactly the same structure as the sequences that are manipulated within a processor. This avoids any translation overheads which can occur between the graph reduction model which provides the synchronisation between concurrently active tasks, and the sequential processes which actually carry out the tasks.

2.3: Introducing Parallelism

Evaluation proceeds by continually applying the operations of classification, dereference and reduction to the sequence representing the main expression, and to some subset of the sequences that become generated during the process. We employ a demand driven strategy by only including a sequence in the subset of active sequences if its label appears in a strict argument position within some already active sequence. Parallelism is introduced by adding a control operator, PAR, into the demand driven model. PAR has rewrite rule

PAR f a => f a [make a active]

where <f a> is a function application in the ongoing evaluation and the argument a can safely be evaluated at the same time as the application <f a>. The 'sparking' of the evaluation of a is not permitted if the processor is approaching its maximum capacity.

In principle the PAR combinator can be introduced as a result of strictness analysis, and this has been a topic of much research [12][10]. However at present we insert this combinator by hand. It is a matter for future investigation to discover if strictness analysis can deliver what is required in all circumstances.

PAR enables us to generate multi-threaded execution on one processor. Threads are spread between processors by a kind of diffusion scheduling: the decision to export or not is a simple heuristic based on the loading of the local processor and that of its immediate neighbours. It has proved efficient to restrict export to those sequences which represent the application of a defined function to some arguments. This is easily marked by the compiler.

3: A prototype PACE architecture

Ultimately we wish to render each PACE processor in VLSI. But for now we plan a simple prototype which can be built from standard MSI components, to demonstrate PACE's viability on a wide range of example programs. We choose MSI circuits because we can more precisely render the architecture we require. Furthermore it is easier to see how well such a design could fit onto silicon, and to judge what effects increased clock rates and improved architectural resources would have on performance.

Figure 1 shows a top-level view of the prototype distributed architecture. A simplified PACE processor is shown in figure 2 and figure 3 shows the internal organisation of the dereference and rewrite unit. A major architectural feature is a sequence-wide FIFO. It is the capacity of this FIFO which determines the number of active threads which can be accommodated on one PACE processor. A FIFO holding 32 entries can easily be provided for the prototype and is a reasonable size to ultimately fit on silicon. The FIFO is fed from three sources: new sequences from rewrites, sequences arriving from other processors and results from the ALU.

The sparking of new threads is inhibited when the FIFO becomes half-full in order that the local processor can continue to accept sequences from other processors. In certain exceptional circumstances it is still possible for the FIFO to become full and possibly generate deadlock. To cater for this situation we allow overflow of the FIFO into main memory and provide a register to point to this overflow list.

The rewrite unit also contains a wide crossbar/ multiplexor. During combinator rewrites this allows an output sequence to be produced in one step from the following: any permutation of fields from the input sequence, up to two fresh labels, a number of fixed constants. During dereference the crossbar is used to combine fields from the input sequence with fields from a stored sequence.

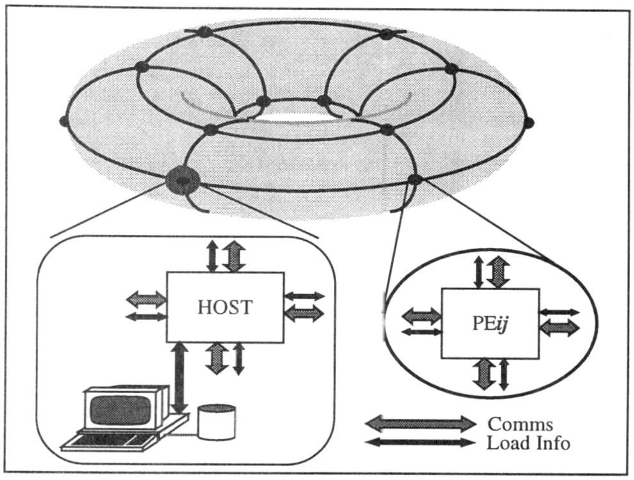

Fig 1: Overview

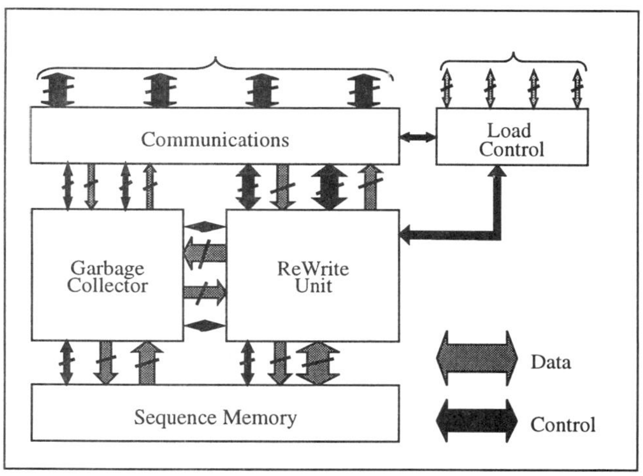

Fig 2: PACE processor

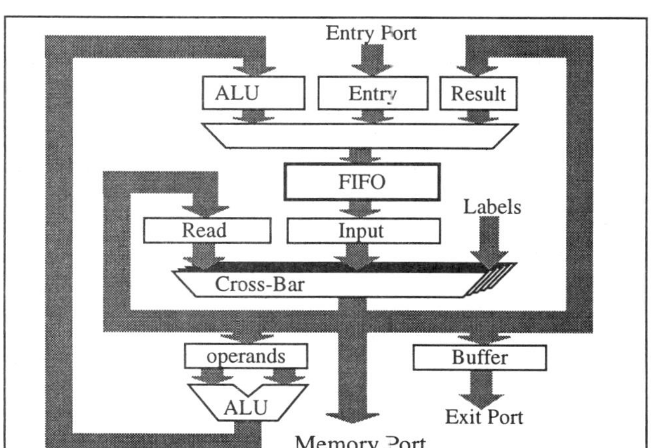

Fig 3: Rewrite/Dereference

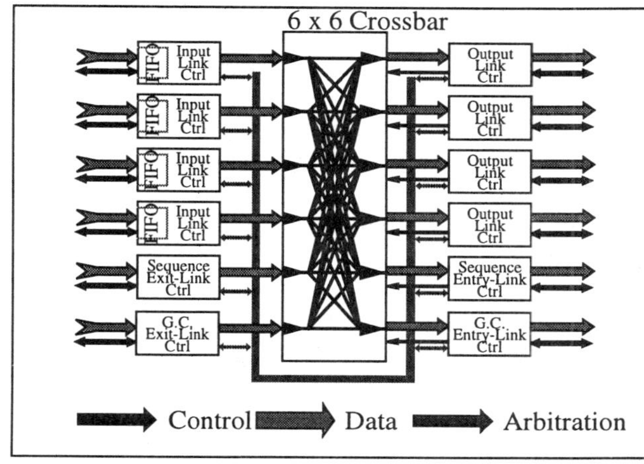

Fig 4: The Communications Unit

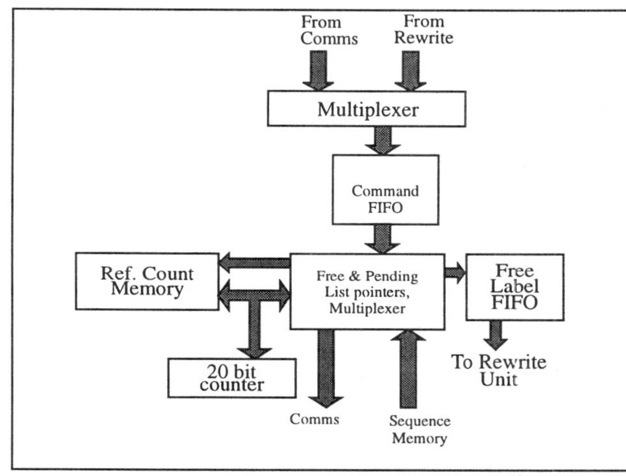

Fig 5: The Garbage Collection Unit

The rewrite unit is constantly aware of its own loading (its FIFO occupancy) and that of its immediate neighbours. When it encounters a PAR combinator, or considers exporting a sequence, this information determines what will occur. If a sequence is to be exported then the communications unit uses the same information to determine which neighbour should receive the sequence.

3.1: The communications unit

As soon as a sequence is identified by the rewrite unit as being destined for another processor it is passed to the communications unit thereby allowing the rewrite unit to immediately continue processing its sequence queue. Figure 4 shows the communications unit. Each unit is a node in a packet-switching network. It consists of a set of six incoming traffic controllers and six outgoing traffic controllers placed on either end of a 6x6 uni-directional crossbar. It provides for through-putting of the four external links as well as connection to the internal rewrite unit and the garbage collector. On the receiving end of each link a FIFO is used as an asynchronous message buffer. Wormhole routing is employed so that, once an open channel is established across the communications unit, dispatch can begin immediately. A link width of 16 bits provides a bandwidth of approximately 1M sequences/sec per link, in each direction. The communications unit is very similar in principle to the Monsoon PARC chip [3].

3.2: The garbage collection unit (GC)

We employ a simple reference-counting scheme in which each PACE GC unit maintains reference counts and a free-list for locally assigned labels. GCs also communicate increments and decrements of non-local labels to other GCs in the system via the communications unit. We do not maintain reference counts on the compiled function definitions and thereby drastically reduce the GC's workload. This also avoids the problem that a simple reference count scheme cannot collect any cyclic structures that are present in the compiled code. We avoid the creation of cycles at run-time by adopting a rewrite rule for the Y combinator which does not "tie the knot".

The GC unit performs three tasks. Firstly it responds to increment and decrement commands by updating the relevant reference count and placing any label whose reference count falls to zero on a pending list. Secondly it maintains a free-list and a supply of fresh labels to the rewrite/dereference unit. Thirdly it processes the pending list to recursively collect data structures. A detailed view of the GC unit is shown in figure 5. Note that the GC has a separate memory in which it manages reference counts for the sequences in main memory. It also has read access to the main sequence memory. FIFOs are used to buffer the communications between the GC and the rewrite/ dereference unit in order to decouple their activities as completely as possible.

4: Simulation results

We have estimated the performance of the PACE architecture using two simulators. The hardware simulation language verilog is being used to model the architecture in considerable detail, in preparation for the construction of a prototype. We know the type of devices which will render each sub-system and have modelled their exact timing at a 25 MHz clock rate. We can thus observe the absolute run-times for the whole machine on small example programs.

A C-simulator is used to model the functionality of the PACE architecture without attempting to model the timings of individual units or devices. The unit of simulation timing is the processing of a sequence at as many PACE processors that have sequences to process. The verilog simulation tells us that sequences take, on average, 5.7 clock cycles to process, and it is this average time which is used to convert C-simulator cycles into wall-clock times. This ratio is surprisingly constant over various programs and gives an average single processor performance of 4.39M sequences processed/sec, of which around 1.4M/sec are combinator rewrites. We show data here for six benchmark programs:

queens(N)	places N queens on an NxN board
matm (N)	multiplies an NxN matrix by itself (by first transposing one copy)
primes(N)	finds all prime numbers [2,N]
treesum(N)	constructs and counts the leaves of a 2**N binary tree
turner(N)	turns N various expression trees into combinator trees, using Turner's abstraction algorithm
nfib(N)	evaluates nfib(N)

Tables 1 and 2 show execution times to allow comparison of the two simulators.

Table 1: runtime in msec from Verilog

program	1 proc	2 procs	8 procs
queens(6)	108.3	55.4	16.7
treesum(11)	48.1	26.6	7.5
matm(30)	31.3	17.2	7.0
nfib(14)	8.6	4.8	1.6

Table 2: runtime in msec from C-simulator

program	1 proc	4 procs	9 procs
queens(6)	107.5	29.7	15.7
treesum(11)	48.0	13.0	6.4
matm(30)	27.6	9.0	4.7
nfib(14)	8.5	2.7	1.3

We can see that the simulators line up reasonably well over the processor range for which verilog can provide us with data. The alignment is also maintained over the different programs, so we do not have to re-calibrate our C-simulator for each program.

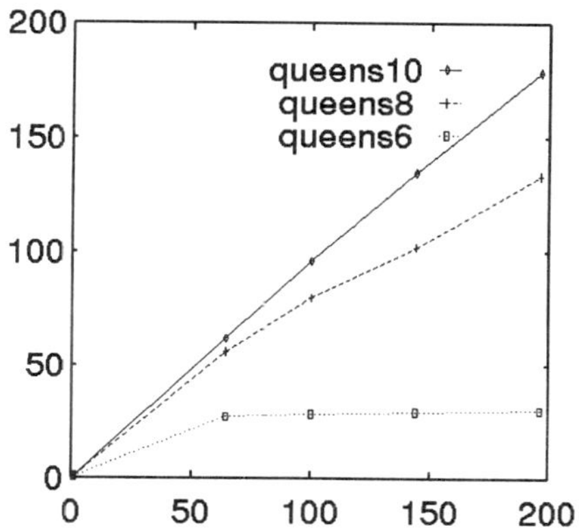

fig 6 : speedup for queens

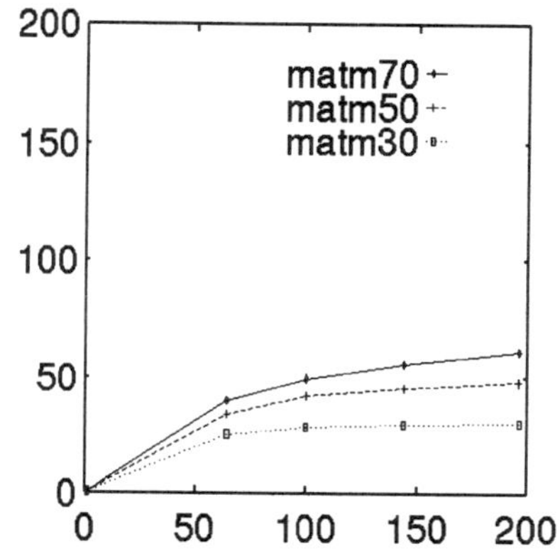

fig 7 : speedup for matm

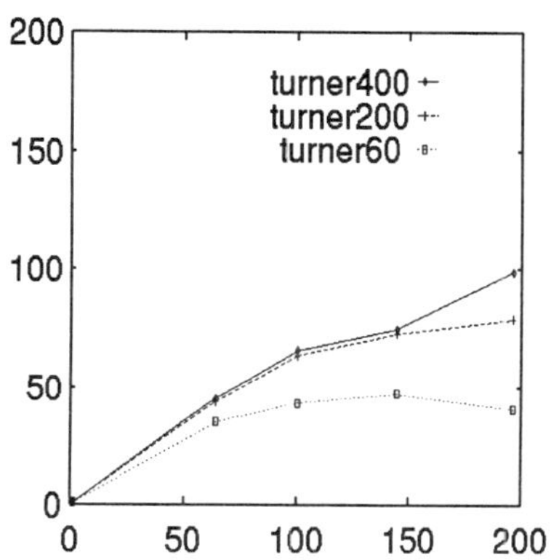

fig 8 : speedup for turner

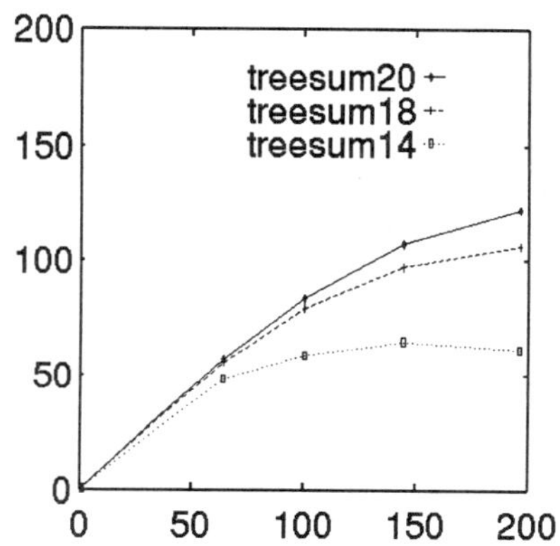

fig 9 : speedup for treesum

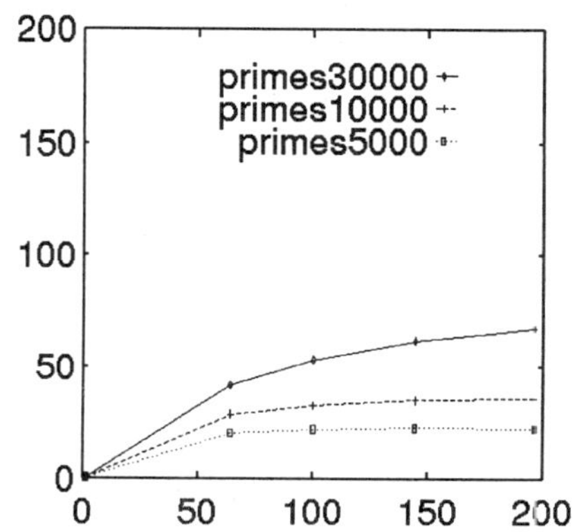

fig 10 : speedup for primes

Figures 6,7,8,9 and 10 give speedup graphs obtained from the calibrated C-simulator for five programs, employing progressively larger problems. As we hoped the speedups that can be obtained steadily improve as the size of the problem is scaled. Unfortunately we cannot scale-up any further for problems like primes and matm, as our machine used for simulation runs out of memory. We would expect improved speedups for larger examples of those programs. However we would not expect the near-linear speedups of queens(10) to be typical, rather we would regard a speedup of 100 from 196 processors as typical. This is a considerable achievement for the generalised approach we are taking. We must remind ourselves that near-linear speedups are really only obtainable in parallel computation in special circumstances, or when careful tuning has been applied.

5: Conclusions

Our results encourage us to conclude that a fine-grained approach to parallelism is practical for SK-combinator graph reduction, provided we build a dedicated machine for the purpose. Our simulations show that our architecture can cope with all the problems inherent in massive parallelism. While running queens(10) on 196 processors there are over 2000 threads in the machine for most of the computation. Many of these threads are short-lived, many make remote references and cause sequences to be exchanged between processors, much exporting of sequences occurs, and there is much garbage collection activity. Nevertheless good speedups can be obtained, because the architecture and the graph rewriting model are in close harmony.

References

[1] Arvind and R.A.Ianucci, "Two Fundamental Issues in Multiprocessing", CSG Memo 226-6, Lab for Computer Science, MIT, 1987.

[2] R.Keller "Overview of Rediflow II Development",Proceedings of the Workshop on Graph Reduction, New Mexico LNCS 279 , 1986.

[3] K.R.Traub, G.M.Papadopoulos, M.J.Beckerle, J.E.Hicks, "Overview of the Monsoon Project", Int. Conf. on Computer Design, 150-155, IEEE 1991.

[4] M.Parkin and D.Yeung, "The MIT Alewife Machine: A Large-Scale Distributed-Memory Multiprocessor", MIT/LCS Technical Memo 454, 1991.

[5] D.A.Turner, "A New Implementation Technique for Applicative Languages", Software - Practice and Experience, Vol 9, 31-49, 1979.

[6] D.A.Turner, "Another Algorithm for Bracket Abstraction", Journal of Symbolic Logic, Vol 44, No 2, 267-270, 1979.

[7] W.R.Stoye, The Implementation of Functional Languages using Custom Hardware", PhD Thesis, University of Cambridge Computer Lab. 1985.

[8] M.Scheevel, "NORMA - a graph reduction processor", Proc. ACM Conference on Lisp and Functional Programming, Aug 1986.

[9] M.D.Cripps, J.Darlington, A.J.Field, P.G.Harrison and M.J.Reeve, "The design and Implementation of ALICE: A Parallel Graph reduction Machine", Proceedings of the Workshop on Graph Reduction, Springer Verlag, 1987

[10] S.L.Peyton-Jones, Parallel Implementations of Functional Languages, The Computer Journal, Vol32(2), 175-186, 1989.

[11] A. Contessa, E.Cousin, C. Coustet, M. Cubero-Castan, G. Durrieu, B. Lecussan, M. Lemaitre, P. Ng, "MaRS, a combinator graph reduction multiprocessor", LNCS 306, 176-192, 1987

[12] E.G.Nocker, J.E.Smetsers, M.C.Eekelen and M.J.Plasmeijer,"Concurrent Clean" PARLE '91 , LNCS 506 , pp 202-219, June 1991.

[13] T.J.Reynolds, M.E.Waite and F.Z.Ieromnimon, "PACE: A prototype design", http:\\cswww.essex.ac.uk, (1995).

Program Comprehension Support for Knowledge-Based Parallelization

Stefan Andel[a] Beniamino Di Martino[a,b] Jan Hulman[a] Hans P. Zima[a]

[a]Institute for Software Technology and Parallel Systems
University of Vienna, Liechtensteinstr. 22,
A-1090 VIENNA, AUSTRIA

[b]Department of Computer Science and Systems,
University "Federico II", via Claudio 21,
80124 NAPLES, ITALY

e-mail: {andel,dimartin,hulman,zima}@par.univie.ac.at

Abstract

Current compilation systems for distributed-memory computers have to integrate new techniques to support the highly complex task of producing efficient programs for parallel systems. Two techniques, program comprehension and expert systems, although developed outside the scope of parallelization domain, are extremely useful to improve the quality of the parallel code generated and to make the parallelization process more convenient and automatic.

In this paper we describe a parallelization environment consisting of three main components: Vienna Fortran Compilation System (VFCS), a tool for recognition of Parallelizable Algorithmic Patterns (PAP Recognizer), and a knowledge-based parallelization support tool (Expert Adviser). After these main components are introduced, the paper focuses on integration issues of PAP Recognizer and Expert Adviser within the framework of VFCS. We outline the salient features of a new parallelization environment. The design of the XPA knowledge base for recognized program concepts (patterns) is presented, and the methodology of knowledge acquisition for program patterns is outlined.

1 Introduction

The current generation of compilers for distributed-memory multiprocessor systems (DMMPs) incorporates advanced program analysis techniques and a variety of program restructuring transformations. However, a compiler in its conventional sense does not, of its own, suffice to support the highly complex and challenging task of producing efficient programs for parallel systems [20]. The restructuring system should be only a part of a sophisticated and integrated programming environment including an extensive set of parallelization supporting tools that help to guide the parallelization process, or at least supply the crucial information for taking important decisions by the user during parallelization.

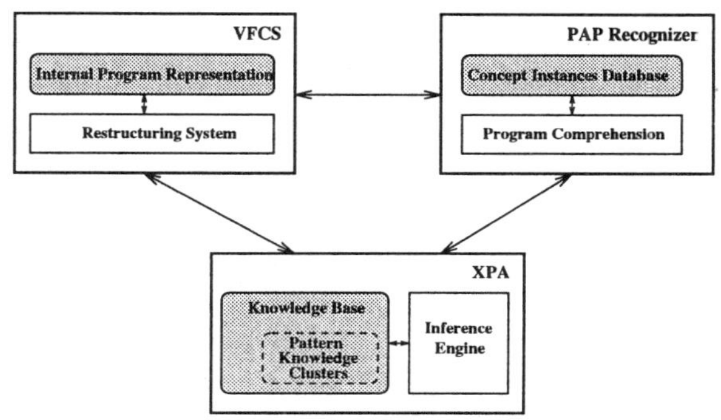

Figure 1: Parallelization environment

In this paper we will present one such parallelization environment. The Vienna Fortran Compilation System (VFCS), a state-of-the-art restructuring system, is extended by a program comprehension tool (PAP Recognizer). In addition, a knowledge-based parallelization support tool (Expert Adviser - XPA) has been integrated with the VFCS. Figure 1 shows the overall structure of the parallelization environment:

- *VFCS* provides a catalog of analysis and restructuring services
- *XPA* supports generation of data distributions and transformation strategies tuned to the target DMMP
- *PAP Recognizer* is able to identify particular program parts as being implementations of (Parallelizable) Algorithmic Patterns

2 Vienna Fortran compilation system

The *Vienna Fortran Compilation System (VFCS)* [3] is a *source-to-source translator* from Vienna Fortran [17] and HPF [11] into Message Passing Fortran

1066-6192/96 $5.00 © 1996 IEEE
Proceedings of PDP '96

(MPF). The parallelization is carried out according to the SPMD programming model. The current system can target several dialects of message passing Fortran running on existing distributed-memory multiprocessor systems, as well as providing a machine-independent target in the form of the Parmacs macros.

The VFCS is being gradually extended by a set of performance prediction and analysis tools. These tools are integrated with the VFCS analysis and transformation subsystems and range from the sequential profiling of the input program (*Weight Finder*) [8], through compile time performance prediction (P^3T and *PEPSY*) [9, 2], up to the selective measurement of resultant parallel programs on the target parallel architecture (*Vienna Fortran Performance Measurement System - VFPMS*). Moreover, based on a post-execution processing of the generated trace files, additional possibilities for performance analysis are available: statistical processing within *MEDEA* optionally using clustering methods, visualization and graphical presentation of parallel program behavior with *ParaGraph* and *Parmon*.

3 Knowledge-based support for VFCS

3.1 Motivation

The parallelization of a program within VFCS is a complex optimization process whereby the user is forced to drive the parallelization session. The most crucial and critical decisions which he must take are related to the specification of a distribution of program arrays and to the selection and application of appropriate program optimization transformations. These decisions require detailed knowledge about the program, compiler features, and target machine characteristics. The user makes decisions on the basis of his previous experience (heuristics), and by exploitation of information from available performance analysis tools. Therefore, decision-making on the basis of a large spectrum of information, ranging from detailed analytical information, via performance parameters, up to human heuristics and known ad-hoc solutions, is required.

It is generally accepted that the representation and exploitation of *explicit* knowledge covering various parallelization aspects within the current parallelizers can enable their future evolution and will make them more automatic and intelligent [18].

So, it is highly desirable to incorporate *expert knowledge* into the present parallelizers. Contemporary parallel compiler technology does not allow its straightforward embedding; for this, technology from the field of artificial intelligence should be used. The present-day *expert system technology* is suitable to organize and represent a large amount of knowledge and information from different sources. The application of expert system technology in the field of parallelization offers a principally new feature: it establishes a platform for the combination of precise analytical and numerical information yielded by the compilation system and performance prediction tools, with human knowledge about parallelization, which is often imprecise and heuristic in its nature.

3.2 Expert Adviser

Based on the rationale mentioned above, a knowledge based tool, the *Expert Adviser* (hereafter referred to as *XPA*) [13, 19], was proposed. The XPA aims to provide:

- *explicit expert knowledge representation and exploitation*
- *intelligent assistance* for the user during parallelization
- partial *automatization* of the parallelization session
- *integration platform* of supporting tools, parallelization paradigms and techniques

XPA was designed as a separate subsystem of the VFCS parallelization environment [12]. The *XPA prototype* has been implemented using the *ProKappa* system that is a professional *expert system development environment*. The XPA has direct access to the internal VFCS program representation and to VFCS transformation subsystem.

Initially, the implementation effort of the XPA prototype has been focused to one of the most crucial problems of parallelization for DMMPs: *automatic data distribution*. At the current time, XPA applies a simple strategy for finding suitable initial data distributions that have to be completed and tuned later.

The XPA consists from two main components: a *knowledge base* and an *inference engine*. The knowledge base comprises *objects* and *rules*. The inference engine performs reasoning over the objects using the rules to deduce new facts or to propose parallelization actions.

One of most important parts of the XPA knowledge base is its own internal representation of the program processed - a *program model*, that is created at the beginning of XPA processing by extraction of relevant information from the VFCS internal program representation. This information is preprocessed, compressed, and converted in the form of ProKappa objects hierarchically interconnected. Besides others, this program model reflects a XPA decomposition of an input program into components (phases) relevant for parallelization. Other objects represent program subroutines, relevant statements, arrays, and array occurrences. The program model is preprocessed using rules from the knowledge base, and it is completed by derived *distribution relevant information*: alignment preferences and alignment conflicts. Finally, also concepts (objects) representing data distributions complete the program model.

The XPA prototype is being gradually extended and refined. The main development direction is to provide the user with intelligent assistance during the VFCS parallelization session considering various target machines [1]. This includes automatic exploitation of information from selected performance analysis tools and integration with a program comprehension tool.

4 Program comprehension within parallelization

4.1 Motivation

The restructuring approach to parallelization, whereby the parallel program is generated by gradual restructuring of the input program, is widely used within current state-of-the-art parallelizers. Recently, a new approach to program parallelization has been suggested which is based on the application of program concept recognition [14, 4].

Program comprehension is the process of discovering concepts related to the semantics in the input code, and assigning them to their realizations within the code itself. This problem has been studied, for instance, in the context of reverse engineering to (partially) automate maintenance and reuse of sequential software [10, 16].

Uses of a concept recognition-based parallelization procedure can range from the automatic selection of a data distribution, via the automatic selection of sequences of optimizing transformations to the sequential code, via the code replacement with optimized parallel libraries, up to the automatic selection of the proper parallel programming paradigm for the given program (related to the target architecture), thus enabling much more flexible approaches to program parallelization than those provided by the SPMD paradigm [4, 5].

The pattern recognition approach to parallelization is usually motivated by the observation that most of the numerical application algorithms that are typically run on DMMPs are composed of only a few (around 100) characteristic programming schemes (called *patterns*) such as e.g. vector and matrix operations, simple recurrences, or relaxation operations. Based on this assumption, it has been claimed that high-level pattern recognition can be usefully applied to entire programs as a *core* of an automatic parallelization system [14].

4.2 Patterns versus complete program

However, we believe that the exclusive application of a pattern recognition approach can lead to serious difficulties, at least due to two reasons:

- the parallelization proposal derived from a pattern is *local* only; serious conflicts among local parallelization proposals can arise
- gaps, not covered by any pattern, can occur in the code, even if there exists a large library of patterns.

The most promising solution consists of a combination of the restructuring and pattern recognition approaches. The restructuring system forms a general frame in which pattern recognition can be applied in order to improve the quality of the target code. We incorporated a pattern recognition tool into the VFCS parallelization environment as described below.

The *comprehension of concepts* in the code, that uses a semantic analysis (at a proper abstraction level), permits powerful knowledge-based program transformations by decrypting the meaning of the program which is often hidden past recognition within the source code by former target-specific transformations and programming styles.

The term *Parallelizable Algorithmic Pattern* (PAP) has been introduced in [4] to refer to a set of identifiable algorithmic properties characterizing a group of concrete algorithms that are parallelizable according to some common strategy.

5 PAP Recognizer

In [7] the implementation of *PAP Recognizer*, a prototype tool that performs recognition of algorithmic patterns, integrated within the VFCS, has been described. It starts from the structural analysis performed by the VFCS front-end, and builds a hierarchical description of the program in terms of concept instances, until one or more parallelizable algorithmic patterns are recognized.

The output of the structural analysis phase, that is syntactic, control flow, data flow and data dependence information on the program, is utilized to build the *Base Internal Representation* of the program, which is stored in the *Concept Instances Database* in the form of *base concepts*.

This base level of the representation is essentially a Program Dependence Graph (PDG), whose nodes represent statements and whose edges represent control and data dependences.

The overall *Internal Program Representation* is generated during the recognition phase performed by the PAP Recognizer. It has the structure of a *Hierarchical PDG* (HPDG), reflecting the hierarchical strategy of the recognition process. The base layer of the HPDG describes the program at the statement and operator level. Starting from the base internal representation, the recognizer performs the concept parsing, following the rules specified by the plans. As long as the parsing process proceeds and more and more abstract concepts are recognized, they are represented as nodes in increasingly higher layers of the HDPG. More specifically, each node representing a concept is linked to the nodes of the lower layer representing subconcepts. Control and data dependence edges for the newly created abstract concept nodes are inherited from those of the composing subconcept nodes, in a way that is characteristic for each concept, and which is determined by the plan which recognizes it. Internal Program Representation is stored in the *Concept Instances Database* which is incrementally updated by the PAP recognizer as the recognition advances.

The tool has been implemented in Prolog: this choice has been mainly driven by its capability to be utilized as a deductive inference-rule engine to perform the hierarchical concept parsing.

The use of a rule-based system as Prolog, and the specification of (inter-statement level) patterns by control and data dependence relations, permits a successful handling of a number of problems arising in the context of Program Comprehension, that can be summarized as follows:

- *syntactic variation*;

- *delocalization*: the implementation of a pattern can be spread throughout the code;

- *implementation variation*: an abstract concept can be implemented in many different ways, and so has to be represented by several and alternative patterns;

- *overlapping implementations*: often the implementations of two or more distinct concepts are merged, so portions of a program may be part of more than one pattern.

The prototype is operational, and able to recognize a few dozen concepts related to numerical computation. It provides as output a graphical browser that permits the visualization of the hierarchical description of the recognized patterns, in the form of a graph, and their implementation within the program code.

For instance, Figure 2 (upper window) shows a Fortran program segment implementing a (*tiled* version of) matrix matrix multiplication algorithm, normalized by the VFCS front end. This version is analyzed by the PAP Recognizer, and Figure 2 (lower window) shows the hierarchical structure of the recognized pattern, in the form of a graph. By clicking on each of the graph nodes, representing a composing subconcept, it is possible to highlight the corresponding code implementing it (as is shown in Figure 2 for the overall concept instance). The matrix multiplication factor arrays and resulting array are also recognized, as are the subscript positions involved in the inner product and in the overall multiplication steps.

6 Integration of PAP Recognizer and XPA

The integration of XPA and the PAP Recognizer has been made under the following constraints:

- restriction to VFCS intrinsic distribution functions and transformations possibilities

- generation of parallelization proposals rather than direct pattern replacement with parallel code

6.1 Parallelization and optimization of recognized code

For every pattern there may exist several good parallel implementations on the given target machine. However, the selection of the implementation for a given recognized pattern depends substantially on the problem size and on the requirements (data distribution) forced by other recognized patterns and by XPA phases. To support such a decision, [14] proposes the use of a run-time table of execution times, parameterized by problem sizes and array distributions. The table is created by pattern benchmarking on the given architecture.

We claim that the use of parameterized tables is not optimal in our parallelization environment because:

- the table quickly grows to an unacceptable size due to the large number of combinations of possible distributions, applicable transformations, and sizes of arrays. Moreover, for every target architecture, a separate table must be created. The decision process requires several time consuming runs through the tables to find good solutions if global program optimization is to be performed.

- most values in the table can be redundant; the table can be significantly reduced by an experienced user. Based on the combination of parallelization knowledge and insight into the table values, the user can formulate statements in the "if-then" forms, that are in fact the concise and compressed pattern parallelization knowledge.

In our exploitation of program comprehension techniques in the context of the knowledge based support for parallelization, we prefer the representation of pattern parallelization knowledge in the form of *expert system rules*.

The output from the application of the PAP Recognizer on the input program specifies the code patterns recognized within the program. Each recognized pattern has a unique *identification*, and it is associated with program code segments that belong to the pattern. The pattern is also parameterized with the actual array dimensions occurring within the pattern.

6.2 Knowledge base for patterns

The pattern identifier serves for a unique identification of the appropriate abstract pattern - the *Pattern Knowledge Cluster (PKC)* in the XPA knowledge base. It is the structure containing the knowledge related to a pattern. The knowledge base comprises a corresponding PKC object for every type of pattern which can be recognized by the PAP Recognizer. Each recognized and parameterized pattern can be seen as an *instance of PKC* in the XPA knowledge base.

The XPA knowledge base for patterns (KBP) is supposed to contain mainly the *medium-level patterns* such as are: vector operations, first order linear recurrences, matrix and vector/matrix operations, two-dimensional reductions, 2D relaxation steps (Jacobi, Gauss-Seidel,...), matrix multiplication, matrix inversion, Gaussian elimination, etc.

At the current stage the PKC *does not* contain the parallel code for pattern replacement but includes rules supporting the generation of suitable parallelization proposals. The rules are parameterized e.g. by array sizes, target architecture configuration, and by ranges of involved loops. Using these rules, XPA is able to derive suitable parallelization proposals for a given PKC instance:

- efficient *local data distributions* (partitioning, alignment, and mapping); several almost optimal distributions should be derivable for most abstract patterns

- *restructuring transformations*; the proposed transformations must be coupled to the proposed data distribution

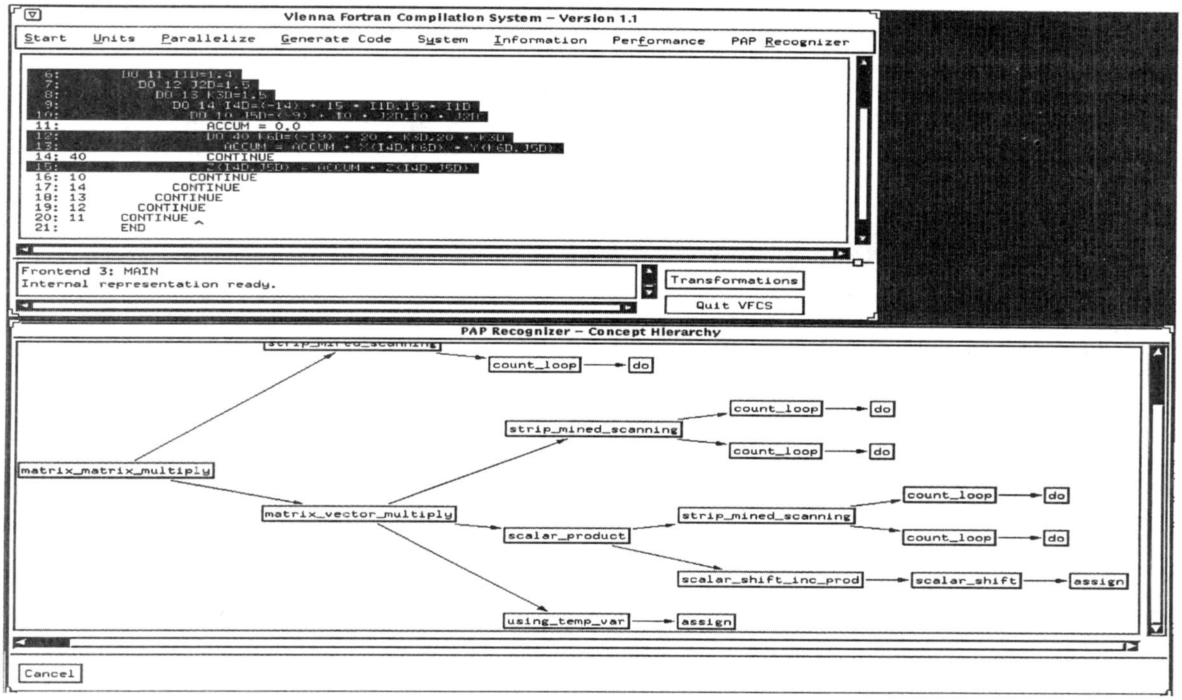

Figure 2: Output of PAP Recognizer for a code segment implementing a tiled version of matrix-matrix mult. PAP

- *estimation of the pattern performance* under various data distributions and transformations to help the XPA at the global optimization task

The performance effect of the transformation application is considered to be local within a pattern. On the other hand, the local data distribution proposal can influence other portions of the program code. It is the responsibility of the XPA to provide the user with intelligent assistance at searching for an optimal combination of local distributions with the aim to achieve an optimal overall performance of the program.

For illustration, consider the Figure 3 that shows the measurement results for the following simplified matrix-matrix multiplication kernel ($C = A \times B$) on an iPSC/860 with 16 processors:

```
        real A(N,N), B(N,N), C(N,N)

        do 10 i=1,N
          do 10 j=1,N
            do 10 k=1,N
10            C(i,j)=C(i,j) + A(i,k) * B(k,j)
```

The figure presents the maximal execution time among all processors. The VFCS communication and masking optimizations had been applied before generating the target program.

This kernel was measured for 7 different data distributions (presented in this figure using Vienna Fortran syntax), and for all 6 possible versions of the algorithm achievable by application of loop interchange transformations. These versions differ in the order of the Fortran do-loops for the indices *i,j,k*, and they are denoted by the corresponding triple. For example, *ijk* version corresponds to the original loop nest, where the outermost loop is referenced by index *i* and the innermost loop by index *k*; the algorithm with *i* and *j* loops interchanged is denoted as *jik*.

Note that the distributions 1,2,3,4 do not replicate any array, while distributions 5,6,7 (totally) replicate array A or B.

About a dozen rules suffice for the derivation of a suitable parallelization proposals for matrix-matrix multiplication pattern. Because of limited space, we present here informally only two of them:

- IF *A or B is to be replicated* THEN
  - *apply loop interchanges to achieve* kji *ordering of loops* AND
  - *select distribution 7 (i.e. (totally) replicate array A, B and C distribute column-wise)*
- IF *neither A nor B is to be replicated* THEN
  - *achieve* kji *ordering of loops* AND
  - *distribute arrays using distribution 1 (equally distribute all arrays block-wise)*

Note that an evaluation of the rule premises may fire particular XPA rules that test other program portions to determine if arrays are to be, or are not to be replicated.

Of course, these rules have to be confirmed also for different array sizes and the number of processors (in

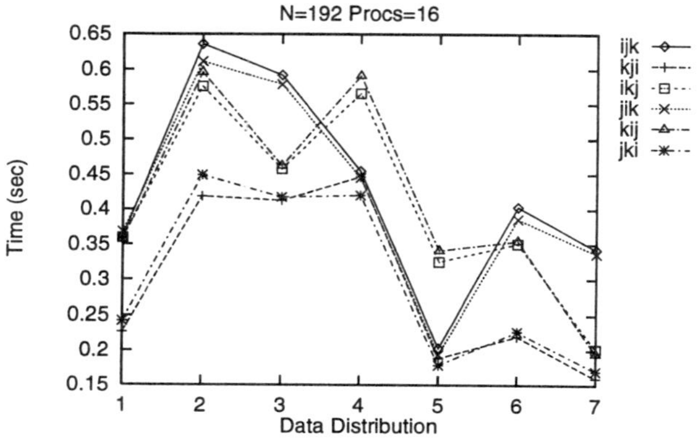

Measured Data Distributions

```
PROCESSORS PB(4,4) RESHAPE PR(16,1), PC(1,16)
1. REAL A(N,N), B(N,N), C(N,N) DIST(BLOCK,BLOCK) TO PB
2. REAL A(N,N) DIST (BLOCK,BLOCK) TO PR
   REAL B(N,N) DIST (BLOCK,BLOCK) TO PC
   REAL C(N,N) DIST (BLOCK,BLOCK) TO PB
3. REAL A(N,N) DIST (BLOCK,BLOCK) TO PR
   REAL B(N,N), C(N,N) DIST (BLOCK,BLOCK) TO PC
4. REAL A(N,N) ,C(N,N) DIST (BLOCK,BLOCK) TO PR
   REAL B(N,N) DIST (BLOCK,BLOCK) TO PC
5. REAL A(N,N) ,C(N,N) DIST (BLOCK,BLOCK) TO PR
   REAL B(N,N) DIST (:,:) TO PB
6. REAL A(N,N) DIST (:,:) TO PB
   REAL B(N,N) DIST (BLOCK,BLOCK) TO PC
   REAL C(N,N) DIST (BLOCK,BLOCK) TO PB
7. REAL A(N,N) DIST (:,:) TO PB
   REAL B(N,N), C(N,N) DIST (BLOCK,BLOCK) TO PC
```

Figure 3: Matrix multiplication on iPSC

fact, they were really confirmed). It is obvious that we may obtain a different set of rules for different target machines.

6.3 Pattern knowledge acquisition, formulation, and representation

The knowledge associated with code patterns cannot often be fully known even to the expert user because the optimal parallelization proposal for the concrete pattern (its impact on performance) is influenced by many factors, e.g.:

- parallelization paradigm, parallelizer features, and target compiler features
- available optimizations, such as loop transformations, mask optimization, communication aggregation and vectorizing
- target machine features: interconnection topology, communication links contention, cashing, vectorizing

The influence of majority of factors cannot be analytically analyzed in details because of their complex interrelations which often cause an unexpected and paradoxical behavior of the target code.

Hence, the most precise and often the only way how to acquire knowledge about a program behavior, is to run and measure the program on the target machine. Although the measurement on the target machine could be very time consuming, we expect that it is an acceptable method for the finite set of available patterns and communication types.

For acquiring of the knowledge related to code patterns we use a semi-automatic knowledge acquisition tool constructed according to ideas described in [15]. It consists of two main components: *measurements* and *collecting* of performance data, and graphical *presentation* of measured data

The experienced user (expert) formulates the conclusions of his analysis of the graphs (as an example see Figure 3) in the form of natural language sentences. The XPA knowledge base developer translates sentences into precise forward-chaining and/or backward-chaining ProKappa rules; these rules are connected to the appropriate knowledge base PKC object using the object methods.

7 Conclusion

In this paper we have described an integrated environment for compiling Fortran programs for massively parallel distributed-memory architectures. The environment includes an advanced parallelizing compiler, a program comprehension tool, and a knowledge-based parallelization support tool. We have argued that such combination of techniques may significantly improve the quality of the parallel code, and it contributes for making a parallelization process more convenient and automatic. Further, it is intended that this system be relatively easy to adapt to different architectures. The environment is currently being developed in the framework of VFCS.

References

[1] Andel S., Chapman B. M., Hulman J., Zima H. P., "An Expert Advisor for Parallel Programming Environments and Its Realization within the Framework of the Vienna Fortran Compilation System", Technical Report TR 95-4, Institute for Software Technology and Parallel Systems, University of Vienna, September 1995.

[2] Blasko R., "Simulation Based Performance Prediction by PEPSY", In *Proc. of the "28th Annual Simulation Symposium"*, April, 1995, Phoenix, USA, IEEE #95TH8049, pp. 341-349.

[3] Chapman B., et al, "Vienna Fortran Compilation System. Version 1.0. User's Guide", Department of Statistics and Computer Science, University of Vienna, Austria, January 1993, 192 pp.

[4] Di Martino B., Iannello G., "Towards Automatic Parallelization through Program Comprehension", Procs. 3^{dh} *IEEE Workshop on Program Comprehension*, Washington (USA), November 1994.

[5] Di Martino B., and Chapman B., "Program Comprehension Techniques to improve Automatic Parallelization", Proc. of *AP'95 - Workshop on Automatic Data Layout and Performance Prediction*, Rice University, Houston (USA), April 1995.

[6] Di Martino B., "Design of a tool for Automatic Recognition of Parallelizable Algorithmic Patterns and description of its prototype implementation", Technical Report TR 95-3, Institute for Software Technology and Parallel Systems, University of Vienna, May 1995.

[7] Di Martino B., Chapman B., Iannello G. and Zima H., "Integration of Program Comprehension Techniques into the Vienna Fortran Compilation System", Proc. of *1995 International Conference on High Performance Computing*, New Delhi (India), December 1995.

[8] Fahringer T., "The Weight Finder - An advanced Profiler for Fortran Programs", Proc. of *AP'93*, Saarbrücken, Germany, 1993.

[9] Fahringer T., "Automatic Performance Prediction for Parallel programs on Massively Parallel Computers", Tecnical Report TR 93-3, Institute for Software Technology and Parallel Systems, University of Vienna, September 1993.

[10] Harandi M.T., Ning J.Q., "Knowledge-Based Program Analysis", *IEEE Software*, January 1990.

[11] High Performance Fortran Forum, "High Performance Fortran Language Specification, Version 1.0", Rice University, Houston, May 1993.

[12] Hulman, J., "Knowledge-Based Support for Transformation Systems", Proc. of *Int. Workshop Algorithms and Software for Parallel Computer Systems*, I. Plander, M. Vajtersic, H.P. Zima, editors, Smolenice, March 4-5, 1993, pp. 95-105.

[13] Hulman J., Andel S., Chapman B., Zima H., "Intelligent Parallelization within the Vienna Fortran Compilation System", Proc. of *Fourth Workshop on Compilers for Parallel Computers*, Delft, Holland, December 1993.

[14] Kessler C.W., Paul W.J., "Automatic Parallelization by Pattern Matching", *Lecture Notes in Computer Science*, (734) Parallel Computation, 1993.

[15] Moritsch H., "Knowledge Acquisition for Automatic Parallelization Based on Performance Test Generation and Evaluation", Internal Report, Institute for Software Technology and Parallel Systems, University of Vienna, 1994.

[16] Wills L.M., "Automated Program Recognition: a Feasibility Demonstration", *Artificial Intelligence*, 45, 1990.

[17] Zima H., Brezany P., Chapman B., Mehrotra P., Schwald A., "Vienna Fortran – a language specification. Version 1.1", ICASE Internal Report 21, ICASE, Hampton, VA, 1992.

[18] Wang K., "Intelligent Program Optimization and Parallelization for Parallel Computers", Technical Report, CSD-TR-91-030, Department of Computer Sciences, Purdue University, April 1991.

[19] Zima H. P., Brezany P., Chapman B.M., Hulman J., "Automatic Parallelization for Distributed-Memory Systems: Experiences and Current Research", Invited paper *EuroArch'93 - European Informatics Congress: Computing System Architecture*, Munich, October 18-19, 1993.

[20] H. P. Zima, B. M. Chapman, "Compiling for Distributed-Memory Systems", *Proc. of the IEEE, Special Section on Languages and Compilers for Parallel Machines*, February 1993.

Developing Distributed Group Communication in pSR

Colin Allison

Division of Computer Science, University of St Andrews, St Andrews KY16 9SS
Scotland
colin@dcs.st-andrews.ac.uk

Abstract

Persistent SR (pSR) is an extended version of the distributed and concurrent programming language SR (Synchronising Resources). Concurrency is extended through persistence in pSR because resources can exist independently of a particular program execution and thus act as shared objects. This paper describes a new extension to pSR, the introduction of groups and group communications, and how they interact with persistent resources. The novelty of this work is that it incorporates groups into a high level programming language. The groups extension raises three issues: how are groups to be expressed at the language level, what are the semantics of group communications, and how are they to be maintained efficiently at the system level? A prototype is built in pSR to enable testing and development. Group semantic options are described and implementation strategies for the maintenance of groups at the system level in a persistent distributed environment are investigated with reference to IP multicast.

1 Introduction

pSR[1] is an extended version of the distributed and concurrent programming language SR[2, 3]. "SR" stands for Synchronising Resources and represents a consolidation of well understood concurrent programming primitives from the last 20 years of research. SR is a multiparadigm language and may be contrasted with other concurrent languages, for example CSP[4] and Occam[5], where a single synchronisation paradigm has been adopted. pSR represents a further consolidation of programming paradigms due to the addition of orthogonal persistence[6]. The addition makes little change to the syntax of the language but extends the scope for concurrency and distribution as pSR resources can exist autonomously and act as shared objects between independent program executions. Although pSR is a multiparadigm language the only pattern of communication it currently supports is one-to-one, or*unicast*. This paper is concerned with extending pSR to support group communication via *multicast*. This is fully in line with pSRs remit as a multiparadigm, concurrent and distributed programming language. The remainder of the paper is organised as follows:

2: multicast and group communication
3: a brief overview of pSR
4: prototyping groups in pSR
5: group semantics
6: supporting groups
7: summary and conclusions

2 Multicast and Group Communication

An interesting consequence of making group communication available is that it changes the way people approach problems and tackle systems organisation. It can simplify the coding of many parallel and distributed algorithms and provides an appropriate logical basis for group computations. Group communication and multicast have been applied in the following areas:

- fault tolerance[7]
- resource discovery and location in distributed environments[11]
- distributed operating systems[10]

1066-6192/96 $5.00 © 1996 IEEE
Proceedings of PDP '96

- shared data objects[8]
- distributed algorithms[9]
- computer supported co-operative work[16]

The value of multicast as a basis for group communications has long been recognised. Boggs wrote in 1983 "VLSI will soon permit low-cost implementation of multicast mechanisms in hardware, and people should be thinking of applications"[11]. More than ten years later the applications are still few, possibly due to the perceived difficulties in programming distributed systems. The motivation of the work described in this paper is to allow the routine use of group communication as a programming primitive in a high-level language that operates in routine computing environments, namely those composed of networked workstations. The novel aspect of group communication in pSR is its integration into a high-level programming language.

2.1 Terminology

Broadcast may be characterised as one-to-all, *unicast* as one-to-one, and *multicast* as any-to-any. Like Boggs[11] we choose to think of broadcast and unicast as special cases of multicast. Multicasting addresses a subset of all possible recipients. For a broadcast the subset is all recipients, and for a unicast the subset is one recipient. Multicast is therefore the most appropriate basis for arbitrary group communication within a system.

We distinguish between true multicast and multiple unicast. A true multicast Mg, is a single message that is picked up by all members of group G, regardless of the size of G. In the multiple unicast scenario N messages are required where N is the size of G.

We must also distinguish between true multicast and filtered broadcasts. In the latter a hardware broadcast is used for all communication, and software filters are constantly employed to select items of interest. This is objectionable because of the high-load it places on the network and all connected hosts. In true multicast the network interface hardware supports multicast addressing and only passes on messages of interest to the hosts software.

Simulated multicast is useful in situations where no true multicast is available but explicit group communication is still desirable as a means of expressing the solution to a problem. It is objectionable as a long-term solution on grounds of poor performance and scalability.

2.2 Architectural support for multicast

Figure 1 shows different architectural levels at which multicast can operate and how they can relate to each other. The lowest level is the hardware level such as a local area network, shared bus or backplane. This is true multicast if the group addresses are hardware addresses and if it costs no more to send a multicast than it does to send a unicast. In shared media networks such as ethernet all transmissions are examined by all nodes to discover the destination address. Address filtering is done by the network interface hardware and does not place any extra load on the host system or the network.

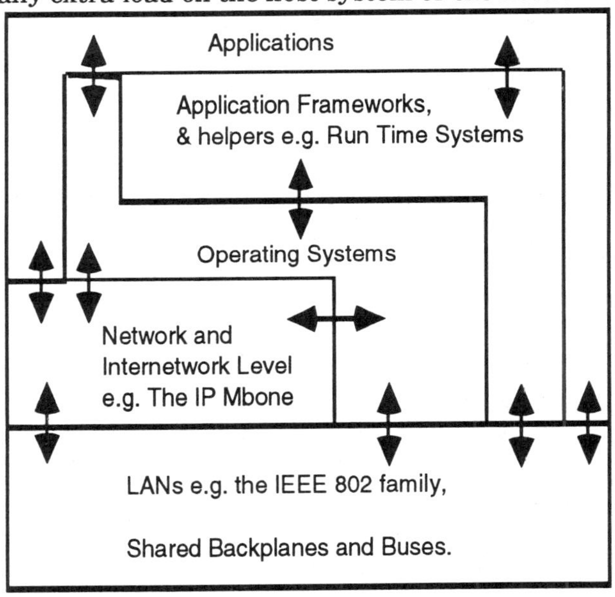

Fig. 1: Architectural Support for Multicast

The hardware level can be directly accessed from the operating system, the network level, application frameworks or even from applications such as network analysers. The IEEE 802 family of LANs (ethernet, token ring, token bus) support multicast addressing. An

802.3 (ethernet) address has 48 bits. Bit 46 indicates if the address is a multicast. There is therefore direct hardware support for 2^{46} multicast addresses.

At the network level multicast must be explicitly supported by routing algorithms and protocols. The experimental MBone (multicast backbone) running over the Internet currently uses a reserved part of the IP address range, 224.0.0.0 – 239.255.255.255, known as Class D addresses, that is, network level multicast addresses. Beyond this agreed address range there are no clear standards yet so not all IP hosts support Class D addresses and very few IP routers do. For an IP host to see the Mbone it must have extensions which support multicast[12]. True (hardware) multicast capability is exploited where possible, for example IP multicast addresses can be mapped directly onto IEEE 802 multicast addresses using the IGMP protocol[12]. The attractions of IP multicast as the basis for group communication in distributed systems are considerable:

- global IP connectivity
- use of true multicast where possible
- routing and optimisation is delegated to the network

The Mbone at present is a hybrid of genuine multicast and unicast links but its efficiency and performance is likely to increase dramatically due to the pressures coming from multimedia applications.

3 A brief overview of pSR

The unit of persistence in pSR is the *resource*. Resources are similar to objects in that they encapsulate a set of code and data entities, but, unlike objects, they do not support inheritance. pSR extends SR by allowing resources to persist and to be shared. Concurrency control policies are implemented by resources as appropriate.

The format of a resource is shown in Fig.2. All communication and synchronisation between resources must reference *operations* which are declared in the specification part. Such references are called *capabilities*. Operations are typed and may be referenced directly by suitably typed capabilities, or less directly by appending the operation invocation to a capability which points to its enclosing resource.

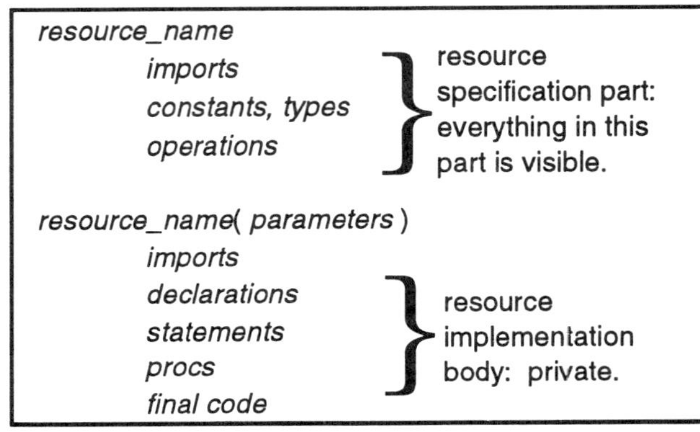

Figure 2 : Resource structure

Multiple resources can exist in a single address space or multiple address spaces, which are called *virtual machines*. A resource cannot span virtual machines. Resources are referenced by suitably typed *capabilities*.

Multiple virtual machines can exist on a single machine or multiple physical machines. A virtual machine cannot span physical machines. Virtual machines are referenced by virtual machine capabilities.

Note the pragmatism of this approach – pSR entities can co-exist relatively happily with standard workstations and operating systems. In Unix for example a pSR virtual machine is a single Un*x process. Nonetheless the approach is powerful enough to allow experimentation with a wide variety of distribution models.

The relationship of physical machines, virtual machines, resources, globals and possible communication paths is shown in Fig. 3. Note the significance of the operation (labelled "op") in the diagram. Operations are central to understanding pSR. They are typed entry points to executable code and are implemented as message queues. They can optionally take parameters and return results. An operation may be serviced by a proc, or by an input block. Semaphores are operations with associated await (P) and signal (V) semantics.

A synchronisation constraint may be explicitly associated with an operation, either *send* or *call*. The default (no constraint) allows either mode of invocation.

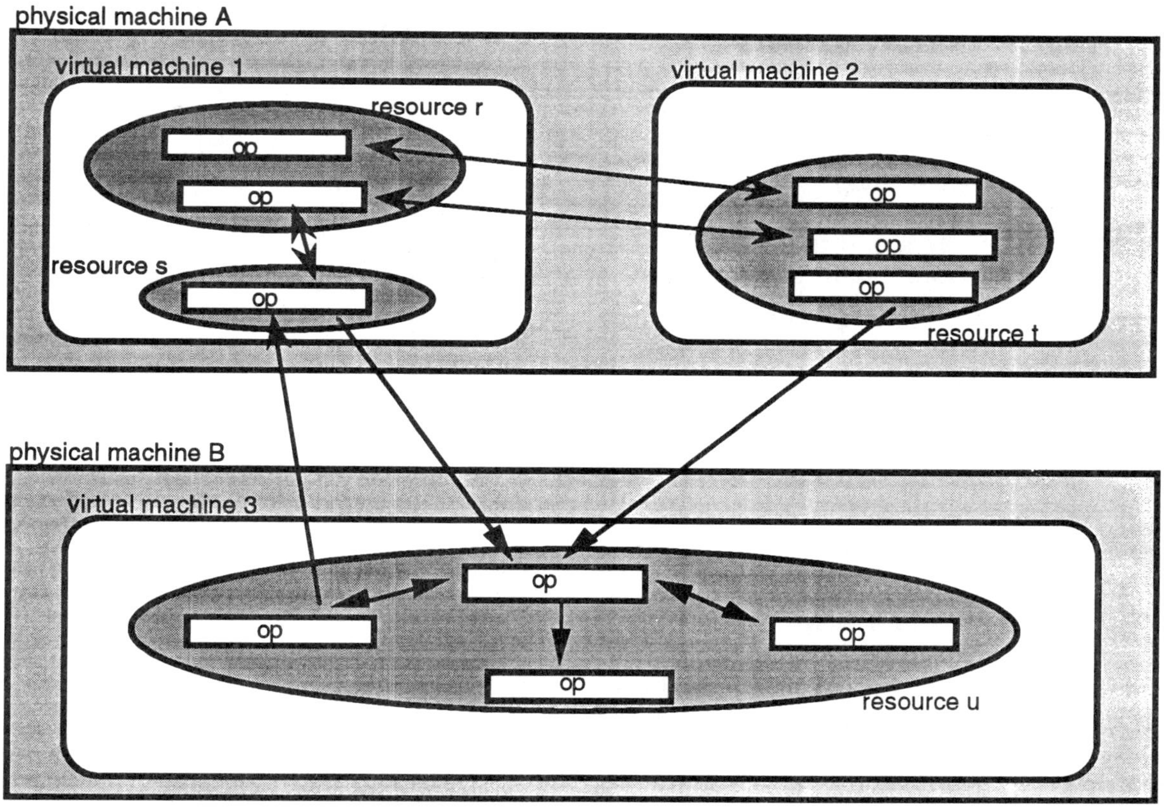

Figure 3: Resource placement and communication paths

Interactions within the same resource are local, interactions between different resources are remote. Basic interaction modes are summarised in Fig. 4.

As combinations of ops, procs and constraints are frequently required to behave as conventional procedures and processes, pSR provides convenient abbreviations. A procedure declaration is an abbreviation for declaring an op with a call constraint serviced by a proc. A process declaration is shorthand for declaring an op with a send constraint, an associated proc, and an initial send to that op.

Invocation	Service	Interaction Mode
call	proc	procedure call
call	in	rendezvous
send	proc	dynamic process creation
send	in	asynchronous message

Figure 4: Interaction moces

To summarise, virtual machines (address spaces) can be created on any reachable physical host, a resource executes within the context of a virtual machine, and synchronisation can take the following forms:

- messages (synchronous or asynchronous)
- procedure call (local or remote)
- process creation (local or remote)
- semaphores (local or remote)

4 Prototyping Groups in pSR

One of the strengths of pSR is its ability to prototype models of distribution. So, while objecting to the use of simulated multicast as a long term solution, the creation of a suite of resources which support group communication is useful for developing a working model and experimenting with group semantics. We initially identify the following basic set of functions as necessary for group communication:

create: creates a new group

destroy: destroys a group

join: apply to join group

leave: apply to leave group

send: send to group

receive: receives group addressed messages

There are broadly two aspects to consider when constructing a prototype: group maintenance, and actual group communication. *Create*, *destroy*, *join* and *leave* are group maintenance functions, whereas *send* and *receive* are communication directives.

4.1 Prototype system model

As we do not have real multicast, a unicast address must masquerade as one. To facilitate this, and some other features, we adopt the notion of a group *owner* or *leader*, who holds an address which *is* the group's address. The resource which *creates* a group is its owner. The onus is on the owner to:

- maintain the group membership list
- simulate multicast
- destroy the group if required

A single resource may be the owner of several groups, but we reject full centralisation in order to more closely model a real distributed group system. However the prototype does support a replicated *global registry* of all groups, held by all resources registered with the group system. While this feature would not necessarily be part of a system based on real multicast, it is useful as a confidence check. We assert as a correctness constraint that all members of all groups must have identical global registries when the system is quiescent with regard to *join*, *leave*, *create* and *destroy* requests. As a further simulation of real multicast a single resource instance, the super group manager, is designated to act as a *well known address* to aid group initialisations.

4.2 Resource types

Three types of resource are used in the prototype: group managers, group clients and a single super manager. Figure 5 shows the relationship between these resources. The overall effect is to allow any arbitrary resource to become a group system client by creating a manager.

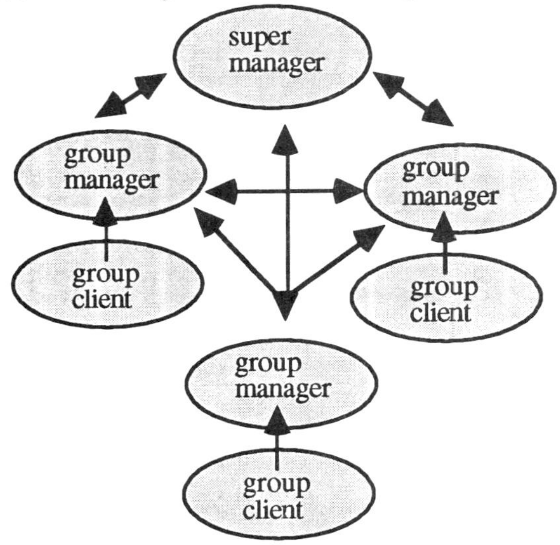

Figure 5: Group managers, group clients and the super manager.

Group clients only interact with the group service via a group manager. A resource becomes a client by spawning a manager to act on its behalf. The manager is driven by the client and is largely reactive. A prospective client first *imports* the group manager resource type and then creates a new instance of the type to operate on its behalf. Each instance of a manager operates on behalf of a single client. This decouples the communications semantics and maintenance functions from the client, thereby facilitating experimentation. When creating a new instance the client acquires the address of its manager in the form of a capability:

```
resource Group_client
  # become aware of Group_manager type
  import Group_manager
  # declare capability variable
  var gm: cap Group_manager
  # create new instance of manager
  # and obtain its address
  gm := create Group_manager()
.....
```

The client then executes concurrently with its manager, carrying out computations and synchronising with the manager when required to by communication needs. The client may join, leave, create and destroy multiple groups via its manager. When the group maintenance subsystem is operational *send* or *call* commands can be made directly to capabilities representing group addresses, where the message is distributed by simulated multicast. Receipt of messages is performed by a routine representing a unicast destination address within a group manager. Messages are buffered by the manager and removed by the client using standard producer-consumer synchronisation. Note that the creation and destruction of groups also rely on the super manager, but that other functions are carried out on a manager-to-manager basis. There is only one instance of the super manager resource and all group managers know where to find it, (although they may know nothing about each other). In the absence of real multicast it simulates a well known network address, an "all groups" address, which all managers can use for group initialisations. Space restrictions preclude further description of the resource types in the prototype.

5 Group Semantics

Point-to-point message semantics cannot simply be extended to groups. For example, *source-ordered* unicast messages provide a clear FIFO mode of communication between two points which satisfies Lamports causality relation[14], i.e. event 1 in resource A clearly precedes event 2 in resource B if the events are separated by a message from A to B. (A messages send time must precede its receive time). However, source-ordering is not sufficient to provide causal ordering in a group system.

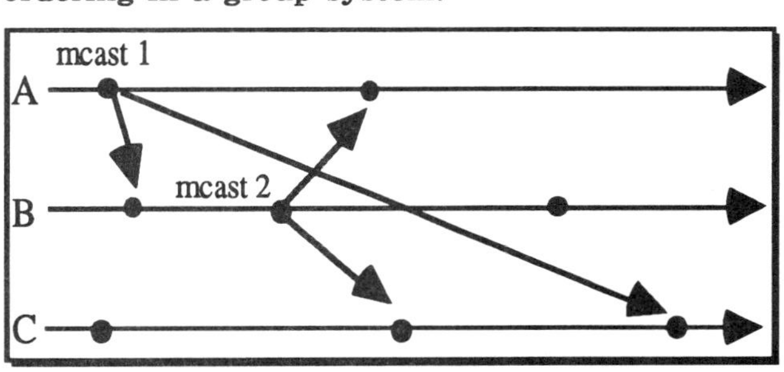

Figure 6: Causality Violation in Group Communication

Figure 6 shows a violation of causality in a multicast system (although all the messages may be source ordered). Resource B's message reaches resource C before C has seen the original message from A. It is possible that B's message was contingent on receipt of A's message, and that C will misinterpret its meaning, throwing the distributed system into an inconsistent state. Mechanisms for achieving causally ordered delivery include pSync[17] and the Birman-Schiper-Stephenson protocol[15]. The latter uses a system of messages tagged by vector clocks which are multicast and then have their delivery delayed by the receiver until the constraints imposed by causality are met. This is easy to add to the pSR prototype. Causal ordering is attractive because distributed systems are inherently partially ordered, and causality provides the minimum synchronisation overhead and does not mask concurrency.

Some applications may require *totally ordered* group communication. For example, a distributed transaction system. The protocol in [15] can be extended to provide a causal and total ordering, and other techniques are known[18].

The prototype pSR system described in Section 4 guarantees that all members of all groups have a consistent view of group memberships *when the system is quiescent*. It is however desirable, in the interests of maintaining a consistent distributed shared state to provide *view synchrony* [19] in a live system. Briefly, view synchrony guarantees that all members of a group always see the same membership list. This means that *joins* and *leaves* must be executed atomically with respect to message delivery and shared view. A crash can be modelled as a *leave*. This can be achieved (at a price) using the causally and totally ordered version of the protocol described in[15], but the topic is still under research[19]. There is a sufficient demand for a view synchronous programming platform to mandate it as a supported option in pSR.

Finally, lightweight, unreliable, unordered group communication is very useful, for example in predicate addressing for resource discovery, and has virtually no overhead. It is the mode of group communication that most closely follows true multicast.

6 Supporting Groups

The real goal of this work is to provide efficient support for the use of groups as a programming paradigm in pSR. We have now seen that group semantics can differ widely and that there are differing degrees of overhead associated with different types of group. In order to keep the support for groups flexible they are modelled in an object-oriented fashion using resources, and the runtime system then provides as efficient a mechanism as possible to support the properties of the defined group resource types. There are two aspects to consider: support at the system level, and the actual extensions to the language.

6.1 pSR and IP multicast

pSR communications are realised by its runtime system which accesses the Internet via a conventional operating system interface, namely BSD sockets. Machines which are Mbone aware support *multicast sockets* and the runtime system is being modified to use these. Ordered broadcasts do not necessarily require multicast but their efficient implementation is greatly simplified by its use. The lowest level of IP multicast is UDP, which provides a stateless, unreliable datagram service. This is adequate for important functions such as resource discovery and location, in which case the runtime system maps such requests into a well known all-groups address. The runtime system is initially being modified to support three predefined types of groups:

- stateless, unreliable delivery, no explicit membership list
- causally ordered
- totally ordered

The longer term aim is to enable efficient support for user defined types drawn from a taxonomy of key group properties.

6.2 Language Extensions

It is highly desirable to alter the language as little as possible and not introduce syntactic noise. Basically, a new capability type, the *group*, is added to the language. Groups are typed when instantiated and must consist of members which are identically typed operations. Typing ensures that the message format is the same, and that the synchronisation restrictions (call or send) are the same. As different types of groups are clearly necessary to satisfy different purposes they are defined as resource types, with their own operational semantics. In particular, join() and leave() may have different meanings for different groups. Non-standard versions of send and call e.g. gsend() and gcall() may also be introduced if necessary.

7 Summary, Status and Conclusions

pSR, a multiparadigm high level programming language with rich support for constructing concurrent and distributed systems, has been briefly described. Group communication has been identified as a highly desirable addition to pSR, and IP multicast as a good means of efficiently implementing it. In order to develop an understanding of group semantics a fully functional and flexible group communication system prototype has been designed and implemented in pSR. It has been shown how pSR can be used to prototype a distributed group system, and how to integrate groups into the language proper. The incorporation of groups into pSR has further strengthened its unique identity as an efficient, high-level, multiparadigm, concurrent and distributed programming language. The prototype system is running satisfactorily on several Sun workstations spanning several LANs.

Integration of groups into pSR raises issues at the system level and at the language level. IP multicast sockets have been adopted at the system level, although this limits participation to resources running on machines with Mbone-aware operating systems. Perhaps the main point behind this effort is the expectation that the Mbone will progressively become more efficient and standardised until it disappears – at which time all IP hosts and routers will support IP multicast.

A new type of capability, the *group*, has been added at the language level. Existing keywords *create*, *send*, *call*, *receive*, *in*, *op* and *proc* can now work with groups. New keywords *join* and *leave* have been added.

The novel aspect of this work is the flexible and efficient provision of *groups* as a programming paradigm in a high level language.

8. Acknowledgements

The author gratefully acknowledges support from the UK JISC New Technologies Initiative, Project 229, and from Sun (UK) Education.

9. References

1. ALLISON C. & LIVESEY M.J., Persistent SR: Adding Persistence to Concurrency in *HICSS'28*, Vol II, IEEE CS Press, (1995),655-664.
2. ANDREWS G. R. & OLSSON R.A., *The SR Programming Language: Concurrency in Practice*, Benjamin/Cummings, 1993.
3. ANDREWS G. R., OLSSON R.A., COFFIN M., ELSHOFF I., NILSEN K., PURDIN T. & TOWNSEND G., An Overview of the SR Language and Implementation. *ACM TOPLAS*, 10,1 (1988), 51 - 86.
4. HOARE C.A.R., Communicating Sequential Processes. *CACM* 21,8 (August 1978), 666-677.
5. MAY D., OCCAM. *SIGPLAN Notices* 18,4(1983), 69-79.
6. ATKINSON M.P., BAILEY P.J., CHISHOLM K.J., COCKSHOTT W.P. & MORRISON R., PS-algol: a language for persistent programming. *10th Australian Computer Conference*, Melbourne, (1983), 70-79.
7. HADZILACOS V. & TOUEG S., Fault Tolerant Broadcasts and Realted Problems in *Distributed Systems*, ed. Mullender,, Addison-Wesley, 1993, 97-145.
8. BAL, H., *Programming Distributed Systems*, Silicon Press, 1990.
9. ANDREWS G. R. Paradigms for Process Interaction in Distributed Programs, *ACM Surveys*, 23,1 (1991), 48-89.
10. KAASHOEK M.F. & TANENBAUM A.S, Group Communication in the Amoeba Distributed Operating System, *Proc. 11th Int'l Conf. on Distributed Computing Systems*, IEEE(1991), 222-230.
11. BOGGS D.R., Internet Broadcasting, *Xerox PARC Report*, CSL-83-3, 1983.
12. DEERING S., Host extensions for IP multicasting, *ARPA Network Working Group Request for Comments* (RFC) 1112, 1989.
13. MONTGOMERY T., Design, Implementation and Verification of the Reliable Multicast Protocol, Masters Thesis, West Virginia University, December 1994.
14. LAMPORT L., Time, clocks, and the ordering of events in a distributed system, *Commun. ACM* 21, *7* (1978),558–565.
15. BIRMAN K. SCHIPER A. & STEPHENSON P., Lightweight causal and atomic group broadcast, *ACM TOCS*, 9,3, (1991), 272-314.
16. ALLISON C. Concurrency Control for Real Time Groupware, in Paul, A.J. & Sobolewski, M. (eds.) *CE94,Concurrent Engineering: Research and Applications, A Global Perspective*, CTC(1994,)163–170.
17. PETERSON L.L, HUTCHINSON, N., & SCHLICHTING, R Preserving and Using Context Information in interprocess communication, *ACM TOCS*, 7,3 (1989), 91-101.
18. CHANG J, & MAXEMCHUK N. Reliable Broadcast Protocols, *ACM TOCS*, 2,3 (1984), 251-273.
19. BABAOGLU O, DAVOLI R, GIACHINI, L & BAKER M.G, RELACS: A Communications Infrastraucture for Constructing Reliable Applications in Large-Scale Distributed Systems, in *HICSS'28*, Vol II, IEEE CS Press (1995),612-621.

A Parallel Processing Environment for Speech Signal Processing Applications

N.R. Garner[1], D.M. Howard[1], P.A. Barrett[2], A.M. Tyrrell[1].
[1]Department Of Electronics, University Of York, Heslington, York, Y01 5DD, UK
[2]BT Laboratories, Martlesham Heath, Ipswich, UK

Abstract

This paper describes a software tool that has been developed for production of speech signal processing systems, but may be easily expanded to include any 1-dimensional signal processing problem with multiple inputs and outputs. The tool allows the user to define an arbitrary set of interconnected signal processing functions that are interlinked by vectors of signal data, this kind of problem is thus expressed in an inherently MIMD format. This user-defined structure is parsed to generate a configuration description that follows a communication based parallel processing format such as that used in Occam. This configuration may be executed either on a serial machine or on a network of transputers using both task and pipeline parallelism. The current system is capable of building a wide range of structures, for applications such as vocoders, speech enhancement, filterbank speech analysis and speech recognition. The parallel version runs on a network of 18 25 MHz T800 transputers. Current efficiency levels are very structure dependent, but for the problems discussed within the paper, efficiencies of around 65 % are achieved.

1. Introduction

This paper describes work being carried out for speech signal processing applications. It reports on novel parallel environment where signal processing 'blocks' can be defined by the user (including specific parameters; such as size of FFT, different windowing types, and number of layers in a Multi-layer Perceptron). These signal processing blocks are then placed onto a large parallel processing network (up to 66 T800 transputers) for efficient implementation. This paper describes the environment designed to enable the user to build up these blocks for the processing network.

It is well known that many signal processing applications are well suited for efficient implementation on parallel machines [6][7]. However, many of these must be 'hand-crafted' onto these machines to achieve the best performance. What is required for signal processing designer is a system that takes some, or all, of this hand-crafting away, and is performed automatically by the system. Such a system is being designed and is detailed in this paper.

The current system has been tailored to be easy to use in any speech processing environment, with emphasis on speech detection, recognition and enhancement. In such areas it may be necessary to experiment with many different signal processing structures. A special Signal Processing Descriptor File (SPDF) has been designed, which contains the user information for a particular signal processing structure. Such a file contains information about the processing elements that have been defined: their function, the input details, their output details, and any compile-time parameters required. These files are parsed by a specially designed parser that produces a configuration description file which is loaded onto the various processors in the network.

A number of standard signal processing functions have been 'hard-wired' into the system to allow larger systems to be built. These include 'standard' signal processing functions such as FFTs, filters, LPC, windowing functions and less 'standard' functions such as multi-layer perceptrons (MLPs) or cepstral transformations. These allow complex systems to be built easily out of simply-defined building blocks. These functional building blocks have a standard C format and new functions are easily added to the compiled code. In addition, combinations of these can be put together to make 'user-standard' functions, for functions that will be

1066-6192/96 $5.00 © 1996 IEEE
Proceedings of PDP '96

used often for a particular application, and will essentially make up a series of libraries.

Finally, the application may be execuated sequentially on virtually any platform with a C compiler, or it may be placed onto a parallel network of transputers [3]. The only difference between sequential and parallel operation is the use of different software libraries and an additional hardware configuration file. The placement of these software processes onto a processing network is very dependent on the hardware available, and the configuration of that hardware. Both spatial (or task) and temporal (or pipeline) parallelism [1][4] are used to produce the 'best' mapping of the software onto the hardware. While this may not always be the best (compared to hand-crafted code), the efficiencies being achieved are good for most applications and combinations of signal processing functions.

2. Signal processing software

This section describes the current state of development of the signal processing software that has been produced as tool for speech research. The software takes a Signal Processing Descriptor File (SPDF) produced by the user and compiles a list of parallel processes, with vector communications, that may implement the description. This configuration description is executed either sequentially or concurrently depending upon the host hardware environment. Much effort has been made to keep the two versions compatible, with 90 % of the source code being common to both - All input and output data is fully compatible between the two versions.

2.1. Description language

The Signal Processing Descriptor File (SPDF) contains the user information for a signal processing structure. Such structures are defined in terms of processes that have an arbitrary list of inputs, outputs and compile-time parameters. The job of defining processes is made easier by allowing a range of user-defined constants. Statements may be entered with any number of separating spaces, tabs and carriage returns. Certain pre-processor type definition statements are preceded with a '$' sign and all statements must be terminated with a semi-colon.

2.1.1. Constants:

Parsing software allows the use of integer, real, Boolean and string constant types, each of which may be expressed as a one dimensional vector. Full bracketed maths may be performed to calculate constant values - Boolean algebra and vector maths are catered for, with the maths type defaulting to the type of the assigned variable, e.g.

```
$INT a(2)=[1,2];              # =[1,2]
$REAL b=1+(3*a[1]);           # =7.0
$STR c="test"+a[0];           # ="test1"
$BOOL d=a(0)||!b    ;         # =TRUE
```

2.1.2. Comments and file inclusion:

Comments are allowed in the datafile, either commenting out the remainder of the line, as shown in the example above, or in between comment braces as shown in the example below. Facilities exist to include the entire contents of another file (this is useful for macro definitions, lists of filter coefficients and standard definitions for functions), e.g.

```
<# include standard definitions
  for signal processing functions
#>
$INCLUDE "std_def.sig";
```

2.1.3. Process description:

The actual interconnected processes are defined as follows:

- Firstly the name of the function or macro is given followed by a set of braces to indicate the beginning of a process definition
- Any parameters that are needed by the function or macro are assigned using their names. A function must have all of its compile-time parameters defined within the process description or an error message will be returned.
- The inputs to the process are defined with the `IN` statement. The input communication is defined by a vector name (which will correspond to an output of the same name from another process) and vector size (which should match the number of elements on the other side of the equality sign).
- The input vector may be used in its entirety or as a subset of elements from that vector. Such a subset is defined in square brackets after the variable name, using a list of elements separated by commas, a range of elements (the first and last of which separated by a colon) or any combination of the two.
- The input statement may or may not be terminated by an iteration descriptor '>' and a number. This number is the number of iterations previous to the current one that the data is taken. By default the process uses input vectors from the current

iteration i.e. a '>0' is not necessary. By this mechansim feedback and multi-rate systems may be produced

- The outputs from a process are given following the OUT statement. As for inputs, a vector size and name are used. This vector name is used by any number of input statements of any process.

A process description for a simple 3-tap FIR filter is given below -

```
$INT size=160; # frame size
$INT f_taps=3; # number of filter taps
$INT n_coeffs=f_taps+1;
$REAL filter_coeffs(n_coeffs)=\
  [-0.125,0.25,-0.5,1];
fir_filter{ taps=f_taps;
  coeffs(n_coeffs)=filter_coeffs;
  IN(f_taps)=ip[size-f_taps:size-1]>1;
  IN(size)=input;
  OUT(size)=output;}
```

The function `filter` requires two parameters:

1. The number of delay taps.
2. The actual filter coefficients.

There are two inputs to the function:

1 The last (number of taps) samples from the previous frame.

2 The current input frame.

The output vector is simply the FIR-filtered output frame.

2.1.4. Conditional parsing:

It is possible to only parse certain statements in the SPDF, depending upon a Boolean expression. This is useful for changing modes of operation of a system, i.e. when a given software structure is fundamentally the same between modes of operation, but the user wishes to conveniently switch between modes without changing the entire file, e.g.

```
#$BOOL use_fft=FALSE;
#could also use !TRUE
$BOOL use_fft=TRUE;
$IF use_fft:
  fft(points=32;
    IN(32)=ip;
    OUT(32)=op;}
```

2.1.5. Macro definitions:

Macros may be defined for a commonly used series of interlinked processes. Once a macro is defined, it may be used like any other function in a process description. An example definition is given below:

```
#polar FFT
{polar_fft{     # start of interface
description
  IN(in_size)=frame;
  OUT(fft_size)=magnitude;
  OUT(fft_size)=angle;}

#macro parameters
$INT in_size=32;
$INT fft_size=in;

# processes used in the macro
  cfft{ points=fft_size;
    IN(in)=frame;
    OUT(fft_size*2)=complex;}
  complex_to_polar{
    IN(fft_size*2)=complex;
    OUT(fft_size*2)=polar;}
  split_data{ items=2;
    IN(fft_size*2)=polar;
    OUT(fft_size)=magnitude;
    OUT(fft_size)=angle;}
} # end of macro definition
```

The first part of the macro definition, after the opening braces and the name, is the interface description, which defines which vectors are to be used as inputs and outputs from / to the outside world. Constants may be defined inside the macro and are in scope anywhere inside it. All other statements inside the macro must be process definitions, having exactly the same format as those described above for normal function definitions. Macros may also be nested in order to create increasingly more complex user functions.

The above macro could be used as shown:

```
$INT size=64;
polar_fft{ in_size=size;
  IN(size)=input;
  OUT(size)=mag;
  OUT(size)=angle;}
```

Here the re-definition of `in_size` causes the macro to be inserted using the new value throughout the definition. Therefore the resultant definitions, which are instantiated into the main program, are given below. Processes internal to the macro have their input and output vector names changed to allow for multiple uses of the same macro in any SPDF, e.g. `complex` becomes `complex_0`

```
cfft{ points=64;
  IN(64)=input;OUT(128)=complex_0;}
complex_to_polar{  IN(128)=complex_0;
  OUT(128)=polar_0;}
split_data{ item=2;    IN(128)polar_0;
  OUT(64)=mag; OUT(64)=ang;}
```

2.1.6. System input / output:

The program needs to know how many inputs and outputs there are to / from the system. These are defined by the reserved keywords `INPUT` and `OUTPUT`:

```
$STR INPUT(2)=["data","reference"];
$STR OUTPUT="op";
```

The parser searches the process definitions for the vector names given. An error message is returned if it cannot find any references to the I/O vector names.

2.2. Available functions

A whole host of ever-expanding functions are available for the user to construct signal processing systems. The current range of 'hard wired' functions include:

- *Adaptive Filter*
- *Autocorrelation and correlation.*
- *Average Data.*
- *Cepstrum from LPC.*
- *Combine and Split Data streams.*
- *Complex to polar conversion* and vice versa.
- *Convert to Boolean Vectors.*
- *Convert to dB*
- *Multiplex and de-multiplex* - may also be used to provide run-time decision logic
- *Normalise and de-normalise*
- *Differentiate and Integrate*
- *Energy* - computes the energy in a frame of data.
- *Signal Limiting.*
- *Maths* - add, subtract, multiply, divide
- *Other Functions* - log, exp, sqrt, cos, sin, tan
- *Fast Fourier Transform* - real and complex
- *Inverse Fast Fourier Transform* -real and complex
- *Generate signal.*
- *Filter* - IIR, FIR structures are allowed.
- *Lateral inhibition.*
- *Linear Predictive Coder (LPC).*
- *Multi-layer Perceptron (MLP).*
- *Peak-picker*
- *Shift and Scale data*
- *Signal Generator.*
- *Statistical Analysis.*
- *Thresholding.*
- *Signal Windows*- hamming, hanning, gaussian etc.
- *Zero-crossing rate*

2.2.1. Library definitions:

There are also various library files of user defined macro structures and useful constants. Currently, the available macro functions include:

- *MEL-scaled filter banks*
- *19-band Vocoder*
- *Spectral-subtraction*
- *5-feature Voice Activity Detector*
- *FFT-based spectrum*
- *Cepstra* - FFT, LPC and MEL-filterbank
- *Polar FFT and IFFT*
- *Inverse noise reduction filter*
- *Neural-net vector quantiser*

2.3. Adding new functions

It is very easy to compile new 'hard-wired' functions into the software, as the definitions which need to be modified are contained in a single header file. The new code module can then be linked into the rest of the code without any problems. A standard interface is used for each signal processing function, with optional extra parameters tagged on at the end. e.g.

```
int filter(float *in, short in_size,
  float *out, short out_size,
  int ntaps, float *coeffs)
```

The function is given a pointer to a floating point input vector and its size, and a pointer to an output vector and its size. Any parameters used are placed at the end, and may take the form of direct or indirect integers, floats or chars. Information must also be supplied for the parser for the names of the function and parameters and to check parameter types, input / output sizes. This is all supplied on one `#define` structure in the parser header file.

3. Exploiting parallelism

Introducing parallel execution to a problem that is expressed in a parallel form should be reasonably easy. Unfortunately, this is not entirely the case, as issues such a reconfigurability, efficiency and process allocation emerge. The parallel design given here goes some way to form a compromise between these issues.

Figure 1 shows a block diagram of how various processes in the system interact. The SPDF parser reads in the user process description from file and passes on the resultant configuration description. The configuration splitter takes the configuration and allocates processes within the description to the processors available. This splitting process is currently manual as no fully automated process allocator has been put together as yet. The output from this stage is an array of smaller configurations. These configurations are transmitted, via the loader, to the data setup process on each processor. This constitutes the initialisation phase of the network. Due to the need for reconfigurability, new SPDFs may be implemented as the user wishes without needing to re-run the whole system.

The execution path starts by reading input data from file and sending it to a data router [2]. This router acts as the nexus of the whole system (it is in fact implemented by many routing processes on each processor) as it controls the dataflow to and from the network. Given appropriate input data, each processor executes its given configuration, and sends any output data, via the router, to the intended processor. The router also takes output data from the network and writes it back to an output file.

The system is also capable of taking frames of data from an transputer ADC port and writing output data back to a similar DAC port. This setup is essential for real-time performance of speech processing algorithms.

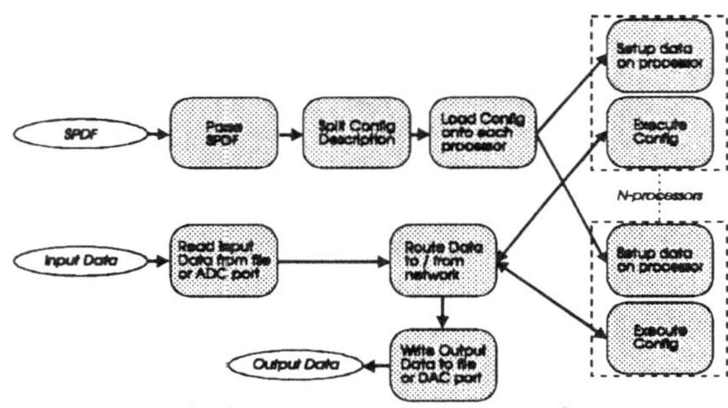

Figure 1: Software block diagram for parallel system.

3.1. Hardware / software placement

Given the simplistic view of how the system is put together from a software point of view, figure 1, it is then necessary to map that software onto the available processing hardware. An examples setup of the system utilises 9 T805 25 MHz Transputer Modules (TRAMs), each with 1 Megabyte of memory. The process to processor mapping for this system is given in figure 2. The main feature of this structure is the ring formed by the HOST TRAM, R1, R2, R3 and R4, which easily controls the passage of data. Spurs come off this ring to the slave processes, S1, S2, S3 and S4, which do the actual processing.

The HOST TRAM, which controls the link between the network and the host PC runs 3 processes:

- A user input / output process that provides menus and interactive support the system functions, plus an interface for file access. This is the top-level process in the system.
- An autonomous Master Input routine, that controls the flow of data and communications around the network. It also waits for commands from the User I/O process and translates these into network communications.
- An autonomous Master Output routine, that takes data and communications from the network and routes it either to the Master Input process or back to the User I/O process.

The 4 routing processors R1, R2, R3 and R4, have 2 processes each, nominally a separate input and output router. Input and Outputs must be performed in such a parallel system to avoid Deadlock, where two processes wish to perform a communication of the same sense with each other. Internal to the router is a dynamically allocated (First In First Out) FIFO buffer that contains all through communications. This allows the system to compute different iteration levels of data at the same time. This shared data buffer is controlled via tightly coupled inter-process communication to avoid simultaneous access. The existing routing software is capable of routing multiple inputs to multiple outputs and a slave spur, although the existing structure is maintained as a simple ring for easy pipelining.

Finally, the 4 slave processors, S1, S2, S3 and S4 do the actual work. Each has the same software kernel and is capable of performing all signal processing functions. Two processes are again used on the slave processors to avoid deadlock and moreover to decouple the execution of processes from the input of new data, that can occur at any time. This decoupling is achieved by use of shared configuration and process data between the two processes, and by using semaphores to prevent either process trying to access the data at the same time. The executing process checks each of the sub-processes its given configuration for full input data at the current iteration level. When this condition is met, the sub-process is called with appropriate input / output arrays and user parameters.

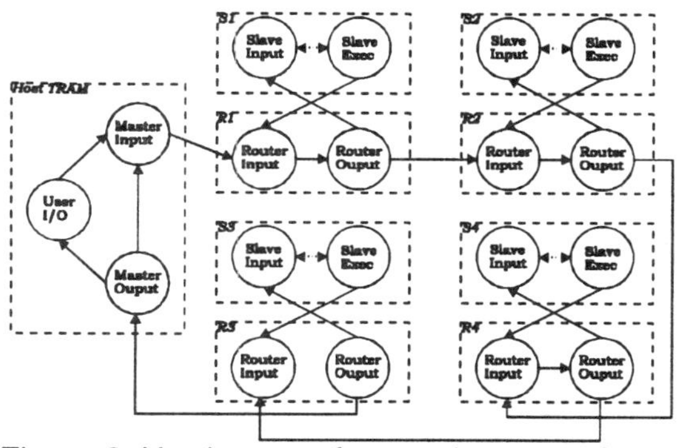

Figure 2: Hardware-software placement for a 4 slave system.

Some internal processes, that the user may require in a configuration, require direct access to the host filing system, in order store and retrieve their own state. Such a process is the MLP which needs to store its topology and its current weights. The routing software allows direct routing of this sort of information to/from the host PC without having to resort to virtual channel routing [5] which can dramatically slow down the system performance.

3.2. Process allocation

The last stage in system development is the allocation of the arbitrary number of interconnected processes to a given number of processors. When doing this, the issues of execution speed and efficiency must be traded off against each other. If a large number of processors are available the efficiency of the system is not as important as speed, if real-time operation is required. In many speech processing applications, a very fast response or hard real-time behaviour is required.

As it stands, the current parallel system exploits spatial (task) and temporal (pipelkine) parallelism. Given the arbitrary process interconnection structure in figure 3, spatial parallelism is exploited by placing any processes that may be executed concurrently on separate processors. This is very inefficient as processor P1 is doing far more work than P3, yet the potential speed-up is equivalent to the number of processors. Such process allocation is very good for banks of filters and for generation of different feature vectors for a speech recognition system.

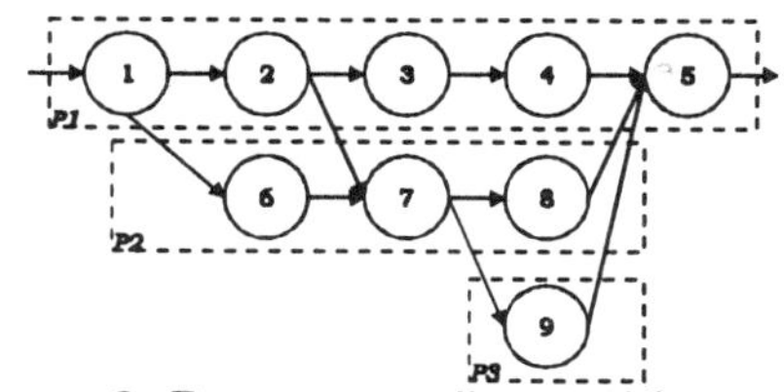

Figure 3: Processes allocated for spatial parallelism.

Another way to increase parallel performance is by temporal parallelism. In this instance, each processor works on a different iteration of data. Process allocation using temporal parallelism (or a pipeline) is shown in figure 4. Such parallelism can be very efficient if each processor takes approximately the same time to compute its processes, with a maximum speed-up of the number of processors. This is more difficult to implement using an arbitrary list of processes as each will take variable time, plus there will need to be some storage of data on each processor to allow for an overflow of data from the previous processor. Such parallelism will be incorporated into the software shortly.

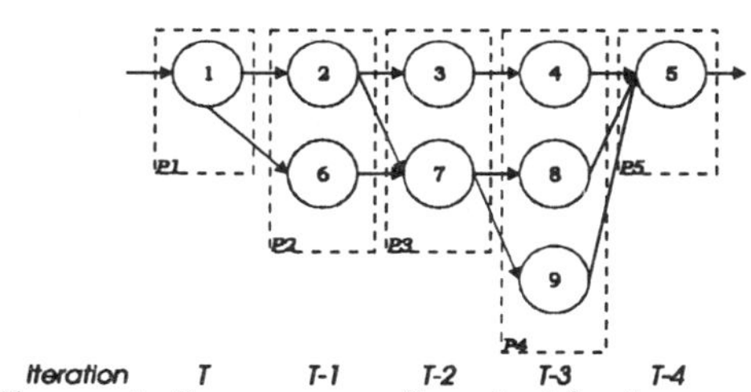

Figure 4: Processes allocated for temporal parallelism (Pipeline)

Knowing what parallelism exists in a problem is important, but does not provide the optimum process allocation for a given problem especially when process execution speed is variable and when exploiting both forms of parallelism simultaneously. One sure, but inefficient way, is to place one process on each processor. This is sufficient for a box of X transputers, while no more than X processes are required. Even when doing this, the time taken for each interprocess communication must be considered, especially for non-adjacent processes. This is especially important for speech signal processing problems where large amounts of data must be communicated, e.g. a 20ms frame of speech, sampled at 8kHz using 16 bits, requires a transmission of 320 bytes (or 2560 serial bits) - 128 μs for a transputer link. In the 4 slave system of figure 2, such data would take 1280 μs to get from input to output assuming no latency and no processing. Thus such a communication requires at least 6.4% of the available frame time. If multiple such communications are required, it can be seen that the communication will be the limiting factor in the speed-up and efficiency of the system. This is why the routing processes must be placed on seperate processors to the executing slave processes.

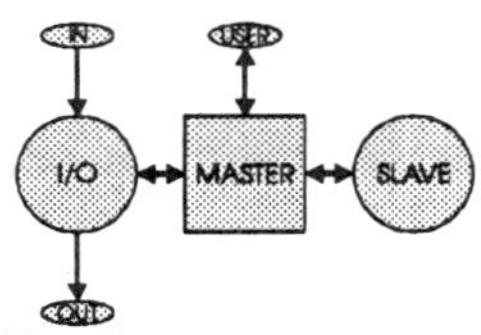

Figure 5: Hardware arrangement for uni-processor operation

Due to these communication considerations, various hardware topologies may be used, to achieve the best performance for a given problem. The most basic of these is the single processor system shown in figure 5. This is a useful starting point to benchmark the other systems, and may be necessary for very communication intensive systems. Figure 6 shows a system that is good for systems that have a resonable amount of spatial parallelism and require an immediate output at the same iteration level as the input. Figure 7 is the most general system that may be used for most problems as it can cater for both forms of parallelism. This structure is analysed in the next section on performance.

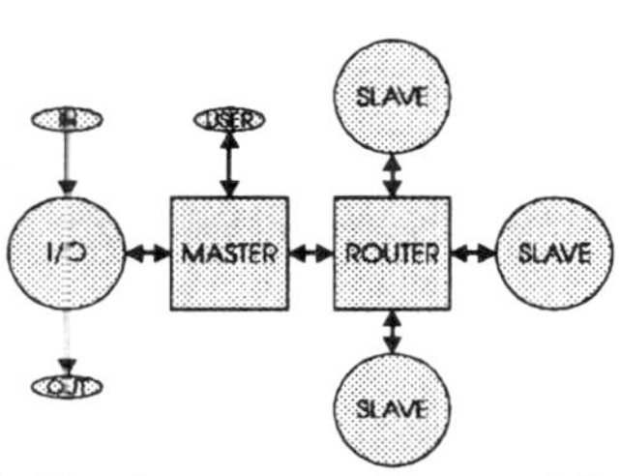

Figure 6: Hardware arrangement for 3 slave units

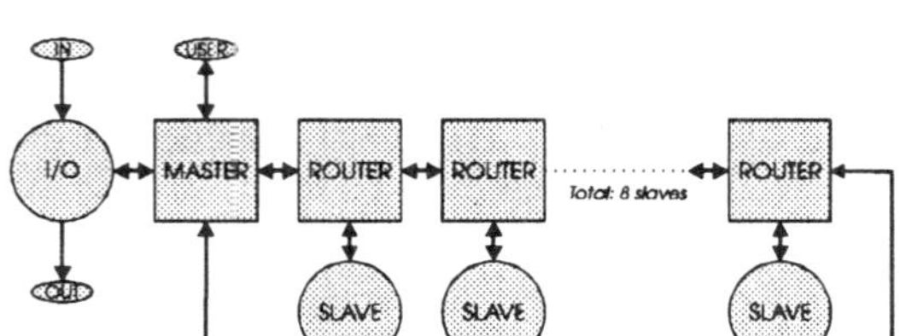

Figure 7: Hardware arrangement for 8 pipelined slave units

4. Performance

The performance of the full parallel processing system, using the hardware topology of figure 7, is analysed in this section using two real signal processing problems. Problem 1, which is depicted in figure 8, is typical of a bandpass filterbank and has a few notable characteristics:

- An input bottleneck; the input data must be transmitted to each of 32 processes.
- Much spatial parallelism in the 32 processes that may be executed in parallel with each other.
- A bottleneck at the output where all data is gathered together to form the final output.
- A maximum pipeline depth of 3.

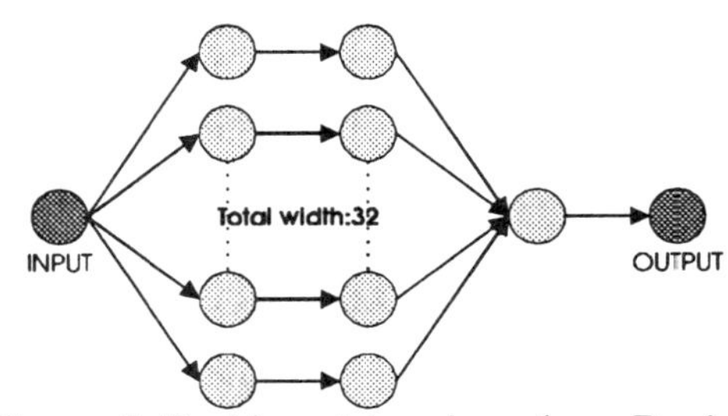

Figure 8: Problem 1 topology (e.g. Bank of Bandpass filters)

Problem 2, as shown in figure 9, is typical of a cascade of signal processing actions and transformations. The main characteristics of this type of problem are:

- Not much spatial parallelism - maximum width is only 2.
- Temporal parallelism may be exploited up to a pipeline depth of 8.

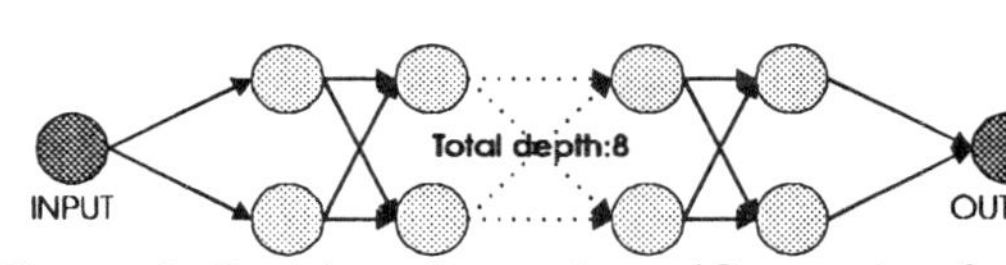

Figure 9: Problem 2 topology (Cascade of signal transformations)

4.1. Results

Each of the problems is analysed in turn using up the maximum of 8 active processors in the network - processors may be easily left idle, however data must still pass through its associated router in all cases, resulting in a degraded communication performance.

4.1.1. Problem 1:

The speed-up achieved, using increasing numbers of processors, for problem 1, is given in figure 10. It may be noticed that the maximum speed-up achieved for the full 8 processors is just under 2.5 - this is an efficiency of only 31%. This is due to the input and output bottlenecks of the problem, causing the speed-up to be very communication dependent. Further speed-up may be achieved by exploiting the temporal parallelism - if a pipeline depth of 2 is used the speed-up increases to 3.2 using only 5 of the processors. This is an efficiency of 64%.

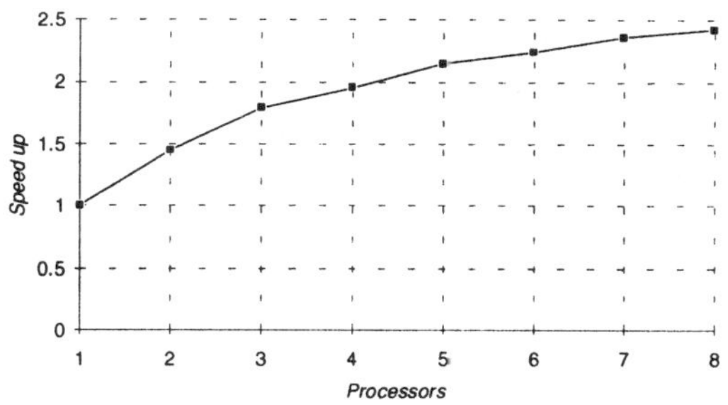

Figure 10: Problem 1 speed-up exploiting task parallelism.

4.1.2. Problem 2:

Problem 2, is easily suited to pipelining, thus figure 11 shows the speed-up achieved via use of this temporal parallelism. Here the maximum speed-up is achieved using a pipeline depth of 5, not the maximum 8. This is due to the inherent communications delay introduced by the routers' internal FIFO buffer, which must contain more data for increasing pipeline depth. However, the maximum speed-up is 3.27 with 5 working processors, hence an efficiency of 65%.

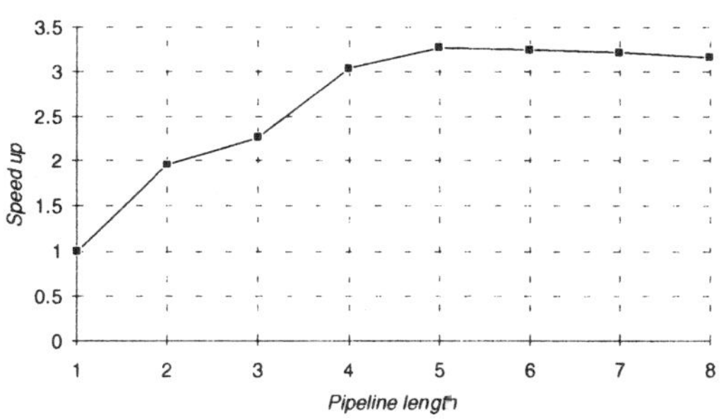

Figure 11: Problem 2 speed-up exploiting pipeline parallelism.

4.1.3. Overall:

It can be seen that reasonable speed-ups may be achieved for real signal processing problems using a mixture of temporal and spatial parallelism, with little benefit of adding more than 8 processors to the problem. The communications bandwidth between processors is not sufficient to allow the problem to become computation rather than communication dependent. As yet, no efficient automatic allocation algorithm has been developed for arbitrary problems, due to the complexity involved with mixing both forms of parallelism. Future work will concentrate on random search methods to generate near-optimum configuration topologies, such as genetic algorithms.

5. Conclusion

In this paper we have presented a novel approach to designing and implementing signal processing functions on a network of parallel processors. A description language has been shown which allows the user to design his/her signal processing system in terms of 'standard' building blocks, giving the appropriate parameters for these functions. These function descriptors are then parsed and converted into code for a parallel processing network, also information is obtained about the required configuration and connectivity for the hardware. The system then places these blocks onto the available hardware, in such a way as to optimise these signal processing functions. Currently speed-ups of up to 5 may be obtained for most problems using up to 8 slave processors - however all problems are heavily communication dependent and thus communication bandwidth is limiting the performance. Efficiences of around 65% are typical.

Work is continuing on the user interface and possible use of pictorial input of data, and on the placement algorithms to optimise the performance of the signal processing functions.

6. References

[1] Flynn, M.J., "*Some computer organisations and their effectiveness*", IEEE Transactions on Computers, C-21, No 9, pp 948-960.

[2] INMOS Limited, "*Occam 2 Reference Manual*", Prentice Hall International, 1988.

[3] INMOS Limited, "*Transputer Development and IQ systems databook*", Inmos, 1991.

[4] DeSegma, A.L., "The Technology Of Parallel Processing...", Prentice Hall, Vol 1, p17, 1989.

[5] INMOS Limited, "*ANSI C toolset - User Guide*", Inmos, 1992.

[6] Lawereins, R. et al., "*GRAPE: a CASE tool for digital signal parallel processing*", IEEE ASSP Magazine, 1990.

[7] Lee, E. et al., "*Gabriel: a design environment for DSP*", IEEE Trans ASSP, 1989, vol 37.

This work is sponsored by BT Laboratories, Martlesham Heath, Ipswich, UK.

InHouse — A User-Oriented Monitoring Approach *

G. Haring, G. Kotsis, S. Musil
Institut für Angewandte Informatik und Informationssysteme
Universität Wien
Lenaugasse 2/8, A-1080 Vienna, Austria

Abstract

In this paper we present a new approach for monitoring and visualization of parallel processing systems. Instead of measuring the system and presenting to the user a variety of performance figures and visualization displays afterwards, in this user-oriented approach the events and features of interest may be selected before instrumentation and measurements. Different techniques for this a priori filtering of events are provided, ranging from a direct manipulative selection in a graphical, hierarchical representation of the program and the architecture, to a textual, rule based selection. Real-Life Metaphors in visualization make this approach particularly suited for so called novice (i.e. non-expert) users, thus suggesting teaching as one of the major fields of application.

1 Introduction

Increasing availability of parallel processing facilities in recent years raises the question of effective and efficient development of parallel software in many fields of application. In the development process of parallel software the critical point is to tune the parallel application to the characteristics of the underlying architecture, so that maximum efficiency is gained. This tuning requires several iterations on program development/modification on the one hand, and observing the program behavior during execution on the target architecture on the other hand. Hence monitoring is a proper methodology to support this *performance oriented* development of parallel programs.

The monitoring process is to give the user insight into the performance behavior of the system, covering both hardware and software aspects. The methodological approach focuses on software monitoring, using event and time oriented instrumentation techniques. The event specification (both predefined and ad hoc user defined) covers various levels of abstraction, ranging from high level language instructions up to the task level.

Much has been published in the area of measuring and visualizing the performance and behavior of parallel programs and systems (see e.g. [2], [8]).

The shortfalls and problems of existing (software) monitoring and visualization approaches can be formulated as follows:

- Instrumenting the program code by hand is an error prone and tedious task. Therefore in most monitoring tools the instrumentation is done automatically, but this causes a loss in flexibility.
- The user typically has no influence on what has to be measured. Selection is only done after monitoring in the visualization phase.
- The execution of parallel programs typically results in large tracefiles. Keeping the amount of information contained in the tracefile as small as possible is crucial for fast visualization and analysis of data.
- The user interfaces of these tools very often seem like an unwanted add-on that is done quickly at the end of the development process. Very many of these interfaces are not well usable, especially for unexperienced users.
- The visualization techniques are not satisfyingly exploited. Often only two dimensional techniques are used to display multidimensional data.

To overcome these shortfalls we propose a user-oriented monitoring and visualization methodology which has been implemented in a tool called InHouse.

InHouse differs from other monitoring tools in that it is directed towards a specific user group, namely the novices to or learners of parallel concepts. This user

*This work is supported by the Austrian Ministry for Science, Research and Arts, (research grant GZ 613.542/1-26/92).

1066-6192/96 $5.00 © 1996 IEEE
Proceedings of PDP '96

group calls for a different approach to monitoring and representing a parallel system on the screen. Intuitive displays are a must and an easy to understand representation of the parallel system ensures that the user will be able to use the tool and explore the concepts of parallelism very soon. Data displays using traditional visualization techniques like Gantt charts or Kiviat diagrams won't be clear for this kind of users as they use identical visual forms for conveying different kinds of information. Furthermore they are very abstract and do not at all help in getting to know the concepts of parallelism.

Existing monitoring tools ([17], ParaGraph [9], Traceview [16], ParMon [19]) are more directed towards the expert user who has a clear understanding of the parallel system. In this case traditional visualization techniques serve the purpose of conveying information to the user well, as they show a lot of information in a compressed form. The experienced user will know that the various displays show different information and interpret them accordingly.

Still there are some monitoring or algorithm animation tools that make use of alternative visualization techniques. For example Brown [3] makes use of sound for algorithm animation. Different sounds mean different states of processors and empirical tests have shown that users are capable of distinguishing a lot of sound patterns after some time. Zabala [22, 23] uses visualization techniques called cave and multiple icons. Both techniques are good for displaying multidimensional data.

2 Studying the User Demands

The learners of parallel concepts do not have a any or only a vague mental model [1] of a parallel system. They maybe have been told that a parallel system has many processors and that things happen faster, but still they lack a clear imagination of what this system will be like. The mental model is only loosely coupled to known concepts of computers. The only thing that these people know is that one can run programs on that kind of machines and that it is possible to measure certain things in order to check whether the program really runs faster than before.

Therefore the users expect the monitoring tool to be usable in two respects: on the one hand the tool must give a clear description of a parallel system and on the other hand it must be easy to use, so that the users can concentrate on fulfilling their tasks and do not have to think about the usage of the system:

Clear Description As the users, who as stated before are not familiar with parallel concepts, need to build up a model of the parallel system with the help of the tool it is important to provide them with a clear description of what is shown on the screen. One of the most intuitive ways to convey new information is by means of known concepts, which share the main features of the new information. By making comparisons and drawing analogies new concepts are learned with a minimum effort. Users want this description to be easily understandable and quickly giving insight. Nothing is more frustrating than not being able to use a tool after half an hour.

Ease of Use The user is already occupied enough with learning the new concepts and selecting measures and objects. It absolutely must not be difficult to use the system. Navigation in the parallel system must be as easy as walking around in one's own flat. The selection mechanisms must be intuitive and well known in order to reduce cognitive workload. Furthermore the elements of the user interface must be used consistently without any modes. Only an easy to use human-computer interface will ensure that the user can focus on the task and not does not have to learn to tackle the system first.

3 Principles and Methods

We have designed the InHouse system according to the following principles:

Hierarchy Since the systematic approach to develop parallel programs implicitly possesses hierarchical features the best idea is to unify all performance information in a regular structure which matches the structure of both the program and the development process. If these requirements are fulfilled then the proposed structure will allow fast access to the performance information as well as to the source code of the program and will support the tuning of the program. The identification of performance problems will be also facilitated. The hierarchy-based model has multiple advantages: it has a regular structure, provides multiple levels of abstraction, supports multiple views, allows an ease way of moving through the different levels.

Architecture Independence In this project a transputer system has been used as parallel architecture and OCCAM as programming language, but the concepts are based on CSP [11, 12, 10] and can therefore be applied for many parallel programming languages and distributed memory multicomputers.

The trace data file contains performance data in a tool independent format. This independence guarantees the tool conception to be proof for future developments and changes in visualization requirements by the user, or display techniques of the workstation equipment. It is even suitable to support the use of hardware monitors for collecting measurement data.

The proposed information structure was designed to support an object-driven software monitor. The approach for solving the monitoring problem is time-based, i.e. after the run of the program, a set of time stamps corresponding to the program objects is available. By a simple mapping of the time stamps to the developed structure the dynamic behavior of the program can be revealed. This structure includes five-level hierarchy representation. Two basic data structures are used for representing the program on each of the hierarchy levels: graph and tree. The proposed structure is independent on the method of monitoring and may be used in software monitors as well as in hardware and hybrid monitors. It is also language and environment independent.

Usability The tool must be easy to use. It must assist the user in understanding the parallel concepts and in accomplishing the tasks without being bothered by a complicated navigation or selection mechanism. Furthermore the look and feel must be consistent.

Information Manipulation Environment This is a specific kind of user interface that has the following features [18]: it is highly visual, metaphor-oriented, application-specific and direct manipulative. An IME ensures the usability of the InHouse system with all its four features.

A highly visual interface is easy to understand. The user will be presented with information in graphical form and will not solely see text on the screen. Graphic representation provide the biggest mental bandwidth [20]. The human brain is specialized for perceiving visual information and can therefore take up more information at once. Furthermore visual concepts are a very general concepts and are not constrainded by standard look and feel components.

A metaphor oriented interaction environment is superbly suited for the purposes of a tool for learners. Metaphors [4, 5, 14, 15] work by explaining facts, which are completely new or rather unusual for the user, by means of some other facts, which are very well known to the user and which share the main features of the facts they shall explain. Empirical tests [21] have shown that for transporting new knowledge so called real world metaphors are suited best.

A problem oriented user interface takes into account the tasks that have to be accomplished and the target users and offers the according representations and interaction techniques. User interfaces for novices will mostly differ from user interfaces for experts and not every application can be pressed into the corset of the desktop metaphor. Furthermore the input and output devices have to fit the used visual representations. What good is a 3D graphics if used solely with a 2D input device and thus awkward to handle?

Direct manipulation is the key interaction technique in Information Manipulation Environments. The user has to be able to interact with the things in the environment as directly as possible. This is the most intuitive way of dealing with the world and should be exploited in a computer human interface, too.

4 Description of InHouse

4.1 Hierarchical Concept

An overview of a system decomposition hierarchy is shown in figure 1. Every level allows a given program to be examined at the level's resolution which is defined through the objects of interest.

The *system level* is the highest level in the hierarchy. On this level the program is treated as a black box, i.e. the resolution on this level is the program as a whole.

The *network level* is the level under the system level. On this level the system is defined through the set of processors and the set of their interconnecting physical links. Thus, the processors and their links define the granularity on this level. All the details about the processes inside given processors are hidden from the user. The processor is treated as a black box, which may or may not communicate with its neighbors through its links. Only the static physical communication channels are represents (i.e. the topology of the network).

On the *process level* the parallel program is represented in terms of communicating processes. The level resolution is defined through the processes, treated as black boxes, and their channels. The details about the process structure are hidden to the user.

Groups of processes or individual processes are objects of interest on this level. In fact, this level implies

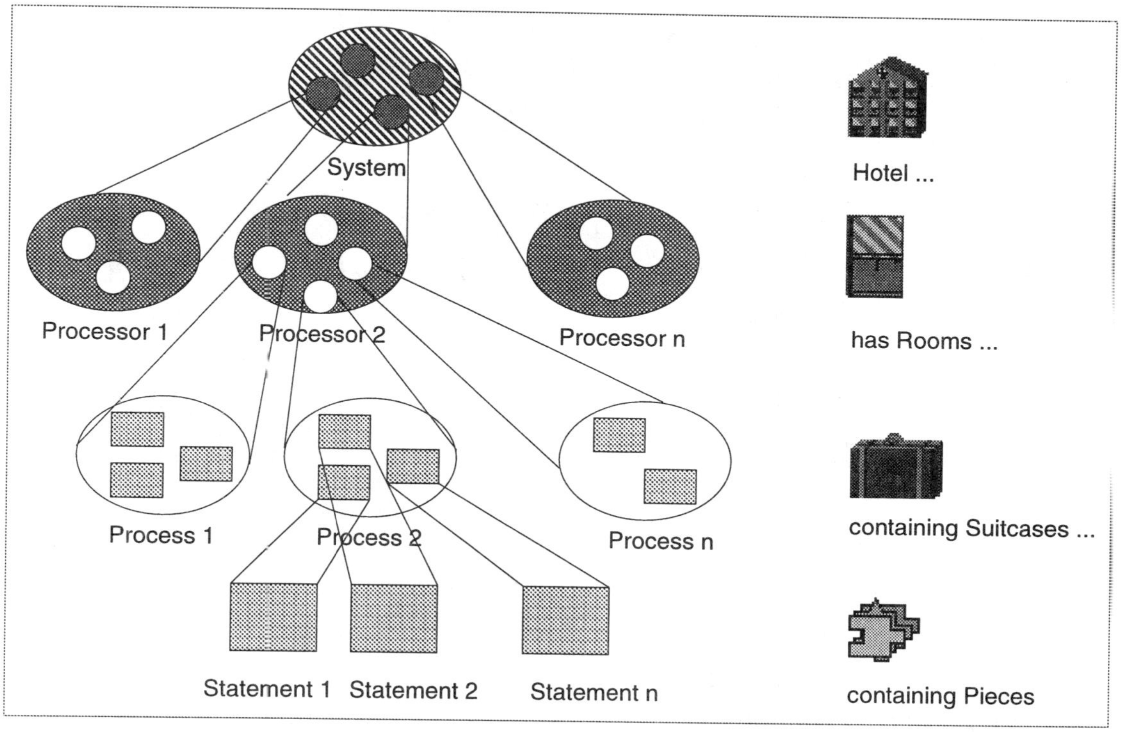

Figure 1: System Hierarchy and Metaphorical Representation

the conceptual solution of the application problem.

At the lowest level, the *command level*, every process is a set of spatially ordered set of commands. The structure of the process representation on this level should reflect this order. All the details about the process structure are visible to the user.

Any command may be treated as an object of interest. Since this granularity would be too fine in most cases, several rules for "packing" sequences of commands into larger objects can be applied. For example, a sequential set of commands which does not include input or output command(s) may be treated as a single object in order to reduce the number of time measurements.

4.2 Scenario, Walk through

Interaction with InHouse can be split into three phases:

1. Object Specification Phase:
   In this phase the users can select which parts of the program shall be monitored and which can be left out. Users shall be able to select the information they are interested in two ways (the meaning of the third way will be explained later). On the one hand there should be a possibility to navigate through a representation of the program and directly select the pieces of interest. On the other hand users should be allowed to select measures they are interested in without having to think about how this measure will be obtained. This will be done by the program. We will call the first way of selection "object selection", the second one "measure selection".

2. Monitoring Phase:
   The source code is instrumented with the probes and run on the target system, thus producing a trace file for later analysis.

3. Visualization Phase:
   The trace file is analyzed and the results are shown in various displays. Different views on the program shall provide the deepest insights and allow for an easy detection of errors or bottlenecks. Again, users shall be allowed to select from a variety of options the displays that seem most useful to them. It is important to notice that only information that has been requested during object specification phase will be available in this phase. So it can happen, that some displays won't be available for a certain program run, as the necessary information for them is not available.

Only two of these three phases call for user interaction, namely Object Specification and Visualization. In the following the InHouse system will be introduced

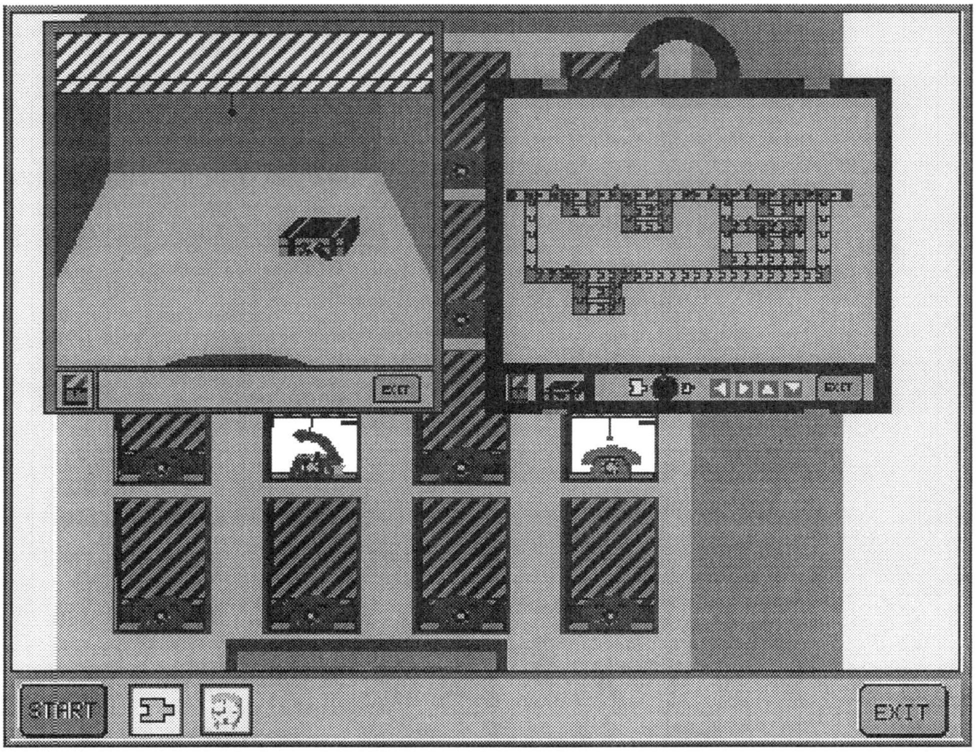

Figure 2: Selection by Direct Manipulation

from the user's point of view. First some general discussion on the user interface is given and then the two for the user most important phases will be explained in more detail.

We decided to design a metaphor based, WIP (Windows, Icons, Pointing), 2 1/2 D IME for the monitoring tool. We used metaphors because we had our design target in mind: explaining something new or unfamiliar to users. As stated before, metaphors are useful in means of transporting new knowledge, if not the only way of learning something radically new.

Our interaction environment is based on the precondition that visual information will be memorized more easily and is an efficient part of intelligent behavior. Therefore most of the system's functions are presented by visual means The goal was to use active and flexible visual elements based on metaphorical semantics, which aren't constrained to specific sets of widgets.

It should be possible to use the tool with what is nowadays a standard hardware equipment in order to allow most students to use the tool. A one button input device is used to provide for usage over a variety of platforms. We use 2 1/2 D only, because real 3D environments require a real 3D input device to be used appropriately. Using a 3D environment with a mouse is not an appropriate form.

The first step in designing the interaction environment was to find an appropriate metaphor for the parallel system. We arrived at a pool of metaphors for representing this structure, which for example included things like tree, city, prison, school or hotel.

We then concentrated on finding out in which metaphor our problem would be represented best and if and how we could bring in the missing parts of the functionality. After some internal discussions assisted by certain techniques and some informal interviews with future users, we arrived at choosing the hotel metaphor, because all other metaphors either lacked functions or had too many features, that were not part of the problem. The hotel was accepted, because it resembled the parallel system hierarchy best and because it allowed an easy and understandable metaphor in order to provide all the demanded functions.

The hotel now stands for the complete parallel system, the rooms represent processors. The size and location of a room currently have no meaning, but could have. Size could show whether this is a processor with small or large computing capability, location on floors could help in representing groups of processors. Processors are connected via hard-links that allow them to exchange messages. The rooms are connected via inhouse telephones. Every room has a phone. During the selection phase a phone will automatically call all its connected partners when selected, thus showing the hardware layout.

The contents of a room are suitcases, which represent the processes that are mapped onto a processor and will be executed there during runtime. We preferred suitcases to pieces of furniture, because furniture is normally placed into a room only once (in a while) whereas the processes (now suitcases) change their location more often. As there is no fixed succession of execution of processes in our parallel system, we can distribute the suitcases randomly in the room and can also allow the user to move them around. Suitcases are currently all the same size, but we could use size for indicating the number of code-lines of a process. Processes are connected via softlinks. We represent the softlinks with suitcase labels of the sort, that are used at airports to send suitcases to the right place. The idea behind that is that suitcases with the same destination can talk with each other.

A literature survey brought us to jigsaw puzzle pieces, that are successively used in visual programming [6, 7, 13], as being the contents of the suitcases. The decision of packing jigsaw pieces into the suitcases might seem strange at first sight, but their characteristics make the choice obvious. They have a fixed sequence and various shapes for indicating types of code constructs.

As specified in the system architecture, there should also be a means to regulate the degree of detail that is shown in the code representation. This was also provided for with the puzzle pieces. The level of detail can be changed interactively in the program, but only for all puzzle piece windows at once. The sets will then be updated accordingly. The current level of detail is also shown in the iconized version of the detail selection panel, so that users always know on which level they operate.

After having found a representation for the parallel system, the selection mechanisms had to be worked out. Object selection meant browsing through the representation of the parallel system and selecting the pieces of interest. Objects therefore had to provide two functions: Open (if necessary) and select. To open a room (entering it), the window blind must be clicked, to select the room the light has to be turned on inside by clicking on the lower part of the window. Suitcases are opened by clicking the lock and are selected by putting them into an upright position. The complete set of puzzle pieces is always shown in the suitcase window when the suitcase is opened. Users can zoom and move around in the set using a certain knob and arrows. Puzzle pieces currently can't be opened to see the underlying codelines. They are selected by simply clicking on them, which makes them blink for a certain time. As stated before, we purposely didn't apply any additional text and relied on colour coding only. We realize that for programs with more processes on more processors (massively parallel programs) labeling the items will be necessary, but we are interested in how long users are still able to remember the colours. Still, we help remembering by showing the mother node(s) (the according suitcase and/or room) in the left hand corner of each window. Telephones and suitcase labels can only be selected. The telephones have a lifted receiver then, the suitcase labels are highlighted. Figure 2 shows a typical screen of direct selection.

Measure selection is done with a selection bar that works like a number lock for bycicles. Every measure is a combination of three items. The first determines the type of the measure, which can be duration or count, the second determines the state of an object (if it can have more than one), which can be idle, waiting, active and communicating respectively. The third item determines from which object, or which group of objects this measure shall be calculated. If an object has to be specified more precisely, an extra window will pop up, that shows all options. For example if a measure for one process (suitcase) is selected all available suitcases sorted after processors will be displayed. Senseless combinations are detected by the system and can't be selected, as a red sign is over the checkbox. If a certain measure has been selected, a green mark will be over the checkbox when this combination is chosen. All items are represented by visual objects

Measure selection and direct selection semantically overlap. Selecting an object directly is like selecting a lot of measures for this object via measure selection, whereas selecting an object via measure selection means selecting an object partially via direct selection. This overlapping has to be made visible to the users. We do this on the one hand by "locking" already selected objects in measure selection, which means that they are shown in the selected state, but can't be deselected. They are "locked" by a lock. On the other hand we show in an animation, which measures already have been selected for this or that object. The animation can be seen when clicking on the icon in the lower left corner of the desired object's window. This small icon will be in selected state if measures have been selected and in unselected state if not. A small

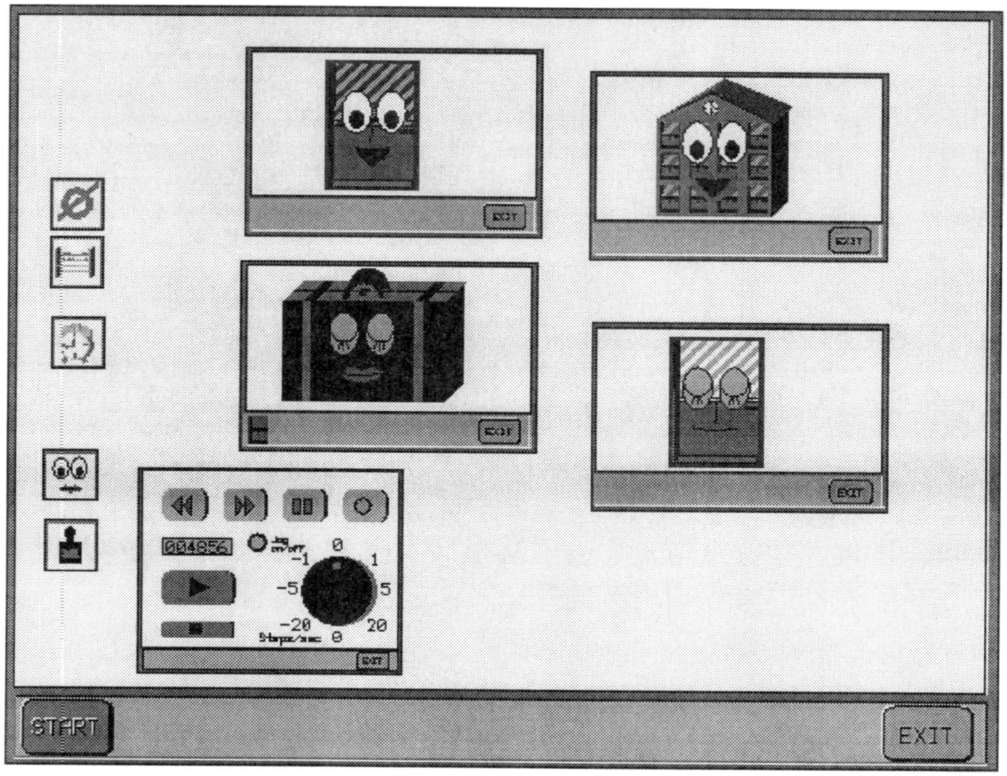

Figure 3: Sample Screen of an InHouse Session

separate window then pops up under the icon, which looks like the icon bar without the handles, and continuously displays the selected measures until exited.

As for the visualization phase the visual elements were reused and thus the represenation for the parallel system. The displays should be as intuitive as possible, as informative as possible and should provide the users with as many displays as possible. It turned out that the displays could be categorized into five different groups.

- Status Information:
  The status of an object at every time during the run will be displayed dynamically. The display of communication partners could also fall within this group.

- Duration Information:
  The duration of idle, waiting etc. periods of a certain object will be displayed in a graphical form, to be viewed statically.

- Counting Information:
  This kind of diplays gives information about how many objects of a kind were active at a time, again dynamically.

- Statistical Information:
  These displays inform the user about the average performance of an object. All data that has been gathered for an object, will be shown in numerical form, if useful assisted by a graphic form. These displays will be static ones.

- Load Information:
  These displays show how much a certain object was used, how large the passed messages were etc. These diplays will be both static and dynamic.

The dynamic displays are regulated with the tape tool. This tool is used like a normal VCR control panel. A jog shuttle is used for regulating the speed of slow motion. The tape tool is an extension to our hotel metaphor, but doesn't spoil the effect, as VCRs can be expected to be found in a hotel nowadays.

We have implemented the status displays. Figure 3 shows a sample screen with the tape tool in use and some status displays open. On the left hand side there are the icons for the five display groups.The users can select status displays on all levels, grouped or single items and then replay the program as often as they want.

5 Conclusions

This project has successfully developed a system for the monitoring of parallel programs that is centered around the user. Users have control over the whole monitoring and visualization process. They actively control what is measured, they control what they want to have visualized and they control the dynamics of this visualization.

An alternative user interface approach has been chosen, that focuses on so-called novice users. Their needs are explicitly supported. Easy comprehension of the parallel concepts is provided by taking up a metaphor based approach, good remembrance by a small visual alphabet, that is used both in the selection and the visualization phase.

Further activities in the realm of monitoring and visualization of results could include the development of an agent-based visualization system. The agent automatically detects bottlenecks and points the user to interesting displays and execution phases.

Furthermore one could try to reuse the globally defined system architecture with another underlying parallel architecture. A design solution for massively parallel systems could also be developed.

From the human computer interaction designer's point of view this project has shown, that there is still a need to define design processes for non-standard, metaphor-based interaction environments, as is the user interface of InHouse. There are no real methods to be found, only some vague guidelines, and it would be a big challenge to work out such a design process, that not only shows what to do, but also how to accomplish the design goals.

References

[1] J.R. Anderson. *Kognitive Psychologie*. Spektrum der Wissenschaft, Germany, 1989.

[2] H. Blaschek, G. Drsticka, A. Ferscha, and G. Kotsis. Visualization of parallel program behavior. Technical report, University of Vienna, Dept. of Appl. Comp. Sci., 1992. Internal Report.

[3] Marc H. Brown and John Hershberger. Color and sound in algorithm animation. *IEEE Computer*, pages 52–63, December 1992.

[4] J.M. Carroll. Metaphors and user interface design. In M. Helander, editor, *Handbook of Human Computer Interaction*, page ?? Elsevier Science Publisher, 1988.

[5] T.D. Erickson. Working with user interface metaphors. In B. Laurel, editor, *The Art of Human Computer Interface Design*, pages 65–73. Addison Wesley, 1990.

[6] E.P. Glinert. Out of flatland: Towards 3-d visual programming. In E.P. Glinert, editor, *Visual Programming Environments, Applications and Issues*, pages 547–554. IEEE Computer Society Press, 1990.

[7] E.P. Glinert, M.M. Blattner, and C.J. Frerking. Visual tools and languages: Directions for the 90ies. In *Proceedings of the IEEE Workshop on Visual Languages*, pages 89–95. IEEE Computer Society Press, 1991.

[8] G. Haring and G. Kotsis, editors. *Performance Measurement and Visualization of Parallel Systems*, volume 7 of *Advances in Parallel Computing, G. R. Joubert, Udo Schendel (Series Eds)*. North Holland, 1993.

[9] Michael T. Heath and Jennifer A. Etheridge. Visualizing the performance of parallel programs. *IEEE Software*, 8(5):29–39, September 1991.

[10] C. A. R. Hoare. *Notes on Communicating Sequential Processes*, volume 14 of *NATO ASI Series F*. Springer, Berlin, Heidelberg, August 1985.

[11] Charles Anthony Richard Hoare. Communicating sequential processes. *Communications of the ACM*, 21(8), August 1978.

[12] Charles Anthony Richard Hoare. *Communicating Sequential Processes*. Series in Computer Science. Prentice Hall International, UK, 1985.

[13] C.M. Holt. Visualizing an algebra of objects. In *Proceedings of IEEE Workshop on Visual Languages*, pages 225–230. IEEE Computer Society Press, 1991.

[14] B. Indurkhya. *Metaphor and Cognition*. Kluwert Academic Press, NL, 1992.

[15] G. Lakoff and M. Johnson. *Metaphors We Live By*. University of Chicago Press, USA, 1980.

[16] Allen D. Malony, David H. Hammerslag, and David J. Jablonowski. Traceview: A trace visualization tool. *IEEE Software*, 8(5):19–28, September 1991.

[17] M. A. Mayoski, E. Luque, R. Suppi, J. Sorribes, and M. A. Senar. Simulation and visualization tools for link-based parallel architectures. In *Proceedings of EUROMICRO 91*, 1991.

[18] S. Musil and M. Tscheligi. *How to Design Non Standard Interaction Environments*. CHI '94 Tutorial Notes, USA, 1994.

[19] E. Pozzetti, G. Serazzi, and V. Vetland. Parmon: Un monitor per programmi paralleli. Technical Report 3/148, Politecnico di Milano, November 1994.

[20] G. Rohr. Using visual concepts. In S. Chang, T. Ichikawa, and P. Ligmenides, editors, *Visual Languages*, pages 325–348. Plenum Press, 1986.

[21] K. Vaananen. Metaphor based user interfaces for multimedia environments. Position paper, Interchi '93 Workshop on Spatial Metaphors for User Interfaces, January 1993.

[22] E. Zabala and R.W. Taylor. Maritxu: Generic visualization of highly parallel processing. In *Programming Environments*, pages 171–180. North Holland, 1992.

[23] E. Zabala and R.W. Taylor. Power tools: New generation data presentation tools. In *Proceedings of HCI'93 People and Computers*, page ?? Cambridge University Press, 1993.

Monitoring Strategies for Hypercube Systems

Dieter Kranzlmüller, Siegfried Grabner, Jens Volkert
GUP Linz
Johannes Kepler University Linz
Altenbergerstraße 69, A-4040 Linz, Austria/Europe
[kranzlmueller | grabner]@gup.uni-linz.ac.at

Abstract

The basis for analyzing and improving the reliability and efficiency of software is a monitoring tool. Besides the usual difficulties of diagnostic tools, parallel computing also introduces the ***probe effect*** *to the monitoring process. This effect describes altered program behaviors observed when delays are introduced into concurrent programs through the use of instrumentation. The probability of the probe effect depends on the amount of overhead that is produced with the monitoring functionality.*

This paper describes the ***E****vent* ***M****onitoring* ***U****tility EMU, which offers an approach for monitoring of distributed memory multiprocessors. The current implementation takes advantage of the hypercube topology for further reduction of the overhead caused by the instrumentation. Therefore EMU contains various monitoring models with different impact on the observed program. The knowledge of these models can help the user to reduce the overhead of the monitor as much as possible.*

Keywords: *parallel debugging, monitoring, probe effect.*

1. Introduction

The quality of sequential as well as parallel software is mainly determined by the criteria reliability and efficiency. With parallel processing the reliability of a program is reduced through errors like deadlocks, stampede effects [14] and race conditions [12], whereas the efficiency suffers from performance bottlenecks and load imbalance [9].

The software lifecycle defines two phases for improving the quality of programs. The reliability is increased through detection and elimination of programming errors during the tedious task of debugging. The performance is improved during the performance tuning phase. Both tasks may be supported by tools, which analyze the runtime behavior of the software.

While diagnostic tools for sequential programs are mostly integrated on-line, the difficulties with time dependencies between concurrent processes force the use of post-mortem tools. Currently only few tools exist for on-the-fly analysis of parallel programs [1].

The basis for the analysis is a monitoring tool, which records all necessary data about a program run. A main problem in instrumenting parallel programs is the so called *probe effect* [11] or *Heisenberg dilatation* [14]. In [4] the *probe effect* is defined as an alteration in the frequency of run-time computational errors observed when delays are introduced in concurrent programs. This means that original bugs vanish when utilization is enabled or program optimization is turned off. The conclusion is that the influence of the instrumentation is the part which determines the quality of the monitor. The best monitor is the one with the lowest interference on the observed program.

This paper presents our **E**vent **M**onitoring **U**tility EMU, which contains facilities and possibilities for recording parallel program behavior of message passing programs. The current implementation is running on an nCUBE 2 distributed memory multiprocessor and derives some advantages from this computer's hypercube topology.

EMU was developed as part of the **M**onitoring **A**nd **D**ebugging environment MAD, which follows two motivations: firstly it helps in testing a program for correctness, secondly it supports achieving a better performance level.

The MAD approach [6] is based on recording of tracefiles with EMU during an initial program run. The results of EMU are fed into ATEMPT - **A T**ool for **E**vent **M**ani**P**ula**T**ion, which produces a partially order graph in time for the representation of interprocess dependencies. The graph is visualized within a graphical user interface and can be inspected and manipulated for the analysis of the recorded program run. The verification of race conditions [7] is done with the trace driven simulator PARASIT [10].

The tracefiles of EMU can also be converted into PICL-format (Portable Instrumented Communication Library [5]) for further analysis with tools like ParaGraph [8]. The

1066-6192/96 $5.00 © 1996 IEEE
Proceedings of PDP '96

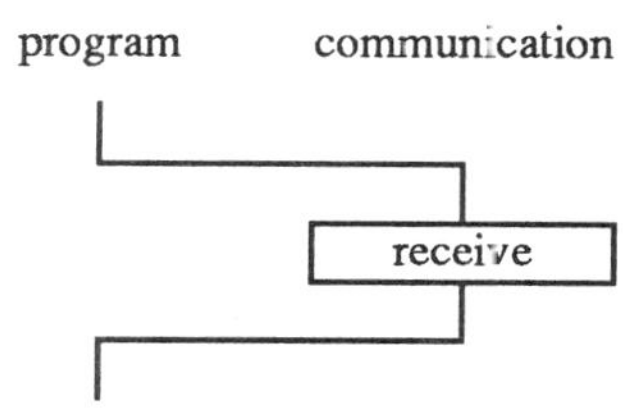

Fig. 1a. Standard communication

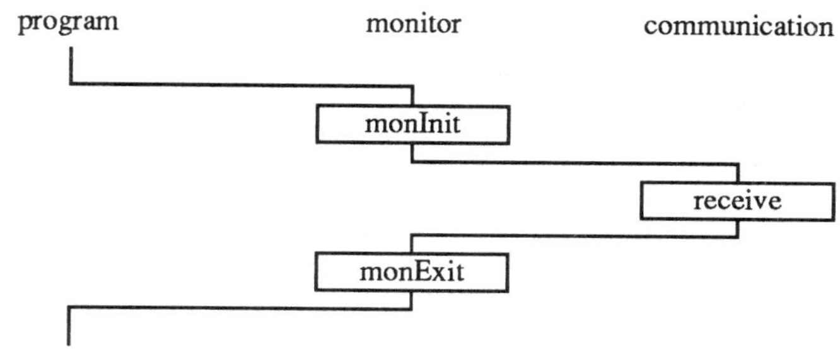

Fig. 1b. Monitored communication

difference between original PICL tracefiles and converted EMU files is the amount of monitoring overhead, which can be reduced with the monitoring strategies described in this paper.

The paper is organized as follows. First we give a short overview about the design principles of EMU. These principles lead to three different characteristics of the monitoring overhead. The connection between the amount of monitoring data and the overhead is described in section 3. Section 4 shows some strategies to reduce the overhead on the hypercube topology. At last the influence of the level of implementation on the resulting monitor is presented. In section 6 we give concrete numbers for the amount of overhead with EMU. We conclude with a summary and our future work.

2. Design principles of EMU

2.1 Monitored communication

The design of the Event Monitoring Utility was mainly based on two goals. On the one hand we wanted to develop a monitor that produces information for error debugging and performance analysis. On the other hand we demanded a monitor, which sufficiently complies with monitoring quality criteria. The main quality factor of a monitor is the overhead needed to produce the trace data. This overhead affects the execution time of the monitored program and the memory consumption on the processing nodes. Therefore our criteria were minimum monitoring overhead in terms of execution delay and memory consumption.

Most important in monitoring of message-passing computers are the communication statements *send* and *receive*. Other events, like variable inspection, produce overhead which is well known from sequential debugging tools and therefore will not be included in this paper.

To determine the monitoring overhead, it is useful to describe how monitoring affects the communication. In standard communication the program switches to the message-passing interface whenever communication routines are called. After performing the appropriate library subroutine, the communication returns to the calling program (see figure 1a). A monitor has to provide the same functionality to the program. In addition it must also generate the needed trace information. This leads us to monitored communication, where all communication routine calls are changed to special monitor routine calls. The monitor routines provide the functionality needed for the monitor and a call to the original communication routine (see figure 1b).

In our monitoring approach the monitoring functionality is divided into two parts, *monInit* and *monExit*. The first part - *monInit*- performs monitoring activities at the initialization of the communication, while the second part - *monExit* - performs the additional monitoring activities at the end of the communication.

The part *monInit* is mainly needed for error-monitoring, which depends on information at the beginning of communication statements for evaluation of the exact point, where an error occurred. If an error occurs in a communication routine and no event attributes are generated at initialization time, it would not be possible to determine that the error occurred exactly in the communication statement. The part *monExit* provides the ability to know when a communication statement is completed.

2.2 The multiprocessor topology

The current implementation of the monitoring system EMU was developed for a nCUBE 2 multiprocessor system. This is a MIMD distributed memory machine with hypercube topology. The message passing is carried out by the network communication unit which performs automatic *cut-through* routing without interference to the computation on the nodes. The path creation algorithm is *e-cube* routing, which is fixed and deadlock free [2].

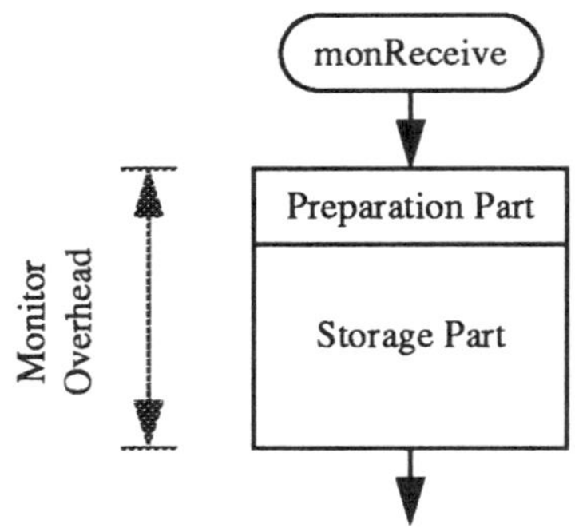

Fig. 2a. Overhead of strategy direct

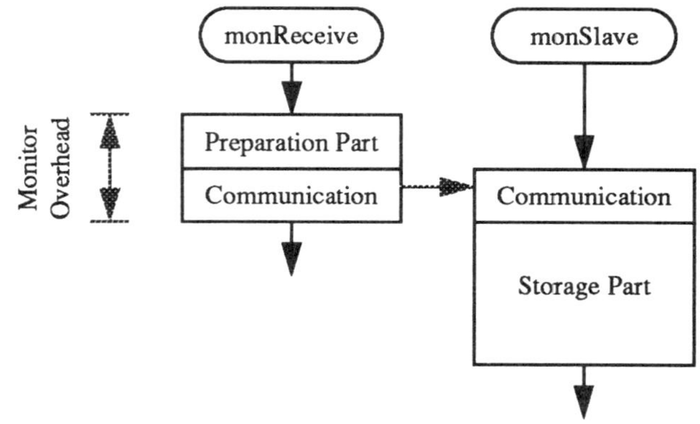

Fig. 2b. Overhead of monitoring node strategies

The topology and the routing algorithm strongly influence the monitoring strategies. The idea is to benefit from hardware features and use them as basis for the monitor implementation. We will show that a reduction of memory consumption and monitoring overhead can be achieved through selecting dedicated monitoring nodes. With these nodes the influence on the program is mostly reduced to the amount of network traffic. With the fixed routing algorithm it is possible to select monitoring nodes where monitoring messages and computation messages never use the same communication link and therefore do not interfere with each other.

3. Amount of data

One of the factors that determine the amount of monitoring overhead is the quantity of data, which have to be produced. This depends on the information which is needed for the post-mortem analysis tool. During the program run data are generated whenever an interesting event happens. An event is defined as an action without duration that takes place at a specific point in time and changes the state of a process [13]. We distinguish the three event classes communication events, global events and trace events.

As we are mainly interested in analyzing the communication structure of message passing programs, the most important group are communication events. They consist of send, receive and test-events. Global events are all events concerning all allocated processors like synchronize statements and global arithmetic functions. Trace events are special events, which are needed for further analysis of the resulting tracefiles. Events for variable inspection or message queue inspection are considered to be trace events.

For further analysis, the monitor must also record additional data about the events, called event attributes. Communication events consist of the following attributes:

- Communication: partner, message type, message length.
- Timing: logical clocks, timestamps.
- Source code information.

The attributes have to be stored in a compact way to keep the resulting tracefiles as small as possible. Due to the facts that more information means more memory consumption and some analysis methods only need a subset of the available information, EMU provides the possibility to select the amount of recorded trace data. The selection is done by choosing the amount of data between *minimum* level and *maximum* level.

The *minimum* level only provides logical clock information as proposed in [3]. The logical clocks concept allows a correct global ordering of events without having a global clock. The main idea of this concept is to transmit information about the partner event as part of a message from the send event to the corresponding receive event.

At the *medium* level the monitor produces simple time stamps to determine computing intervals between the communication. This gives the user the ability to obtain information about the delay between to events and therefore about the computation time. All possible information is produced on the *maximum* amount level, which extends the prior levels mainly by exhaustive timing. With these data it is possible to evaluate the computation time between two successive events and the communication and blocking time of an event.

4. Strategies for monitoring

4.1 Monitoring activities

Another main part of the monitoring overhead is the time consumption when storing the produced data. In our approach this time is mainly affected through the monitoring strategy, which divides the monitoring process into

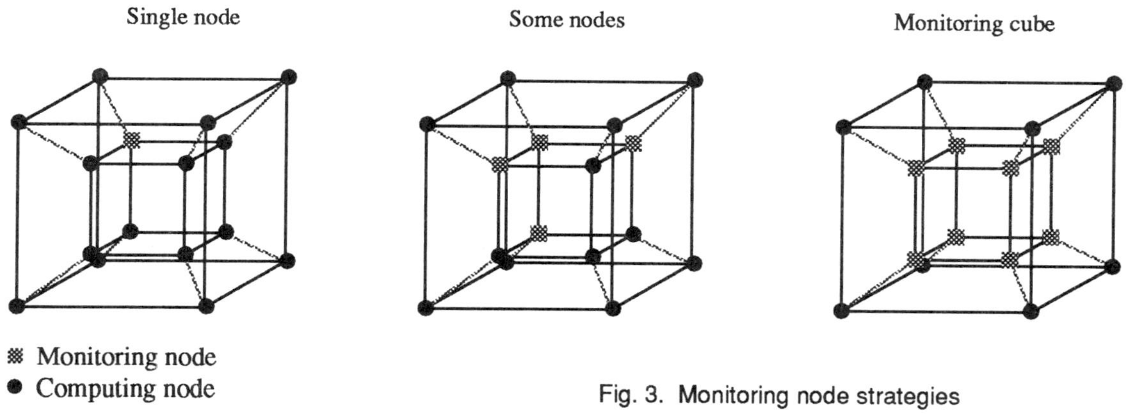

Fig. 3. Monitoring node strategies

two parts. A first part prepares the data and therefore must be fully integrated in the computing process. A second part takes the prepared data, generates additional information and stores the event data for further processing.

The interesting question is how much the computing process is delayed while the monitor stores the gathered information. As there is no possibility that the first part - the *preparation part* - is separated from the computing process, the only solution to this problem is to move the *storage part* from the computing process to a separate monitoring process. This can be achieved with our monitoring strategies.

4.2 Monitoring strategies

The simplest method is the *direct* monitoring strategy. It includes all monitoring functionality in the computing process, which means that the *storage part* delays the actual running program. The monitoring functionality directly affects the monitoring overhead (see figure 2). This is the usual way a monitor is implemented, e.g. the tracing functionality of PICL [5].

For the model *direct* the *preparation part* is the collection of the event attributes as specified by the amount level above. The *storage part* takes all information and performs the necessary I/O-statement for the appropriate tracefile access. The time for the disk access depends on several factors, some machine dependent and some user dependent. The most important factors are:

- I/O-buffer size
- I/O-flushing on/off

The I/O-buffer size determines how many trace events are collected before they are actually written to the tracefile. This buffer can be increased if more memory is available. A collection of monitoring events is only useful, if the traced program runs correct and therefore no error monitoring is needed. If the debugger is used for the location of errors in the communication statements, it must be possible to write all information immediately to provide the user with all necessary event data until the state of abortion. With the flushing mechanism it is possible to select, if buffering is enabled or disabled.

Another factor in tracefile access is the network traffic generated for transferring data to the hard disk, which influences the actual running program. This part strongly depends on the operating system and on the hardware. With the current available information it is not possible to specify exactly the quantity of this influence.

The delay for storing the data with the *direct strategy* can be decreased with the strategy *monitoring process*. This strategy makes use of the multitasking paradigm, where the monitoring process can use the idle time of the computing process for tracefile activities. The greatest advantage of the *process* strategy is obtained, if the computing process has a lot of idle time. Then the monitoring process on the same processor can use this time to perform the storage activities.

The other monitoring strategies - *single node*, *some nodes*, *monitoring cube* - are designed to split off the *storage part* from the *preparation part*. There dedicated monitoring slave nodes provide the functionality to perform the storage of the generated event data, while the computing nodes only have to prepare the data and transmit them to the appropriate slave node (see figure 2b).

The model *single node* only provides one monitoring node for all computing slaves. The disadvantage of this model is that monitor communication increases network traffic, which again means intrusion upon the running program.

A possible solution to reduce this influence is the use of more than one monitoring slave. This is obtained with the strategy *some nodes*, where the *storage part* of the monitor is done on several monitoring slaves. The advantage of

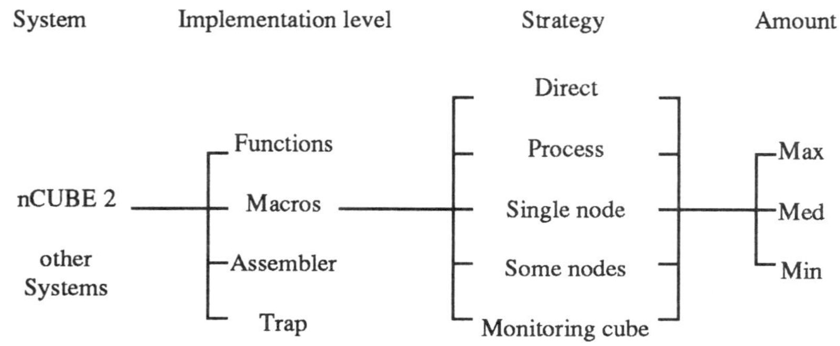

Fig. 4. EMU monitoring scheme

this model is that the communication links between neighboring computing and monitoring nodes are only used for monitor communication and do not affect network traffic between computing nodes. The network traffic only influences computing nodes which do not have a monitoring node in their neighborhood.

Further improvements to this situation can be made by choosing the monitoring strategy *monitoring cube*, where each computing node has a dedicated monitoring node and a reserved link to this node for the monitor communication. The disadvantage of the *monitoring cube* strategy is the loss of half of the processors.

The *monitoring cube* is the only strategy where the communication part is never delayed due to network traffic. The reason is the appropriate selection of a monitoring node for a computing node. If the node-id determined through grey-coding only differs in one bit, the routing of monitoring messages is fixed on one dedicated channel between the computing node and the monitoring node [2]. Figure 3 shows the strategies, which make use of monitoring slave nodes.

5. Level of implementation

Another differentiation about the monitoring overhead can be made concerning the level of implementation. Although high-level programming languages provide a greater portability, they also consume more memory and execution time than low level assembler implementations. We distinguish between the four levels functions, macros, assembler and trap level.

On the function level, the traced statements are replaced with the monitoring statements by a parser of the MAD environment. On the macro level this substitution is done through the C-language precompiler, which replaces the original statements with our own monitoring macros. The facilities of the function and macro levels are mostly hardware independent or need only small adjustments for different hardware systems. We designed this portability concept with an eye on other architectures. The main task in porting the monitor will be to find ideas that include hardware features of the architectures in the strategies.

The compiler influences of the first two levels will be decreased with the use of low-level languages. The assembler level provides a special communication library which replaces the original message passing interface at program link-time. At the trap level, the interrupt service routine is replaced whenever a communication statement is called at run-time. This is the fastest possibility of software monitors. Further improvements are only possible with hardware assisted monitoring tools.

6. Results

6.1 Current implementation

With all the criteria above we implemented the current version of EMU. The availability of a mechanism for selecting the amount of generated data and the possibility of choosing the appropriate monitoring strategy allows the user a lot of flexibility in controlling the monitoring overhead.

On the other hand the different implementation levels allow a certain portability of the tool as well as best performance with lower level programming languages. The whole monitoring scheme is sketched in figure 4.

At present all levels of amount and all strategies are only implemented for the macro implementation level. Therefore the following measurements are only provided for this level. It is clear, that these timings are further improved with the low-level implementations. Nevertheless the numbers present a first possibility to compare the different monitoring strategies.

6.2 Amount of event data

The actual times of the current implementation for producing the event data are shown in table 1. This table contains the three levels of amount, each with *monInit* and *monExit* and the total time needed by the monitor overhead. These times are valid for all monitoring strategies, because each strategy contains the preparation part.

Table 1: Amount level measurement

Level	monInit	monExit	total
Min	1.6 μs	39.9 μs	41.5 μs
Med	28.1 μs	39.9 μs	68.0 μs
Max	35.4 μs	66.5 μs	101.9 μs

6.3 Monitoring strategies

The following table 2 shows average times needed for disk-access to write the prepared event data to disk. The times are given for all levels of amount with the appropriate number of event data bytes needed. The first line shows the times with file flushing enabled - each record is immediately written to the file, the second line with flushing disabled and the default buffer size of 1024 bytes.

Table 2: Average storage times

Flushing	Min	Med	Max
On	16383.5 μs	17229.4 μs	27172.8 μs
Off	435.6 μs	491.7 μs	794.8 μs
Bytes	22	26	42

The following measurements were produced with the monitoring cube strategy. For the other node strategies this is the best reachable case. The timings for the communication part are given in table 3.

Table 3: Average communication times

Error		Min	Med	Max
On	Init	94.5 μs	105.4 μs	110.0 μs
	Exit	108.3 μs	111.3 μs	111.6 μs
	total	202.8 μs	216.7 μs	221.6 μs
Off	total	89.8 μs	90.6 μs	90.9 μs
Bytes		25	29	45

There has to be made a distinction for error monitoring enabled and disabled. With error monitoring disabled the monitoring process has to send only one message after the traced communication statement (*monExit*). If this feature is enabled, an additional message is transmitted before the initialization phase of the communication (*monInit*). The number of bytes shows the amount of produced monitor data.

6.4 Examples

The following paragraphs present monitoring overhead measurements for two parallel implementations. The first one is a Gaussian elimination on a nCUBE 2 with 2^3=8 processors. The problem size is rather small with only 100x100 matrix elements.

The second example is a parallel implementation of the Householder tridiagonalization algorithm. The problem size is the same as above, but the parallel tasks are much more computational and communication intensive. Table 4 contains the measurements of the implemented algorithms in percent of execution time. The table shows only the three strategies *direct*, *process* and *monitoring cube*. The two strategies *single node* and *some nodes* are not included, because they influence the amount of network traffic.

Since the amount of monitoring overhead depends on the generation of data at communication events, a most interesting point is the number of send and receive events and the bytes that are transferred. These numbers are included in table 4 in the last four rows.

Table 4: Example implementations

		Gaussian Elimination	Householder Tridiagonal-ization
monitor over-head	direct	11,41%	6,71%
	process	9,02%	4,15%
	cube	3,25%	0,77%
send	number	114	6500
	bytes	90740	1515992
receive	number	799	12480
	bytes	284652	4015416

7. Conclusion and future work

The results of section 6 lead us to the conclusion that the amount of traced data has only little influence on the monitoring overhead during the preparation part, since most of the time is consumed when storing the monitored data to the disk.

The worst case is the strategy *direct*, because time consumption for tracefile access and memory consumption for monitoring functionality directly affect the computing process and produce a large monitoring overhead. This situation is improved with the *process* strategy by performing the monitoring functionality at the idle states of the computing process. However, the memory consumption is a little higher than with *direct* monitoring.

The strategy with one monitoring slave node relaxes the situation of time and memory consumption on the computing nodes, but produces additional network traffic and therefore may significantly influence the overall performance of the investigated program. The network traffic can be decreased with the use of more than one monitoring slave in strategy *some*. The disadvantage of this strategy is the loss of computing power with the dedicated monitoring processors.

The best strategy concerning monitoring overhead is the *monitoring cube* strategy, where each computing node has direct access to a monitoring slave. The main disadvantage of this strategy is the loss of half the hypercube.

All strategies show certain advantages and disadvantages. On parallel computers with many processors the use of dedicated slave nodes allows the minimum possible monitoring overhead and therefore has little influence on traced programs. With few processors the strategy *direct* allows monitoring, but the user has to be aware that this may have intrusive effects on program behavior. With EMU the program developer has the possibility to select the best fitting strategy with respect to the program behavior and the computing environment.

A main goal of our future work will be further minimization of the monitoring overhead on the assembler and trap level. We will improve the performance monitoring facility with an eye on the visualization of blocking reads due to network traffic. Investigations about the use of parallel I/O accesses will lead to further improvements of the *storage part*.

Acknowledgment

This work is partially sponsored by the Austrian Ministry for Science and Research (BMWF), project CEI-PACT, subproject Work Package 7: "Execution Environment for Parallel Programs".

References

[1] T. Born, W. Obelöer, L. Schäfers, C. Scheidler, "The Monitoring Facilities of the Graphical Parallel Programming Environment TRAPPER", Proc. of the Euromicro Workshop on Parallel and Distributed Processing, San Remo, Italy, pp. 555-562, Jan. 1995.

[2] W.J. Dally, C.L. Seitz, "Deadlock-Free Message Routing in Multiprocessor Interconnection Networks", IEEE Transactions on Computers, Vol. C-36, No. 5, pp. 547-553, May 1987.

[3] C. J. Fidge, "Partial orders for parallel debugging", Proc. Workshop on Parallel and Distributed Debugging, ACM, pp. 183-194, 1988.

[4] J. Gait, "A Probe Effect in Concurrent Programs", IEEE Software - Practise and Experience, Vol. 16(3), pp. 225-233, March 1986.

[5] G. A. Geist, M.T. Heath, B.W. Peyton, P.H.Worley, "A Users' Guide to PICL - A Portable Instrumented Communication Library", ORNL/TM-11616, Oak Ridge National Lab, Aug. 1990.

[6] S. Grabner, D. Kranzlmüller, J. Volkert, "Debugging of Concurrent Processes", Proc. of EUROMICRO PDP 95 Workshop, Sanremo, Italy, January 1995.

[7] S. Grabner, "Fehlersuchstrategien für Programme auf Rechner mit verteiltem Speicher", Ph.D. Thesis, GUP, Johannes Kepler University Linz Austria, 1995, [to app.].

[8] M. T. Heath, J.E. Finger, "ParaGraph: A Tool for Visualizing Performance of Parallel Programs", Technical Report Oak Ridge Natl. Lab., Sept. 1993.

[9] D. Kranzlmüller, S. Grabner, J. Volkert, "Combining the Benefits of Error-Debugging and Performance Evaluation", Proc. of PCAT'94 Conference, Wollongong, Australia, pp. 79-88, Nov. 1994.

[10] D. Kranzlmüller, S. Grabner, J. Volkert, "PARASIT - Parallel Simulation Tool", ACPC Technical Report Series, TR 95-2, Linz, Austria, Dec. 1994.

[11] C. E. McDowell, D.P. Helmbold, "Debugging Concurrent Programs", ACM Computing Surveys 21 (4), pp. 593-622, Dec. 1989.

[12] R.H.B. Netzer, B.P. Miller, "Optimal Tracing and Replay for Debugging Message-Passing parallel programs", Proc. of Supercomputing'92, Minneapolis, MN, pp. 502-511, Nov. 1992.

[13] M. van Rick, B. Tourancheau, "The Design of the General Parallel Monitoring System", Progr. Environments for Parallel Comp., IFIP, North-Holland, pp. 127-137, 1992

[14] D.F. Snelling, G.-R. Hoffmann, "A comparative study of libraries for parallel processing", Proc. of the Intl. Conference on Vector and Parallel Processors", in Computational Science III, Parallel Computing, Vol. 8, (1-3), pp. 255-266, 1988.

Using ITL and Tempura for Large-Scale Specification and Simulation

Antonio Cau[†] Hussein Zedan[†] Nick Coleman Ben Moszkowski

School of Computing and Mathematical Sciences
Liverpool John Moores University
Liverpool L3 3AF, UK

Department of Electrical and Electronic Engineering
University of Newcastle upon Tyne
Newcastle NE1 7RU, UK

Abstract

ITL and Tempura are used for respectively the formal specification and simulation of a large scale system, namely the general purpose multi-threaded dataflow processor EP/3. This paper shows that this processor can be specified concisely within ITL and simulated with Tempura. But it also discusses some problems encountered during the specification and simulation, and indicates what should be added to solve those problems.

1 Introduction

There has been a considerable debate about the use and relevance of formal methods in the development of computing systems (both software and hardware). Some claim that formal methods offer a complete solution to the problems encountered in such development. Others put the claim that formal methods are of little or no use, or that their utility is severely hindered by their cost.

However, it would be over-enthusiastic to claim that a formal development technique could provide a panacea for the problem involved in developing useful computer systems. Indeed, there are too many aspects which are not amenable to formal representation or reasoning. For example, it is hard to envisage a way in which the process of requirements elicitation could be totally formalised; it is true that some requirements can be denoted using a formal notation, and possible inconsistencies found, but the completeness of the requirements (with respect to client's intentions) cannot be formally proven.

As digital devices are deployed in a growing number of high integrity applications there is increased anxiety about the dependability of such systems. Furthermore, the rapid growth of the VLSI market has meant that manufacturers are under pressure to deliver increasingly complex, reliable and cost-effective products within a short time scale. Formal techniques have clearly had an impact on the design of safety critical systems, and have been shown to be commercially advantageous as demonstrated in the production of Inmos IMS T800 floating point unit [8]. We believe that using formal techniques in the production of systems should be viewed as a means of delivering correctness (with respect to requirements) and hence enhanced quality.

One such formal technique is ITL which has been developed over a range of years and has been applied to a various number of systems. However it has not been applied to the design of large scale hardware systems. The aim of this paper is an analysis and discussion of the benefits of the use of ITL and its associated executable language Tempura [10] for such large scale hardware systems. Our chosen hardware is a general-purpose multithreaded dataflow computer known as EP/3 (Event Processor/3) [3]. EP/3 is intended primarily as a vehicle for exploratory research in high-performance computer structures.

1.1 Related work

There have been a plethora of formalisms proposed and used in conjunction with digital system specification and verification. A complete overview of these formalisms is outside the scope of the present paper, however, in this section we will only highlight some of the well known formalism classes used in this field.

A number of hardware specific calculi have been developed and used. Some of these are supported by theorem proving or other checking tools. Barrow's seminal work on VERIFY [1] (a Prolog program for checking the correctness of finite state machines) and Milne's Circle (a calculus based on CCS) [9] for specifying and analysing circuit behaviour.

General purpose logics have been proposed. The

*Supported by EPSRC Research Grant GR/K25922

[†]Current address: Department of Computer Science, de Montfort University, Leicester LE1 9BH, UK

1066-6192/96 $5.00 © 1996 IEEE
Proceedings of PDP '96

Boyer-Moore theorem prover is a notable example [2]. Recently, CLInc has demonstrated that Boyer-Moore can be used successfully for non-trivial hardware verification cases. Higher order logic was first used by Hanna and Daeche who developed the VERITAS theorem proving system [6]. HOL [5] is also a machine-oriented formulation of higher logic based on Church's lambda calculus.

Algebraic specification languages have also been used; a notable example is the use of OBJ specifications with hardware. OBJ-T [13] version of the language was used to specify and test hardware building blocks. UMIST OBJ [4] has also been used to specify simple devices with theorem proving support from REVE [7].

Computer hardware description languages were the first textual descriptive techniques to be used in the design of hardware. Examples include ELLA [12] and VHDL.

Many ideas originating from reactive systems theory including temporal logics, are relevant to the specification and verification of synchronous and asynchronous digital systems. Although propositional temporal logic can be used for reasoning about hardware, interval temporal logic is particularly interesting for hardware verification.

To our best knowledge, there have not been any serious attempt to specify, verify and design a large-scale hardware in interval temporal logic.

1.2 Paper Organisation

In Section 2 we will describe the EP/3 processor architecture and in section 3 we will present an overview of ITL and its associated programming language Tempura. The specification and simulation of EP/3 in ITL are discussed in section 4. We give our evaluations in section 5 and indicate future work.

2 The EP/3 Processor

The system used in this case-study is the Event Processor [3]. Its processing elements are based on the multithreaded principle, in which a main memory is available for explicit storage of data (known as static operands), in addition to the normal circulation of tokens (flow operands). The processors are designed for individual high speed (150MHz with ≈ 1 cycle instruction execution) with the facility for assembly into a small multiprocessing array with shared memory. The latter aims at almost 100% load-balancing efficiency by dynamic scheduling at instruction level.

For the purpose of this case-study, a single processing element will be described, as shown in figure 1. It consists of a circular pipeline in which the 8 units communicate via highways[1]. Each unit will be described

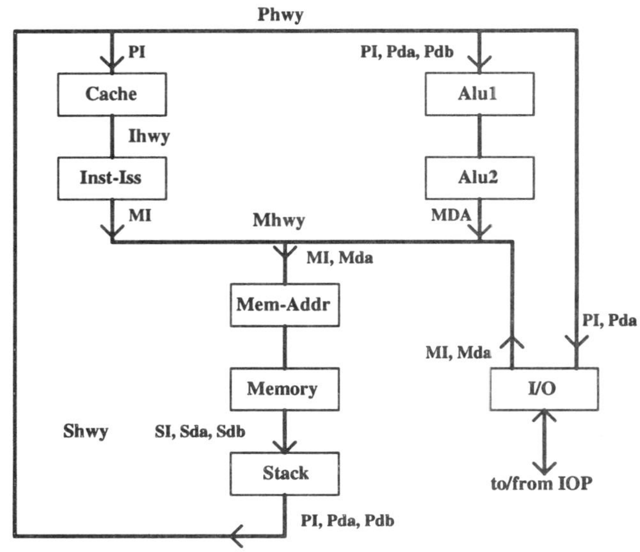

Figure 1: *The EP/3 processor*

below.

1: The Instruction Issue unit (Inst-Iss) receives instructions from the Cache unit. It will decode these instructions and issue these decoded instructions onto the MI field of the memory highway (Mhwy). All instructions consists of a Command Field and a Destination Field. In the case of multi-target instructions, the Inst-Iss unit will issue the instruction once for each destination, using separate cycle for each. An Interlock signal from the control highway (Zhwy) will prevent any further input into the Inst-Iss unit during this time.

2: The Alu1 unit receives executable parcels of work from the Stack unit via the processor highway (Phwy). These parcels consist of a command field PI and data operands Pda and Pdb. If the PI is a logical or arithmetic command then the Alu1 unit will calculate the low-order of the result within one cycle and send this to the Alu2 unit together with the command otherwise it will send one of the operands plus the command field to the Alu2 unit.

3: The Alu2 unit receives an operand and a command from the Alu1 unit. If the command is a shift or rotate instruction it will execute it on the operand within one cycle and send the result onto the Mda field of the Mhwy otherwise it will complete the high-order

[1] Note: the Zhwy in figure 1 is omitted because it is connected to each unit.

of an arithmetic operation from the Alu1 unit and send the result onto the Mda field of the Mhwy.

4: The Memory Address unit (Mem-Addr) receives from the Mhwy the instruction and its flow operand. The Mem-Addr unit calculates the effective address of the static operand. This address together with the instruction and the flow operand are sent to the Memory unit.

5: The Memory unit will fetch the contents of the address received from the Mem-Addr unit and will issue them (Sdb) together with the instruction (SI) and the flow operand (Sda) onto the stack highway (Shwy).

6: The Stack unit receives complete executable parcels of work destined for the Alu units via the Phwy, but in order to buffer variations in the rate of flow between the Mhwy and Phwy the Stack unit is interposed. If the Interlock signal from the Zhwy is present it will store the parcel, and wait until some future time when the Phwy is clear but nothing is present on the Shwy. It will then issue any stored instruction parcels. In the absence of an Interlock signal, the Stack unit will pass the input parcel from the Shwy straight through to the Phwy. The Stack unit also plays a special role during cache and i/o operations (see the description of the I/O unit).

7: The Cache unit receives via the Phwy instructions PI. The destination field of PI is used by the Cache unit to fetch the corresponding target instruction which is sent to the Inst-Iss unit. When a target instruction is requested which is not present in the Cache unit, a stream of memory accesses must be made to fill the relevant cache block. This loading function will be performed by the I/O unit.

8: The I/O unit is an interface to an external I/O processor IOP. It accesses the Memory unit by issueing dummy instructions, together with a flow operand, onto the Mhwy. These cause the Memory unit either to read out a word onto Sdb, or to write the flow operand. In the case of a read, the data issued by the Memory unit enters the Stack unit. A second function performed by the I/O unit is related to cache loading. When a target instruction is requested which is not present in the Cache unit, a stream of memory accesses must be made to fill the relevant cache block. Since the I/O unit already contains hardware for generating memory accesses, it is convenient to use the unit for this purpose. The PI field is therefore carried into the I/O unit, which contains the cache tag memory and address comparator. When a cache miss is detected by the I/O unit, the Interlock signal is asserted and several consecutive memory accesses are made onto the Mhwy. The requested data is passed out of the Memory unit into the Stack unit, as before. I/O and cache operations are identified by a special tag on the Mhwy and Shwy; this causes the Stack unit to ignore any such data.

I/O transfers and cache loading each involve serial operations, and are somewhat too complex to handle with hardwired control. The I/O is therefore microcoded.

3 Interval Temporal Logic and Tempura

This section describes the syntax and informal semantics of the Interval Temporal Logic (ITL) and gives the syntax of the executable part of ITL, i.e., the Tempura language. For a more succinct exposition and the formal semantics see [10].

An interval is considered to be a finite sequence of states, where a state is a mapping from variables to their values. The length of an interval is equal to one less than the number of states in the interval (i.e., a one state interval has length 0).

The syntax of ITL is defined in Table 1 where a is a static variable (doesn't change within an interval), A is a state variable (can change within an interval), v a static or state variable, g is a function symbol, p is a predicate symbol.

Table 1: Syntax of ITL

	Expressions
$exp ::=$	$a \mid A \mid g(exp_1, \ldots, exp_n) \mid \imath a\colon f$
	Formulas
$f ::=$	$p(exp_1, \ldots, exp_n) \mid exp_1 = exp_2 \mid \neg f$ $\mid f_1 \wedge f_2 \mid \forall v\colon f \mid \textit{skip} \mid f_1 \,;\, f_2 \mid f^*$

The informal semantics of the most interesting constructs are as follows:

- $\imath a\colon f$: the value of a such that f holds.
- $\forall v\colon f$: for all v such that f holds.
- ***skip***: unit interval (length 1).
- $f_1 \,;\, f_2$: holds if the interval can be decomposed ("chopped") into a prefix and suffix interval, such that f_1 holds over the prefix and f_2 over the suffix.
- f^*: holds if the interval is decomposable into a finite number of intervals such that for each of them f holds.

Frequently used abbreviations are listed in table 2.

Tempura is an executable subset of ITL, its syntax resembles that of ITL. It has as data-structures

Table 2: Frequently used abbreviations

$f_1 \supset f_2$	$\stackrel{\text{def}}{\equiv} \neg(f_1 \wedge \neg f_2)$
$f_1 \vee f_2$	$\stackrel{\text{def}}{\equiv} \neg(\neg p_1 \wedge \neg p_2)$
$f_1 \equiv f_2$	$\stackrel{\text{def}}{\equiv} (f_1 \supset f_2) \wedge (f_1 \supset f_2)$
$\exists v\colon f$	$\stackrel{\text{def}}{\equiv} \neg\forall v\colon \neg f$
$\bigcirc f$	$\stackrel{\text{def}}{\equiv} \textit{skip} \,;\, f$ (next f)
$\Diamond f$	$\stackrel{\text{def}}{\equiv} \textit{true} \,;\, f$ (sometimes f)
$\Box f$	$\stackrel{\text{def}}{\equiv} \neg\Diamond\neg f$ (always f)
$\circledast f$	$\stackrel{\text{def}}{\equiv} \neg \bigcirc \neg f$ (weak next f)
if f_0 *then* f_1 *else* f_2	$\stackrel{\text{def}}{\equiv} (f_0 \wedge f_1) \vee (\neg f_0 \wedge f_2)$
$A := exp$	$\stackrel{\text{def}}{\equiv} \bigcirc A = exp$
more	$\stackrel{\text{def}}{\equiv} \bigcirc\, \textit{true}$ (non-empty interval)
empty	$\stackrel{\text{def}}{\equiv} \neg \textit{more}$ (empty interval)
fin f	$\stackrel{\text{def}}{\equiv} \Diamond(\textit{empty} \wedge f)$
while f_0 *do* f_1	$\stackrel{\text{def}}{\equiv} (f_0 \wedge f_1)^* \wedge \textit{fin}\ \neg f_0$
repeat f_0 *until* f_1	$\stackrel{\text{def}}{\equiv} f_0 \,;\, (\textit{while}\ \neg f_1\ \textit{do}\ f_0)$

integers and booleans and the list construct to built more complex ones. The standard operations on expressions are available like $+, -, *, /, div, mod, =, >$ $, or, and,$. The basic statements are as follows with b a formula without temporal operators (with the corresponding ITL construct in parentheses behind it): f_1 *and* f_2 ($f_1 \wedge f_2$), $A := exp$ ($A := exp$), *more* (*more*), *empty* (*empty*), *sometimes* ($\Diamond$), *always* ($\Box$), *true* (*true*) , *false* (*false*), *if* b *then* f_1 *else* f_2 (*if* b *then* f_1 *else* f_2), *while* b *do* f (*while* b *do* f), *repeat* b *until* f (*repeat* b *until* f). See [10] for more statements. With the *define* $name(p_1, \ldots, p_n) = f$ and *define* $name(p_1, \ldots, p_n) = exp$ one can define "procedures" and functions (recursive definitions are allowed).

4 The Specification and Simulation of the EP/3

This section describes some parts of the specification of the EP/3 in ITL. The whole specification consists of a temporal formula of about 3400 lines, so this won't be given.

4.1 The Specification

The description of the processor from which we started to write the formal specification, consisted of what is given in section 2 plus a Pascal program that simulates the processor. The first formal specification was therefore of sequential nature, i.e., the units of the processor were sequentially composed. This however was not a faithful specification of the processor because each unit should work in parallel. Luckily the specification was such that the transformation into a "parallel" version was not so difficult. Only the interlock signal caused some difficulties. The specification of the processor is a big ITL formula of about 3400 lines. The general structure of the formula is as follows:

```
epsim(IO) ≝
∃Stopped, Zlocka, Zlockb, Zvalid, Zioreq,
   Phwy, Ihwy, Mhwy, Shwy : (
   init()  ∧
   repeat(
     skip  ∧
     cache(Phwy, Zlockb ∨ Zlocka,   Ihwy)  ∧
     instis(Ihwy, Zlocka, Zvalid, Zioreq,
            Mhwy, Zlockb, Stopped)  ∧
     alu(Phwy, Zlockb ∨ Zlocka, Zioreq,
            Mhwy, Zvalid)  ∧
     io(IO, Phwy, Zvalid, Zlockb,
            Mhwy, Zioreq, Zlocka)  ∧
     mem(Mhwy,   Shwy)  ∧
     stk(Shwy, Zlockb ∨ Zlocka,   Phwy)
   ) until Stopped
)
```

The `init()` formula initializes the values of the variables. The `repeat ( S ) until Stopped` repeats "executing" the `S` formula until `Stopped` is true which is the case if an stop instruction is executed by the processor. The `S` formula is an $\wedge$ (and) formula of 7 sub-formulas which means that these sub-formulas are "executed" in parallel.

- The *skip* formula describes that we use an interval of two states namely the state of the processor before and after each clock cycle.
- The *cache*(*Phwy*, *Zlockb* $\vee$ *Zlocka*, *Ihwy*) formula describes the behavior of the Cache unit. It has as inputs the processor highway *Phwy* and the interlock signal which consists of the logical or of respectively the lock signal *Zlocka* issued by the I/O unit and the lock signal *Zlockb* issued by the Inst-Iss unit. This means that both units can lock the pipeline. The Cache outputs on the instruction highway *Ihwy*.
- The *instis*(*Ihwy*, *Zlocka*, *Zvalid*, *Zioreq*, *Mhwy*, *Zlockb*, *Stopped*) formula describes the behavior of the Inst-Iss unit. It has as inputs the instruction

highway *Ihwy* and the lock signal *Zlocka* from the I/O unit. It has furthermore as input the signal *Zvalid* from the Alu unit indicating if data is valid, and the signal *Zioreq* from the I/O unit indicating if it is allowed to output on the memory highway *Mhwy*. It issues also the lock signal *Zlockb* for interlocking. If the stop instruction is issued the *Stopped* signal will be on.

- The *alu*(*Phwy*, *Zlockb* ∨ *Zlocka*, *Zioreq*, *Mhwy*, *Zvalid*) formula describes the behavior of the Alu1 and Alu2 unit. It is defined as

  ∃*Alu2in*: (
    alu1(*Phwy*, *Zlockb* ∨ *Zlocka*, *Alu2in*) ∧
    alu2(*Alu2in*, *Zlockb* ∨ *Zlocka*, *Zioreq*,
      Mhwy, *Zvalid*)
).

  So the Alu1 unit has as inputs the processor highway *Phwy* and the interlock signal *Zlockb* ∨ *Zlocka*. It outputs *Alu2in* to the Alu2 unit[2]. The Alu2 unit has as further inputs the interlock signal *Zlockb* ∨ *Zlocka* and the signal *Zioreq* from the I/O unit indicating if it is allowed to output on the memory highway *Mhwy*. It outputs furthermore the signal *Zvalid* indicating if the computed data is valid.

- The *io*(*IO*, *Phwy*, *Zvalid*, *Zlockb*, *Mhwy*, *Zioreq*, *Zlocka*) formula describes the behavior of the I/O unit. It has as inputs the stream *IO* from the external I/O processor IOP, and the processor highway *Phwy*, and the signal *Zvalid* from the Alu unit, and the lock signal *Zlockb* from the Inst-Iss unit. It outputs on the memory highway *Mhwy* and it generates the signal *Zioreq* during this output preventing that the Alu and the Inst-Iss unit generate output on the *Mhwy*. It also generates the lock signal *Zlocka* for interlock.

- The *mem*(*Mhwy*, *Shwy*) formula describes the behavior of the Mem-Addr and Memory unit. It is defined as

  ∃*Mem2in*: (
    mem1(*Mhwy*, *Mem2in*) ∧
    mem2(*Mem2in*, *Shwy*)
).

  mem1(*Mhwy*, *Mem2in*) describes the Mem-Addr unit and has as input the memory highway *Mhwy* and as output *Mem2in* to the Memory unit. The Memory unit is described by the *mem2*(*Mem2in*, *Shwy*) formula and has as output the stack highway *Shwy*.

- The *stk*(*Shwy*, *Zlockb* ∨ *Zlocka*, *Phwy*) formula describes the behavior of the Stack unit. It has as inputs the stack highway *Shwy* and the interlock signal *Zlockb* ∨ *Zlocka* and it outputs on the processor highway *Phwy*.

[2] The current specification of the Alu units is such that Alu1 computes the arithmetic and logical operations as opposed to the informal specification of section 2

4.2 The Simulation

We will simulate the execution of a small machine code program on the processor. This program consists of two threads running in parallel on the processor, one thread subtracts from 0 the value 31 and the other thread adds 31 to 0. The machine code program is as follows:

```
1.      QA   F1,Z /X2 /X1
2. X1   S    F2,F1
3.      WS   F2,Y1 /END
4. X2   A    F3,F1
5.      WS   F3,Y2 /END
6. END  STOP
7. Z    DCW  31
8. Y1
9. Y2
```

The program performs the following: 1. load flow F1 with the value of Z (i.e., 31) and "goto" /X1 and /X2 , 2. subtract from flow F2 the value of flow F1, 3. write the value of flow F2 to Y1 and goto END, 4. add to flow F3 the value of flow F1, 5. write the value of flow F3 to Y2 and goto END, 6. stop the computation, 7. the variable Z (with value 31), 8. the variable Y1, 9. the variable Y2. The stages of the pipeline are illustrated in figure 2 where

A	is	Cache and Alu1
B	is	Inst-Iss and Alu2
C	is	Mem-Addr
D	is	Memory
E	is	Stack

and the numbers correspond to the instructions.

At stage 1 the Inst-Iss unit gets the first instruction from the Cache and because the instruction has two destinations this instruction is split into two instructions (1.1 and 1.2), it first issues the instruction with the first destination to the Mem-Addr unit (stage 2) and then the same instruction with the second destination (stage 3). Meanwhile the Mem-Addr has send the first instruction to the Memory (stage 3) where the contents of the *Z* variable are fetched. The contents of the flows and the value of the *Z* variable are sent to the Stack unit (stage 4) and the Memory unit fetches the contents of the *Z* variable for the second instruction.

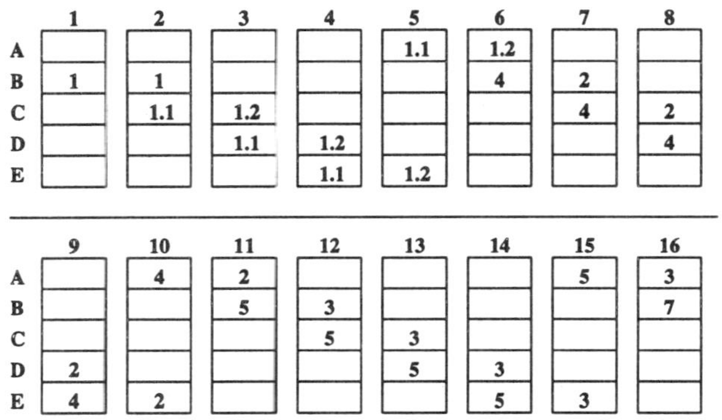

Figure 2: *The stages of the pipeline during execution.*

The Stack sends the first instruction to the Alu1 and the Cache (stage 5). The Cache fetches the destination instruction where to the Alu unit should send the result of the first instruction (this instruction is `4. X2 A F3,F1`) and sends it to the Inst-Iss unit (stage 6). At stage 7 this instruction is sent to the Mem-Addr unit together with the result of the Alu unit (flow F1 is loaded with the contents of the Z variable). Meanwhile the Cache has fetched the destination instruction for the second instruction (namely 2. X1 S F2,F1) and this is sent at stage 8 to the Mem-Addr unit together with the result of the Alu1 unit (the same as the first instruction). These two "destination" instructions migrate through the Mem-Addr, the Memory and the Stack unit (stages 7-10) towards the Alu1 unit and the Cache. The same procedure as before is followed: the Cache fetches the destination instruction and the Alu unit computes the result. For the first instruction this result is "add the contents of flow F1 to the contents of flow F3 and write them to flow F3" (stage 12) and the destination instruction is `5. WS F3,Y2 /END`. For the second instruction this result is "subtract the contents of flow F1 from flow F2 and write them to flow F2" (stage 13). The two destination instructions again migrate through the Mem-Addr and the Memory unit. The Memory unit writes at the arrival of the first instruction (stage 13) the contents of flow F3 to variable $Y2$ and at the arrival of the first instruction (stage 14) the contents of flow F2 to variable $Y1$. The two instructions then migrates through the Stack to arrive at the Alu1 and the Cache unit (stages 15-16) where the Cache fetches the destination instruction of the first instruction, i.e., `6. END STOP` and sends it to the Inst-Iss unit (stage 16). Because this is the halt instruction the processor stops. The output as generated by the simulator is shown in the appendix.

This sample machine program works fine on the processor but there is a problem. This problem is you can already observe when you execute the following program:

```
1. X  AS F0,Y /X /X
2. Y  DCW 1
```

This program adds 1 to flow F0 and then sends the result twice to itself (it constructs a binary tree of adding instructions).

The stages of the pipeline are illustrated in figure 3. Whenever an instruction enters the Inst-Iss (B) it will be split into 2 instructions. Because the pipeline has a length five this will eventually result in a situation (for instance stage 12) that there is "no room" in the pipeline; the instruction (i.e., 1.2.1) in the Stack (E) unit will then be put on the stack. In this example because the stack is of finite length, this will result eventually in a stack overflow. On operating system level this problem should then be solved.

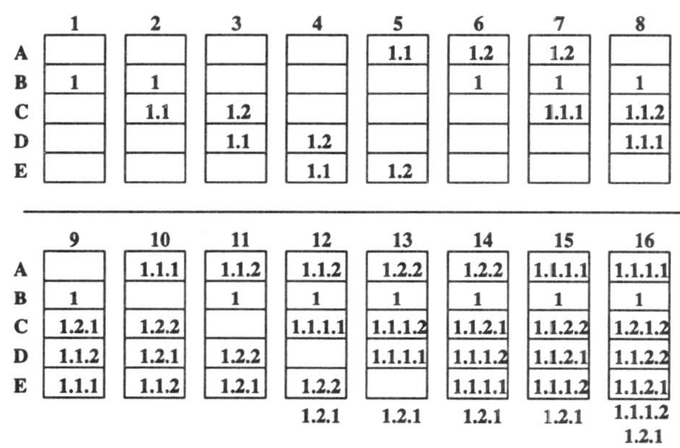

Figure 3: *The stages of the pipeline during execution.*

5 Evaluation and Future Work

This section evaluates ITL and Tempura as vehicle for the specification and simulation of large scale systems. It also indicates future work.

5.1 Evaluation

ITL and Tempura are suitable for the specification and simulation of the EP/3, i.e., for large scale systems. But the following problems were encountered during the specification of the processor:

- In ITL/Tempura only integers, booleans and lists are available as data-types. One would like to have the data-structures of Pascal like records, reals, files etc. Although these could be simulated using lists, it would ease usability if these data-types were explicitly expressed.

- The units of the processor communicate with each other over the highways. This is modeled with shared variables. The use of special kind of variables like channels is more appropriate. Plus allowing communication actions to be explicitly expressed.

- In normal programming languages like Pascal, a program like `if y>0 then x:=x+1` the value of `x` increases by 1 if `y>0` and `x` doesn't change otherwise. In ITL/Tempura the information that `x` doesn't change has to be coded explicitly: `if y>0 then x:=x+1 else x:=x`, i.e., one has to state explicitly that a variable doesn't change. If one has to update one memory cell, this will be a very costly operation. This is the so-called framing problem.

- Within ITL/Tempura is it hard to model timing constrains like delay or time-out. In the specification of the processor each clock cycle corresponds to a state in ITL, i.e., the length of the interval corresponds to the number of cycles of the processor. We couldn't model properties like: the Alu unit computes the result within 1 clock cycle.

A problem that did not show up in this example is whether to extend Tempura (the executable part of ITL) with high level constructs like the "or" for non-determinism. The advantage is that more specifications become executable but a disadvantage is that the simulator becomes then very complicated. It may be better to construct a refinement tool that refines a high level specification (written in ITL) into a executable specification (written in Tempura).

5.2 Future work

Future work will consists in extending ITL/Tempura with more data-structures and data-types, and constructs for the description of communicating and timing constrains. Furthermore the framing problem should be solved, this will result in an increase of the speed of the simulator because an update of the memory would then only cost 1 statement instead of as many as there are memory cells. Also we will investigate the use of the PVS[11] system as refinement tool for high level specifications written in ITL to executable specifications written in Tempura.

An issue that isn't addressed in this paper is the correctness of the EP/3, i.e., the proof that certain properties like the pipeline doesn't "overwrite" an unit when there is for some reason "no room" in the pipeline. This kind of properties should be formalized within ITL. With the proof system of ITL these properties then can be proven.

References

1. H. Barrow. Proving the correctness of hardware designs. In *VLSI Design*, pages 64–77, July 1984.
2. R. Boyer and J. Moore. *A Computational Logic*. Academic Press, 1979.
3. J. Coleman. A high speed data-flow processing element and its performance compared to a von Neumann mainframe. In *IEEE 7th Int'l. Parallel Processing Symp*, pages 24–33, Newport Beach, California, 1993.
4. R. Gallimore, D. Coleman, and V. Stavridou. UMIST OBJ: a language for executable program specifications. *Comp. J.*, pages 413–421, 1989.
5. M. Gordon. HOL: A machine oriented formulation of higher order logic. Technical Report Report 68, University of Cambridge, 1985.
6. F. Hanna and N. Daeche. Specification and verification using higher order logic. In *Proc. of 7th Intern. Symp. on Computer Hardware Description Languages and Applications*, pages 418–443, 1985.
7. P. Lescanne. Computer experiments with the REVE term rewriting system generator. In *Proc. 10th ACM Symp. on PPL*, 1983.
8. D. May, G. Barrett, and D. Shepherd. Designing chips that work. In C. Hoare and M. Gordon, editors, *Mechanised Reasoning and Hardware Design*, pages 3–18. Prentice Hall, 1992.
9. G. Milne. Circal: a calculus for circuit description. *INTEGRATION. VLSI J.*, pages 121–160, 1983.
10. B. Moszkowski. *Executing Temporal Logic Programs*. Cambridge Univ. Press, Cambridge, UK, 1986.
11. S. Owre, J. Rushby, and N. Shankar. PVS: A prototype verification system. In D. Kapur, editor, *International Conference on Automated Deduction*, volume LNAI 607, pages 748–752, Saratoga, NY, June 1992. Springer Verlag.
12. Praxis Systems. *The ELLA User Manual*, 2.0 edition, 1986.
13. A. Sampaio and K. Parsaye-Ghomi. The formal specification and testing of expanded hardware building blocks. In *Proc. Computer Science Conf*, Rolla, MO, 1981.

A Simulator output of first example

The simulator has a more detailed output namely the values of the registers of the various units of the processor before the start of the cycle. The format is as follows of the output is given in table 3.

Table 3: *Format of the simulator output*

```
Cyc Zlck Zirq Zvld
NR   B    B    B
---------ralu1in ralu1s F3-------F2-------F1-------F0-ralu1a --ralu1b
 7 6 5 4 3 2 1 0    B     3 2 1 0  3 2 1 0  3 2 1 0  3 2 1 0  3 2 1 0
------------rii1 -rii1s -----------------------------ralu2 rii1dest
 7 6 5 4 3 2 1 0    B     3 2 1 0  3 2 1 0  3 2 1 0  3 2 1 0     D
---------rmem1in rmem1s -----------------------------rmem1
 7 6 5 4 3 2 1 0    B     3 2 1 0  3 2 1 0  3 2 1 0  3 2 1 0
---------rmem2in rmem2s -----------------------------rmem2 --rmem2b
 7 6 5 4 3 2 1 0    B     3 2 1 0  3 2 1 0  3 2 1 0  3 2 1 0  3 2 1 0
---------rstk1in rstk1s -----------------------------rstk1 --rstk1b
 7 6 5 4 3 2 1 0    B     3 2 1 0  3 2 1 0  3 2 1 0  3 2 1 0  3 2 1 0
```

where NR is a positive integer, B a boolean and D one of the values 0, 1 or 2 (the destination index). The first line describes the registers comprising the Alu1, i.e., the instruction, the active, the flow and the static operand registers. The second line describes the registers comprising the Inst-Iss and the Alu2. The third line describes the registers comprising the Mem-Addr. The fourth line describes the registers comprising the Memory. And the fifth and last line describes the registers comprising the Stack.

The output generated by the simulator of the most interesting cycles is given in the following table. Stage i (in figure 2) corresponds with cycle $20 + i$. Variables $Z, Y1$ and $Y2$ corresponds to respectively Memory locations 00000020, 00000024 and 00000028.

```
21  .  .  .
0000000000000000  .  00000000 00000000 00000000 00000000 00000000
81100020F012F108  T  00000000 00000000 00000000 00000000     0
0000000000000000  .  00000000 00000000 00000000 00000000
0000000000000000  .  00000000 00000000 00000000 00000000 00000000
0000000000000000  .  00000000 00000000 00000000 00000000 00000000

22  T  .  T
0000000000000000  .  00000000 00000000 00000000 00000000 00000000
81100020F012F108  T  00000000 00000000 00000000 00000000     1
81100020F0000012  T  00000000 00000000 00000000 00000000
0000000000000000  .  00000000 00000000 00000000 00000000 00000000
0000000000000000  .  00000000 00000000 00000000 00000000 00000000

23  .  .  T
0000000000000000  .  00000000 00000000 00000000 00000000 00000000
81100020F012F108  .  00000000 00000000 00000000 00000000     0
81100020F1000008  T  00000000 00000000 00000000 00000000
81100020F0000012  T  00000000 00000000 00000000 00000000 00000000
0000000000000000  .  00000000 00000000 00000000 00000000 00000000
Reading from Memory[00000020] the value 0000001F

24  .  .  .
0000000000000000  .  00000000 00000000 00000000 00000000 00000000
81100020F012F108  .  00000000 00000000 00000000 00000000     0
81100020F0000012  .  00000000 00000000 00000000 00000000
81100020F1000008  T  00000000 00000000 00000000 00000000 00000000
81100020F0000012  T  00000000 00000000 00000000 00000000 0000001F
Reading from Memory[00000020] the value 0000001F

25  .  .  .
81100020F0000012  T  00000000 00000000 00000000 00000000 0000001F
81100020F012F108  .  00000000 00000000 00000000 00000000     0
81100020F0000012  .  00000000 00000000 00000000 00000000
81100020F0000012  .  00000000 00000000 00000000 00000000 00000000
81100020F1000008  T  00000000 00000000 00000000 00000000 0000001F

26  .  .  .
81100020F1000008  T  00000000 00000000 00000000 00000000 0000001F
0231F1168F300028  T  00000000 00000000 00000000 00000000     0
81100020F0000012  .  00000000 00000000 00000000 00000000
81100020F0000012  .  00000000 00000000 00000000 00000000 00000000
0000000000000000  .  00000000 00000000 00000000 00000000 00000000

27  .  .  T
0000000000000000  .  00000000 00000000 00000000 00000000 00000000
0321F10C8F200024  T  00000000 00000000 00000000 00000000     0
02310000F1000016  T  00000000 00000000 0000001F 00000000
81100020F0000012  .  00000000 00000000 00000000 00000000 00000000
0000000000000000  .  00000000 00000000 00000000 00000000 00000000

28  .  .  T
0000000000000000  .  00000000 00000000 00000000 00000000 00000000
81100020F012F108  .  00000000 00000000 00000000 00000000     0
03210000F100000C  T  00000000 00000000 0000001F 00000000
02310000F1000016  T  00000000 00000000 0000001F 00000000 0000001F
0000000000000000  .  00000000 00000000 00000000 00000000 00000000

29  .  .  .
0000000000000000  .  00000000 00000000 00000000 00000000 00000000
81100020F012F108  .  00000000 00000000 00000000 00000000     0
81100020F0000012  .  00000000 00000000 00000000 00000000
03210000F100000C  T  00000000 00000000 0000001F 00000000 0000001F
02310000F1000016  T  00000000 00000000 0000001F 00000000 0000001F

30  .  .  .
02310000F1000016  T  00000000 00000000 0000001F 00000000 0000001F
81100020F012F108  .  00000000 00000000 00000000 00000000     0
81100020F0000012  .  00000000 00000000 00000000 00000000
81100020F0000012  .  00000000 00000000 00000000 00000000 00000000
03210000F100000C  T  00000000 00000000 0000001F 00000000 0000001F

31  .  .  .
03210000F100000C  T  00000000 00000000 0000001F 00000000 0000001F
8F300028F11C7F00  T  00000000 00000000 0000001F 00000000     0
81100020F0000012  .  00000000 00000000 00000000 00000000
81100020F0000012  .  00000000 00000000 00000000 00000000 00000000
0000000000000000  .  00000000 00000000 00000000 00000000 00000000

32  .  .  T
0000000000000000  .  00000000 00000000 00000000 00000000 00000000
8F200024F11C0231  T  00000000 00000000 0000001F 00000000     0
8F300028F100001C  T  0000001F 00000000 0000001F 00000000
81100020F0000012  .  00000000 00000000 00000000 00000000 00000000
0000000000000000  .  00000000 00000000 00000000 00000000 00000000

33  .  .  T
0000000000000000  .  00000000 00000000 00000000 00000000 00000000
81100020F012F108  .  00000000 00000000 00000000 00000000     0
8F200024F100001C  T  00000000 FFFFFFE1 0000001F 00000000
8F300028F100001C  T  0000001F 00000000 0000001F 00000000 0000001F
0000000000000000  .  00000000 00000000 00000000 00000000 00000000
Writing to Memory[00000028] the value 0000001F

34  .  .  .
0000000000000000  .  00000000 00000000 00000000 00000000 00000000
81100020F012F108  .  00000000 00000000 00000000 00000000     0
81100020F0000012  .  00000000 00000000 00000000 00000000
8F200024F100001C  T  00000000 FFFFFFE1 0000001F 00000000 FFFFFFE1
8F300028F100001C  T  0000001F 00000000 0000001F 00000000 00000000
Writing to Memory[00000024] the value FFFFFFE1

35  .  .  .
8F300028F100001C  T  0000001F 00000000 0000001F 00000000 00000000
81100020F012F108  .  00000000 00000000 00000000 00000000     0
81100020F0000012  .  00000000 00000000 00000000 00000000
81100020F0000012  .  00000000 00000000 00000000 00000000 00000000
8F200024F100001C  T  00000000 FFFFFFE1 0000001F 00000000 00000000

36  .  .  .
8F200024F100001C  T  00000000 FFFFFFE1 0000001F 00000000 00000000
7F0000000000001F  T  0000001F 00000000 0000001F 00000000     0
81100020F0000012  .  00000000 00000000 00000000 00000000
81100020F0000012  .  00000000 00000000 00000000 00000000 00000000
0000000000000000  .  00000000 00000000 00000000 00000000 00000000
Stop Instruction Executed
Done!  Computation length:  36.  Total Passes:  160.
Total Reductions: 2045605 (1725696 successful).
Cumulative Statistics
Total Cycles = 36 Processing Cycles = 34 during which
Instructions Executed = 6 Mean Cycles / Instruction = 5
```

Propagation of I/O-Variables in Massively Parallel Processor Arrays

Dirk Fimmel

Department of Electrical Engineering
University of Technology
Dresden, Germany

Renate Merker

Department of Electrical Engineering
University of Technology
Dresden, Germany

Abstract

In this paper the underlying design method for massively parallel processor arrays allows to exploit parallelism in a broader range because of not considering the I/O-variables during the design process of a full size array. As a consequence of this approach a reallocation of the I/O-ports of the I/O-variables at the boundary processors of the processor array is necessary.
Algorithms are described for the reallocation of the I/O-ports at the array boundaries leading to a minimal additional latency and taking systolic constraints into account. Integer linear programming is used to solve the arising optimization problems.

1 Introduction

The design of massively parallel processor arrays such as systolic arrays was introduced about 15 years ago in order to speed up time consuming computations [6, 8]. Since then a lot of work has been done on the creation of automatic design systems of massively parallel processor arrays for real-time applications in order to ensure an optimal and correct design [1, 2, 3, 4, 5, 11, 12].
Usually, in existing design systems the algorithm is represented as a system of affine recurrence equations defined in different computation spaces. In these equations so called recurrent variables, which are both defined and used, as well as so called I/O-variables, which can only be used or defined, occur. Many algorithms for instance in digital filter design and image processing can be represented as systems of affine recurrence equations.

Generally, a design system for massively parallel processor arrays contains tools such as an embedding of all variables of the equations into a common index space, a reindexing of the computation spaces, an uniformization of the dependencies of the variables and an affine space time mapping of the computation spaces into full size arrays [1, 12]. Sometimes tools for a hardware adaptation of the full size array are included [12]. The design trajectory underlying this paper does not contain an embedding of the I/O-variables into a common index space [10]. This is because of the ommission of I/O-variables from the tools for the generation of the full size array. This is possible, since the I/O-variables do not cause any variable dependence. The advantage of this strategy is a wider search space for the space time mapping in order to exploit the parallelism in a broader range.

The interface of massively parallel processor arrays is usually restricted to boundary processors. This leads to the task of a reallocation of the I/O-ports of the I/O-variables at the boundary processors of the processor array. Such processors are called input(I)- or output(O)-ports, where input(I)- or output(O)-variables are, respectively, first used or finally computed.
In existing design trajectories such as [1, 12] another approach is used. Here the embedding of the I/O-variables into a common index space is applied under the constraint that after space time mapping the I/O-ports of the I/O-variables will be in the boundary processors. A propagation of the I/O-variables to the I/O-ports is not necessary. The disadvantages of this approach is a considerably limited search space for the generation of the full size array. In another approach [4] the reallocation of I/O-ports of the I/O-variables at the array boundaries is considered without minimizing the arising latency.

In this paper a time minimal reallocation of the input ports of the input variables at the array boundary processors is described. (The investigation of the output variables follows analogously and is omitted here.) To this end we consider the full size processor array as a control space [12]. At first, initialization subspaces as convex subdomains of this control space are

1066-6192/96 $5.00 © 1996 IEEE
Proceedings of PDP '96

determined, which represent the set of input ports for the input variables and the appropriate time instances for using these input ports. These initialization subspaces are fixed by the propagation vectors of the input variables in the control space. Next reallocation vectors, i.e. vectors describing the propagation of the input variables from the array boundaries to the processors of the initialization subspaces, are derived which minimize the latency caused by the reallocation. Generally, the resulting reallocation vectors differ from the propagation vectors of the input variables in the control space.

Integer linear programming is used to solve the optimization problems which arise. The proposed tools will be described for n-dimensional index spaces.

This paper is organized as follows: Section 2 covers basic notations and definitions. In section 3 the determination of the initialization spaces for the input data is explained. In section 4 an algorithm is introduced which derives the best reallocation vector with respect to the minimal latency and the systolic constraints. To reduce the achieved latency further, a partitioning of the initialization spaces into subspaces is proposed in section 5. An example follows in section 6 and the conclusion in section 7.

2 Basic definitions

First, we will define the class of algorithms we consider in the underlying design trajectory:

Definition 1 (Systems of Affine Recurrence Equations (SARE)) *A system of recurrence equations is a set of equations of the following form:*

$$y_i[f_i(\hat{I})] = F_i(..., y_j[g_{ji}(\hat{I})], ...), \quad 1 \le i,j \le l, \quad (1)$$

where $\hat{I} \in \hat{\mathcal{I}}_i \subset \mathbb{Z}^n$ *is an index point in the convex index space* $\hat{\mathcal{I}}_i = \{\hat{I} \mid \mathbf{A}_i\hat{I} \ge \mathbf{a}_{0i}\}$,
$\mathbf{A}_i \in \mathbb{Q}^{m_i \times n}, \mathbf{a}_{0i} \in \mathbb{Q}^{m_i}$,
the variables $y_i[f_i(\hat{I})]$ *are indexed variables with the affine index functions* $f_i(\hat{I}) = \mathbf{M}_i\hat{I} + \mathbf{m}_{0i}$,
$\mathbf{M}_i \in \mathbb{Z}^{l_i \times n}, \mathbf{m}_{0i} \in \mathbb{Z}^{l_i}$, *and*
F_i *are arbitrary functions.*

The convex index spaces $\hat{\mathcal{I}}_i$ are polytops, i.e. bounded polyhedrons, since we assume finite computations. Variables which will be defined *and* used in (1) are called recurrent variables. Variables which will only be used *or* defined in (1) are called I/O-variables.

The convex index spaces $\hat{\mathcal{I}}_i$ are transformed into convex computation spaces $\mathcal{I}_i$ after applying the tools reindexing, uniformization and space time mapping to the SARE. The first coordinate of the computation spaces is the time axis and the remaining n-1 coordinates form the processor space.

The convex union of the computation spaces leads to the control space [12], using the constant extremal values of the time instances as time bounds.

Definition 2 (Control space) *The control space* $\mathcal{I}$ *for the set of computation spaces* $\mathcal{I}_i$ *is defined as follows:*

$$\mathcal{I} = \{\begin{pmatrix} t \\ \mathbf{p} \end{pmatrix} \mid \begin{pmatrix} 1 & \mathbf{0} \\ -1 & \mathbf{0} \\ \mathbf{0} & \mathbf{S} \end{pmatrix} \begin{pmatrix} t \\ \mathbf{p} \end{pmatrix} \ge \begin{pmatrix} t_{min} \\ -t_{max} \\ \mathbf{s}_0 \end{pmatrix}\}, \quad (2)$$

where $\mathcal{P} = \{\mathbf{p} \mid \mathbf{Sp} \ge \mathbf{s}_0\} = convHull(\bigcup_{i=1}^{m} proj_t(\mathcal{I}_i))$, $\mathbf{S} \in \mathbb{Q}^{m \times n-1}$, $\mathbf{s}_0 \in \mathbb{Q}^m$, $\mathbf{p} \in \mathbb{Z}^{n-1}$, *is the processor space, and* $\mathcal{T} = \{t \mid \begin{pmatrix} 1 \\ -1 \end{pmatrix} t \ge \begin{pmatrix} t_{min} \\ -t_{max} \end{pmatrix}\} = convHull(\bigcup_{i=1}^{m} proj_{\mathbf{p}}(\mathcal{I}_i))$, $t, t_{min}, t_{max} \in \mathbb{Z}$, *is the time interval. The function* $convHull()$ *denotes the integer convex hull of a polytop* [9] *and* $proj_t()$ *the projection of a polytop into the direction of the coordinate* t.

Since the projection of a polytop is not exact with respect to integer points [12], it is necessary to build either the integer convex hull of the polytop first or to introduce some cutting planes into the projected polytop.

In the following some mathematical functions will be introduced in order to simplify the further descriptions.

Definition 3 (Cylinder extension) *The cylinder extension of a polytop* $\mathcal{I} = \{I \mid \mathbf{A}I \ge \mathbf{a}_0\}$ *into the direction of* $\mathbf{v} \in \mathbb{Q}^n$ *yields an open convex polyhedron:*

$$\begin{aligned} \mathcal{I}^* &= cylExt(\mathcal{I}, \mathbf{v}) = \{I \mid \mathbf{A}^*I \ge \mathbf{a}_0^*\} \\ &= \{I \mid I = J + u\mathbf{v}, J \in \mathcal{I}, u \in \mathbb{Q}\}. \end{aligned} \quad (3)$$

Definition 4 (Normal form of linear integer half spaces) *We call* $\mathcal{H}$ *a linear integer half space given in normal form, if* $\mathcal{H} = \{I \mid \mathbf{a}_h^T I \ge a_{h0}\}$, $\mathbf{a}_h \in \mathbb{Z}^n, a_{h0} \in \mathbb{Z}$.

Remark: Every half space defined by an inequality with rational coefficients and a rational constant can be transformed into its normal form by a multiplication of the inequality with the *least common multiple* of the denominators of the coefficients and the constant.

Proposition 1 (Integer complement of a linear integer half space in normal form) *For a linear integer half space $\mathcal{H} = \{I \mid \mathbf{a}_h^T I \geq a_{h0}\}$ in normal form the integer complement is given by:*

$$\mathcal{H}^* = \mathbb{Z}^n \backslash \mathcal{H} = \{I \mid -\mathbf{a}_h^T I \geq -\lceil \frac{a_{h0}}{gcd(\mathbf{a}_h)} - 1 \rceil gcd(\mathbf{a}_h)\} \quad (4)$$

Proof: The integer complement of $\mathcal{H}$ is characterized by $\mathcal{H}^* = \mathbb{Z}^n \backslash \mathbf{H} = \{I \mid \mathbf{a}_h^T I < a_{h0}\}$ which we have to transform into its normal form $\mathcal{H}^* = \{I \mid -\mathbf{a}_h^T I \geq a_{h0}^*\}$. Using the *gcd-theorem* [9] (that every diophantine equation $\mathbf{a}_h^T I = a_{h0}$ has an integer solution I if and only if $\frac{a_{h0}}{gcd(\mathbf{a}_h)}$ is integer) only one a_{h0}^*, with $a_{h0} - gcd(\mathbf{a}_h) \leq a_{h0}^* < a_{h0}$, satisfying the gcd-theorem, can be derived. It is easy to see that $a_{h0}^* = \lceil \frac{a_{h0}}{gcd(\mathbf{a}_h)} - 1 \rceil gcd(\mathbf{a}_h)$. We get $\mathcal{H}^* = \{I \mid \mathbf{a}_h^T I \leq \lceil \frac{a_{h0}}{gcd(\mathbf{a}_h)} - 1 \rceil gcd(\mathbf{a}_h)\}$ which leads to (4).
□

3 Initialization space of an input variable

Let us consider an input variable of an equation in the SARE (1). Obviously, the input variable is used at the index points $\hat{I}$ of the index space $\hat{\mathcal{I}}_i$ of the equation and after the mapping process at the index points I of the computation space $\mathcal{I}_i$. It is well known, that a propagation vector for the input variable in the appropriate space can be derived by using the property of the input variable's *Null space propagation* [7].

Remark: If the right Null space of the considered matrix $\mathbf{M}_i$ is k-dimensional the variable has to be propagated in k directions in order to feed the variable instance only once into the processor array. In our reallocation procedure we take only the first propagation vector in the order of propagations into account. The choice of the propagation vector influences the optimization of the reallocation of the I/O-ports and has to be treated as an optimization problem, too, which will not be discussed in this paper.

Next we determine that part of the computation space $\mathcal{I}_i$ where the input variable propagated through the computation space with the propagation vector $\mathbf{w}$ will be used first. We call this space *initialization space* $\mathcal{J}$. Usually the initialization space is not convex. Therefore, we divide the initialization space $\mathcal{J}$ into disjoint convex initialization subspaces $\mathcal{J}_j$. The union of the convex initialization subspaces contains all integer points of the initialization space.

Theorem 1 (Initialization space) *Let $\mathcal{I}_i = \{I \mid \mathbf{A}I \geq \mathbf{a}_0\}$ be a computation space, and $\mathbf{w}$ be a propagation vector of an input variable, then the set of convex initialization subspaces $\mathcal{J}_j$, $1 \leq j \leq k$, with $\mathcal{J} = \bigcup_{j=1}^{k} \mathcal{J}_j$, are given by:*

$$\begin{aligned} \mathcal{J}_j = \{I \mid \mathbf{A}I \geq \mathbf{a}_0 \wedge \mathbf{a}_h^T I \geq a_{h0} + \mathbf{a}_h^T \mathbf{w} \wedge \\ \wedge -\mathbf{a}_j^T I \geq -\lceil \tfrac{(a_{j0} + \mathbf{a}_j^T \mathbf{w})}{gcd(\mathbf{a}_j)} - 1 \rceil gcd(\mathbf{a}_j) \wedge \\ \wedge \mathbf{a}_j^T \mathbf{w} > 0 \wedge \mathbf{a}_i^T \mathbf{w} > 0 \wedge 1 \leq h < j\}, \end{aligned} \quad (5)$$

where $\mathbf{A} = \begin{pmatrix} \mathbf{a}_1^T \\ \vdots \\ \mathbf{a}_m^T \end{pmatrix}$ *and* $\mathbf{a}_0 = (\ a_{10} \ \cdots \ a_{m0}\ )^T$.

Proof: We consider the inequality $\mathbf{a}_1^T I \geq a_{10}$ and assume that $\mathbf{a}_1^T \mathbf{w} > 0$. Then all $I \in \mathcal{I}_i$ satisfying $\mathbf{a}_1^T I < a_{10} + \mathbf{a}_1^T \mathbf{w}$ are elements of the initialization space $\mathcal{J}$. Using Proposition 1 we get $\mathcal{J}_1 = \{I \mid \mathbf{A}I \geq \mathbf{a}_0 \wedge \mathbf{a}_1^T I \geq -\lceil \frac{(a_{10} + \mathbf{a}_1^T \mathbf{w})}{gcd(\mathbf{a}_1)} - 1 \rceil gcd(\mathbf{a}_1)$. The same follows for all j, $1 < j \leq k$, with $\mathbf{a}_j^T \mathbf{w} > 0$. The intersection of the half spaces $\mathcal{H}_h = \{I \mid \mathbf{a}_h^T I \geq a_{h0} + \mathbf{a}_h^T \mathbf{w}\}$, $1 \leq h < j$, and the computation space $\mathcal{I}_i$ ensures disjoint initialization subspaces $\mathcal{J}_j$.
□

Remark: Any order of building the initialization subspaces $\mathcal{J}_j$ produces a correct separation of the initialization space $\mathcal{J}$. However, the order has some effect on the determination of an optimal propagation of the variables from the boundary processors to the initialization space.

4 Determination of an optimal reallocation vector

For a given initialization space we will determine a reallocation vector $\mathbf{v} \in \mathcal{I}$ which realizes the propagation of the input variables from the array boundaries to the initialization space. The first component of the reallocation vector $\mathbf{v}$ is the time component t_v, representing the number of registers in the processor connection and the remaining components form the displacement vector $\mathbf{p}_v$, representing the connection between the processors in the processor array.

We consider each initialization subspace separately in order to explore all optimization possibilities during the determination of the reallocation vectors. In the process of determining the reallocation vectors we use four criteria to decide whether a reallocation vector is valid and one criterion to find out the optimal reallocation vector with respect to a minimal latency for the reallocation. The four criteria for a valid reallocation vector can be characterized as follows.

First, displacement vectors are permitted only between processors in a *Moore neighborhood* (this is the eight neighborhood for a two dimensional displacement vector) in the processor array. This property is called the systolic constraint.

Secondly, a reallocation vector has to satisfy the causality constraint, i.e. its time component must be greater than zero.

Third, the unicity constraint requires a unique definition of the variable instances for every integer point of the control space. This results directly in the constraint: $\forall I \in \mathcal{J}_j : I - \mathbf{v} \notin \mathcal{J}_j$, where $\mathcal{J}_j$ is a initialization subspace.

Fourthly, for each displacement vector we choose the minimal of all valid time components in order to get a minimal number of registers and the minimal latency for the reallocation.

The four criteria are used in the following way: We determine all displacement vectors satisfying the Moore neighborhood and compute for each of them the minimal time component satisfying the second and third criteria.

The time component is established for every possible displacement vector by solving the following integer linear program:

Theorem 2 (Valid reallocation vector) *For a given displacement vector* $\mathbf{p}_v$, *a time component* t_v *satisfying* $t_v > 0$ *and* $\forall I \in \mathcal{J}_j : I - \mathbf{v} \notin \mathcal{J}_j$, *with* $\mathcal{J}_j = \{I \mid \mathbf{A}_j I \geq \mathbf{a}_{j0}\}$, *can be determined by solving the integer linear program:*

$$\begin{array}{ll} \textit{maximize} \;\; t_v & \\ \textit{subject to} & \\ \quad \mathbf{A}_j I \geq \mathbf{a}_{j0} & I \in \mathbb{Z}^n \\ \quad \mathbf{A}_j I + \mathbf{A}_j \begin{pmatrix} t_v - 1 \\ \mathbf{0} \end{pmatrix} \geq \mathbf{a}_{j0} + \mathbf{A}_j \begin{pmatrix} 0 \\ \mathbf{p}_v \end{pmatrix} & t_v \in \mathbb{Z} \\ \quad t_v \geq 1 & \end{array} \tag{6}$$

Proof: If t_v^* is the maximal value satisfying $\exists I \in \mathcal{J}_j : I + (\, t_v^* \;\; \mathbf{p}_v \,)^T \in \mathcal{J}_j$, then is $t_v = t_v^* + 1$ the minimal value satisfying $\forall I \in \mathcal{J}_j : I + (\, t_v \;\; \mathbf{p}_v \,)^T \notin \mathcal{J}_j$, which leads to (6).

□

The result is a set $\mathcal{V}$ of permissible reallocation vectors $\mathbf{v}$. The set can be reduced using a more restrictive neighborhood or by considering only the existing propagation vectors as possible reallocation vectors in order to restrict the number of channels in the processor array.

Now we select one reallocation vector $\mathbf{v} \in \mathcal{V}$ for every initialization subspace satisfying the criterion that the additional time caused by the reallocation is minimal. To this end we compute for every $\mathbf{v} \in \mathcal{V}$ the minimal time instance when a variable instance has to be fed into a boundary processor. This task can be expressed as an optimization problem too. Then we select the reallocation vector $\mathbf{v}$ with the greatest minimal time instance.

Theorem 3 (Minimal input time as a function of a reallocation vector) *For a given reallocation vector* $\mathbf{v}$, *for a processor space* $\mathcal{P} = \{\mathbf{p} \mid \mathbf{S}\mathbf{p} \geq \mathbf{s}_0\}$ *and for a initialization subspace* $\mathcal{J}_j = \{(\, t \;\; \mathbf{p} \,) \mid \mathbf{A}_j (\, t \;\; \mathbf{p} \,)^T \geq \mathbf{a}_{j0}\}$, *the minimal time* t_{j0}, *that a variable instance has to be fed into the processor array, will be determined by solving the integer linear program:*

$$\begin{array}{ll} \textit{minimize} \;\; t^* & \\ \textit{subject to} & \\ \mathbf{A}_j \begin{pmatrix} t^* \\ \mathbf{p}^* \end{pmatrix} - \mathbf{A}_j \mathbf{v} n \geq \mathbf{a}_{j0} & t^*, n \in \mathbb{Z} \\ \mathbf{S}\mathbf{p}^* \geq \mathbf{s}_0 & \mathbf{p}^* \in \mathbb{Z}^{n-1} \\ n \geq 0 & \end{array} \tag{7}$$

Proof: Let us assume, that the input port for a variable instance is $\mathbf{p} \in \mathcal{P}$. Then, the processor $\mathbf{p}^* \in \mathcal{P}$ is the input boundary processor, if $\mathbf{p}^* = \mathbf{p} - n\mathbf{p}_v$, where $n \in \mathbb{Z}$ is the maximal value satisfying $\mathbf{p}^* \in \mathcal{P}$. With $\begin{pmatrix} t \\ \mathbf{p} \end{pmatrix} - n \begin{pmatrix} t_v \\ \mathbf{p}_v \end{pmatrix} = \begin{pmatrix} t^* \\ \mathbf{p}^* \end{pmatrix}$ and $t_v > 0$ follows, that the search for a maximal value $n \in \mathbb{Z}$ can be replaced by the search for a minimal $t^* \in \mathbb{Z}$, which leads to (7).

□

Remark: Instead of taking the reallocation vector with the greatest minimal time instance into account we can take one of the reallocation vectors associating minimal input time instances greater than $t_{min} \in \mathcal{T}$ in order to keep the latency of the processor array.

The proposed method can be enhanced by dividing the initialization subspaces into partial subspaces and by choosing a separate reallocation vector for each partial subspace. The partitioning of a initialization subspace into two partial subspaces will be considered in the next chapter.

5 Partitioning of initialization subspaces

The additional time caused by the reallocation of the input ports at the array boundaries described above can be considerable large. To keep the additional latency minimal, reallocation vectors in different directions are used to realize a reallocation of the I/O-ports of one initialization subspace at their nearest boundary processors.
To this end the initialization subspace are divided into partial subspaces with different reallocation vectors. In the following a general method for determining a partitioning hyperplane $\mathcal{H} = \{I \mid \mathbf{b}^T I = b_0\}$ for the initialization subspace is proposed. The method is based on a search procedure for a minimal scheduling in systolic array design [13].

Theorem 4 (Partitioning of initialization subspaces) *For a given a processor space $\mathcal{P} = \{\mathbf{p} \mid \mathbf{S}\mathbf{p} \geq \mathbf{s}_0\}$ and the reallocation vectors $\mathbf{v}_1 = (t_{v1} \quad \mathbf{p}_{v1}^T)^T$ and $\mathbf{v}_2 = (t_{v2} \quad \mathbf{p}_{v2}^T)^T$ a hyperplane can be created which divides an initialization subspace into two partial subspaces using different reallocation vectors (in order to minimize the additional latency) by solving the following integer linear programs:*

$$\begin{array}{llll} \textit{minimize} & -\mathbf{s}_0^T(\mathbf{y}_1+\mathbf{y}_2) & & \\ \textit{subject to} & & & \\ \mathbf{y}_1^T\mathbf{S} = \mathbf{p}_b & \mathbf{y}_1 \geq \mathbf{0} & \mathbf{y}_1 \in \mathbb{Q}^m & \\ \mathbf{y}_2^T\mathbf{S} = -\mathbf{p}_b & \mathbf{y}_2 \geq \mathbf{0} & \mathbf{y}_2 \in \mathbb{Q}^m & \\ -\mathbf{p}_b^T\mathbf{p}_{v1} \leq -1 & & \mathbf{p}_b \in \mathbb{Z}^{n-1} & \\ \mathbf{p}_b^T\mathbf{p}_{v2} \leq 1 & & & \end{array} \quad (8)$$

$$\begin{array}{lll} \textit{maximize} & n & \\ \textit{subject to} & & \\ \mathbf{S}\mathbf{p}_1 \geq \mathbf{s}_0 & & \mathbf{p}_1 \in \mathbb{Z}^{n-1} \\ \mathbf{S}\mathbf{p}_2 \geq \mathbf{s}_0 & & \mathbf{p}_2 \in \mathbb{Z}^{n-1} \\ \mathbf{p}_b^T\mathbf{p}_1 + \mathbf{p}_b^T\mathbf{p}_{v1}n = b_0 & & n, b_0 \in \mathbb{Q} \\ \mathbf{p}_b^T\mathbf{p}_2 + \mathbf{p}_b^T\mathbf{p}_{v2}\frac{t_{v1}}{t_{v2}}n = b_0 & & \\ n \geq 0 & & \end{array} \quad (9)$$

The resulting partitioning hyperplane is given by: $\mathcal{H} = \{I \mid \mathbf{b}^T I = b_0\}$, *with* $\mathbf{b} = (\ 0 \quad \mathbf{p}_b^T\ )^T$.

Proof: The first part of (8) is the dual linear program to the following:

$$\begin{array}{lll} \textit{maximize} & \mathbf{p}_b^T(\mathbf{p}_1 - \mathbf{p}_2) & \\ \textit{subject to} & & \\ \mathbf{S}\mathbf{p}_1 \geq \mathbf{s}_0 & \mathbf{p}_1 \geq \mathbf{0} & \mathbf{p}_1 \in \mathbb{Q}^{n-1} \\ \mathbf{S}\mathbf{p}_2 \geq \mathbf{s}_0 & \mathbf{p}_2 \geq \mathbf{0} & \mathbf{p}_2 \in \mathbb{Q}^{n-1} \end{array}$$

which yields the maximal count of interconnections in the direction of $\mathbf{p}_b$ through the processor array. The constraints $\mathbf{p}_b^T\mathbf{p}_{v1} \geq 1$ and $\mathbf{p}_b^T\mathbf{p}_{v2} \leq 1$ ensure the direction of the reallocation vectors in both half spaces created by the partitioning hyperplane.
The second integer linear program (9) computes the optimal location of the hyperplane with the normal vector $\mathbf{b} = (\ 0 \quad \mathbf{p}_b^T\ )^T$. The additional time for the reallocation of the input ports will be minimal if the maximal propagation time for the input variables, which are used at the index points on the partitioning hyperplane, is equal for both propagation directions. This corresponds with $nt_{v1} = mt_{v2}$, whereas n and m are the maximal values satisfying $\exists \mathbf{p}_1, \mathbf{p}_2 \in \mathcal{P} : \mathbf{p}_b^T\mathbf{p}_1 + \mathbf{p}_b^T\mathbf{p}_{v1}n = \mathbf{p}_b^T\mathbf{p}_2 + \mathbf{p}_b^T\mathbf{p}_{v2}m = b_0$, which leads to (9).
The normal vector $\mathbf{b}$ of the hyperplane is perpendicular to the time axis since the partitioning of the initialization subspace has to be time invariant.
□

The two partial subspaces of the initialization subspace are defined by the intersection of the half spaces $\mathcal{H} = \{I \mid \mathbf{b}^T I \geq b_0\}$ or $\mathcal{H}^* = \{I \mid -\mathbf{b}^T I \geq -\lceil \frac{b_0}{gcd(\mathbf{b})} - 1 \rceil gcd(\mathbf{b})\}$ (see Proposition 1) respectively and the initialization subspace $\mathcal{J}_j$.

Remark: One of the partial subspaces generated by the dividing hyperplane can be empty. Then the dividing of the initialization subspace does not have any effect.

The consideration of n reallocation vectors for one initialization subspace leads to $(n+1)n/2$ partitioning hyperplanes which yields some half spaces. The intersection of the half spaces concerning one reallocation vector and the initialization subspace defines the partial subspace associated to this reallocation vector.

Finally, we compute the reallocation space which is a subspace of the computation space where the input variables will be propagated from the array boundaries to the initialization subspaces.

Proposition 2 (Reallocation space) *For a control space $\mathcal{I}$, a computation space $\mathcal{I}_i$, an initialization subspace $\mathcal{J}_j = \{I \mid \mathbf{A}I \geq \mathbf{a}_0\}$ and a reallocation vector $\mathbf{v}$, the reallocation space $\mathcal{J}_p$ is determined by:*

$$\mathcal{J}_p = cylExt_t(\mathcal{I}) \cap cylExt_{\mathbf{v}}(convHull(\mathcal{I}_i)) \cap \mathcal{U}, \quad (10)$$

where $\mathcal{U}$ is an open polyhedron defined by: $\mathcal{U} = \{I \mid \mathbf{a}_i^T I \geq a_{i0} \wedge \mathbf{a}_i^T \mathbf{v} < 0\}$, *where*

$$\mathbf{A} = \begin{pmatrix} \mathbf{a}_1^T \\ \vdots \\ \mathbf{a}_m^T \end{pmatrix} \textit{ and } \mathbf{a}_0 = (\ a_{10} \quad \cdots \quad a_{m0}\ )^T.$$

6 Example

We illustrate the methods of the reallocation process with an example. Suppose, that
a control space $\mathcal{I}$:

$$\mathcal{I} = \{ \begin{pmatrix} t \\ p \end{pmatrix} \mid \begin{pmatrix} 1 & 0 \\ -1 & 0 \\ 0 & 1 \\ 0 & -1 \end{pmatrix} \begin{pmatrix} t \\ p \end{pmatrix} \geq \begin{pmatrix} 1 \\ -10 \\ 1 \\ -10 \end{pmatrix} \},$$

a computation space $\mathcal{I}_i$:

$$\mathcal{I}_i = \{ \begin{pmatrix} t \\ p \end{pmatrix} \mid \begin{pmatrix} 1 & 0 \\ -1 & 0 \\ 0 & 1 \\ 0 & -1 \\ 1 & -1 \end{pmatrix} \begin{pmatrix} t \\ p \end{pmatrix} \geq \begin{pmatrix} 1 \\ -5 \\ 2 \\ -10 \\ -7 \end{pmatrix} \},$$

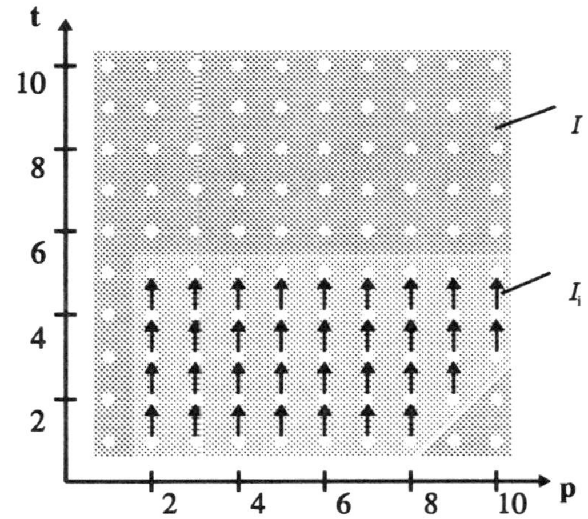

Figure 1: *control space $\mathcal{I}$ with computation spaces $\mathcal{I}_i$*

a variable $y[f(I)]$, where $f(I) = \begin{pmatrix} 0 & 1 \end{pmatrix} \begin{pmatrix} t \\ p \end{pmatrix} + 5$, and the propagation vector
$\mathbf{w} = (1 \quad 0)^T \in nullSpace((\; 0 \quad 1 \;))$ are given.

The initialization subspaces are computed according to Theorem 1, whereas the redundant inequalities are omitted.
The resulting initialization subspaces $\mathcal{J}_1$ and $\mathcal{J}_2$ shown in figure 2 are the following:

$$\mathcal{J}_1 = \{ \begin{pmatrix} t \\ p \end{pmatrix} \mid \begin{pmatrix} 1 & 0 \\ -1 & 0 \\ 0 & 1 \\ 1 & -1 \end{pmatrix} \begin{pmatrix} t \\ p \end{pmatrix} \geq \begin{pmatrix} 1 \\ -1 \\ 2 \\ -7 \end{pmatrix} \},$$

$$\mathcal{J}_2 = \{ \begin{pmatrix} t \\ p \end{pmatrix} \mid \begin{pmatrix} 1 & 0 \\ 0 & -1 \\ 1 & -1 \\ -1 & 1 \end{pmatrix} \begin{pmatrix} t \\ p \end{pmatrix} \geq \begin{pmatrix} 2 \\ -10 \\ -7 \\ 7 \end{pmatrix} \}.$$

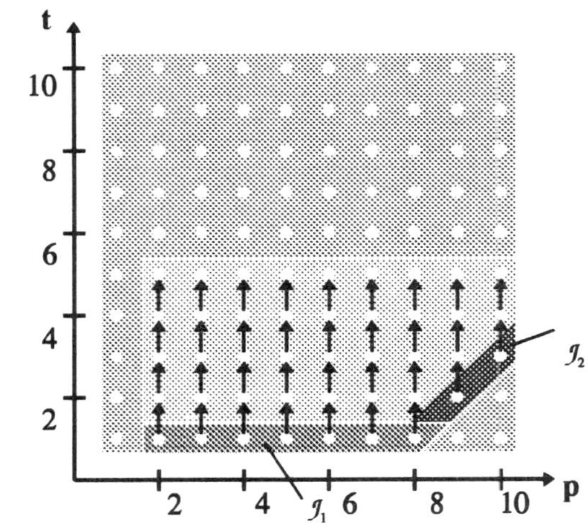

Figure 2: *initialization subspaces*

There are only two systolic displacement vectors in one-dimensional processor spaces: $\mathbf{p}_{v1} = 1$ and $\mathbf{p}_{v2} = -1$. We generate the set of valid reallocation vectors for each initialization subspace separately by solving the integer linear program of Theorem 2. The program for the initialization subspace $\mathcal{J}_1$ and the displacement vector $\mathbf{p}_{v1}$ is the following:

maximize t_v
subject to

$$\begin{pmatrix} 1 & 0 \\ -1 & 0 \\ 0 & 1 \\ 1 & -1 \end{pmatrix} \begin{pmatrix} t \\ p \end{pmatrix} \geq \begin{pmatrix} 1 \\ -1 \\ 2 \\ -7 \end{pmatrix}$$

$$\begin{pmatrix} 1 & 0 \\ -1 & 0 \\ 0 & 1 \\ 1 & -1 \end{pmatrix} \begin{pmatrix} t \\ p \end{pmatrix} + \begin{pmatrix} 1 & 0 \\ -1 & 0 \\ 0 & 1 \\ 1 & -1 \end{pmatrix} \begin{pmatrix} t_v - 1 \\ 0 \end{pmatrix} \geq$$

$$\geq \begin{pmatrix} 1 \\ -1 \\ 2 \\ -7 \end{pmatrix} + \begin{pmatrix} 1 & 0 \\ -1 & 0 \\ 0 & 1 \\ 1 & -1 \end{pmatrix} \begin{pmatrix} 0 \\ 1 \end{pmatrix}$$

$t_v \geq 1$

The result is $t_v = 1$. In the same way we obtain the sets of valid reallocation vectors $\mathcal{V}_1 = \{\mathbf{v}_{11}, \mathbf{v}_{12}\} = \{(1 \quad 1)^T, (1 \quad -1)^T\}$ for $\mathcal{J}_1$ and $\mathcal{V}_2 = \{\mathbf{v}_{21}, \mathbf{v}_{22}\} = \{(2 \quad 1)^T, (1 \quad -1)^T\}$ for $\mathcal{J}_2$ respectively.
We choose the optimal reallocation vector with respect to a minimal additional latency for every initialization subspace by solving the integer linear program of Theorem 3. The computation of the minimal time instance is shown for the reallocation vector $\mathbf{v}_{11}$:

$$
\begin{aligned}
&\textit{minimize} \quad t \\
&\textit{subject to} \\
&\begin{pmatrix} 1 & 0 \\ -1 & 0 \\ 0 & 1 \\ 1 & -1 \end{pmatrix} \begin{pmatrix} t \\ p \end{pmatrix} - \begin{pmatrix} 1 & 0 \\ -1 & 0 \\ 0 & 1 \\ 1 & -1 \end{pmatrix} \begin{pmatrix} 1 \\ 1 \end{pmatrix} n \geq \\
&\qquad \geq \begin{pmatrix} 1 \\ -1 \\ 2 \\ -7 \end{pmatrix} + \begin{pmatrix} 1 & 0 \\ -1 & 0 \\ 0 & 1 \\ 1 & -1 \end{pmatrix} \begin{pmatrix} 0 \\ 1 \end{pmatrix} \\
&\begin{pmatrix} 1 \\ -1 \end{pmatrix} p \geq \begin{pmatrix} 1 \\ -10 \end{pmatrix} \\
&n \geq 1
\end{aligned}
$$

The result is $t = t_{11} = -6$. The minimal input time instances for the other reallocation vectors are: $t_{12} = -7$, $t_{21} = -13$ and $t_{22} = 1$. We could choose the reallocation vectors $\mathbf{v}_{11}$ and $\mathbf{v}_{22}$ in order to yield the minimal additional latency of seven time steps.

A better result can be achieved by a partitioning of the first initialization subspace $\mathcal{J}_1$ into two partial subspaces. To this end we generate the partitioning hyperplane by solving the integer linear programs of Theorem 4:

$$
\begin{aligned}
&\textit{minimize} \quad -(1 \quad -10)(\mathbf{y}_1 + \mathbf{y}_2) \\
&\textit{subject to} \\
&\mathbf{y}_1^T \begin{pmatrix} 1 \\ -1 \end{pmatrix} \leq p_b \quad \mathbf{y}_1 \geq \mathbf{0} \quad \mathbf{y}_1 \in \mathbb{Q}^2 \\
&\mathbf{y}_2^T \begin{pmatrix} 1 \\ -1 \end{pmatrix} \leq -p_b \quad \mathbf{y}_2 \geq \mathbf{0} \quad \mathbf{y}_2 \in \mathbb{Q}^2 \\
&-p_b(1) \leq -1 \qquad\qquad p_b \in \mathbb{Z} \\
&p_b(-1) \leq 1
\end{aligned}
$$

The last inequalities already imply that $p_b = 1$. (The results for the other variables are $\mathbf{y}_1 = (1 \quad 0)^T$ and $\mathbf{y}_2 = (0 \quad 1)^T$). Now we compute the constant b_0 of the hyperplane.

$$
\begin{aligned}
&\textit{maximize} \quad n \\
&\textit{subject to} \\
&\begin{pmatrix} 1 \\ -1 \end{pmatrix} p_1 \geq \begin{pmatrix} 1 \\ -10 \end{pmatrix} \quad p_1 \in \mathbb{Z} \\
&\begin{pmatrix} 1 \\ -1 \end{pmatrix} p_2 \geq \begin{pmatrix} 1 \\ -10 \end{pmatrix} \quad p_2 \in \mathbb{Z} \\
&1p_1 + 1(1)n = b_0 \qquad b_0, n \in \mathbb{Q} \\
&1p_2 + 1(-1)\tfrac{1}{1}n = b_0 \\
&n \geq 0
\end{aligned}
$$

We get $b_0 = \frac{11}{2}$ (and $n = \frac{9}{2}$). Hence the partitioning hyperplane results in:

$$\mathcal{H} = \{I \mid (\ 0 \quad 1\ ) I \geq 11/2\}$$

The initialization subspace $\mathcal{J}_1$ is divided by $\mathcal{H}$ into $\mathcal{J}_{11}$ and $\mathcal{J}_{12}$.

The generated partial subspaces of $\mathcal{I}_1$ are:

$$\mathcal{J}_{11} = \{\begin{pmatrix} t \\ p \end{pmatrix} \mid \begin{pmatrix} 1 & 0 \\ -1 & 0 \\ 0 & 1 \\ 0 & -1 \end{pmatrix} \begin{pmatrix} t \\ p \end{pmatrix} \geq \begin{pmatrix} 1 \\ -1 \\ 2 \\ -5 \end{pmatrix}\},$$

$$\mathcal{J}_{12} = \{\begin{pmatrix} t \\ p \end{pmatrix} \mid \begin{pmatrix} 1 & 0 \\ -1 & 0 \\ 1 & -1 \\ 0 & 1 \end{pmatrix} \begin{pmatrix} t \\ p \end{pmatrix} \geq \begin{pmatrix} 1 \\ -1 \\ -7 \\ 11/2 \end{pmatrix}\}.$$

Now we achieved an additional latency of four time steps only.

The resulting reallocation spaces $\mathcal{J}_{p11}$, $\mathcal{J}_{p12}$ and $\mathcal{J}_{p2}$ are shown in figure 3.

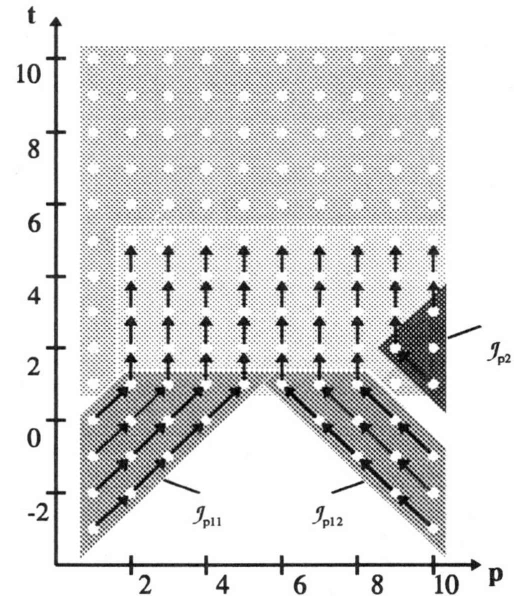

Figure 3: *reallocation spaces*

7 Conclusion

In the paper the reallocation of the I/O-ports of the I/O-variables at the array boundaries of the processor array have been considered. We have developed methods for an optimal reallocation under the constraints keeping the properties of the processor arrays and with respect to a minimal arising latency. With the developed hyperplane method we achieved reallocation vectors realizing a minimal additional latency without any additional hardware. Some integer linear programming has been used to achieve optimal results. The tools will be implemented as part of the synthesis system for massively parallel processor arrays DESA [10].

Open problems are the application of the proposed tools to a hardware adapted processor array instead of the full size array as well as the combination of the considered optimization problem of finding reallocation vectors with the search for propagation vectors of the Null space propagation of the I/O-variables to further reduce the time and hardware costs.

Acknowledgements

The research was supported by the "Deutsche Forschungsgemeinschaft", in the project A1/SFB358.

References

[1] D. Baltus: "Efficient Exploration of Affine Space-Time Transformations for Optimal Systolic Array Synthesis", *PhD thesis*, MIT 1994

[2] P. Held, P. Dewilde, E.F. Deprettere, P. Willage: "HIFI: From Parallel Algorithm to Fixed-Size VLSI Processor Array", in *Application-Driven Architecture Synthesis*, F. Cathoor, L. Svensson (eds.), Kluwer Academic Publishers, pages 71-94, 1993

[3] R.M. Karp, R.E. Miller, S. Winograd: "The organization of computations for uniform recurrence equations", *J. of the ACM*, vol.14, pages 563-590, 1967

[4] A.A.J. de Lange, A. van der Hoeven, P. van Prooijen: "Hierarchical Parameterized Synthesis of Semi-Regular VLSI Processor Arrays", in *Algorithms and Parallel VLSI Architectures*, 1991

[5] C.M.H. Leverge, P. Quinton: "A language-oriented approach to the design of systolic chips", in *Algorithms and Parallel VLSI-Architectures*, A.J. van der Veen, E.F. Deprettere (eds.) Elsevier Science Publisher B.V., volume A, pages 309-327, 1991

[6] D.I. Moldovan: "On the Design of Algorithms for VLSI Systolic Arrays", *Proceedings of the IEEE*, pages 113-120, January 1983

[7] S.K. Rao: "Regular Iterative Algorithms and their Implementations on Processor Arrays", *PhD thesis*, Stanford University, 1985

[8] P. Quinton: "Automatic Synthesis of Systolic Arrays from Uniform Recurrent Equations", *IEEE 11-th Int. Symp. on Computer Architecture*, Ann Arbor, pages 208-214, 1984

[9] A. Schrijver: *Theory of Linear and Integer Programming*, John Wiles & Sons, New York, 1986

[10] A. Schubert, R. Merker, H. Schreiber: "Systematic Generation of a Variety of Processor Arrays", in *Parcella '94*, Mathematical Research, Chr. Jesshope, V. Jossifov, W. Wilhelmi (eds.), vol. 81, Akademie-Verlag 1994, pages 267-276, 1994

[11] M.F.X.B. van Swaaij, F.V.M. Catthor, H.J. de Man: "Nonlinear transformations for high level regular array ASIC synthesis", *J. VLSI Signal Processing*, vol.4, pages 259-268, 1992

[12] J. Teich: "A Compiler for Application-Specific Processor Arrays", *PhD thesis*, Univ. of Saarland, Verlag Shaker, Aachen 1993

[13] L. Thiele: "Resource Constraint Scheduling of Uniform Algorithms", in *Proc. Application-Specific Array Processors 1993*, L. Dadda, B. Wah (eds.), pages 29-40, 1993

❖ SESSION 10 ❖

Parallel Performance, Models, and Simulation

Chair

A. Tyrrell

Deblocking Event Algorithm: a New Approach to Conservative Parallel Discrete Event Simulation

V. Sánchez, A. Bautista, F. Tirado
Dpto.Informática y Automática U.C.M.
Facultad CC. Físicas. Ciudad Universitaria S/N. Madrid 28040
E-Mail: victor@dia.ucm.es | alfredob@dia.ucm.es

Abstract.

This paper presents a new approach to perform distributed event driven simulation that we have named the Deblocking Event algorithm. This algorithm adopts the conservative paradigm, but takes into account the structural properties of the simulation network to reduce the overhead that inherently have any distributed simulation scheme. At the same time, the algorithm keeps a high degree of activity in the network of processes that performs the simulation, what means that the scheme obtains almost all the parallelism inherent to the problem. First, the distributed parallel simulation problems and the classical approaches proposed to solve them are reviewed in the paper. Then the properties of a simulation network are mathematically characterized. Finally the Deblocking Event algorithm and some results about overhead reduction and degree of activity in the network of processes are presented.

1. Introduction.

Parallel discrete event simulation (PDES) has been a topic of intensive research during the last fifteen years, and it is still an open problem. In this kind of simulation the system to simulate is modelled as a set of logical processes (LPs). Each LP simulates a part of the physical model called physical process (PP). In order to evaluate the whole system in a multiprocessor, groups of LPs are mapped onto each processor and are executed. Each LP has a state, consisting of a set of private variables, and a local clock, which register the simulated time reached at that LP. Interactions among PPs, causing the change of the state of an LP indirectly by others LPs, are carried out interchanging time-tagged messages (called events) among the related LPs. We suppose that each LP can predict its behaviour until the simulated time t+LA, when it knows the values of its inputs until the simulated time t. Parameter LA is known as lookahead, and we suppose that it is greater than zero.

With this approach the execution of the model consist of a set of LP evaluations. Each LP evaluation is an execution of the following loop:

I. To synchronize the process with the rest of the model.
II. To update the state variables corresponding to the LP's inputs, as well as the local clock, with received messages.
III. To evaluate the LP, what probably modifies its state.
IV. To send events for each changed state variable corresponding to an LP's output, as the event oriented simulation philosophy imposes. Messages are sent to every LP in the network that must be informed of the state variations produced at the evaluated LP.

The synchronization phase is critical, because it includes all operations performed in order to avoid that the simulation could introduce causality errors. A causality error arises at LPi if it receives from LPj an event with a time tag greater than its local time. This would mean that LPi has been evaluated without taking into account all previous interactions with other LPs, and in consequence, the results of the simulation would be probably erroneous. In [1] it can be found an interesting study about factors involved in PDES performance, among them the synchronization requirement.

In a parallel simulation LPs can be evaluated in multiple different sequences, but only some of them leads to the correct evaluation of the model. A synchronization mechanism must provide a correct evaluation of the model, just selecting a sequence of LPs evaluations without causality transgressions, or just rectifying possible causality transgressions, if they are

1066-6192/96 $5.00 © 1996 IEEE
Proceedings of PDP '96

allowed. This property is named accurateness in Reynolds terminology [2].

Another important goal of any synchronization mechanism for PDES is to allow LPs to be evaluated in an order that extracts the maximum parallelism. This property is called aggressiveness in Reynolds terminology. Related to aggressiveness there is another property of a synchronization mechanism called risk, that measures the possibility of causality violations that it introduces in the evaluation of the system.

Further, another desirable property of a synchronization mechanism is that its associated overhead will be minimum. This overhead has two components:

- The work performed to compute global values, or to send extra events that synchronize processes. That could be called common overhead, because it is carried out periodically during the system evaluation.
- The work performed to recover the systems from causality violations, or from deadlocks. That could be called uncommon overhead, because it is associated to those points of the system evaluation where the mentioned anomalies are detected.

There is a relation among these former factors that could be expressed as follows: "*The bigger the aggressiveness and the accurateness of a synchronization scheme, the bigger the riskness and the associated overhead due to recovering from errors*".

Several synchronization methods has been proposed by PDES researchers, that can be classified in two main groups:

Conservative protocols *(non aggressive, non risk, and accurate protocols):* These synchronization schemes allow evaluation of LPs only if it is warranted that this evaluation will not lead to a causality violation, so they are accurate by construction. Usually these algorithms are based on the *local causality constraint* (LCC) [3] that can be enunciated as follows: "Each LP sends an event <out1,t1> if it is sure that it will not send any event <out2,t2> , where t2<t1, in the future". As a consequence of the LCC, an LP only can be evaluated and produce messages if the values of all of its inputs are known at the local simulation time.

The problem is that the LCC reduces the parallelism, because it imposes artificial restriction to the LP's evaluation, and what is more important, it could lead to deadlocks in the network of LPs. Solutions to this problem are:

- To modify the event driven simulation philosophy, sending messages from LPi to LPj even if the evaluation of LPi does not change the LPj state. Those messages, that transmit information about inactivity, are called null events [4].
- To introduce a deadlock detection/recovery mechanism, that detects deadlock and computes the minimum global time of all events prepared to be sent. Communicating this safe horizon time to each LP, the simulation is allowed to continue until it is reached ([5], [6]).

Both solutions introduce overhead in the system evaluation because of extra communications in the former and because of computation of the global minima in the second.

Optimistic protocols *(aggressive, risk, and accurate protocols):* These synchronization schemes allow evaluation of LPs without any restraint. This results in a synchronization that allows to obtain the maximum parallelism in the execution of the model. However this kind of synchronization could exceed the maximum available parallelism, and possibly lead to causality violations. Since an event is processed when it is available, evaluation of events that causes causality violations produce faults (fault points). To guarantee accurateness, the synchronization mechanism provides ways to detect and recover from these violations, usually based on storing the execution history of the system which allows rolling back the simulation to the fault point. The roll back procedure is not the only source of overhead; because of limits in the storage capacity of machines, safe parts of the history database of the simulation (that is, parts without risk of being modified because a causality violation) must be deleted from it. The best known of these protocols is the "time warp" algorithm ([7], [8]). A pictorially representation of the behaviour of both approaches can be seen in Fig. 1, where the parallelism reachable by both synchronization schemes along the simulation of an LP's network is represented.

Neither of these classes of synchronization algorithms has been proved to be strictly better than the other. An interesting discussion about both synchronisation algorithms and their properties can be found in [3] and [9]. A formal analysis of both approaches is presented in [10].

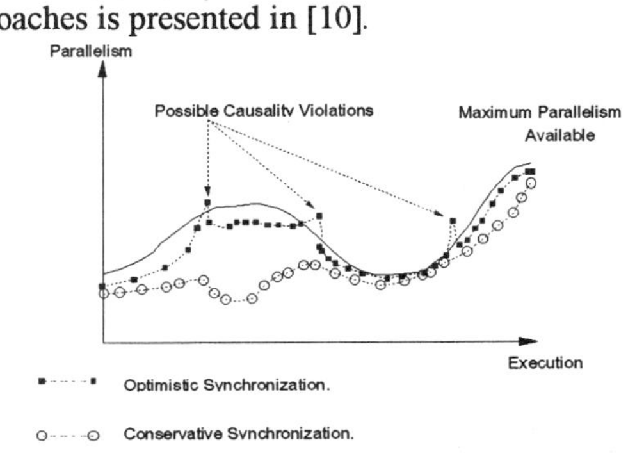

Fig. 1: Synchronization schemes behaviour.

We are interested in PDES on a message passing distributed memory machine. Our objective has been to design an efficient synchronization mechanism for PDES with the following characteristics:

- The distributed scheme should not have to calculate global values, because it is expensive computationally on distributed memory machines. This led us to choose a conservative simulation scheme based on null events.
- The scheme should reduce the message traffic overhead as much as possible, because communications are expensive in distributed memory machines.
- It would be desirable for the scheme that it allows to take advantage of LA to increase the efficiency of the simulation algorithm. In [11] it is emphasized the importance of LA in the performance of conservative synchronization schemes for PDES.

The outline of this paper is as follows: section 2 justifies mathematically the proposed conservative synchronization scheme. Section 3 explains the simulation algorithms that implement this synchronization scheme. Section 4 presents the pre-processing requirements of the network of LPs imposed by the synchronization scheme. Section 5 studies the algorithm that take advantage of lookahead on loops. Section 6 shows some experimental results comparing the overhead and the parallelism degree of the proposed PDES algorithm vs. the classical null event approach. Last section is devoted to conclusions.

2. A new PDES synchronization approach.

As we have mentioned in section 1, a simulation scheme that adopts LCC can lead to deadlock situations. In this section we are going to find out the minimum requirements for a network of LPs to be active (i.e. not deadlocked) when LCC is applied. To reach this goal we are going to present a model of activity of an LP 's network.

Dependencies among LPs in PDES can be modelled by means of a graph where each node represents an LP, and each arc a dependence of the destination from the origin. An immediate representation of a graph can be achieved by means of binary matrices. This is not a computationally efficient representation, but is useful to demonstrate in an easy way the validity of our proposal.

We have chosen a representation of a network of n LPs connected by m channels (CH) by way of two binary matrices I∈{nxm} and O∈{nxm} where:

I is the input matrix: I[i,j]=1 *if CHj is an input to LPi*; 0 *otherwise*.

O is the output matrix: O[i,j]=1 *if CHj is an output from LPi*; 0 *otherwise*.

Row i of I (I[i]) has the following meaning: *"LPi satisfies LCC if CHj is not empty for all j where I[i,j]=1"*. In a similar way row i of O has the following meaning: *"CHi receives an event when LPj is evaluated if $O^t[i,j]=1$"*.

We define the matrix product in the classical way but using the logical (OR), (AND) operators instead of the arithmetic (+), (·). Performing $I^t \cdot O$ (where I^t is the transpose of matrix I) we obtain a matrix D that express the dependency among channels:

D[i,j]=1 *if CHj is an output from the same LP that has CHi as one of its inputs;* 0 *otherwise* .

The meaning of D is the following: *"CHj will receive events from its source LP if and only if CHi is not empty for all i where D[i,j]=1"*. In other words, D expresses the dependency among channels separated by one LP. Multiplying D by itself we obtain the dependency of channels separated by two LPs. Generalizing D^k will express the dependency among channels separated by k LPs.

The state of the network of channels can be characterized by means of a binary vector S with m components, that could be interpreted as follows:

S[i]=1 *if CHi holds some event (that is, CHi is active);* 0 *otherwise* .

Starting from an initial state S_0, the next state could be obtained in the following way (it has been assumed that evaluation of any LP only requires that all of its inputs are active, and produces events at all of its outputs):

$$\overline{S_1[i]} = \sum_{\forall j} (D^t) \; [i,j] \cdot \overline{S_0[j]}$$

In general the state of the network after k evaluations of the whole system will be:

$$\overline{S_k[i]} = \sum_{\forall j} (D^t)^k \; [i,j] \cdot \overline{S_0[j]}$$

Matrix D stores structural information about dependencies among channels, that could be used to design a PDES synchronization algorithms that, fulfilling LCC requirement, will not block. The question is: *"What is the minimum set of channels that must be kept active to ensure that the system is not blocked?"*. The answer is difficult to find because of the complexity of matrix D. The analysis of matrix D could be simplified, just by applying several reduction rules that preserve the structural information of the original matrix.

Rule 1: If two columns of matrix D are equal, this means that both have the same dependence, so they are equivalent and one can be deleted keeping the other as a representative of both. When CHi and CHj are equivalent, and CHj is selected as representative of both, successors of CHi must be included as successors of CHj, to avoid losing information. This is achieved by performing:

D[j,k]=D[i,k]+D[j,k] (for k=0...m-1).

After doing this operation, CHi can be deleted. An example of the application of this rule can be seen in Fig. 2 where CH_1 and CH_2 are equivalent, and CH_2 is deleted.

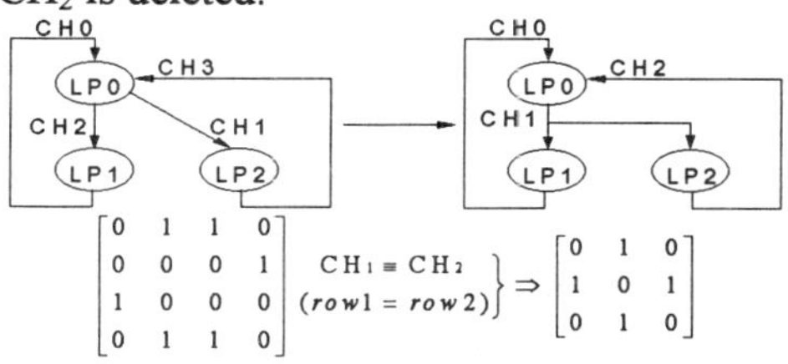

Fig. 2: Example of application of rule 1.

Rule 2: If a column in matrix D has all of its elements equal to 0, this means that the channel corresponding to that column does not depend on other channels, so it is always active independently of the state of the rest of the network. Let us assume that channel i is independent, and channel j depends on channel i. This dependence can be expressed as follows:

if (channel$_i$ is active) and (other conditions)
then channel$_j$ will be active in the future.

Taking into account that channel i is always active, the previous condition can be reduced to:

if (other conditions)
then channel$_j$ will be active in the future.

In other words, independent channels do not affect to the future state of other channels in the network, so they can be deleted from matrix D.

In Fig. 3 rule 2 is applied two times to the initial matrix D.

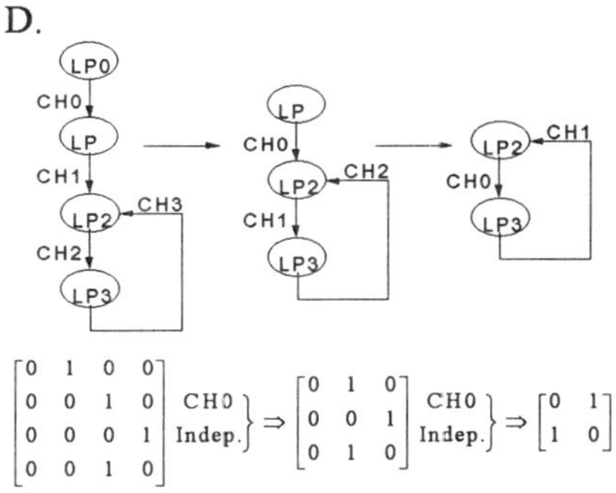

Fig. 3: Example of application of rule 2.

Rule 3: If a channel i depends on a set of channels $\{j_1, ..., j_k\}$ then row i and column i can be deleted from D, but previously all successors of i must be converted to successors of $\{j_1, ..., j_k\}$. This rule is supported by the following argument:

Let us assume that CHx is a successor of CHi, then:

if (channels$\{j_1, ..., j_k\}$ are active)
then channel i will be active.
if (channel i will be active) and (conditions)
then channel x will be active.

So:

if (channels$\{j_1, ..., j_k\}$ are active) and (conditions)
then channel x will be active.

In other words, the activity of x depends on the activity of $\{j_1,...,j_k\}$.

This rule is applied in two steps:

i) $D[j_p, q] = D[j_p, q] + D[i, q]$; $q=\{0...m-1\}$. $j_p \in \{j_1, ..., j_k\}$.

ii) Delete row and column i.

This rule is only applied to channels that do not depend on themselves, because in that case the elimination of a channel will cause information loss. An example of application of rule 3 can be seen in Fig. 4.

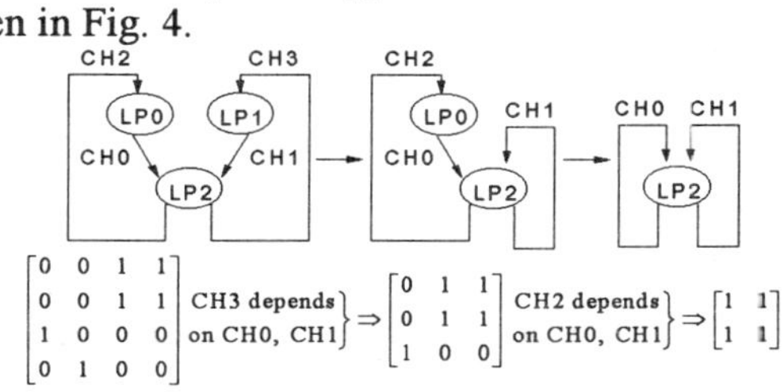

Fig. 4: Example of application of rule 3.

Applying rules 1, 2, 3 to matrix D of an LP's network, dependencies among channels can be reduced to the minimum. Using the reduced matrix, it is easy to find out the set of channels that ensures a reduced deadlock-free system. This set matches the minimum number of channels that keep the original system active.

A consequence of this formal method, due to rule 3 that can be applied to each channel that does not depend on itself (that is acyclic channels), is that only a subset of cyclic channels must be active to ensure that the system is deadlock-free. We have named critical channels to the channels in this subset.

For example let us apply rules 1,2,3 to the network depicted in Fig. 5. Applying rule 1 to matrix D, the following equivalencies are obtained:

- $CH_2 \equiv CH_3$; $CH_8 \equiv CH_9$; $CH_5 \equiv CH_6 \equiv CH_7$; $CH_{12} \equiv CH_{11}$.

Applying rule 2 the following deletions are produced

- CH_0 , CH_1 , CH_2, CH_3 are independent.

Applying rule 3 the following implications are found:

- $CH_8 \Rightarrow CH_4$, $CH_{11} \Rightarrow CH_5$, CH_{10}.

Finally, the reduced matrix will be the following:

$$\begin{bmatrix} 0 & 1 \\ 1 & 0 \end{bmatrix} \begin{matrix} (\text{row}_0 \text{ represents } CH_8) \\ (\text{row}_1 \text{ represents } CH_{11}) \end{matrix}$$

That means that if CH_8 and CH_{11} are maintained active, the whole system will be deadlock-free.

$$D = \begin{bmatrix} 0 & 0 & 0 & 0 & 0 & 0 & 0 & 0 & 0 & 0 & 0 & 0 & 0 \\ 0 & 0 & 0 & 0 & 0 & 0 & 0 & 0 & 0 & 0 & 0 & 0 & 0 \\ 1 & 0 & 0 & 0 & 0 & 0 & 0 & 0 & 0 & 0 & 0 & 0 & 0 \\ 1 & 0 & 0 & 0 & 0 & 0 & 0 & 0 & 0 & 0 & 0 & 0 & 0 \\ 0 & 0 & 1 & 0 & 0 & 0 & 0 & 0 & 1 & 0 & 0 & 0 & 0 \\ 0 & 1 & 0 & 1 & 0 & 0 & 0 & 0 & 0 & 0 & 0 & 1 & 0 \\ 0 & 1 & 0 & 1 & 0 & 0 & 0 & 0 & 0 & 0 & 0 & 1 & 0 \\ 0 & 1 & 0 & 1 & 0 & 0 & 0 & 0 & 0 & 0 & 0 & 1 & 0 \\ 0 & 0 & 0 & 0 & 1 & 1 & 0 & 0 & 0 & 0 & 0 & 0 & 0 \\ 0 & 0 & 0 & 0 & 1 & 1 & 0 & 0 & 0 & 0 & 0 & 0 & 0 \\ 0 & 0 & 0 & 0 & 0 & 0 & 1 & 0 & 0 & 1 & 0 & 0 & 0 \\ 0 & 0 & 0 & 0 & 0 & 0 & 1 & 0 & 0 & 1 & 0 & 0 & 0 \\ 0 & 0 & 0 & 0 & 0 & 0 & 1 & 0 & 0 & 1 & 0 & 0 & 0 \end{bmatrix}$$

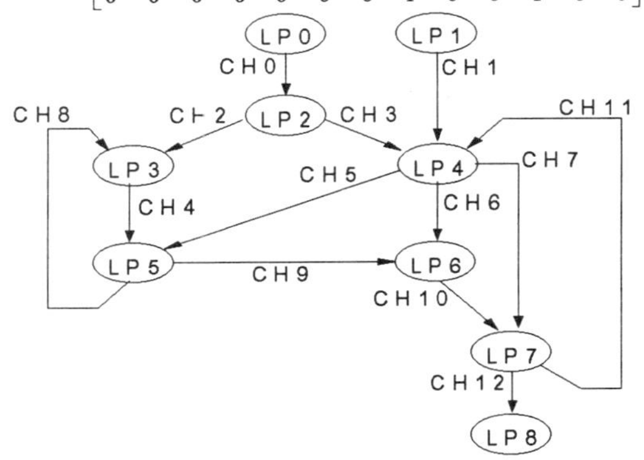

Fig. 5: LPs network and its channel dependence matrix.

3. The deblocking event algorithm.

In this section we introduce a new approach to distributed simulation, based on ensuring that the critical channels of the network of LPs are kept active along the whole simulation time. To reach this requirement extra traffic of events must be introduced: when an LP is evaluated with no change as consequence, some unnecessary messages (equivalent to null events) must be sent if there is any possibility that a critical channel goes inactive. Because critical channels are always included in cycles, the extra traffic to maintain active critical channels is confined to cyclic subsets of LPs. Several authors ([12], [13]) have propose the technique of confining extra traffic to cyclic subsets of LPs, where the risk of deadlock is present. Further on, our approach try to reduce the extra traffic into the cycles almost to the minimum necessary to keep the activity of the network of LPs.

Let us classify LPs into two categories: those having cyclic channels as inputs (CLP), and those whose input channels are all acyclic (ALP). In addition we will distinguish three classes of events:

- ***Normal Events:*** They are events in the classical sense: messages sent among LPs carrying information about changes in the state of the system. They are evaluated in the way that the event driven philosophy imposes: sending new normal events, if any change is produced, over the corresponding channels.
- ***Deblocking Events:*** They are a new kind of events introduced to ensure that critical channels are kept active. When these events are evaluated by any CLP, a deblocking event is produced at each of the output channels, even if the state of the channel does not change. If a deblocking event is evaluated by an ALP, then normal events are queued only at those outputs whose state has changed. We must emphasize that any deblocking event sent over a channel whose state does not change, is equivalent to a null event in the classical conservative algorithms.
- ***Anti-Deblocking Events:*** They are also a new kind of events introduced to avoid the proliferation of deblocking events inside the network of LPs. It must be noticed that when a deblocking event is evaluated by an CLP, new deblocking events are produced at the outputs of the process. This means that the number of deblocking events would rise exponentially. To avoid this increment of deblocking events, each time that one of them is processed by a CLP, an anti-deblocking event is introduced to each cyclic input channel, except those containing processed deblocking events. When any deblocking event is queued at a cyclic channels, it is annihilated if there is already an anti-deblocking event inside the queue.

The algorithms carried out by CLPs and ALPs are different and can be expressed in this way (in pseudo-code):

PROC CLP(inputs, outputs)

```
While(End_of_simulation=FALSE)
  Compute min=minimum time of input events
  Select input events with time equal to min as those to be
     consumed
  If there are deblocking events to be consumed
    Introduce anti-deblocking events at all cyclic input
       channels, except those containing deblocking
       events to be evaluated.
  Actualize the state and local clock of the LP
  Execute the model
  If any deblocking event is going to be consumed
    Send deblocking events to all outputs
  Else
    For each changed output
       Send normal event
  Consume selected events
```

PROC ALP(inputs, outputs)

While(End_of_simulation=FALSE)

Compute min=minimum time of input events

Select input events with time equal to min as those to be consumed

Actualize the state and local clock of the LP

Execute the model

For each changed output

Send normal event

Consume selected events

Before the evaluation the network of LPs must be properly initialized, performing the following actions:

- To detect, from the description of the network of LPs, the type of each channel (linear, cyclic, critical), and select the algorithm appropriate to each process (ALP, CLP).
- To inject deblocking events in critical channels, to ensure that the system will not block.

To carry out the initialization of the network we have developed a distributed method, based on a pre-simulation of the network that detects linear, cyclic and critical channels. Subsequently the selection of the algorithm to be executed, and the injection of deblocking events can be made locally in each LP.

4. Distributed pre-processing of the network of LPs.

For the proposed algorithm, some pre-processing of the model is needed to extract the structural properties of the network. After these pre-processing operations, each LP must know locally the type of each of its inputs (linear, cyclic or critical). If any of the inputs of an LP is cyclic or critical, it must perform the CLP algorithm. On the other hand, if all of the inputs of an LP are linear, it must perform the ALP algorithm. Finally, every LP must initialize its critical inputs, queuing a deblocking event.

The pre-processing of the network is performed in two phases. The first phase find out the set of cyclic channels and the second phase find out the critical channels. In the procedure associated to the first phase, each LP interchanges with others special messages containing information about the predecessors of the channels. So if LPi consumes a message from any of its inputs, it sends another message over each of its outputs with the following information about its predecessors:

$$\forall \, CH_k \in \text{outputs}(LP_i)$$

$$\text{predecessors}(CH_k) = \text{inputs}(LP_i) \cup \left(\bigcup_{\forall CH_j \in \text{inputs}(LP_i)} \text{predecessors}(CH_j) \right)$$

The first pre-processing phase begins with by source LPs (i.e., LPs without inputs) sending messages recording that their output channels have no predecessors. Subsequently those source processes send over each output a special event to indicate that the first pre-processing phase has finished locally. All channels are supposed to be linear initially. When a message is received from channel i indicating that it is predecessor of itself, the channel is recognized as cyclic. When an LP receives the final message at all of its linear inputs, it sends final messages over all of its outputs, and then it remains waiting to receive a final message at the rest of its inputs. After that, the LP finish the first pre-processing phase locally.

The second pre-processing phase works similarly, but in this case the messages register the set of LPs that they have crossed (the message set, MS). The channels can record one of these sets (the channel set, CS). Each time that a channel receives a message, its MS is recorded at the corresponding CS only if:

- Card {MS}< Card {CS}
- Destination LP of the channel ∈{MS}

At the end of the second phase a channel is recognized as critical if its destination LP is included in its CS. Initially CSs do not include the destination LP of the corresponding channel, and its cardinal is ∞.

Because of its distributed nature, the incidence of the initialization phase over the whole simulation time is negligible.

5. Dynamic computation of lookahead in cyclic subsets of LPs.

As we remarked in section 1, the lookahead of the models is crucial to obtain good results in conservative simulation. In addition lookahead prediction inside cycles is critical [11]: if there is a loop of LPs where the accumulated lookahead along the cyclic path is much smaller than the arrival period of events introduced in the loop from the outside, it is possible to produce a lot of overhead traffic across the loop of LPs, only to transmit information of inactivity. To avoid this effect some authors [11] propose a mechanism to predict the lookahead of the model dynamically. This mechanism is based on creating an auxiliary linear network of processes from the initial cyclic network determined by the model. In consequence this solution implies an overhead consisting on evaluating three times the number of processes of the original network.

The deblocking event scheme also allows to compute the lookahead in cycles dynamically, but does not suppose an important overhead . The idea is to use the deblocking events, that are crossing incessantly the loops in the network of processes, to compute the minimum time of the events that are going to be injected in the loops from the outside. Also the deblocking events must determine if a cyclic subset of

LPs is inactive, i. e. the state of all channels does not change. If a loop is inactive, the time of the deblocking events crossing that loop can be incremented to the time of the first event that is going to be injected into the loop from the outside.

To allow the dynamic computation of the lookahead inside loops, more information must be included within the deblocking events: the number of the critical channel where they were introduced initially, and a lower bound of time (LBT) of events coming after the deblocking event. So a deblocking event will be a tuple of four elements $< value, time >^{Channel}_{LBT}$.

Fig. 6 shows an example of computing lookahead in a loop of processes using deblocking events.

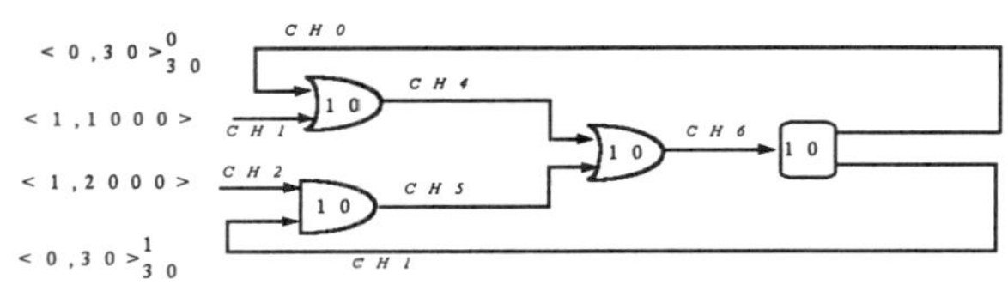

Fig. 6: Initial state of a cyclic set of LPs (deblocking events). Each LP has marked its model delay.

After crossing their loops twice, deblocking events number 0 and 1 detect that no changes are produced inside, so their LBT can be updated to 1000 and 2000 respectively. When the deblocking events join at the LP that simulates the OR gate in the middle of the circuit, as no change is produced at any of its inputs, the time of the event resulting on the evaluation, is set to the minimum LBT at the inputs, plus the lookahead associated to the LP for this evaluation. The new formula to compute the time of events produced by the evaluation of LPi is:

$$time = min \begin{Bmatrix} time \text{ at changing inputs} \\ LBT \text{ at not changing inputs} \end{Bmatrix} + lookahead$$

This simple mechanism allows to take advantage of the lookahead at loops in an efficient way, so reducing the extra traffic due to the synchronization scheme.

6. Experimental results.

In order to verify if our approach fit the requirements that we impose to a PDES synchronization algorithm, we have simulate networks such as that presented in Fig. 5, where LPs have the following behaviour:

- An LP is active if all of its inputs are not empty (LCC).
- When an LP is active, it can be evaluated and consumes input events with time equal to the simulation time at the LP.
- Each LP has a "null event percentage" (NEP). The meaning of NEP is the ratio of evaluations that does not change the outputs of the LP. When an LP is evaluated, it computes a random number R. If R>NEP then LP changes its outputs (that is, produce events that are sent over every output). In other case no change is produced at the outputs.
- LPs with no inputs produce changes at their outputs always, so they are event producers.

In our experiments all LPs in the network have the same NEP. We have performed several simulations of the model changing the NEP of LPs in the network.

To measure the activity of the network at a simulation point we use the formula:

$$\text{Activity} = \frac{\text{Number of active LPs}}{\text{Number of LPs}}$$

The average activity of the network is computed from several values of activity sampled along a simulation period. The evolution of the average activity along a large simulation for several values of NEP is presented in Fig. 7.

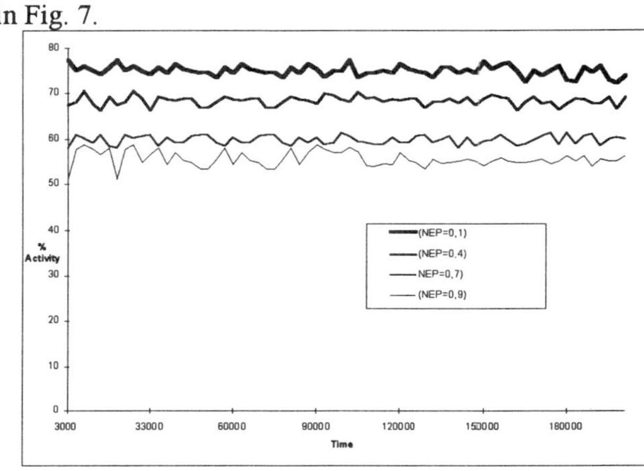

Fig. 7: Activity of LPs in the network of Fig. 5 during a simulation for several values of NEP.

Networks with lower NEP have a larger number of normal events, so the activity of the network is higher than in the case of greater values of NEP. But even for high values of NEP the activity of the network is kept over 50%, due to the presence of deblocking events.

Deblocking events introduce in the system unnecessary traffic when they are involved in evaluations that do not produce changes in the outputs. But in the classic null event algorithm the unnecessary traffic is much higher, because not only evaluations that involve special events (i. e. deblocking events), but all evaluations that do not produce changes at the outputs of an LP, result in extra traffic generation. In Fig. 8 it is depicted the percentage of extra traffic generated during the simulation of the network, for several values of NEP and for the deblocking event and the classical null event algorithms (tagged as "with deblock" and "without deblock" respectively).

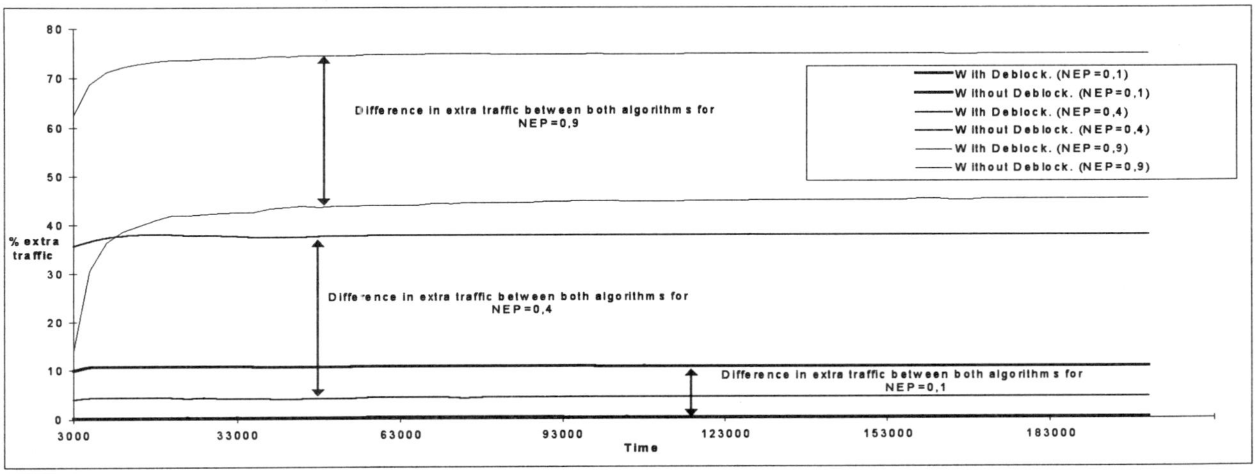

Fig. 8: Percentage of extra traffic in the LP's network during a simulation for several values of NEP using the classical null event and the deblocking event algorithms.

In both cases, the amount of extra traffic increases as NEP increases, because more evaluations produce no changes at the outputs of LPs. But using deblocking events, the amount of extra traffic is clearly smaller than using the classical null events algorithm. This is due to the restriction that our approach imposes to the production of unnecessary traffic: only evaluations that involve deblocking events could produce this kind of traffic.

7. Conclusions.

We have presented a conservative PDES synchronization algorithm that uses structural information about the LP's network to reduce the overhead due to unnecessary event traffic in the network. The algorithm keep a significant number of LPs active during the simulation and , what is more important, performing a useful work.

The algorithm takes advantage of lookahead inside loops of LPs dynamically, so increasing the efficiency of the simulation.

REFERENCES

[1] BAILEY, M. L., BRINER, J. V., CHAMBERLAIN, R. D., "Parallel Logic Simulation of VLSI Systems". ACM Computing Surveys, Vol. 26, N° 3, pp. 255-294 (September 1994).

[2] REYNOLDS, P. F., Jr., 1988 "A Spectrum of Options for Parallel Simulation". Proceedings of 1988 Winter Simulation Conference, pp. 325-332.

[3] FUJIMOTO,R.M. 1990 "Parallel Discrete Event Simulation". Communications of the ACM, Vol. 33, N° 10, pp. 30-53.

[4] MISRA,J. 1986 "Distributed Discrete-Event Simulation". ACM Computing Surveys, March, pp. 39-65.

[5] CHANDY,K., MISRA,J. 1981 "Asynchronous Distributed Simulation Via a Sequence of Parallel Computations". Comm. ACM. Vol. 24, N° 11, pp. 198-206 .

[6] CHANDY,K., MISRA,J., A.L.M.HAAS. 1983. "Distributed Deadlock Detection". ACM Trans. on Computer Science, Vol. 1, N° 5, pp. 144-156.

[7] JEFFERSON,D. 1985 " Virtual Time". ACM Trans. on Programming Languages and Systems, Vol. 7, N° 3, pp. 404-425.

[8] FUJIMOTO,R.M. 1989 "Time Warp on a Shared Memory Multiprocessor". Proc. International Conference on Parallel Processing, Vol. III, pp. 242-249.

[9] FERSCHA, A., TRIPATHI, S. K., "Parallel and Distributed Simulation of Discrete Event Systems". Technical Report CS-TR-3336, Computer Science Department, University of Maryland (August 1994).

[10] LIN, Y.-B., "Understanding the Limits of Optimistic and Conservative Parallel Simulation". PhD. Dissertation. Department of Computer Science and Engineering. University of Washington (1990).

[11] FUJIMOTO,R.M. 1988 "Lookahead in Parallel Discrete Event Simulation". Proc. International Conference on Parallel Processing. pp. 34-41.

[12] YU, M., GHOSH, SUMIT, DeBENEDICTIS, E., "A Non-Deadlocking Conservative Asynchronous Distributed Discrete Event Simulation Algorithm". Proceedings of the SCS Multiconference on Advances in Parallel and Distributed Simulation, pp. 100-111 California, January 1991.

[13] GHOSH, S., YU, M.-L. 1995 "An Asynchronous Distributed Approach for the Simulation of Behaviour-Level Models on Parallel Processors". IEEE Transactions on Parallel and Distributed Systems, Vol. 6, N° 6, pp.639-652.

Distributed Simulation of ECATNets : A Conservative Approach

K.Djemame, D.C.Gilles, and L.M.Mackenzie

Computing Science Department
University of Glasgow
Glasgow G12 8QQ, Scotland
{karim,dcg,lewis}@dcs.gla.ac.uk

M.Bettaz

Computing Science Institute
University of Constantine
25000 Constantine, Algeria
bettaz@ist.cerist.dz

Abstract

ECATNets (Extended Concurrent Algebraic Term Nets) are a kind of High-Level Algebraic Nets used for specifying various aspects of distributed and parallel systems. In this paper, we address the problem of developing parallel simulation techniques to analyze ECATNets. Distributed Discrete Event Simulation (DDES) is used to develop a a simulation framework for studying their behaviour. The ECATNet model to be simulated is partitioned into several connected subnets. The various subnets are simulated in parallel by several Logical Processes. We develop and discuss a distributed simulation protocol based on the conservative approach to execute discrete-event simulations of ECATNets.

1 Introduction

Petri nets [17, 31, 30] are a graphical and mathematical tool applicable to many systems. They are a promising tool for describing and studying information processing systems that are characterized as being concurrent, asynchronous, distributed, parallel, nondeterministic and/or stochastic. ECATNets are a kind of High-Level Algebraic Nets. They are proposed as a way for specifying and modelizing various aspects of distributed and parallel systems. They are built around a combination of three formalisms. The first two formalisms constitute a net/data model, and are used for defining the syntax of the system, in other terms to capture its structure. The net model, which is a kind of advanced Petri net [19], is used to describe the process architecture of the system; the data model, which is an algebraic formalism [10], is used for specifying the data structures of the system. The third formalism, which is a rewriting logic [15], is used for defining the semantics of the system, or in other words to describe its behaviour. According to this logic, the system behaviour may be explained by formal reasoning. Transforming our logic into a rewriting system [26] may be used for rapid prototyping and automatic proving of a system under design. The reader interested in more details about ECATNets, their formal definition, motivation and relation to other works may consult [23, 1, 25, 27]. Previous works [2, 26, 3, 24, 4] showed how ECATNets are used for specifying and validating applications from the area of distributed and parallel systems. The achieved models had two drawbacks: the occultation of the problem of time and a bad exploitation of the parallelism inherent to the studied models. In a previous paper [18], we presented an approach for the treatment of time in ECATNets, by introducing in each transition a firing delay to perform the operations "remove/deposit tokens". Simulation can not only perform the validation of these models, but can evaluate their performances as well. Simulation may also be amenable to parallel execution in order to exploit the inherent parallelism of these models. It is worth mentioning that we are dealing with the parallelism at two levels: the inter-module level, where the parallelism is achieved by partitioning the "initial" models w.r.t. a "separation of concern" strategy; the "intra-module" where parallelism is permitted by the use of our rewriting logic.

1.1 Approaches to DDES in the literature

In discrete simulation, the inherently sequential nature of the global event list manipulation limits the potential parallelism of simulation models [28]. By eliminating the global event list, additional parallelism can be obtained. Using multiple processors can not only appear to be a promising approach for a better modelling, but can also improve the simulation execution time, because simulation of complex (discrete event) systems is usually exceedingly slow. Distributed Discrete Event Simulation (DDES) refers to the execution of a single discrete event simulation program on a parallel computer. The system being modeled is viewed as being composed of some number of Physical Processes (PPs) that interact at various points in simulated time. The simulator is constructed as a set of Logical Processes (or simply LPs), one per physical process. An event is represented by a timestamped message, Logical Processes exchange timestamped event messages to interact. However, relationship between events may exist, so concurrent execution of these events must be synchronized, otherwise *causality errors* can occur. So a certain sequencing constraints must be maintained in order for the computation to be correct. DDES falls into two categories [29]: *conservative* and *optimistic*. The conservative mechanisms strictly avoid the possibility of any causality error ever occurring [16]. The optimistic mechanisms use a detection and recovery approach, this means that causality errors are detected and a rollback mechanism is invoked to recover. The most well-known optimistic protocol is the Time-Warp mechanism based on the virtual time paradigm [9]. Recently, [12] proposed a new DDES protocol called *probabilistic*, a performance efficient compromise between the two classical approaches. Notions such as causality, virtual time, clock synchronization, organization and exploitation of timestamps, and a lot of related

1066-6192/96 $5.00 © 1996 IEEE

Proceedings of PDP '96

concepts are reported in [20, 21, 16, 9, 29]. The idea in [22] is meanwhile a standard concept in many models of concurrent computation. Distributed Discrete Event Simulation (DDES) refers to an implementation for a machine with communication based on message passing (loosely coupled multiprocessor) whereas Parallel Discrete Event Simulation (PDES) refers to an implementation for a shared memory machine (tightly coupled multiprocessor).

1.2 Related Work

The simulation protocols we are proposing for ECATNets distributed simulation differ significantly from the protocols developed in [7, 5]. The work in [7] was performed in the context of "Petri net driven execution" of distributed programs, where the firing of a transition causes the invocation of a procedure, with the net itself used to determine the flow of control. Each transition firing results in a procedure execution, which yields an amount of overhead less important for execution of distributed programs than in the simulation context. In addition to that, the nets assumed are untimed, so there is no notion of simulated time. [5] describes a distributed simulator of high order Petri nets, showing how the inherent parallelism can be used to obtain a fast simulator. The simulator is a component of a suite of tools which allow the construction of specifications of embedded systems. The contributions of parallel simulation in the area of Petri nets and reported in the literature include [13, 14, 6, 11]. They all deal with Timed and/or Stochastic nets. It is worth mentioning that concerning simulation techniques for high level nets with arc inscriptions, the enabling test and the firing operations are substantially more complex. In [8], we proposed an optimistic distributed simulation protocol which is expected to improve the ability of efficiently simulate the behaviour of systems modelized by ECATNets over a period of time. The approach we present in this paper is *conservative*.

1.3 Paper Organization

This paper is organized in the following way: in section 2, we review some basic notions about syntactic and semantic aspects of ECATNets. In section 3, the use of ECATNets is illustrated by a complete example. Section 4 presents the synchronization and simulation algorithm based on the conservative approach for ECATNets distributed simulation. In section 5, we end by giving some concluding remarks.

2 Algebraic Term Nets

2.1 Basic concepts

The graphical representation of a generic ECATNet is given by figure 1. IC, DT and CT are multisets of (equivalence classes of) terms. The terms are defined by an algebraic specification of an abstract data type given by the user [10]. TC (Transition Condition) is a boolean expression which may contain variables occurring in IC (Input Condition), DT (Destroyed Tokens) and CT (Created Tokens). Each place is associated with a capacity C(p) defined as a multiset of closed (equivalence classes of) terms. The marking M(p) of a place p of the net, which is itself a multiset of closed terms, is defined w.r.t. the capacity (which may be infinite).

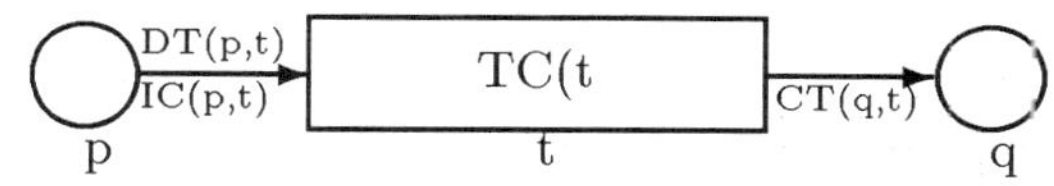

Figure 1 A generic ECATNet

A transition t is fireable when various conditions are simultaneously true. The first condition is that every IC(p,t) for each input place p is enabled. The second condition is that TC(t) is true. Finally the addition of CT(p,t) to each output place p must not result in p exceeding its capacity when this capacity is finite. When t is fired, DT(p,t) is removed from the input place p and simultaneously CT(q,t) is added to the output place q. Transition firing and its conditions are expressed by rewrite rules which are strongly depending on the form of the syntactic notation used for representing IC. Those rewrite rules together with a set of deduction rules define a rewriting logic [15] which gives the semantics of the net. Examples on concrete instantiations and practical use of these metarules may be found in [2, 3, 24, 4].

2.2 Aspect of Time

A lot of properties of systems involving time, particularly issues of performance evaluation and simulation, can be covered by decorating Petri nets with requirements on timing: occurrence of transitions or residence of tokens in places are assumed to take a distinguished amount of time. These extensions have been widely adopted, either for necessity or for convenience purpose. In [18], we have chosen to introduce in each transition a (marking) related rate, leading to take into account a firing delay "d" to perform the operations "remove/deposit tokens". This choice allows to preserve the incremental approach used for defining ECATNets and preserves the semantic framework defined in terms of rewriting logic. Note that there are two kinds of transitions. *Timed* transitions are specified by annotating each timed transition t_i with a firing rate λ_i. Let λ : T$\rightarrow \mathcal{R}$ assigns firing delays λ_i to T-elements $t_i \in$ T. Zero delays are associated with transitions that are called *immediate*. ECATNets enriched with temporal specification are then suitable to discrete simulation. This is an important step in their quantitative performance evaluation. In this sense, the use of transition timed Petri net formalism provides a substantial contribution to the implementation of efficient, general purpose discrete event simulation techniques.

3 An Example of Modelling with ECATNets

This example, borrowed from [27], deals with the behaviour of the Ethernet transmitting station. It comprises four modules (figures 2..5), each module is specified by an ECATNet model. The first module deals with the functions of formating and transmitting starting. The second module is relative to the functions of transmission with success and acknowledgment. The third module treats essentially the functions of collision handling and acknowledgment. The fourth module is relative to the retransmission function. The transmitter station transmits one frame at a time. The user is not allowed to request the transmission of a new frame before receiving the ackowledgment of the previous frame. The formating function starts when a token

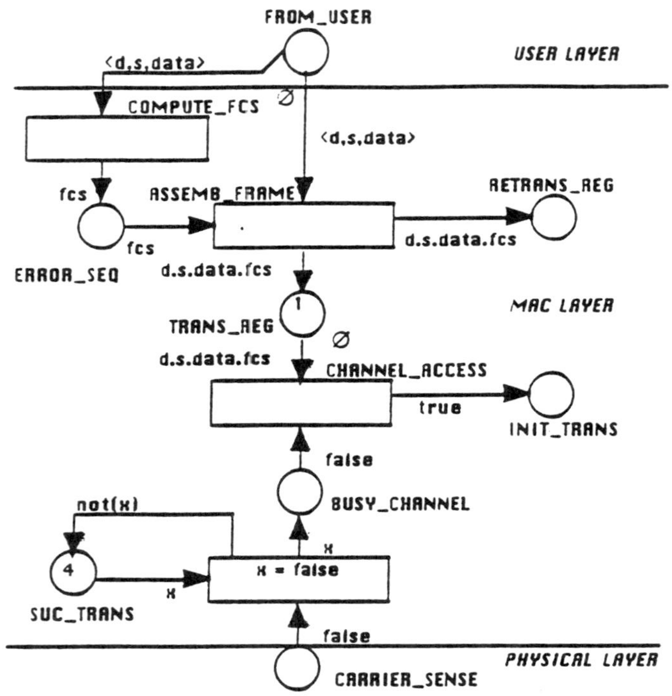

Fig.2 Starting of transmission

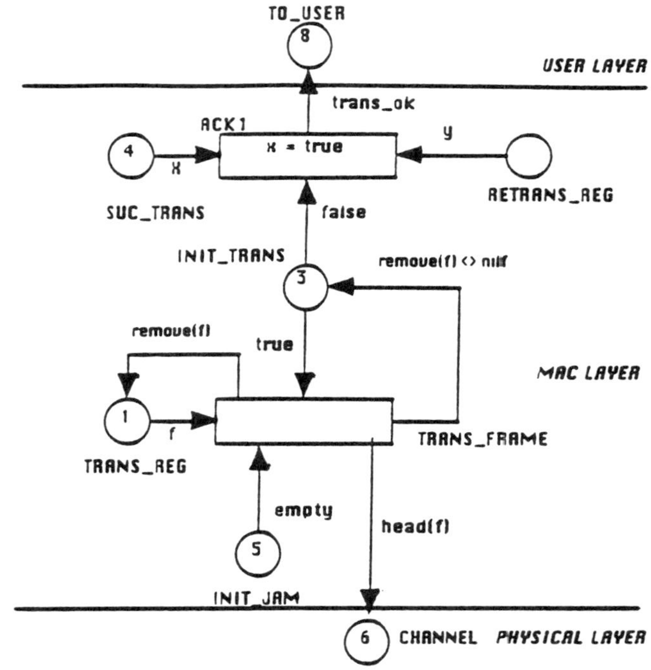

Fig.3 Transmission with success

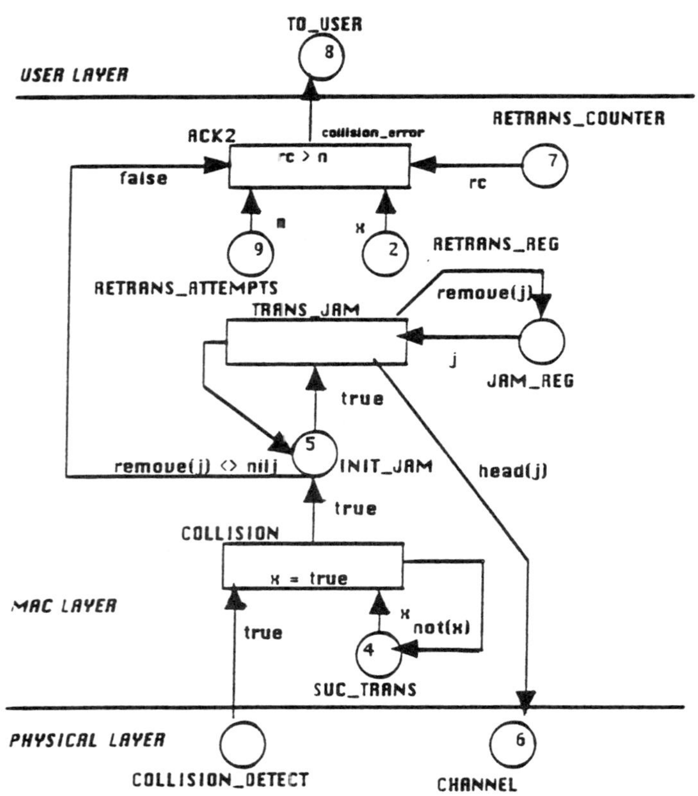

Fig.4 Collision Handling

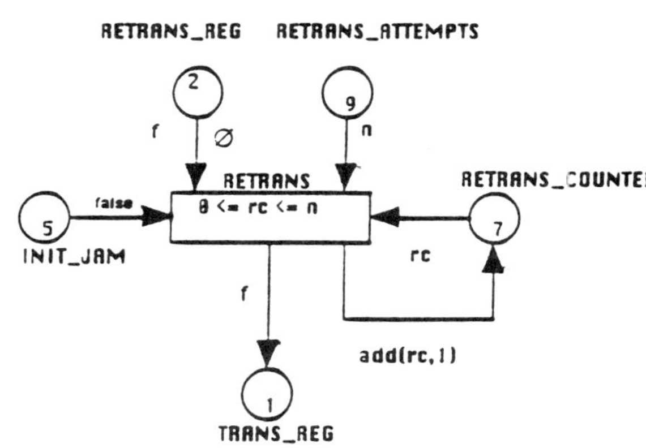

Fig.5 Retransmission

of type "d,s,data" is deposited in place FROM_USER. This token is considered as a primitive transfered from the user layer to the MAC layer for requesting the transmission of data "data", from a source "s" to a destination "d". The place FROM_USER is an interface between the two layers. The frame "d.s.data.fcs" is then deposited as soon as it is composed in a transmission register (TRANS_REG). The formating function is consisting of the concatenation of sequences of bits corresponding to the addresses "d" and "s", to the data "data", and to the error control sequence "fcs" previously computed. On the other hand, the layer MAC is listening to the medium (CARRIER_SENSE) in order to avoid any collision occurring with a current transmission. The place CARRIER_SENSE is an interface between the layer MAC and the physical layer. When the medium becomes free (a token "false" is present in place CARRIER_SENSE), it waits a certain amount of time corresponding to the interframe spacing delay. Then, considering that the transmission may terminate with success (deposit of a token "false" in place BUSY_CHANNEL and a token "true" in place SUC_TRANS), it takes possession of the medium (CHANNEL_ACCESS) and the transmission starts (deposit of a token "true" in INIT_TRANS).

When a transition (eg. transition DELAY (fig.2)) is enabled to fire at time *Tsim* and a firing delay *d* is associated with this transition, then :

- at time *Tsim* appropriate tokens are removed from its input places (CARRIER_SENSE and SUC_TRANS);
- from time clock to time *Tsim+d*, the transition is considered to be firing;
- at time *Tsim+d* appropriate tokens are deposited in its output places (SUC_TRANS and BUSY_CHANNEL).

In module "Retransmission", the random waiting time before retransmission leads to a *backoff* state.

4 A Conservative Distributed Simulation Framework for ECATNets

In the conservative mechanisms, each Logical Process is an execution model which contains a section of code, a portion of the system modeled state, a local clock (which denotes how far the process has progressed) and input/output links. Input links are characterized by queues of timestamped messages received from other Logical Processes, sorted on time of occurrence. *Loohahead* is required in conservative mechanisms to avoid deadlock situation [16]. It is the processor's ability to predict what will happen, or more importantly, what will not happen in the simulated time as regards to its behaviour and when next it may affect other processors.

The initial ECATNet model to be simulated is partitioned using the "separation of concern" strategy. We obtain a set of modules, each module corresponds to a subnet to be simulated by a Logical Process. There are fixed communication channels between Logical Processes, timestamped messages are exchanged via these channels for LPs synchronization. As shown in [6], three events may occur when constructing a distributed discrete event simulator of (timed) Petri nets : **Start_firing, End_firing** and **Tokens_deposited**.

- **Start_firing** : if transition t is enabled to fire at *Tsim*, for every t's input place remove appropriate token. The event **Token_deposited** is inserted into the event-list at each t's output place with timestamp *Tsim+d*, where *d* is the firing delay associated with t. The event **End_firing** with timestamp *Tsim+d* is inserted into the event-list.
- **End_firing** : when t ends firing at *Tsim*, t's input places are checked. If the enabled conditions are satisfied (each of t's input places has the appropriate token), t is refired (an event **Start_firing** is inserted into the event-list at time *Tsim*).
- **Tokens_deposited** : when tokens arrive at place p at *Tsim*, its marking is updated. This deposit may enable any of p's output transitions. If p's output transition is enabled, the event **Start_firing** at *Tsim* is inserted into the event-list.

The events **Start_firing** and **End_firing** are always inserted into LP's event-list. However, when the event Start_firing is processed, if the firing transition t and its output place p are assigned to the same LP, the event **Tokens_deposited** is inserted into the event-list, otherwise the event is sent as a timestamped message to the LP p is assigned to.

4.1 Lookahead computation

If a transition starts firing, an LP can predict exactly when the tokens generated by this firing are deposited. We use a *time window* to prevent incorrect computations from propagating too far ahead into the simulated time. This is to highlight lookahead that exists in Petri nets simulation. Lookahead provides a window [*Tsim*, *W(Tsim)*] such that all events with timestamps in the window can be executed safely and without further communication between LP's. We refer to [6] to compute lookahead. First, we find δ_{min}, the minimum firing time among all the LP's enabled transitions. This LP will send a timestamped Tokens_deposited message to another LP when the transition to fire t has an off-LP output place. Second, we find E_{min}, the value of the least timestamp on any event in the event-list. As the event-list is sorted on the time of occurrence of events, E_{min} is the event's timestamp in the head of the list. If the list is empty, we take $E_{min} = \infty$. Third, we compute $E_{min} + \delta_{min}$ which provides the desired uppon bound. We suppose that each LP call a routine **BOUND_NEXTMSGTIME()** which returns the value $E_{min} + \delta_{min}$. We then compute W(Tsim) = Min[BOUND_NEXT MSGTIME()] among all LPs.

4.2 ECATNet Partitioning

A natural decomposition of the "initial" ECATNet model into LPs is a spatial partitioning into different subnets. The "separation of concern" strategy is suitable for representing complex systems ECATNets models and for the inter-module parallelism achievement, but does not necessarily lead to a good parallel simulation partitioning. The first drawback is the redundant representation of places and the corresponding arcs in adjacent LPs. The second drawback is related to the firing of a transition. A transition t fires when all the enabling conditions are satisfied, by checking first its input places in the same LP. This transition may have one or more input places in different LPs. Since a LP only has information on its local marking, it needs to exchange messages with other LPs to obtain information concerning the marking of t's input places. Another difficult case is when several transitions share input places. Such places are called *decision places*. Therefore, it is necessary to develop a distributed conflict resolution strategy to decide which transition is going to fire among the enabled transitions. In such case, the synchronization and communication needed to implement the simulation properly are rather more complex.

Separation of subnets We first consider the places which are relevant for each subnet. If P, T and A are respectively the set of places, the set of transitions and the set of arcs of the "intial" ECATNet model, the partition is a set of n subnets such that :
$ECATNet_i = (P_i, T_i, A_i, \lambda_i)$ where $\cup P_i$ = P, $\cup T_i$ = T, $A_i \subset (P_i \times T_i) \cup (T_i \times P_i)$, i=1..n.

λ_i is the set of rates of local transitions in T_i. We did not consider the multisets of terms IC, DT, CT and the boolean expression TC. They are defined as in the "initial" model and appear in the graphical representation of the subnets. The transitions remain in the same subnets, the duplicated places have to be assigned to the relevant subnet.

4.3 The Communication Interface

Definitions A place $p_i \in P_i$ in LP_i is said to be a member of the set of *output places* (OP_i) of LP_i if there exists a transition $t_j \notin LP_i$ which p_i is an input place. A transition $t_i \in T_i$ in LP_i is said to be a member of the set of *input transitions* (IT_i) of LP_i if there exists a place $p_j \notin LP_i$ which t_i is an output transition. We define in exactly the same manner *input places* and *output transitions* by interchanging places and transitions. *A communication arc* is an arc connecting a place (transition) in LP_i to a transition (place) in LP_j. If there is a communication arc from an *output place* p to an *input transition* t, there also exists an additional communication arc from t to p. These unidirectional channels are motivated by *decision places* which have to interact with their output transitions before choosing the transition to fire.

For each *input transition* t in subnet i, define :
$P_{t_{in}}$ = list of places to indicate which (input) places are related to t and the kind of relation that exists. $P_{t_{out}}$ is defined for each *output transition* in the same manner by interchanging input by output.

For each *output place* p in subnet i, define :
$T_{p_{out}}$ = list of transitions to indicate which (output) transitions are related to p and the kind of relation that exists. $T_{p_{in}}$ is defined for each *input place* in the same manner by interchanging output by input.

Example: Let's take the example of section 3, the modular specification of the Ethernet transmitting station. The partition is a set of four subnets, each subnet is simulated by an LP. The set of duplicated places (labelled 1..9) is partitioned among the subnets as follows (figure 6):
Subnet 1 : TRANS_REG(1), SUC_TRANS(4)
Subnet 2 : INIT_TRANS(3), CHANNEL(6), TO_USER (8)
Subnet 3 : INIT_JAM(5)
Subnet 4 : RETRANS_REG(2), RETRANS_COUNTER (7), RETRANS_ATTEMPTS (9)

RETRANS_REG is an input place in $subnet_4$, SUC_TRANS is an output place in $subnet_1$. ACK1 is an input transition in $subnet_2$, ASSEMB_FRAME is an output transition in $subnet_1$. (ASSEMB_FRAME, RETRANS_REG), (SUC_TRANS, ACK1) are communication arcs, (ACK1, SUC_TRANS) is an additional one. The set of LP_i, i=1..4 exchange messages via communication channels. A Token_deposited message is sent from LP_1 to LP_4 when transition ASSEMB_FRAME fires. In LP_2, transition ACK1 has local informations about its input place INIT_TRANS, and has to obtain informations about the marking of places SUC_TRANS and RETRANS_REG from LP_1 and LP_4 respectively.

4.4 The Algorithm

4.4.1 Types of Messages

Five messages are exchanged between LPs for synchronization. The form of these messages is (Type_message, source, destination, timestamp, type_token). *Source* and *destination* are either a place (in LP_i) or a transition (in LP_j) depending on the communication arc. Type_token is the abstract data type of the token moved among subnets.

- **Tokens_available**(p,t,T0,M(p)) : this message is sent from the output place p at time T0 to inform transition t $\in T_{p_{out}}$ that the marking of place p is M(p).
- **Tokens_requested**(t,p,T1,IC(p,t)): the input transition t waits for Tokens_available messages from all the places p $\in P_{t_{in}}$, then processes T1 = MAX(T0), the latest timestamp among these messages.It sends a Tokens_requested message as a reply if its enabling conditions are satisfied (TC(t) is true and IC(p,t) is enabled). Otherwise, it sends a message to p to inform that it does not need the token.
- **Tokens_allowed**(p,t,T2,DT(p,t)): p waits for a reply for each Tokens_available sent and collects Tokens_requested messages. It then processes T2 = MIN(T1) and executes a conflict resolution algorithm for choosing the transition t to be fired. A Tokens_allowed message is sent to such transition.
- **Tokens_consumed**(t,p,T2,DT(p,t)): the input transition t collects a Tokens_allowed message from all its places p $\in P_{t_{in}}$ and then sends a Tokens_consumed message with timestamp T2 to such places. It processes T3, the time of the end of its firing (T3 = T2 + firing_delay)
- **Tokens_deposited**: when t fires, a message Tokens_deposited(t,q,T3,CT(q,t)) may be inserted into the local event-list if t has any output places in the same LP or sent as a message to another LP where q $\in P_{t_{out}}$.

Lookahead is computed at the time the transition to fire is known. The LP first checks whether the local

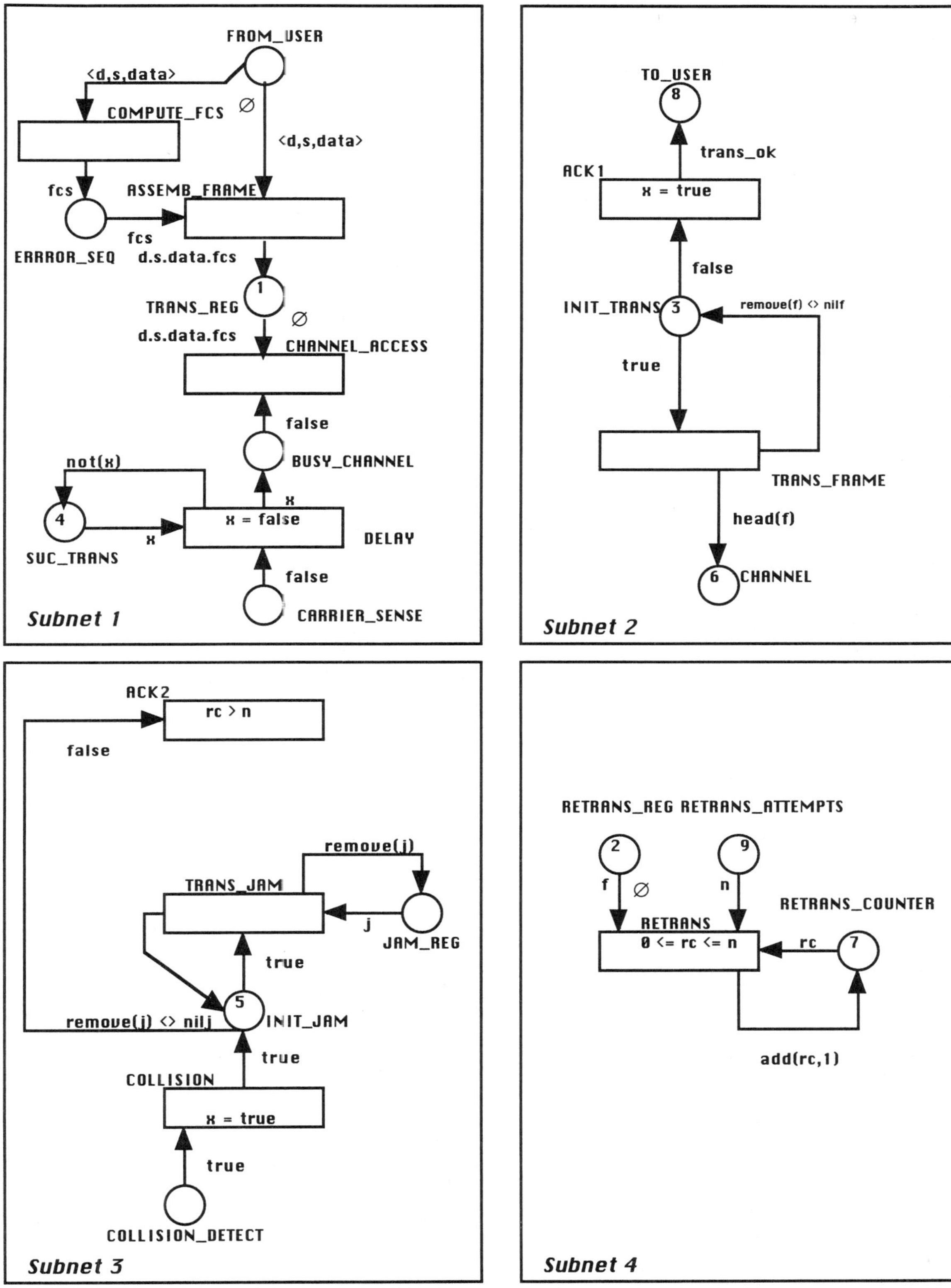

Figure 6 ECATNet Partition (The ETHERNET transmitting station)

firing is possible. If the local enabling conditions of transition t are satisfied because t's input places are assigned to the same LP, no communication with other LPs is necesssary. Otherwise, t has to wait for any Tokens_available messages sent from p $\in P_{t_{in}}$. As soon as the marking of place p is updated because of the process of an event Tokens_deposited, p has to inform t $\in T_{p_{out}}$ so that t can compete for the available tokens. However, the place p can ignore some of its output transitions that might not fire because p knows the relation that exists between these transitions which are related to it.

4.4.2 Algorithm

1. Initial Marking: for every initial token, insert a Tokens_deposited event in the appropriate LP's event list, with timestamp = 0.

2. Set i = 1, set $step_i$ = 0.

3. For every LP, check local firing conditions. In case where no transition is enabled, apply comunication protocol described in sec.5.4.1. Call BOUND_NEXT MSGTIME(). Compute W($step_i$), every LP learns the value of W($step_i$).

4. Every LP is going to simulate its subnet up to W($step_i$);
Input message MSG from input queue;
Case Tokens_deposited : generate event Start_firing if conditions satified;
Case Start_firing : generate event Tokens_deposited into LP's event list, send message Tokens_deposited in case of an off-LP output place;
Case End_firing : generate event Start_firing if conditions satisfied.

5. The LPs synchronize globally. Every LP may receive all messages sent to it during the processing of window [$step_i$, W($step_i$)]. Every message received is inserted into the event-list.

6. Define $step_{i+1}$ = W($step_i$), i= i+1, check termination conditions, repeat the above process (return to step 3) if not end of simulation.

4.4.3 Conflict Resolution Strategy

When multiple transitions sharing input places become enabled at the same time and compete for tokens, a decision must be made about which transition (or set of transitions) to fire. Different methods exist to solve this conflict:

- The user may specify priorities for transitions: $\Pi : T \rightarrow N$ assigns priorities π_i to T-elements $t_i \in T$.

- the decision place p selects randomly according to a probability distribution defined by the user one or more transitions that it would like to fire and offers them tokens via a Tokens_allowed message if these transitions $\in T_{p_{out}}$. If a transition t is lucky enough to receive Tokens_allowed messages from all places p $\in P_{t_{in}}$, it then fires. Otherwise, it replies by sending a message that it cannot use any of the tokens. Its input places try again later in simulation time by sending another Tokens_available message.

Note that the marking's update of place p may lead to the enabling and the firing of several output transitions at the same time.

4.5 Efficient Partitioning

Let us recall that the partitioning of the "initial" model has a strong impact on the DDES performance. When the transitions sharing places are assigned to the same LP with their input places, the distributed conflict resolution protocol is avoided. In case where transitions with their input places are not assigned to the same LP or several transitions share input places, four messages (Tokens_available, Tokens_requested, Tokens_allowed, Tokens_consumed) are exchanged between LPs since arcs $\in$ (P $\times$ T) have a severe consequence on the efficient computation of enabling and firing of transitions. Obviously, this will lead to substantial overhead in the distributed simulation and the amount of messages inherent to this protocol can prevent efficiency. Another partitioning technique has to be investigated starting from the subnets we obtain using the "separation of concern" strategy in order to improve distributed simulation performance.

5 Conclusion

In this paper, we addressed the problem of developing a conservative distributed simulation technique for ECATNets. The use of simulation exploits the syntactic aspect of ECATNets leading to a user-friendly interface. The conservative distributed simulation protocol we proposed is expected to improve the ability of efficiently simulate the behaviour of ECATNet models over a period of time. We developed a proper communication protocol among LPs in order to implement a distributed conflict resolution strategy for transitions sharing input places. Obviously, such conflict resolution strategy may induce substantial overhead in the distributed simulation in a message-passing environment. Starting from the "separation of concern" strategy, simulating transitions together with all their input places by a single Logical Process should reduce the communication overhead and attain a better performance. This protocol is currently implemented on the Thinking Machine CM-200 available at the EPCC (Edinburgh Parallel Computer Center) using C*, the CM's C-based parallel language. Simulation results will be presented in the final version of this paper. We are also planning to assess the overall performance of both simulation approaches: conservative and optimistic.

Ackowledgement This work is partially supported by a grant from the Algerian Ministry of Higher Education and Scientific Research under research contract number B2501-01-05-94, and by a grant from the British Council under the Anglo-Algerian SATELLITE Programme. The authors would like to thank the EPCC for providing access to the computing facilities.

References

[1] BETTAZ M., MAOUCHE M., SOUALMI M. and BOUKEBECHE M. Using ECATNets for specifying communication software in the OSI framework. In *Proceedings of ICCI'92*, pages 410–413. IEEE, 1992.

[2] BETTAZ M., MAOUCHE M., SOUALMI M. and BOUKEBECHE M. Compact modeling and rapid prototyping of communication software with ECATNets: a case study. *Simulation Series*, 25(1):149–154, 1993. SCS and IEEE.

[3] BETTAZ M., MAOUCHE M., SOUALMI M. and BOUKEBECHE M. Protocol specification using ECATNets. *Networking and Distributed Computing*, 3(1):7–35, 1993. Hermes, Paris.

[4] BETTAZ M., MAOUCHE M., SOUALMI M. and BOUKEBECHE M. On reusing ATNet modules in protocol specification. *JSS*, 27(2), nov 1994.

[5] BUTLER B., ESSER R. and MATTMANN R. A distributed simulator for High Order Petri Nets. *Lecture Notes in Computer Science*, 483:47–63, 1990.

[6] NICOL D. and ROY S. Parallel Simulation of Timed Petri Nets. In *Proceedings of the 1991 Winter Simulation Conference*, pages 574–583. B.NELSON, D.KELTON, G.CLARK (Ed.), 1991.

[7] TAUBNER D. On the implementation of Petri Nets. *Lecture Notes in Computer Science*, 340:418–439, 1988.

[8] DJEMAME K., BETTAZ M., D.C.GILLES and L.M.MACKENZIE. Time warp simulation of ECATNets. In *Proceedings of 7th European Simulation Symposium*. SCS, oct 1995. (To appear).

[9] JEFFERSON D.R. Virtual time. *ACM Trans. on Programming Languages and Systems*, 7(3):404–425, jul 1985.

[10] EHRIG E. and MAHR B. *Fundamentals of Algebraic Specifications*. EATCS Monographs on Theoretical Computer Science, Springer-Verlag, 1985.

[11] CHIOLA G. and FERSCHA A. Distributed Simulation of Timed Petri nets: Exploiting the net structure to obtain efficiency. *Lecture Notes in Computer Science*, 691:146–165, 1993.

[12] CHIOLA G. and FERSCHA A. Performance Comparable Design of Efficient Synchronization Protocols for Distributed Simulation. In *Proceedings of MASCOTS'95*, pages 59–65, Durham, North Carolina, jan 1995. IEEE.

[13] THOMAS G.S. and ZAHORJAN J. Parallel Simulation of Performance Petri Nets: Extending the domain of parallel simulation. In *Proceedings of the 1991 Winter Simulation Conference*, pages 564–573. B.NELSON, D.KELTON, G.CLARK (Ed.), 1991.

[14] AMMAR H. and DENG S. Parallel Simulation of Petri Nets using spatial decomposition. In *Proceedings of the 1991 IEEE International Symposium on Circuits and Systems*, pages 826–829, Singapore, jun 1991.

[15] MESEGUER J. Conditional rewriting logic as a unified model of concurrency. *TCS*, 96, 1992.

[16] MISRA J. Distributed discrete event simulation. *ACM Computing Surveys*, 18(1):39–65, mar 1986.

[17] PETERSON J.L. *Petri Net Theory and the Modeling of Systems*. Englewood Cliffs, NJ: Prentice-Hall, 1981.

[18] DJEMAME K. and BETTAZ M. On the parallel simulation of ECATNets. Technical report, Computing Science Institute, University of Constantine, Algeria, jun 1994.

[19] JENSEN K. and ROZENBERG G.(Ed.). *High-Level Petri Nets*. Springer-Verlag, Berlin, 1991.

[20] CHANDY K.M. and MISRA J. Distributed simulation: A case study in design and verification of distributed programs. *IEEE Trans. on Software Engineering*, SE-5(5):440–453, sep 1979.

[21] CHANDY K.M. and MISRA J. Asynchronous distributed simulation via a sequence of parallel computations. *Communications of the ACM*, 24(11):198–206, apr 1981.

[22] LAMPORT L. Time, clocks, and the ordering of events in a distributed system. *Communications of the ACM*, 21(7):558–565, jul 1978.

[23] BETTAZ M. An association of algebraic term nets and abstract data types for specifying real communication protocols. *Lecture Notes in Computer Science*, 534:11–30, 1991.

[24] BETTAZ M. Specification hautement compacte et modulaire de l'ETHERNET: la station emettrice. In *Proc. of CFIP'93*. Montreal, HERMES, Paris, 1993.

[25] BETTAZ M. and CHOUTRI A. Algebraic Term Nets: a formalism for specifying communication software in the OSI framework. In *Proceedings of the Unified Computation Laboratory*, pages 293–305. Oxford University Press, 1992.

[26] BETTAZ M. and MEHEMMEL A. Modeling and proving of truly concurrent systems with CATNets. In *Proceedings of Euromicro Workshop on Parallel and Distributed Processing*, pages 265–272. IEEE, 1993.

[27] BETTAZ M. and MAOUCHE M. How to specify non determinism and true concurrency with Algebraic Term Nets. *Lecture Notes in Computer Science*, 655:164–180, 1993.

[28] GARZIA M. Discrete event simulation methodologies and formalisms. *Simulation Digest*, 21(1):3–13, 1990.

[29] FUJIMOTO R. Parallel discrete event simulation. *Communications of the ACM*, 33(10):31–53, oct 1990.

[30] MURATA T. Petri Nets: Properties, analysis and applications. *Proceedings of the IEEE*, 77(4):541–580, apr 1989.

[31] REISIG W. *Petri Nets*. EATCS Monographs on Theoretical Computer Science, Springer-Verlag, 1985.

The Abingdon Cross Benchmark on the two PAPRICA Systems*

Alberto Broggi
Dipartimento di Ingegneria dell'Informazione
Università di Parma
Parma, ITALY, I-43100
broggi@CE.UniPR.IT

Abstract

This work presents the results of the Abingdon Cross Benchmark on the two PAPRICA systems, which are here briefly described focusing especially on their different architectural solutions. Starting from some considerations on their computational paradigm and hardware characteristics, the most efficient algorithm for the Abingdon Cross benchmark is discussed.

The algorithm has been implemented on the two systems taking advantage of specific ad-hoc *optimizations; the final* Quality Factor *is derived for both architectures and compared against that of other different non-commercial systems developed worldwide.*

1 Introduction

The PAPRICA project [5, 4, 7] started in 1988, aimed to the development of an experimental VLSI architecture devoted to the efficient handling of data with a two-dimensional structure. The main goal of the project was to develop a subsystem that could operate as an attached processing unit to a standard workstation and, in perspective, as a specialized *low-cost* processing module in dedicated systems devoted to low level image analysis, and/or cellular neural networks emulation.

The two PAPRICA prototypes follow the SIMD classification: both of them are composed of a high number of Processing Elements (PEs), each one processing different data according to the same algorithm. The computational paradigm implemented on such systems is based on binary mathematical morphology; in other words, the processing of 2D non-binary data structures is performed one-bit at a time. In order to obtain always the maximum efficiency from the hardware, the PAPRICA systems feature in fact single-bit processing units, as well as the possibility to execute more than one operation in pipeline. Moreover, since one of the goals of the project is to keep the cost of the system low, the architecture cannot integrate a large number of PEs, and each PE can only own a small amount of internal memory.

Generally (e.g. in image processing applications) the number of PEs is far smaller than the number of image pixels, thus requiring a sort of *virtualization* of the Processing Array (PA). This is done utilizing an external memory [13, 9, 11] (hereinafter referred to as Image Memory, IM): the PA is loaded from the external memory with a sub-window of the data set; then the computation is performed until a special instruction is reached; finally, the results are stored back again into the external memory. These steps are iterated until all the sub-windows have been processed. Then the first sub-window is reloaded again into the PA and the computation is resumed. According to this solution, data flow back and forth from the IM to the PA and viceversa through the data-bus.

The logical organization of the data-bus, the external organization of the PEs, and the size of their accessible neighborhood are the features that differentiate the two considered PAPRICA prototypes.

1.1 The First PAPRICA Prototype

In the first PAPRICA prototype, the PA is composed of an array of 4 × 4 full custom ICs (1.5 μm CMOS, 45 mm^2, $\simeq$ 35000 transistors), each of them containing a sub-array of 4 × 4 PEs. In the present implementation, the PA is a 16 × 16 square matrix of 1-bit PEs each one with full 8-neighbors connectivity [9, 6, 11]; each PE has an internal memory composed of 64 bits;

*This work was partially supported by CNR Progetto Finalizzato Trasporti under contract number 91.01031.PF93.

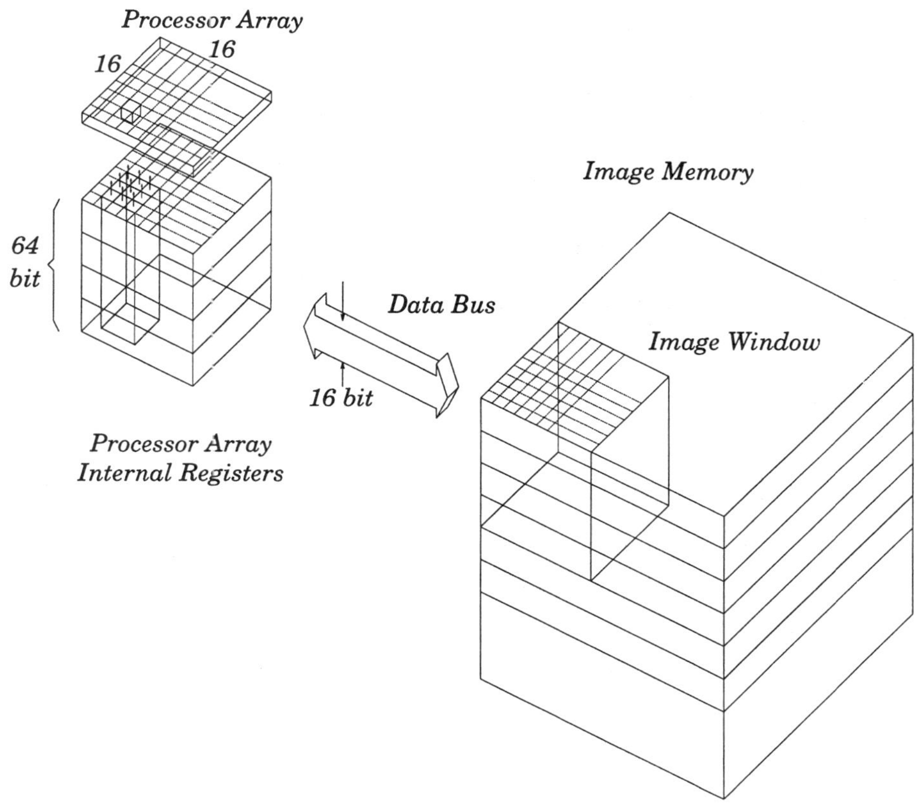

Figure 1: The logical organization of the first PAPRICA prototype

data flow between the IM and the PA through a 16-bit data bus. A block diagram depicting the logical organization of the PAPRICA-1 prototype is shown in figure 1.

In the current implementation, the PAPRICA co-processor is integrated on a single VME board (6U) connected to a SPARC-based workstation. It comprises 5 major functional parts:

1. the Program Memory, storing up to 256k instructions;

2. the Image Memory (up to 8 MBytes of static RAM), whose 16-bit memory fetch time is 150 ns;

3. the Processor Array, whose PE cycle time is 250 ns;

4. the Frame Grabber device, able to grab and store into PAPRICA Image Memory 512 × 512 8 bit/pixel grey-tone images at video rate (25 frames/s);

5. the Control Unit, which manages the activity of the whole system.

1.2 The Evolution of the Project: PAPRICA-3

The intensive use [1, 2] of the first prototype as well as some theoretical studies [7, 3] have pointed out some architectural problems.

- The low amount of internal memory does not allow to store internally a large amount of intermediate results, as often needed by computation intensive problems, thus requiring I/O operations to store the intermediate data in the external memory.

- The data transfer between the IM and the PA takes place on a 16 bit data bus: in a single cycle 16 bits (belonging to the same image pixel) are transferred in parallel. Unfortunately in many cases (almost all the real ones) the word parallelism of the data to be transferred is not a multiple of 16. This means that a significant amount of time is wasted transferring unnecessary data back and forth from the IM to the PA.

- The first prototype was conceived to run DRC algorithms and thus its instruction set follows a sort of CISC-oriented implementation, including also specific instructions needed to solve that kind of tasks. The evaluation of the performances has led to the consideration that the instruction set should evolve toward a RISC implementation. Moreover, since the complexity of the instruction set determines the PE size, the RISC choice allows the integration of a higher number of PEs on a single chip.

- Finally, the possibility to enlarge the neighborhood involved in morphological operations has been investigated.

The above considerations led to the design of a different architecture: as shown in figure 2.a, the PAPRICA-3 system features a *linear* array of Q single-bit PEs, connected to an external image memory via a bidirectional Q-bit bus. Therefore each memory access transfers a complete vector of Q pixels at a time, 1 bit per pixel. The rationale behind this system is that the size of the PA matches exactly the width of the input image, thus reducing the PE virtualization mechanism problem which has been proven to be a critical design issue in 2D arrays [7]. The foreseen values of Q for the first hardware implementation (now under development) will range from a minimum of 64 to 256.

Data are transferred into the PEs internal registers, processed, and explicitly stored back into memory according to a RISC-oriented processing paradigm. The PE neighborhood has been augmented to include also the 4 cells in the 4 main directions at a distance 2 from the central cell (reduced 5×5 neighborhood, as shown in figure 2.b). For this reason a number of registers (*Morphological Registers (MOR)*) have a structure which is more complex than that of a simple memory cell and are in reality composed of 5 1-bit cells with a `S`$\rightarrow$`N` shift register connection. Besides the MOR, each PE owns also a number of *Logical Registers (LOR)* which may be used for intermediate storage and for all operations which do not require the use of neighboring values.

2 The Abingdon Cross benchmark

The main target of the Abingdon Cross benchmark [10] is to compare the performance of different computer architectures devoted to image processing.

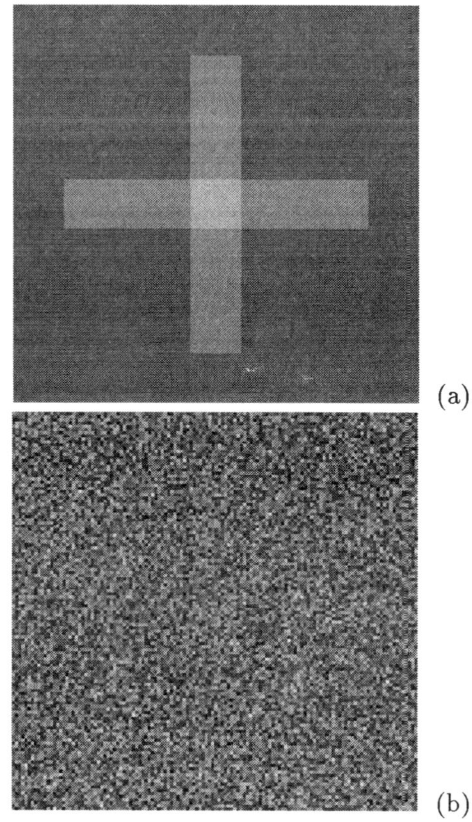

Figure 3: *a*) synthetic cross; *b*) white gaussian noise.

This benchmark has been defined to be implemented on any computer architecture, regardless of its computational paradigm. The target of this benchmark is the determination of the computational time required by the filtering of a 8 bit/pixel test image; the filter consists of the determination of the skeleton of a synthetic cross (figure 3.a) added with white gaussian noise (figure 3.b).

There are no constraints at all on the implementation of the Abingdon Cross benchmark, but obviously the best performances are achieved when the algorithm matches the computer architecture and the computational paradigm. Moreover the design of the algorithm can take advantage of the knowledge of the key parameters used in the synthesis of the test image.

1. Number of gray levels: 256 (8 bit/pixel);

2. Linear image size: N;

3. Mean value of the added gaussian noise: 0;

4. Signal to noise ratio: 0 dB.

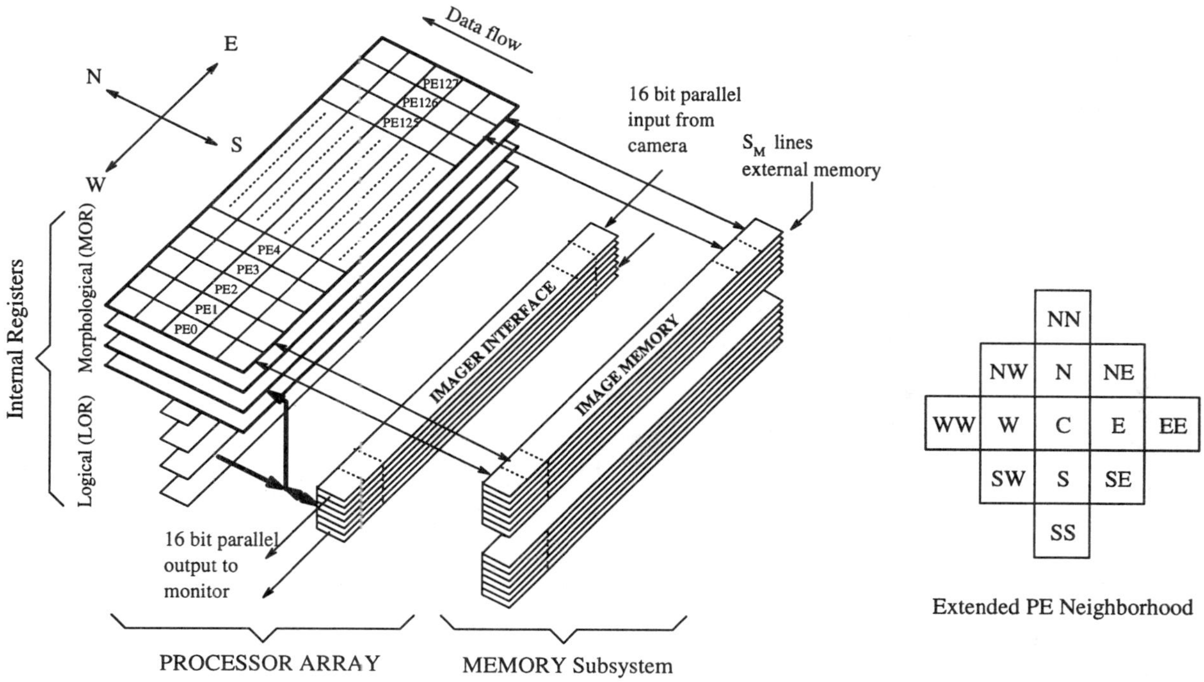

Figure 2: *(a)* structure of the Processor Array; *(b)* PE neighborhood.

5. Size of cross relative to the image size: arm length: $\frac{3}{4}N$; arm width: $\frac{N}{8}$;

An example of a test image with $N = 128$ generated according to the specifications described in [15] (256 gray levels; background level: 128; cross arms level: 160; arms intersection: 192; noise standard deviation: 32) is shown in figure 4.a. The final target of the Abingdon Cross benchmark is the determination of the *Quality Factor* performance index, which is defined as the ratio between the linear size of the test image (N, generally 128 or 512) and time required to filter it (T):

$$QF \triangleq \frac{N}{T} \,. \tag{1}$$

Moreover, for commercial systems the *Price-Performance Factor* is also defined, but since the two PAPRICA systems are non-commercial research prototypes, only the Quality Factor is considered.

3 The Algorithm

Since both PAPRICA-1 and PAPRICA-3 systems are composed of single bit PEs, the processing of binary images is preferred with respect to the handling of data structures with higher word parallelism. Moreover, due to the specific instruction set implemented on such systems, high performances are obtained when the algorithm is based on morphological [8, 14] operations, namely when only the configuration of a reduced neighborhood is considered in the processing of each image pixel.

The above considerations lead to the subdivision of the algorithm into two main steps:

(a) image binarization, and

(b) morphological processing.

3.1 Image Binarization

Concerning step *(a)*, different approaches have been considered, including the application of: (i) a fixed threshold, (ii) an adaptive one (based on a given neighborhood), (iii) a set of two thresholds together with a hysteresis process. However, since step *(b)* plays the most important role in the algorithm, the simplest implementation (fixed threshold) has been chosen for step *(a)*.

3.2 Morphological Processing

As already justified above, the second step of the filter consists of a set of morphological operations whose im-

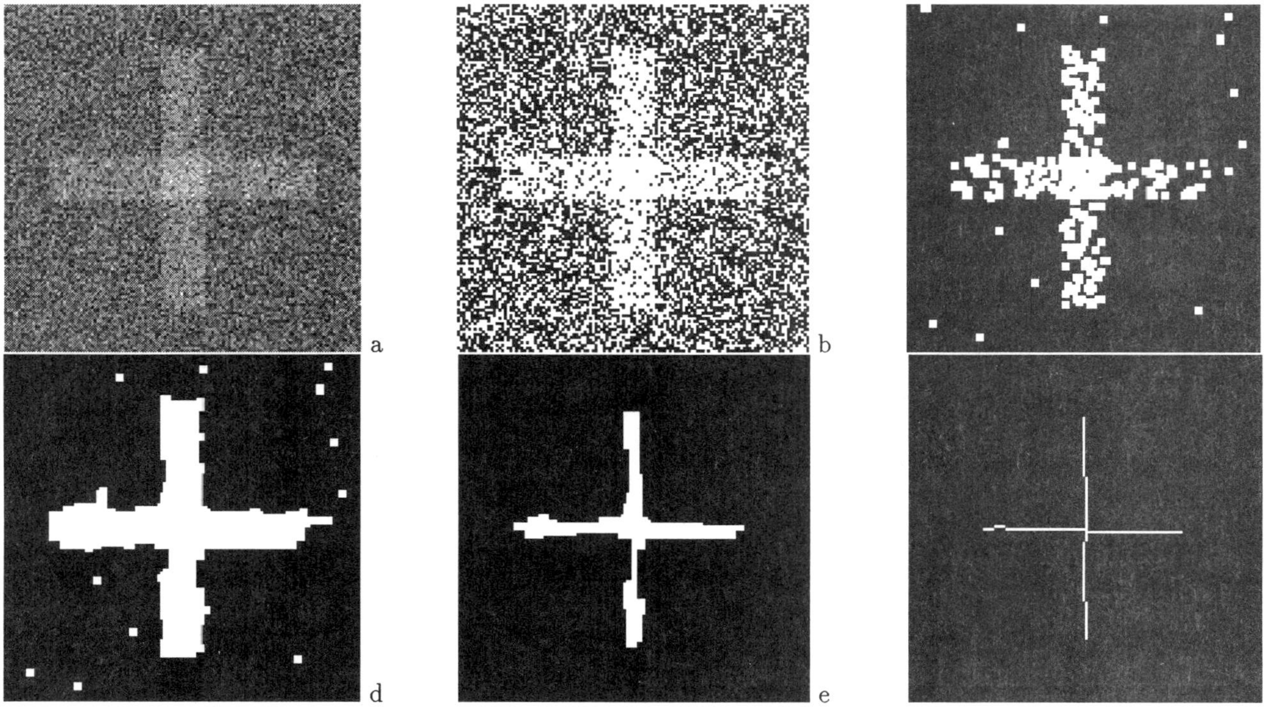

Figure 4: The Abingdon Cross benchmark on a 128 × 128 image: *a*) input image; *b*) thresholded image; *c*) after one morphological opening with the 3×3 anisotropic structuring element; *d*) after one morphological closing with a 7×7 anisotropic structuring element; *e*) after four morphological erosions with the 3×3 anisotropic structuring element; *f*) after three thinning iterations.

plementation on the PAPRICA systems is extremely efficient. The morphological step of the algorithm is based on:

- a morphological opening [8] (an erosion followed by a dilation) with the 3×3 anisotropic structuring element 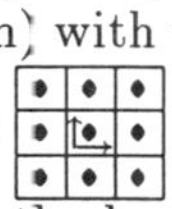, aimed to the elimination of the noise in the background;
- a morphological closing (a dilation followed by an erosion) with the 7×7 anisotropic structuring element 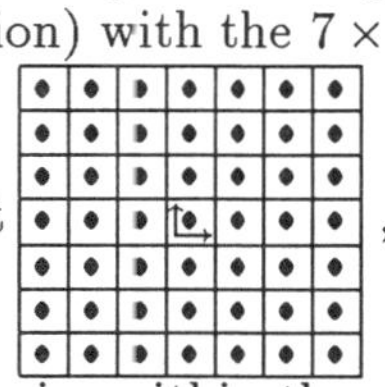, aimed to the elimination of the noise within the cross;
- a fixed number of erosions (again with the 3×3 anisotropic structuring element) aimed to the reduction of the arms width. The number of iterations depends on the image linear size: in the case of $N = 128$, 4 erosions are performed.
- finally, a thinning filter [12] is iterated until the image consists of lines with single-pixel width. For $N = 128$, 3 to 4 iterations are performed, depending on the specific noise conditions.

The complete sequence of intermediate results of the algorithm for the Abingdon Cross Benchmark is depicted in figure 4.

4 Benchmarking PAPRICA-1 system

In the implementation of point *(b)*, an optimizing technique [3] has been exploited: it is based on the consideration that the data bus, which links the IM and the PA, has a 16 bit parallelism, thus during the transfer of a p-bit image (with $1 \leq p \leq 16$), the data bus efficiency is $\frac{p \times 100}{16}\%$. A low bus efficiency is measured for example during the execution of the thinning filter, since both the data loading and the data saving involve the transfer of a single-bit (binary) images over the 16-bit data bus; this produces the lowest bus efficiency (about 6%).

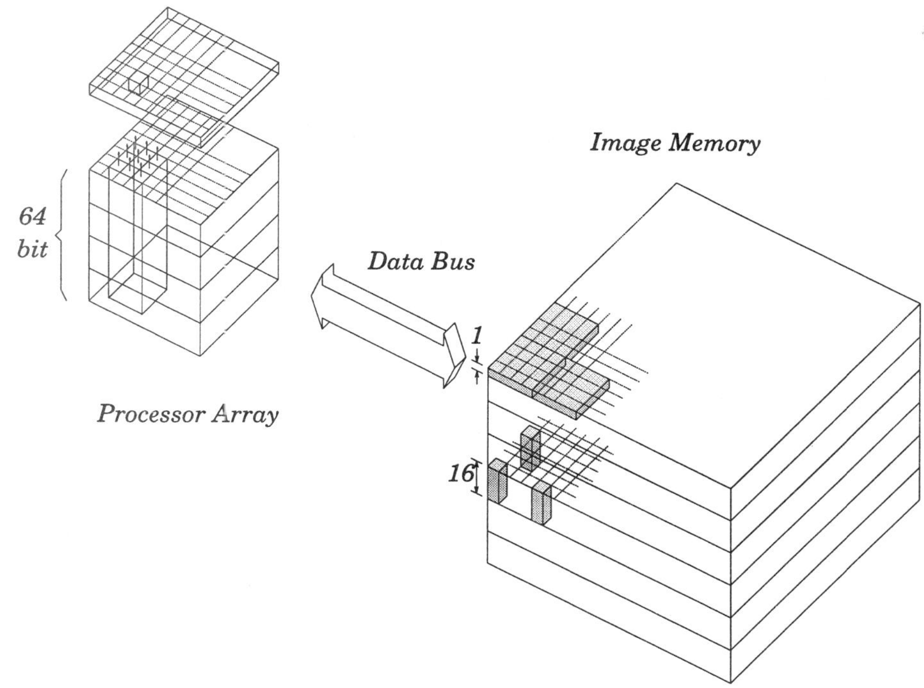

Figure 5: The result of the data packing procedure

The goal of the optimization technique is the improvement of the data bus efficiency, which is achieved by a data packing procedure [3]. The data packing, performed immediately after the thresholding step, reads the result of the binarization process (a $N \times N \times 1$ image) from the PA and writes a $\frac{N}{4} \times \frac{N}{4} \times 16$ image into the IM. Besides improving the bus efficiency (now during the saving of the binarized result into the image memory a single data transfer consists of 16 bit, and thus the bus efficiency reaches 100%), it also decreases the image linear dimensions from N to $\frac{N}{4}$, and increases the pixels' neighborhood accessed by an individual read instruction (for details see [3]). An example of the packing of 3 image subwindows is depicted in figure 5, which shows that the data of a single sub-window are stacked in 16-bit columns.

The total processing time for $N = 128$ is about 110 ms. The quality factor, as defined by equation (1), becomes $QF = 1.1\ 10^3$.

5 Benchmarking PAPRICA-3 system

The data packing optimization used for the implementation of the algorithm on PAPRICA-1 system was explicitly designed to overcome the low efficiency of the data bus during the transfer of data structures with a parallelism lower than 16. Conversely, the different logical organization of the IM in the PAPRICA-3 system allows to transfer on the data bus only the significant information, thus providing always the maximum bus efficiency. In this case no data packing is needed, and the image is processed in plain format.

Another advantage offered by the architecture of the PAPRICA-3 system is the enhanced neighborhood accessible with a single morphological operation. This fact allows to decrease the number of morphological instructions.

Furthermore, a specific hardware enhancement allows to decrease drastically the number of memory accesses. When a new image line is loaded from the IM to the PA, the morphological registers are shifted one position north; the processing begins and the result is saved back into the IM (see figure 6). When the processing is based on a neighborhood wider than 5 consecutive lines, the above process must be iterated: a filter based on a 9×9 neighborhood needs two iterations.

In order to reduce the number of accesses to the IM, the PA has been enhanced by the possibility to load a new image line also from the logical registers, as shown in figure 7. Thanks to this feature, the intermediate saving and successive reloading of temporary

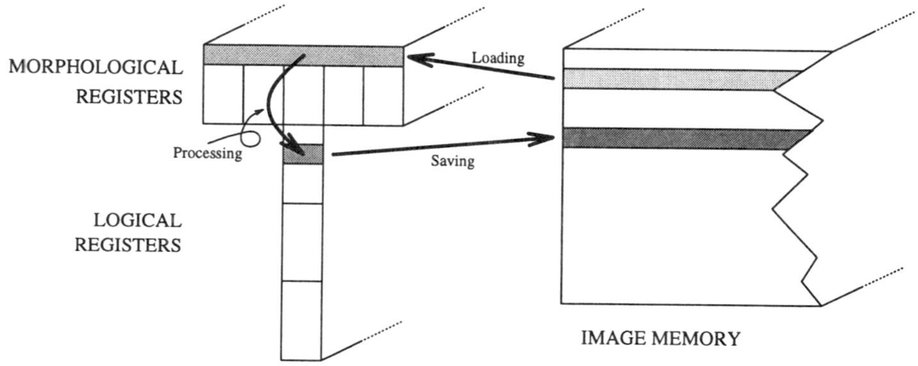

Figure 6: An image line is loaded from the IM into the PA morphological registers, which are shifted one position; the result of the processing is generally stored into the logical registers; and finally it is saved back again into the IM.

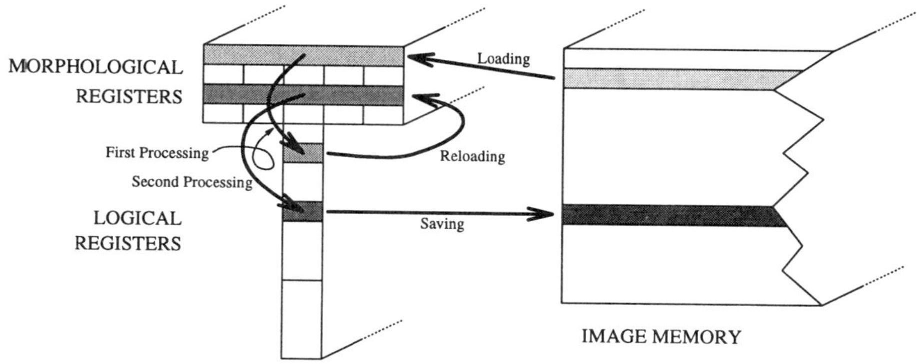

Figure 7: In this case, after the first processing, the result is no more saved back into the IM, but it is reloaded into the PA morphological registers for further processing. This facility emulates the presence of a wider neighborhood.

results to/from the IM are replaced with a faster and more efficient internal data transfer between the PA registers. In fact in this way, if the number of morphological registers is sufficiently high, data remain into the PA chip. Nevertheless, since only 16 morphological registers are available, in the implementation of the Abingdon Cross benchmark, one intermediate transfer to and from the IM is anyway required.

Since the PAPRICA-3 hardware system is currently still under development, a software simulator (at the system level) has been used to derive the Abingdon Cross Quality Factor. In order to produce results comparable to the ones derived for the first PAPRICA-1 system (with $16 \times 16 = 256$ PEs), in the simulator the number of PEs has been fixed to 256, thus the size of the test image is 256×256. Two different results have been obtained, assuming different values for the memory access time T_M and the instruction execution time T_C:

a) a conservative solution: $T_M = 100$ ns and $T_C = 20$ ns;

b) a desirable one: $T_M = 50$ ns and $T_C = 10$ ns.

In case a), the total time required to filter a 256×256 test image is 4.68 ms, thus providing a Quality Factor of about $5.47\ 10^4$. In case b) the time is reduced to 2.34 ms, while the Quality Factor becomes $1.1\ 10^5$.

6 Conclusions

Table 1 presents the results shown in [10] for non-commercial machines only, together with the results for the PAPRICA-1 and PAPRICA-3 systems.

This results are in accordance with the theoretical studies on the architectural solution (discussed in [5]), which forecast a speed-up of 2 orders of magnitude thanks to the different IM logical organization and to

Machine	Quality Factor
CLIP4 (96 × 96)	7.3 10^3
Cyto III	1.0 10^2
DIP	4.7 10
PHP	7.1
POP II	2.9
VAP	1.8 10
WARP	5.0 10^2
PAPRICA-1	1.1 10^3
PAPRICA-3	5.47 10^4 - 1.1 10^5

Table 1: The quality factor for some non-commercial machines

the possibility to decrease the computational overhead caused by the PA virtualization.

Acknowledgments

The author would like to thank Luca Giovanelli and Gian Luca Porcari for their useful help.

References

[1] A. Broggi. A Novel Approach to Lossy Real-Time Image Compression: Hierarchical Data Reorganization on a Low-Cost Massively Parallel System. *Real-Time Imaging Journal*, 1(2), 1995.

[2] A. Broggi. Parallel and Local Feature Extraction: a Real-Time Approach to Road Boundary Detection. *IEEE Transactions on Image Processing*, 4(2):217–223, February 1995.

[3] A. Broggi. Word Parallelism vs Spatial Parallelism: a performance optimization technique on the PAPRICA system. In *Proceedings 3rd EuroMicro Workshop on Parallel and Distributed Processing*, pages 236–243, Sanremo, Italy, January, 25-27 1995.

[4] A. Broggi, G. Conte, F. Gregoretti, C. Sansoè, and L. M. Reyneri. The PAPRICA Massively Parallel Processor. In *Proceedings MPCS - IEEE International Conference on Massively Parallel Computing Systems*, pages 16–30, Ischia, Italy, May 2-6 1994.

[5] A. Broggi, G. Conte, F. Gregoretti, C. Sansoè, and L. M. Reyneri. The Evolution of the PAPRICA System. *Integrated Computer-Aided Engineering Journal - Special Issue on Massively Parallel Computing*, 1995. In press.

[6] T. Fountain. *Processor Arrays: Architectures and applications.* Academic-Press, London, 1987.

[7] F. Gregoretti, L. M. Reyneri, C. Sansoè, A. Broggi, and G. Conte. The PAPRICA SIMD array: critical reviews and perspectives. In L. Dadda and B. Wah, editors, *Proceedings ASAP'93 - IEEE Computer Society International Conference on Application Specific Array Processors*, pages 309–320, Venezia, Italy, October 25-27 1993.

[8] R. M. Haralick, S. R. Sternberg, and X. Zhuang. Image Analysis Using Mathematical Morphology. *IEEE Transaction on Pattern Analysis and Machine Intelligence*, 9(4):532–550, 1987.

[9] NCR Corporation, Dayton, Ohio. *Geometric Arithmetic Parallel Processor*, 1984.

[10] K. Preston. The Abingdon Cross Benchmark Survey. *Computer*, pages 9–18, July 1989.

[11] S. Reddaway. DAP - A Distributed Array Processor. In *1st Annual Symposium on Computer Architectures*, pages 61–65, Florida, 1973.

[12] A. Rosenfeld. A characterization of parallel thinning algorithms. *Information Control*, 29:286–291, 1975.

[13] L. A. Schmitt and S. S. Wilson. The AIS-5000 Parallel Processor. *IEEE Transactions on Pattern Analysis and Machine Intelligence*, 10(3):320–330, May 1988.

[14] J. Serra. *Image Analysis and Mathematical Morphology.* Academic Press, London, 1982.

[15] W. B. Teeuw and R. P. W. Duin. An algorithm for benchmarking an SIMD pyramid with the Abingdon Cross. *Patt. Rec. Letters*, 11:501–506, 1990.

Performance Evaluation of Automatically Generated Data-Parallel Programs

L. Massari

DIS
Università di Pavia
via Ferrata 1
27100 Pavia, ITALIA

Y. Mahéo

IRISA
Campus de Beaulieu
Avenue du Général Leclerc
35042 Rennes Cedex, FRANCE

Abstract

In this paper, the problem of evaluating the performance of parallel programs generated by data-parallel compilers is studied. These compilers take as input an application written in a sequential language augmented with data distribution directives and produce a parallel version, based on the specified partitioning of data.

A methodology for evaluating the relationships existing among the program characteristics, the data distribution adopted, and the performance indices measured during the program execution is described. It consists of three phases: a "static" description of the program under study, a "dynamic" description, based on the measurement and the analysis of its execution on a real system, and the construction of a workload model, by using workload characterization techniques. Following such a methodology, decisions related to the selection of the data distribution to be adopted can be facilitated.

The approach is exposed through the use of the PANDORE *environment, designed for the execution of sequential programs on distributed memory parallel computers. It is composed of a compiler, a runtime system and tools for trace and profile generation. The results of an experiment explaining the methodology are presented.*

1 Introduction

Performance evaluation activities are required in many studies, involving the design and the tuning of a system, as well as the debugging of its performance. Whatever is the objective of the study, the workload, that is the set of programs submitted to the system, is one of the major components which determine system performance, in that strict relationships exist between the obtained performance and the hardware and software components of the system itself. Workload characterization is the basis of every performance evaluation study, in that it provides systematic methods for a quantitative description of the load which, together with the systems architectural aspects, is responsible of the performance.

In parallel environments, in particular, the performance evaluation process is more crucial and difficult than in sequential ones. The analysis and characterization of the workload in parallel systems require special care because of their complex architectures, the large number of hardware and software components interacting, and the new programming paradigm adopted.

In this paper, we study the problem of evaluating the performance of parallel programs generated by data-parallel compilers. Such compilers that takes as input an application written in a sequential language augmented with data distribution directives like HPF [9] and produce a parallel version, based on the specified partitioning of data (*e.g.* [12, 18, 1]).

The "parallelizing" compiler represents one of the most important system's software component influencing the program execution. However, even if the compiler manages in a transparent way code distribution, data distribution and communication among tasks, the parallelization decisions are definitively left to the user who specifies the partitioning of the data and their mapping onto the available processors. These factors highly influence the performance attained by the system.

The paper is organized as follows. In Sect. 2, the motivations for such a study and the problems related to the selection of the appropriate data distribution are presented. A methodology for the evaluation of the relationships existing between the workload characteristics and the obtained performance is proposed. In Sect. 3, the environment used for the automatic generation of data parallel programs is briefly described, together with the profiler tool providing measurements of the program execution. Finally, an experiment showing the feasibility of the approach is presented in Sect. 4.

2 Performance Evaluation of Data Parallel Programs

From the performance point of view, the major characteristic of a data parallel program is the dependence of the obtained performance from the specified data distribution, which influences computation, as well as communication activities. Optimal system

1066-6192/96 $5.00 © 1996 IEEE
Proceedings of PDP '96

performance is obtained by balancing the computation activity among different processors but also by minimizing communication traffic, and achieving a large degree of parallelism.

As already pointed out, the user is still responsible for decisions related to data distribution. Hence, due to the large number of distributions available and to the number of parameters affecting such decisions, an help in selecting the appropriate data decomposition which maximizes performance has emerged as an essential requirement. This help can benefit to the user, who has to choose the distribution, or it can serve the development of automatic data management in parallelizing compilers (see [6, 16]).

2.1 Methodology

Generally, depending on the objective of the study and on the availability of the system, different methods can be applied for performance evaluation [11]. They range from the construction of models having an analytical solution, to very detailed simulation models, to measurement based approaches. The major benefit in using performance modeling is when measurements are not available, for example, in performance prediction studies or during design activities. A number of studies have been done in the framework of data-parallel compilers to statically estimate the performance of the generated parallel programs [7, 2]. However, also in this case, an interaction with performance measurement activity is required in order to test if the model is realistic, or to verify the validity of the parameterization of the model and to drive its input.

When the system is available, a measurement-based study is generally carried out; measurements represent the basis for the workload characterization process (see [5, 8]). Following this approach, the performances of the real system are obtained: they contain also the influence of hardware and software components which would be otherwise difficult to capture even in a very detailed model. When dealing with programs generated by a parallelizing compiler, in particular, many are the decisions to be taken and the factors which interact and which make a measurement based approach particularly suitable.

Thus, the approach that we propose is based on various statistical analyses of the data measured during the program execution. The aim is to relate the program characteristics with that of the data partitioning and mapping, in order to optimize performance. Three phases have been identified. First, the program under study can be statically described by means of a few parameters. Then, a "dynamic" description, based on the measurement and the analysis of its execution on a real system is obtained. Finally, workload characterization techniques are applied to the obtained workload for constructing a model. In what follows, the three phases are described in more detail.

By statically analyzing the program structure, a workload description in terms of parameters that can affect the choice of the data distribution can be obtained. The attention has been focused on DO loops, and on array data structures, because the most part of scientific codes are based on loops working on data arrays, and the major part of the parallelism inherent in an application resides in them. Indeed, efficient code has to be generated especially for such structures; they form also the major source of performance degradation in numerical applications, due to communication.

Parameters which are strictly related to the loop structure, and others which characterize the whole program have been defined. As an example, the loop can be defined by the size of each of the referenced arrays, by the order of the index in the nested loops, and by the depth of the loop. The selected data distribution, which can be identified by the size of the blocks into which the data structures are partitioned, and the mapping strategy adopted are other parameters characterizing the program. Finally, the number of allocated processors can be chosen as a parameter reflecting the influence of the system hardware configuration.
Note that the parameter selection is a critical point, in that they have to accurately describe the program characteristics.

Once the program under study has been defined according to some of the previously described parameters, the second phase deals with the measurement and the analysis of its execution on a real architecture. In order to trace the program execution, appropriate monitoring instrumentation is required (see [17, 18]). Very low level data, related for example to the start and to the end of an event, are produced by monitoring tools and collected into trace files. The generally huge amount of data obtained makes them difficult to interpret. At this point, a pre-elaboration phase is needed in order to derive a more intuitive and compact description of the program behavior. Starting from measurements collected by the monitoring tools, a set of higher-level parameters are identified, describing the behavior of the program in terms of computation and communication activities. Such parameters deal, for example, with the number of messages exchanged the execution, computation and communication times.

At the end of these two phases, the whole program execution can globally be represented by a set of n parameters, that is, those related to its "static" structure and to the system configuration, and those reflecting its "dynamic" behavior, that is, measured.

Each execution of the program is a *workload component*, which can be represented as a point in a n-dimensional space [8]. Then, the *workload* processed by the system is constituted by a collection of workload components, obtained varying the values of the parameters, for example, changing the dimension of the blocks into which data have been distributed, the mapping policy, or the problem dimension.

The aim and the core of the methodology, at this point, is to construct a model of the workload, that is, a compact representation able to capture and reproduce the behavior of the system. Workload characterization techniques have to be applied, so that "typical" behaviors of the program can be identified; multidimensional analysis techniques are required for this purpose. A description of the techniques applied for workload characterization is presented in the next section.

2.2 Workload Characterization

The characteristics of the workload have to be studied by applying different statistical analyses. A complete description of workload characterization techniques applied to performance evaluation studies of various system architectures, can be found in [5, 4].

The idea in our study is to find relationships among the program, the system configuration, and the achieved performance.

In order to reduce the number of parameters, and thus the complexity of the analysis, the correlation among the parameters can be analyzed. The correlation matrix helps in selecting the most appropriate parameters by expressing the dependencies among them: a correlation index between two parameters close to one reflects an equivalent behavior. Just one parameter amongst the highly correlated parameters can then be considered for the description of the application, hence reducing the dimension of the n-dimensional space.

Clustering analysis (see [10]) revealed very important for the identification of workload components having "similar" behavior, and is most commonly applied to the workload characterization problem.

The workload is considered as a set of points (components) in a space with a number of dimensions equal to the number of parameters used to describe each component.

Clustering algorithms partition the workload into clusters, such that components with similar characteristics belong to the same cluster. These algorithms have to identify the partition which better represents the characteristics of the original measurements. The goodness of a partition is given by an optimality measure, based on a selected metric, for example the euclidean distance.

Then, according to some specified criteria, a few components are extracted from every cluster and are considered as the representatives of the measured workload. The centroid, that is, the geometric center of the clusters, is generally chosen.

The partitioning of the workload means that "typical" behaviors can be identified among the various program executions. This gives the possibility to relate the static parameters describing the program and the system configuratio, with the dynamic ones, that is, with the performance indices. Centroids represent a model of the workload; hence, once the static configuration of the program has been chosen, the corresponding performance indices can be "expected".

Furthermore, clustering algorithms provide an analysis of the behavior of the components belonging to a cluster. Basic statistics, such as minimum, maximum, average values and standard deviation give a first idea of the "average" behavior of the program. For example, when considering parameters related to communication activities, a very high value of the standard deviation, compared with the mean value, is a synonym of variabilities. This means that unbalanced conditions due to uneven work or data distribution are detected.

In Sect. 4, the application of our methodology is described through a test example.

In the following section, the environment used for parallelizing the program and for monitoring its execution is presented.

3 The Pandore Environment

PANDORE is an environment designed for the execution of sequential programs on distributed memory parallel computers [1]. It is composed of a compiler, a runtime system and tools for trace and profile generation.

3.1 The Language

The PANDORE language is based on a sequential imperative language using a subset of C (excluding pointers) as a basis. We have added a small set of simple and well-defined data distribution features in order to describe frequently used decompositions.

A PANDORE program is a sequential program which calls distributed phases. The sequential part is in charge of all I/O operations and is executed on the host processor (if exists) or on one specific node of the distributed computer. Each distributed phase is spread over the processors of the target machine and is executed in parallel according to the owner-writes rule.

Distributed phases are declared like procedures preceded by the keyword `dist`. To each formal parameter of the distributed phase is assigned a distribution. The distributed parameter list allows the specification of the partitioning and the mapping of the data used in the distributed phase.

The array is the only data type that may be partitioned, scalars are replicated. The means to decompose an array is to split it into blocks. The specification of the partitioning for a d-dimensional array is given by the construct `block` $(t_1, ..., t_d)$ where t_i indicates the size of the blocks in the ith dimension.

Then, the mapping of the blocks onto the architecture will be achieved in a regular or cyclic way according to the mapping parameters (`regular` or `wrapped`). In PANDORE, we consider only one dimensional processor arrays whose size is not specified in the source code but used as a parameter by the compiler. As we allow the mapping of multidimensional decompositions, it is needed to indicate the order for the mapping of blocks by providing an ordered list of dimension numbers: for instance, `(1,0)` states for column first, `(0,1)` states for row first.

The last specification given in the parameter list concerns the transfer mode for values between the caller and the distributed phase: allowed modes are `IN`, `OUT` and `INOUT`. This specification is similar to the one found in Ada or Fortran90.

For example the formal parameter declaration

```
int A[N][N] by block(1,N) map wrapped(0,1) mode INOUT
```

states that array **A** is decomposed into **N** lines mapped cyclically onto the processors. The value of the elements of the array must be transferred from the host at the beginning of the distributed phase and must be sent back to it at the end of the phase.

3.2 The Compiler and the Runtime System

From the source program, the PANDORE compiler automatically generates a machine independent SPMD code according to the owner-writes rule: a processor modifies only the variables that have been assigned to it by the distribution specification.

Two compilation schemes are embedded in the compiler. For reductions and parallel loops, the compiler applies an optimized scheme [14] performing loop bounds reduction and message vectorization, based on static domain analysis. For statements that cannot be optimized, the compiler relies on the well-known *run-time resolution* technique: masks and communication operations are introduced at the statement level to fetch distant data and select the processor responsible for the computation.

An original distributed array management based on paging [15] has been developed to support both schemes. Each block of a distributed array is decomposed into pages so that the array is represented on a processor by a table of pages that contains both *local pages* (pages of the blocks owned by the processor) and *distant pages* (copies of pages owned by other processors). Such a management leads to both efficient accesses and reasonable memory overhead.

The code generated by the compiler is a SPMD *C* code containing calls to the runtime system. The goal of the runtime system is to implement memory and process management, communication of data elements between processes, and distributed data accesses. It is build upon a virtual machine that permits the execution of PANDORE programs on a wide range of parallel platforms.

3.3 The Pandore Profiler

The PANDORE profiler allows the user to collect a number of quantitative measures on his program's execution with minimal intervention. It may be complemented by a trace generator for more qualitative measurements [3]. The use of profiling restrains the amount of storage needed; the number of counters to be updated is of the order of the number of variables declared in the source program. Sensors are inserted in modified versions of some runtime primitives, thus the compiler generates a similar code whether an instrumentation is demanded or not. An enhancement of mere profiling is actually used: in addition to their occurrences, the durations of events may also be cumulated [13]. Measurements are performed on each node and counters are brought back to the host at the end of the execution and then written down into a file that can be exploited by appropriate tools.

The links between the source and the evaluation results are established two different ways: first the user bounds fragments of the distributed phases he wants to be evaluated by defining some *instrumentation zones*, typically loop nests. Moreover, output figures are associated with objects of the source program such as arrays, scalars or conditional statements.

Twelve types of information are available that can be divided in two categories:

- *Information relative to each instrumentation zone*

  For each distributed variable v and each couple of processors (p_1, p_2), the number of messages from p_1 to p_2 required for the assignment of v is computed as well as the corresponding volume transferred and the cumulated waiting time on p_2. Identical information is collected for broadcast messages due to assignments to replicated scalars and due to the evaluation of conditional expressions.

  For the entire zone, the number of local accesses to a distributed array element and the number of accesses that required communication is computed for each processor. Identically, the number of purely local assignments and the number of assignments that required distant data is reported.

  The execution time for the zone is also given.

- *Information relative to each distributed phase*

  For each distributed variable, the time spent receiving the corresponding initial value from the host is reported for each processor. The waiting part of this time is also given.

  Different times are measured globally for the phase: the time for the triggering of the phase by the host, the time for transferring **IN** variables from the host, the time for executing the statements of the phase and the time for transferring **OUT** variables back to the host.

4 Experiments

In order to test the feasibility of the proposed methodology, a few experiments have been carried out based on data obtained using the profiler integrated into the PANDORE environment, described in the previous section. An iPSC/2 with 32 nodes has been chosen as target architecture. As a test program, the Jacobi algorithm has been considered (see Fig. 1). Following the methodology presented in Sect. 2.1 raw data collected by the profiler have been analyzed, by applying various statistical techniques.

The algorithm has been statically described as follows: the size of the array (`Size`) has been chosen for the definition of the loop, while the number of allocated processors (`Npr`) and the number of blocks (`NBl`) into which the array are partitioned represent the data distribution policy.

Different runs of the algorithm have been executed, and monitored using the PANDORE profiler, obtaining 32 components for the workload. Each workload component has been obtained by executing the algorithm varying from 2 to 16 the number of allocated processors, the problem size, and the number of blocks allocated per processor.

At the beginning, 10 parameters have been extracted from the measurements for the description of the achieved performance. They are (see Sect. 3.3) the mean number of messages exchanged between a couple of processors (NM), the waiting time (Wait), the execution time for the zone (Tex), the time for the triggering of the phase (Trigg) by the host, the time for transferring variables from the host (Tin) and back to the host (Tout) and parameters related to the number of accesses (NRL, NRD, NAD, NAR).

```
#define N      256
#define P      4
 ...
dist jacobien(double B[N][N] by block(N/P,N)
                            map wrapped(0,1)
                            mode INOUT
          )
double A[N][N] by block(N/P,N) map wrapped(0,1);
{
 int i,j;
  for (i=1; i<(N-1); i++)
     for (j=1; j<(N-1); j++) {
        A[i][j] = ( B[i-1][j] + B[i+1][j] +
                    B[i][j-1] + B[i][j+1] ) +
                    V * B[i][j] ;
     }
}
```

Figure 1: The Jacobi algorithm considered.

The pre-analysis phase dealt with the definition of the relevant parameters able to capture the parallel characteristics of the load. Indeed, each component, has been represented in a 11-dimensional space.

The aim of the experiments was to analyze the average behavior of the program; the value of the parameters for each component have been computed by averaging the values on all the processors on which the data have been distributed.

Analyzing the correlation matrix (see Fig. 2), 4 highly correlated parameters have been discovered. In the further analysis, only 7 parameters, namely, the number of processors, the array size, the number of blocks per processor, the number of exchanged messages, the execution time, and the I/O times, have been considered (see Fig. 3).

Cluster analysis yield an optimal partition of the workload into 2 clusters, whose statistics are shown in Fig. 4. As can be seen, cluster 1 contains the major part of the workload components, and is characterized by low execution times and number of exchanged messages.

Looking at the composition of each cluster, we can see that, independently on the number of the allocated processors, cluster 2 groups executions with high problem size and high number of blocks per processor. Then, we can conclude that the performance obtained when executing the jacobi algorithm with high problem size and a partitioning of the data in small blocks are independent on the number of allocated processors.

5 Conclusions and Future Work

A methodology for evaluating the relationships existing among the program characteristics, the data distribution adopted and the measured performance indices has been presented. The results of an experiment in which the Jacobi algorithm has been analyzed, have been shown.

Following such methodology, decisions related to the selection of the data distribution to be adopted can be facilitated.

The methodology has to be tested on real application programs. Then, a more detailed description of the loop has to be studied, reflecting, for example, the dependences among the statements, can be useful for representing the influence that such factors have on the selected data distribution. If different experimentations are carried out while varying the data distribution, the data mapping and the problem description, groups of programs with similar performance behavior can be identified. Then, given the program description, a prediction of the performance can be obtained, based on the specified data distribution.

References

[1] F. André, M. Le Fur, Y. Mahéo, and J.-L. Pazat. The Pandore Data Parallel Compiler and its Portable Runtime. In *International Conference and Exhibition on High-Performance Computing and Networking, HPCN Europe'95*, number 919 in Lecture Notes in Computer Science, Milan, Italy, May 1995. Springer Verlag.

[2] V. Balasundaram, G. Fox, K. Kennedy, and U. Kremer. A Static Performance Estimator to Guide Data Partitioning Decisions. In *3rd ACM SYGPLAN Symposium on Principles and Practice of Parallel Programming*, Williamsburg, VA USA, June 1991.

[3] C. Bareau, Y. Mahéo, and J.-L. Pazat. Parallel Program Performance Debugging with the Pandore II Environment. *Parallel Computing*, September 1993.

[4] M. Calzarossa and L. Massari. Measurement-Based Approach to Workload Characterization. In G. Haring, R. Marie, and G. Kotsis, editors, *Performance and Reliability Evaluation. Tutorials Papers at the 7th International Conference on Modelling Techniques and Tools for Computer Performance Evaluation*, OCG Schriftenreihe, pages 123–148. Oldenbourg Verlag, 1994.

[5] M. Calzarossa and G. Serazzi. Workload Characterization: A Survey. *Proc. of the IEEE*, 81(8):1136–1150, 1993.

[6] B. Chapman, T. Fahringer, and H.P. Zima. Automatic Support for Data Distribution on Distributed Memory Multiprocessor Systems. In U. Banerjee, D. Gelernter, A. Nicolau, and D. Padua, editors, *Proc. Sixth International Workshop on Languages and Compilers for Parallel Computing*, number 768 in Lecture Notes in Computer Science, pages 184–199. Springer-Verlag, 1993.

[7] T. Fahringer and H. Zima. A Static Parameter Based Performance Prediction Tool for Parallel Programs. In *International Conference on Supercomputing*, Tokyo, Japan, July 1993. ACM Press.

[8] D. Ferrari, G. Serazzi, and A. Zeigner. *Measurement and Tuning of Computer Systems.* Prentice-Hall, Inc., 1983.

[9] High Performance Fortran Forum. High Performance Fortran Language Specification, Version 1.0. Technical report, Rice University, Huston, Texas, 1993.

[10] J.A. Hartigan. *Clustering Algorithms.* John Wiley & Sons, New York, 1975.

[11] P. Heidelberger and S.S. Lavenberg. Computer Performance Evaluation Methodology. *IEEE Trans. on Computers*, C-33(12):1195–1220, 1984.

[12] S. Hiranandani, K. Kennedy, and C-W. Tseng. Compiling Fortran D for MIMD Distributed-Memory Machines. *Communications of the ACM*, 35(8), August 1992.

[13] C. Kesselman. *Tools and Techniques for Performance Measurement and Performance Improvement in Parallel Programs.* PhD thesis, UCLA, July 1991.

[14] M. Le Fur, J.-L. Pazat, and F. André. An Array Partitioning Analysis for Parallel Loop Distribution. In *International Conference on Parallel Processing, Euro-Par'95*, Stockholm, Sweden, August 1995. Springer Verlag.

[15] Y. Mahéo and J.-L. Pazat. Distributed Array Management for HPF Compilers. In *High Performance Computing Symposium*, Montreal, Canada, July 1995.

[16] J. Ramanujam and P. Sadayappan. Compile-Time Techniques for Data Distribution in Distributed Memory Machines. *IEEE Trans. on Parallel and Distributed Systems*, 2(4):472–482, October 1991.

[17] P.H. Worley. A New PICL Trace File Format. Technical Report TM-12125, Oak Ridge National Laboratory, 1992.

[18] H. Zima and B. Chapman. Compiling for Distributed-Memory Systems. *Proc. of the IEEE*, 81(2):264–287, 1993.

	Npr	Size	NBl	NM	Wait	Tex	Tin	Tout	NRL	NRD	NAD
Npr	1.00	0.00	0.00	0.04	0.49	0.44	-0.59	0.45	-0.58	0.04	-0.58
Size	0.00	1.00	0.00	0.38	0.35	0.44	0.58	0.49	0.58	0.38	0.58
NBl	0.00	0.00	1.00	0.87	0.42	0.45	0.01	0.33	-0.01	0.87	0.00
NM	0.04	0.38	0.87	1.00	0.62	0.68	0.18	0.55	0.16	1.00	0.18
Wait	0.49	0.35	0.42	0.62	1.00	0.99	-0.21	0.83	-0.21	0.62	-0.20
Tex	0.44	0.44	0.45	0.68	0.99	1.00	-0.14	0.83	-0.14	0.68	-0.12
Tin	-0.59	0.58	0.01	0.18	-0.21	-0.14	1.00	-0.04	0.99	0.18	0.99
Tout	0.45	0.49	0.33	0.55	0.83	0.83	-0.04	1.00	-0.05	0.55	-0.04
NRL	-0.58	0.58	-0.01	0.16	-0.21	-0.14	0.99	-0.05	1.00	0.16	1.00
NRD	0.04	0.38	0.87	1.00	0.62	0.68	0.18	0.55	0.16	1.00	0.18
NAD	-0.58	0.58	0.00	0.18	-0.20	-0.12	0.99	-0.04	1.00	0.18	1.00

Figure 2: Correlation matrix.

Npr	Size	NBl	NM	Tex	Tin	Tout
16	128	1	236.25	2960.40	77.02	63.85
16	128	2	488.25	6961.27	95.80	2115.51
16	128	4	992.25	14693.36	42.19	2472.90
16	128	8	1984.50	19382.80	42.29	2162.21
16	256	1	476.25	13169.92	152.69	151.59
16	256	2	984.25	30699.33	180.96	7571.21
16	256	4	2000.25	64488.50	134.20	8231.70
16	256	8	4032.25	131149.64	137.57	8556.59
8	128	1	220.50	2024.08	81.45	148.48
8	128	2	472.50	4124.83	100.27	1212.01
8	128	4	976.50	8086.10	125.39	1475.52
.						
.						

Figure 3: Workload components.

1 th cluster of 2			n. of observations= 23.0000	
param.	center	min	max	st.dev
Npr	7.130	2.000	16.000	5.286
Size	166.957	128.000	256.000	60.220
NBl	3.043	1.000	8.000	2.549
NM	796.457	126.000	1984.500	608.624
Tex	7370.958	1411.711	19382.811	5579.477
Tin	257.511	42.192	946.695	248.937
Tout	1231.401	63.854	3622.539	872.672

2 th cluster of 2			n. of observations= 9.0000	
param.	center	min	max	st.dev
Npr	8.444	2.000	16.000	6.064
Size	256.000	256.000	256.000	0.000
NBl	5.556	2.000	8.000	2.404
NM	2712.861	984.250	4032.250	1208.181
Tex	44796.430	7039.291	131149.641	38947.316
Tin	441.284	134.206	964.395	328.209
Tout	4743.210	2250.381	8556.596	2654.015

Figure 4: Statistics of the two clusters obtained.

Performance of Shared Cache on Multithreaded Architectures *

Yunn-Yen Chen
ATC, Comp. & Comm. Research Lab.
Industrial Tech. Research Inst.
Hsin-chu, Taiwan, R.O.C.

Jih-Kwon Peir
Dept. of Comp. & Info. Sciences
Univ. of Florida
Gainesville, FL, 32611

Chung-Ta King
Dept. of Comp. Science
National Tsing Hua Univ.
Hsinchu, Taiwan, R.O.C.

Abstract:

In this paper, we use trace-driven simulation technique to study the performance impact to the storage hierarchy system on a multithreaded execution environment. Particularly, we examined the effects of different multithread scheduling techniques on cache performance using several program traces representing typical server/workstation workload mix. A *MRU-priority* scheduling scheme is proposed as the baseline scheduling scheme to study the performance effects. We found that the cache performance can be improved over the traditional round-robin scheduling method when the thread with the MRU hit is given a higher priority. With a direct-map cache, the absolute hit ratio can be improved 7% more than the original ratio. we also studied the performance effects on cache memory with a varying number of concurrent threads. The results showed that both the cache size and the set associativity need to increase according to the number of threads in order to maintain comparable cache performance. The main contribution of this paper is provide the performance comparison between two simple schemes which are easy to implement with the proposed baseline scheme.

1 Introduction

Memory latency has been one of the major performance bottlenecks in traditional or modern pipeline computer systems. There are two mechanisms to tolerate the memory latency. The first one is to reduce the latency by adding a small fast cache memory into the processor's storage hierarchy [6, 19]. Due to program locality, majority of references will access the fast cache memory under proper cache management. The other mechanism is to hide the main memory latency using the dataflow execution model [4, 8]. In such a model, multiple execution contexts exist in the processor pipeline. When the currently active context needs to access the memory, the processor switches to another context for execution. In this way, the memory latency in serving the first context is overlapped with (or hidden in) the execution of the second context.

Recently, the emergence of the *multithreaded* (or *multistreamed*) computers has made it possible to incorporate the latency tolerance of the dataflow concept into the traditional pipelined Von Neumann architecture [11, 13]. In a multithreaded computer, multiple program counters are usually maintained, each is associated with one independent executing thread. In order to minimize the context switching overhead, multiple register files are provided so that saving of register contents is not needed during context switching. As a result, context switching can be done within a few cycles.

There are a number of research and commercial projects focusing on the design of the multithreaded systems such as, Tera [1], Alewife [3], J-machine [7], MASA [9], IBM Empire [12], *T [16], CPC [21], etc. However, there are relatively fewer studies on the performance impact to the storage hierarchy in this type of systems. Two previous works by Agarwal [2] and Saavedra-Barrera et al. [18] used analytical methods in their attempt to estimate cache performance in a multithreaded environment. They both assumed that the executing threads have identical miss ratio and calculated the cache "interference" among multiple threads. Spee et al. [21], on the other hand, used two parallel programs, Linpack and Quicksort, to simulate cache performance under different number of threads.

In this paper, we apply trace-driven simulation to study cache performance on multiple independent threads. We consider a multithreaded uniprocessor environment with a shared cache for all the threads. The threads we selected represent a typical workload mix in a server/workstation environment. The traces are generated through the MITFAB tracing tool [5]).

We report in this paper the results of two experi-

*This work is a partial result of the project number 37H1100 conducted by the ITRI under sponsorship of the Ministry of Economic Affairs, R.O.C.

1066-6192/96 $5.00 © 1996 IEEE
Proceedings of PDP '96

ments. The first experiment is to simulate cache performance using different thread scheduling policies. We applied two conventional schemes. The first scheme is to switch threads on every instruction in a round-robin fashion (*switch-on-instruction*). The second scheme is to switch threads whenever a cache miss is encountered (*switch-on-miss*). The results showed very little difference between these two schemes. We also tried a new multithreaded scheduling scheme which selects the next thread based on the cache hit position[1] (i.e. the MRU position, the next to the MRU position etc.) of the first instruction to be executed. Comparing with the switch-on-instruction method, we observed a 7.3%, 4.1%, and 2.7% increase in hit ratios on a direct-map cache, a 2-way set-associative cache, and a 4-way set-associative cache, respectively.

The second experiment is to simulate cache performance by varying the number of independent threads. The results indicate that both cache size and set-associativity are very important in influencing cache performance. When the number of threads increases, both the cache size and set-associativity need to increase accordingly to obtain a comparable performance. For example, when 2 threads execute with a 4K bytes, 2-way set-associative cache, the increase of miss ratio is 3.72% comparing to the combined miss ratio of the two threads executed sequentially. When the number of threads increases to four and eight, the increase of miss ratios are equal to 3.84% and 3.74% with a 8K bytes 4-way cache and a 16K bytes 8-way cache, respectively.

We will first give the background information and discuss some related works in the next section. In Section 3, the tracing facility and the workloads we selected in this study will be discussed. The new thread scheduling scheme will be defined in detail in Section 4. The results of multithreaded cache performance under different scheduling techniques will be discussed in Section 5. Cache performance comparison with varying number of concurrent threads and the implementation of the new scheme will also be given. Finally, we will summarize this work in Section 7.

2 Background and Related Work

Multithreaded architectures can be traced back to the CDC 6600 introduced in the mid-60s. The essence of this architecture is to allow processors performing fast context switching to maintain high processor utilization. For instance, due to the data dependence, a memory reference with long access latency may stall the execution of the current thread. When this situation is encountered, the processor can switch to another thread to keep the pipeline from stopping.

The first multithreaded multiprocessor was built by Denelcor, which was named HEP [20]. Each processor of HEP allows up to 128 user threads (called *processes* in HEP terminology). On each cycle, an instruction from a different thread is executed. In order to allow fast context switching, these threads share a common set of registers. A minimum of eight *active* threads that are not waiting for a memory reference are required to keep the execution pipeline full. A full/empty bit is attached to each register and data memory location to provide proper synchronization functions. Tera [1] can be considered as a descendant of HEP. A full system is constructed with a $16 \times 16 \times 16$ toroidal mesh. Tera has a much deeper pipeline design to accommodate fast cycle time. On the average, it requires up to 70 active threads to maintain a full execution pipeline. a total 128 threads with their own independent program counter and register sets are designed in Tera to allow context switching in a single cycle.

Recently, there are several projects to combine the dataflow execution model with the traditional Von Neumann architectures. Examples include MIT P-RISC [15], the IBM Empire [12], and the MIT/Motorola *T [16]. The common trait of this type of architecture is to multiplex many threads. When one thread issues a remote load request, the processor switches to work on another thread. Multiple remote loads can be active at the same period and responses can be received out of order. Therefore, each remote load is attached with a thread identifier called *continuation*. This is very similar to the *color token* idea in the dynamic dataflow architecture. Each thread can be any size and executed under the control of the program counter. A regular computation thread is normally long and will not encounter a context switching unless the required data is not in the local registers or memory. Cache has not been implemented in this type of systems. Memory latency is tolerated by switching among a large number of parallel executing threads in the processor.

The multithreading concept can also find applications in traditional high-performance Von Neumann processors, usually at a very fine-grain level. For example, with the inclusion of the write buffer design, the thread issuing a write operation can resume its execution immediately after the updated data is put into the write buffer. The actual write to the memory can be viewed as a thread executing in parallel with the parent thread. Furthermore, a few recent experimental systems have incorporated an explicit multithreaded design into Von Neumann processors. For

[1] Note that LRU replacement scheme is assumed throughout this paper, except the scheduling scheme.

example, Alewife [3] is designed to have four program counters, each has an associated processor status register and a set of general-purpose registers called a *task frame*. Context switching will occur when a remote memory access or a synchronization attempt is encountered. The overhead for context switching is 11 cycles. The J-Machine [7] implements in each processor three execution levels: background, priority-0, and priority-1. Separate registers are provided to support rapid switching among these three levels.

Cache memory is a proven technique to reduce memory latency and has been implemented in all the known high-performance microprocessors today. Cache performance on a multithreaded processor has been reported in [2, 18, 21]. Analytical modeling methods were used in the first two works. Saavedra-Barrera et al. assumed an evenly partitioned shared cache among multiple threads in their attempt to model the cache performance. Under this assumption, the extrinsic interference among multiple threads is not considered. Argawal made similar assumptions that all the threads have the same fixed cache miss ratio. Such an assumption may reflect a parallel program workload under the Single-Program-Multiple-Data (SPMD) model of computation. However, the model may be inaccurate when the threads are independent and vary significantly. When the number of threads increases, a noticeable cache performance degradation on a direct-map cache were observed in the two above-mentioned studies.

Cache performance in a Cyclic Pipeline Computer (CPC) has been studied [21]. In CPC, both the functional units and the memory are pipelined and shared among multiple instruction threads. Unlike HEP, the CPC does not have additional hardware to switch instruction threads during execution. Instead, a fixed number of threads are given to execute in fixed "time slots" in the pipeline. Two thread scheduling methods, switch-on-fixed-interval and switch-on-miss are studied. Using the parallel workload Linpack and Quicksort, they reported that set associativity is a very important factor in designing multithreaded processors.

3 Tracing Environment

Trace-driven simulation method is used in this study. Multiple thread traces are generated through MITFAB tracing tool, it is started to develop while the author was at National Tsing-Hua University. One preliminary version of MITFAB was modified when the author was with University of Florida, this version was named as *Florida Tracing Facility*. MITFAB can start multiple processes in a UNIX environment and collect both instruction execution and data reference sequence from each process. In order to avoid saving the long traces,

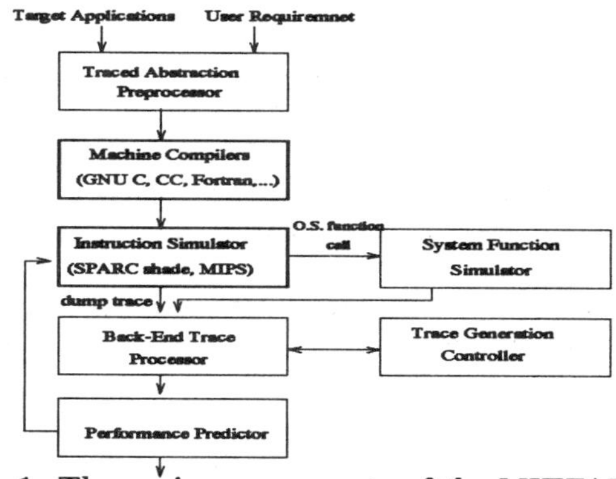

Figure 1: The major components of the MITFAB tracing tool.

a cache performance model has been incorporated into. This way only limited buffer space is required to save temporarily a window of the execution trace for each process. An execution process is stopped when the associated buffer space becomes full. This process will be reactivated later when the current window of the execution trace is exhausted by the cache performance model. As a result, MITFAB is able to simulate multiple execution threads by managing a relatively small buffer space.

Figure 1 depicts the structure of MITFAB. MITFAB consists of seven major components: trace abstraction preprocessor, target machine compilers, instruction simulators, system function simulator, back-end trace processor, trace generation controller and performance predictor.

The target source code is first processed by the *trace abstraction preprocessor*. Trace abstraction preprocessor allows users to specify a set of program behavior parameters to be monitored. These parameters include degree of parallelism, distance of branches, number of iterations in a loop, cache hit/miss ratios, etc. According to the requirements, the preprocessor makes proper insertions into the source code to inform the machine compiler to link appropriate system function routines and/or tracing facility libraries developed for MITFAB. One such example is to link a function routine to dump the execution trace into a pre-assigned buffer for the trace collection purpose. A *machine compiler* is then invoked to generate object code for the source workload as well as all the necessary system routines.

The *instruction simulator* generates the user-level trace by executing the user-level object codes. Any system call and privilege instruction are handled by the *system function simulator*. Whenever a "Dump Trace" instruction is executed, the *back-end trace processor* will be invoked to insert the traces into respective buffers. The back-end trace processor works closely with the *trace generation controller* which performs functions like workload profiling, trace filtering and re-structuring, trace compression, etc. When the buffer at the back-end trace processor is full, the collected traces begin to be consumed by the *performance predictor*. Various trace-driven performance models can be implemented. For the purpose of this study, several cache models are integrated in the performance predictor. The instruction simulator will be reactivated after all the traces in the buffer have been consumed by the performance predictor.

In this paper, we chose *SPARC Shadow* tool as the target machine instruction simulator [10]. Due to the lack of the UNIX source code, we focused on simulating the cache behaviors of multiple user-level execution threads. The format of the trace consists of four fields: program counter, instruction code, effective address, and a few associated flags. The back-end trace processor filters the traces into memory reference threads according to the SPARC processor specification. For example, assume the memory accessing granularity is 4 bytes, the back-end trace processor will generate two memory references for Load Double word (LDD) instruction.

In order to study the cache behavior in a multithreaded environment, we selected nine benchmark programs (Table 1). These nine programs represent a reasonable workload mix in a typical server/workstation environment. We selected four Unix system routines including text processing (*Latex*), an e-mail package (*elm*), a Gnu C compiler (*cc1*), and a set of Unix system utility programs (*sysutl*); three computational intensive programs: matrix multiply (*matmul*), fluid dynamics (*adi*), and gaussian elimination (*gauss*); as well as two popular VLSI CAD programs: circuit simulation (*spice*), and logic minimization (*espresso*). The number of references of each trace range from 11 to 16 million as shown in Table 1. The required data spaces for *matmul*, *adi*, and *gauss* are 230K, 228K, and 250K bytes respectively. Due to their dynamic memory allocation nature, it is difficult to report the exact data sizes required for the other programs. But, they all require a data space larger than the simulated cache size. To make observation clear, we terminate the simulation when one of the reference streams ends.

4 Scheduling Multiple Independent Threads

The main question arising in a multiple contexts execution system is when and how to switch a context. In this section we will describe three multithread scheduling techniques.

- Round-robin scheduling at every instruction (*switch-on-instruction*): switch threads after executing each instruction in a round-robin fashion.
- Round-robin scheduling on cache miss (*switch-on-miss*): switch threads when a cache miss is encountered.
- Priority scheduling (*MRU-priority*): after each instruction execution, select the next thread to be executed based on the cache access position of the next ready-to-execute instruction in each thread.

Round-robin scheduling at every instruction among the execution threads are adapted in several previous designs[20, 21]. Switching the execution among multiple threads at every instruction may alleviate the long memory access latency problem. It may also decrease the pipeline hazards due to dependence interlocks. However, when multiple threads share a common cache, the locality of access is likely to be reduced due to the mixture of working sets among multiple execution threads.

The second approach of the round-robin scheduling is only to switch thread execution when a cache miss happens. Certain miss penalty need to be paid to bring in the cache line from memory or from other higher-level storage hierarchy system. In a single thread execution, the processor may "stall" until the needed data is returned from memory.[2] To take advantage of multithread execution, the processor can switch to execute the next thread so that the processor stall can be reduced or eliminated. Round-robin scheduling on cache miss may also help the performance of the shared cache since consecutive memory references from the same thread are executed sequentially until cache miss is encountered.

In order to maximize the shared cache performance, the MRU-priority scheduling scheme attempts to minimize the cache interference by selecting appropriate execution threads. Let R_i represents the ith thread. r_i is the first reference of R_i yet to be scheduled for execution. p_{r_i} indicates the hit position of r_i defined relatively from the MRU to the LRU position, i.e. MRU is equal to 1, the position next to MRU is equal to 2, and so on. Obviously, the miss position is equal to the set-associativity plus 1. We define a *MRU-priority scheduling* scheme to be one which selects thread k for execution, where $p_{r_k} = Minimum_{i=1}^{TotalThreads} (p_{r_i})$.

[2] More advanced processors do allow "non-stop" cache design with complicated hardware logic [14]. The processor starts executing the next instruction even when a cache miss happens. Again, this takes the multithread concept at a very fine-grain level.

Name	References	Description
matmul	11225307	Multiply two 140*140 matrices
adi	15431937	Partial equation solver using finite difference method, whose data size is 95*95. This program is selected from [17]
spice	13575900	SPICE program simulates a small circuit. This program is selected from DLX benchmark suite, runs "small.inp" file.
gauss	15586204	Gauss elimination to solve a linear equation, whose data size is 120*120. This program is selected from [17]
espresso	12883022	Logic minimization program runs example Z5xpl with -Dexact option, the example has 7 inputs, 10 outputs, and 128 product terms.
sysutl	14659480	UNIX system utilities such as cp, ls, mv, rm, and cat with options
latex	12536854	Latex to process a two page document.
cc1	14482744	The first phase of Gnu C compiler to compile a 400-lines program
elm	16149230	An interactive mail processing program

Table 1: Selected workloads for multithreaded cache study

Basically, the MRU-priority scheduling scheme will select the thread which has the least impact on the cache content. When a reference hits the MRU position, no MRU update is required and the entire cache contents keep intact after the execution of the selected reference. As a result, the cache content for other threads will not be affected. If a reference hits the position next to the MRU position, then only the MRU cache line of the same set gets affected. The MRU line has to be moved to the next position as a result of the reference. Similarly, when a reference hits the third position, there will be two lines ahead of the referenced line in the same set. The MRU-LRU positions of these two lines will be changed.

Intuitively speaking, the total number of references to the MRU position should increase according to the MRU-priority scheduling scheme. This is due to the fact that the references with MRU hit will be scheduled earlier to reduce the adverse effect on cache memory for the following thread execution. The references hit the next-to-MRU position can be scheduled only when no instruction at the top of each execution thread has MRU hit. However, it is also possible that some references which hit MRU position in the original round-robin scheduling execution may slide to other positions in the MRU-priority scheme. This is due to the fact that the entire sequence between the two scheduling schemes are quite different. We have conducted trace-driven simulation to evaluate the cache hit/miss ratios for all three scheduling schemes. The results will be given in the next section.

5 Performance Evaluation on Multi-threaded Cache

In this section, we will report the multithreaded cache performance using the selected nine applications. Each application will generate an independent execution thread. No address sharing exists among the threads. The locality behaviors of the applications are quite different. The cache performance of each individual thread varies significantly.

5.1 Multithread Scheduling Schemes

In order to test the MRU-priority scheduling scheme, we simulated caches that have a fixed number of sets (64) with 64 bytes per line. This way the hit ratios to the MRU-to-LRU position in each set can be obtained. The actual set associativity is determined according to the cache size. For example, under our assumption, a direct-map cache has 4K bytes. For a 16K byte cache, the set-associativity becomes 4. The cache hit ratio for each individual application(*i.e.,* only one application runs on the cache) is given in Table 2. Each column represents the hit ratios to the particular position, i.e. the MRU position, the position next to MRU (2), and so on. Assume a 16K bytes, 4-way cache, the hit ratio of each application is equal to the sum of the hit ratios in the first 4 columns of the corresponding row. The nine programs are sorted based on the miss ratios of a 4-way set-associative design as indicated in the last column.

We can see that all the nine threads have high hit ratios on the MRU position except for Gaussian elimination. *Gauss* is implemented by using pivoting, so it performs poorly because of the large data space and non-stride-1(non-continuous memory access) access in nature. Matrix multiply performs relatively poor in the MRU hits. This is because we use a non-optimized version which has one non-stride-1 access out of every four accesses in the inner-product loop. But, the hit to the 2nd and 3rd position is higher than other threads. Consider a 16K bytes 4-way set-associative cache, the first

Name	MRU	2	3	4	5	6	7	8	9	10^+	4-way miss
spice	0.915	0.052	0.015	0.007	0.004	0.002	0.002	0.001	0.001	0.002	0.012
cc1	0.902	0.066	0.015	0.005	0.003	0.002	0.001	0.001	0.001	0.005	0.012
espresso	0.916	0.053	0.010	0.005	0.003	0.003	0.002	0.002	0.001	0.005	0.016
sysutl	0.906	0.053	0.016	0.007	0.003	0.002	0.001	0.001	0.001	0.010	0.018
matmul	0.728	0.151	0.091	0.012	0.001	0.001	0.001	0.000	0.000	0.016	0.019
latex	0.899	0.060	0.014	0.006	0.003	0.002	0.001	0.001	0.001	0.012	0.021
elm	0.888	0.049	0.017	0.008	0.005	0.004	0.003	0.002	0.002	0.022	0.037
adi	0.879	0.023	0.008	0.007	0.005	0.006	0.008	0.011	0.013	0.041	0.083
gauss	0.498	0.028	0.015	0.007	0.009	0.017	0.026	0.066	0.118	0.217	0.452

Table 2: Cache hit ratios for each individual trace

6 threads have 98% or higher hit ratios. The two numerical programs *adi* and *guass* from [17] produce high miss ratios of 8.3% and 45.2%.

The results of the three multithread scheduling strategies are shown in Table 3. Generally speaking, the MRU-priority scheme performs better than the other two schemes, and there is very little difference in the hit ratios between the switch-on-instruction scheme and the switch-on-miss scheme. For the MRU-priority scheduling, we observe a 7.3% increase in MRU hits comparing with a regular round-robin scheduling. This is due to the fact that many references originally hit a non-MRU position are now changed to an MRU hit. The hit ratios to the other positions decrease for the MRU-priority scheduling. Again, this is because a good percentage of references in these positions are moved away to hit other positions, especially to the MRU position.

In order to compare the change of hit positions between the MRU-priority scheduling and the switch-on-instruction scheduling schemes, we simulated the percentage of changes of each position between these two methods. Figure 2 depicts the results. One can see that for the MRU position, majority of hits (50.1%) stay unchanged between the two scheduling methods. However, there are 22.8% gain from other positions while 15.5% loss to other positions. As a result, a net gain of 7.3% can be obtained. For the second position, there is a net loss of 3.2%. This is due mainly to the fact that 9.4% of the original references have moved to the MRU hit in the MRU-priority scheduling while only 6.1% are moved from the MRU position into the second position. When we consider a 8K bytes 2-way set-associative cache, the MRU-priority scheduling method will increase the cache hit ratio by 4.1%.

5.2 Cache Performance with Different Number of Threads

The second experiment is to study the impact on cache performance with different number of threads.

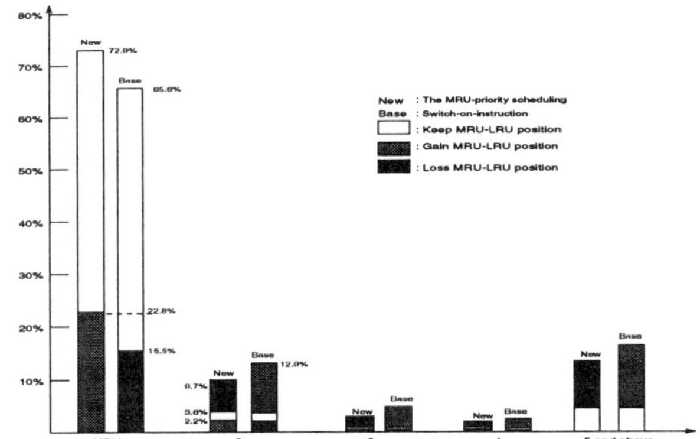

Figure 2: Comparison of hit ratios gain/loss between MRU and switch-on-inst. scheduling

When experimenting with fewer threads, we selected those threads with better individual cache performance (i.e. from the top of Table 2). For example, *spice* and *cc1* were selected in simulating the two-thread case. We considered three different cache sizes: 4K, 8K, and 16K bytes in the simulation with set associativities ranging from direct-map to 8-way. The switch-on-instruction scheduling was used. The line size is still 64 bytes.

Since the size and the cache behavior of each thread may vary significantly, we define a normalized *extra miss ratio* in order to compare the results among different number of threads.

$$\textit{Extra Miss Ratio} = \textit{Simulated Multithread Miss Ratio} - \frac{\sum_{i=1}^{TotalThreads} Miss_i}{\sum_{i=1}^{TotalThreads} Ref_i}$$

The second term on the right-hand side of the equation is a weighted average miss ratio of the simulated multiple threads. The extra miss ratio represents the difference in terms of the cache performance between sequential execution of the multiple threads and the simulated multithread execution.

Figure 3 plots the results of extra cache misses with different number of threads on various cache topolo-

Scheme	MRU	2	3	4	5	6	7	8	9	10^+
switch-on-inst.	65.6	12.9	3.6	1.6	1.1	0.8	0.8	0.9	1.1	11.6
switch-on-miss	66.7	12.3	3.4	1.7	1.0	0.8	0.8	1.0	1.1	11.2
MRU-priority	72.9	9.7	2.6	1.2	0.9	0.8	0.8	1.0	1.0	9.1

Table 3: The cache hit ratios for the three scheduling techniques

gies, in which 'w' represents set associativity and 't' is the thread number. We can easily observe that the extra miss ratio increases with the number of threads. The top three curves represent the extra miss for the 8-thread results. The next three curves are for the 4-thread cases. Finally, the lower three curves indicate the extra misses for the 2-thread runs. The results are obvious because when the number of threads increase, the working set increases accordingly. With the same cache size, the extra miss ratio must also increase.

The second observation is the importance of the set associativity. When the cache size and the number of thread are the same, caches with higher set associativity reduces the extra miss ratio. This reduction of extra miss ratio becomes more noticeable when the set associativity matches the number of thread. For example, we observe a relatively large gap between the second and the third curves. These two curves represent the extra miss ratios of 8-thread cases with 4-way and 8-way caches. We also observe that overly designing the cache set associativity does very little help in reducing the extra miss ratio. This situation can be seen by the small gap between the fifth and the sixth curves.

Finally, both the cache size and the set associativity need to increase with the number of threads in order to maintain the same level of cache performance. For example, the extra miss ratio of 2-thread case running on a 2-way, 4K cache is equal to 3.72%. When the number of threads, the cache size, and the set associativity are all doubled, the extra miss ratio is 3.84%. Similarly, when these three parameters are all doubled again, the extra miss ratio becomes 3.74%. This is due to again the fact that the disjoint of the working space of the multiple threads. Both the cache and the set associativity need to be doubled in order to obtain a comparable performance when the thread is doubled.

6 Summary

Trace-driven simulation has been applied to study cache performance in a multithreaded environment. Three thread scheduling schemes were simulated. The results showed that the MRU-priority scheduling had the best cache performance. The impact on cache performance in terms of the number of active threads was also studied. The results indicated that both the cache size and the set associativity should be increased according to the number of threads in order to obtain a comparable cache performance.

Multithreaded architectures will become more mature in the next few years. How can we incorporate the traditional cache design into the multithreaded architecture is still a very challenging issue. This study has demonstrated a comprehensive thread scheduling technique to improve cache performance. Detail implementation issues still need to be worked out in order to take the advantage of the proposed scheduling technique.

References

[1] R. Alverson, D. Callahan, D. Cummings, B. Koblenz, A. Porterfield, and B. Smith, "The Tera Computer System," *Proc. of International Coference on SuperComputing,* pp. 1–6, 1990.

[2] A. Argawal, "Performance Tradeoffs in Multithreaded Processors," *IEEE Trans. on Parallel and Distributed Systems,* vol. 3, no. 5, pp. 525–539, 1992.

[3] A. Argawal, D. Chaiken, G. D'Souza, K. Johnson, D. Kranz, J. Kubiatowicz, K. Kurihara, B. H. Lim, G. Maa. D. Nussbaum, M. Parkin, and D. A. Yeung, "The MIT Alewife Machine: A Large-Scale Distributed-Memory Multiprocessor," *Proc. Workshop Multithreaded Computers, Supercomputing 91,* 1991.

[4] Arvind, D. E. Culler, R. A. Iannucci, V. Kathail, K. Pingali, and R. E. Thomas, "The Tagged Token Dataflow Architecture," Technical report, MIT Laboratory for Computer Science, 545 Technology Square, Cambridge, MA 02139, 1984.

[5] Yunn-Yen Chen, "*MITFAB*: A Monitoring and Interfacing Tracing Facility Architecture Benchmarking,", *1995 Workshop on High Performance Multiprocessor Systems,* pp. 77–81, National Chiao-Tung University, Hsin-chu, Taiwan.

[6] C. Conti, "Concepts for Buffer Storage," *IEEE Computer Group News,* Vol. 2, No. 8, pp. 9–13, March 1969.

[7] W. Dally, L. Chao, A. Chien, S. Hassoun, W. Horwat, J. Kaplan, P. Song, B. Totty and S.

	4K	8K	16K
2w-2t	3.72	2.86	1.72
2w-4t	7.87	4.93	3.01
2w-8t	12.83	10.06	7.6
4w-2t	3.04	2.13	1.57
4w-4t	5.94	3.84	2.56
4w-8t	10.72	8.19	6.77
8w-2t	2.62	1.92	0.91
8w-4t	5.67	3.66	2.08
8w-8t	8.92	5.29	3.74

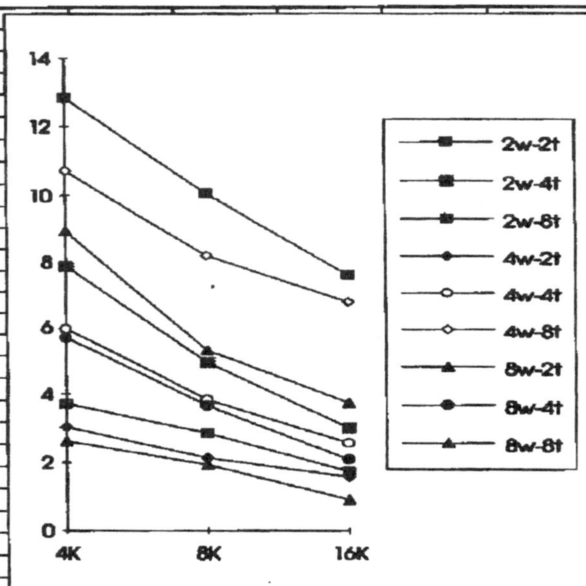

Figure 3: Extra miss ratios for different number of threads

Wills, "Architecture of a Message-Driven Processor," *Proc. of the 14th Annual International Symposium on Computer Architecture,* pp. 189–196, June 1987.

[8] J. B. Dennis, "Data Flow Supercomputers," *IEEE Computer,* pp. 48–56, Nov. 1980.

[9] R. A. Halstread and T. Fujita, "A Multithreaded Processor Architecture for Parallel Symbolic Computing," In *Proc. of 15th International Symposium on Computer Architecture,* pp. 443–451, 1988.

[10] Peter Hsu, "Shadow User Manual," Sun Microsystems.

[11] Kai Hwang, Advanced Computer Architecture – Parallelism, Scalability, Programmability, McGraw-Hill Readings, 1993.

[12] R. A. Iannucci, "Toward a Dataflow/Von Neumann Hybrid Architecture," In *Proc. of 15th International Symposium on Computer Architecture,* pp. 131–140, 1988.

[13] R. Iannucci, A. Agarwal, Bill Dally, G. Papadopoulos, B. Smith, "Architectural and Implementation Issues for Multiprocessing," *Computer Architecture News,* Vol. 22, No.1, pp. 3–18, March 1994.

[14] D. Kroft, "Lookup-free Instruction Fetch/Prefetch Cache Organization," In *Proc. of 8th International Symposium on Computer Architecture,* pp. 81–87, 1981.

[15] R. S. Nikhil and Arvind, "Can Dataflow Subsume Von Neumann Computing," In *Proc. 16th Annual International Symposium on Computer Architecture,* pp. 262–272, 1989.

[16] R. S. Nikhil, G. M. Papadopoulos, Arvind, "*T: A Multithreaded Massively Parallel Architecture,", In *Proc. of 19th International Symposium on Computer Architecture,* pp. 156–167, 1988.

[17] William H. Press, Brian P. Flannery, Saul A. Teukolsky, and William T. Vetterling, Numerical Recipes: The Art of Scientific Computing, Cambridge University Press, 1985.

[18] R. Saavedra-Barrera, D. E. Culler, and T. von Eiken, "Analysis of Multithreaded Architectures for Parallel Computing," in *Proc. of 2nd ACM Symp. on Parallel Algorithms and Architectures,* pp. 169–178, 1990.

[19] A. J. Smith, "Cache Memories," *ACM Computing Surveys,* vol. 14, No. 3, pp. 473–530, Sep. 1992.

[20] R. J. Smith, "Architecture and Applications of the HEP Multiprocessor Computer System," In *SPIE,* vol. 298, pp. 241–248, 1981.

[21] P. Spee, W. F. Wong and E. Goto, "Effects of Multiple Instruction Stream Execution on Cache Performance," *International Journal of High Speed Computing,* vol. 3, no. 2, pp. 135–155, 1991.

Author Index

Offices of the IEEE Computer Society

Headquarters Office
1730 Massachusetts Avenue, N.W.
Washington, DC 20036-1903
Phone: (202) 371-0101 — Fax: (202) 728-9614
E-mail: hq.ofc@computer.org

Publications Office
P.O. Box 3014
10662 Los Vaqueros Circle
Los Alamitos, CA 90720-1264
Membership and General Information: (714) 821-8380
Publication Orders: (800) 272-6657 — Fax: (714) 821-4010
E-mail: cs.books@computer.org

European Office
13, avenue de l'Aquilon
B-1200 Brussels, BELGIUM
Phone: 32-2-770-21-98 — Fax: 32-2-770-85-05
E-mail: euro.ofc@computer.org

Asian Office
Ooshima Building
2-19-1 Minami-Aoyama, Minato-ku
Tokyo 107, JAPAN
Phone: 81-3-408-3118 — Fax: 81-3-408-3553
E-mail: tokyo.ofc@computer.org

IEEE Computer Society

IEEE Computer Society Press Publications

CS Press publishes, promotes, and distributes over 20 original and reprint computer science and engineering texts annually. Original books consist of 100 percent original material; reprint books contain a carefully selected group of previously published papers with accompanying original introductory and explanatory text.

Submission of proposals: For guidelines on preparing CS Press books, write to Manager, Press Product Development, IEEE Computer Society Press, P.O. Box 3014, 10662 Los Vaqueros Circle, Los Alamitos, CA 90720-1264, or telephone (714) 821-8380.

Purpose

The IEEE Computer Society advances the theory and practice of computer science and engineering, promotes the exchange of technical information among 100,000 members worldwide, and provides a wide range of services to members and nonmembers.

Membership

All members receive the monthly magazine *Computer*, discounts, and opportunities to serve (all activities are led by volunteer members). Membership is open to all IEEE members, affiliate society members, and others interested in the computer field.

Publications and Activities

Computer Society On-Line: Provides electronic access to abstracts and tables of contents from society periodicals and conference proceedings, plus information on membership and volunteer activities. To access, telnet to the Internet address info.computer.org (user i.d.: guest).

***Computer* magazine:** An authoritative, easy-to-read magazine containing tutorial and in-depth articles on topics across the computer field, plus news, conferences, calendar, interviews, and product reviews.

Periodicals: The society publishes 10 magazines and seven research transactions.

Conference proceedings, tutorial texts, and standards documents: The Computer Society Press publishes more than 100 titles every year.

Standards working groups: Over 200 of these groups produce IEEE standards used throughout the industrial world.

Technical committees: Over 29 TCs publish newsletters, provide interaction with peers in specialty areas, and directly influence standards, conferences, and education.

Conferences/Education: The society holds about 100 conferences each year and sponsors many educational activities, including computing science accreditation.

Chapters: Regular and student chapters worldwide provide the opportunity to interact with colleagues, hear technical experts, and serve the local professional community.

Revised 11/15/95